CONTENTS

NOTES

In 2013, Sage renamed the Sage Simply Accounting program to Sage 50 Accounting, Canadian Edition. The US Edition of Sage 50 Accounting replaces Sage Peachtree.

PREFACE

Using Sage 50 Accounting 2016 provides full coverage of Sage 50 Accounting 2016 (Pro and Premium versions). The Student version (Release 2016.2) is also a Premium version program, so all users can learn the program using the same release the author used to create the data files, screens and keystrokes. Although we do not address the Quantum version of Sage 50, the book is also compatible with this version. Because Sage offers the Sage 50 Student version program only as a download from its Web site, we provide detailed instructions for downloading, installing and activating the Student version in Appendix A of this text.

As in last year's edition, the keystrokes and source documents are integrated throughout each chapter, printed in colour with check boxes. All source documents are numbered.

No topics were added in this edition, but we created one new application: Northern Lights (payroll setup application in Chapter 9). Appendix M on the Student DVD (Online Accounting with Sage One) has been expanded with instructions for integrating Sage One and Sage 50 data files.

But we maintained the aspects of previous editions that have been well received:

- a diversity of companies and business situations, including non-profit, service and inventory businesses
- comprehensive and current tax coverage for different provinces, including GST, HST, PST and QST, and tax remittances
- a realistic approach
- easy-to-follow, step-by-step keystroke instructions and screen illustrations, updated for Version 2016
- current information that has been updated to reflect the business realities in 2016
- several company setup chapters increasing in complexity and a separate setup for payroll, all with keystroke instructions
- separate chapters for basic and advanced Accounts Receivable and Payable topics
- comprehensive company profiles and realistic source documents throughout the text to give you the "feel" of real companies

The Student DVD with Data Files included with the text has the following resources:

- Pro and Premium version data files for all applications (except Chapters 7, 16 and 17)
- review questions and cases for each chapter (Appendix D)
- additional appendices with supplementary materials (Appendices E – N)
- the interactive Accounting Cycle Tutorial, which introduces basic accounting terms and concepts

We continue to provide options for automatically installing data from the Student DVD: backup data files for both Premium and Pro versions, and full Premium version data files for the source document applications in the text. Supplementary files are provided only as backup files. Of course, we still include detailed instructions on restoring backups. These alternatives have additional

advantages — if computer speed and time permit, users can install the full data files; otherwise, the smaller backup files can be copied quickly or backup files can be restored to your hard disk directly from the DVD one at a time. Premium version users can install both the full and backup sets of files. Backup files may be restored as often as needed without reinstalling.

The removable page-length bookmark attached to the back cover has a mini index and a ruler-marked edge to help you refer to specific lines on a page. This bookmark should help to manage page-flipping, which is inevitable because most keystrokes for a transaction go beyond the page with the transaction.

As in the past, we work with module windows in the Enhanced view throughout the text, create user-specific customized shortcuts to access journals in other modules and use the industry-specific terms for the different applications. Classic View margin notes like the following are included for users who prefer this approach:

 CLASSIC VIEW
Notes for Classic view users

These notes describe how icons, keystrokes or terms in the Classic view are different from those in the Enhanced view.

The basic organization of the text is unchanged. Part One provides an overview and introduction to Sage 50 and sales taxes. Data applications that can be completed with both Pro and Premium versions are located in Part Two. We introduce the six ledgers of Sage 50 (General, Payables, Receivables, Payroll, Inventory and Division) in separate applications. Budgeting and bank deposits and account reconciliation are covered in two more applications. Advanced Receivables and Payables features (orders and quotes, tax remittances, credit card payments, transactions with foreign customers and suppliers and Internet links) are demonstrated in two more chapters. An online banking simulation (in Appendix I on the Student DVD) allows you to download a bank statement that integrates with data from the text. The required data files for all these chapters are set up in advance, and for each new type of transaction we provide detailed keystrokes and matching screens.

Four applications cover setting up a computerized accounting system using Sage 50. Again, detailed instructions with screen illustrations are given for each setup as you learn to design, convert and implement a complete accounting system.

- Chapter 4: set up a non-profit organization that uses only the General Ledger
- Chapter 7: set up an organization using the General, Payables and Receivables ledgers
- Chapter 9: add payroll to a data file that already has the General, Payables and Receivables ledgers
- Chapter 16: set up a comprehensive retail organization that uses the General, Payables, Receivables, Payroll and Inventory ledgers

In the final application in Part Two (Stratford Country Inn, Chapter 17), you set up a computerized accounting system on your own. All source documents in this chapter are realistic and descriptive.

Time & Billing and Departmental Accounting, advanced features available only in the Premium version, are covered in Part Three. Separate chapters and

data files are prepared for these. All Part Three pages are edged with a blue stripe so that you can find them quickly.

For reference or further study, we include three appendices in Part Four of the text and 11 more on the Student DVD in PDF format — placing them on the DVD allows us to cover additional and advanced features of the program. The appendices on the Student DVD are available for you to read or print. These supplementary appendices are provided as reference material that should prove to be useful in any working environment.

USING THIS BOOK

The accounting applications in this text were prepared using Sage 50 Premium Accounting, Canadian Edition (Release 2016.2) and Sage 50 Pro Accounting, Canadian Edition software published by The Sage Group PLC. The Windows 10 operating system was used to create and test the screen images and keystrokes.

You must have a hard disk and DVD drive or a network system with Windows installed. If you do not have your own copy of the Sage 50 program, you can download the Student Premium software from the Sage Web site (refer to page xiii and Appendix A). Network system users should work with the site administrator to ensure complete data access.

In addition, you should have a standard accounting text for reviewing accounting principles. The text provides some accounting principles and procedures, and the Review of Basic Accounting (Appendix N) and the Accounting Cycle Tutorial on the Student DVD also provide an introduction. However, these are not intended to replace the breadth and depth of most standard accounting texts. You should also consult the Help features of Sage 50 described in Chapter 1, because they also include information about accounting procedures.

The text is as simple and straightforward as we could make it, but familiarity with computers and some fundamentals of troubleshooting will make your progress through this text easier.

Student Resources

The Student DVD with Data Files

The Student DVD has an autorun feature that should open the Student DVD home page automatically when you insert the DVD into your DVD drive. From this home page you can choose to install data files, view the supplementary appendices (PDF format), run the Accounting Cycle Tutorial or browse the DVD. The Student DVD home page will remain open for you to make another selection until you close it.

Complete instructions for installing and accessing the files on the Student DVD are provided in Chapter 1.

Separate data sets with separate installation programs will help you install the data set you need and make it easy for all users to follow the text. To choose the correct data set, you must know what version of Sage 50 you are using. You can get this information from the program package or program CD (if you are using a retail version) or from the Welcome and Select Company window in the program (see page 8). SAGE 50 PRO ACCOUNTING or SAGE 50 PREMIUM ACCOUNTING appears in the Home window for all data files. If you accepted the default installation settings, the program folder name in Program Files also matches the version. The Student version is a Premium version program, Release 2016.2.

The following chart will help you install the data set you need from the Install Data screen:

FOR VERSION	Pro Version 2016
CLICK INSTALL BUTTON	Install Pro Version Backup Files
DATA SET (FOLDER ON DVD)	Pro_Backup_Version

FOR VERSIONS	Student Version 2016, Premium Version 2016 and Quantum Version 2016
CLICK INSTALL BUTTON	Install Premium Version Full Files
DATA SET (FOLDER ON DVD)	Premium_Full_Version_Data

or

CLICK INSTALL BUTTON	Install Premium Version Backup Files
DATA SET (FOLDER ON DVD)	Premium_Backup_Version

All installation programs create a data folder named SageData16 on drive C (Local Disk C: or [OS] C:). If you need to work with another location for your data files, refer to page 6 in this text. You can install the data as often as you need to. We recommend renaming the previous folder to prevent overwriting all your previous files that may include data you want to keep. If you started by installing the backup files, you will not need to reinstall them because they remain unchanged.

You can restore backup files directly from the Student DVD to your hard disk. However, we recommend installing the backup files to your hard disk and keeping the original DVD safe for later use.

If you are using Sage 50 Quantum Accounting, the Sage 50 Upgrade Company wizard will convert the Premium data files when you open them or restore them. Because the DVD files remain unchanged, you can install the same files later and use the Premium version.

Supplementary Data Files

In addition to the data files needed to work through the keystroke applications in the text, we provide supplementary files with all installation options. Backup files are included for online bank reconciliation (Appendix I on the Student DVD) and importing accounting transactions from an Accountant's Copy (Chapter 12). These backup files will be located in the BANK and ACCOUNTANT folders in SageData16, respectively, when you install the data files. The ACCOUNTANT folder also has the text file that you import. The LOGOS folder includes company and inventory logos for the setup chapters and new inventory items.

Passwords

We have not added passwords to any data files to ensure maximum accessibility. However, if you are using the program in a multi-user or network environment that includes users and passwords, you will need to enter your user name and password before you can open the data files. Ask your instructor or site administrator for the user name and password that you should use. Refer to Chapter 16, page 686, and Appendix G on the Student DVD for instructions on working with passwords.

Working with Different Versions of Sage 50

Windows Version

We used Windows 10 for all screenshots and keystrokes in this text and to create and test the data files. Fortunately, the screens and functionality of Sage 50 are the same for different versions of Windows. They differ only at the interface between Windows and Sage 50 — in the screens for browsing, opening and saving files. Sage 50 is also compatible with Windows 7 and Windows 8.

Pro Version

Although we have written this text primarily for the Premium version and show Premium version screens, you can use the Student DVD data files with the Pro, Premium and Quantum versions of Sage 50, Release 2016.2 or later, and with the Premium Student version (2016 only).

Therefore, we have tried to make version differences, such as differences in features, terminology and labels, as clear as possible. We use margin notes identified by a specific Pro version heading and icon:

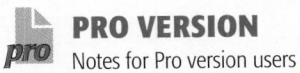

PRO VERSION
Notes for Pro version users

These notes for Pro version users describe how screens, terms or keystrokes in the Pro version are different from those in the Premium version.

Student Version of Sage 50

The Student Premium version of Sage 50 must be downloaded from the Sage Web site (**sage.com/ca/about-us/education**). All copies of the 2016 Student version program have the same **serial number — 242P1U2-1000011**. Detailed instructions for downloading, installing, registering and activating your Student version of Sage 50 are provided in Appendix A. The installation procedure is the same for the regular retail CD version of the program. Only the activation process — also described in Appendix A — is different.

Students needing help with the program should work with their instructor. Additional help for students is available online from the student forum that you access from the following Web site: **sagecity.na.sage.com**. For more information about accessing this site and posting your questions, refer to Appendix A in this text, pages A-10–A-12.

About the Student Version Program

The Student version is a fully functional Premium version that remains valid for 14 months after installation, but you cannot restore or open data files from previous versions with it. If you have already installed a Trial version, the date you installed it will count toward this 14-month limit. You can install only one version of Sage 50 Accounting 2016 on your computer. If you are using the Pro version or a Trial version and you want to install the Student Premium version, you must first completely uninstall the Pro or Trial version from the Control Panel in Windows (refer to Appendix A, page A–10). After you use a data set with the Student version for 14 months, you must use a regular retail licensed version of the program to access that data.

None of the data files were created with a Student or Trial version, so the data itself will not expire. If you have used the data with a Student version for 14 months, however, you may see a data expired message.

If you see a message that the program has expired when you try to install it or open a data set, and you have not yet used the program for 14 months, you should refer to page A–10 and ask your instructor for assistance.

The differences between the Student version and the retail Premium version are very small, but where they occur we have identified them with margin notes as shown here:

STUDENT VERSION
Notes for Student version users

These notes describe how the Student version differs from the regular or retail Premium version.

Earlier Versions

If you try to access the data files with earlier versions of Sage 50 Accounting (2016.0 and earlier), Sage 50 displays an error message. In this case, you should download and install the Student version. Refer to Appendix A for information on downloading and installing the Student version.

Later Versions

Although the data files can be used with later versions of the software, you may see changes in screens, keystrokes and payroll tax amounts. Before you open a data file with a later version, the Sage 50 conversion wizard will update the data file to match the later version you are using. Always refer to the manuals and update notices for later versions. Once the file has been updated, you will no longer be able to use it with the earlier version or release, unless you reinstall the data files from the Student DVD.

For this reason, we recommend that you turn off the Automatic Updates feature so that you do not update your program beyond Release 2016.2 until you have finished working with the data files in the text. For the 2016 program, selecting automatic updates is a user preference. Refer to Chapter 4, page 80, for information on turning off automatic updates. Automatic updates are not available for the Student version.

Quantum Version

This text can be used with Sage 50 Quantum Accounting. All the features covered in the text are available in the Quantum version, though you may see small variations in the screens. The Quantum version includes features that are not available in the Premium version — these advanced features are not covered in this text. If you are using the Quantum version, the Sage 50 data conversion wizard will convert the Premium data files when you open them or restore them. Because the DVD files remain unchanged, you can install and use the same files later with the Premium version.

Working Through the Applications

Keystroke Instruction Style

We have incorporated different paragraph styles for different kinds of statements in the text to help you identify the instructions that you must follow to complete the transactions correctly and see the screens that we present. These different styles are illustrated below:

Press   (enter) or **press** the **Add button** to start the Add Account wizard. (Keystroke command line — command word is in bold and the object of the command, what you press, is in colour. Commands are indented and spaced apart. Additional text or information for the line is shown in plain text.)

Type   `Foothills Hardware` (Keystroke command line with text you type in a special font.)

Or, you can click the Comment field to advance the cursor. (Alternative keystroke sequence that you may want to use later. Paragraph is indented in block style and plain text style is used.)

Regular text is presented in normal paragraphs, like this one. **Key words** are shown in colour to make it easy to identify the topics. Names of icons, fields, text and tool buttons that you will see on-screen have all initial letters capitalized (for example, Adjust A Previously Posted Invoice tool or E-mail Confirmation Of Invoices And Quotes). Account names included in regular text paragraphs are italicized (for example, *Revenue from Sales* or *Cost of Goods Sold*).

☑ **Purchase Invoice #DS-642**   **Dated May 1/18**

1   From Data Savers, $1 320 plus $198 HST for off-site data backup and restoration services for one year. Invoice total $1 518. Terms: net 30. (Source document — with all text in colour — that you should enter using Sage 50. The ✓ in the check box indicates that keystroke instructions are provided. The number in colour in the lower part of the check box shows the source document number. All source documents are numbered in sequence.)

☐ **Cash Purchase Invoice #BC-6110**   **Dated May 12/18**

19   From Bloomers, $1 280 plus $192 HST for batch of tree saplings to grow for future sales. Invoice total $1 472 paid in full by cheque #180. (Source document — with all text in colour — that you should enter on your own using Sage 50. No keystroke instructions are provided — the upper part of the check box is empty and the lower part contains the source document number in colour.)

In addition to the different types of margin notes already described for the Pro and Student versions and the Classic view, the text includes regular margin Notes that contain additional important information for all users and Warning notes when extra attention is needed:

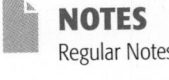 **NOTES**
Regular Notes

Regular Notes for all users providing additional general information.

 WARNING!
Warning notes

Warning notes point out common errors or things to watch out for!
All users should read these notes carefully.

Order of Applications

Setup applications are introduced early in the text. Advanced users should have no difficulty working through the applications in the order given and may even choose to skip some applications. However, at a minimum, we recommend working through all keystroke transactions (the ones with a ✓ in the check box beside them) so that you become familiar with all the journals before starting the more comprehensive applications.

There are alternatives if the text is used at introductory and advanced levels for different courses. In this case, students can complete the General, basic Payables, basic Receivables, Payroll and Inventory transaction applications (Chapters 3, 5, 6, 8 and 10) in the introductory course and the remaining chapters later. Chapters 11 and 12 may be completed at any time after Chapter 6 because these chapters do not have payroll or inventory transactions. Chapters may also be completed in a different sequence, as outlined below and on the following page:

1. Read and work through the two Getting Started chapters in Part One.
2A. Complete the ledger applications in order: Muriel's Murals (General), Groen Fields (basic Payables), Phoebe's Photo Studio (basic Receivables), Helena's Academy (Payroll), Flabuless Fitness (Inventory), Andersson Chiropractic Clinic and Maple Leaf Rags (advanced features of the first three ledgers) and Shady Corners* (Division or Project).
2B. (Premium version only) Complete the Part Three applications in any order: Ryder's Routes (Time & Billing) and Able & Associates (departmental accounting).
3. Complete Tesses Tresses (Chapter 15, account reconciliation and deposit slips) and Village Galleries (Chapter 14, budgeting).
4. Complete the four setup applications in order: Love It Again (General), Air Care Services (three ledgers), Northern Lights (adding the Payroll ledger) and VeloCity (five ledgers).
5. Complete the Stratford Country Inn setup application with realistic source documents. Users may want to attempt this setup with the help of the setup wizards from the Setup menu in the Home window.
6. Complete the cash-basis accounting application in Appendix H at any time after Chapter 6.
7. Complete the setup for some of the other chapters based on the company information provided at the start of the chapter.

* Shady Corners (Division Ledger, Chapter 13) may be completed at any time after these chapters because it does not introduce keystrokes required for any other application. Later chapters may be completed before Shady Corners.

This order is shown graphically in the chart on the following page:

AN ALTERNATIVE SEQUENCE FOR WORKING THROUGH THE APPLICATIONS

Getting Started	Ledger Applications	Advanced Features	Setup

Getting Started (**1**)

⇩

GST, HST and PST (**2**)   ⇨   Muriel's Murals (**3** General)

⇩

Groen Fields (**5** Payables)

⇩

Phoebe's Photo Studio (**6** Receivables)   ⇨ ⇨ ⇨ ⇨ ⇨ / ⇦ ⇦ ⇦ ⇦ ⇦   Phoebe's Photo Studio (**Appendix H** Cash-Basis Accounting)

⇩

Helena's Academy (**8** Payroll)

⇩

Flabuless Fitness (**10** Inventory)   ⇨   Andersson Chiropractic Clinic (**11** Advanced A/P & A/R)

Shady Corners (**13** Allocations & Electronic Payments)   ⇦ / ⇨   Maple Leaf Rags (**12** Advanced A/P & A/R)

Village Galleries (**14** Budgeting)   ⇨ ⇨   Love It Again (**4** General)

⇩

Tesses Tresses (**15** Account Reconciliation)   Air Care Services (**7** General, Payables, Receivables)

⇩

Ryder's Routes (**18** Premium – Time & Billing)   Northern Lights (**9** Payroll)

⇩

Able & Associates (**19** Premium – Departmental Accounting)   VeloCity (**16** General, Payables, Receivables, Payroll, Inventory)

⇩

Stratford Country Inn (**17** Challenge Application)

NOTES

Each box includes the chapter or application title, the chapter number and the topic being introduced.

Applications within the same box may be completed in any order.

Organization within Chapters

The chapter material is organized the same way for all chapters. After stating the objectives of the chapter, a comprehensive company profile is provided to bring the business to life. This profile includes a description of the business's primary activities; its customers, suppliers, employees and inventory; historical financial data for all the modules in Sage 50 used by this company; and accounting procedures relevant to this company.

After the profile, we provide the instructions for completing the chapter. The keystroke section follows with detailed instructions for setting up the company files or instructions for each new type of transaction. For the setup chapters, the transactions follow the keystroke section. Otherwise, the keystrokes and transactions are presented together — the instructions for each new type of transaction follow immediately after the transaction.

Instructions and descriptions for reports for the module and features covered in a chapter appear at the end of the chapters.

Review questions and cases for all chapters can be found in Appendix D on the Student DVD.

Supplements

The Student Text Enrichment Site

A text enrichment site accompanies this text: **pearsoncanada.ca/text/ purbhoo2016**. This site has an online banking simulation for VeloCity in Chapter 16, including the bank statement that you can download for reconciliation. Instructions for accessing the site and completing the simulation are in Appendix I on the Student DVD.

Instructor Supplements

- **Solutions**   Solutions for all applications in the text are available as Sage 50 Premium Accounting backup files. These files have all the source document transactions in the text completed. The files must be restored with the Sage 50 program and all reports may be displayed or printed.

- **Additional Setup Files**   Backup files for the setup chapters (Chapters 4, 7, 9, 16 and 17) are provided with setup completed and ready for entry of source documents. Two additional files are provided for Chapter 16 — for journal entries beginning in the second and third month of the applications. Files for bank reconciliation are also included: February bank reconciliation for Tesses Tresses; Case 8 in Appendix D for VeloCity; and Case 2 in Appendix D for Stratford Country Inn. Appendix D is on the Student DVD. These additional files are provided with the Solutions.

- **Instructor's Manual**   The Instructor's Manual is offered in two parts. The first is a file in PDF format with information about all the instructor resource materials, teaching and testing suggestions and some troubleshooting tips. The second part, Answers to Review Questions and Cases, includes answers to all the end-of-chapter questions and cases

(Appendix D on the Student DVD). This part is available as a PDF and a Microsoft Word document so that instructors may choose or modify individual answers.

- **Test Item File**   Multiple-choice tests (with over 500 questions) organized by textbook chapter and several applied tests that require students to set up company files and enter source documents using Sage 50 are provided. The applied tests have alternate versions and may be completed as intermediate or end-of-course tests. All test files are provided in Microsoft Word format and may be modified by instructors. Solutions are included for all test items. For increased flexibility, the applied test solutions are Sage 50 backup files at two stages of completion: with the setup completed but history not finished and with all source transactions completed. The setup solution files may be given as separate tests (entering source transactions only) or they may be modified to create your own tests.

- **Source Documents**   Source document files for all chapters are available. These PDF-formatted source document files do not include any keystrokes.

All instructor supplements except the source document files are available for download from a password-protected section of Pearson Canada's online catalogue **catalogue.pearsoned.ca**. Navigate to the catalogue page for this text to view a list of the supplements that are available. Contact your local sales representative for details and access.

ACKNOWLEDGMENTS

So many people have been instrumental in providing ongoing support during the past year it is difficult to remember all the details. Having constancy in the team makes everything go more smoothly.

Avinash Chandra, I value tremendously your commitment to the Purbhoo book, making it a priority. Anthony Leung, senior designer at Pearson — your dedication to making the inside and outside of the book look great is truly appreciated. Anthony has been working on my books since I started writing them and he first joined Pearson, so we have worked together for a long time. As usual, we give you short turnaround times, and you always perform, creating new, and I think interesting, designs for the outside and inside of the book and changing them on the fly as needed.

Patricia Ciardullo started as program manager and provided her usual friendly and supportive backing. Trish, it was good to work with you and I will miss you, but you left me in good hands with Richard di Santo. Michael Kelley, still the technical expert, thank you for another eleventh-hour rescue.

Megan Farrell, acquisitions editor, manages the contracts with Sage and the contacts with sales representatives and instructors — their questions and the errors they found provide important feedback.

I trust — a word I do not use lightly — Leanne Rancourt in her many roles: developmental editor, copy editor and production editor. As before, she has proved to be an invaluable resource — professional, efficient and effective — fixing errors while remaining open to suggestions. Once again, thank you, it has been a pleasure. Together with Söğüt Y. Güleç who carefully proofread the entire manuscript, they fine-tuned the wording, caught some fairly blatant mistakes and are still correcting my punctuation. They help make each text better than the one before.

As always, the remaining errors are my responsibility, but without the efforts of this team there would be many more.

Several individuals at Sage — Nancy Harris, Melissa Lutman, Joel Reisler and Jim Collins — have been helpful throughout this project, providing access to the Sage resources needed to create this text and technical support. Edward Mortimer from Sage arranged access and helped me understand the links between Sage 50 and Sage One.

We are also grateful for the cooperation of Sage Payment Solutions and Beanstream — by allowing me access to these programs, they made it possible for the students to see how Sage 50 reaches further into the real world of business.

The job of writing the content is mine, but this large cast of contributors makes the output more professional and assures me that they are there to help.

And finally, thank you to friends for walks in the park, dinner and theatre nights and afternoon coffees. And to my family for visits, including muffin-making mornings with Ella and Erin. They reminded me of the important things in life during a stressful year.

Mary Purbhoo

Part 1
Getting Started

CHAPTER ONE

Getting Started

*After completing
this chapter, you
should be able to*

OBJECTIVES

- ■ *start* the Sage 50 program
- ■ *open* a working copy to access the data files for a business
- ■ *restore* backup files to access data files for a business
- ■ *understand* the help feature in Sage 50
- ■ *save* your work
- ■ *back up* your data files
- ■ *finish* your session
- ■ *change* default date format settings

⚠ WARNING!

In 2013, Sage Simply Accounting was renamed Sage 50. You will be unable to open the data files with Sage 50 Accounting 2015 or earlier releases of Sage 50 Accounting 2016.

The Student DVD with Data Files will be referred to as the Student DVD throughout the text.

📄 NOTES

The instructions in this chapter for starting the program and copying files refer to Windows 10 procedures. If you are using a different version of Windows, please refer to Sage 50 and Windows Help and manuals for assistance with these procedures.

Sage 50 works best when Internet Explorer is your default browser and you keep your Internet connection open.

GETTING STARTED

Data Files and Abbreviations

The applications in this workbook were prepared using Windows 10 and the Sage 50 Premium Accounting and Sage 50 Pro Accounting (Release 2016.2) software packages produced by Sage. Before 2013, this program was named Sage Simply Accounting (Premium and Pro). You will be unable to open the data files with any version or release of Sage 50 Accounting earlier than 2016, Release 2. Automatic updates have been turned off within the data files for this text. Later releases and versions of the software use later income tax tables and may have changes in screens or keystrokes. If you have a version other than Release 16.2, you can download and install the Sage 50 Premium Accounting – Student Version program to work through the applications. Refer to Appendix A if you are installing the Student version.

The instructions in this workbook have been written for a stand-alone PC with a DVD drive and a hard drive with Windows correctly installed. Your printer(s) should be installed and accessible through the Windows program. Refer to the corresponding manuals for assistance with these procedures.

This workbook reflects the author's approach to working with Sage 50. There are alternative approaches to setting up company accounts and working with the software. Refer to Sage 50 and Windows Help and manuals for further details.

DATA APPLICATION FILE NAMES AND LOCATIONS (All folders and files are located in C:\SageData16\)

Company	Full File Installation	Backup File Installation	Chapter
Getting Started	START\START.SAI	START1.CAB	1
Muriel's Murals	MURALS\MURALS.SAI	MURALS1.CAB	3
Love It Again	TEMPLATE\SKELETON.SAI plus user setup	SKELETON1.CAB plus user setup	4
Groen Fields	FIELDS\FIELDS.SAI	FIELDS1.CAB	5
Phoebe's Photo Studio	PHOTO\PHOTO.SAI	PHOTO1.CAB	6
Air Care Services	user setup required	user setup required	7
Helena's Academy	HELENA\HELENA.SAI	HELENA1.CAB	8
Northern Lights	NORTHERN\NORTHERN.SAI plus user setup	NORTHERN1.CAB plus user setup	9
Flabuless Fitness	FLABULESS\FLABULESS.SAI	FLABULESS1.CAB	10
Andersson Chiropractic Clinic	ANDERSSON\ANDERSSON.SAI	ANDERSSON1.CAB	11
Maple Leaf Rags	MAPLE\MAPLE.SAI	MAPLE1.CAB	12
Shady Corners	SHADE\SHADE.SAI	SHADE1.CAB	13
Village Galleries	VILLAGE\VILLAGE.SAI	VILLAGE1.CAB	14
Tesses Tresses	TESS\TESS.SAI	TESS1.CAB	15
VeloCity	user setup required	user setup required	16
Stratford Country Inn	user setup required	user setup required	17
Ryder's Routes (Prem.)	RYDER\RYDER.SAI	RYDER1.CAB	18
Able & Associates Inc. (Prem.)	ABLE\ABLE.SAI	ABLE1.CAB	19
Phoebe's Photo Studio (Cash-Basis)	CASH\PHOTO-CASH.SAI	CASH1.CAB	Appendix H

NOTES
Applications in Chapters 1 through 17 can be completed with both the Pro and the Premium versions. For the applications in Chapters 18 and 19 you must use the Premium version.

Data files for the applications in Chapters 4, 7, 9, 16 and 17 — the setup chapters — are not set up in advance. You must create those files on your own.

In addition to the data files, the Student DVD includes data files for cash-basis accounting in Appendix H (CASH folder or CASH1.CAB backup file) and a backup file VELOBANK1.CAB (Bank folder) for online banking in Appendix I. Appendices H and I are on the Student DVD as PDF files.

The applications increase in complexity. Each one introduces new ledgers, setups or features as indicated in the following chart:

DATA APPLICATION	GL	AP	AR	PAY	INV	DIV	OTHER
Muriel's Murals	*						
Love It Again	*						2
Groen Fields	*	*					
Phoebe's Photo Studio	*	*	*				3
Air Care Services	*	*	*				2, 3
Helena's Academy	*	*	*	*			
Northern Lights	*	*	*	*			2
Flabuless Fitness	*	*	*	*	*		3
Andersson Chiropractic Clinic	*	*	*				
Maple Leaf Rags	*	*	*				3, 4, 7
Shady Corners	*	*	*	*	*	*	3, 4, 7, 9
Village Galleries	*	*	*	*	*		3, 5, 7
Tesses Tresses	*	*	*		*		6
VeloCity	*	*	*	*	*		2, 3, 4, 7
Stratford Country Inn	*	*	*	*	*		1, 3, 7, 8
Ryder's Routes	*	*	*	*	*		PREMIUM 1
Able & Associates Inc.	*	*	*	*	*		PREMIUM 2
Phoebe's Photo Studios (Appendix H)	*	*	*				10

LEDGERS

GL = General Ledger
AP = Accounts Payable
AR = Accounts Receivable
PAY = Payroll
INV = Inventory
DIV = Division or Project Allocations

Other:
1 All realistic source documents (most chapters have some realistic source documents)
2 Setup application with keystrokes 5 Budgeting 8 Setup application without keystrokes
3 Credit cards 6 Account reconciliation 9 Electronic payments
4 Internet links 7 Foreign currency transactions 10 Cash-basis accounting

PREMIUM 1 Time & Billing; Build from Bill of Materials; Inventory locations (Premium version only)
PREMIUM 2 Departmental Accounting (Premium version only)

The Sage 50 Program

Sage 50 is an integrated accounting program with many features that are suitable for small and medium-sized businesses. It includes several ledgers and journals that work together so that data entered in one part of the program will be linked to and available in other parts of the program. Ledgers are automatically updated from journal entries, and reports always include the most recent transactions and ledger changes. A business can use one or more of the accounting modules: General, Payables, Receivables, Payroll, Inventory, Project and, for the Premium and Quantum versions, Time & Billing. You need to set up only the features you use. Thus, if payroll is not used, there is no need to set up the Payroll module, and it can be hidden from view. A more complete description of the program and its features is presented in Chapter 16, pages 621–622.

Sage 50 Program Components

When you select the Typical Installation option, several components will be installed:

- **Sage 50 Program**: the program that you will need to perform the accounting transactions for your company.
- **Sample Data**: complete records for a sample company — Universal Construction.
- **Templates**: predefined charts of accounts and settings for a large number of business types.
- **Customizable Forms**: a variety of commonly used business forms.
- **Microsoft Office Documents**: a variety of Microsoft Office documents designed for integrated use with Sage 50.
- **Manuals** & **Tutorials**: documentation and videos to help you learn the program.
- **Add-in for Microsoft Outlook**: a program link that connects your data with Microsoft Outlook.

The Student Data DVD

Before you begin the applications, you must copy the data to your hard drive. The Student DVD has both full data files and Sage 50 backup files. The full data files are large and will take longer to install, so we provide only backup files for supplementary data files (refer to page xii) and for Pro users. Furthermore, you cannot work from CD or DVD files because they are read-only files. Keep the Student DVD in a safe place in case you need to start over from the original files. The following instructions will copy all the files to your hard drive and create the necessary folders.

Installing Your Data

The Student DVD contains Pro and Premium versions of the data files and several supplementary files for the book. It also has programs that will automatically copy the data to a new SageData16 folder on your hard drive (drive C:). If you want to use a different location for your data files, proceed to page 6.

You must work with the correct version of the data set. If you are working with the Pro version, install the Pro data files — you cannot open Premium version files. If you are working with the Premium (or Student) version, install the Premium data files.

If you are using the **Pro version**, refer to the Pro Version margin notes throughout the text for the differences between the Pro and Premium versions for 2016.

NOTES
For assistance with installing the Sage 50 program, refer to Appendix A.

NOTES
You can access the Sample Data file from the Sage 50 Welcome Select Company screen on page 8.

PRO VERSION
pro The Pro version does not have the add-in for Microsoft Outlook.

NOTES
Sage 50 writes directly to your working data file as you enter transactions. Therefore, you cannot use read-only files as your working copy. All CD and DVD files are read-only files, so you cannot open the Sage 50 data files from the Student DVD.

WARNING!
Unless you have experience working with Windows folders, we recommend using the auto-install feature on the Student DVD to install your data set.

Insert the **Student DVD** into your DVD drive. The home page appears:

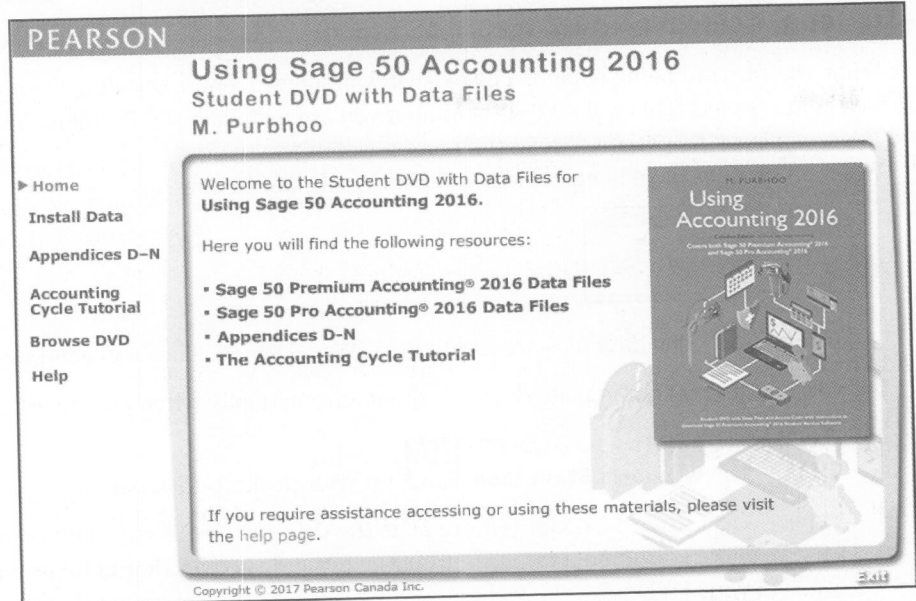

This page has your options for installing data files and viewing the additional resources and allows you to access these options from the left-hand side pane.

Click **Install Data** to open your data installation options:

All data installation options will create the SageData16 folder on your hard drive — This PC — OS C: or Local Disk C:, and all files will be placed in this new folder.

The **Install Premium Version Full Files** option (~2 GBytes) will copy folders and files for each company data set in the primary keystroke chapters. In addition, you will have backup files for online banking and importing entries from an accountant. This installation requires substantially more time for copying the files.

The **Install Premium Version Backup Files** option (~60 MBytes) will install backup files for all the applications in the text except the setup chapters. When you restore these with Sage 50, the default location will be the same as that for the Full File Installation option. If you are working on a slower computer, we recommend this option.

The **Install Pro Version Backup Files** option will install backup files for the applications for Pro users. Pro version files are provided only in backup format.

Instructions for restoring backup files begin on page 24.

Click **Install Pro Version Backup Files** to copy the data set for Pro 2016.

The Premium, Student Premium and Quantum versions use the same data files.

NOTES
A black DOS Command screen will scroll through all the files as they are being copied to your hard drive. There are thousands of individual files in the full version data set, so this will take some time.

All data files will be copied to C:\SageData16\, the starting point we use throughout the text.

If you reinstall the files, you will be prompted to replace the older files. Your options are to replace all (type A), replace just this one file (type Y) or do not replace this one file (type N). Press (enter) after making your choice. Choosing All (typing A) will automatically replace all the files and you will not get this same prompt for each of the thousands of individual files.

NOTES
Keystroke instructions that you must use have highlighted text in indented paragraphs, like the ones on this page starting with **Click**, **Type** and **Close**.

The command words are in **bold black** type and the object of the command is in **colour**.

Text you should type or key uses the `Courier font` after the command word **Type**.

Additional key words are also in **colour**.

NOTES
Alternative instructions or commands that you may need to use are given in indented paragraphs without highlighting, like the paragraph beside this note, beginning with "You can copy the files to."

PRO VERSION
pro The desktop shortcut is labelled Sage 50 Pro Accounting Version 2016.

Click   **Install Premium Version Full Files**, or

Click   **Install Premium Version Backup Files**.

While the files are being copied, a black DOS window will open, scrolling through all the files being copied. This will take some time if you are installing the Premium Version Full Files, so please be patient. (Read the margin Notes.)

When all the files have been copied, you get a confirmation message:

Click   **OK**. The data files are located in C:\SageData16. The DOS window closes.

If the Student DVD home page does not open automatically when you insert the Student DVD,

Click   the **Windows Start icon** [icon] on your desktop task bar.

Type   `d:\start.exe` (where D: is the drive letter for your DVD drive). The Search field opens automatically, and this file should be available on your DVD.

Click   **D:\START.EXE** to open the installation options on the previous page.

You can also view the supplementary files on the DVD. You can save these PDF files to your hard drive or print them if you want.

Click   **Appendices D–N** in the left navigation bar and then **click** the **file** you want.

Close   the **PDF file** when you have finished viewing or printing it.

Click   **Exit** to close the Student DVD window.

All the data files for the book are now located in the new SageData16 folder in drive C:. We will use the shorthand C: instead of This PC\C:, Local Disk C: or OS C:. We will open and restore the backups from this folder and use it as our working data folder.

Working with Other File Locations

You can copy the files to a different location by copying the data from the DVD just as you would copy other files to your hard drive. Choose the correct version of the data set (Pro or Premium), and be sure to copy the entire folder for each data set to include both the SAJ folder and the .SAI file. These must be kept together for Sage 50 to be able to open the data file.

You cannot open a Sage 50 data file directly from a CD or DVD, but you can restore a Sage 50 backup file from a CD or DVD. You must save the file on your hard drive before you can work with the data.

You can also work on a removable USB drive in Sage 50 because this is a rewritable medium, but working from a hard disk drive is faster and is the preferred method.

Starting Sage 50

A Sage 50 shortcut icon was added to your desktop when you installed the program.

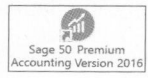

Double-click , the Sage 50 program shortcut on your desktop.

From this shortcut, you can pin the program to your Windows 10 Start page.

    Right-click the **Sage 50 shortcut** to open pop-up menu:

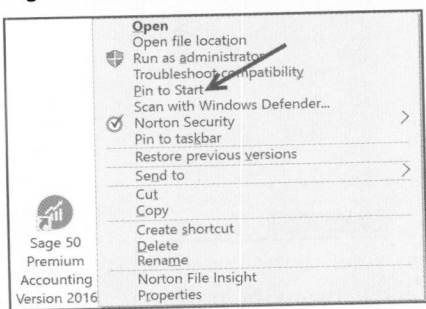

    Click   **Pin To Start**. You can now start Sage 50 from the Windows Start page (Tablet mode). A shortcut has been added here for the program:

    Click   **Sage 50 Premium Accounting Version 2016**.

If you are not viewing your screen in Tablet mode, you will begin from ▦ (the Windows Start logo) in the task bar.

    Click   ▦ to expand the traditional Start menu; all applications you have pinned to the Start page are in alphabetic order with their program icons. The shortcut you created earlier will also be included here.

    Click   **All Apps** to expand the list (or click the Sage 50 Premium Accounting Version shortcut you added here to start the program):

    Scroll down the list of Apps to Sage. **Click Sage** and then **point to Sage 50 Premium Accounting Version 2016**:

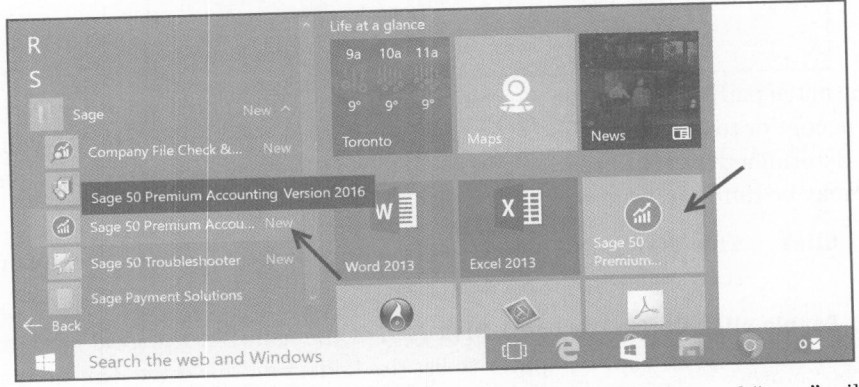

    Click   **Sage 50 Premium Accounting Version 2016**. The word "new" will appear beside the program name if you have recently installed it.

NOTES
We intentionally use large arrow pointers in our screenshots.

NOTES
From this pop-up menu, you can also pin a shortcut to the desktop task bar and then click this shortcut to start the Sage 50 program.

PRO VERSION
pro The Start page shortcut is also labelled Sage 50 Pro Accounting Version 2016.

PRO VERSION
pro You will click Sage and then click Sage 50 Pro Accounting Version 2016.

NOTES
The Select Company window includes the version you are using. This window has Premium added to the program name.

The Select Company window option is located in the View menu (refer to Chapter 4, page 82).

⚠ WARNING!
You will be allowed to use the retail version of the program only for a limited time before entering the registration validation codes.

Remember to activate Payroll as well. Refer to Appendix A in this text. You must have a payroll ID code in order to use the Payroll features of the program.

You must register and activate the Student version before you can use it, but you will not need to activate payroll.

Refer to Appendix A for information about registering and activating your program.

NOTES
Your screens may look different if you have selected different viewing options, such as displaying the folders as icons, details or lists. The viewing options can be changed from the View icon drop-down menu.

⚠ WARNING!
Each application has many files containing different parts of the accounting information. All files must be contained in the same folder. If any file is missing, you will be unable to access the information. The auto-install procedure keeps the necessary files together.

NOTES
The path for the most recently used company file will be used initially. Therefore, we cannot be certain what your screen will have in the path field. Our instructions should direct you to the data files from any location.

We provide the complete path and extensions for files. These are folder options in Windows.

You will open the registration screen the first time you use the program. Otherwise, you will open the Sage 50 Welcome and Select Company screen:

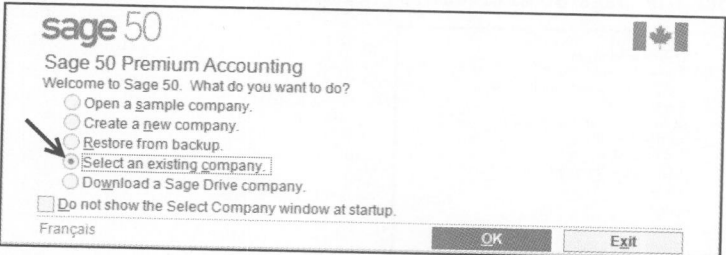

If you have not yet registered the program, refer to the boxed notes in Appendix A, pages A-3–A-4 in the text. Until you register and activate the program, you will be allowed to use the program only for a limited time. The Student version must be activated before you can use it. Refer to Appendix A, pages A-5–A-6 and A–9.

If you are restoring the Premium or the Pro version backup file, refer to page 24 for instructions.

Opening a Data File

The opening Sage 50 Welcome and Select Company screen gives you several options: working with the sample company files, creating new company files, restoring backup files or working with existing data files on your own computer or through a Sage Drive Internet connection. The next time, because we will have worked with the program before, the option to Open The Last Company You Worked On will be added with the name of the file you used (refer to page 24). If you choose this option when you use the same data set for several work sessions, you will bypass the Open Company window (the next screen on this page).

If you are restoring backup files, refer to the instructions starting on page 24.

> **Click**   **Select An Existing Company. Click OK.**

The Sage 50 – Open Company window appears next. Our screen uses the Tiles view:

The initial path will be for the file you used most recently, and it will be selected for you to accept or to change. If this is the first time you are opening a data file, your path will be determined by your program and system settings. Therefore, the folder on your screen may be different from ours.

> **Click**   **This PC** in the left pane list or in the file path field on top to open the screen above.

> **Double-click OS (C:)** or **Local Disk (C:)** or the name for the local hard drive C: on your computer to list the folders on this drive. Our next screen uses the Details view for the folders:

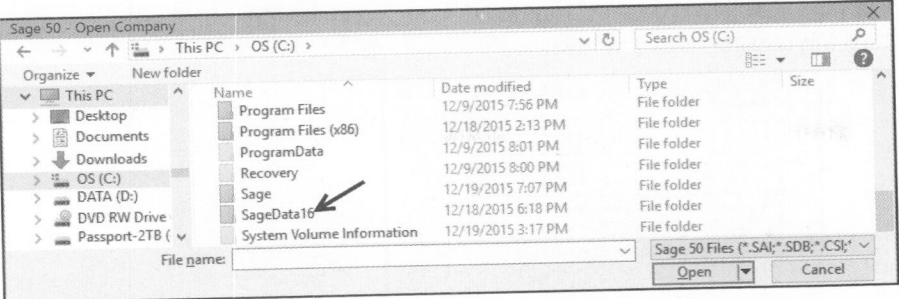

Click   **SageData16**. (Click the SageData16 folder icon ![SageData16] if your viewing mode is icons.) Then **click Open** for the files you installed from the Student DVD. We used the List view for folders in the next screen:

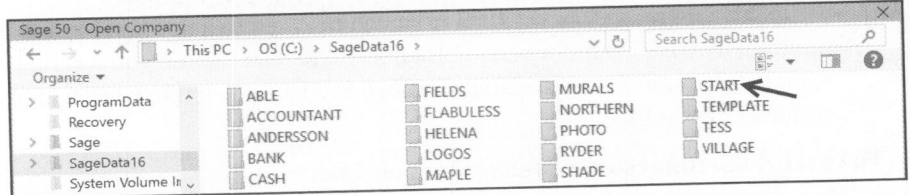

Click   **START** (or its folder icon ![START]) and then **click Open**:

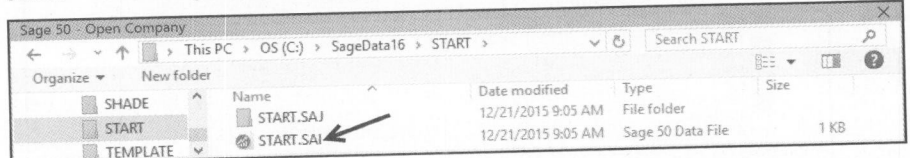

You can gain access to the company records only from the ***.SAI** file. Sage 50 recognizes this file extension as a Sage 50 format. The remaining data files for the company are in the SAJ folder. Both the .SAI file and the SAJ folder that are part of the data set must be located in the same folder. The complete data path [This PC>OS(C:)> SageData16>START] is added to the path field near the top of the screen. START is now the folder named in the Search field.

Click   **START** (or the start icon ![START.SAI]), or click **START.SAI** (if you show file extensions) to select it and add it to the File Name field:

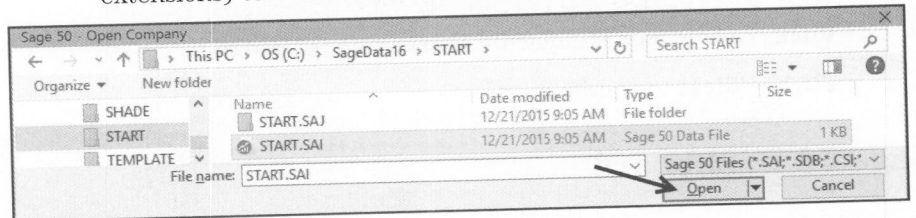

Click   **Open** to open the session date screen:

Click   **OK** to accept the date and open the Home window. The session date is explained in Chapter 3.

NOTES
We use the default location for the data files from the automatic installation. If you installed the files to a different location, choose the drive and location for your setup.

PRO VERSION
pro You will have folders only for ACCOUNTANT, BANK and LOGOS. All data files are available as backup files. Refer to page 24 for instructions on restoring backup files.

NOTES
Showing the complete file path as we do is a Windows option. The open folder is named in the Search field.

WARNING!
If you are not showing file extensions, you will click START. Do not click the START.SAJ folder. The folder has a small folder icon ![folder] beside the name. The .SAI file you need has a Sage 50 program icon ![sage50] beside the name.

NOTES
The session date is explained in Chapter 3, where you will also learn how to change the session date.
The session date drop-down list includes the current session date, the end of the fiscal period and the start of the next fiscal period. The list for any date field includes the dates commonly selected.

If passwords have been set up for the file, you will open the password entry screen before the session date window:

NOTES

We have not set passwords for any data files in this text, but your site administrator for the network may have done so. Refer to Appendix G for more information about passwords.

Ask your instructor or site administrator for the name and password to use. Enter your user name and password. Open the file in Single-User Mode. Click OK to open the session date screen. Refer to Chapter 16, page 686, and Appendix G on the Student DVD.

If you get a message that the data has been updated to a new file format, your program may be an earlier version than 2016, Release 2, and you will be unable to open the data file. You can install the 2016 Student version to work with this text (refer to Appendix A).

PRO VERSION

You may get an additional message about upgrading to the Premium version of Sage 50. Choose Do Not Show This Message Again.

The Sage 50 Getting Started Welcome screen opens:

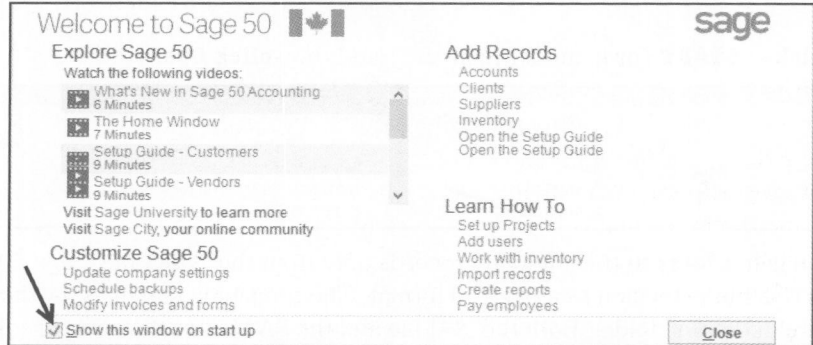

NOTES

The contents of the Getting Started screen will change to match the industry or business type of your company data set.

This screen outlines various options for getting assistance with the program. These include brief video tutorials and instructions for some basic steps you might need when setting up data files for a new company. You will start with this screen each time you open a data file in Sage 50, unless you have turned it off. After reading the options, you can close this screen now so that it will not appear each time you open this file. For other data files in this text, we have already turned off the selection.

PRO VERSION

The terms do not change. Customers and Vendors will replace Clients and Suppliers on the Getting Started screen.

> **Click** **Show This Window On Start Up** to remove the ✓.

> **Click** **Close** to continue.

Sage 50 Dashboard

The main Sage 50 Dashboard Home window on page 11 should now be open.

PRO VERSION

The program name is Sage 50 Pro Accounting. Purchase Invoice replaces Supplier Invoice, and Sales Invoice replaces Client Invoice.

The **title bar** is at the top of the Home window, and it contains the file name, START.SAI (or START); the Control Menu icon on the left-hand side; and the size buttons on the right-hand side. The **main menu bar** comes next, followed by the program name, Sage 50 Premium Accounting, and the **tool bar**. Tool buttons provide quick access to commonly used menu items and the **search** function. The Search field enables you to look up information in any journal or ledger. Different windows in the program have different buttons on the tool bar. Below the tool bar you will find the company name, Start Co., and the command to **Switch To Classic View** (refer to page 14).

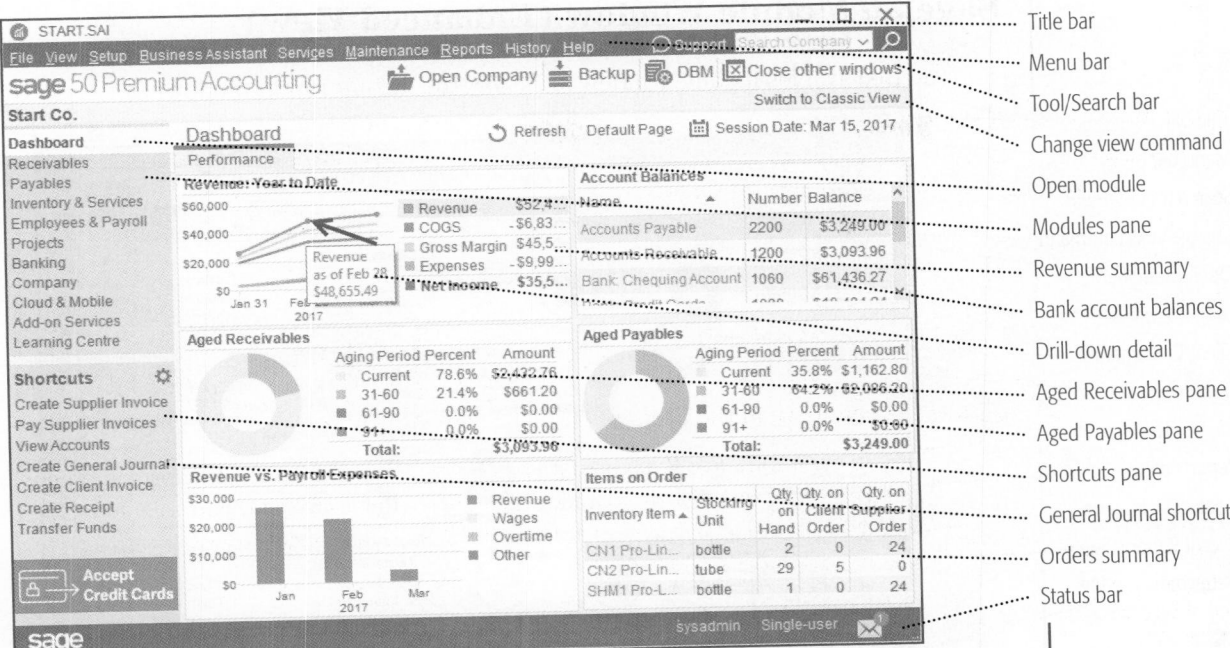

Title bar
Menu bar
Tool/Search bar
Change view command
Open module
Modules pane
Revenue summary
Bank account balances
Drill-down detail
Aged Receivables pane
Aged Payables pane
Shortcuts pane
General Journal shortcut
Orders summary
Status bar

The **Modules pane** on the left-hand side of the window or navigation pane lists all the modules set up for this company. It also provides direct one-click access to the Cloud & Mobile module for sharing company data with accountants or employees and sharing data with the Sage One Accounting program. Through an Internet connection, the link to Add-on Services will provide more information about payroll, cheque printing, Sage University and direct payments.

The Dashboard provides several key performance indicators in the various panes, including both graphic views and tables. Account balances for all bank, credit card, receivable and payable accounts indicate the cash position of the company. The first graph — for Revenue — has revenue, cost of goods sold and other expense information, providing both gross margin income and net income for the fiscal year to date. The Receivables and Payables graphs are pie charts with the totals divided among the different aging periods defined for the business. The proportion of the total that is overdue in each case is immediately apparent. The final two charts on the Dashboard report the relation between payroll expenses and total revenue and the items on order. This particular company has no employees, so the payroll expenses are zero.

Point to the **Revenue line** to access the amount details represented in this line.

Point to some **other segments** to expand the details for them.

For all graphs, details for part of a graph will appear in a bubble when you point to that part, as in the screen on this page with the detail for revenue as of February 28. Clicking any part of a graph will open the detailed Sage 50 report for that information.

Sage 50 reports are covered further in later chapters for each module.

Click   **Cloud & Mobile** in the Modules pane on the left-hand side to access the data-sharing features of the program.

Click   **Add-on Services** in the Modules pane of the window to learn more about these features. Remember, you must be connected to the Internet to access the additional information from the Learn More links.

Click   **Receivables** in the Modules pane.

NOTES
Sage One is covered in Appendix M on the Student DVD.

Sage 50 Module Window (Enhanced View)

The Receivables module window is usually the default Home window:

Title bar ·············
Menu bar ·············
Search tool ·············
Change View command ·············
Open module ·············
Ledger icon ·············
Client/Customer list ·············
Tasks pane ·············
Journal activity icons ·············
Reports pane ·············
Related Tasks pane ·············
Recent Reports list ·············
Status bar ·············

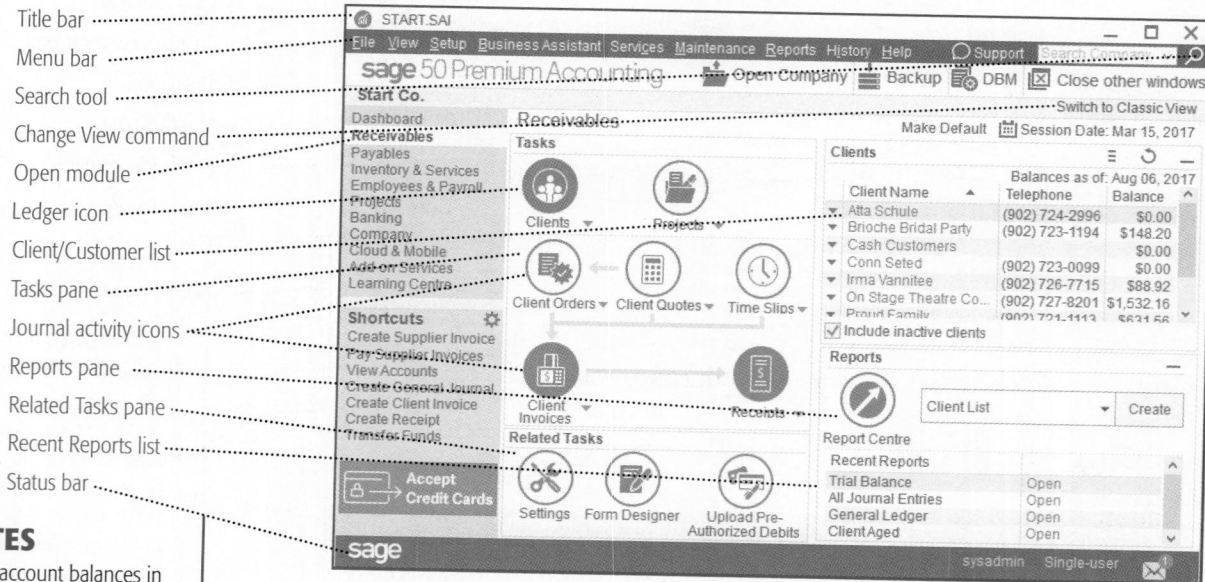

The module Home window is divided into several panes. The **Modules pane** lists all the modules available for this company data set. The open module — Receivables in this illustration — has a lighter background. The Receivables module is the default Home window for most of our chapters, but you can choose any module as the Home window. Activities for the module are represented by separate icons. The Modules pane also has access to the **Learning Centre**. To access a function or activity, click the related icon.

Below the list of modules, the **Shortcuts pane** allows one-click access to as many as 10 different tasks and activities that you set up or customize for each user.

The next column has all the icons you need to complete the activities for the module. The **upper Tasks pane** has the **ledger icon** that allows you to create and modify customer records from the Clients (Customers) window and Project records in the Projects window. The **lower Tasks pane** has the icons for **journal activities** or **transactions**. Use these icons to enter the accounting transactions in this text. Clicking the icon opens the journal directly for that type of transaction.

In the Premium version, the icon labels change to suit the type of company. For the service company illustrated here, the ledger icon is labelled Clients.

Many ledger and journal icons have a **shortcuts drop-down list arrow**. Clicking an entry in an icon shortcuts list will access the activity directly and bypass the main task window. For example, you can begin adjusting an invoice to make a correction if an entry was posted in error, bypassing the first step of opening the journal.

Click   the **shortcuts drop-down list arrow for Client Invoices** ▼:

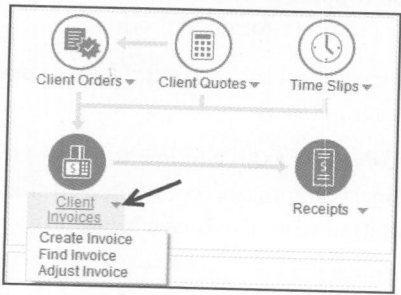

Click   some **other shortcuts list arrows** for the different options.

Below the ledger and journal icons, you will find the **Related Tasks pane**. From the icons in this pane, you can perform other ledger-related activities, such as entering settings for the open ledger.

The right-hand column also has three panes. The first has a **list of ledger accounts** for the selected module. For the Receivables module, the list has clients or customers with the phone number and outstanding balance. The Payables module window will have the list of suppliers or vendors. You can hide the phone and account balance details.

Below the list of customers or clients, the **Reports pane** allows quick access to all reports for the ledger from the **Reports drop-down list** and to the **Report Centre**, from which you can access all reports. Reports that you displayed most recently are listed in the **Recent Reports** section. Clicking a report in this list will open it with the report options you selected most recently.

The **status bar** appears last. In the Enhanced View, the status bar includes the user's name and **messages** icon.

To work with another module, click the module you want in the Modules pane list.

Sage 50 on the Windows Desktop

Click   **Make Default** beside the Receivables module heading. (Click Receivables in the Modules pane list first if necessary.)

Now each time you open this data file, the Receivables module will be the starting point — Default Page has replaced Make Default.

Click   **Create General Journal** in the Shortcuts pane list. This will open the General Journal with the Receivables Home window in the background.

Click   the **Entry menu**. Our next screen has these settings with the desktop in the background:

NOTES

In other windows, the status bar describes the purpose of the icon or field that has the pointer. In the screenshot on this page, the General Journal journal window has Recalls A Saved Recurring Transaction in the status bar.

NOTES

Many Sage 50 windows include a Home window tool that brings the default Home window to the front without closing the other windows.

We used Windows 10 to illustrate this desktop. The Help/Search option hides the minimize size control button in the journal window. In later screenshots, we edited images to show this button.

If you have a different version of Windows or use different Windows settings, your desktop may look different.

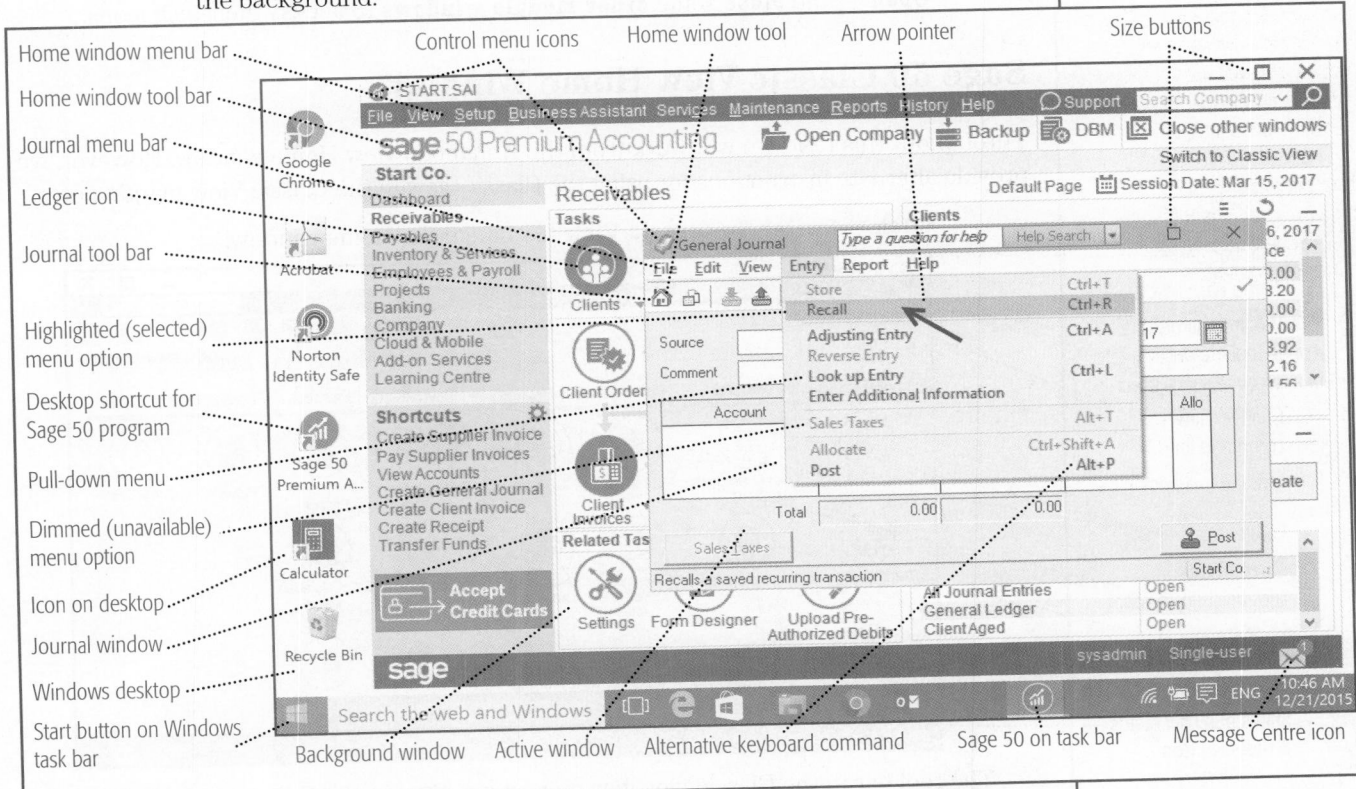

If you have messages from Sage for your account, the Message Centre icon will have a number on it. Connect to the Internet and click this icon to access your messages.

NOTES

When you point to the Sage icon on the Windows task bar, two Sage 50 windows will pop up: the Home window and the journal window. Clicking the pop-up makes it the active window.

When you click Sage 50 on the Windows task bar, you see the two pop-ups for the windows you currently have open:

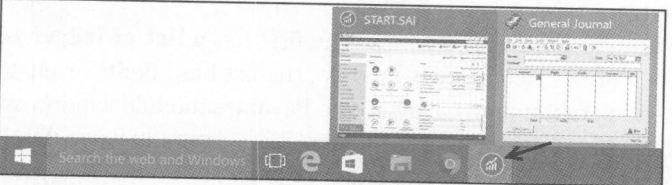

Click   ☒ to close the Journal window and return to the Home window.

Click   **Employees & Payroll** in the Modules pane.

This module now becomes the Home window, so its icons for ledger and journal activities are displayed. The ledger icon is now labelled Employees:

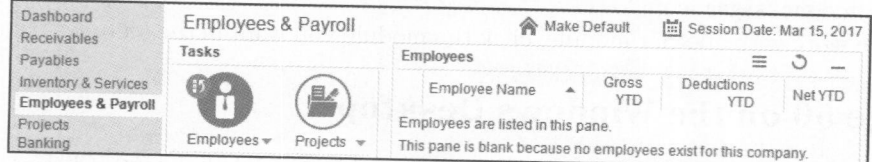

In this module, the backward curved arrow symbol 🔄 informs us that the Payroll Ledger is not set up — the history is not finished. When ledgers are not finished, you can add and change historical data. When you create new company data files, all ledgers have this symbol.

Your Muriel's Murals Home window (in Chapter 3) will be the Company Module with access only to the General Ledger and journals — Chart of Accounts and General Journal. Icons for unused features and ledgers that are not set up will be hidden.

Open   and **close** some **other module windows** to access their task icons.

Sage 50 Classic View Home Window

Throughout this text, we will work from the Enhanced view Home window. However, we provide alternate instructions for using the Classic view in the Classic View margin notes.

Click   **Switch To Classic View** to change the Home window:

Title bar ·············
Menu bar ·············
Program name/version & Tool buttons line ···
Company name & Change View command line ···
Module headings ···
Ledger icons ···
Open history (not-finished) symbol ···
Journal icons ···
Arrow pointer ···
Status bar, user status & message icon ···

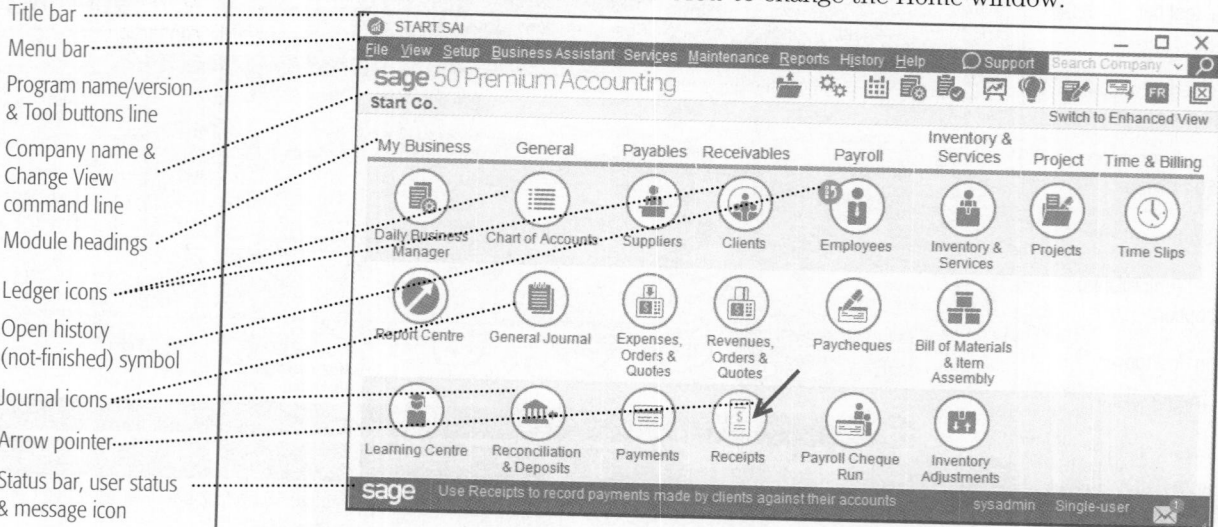

The tool bar in the Classic view has more items than in the Enhanced view. The **ledger** or module names come next with their respective icons filling up the major part of the window. The ledger icons in the top row are below the ledger or module name,

and the **journal icons** are under their respective ledgers in the last two icon rows of the window. All journals and ledgers can be accessed from the icons in this single Classic view Home window. Below the journal icons we have the **status bar**. In this example, the status bar describes the purpose of the Receipts Journal because the pointer is on the Receipts icon.

The icons in the **My Business tab column** allow quick access to the Daily Business Manager (covered in Chapter 11), Report Centre and Learning Centre.

> Hold the mouse pointer on a tool button for a few seconds to display the name or function of the tool button and the keyboard shortcut if there is one. Hold the mouse over an icon to open its description or function in the status bar at the bottom of the window.

Click   **Switch To Enhanced View** to change back to the Receivables window.

Sage 50 Help Features

Sage 50 provides program assistance in several different ways. You can display or print Help information on many topics. General accounting information, advice topics and Sage 50 software assistance are included. You can access Help from the Home window at any time.

The most immediate form of help comes from the **status bar** at the bottom of many program windows. It offers a one-line description of the icon or field that the mouse is pointing to. As you move the mouse around the screen, the status bar information changes accordingly. The message in the status bar is connected to the mouse position only. This may not be the same as the position of the cursor or insertion point, which is located wherever the mouse was when you last clicked the mouse button.

Many settings or options windows include a **Help button** that offers context-sensitive help for the procedure you are using.

Sage 50 Help can be accessed in several ways.

Start   your **Internet connection**.

Click   **Learning Centre** in the Modules pane:

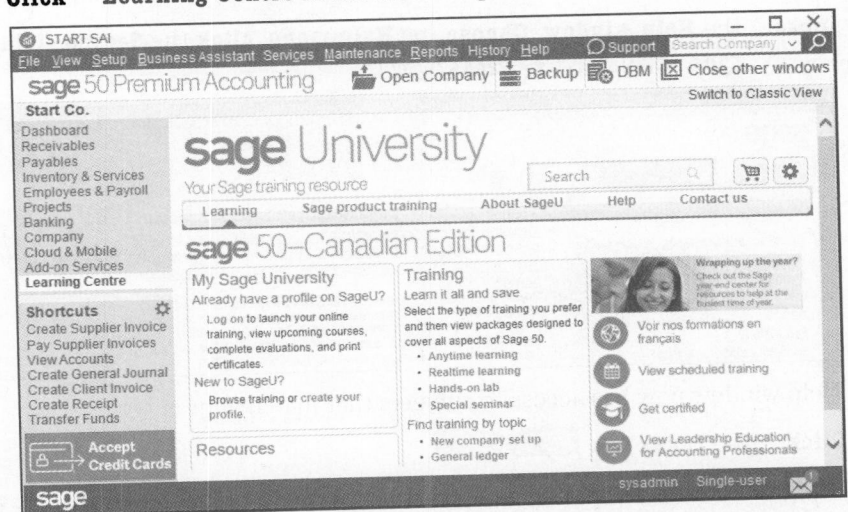

From this Web page you can learn about courses and training available from Sage U (Sage University).

You can also use the program's built-in Help, with or without Internet access.

NOTES
The Support Info button on the About Sage 50 screen (from the Help menu) has your complete registration details.

Click   the **Help menu** in the Home window:

The options on this menu include access to the online community for help, the Learning Centre and its tutorials, a description of new features and the Getting Started Guide. In addition, you can update the program to a later release, upgrade the program to Premium from Pro (or to Quantum) and get the version number and serial number for your program (About Sage 50 Premium Accounting).

NOTES
If your Internet connection is active and Internet Explorer is your default browser, you will have access to online help information. Most Help features do not require an Internet connection.
Internet Explorer is the preferred default browser for working with Sage 50.

Choose the **Help menu** and **click** 🔍 in the **Search field**:

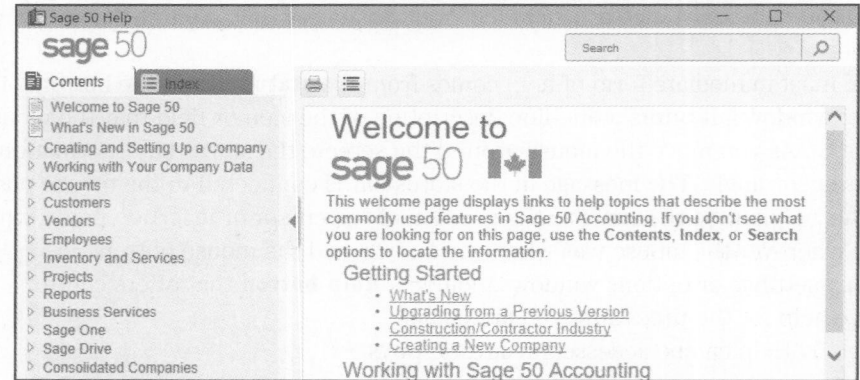

The Help Welcome screen opens with the **Contents tab** 📄 Contents list of topics and links to several introductory topics and sources of assistance in the information pane.

Close   the **Help window**. **Choose** the **Help menu**, **click** the **Search field** and **type** payments **Press** (enter):

NOTES
If a topic has subtopics, it will have a book icon or arrow; then you must choose a subtopic with the question or page icon to display the help information. If there are still multiple entries, there will be an additional book icon or arrow and you can choose from the list that Sage 50 offers at this stage.

The Help window now has access to subjects that match your entry.

Click   the **Index tab** 📄 Index .

The navigation pane now has an alphabetic list of topics. Payments is a major topic with subtopics, so the contents of the information pane have not changed.

Major topics are marked with an arrow ▷ . As soon as you click a subtopic below payments, the information pane will have details about that topic.

Click   the **Search Index field** and **type** payments:

NOTES
Subtopics on this screen do not have an arrow or page icon beside them.

The navigation pane now has a different alphabetic list of topics related to payments — many have subtopics. As soon as you click a subtopic, the information pane will have details about that topic.

Close   the **Help window**. The next section describes the same Help features without Internet access.

Close   your **Internet connection** for the next group of screenshots.

Choose the **Help menu** and **click** 🔍 in the **Search field**:

Without online help selected, the **Search tab** is the starting point and the information pane is on the right, as before. Initially, the topic fields will be blank. The tool bar is different in the two methods. Both include the Print icon. The remaining icons — for Hide, Back, Forward, Font, Home and Options — are all missing in online help windows. The online version has the **Expand All** tool ▤; the **Search field** [Search 🔍] replaces the Search tab.

The Search tab has a field for entering the terms you want to search for.

Type   a **keyword** in the text box below Type In The Keyword To Find.

Click   **List Topics** to see an alphabetic list of entries containing the keyword.

Click   the **entry** you want.

Click   the **Display button** to view the information you need.

Close   the **Help window**. **Choose** the **Help menu**, **click** the **Search field**, **type** payments and **press** (enter):

When you enter a search term in the Help menu Search field, the Index tab screen opens with the alphabetic list of topics, beginning with the term you typed. As soon as you choose a subtopic under Payments, the contents of the information pane will change.

Scroll down and **click Making To Vendors**. **Click Display** to learn about this topic:

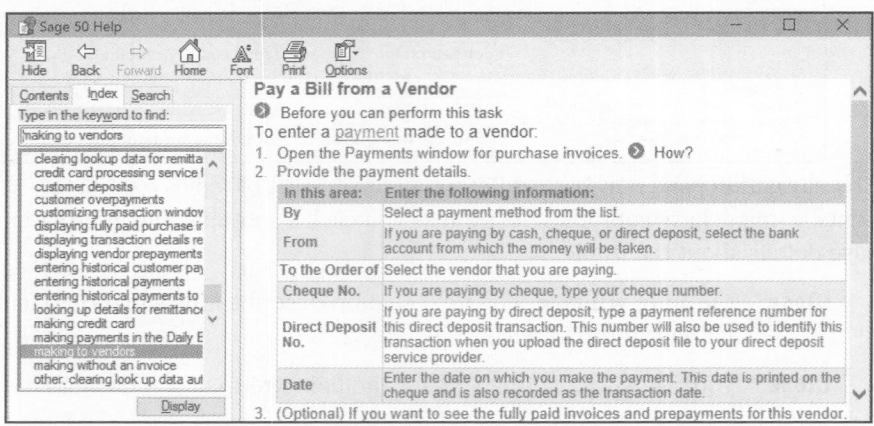

Click   the **Contents tab** in the Options pane to open a list of topics in the left-hand side options or navigation pane:

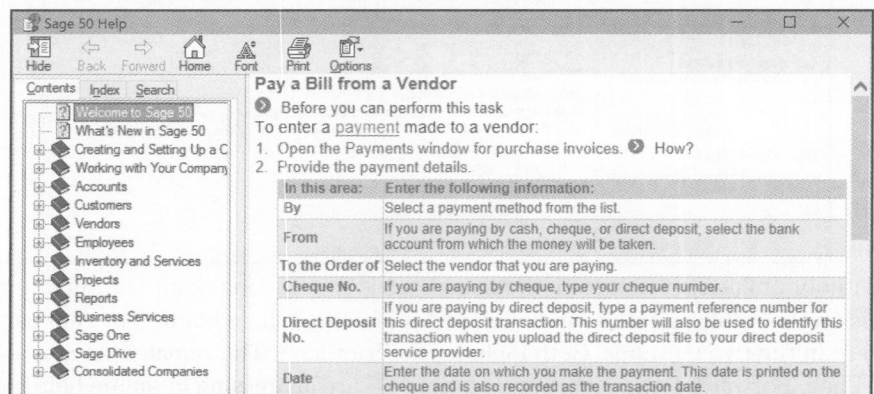

As before, until you choose a different subtopic, the contents of the information pane do not change.

Although the two approaches provide the same help information, the icons are different. **Expand All** — the second online tool 🔲 — expands all topics in the information pane, which serves the same function as 🔘 .

Without online help, the window may include a Show All option.

Icons in the left-hand side contents pane also look different with and without online help. Major topics in the Contents menu have a **book icon** 📖 beside them (or an **arrow icon** ▷ in the online version).

Click   **Vendors** or click 📖 (or ⊞ or ▷ in the online help version) beside Vendors in the Table of Contents pane to open a list of subtopics.

When a topic has a **question icon** ❓ (or a page icon 📄 in the online version) beside it, there is detailed help on that subject. Click a topic or the question icon to display information on that subject in the right-hand side information display pane of the Help window.

The book icon beside Vendors has changed to an **open book** icon 📖 ; in the online version, the arrow is removed or changed to ◢ . The second list of topics has both question (or page) icons for the detail level and book (or arrow) icons that indicate another level of subtopics.

Clicking a circled arrow 🔘 beside a heading in the information pane — like the ones before How? and Before You Can Perform This Task on this page — will expand the list of

NOTES

The information from your previous search always remains on display until you choose to display another topic.

topics. Clicking the **Expand All tool** ▤ in the online version will give the details for both at the same time. Clicking an underlined subtopic will open detailed information for that topic.

> Click a book title (or 📖) to close the book and hide the list of subtopics.

> **Click** Purchases and **click** 📕 or ▷ to view the second list of subtopics.

> **Click** Purchase Orders and **click** 📕 or ▷ to view the next list of subtopics.

> **Scroll down** and **click Entering A Purchase Order** (with ❓ or 🗐 beside it):

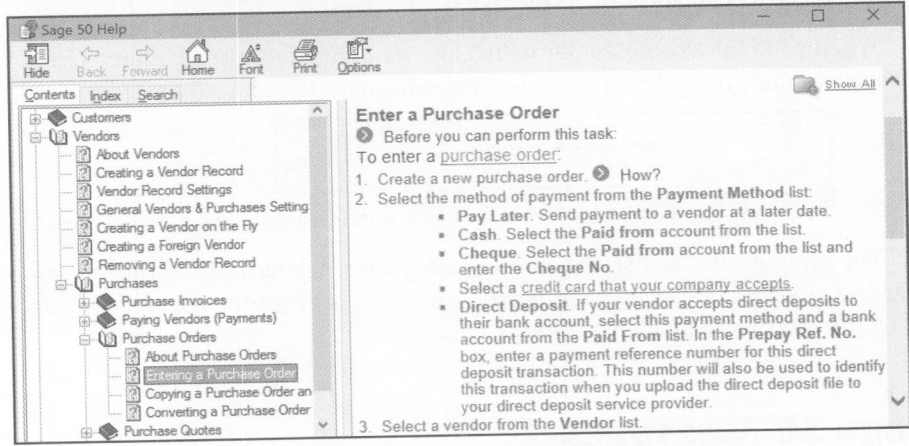

> **Search** for **information** on other topics in the different option screens.

> **Close** the **Help windows** when finished. **Click Receivables** in the Modules pane.

Sage 50 Advice

Sage 50 also includes **Advice** on a number of topics.

> **Choose** the **Business Assistant menu**, then **click Business Advice** and **All Modules**:

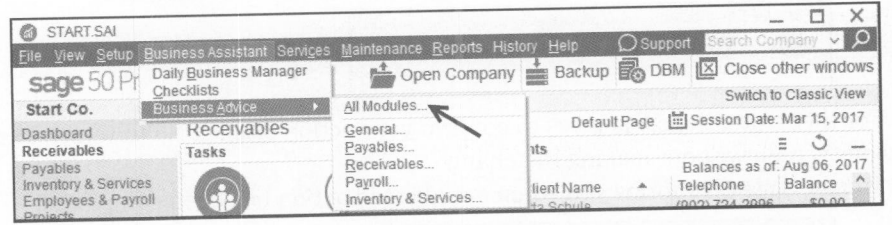

A list of topics opens:

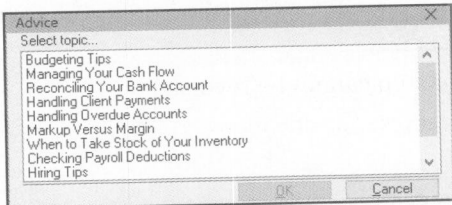

These topics provide general business information or accounting practices.

> **Click** the **topic** you want and then **click OK**. **Close** the **advice report windows** when finished.

A final source of general assistance is available as **automatic advice**. This feature can be turned off from the Setup menu — User Preferences, View options, in the Home

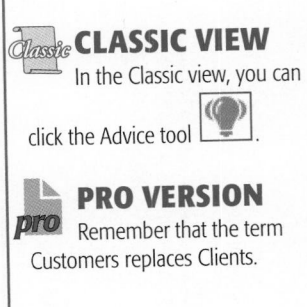

CLASSIC VIEW
In the Classic view, you can click the Advice tool 💡.

PRO VERSION
Remember that the term Customers replaces Clients.

window (refer to page 81) — if it is not needed. We recommend leaving it on. When it is turned on, Sage 50 will provide important warning statements.

For example, for a customer who has exceeded the credit limit, the related Advisor warning will open:

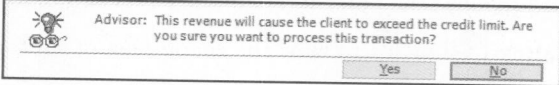

To proceed, you must make a decision in order to close the advice screen. In this case, you can click Yes to proceed with the sale or No to return to the invoice and make a change (perhaps by asking for a deposit).

When you choose a customer with a history of making late payments (Irma Vanitee in this data file), the Advisor provides that information:

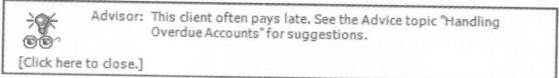

To close this message, click the Advisor icon as indicated [Click Here To Close].

The program also advises when year-end is approaching and it is time to complete year-end adjustments, when your chequing account is overdrawn or when inventory items reach the reorder point.

NOTES

If you try to post a pay-later sale (client invoice) for any of the listed customers for $10 000, you will get the message about credit limits.

If you try to enter a sale to Irma Vanitee, you will get the message about the customer who pays late.

Sage 50 Messages

Sage 50 provides a number of different messages when you are working with the program. Some messages serve as warnings that you have made an error:

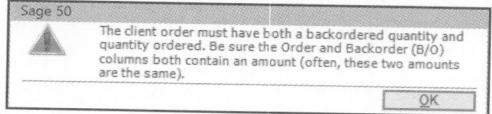

In this case, click OK to return to your previous screen and make the necessary corrections.

Sage 50 also asks you to confirm decisions that cannot be reversed:

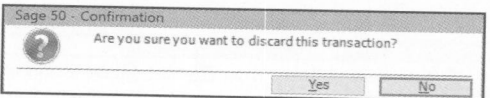

For these situations, click Yes to confirm your action or click No to return to the previous screen without making the change.

Finally, Sage 50 informs you when a requested action has been completed:

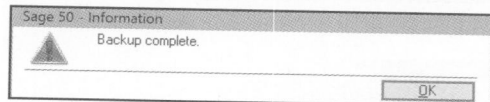

Click OK to continue — the completed step cannot be reversed.

Date Formats and Settings

Before closing the program we will review date format settings. Date accuracy is very important because dates are used for discounts, payment terms and many reports.

Sage 50 has date format control settings within each file that are independent of the display date settings for Windows. When you enter dates using a series of two digits for month, day and year, it is important to know how these will be interpreted. For example,

when you type 12-06-05, this date may be June 12, December 6 or June 5 in the year 2005, 1905, 1912 or 2012, depending on whether month, day or year comes first and whether your computer defaults to 1900 dates or is preset for 2000 dates.

Fortunately, Sage 50 allows you to enter and display dates as text. Thus, you can type June 5, 2012, in a date field. And if you want, you can display this date as Jun 05, 2012, even if you enter numbers in the date field. Sage 50 uses three letters to display the month when the text option is selected.

All date fields also have a **Calendar icon** 📅 that you can click to access a month-by-month calendar from which you can select a date. These two options will help you avoid making date errors from incorrect orders. To access the date settings,

Click   the **Settings icon** ⚙ in the Related Tasks pane, or **choose** the **Setup menu**, then **click Settings**. **Click Company** in the list of modules on the left to open the main Company Settings window.

Each entry in the list opens the Settings screen for a different part of the program.

Click   **Date Format** to open the Settings window for dates:

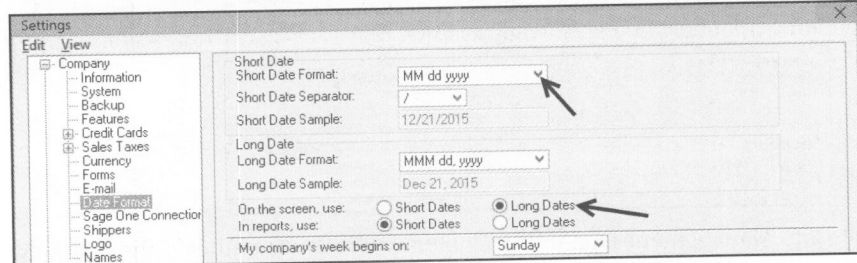

Each field has a drop-down list of format options. The **Short Date Format** uses two digits each for month and day. For the year, you can choose two or four digits. You can begin the date with month, day or year — the Short Date Format illustrates which comes first. The **Short Date Separator** character may be a slash, dash or period. This is the character that will appear on the screen regardless of how you entered the date. The sample illustrates the appearance for the current date from your selections.

The **Long Date Format** displays the month as a three-letter text abbreviation. Either the month or the day can be the first character in the long date style. The sample has the current date with your selected format.

The next section allows you to select the short or long date styles for your screen and reports. You can select different date styles for your reports and screen displays.

We will use the long date format settings on screen for all files to avoid any confusion about dates when the numeric entry might be ambiguous. For reports you can use long or short date formats. For the files we provided in the data set, the month-day-year order is already selected for short and long formats.

To change the date format settings,

Click   the **Short Date Format field list arrow** for the format options.

Click   **MM dd yyyy**. Be sure that Month (MM) is the first part of the entry.

Click   the **Long Date Format field list arrow** to view the format options.

Click   **MMM dd, yyyy**.

Click   **Long Dates** beside the option On The Screen, Use. **Click OK** to save the settings.

NOTES

Sage 50 allows you to enter earlier session dates but warns you first. If you have advanced the date incorrectly, you can reverse the decision as long as you have not advanced to a new fiscal year. Warnings are also given when you advance the date by more than one week or when you try to advance to a new fiscal period. These warnings should serve as signals that you may have made a mistake.

CLASSIC VIEW

Right-click the Chart of Accounts icon and then click the Settings tool icon ⚙ to open the General Settings window. Click Company.

NOTES

When you click the ⊞ beside Company, the list expands beneath the heading. You can click Date Format in either list to open the Date Format Settings window.

Company settings are described in detail in Chapters 4 and 7.

NOTES

Sage 50 displays only the first three letters of a month when you choose the long or text date format (entered as MMM in the selection list). Therefore, Oct is displayed for October; Jun will be displayed for June, and so on.

NOTES

Showing a four-digit year will ensure that you know whether you are using 1900 or 2000 year dates.

A final date option allows you to indicate the normal first weekday for the business.

Saving and Backing Up Your Work

Sage 50 saves your work automatically when you are working with the program. For example, when you post a journal entry or when you display or print reports, Sage 50 writes all the journal transactions to your file to compile the report you want. When you exit from the program properly, Sage 50 also saves all your work.

On a regular basis, you should also make a backup copy of your files. The Backup command is described in detail in Chapter 3.

Making Backups from the Data Management Icon

PRO VERSION
The Pro version does not have the option to consolidate companies.

Close   any other open **windows**. (**Click** the **Close Other Windows tool** .)

Click   **Company** in the Modules pane.

Click   the **Data Management icon shortcuts list arrow**:

NOTES
Refer to page 49 for more information about the Backup wizard.

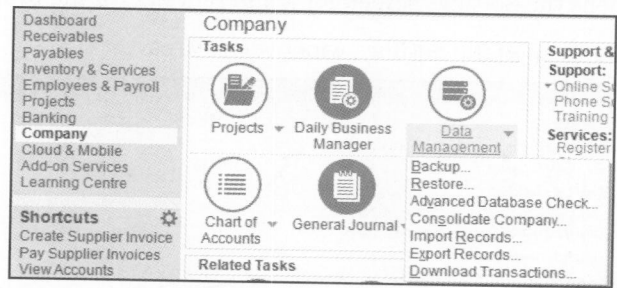

The Data Management icon in the Company window includes a shortcuts menu with options to back up and to restore a data file. It also has direct access to other functions, including exporting and importing records (covered in Appendix J on the Student DVD), checking your database for inconsistencies and fixing them if they are minor, and consolidating data from multiple companies.

Click   the **Data Management icon** to start the Backup wizard, or **click Backup** on the icon's shortcuts list.

You can also start the backup procedure from any Home window.

Click   the **Backup tool** or **choose** the **File menu** and **click Backup** to start the Backup wizard.

The wizard will create a separate backup folder inside your current working folder so that the backup will remain separate from your working copy.

NOTES
You may want to use the Save A Copy or Save As command when you are unsure how a journal entry will be posted and you want to experiment with different methods of entering the same transactions.

Saving a Copy of Your Data File

While **Backup** creates compressed copies of the files that must be restored with the Restore command before you can use them, the next two options create new complete working copies of your data files that can be opened directly. Both save the file under a different file name so that you will have two working copies of the files — the original and the copy. You can create backups on a CD but not on a DVD with the Backup command.

Save As makes a copy, closes the original file and lets you continue to work with the new copy. Because the new file becomes your working file, you can use Save As to copy to any medium that you can also work from in Sage 50 — your hard drive or a removable memory stick or flash drive, but not a CD. **Save A Copy** makes a copy of the file and then allows you to continue working with the original file. You can use Save A Copy to save your files to a CD (but not to a DVD). You must copy the CD files back to your hard drive, and you may need to remove the read-only property before working with these files.

NOTES
If you need to remove the read-only property, right-click the file name or icon in the Computer window and choose Properties from the pop-up menu. Click Read-Only to remove the ✓.

Because the data files are very large, we recommend using the Backup procedure described in Chapter 3 rather than Save As or Save A Copy for regular backups.

Choose the **File menu** and **click Save A Copy** to open the file name window.

You can save the copy in the same folder as the original by entering a different file name or, if you want to use the same name, you must use a different folder. We recommend using different folders.

Click   a **different folder in the file path** to change folders.

Double-click   a **folder** in the name and folders pane to open it.

To create a new folder inside the one that you have open,

Click   **New Folder** (in the tool bar). **Click Browse Folders** first if necessary to reveal the New Folder option. **Type** a **new name** to replace New Folder, the selected text. **Click** the **folder's icon** or **name** to select it. **Click Open**.

Double-click   the file name **NEW** or **NEW.SAI** if you show file extensions.

Type   the **new file name**. **Click Save**. You will return to your original file and you can continue working.

To save the file under a different name and work with the new file, use **Save As**.

Choose the **File menu** and **click Save As** to open the file name window.

The remaining steps are the same as Save A Copy. Change folders, create a new folder, rename the folder, open the new folder, type a file name for the copy and click Save. Remember to return to your original working copy before entering any transactions if you use the Save As command.

You can also back up all your data files at the same time by using Windows (in the Windows Explorer or Computer windows) Copy and Paste commands. In this way, you can save the files to a different folder on your hard drive or on a CD.

Finishing a Session

Choose the **open window Control Menu icon** and **click Close** or **click** ☒ to close the journal input form or display window you are working in.

Click   the **Close Other Windows tool** ☒ if you have several windows open. You will return to the main Home window.

Choose the **Sage 50 Control Menu icon** 🏠 and **click Close**, or **click** ☒ or **choose** the **File menu** and **click Exit** to close the Home window. The backup prompt will open:

For this practice file, you do not need to create a separate backup file.

Click   **No** to close the backup prompt. Your work will be saved again automatically when you complete this step. You should now be in the Windows desktop.

NOTES
You can also use the Windows Copy command to make CD copies of your data, but you must close the Sage 50 data file before you start to copy. Remember to copy the data folders when you copy from Windows to ensure that you keep all necessary files (the .SAI file and the SAJ folder) together.

You must use a DVD-writing program to copy your data files to a DVD.

You cannot open the data files from the CD or DVD. You must first copy them back to your hard drive and you may need to remove the read-only property.

NOTES
All our data files are set up with the option to prompt you to back up the company data when you close the file.

Opening a Data File from a Backup

Double-click 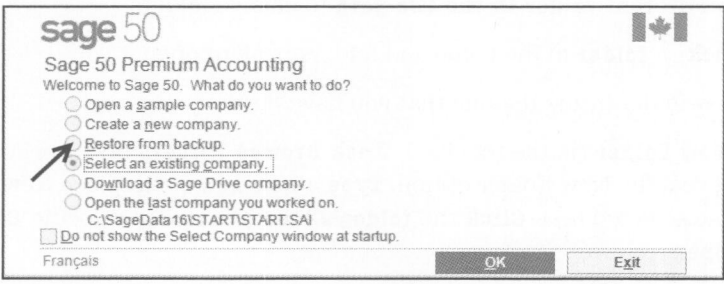, the desktop icon, or the **Sage 50 program** button on the Start window to open the Welcome and Select Company window.

This is the same opening window as on page 8:

This is the same opening window as on page 8:

sage 50

Sage 50 Premium Accounting
Welcome to Sage 50. What do you want to do?
- ○ Open a sample company.
- ○ Create a new company.
- ○ Restore from backup.
- ⊙ Select an existing company.
- ○ Download a Sage Drive company.
- ○ Open the last company you worked on.
  C:\SageData16\START\START.SAI
- ☐ Do not show the Select Company window at startup.

Français   OK   Exit

The opening window gives you several options: working with the sample company files, creating new company files, restoring backup files or working with existing data files. If you have worked with the program before, the option to **Open The Last Company You Worked On** appears with the name of the file you used most recently, as in our example. We need to restore a backup file.

If your working files are lost or damaged, you will also need to restore backup files. You can also restore files from the Home window File menu of any data file, including the Sample Company file, or from the Company window Data Management shortcuts list.

Click   **Restore From Backup**.

Click   **OK** to start the Sage 50 Restore From Backup wizard:

Restore from Backup

Use the Restore wizard to restore files that have been saved with the Backup command on the File menu.
If you saved your backup on a disc, insert it into the appropriate drive now. If you saved the backup on any portable media device, such as a flash drive or external hard drive, plug it into your computer now. If you have saved the backup on a network location, ensure you can connect to that folder.

< Back   Next >   Cancel

Click   **Next** to begin:

Select Backup File

There are no backup files at your last backup folder:
C:\SAGEDATA16\START\Backup
Click Browse to select a backup file from a different folder (directory).
Select a backup file
[   ]   Browse...
Scheduled Backup Files Found
[   ]

< Back   Next >   Cancel

The first time you restore a backup, no default location or backup files are entered.

Click   **Browse** to open the folder you worked in most recently.

The folder names in your Select field and Browse windows may be different from ours. Sage 50 uses a folder under Libraries\Documents as the default location for files so you may have this as the selected folder initially. If you have opened another data file, the folder where that file is stored may be entered. To ensure consistency in file names and locations for our instructions, we always work with the folder we created when installing the data files, that is, C:\SageData16.

Click   **This PC** in the path field at the top of the screen or in the left pane list of links, drives and folders. All your computer drives will be listed:

NOTES
The first time you start the program, the option to Open The Last Company You Worked On will not be included. Refer to the Welcome and Select Company screen on page 8.

NOTES
You can start the Restore wizard from any open Sage 50 data file. From any Home window, choose the File menu and click Restore to start the Restore wizard.
Or, from the Company module window, start the wizard from the Data Management icon shortcuts list. Click the icon's list arrow and choose Restore (refer to page 22).

NOTES
By default, Sage 50 assumes that backup files are in a Backup folder within the folder you recently used.

Double-click OS(C:) to list the files and folders in this drive:

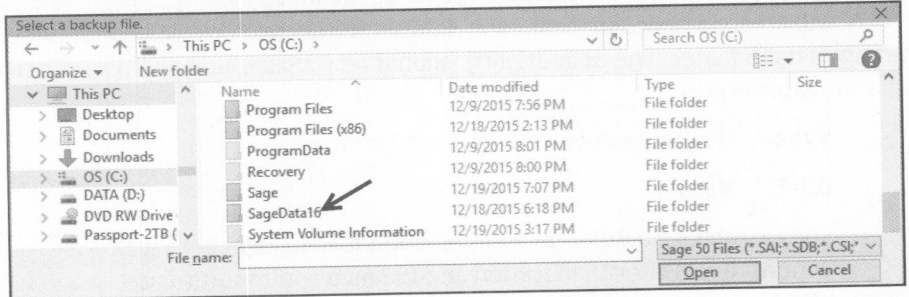

Click   SageData16 to select it, or click the SageData16 folder icon 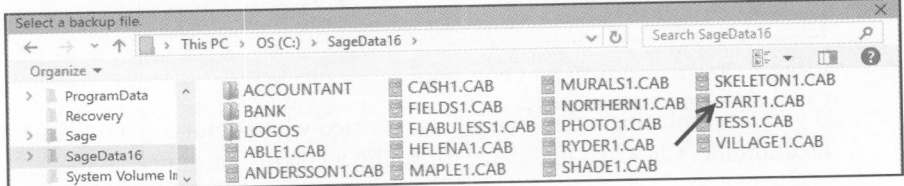 .

Click   Open to list the files you copied from the Student DVD:

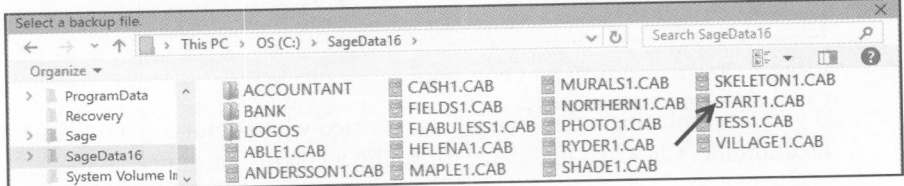

Only Sage 50 format backup files and folders are listed because we are working with the Restore Backup wizard.

Click   START1.CAB to select it or click the START1.CAB icon [START1.CAB] if you are in icon view. (Click **START1** if you are not showing file extensions.) START1 is added to the File Name field.

Click   Open. You will return to the wizard with your backup files listed in the Select A Backup File text box and START1.CAB selected:

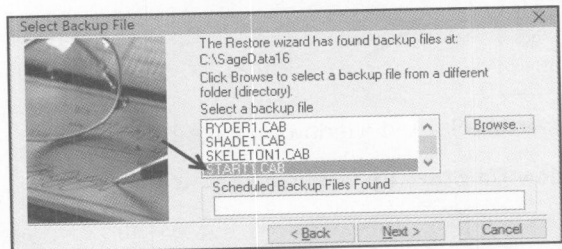

Click   Next to continue. The screen will have the selections you have made:

NOTES
Your screens may look different if you have selected different viewing options such as displaying the folders as lists or icons. The viewing options can be changed from the Views icon drop-down menu.

NOTES
We use the default location for the data files from the automatic installation. If you installed the files to a different location, choose the drive and folder for your setup.

PRO VERSION
pro The first backup file listed is ANDERSSON1.CAB — you will not have entries for ABLE and RYDER.

WARNING!
If you are not showing file extensions, click START1. The file name has a filing cabinet icon beside it [icon] (like the ones on this page).

NOTES
The dates on this screen may be entered with the day before the month — the format may be controlled by your Windows settings.

NOTES
The original name and location — the ones we used to create the initial backup file — will be the default ones used when you restore a backup. The default for the restored file will be C:\SageData16\START\START.SAI.

If the information is incorrect, click Back to return to the file selection screen.

Click **Next** to continue if the information is correct:

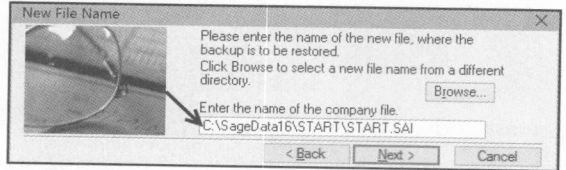

At this stage, you should enter the name of the file you are restoring. If you have created the backup from your own file, the name and location of the original file from which you created the backup are entered as the default.

We will create a new folder for each data set in this text. We will continue to work in the SageData16 folder. The default entry should be C:\SageData16\START\START. If a different name is entered,

Type C:\SageData16\START\START

Click **Next**.

You can choose a different location and file name by clicking Browse to access your folders. Enter the location and file name you want to use.

Sage 50 asks for confirmation because you are using folder and file names that are new. Sage 50 will create the new folders and files for you:

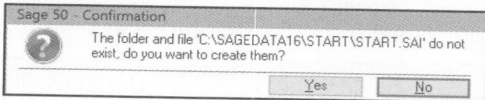

Click **Yes** to confirm and continue.

If you are replacing a file, you will be warned when you type the file name and location file. Click Yes if you are replacing a corrupt or unusable file.

Sage 50 now has all the data required to complete the restore process:

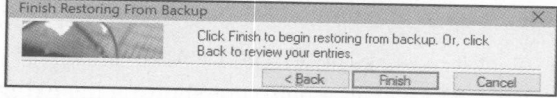

This is your last chance to change information by clicking Back.

Click **Finish** to begin restoring the file. The next screen prompts you to enter the session date:

Click **OK** to open the Getting Started window on page 10.

Click **Show This Window On Start Up** to remove the ✓.

R E V I E W

The Student DVD with Data Files includes Review Questions for this chapter.

GST, HST and PST

After completing
this chapter, you
should be able to

OBJECTIVES

- ***understand*** the terms relevant to the federal Goods and Services Tax
- ***understand*** the different methods of calculating the GST
- ***understand*** Harmonized Sales Tax in relation to GST
- ***understand*** how to file for GST or HST remittances or refunds
- ***understand*** other provincial sales taxes in relation to GST

GENERAL TAX INFORMATION

Definition of Goods and Services Tax: GST

The Goods and Services Tax (GST) is levied by the federal government at the rate of 5 percent on most goods and services in Canada. Retailers pay the GST to their wholesalers and vendors but are allowed to deduct any GST they pay from the GST they collect from customers. Retailers remit the difference, GST owing, to the Receiver General for Canada or claim a refund with monthly or quarterly returns.

GST Registration   Any business with annual sales exceeding $30 000 per year must register for GST collection and must collect GST on all applicable sales. Registration is optional for most smaller businesses. Businesses that are not registered for GST do not charge GST on sales to their customers, but they also cannot recover the GST they pay on business-related purchases.

Collecting the GST   The business must collect GST for those goods and services sold that are not zero rated or tax exempt. The business must remit GST at regular intervals, filing GST returns monthly, quarterly or annually and paying instalments, depending on annual income and GST owing.

Zero Rated Goods and Services   Zero rated goods and services are those on which the tax rate is zero. These goods include basic groceries, prescribed medical devices, prescribed drugs, exported goods and services, agricultural products and fish products. A business selling only zero rated goods and services does not collect GST on sales, but it can still claim a refund for GST it pays for purchases.

> **NOTES**
> Provinces may or may not include GST in the price on which they calculate Provincial Sales Tax (PST). Provincial tax rates vary from province to province. See pages 30 and 32.

> **NOTES**
> GST collected on sales is reduced by the GST on sales returns.

Tax Exempt Goods and Services   Tax exempt goods and services are those on which tax is not collected. These goods and services include health care, dental care, daycare services and rent on personal residences. Most educational and financial services are also included in this group. These businesses are not able to claim refunds for GST paid for business purchases related to selling tax exempt goods and services.

Paying the GST   A business must pay GST for purchases made for business purposes, unless the goods or services purchased are zero rated or tax exempt. The business can use the GST paid as an input tax credit by subtracting the amount of GST paid from the amount of GST collected and remitting GST owing or claiming a refund. GST amounts paid on purchases for personal use do not qualify as input tax credits.

Bank and Financial Institution Services   Most bank products and services are not taxable. Exceptions include safety deposit box rentals, custodial and safekeeping services, personalized cheques, self-administered registered savings plan fees, payroll services, rentals of night depository, rentals of credit card imprinters and reconciliation of cheques. Banks remit the full amount of GST they collect from customers. Because most bank services are not taxable, banks cannot claim input tax credits for GST they pay on business-related purchases.

GST on Imported and Exported Goods   GST is not charged on exported goods. Customers in other countries who import goods from Canada do not pay GST. However, businesses in Canada must pay GST on the items they import or purchase from other countries. The GST is collected by the Canada Revenue Agency (CRA) when the goods enter Canada based on the purchase price (plus import duty) and current exchange rates. Businesses must pay this GST and other import duties before the goods are released to them.

Administering the GST

The federal government has approved different methods of administering the GST; the regular method is most commonly used.

The Regular Method

The regular method of administering the GST requires the business to keep track of GST paid for all goods and services purchased from vendors (less returns) and of GST collected for all goods and services sold to customers (less returns). It then deducts the GST paid from the GST collected and files for a refund or remits the balance owing to the Receiver General on a monthly or quarterly basis.

Accounting Examples Using the Regular Method (without PST)

SALES INVOICE Sold goods to customer for $200 plus $10 GST collected (5%). Invoice total, $210.

Date	Particulars	Debit	Credit
02/15	Accounts Receivable	210.00	
	GST Charged on Sales		10.00
	Revenue from Sales		200.00

PURCHASE INVOICE Purchased supplies from vendor for $300 plus $15 GST paid (5%). Invoice total, $315.

Date	Particulars	Debit	Credit
02/15	Supplies	300.00	
	GST Paid on Purchases	15.00	
	Accounts Payable		315.00

The GST owing is further reduced by any GST adjustments — for example, GST that applies to bad debts that are written off. If the debt is later recovered, the GST liability is also restored as an input tax credit adjustment.

Other Methods of Calculating GST

Certain small businesses may be eligible to use simpler methods of calculating their GST refunds and remittances that do not require them to keep a separate record for GST on each individual purchase or sale. The simplified accounting method, the streamlined accounting method and the quick method are examples of these alternatives.

Calculating GST Refunds or Remittances

The following example uses the regular method for a retailer who is filing quarterly:

Quarterly Total Sales (excluding GST)	$50 000.00	
Quarterly Total Qualifying Purchases	29 700.00	
5% GST Charged on Sales		$2 500.00
Less: 5% GST Paid on Purchases		
Cash Register (cost $1 000)	50.00	
Inventory (cost $25 000)	1 250.00	
Supplies (cost $500)	25.00	
Payroll Services (cost $200)	10.00	
Store Lease (cost $3 000)	150.00	
Total GST Paid		− 1 485.00
GST Remittance		$1 015.00

GST Remittances and Refunds

The business must file returns that summarize the amount of GST it has collected and the amount of GST it has paid. The CRA may require reports monthly, quarterly or yearly, depending on total sales. Yearly reports usually require quarterly instalments.

GST Collected on Sales	>	GST Paid on Purchases	=	GST Owing
GST Collected on Sales	<	GST Paid on Purchases	=	GST Refund

Accounting Examples for Remittances

Usually a business will make GST remittances because sales usually exceed expenses — the business operates at a profit. The following example shows how the GST accounts are cleared and a liability (*Accounts Payable*) is set up to remit GST owing to the Receiver General for Canada. In this case, the usual one, the Receiver General becomes a vendor for the business so that the liability can be entered and the payment made.

Date	Particulars	Debit	Credit
03/31	GST Charged on Sales	2 500.00	
	GST Paid on Purchases		1 485.00
	A/P - Receiver General		1 015.00
03/31	A/P - Receiver General	1 015.00	
	Chequing Bank Account		1 015.00

NOTES
Under the quick method, the GST remittance or refund amount is based on a flat-rate percentage of total sales, including GST. The remittance rate varies for different types of businesses. GST paid on purchases of capital is an input tax credit to reduce the amount owing (or increase the refund).
These alternative methods of calculating GST are not used in the applications in this workbook.

NOTES
The rules concerning the GST may change periodically, as in the 2006 federal budget when the rate changed from 7 percent to 6 percent. In the 2007 budget, the rate was reduced again to 5 percent. Always refer to current guidelines.

Accounting Examples for Refunds

The example below shows how the GST accounts are cleared and a current asset account (*Accounts Receivable*) is set up for a GST refund from the Receiver General for Canada. In this case, the Receiver General owes money to the business; that is, it acts like a customer, so a customer record is set up to record and collect the refund.

Date	Particulars	Debit	Credit
03/31	GST Charged on Sales	1 500.00	
	A/R - Receiver General	500.00	
	GST Paid on Purchases		2 000.00
04/15	Chequing Bank Account	500.00	
	A/R - Receiver General		500.00

Harmonized Sales Tax: HST

Five provinces have adopted the Harmonized Sales Tax (HST) method of taxing goods and services: Prince Edward Island, Ontario, New Brunswick, Nova Scotia and Newfoundland and Labrador. When HST applies, the GST and provincial taxes are harmonized at a single rate. In all provinces, 5 percent of the HST rate is the federal portion, or GST, while the remainder is the provincial portion. Provincial retail sales tax rates vary from one province to another, so the HST rates also vary. In Prince Edward Island, the HST rate is 14 percent (9 percent provincial); in Ontario, New Brunswick and Newfoundland and Labrador, the HST rate in 2016 is 13 percent (8 percent provincial); and in Nova Scotia the rate is 15 percent (10 percent provincial). The HST replaces the separate GST and PST, and unlike those separate taxes, it is administered entirely at the federal level. This removes some administrative work both from the provincial Ministries of Finance and from the businesses that charge taxes to their customers. They have only one tax to calculate and remit.

The full 13, 14 or 15 percent Harmonized Sales Tax operates much like the basic GST: HST is applied at each level of sale and resale, and manufacturing; has the same business registration requirement of annual sales exceeding $30 000; is applied to the same base of goods and services; and is collected in the same way. HST returns and remittances are also calculated in the same way as GST returns and remittances. The business remits any excess of HST collected over HST paid for its business expenses, or claims a refund when HST paid exceeds the HST collected from customers.

The following example illustrates the application in Ontario (or New Brunswick or Newfoundland and Labrador), where the HST rate is 13 percent:

> **Ontario** business sold goods on account for $565, including $500 base price and HST at 13% ($65).
>
> HST = (0.13 × 500) = $65
> Total amount of invoice = $565

Date	Particulars	Debit	Credit
02/15	Accounts Receivable	565.00	
	HST Charged on Sales		65.00
	Revenue from Sales		500.00

A single remittance for the full 13 percent is made to the Receiver General; the provincial portion of the HST is not tracked or collected separately by the business.

> **NOTES**
> Prices shown to customers may have the HST included (tax-inclusive pricing), but they must show either the amount of HST included in the price or the HST rate. Most retailers show prices before taxes are included.

The following examples show the journal entries for an HST remittance and an HST refund:

Remittance: A **New Brunswick** business calculates and pays HST owing

For Sales of $50 000 plus 13% HST; qualifying purchases of $30 000 plus 13% HST

Date	Particulars	Debit	Credit
03/31	HST Charged on Sales	6 500.00	
	A/P - Receiver General		2 600.00
	HST Paid on Purchases		3 900.00
04/15	A/P - Receiver General	2 600.00	
	Chequing Bank Account		2 600.00

Refund: A **New Brunswick** business qualifies and applies for an HST refund

For Sales of $30 000 plus 13% HST; qualifying purchases of $42 000 plus 13% HST

Date	Particulars	Debit	Credit
03/31	HST Charged on Sales	3 900.00	
	A/R - Receiver General	1 560.00	
	HST Paid on Purchases		5 460.00
04/15	Chequing Bank Account	1 560.00	
	A/R - Receiver General		1 560.00

Goods and Services Exempt for HST

Under the HST method, all items that are exempt for GST or are zero rated are also exempt for HST or are zero rated for HST. In addition, each province has decided that some items will be exempt for HST and subject only to GST. For example, books and children's clothing are exempt for HST but not for GST. For these goods, the customer pays only the 5 percent GST portion of the tax. At the retail level, for these special items a separate tax code for GST only is applied. When the business files its HST return, it will remit the HST collected plus the GST collected less the amounts of GST plus HST paid on qualifying business-related purchases on a single return.

The following example shows these calculations for a bookseller who also sells music CDs in Nova Scotia. HST at the rate of 15 percent (including a provincial portion of 10 percent) applies to the sale of CDs, while GST at the rate of 5 percent applies to the sale of books.

Quarterly Total Sales (excluding taxes)	$92 000	
Quarterly Total Qualifying Purchases (excluding taxes)	$52 000	
HST Charged on Sales (15% × 41 000)	$6 150	
GST Charged on Sales (5% × 51 000)	2 550	
Total GST/HST collected		$8 700
Less: GST Paid on Purchase of books for resale (5% × 21 000)	1 050	
HST Paid on other Purchases (15% × 31 000)	4 650	
Total HST Credits		−5 700
HST Remittance		$3 000

NOTES
The quick method may also be used by small businesses registered for HST, and it operates in the same way as for GST alone.

NOTES
Instead of applying different tax rates, retailers who sell PST exempt goods may also charge the full HST rate but provide an immediate point-of-sale rebate to the customer for the provincial portion. They will then claim an adjustment for the rebate amount on their HST return to reduce the amount remitted.

The net effect of the two methods is the same for the customer and for the merchant.

GST and Provincial (Retail) Sales Taxes

The rules governing provincial sales taxes vary from province to province in terms of the tax rate, the goods and services that are taxed and whether Provincial Sales Tax (PST) is applied to the GST as well as to the base purchase price (that is, whether GST is taxable). In May 2016, no provinces charged PST on GST. The following examples assume that the item sold has both GST and PST applied.

Although GST is applied at each level of sale and resale (including the stages of manufacturing), PST is a retail sales tax and, therefore, is paid only by the final consumer of a product or service. Therefore, it is generally referred to as a Retail Sales Tax by the provincial governments, and the terms RST and PST are equivalent. Thus, a business purchasing inventory to sell to customers will not pay PST on these purchases. When the same business buys supplies or services for its use in conducting business, it must pay PST because it has become the final consumer of these goods or services.

PST applies only to sales within a province, not to sales to customers in a different province or in a different country. HST and GST do apply to interprovincial sales. If the consumer's province applies HST, the consumer pays HST on purchases from other provinces. All consumers in Canada pay GST.

Alberta, the Northwest Territories, Yukon and Nunavut

Alberta, the Northwest Territories, Yukon and Nunavut do not have Provincial Sales Taxes. Customers in these regions pay only the 5 percent GST on their purchases. Thus, the examples provided earlier without PST illustrate the application of GST for these regions.

PST in Manitoba, Saskatchewan, British Columbia and Quebec

These four provinces apply PST to the base price of the sale, the amount without GST included. In Manitoba and British Columbia, the retail sales tax rate is 8 percent; in Saskatchewan, the rate is 5 percent; in Quebec, the rate is 9.975 percent. The following example illustrates the application in Manitoba:

Manitoba business sold goods on account for $500. GST charged is 5% and PST charged is 8%.

GST = (0.05 × 500) = $25
PST in Manitoba = (0.08 × 500) = $40
Total amount of invoice = $500 + $25 + $40 = $565

Date	Particulars	Debit	Credit
02/15	Accounts Receivable	565.00	
	GST Charged on Sales		25.00
	PST Payable		40.00
	Revenue from Sales		500.00

The full amount of PST collected on sales is remitted to the provincial Minister of Finance (less any applicable sales tax compensation).

Part 2
Applications

Muriel's Murals

**After completing
this chapter, you
should be able to**

OBJECTIVES

- *access* the data files for the business
- *open* the General Journal
- *enter* transactions in the General Journal
- *edit* and *review* General Journal transactions
- *post* transactions
- *create* new General Ledger accounts
- *adjust* journal entries after posting
- *display* and *print* General Ledger and General Journal reports
- *display* and *print* comparative financial reports
- *customize* reports
- *back up* your data files
- *advance* the session date
- *finish* an accounting session

COMPANY INFORMATION

Company Profile

NOTES
Muriel's Murals
66 Collage Avenue
Edmonton, AB T4P 4C2
Tel 1: (780) 763-4127
Tel 2: (800) 455-4127
Fax: (780) 765-4842
Business No.: 743 647 397

Muriel's Murals is owned and operated by Muriel Missoni in Edmonton, Alberta. She shares studio space with her sister Maria, owner of Missoni Marbleworks. While studying art and interior design at university and community college, Missoni learned that she enjoys the physical aspects of art as well as the creative parts. Therefore, she started her own business as an interior painter specializing in unique wall textures, collages and murals for private homes and public places. For customers who want three-dimensional wall friezes, she collaborates with Maria, her sister the sculptor, who creates moulds for plaster appliques based on Muriel's drawings. Muriel applies and paints the plaster friezes. Her superior colour sense has encouraged her to keep an inventory of base paints that she can colour as needed. Her customers, especially those with young children, appreciate her insistence on VOC-free paints and cleaning products (free of volatile organic compounds) and are willing to pay the premium prices for the

non-toxic products. For large murals, she enlists the assistance of senior art college students who work from her drawings.

Some of her customers have set up accounts with Muriel's Murals, and she has set up accounts with her regular vendors and suppliers.

To convert her accounting records to Sage 50 in April, she has used the following:

- Chart of Accounts
- Trial Balance
- Accounting Procedures

CHART OF POSTABLE ACCOUNTS

MURIEL'S MURALS

ASSETS
1080 Chequing Account
1200 A/R - Alberta Jasper
1220 A/R - Kananaskis Mall
1240 A/R - Silver Birch Inn
1320 Prepaid Insurance
1360 Paint & Supplies
1540 Computer Equipment
1550 Tools & Equipment
1570 Van ▶

▶LIABILITIES
2100 A/P - Foothills Hardware
2120 A/P - Western Sky Interiors
2180 A/P - Chinook Promotions
2650 GST Charged on Services
2670 GST Paid on Purchases

EQUITY
3100 M. Missoni, Capital
3150 M. Missoni, Drawings
3600 Net Income ▶

▶REVENUE
4100 Revenue from Painting
     Contracts
4150 Revenue from Consultation
4200 Interest Revenue

EXPENSE
5020 Advertising & Promotion
5040 Bank Charges
5060 Hydro Expense
5080 Interest Expense ▶

▶5100 Maintenance & Repairs
5110 Paint & Supplies Used
5120 Rental Expenses
5140 Telephone Expenses
5160 Wages Expenses

NOTES: The Chart of Accounts includes only postable accounts and the Net Income or Current Earnings account. Sage 50 uses the Net Income account for the Income Statement to calculate the difference between revenue and expenses before closing the books.

TRIAL BALANCE

MURIEL'S MURALS

April 1, 2018		Debits	Credits
1080	Chequing Account	$ 34 000	
1200	A/R - Alberta Jasper	2 400	
1220	A/R - Kananaskis Mall	3 600	
1320	Prepaid Insurance	2 100	
1360	Paint & Supplies	2 050	
1540	Computer Equipment	2 500	
1550	Tools & Equipment	14 500	
1570	Van	32 000	
2120	A/P - Western Sky Interiors		$ 1 200
2650	GST Charged on Services		1 500
2670	GST Paid on Purchases	940	
3100	M. Missoni, Capital		80 160
3150	M. Missoni, Drawings	900	
4100	Revenue from Painting Contracts		21 000
4150	Revenue from Consultation		4 000
5020	Advertising & Promotion	2 000	
5040	Bank Charges	160	
5060	Hydro Expense	300	
5100	Maintenance & Repairs	400	
5110	Paint & Supplies Used	4 400	
5120	Rental Expenses	1 650	
5140	Telephone Expenses	360	
5160	Wages Expenses	3 600	
		$107 860	$107 860

Accounting Procedures

GST

Muriel's Murals has chosen the regular method for remittance of the Goods and Services Tax (GST). Missoni records the GST collected from customers as a liability (credit) in the *GST Charged on Services* account. She records GST that she pays to vendors in the *GST Paid on Purchases* account as a decrease (debit) to her liability to the Canada Revenue Agency. Her GST remittance or refund is calculated automatically in the *GST Owing (Refund)* subtotal. These accounts are included in the display or printout of the Balance Sheet. Missoni files her GST remittances or requests for refunds with the Receiver General for Canada on the last day of each fiscal quarter. (For details, please read Chapter 2 on the Goods and Services Tax.)

INSTRUCTIONS

1. **Open** or **restore** the **data for Muriel's Murals**. Keystroke instructions begin below.

2. **Enter** the **source documents for April** in the General Journal in Sage 50 using the Chart of Accounts and Trial Balance for Muriel's Murals. The procedures for entering each new type of transaction for this application are outlined step by step in the Keystrokes section with the source documents. These transactions have a ✓ in the completion check box beside the source document. The source documents are numbered — the number is placed below or in the lower part of the check box.

3. **Print** the **reports** on the following form after you have completed your entries. Keystrokes for reports begin on page 53.

REPORTS

Accounts

☐ Chart of Accounts
☐ Account List
☑ General Journal Entries: Apr 1 to Apr 30

Financials

☑ Comparative Balance Sheet dates: Apr 1 and Apr 30 with difference in percentage
☑ Trial Balance date: Apr 30
☑ Income Statement from Jan 1 to Apr 30
☑ General Ledger accounts: 1080 2650 3100 4100 from Apr 1 to Apr 30

KEYSTROKES

Opening Data Files

Double-click the **Sage 50 desktop shortcut** , or the Sage 50 shortcut on the Windows Start page.

Click   **Select An Existing Company** and **click OK**.

Locate the folder **C:\SageData16** where you installed the data.

Double-click the **SageData16 folder** to open it.

Double-click the **MURALS folder** to open it.

Click   **MURALS** or **MURALS.SAI** to select the file you need. **Click Open**.

Refer to Chapter 1, page 8, for detailed instructions on opening data files.

The next screen asks (prompts) you to enter the session date for this work session:

```
Sage 50 - Session Date                    ×
Date for this Session:  Apr 01, 2018  ⌄  ▦
☐ Do not show this message again
        OK              Cancel
```

The date format on your screen is controlled by the Date Format Settings options in Sage 50, not by the format you use to enter the date. (Refer to page 20.)

The **session date** is the date of your work session — the date on which you are recording the accounting transactions on the computer. A business with a large number of transactions may record these transactions at the end of each day. One with fewer transactions may enter them once a week. In this workbook, transactions are entered once a week for most applications, so we update the session date one week at a time. The session date may or may not be the same as the date on which the transaction actually took place.

The session date for your first session is April 7, 2018. Since this is not the default on the screen, you must change the date. Every date field has a Calendar icon.

Click   the **Calendar icon** ▦ to open the calendar:

```
‹          April 2018              ›
Sun  Mon  Tue  Wed  Thu  Fri  Sat
  1    2    3    4    5    6    7
  8    9   10   11   12   13   14
 15   16   17   18   19   20   21
 22   23   24   25   26   27   28
 29   30    1    2    3    4    5
```

The calendar has the current session date highlighted with a blue background. The calendar for any date field also has the range of dates that will be accepted based on the settings chosen for the company files. The arrows allow you to move forward to a later month ▶ or back to a previous month ◀. The calendar stops at the dates that indicate the range you may use. Click a date on the calendar to enter it or use one of the following alternative formats. For consistency, we use the same order of month, day and year throughout the text. Entering the year is optional in most date fields.

- use different characters to separate numbers: 04-07-18 or 04/07/18
- omit leading zeros or the year: 4/7/18 or 4-7
- leave spaces between numbers instead of separating characters: 04 07 18 or 4 7
- type lower or upper case text: April 7, 2018 or APRIL 7, 2018
- use three-letter abbreviations for the month: Apr 7 -18 or apr 7 18
- use three-letter abbreviations for the month with the day first: 7 apr or 7Apr
- other non-alpha or non-numeric separating characters may also be used
- in most date windows, you can omit the year

We will use a variety of date formats throughout this workbook, but we always use the text format for dates on-screen to minimize entering incorrect dates. Using the calendar to choose a date or using a text version to enter a date will prevent an incorrect date entry.

Click   **7** on the April date calendar or

Type   april 7 or 7apr

Click   **OK**.

NOTES
Many screens include a Cancel button. If you click Cancel, you will return to your previous screen without entering any changes.

NOTES
When you click ◀ , the dimmed back arrow in the date calendar, nothing happens because the earliest date you can use for Muriel's Murals is April 1.

NOTES
When you enter the date as text, the date is not ambiguous, so you can enter the day first. Similarly, you do not need to leave a space between the month and day because there is no ambiguity.

NOTES
Refer to Chapter 1, page 20, and Chapter 4, page 78, for instructions on changing date format settings.

NOTES
Keystrokes that you must follow have command statements like:
    Type   april 7
or
    Click OK
Instruction lines are indented; command words are in **boldface**; text you type uses a special font (Courier); and things that you must click on or select are in **colour and bold**. This format makes it easy to find the instruction statements in the text.

The Company module Home window opens:

For Muriel's Murals, the Company module is the default page. Only the General ledger and journal can be accessed for this file. When ledger icons are hidden, all main menu options related to those ledgers are also hidden or unavailable. (Click ▢ to maximize the window if necessary.) The Home window has the title bar on top with the file name, control menu icon and size buttons; the main menu bar comes next with the Chat With Support tool (Help menu) and Search function and tool (Edit menu) on the far right. The tool bar follows with the program name and tool buttons that permit quick access to commonly used menu items. The Home window tools (with their alternative pull-down menu locations) include Open Company and Backup (File menu), DBM — Daily Business Manager — (Business Assistant menu) and Close Other Windows (View menu).

The major part of the window is divided into three columns of panes or sections — the **Modules** and **Shortcuts** panes on the left; **Tasks** in the middle with Ledger and Journal icons and **Related Tasks**; and the **Support** and **Reports** panes on the right. Instead of ledgers in the upper Tasks pane, the Company window has access to the **Daily Business Manager** and **Data Management** tasks, such as backing up files, restoring files and checking for database errors. For the Company module, the upper right pane has access to support services for Sage 50. For other modules, this pane lists the ledger accounts. The session date and the change date Calendar icon are located above the Support pane.

Below these panes is the status bar with the user name (sysadmin) and status (Single-user) and message icon. In most windows, the status bar describes the purpose of the field or icon that has the pointer on it.

Entering General Journal Transactions

All transactions for Muriel's Murals are entered in the General Journal in the Tasks pane, indicated by the General Journal icon:

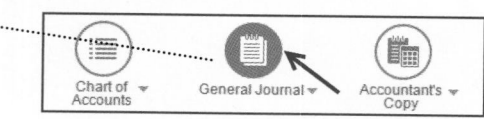

Click   the **General Journal icon** in the Tasks pane of the Company module Home window to open the General Journal.

The General Journal input form opens on your screen:

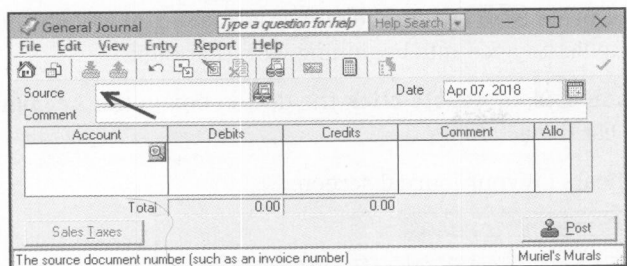

You are now ready to enter the first transaction in the General Journal input screen.

> ✓ **Purchase Invoice #FH-161**   **Dated April 2, 2018**
> 1 From Foothills Hardware, $795 plus $39.75 GST paid for cordless power drill with sander attachments. Purchase invoice total $834.75. Terms: net 30 days.

The cursor, a flashing vertical line, is blinking in the Source field, ready to receive information — up to 20 characters, including spaces. The Source field identifies the reference document from which you obtain the information for a transaction, in this case the invoice number.

> **Type**   FH-161
>
> **Press**   ⏽tab⏽ to advance to the Look Up Entry icon 📇 . **Press** ⏽tab⏽ again.

The cursor advances to the next field, the Date field. You should enter the transaction date here. The program enters the session date by default. It is highlighted, ready to be accepted or changed. Because the work was completed on April 2, 2018, the session date of April 7 is incorrect and must be changed.

> **Type**   04-02
>
> **Press**   ⏽tab⏽ to move to the Calendar icon 📅 .

The text form of the date is displayed, even though we entered the date as numbers. The year is added to the date.

> If you click the Calendar icon in the Date field now, the session date is on a white background with a frame around it. The current transaction date has a solid blue background.
>
> **Press**   ⏽tab⏽ again to accept the date and advance to the Comment field.

In the Comment field, you should enter a description of the transaction to make the permanent record more meaningful. You may enter up to 85 characters, including spaces.

> **Type**   Foothills Hardware **Press** ⏽tab⏽ .

The cursor moves forward to the first line of the Account field, creating a dotted box for the first account.

Sage 50 organizes accounts into financial statement sections or categories using the following boundaries for numbering:

- 1000–1999 Assets
- 2000–2999 Liabilities
- 3000–3999 Equity
- 4000–4999 Revenue
- 5000–5999 Expense

This system makes it easy to remember the first digit of an account. Double-clicking the Account field will display the list of accounts. If you type the first digit of an account

NOTES
Many fields that allow you to select an account or other information from a list have the Select or List icon to provide quick access to the list. Showing the List icon is an option that you select as a user preference setting.
Other fields have list arrows that provide a drop-down or pop-up list.

NOTES
If the cursor is in the Account field, you can also press (enter) to open the Select Account list.

NOTES
Command statements that are indented but do not have the boldfaced command words provide alternative keystrokes or optional instructions.
"You can also double-click…" is an example of an alternative command statement.

number then double-click or press (enter) while the cursor is flashing in any account field, the program will advance the list to accounts beginning with that digit.

> **Click** the **List icon** 🔍, or **double-click** the dotted box in the **Account column** to list the accounts.

The list of accounts appears on your journal screen:

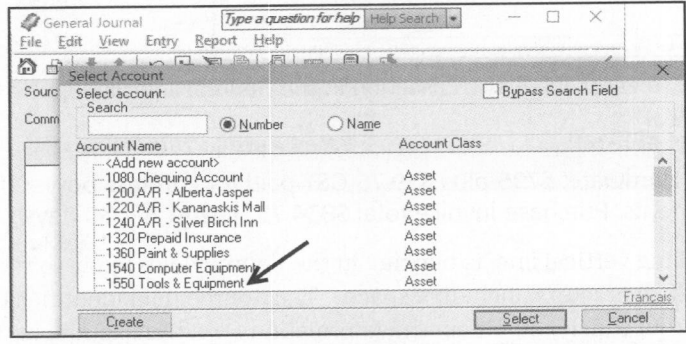

The beginning of the account list is displayed. The list includes only postable accounts — those that can be debited or credited in journal entries. The cursor is in the Search field. If you want to place the cursor in the account list directly from the Account field, you can choose the **Bypass Search Field** option. We will not select this option. Typing a number in the Search field selects the first account with that number. Following usual accounting practice, we enter the account to be debited first.

> **Click** **1550 Tools & Equipment** to select this asset account.
>
> **Click** the **Select button**. (A selected button has a darker frame or an inner dotted box.)

You can also double-click a selected account or press (enter) to add it directly to your journal entry form. Instead of using the selection list, you can find the number in the Chart of Accounts, type it in and press (tab).

Because the account number and name have been added to your input form, you can easily determine whether you have selected the correct account. If the screen does not display the entire account title, you can display the rest of the account title by clicking anywhere on the part that is showing, or you can maximize the journal window.

Your cursor is now positioned in the Debits field. The amount 0.00 is selected, ready to be changed. All journals include a **Windows Calculator tool** that opens the calculator directly for easy calculation of amounts, if needed.

Click the Display The Windows Calculator tool 🖩 to open the calculator. You can leave it open in the background for easy access.

Type amounts without dollar signs. You do not need to type decimals when you enter whole numbers. Sage 50 ignores any non-numeric characters that you type in an amount field.

> **Type** 795
>
> **Press** (tab).

The cursor moves to the Comment field. You can add a comment for each account line in the journal. Account line comments are optional. You can add a comment for each line, for some lines or for none of the lines, but the extra details will be included in the journal report and will give you more information about the transaction.

> **Type** power drill & attachments

Press ⟨tab⟩. Your input form is partially completed:

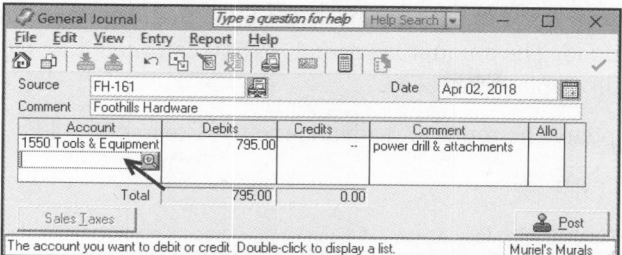

The cursor has advanced to the next line of the Account field, creating a dotted box and List icon for the next account for this transaction — the liability account *GST Paid on Purchases*. Remember, liability accounts start with 2. However, we will type 3 to include the end of the 2000-level accounts in the selection list.

Type 3

Click the **List icon** to advance your list to the 3000 accounts:

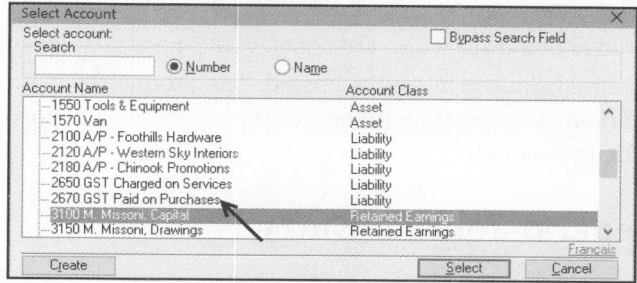

We have bypassed the Search field and selected the first account with the number we typed. This method quickly moves you to a later position in the list.

Click **2670 GST Paid on Purchases** from the displayed list to highlight it. If necessary, click a scroll arrow (⟨▼⟩ or ⟨▲⟩) to move through the account list to include *2670* in the display.

Press ⟨enter⟩.

Again, the account number and name have been added to your transaction form. The cursor has advanced to the Credits field, which has 795.00 as the default amount because this amount will balance the entry. The amount is highlighted to indicate that you may edit it. This is a compound entry. You must change the amount to separate the GST, and you must delete the credit entry because the GST account is debited.

Press ⟨del⟩ to delete the credit entry.

Click the **Debits field** on the second journal line below 795.00 to move the cursor.

Type 39.75

Press ⟨tab⟩ to advance to the optional Comment field.

Type GST @ 5%

Press ⟨tab⟩. The cursor moves to the next line in the Account field.

Press ⟨enter⟩ to open the Select Account list. The cursor is in the Search field.

Type 2

The list advances to the 2000 accounts. The liability account *2100 A/P - Foothills Hardware*, the account we need, is selected because it is the first 2000-level account.

NOTES

If you know that the account you need is closer to the end of its numbered section, typing the next higher number takes you to the end of the section you want. For example, typing 3 advances to 3100 and includes 2670 in the display. In this way, your account is more likely to be included in the display. Typing 2 will open the list with 2100 at the end and you will have to scroll down to find 2670.

NOTES

Typing a negative number (adding a minus sign) in the Credits field will move the number to the Debits field. Typing a negative number in the Debits field will create a Credit entry.

Click **Select** to enter it and return to the journal.

The cursor advances to the Credits field again, where 834.75, the amount that will now balance the entry, is added. The amount is correct, so you can accept it. The total for the Credits column is still displayed as zero.

Press (tab) to update the totals and advance to the Comment field.

Type `terms: net 30`

Your input form is now completed:

The Sales Taxes button will be covered in Chapter 5. Sales taxes are not set up for Muriel's Murals, so the button remains dimmed.

Until the debits and credits of a transaction are equal, you cannot post an entry. Once the entry is complete and balanced, it can be posted. The Store (icon) tool, for recurring entries, is also darkened. Before you proceed either to store or to post an entry, you should review the transaction.

Reviewing the General Journal Entry

Choose the **Report menu** and then **click Display General Journal Entry**:

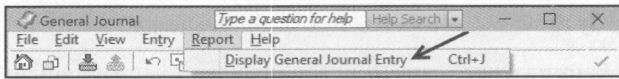

The journal entry that will be posted for the transaction is displayed:

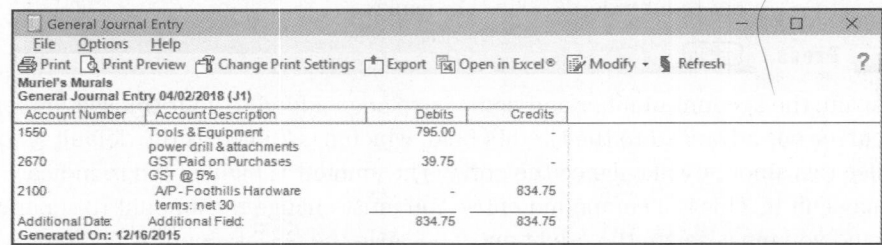

Click the **Maximize button** ☐ to change your display to full screen size if your transaction does not fit in your display window.

To return to your input form,

Click ☒ or **choose** the entry's **Control Menu icon** ☐ and **click Close**.

CORRECTING THE GENERAL JOURNAL ENTRY BEFORE POSTING

Press (tab) to advance to the field that has the error. To move to a previous field, **press** (shift) and (tab) together (that is, while holding down (shift), **press** (tab)). The field will be highlighted, ready for editing. **Type** the **correct information** and **press** (tab) to enter it.

You can also use the mouse to **point** to a field and **drag through** the **incorrect information** to highlight it. You can highlight a single number or letter or the entire field. **Type** the **correct information** and **press** (tab) to enter it.

continued...

NOTES

NOTES
We will use the Store tool and the Sales Taxes button in the Groen Fields application (Chapter 5).

NOTES
Pressing (ctrl) + J will also display the journal entry in any journal. Refer to Appendix B for a list of Sage 50 keyboard shortcuts.

NOTES
If your display includes scroll arrows, you can use them to include more of your transaction.
We use the short date format as the default for dates in reports, but we use the same order: month, day, year.

NOTES
The Additional Date and Additional Field can be used to add more information to a journal entry. The Additional Information feature is available in all journals and will be introduced in Chapter 11.

NOTES
Refer to page 45 for assistance with correcting errors after posting.

CORRECTING THE GENERAL JOURNAL ENTRY BEFORE POSTING (CONTINUED)

To correct an account number, **click** the **incorrect account number** (or name) to select the field. **Press** (enter) to display the list of accounts. **Click** the **correct account**. **Click Select**. **Press** (tab) to advance the cursor and enter the correction.

Click an **incorrect amount** to highlight it. **Type** the **correct amount** and **press** (tab).

You can insert a line or remove a line by clicking the line that will be moved down or removed. Then **choose** the **Edit menu** and **click Insert Line** or **Remove Line**.

To discard the entry and begin again, **click** ⊠ (Close) to close the journal or **click** ↰ (Undo on the tool bar) to open a blank journal window. When Sage 50 asks whether you want to discard the entry, **click Yes** to confirm your decision.

Posting

Once you are sure that all the information is correct, you are ready to post the entry.

Click   the **Post button** 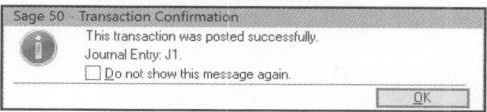 in the lower right-hand corner of the General Journal (the one that looks like a stamp) or **choose** the **Entry menu** and then **click Post**.

We have chosen the option to confirm when a transaction is posted successfully, so a confirmation message will open each time you post or record a transaction:

> Sage 50 - Transaction Confirmation
> ⓘ This transaction was posted successfully.
>   Journal Entry: J1.
>   ☐ Do not show this message again.
>   [OK]

Click   **OK** to open a new blank General Journal input form.

You can now enter the next transaction for this session date.

Adding a New Account

The bank credit memo on April 3 uses an account that is not listed in your Chart of Accounts. Often a company will need to create new accounts as it expands or changes direction. These future needs are not always foreseen when the accounts are first set up. You must add the account *2300 Bank Loan* to enter the bank credit memo transaction.

Bank Credit Memo #AT-C3104   **Dated April 3, 2018**

From Alberta Trust Company, $8 000 bank loan secured for purchase of new customized work table. Loan deposited into bank account. Create new Group account 2300 Bank Loan.

First, enter the Source for the memo.

Type   AT-C3104

Press   (tab) **twice** to advance to the Date field. The date of the previous journal entry becomes the default date until you close the journal.

Click   the **Calendar icon** 🗓 and then **click 3**.

Press   (tab) to advance to the Comment field.

Type   Alberta Trust - new loan

Double-click the **Account field**.

Double-click **Chequing Account**.

⚠ WARNING!
Don't post the transaction until you make sure that it is correct. Always review a transaction before posting it.

📄 NOTES
This confirmation does not mean that you have entered the correct details, only that the entry could be posted – debits and credits were equal and data for required fields (Source and Date) were included.

📄 NOTES
You can add new accounts from the Account field in any journal, from the Accounts window or any General Ledger window. The General Ledger and Accounts windows are introduced in Chapter 4.

📄 NOTES
When you close the journal and open it later, the session date becomes the default again.

Type	8000 (the amount of the loan) as the debit part of the transaction.
Press	⬚tab⬚ to advance to the Comment field for the account.
Type	`loan for customized work table`
Press	⬚tab⬚ to advance to the Account field on the second journal line.
Click	the **List icon** or **press** ⬚enter⬚ to open the Select Account list.
Click	**Add New Account**, the first entry in the list, and **click Select** or **click** the **Create** button.

This will begin the wizard for adding a General Ledger account:

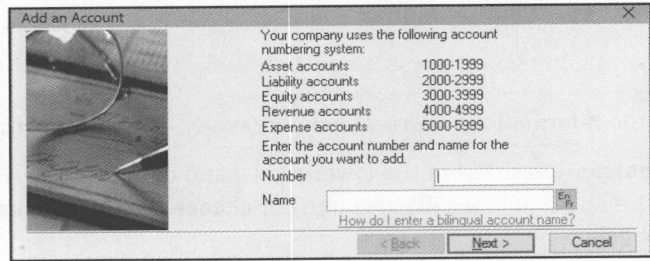

The first screen prompts you for the account number and name. The cursor is in the Number field.

Type	2300 **Press** ⬚tab⬚.
Type	`Bank Loan`
Click	**Next** or **press** ⬚enter⬚ to continue.

The next screen asks for the **GIFI code**. This is the four-digit account number assigned by the Canada Revenue Agency for this category of account to use in electronically filed business returns. GIFI codes are not used in this workbook. They are described in Appendix K.

Click	**Next** to skip this screen and continue.

The next screen asks whether this account is to be used as a **Heading** or **Total** in the financial statements. *Bank Loan* is an ordinary postable account that has a balance, so the default selection, No, is correct. A partial Balance Sheet illustrates account types.

Click	**Next** to accept the default and continue.

The following screen deals with another aspect of the **account type**. Accounts may be **subtotalled** within their group of accounts. For example, if you have several bank accounts, you will want your Balance Sheet report to include the total cash deposited in all of them together. Different account types will be explained fully in the Love It Again application (Chapter 4), where you will set up the accounting records for a new company.

Bank Loan is a Group account. It is not subtotalled with any other account, so the default selection, No, is correct.

Click	**Next** to continue.

The next wizard screen refers to the **account class**. Account classes are explained in Chapter 7. The default selection is the name of the section. Therefore, for account *2300*, Liability is the section and the default class. Generally, you can accept the default selection.

Click	**Next** to continue.

⚠ WARNING!
Enter account numbers carefully. You cannot change them after you post to the account in a journal entry.

📝 NOTES
Next is selected, so you can press ⬚enter⬚ repeatedly to advance through the wizard screens that you do not need to change.

⚠ WARNING!
Account types must be set correctly or you will get the error message that accounts are not in logical order when you try to display financial reports. If one of these messages opens, you can edit the account type. Refer to Chapter 4, page 88, for help with creating and editing accounts.

Now you are being asked whether you want to **allocate** the balance of the account to different projects or divisions. Projects are not set up for Muriel's Murals, so the default selection, set at No for Balance Sheet accounts, is correct.

> **Click**   **Next** to continue.

The next setting screen asks whether you want to include or **omit** this account **from financial statements** when it has a zero balance. Choosing Yes means that if the balance in this account is zero, the account will not be included in your financial statements. If you choose No, the account will be printed even if it has a balance of zero. Some accounts, such as *Chequing Account*, should always be printed in financial statements. In Chapter 4 we explain this setting. The default setting, to include accounts (not to omit), is never wrong.

> **Click**   **Next** to continue to the final screen with the selections you have made:

> **Check**   your **work**. If you need to make corrections, **click Back** until you reach the screen with the error. **Make** the **correction** and **click Next** until you reach this final screen again.

When all the information is correct, you must save the new account information.

> **Click**   **Finish**.

You will return to the General Journal window with the new account added to the account field. The cursor has not yet advanced, so you can change your account selection if you need to.

> **Click**   the **Credits field**. The balancing amount, $8 000, is added.
>
> **Press**   (tab) to accept the amount and advance to the Comment field.
>
> **Type**   Alberta Trust loan
>
> **Display**   the **journal entry** to verify whether it is correct.
>
> **Close**   the **display**. **Make corrections** if you find errors.
>
> **Click**   **Post** [Post] to save the information. **Click OK** to confirm.
>
> **Enter**   the **next sale transaction** on your own.

3
Sales Invoice #MM-40   **Dated April 3, 2018**
To Alberta Jasper, $3 500 plus $175 GST charged to design and paint animal theme mural in nursery as per contract. Sales invoice total $3 675. Terms: net 30 days.

Adjusting a Posted Entry

Sometimes after posting a journal entry you discover that it had an error. You can make corrections directly in the General Journal by adjusting the previously posted entry. Sage 50 allows you to make the correction by adjusting the entry without completing a reversing entry. The program creates the reversing and correcting journal entries when you post the correction so that the audit trail is complete. The purchase from Foothills Hardware on April 2 was posted with an incorrect amount. The General Journal should still be open.

NOTES
For Muriel's Murals, the title for Projects is changed to Job Sites.

NOTES
Some reports have omitting accounts with zero balances as a report option.

NOTES
You can use the wizard in any account field to create a new account at any time. You do not need to use the account after creating it when you return to the journal.

NOTES
A check box without a ✓ indicates that keystroke instructions are not provided for this source document.
The lower part of the check box contains the source document number (**3**).
If you use MM-xx as the source for sales, you can apply the report filter we describe in Appendix E.

☑ / 4   **Memo #1**   **Dated April 4, 2018**

From Owner: The invoice from Foothills Hardware was entered incorrectly. The cost of the drill was $820 plus $41 GST paid. The revised purchase invoice total is $861. Adjust the posted invoice to make the correction.

Click   the **Adjust A Previously Posted Entry tool** 🖼 in the tool bar, or

Choose   the **Entry menu** and **click Adjusting Entry**.

The Search screen opens:

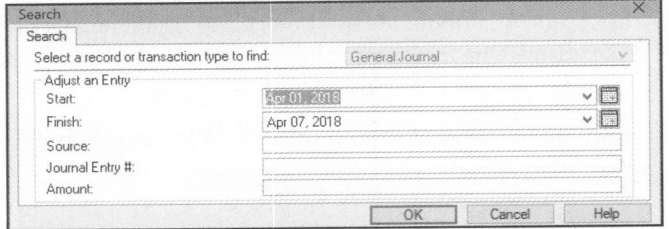

NOTES
Pressing ⌨ ctrl + A will also start the adjust entry process in any journal when the option is available.

The Adjust An Entry and Search functions are combined. Because we selected the Adjust option, the Select field on the screen is dimmed, but General Journal is indicated as the search area. You can select a range of journal entry dates to search. The date we converted the data files to Sage 50 and the session date are the default start and finish dates for the list. If you know the source, journal entry number or amount, you can enter it in the Source, Journal Entry # or Amount field, respectively, and access the transaction entry directly by clicking OK. You must enter the exact source, journal entry number or amount for these searches.

We can accept the default dates because they include the transaction we need.

Click   **OK** to list the journal entries:

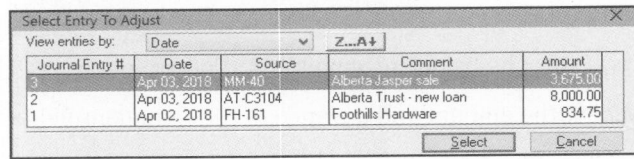

All journal entries are listed, with the most recent one at the top of the list (Z...A↓ order for Date). You can choose the way the journal entries are sorted.

Click   the **list arrow** beside the Date entry for **View Entries By**:

NOTES
You should choose the order that makes it easiest to find your entry. That will depend on what information you entered and what you remember as well as how many entries you have.

You can organize the list of entries by journal entry number, date, source number, comment or amount. The Z...A↓ button lets you choose ascending or descending order.

Click   **Journal Entry #**.

Click   Z...A↓ to reverse the order. The one we want is now first in the list and the button label has changed A...Z↓.

Click   **Journal Entry #1**, **FH-161** to select it.

Click   **Select** or **double-click** to open the journal entry as it was posted:

NOTES
Although Journal Entry #1 is highlighted, the cursor is still on the A...Z↓ button, so pressing ⌨ enter does not open the journal because of the keystroke sequence we used.
You can also double-click anywhere on the line for an entry to open the transaction.

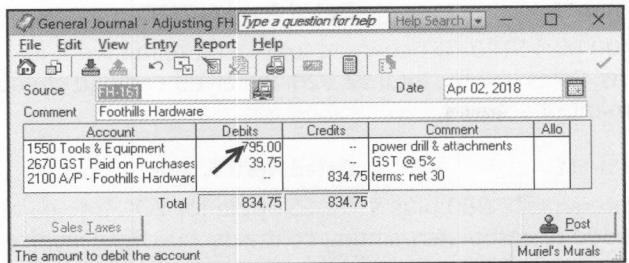

All fields may now be edited, just as if you had not yet posted the transaction. The title bar entry has changed to General Journal – Adjusting FH-161. This full title will be included if you expand the journal window size.

> **Click** **795.00**, the amount in the Debit column for *Tools & Equipment*, to select it for editing.
>
> **Type** 820
>
> **Click** **39.75** or **press** ⬇ to select the Debit column amount for *GST Paid on Purchases*.
>
> **Type** 41
>
> **Click** **834.75**, the Credit column amount for *A/P - Foothills Hardware*.
>
> **Type** 861 **Press** (tab) to update the totals with the correct amounts.

We will also modify the source to differentiate this correct entry from the original.

> **Click** the **Source field** before the current entry (**before F**). **Type** (COR)

We will not change the date for this correction because the date affects the payment due date and the original date was correct.

> **Review** the **entry** to display the correct transaction and **close** the **display**. **Make corrections** if necessary.
>
> **Click** Post 🗳 *Post* . **Click OK** to confirm the posting. The entry is J5. (J4 is the reversing entry created by the program.)

When you display the General Journal Report with Corrections selected (refer to page 61), the three entries for the purchase invoice — the original incorrect entry, a reversing adjusting entry created by the program (ADJFH-161) and the correct entry (COR) FH-161 — are included, providing a complete audit trail for the transaction and correction. Refer to the partial General Journal Report display on page 61.

REVERSING A GENERAL JOURNAL ENTRY AFTER POSTING

If you need to reverse an entry instead of making changes to it, **click** the **Reverse Entry tool** 🗒 in the tool bar of the General Journal – Adjusting window, or **choose** the **Entry menu** and **click Reverse Entry**. You must confirm your decision before the action is taken. **Click Yes** to confirm and continue. Sage 50 does not delete the original entry. Instead it adds the reversing entry to the journal report for a complete audit trail. You can hide reversing entries in journal reports by not showing corrections.

> **Continue** with the **journal entries** for the April 7 session date.

5 | **Payment Cheque #48**   **Dated April 5, 2018**
To Western Sky Interiors, $1 200 in payment of invoice #WSI-129.

6 | **Receipt #20**   **Dated April 5, 2018**
From Alberta Jasper, cheque #828 for $2 400 in payment of invoice #MM-37.

NOTES
Usually clicking a number in a field will select the entire number. Sometimes, however, depending on exactly where you click, only part of the number is selected or an insertion point is added. Double-clicking will always select the entire number in the field so that you can edit it.

WARNING!
You can change the date for the final correct entry but not for the adjusting or reversing entry.
Dates should be changed only when they were incorrect because they affect the terms for sales and purchases.

NOTES
If you use Cheque #*xx* as the source for cheques, you can apply the report filter we describe in Appendix E.

Cash Sales Invoice #MM-41   **Dated April 6, 2018**

7

To Rolf Kleinje, $2 400 plus $120 GST charged for plaster repair work and repainting two rooms. Sales invoice total $2 520. Received certified cheque #AT-603 in full payment of account.

Purchase Invoice #WSI-611   **Dated April 6, 2018**

8

From Western Sky Interiors, $2 080 plus $104 GST paid for VOC-free paint and colour additives needed to complete painting contracts. Purchase invoice total $2 184. Terms: net 30 days.

Advancing the Session Date and Backing Up Files

When you have finished all the entries for the April 7 session date, the date for the next transaction is later than April 7. Therefore, you must advance the session date before you can continue. If you do not advance the date before posting the April 8 transaction, you will receive an error message.

Before advancing the date, however, close all open windows and then save and back up your work because you have already completed one week of transactions. Although Sage 50 saves automatically each time you post an entry or exit the program, it is important to know how to save and back up your work directly to a separate file and location or disk because your working files may become damaged and unusable.

Click   ⊠ or **choose** the **File menu** for the journal and **click Close** to close the General Journal.

To save a working copy of the file under a different file name, choose the File menu and click Save A Copy to continue working with the original file or Save As to open a new working copy of the file.

You are now ready to advance the session date to April 14.

Click   the **Calendar icon** 📅 beside **Session Date: Apr 07, 2018** on the right-hand side of the Home window:

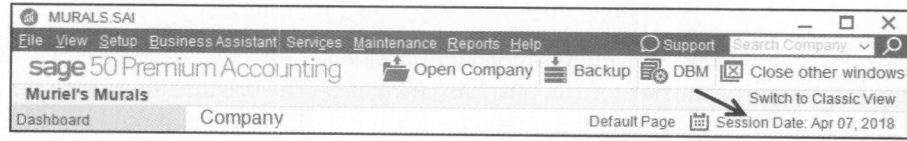

Or, **choose** the **Maintenance menu** and **click Change Session Date**:

The Change Session Date window opens with the current session date highlighted:

Type   04-14-18   (or click the calendar icon and click 14).

Click   **OK** to accept the new date.

A Sage 50 message advises you that you have not yet backed up your work:

NOTES
We have set up the data files for Muriel's Murals so that future-dated transactions are not allowed.

NOTES
Refer to page 22 for information on the Save As and Save A Copy commands.
A complete data set is more than 30 Megabytes in size, while its backup file is about 2 Megabytes. The Save As and Save A Copy options require more disk storage space because the copy is not compressed.

WARNING!
You must close all windows before you can advance the session date or before you make a backup.
You can click ⊠, the Home window Close Other Windows tool, or close each window separately. You also must be working in single-user mode to change the session date.

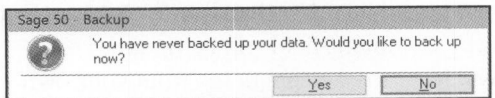

The data files for this workbook have been prepared with the default warning to back up your work weekly. Since we also advance the session date by one week at a time, you will be reminded to back up each time you advance the session date.

Click   Yes to proceed with the backup. The next screen asks for a file name for the backup:

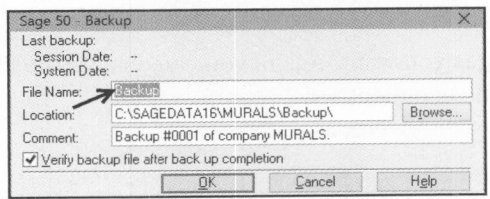

Sage 50 will create a file named Backup1 inside a new Backup subfolder of the folder that contains your working data files. You can edit the file name, location and comment. The name Backup is selected, so you can change the name.

Type   MURALS

If you want to change the location of the backup, click Browse, select a folder and file name and click OK.

Click   OK to proceed.

When you name a new folder, an advisory message opens:

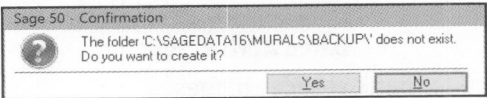

The program recognizes that the folder name is new and offers to create the folder. If you have typed the correct name and location,

Click   Yes to accept the information and continue.

The backup file is different from the one you create by copying or using the Save A Copy or Save As command. The Save A Copy and Save As commands create a complete working copy of your data that you can access with the Sage 50 program directly. Backup creates a compressed file that must first be restored before you can use it to enter transactions. This backup file (MURALS1.CAB) has 1 and the .CAB file extension added to the name.

After a brief interval, a message confirms that the backup is complete:

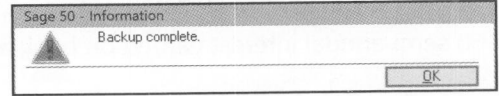

Click   OK to proceed. You may now enter transactions for this session date.

If you have already created a backup for this data file, or when you change the session date again, you will be advised of the most recent backup date when you are prompted to back up again:

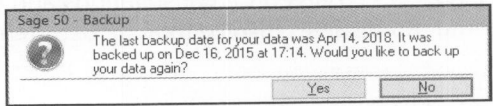

Click   Yes to continue.

NOTES
You cannot create backups when working in multi-user mode.

WARNING!
Be sure to back up each time you are prompted to do so or each time you advance the session date. If your files are damaged, your work will be lost unless you have a backup.

NOTES
For later backups, the backup message will have the previous backup file name and date. In this case the backup # will also be increased — refer to the example on page 50.

WARNING!
You cannot use the same name for the backup and the file if they are in the same folder. If you want to use the same name, you must use a different folder. By using the Backup folder, we can name the backup file MURALS.

NOTES
If you do not show file extensions, the backup will be named MURALS1.

Sage 50 will provide the same file name and location that you used for your most recent backup. The backup number in the Comment field will be updated.

Your backup information screens will have the system dates from your own computer:

NOTES
When you change the session date again, the prompt to back up the file will include the session date and calendar date and time of the previous backup.

Click **OK**, or **make** the **changes** you want. Again, you can change the file name, its location or the comment.

Click **OK**.

WARNING!
We recommend updating the backup name by adding a date or number to the name. For example, type MURALS-2 for the next backup, then MURALS-3 and so on. This will provide backups for different stages to return to if you later find errors.

If you use the same backup file name, you will be asked to replace the previous file:

Clicking No will result in the message that the backup was unsuccessful. Then click OK to return to the Backup File Name screen.

Click Yes to continue with the replacement or click No to enter a different name.

Enter the **remaining transactions for April** and **advance** the **session date** as needed.

9

Bank Debit Memo #AT-D3691　　　　**Dated April 8, 2018**

From Alberta Trust Company, $49 for bank service charges.

10

Purchase Invoice #WMM-4499　　　　**Dated April 10, 2018**

From West Mall Mechanical, $840 plus $42 GST paid for maintenance work on van. Purchase invoice total $882. Terms: net 10 days. Create new Group account 2190 A/P - West Mall Mechanical.

11

Memo #2　　　　**Dated April 11, 2018**

Missoni paid her business hydro and telephone bills from her personal chequing account. She wrote cheque #49 for $361.20 to reimburse herself for these expenses. The hydro bill was $160 plus $8.00 GST and the telephone bill was $184 plus $9.20 GST.

12

Bank Credit Memo #AT-C3421　　　　**Dated April 11, 2018**

From Alberta Trust Company, $160 semi-annual interest earned on bank account.

13

Receipt #21　　　　**Dated April 12, 2018**

From Kananaskis Mall, cheque #58821 for $3 600 in full payment of invoice #MM-38.

14

Sales Invoice #MM-42　　　　**Dated April 14, 2018**

To Kananaskis Mall, $2 500 plus $125 GST charged for consultations and design for additions to existing park theme mural. Sales invoice total $2 625. Terms: net 30 days.

SESSION DATE – APRIL 21, 2018

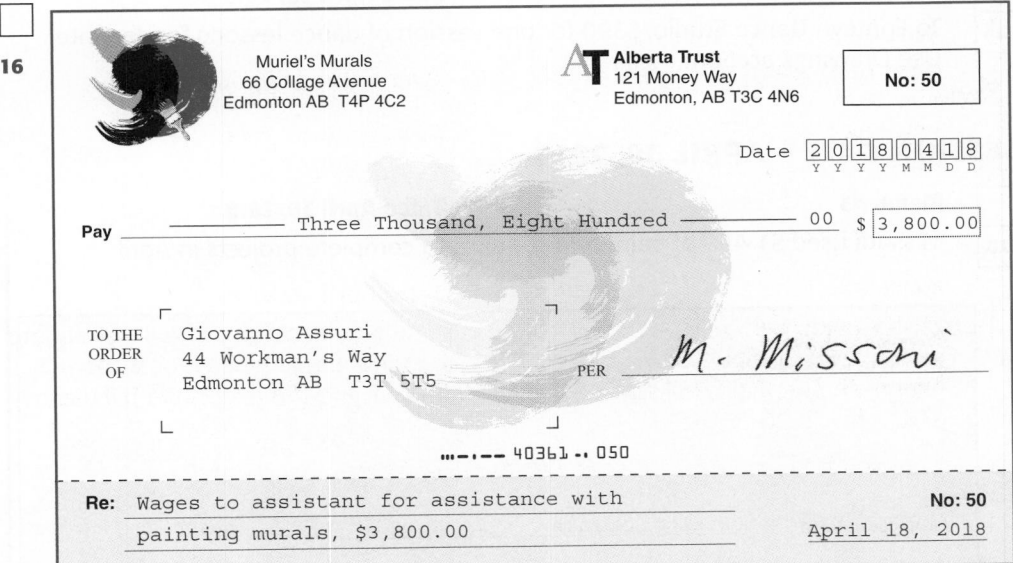

15

To: Muriel's Murals
66 Collage Avenue
Edmonton, AB
T4P 4C2

DEVON
Equipment Co.

68 CUTTERS ROAD EDMONTON, AB T4C 3N6

TEL: 780-775-6116

No: DE-1141

Date: April 15, 2018

Description of item	
Large stainless steel work table with power supply	8,000.00

GST # 651 034 271	**Terms:** net 30 days	**Subtotal**	8,000.00
Signature *M. Missari*		**GST**	400.00
		Total	$8,400.00

16

Muriel's Murals
66 Collage Avenue
Edmonton AB T4P 4C2

AT Alberta Trust
121 Money Way
Edmonton, AB T3C 4N6

No: 50

Date 2 0 1 8 0 4 1 8
Y Y Y Y M M D D

Pay ———— Three Thousand, Eight Hundred ———— 00 $ 3,800.00

TO THE
ORDER
OF

Giovanno Assuri
44 Workman's Way
Edmonton AB T3T 5T5

PER *M. Missari*

⑆⑈ 40361 ⑈ 050

Re: Wages to assistant for assistance with
painting murals, $3,800.00

No: 50
April 18, 2018

17

Sales Invoice #MM-43   **Dated April 19, 2018**

To Lindbrook Estates, $1 600 plus $80 GST charged for consultation and design
of frieze and mural for home office. Sales invoice total $1 680. Terms: net
10 days. Create new Group account 1280 A/R - Lindbrook Estates.

18

Payment Cheque #51   **Dated April 20, 2018**

To West Mall Mechanical, $842 in payment of account. Reference invoice
#WMM-4499.

Sales Invoice #MM-44   **Dated April 20, 2018**

19 To Sherwood Park Estates (new customer), $6 000 plus $300 GST charged to prepare and paint bedroom walls and ceilings, as per contract. Sales invoice total $6 300. Terms: net 10 days. Create new Group account 1260 A/R - Sherwood Park Estates.

Receipt #22   **Dated April 21, 2018**

20 From Lindbrook Estates, cheque #189 for $1 680 in payment of invoice #MM-43.

SESSION DATE – APRIL 28, 2018

Sales Invoice #MM-45   **Dated April 24, 2018**

21 To Silver Birch Inn, $4 100 plus $205 GST charged to paint mural in dining room as per contract. Sales invoice total $4 305. Terms: net 30 days.

Purchase Invoice #BT-2194   **Dated April 25, 2018**

22 From Beaumont Tekstore, $810 plus $40.50 GST paid for external hard drive for computer. Purchase invoice total $850.50. Terms: net 10 days. Create new Group account 2220 A/P - Beaumont Tekstore.

Cash Purchase Invoice #BAA-719   **Dated April 25, 2018**

23 From Bon Accord Advertising, $400 plus $20 GST paid for printing and copying advertising flyers. Purchase invoice total $420. Terms: cash on receipt. Invoice paid in full with cheque #52.

Cheque #53   **Dated April 28, 2018**

24 To Fonteyn Dance Studio, $390 for one session of dance lessons for daughter. Use Drawings account.

SESSION DATE – APRIL 30, 2018

Memo #3   **Dated April 30, 2018**

25 Missoni used $1 450 of paint and supplies to complete projects in April.

26

Sherwood Park Estates
900 Sherwood Park Rd.
Edmonton, AB
T4J 4S6

No: 223

Date 2 0 1 8 0 4 3 0
Y Y Y Y M M D D

Pay to the order of   Muriel's Murals $ 6,300.00

———————— Six thousand three hundred ———————— 00 /100 **Dollars**

R **Royal Bank**
   69 Royalty Avenue
B Edmonton, AB T3P 7C6

Robin Sherwood
Signature

⑈⸺ 393214 ⸺⑈ 0223

Re: Receipt #23 Reference Invoice #MM-44,   No: 223
    $6,300.00 on full payment of account. $6,300.00   April 30, 2018

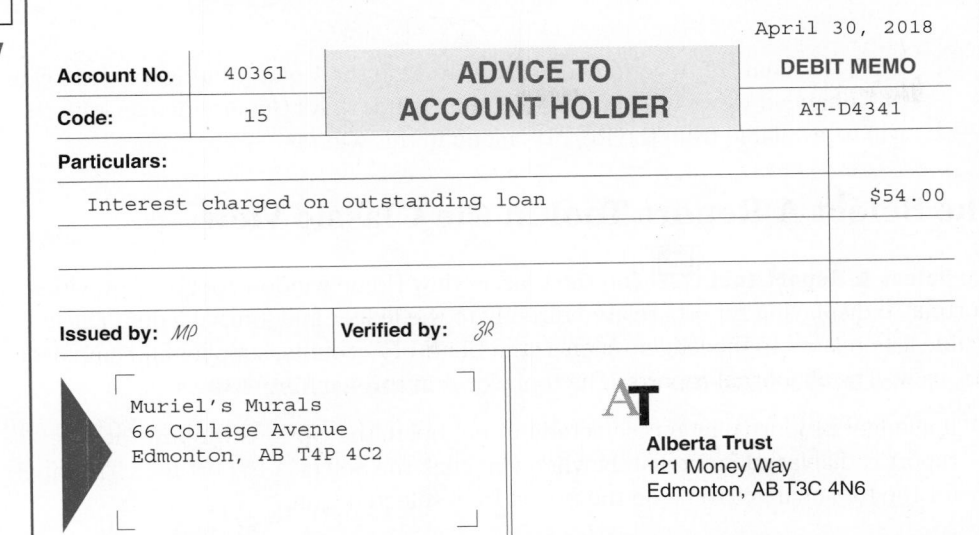

27

| April 30, 2018 |
| DEBIT MEMO |

| Account No. | 40361 | **ADVICE TO ACCOUNT HOLDER** | **DEBIT MEMO** |
| Code: | 15 | | AT-D4341 |

Particulars:

| Interest charged on outstanding loan | $54.00 |

Issued by: *MP*   **Verified by:** *3R*

Muriel's Murals
66 Collage Avenue
Edmonton, AB T4P 4C2

AT

Alberta Trust
121 Money Way
Edmonton, AB T3C 4N6

28

Memo #4   **Dated April 30, 2018**

Cheque #51 for $842 to West Mall Mechanical was recorded with an incorrect amount. The cheque amount was $882. Adjust the entry to change the amount.

Displaying General Reports

A key advantage to using Sage 50 rather than a manual system is the ability to produce financial reports quickly for any date or time period. Sage 50 allows you to enter accounting data accurately so you can prepare the reports you need for reporting to government and investors and for business analysis.

Reports that are provided for a specific date, such as the Balance Sheet, can be produced for any date from the time the accounting records were converted to the computerized system up to the latest journal entry. Reports that summarize a financial period, such as the Income Statement, can be produced for any period between the beginning of the fiscal period and the latest journal entry.

Reports are available from multiple locations: the Accounts window, the Home window Reports menu, the Select A Report tool in the Classic view, and from the Reports list and the Report Centre in the Reports pane of the Home window.

The Reports Menu

From the Home window Reports menu, most General Ledger reports are located under the Financials submenu option:

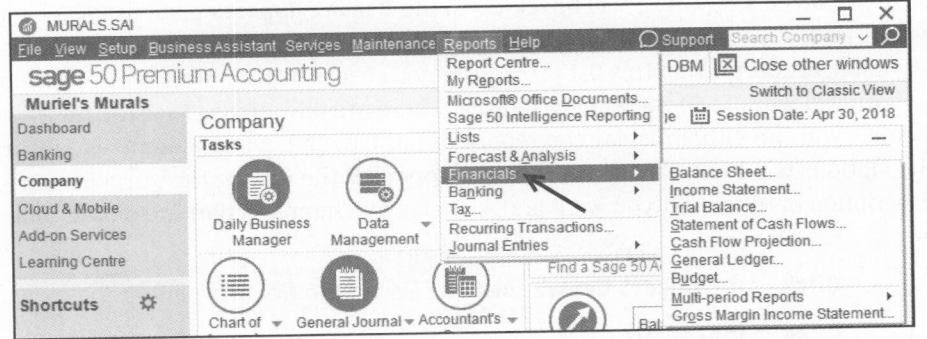

NOTES
Report analysis is beyond the scope of this text.

NOTES
If you have data for more than one fiscal period, you can display and print reports for the previous fiscal periods.

NOTES
The Home window Reports menu has only the General Ledger reports because the other ledgers are hidden.

PRO VERSION
pro Sage 50 Intelligence, Forecast & Analysis, Multi-Period reports and Time & Billing reports are not available in the Pro version.

Accounts Window Reports Menu

Click the Chart of Accounts icon 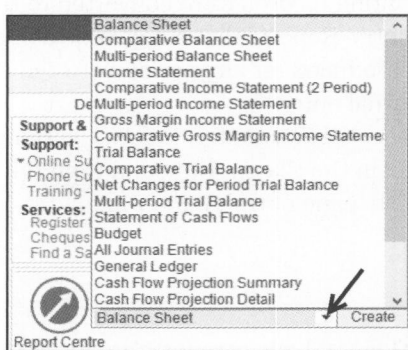 in the Home window (Classic view or Enhanced view) to open the Accounts window. All General Ledger reports will be available from the Reports menu in this window.

The Select A Report Tool in the Classic View

The **Select A Report tool** (on the Classic view Home window tool bar) provides a shortcut to displaying reports related directly to the ledger and journal icons. These include lists related to the ledgers such as the Chart of Accounts, supplier and employee lists, as well as all journal reports. The tool works in three different ways:

1. If a ledger or journal icon is selected but not open, the Options window for that report is displayed immediately when you click the Select A Report tool. The label for the tool changes to name the report for a selected icon.

2. If no icon is highlighted, clicking the Select A Report tool produces the Select Report window that lists all journal reports and ledger lists. Click the list arrow ✔ and choose a report from this list. Click Select to display the report options window.

3. When the Accounts window is open, clicking the **Reports tool** provides a Select A Report window that lists all General Ledger reports. Click the list arrow ✔, choose from this list and click Select to display the report or its options window. In other ledger windows, the reports list will include the reports related to that ledger.

The Reports Pane and Report Centre

The Reports pane allows access to reports in three ways: from the Report Centre, from the list of recently viewed reports or from the drop-down list of reports for the module you have open. The Company module Reports list has Financial and Accounts reports:

Balance Sheet
Comparative Balance Sheet
Multi-period Balance Sheet
Income Statement
Comparative Income Statement (2 Period)
Multi-period Income Statement
Gross Margin Income Statement
Comparative Gross Margin Income Statemen
Trial Balance
Comparative Trial Balance
Net Changes for Period Trial Balance
Multi-period Trial Balance
Statement of Cash Flows
Budget
All Journal Entries
General Ledger
Cash Flow Projection Summary
Cash Flow Projection Detail
Balance Sheet   Create
Report Centre

Clicking a report in this list will display it with the default report settings. Once you have displayed a report, it will be added to the **Recent Reports** pane list. Clicking the report in this list will display it with the settings you used most recently. If you have modified a report, using this list provides quick access to your modified report.

We will work from the **Report Centre**. There are advantages to using the Report Centre: you can either display the report with the default settings immediately or display the Options windows. Furthermore, before opening the report, the purpose and a brief description of the report you want and a display of a sample report are on the same screen.

Click   the **Report Centre icon** in the Reports pane.

Click   **Financials** in the Select A Report Type list:

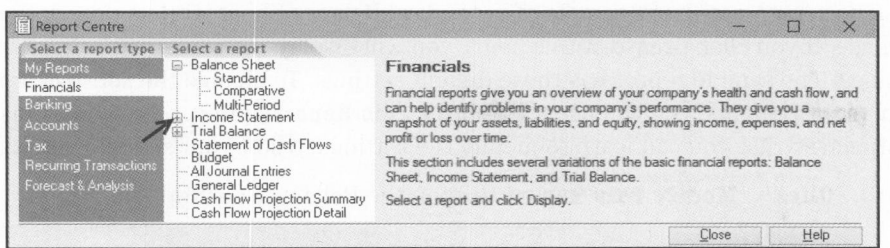

As from the Reports menu, reports for ledgers that are hidden are not available. Financial reports are selected when you start from the Company module Home window, and a list of the different financial reports is added. Several of the reports have a ⊞ beside them, indicating that there are different forms of the report. A brief explanation of Financial Reports appears.

Read   the **description**.

Click   the ⊞ beside each report type to expand the list.

Click   **Balance Sheet** to display a general description of Balance Sheet reports:

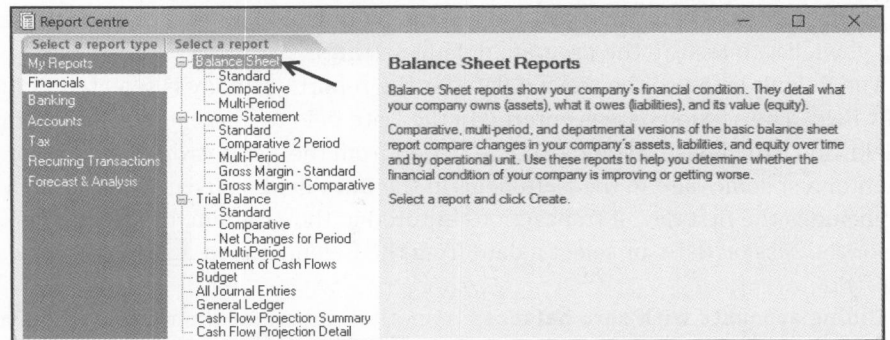

Because Balance Sheet is selected, the description now applies to that report. Standard (single-period) and Comparative (two-period) reports are available. When you have data for more than two months, you can also display Multi-Period Balance Sheets to compare reports for periods ranging from one to 12 months.

Displaying the Balance Sheet

The Balance Sheet informs you of the financial position of the business on the date you select for the report. You can display the Balance Sheet at any time.

Click   **Standard** below Balance Sheet:

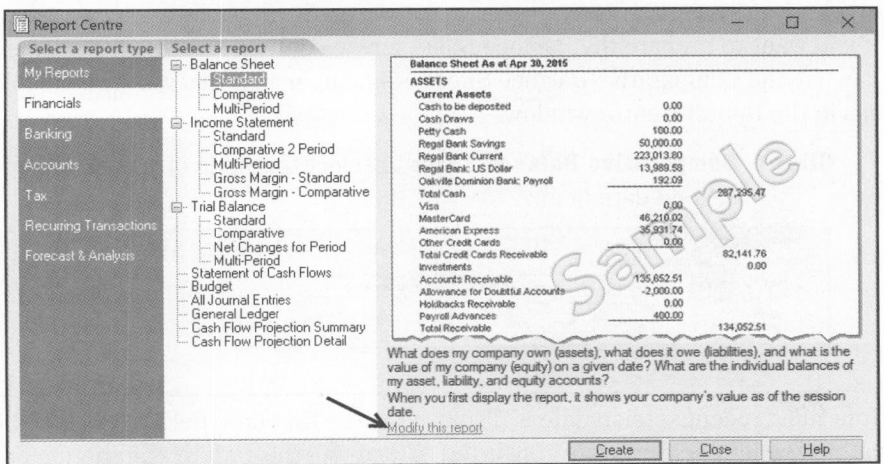

The screen now has a sample of a standard Balance Sheet with its description and purpose. If you click **Create** at this point, you will display the report with the default settings. The sample report has these default settings. To change the settings or to display the defaults, you can use the **Modify This Report** option. We will use this approach so that you can learn to modify the settings to suit your specific needs.

Click   **Modify This Report** to open the Balance Sheet options window:

You can also choose the Reports menu, then choose Financials and click Balance Sheet. The report options window will open.

Default Report Options appears as the template the first time you view a report. The next time you open this window, the **Last Used Report Options** will display as the template. This selection allows you to open the same report without re-entering dates and other options. At any time you can choose **Default Report Options** on the Template drop-down list to restore the program default settings.

The default is to use the session date for the report — Today is selected in the **As At** field. The session date is entered in the Date field to match the selection in the As At field. You can choose a standard time period from the As At drop-down list, or you can enter a specific date in the Date field. In the **Date** field, you can select from a list that includes the first day of transactions entered in the program, the latest transaction date or the session date, or select a date from the Calendar icon 🗓 to the right of the Date field.

Hiding accounts with zero balances is another option for the report. When you choose to omit zero balance accounts in the General Ledger (refer to page 91), you must select the option for each account individually, and the selection will apply to all reports that include this account. Here, you can choose the option selectively for different reports, and it will apply to all accounts in the report, overriding the ledger option.

Click   the **As At field list arrow** to access the predefined date options:

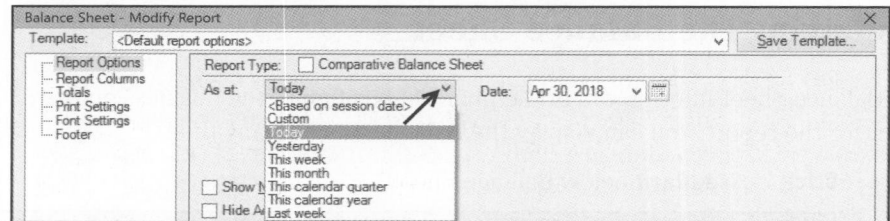

If you want to prepare the Balance Sheet for two different dates at the same time, you can use the Comparative Balance Sheet. Remember that this was also one of the options in the Report Centre window.

Click   **Comparative Balance Sheet** to select this style of report and open the second date field:

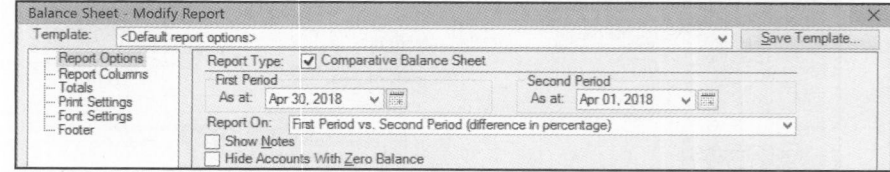

Your most recent session date is displayed in the first date field. The second date is the date on which the files were converted to Sage 50, the earliest transaction date.

Press   `tab` to highlight the first date if you want to change it.

Click   the **Calendar icon** 🔲 to the right of the date (As At) field.

To enter a date, click 🔲 and choose a date, select a date from the list or type the date you want using any accepted date format.

Press   `tab` or **press** `tab` **twice** if you type the date.

Type   the **second date** or choose from the date list or calendar.

Click   the **Report On field** to display the report types in the drop-down list:

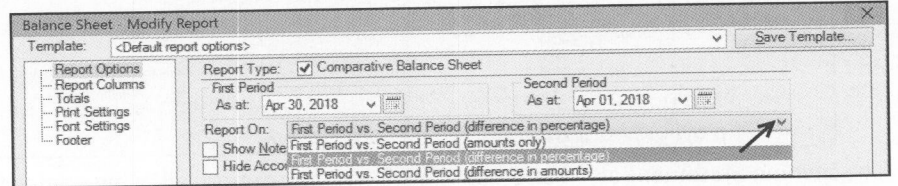

Choose **Amounts Only** if you want only the dollar balances for both dates. Choose **Difference In Percentage** if you want the dollar balances as well as the increase in percentage from the second, earlier period amount to the first, later period amount. Choose **Difference In Amounts** if you want the dollar balances together with the difference between them in dollars. The second, earlier period amount is subtracted from the first, later period amount to calculate the difference.

Click   the report **contents** you want.

Click   **OK** to display the Balance Sheet.

From any displayed report, you can change report options to create different reports.

Click   the **Modify tool** 🔲 and **choose Report Options** or **choose** the **Options menu** and **click Modify Report** to re-open the report options screen.

Click   ❌ when you have finished to return to the Report Centre.

Displaying the Income Statement

The Income Statement is a summary of how much a business has earned — after expenses — in the interval you select for the statement. You can view the Income Statement at any time from the Report Centre or the Reports menu. We will continue from the Report Centre. The Income Statement list should still be expanded with the options — to display a Standard (single-period), Comparative (two-period) or Multi-Period statement. If inventory costs are tracked, Gross Margin Statements that separate the cost of goods sold from other expenses can also be displayed when inventory is sold.

Click   **Income Statement** and then **Standard** under Income Statement in the Select A Report list to display the report sample.

Click   **Modify This Report** to open the report options window:

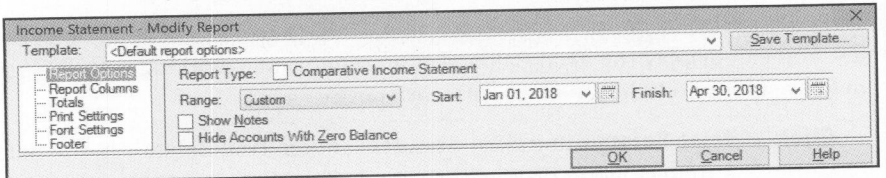

From the Home window, choose the Reports menu, then choose Financials and click Income Statement to open the Modify Report window.

NOTES
If you want a single Balance Sheet only, do not click Comparative Balance Sheet (the check box does not have a ✓ in it). Your most recent session date is displayed by default and highlighted. Choose from the calendar, choose from the date field list or type in the date you want. Click OK to display the Balance Sheet.
If you have accounting data for more than one fiscal period, you can display reports for the previous period as well as for the current period.

NOTES
The date list provided by the list arrow includes the earliest transaction date, the latest session date and the latest transaction date. The earliest transaction date and session date are frequent choices for the start and finish dates in reports.

NOTES
All reports include the option to modify them, so you can change your report options easily. Modifying reports is covered more extensively in Appendix E on the Student DVD.

PRO VERSION
The Pro version does not have the entries for Totals and Footer below Report Options or the option to Show Notes.

NOTES
The default report range is for the fiscal year up to the session date.

As with the Balance Sheet, you can hide accounts with zero balances. You can select the range of dates for the statement from the Range field list or from the Start and Finish field drop-down lists. You can also enter your own choices for the date range (Custom) by typing them in the Start and Finish fields or selecting other dates from the Calendar for those fields. The default range is the fiscal year to date.

Click the **Range field list arrow**:

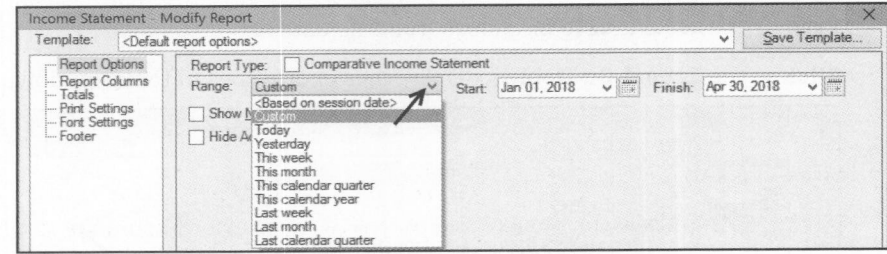

The Income Statement also has a comparative report option, allowing comparisons between two different periods. You might want to compare the income for two months, quarters or years. For the comparative report, you have the same amount and difference options as the Balance Sheet.

NOTES
If you have data for two fiscal periods, the dates for these two periods will be the defaults for comparative income statements.

Click **Comparative Income Statement** to select this option:

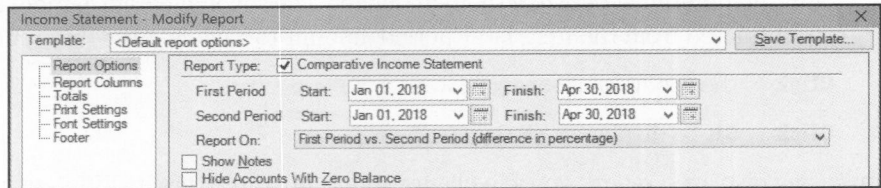

By default, the fiscal start date is provided as the start date for the first period and the second period, and the session date is the finish date for both periods when you select the comparative report.

You must enter beginning and ending dates for the period (or periods) you want your Income Statement to cover. You may accept the defaults, choose a date from the calendar, choose from the date field list or type in the dates.

NOTES
When other modules are used, the Home window Reports menu in the Premium version includes a Business Reports option with several analysis reports. One of these is a Comparative Income Statement – YTD To Last Year. The menu label for these reports changes to match the industry type.

Click the **Start date field** and **enter** the **date** on which your Income Statement period begins.

Press ⟨tab⟩ (**twice** if you type the date).

Enter the **date** that your Income Statement period ends.

Enter the **Start** and **Finish dates** for the second period and **choose** the report **content** for comparative reports.

Click **OK**. **Click** ☒ to close the display window when you have finished.

Displaying the Trial Balance

The Trial Balance has account balances for all postable accounts in debit and credit columns. You can display the Trial Balance at any time while working with the software and have the option to hide accounts with zero balances.

Click **Trial Balance** and then **Standard** under Trial Balance in the Select A Report list to display the sample Trial Balance.

Click **Modify This Report** to open the report options window:

From the Home window choose the Reports menu, then choose Financials and click Trial Balance to open the report options window.

Click   the **default date** and **enter** the **date** for which you want the Trial Balance or choose from the calendar.

Choose   whether you want to **hide accounts with zero balances**.

Click   **OK** to display the Trial Balance.

Click   ☒ to leave the display and return to the previous screen or window.

Displaying the General Ledger Report

The General Ledger Report lists all transactions and account balances for one or more accounts in the selected interval. You can display the General Ledger at any time.

Click   **General Ledger** in the Select A Report list to display the sample report.

Click   **Modify This Report** to open the report options window:

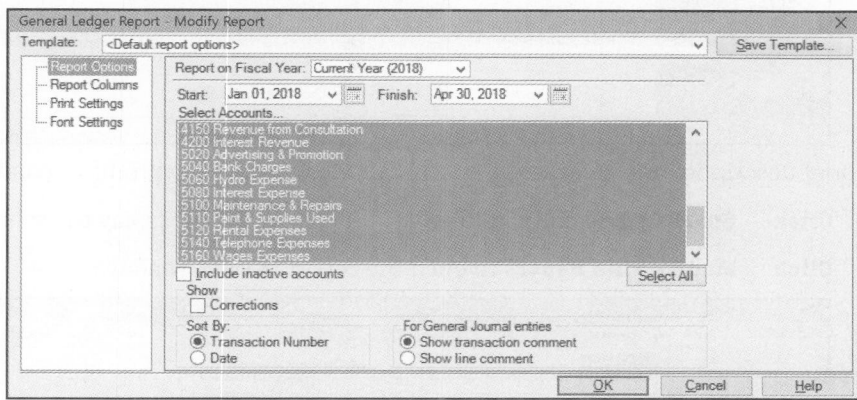

From the Home window choose the Reports menu, then choose Financials and click General Ledger to display the report options.

The General Ledger Report can be sorted in order of the transaction number (journal entry number) or the transaction date. The report includes account balances and transaction or account line comments. The earliest transaction and session dates are the default Start and Finish dates. All accounts are selected for the report initially. You can include or omit the corrections (adjusting and reversing entries) you made to journal entries with the **Show Corrections** option.

Click   an **option** to select it or to change the default choices.

Enter   the **starting date** for your General Ledger Report, choose a date from the calendar or choose a date from the Start field drop-down list.

Press   ⌨tab⌨ (**twice** if you type the date).

Enter   the **ending date** for your General Ledger Report.

The **Select All** option works like a toggle switch. When all accounts are selected, clicking Select All will remove all selections. With one or more accounts selected or with no selections, clicking Select All will include all accounts for the reports.

NOTES
The Trial Balance is also available in two other formats from the Report Type drop-down list: a Comparative Report with the same options as the Balance Sheet, and a report that includes the Net Changes for the selected period — with the debit and credit amounts between the two dates that create the difference.
Click the selection you want, enter the first and second dates, choose the report contents from the Report On list and click OK.

NOTES
When you do not show corrections, only the final correct entry is included in reports. In that case, sorting by date will place the adjusting entries in the correct chronological position.

Click   the **account**, or **press** and **hold** `ctrl` and **click** the **accounts** you want in order to include several individual accounts.

Use the scroll arrows to list more accounts if the one you want is not visible. Click Select All twice to clear all selections.

To select several accounts in a row, click the first one and then press and hold `shift` and click the last one you want to include in the list.

Choose the sorting method (date or journal entry) and the type of comment (transaction or account line) to include in your report.

Click   **OK** to view the report.

Click   ⊠ to close the **display window** after viewing it.

Displaying the Chart of Accounts

The Chart of Accounts is a list of all accounts with the account number, name and account type and class.

Click   **Accounts** in the Select A Report Type list (the list on the left) to expand the Select A Report list:

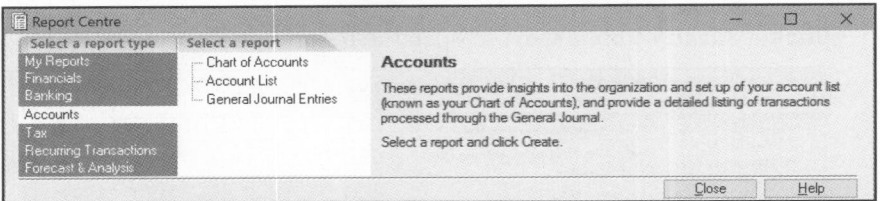

A brief description for the class of Accounts reports appears with the expanded list.

Click   **Chart Of Accounts** in the Select A Report list to display the sample.

Click   **Modify This Report** to open the report options window:

Or, choose the Reports menu, then choose Lists and click Chart Of Accounts to display report options.

Choose   the **year** (in the Select Fields list).

The default report will include the account number, name, type and class.

Click   **OK** to display the chart. **Close** the **display** when you have finished.

Displaying the Account List

If you want to display the Chart of Accounts with account balances or other selected details, you can use the Account List. For example, you could create an account list with only GIFI numbers or account balances as the additional information.

Click   **Account List** in the Select A Report list to display the sample.

Click   **Modify This Report** to open the report options window:

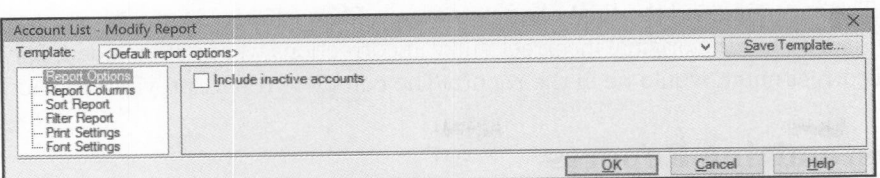

From the Home window, choose the Reports menu, then choose Lists and click Accounts to display the report options.

Click   **OK** to view the report. The default report includes the account number and name, balance, account type and account class.

Click   ☒ to close the **display window** after viewing it.

Displaying the General Journal

Click   **General Journal Entries** in the Select A Report list to display the sample.

Click   **Modify This Report** to open the report options window:

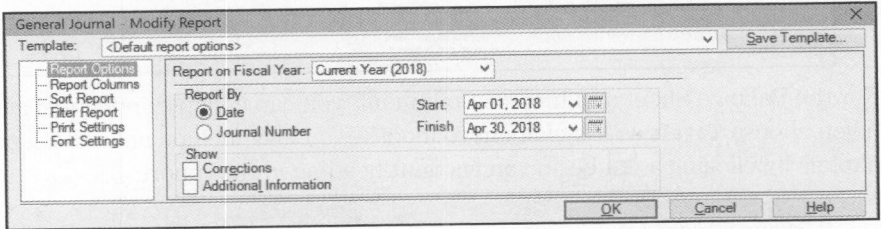

Or, choose the Reports menu, then choose Journal Entries and click General to display the report options.

Journal reports may omit correcting or adjusting entries or may include them to provide a complete audit trail. You may select entries for the report either by the (posting) **Date** of the journal entries or by journal entry number. When you choose **Journal Number**, you must enter the first and last numbers for the entries you want to display. If you do not know the journal numbers, the date method is easier. Furthermore, your journal entry numbers might not match the ones we use if you have made any additional or correcting journal entries. Therefore, all reports in this workbook are requested by date — the default setting.

The earliest transaction and the latest session date are given by default for the period of the report.

    Click   **Corrections** to include the adjusting entries.

You can choose any dates for the Journal Report between the earliest transaction date and the last journal entry, including postdated entries if there are any.

    Accept April 1 and **April 30** as the dates for your Journal Report and **click OK**:

NOTES
You can select different details for the Account List Report by modifying the Report Columns. Refer to Appendix E on the Student DVD.

CLASSIC VIEW
From the Home window, right-click the General Journal icon to select it.
Click the Select A Report tool on the tool bar, to open the report options.

PRO VERSION
The Pro version does not have the option to report on different fiscal years.

NOTES
Since we have only General Journal entries for Muriel's Murals, this report will be the same as the one for All Journal Entries that you select from the Financials report list.

WARNING!
If you do not choose Show Corrections, the journal report will include only the latest corrected version of all entries. Showing the corrections will include the original incorrect entry, the reversing entry and the final correct one, thus providing a complete audit trail.

NOTES
From the Options menu in a displayed report, you can use the Find In This Report option to search for specific information. When you select the option, a Find field opens at the bottom of the report for you to enter the text you want to find. The Options menu also has a Find Next entry so you can continue searching for the next occurrence of the text.

NOTES
Sometimes, depending on who will need the report, you may want to omit the corrections.

NOTES
For example, you could create a journal report that displays only cheques by filtering on the Source field to match the word Cheque (or the entry you used for these transactions). We explain this in Appendix E on the Student DVD.

NOTES
You can easily rearrange columns by dragging a column heading to a new position, or change the width by dragging a column margin.

PRO VERSION
pro The option to show only totals or to collapse the amounts is not available in the Pro version.

NOTES
Clicking ⊞ beside a collapsed amount will expand the account display again.

You can collapse all amounts at once by clicking Show Totals Only. Clicking Show All Amounts will expand the totals and restore all individual amounts.

The reversing and the final corrected entry (J4 and J5) for Memo #1 on page 46 are included. J1 has the original incorrect entry. If corrections were not included, only J5, the final correct entry, would be in the report. The complete report provides the audit trail.

Customizing Reports

When we selected dates, comparative options or correcting journal entries, we were customizing reports. Modify Report windows also include customization options in the pane on the left. You can change the **columns** or fields in the report, sort reports and filter them. **Sorting** reports changes the order in which data are presented, while **filtering** reports selects the records to include according to the data fields used as selection criteria. Printing options may also be modified.

Reports already on display may also be modified. You can choose the elements you want to change from the **Modify tool** drop-down list:

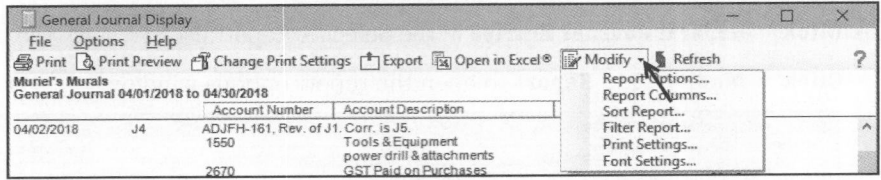

For the Balance Sheet and Income Statement, you can collapse individual amounts when you choose **Totals** as the element to modify. You may include only totals, or only some totals by clicking a ⊟ beside an account heading in the report:

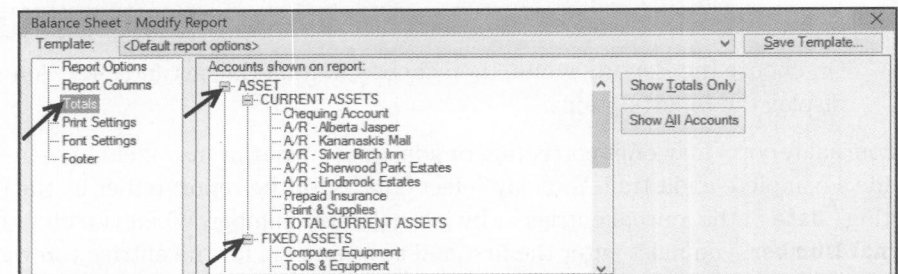

The ⊟ will change to a ⊞ when the amounts have been collapsed.

You can also modify columns directly in the display. For example, you can widen a column by dragging the header margin to the right or remove a column by dragging it to the left. Clicking a column head will sort the report by the contents of that column, if the report can be sorted. Report modifications are covered further in Appendix E.

      Close   the **displayed report** when finished.

Drill-Down Reports

Some reports can be accessed from other reports that you have opened or displayed. These are cross-referenced or drill-down reports.

Whenever the pointer changes to 🔍 (a magnifying glass icon with a plus sign inside it), the additional reports can be displayed. When the other ledgers are used, detailed customer, vendor and employee reports are available from the General Ledger Report and from the General Journal.

      Move   the **mouse pointer** over various items in the first report. The type of second report available may change. The name of the second report will appear in the status bar.

Double-click while the magnifying glass icon is visible to display the second report immediately. The first report stays open in the background.

The General Ledger Report for a specific account can be accessed from the Balance Sheet, Income Statement, Trial Balance, Chart of Accounts or General Journal when you double-click an account number, name or balance amount. The General Ledger record for an account can be accessed from the General Ledger Report.

From any Journal Report, you can open the original transaction by clicking the Source or Comment.

While you have the additional drill-down report displayed, you may print it or drill down to other reports. (Refer to Printing General Reports below.)

Close the **second report** and then **close** the **first report** when you have finished viewing them. **Close** the **Report Centre**.

Printing General Reports

Display the **report** you want to print by following the instructions in the preceding pages on displaying reports.

There are overall print settings for the company file. These are available from the Home window and from any open report. From the displayed report,

Click the **Change Print Settings tool** [icon] or **choose** the **File menu** and **click Reports & Forms**.

The Report & Form Options screen opens:

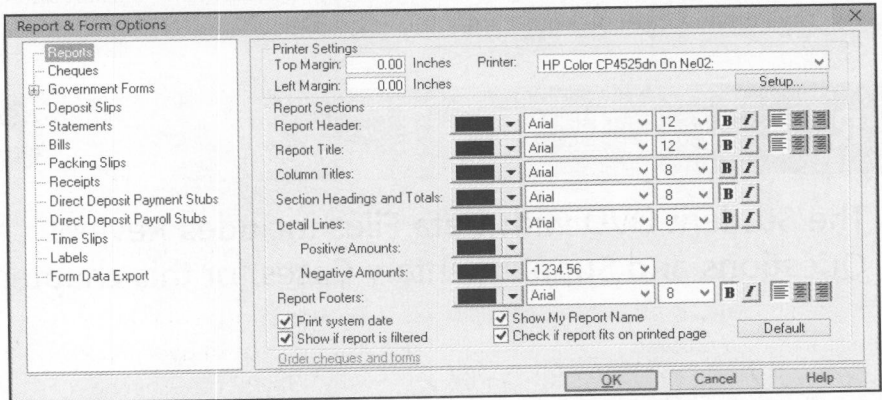

From the Home window, choose the Setup menu and click Reports & Forms.

These settings become the defaults for all company reports.

From this window, you can select a printer, set the margins and choose the default style for different parts of the report. You can also add the computer system date to the report and indicate whether the report is filtered. The Default button will restore the original program default settings for the report.

Choose your **printer** from the drop-down list in the Printer field.

Click **OK** to save your changes and return to the display or **click Cancel** if you do not want to save the changes you made.

If you want to change the appearance only for the displayed report, you should modify the displayed report. The Modify Report windows include Print Settings and Font Settings as elements that you can modify separately for each type of report.

WARNING!
Always check that the correct printer is selected before printing reports. The printer selection is saved with the data file and may be incorrect for your setup.

PRO VERSION
pro Packing Slips and Time Slips will not appear on the list in the Pro version. The term Invoices replaces Bills.

NOTES
From the Setup or other option buttons, you can choose advanced settings for the report and printer.

NOTES
Refer to Appendix E for more detail on modifying Print Settings for individual reports.

Finishing a Session

Finish the last transaction you are working on for this session.

> **Click**   ⊠ to close the transaction window (such as journal input or display) to return to the Home window.

You can click the Close Other Windows tool ⊠ in the Home window if you have more than one open window. To restore the Home window,

> **Click**   the **Home window tool** in an open journal window. Or,

> **Click**   the **Sage 50 button** on the desktop task bar.

> **Click**   the **Close Other Windows tool** ⊠ in the Home window.

> **Click**   ⊠ or **choose** the **File menu** and **click Exit** to close the program.

A message asks if you want to back up the data file first:

```
Sage 50 - Backup
 (?)         Do you want to back up this company before closing?
                    ● Yes      ○ No
 ☐ Do not ask me again.
               [    OK    ]  [  Cancel  ]  [   Help   ]
```

If you did not back up the file after the last set of transactions, you should do so now.

> **Click**   **OK** to start the backup procedure. Follow the instructions on pages 48–49 to complete the backup.

After the backup is complete, the file will close.

Sage 50 will automatically save your work when you finish your session and exit properly. You can now turn off your computer — or take a coffee break.

REVIEW

The Student DVD with Data Files includes Review Questions and Supplementary Cases for this chapter.

It Again

OBJECTIVES

After completing this chapter, you should be able to

- *plan* and *design* an accounting system for a non-profit organization
- *prepare* a conversion procedure from manual records
- *understand* the objectives of a computerized accounting system
- *create* company files using the Skeleton starter file
- *change* the default home window
- *set up* the organization's accounts
- *enter* historical account information
- *finish* entering accounting history to prepare for transactions
- *enter* fiscal end adjusting transactions
- *close* the books and start a new fiscal period
- *enter* transactions for a previous fiscal period

COMPANY INFORMATION

Company Profile

NOTES
Love It Again
4-A Charity Blvd.
Toronto, ON M4G 2T2
Tel: (416) 885-8967
Fax: (647) 885-8967
Business No.: 127 362 644
RR0001

It Again is a store associated with a charitable organization that raises awareness of and supports research on heart disease in children, and encourages organ donations for heart transplants. Most of the store's merchandise is donated. Thus, in addition to the charitable aspect of the business, it promotes an ecologically friendly environment by preventing usable goods from entering landfill sites.

The store sells gently used children's clothing, toys, books, furniture and strollers. Used car seats and cribs are not accepted because of the high safety standards associated with these items. Special-occasion clothing is especially desirable because it is generally more costly to purchase and less worn. Repeat customers frequently donate merchandise. The store also purchases discontinued items such as out-of-print books or end-of-season clothing at reduced prices, floor models or slightly marked but otherwise undamaged goods. All items are priced to sell to encourage faster turnover and return customer visits. Merchandise that is not sold within a short period of time is donated to local shelters that

accommodate families or to organizations that support newly arrived immigrant and refugee families.

As a charity, the store makes every effort to minimize expenses. Overseen by a board of directors, the store pays only the salaried manager, Jeremy Fischer, who is assisted by a volunteer sales staff. These volunteers are often parents of children who have experienced heart-health issues.

Funds from the sale of items that were purchased are subject to HST at 13 percent (or GST at 5 percent for children's clothing and books). Donated items are not taxed on resale.

Volunteers handle all the day-to-day sales. The organization does incur some expenses: the manager's salary, rent, a computerized cash register to record all sales and donations, office supplies, promotional materials, telephones and so on.

The bank account has been set up for regular deposits and to write cheques for expenses. Some cash is also kept on hand at the store to make change for on-site sales and for incidental purchases. Most of the cash and cheques received are deposited immediately for security purposes, but for the sake of reducing the length of the exercise, monthly sales summaries and bank deposits are recorded.

Love It Again has decided to start using Sage 50 to keep the accounting records in August 2018, partway through its current fiscal year. The charity requires only General Ledger accounts. The following information is available to set up the accounts using the General Ledger:

- Chart of Accounts
- Income Statement
- Balance Sheet
- Trial Balance
- Accounting Procedures

CHART OF ACCOUNTS

LOVE IT AGAIN

ASSETS
- 1000 CURRENT ASSETS [H]
- 1020 Bank: Love It Again [A]
- 1100 Cash on Hand [A]
- 1150 Total Cash [S]
- 1190 Prepaid Expenses
- 1200 Purchased Clothing
- 1210 Purchased Books
- 1220 Other Purchased Items
- 1300 Office Supplies
- 1310 Other Supplies
- 1320 T-shirts
- 1390 TOTAL CURRENT ASSETS [T]

- 1500 FIXED ASSETS [H]
- 1510 Fax/Telephone
- 1520 Computers
- 1530 Store Furniture & Shelving
- 1590 TOTAL FIXED ASSETS [T] ▶

▶LIABILITIES
- 2000 CURRENT LIABILITIES [H]
- 2100 Bank Loan
- 2200 A/P - Kids Stuff
- 2300 A/P - Kids In Motion
- 2350 A/P - Wearable Designs
- 2400 A/P - Places For Us
- 2550 GST Charged on Sales [A]
- 2560 HST Charged on Sales [A]
- 2570 GST Paid on Purchases [A]
- 2580 HST Paid on Purchases [A]
- 2590 GST/HST Owing/Refund [S]
- 2690 TOTAL CURRENT LIABILITIES [T]

EQUITY
- 3000 EQUITY [H]
- 3560 Accumulated Surplus
- 3600 Net Income [X]
- 3690 TOTAL EQUITY [T] ▶

▶REVENUE
- 4000 REVENUE [H]
- 4020 Revenue: Donated Items
- 4040 Revenue: Purchased Clothing & Books
- 4080 Revenue: Other Purchases
- 4100 Revenue: Donations
- 4390 TOTAL REVENUE [T]

EXPENSE
- 5000 OPERATING EXPENSES [H]
- 5020 Rental Expense
- 5200 Supplies Used
- 5240 Postage Expense
- 5280 Maintenance Expenses
- 5300 Utilities Expenses
- 5320 Publicity & Promotion
- 5400 Wages - Manager
- 5420 Miscellaneous Expenses
- 5490 TOTAL OPERATING EXPENSES [T] ▶

▶5500 COST OF GOODS SOLD [H]
- 5510 Cost of Purchased Clothing & Books
- 5520 Cost of Other Purchases
- 5690 TOTAL COST OF GOODS SOLD [T]

NOTES: The Chart of Accounts is based on the current expenses and accounts. Account types are marked in brackets for subgroup Accounts [A], Subgroup totals [S], Headings [H], Totals [T] and Current Earnings [X]. All unmarked accounts are postable Group [G] accounts. The explanation of account types begins on page 84.

INCOME STATEMENT

LOVE IT AGAIN

For the Ten Months Ending July 31, 2018

Revenue

4000	REVENUE	
4020	Revenue: Donated Items	$ 22 600.00
4040	Revenue: Purchased Clothing & Books	41 200.00
4080	Revenue: Other Purchases	33 400.00
4100	Revenue: Donations	9 800.00
4390	TOTAL REVENUE	$107 000.00
	TOTAL REVENUE	$107 000.00

Expense

5000	OPERATING EXPENSES	
5020	Rental Expense	$18 000.00
5200	Supplies Used	320.00
5240	Postage Expense	1 850.00
5280	Maintenance Expenses	5 200.00
5300	Utilities Expenses	4 800.00
5320	Publicity & Promotion	1 230.00
5400	Wages - Manager	42 000.00
5490	TOTAL OPERATING EXPENSES	$73 400.00
	TOTAL EXPENSE	$73 400.00
	NET INCOME	$33 600.00

BALANCE SHEET

LOVE IT AGAIN

August 1, 2018

Assets

1000	CURRENT ASSETS		
1020	Bank: Love It Again	$46 380.00	
1100	Cash on Hand	1 220.00	
1150	Total Cash		$47 600.00
1190	Prepaid Expenses		290.00
1200	Purchased Clothing		7 110.00
1210	Purchased Books		4 790.00
1220	Other Purchased Items		14 200.00
1300	Office Supplies		380.00
1310	Other Supplies		1 120.00
1320	T-shirts		360.00
1390	TOTAL CURRENT ASSETS		$75 850.00
1500	FIXED ASSETS		
1510	Fax/Telephone		390.00
1520	Computers		4 560.00
1530	Store Furniture & Shelving		8 600.00
1590	TOTAL FIXED ASSETS		$13 550.00
	TOTAL ASSETS		$89 400.00

Liabilities

2000	CURRENT LIABILITIES		
2100	Bank Loan		$ 14 000.00
2200	A/P - Kids Stuff		904.00
2300	A/P - Kids In Motion		1 260.00
2350	A/P - Wearable Designs		339.00
2550	GST Charged on Sales	$2 060.00	
2560	HST Charged on Sales	4 342.00	
2570	GST Paid on Purchases	-605.00	
2580	HST Paid on Purchases	-4 795.00	
2590	GST/HST Owing/Refund		1 002.00
2690	TOTAL CURRENT LIABILITIES		$17 505.00
	TOTAL LIABILITIES		$17 505.00

Equity

3000	EQUITY	
3560	Accumulated Surplus	$ 38 295.00
3600	Net Income	33 600.00
3690	TOTAL EQUITY	$ 71 895.00
	TOTAL EQUITY	$ 71 895.00
	LIABILITIES AND EQUITY	$89 400.00

TRIAL BALANCE

LOVE IT AGAIN

August 1, 2018	Debits	Credits	August 1, 2018	Debits	Credits
1020 Bank: Love It Again	$46 380.00		▶ 2570 GST Paid on Purchases	$ 605.00	
1100 Cash on Hand	1 220.00		2580 HST Paid on Purchases	4 795.00	
1190 Prepaid Expenses	290.00		3560 Accumulated Surplus		$ 38 295.00
1200 Purchased Clothing	7 110.00		4020 Revenue: Donated Items		22 600.00
1210 Purchased Books	4 790.00		4040 Revenue: Purchased		
1220 Other Purchased Items	14 200.00		Clothing & Books		41 200.00
1300 Office Supplies	380.00		4080 Revenue: Other Purchases		33 400.00
1310 Other Supplies	1 120.00		4100 Revenue: Donations		9 800.00
1320 T-shirts	360.00		5020 Rental Expense	18 000.00	
1510 Fax/Telephone	390.00		5200 Supplies Used	320.00	
1520 Computers	4 560.00		5240 Postage Expense	1 850.00	
1530 Store Furniture & Shelving	8 600.00		5280 Maintenance Expenses	5 200.00	
2100 Bank Loan		$14 000.00	5300 Utilities Expenses	4 800.00	
2200 A/P - Kids Stuff		904.00	5320 Publicity & Promotion	1 230.00	
2300 A/P - Kids In Motion		1 260.00	5400 Wages - Manager	42 000.00	
2350 A/P - Wearable Designs		339.00		$168 200.00	$168 200.00
2550 GST Charged on Sales		2 060.00			
2560 HST Charged on Sales		4 342.00 ▶			

Accounting Procedures

HST

Registered charities have two options with respect to the GST and HST. Like regular for-profit businesses, they can register, charge taxes on sales, membership fees and so on, and claim taxes paid as input tax credits to reduce the liability to the Receiver General. The second option does not require collection of taxes but permits a Public Service Bodies' (PSB) rebate of taxes paid. Love It Again charges GST and HST because it sells merchandise. No taxes are charged on donated goods, but other sales are subject to regular tax charges. HST and GST paid toward operating expenses are deemed as input tax credits (ITCs). Other expenses, such as the cost of merchandise, are not ITCs.

Tax returns are prepared by debiting *GST* and *HST Charged on Sales* and crediting *GST* and *HST Paid on Purchases*. If a refund is due, it is entered as an *Accounts Receivable* debit entry that can be cleared when the rebate is received. After the remittance, the tax accounts will have residual balances that are cleared at year-end and recorded as income.

Bank Accounts

The proceeds from the sale of merchandise are entered into the *Cash on Hand* account. This account is also used for some small day-to-day purchases. Donation receipts are deposited directly to the *Bank: Love It Again* account. Cheques to suppliers for merchandise and operating and administrative expenses are also written from this bank account. Transfers of surplus cash — amounts not needed to make change for customers — are made regularly from *Cash on Hand* to *Bank: Love It Again*.

NOTES

HST does not apply to the sale of books or children's clothing — only GST applies to these sales. Therefore, Love It Again has both GST and HST accounts.

A charity must register for GST/HST to receive the PSB rebate. The federal portion of the rebate — 50 percent of the 5 percent GST paid (form GST66) — is separated from the provincial portion — 82 percent of the 8 percent PST paid (Ontario form RC7066SCH). We have completed the rebate and net tax calculations for Love It Again.

The provincial rebate percentage varies among the different provinces and for different types of non-profit organizations.

INSTRUCTIONS

1. **Set up** the **company accounts for Love It Again** in the General Ledger in Sage 50 using all the information provided in this application. Detailed keystroke instructions follow.

2. **Back up your work frequently** when working through this application to keep your backups updated.

   You may finish your session at any time while completing the setup. Simply open the Love It Again data file again, accept the session date and continue from where you left off.

   If you are using a different location for your data files, substitute the appropriate data path, including the drive and folder, for your data setup.

3. **Enter** the **source documents** that begin on page 96 in the General Journal in Sage 50 using the Chart of Accounts and other information provided.

4. **Print** the **following reports** after you have completed your entries — choose Previous Year (2018) as the reporting period:

   a. General Journal from July 1 to September 30
   b. Comparative Balance Sheet at September 30 and October 1 (amounts)
   c. Income Statement for the period October 1, 2017, to September 30, 2018

WARNING!
You must choose 2018 as the year for journal entries because there is no data for October 1, the default date for the Journal Report.

KEYSTROKES FOR SETUP

The following are the five key stages in preparing the Sage 50 program for use by a company:

1. creating company files
2. preparing the system
3. preparing the ledgers
4. printing reports to check your work
5. backing up your files and finishing the company history

   The following keystroke instructions are written for a stand-alone PC with a hard drive. The keystroke instructions provided in this application demonstrate one approach to setting up company accounts. Always refer to the Sage 50 and Windows manuals and Help for further details.

Creating Company Files

The instructions we provide assume that you installed the Sage 50 data files on your hard disk in drive C: in the SageData16 folder.

Sage 50 provides both templates and starter files to make it easier to create files for a new company. These files contain different sets of accounts that match the needs of different kinds of businesses. By starting with one of these files, you eliminate the need to create all the accounts for your business from scratch.

There are many templates that work with the setup wizards to define not only accounts but also a number of settings for the different ledgers. These settings and accounts are suited to the type of business named by the files.

NOTES
Using subsequent versions of Sage 50 may result in different screens and keystrokes from those described in this application.

NOTES
You must work in single-user mode to set up new company files. Access to most settings is restricted in multi-user mode.

NOTES
The non-profit template has many more accounts, modules and features than are needed for Love It Again. This file, therefore, would require substantially more modification to make it match the company profile in this chapter.

NOTES

We want to illustrate different ways of creating company files. Therefore, the method of creating your company files from scratch is described in the Air Care Services setup application in Chapter 7.

Before 2016, the two Sage 50 starter files — Skeleton and Integration (Integration Plus) — could be updated to a later version of Sage 50. These files contain only a set of basic accounts. The Skeleton starter has only General Ledger accounts, whereas the Integration Plus starter is suitable for a variety of business types because it has the basic linked accounts for all the ledgers.

Both files are from an earlier version of the program (Simply Basic 2005) that cannot be updated with Sage 50 2016, so we created a Sage 50 Pro 2016.2 version copy of the Skeleton file to use with this text. We placed this file in the SageData16 folder with the other data files. Furthermore, the Student version program cannot open or update any data files from versions older than 2016 (Release 2).

The Skeleton starter files are best suited to the Chart of Accounts for Love It Again. These files contain only a few General Ledger accounts, headings and totals. They contain no linked accounts that link General Ledger accounts to the subsidiary ledgers. This is appropriate for Love It Again, which uses only the General Ledger.

You will have to customize any starter file to your particular company. Rarely are accounts and features identical for any two businesses.

The starter files are located in the TEMPLATE folder in the Sage 50 Premium Accounting Version 2016 folder — the folder that contains your Sage 50 program.

We will open the SKELETON.SAI file we updated from the SageData16\TEMPLATE folder.

Start   the **Sage 50 program** to access the Select Company window.

Click   **Select An Existing Company** to access the Open Company window:

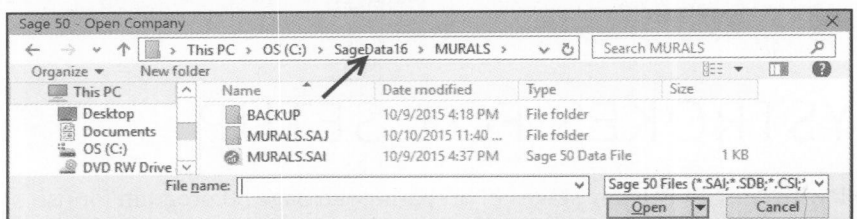

NOTES

If you are using backup files, restore SageData16\ SKELETON1.CAB or SKELETON1 to SageData16\AGAIN\AGAIN. Sage 50 will create the necessary new folder. Refer to page 24 for assistance with restoring backup files.

If you start from the backup file, you will not need to complete the additional step of saving the file after the Upgrade wizard has completed.

Click   **SageData16** in the file path field to return to this folder and display all the folders you installed from the Student DVD.

Double-click   **TEMPLATE** to open this folder.

Click   **SKELETON** (or **SKELETON.SAI**) to select this data file. **Click Open** to start the Upgrade Company Wizard:

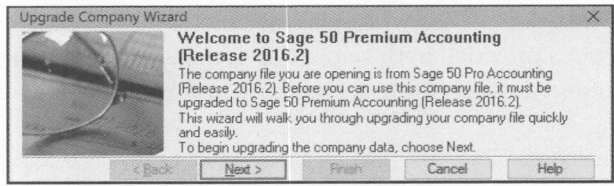

The Pro version Skeleton starter file must be converted to Premium Release 2016.2.

Read   the **introduction** to the wizard and **click Next** to continue:

PRO VERSION

The file will not be converted. You will begin with the Session Date screen on page 71 immediately, also skipping the selection of the type of company.

This screen has the name and location of the working file and the version changes that will be made if you proceed.

Click   Next:

You can now back up the Skeleton file before proceeding. The program will check your data file for problems and repair them if you choose this option.

Click   Next to open the final warning about converting files:

This final screen warns you of the changes you are making. After this step you cannot cancel the conversion. File conversions cannot be reversed — once you convert a file you will be unable to open it in the earlier version.

Click   Finish to begin the conversion.

You will now be asked to indicate the type of company you are working with. Different company types have different icon and journal labels in the Premium version.

Click   the list arrow beside Other, the default entry, to list the types:

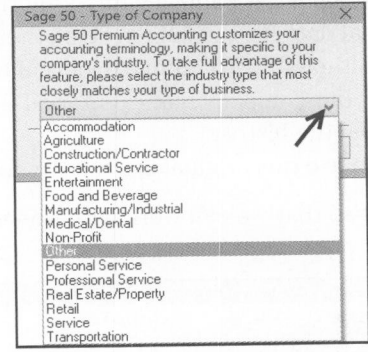

Click   Non-Profit and then **click OK**.

The Session Date window appears with January 1, 2000, as the session date:

Click   OK to accept the date for now. We will update it later.

The Getting Started Welcome screen and the Daily Business Manager will now open. One window may be open in the background behind the other.

Click   Show This Window On Startup to remove the ✓, then **click** the **Close button** to close the Getting Started window.

Click   ⊠ to close the Daily Business Manager window.

 WARNING!
If you make a backup at this stage, it will be a Premium Version Release 2016.2 backup.

NOTES
When you upgrade to a later release, you will be reminded about payroll tax changes because new releases of Sage 50 are tied to tax table changes that usually occur every six months.

NOTES
Clicking the Sage 50 icon on your Windows desktop task bar will let you know which Sage windows are open. Click the one you need to make it active and bring it to the front so that you can close it.

PRO VERSION

pro Sage 50 Pro Accounting is
displayed as the program name.
The ledger icon labels are
Customers and Projects. Sales
Invoices replaces Statements and
Sales replaces Supporter for the
Quote and Order labels.

The Home window opens and all ledgers are available in the list of modules.

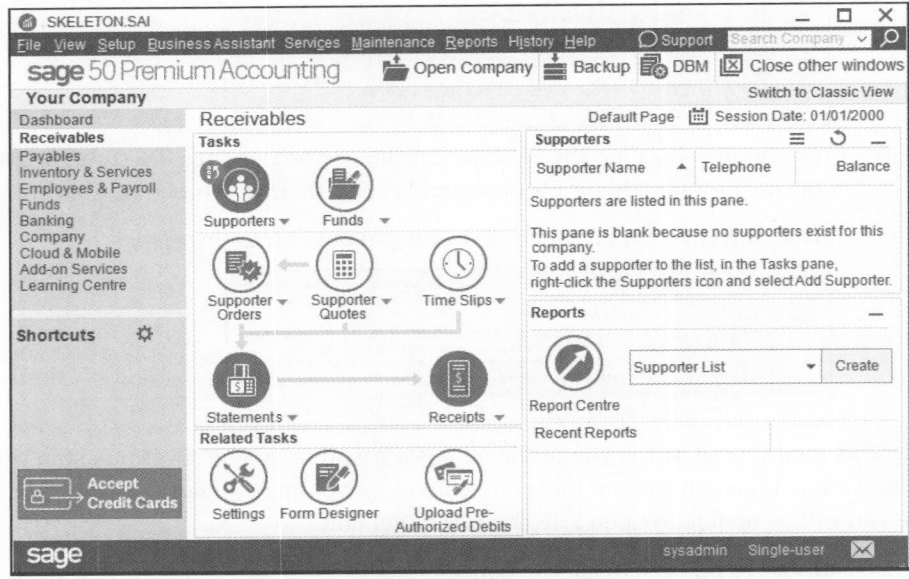

The ledger icon is labelled Supporters because we selected Non-Profit as the company type. For other types of companies, this icon may be labelled Customers or Clients. Projects are labelled Funds for non-profit companies.

PRO VERSION

pro The open history symbol
appears with the Customers icon.

The ledgers are not set up. An open history symbol appears on Supporters, the ledger icon, indicating that you can enter historical data for the ledger. The other modules have the same symbol on ledger icons. Although you can make journal entries at this stage, you should first save this file under your company name, enter all the necessary company information and finish entering the history.

First we will copy the template files so we can use this original again if we need to.

> **Choose** the **File menu** and **click Save As** so that we can work with the new copy:

The Save As window opens. The path <C:\SageData16\TEMPLATE> indicates the location of the open SKELETON file. NEW.SAI (or NEW) is the default name for the new data file. We need to delete the name NEW and create a new data folder for Love It Again, but we want this under the SageData16 folder level.

> **Click** **SageData16** in the file path field. We need to return to the SageData16 folder where we will create the new data folder.

> **Delete** **NEW** (or **NEW.SAI**) in the File Name field.

> **Click** **Browse Folders** if necessary to expand the window and include the New Folder option:

> **Click** **New Folder**. The name New Folder is selected as the folder name, so we can change it. **Type** AGAIN

> **Click** the **AGAIN folder** and **click Open** or **double-click** the **AGAIN folder**:

NOTES

For consistency, we use
upper case for the names of all
files and folders, but you may
choose to type the names in lower
case. The screen display may
sometimes be in upper case even
though you entered a lower case
name.

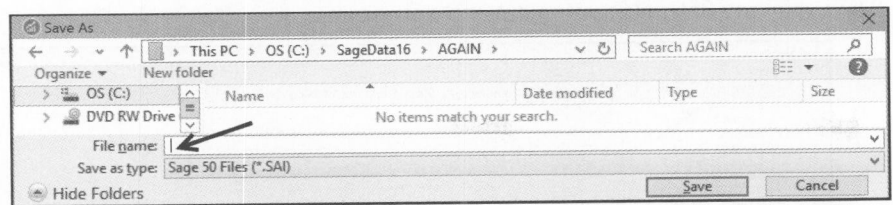

We can now enter the name for the new company file. NEW.SAI may be selected.

> **Click** the **File Name field**. **Type** AGAIN and **click Save**.

Now the same Home window is open, but it has the file name AGAIN.SAI (or AGAIN) in the title bar:

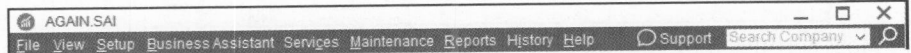

The Receivables module is the default for the Home window. We will change this default because Love It Again does not use this module.

Changing the Default Home Window

Love It Again uses only the General Ledger (Company module), so we will make this the Home window. The Receivables module has Default Page beside the name.

> **Click** **Company** in the list of modules on the left to change the Home window.

Now we have the Chart of Accounts and the General Journal available. The message beside Company has changed to Make Default. Clicking this option for any module will select the displayed module as the default Home window.

> **Click** **Make Default**. The Company heading now has Default Page beside it:

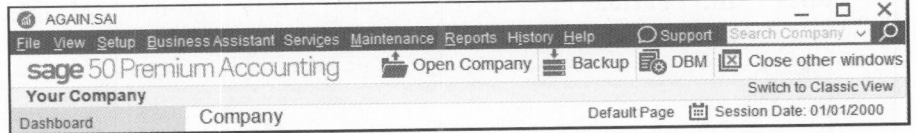

Preparing the System

Before entering financial records for a new company, you must prepare the system for operation. This involves changing the default settings to reflect the Love It Again company information, such as the company name and address, fiscal dates, screen display preferences and Chart of Accounts. Some initial defaults will not be suitable for Love It Again. You must also provide other information, such as the printer(s) that you will be using and the printing formats. This process of adding, deleting and modifying information is called customizing the system.

Changing Company Default Settings

> **Click** the **Settings icon** [Settings] in the Related Tasks pane, or **choose** the **Setup menu** and **click Settings**:

NOTES
The not-finished symbol appears on the Chart of Accounts icon in the Company module window.

NOTES
You cannot complete the setup in multi-user mode.

NOTES
The Sage 50 Setup menu includes a Setup Guide for modifying and creating ledger records. We will use this method to edit or modify the accounts.
The Setup menu also has wizards for linked accounts, adding users and updating HST. Because none of these wizards modify the company settings, we cannot use them to complete the setup.

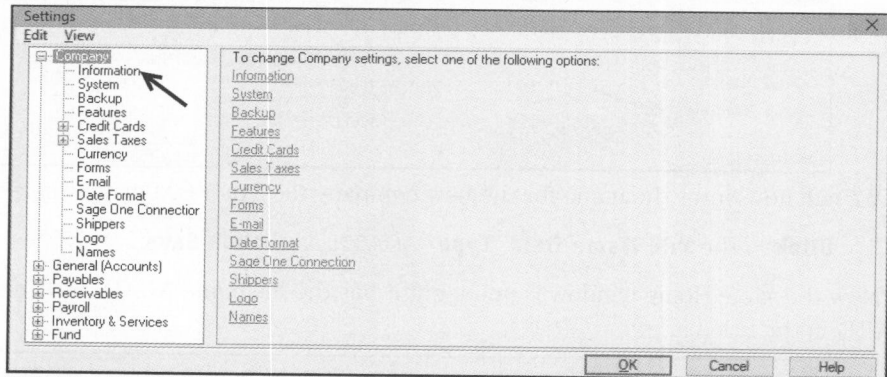

NOTES
If another module is open when you choose Settings, the settings for that ledger will open first. Click Company and then click Information to open the Information screen.

NOTES
Clicking the ⊟ beside a module name will collapse the expanded list.

WARNING!
The initial date format for this file is day/month/year. This is evident from the Fiscal End date.

NOTES
You can personalize your files by adding your own name to the Name field (e.g., Love It Again – Sabeena) so that all reports printed will include your name for easy identification.

The Company Settings main menu window opens:

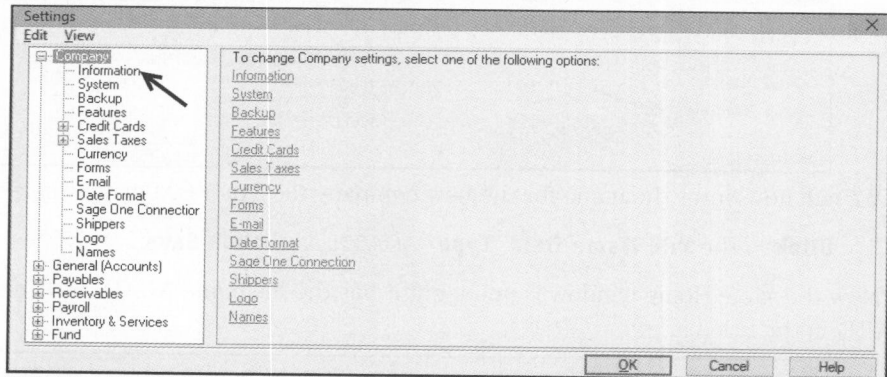

Most settings for a data file are entered from this central Settings screen. Some apply to features and modules not used by Love It Again. We will skip the screens that do not apply; they will be introduced in later chapters.

The modules are listed on the left. The remaining modules have a ⊞ beside them indicating they also have multiple settings. The larger right-hand pane begins with the same expanded list of entries for the selected module as the expanded list on the left. The open Company module has a ⊟ beside it.

Clicking a ⊞ beside an entry will expand the list and change the icon to ⊟. Clicking an entry in the list on the left without a ⊞ beside it or in the list on the right-hand side will open the options window for that entry.

Entering Company Information

Company settings apply to all modules of the company for all users of the data file.

Click   **Information** (in either the left-hand side or right-hand side list) to open the Company information screen:

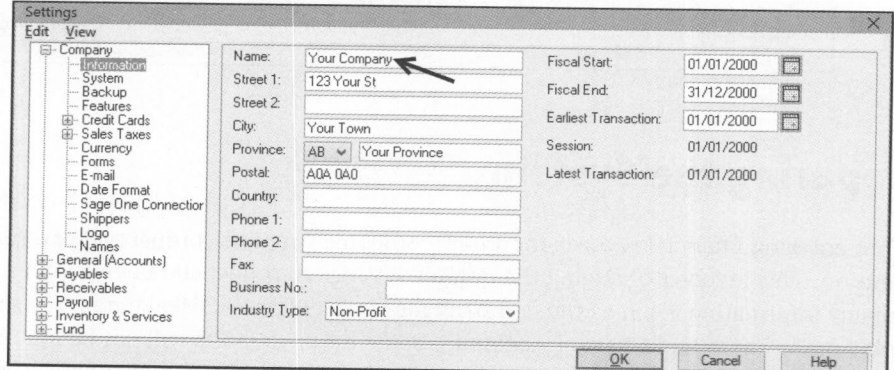

The Name field contains the information "Your Company" to let you know that this is where you should enter the name of your company.

Press   ⌷ tab ⌷ or **drag through Your Company** to select this text.

Type   Love It Again (add your own name). **Press** ⌷ tab ⌷.

The cursor moves to the Street 1 field, the first address field. You can enter the address immediately because the current contents are already highlighted.

Type   4-A Charity Blvd.

Press   ⌷ tab ⌷ to advance to the second street address line (Street 2 field).

Press   ⌷ tab ⌷ again to leave this field blank. The cursor advances to and highlights the contents of the City field.

Type   Toronto **Press** ⌈tab⌉ .

The cursor advances to the Province code field. It, too, is ready for editing.

Typing the first letter of the province name will enter the first province beginning with that letter. Typing the same letter again or clicking the list arrow will advance the list to the next province starting with the same letter. You can also select a code from the drop-down list.

Type   O **Press** ⌈tab⌉ to advance to the province name field. ON and Ontario are entered as this is the only province beginning with "O."

Press   ⌈tab⌉ again to accept Ontario as the province.

The cursor is now placed in the highlighted Postal (postal code) field. You do not have to type the capitals or spaces in postal codes.

Type   m4g2t2

The program automatically corrects the postal code format when you enter a Canadian postal code pattern.

In this case, all addresses will be in Canada, so we can leave the Country field blank. Now enter the telephone and fax numbers for the business. There is only one phone number, so the Phone 2 field will remain blank. You do not need to type brackets or hyphens for phone numbers. Sage 50 will correct the format when you enter a seven- or ten-digit phone number.

Click   the **Phone 1 field**. The postal code format is corrected.

Type   4168858967

Click   the **Fax field**. The telephone number format is corrected.

Type   6478858967

Press   ⌈tab⌉ to move to the Business No. field.

All companies must use a single Canada Revenue Agency business number that also serves as the HST registration number. All business numbers have an Rx extension that indicates the business area for tax purposes.

Type   127362644 RR0001 **Press** ⌈tab⌉ .

There are a number of types of companies to choose from in the program. We selected the type when we upgraded the data file. You can select from the **Industry Type** list to change the type. Changing the company type will also change the icon labels.

Sage 50 will accept dates after January 1, 1900. You can store 100 years of accounting records.

The **Fiscal Start** field contains the date at which the current fiscal year begins. This date usually defines the beginning of the fiscal year for income tax purposes.

The **Fiscal End** is the date at which the company closes its books, usually one year after the fiscal start, and the end of the fiscal year used for income tax reporting purposes. For Love It Again, the fiscal end is two months after converting the files to Sage 50.

The **Earliest Transaction** date is the date on which the company converts its manual accounting records to the computerized system. Entries before this date are historical entries. The earliest transaction date must not be earlier than the fiscal start and not later than the fiscal end. The earliest transaction date will be the first session date when you are ready to enter journal transactions. Sage 50 automatically advances the earliest transaction date when you start a new fiscal year.

NOTES
From the Fiscal End Date entry, 31/12/2000, you can tell that the date order is day-month-year. You cannot determine the order from the Start and Earliest Transaction dates.

WARNING!
Type the date as text to avoid number confusion, such as entering Jan 10 instead of Oct 1. Type 2017 and 2018 (use four digits) for the year. If you type 17 and 18, Sage 50 may enter 1917 and 1918 – this entry is controlled by Windows settings.

NOTES
When you view the Company Information again, the session and latest transaction dates will have been updated to match the new fiscal dates.

PRO VERSION
There is no warning about changing the industry type because the terminology does not change in the Pro version.

WARNING!
You must save the new fiscal dates before changing the Do Not Allow Transactions Before date.

PRO VERSION
The option to enter transactions in a later fiscal or calendar year is not available.

NOTES
Refer to Appendix N on the Student DVD for more information on accrual- and cash-basis accounting. Refer to Appendix H on the Student DVD for an exercise with keystrokes that uses cash-basis accounting in Sage 50.

PRO VERSION
The terms Purchases and Sales will replace Expenses and Revenues.

The **default date format** for this file is day-month-year. We will enter the fiscal dates in text form and then change the date format for the file. By entering text with four digits for the year initially, we will ensure that we enter the date correctly.

Press (tab) to advance to the Fiscal Start field.

Type oct 1 2017 **Press** (tab) **twice**.

Sage 50 entered 01/10/2017 as the fiscal start. The cursor is in the Fiscal End field.

Type sep 30 2018 **Press** (tab) **twice**.

Sage 50 has entered 30/09/2018 as the fiscal end. The cursor is now in the Earliest Transaction field.

Type aug 1 2018

The session date and the latest transaction date will change automatically as you complete journal entries and advance the session date from the Home window. When the **latest transaction date** is later than the session date, it indicates there are postdated journal transactions.

You cannot change the fiscal start or earliest transaction date after finishing the history and making journal entries. The company name, address and fiscal end date can be edited at any time. Return to any field with errors to correct mistakes.

You will need to save the fiscal dates before completing the next step.

Click **OK**. If you change the industry type from this Information screen, the Sage 50 message requires confirmation before making the change:

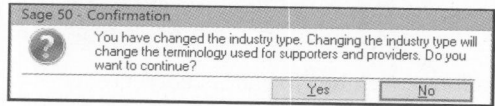

Click **Yes** to accept the changes.

Setting System Defaults

Click the **Settings icon**, or **choose** the **Setup menu** and **click Settings** to resume.

Click **System** in the list under Company to access the options:

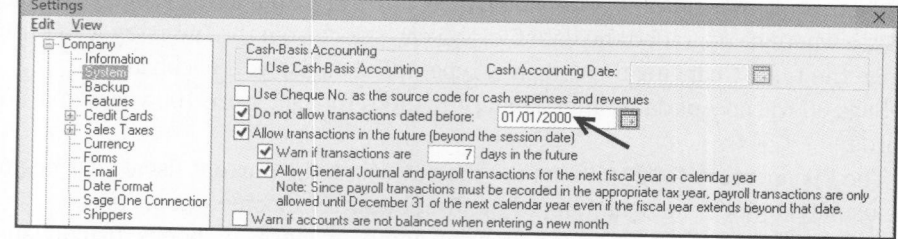

The Company System settings apply to all modules of the program.

This screen has several important settings. The first refers to whether the business is using **cash-basis accounting** instead of the default, **accrual-basis accounting**. The cash basis of accounting records revenues and expenses on the date the money is paid or received. In the accrual method, revenues and expenses are recorded on the transaction date (matching principle). To change to the cash-basis method, click the check box and enter the date on which the change is to take effect. This text uses the accrual basis. Do not change this setting.

The next option relates to the use of the **Cheque Number As The Source Code For Cash Expenses And Revenues** in account reconciliation. Since Love It Again uses only

the General Ledger, this option does not apply. When you are using the Payables and Receivables ledgers, you should turn on this option.

The next option, **Do Not Allow Transactions Dated Before**, permits you to lock out transactions before the date you enter here to prevent posting incorrectly to an earlier date. Similarly, you should generally not **allow posting to future periods**, beyond the session date, unless you are entering a series of postdated transactions. You can add a warning for dates beyond a certain period as well. You can activate these features for specific transactions when needed by changing the settings so that you do not post with incorrect dates. We will restrict transactions before the earliest transaction date and not allow postdated transactions. Transactions before the earliest transaction date are not allowed after you finish the history.

Remember that the date format is still day-month-year.

> **Ensure** that **Do Not Allow Transactions Dated Before** has a ✓.
>
> **Drag through** the date **01/01/2000**.
>
> **Type** aug 1 (Sage 50 will add the year from the fiscal date information.)
>
> **Click** **Allow Transactions In The Future** to remove the ✓ and not allow postdating.

Since Sage 50 allows journal entries before the company setup details are completed, you can add a reminder **warning** as you continue to work with an incomplete and **unbalanced account history**. If you choose to post journal entries before completing the history, you should turn on the warning.

Setting Backup Options

> **Click** **Backup** in the list under Company:

This screen has several options for backing up company files. You can select the **frequency** with which you **back up** your data. Since we usually advance the session date weekly, we will choose Weekly as the backup frequency as well. The program prompts you to back up according to this entry.

> **Click** the **Display A Backup Reminder field list arrow** and **choose Weekly**.

If you want a specific number of days as the interval between backups, choose Other and type the number in the Number Of Days field that opens.

The next option will provide a **reminder** to back up the file each time you close the company file. Leave the option selected because you should back up data files regularly.

You should **verify** the backup files regularly to ensure there are no errors that will prevent you from restoring the data later.

You can **schedule automatic backups** by choosing the frequency, the backup file location and the **number of old backup files** that should be saved.

Choosing Company Features

Sage 50 includes a number of features that are not used by Love It Again — they do not apply to the General Ledger. We can turn them off to reduce the complexity of the screens and setup.

WARNING! The date you enter for Do Not Allow Transactions Dated Before must not be earlier than the Earliest Transaction Date on the Company Information screen.

If the check box is not checked, you can leave the date field blank. You can also enter the date later.

If you did not save the new fiscal dates, you will get an error message if you enter Aug 1 2018 — the original fiscal year 2000 will restrict the date allowed.

NOTES Refer to page 104 for details on allowing transactions in a previous year.

NOTES Sage 50 forces the General Ledger to remain balanced, so this warning does not apply to Love It Again (refer to page 95).

PRO VERSION

Packing slips are not available in the Pro version. The terms Vendors, Customers and Project replace Providers, Supporters and Fund.

Click **Features** in the list below Company in the left-hand side panel:

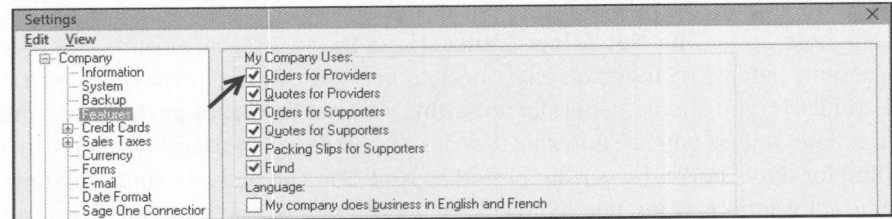

Orders, quotes and packing slips do not apply to General Ledger transactions. The final option refers to languages used. To create forms in both languages, you must choose the option to conduct business in English and French. The Settings option makes the language switch available for many name fields so you can enter names in both languages. The working language for the program is controlled from the View menu (refer to pages 82–83), not from the Features setting.

> **Click** **each check box** or **feature** to change all settings. This will remove all checkmarks and add one to **My Company Does Business In English And French**, the final option.

Credit cards, sales taxes, currency, e-mail and form numbers, such as for invoices and quotes, do not apply to the General Journal transactions entered by Love It Again. Love It Again does not use Shippers or the additional Names fields in the General Ledger, so you can skip these screens as well.

Changing Date Formats

The date formats for the starter file are different from the formats we used for other files. To avoid entering incorrect dates, we will choose the same format that we used for our other data files. We need to change the default setting so that the month appears first. You can choose any separator character you want.

> **Click** **Date Format** in the list below Company in the left-hand side panel:

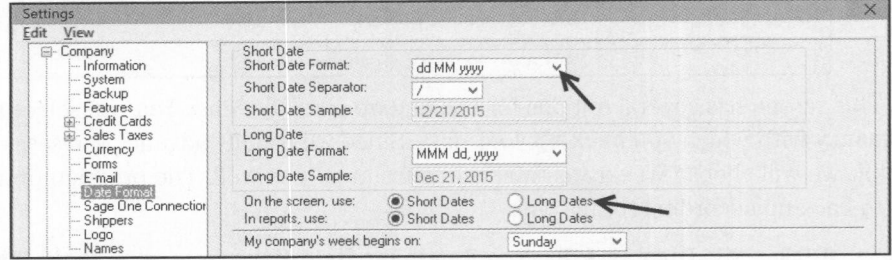

> **Choose** **MM dd yyyy** from the Short Date Format drop-down list.

> Choose another separator symbol from the Short Date Separator list, if you want.

On the screen we choose the long form for dates, that is, text style, to make them as clear as possible. You can choose long or short dates for reports.

> **Click** **Long Dates** beside the option for On The Screen, Use.

You can also enter the day that is normally the first day of the business week.

NOTES

The entry for Week Begins On is used for reports that have This Week To Date as an option for the date range.

Adding a Company Logo

Next we will add the company logo. This logo can be added to invoices or other company documents created in Sage 50.

Click   Logo:

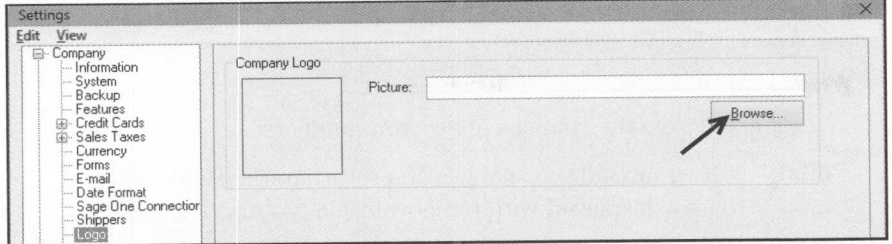

Click   Browse. Click This PC (or Computer) in the left pane. **Double-click C:\.** Then **double-click SageData16** and **LOGOS** to locate the folder with company logos.

Click   AGAIN.BMP (or **AGAIN**) and **click Open** to return to the Logo Settings with the image and file name added:

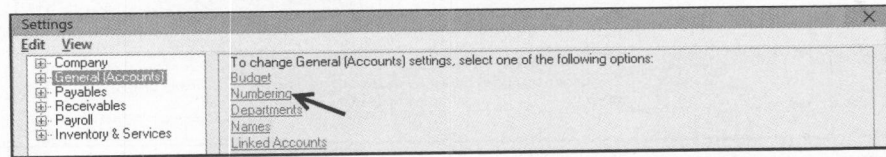

Setting General Defaults

To change the settings for the General Ledger for Love It Again,

Click   General (Accounts) in the list on the left:

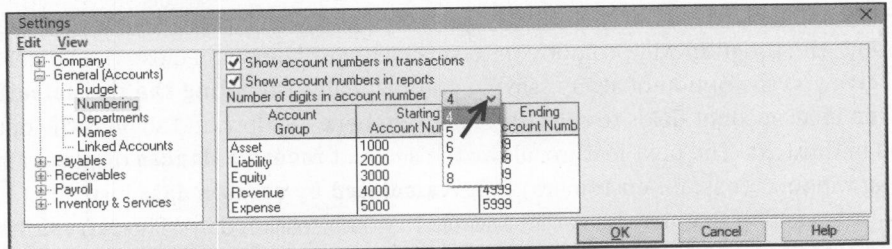

If you want Sage 50 to prepare budget reports, clicking **Budget** will open the Budget setup options and allow you to enter budget amounts for revenue and expense accounts and prepare budget reports. You can activate budgeting at any time.

Love It Again does not have different **Departments** to track expenses, so we do not need to turn on this option.

Click   Numbering:

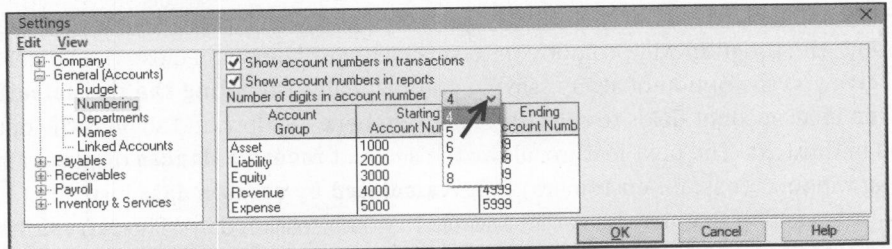

From the **Numbering** option, you can choose not to use account numbers in your reports and journal transactions when the account names are unique; that is, there is no duplication of names. We use account numbers in all the applications in this text.

You can also choose the **number of digits** for your account numbers. Each digit you add to create five- to eight-digit numbers will add an extra zero to the starting and ending number for the account group. For example, when you use six-digit numbers, the Asset accounts will range from 100 000 to 199 900, and the Liabilities accounts will range from 200 000 to 299 900. Using extra digits allows you to create more accounts.

We use four-digit account numbers in this text. You do not need to change the settings for the other ledgers — they are not used by Love It Again.

If you changed the number of digits, you must confirm that decision before you can make additional Settings changes.

NOTES
If you need to insert additional accounts, adding a digit to the account number creates room between adjacent account numbers.

Sage 50 prompts you to confirm with a message about saving your changes:

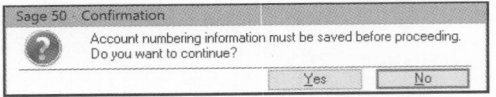

Click Yes to save the changes to account numbers.

Click   **OK** to save all the changes and return to the Home window. The session date is displayed with the new format — Aug 1, 2018.

Changing User Preference Settings

User preferences apply to individual users and indicate the way that person prefers to work with the data files. They do not affect the accounting processes. If you have multiple users who access the files, each user can set his or her own preferences.

All user preference settings can be changed at any time by clicking an option again.

Choose the **Setup menu**, then **click User Preferences**:

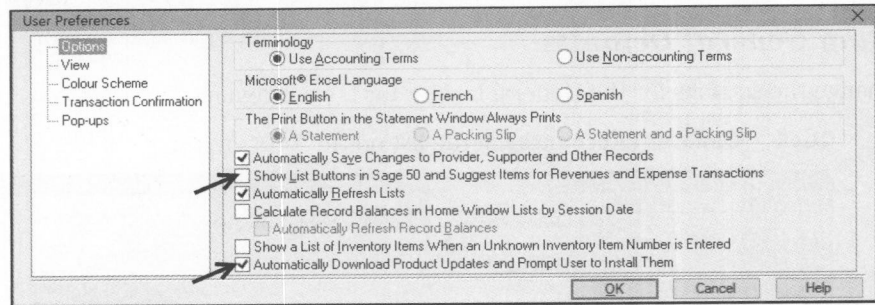

PRO VERSION
pro The Automatically Refresh Lists option is not on the list because it refers to the multi-user options.
Packing slips are not available in the Pro version.

NOTES
Appendix B lists equivalent accounting and non-accounting terms.

NOTES
The Excel language option will apply only if you have installed a non–English language version of the Excel program.

NOTES
Many account input fields, like the Account field that you saw in the General Journal in Chapter 3, have list buttons or icons. Other fields have list arrows that provide a drop-down or pop-up list to select from. Inventory and allocations are covered in Chapters 10 and 13, respectively.

NOTES
The Refresh Lists option applies only to the multi-user version of Sage 50 Premium.

The first feature refers to the language used by the program. We use **accounting terms** throughout this workbook. If you choose non-accounting terms, the Payables Ledger will be named Vendors and Purchases in menus and so on. To follow the instructions we provide, you should **Use Accounting Terms**. You can also choose the **language** of your **Excel** program — exported reports will use the language chosen here.

Some invoice windows include a **Print button**. If you print these invoices, you can set whether the invoice, packing slip or both will be printed as the default.

If you choose not to **automatically save changes** when you close a ledger record window, the program will prompt you to save changes when you close the ledger record and give you the option of always saving automatically. **Including the list selection button** in all account fields to select account numbers, vendors and so on is the option used in this text. The next feature allows the account **record balances** displayed in the Home windows (e.g., for customers) to be **calculated by session date** instead of by the latest transaction that may be earlier or later than the session date. The **refresh lists automatically** option applies when working in multi-user mode. You can select to show **inventory item lists** whenever a new item is entered in the item field. When you use the Project (Fund) feature, you can always **apply allocations** to the entire transaction. We turned off Fund in the Features Settings for this company (page 78), so this option has been removed. The final setting refers to program updates. When you **automatically download product updates**, you will include later tax tables and your screens and payroll tax calculations may be different from the ones we have in the text. You should not download updates while working with this text. In an ongoing business, updates should always be installed regularly.

Click   **Show List Buttons In Sage 50 And Suggest Items....**

Click   **Automatically Download Product Updates And Prompt...** to **turn off** this option. **Do not click** the **check box if the ✓ is already removed**.

Changing the View Settings

Several important display or appearance options are controlled from the View option.

> **Click   View**:

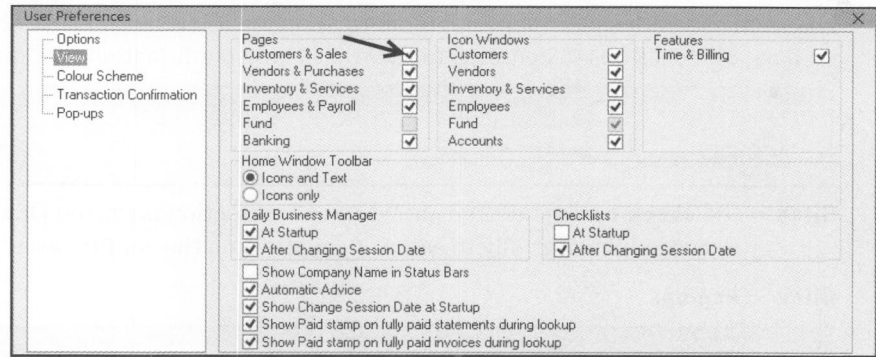

You can **hide**, that is, not display, the icons for **modules** or **pages** that you are not using. We must hide the modules that are not used before finishing the history.

The **Icon Windows** check boxes allow you to hide the accounts icon window for the ledgers. Selecting the Chart of Accounts icon (or other ledger icon) with this option on will display the first ledger record instead of the list of accounts. Icon windows can be hidden separately only if the module pages are not hidden.

> **Click**   the **Pages check box for Customers & Sales** to remove the ✓. The ✓ for Icon Windows is also removed.
>
> **Repeat**   this step for **Vendors & Purchases**, **Inventory & Services** and **Employees & Payroll**. The **Time & Billing Feature** ✓ is automatically removed when you remove both Customers and Employees.
>
> **Do not remove** the ✓ for **Banking**.

The next two options refer to the appearance of the **tool bar** in the Home window. You can display the tools with text or as icons only. The Classic view Home window tool bar never includes text. In our data files, we include the text with the icons.

Sage 50 has reminders about upcoming activities such as payments that are due, discounts available and recurring entries. The **Checklists** and the **Daily Business Manager** can remind you of these activities each time you start the program, each time you advance the session date or both. Love It Again does not use these lists.

> **Click**   **At Startup** and **click After Changing Session Date** for **Daily Business Manager** to **remove** the ✓s.
>
> **Click**   **After Changing Session Date** for **Checklists** to **remove** the ✓.

You can **Show Company Name In Status Bars** or omit this detail. We show the name.
Automatic Advice provides advisory messages automatically while you are entering transactions, as, for example, when customers exceed credit limits or the chequing account is overdrawn. Clicking removes the ✓ and the feature. Leave Advice turned on.

We also select to **show the session date** each time we start a work session. If your company has several users who log on frequently during a single day, bypassing this step would be efficient. In that case, the system administrator would update the session date for all users at the start of each business day.

Showing the **Paid Stamp** on invoices and payments is another option. If you hide the Vendors & Customers pages, these options will be dimmed because they no longer apply.

> **Click**   **Colour Scheme**. You can choose backgrounds from a variety of colours and patterns for the different journal windows.

---

pro **PRO VERSION**
There is no Time & Billing feature in the Pro version, so you will not need to hide it. The term Project replaces Fund.

Classic **CLASSIC VIEW**
There are two lists: Modules and Icon Windows. Time & Billing is added to the Modules list. Banking is not included in the lists.

NOTES
When you hide modules and icon windows, all information about icon positions is removed. Sage 50 advises you of this when you display the records in the account windows by icon instead of by name. When you view a page, you can hide its icon window separately.

WARNING!
If you do not hide the remaining modules, you will be unable to complete the final setup step of finishing the history because essential information for those modules is missing.

WARNING!
Do not hide the Banking page. If you hide this page, you will be unable to access the General Journal.

NOTES
Fund is already removed from the list of pages because we turned off the feature.

NOTES
You can access Checklists and the Daily Business Manager at any time from the Business Assistant menu, even if the automatic display for them is turned off. You can turn on the automatic display again at any time from this User Preferences View settings screen.
Checklists are covered in Chapters 12 and 15; the Daily Business Manager is covered in Chapter 11.

NOTES
Remember that these are user preferences — each user can change these settings for personal preferences. User setup is described in Chapter 16 and Appendix G.

Confirming Posting of Transactions Settings

We will choose to have the program advise when transactions are successfully recorded.

Click   **Transaction Confirmation**.

If warning about losing icon position information opens (refer to margin Notes on page 81), click Yes to continue to the transaction confirmation window:

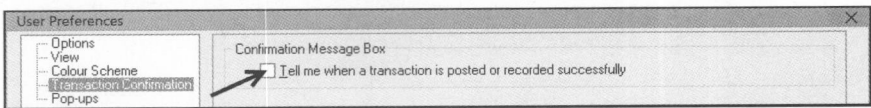

Click   the **check box** beside Tell Me When A Transaction Is Posted Or Recorded Successfully to add a ✓ and turn on the confirmation.

Click   **Pop-ups**:

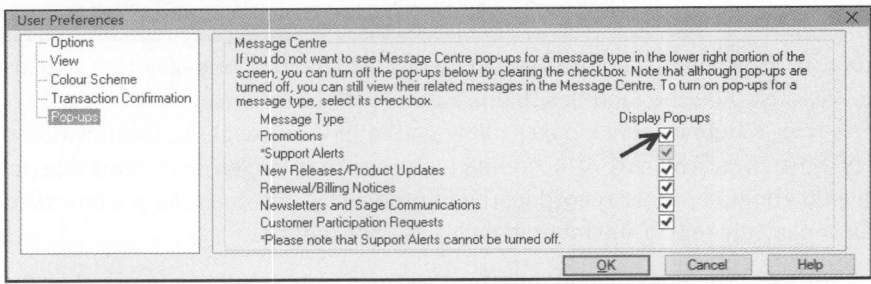

NOTES
We have turned off pop-ups for the data files we provided on the Student DVD.
Support Alerts is dimmed — you cannot turn off the display of these messages.

On this screen you control the types of messages Sage 50 will provide. Clicking a check box will prevent that type of message from appearing for this data file.

Click   the **messages** that you do not want in order to remove the ✓s.

Click   **OK** to save the settings and return to the updated Home window:

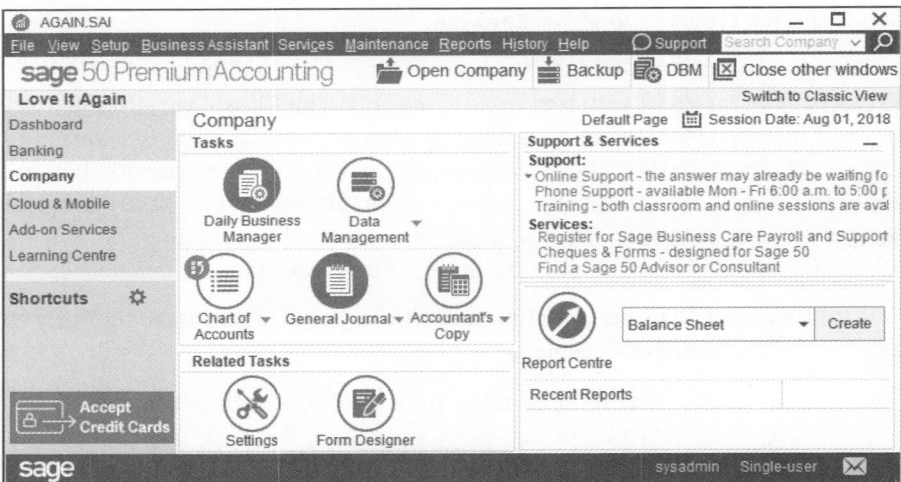

The unused modules (hidden pages) have been removed from the Modules pane list and the session date is displayed in the long date format we selected for the screen.

Changing View Menu Settings

Click   the **View menu**:

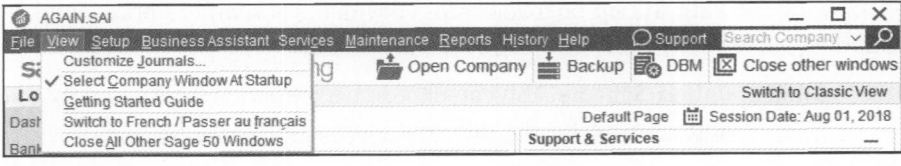

The View menu controls some appearance options for the program. Each journal may be customized by hiding optional fields that are not used.

You can also change the order in which journal fields are accessed from the ⌜tab⌟ key, that is, which field is next when you press ⌜tab⌟. You can **customize all journals** from this menu or you can use the customize option within individual journals.

> To customize a journal, choose the View menu and click Customize Journals. Click the journal you want. Click Columns or Tabbing Order and click the columns or details you want to change. Hidden fields may be restored at any time by clicking their names again.
>
> Click OK to save the changes and return to the Home window.

The Customize Journal tool ⊞ and View menu option in each journal provide the same options as the Home window View menu Customize Journals screen.

> You can also customize the order and size of journal columns. To change the order, drag a column heading to the location you want. To change the column size, point to the edge of the column heading; when the pointer changes to a double-headed arrow ⊞, drag the column margin to its new size.

The next choice on the main View menu refers to the **Welcome and Select Company window** that appears when you first start Sage 50. There are advantages to showing this window. If you regularly use the same data file, you can bypass the Open Company file window and open your data file with a single step by selecting Open The Last Company You Worked On. Similarly, you can restore a backup file from this window without first opening another data file. The View menu setting acts as a toggle switch, and you can change it at any time.

Sage 50 is a fully bilingual program. You can **switch the program language** (choose to work in French or in English) from the View menu with this toggle switch. When you are working in French, the View menu (now renamed *Vue*) option changes to *Passer A L'Anglais*/Switch To English.

You can also switch languages by clicking ⌜FR⌟ in the Classic view tool bar.

The final View menu option allows you to **close all other Sage 50 windows** in a single step, leaving only the Home window open. This menu choice is the same as the one provided by the Home window tool bar icon ⌜⌧⌟.

Changing the Printer Defaults

You may select a different printer for customized forms, or you may want to change the format of the printed reports.

The following instructions should assist you in making the selections you need.

> **Choose** the **Setup menu** and **click Reports & Forms**:

Printer selections are saved with each company file. If you use the file with another computer system or program installation, they may be incorrect. Sage 50 allows you to set up different printers and settings for reports, cheques, invoices, labels and so on. Many companies use different printers for their reports and preprinted forms and invoices. Even if you use one printer, you may want to adjust fonts, margins and form selections for each type of printed report or statement.

Choose the printer you will use for reports from the list provided by the arrow beside the field. All printers installed on your computer should be on the list. Change the page margins if necessary. For each part of the report, choose font, type size, colour and how to display positive and negative numbers by clicking the list arrows beside these fields. You can experiment to find the combination that will best fit the reports on the page. By default, reports include the computer system date and a message indicating whether filtering is applied.

To modify the printer setup for other outputs, click the relevant form in the list. You can modify printer setup information at any time by returning to this screen.

Additional printer settings may be available from the Setup button screen for print quality, paper source, paper size, two-sided printing, orientation and so on. The screens and options will vary from printer to printer.

Click   Cancel to exit without making changes and return to the Home window, or click OK to leave each dialogue box and save the change.

Preparing the Ledgers

The third stage in setting up an accounting system involves preparing each ledger for operation. For Love It Again, this stage involves the following steps:

1. organizing all accounting reports and records (this step has been completed)
2. modifying some existing accounts (you will not need to delete any accounts)
3. creating new accounts
4. entering historical account balance information

Defining the Skeleton Starter Files

When you created the company files for Love It Again in stage one, Creating Company Files (page 69), some preset accounts were provided.

Print   the **Chart of Accounts** for the current year to prepare for the next stage.

Accounts are organized by **section**: Assets, Liabilities, Equity, Revenue and Expense. The chart also has the **account type** — such as Heading (H), Subgroup total (S), Total (T), subgroup Account (A), Group account (G) and Current Earnings (X) — and the Account Class. Account type is a method of classifying and organizing accounts within a section or subsection of a report.

Initial account numbers for each account are also in the Chart of Accounts.

We are using only four digits for account numbers, so the accounts in this chart follow the sectional boundaries as in Chapter 3:

*   1000–1999   Assets
*   2000–2999   Liabilities
*   3000–3999   Equity
*   4000–4999   Revenue
*   5000–5999   Expense

The Format of Financial Statements

When setting up the complete Chart of Accounts for Love It Again, it is important to understand the composition and format of financial statements in Sage 50. The chart on this page summarizes the application of the following rules in Sage 50.

The Balance Sheet is divided into three **sections**, each with **headings**: Assets, Liabilities and Equity. The Income Statement is divided into two sections with headings: Revenue and Expense.

Each section of the financial statements can be subdivided into groups. Assets can be divided into groups such as CURRENT ASSETS, INVENTORY ASSETS and PLANT AND EQUIPMENT. Liabilities can be divided into groups titled CURRENT LIABILITIES and LONG TERM DEBT. Equity, Revenue and Expense sections can also be divided. Groups may be further divided by creating subgroups.

Sage 50 requires that all accounts, including group headings, subgroup totals and group totals, be assigned numbers even if you do not use account numbers in transactions or reports. This is different from manual accounting, in which numbers are assigned only to postable accounts. Predefined section headings and section totals (e.g., ASSETS, TOTAL ASSETS and LIABILITIES), however, are not assigned numbers by the program.

ORGANIZATION OF ACCOUNTS

BALANCE SHEET

Type	Number	Account Name	Amount	Amount
ASSETS [section heading]				
H	**1000**	**CURRENT ASSETS**		
A	1020	Bank: Love It Again	xxx	
A	1100	Cash on Hand	xxx	
S	1150	Total Cash		xxx
G	1190	Prepaid Expenses		xxx
G	1200	Purchased Clothing		xxx
		—		
		—		
T	**1390**	**TOTAL CURRENT ASSETS**		**xxx**
H	**1500**	**FIXED ASSETS**		
G	1510	Fax/Telephone		xxx
G	1520	Computers		xxx
		—		
T	**1590**	**TOTAL FIXED ASSETS**		**xxx**
TOTAL ASSETS [section total]				xxx
LIABILITIES [section heading]				
H	**2000**	**CURRENT LIABILITIES**		
G	2100	Bank Loan		xxx
G	2200	A/P – Kids Stuff		xxx
		—		
T	**2690**	**TOTAL CURRENT LIABILITIES**		**xxx**
TOTAL LIABILITIES [section total]				xxx
EQUITY [section heading]				
H	**3000**	**EQUITY**		
G	3560	Accumulated Surplus		xxx
X	3600	Net Income		xxx
		—		
T	**3690**	**TOTAL EQUITY**		**xxx**
TOTAL EQUITY [section total]				xxx
LIABILITIES & EQUITY				xxx

INCOME STATEMENT

Type	Number	Account Name	Amount	Amount
REVENUE [section heading]				
H	**4000**	**REVENUE**		
G	4020	Revenue: Donated Items		xxx
G	4040	Revenue: Purchased Clothing & Books		xxx
		—		
		—		
T	**4390**	**TOTAL REVENUE**		**xxx**
TOTAL REVENUE [section total]				xxx
EXPENSE [section heading]				
H	**5000**	**OPERATING EXPENSES**		
G	5020	Rental Expense		xxx
G	5200	Supplies Used		xxx
		—		
		—		
T	**5490**	**TOTAL OPERATING EXPENSES**		**xxx**
H	**5500**	**COST OF GOODS SOLD**		
G	5510	Cost of Purchased Clothing & Books		xxx
G	5520	Cost of Other Purchases		xxx
		—		
T	**5690**	**TOTAL COST OF GOODS SOLD**		**xxx**
TOTAL EXPENSE [section total]				xxx
NET INCOME				xxx

Type
H = Group **H**eading
T = Group **T**otal
G = Postable **G**roup Account
A = Postable Subgroup **A**ccount
S = Group **S**ubtotal
X = Current Earnings Account

Financial Statement Sections

These four rules apply to financial statement sections in Sage 50:

1. Each of the five financial statement sections has a **section heading** and a **section total**. You cannot change the titles for these headings and totals.

2. A **section total** is the total of the individual group totals within that section. The program will calculate section totals automatically and print them in the financial statement reports. The five section totals are
    - TOTAL ASSETS
    - TOTAL LIABILITIES
    - TOTAL EQUITY
    - TOTAL REVENUE
    - TOTAL EXPENSE

3. The Liabilities and Equity section totals are also automatically added together on the Balance Sheet. **LIABILITIES AND EQUITY** is the sum of TOTAL LIABILITIES and TOTAL EQUITY.

4. In the Income Statement, **NET INCOME**, the difference between TOTAL REVENUE and TOTAL EXPENSE, is automatically calculated and listed under TOTAL EXPENSE on the Income Statement.

Financial Statement Account Groups

Financial statement sections are further divided into user-defined account groups made up of different types of accounts. The following rules apply to account groups in Sage 50:

1. Each group must start with a **group Heading (H)**, which will be printed in boldface type. A heading is not considered a postable account, cannot be debited or credited through transaction entries and cannot have an amount assigned to it.

2. Groups contain one or more user-defined **postable accounts**. Postable accounts are those that can be debited or credited through journal transaction entries. Postable accounts may have an opening balance.

> **NOTES**
>
> Although omitting postable accounts in a group (between the Heading and Total) does not create an error message, it is not logical to have this account setup.

3. Postable accounts may be **subgroup Accounts (A)** or **Group accounts (G)**. Subgroup account balances appear in a separate column to the left of the group account balances, which are in the right column.

4. Postable subgroup accounts must be followed by a **Subgroup total (S)** account. A subgroup total is not a postable account and cannot be given an opening balance. The program automatically calculates a subgroup total by adding all preceding subgroup postable account balances that follow the last group, subgroup total or heading account. Subgroup total balances always appear in the right column. For Love it Again, *GST Charged on Sales, HST Charged on Sales, GST Paid on Purchases* and *HST Paid on Purchases* are subgroup accounts followed by the subgroup total *GST/HST Owing (Refund)*. The bank and cash accounts are also subtotalled.

5. Each group must end with a **group Total (T)**. All amounts in the right-hand column, for postable group and subgroup total accounts, are added together to form the group total. A group total is not a postable account. The program automatically calculates this total and prints it in boldface type.

The chart on the previous page summarizes the application of these rules.

The Current Earnings (X) Account

There are two linked accounts for the General Ledger — **Retained Earnings** and **Current Earnings**, or Net Income. Both accounts are required and appear in the EQUITY section of the Balance Sheet. You do not need to change the links for these accounts.

The *Current Earnings* account is the only **Type X** account in the Chart of Accounts. This account is calculated as follows:

Current Earnings = Total Revenue – Total Expense

Current Earnings is not a postable account, but it appears with other Equity accounts in the Balance Sheet and on the Income Statement as Net Income. It cannot be removed, but its title and number can be modified (refer to Editing General Ledger Accounts, page 88). *Current Earnings* is updated from any transactions that change revenue and expense account balances. At the end of the fiscal period when closing routines are performed, the balance of this account is added to *Retained Earnings* (or its renamed account) and then reset to zero.

For Love It Again, a charitable organization, the *Retained Earnings* account will be renamed *Accumulated Surplus*. *Current Earnings* will be renamed *Net Income*.

Preparing the General Ledger

As a first step, we must identify the changes needed in the Skeleton preset accounts to match the accounts needed for Love It Again. These changes are outlined below:

1. Some starter accounts provided by the program require no changes. For the following accounts, the account title, the initial account number and the account type are the same as those in the financial statements:

CURRENT ASSETS	1000	Type H
TOTAL CURRENT ASSETS	1390	Type T
CURRENT LIABILITIES	2000	Type H
TOTAL CURRENT LIABILITIES	2690	Type T
REVENUE	4000	Type H
TOTAL REVENUE	4390	Type T

2. The following accounts have account titles or names that need to be changed. You must also change the account type for *Bank 1020*. (Account numbers are correct.)

FROM (SKELETON ACCOUNTS)			TO (LOVE IT AGAIN ACCOUNTS)
Account Name	Number	Type	Account Name (Type)
Bank	1020	Type G	Bank: Love It Again (Type A)
Accounts Receivable	1200	Type G	Purchased Clothing
Accounts Payable	2200	Type G	A/P - Kids Stuff
EARNINGS	3000	Type H	EQUITY
Retained Earnings	3560	Type G	Accumulated Surplus
Current Earnings	3600	Type X	Net Income
TOTAL EARNINGS	3690	Type T	TOTAL EQUITY
General Revenue	4020	Type G	Revenue: Donated Items
EXPENSES	5000	Type H	OPERATING EXPENSES
General Expense	5020	Type G	Rental Expense

3. The following account requires changes in both the account name and the number:

FROM (SKELETON ACCOUNTS)			TO (LOVE IT AGAIN ACCOUNTS)	
Account Name	Number	Type	Account Name	Number
TOTAL EXPENSES	5390	Type T	TOTAL OPERATING EXPENSES	5490

NOTES
You will not need to delete any of the preset accounts for Love It Again.

NOTES
Remember that Type G accounts are Group Accounts and Type A accounts are Subgroup accounts.

Using the Setup Guide to Edit General Ledger Accounts

We will use the Setup Guide to modify the predefined accounts so that they match the ones used by Love It Again.

Click   the **Setup menu** and **click Setup Guide**:

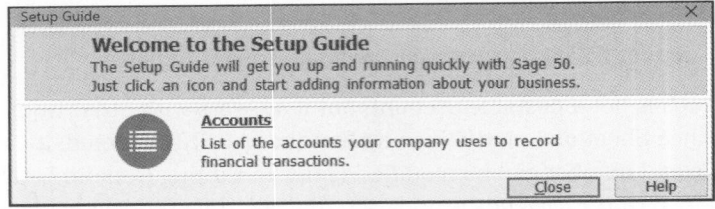

Click   **Accounts**:

NOTES

When other modules are used, you can enter and modify records for them. We use the Guide to modify customer records in Chapter 6.

NOTES

The Opening Balance field for the Group Heading *CURRENT ASSETS* has -- entered instead of $0.00. This entry indicates that you cannot enter a balance for the account. Subgroup Totals will also have the option for an opening balance removed.

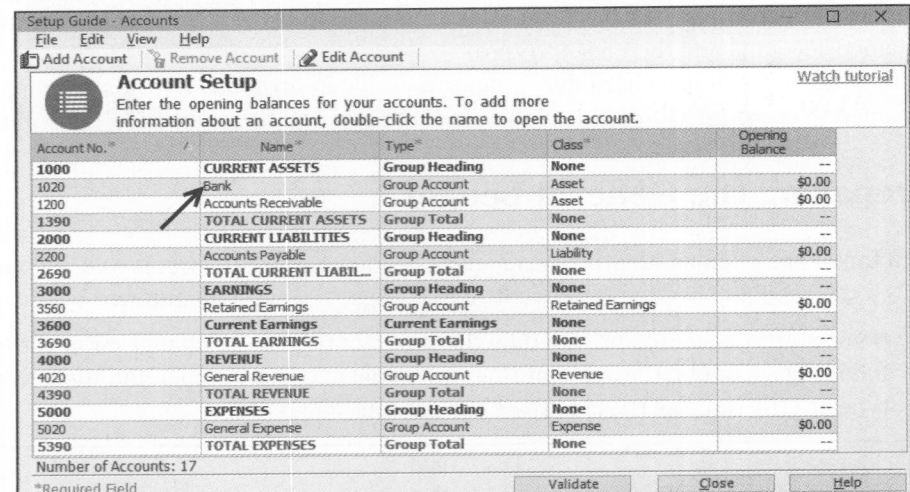

Compare this list and the Chart of Accounts you printed with the Love It Again Chart of Accounts, Balance Sheet and Income Statement provided in this application. Some accounts are the same, some account numbers match, but the names do not and some accounts you need are not yet in the program. You have to customize the accounts for Love It Again. The required changes are outlined on the preceding page.

The Guide allows us to edit a few details for all accounts from a single screen: the account number, name, type, class and opening account balance. We can also add and remove accounts from this screen.

Click   **Bank** in the Name field to highlight it for editing.

Type   Bank: Love It Again

Click   the **list arrow beside Group Account** in the Type field:

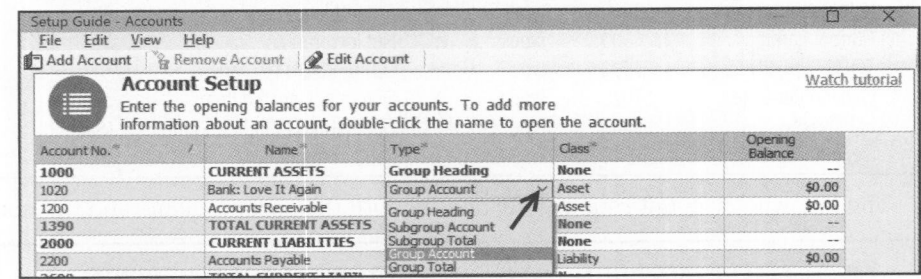

Click   **Subgroup Account**.

Make   the **remaining account changes** on page 87 by clicking the appropriate field and typing the new information.

NOTES

You do not need to change the Type for any of the remaining accounts.

Click   Close. Sage 50 advises that there is an error in the Chart of Accounts:

> **Sage 50 - Information**
>
> ⚠ Your accounts are not in logical order. The reason is: there is a missing Subgroup Total before account '1200 Accounts Receivable'.
> Until this issue is resolved, you cannot open some of your reports.
>
> [Continue]   [Cancel]

Without the subgroup total, we have not followed the rules for Groups (page 86, rule 4). The accounts are not in logical order — a subtotal is missing. Periodically you can check the validity of accounts while you are editing or adding accounts (by clicking **Validate**) to determine whether you have made errors in your account type sequence that will prevent you from finishing the account history. When we add the subgroup account, *Cash on Hand,* and the Subtotal, *Total Cash*, the accounts should be in logical order and the error will be corrected.

Click   Continue to accept the error for now. **Click Close** to leave the Setup Guide.

Creating the Chart of Accounts: The Accounts Window

After modifying the predefined Skeleton accounts, the next step is to identify the accounts that you need to create or add to the preset accounts. Again, you should refer to the company Chart of Accounts on page 66 to complete this step.

The chart that follows has the accounts that you will need to create. The chart includes account names, account numbers, account types and the option to omit printing zero balances. It lists both postable (group and subgroup) and non-postable accounts (subgroup totals, group headings and group totals).

You are now ready to create the accounts in the Love It Again files.

NOTES
Clicking Cancel will return you to the Guide so you can make corrections.

CHART OF ACCOUNTS TO BE CREATED

Account: *Number	*Name	Type	Omit	Account: *Number	*Name	Type	Omit
1100	Cash on Hand	[A]	No	▶ 2580	HST Paid on Purchases	[A]	No
1150	Total Cash	[S]		2590	GST/HST Owing/Refund	[S]	
1190	Prepaid Expenses		Optional	4040	Revenue: Purchased Clothing & Books		No
1210	Purchased Books		Optional	4080	Revenue: Other Purchases		No
1220	Other Purchased Items		Optional	4100	Revenue: Donations		No
1300	Office Supplies		Optional	5200	Supplies Used		Optional
1310	Other Supplies		Optional	5240	Postage Expense		Optional
1320	T-shirts		Optional	5280	Maintenance Expenses		Optional
1500	FIXED ASSETS	[H]		5300	Utilities Expenses		Optional
1510	Fax/Telephone		Optional	5320	Publicity & Promotion		Optional
1520	Computers		Optional	5400	Wages - Manager		Optional
1530	Store Furniture & Shelving		Optional	5420	Miscellaneous Expenses		Optional
1590	TOTAL FIXED ASSETS	[T]		5500	COST OF GOODS SOLD	[H]	
2100	Bank Loan		Optional	5510	Cost of Purchased Clothing & Books		Optional
2300	A/P - Kids In Motion		Optional	5520	Cost of Other Purchases		Optional
2350	A/P - Wearable Designs		Optional	5690	TOTAL COST OF GOODS SOLD	[T]	
2400	A/P - Places For Us		Optional				
2550	GST Charged on Sales	[A]	No				
2560	HST Charged on Sales	[A]	No				
2570	GST Paid on Purchases	[A]	No ▶				

Account Types: A = Subgroup Account   S = Subgroup Total
G = Group Account   H = Heading   T = Group Total
* Account number and account name are required fields.

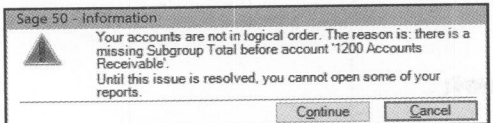

From the Chart of Accounts icon [Chart of Accounts ▾] drop-down list, you can begin all ledger account record–related changes. You can also make many of these changes from the Setup Guide, but you will not have access to all ledger fields.

Click   the **Chart of Accounts shortcuts list arrow**:

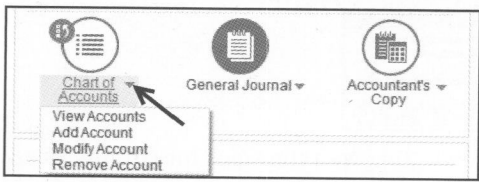

Click   the **Chart of Accounts icon** to open the Accounts window or **click View Accounts** from the Chart of Accounts shortcuts list.

Both methods will open the Accounts window.

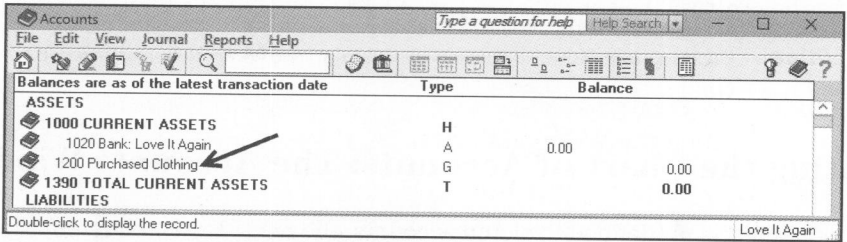

From this window, you can perform all ledger account–related activities. The tool buttons and menu options give access to the individual ledger records, and you can modify, delete, add records, display reports, access help and so on.

Click the Maximize button so that the Accounts window fills the screen. This will allow you to display more accounts and keep the Accounts window in view in the background while you are creating or editing accounts. To return the window to normal size, click , the Restore button.

Several tools control the appearance of the Accounts window. The preset accounts should be displayed in the **Type** format. You can also display accounts in the Accounts window in the large or small **Icon** format with icons representing each account. In the Icon view, you can rearrange icons by dragging so that frequently used accounts appear at the top for easier access. New accounts are automatically added at the bottom of the screen, but they can be moved to the desired location.

Viewing accounts by **Name** will include the account numbers, names and balances in debit and credit columns. Accounts remain in numerical order as accounts are added.

For entering new accounts and editing a large number of existing accounts, it is easier to work with the accounts listed in numerical order. New accounts are inserted in their correct order, providing a better view of the progress during the setup phase. The addition of account type in the Type view is helpful for checking the logical order of accounts as they are created. You can change the Accounts window view at any time.

If you do not display the accounts by Type, you should change the viewing option.

Click   the **Display By Type tool** or **choose** the **View menu** and **click Type**.

When others are using the same data file, you can click the **Refresh tool** to update your data file with changes that other users have made to accounts. In single-user mode, the tool is dimmed.

We should check that the accounts are in proper sequence; that is, they follow the rules outlined on pages 84–86.

Click   the **Check Validity Of Accounts tool** or **choose** the **File menu** and **click Check The Validity Of Accounts**:

PRO VERSION

The Refresh tool is not on the tool bar.

NOTES

To edit an account from the Accounts window, double-click the account you want to change or click the account to select it and then either click the Edit tool or choose the File menu and click Open or press *ctrl* + O.

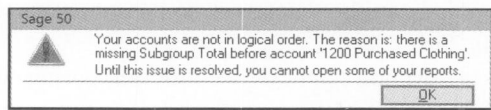

You will get this same information when you click the **Validate button** in the Setup Guide before adding the new accounts.

Click **OK** to return to the Accounts window.

Creating New Accounts in the General Ledger

You are now ready to enter the information for the first new account, *Cash on Hand*, using the chart on page 89 as your reference. The following keystrokes will enter the account name, number, type and option to include or omit zero balance accounts.

We are entering new accounts from the Accounts window, and it should still be open.

Click the **Create tool** on the Accounts window tool bar or **choose** the **File menu** and **click Create**.

You will display the new account window:

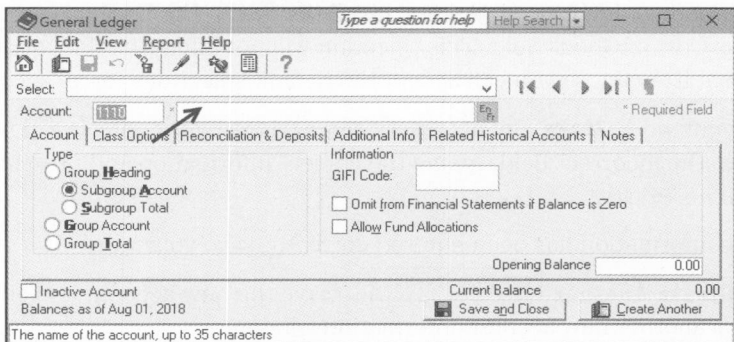

You can also open this ledger record from the Setup Guide by clicking Add Account at the top of the Guide or by double-clicking the blank line below the account list.

Or, you can press ⌨ *ctrl* + N to open a new account ledger form from the Accounts window or from any account's General Ledger window.

The tabs that appear in the ledger depend on the account section as defined by the account number. If no number is entered initially, only the tabs that apply to all accounts appear. We will create the first account that was not in the Skeleton Chart of Accounts, *Cash on Hand*. The account type is selected as the most likely option for logical account order. The default account type depends on the account record you used most recently. For example, group total accounts are often followed by a group account. The cursor is in the Account number field and the field is selected for editing. Sage 50 will not allow duplicate account numbers.

Two fields are required for accounts: the number and the name. An * appears beside a **required field** as long as it remains blank. Sage 50 may enter an account number and type that is the most likely next entry based on the previous selection. If an account number is entered as a default, the * will be removed. After the error message about logical order, account 1200 is selected in the Accounts window so that you can correct the error. Its preceding account is a Subgroup account, so another Subgroup account is expected. The account number will be selected for editing.

Sometimes, it may be appropriate to print an account with a zero balance, although zero balance accounts usually do not need to be printed. In Sage 50, you have the option to **omit accounts with zero balances** from financial statements. You may select this option in the General Ledger or in the options windows for financial reports.

NOTES
Only one error is listed, the first one encountered in checking the Chart of Accounts for validity of account order. After you correct the first error, the second error will be listed, if there is one.

PRO VERSION
The Pro version does not have 🛈, the Refresh tool.
The Notes tab is also not available in the Pro version.

NOTES
The Account number field will be blank when you add a new account from the Setup Guide. Therefore, the ledger will not have all the tabs until you enter an account number.

NOTES
When no number is entered, only the Account, Class Options and Additional Information tabs are available. When you enter a 4000- or 5000-level account number, the Budget tab will be added. The Reconciliation & Deposits tab is included for all Balance Sheet accounts.

NOTES
Some reports have the option to hide zero balances for all the accounts in the report. If selected in a report, this option will override the ledger account selection of showing zero balances.

NOTES
GIFI codes and exporting GIFI reports are covered in Appendix K.

Information you enter on the Notes tab screen can be added to the financial statements (refer to the Modify Report screenshots on pages 56–58).

NOTES
Depending on your previous step or cursor position, you may have a different initial account number and type.

NOTES
Remember that if you do not use account numbers in transactions or reports, the account names must be unique.

NOTES
Account class (Class Options tab) is introduced in Chapter 7.

NOTES
If you want to end your session, close the General Ledger window and close the Accounts window to return to the Home window.

WARNING!
Before you finish the history, the opening balance can be edited. The Current Balance has no data input field because you cannot edit it. Initially it is the same as the opening balance, but it changes when you add journal entries. Because you can enter journal transactions before finishing the history, this distinction is very important. The balance in the Accounts window is the current balance, which may not be the same as the opening balance.

After you finish the history, the Opening Balance field is removed.

The balances of bank accounts should always be displayed, so do not select Omit From Financial Statements If Balance Is Zero.

We are not using **GIFI** codes (Canada Revenue Agency's account numbering system for electronic report filing) or fund or project allocations, so we can leave these options unchanged. The current balance is displayed, but you cannot edit it. It is updated when you enter an opening balance and journal entries. The opening account balance will be added later (refer to Entering Historical Account Balances below). There is no additional account information. We are not using Account Reconciliation, so we can skip this tab screen. The Related Historical Accounts tab screen has the relationship between different account numbers that are used for the same account in multiple fiscal periods. They do not apply until you have data for more than two fiscal periods.

Type 1100 **Press** (tab) to advance to the Account name field.

Type Cash on Hand

Click **Subgroup Account** to change the account type if necessary.

The bank and cash accounts together will be subtotalled.

Sage 50 enters an **Account Class** automatically (Class Options tab screen). For most accounts, the section heading is used (Assets, Liabilities, etc.). For Expense accounts, the default class is Cost of Goods Sold. This selection will not affect the financial statements for Love It Again, so you can accept the default selections for all accounts.

Check your work. **Make** any necessary **corrections** by pressing (tab) to return to the incorrect field, typing the correct information and pressing (tab) if necessary.

When the information has been entered correctly, save your work.

Click **Create Another** [Create Another] to save the new account and advance to another new account information window.

Both the number and name fields are now marked with an *.

Create the **remaining accounts** from page 89.

Subgroup totals, group headings and group totals — the non-postable accounts — will have the Balance fields removed when you choose these account types.

Click **Save And Close** [Save and Close] to save the final account.

Display or **print** the **Chart of Accounts** to check the accuracy of your work.

If you find mistakes, edit the account information as described in the Editing General Ledger Accounts section on page 88.

Entering Historical Account Balances

Before completing this step, we will create one more account to use as a test account for our Trial Balance. If you close the General Ledger before entering all the account balances, or if the total debits and credits are not equal, the program forces the Trial Balance to balance by adding the required debit or credit amount to another account.

This automatic adjustment may compensate for other errors in amounts, and you may be able to finish the history with errors in opening balances. You cannot change these balances after finishing the history. To detect this problem, we will create a test account and put all the adjustments into it. If all the balances are entered correctly, the test account will have a zero balance and we can remove the account.

Create the new Group account **1005 Test Account**.

You are now ready to enter the opening historical account balances for all postable (type G or A) accounts. The opening balances for Love It Again can be found in the Trial Balance on page 68. Accounts with zero balances are not included in the Trial Balance. You should skip these accounts when entering account balances.

You can enter opening balances from the Setup Guide or you can start from the Modify Account shortcut in the Chart of Accounts drop-down shortcuts list. We will include both methods.

Entering Opening Account Balances from the Setup Guide

Click   the **Setup menu** and **click Setup Guide**. **Click Accounts**:

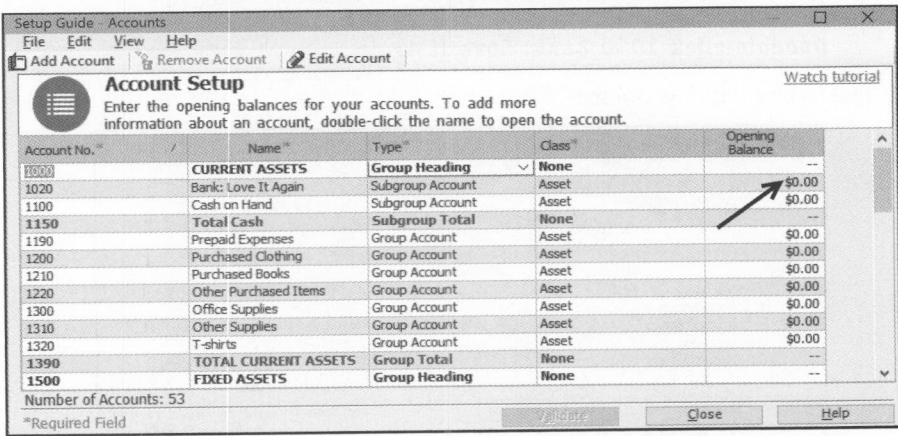

The Balance field is not available for Heading, Total and Subtotal accounts. The postable Group and Subgroup accounts initially have a zero balance.

Click   **$0.00** in the Opening Balance field for Bank: Love It Again.

Type   46380 **Press** ⊥ to select the balance for the next account.

Enter   the remaining account **balances** from the Trial Balance on page 68. Remember that *GST Paid on Purchases* and *HST Paid on Purchases* have a debit balance (add a minus sign).

Double-click any account line to open the ledger record if you need to change other details for the account. (Refer to the screenshot on page 90.)

If you close the Setup Guide before entering all the account balances, or the Trial Balance is still unbalanced, you will be asked to correct the discrepancy:

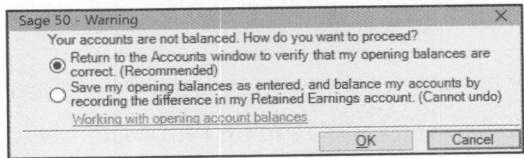

You can either return to the Guide to make a correction or add the difference to the Retained Earning account.

Make   **your selection** and **click OK**. **Click Close** when finished to leave the Setup Guide.

Entering Opening Account Balances from the Search Window

Click   the **Chart of Accounts shortcuts list arrow**.

Click   **Modify Account**.

NOTES
You can advance to a later part of the account list by typing the first number in the Search field. You can also search by account name by choosing this option.

This Search window that opens is similar to the one in the General Journal that starts the Adjust Entry feature. Accounts is selected as the search field area:

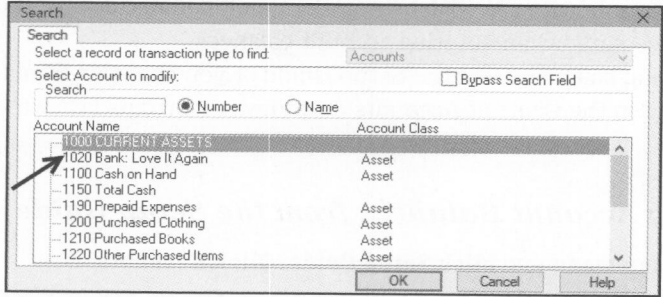

Doouble-click 1020 Bank: Love It Again.

The ledger window opens:

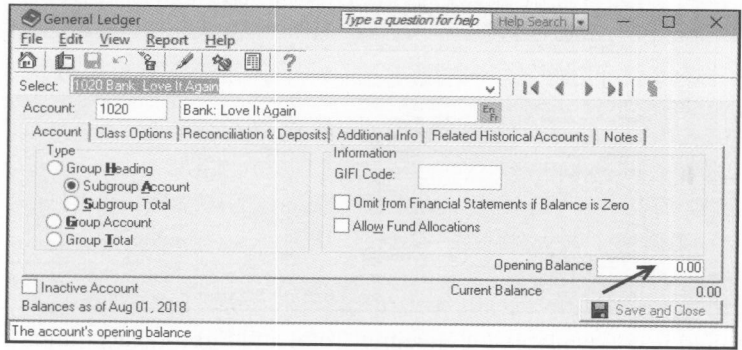

Click   the **Opening Balance field** to highlight it.

Type   46380 **Press** tab .

The Current Balance is updated, but you cannot change it directly. Sage 50 updates this balance automatically from journal entries.

To open a different ledger record, you can click the **Next Account tool** to open the ledger record for the next account in numerical sequence, or select an account from the **Select drop-down list**:

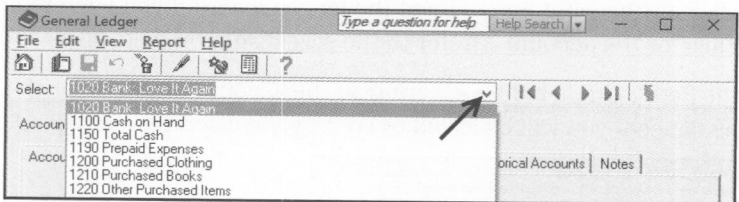

Enter   the **balances** for the remaining accounts in the Trial Balance on page 68.

Remember that *GST Paid on Purchases* and *HST Paid on Purchases* have a debit balance (add a minus sign).

If you close the General Ledger window before entering all the account balances, or the Trial Balance is still unbalanced, you will be asked to correct the discrepancy:

The message asks you to choose an account for the difference — an adjusting, balancing entry that will place the Trial Balance in balance. Choose *Test Account* from the drop-down list of accounts. Unlike the similar warning from the Guide, here you can choose any account from the drop-down list or accept the default. If this warning appears,

---

⚠ WARNING!
Remember to enter the amounts for GST and HST Paid on Purchases with a minus sign to create a debit entry.

📄 NOTES
The default account for the balancing entry is the Retained Earnings linked account – renamed Accumulated Surplus in our example.

📄 NOTES
When all account balances are correct and the Test Account has a zero balance, you can remove it. Open the Chart of Accounts window and click Test Account, or open its ledger record.
Or, click the account in the Setup Guide Accounts window.
Click the Remove tool 🗑. and confirm that you want to remove the account by clicking Yes.

Choose account **1005 Test Account** from the drop-down list. **Click OK**.

Close   the **Ledger window** to return to the Accounts window after entering all the accounts and balances.

Display or **print** the **Chart of Accounts**, **Trial Balance**, **Balance Sheet** and **Income Statement** to check the accuracy of your work.

Choose the **Reports menu** in the Accounts window and **click Trial Balance** (or Balance Sheet or Income Statement).

Check   all your **opening balances** carefully and **edit** any accounts with errors in **amounts** or **names** before finishing the history.

Close   the **Accounts window** and any other open windows to return to the Home window.

Compare your reports with the information on pages 66–68 to be sure that all account numbers, names and balances are correct. The balance for *Test Account* should be zero. Make additional corrections if necessary.

Finishing the History

Making a Backup Copy

By having a backup copy of your files before finishing the history, you will be able to make changes easily, if you find an error, without having to repeat the entire setup from scratch. After the ledger history is finished, the program will not permit you to make certain changes, such as opening account balances and fiscal dates. You cannot change the account number for an account after making a journal entry to the account.

You should back up your unfinished open history files to a different folder so they can be easily identified (e.g., NF-AGAIN).

Choose the **File menu** and **click Backup**, or **click** the **Backup tool** 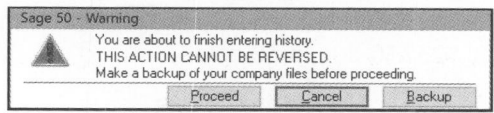.

Create a **backup copy** by following the instructions. Refer to page 48 and page 246 if you need help.

Finishing the General Ledger History

You should be in the Home window.

Choose the **History menu** and **click Finish Entering History**.

A caution about making a backup first appears:

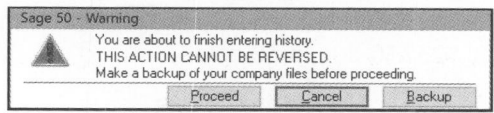

If you have not made a backup copy yet, click Backup and do so before proceeding. If you have made your backup copy, you should continue.

Click   **Proceed**.

WARNING!
If an account was used in journal entries, you can change account numbers only after two fiscal periods have passed without additional transactions.

WARNING!
You can finish entering the history when the Trial Balance is in balance. Afterward, you cannot change opening balances, even if they are incorrect. You will need to make adjusting entries. Sage 50 always keeps the Trial Balance balanced. Therefore, checking for a zero balance in the Test Account can stop you from proceeding with incorrect account balances.

WARNING!
You cannot change the Fiscal Start date or the opening balance for an account after finishing the history.
Back up the not-finished Love It Again files before proceeding. Refer to Chapter 3 if you need further assistance.

WARNING!
You must close all other windows before making a backup or before finishing the history.

WARNING!
You can verify that the file is correct before making a backup — choose the Finish History option. If the option to proceed is available, click Backup on this screen or click Cancel, make the backup and then finish the history.

NOTES
The first error on this screen states that accounts are not in logical order.

The remaining messages refer to missing linked accounts for modules that are not used but are also not hidden.

A different screen at this stage indicates that you have errors that must be corrected before you can continue:

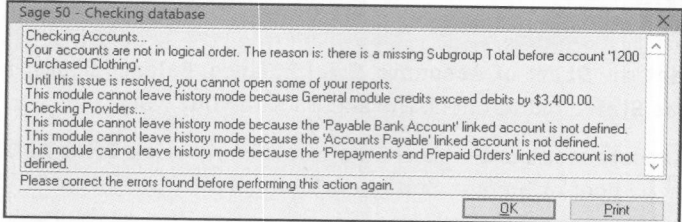

The message describes the mistakes you must correct. If your accounts are out of order, you cannot finish entering the history. If you did not hide the unused modules, you cannot finish entering the history because some essential linked accounts for these modules are not defined.

Read the error description carefully. Print the message for reference when you make corrections. Click OK to return to the Home window.

Make the necessary corrections. Remember to replace your previous unfinished history backup file. Then try again to finish the history.

The open or not-finished history symbol has been removed from the Chart of Accounts icon. In the Setup Guide Accounts window, the Current Balance field has replaced the Opening Balance, but you cannot change these amounts.

You can now exit the program or continue by entering the source documents. Remember to advance the Session Date. Enter all transactions for Love It Again in the General Journal.

NOTES
If you unhide (view) the unused modules now, they will have the not-finished icon on the ledger icons. If you want to set them up later, you must first unhide or view them, as we do in Chapter 9.

SOURCE DOCUMENTS

SESSION DATE — AUGUST 7, 2018

NOTES
The HST rate in Ontario is 13 percent.

1   **Cheque Purchase Invoice #PFU-4877**   **Dated August 2/18**
From Places For Us, $1 800 plus $234 HST for monthly rent. Invoice total $2 034 paid by cheque #3421. Terms: payable on first day of each month.

2   **Purchase Invoice #BC-10116**   **Dated August 2/18**
From Bell Canada, $145 plus $18.85 HST for monthly telephone and Internet service. Invoice total $163.85. Terms: net 15. Create new Group account 2140 A/P - Bell Canada.

3   **Purchase Invoice #WD-2919**   **Dated August 4/18**
From Wearable Designs, $210 plus $27.30 HST for new store uniform T-shirts for volunteer sales staff. Invoice total $237.30 due in 30 days.

4   **Memo #1**   **Dated August 4/18**
From Fischer: Give T-shirts to volunteer sales staff. Cost of T-shirts given out is $210. Reduce T-shirt asset account and charge the cost to Miscellaneous Expenses account.

NOTES
In most businesses, the Cash on Hand balance is usually small and is used only for paying small amounts. In this application, we are using the Cash on Hand account to record merchandise sales and to pay for any purchases that normally would require cash or credit card payments.

5   **Cash Purchase Invoice #PI-2168**   **Dated August 6/18**
From Picture It, $110 plus $14.30 HST for printing large poster to place in store window to solicit Halloween costumes and other donations. Invoice total $124.30 paid from Cash on Hand.

SESSION DATE — AUGUST 14, 2018

6

Purchase Invoice #KS-9493   **Dated August 8/18**

From Kids Stuff, $900 plus $45 GST for children's clothing from store liquidation sale. Invoice total $945. Terms: net 20 days.

7

Purchase Invoice #KIM-10990   **Dated August 8/18**

From Kids In Motion, $1 100 plus $143 HST for toys that were returned and strollers that were discontinued styles or slightly marked floor models. Invoice total $1 243. Terms: net 30 days.

8

Cash Purchase Invoice #LT-4632   **Dated August 10/18**

From Loonie-Toonies, $150 plus $19.50 HST for holiday decorations for store. Invoice total $169.50. Paid from Cash on Hand. (Debit Other Supplies account.)

9

It Again
4-A Charity Blvd.
Toronto, ON
M4G 2T2

No: 3422

Date | 2 0 1 8 0 8 1 2 |
Y Y Y Y M M D D

Pay to the order of   Bell Canada $ 163.85

———— One hundred sixty-three dollars ————   85 /100 **Dollars**

TD-CT
2544 Yonge St.
Toronto, ON M4P 1A6

Jeremy Fischer

,· — — 03544· 5499 388 3422

Re: pay invoice # BC-10116 $163.85   **No: 3422**
                                          August 12, 2018

SESSION DATE — AUGUST 21, 2018

10

Funds Raised Form #FR-18-08   **Dated August 16/18**

Received $3 000 in donations to purchase new computer for store. Amount deposited to Bank: Love It Again.

11

Purchase Invoice #DC-5306   **Dated August 17/18**

From Data Connections, $2 600 plus $338 HST for new computer with point-of-sale software. Invoice total $2 938. Terms: net 25 days. Create new account 2420 A/P - Data Connections.

12

Cheque Purchase Invoice #P-44982   **Dated August 17/18**

From Pizzaz, $650 plus $84.50 HST to repair and repaint store sign — replace the word Love with heart logo. Invoice total $734.50 paid by cheque #3423.

SESSION DATE — AUGUST 28, 2018

13

Cash Purchase Invoice #PH-9976   **Dated August 24/18**

From Pizza House, $320 plus $41.60 HST for pizza and soft drinks to show appreciation to volunteers. Invoice total $361.60. Paid from Cash on Hand.

14	**Payment Cheque #3424**	**Dated August 26/18**

To Wearable Designs, $576.30 in payment of account. Reference invoice #WD-2919 and #WD-1813.

15	**Bank Debit Memo #HB-3881**	**Dated August 28/18**

From Heartfelt Bank, $45.50 in bank charges for cheques and statement preparation. Create new Group account 5010 Bank Charges.

16	**Bank Debit Memo #HB-3996**	**Dated August 28/18**

From Heartfelt Bank, $4 200 for payroll including all payroll expenses to pay store manager Jeremy Fischer wages for one month.

Advancing the Session Date

Sage 50 warns you as you approach the end of a fiscal period because important end-of-period adjusting entries are usually required.

Change the **session date** to **August 31**.

An Advisor message about preparing for year-end opens. Sage 50 displays this message about one month before the end of the fiscal period:

> Advisor: Now is a good time to prepare for your company's year end. Refer to the Help for more information.
>
> [Click here to close.]

Click to close the **Advisor**, **back up** your **data files** and **continue** with the **transactions** for August 31.

No taxes are charged on sales of donated goods. Children's clothing and books are subject to 5% GST, while HST at 13% is charged on sales of other purchased items.

17		

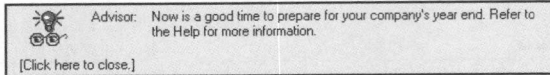

SALES SUMMARY FORM: FR-18-09

It Again
4-A Charity Blvd.
Toronto, ON
M4G 2T2

Date: August 31, 2018

Comment: Summary of cash receipts sales in August 2018

Description	Amount
Sales of donated items	$4 200.00
Sales of purchased clothing & books	4 300.00
Sales of other purchased items	8 680.00
GST on books and clothing sold	215.00
HST on sales of other purchased items	1 128.40

Received in cash by August 31, 2018

Signature: *Jeremy Fischer*

| | Total | **$18 523.40** |

18	**Memo #2**	**Dated August 31/18**

From Fischer: Deposited $18 200 from Cash on Hand (receipts from sales) to Bank: Love It Again.

Payment Cheque #3425   **Dated August 31/18**

19 To Kids Stuff, $1 849 in full payment of account. Reference invoices #KS-9493 and #KS-6279.

SESSION DATE — SEPTEMBER 15, 2018

When you change the session date to September 15, you will receive a date warning:

Normally a business would advance the session date by a shorter period, so the warning helps you avoid entering the wrong session date.

Click   OK to confirm that you entered the date you intended.

Cheque Purchase Invoice #PFU-9328   **Dated September 1/18**

20 From Places For Us, $1 800 plus $234 HST for monthly rent. Invoice total $2 034 paid by cheque #3426. Terms: payable on first day of each month.

Purchase Invoice #BC-18588   **Dated September 2/18**

21 From Bell Canada, $145 plus $18.85 HST for monthly telephone and Internet service. Invoice total $163.85. Terms: net 15.

Payment Cheque #3427   **Dated September 2/18**

22 To Kids In Motion, $2 503 in full payment of invoice #KIM-10990 and #KIM-8697.

Payment Cheque #3428   **Dated September 12/18**

23 To Bell Canada, $163.85 in full payment of invoice #BC-18588.

Funds Raised Form #FR-18-10   **Dated September 13/18**

24 Received $4 000 plus $520 HST for advertising on the charity's Web site. Total revenue received $4 520 deposited to Bank. Create new account: 4180 Revenue: Advertising.

SESSION DATE — SEPTEMBER 29, 2018

Memo #3   **Dated September 19/18**

25 From Fischer: Presented Sunni Husein with $200 gift certificate for Volunteer Extraordinaire Award. Create new Group account 5430 Employee Gifts. Paid for gift certificate from Cash on Hand.

Bank Debit Memo #HB-8310   **Dated September 20/18**

26 From Heartfelt Bank, $240 plus $31.20 HST for payroll services for one year. Total withdrawal from chequing account was $271.20. Create new expense account 5380 Payroll Services.

Bank Debit Memo #HB-9778   **Dated September 28/18**

27 From Heartfelt Bank, $4 200 for payroll, including all payroll expenses, to pay store manager Jeremy Fischer wages for one month.

Funds Received Form #FR-18-11   **Dated September 29/18**

28 Received $800 in donations. Amount deposited to Bank: Love It Again account.

NOTES
The year-end advisor may appear again when you advance the date to September 29.

Cash Purchase Invoice #CP-2   **Dated September 29/18**

29

From Canada Post, $200 plus $26 HST for postage to mail donation receipts. Invoice total $226. Paid from Cash on Hand.

Adjusting Closing Entries

NOTES

Adjusting entries always involve an Income Statement and a Balance Sheet account. For example, you might debit Supplies Used (Income Statement account) and credit Supplies (asset account on the Balance Sheet), or debit Unearned Revenue and credit Customer Prepayments.

Two source document entries — adjustments for the remaining supplies — provide the details for these year-end adjustments for Love It Again. For other businesses, adjusting entries include depreciation entries, inventory adjustments, adjustments for prepaid expenses that have expired, accrued wages and so on. Most adjusting entries do not have an external source document that reminds you to complete them, and most of them are General Journal entries.

Change the **session date** to **September 30**.

When you advance the session date further to a date very close to the end of the fiscal period, September 30 in this case, the year-end Advisor message appears again.

Close the **Advisor window** and **back up** your **data files** and **continue** with the remaining **transactions**.

Sales Summary Form #FR-18-12   **Dated September 30/18**

30

Summary of sales receipts during the month.

Revenue from donated items	$2 500
Revenue from purchased clothing & books	7 200
Revenue from other purchased items	8 000
GST @ 5%	360
HST @ 13%	1 040

Total $19 100 deposited to Cash on Hand.

Memo #4   **Dated September 30/18**

31

From Fischer: Deposited $18 500 from Cash on Hand (receipts from sales) to Bank: Love It Again.

32

NOTES

Donated items are not included in these costs — no purchase cost is associated with them.

It Again
4-A Charity Blvd.
Toronto, ON
M4G 2T2

M E M O #5

Date: September 30, 2018
From: Jeremy Fischer
Re: Adjustments required for year-end (cost of goods sold,
         supplies used and prepaid expenses expired)

Cost of books sold	$1 990
Cost of clothing sold	4 155
Cost of purchased items sold	8 200
Office supplies used	120
Other supplies used	680
Prepaid utilities	290

Authorization: JF

33 | **Bank Debit Memo #HB-10921**   **Dated September 30/18**

From Heartfelt Bank, withdraw $14 200 from chequing account to repay loan for $14 000 plus $200 interest. Create new Group account 5100 Interest Expense.

34 | **Bank Debit Memo #HB-10998**   **Dated September 30/18**

From Heartfelt Bank, $45.50 in bank charges for cheques and statement preparation. Create new Group account 5010 Bank Charges.

35

 It Again
4-A Charity Blvd.
Toronto, ON
M4G 2T2   M E M O #6

```
Date:   September 30, 2018
From:   Jeremy Fischer
Re:     Final account adjustments required to clear outdated
        inventory of supplies and other goods
        (all items donated to family shelters)

Cost of purchased books donated              $   570
Cost of purchased clothing donated             1 280
Cost of other purchases donated                1 990
```

Authorization: *JF*

KEYSTROKES FOR CLOSING
Starting a New Fiscal Period

Starting a new fiscal period is not a reversible step, so you should prepare a complete set of financial reports and make a backup of the data set as instructed in the next memo.

36 ✓ | **Memo #7**   **Dated September 30/18**

All accounts for the year are settled, so the books can be closed. Make a backup of the data files. Start a new fiscal period to close the books.

> **Print** all the **financial reports** for Love It Again for September 30, 2018.

> **Back up** your **data files** with a file name that indicates it is the year-end copy.

There are two methods for beginning a new fiscal year. The first is the method we have been using to change the session date.

> **Choose** the **Maintenance menu** and **click Change Session Date** or **click** , the Calendar icon beside Session Date.

The first date of the new fiscal period is always on the drop-down list of dates in the Session Date window. The program will not accept any dates later than October 1, 2018.

> **Type** October 1, 2018 or choose this date from the date field list or Calendar icon.

NOTES
You cannot start a new fiscal period in multi-user mode.

⚠ **WARNING!**
You should advance to the new fiscal period in two steps. First advance to the last day of the current fiscal period, and then advance to the first day of the new fiscal period. This control feature prevents you from advancing by mistake and losing important data or forgetting year-end adjusting entries.

⚠ **WARNING!**
Initially, from the last day of the fiscal period, you cannot advance the session date past October 1, the first day of the new fiscal period.

Click **OK**. Because this step is not reversible, Sage 50 provides a warning:

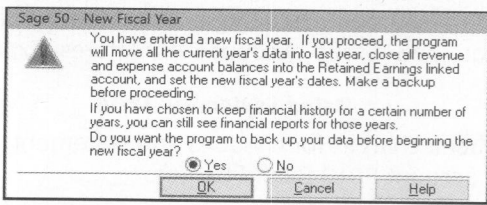

The expense and revenue amounts will be transferred to the capital account, but historical data will be saved in the data file.

Read the **warning** carefully.

The warning describes the changes about to take place in the data set. All revenue and expense accounts are reset to zero at the start of the new fiscal year. Their balances are closed out to the linked *Accumulated Surplus (Retained Earnings)* account, and the linked *Net Income (Current Earnings)* account is reset to zero to begin a new Income Statement. All previous-year entries that are not cleared are stored as data for the previous year. The program also updates the fiscal dates for the company by one year. The new fiscal end date becomes the final date allowed as a session date.

At this stage you can choose to back up the data files, continue with the date change or cancel the date change by clicking No.

Click **Cancel** to return to the Session Date window and then **click Cancel** again to close the Change Session Date screen. We will use the second menu option to change to a new fiscal year.

Choose the **Maintenance menu** and **click Start New Year**.

The next screen asks whether you want to start a new fiscal or calendar year:

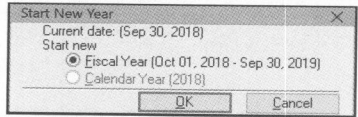

The default will be the period that starts first. Start New Fiscal Year is correctly selected.

Click **OK** to continue.

A similar warning advises you to make a backup before proceeding:

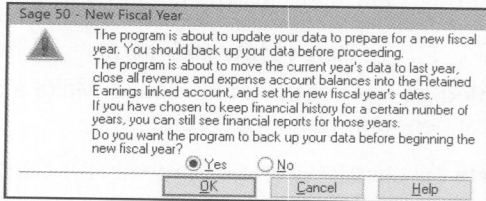

The default setting, again, is to make a backup before continuing. If you have not yet made a backup, do so now. If you do not want to begin a new year, you can click Cancel and the old dates will remain in effect.

Click **No** because you have already backed up your files.

Click **OK** to begin the new fiscal period.

The message confirms that the new year has been started:

NOTES
If the history is not finished when you choose to start a new fiscal year, the program will ask if you have finished entering the history and give you a chance to do so. You must finish the history before you can start a new fiscal period.

If you still have errors in your not-finished file, Sage 50 will list the errors that you must correct, as in the message on page 95, before you can finish the history and start a new fiscal period.

NOTES
The new calendar year entry, 2018, (that is, January 1, 2018) is earlier than the earliest date allowed in our data file (July 1, 2018), so the new Calendar Year option is dimmed. The start of the new fiscal year (October 1, 2018) also precedes the date for the next calendar year (January 1, 2019), so this option is selected.

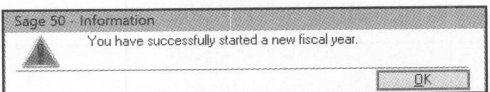

Click **OK** to close the message and display a warning about clearing data:

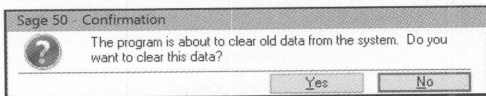

You have the option of retaining the old data or clearing it. Journal entries from the previous year are never cleared, and Income Statement and Balance Sheet details for the previous year are also retained.

Click **Yes** because Love It Again has no other data. If in doubt, choose No.

Another message now appears:

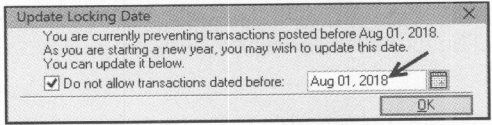

You must now change the earliest date for which you will allow transactions. We should not allow any transactions to the previous fiscal period so that the historical records cannot be altered in error.

Drag through **Aug 01, 2018**, the date entered.

Type 10/01

Click **OK** to continue. Close the message about payroll updates if it appears.

When you have more than one fiscal period, most financial reports offer comparisons with the previous year as an option. Journal reports and other reports are available for both periods — the Report On Fiscal Year field is available with Current Year and Previous Year options in a drop-down list.

Print the **Comparative Trial Balance** and **Balance Sheet** for September 30 and October 1.

Notice the changes in the capital accounts on the Balance Sheet. The *Net Income* balance for September 30 has been added to the *Accumulated Surplus* account to create the October 1 balance in the *Accumulated Surplus* account.

Print the **Comparative Income Statement for the previous year** (Oct. 1, 2017, to Sep. 30, 2018) and the **current fiscal year to date** (Oct. 1, 2018, to Oct. 1, 2018).

The Income Statement for the current year has no income or revenue. All accounts have a zero balance because you have not recorded any transactions for the new fiscal year.

The files are now ready for transactions in the new fiscal period. When you check the Company Information, the fiscal dates are updated and information about last year's dates has been added.

Choose the **Setup menu** and **click Settings**, or **click** the **Settings icon** .

NOTES

If you choose to clear old data, the program will clear the information you selected for the periods you entered in the Automatically Clear Data screen. Refer to Chapter 15, page 617.

We describe how to clear data from company files in Chapter 15.

WARNING!

If you have cleared paid invoices, these details will be unavailable for reports. Comparative Income Statements and Balance Sheets are always available for the two fiscal periods.

NOTES
After you start a new fiscal period, you cannot change the Fiscal Start date.

NOTES
The program assumes a fiscal year of one year, so the fiscal end will be advanced by 12 months.

NOTES
In Chapter 12, we show how to create a copy of your data for your accountant to update and how to import the transactions your accountant has completed for your company.

NOTES
Type the date in the Date field. You will be unable to select September 30 from the date field calendar.
Because the session date is Oct. 1, 2018, and we do not allow future-dated transactions, Oct. 1 is the only date allowed for journal entries until we advance the session date.

Click **Company** if necessary and then **click Information**:

The new Fiscal Start is October 1, 2018, and the new Fiscal End is September 30, 2019. Sage 50 automatically updates the Fiscal End by 12 months, but you can edit the Fiscal End date if the fiscal period is shorter. In fact, this is the only date that you can edit after you have finished the history for a data file. The Earliest Transaction Date has also been updated to October 1, 2018. The dates for the previous fiscal period (Last Year Dates) are provided for reference.

Click **Cancel** to close the Company Information window.

Entering Transactions for an Earlier Fiscal Period

Sometimes not all the information required is available before the books are closed for the fiscal period. However, it may be necessary to close the books (start a new fiscal period) so that transactions in the new year can be entered. The details of the adjusting entries can be calculated by an accountant who does not have the information until after a business has started entering transactions for a new year. Sage 50 allows you to post transactions to the previous year (but not to future fiscal periods) so that the financial statements for both the previous year and the current year will be correct.

✓ 37	**Memo #8**	**Dated September 30/18**

After starting the new fiscal period, Fischer discovered a donation cheque #488129 for $500 that has not been recorded and should be added to the revenue for the previous fiscal period. We closed the books before making the entry. Read the margin Notes.

Open the **General Journal**. **Type** `Memo 8` in the Source field.

Click the **Date field** and **type** `Sep 30`

Enter the **remaining information** to complete the transaction.

Click the **Post button**. Sage 50 blocks the transaction:

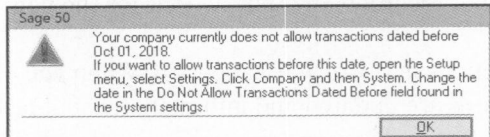

Before the program allows the entry, we must change the System Settings. We indicated that transactions earlier than Oct. 1, 2018, should not be allowed.

Click **OK** to close the message. **Close** the **journal** to discard the entry. **Click** **Yes** to confirm that you want to discard the entry.

Choose the **Setup menu** and **click Settings** or **click** the **Settings icon** [Settings].

Click **Company** if necessary and then **click System**.

This will access the Settings field we need:

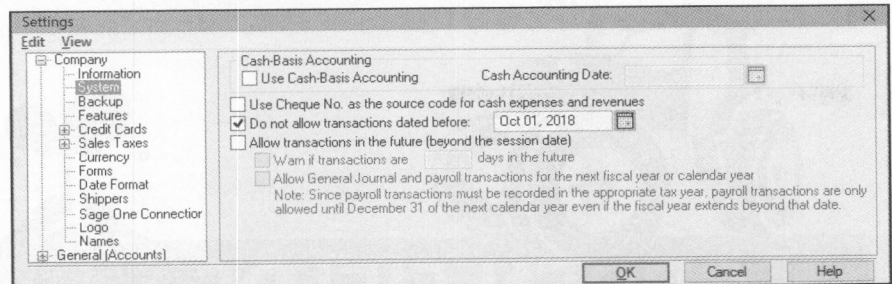

This is the same Settings screen we saw earlier, but now we must allow transactions in the previous period.

Click   **Do Not Allow Transactions Dated Before** to **remove** the ✓.

Click   **OK**.

Enter   **Memo #8** again.

Review and then **post** it. This time you must confirm before the entry is posted:

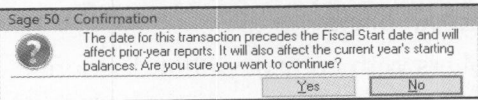

Because the transaction date is in a previous month or period, you are advised that prior period reports may be affected by the transaction. The warning gives you a chance to correct the date if it was incorrect. But we want to proceed. After completing the transaction, we will change the System Settings again to avoid mistakenly posting to the previous year.

Click   **Yes** to continue with posting.

Close   the **General Journal**.

Click   the **Settings icon** or **choose** the **Setup menu**, then **choose Settings** and **click Company** and **System**.

Click   **Do Not Allow Transactions Dated Before** to **add** the ✓.

Enter   **Oct 1** as the date and **click OK**.

Finish   your **session** by backing up and closing the files for Love It Again.

NOTES
The warnings in Sage 50 make it difficult to post to the wrong year by mistake.

NOTES
To display and print reports after starting a new fiscal period, you must choose Previous Year (2018) to view the transactions for August and September.

R E V I E W

The Student DVD with Data Files includes Review Questions and Supplementary Cases for this chapter.

GROEN FIELDS

OBJECTIVES

- **open** the General and Payables journals
- **enter** supplier- or vendor-related purchase transactions
- **enter** supplier-related payment transactions
- **enter** partial payments to suppliers
- **enter** payments to suppliers with early payment discounts
- **enter** cash purchase transactions
- **enter** sales taxes in the General Journal
- **create** shortcuts in the Home window
- **store** recurring purchase transactions
- **add** new supplier accounts
- **edit** supplier accounts
- **edit** and **review** transactions in the journals
- **recall**, **use** and **edit** stored purchase transactions
- **adjust** and **reverse** purchase invoices and payments after posting
- **understand** Payables Ledger linked accounts
- **display** and **print** payables transactions and reports

*After completing
this chapter, you
should be able to*

COMPANY INFORMATION

Company Profile

NOTES
Groen Fields
RR #2
Truro, NS B2N 5B1
Tel 1: (902) 454-6111
Tel 2: (800) 454-6000
Fax: (902) 454-6990
Business No.: 186 522 333

Groen Fields, located outside of Truro, Nova Scotia, is owned by Arjen Groen and Ryan Field. (Arjen is a cousin of Julie and Jules Jardin, who own Shady Corners in Halifax. Groen is the Dutch name/translation and equivalent of the English name Green, and is often pronounced "green.") The nursery and tree farm supplies a number of garden centres in the area with annual bedding plants, perennials and ornamental trees. Most of the plants are grown from their own seed supplies, and the greenhouse allows Groen Fields to start the annual bedding plants in time for spring sales and garden planting. Trees and specialty plants are

purchased when they are still small and then grown to the more mature sizes desired by customers. They also sell packaged seeds harvested from their own flowers.

Arjen Groen, together with his partner Ryan Field, manage the day-to-day activities of the business. Both specialized in horticulture at the Nova Scotia Agricultural College at Dalhousie University, where they met as undergraduates. Field continued his studies in Business Administration while Groen went on to complete a Master's degree in Agriculture. Most of the day-to-day farming work is carried out by their employees. One full-time manager looks after the greenhouse plants and lives in the main farmhouse during the winter. During the summer months, the manager shares the freshly painted three-bedroom bungalow with four co-op students from the Agricultural College. They prepare their own meals, but all other expenses are covered by the owners. The payroll is managed by the bank for a small fee.

Groen Fields has set up accounts with regular vendors or suppliers, such as the suppliers of seedlings, as well as the utility companies. Some suppliers offer discounts for early payment. Cleaning and maintenance of the office space in the large farmhouse and the bungalow are done professionally once a week by Spotless Company, and the owners have maintenance contracts for repairs of their farm equipment and delivery vehicles.

The nursery is classified as an agricultural business for tax purposes and charges HST on all sales and pays HST on most purchases. Some business-related purchases, however, are zero rated.

Field currently manages all the accounting records for the nursery and has just closed the books for the income tax year on April 30. Using the following information, Field has finished converting the manual records to Sage 50 for the new year beginning May 1, which is also the start of the planting season and Groen Fields' busiest month:

- Chart of Accounts
- Post-Closing Trial Balance
- Supplier Information
- Accounting Procedures

NOTES

HST, Harmonized Sales Tax, is charged instead of GST and PST in Nova Scotia. HST at 15 percent includes both GST at 5 percent and PST at 10 percent. Refer to the Accounting Procedures on page 109 and Chapter 2 for further details. For zero rated goods, the HST rate is 0.0 percent.

CHART OF POSTABLE ACCOUNTS

GROEN FIELDS

ASSETS
1080	Chequing Bank Account
1300	Seed Supplies
1310	Fertilizer
1320	Plant Care Supplies
1330	Office Supplies
1420	Annual Bedding Plants
1440	Perennial Plant Stock
1460	Tree Inventory
1480	Planters and Hangers
1510	Computer Software
1520	Computer Equipment
1540	Office Furniture
1560	Farming Equipment ▶

▶1570	Greenhouse
1580	Buildings & Property

LIABILITIES
2100	Bank Loan
2200	Accounts Payable
2650	HST Charged on Sales
2670	HST Paid on Purchases
2850	Mortgage Payable

EQUITY
3100	GF, Capital
3150	GF, Drawings
3600	Net Income ▶

▶REVENUE
4100	Revenue from Sales

EXPENSE
5020	Advertising and Promotion
5040	Bank Charges
5050	General Expense
5060	Cleaning Expenses
5070	Maintenance and Repairs
5080	Cost of Goods Sold
5090	Purchase Discounts
5100	Entertainment Expense
5110	Supplies Expense
5120	Hydro Expense ▶

▶5130	Data Management
5140	Interest Expense
5150	Soil Treatment Expenses
5160	Property Taxes
5190	Telephone and Internet
5220	Payroll Services
5240	Wages

NOTES: The Chart of Accounts includes only postable accounts and the Net Income or Current Earnings account. Sage 50 uses the Net Income account for the Income Statement to calculate the difference between revenue and expenses before closing the books.

POST-CLOSING TRIAL BALANCE

GROEN FIELDS

May 1, 2018			Debits	Credits
1080	Chequing Bank Account		$ 59 640.00	
1300	Seed Supplies		1 230.00	
1310	Fertilizer		780.00	
1320	Plant Care Supplies		2 145.00	
1330	Office Supplies		895.00	
1420	Annual Bedding Plants		5 890.00	
1440	Perennial Plant Stock		8 995.00	
1460	Tree Inventory		4 885.00	
1480	Planters and Hangers		2 255.00	
1500	Computer Software		5 295.00	
1520	Computer Equipment		8 310.00	
1540	Office Furniture		2 490.00	
1560	Farming Equipment		73 400.00	
1570	Greenhouse		120 500.00	
1580	Buildings & Property		625 800.00	
2100	Bank Loan			$120 000.00
2200	Accounts Payable			3 225.00
2650	HST Charged on Sales			4 555.00
2670	HST Paid on Purchases		2 465.00	
2850	Mortgage Payable			450 000.00
3100	GF, Capital			347 195.00
			$924 975.00	$924 975.00

SUPPLIER INFORMATION

GROEN FIELDS

Supplier Name (Contact)	Address	Phone No. Fax No.	E-mail Web Site	Terms Tax ID
Bloomers (C. D. Budd)	RR #3 Clyde River, NS B0W 1R0	Tel: (902) 544-6292 Fax: (902) 544-5217	budd@bloomers.com bloomers.com	2/10, n/30 385 345 865
Crop Savers (Gen Nitro)	910 Main Street Greenfield, NS B0T 1E0	Tel 1: (902) 622-3188 Tel 2: (800) 622-2881	GN@cropsavers.com cropsavers.com	1/10, n/30 901 200 862
Data Savers (N. T. Buggs)	4 Industrial Road Truro, NS B2C 8J6	Tel: (902) 721-5121 Fax: (902) 721-5522	ntbuggs@datasavers.com datasavers.com	net 30 567 321 447
Dust Busters (Joan Waters)	60 Water Street Dartmouth, NS B2W 6R9	Tel 1: (902) 366-1551 Tel 2: (877) 366-1500	waters@dustbusters.com dustbusters.com	net 1 345 667 211
Intertel (Les Chatter)	2 Communicate Road Truro, NS B2A 2K4	Tel: (902) 456-2355	chatter@intertel.ca intertel.ca	net 7
NS Gas (N. Bridge)	355 Pipeline Road Truro, NS B2A 5B1	Tel: (902) 454-8110	nbridge@naturalgas.com naturalgas.com	net 7
NS Hydro (N. Ergie)	83 Water Street Truro, NS B2W 6S9	Tel: (902) 455-5120	n.ergie@nshydro.ns.ca nshydro.ns.ca	net 7
Rural Property Repairs (Hy Drangea)	71 Ridge Way Currys Corner, NS B0N 1H0	Tel: (902) 499-3481 Fax: (902) 499-3482	hd@RPR.com RPR.com	1/20, n/30 124 653 779
Spotless Company (Dee Tergent)	49 Scrub Street Truro, NS B2G 1V0	Tel: (902) 454-6611 Fax: (902) 454-3216	dtergent@spotless.com spotless.com	1/30, n/60 481 532 556
Yardworks Inc. (J. Bigge)	20 Oceanview Drive Sydney, NS B1P 2L2	Tel 1: (902) 777-2346 Tel 2: (888) 337-4599	jbigge@yardworks.com yardworks.com	net 10 288 411 755

OUTSTANDING SUPPLIER INVOICES					

GROEN FIELDS

Supplier Name	Terms	Date	Inv/Chq No.	Amount	Total
Crop Savers	1/10, n/30	Apr. 26/18	CS-1044	$ 800	$ 800
Data Savers	net 30	Apr. 6/18	DS-361	$1 200	$1 200
Rural Property Repairs	1/20, n/30	Apr. 25/18 Apr. 25/18	RPR-1341 Chq #3394 Balance owing	$1 725 500	 $1 225
			Grand Total		$3 225

Accounting Procedures

The Harmonized Sales Tax (Provincial Sales Tax and Goods and Services Tax)

In Nova Scotia, federal and provincial taxes are combined in the Harmonized Sales Tax, or HST, a single tax at the rate of 15 percent. The HST is applied to most goods and services. Groen Fields uses the regular method for calculating and remitting the HST. All items sold by the farm have HST added to them. At the end of each quarter, the HST liability to the Receiver General is reduced by any HST paid to suppliers on purchases. Some items, such as large farm equipment and fertilizer and seeds purchased in large quantities, are zero rated for HST purposes. Groen Fields' *HST Owing (Refund)* subgroup total account has the amount of HST that is to be remitted to the Receiver General for Canada on the last day of each quarter. (For details, please read Chapter 2 on the GST and HST.)

Open-Invoice Accounting for Payables

The open-invoice method of accounting for invoices allows a business to keep track of each individual invoice and partial payment made against the invoice. This is in contrast to methods that keep track only of the outstanding balance by combining all invoice balances owed to a supplier. Sage 50 uses the open-invoice method. Fully paid invoices can be cleared (removed) periodically; outstanding invoices cannot be cleared.

Discounts

When discounts for early payment are offered by suppliers, Groen Fields takes advantage of them by paying invoices before the discount period ends. When the payment terms are set up correctly for the supplier and invoice, and dates are entered correctly, discounts are calculated automatically by Sage 50 and credited to *Purchase Discounts*, a contra-expense account that has a credit balance and reduces overall expenses.

Purchase of Inventory Items and Cost of Goods Sold

Inventory items and supplies purchased are recorded in the appropriate inventory or supplies asset account. Periodically, these are counted to determine the value of items remaining and the cost price of inventory sold and supplies used. The manager then issues a memo to reduce the inventory or supplies asset account and to charge the cost price to the corresponding expense account. For example, at the end of each month the *Annual Bedding Plants* asset account (*1420*) is reduced (credited) and the *Cost of Goods Sold* expense account (*5080*) is increased (debited) by the cost price of the amount sold.

NOTES

For zero rated goods the HST rate is 0 percent. None of the sales are zero rated.

Most bank services and other financial institution services are exempt from HST charges. Bank payroll services are subject to HST charges.

Provincial sales tax is not levied as a separate tax in Nova Scotia. PST will be introduced in Chapter 6.

NOTES

Discounts for early payment may be calculated on pretax amounts or on the full invoice amounts. This choice is entered in the ledger settings for the vendor or supplier.

INSTRUCTIONS

1. **Enter** the **source documents for May** in Sage 50 using the Chart of Accounts, Trial Balance, Supplier Information and Accounting Procedures for Groen Fields. The procedures for entering each new type of transaction for this application are outlined step by step in the Keystrokes section with the source documents. These transactions are indicated with a ✓ in the upper part of the completion check box beside the source document. Source document numbers are included below or in the lower part of the check box.

2. **Print** the **reports** indicated on the printing form below after you have completed your entries. Instructions for reports begin on page 144.

REPORTS

Accounts
- [ ] Chart of Accounts
- [ ] Account List
- [ ] General Journal Entries

Financials
- [✓] Comparative Balance Sheet dates: May 1 and May 31 with difference in percentage
- [✓] Income Statement from May 1 to May 31
- [✓] Trial Balance date: May 31

- [ ] All Journal Entries
- [✓] General Ledger accounts: 1420 4100 5080 from May 1 to May 31

Banking
- [ ] Cheque Log Report

Payables
- [ ] Supplier List
- [✓] Supplier Aged Detail for all suppliers May 31
- [ ] Aged Overdue Payables

- [✓] Purchases Journal Entries: May 1 to May 31
- [✓] Payments Journal Entries: May 1 to May 31

Mailing Labels
- [ ] Labels

KEYSTROKES

Opening Data Files

> **Open** **SageData16\FIELDS\FIELDS** to access the data files for Groen Fields. Refer to page 8 if you need assistance with opening data files.

You are prompted to enter the session date, which is May 7, 2018, for the first group of transactions in this application.

> **Type** May 7 18

> **Click** **OK** to enter the first session date for this application.

The Payables module appears. This is the default page for Groen Fields.

NOTES
If you are working from backup files, restore SageData16\FIELDS1.CAB or FIELDS1 to SageData16\FIELDS\FIELDS. You should create the new folder. Refer to Chapter 1, page 24, if you need assistance with restoring files.

Accounting for Purchases

All supplier-related transactions can be entered from the Payables module window. Purchases from suppliers are entered in the Purchases Journal, which is accessed from the Purchase Invoices icon:

NOTES
Access to the Receivables, Payroll, Inventory and Division ledgers is hidden because these ledgers are not set up or ready to use.

PRO VERSION
pro Pro replaces Premium in the title bar. The term Vendors will replace Suppliers for all icon labels and fields.

CLASSIC VIEW
In the Classic view Home window, click the Purchases icon to open the Purchases Journal.

PRO VERSION
pro The Refresh tool applies to multi-user mode and does not appear in the Pro version.

NOTES
When the other features are not hidden, you will have a pull-down menu for Transaction types that includes quotes and purchase orders.
When payment is by cheque, a drop-down list of bank accounts is available. These topics are covered in later chapters.

The first transaction is a normal purchase invoice that will be paid later.

| ✓ 1 | **Purchase Invoice #DS-642** | **Dated May 1/18** |

From Data Savers, $1 320 plus $198 HST for off-site data backup and restoration services for one year. Invoice total $1 518. Terms: net 30.

Click the **Purchase Invoices icon** to open the Purchases Journal input form:

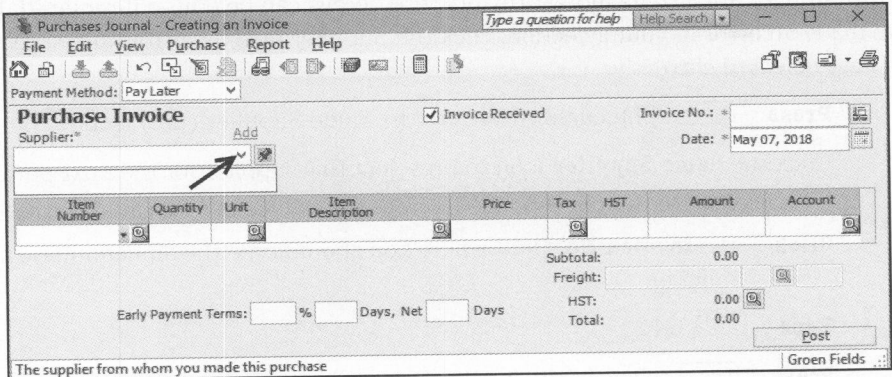

Move the mouse pointer across the various tool buttons and input fields and observe the labels and status bar messages.

Creating An Invoice is included in the title bar label and the option to Pay Later is correct because this is a credit purchase. Payment methods include cheque, cash, direct deposits and credit cards (when these are set up).

Most tool buttons should already be familiar. The Calculator tool button appears in the tool bar of the Purchases Journal and all other journal windows.

Several tool buttons have been added to the Purchases Journal window: Look Up An Invoice, Look Up Previous and Next Invoice, Track Shipments, Printer Settings, Print Preview, E-mail and Print.

Each tool will be discussed when used. The Projects or Divisions module is hidden, so there is no column for it in the journal.

Required fields are marked with * (an asterisk), as they are in other journals and ledgers.

WARNING!
You must click the list arrow to open the supplier list. Clicking the field will place an insertion point to prepare for typing a name.

Click the **Supplier** (or Vendor) **field list arrow** to expand the supplier list:

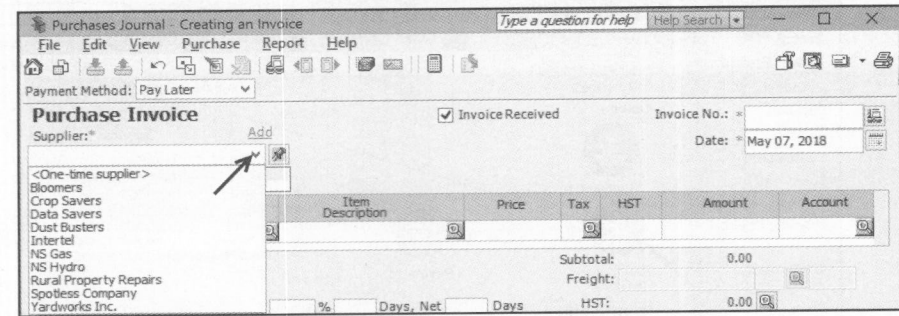

Whenever you have a downward pointing arrow ☑ beside a field, you can make a selection from a drop-down list. Type the first letter of the supplier's name to advance to the names beginning with that letter. When you type in the Supplier field, the program fills in a name from the supplier list by trying to match the letters you type.

Click **Data Savers**, the supplier for this purchase, to select and enter it.

The supplier's name and address have been added to your input form, making it easy to check whether you have selected the correct supplier. Many other details have also been added by default from the supplier's record. The tax code and the account number usually stay the same for a supplier, so they are set up as defaults. The payment terms for the supplier are also included. Any of these details can be edited if required. If you have made an error in your selection, click the Supplier field list arrow and start again. If you have selected correctly,

Press ⌨ tab . The cursor moves to the Same Supplier (pin) icon 📌.

Click the **Same Supplier** icon to preselect this supplier for the next purchase. When selected, the pin is pushed in 📌. Click it again to turn off the selection.

Click the **Invoice No. field** where you should type the alphanumeric invoice number.

Type DS-642

Press ⌨ tab to select the Invoice Lookup icon.

Press ⌨ tab again to advance to the Date field.

Enter the date the transaction took place, May 1, 2018. The session date appears by default, in long (text) format according to the settings for the company file. It is highlighted, ready to be accepted or changed. You need to change the date.

Type may 1

Many of the invoice fields (Item Number, Quantity, Unit, Item Description and unit Price) pertain mainly to inventory items. Because we are not using the Inventory Ledger for this application, you can skip the inventory-related fields. Any information you type in these fields does not appear in the journal report. You can add a description in the Item Description field.

Click the **Item Description field**.

Type data backup service

If necessary, you can select a different tax code. To access the codes set up and available,

Click the **Tax field List icon** 🔍 to open the list of tax codes for Groen Fields:

NOTES
If you use the same supplier for consecutive purchases, preselecting the supplier can save data entry time. You can still select a different supplier from the list. The pin will remain selected, so you can enter multiple purchases from the next supplier as well.

NOTES
The year is automatically added when you enter the month and day in the Date field of the Purchases Journal.

NOTES
Inventory is introduced in Chapter 10.
When orders and quotes are used, fields for these features will be added to the journal. (Refer to Chapter 11.)

NOTES
When you are selling multiple quantities of an item, you can enter the quantity in the Quantity field and the unit price in the Price field. Sage 50 will then calculate the total amount.

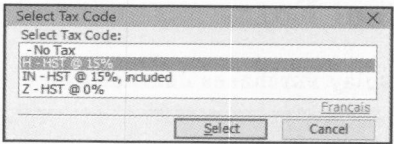

The selected tax code is H, that is, HST is charged on the purchase at 15 percent, and the tax is not included in the price. You can select a different code if needed, but in this case the tax code is correct.

Click   **Cancel** so that the selection remains unchanged.

Click   the **first line of the Amount field**, where you will enter the total amount for this purchase.

Type   1320

Press   tab .

The cursor moves to the Account field. The Account field for this purchase refers to the debit part of the journal entry, normally the acquisition of an asset or the incurring of an expense. It could also be used to decrease a liability or to decrease equity if the purchase were made for the owner's personal use. When you work in the subsidiary Payables journal, Sage 50 will automatically credit your *Accounts Payable* **control account** in the General Ledger for the purchase. In fact, you cannot access *Accounts Payable* directly when the Payables Ledger is set up and linked. If you click the Account List icon, this account is not included.

In this example, the business has incurred an expense and the correct account, *Data Management,* is entered as the default for this supplier.

To select a different account, click the List icon 🔍 for the Account field, double-click the Account field or press enter to open the Select Account screen. You can also add a new account from the Select Account screen.

Press   tab to advance the cursor to the next invoice line. You can now enter additional purchases from this supplier if there are any.

Sage 50 uses the tax code to calculate and enter the tax amount automatically in the HST field when you enter the amount for the purchase.

Your screen has been updated with this information:

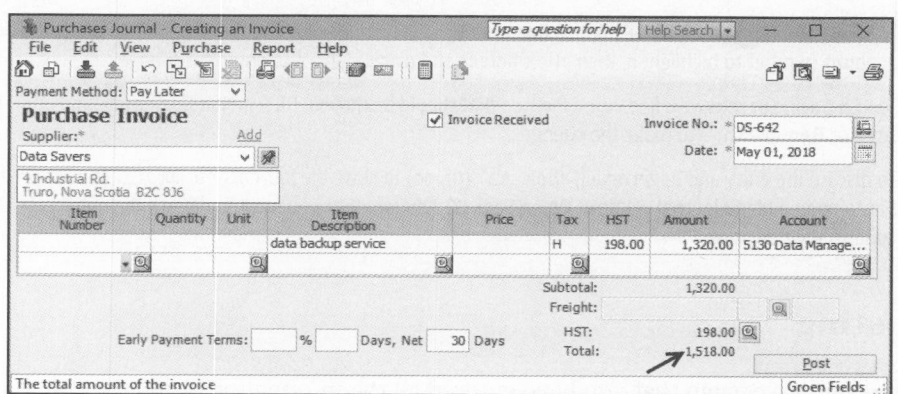

The payment terms have been set up as defaults for this supplier and are entered automatically. They can be edited if needed for specific purchases, but in this case they are correct. There is no discount, and full payment is due in 30 days. The **subtotal** (amount owing before taxes) and the **total** amounts are calculated and added automatically, so the entries for this transaction are complete and you are ready to review the transaction. By reviewing the journal entry, you can check for mistakes.

NOTES

For this application, the sales tax rate is set to 15 percent, the harmonized single tax rate for Nova Scotia. For provinces that have a separate or no provincial sales tax, the rate is 5 percent and tax codes will display as GST @ 5%.

Since the provincial and federal retail sales taxes are harmonized, there is no separate amount for PST. When PST is applicable and is set up in the defaults for the company, the program will calculate PST as well, based on the tax rates and codes entered for PST.

NOTES

Typing negative amounts will generate a credit entry with a debit for Accounts Payable. This is similar to entering a negative amount in the General Journal to switch debits to credits and vice versa.

NOTES

The account name may not fit in the account column if the column is very narrow. To change the width of a column, point to the heading column margin. When the pointer changes to a double-sided arrow, drag the margin line to the new location. Make a journal window wider by dragging the side frame. You can also maximize a journal window to occupy the entire screen.

NOTES
Pressing ⌃ctrl + J will also display the journal entry.

Reviewing the Purchases Journal Entry

Choose the **Report menu** and **click Display Purchases Journal Entry**:

Account Number	Account Description	Debits	Credits
2670	HST Paid on Purchases	198.00	-
5130	Data Management	1,320.00	-
2200	Accounts Payable	-	1,518.00
Additional Date:	Additional Field:	1,518.00	1,518.00

Groen Fields
Purchases Journal Entry May 01, 2018 (J1)
Generated On: Dec 20, 2015

Note that Sage 50 automatically updates the *Accounts Payable* **control account** because the Payables and General ledgers are linked or fully integrated. Even though you did not enter account *2200*, Sage 50 uses it because it is defined as the linked account to which all purchases should be credited. In fact, you cannot select *Accounts Payable* directly for posting when it is used as a linked account. *HST Paid on Purchases*, the linked tax account, is also automatically updated. Using the Purchases Journal instead of the General Journal to enter purchases is faster because you need to enter only half the journal entry. You should use this journal for purchases because the program credits the account of the selected supplier directly, prevents you from choosing an incorrect payables account and updates the total payables and tax amounts directly. The automatic selection of tax codes and accounts and calculation of tax amounts also makes the transaction simpler to enter and increases accuracy.

Close the **display** to return to the Purchases Journal input screen.

CORRECTING THE PURCHASES JOURNAL ENTRY BEFORE POSTING

Move to the field that has the error. **Press** ⌨tab to move forward through the fields or **press** ⌨shift and ⌨tab together to move back to a previous field. This will highlight the field information so you can change it. **Type** the **correct information** and **press** ⌨tab to enter it.

You can also use the mouse to **point** to a field and **drag through** the **incorrect information** to highlight it. **Type** the **correct information** and **press** ⌨tab to enter it.

If the supplier is incorrect, reselect from the supplier list by **clicking** the **Supplier field list arrow**. **Click** the name of the **correct supplier**. If the supplier terms or account are now incorrect, you should reverse the entry instead. Refer to page 139.

Click an **incorrect amount** to highlight it, **type** the **correct amount** and **press** ⌨tab to enter the change.

To select a different account, **click** the **Account List icon** to display the list of accounts. **Click** the **correct account** number to highlight it, then **click Select** and **press** ⌨tab to enter the change.

To insert a line or remove a line, **click** the **line** that should be moved. **Choose** the **Edit menu** and **click Insert Line** or **Remove Line** to make the change.

To discard the entry and begin again, **click** ☒ (**Close**) to close the journal or **click** ↺ (**Undo**) on the tool bar to open a blank journal window. When Sage 50 asks whether you want to discard the entry, **click Yes** to confirm your decision.

Posting

When you are certain that you have entered all the information correctly, you must post the transaction to save it.

Click the **Post button** ⌐Post⌐ or **choose** the **Purchase menu** and **click Post** to save your transaction.

Click **OK** to confirm successful posting.

A new blank Purchases Journal form appears on the screen.

NOTES
Other linked accounts for the Payables Ledger include a bank account, a freight expense account and a purchase discounts account. Each linked account will be explained when it is used in this workbook.

NOTES
Using the Payables journals also makes it less likely to reverse debit and credit amounts in error.

NOTES
To correct a Purchases Journal entry after posting, refer to page 127 and Appendix C.

NOTES
You can press ⌨alt + P to post the journal entry.

Storing a Recurring Journal Entry

The second transaction is the recurring purchase of soil treatment. Businesses often have transactions that are repeated regularly. For example, loan payments, bank charges and rent payments usually occur on the same day each month; supplies may be ordered daily or weekly; insurance payments may be less frequent but nonetheless regular. Groen Fields is invoiced weekly for the treatment service. By storing an entry and indicating the frequency, it can be recalled when it is needed without re-entering all the information.

> ✓
> 2
>
> **Purchase Invoice #CS-1243**   **Dated May 1/18**
> From Crop Savers, $640 for soil testing and follow-up fertilizer treatment plus $96 HST. Invoice total $736. Terms: 1/10, n/30. Store as a weekly recurring entry.

The Purchases Journal should still be open with the correct payment method and date.

Choose	**Crop Savers** from the supplier list. Or,
Click	the **Supplier field** and **type** C
Click	the **Invoice field**.
Type	CS-1243
Enter	a **description** for the purchase.

The tax code is correct; HST is charged on this service. The payment terms and account are also correct by default.

Click	the **Amount field**, **type** 640 and **press** `tab` to complete the transaction.
Choose	the **Report menu** and **click Display Purchases Journal Entry** to review the entry.
Close	the **display** and **make corrections** if necessary.
Click	the **Store tool** 🖳 on the tool bar or **choose** the **Purchase menu** and **click Store** to open the Store Recurring Transaction screen:

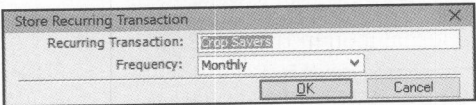

Sage 50 enters the supplier and Monthly as the default name and frequency for the entry. The cursor is in the name field. You can type another descriptive name to change it. Be sure to use one that you will recognize easily as belonging to this entry. The default frequency is incorrect since the invoices for soil treatments are received weekly.

Click   **Monthly** to list the choices for the recurring frequency:

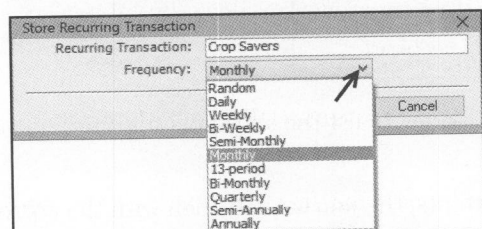

The frequency options are Random (for irregular purchases), Daily, Weekly, Bi-Weekly, Semi-Monthly, Monthly, 13-Period, Bi-Monthly, Quarterly, Semi-Annually and Annually.

NOTES
Typing the first letter of a supplier name in the Supplier field will add the first supplier name beginning with that letter. Because Crop Savers is the first supplier name starting with "C," it will be entered.

NOTES
The procedure for storing entries is the same for all journals when the option is available. Choose Store, assign a name to the entry, then choose a frequency and click OK to save it.
The shortcut for storing a transaction is `ctrl` + T.

NOTES
The recurring frequency options are Daily, Weekly (52 times per year), Bi-Weekly (26 times per year, or every two weeks), Semi-Monthly (24 times per year), Monthly (12 times per year), 13-Period (13 times per year, or every four weeks), Bi-Monthly (six times per year, or every two months), Quarterly (four times per year, or every three months), Semi-Annually (twice per year, or every six months), Annually (once per year) and Random (irregular intervals using the session date when the entry is recalled).

> **Click** **Weekly**.

When you recall the stored entry, Sage 50 will advance the default journal date according to the frequency selected. The session date is entered if the Random frequency is chosen.

> **Click** **OK** to return to the Purchases Journal window.

The **Recall tool** ![icon] is now darkened and can be selected because you have stored a journal entry. The journal title bar label has also changed — to Using Recurring Crop Savers.

CORRECTING A STORED JOURNAL ENTRY

If you notice an error in the stored journal entry before posting, you must first **correct** the **journal entry** in the Purchases Journal window, then **click Store**. When asked to confirm that you want to overwrite or replace the previous version, **click Yes**.

If you edit the journal entry after storing it and do not want to store the changed entry, Sage 50 will warn you that the entry has changed. **Click Yes** to proceed.

Posting

When you are sure that you have entered all the information correctly and you have stored the entry, you must post the transaction to save it.

> **Click** the **Post button** ![Post] or **choose** the **Purchase menu** and **click Post** to save your transaction. **Click OK** to confirm successful posting.

A new blank Purchases Journal form appears on the screen. The Recall tool is now available so we can recall the purchase we stored. Our next transaction is a payment, however, not a purchase.

> **Close** the **Purchases Journal window** to return to the Payables window.

Accounting for Payments

Payments are made from the Payments Journal icon in the Tasks pane:

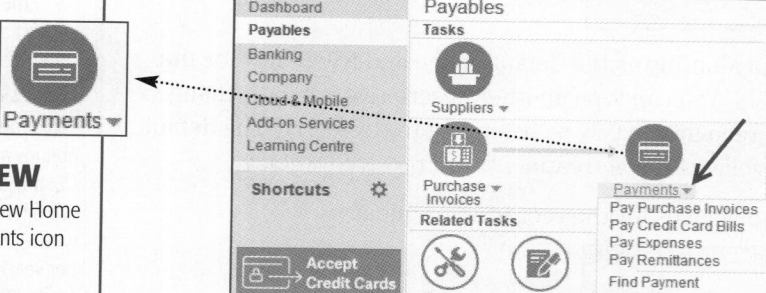

> **Click** the **Payments icon list arrow** to list the shortcuts for different payment types.

When you click on one of these shortcuts, the journal will open with the correct type of transaction preselected.

> **Click** **Pay Purchase Invoices** to open the Payments Journal:

CLASSIC VIEW

From the Classic view Home window, click the Payments icon ![Payments icon] to open the Payments Journal. Pay Invoices will be selected as the default type of transaction.

PRO VERSION

pro The term Vendors replaces Suppliers.

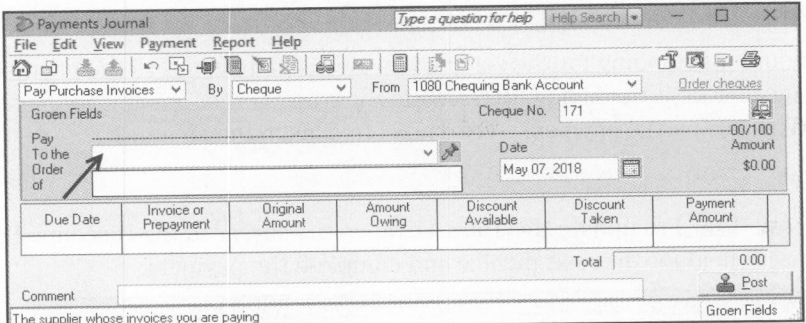

Pay Invoices is selected as the type of payment in the type of Pay transaction field because we made this selection in the Home window. Pay Invoices is also the default transaction type when you click the Payments icon. Cheque appears as the method of payment in the By field, and *1080 Chequing Bank Account* is the account the payment is made from. These defaults are correct for the first payment.

✓ 3   **Payment Cheque #171**   **Dated May 2/18**
To Data Savers, $780 in partial payment of account. Reference invoice #DS-361.

Click   the **To The Order Of** (Supplier) **field list arrow** to open the familiar list of suppliers displayed in alphabetic order.

Click   **Data Savers** (or **type** D) to choose and enter the supplier to whom the payment is made.

The journal is updated with the outstanding invoices for the supplier:

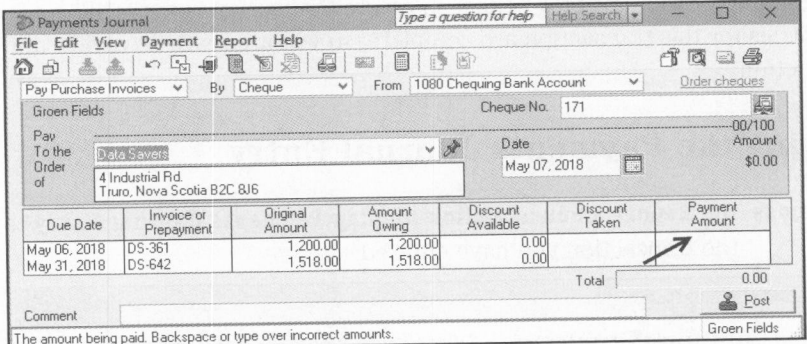

The addition of the supplier's name and address make it easy to determine whether you have selected correctly. If you need to change the supplier, click the Supplier field list arrow again to select from the supplier list. The cheque number is entered in the Number field. The next cheque number appears according to the settings for the company. It is correct, so you can accept it. Normally the cheque number should be correct. It can be edited, if necessary, for reversing or correcting entries.

The default session date is entered and is incorrect; you must change it.

Click   the **Calendar icon** for the Date field.

Click   **2** in the May section. **Press** *tab*.

The year will be added correctly when you type the month and day in the Payments Journal Date field.

The cursor moves to the Due Date field for the first outstanding invoice. All outstanding invoices, including both the amount of the original invoice and the balance owing for the selected supplier, are listed on the screen.

Press   *tab* to advance to the Discount Taken field. Since there is no discount, the field is blank and you can skip it.

Press   (tab) again.

The amount outstanding for the selected invoice is highlighted as the payment amount. You can accept the highlighted amount or type another amount for partial payments. This is a partial payment, so we need to change the amount.

Type   780

Press   (tab) to update the Total, advance the cursor to the Discount Taken field for the next invoice and complete the payment:

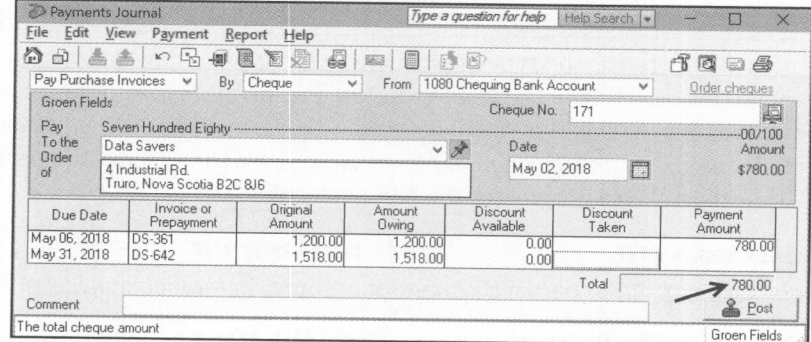

The upper cheque portion of the form is completed automatically. There is no field for account numbers in the Payments Journal — you need to enter only the amount of the payment on the appropriate invoice line.

As you pay invoices in the subsidiary Payments Journal, you do not enter any accounts, so you cannot make an incorrect selection. Sage 50 chooses the default linked accounts defined for the Payables Ledger to create the journal entry.

The entries for this transaction are complete, so you are ready to review and post your transaction.

Reviewing the Payments Journal Entry

Choose the **Report menu** and **click Display Payments Journal Entry** to display the transaction you have entered:

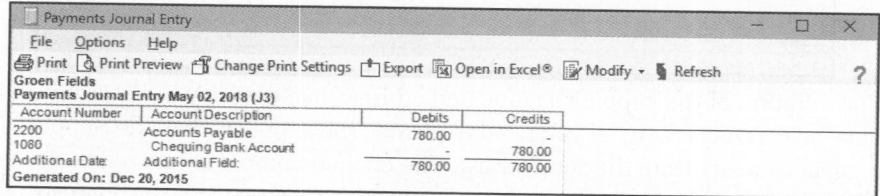

Sage 50 automatically creates a related journal entry when you complete a Payments Journal entry. The program updates *Accounts Payable* and *Chequing Bank Account* because the Payables and General ledgers are fully linked. *Chequing Bank Account* has been defined as the default Payables linked account to which payments are credited. The payment is also recorded to the supplier's account to reduce the balance owing.

Close the **display** to return to the Payments Journal input screen.

You can print the cheque, but you must do so before posting. However, you should check that you have selected the correct printer and forms for printing cheques (refer to Chapter 4, page 83) and make corrections first, if necessary.

Make **corrections. Click** the **Print tool** if you want to print the cheque.

Posting

When you are certain that you have entered all the information correctly, you must post the transaction to save it.

Click   the **Post button** [🖊 Post] (or **choose** the **Payment menu** and **click Post**) to save your transaction and then **click OK** to confirm.

Entering Cash Purchases

The property tax statement on May 2 is to be paid immediately on receipt of the assessment notice. Instead of recording the purchase and payment separately, you can record the payment with the purchase in the Payments Journal. This transaction also involves a company that is not listed as a supplier, so you must add Truro City Treasurer to the supplier list to record the transaction.

Suppliers can be added directly from the Payables Ledger or from the supplier field in the Purchases Journal or the Payments Journal. We will add the new supplier from the Payments Journal. The Payments Journal should still be open.

✓	**Cash Purchase Invoice #Truro-18** **Dated May 2/18**
4	From Truro City Treasurer (use Quick Add for the new supplier), $1 425 for annual property taxes. Paid by cheque #172.

The date and the cheque number are correct. The date is unchanged from the previous Payments Journal transaction. The next available cheque number is entered by default, and the bank account is selected for the payment. Cheque numbers are updated in sequence for both invoice payment entries and cash purchases.

Click   **Pay Purchase Invoices** to list the options for payment transactions:

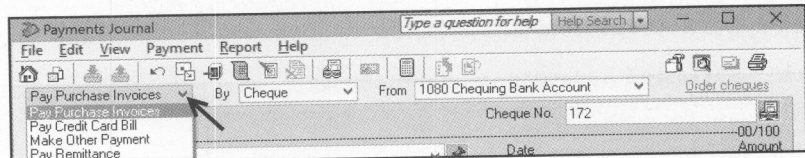

Click   **Make Other Payment** in the drop-down list.

If you have closed the Payments Journal, you can open the form for cash purchases from the Home window. Click the Payments icon list arrow and click **Pay Expenses** (refer to page 116). In this case, you must enter May 2 as the date.

WARNING!
If you have closed the Payments Journal, the session date will be entered and you must change it to May 2.

PRO VERSION
The term Vendor is used instead of Supplier in all journals.

NOTES
The Continue option will add the supplier's name to journal entries for purchase invoices entered in the Purchases Journal, but not for Other Payments entered in the Payments Journal.
If you create a partial supplier record with Quick Add, you can add more supplier details later by editing the record.

NOTES
When you display the list of All Accounts and scroll down, Accounts Payable (account 2200) is not included.

Journal input fields are added to the payment form:

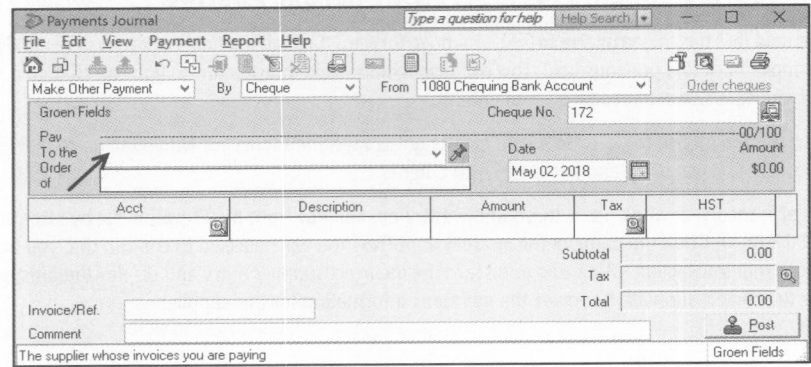

Click   the **To The Order Of (Supplier) field** to move the cursor.

Type   Truro City Treasurer and then **press** tab to display the options for a new name:

The program recognizes that the name is new and gives you four options. **Continue** will add the name to the journal and the Journal Report and apply the default settings for the ledger. This option will not create a supplier record or include the name in the Supplier list. **Quick Add** will create a partial record with only the supplier's name and will apply the default settings for the ledger. **Full Add** will open a new ledger record for the supplier where you can add complete details. **Cancel** will return you to the journal. You can then type or choose another name if the one you typed was incorrect.

If you are making a cash purchase and you will not be making additional purchases from this supplier, you can choose **One-Time Supplier** from the Supplier list instead of adding the supplier. Type the supplier's name and address in the text box area below the To The Order Of field. The default settings for the ledger will apply to the invoice, but you can change them if needed. The transaction will be included in the GST/HST report, but the supplier's name will not appear in supplier lists or in the journal reports.

We want to add a partial record for the new supplier.

Click   **Quick Add** to return to the Payments Journal.

The supplier's name is added to the journal. Because an account is not set up for the supplier, you must enter the asset or expense account that is debited for the transaction.

Click   the **Account field List icon** to open the Select Account list.

Click   **Suggested Accounts** to modify the list:

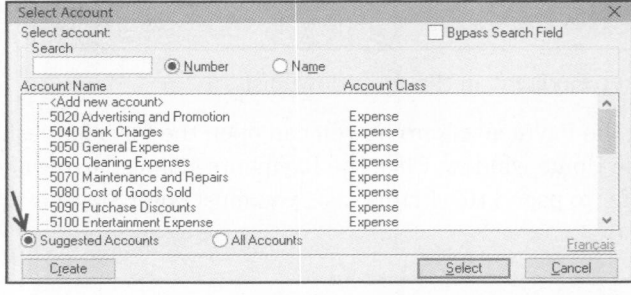

The list now has only the expense accounts, the ones used most often for purchases. This list is easier to work with because it is shorter. When you enter sales in the Sales Journal, the suggested accounts will list only revenue accounts.

> **Scroll down** and **click 5160 Property Taxes**.
>
> **Click** **Select** to add the account and advance to the Description field.
>
> **Type** annual property taxes
>
> **Press** (tab) to advance to the Amount field.
>
> **Type** 1425 **Press** (tab).

Since no sales tax is charged on property taxes, the default entry of No Tax is correct.

> **Click** the **Invoice/Ref. field**.
>
> **Type** Truro-18 **Press** (tab) to advance to the Comment field.

The comment will become part of the journal record, so you should include it.

> **Type** Truro-18, annual property taxes

The subtotal and total amounts are entered automatically — in this case they are the same because no taxes are added. Your payment form is completed and you are ready to review it:

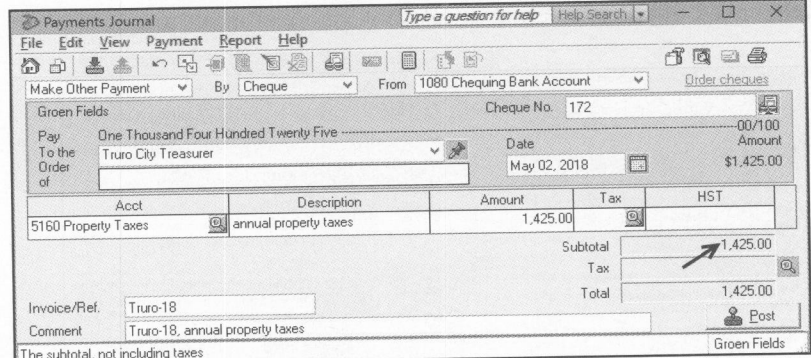

Choose the **Report menu** and **click Display Payments Journal Entry**:

Account Number	Account Description	Debits	Credits
5160	Property Taxes	1,425.00	-
1080	Chequing Bank Account	-	1,425.00
Additional Date:	Additional Field:	1,425.00	1,425.00

Generated On: Dec 20, 2015

The program has automatically credited *Chequing Bank Account*, the Payables linked bank account, for the cash purchase instead of *Accounts Payable*.

> **Close** the **display** when you have finished.
>
> **Make** any **corrections** necessary. Double-click an incorrect entry and type the correct details.
>
> **Click** the **Post button** [Post] to save the **entry** when you are certain that it is correct. **Click OK**.
>
> **Close** the **Payments Journal** to return to the Home window.

Balance amounts in the Suppliers list pane have been updated to include the transactions we have recorded.

NOTES
You can use keyboard shortcuts to copy text. Click the text you want to copy and press (ctrl) + C. Then click the field you want the text copied to and press (ctrl) + V.

NOTES
The Invoice/Ref. number is not added to the journal entry for Other Payment transactions, so we repeat it in the Comment field.

NOTES
If the purchase has taxes added, choose the tax code from the Tax field List icon selection list.

NOTES
You can preview this expense payment, just as you can preview invoice payment cheques. Two copies of the invoice details are added to the upper cheque portion.

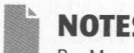
NOTES
Entering cash purchases in the Payments Journal as an Other Payment or in the Purchases Journal is a personal preference.

NOTES
BuyMore
☑ Terms: net 1
Expense account: 5020
Tax code: H - HST @ 15%

PRO VERSION
Click Add Vendor in the Vendors shortcuts list.

Classic **CLASSIC VIEW**
From the Classic view Home window, click the Suppliers icon to open the Suppliers window. Then click the Create tool , or choose the File menu and click Create, or press *ctrl* + N. Close the Suppliers window after saving the new record.

PRO VERSION
The Refresh tool does not appear in the Pro version. The term Vendor replaces the term Supplier in all fields.

NOTES
If you are missing any information for a supplier, you can leave the field blank and enter the details later by editing the record. Refer to page 136.
Although the extra fields are not required, entering the details in the ledger record will speed up journal entry when you choose the supplier.

Adding a New Supplier Record

Cash purchases and new suppliers may be recorded in the Payments Journal or the Purchases Journal. We will record the next cash purchase in the Purchases Journal after we add a full record for the supplier. You can create a new supplier record on the fly, as in the previous transaction, by choosing Full Add, or you can open the Payables Ledger for a new supplier record from the Add Supplier option in the Suppliers shortcuts list. For the next purchase, we will use the ledger option to enter a complete new record.

Memo #12   **Dated May 3/18**
Add a new record for BuyMore (contact B. S. Fullovit)
Located at 447 Slick St., Halifax, NS B3B 8J5
Tel: (902) 564-8907
E-mail: fullovit@buymore.ca

Click   the **Suppliers icon shortcuts list arrow**:

Click   **Add Supplier** to open the Payables Ledger input form:

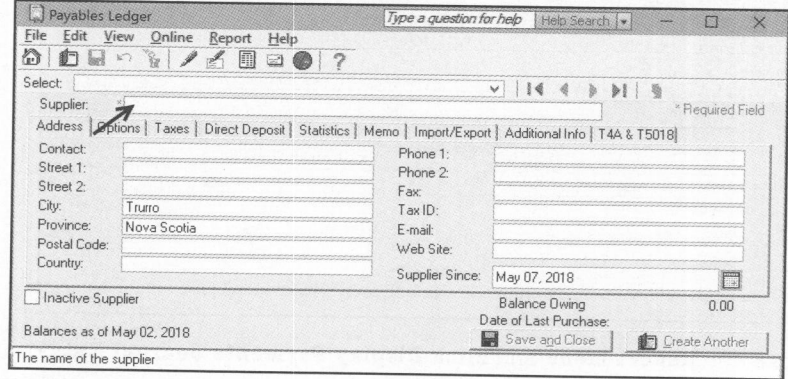

You are ready to enter the new supplier. The Supplier Address tab information screen appears first. Note that **required fields** have an * beside them as they do in the General Ledger. The supplier name is the only required field. As soon as you begin to type in the field, the * is removed.

Type   BuyMore **Press** *tab* .

The cursor advances to the Contact field, where you enter the name of Groen Fields' contact person at BuyMore. This field can also be used to enter a third address line if two street lines are insufficient. This field or any other may be left blank by pressing *tab* or clicking the next field for which you have information.

Type   B. S. Fullovit

Press   *tab* . The cursor moves to the Street 1 field.

Type   447 Slick St.

The Street 2 field can be used for a second address line, if there is one.

By default, the program has entered the city, province and country from the Payables Ledger Address settings. We need to change the city.

Double-click Truro in the City field and **type** `Halifax`

Click   the **Postal Code field** to move the cursor. The default entry for Province is correct.

When you enter a Canadian postal code, you do not need to use capital letters or leave a space within the postal code. The program makes these adjustments for you.

Type   `b3b8j5` **Press** `tab`.

The format of the postal code has been corrected automatically. The cursor moves to the Country field. You can leave this field blank.

Press   `tab`. The cursor moves to the Phone 1 field.

You do not need to insert a dash, space or bracket when you enter a telephone number. Telephone and fax numbers may be entered with or without the area code.

Type   `9025648907` **Press** `tab`.

The format for the telephone number has also been corrected automatically. The cursor advances to the Phone 2 field for the supplier's second phone number. We do not have additional phone or fax numbers at this time. They can be added later when they are obtained. The Tax ID number refers to the business's federal tax or GST registration number. Adding e-mail and Web site information allows you to send purchase orders by e-mail and connect to the supplier's Web site directly from Sage 50. Type e-mail and Web addresses just as you enter them in your Internet program.

Click   the **E-mail field**. **Type** `fullovit@buymore.ca`

The date in the Supplier Since field is the session date or the date of the earliest transaction you enter for this supplier in Sage 50. You can enter a different date if this is appropriate. The Date Of Last Purchase is added automatically by the program based on the transactions you enter for the supplier.

Press   `tab` **twice** to advance to the Supplier Since date field.

Type   `May 3`

The last option concerns the supplier's status. You can make a supplier inactive and remove the name from the selection lists and reports. Suppliers that you will not use again can be made inactive.

Click   the **Options tab** to open the next supplier information screen:

The Options screen has several important fields. In the first part of the Options screen, you can choose the default account and preferred language (English or French) for the supplier. Forms you send to that supplier will be in the selected language, although your own screens will not change. Although the default account field is named

Expense Account — often an expense account is the default — you may select any postable account. If you usually buy the same kinds of goods from a supplier, entering a default account saves time and prevents errors when completing journal entries. BuyMore provides promotional materials.

> **Click** the **Expense Account list arrow** to list the accounts available.

> **Scroll down** and **click 5020 Advertising and Promotion**.

In the **Early Payment Terms** section of the ledger, you can enter the discount for early settlement of accounts and the term for full payment. Discounts may be calculated on the amount before taxes or on the full invoice (after-tax) amount. Three fields are used to enter the discount. The first has the discount rate as a percentage, and the second holds the number of days over which the discount remains valid. In the final field, enter the number of days in which net payment is due. According to the source document, immediate payment is expected.

> **Click** the **Net Due In _____ Days field** (Early Payment Terms section).

> **Type** 1

The next fields appear as check boxes. There are no discounts from this supplier. Leave the check box for Calculate Discounts Before Tax blank.

Selecting **Print Contact On Cheques** will add the name of the contact person to the cheques written to the supplier. If the Contact field contains address information, check this box; otherwise, leave it unchecked — cheques are usually made payable to the business name.

The next option allows you to choose **Print or E-mail Purchase Orders For This Supplier** as the default setting, but you can change the selection for individual purchase orders if necessary. If you usually e-mail the orders, you should also check the **E-mail Confirmation Of Invoices And Quotes** option by clicking it.

If you want to synchronize lists in Sage 50 with Microsoft Outlook, click the **Synchronize With Microsoft Outlook** check box.

The next input screen defines the tax options for this supplier.

> **Click** the **Taxes tab** to open the screen:

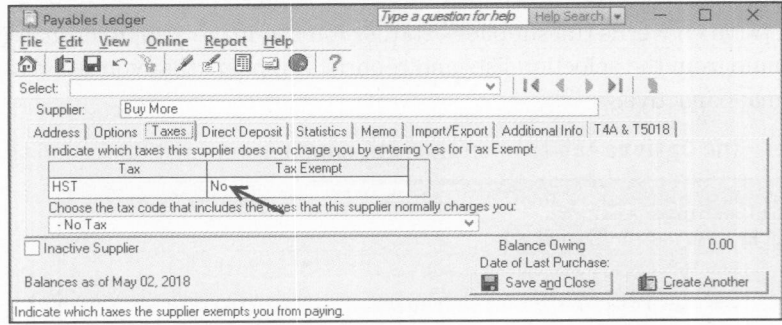

All the taxes Groen Fields usually pays are set up for the company and appear on the list. HST is the only applicable tax. The default option is to pay the tax — the option under Tax Exempt is set at No — that is, Groen Fields is not exempt from taxes on purchases from this supplier. Clicking No will change the tax exemption setting to Yes. This change would be appropriate for suppliers that do not provide goods or services, such as the Receiver General. Refer to Chapter 2 for further information about taxes.

To enter a default tax code for purchases from the supplier, we can choose a code from the drop-down list in the next field. The default setting, No Tax, is incorrect.

> **Click** **No Tax** to open the list of the available codes:

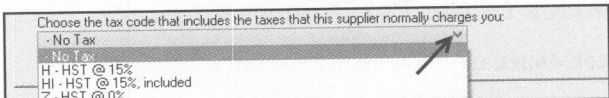

Four codes are defined for Groen Fields: **No Tax** and **Z** (zero rated – HST @ 0%) for suppliers from which purchases are exempt from tax; **H** for suppliers of normal taxable goods or services when HST is not included in the price; and **HI** for suppliers of taxable goods such as gasoline or liquor when the tax is included in the purchase price.

BuyMore charges HST but does not include it in the price.

> **Click**   **H - HST @ 15%**.

The remaining input screens will be introduced in later applications. The **Direct Deposit** tab screen holds the details for automatic payments from your bank account, the **Statistics** tab screen stores cumulative historical transactions, the **Memo** tab screen allows you to add messages to the Daily Business Manager and the **Import/Export** tab screen allows you to specify corresponding inventory item codes for your business and your suppliers. The **Additional Info** tab screen has customizable fields for other information. You can prepare **T4A** and **T5018 Slips** for suppliers and subcontractors (for contract and construction services) — this does not apply to Groen Fields.

Check your work carefully before saving the information because the options you select will affect the invoices directly.

CORRECTING A NEW SUPPLIER ACCOUNT

Move to the field that has the error by **pressing** (tab) to move forward through the fields or **pressing** (shift) and (tab) together to move back to a previous field. **Type** the **correct information**.

You can also highlight the incorrect information by dragging the cursor through it. You can now type the correct information.

After a field has been corrected, **press** (tab) to enter the correction.

To open a different tab screen, **click** the **tab** you want.

When you are certain that all the information is correct,

> **Click**   **Save And Close** [Save and Close] to save the supplier information and return to the Home window.

Entering Vendor Records from the Purchases Journal

Click the Purchase Invoices icon [Purchase Invoices] to open the journal and click the Supplier field.

Type the new supplier's name in the Supplier field. Click the Add link (just above the Supplier field) to open a ledger record at the Address tab screen.

Or, press (tab) after typing the name. The program recognizes the name as new:

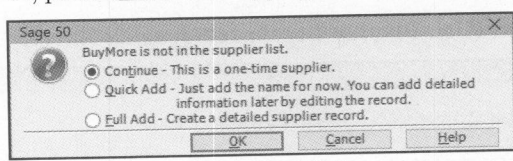

Click Full Add to open a Payables Ledger record at the Address tab screen. The new supplier name will be entered as you typed it in the Supplier field. Enter the remaining details for the supplier as described above. Click the Save And Close button to return to the invoice. The supplier's address, tax code and expense account will be added to the invoice form.

NOTES
When the tax exempt settings are No, you can change the tax codes in the journals and the tax calculations will be correct. If the tax exempt settings are Yes, you can change the codes but no taxes will be calculated.

NOTES
The Daily Business Manager is covered in Chapter 11, and the Import/Export options are explained in Appendix J on the Student DVD. Direct deposits are covered in Chapter 13.
We use the Additional Info tab fields for the Payroll Ledger in Chapter 9.

Classic **CLASSIC VIEW**
From the Classic view Home window, click the Purchases icon [Purchases] to open the Purchases Journal.

NOTES
If you click the Add link before typing the name, add the name when the ledger record opens.

Entering Cash Purchases in the Purchases Journal

Open the **Purchases Journal**.

✓	**Cash Purchase Invoice #BM-3492**	**Dated May 3/18**
6		

From BuyMore, $1 200 plus $180 HST for updating online sales catalogue. Terms: cash on receipt. Invoice total $1 380 paid in full by cheque #173.

Choose **BuyMore** from the Supplier drop-down list. **Press** (tab).

We can now enter the transaction details, as we did for previous purchases. We need to change the payment method because this is a cash purchase.

Click **Pay Later** in the Payment Method field for the payment options:

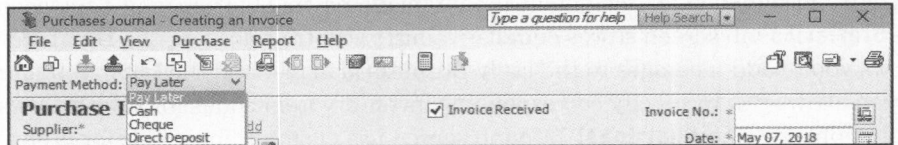

The payment options are the same as those in the Payments Journal for Other Payments, with the addition of Pay Later.

Click **Cheque**.

A cheque number field with the next cheque number is added in the upper right-hand corner of the invoice form. The cheque number is updated automatically. The account number and payment terms are added from the supplier record information we entered. You need to add the invoice number, transaction date and amount.

Click the **Invoice No. field** and **type** BM-3492

Click the **Calendar icon** and **choose May 3**.

Click the **Amount field**.

Type 1200 **Press** (tab). Add a description to complete the invoice:

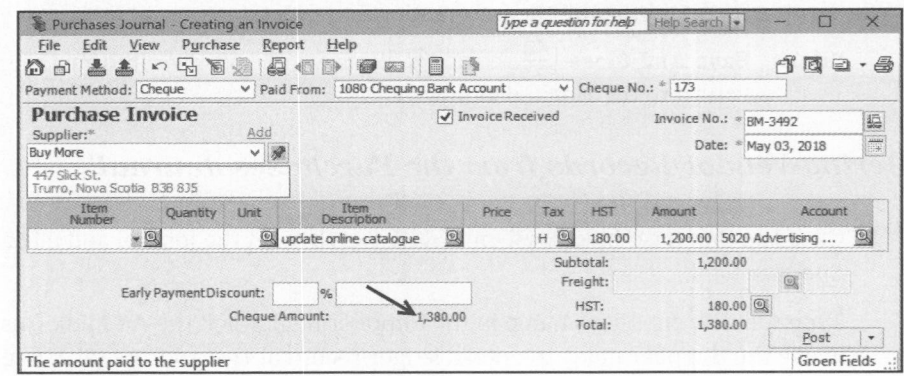

You should review the journal entry before posting it.

Choose the **Report menu** and **click Display Purchases Journal Entry**:

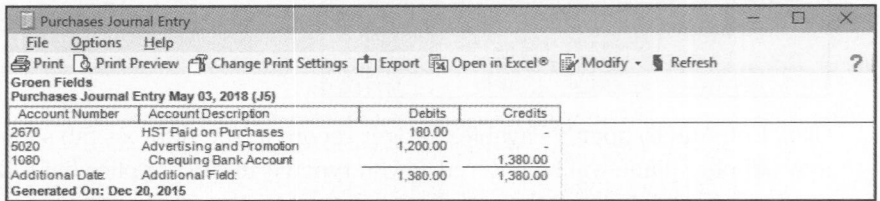

This journal entry is the same as the one from the Payments Journal when we chose Make Other Payment. *Chequing Bank Account* is credited instead of *Accounts*

Payable. The supplier record is updated for the transaction by including both an invoice and a payment for the same date. Because the journal entries are the same, the method you choose for entering cash purchases — either in the Purchases Journal or as Other Payments in the Payments Journal — is a personal preference.

Close   the **display**.

Check   the **invoice** for errors and **make corrections**, just as you would for regular purchases. When the information is correct,

Click   **Post** `Post ▼` to save the transaction. **Click OK**.

Adjusting a Posted Invoice

In the same way that you can correct or adjust a previously posted entry in the General Journal, you can edit a Purchases Journal invoice after posting. Sage 50 will create the necessary reversing entry when you post the revised invoice.

✓	**Memo #13**	**Dated May 4/18**
7	From Owner: Adjust invoice #DS-642. The invoice from Data Savers included a one-time charge of $350 plus $52.50 HST to restore system and recover data after data was compromised. The corrected invoice total is $1 920.50.	

The Purchases Journal should still be open.

Click   the **Adjust Invoice tool** 📇 or **choose** the **Purchase menu** and **click Adjust Invoice** to open the Search Purchase Invoices screen:

This is similar to the Search screen for the General Journal, but you have the additional option of searching for invoices by the name of the supplier. The program enters default start and finish dates. These dates can be edited like any other date fields, or you can choose dates from the calendars. The default dates include all transactions for the journal, so we can accept them.

We will search all invoices by accepting the default to Search All Suppliers.

If you know the invoice number, journal entry number or amount, you can enter this in the corresponding field and click OK to select the invoice directly.

Click   **OK** to open the requested list of Purchases Journal invoices:

Date	Supplier	Invoice #	Journal Entry #	Original Amt
May 03, 2018	Buy More	BM-3492	5	1,380.00
May 01, 2018	Crop Savers	CS-1243	2	736.00
May 01, 2018	Data Savers	DS-642	1	1,518.00

View invoices by: Date   Z...A+   Select   Cancel

Invoices are presented in order with the most recent one listed first and selected. The invoice that we need is Journal Entry #1, DS-642. You can change the order of the listed transactions by selecting from the **View Invoices By** drop-down list. You can view the list by date, supplier, invoice number, journal entry number or amount. And you can reverse the order of any list by clicking the `Z...A+` button.

NOTES
The Post button now includes a list arrow with a drop-down list: `Post ▼` ✓ Post / Print & Post

You can select Print & Post instead of Post as your default. With this selection, you will print the cheque automatically when you enter the invoice.

This option is available only for cash purchases because the printed invoices include cheques.

NOTES
You can also press `ctrl` + A to open the Adjust Invoice window from any journal. Refer to Appendix B for a list of keyboard shortcuts.

NOTES
From the Home window, you can choose Adjust Invoice from the Purchase Invoices drop-down shortcuts list to open the Search window.

NOTES
Searching by Invoice Number is the equivalent of searching by Source in the General Journal.

NOTES
The cash purchases entered in the Payments Journal are not included in this list. You can adjust these transactions from the Payments Journal after choosing Make Other Payment, or from the Payments icon Adjust Payment shortcut (refer to page 129).

NOTES

The Post button for Pay Later invoices does not have a list arrow with the option to print.

You can still print the invoice from the File menu Print option or from the Print tool.

NOTES

Adjusting Invoice DS-642 has replaced Creating An Invoice in the journal's title bar.

Click   **DS-642**. (Click anywhere on the line to highlight the invoice.)

Click   **Select** or **double-click** the **entry** to recall the selected transaction:

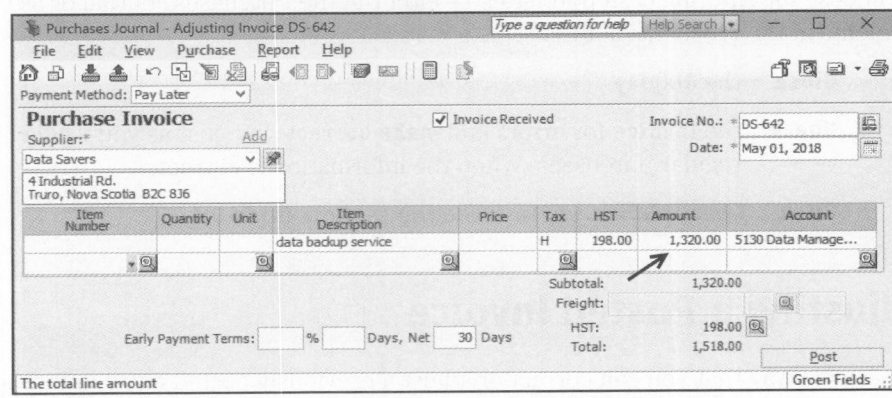

All fields are available for editing. We need to edit the amount.

Click   **line 2** in the Amount field below 1320.

Type   350

Press   ⌨ tab to update the tax code and amount, totals and account.

Add   an appropriate **description**.

You can add -R to the invoice number to complete the revised invoice:

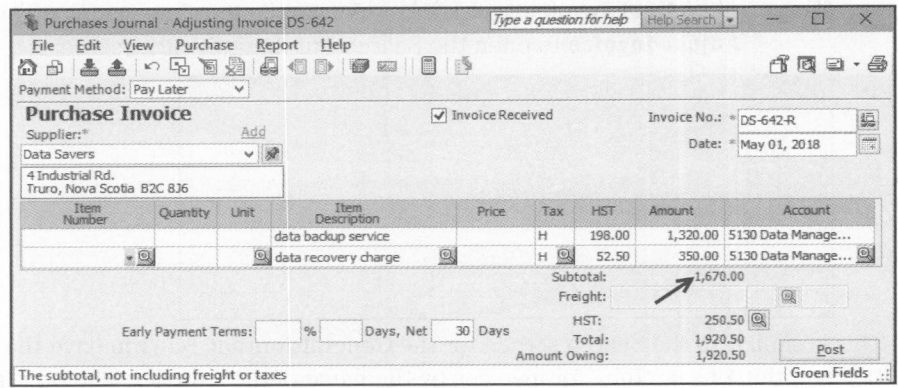

If you change the supplier, Sage 50 warns you and requires confirmation:

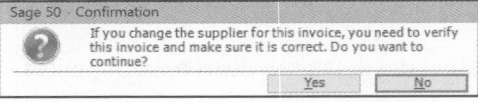

Before posting the revised transaction, review it for accuracy.

Choose the **Report menu** and **click Display Purchases Journal Entry**:

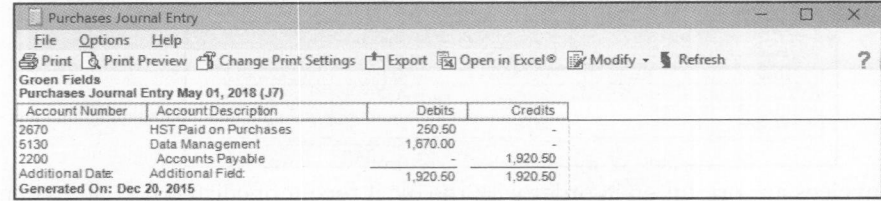

NOTES

When you change the supplier, the default settings for the previously selected supplier will still be used. Check your entry carefully before posting.

To change the supplier, it is easier and safer to reverse the invoice and then enter it correctly. Refer to page 139.

NOTES

Dates should be changed only if they were incorrect. If you edit the date, the final correct entry will be posted with the revised date and will affect the payment terms. To include all three entries in the journal report, Corrections must be selected (refer to pages 147–148).

Although only one journal entry is displayed , three entries are posted — J1, the first one that was incorrect, J6, the second created by Sage 50 to reverse the incorrect entry, and J7, the final correct one that is displayed. All use the original posting date. The previous transaction we posted was entry #5 (refer to the screenshot on page 126).

Close the **report display** when you have finished and **make** additional **corrections** if necessary.

Click the **Post button** [Post] , **click OK** and **close** the **Purchases Journal**.

CORRECTING CASH PURCHASES AND PAYMENTS FROM THE PAYMENTS JOURNAL

Purchases entered as Other Payments in the Payments Journal do not appear on the Search Purchase Invoices list from the Purchases Journal. You can, however, adjust these other payments from the Payments Journal as follows:

- **Click** the Home window **Payments icon** [Payments ▼] **shortcuts list arrow**, and **click Adjust Payment**.

- **Select** your search parameters: the **date range**, **supplier** or **cheque number**. **Click OK**.

- **Click** the **cheque/invoice** you want to adjust. All cheques used to pay invoices and cash purchases will appear on this list.

- **Double-click** the **entry** or **click Select** to open the cheque.

- **Make** the **corrections**. **Review** your **entry** and **post** the revised transaction.

- If the **Payments Journal** is already open, **click Make Other Payment** from the transaction list if you want to adjust a cash purchase payment.

- **Click Pay Invoices** from the transaction list if you want to adjust a cheque used to pay invoices.

- **Click** the **Adjust Payment** or **Adjust Other Payment tool** [icon] or **choose** the **Payment menu** and **click Adjust Payment** or **Adjust Other Payment**.

- **Select** your search parameters. **Click OK** to open the list of cheques. Your list will include either payment or cash purchase (other payment) cheques, depending on the type of transaction you started from.

- **Make** the **corrections**. **Review** your **entry** and **post** the revised transaction.

Refer to page 137 for detailed instructions on correcting a payment cheque.

Entering Discounts for Early Payments

Entering discounts for early payments is very much like entering regular payments. The discounts are entered automatically when the invoices and dates are correct and the discount period has not expired.

✓
8

Payment Cheque #174   **Dated May 4/18**

To Crop Savers, $792 in payment of account, including $8 discount for early payment. Reference invoice #CS-1044.

Click the **Payments icon** to open the Payments Journal.

Choose Crop Savers from the list to display the outstanding invoices:

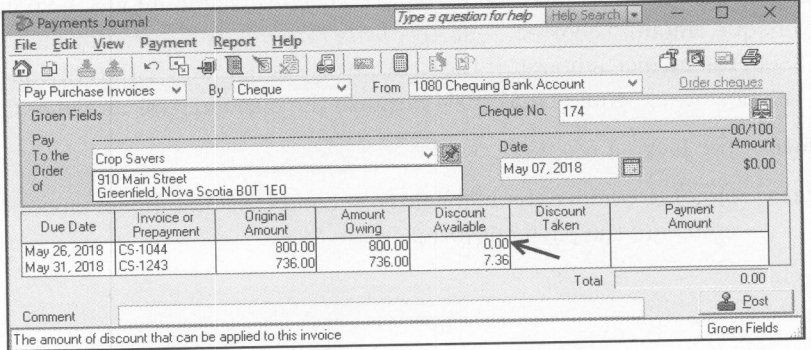

Initially, no discount is available for invoice #CS-1044 because the session date is beyond the discount period — that is, more than 10 days past the April 26 invoice date.

The discount for the second invoice is available because the session date lies within the 10-day discount period.

> **Enter** **May 4** as the date of the payment. **Press** (tab).

Both discounts are now available because the payment date falls within the 10-day discount period for them:

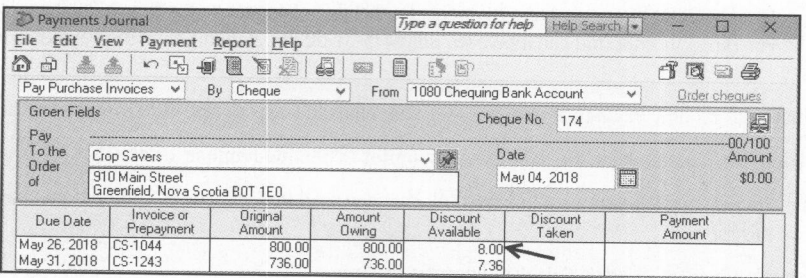

> **Press** (tab) **twice** to advance to the Discount Taken field and enter the amount.

> **Press** (tab) to advance to the Payment Amount field and accept the discount.

The discount has been subtracted from the invoice amount.

> **Press** (tab) to accept the amount in the Payment Amount field and update the total and the cheque portion of the journal:

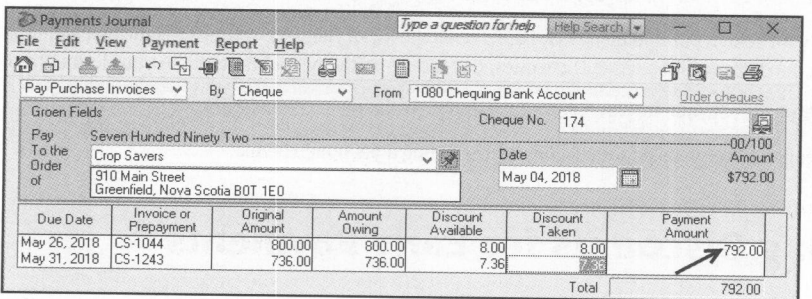

> **Press** (ctrl) **+ J** to display the payment as you have it entered so far:

Account Number	Account Description	Debits	Credits
2200	Accounts Payable	807.36	-
1080	Chequing Bank Account	-	792.00
5090	Purchase Discounts	-	15.36
Additional Date:	Additional Field:	807.36	807.36

Groen Fields
Payments Journal Entry May 04, 2018 (J8)

At this stage, a discount amount is entered for the second invoice, but this invoice is not being paid. Therefore, you must delete this discount entry to avoid adding it to the invoice.

If you do not delete this second discount, your entry will be posted with both discount amounts included — the total *Purchase Discounts* amount is $15.36 instead of $8.00. The cheque amount is correct, but *Accounts Payable* is reduced by $807.36 instead of $800, the invoice amount. If the next invoice is not paid within the discount period, its balance owing would be $728.64 because the discount was already taken.

> **Close** the **journal display**.

> **Press** (del) to remove the highlighted second Discount Taken amount and complete the payment form:

WARNING!

If a second discount amount is displayed, you must delete it. It will be included in the journal entry even though the total payment and cheque amount appear correct. If you post at this stage, the discount will be accepted and included.

WARNING!

Do not press (tab) after deleting the discount because this will add an amount paid for the second invoice. To be safe, you should click somewhere in the upper cheque portion of the form.

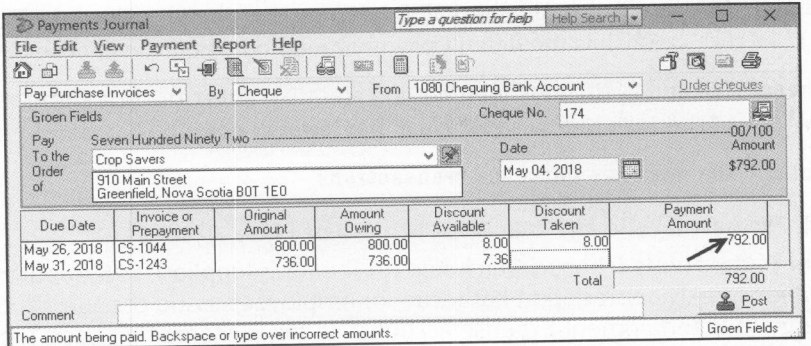

NOTES
If a second discount is not displayed, you can skip the step of deleting the discount amount.

When you point to the Amount field, the status bar message advises you how to enter or change the amounts.

Choose the **Report menu** and **click Display Payments Journal Entry** to review the transaction before posting:

In the related journal entry, the program has now updated the General Ledger *Accounts Payable* control account for the full amount of the invoice and reduced the balance owing to the supplier by the same amount. The amount taken from *Chequing Bank Account* is the actual amount of the payment, taking the single discount amount into consideration. The discount amount is automatically debited to the linked *Purchase Discounts* account. *Purchase Discounts* is a contra-expense account. It has a credit balance, so it reduces total expense and increases net income.

Close the **display** to return to the Payments Journal input screen and **correct** your **work** if necessary. (Refer to page 119 for assistance.)

Post the **transaction**. **Click OK**. **Close** the **Payments Journal**.

Using Continue to Enter New Suppliers

Sometimes you may want to include the name of a supplier in the journal record without creating a supplier record. In these situations, you can use the Continue feature. For the cheque to Anything on Paper, a cash purchase, we will use this approach.

☑ 9 | **Cash Purchase Invoice #AP-5899**   **Dated May 7/18**

From Anything on Paper (choose Continue), $320 plus $48 HST to create and print packages for selling seeds (use Seed Supplies account). Invoice total $368 paid in full by cheque #175.

NOTES
When you choose One-Time Supplier, you can type the supplier's name in the Address field. The supplier's name will not be included in journal reports.

Click the **Purchase Invoices icon** [Purchase Invoices▾] to open the Purchases Journal.

Click the **Supplier field** and **type** `Anything on Paper`

Press (tab) to open the message about a new supplier name:

NOTES
When you choose Continue for a new supplier in the Make Other Payment Journal, the name is not added to the journal entry.

Click   **OK** to return to the journal. (Continue was already selected.) **Press** (tab). Cash is the default payment method when you choose Continue.

Choose   **Cheque** as the Payment Method and then **enter** the **remaining details** of the cash purchase as usual. **Review** and **post** the **transaction**.

Enter   the next **two purchase transactions**.

10

Cash Purchase Invoice #BF-100   **Dated May 7/18**

From Better Foods (choose Quick Add for the new supplier), $95 to purchase food for weekly appreciation barbecue for employees. Issue cheque #176. Charge to Entertainment Expense account. No tax is charged on basic groceries. Store this transaction as a weekly recurring entry.

11

Purchase Invoice #SC-701   **Dated May 7/18**

From Spotless Company, $180 plus $27 HST for weekly cleaning of office. Purchase invoice total $207. Terms: 1/30, n/60. Store as a weekly recurring transaction.

Close   the **Purchases Journal**.

Entering Sales Taxes in the General Journal

The sales summary on May 7 is entered in the General Journal because Groen Fields does not use the Receivables Ledger. When you set up and link sales tax accounts, you can add General Journal sales tax entries to the tax reports. A Sales Taxes button becomes available when you use one of these linked tax accounts in the General Journal. Groen Fields has two linked tax accounts, *HST Charged on Sales* and *HST Paid on Purchases*.

The General Journal is accessed from the Company module window that we used in the previous two chapters.

> To open the Company module window, click Company in the list of modules in the upper left-hand Modules pane. Click the General Journal icon.

Instead, we will create a shortcut to open the General Journal.

Creating Shortcuts

Click   the **Shortcuts icon** in the Shortcuts pane below the modules:

The Customize Shortcuts window opens:

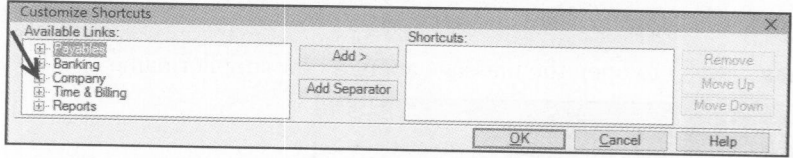

Click   the ⊞ beside **Company** to expand the list of Company tasks:

NOTES
Pay Later is not an option when you choose Continue or One-Time Supplier. Only immediate payment is allowed – Cash and Cheque. Cash is the default.

NOTES
Only 50 percent of entertainment expenses may be claimed for income tax. The total food bill was $190.

⚠ WARNING!
Remember to select Pay Later as the payment method for the Spotless Company invoice and to store the entry before posting.

 CLASSIC VIEW
Users who are more familiar with Sage 50 may prefer to work from the Classic view. You can access all journals and ledgers from a single Classic view Home window, but you cannot add shortcuts.

pro **PRO VERSION**
The entry for Time & Billing is not in the list of links.

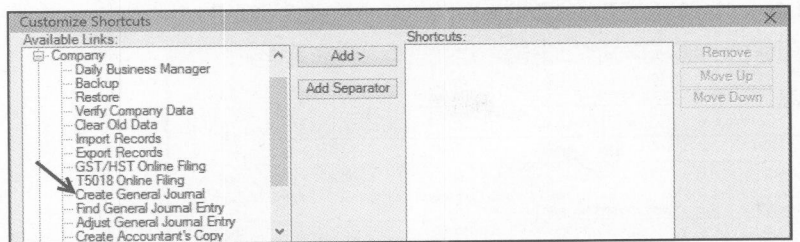

You can create up to 10 shortcuts for each user. The expanded list for each module has the items for which you can create shortcuts. Once you create it, you can click the name in the Shortcuts pane to access that journal or task directly.

Click   Create General Journal in the list of Company tasks.

Click   Add > to move this task to the Shortcuts box:

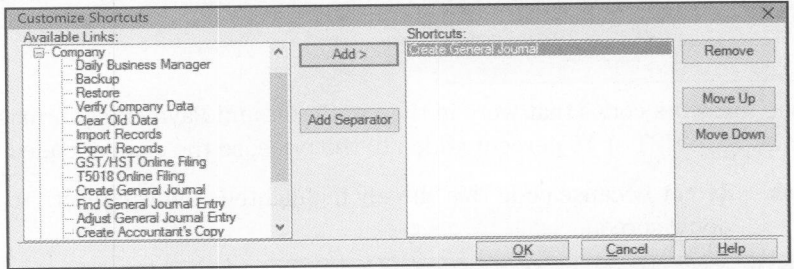

Click   OK to return to the Home window. Create General Journal now appears in the Home window Shortcuts pane:

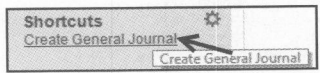

Follow the keystroke instructions for the General Journal from the Muriel's Murals application starting on page 38.

> ✓
> **12**

Cash Sales Summary #34   **Dated May 7/18**

From garden centres, $13 800 plus $2 070 HST for hardy spring annual bedding plants and hanger and planter arrangements. Total receipts $15 870 deposited in bank. Use the shortcut for the General Journal.

Click   Create General Journal in the Shortcuts pane. The General Journal opens immediately. This shortcut will be available in the Home window for all modules.

Enter the **Source** and **Comment** for the sale. The session date is correct.

Choose   Chequing Bank Account as the account to be debited and **type** 15870 as the amount. **Enter** an appropriate **Comment** for the account.

Choose   HST Charged on Sales as the account. Advance to the credit column.

Type 2070 as the amount to be credited. **Press** (tab) to update the entry and continue:

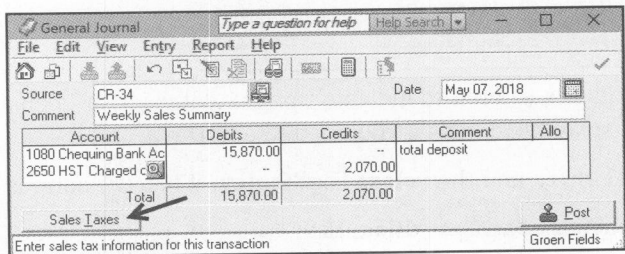

The **Sales Taxes** button became available as soon as you entered the tax amount.

NOTES
You can remove a shortcut if it is not needed. Just click the Shortcuts icon in the Home window. Click the shortcut in the Shortcuts pane and click Remove and OK.

NOTES
Use the General Journal for sales in this application. We will introduce the Sales Journal in Chapter 6.

NOTES
Follow the keystroke instructions for the General Journal from the Muriel's Murals application starting on page 38.

NOTES

HST Charged on Sales is the linked tax account for sales. When you enter HST Paid on Purchases as the account, Purchase will be selected as the default transaction type because this account is linked to the Payables module.

Click the **Sales Taxes button** to open the tax detail screen:

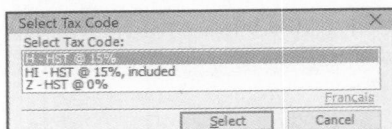

Because you entered *HST Charged on Sales* as the account, the transaction is recognized as a sale (Revenue). You can change the transaction type if it is not correct. The account and tax amount are already entered. We need to add the tax code.

Click the **List icon** in the Tax Code field to open the Tax Code list:

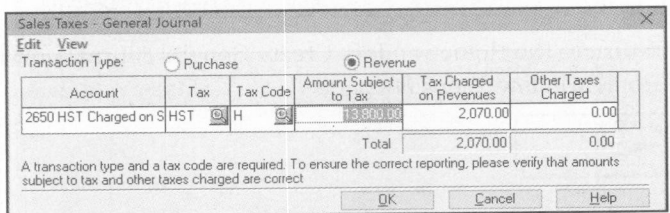

The same three tax codes that were in the Purchases and Payments journals are available. Sales have HST at 15 percent added to the price, so the correct code is H.

Click **Select** because code H is already highlighted. You will return to the tax detail screen:

Because the tax amount was already entered, the sales amount — the Amount Subject To Tax — is calculated as soon as you select the tax code. The sales amount is correct, so we can continue. If the amount is not correct because there are other taxes included, you can edit the default amount and enter an amount for Other Taxes Charged.

Click **OK** to return to the journal.

Enter a **Comment** for the tax line and then add the final account line — **choose** account **4100**, accept the amount and **add** an appropriate **comment** to complete your journal entry:

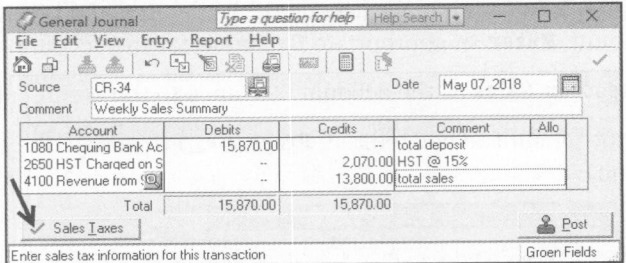

The Sales Taxes button has a ✓ on it to indicate that tax details have been added. Click the button again to display the details if you need to edit them.

Review the **journal entry** and then **close** the **display**. When the entry is correct,

Click the **Post button** . **Click OK**.

If you forgot to enter the tax codes for *HST Charged on Sales*, Sage 50 warns you and asks for confirmation that you do not want to add tax details:

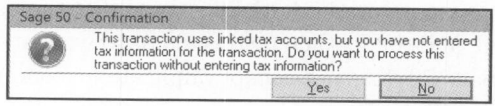

If you forgot to add the tax details, click No to cancel posting and open the Sales Taxes window. Add the missing details and then post the journal entry.

Close   the **General Journal** to return to the Home window.

Advance the **session date** to **May 14**. **Back up** your **data file** when prompted.

Recalling a Stored Entry

The first journal entry for the May 14 session date is the recurring purchase from Crop Savers. Since we have stored this purchase, we do not need to re-enter all the information.

Purchase Invoice #CS-2100   **Dated May 8/18**

From Crop Savers, $640 for soil testing and follow-up fertilizer treatment plus $96 HST. Invoice total $736. Terms: 1/10, n/30. Recall stored entry.

Click   the **Purchase Invoices icon** 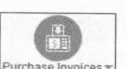 to open the Purchases Journal.

Click   the **Recall tool** in the tool bar (or **choose** the **Purchase menu** and **click Recall**) to display the Recall Recurring Transaction dialogue box:

NOTES
You can press _ctrl_ + R to recall a stored entry.

The stored entries are listed in order according to the next date that they will be repeated. If you want, you can display the stored entries in a different order.

Click   the **View Recurring Transactions By list arrow** for your options:

You can choose to view the stored entries in order by Transaction Name (which is the supplier's name if you did not change the default), Frequency (how often the transaction is repeated), the Date Last Posted or the Next Due Date. If you have a large number of stored entries it may be easier to find the one you need with a different order. You can also reverse the order for any of the order selections with the ⎡A...Z↓⎤ button. For our stored entries, the default selection, Next Due Date, placed the one we want first. Do not change the default.

From the Recall Stored Entry dialogue box you can remove an entry that is incorrect or no longer needed. Click an entry to select it. Click Remove and then click Yes to confirm that you want to delete the entry. (Refer to page 443.)

Crop Savers, the name of the entry we want to use, should be selected because it is the recurring entry that is due next.

Click   **Crop Savers** if it is not already selected.

Click   **Select** or **press** _enter_ to return to the Purchases Journal.

The stored entry is displayed just as we entered it initially, except that the date has been advanced by one week, as needed, and the Invoice field is blank so we can enter a new invoice number. Remember that Sage 50 does not accept duplicate invoice numbers.

Click   the **Invoice No. field** to move the cursor.

Type   CS-2100 to complete the entry. You should review it before posting.

Choose   the **Report menu** and **click Display Purchases Journal Entry**.

Close   the **display** when finished and **make** any necessary **corrections**.

Click   the **Post button** [Post]. **Click OK** and then **close** the **journal**.

Editing Supplier Information

The Home window Suppliers pane has the option to hide or display account phone numbers and balances. There may be times when it is appropriate to hide these details for security purposes.

Click the ▤ icon above the Suppliers list for the options:

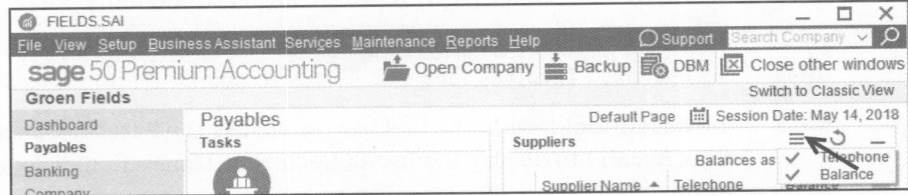

Checkmarks indicate that the information is displayed.

> **NOTES**
> You can open the Suppliers window by clicking the Suppliers icon in the Home window in either the Classic or the Enhanced view. From the Suppliers window, double-click the supplier you want to open the record at the Address tab screen.

To hide the additional details, click the ▤ icon and click the detail you want to hide. To restore the detail, click this button and the option to add the ✓.

To refresh or update the supplier balance amounts, click ↻.

Click ▭ to hide the entire suppliers list. Click ▣ to restore the list.

Sometimes a supplier record must be revised after it is saved because the initial information has changed or because information initially unavailable is now known. We need to edit the record for NS Gas to add the default expense account.

> **NOTES**
> You can use the Refresh icon to update supplier balances when you choose not to refresh lists automatically (refer to page 80).

✓	**Memo #14**	**Dated May 9/18**
14	From Owner: Edit the supplier record for NS Gas to include a default expense account. Create a new Group account 5170 Heating Expense.	

Supplier records are accessed from the Suppliers icon shortcuts list, the Suppliers list pane or the Suppliers window. The list arrow beside the supplier in the Suppliers list pane has shortcuts for several tasks for the selected vendor. The journal or ledger will open with that supplier and task already selected. The drop-down shortcuts list with the Suppliers icon also has several options. Both lists provide access to supplier records:

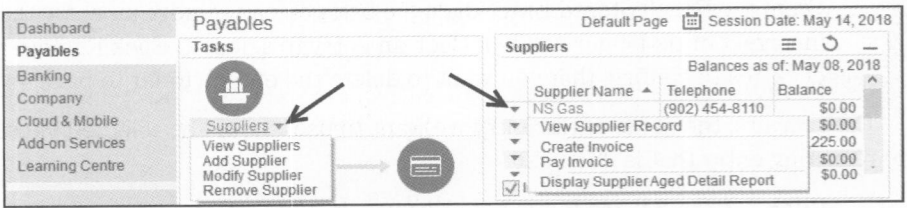

Click   **NS Gas** in the Suppliers list (or click its list arrow and select View Supplier Record) to open the Address tab information screen. Or,

Click   the **Suppliers icon shortcuts list arrow** and **click Modify Supplier** to open the Search Suppliers window:

Each supplier on record is listed on the Search Suppliers selection window. Suppliers is entered as the search area. Anything on Paper is not listed.

Double-click NS Gas to open the Address tab information screen.

Click   the **Options tab** to access the Expense Account field:

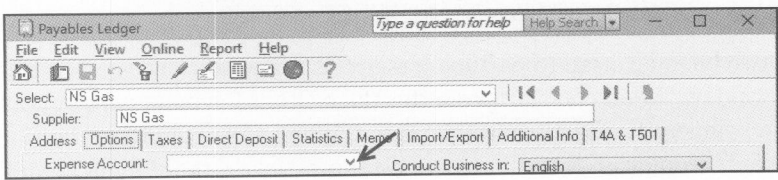

Click   the **Expense Account field**.

You can choose an account from the list provided by the list arrow, type the account number or add a new account. We need to create an account.

Type   5170 **Press** (tab) and then **click Add** to start the Add An Account wizard. **Enter Heating Expense** as the account name and accept the remaining default settings. **Click Finish** to return to the ledger.

Click   **Save And Close** [Save and Close] to close the Payables Ledger (supplier record) window and return to the Payables module window.

Click   **Pay Expenses** from the Payments icon shortcuts list to open the Payments Journal or **click** the **Purchase Invoices icon**.

Enter   the **cash purchase from NS Gas**; the account will appear automatically.

Cash Purchase Invoice #NSG-559932   **Dated May 9/18**

15

From NS Gas, $200 plus $30 HST for monthly supply of natural gas on equal billing method. Invoice total $230 paid in full by cheque #177. Because equal billing applies, store as a monthly recurring entry.

Adjusting a Posted Payment

Just as you can correct a purchase invoice after posting, you can correct a cheque that has been posted.

Choose Pay Purchase Invoices from the Payments transaction list in the Payments Journal. Open the Payments Journal first if necessary.

Memo #15   **Dated May 9/18**

16

From Owner: Adjust cheque #171 to Data Savers. The numbers were transposed. The correct cheque amount was $870 in partial payment of invoice #DS-361.

PRO VERSION
pro Click the Vendors icon shortcuts list arrow and click Modify Vendor.

NOTES
Remember that although the field is named Expense Account, you can choose any postable account as the default for the supplier. You can also select a different account in the journal if necessary.

NOTES
Pressing [ctrl] + A will also open the Search window to begin the adjusting procedure.

NOTES
When you choose Adjust Payment from the Home window Payments icon shortcuts list, you will list all cheques — those used to pay invoices and those for other payments.

NOTES
Cash purchases entered in the Payments Journal are not included in this list. You can adjust these transactions from the Payments Journal after you select Make Other Payment (refer to page 129).

Click   the **Adjust Payment tool** 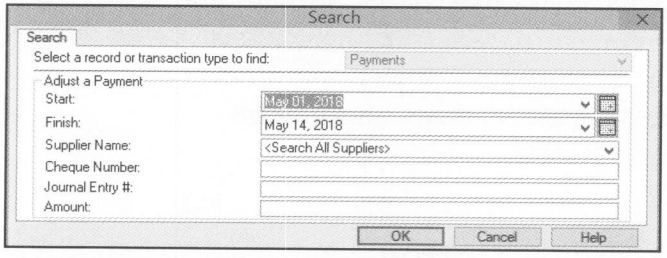 or **choose** the **Payment menu** and **click Adjust Payment** to open the Search screen for Adjust Payments:

Again the familiar Search window for the selected journal opens.

Click   **OK** to list the cheques already posted for this date range:

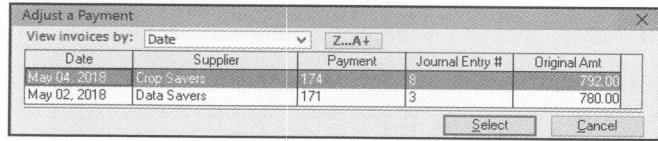

Only the two cheques used to pay invoices are listed because we started from the Pay Invoices window. When you start from the Make Other Payment window, only the cash purchase payment transactions will be listed. When you begin from the Home window Payments icon drop-down shortcuts list, both Make Other Payment and Pay Invoices transactions will be listed.

Double-click   **Data Savers** to open the cheque we posted:

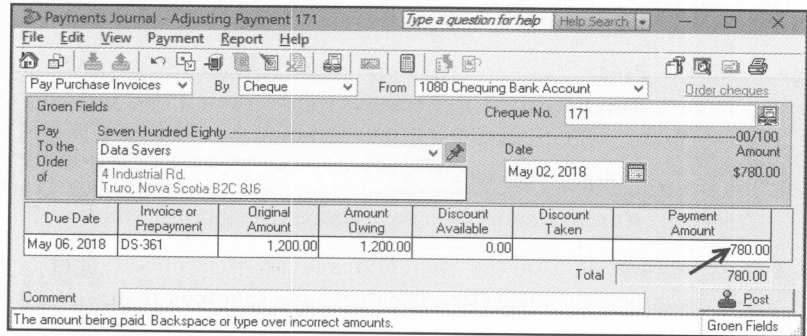

The cheque appears as it was completed. You can edit all the details (except the supplier).

Click   **780.00** in the Payment Amount field.

Type   870

Click   the **Comment field**.

Type   previous chq amount incorrectly entered

Check   your **work** carefully. **Click Post** to save the changes:

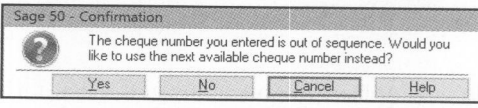

A message about the cheque number being out of sequence appears because we have already used this cheque number. The cheque number is correct so we should continue without changing it.

NOTES
If you cannot reprint the cheque using the same cheque number, you should click Yes to change the number.

Click   **No** to accept the number and continue.

Sage 50 will create the intermediate entry that reverses the original payment, and the original entry is also saved for a complete audit trail.

If you change a payment by selecting a different supplier, Sage 50 advises you that the original payment will be reversed and a new one created:

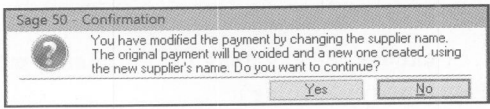

Click Yes to accept the changes or No to cancel the supplier change.

Enter the next group of three **transactions**.

17	**Cash Purchase Invoice #NSH-45321** **Dated May 9/18** From NS Hydro, $240 plus $36 HST for one month of hydro service. Invoice total $276 paid in full by cheque #178.
18	**Payment Cheque #179** **Dated May 9/18** To Crop Savers, $728.64 in payment of account, including $7.36 discount for early payment. Reference invoice #CS-1243.
19	**Cash Purchase Invoice #BC-6110** **Dated May 12/18** From Bloomers, $1 280 plus $192 HST for batch of tree saplings to grow for future sales. Invoice total $1 472 paid in full by cheque #180.

Reversing a Posted Purchase Entry

The cash purchase entered for Bloomers selected an incorrect supplier. We will reverse this entry rather than adjust it because the default details such as account or payment terms may also be incorrect. These details do not change when you adjust the invoice by selecting a different supplier. Refer to the confirmation message on page 128.

Any journal that has an Adjust option also has the option to reverse an entry. You can also use the Lookup feature to begin.

The journal you used to enter the purchase should still be open, either the Payments Journal with Make Other Payment selected or the Purchases Journal. In each case, you can follow the steps below.

✓ **20**	**Memo #16** **Dated May 12/18** Cash Purchase Invoice #BC-6110 was entered for an incorrect supplier and account. The purchase was from Better Crop Tree Farms, a new supplier. Reverse the original entry.

Click the **Look Up Other Payment tool** 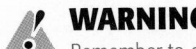 in the Payments Journal with Make Other Payment selected, or the **Look Up An Invoice tool** in the Purchases Journal. Or,

Click the **Adjust Other Payment (Adjust An Invoice) tool** 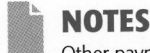 to open the Search screen.

Click **OK** to list the cheques (or purchases) already posted.

Double-click **Bloomers** to open this cash purchase. The entry (in the Purchases Journal) has a Paid stamp on it. This is a User Preference View option (refer to page 81).

The Reverse tool [icon] in the tool bar is now available:

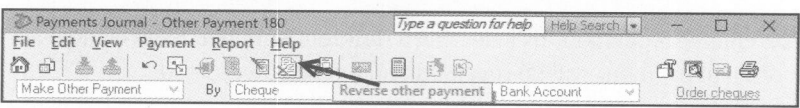

Click   the **Reverse tool** [icon], or **choose** the **Payment** (or **Purchase**) menu and **click Reverse Other Payment** (or **Invoice**):

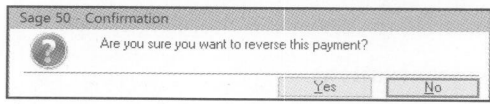

Click   **Yes** to confirm that you want to continue with reversing the entry.

Sage 50 will create the entry that reverses the original one automatically. Both the original and the reversing entry are included in the journal report when you choose Show Corrections.

Click   **OK**. Sage 50 confirms that the entry was successfully reversed.

Enter   the **purchase** for the correct supplier and date this time.

> **21**   **Cash Purchase Invoice #BC-6110**   **Dated May 12/18**
> From Better Crop Tree Farms (use Full Add for the new supplier), $1 280 plus $192 HST for tree saplings. Invoice total $1 472 paid in full by cheque #181.

Changing a Stored Entry

The next entry is the purchase from Spotless Company. Going forward, Groen Fields will be invoiced on a monthly basis and at a different rate. Therefore, we need to update the stored entry. If a change is for a single purchase and will not be repeated, edit the entry after recalling it but do not store the entry again.

> **22**   **Purchase Invoice #SC-1219**   **Dated May 14/18**
> From Spotless Company, $1 200 plus $180 HST for one month of office cleaning as per new contract. Purchase invoice total $1 380. Terms: 1/30, n/60. Recall the stored transaction. Edit the amount and store the revised transaction as a monthly recurring entry.

Click   the **Purchase Invoices** icon [Purchase Invoices] in the Payables window to open the journal.

Click   the **Recall tool** [icon] on the tool bar, or **choose** the **Purchase menu** and **click Recall** to display the Recall Recurring Transaction dialogue box.

Double-click   **Spotless Company**, the entry we want to use to display the purchase entry with the new date.

Click   the **Invoice No. field** so you can add the invoice number.

Type   SC-1219

Click   **180.00**, the Amount, to highlight it so that you can edit it. Double-click if necessary to select the amount.

Type   1200

Press   tab   to enter the change.

Review the **journal entry** as usual to make sure that it is correct before proceeding.

Click the **Store button** 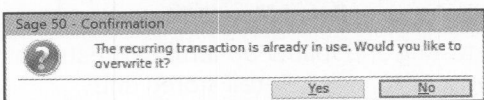, or **choose** the **Purchase menu** and **click Store**.

Choose **Monthly** as the new frequency and accept the name without change.

Sage 50 now asks you to confirm your changes:

> **Sage 50 - Confirmation**
>
> ? The recurring transaction is already in use. Would you like to overwrite it?
>
> [Yes] [No]

Click **Yes** to confirm that you want to replace the previous stored version and return to the Purchases Journal.

Click the **Post button** [Post] to save the entry. **Click OK** and **close** the **Journal**.

Enter the **remaining journal transactions** for May.

23

Cash Purchase Invoice #BF-101   **Dated May 14/18**

From Better Foods, $95 to purchase food for weekly barbecue for employees. Issue cheque #182. Recall stored entry.

NOTES
You can press ctrl + R to recall a stored entry.

24

DUST BUSTERS WWW.DUSTBUSTERS.COM	**Invoice:** DB-4857
60 Water Street Dartmouth, NS B2W 6R9	**Delivery Date:** May 14, 2018
Phone: (902) 366-1551 Toll free: (877) 366-15001	**Sold to:** Groen Fields RR #2 Truro, NS B2N 5B1 (902) 454-6111

Your Hydration Experts

Date	Description	Tax Code	Amount
May 14/18	Repairs to irrigation system	1	700.00
May 14/18	Install additional drip irrigation pipe	1	1 300.00
	Received cheque #183 in full payment		

Thank you.

Signature *Arjen Groen*

Payment Terms: Net 1 days	**HST**	300.00
Business No.: 345 667 211	**TOTAL**	2 300.00

25

Bank Debit Memo #AT-53186   **Dated May 14/18**

From Agri-Trust Credit Union, withdrawals from bank account for bi-weekly payroll:

Wages, including payroll taxes	$3 400.00
Payroll services	40.00
HST Paid on Purchases (payroll services)	6.00

NOTES
Use the General Journal for the payroll transaction in this application.
Remember to enter the sales tax code for the payroll services charge.

<table>
<tr><td>26</td></tr>
</table>

Cash Sales Summary #35   **Dated May 14/18**

From garden centres, $16 400 plus $2 460 HST for early spring bedding plants and planter arrangements. Total receipts $18 860 deposited in bank.

SESSION DATE – MAY 21, 2018

<table>
<tr><td>27</td></tr>
</table>

Purchase Invoice #CS-2987   **Dated May 15/18**

From Crop Savers, $640 for soil testing and follow-up fertilizer treatment plus $96 HST. Invoice total $736. Terms: 1/10, n/30. Recall stored entry.

<table>
<tr><td>28</td></tr>
</table>

Cash Purchase Invoice #YI-345   **Dated May 16/18**

From Yardworks, Inc., $26 000 for rototiller and tractor to prepare adjacent fields for business expansion. Invoice paid in full by cheque #184.

> **NOTES**
> Large farm equipment purchased for business is zero rated for tax purposes.

<table>
<tr><td>29</td></tr>
</table>

INTERTEL

2 Communicate Rd.
Truro, NS
B2A 2K4

www.intertel.ca
chatter@intertel.ca

Account Inquiries: (902) 456-2355

Account Number
902 454-6111

Account Address

Groen Fields
RR #2 Truro, NS
B2N 5B1

Billing Date: May 17, 2018

ACCOUNT SUMMARY

```
Current Charges (April 13 - May 12)
    Business phone complete package       80.00
    Mobile phone services                110.00
    Internet service                      55.00
                                         245.00

    HST (93436 8699)                      36.75
Total Current Charges                    281.75

Previous Charges
    Amount of last bill                  281.75
    Payment Received April 19 — thank you 281.75
    Adjustments                            0.00
    Balance Forward                        0.00
```

Paid in full by cheque #185

Arjen Groen 05/17/18

| Invoice: IT 557121 | PLEASE PAY THIS AMOUNT UPON RECEIPT ➡ | $281.75 |

<table>
<tr><td>30</td></tr>
</table>

Cash Purchase Invoice #BF-102   **Dated May 17/18**

From Better Foods, $95 to purchase food for weekly barbecue for employees. Issue cheque #186. Recall stored entry. Edit the date and replace the stored entry.

<table>
<tr><td>31</td></tr>
</table>

Cash Purchase Invoice #IFI-8250   **Dated May 18/18**

From Industrial Fuels Inc. (use Full Add for the new supplier), $1 260 including HST to fill diesel fuel tank on property. The diesel fuel supplies all farm vehicles. Issue cheque #187. Create new expense account, 5180 Fuel Expense.

> **NOTES**
> Industrial Fuels Inc.
> Terms: net 1
> Tax Code: HI
> Expense Account: 5180 Fuel Expense

<table>
<tr><td>32</td></tr>
</table>

Purchase Invoice #RPR-9257   **Dated May 18/18**

From Rural Property Repairs, $1 500 plus $225 HST to repair broken glass panes in greenhouse. Invoice total $1 725. Terms: 1/20, n/30.

33

Groen Fields
RR #2
Truro, NS B2N 5B1
(902) 454-6111

GROEN FIELDS

Agri-Trust Credit Union
55 Freedom Ave.
Truro, NS B2C 6S0

No: 188

Date 2 0 1 8 0 5 1 8
      Y Y Y Y M M D D

Pay ——— Seven hundred twenty-eight dollars & 64 cents ——— $ 728.64

TO THE
ORDER
OF

Crop Savers
910 Main Street
Greenfield, NS B0T 1E0

PER   *Arjen Groen*

⑆⑈——— 21292⑉⑆60385 188

Re: pay invoice #CS-2100 $728.64   No: 188
     Includes $7.36 discount   May 18, 2018

NOTES
Remember to delete the discount taken amount for the second invoice.

34

Cash Sales Summary #36   **Dated May 21/18**

From garden centres, $17 300 plus $2 595 HST for annual bedding plants, hanger and planter arrangements, perennials and ornamental trees. Total receipts $19 895 deposited in bank.

SESSION DATE – MAY 28, 2018

35

Purchase Invoice #CS-3429   **Dated May 22/18**

From Crop Savers, $900 for soil testing and follow-up fertilizer treatment plus $135 HST. Invoice total $1 035. Terms: 1/10, n/30. Recall stored entry. Change the amount and store the revised transaction as a bi-weekly recurring entry.

36

Purchase Invoice #DS-3168   **Dated May 23/18**

From Data Savers, $500 for updating Web site plus $75 HST. Invoice total $575. Terms: net 30 days.

37

Payment Cheque #189   **Dated May 24/18**

To Crop Savers, $728.64 in payment of account, including $7.36 discount for early payment. Reference invoice #CS-2987.

38

Bank Debit Memo #AT-99553   **Dated May 28/18**

From Agri-Trust Credit Union, withdrawals from bank account for bi-weekly payroll. Create new Group account 5250 Salaries.

Wages, including payroll taxes	$3 400.00
Salaries	4 000.00
Payroll services	70.00
HST Paid on Purchases (payroll services)	10.50

NOTES
Remember to enter the sales tax code for the payroll services charge.

39

Cash Purchase Invoice #BF-103   **Dated May 28/18**

From Better Foods, $95 to purchase food for weekly barbecue for employees. Issue cheque #190. Recall stored entry. Edit the date and re-store the entry.

40

Cash Sales Summary #37   **Dated May 28/18**

From garden centres, $18 400 plus $2 760 HST for annual bedding plants, hanger and planter arrangements, perennials and ornamental trees. Total receipts $21 160 deposited in bank.

SESSION DATE – MAY 31, 2018

41

Purchase Invoice #B-8995   **Dated May 31/18**

From Bloomers, $600 plus $90 HST for seedlings to start growth for future sales. Invoice total $690. Terms: 2/10, n/30.

42

Bank Debit Memo #AT-100223   **Dated May 31/18**

From Agri-Trust Credit Union, withdrawals for bank charges and loan and mortgage payments:

Bank charges	$ 65
Mortgage payment (included $2 250 interest and $250 principal)	2 500
Loan payment (included $90 interest and $2 000 principal)	2 090

43

Memo #17   **Dated May 31/18**

From Owner: Make adjusting entries to reflect inventory sold and supplies used during May. The end-of-month inventory counts indicate the following amounts were used or sold:

Trees sold	$3 900
Bedding plants sold	4 800
Perennials sold	4 320
Planters sold	1 300
Seed inventory and supplies sold	900
Fertilizer used	520
Plant care supplies used	1 350

NOTES

Charge used inventory to Cost of Goods Sold, fertilizer to Soil Treatments and plant care supplies to Supplies Expense.

44

Groen Fields
RR #2
Truro, NS B2N 5B1
(902) 454-1611

GROEN FIELDS

Agri-Trust Credit Union
55 Freedom Ave.
Truro, NS B2C 6S0

No: 191

Date 2 0 1 8 0 5 3 1
     Y Y Y Y M M D D

Pay One thousand, five hundred seventy-one dollars & 13 cents $ 1,571.13

TO THE
ORDER
OF

Spotless Company
49 Scrub St.
Truro, NS B2B 2M6

PER *Arjen Groen*

⑊━━━ 21292 ⑊ 60385 191

Re: pay invoice #SC-701 and #1219 $1,571.13   **No: 191**
     Includes $15.87 discount   May 31, 2018

Displaying Supplier Reports

PRO VERSION

The term Vendor will replace Supplier in all report names and fields.

Grouped lists are not available.

Like General Ledger reports, supplier-related reports can be displayed and printed from multiple starting points: the Suppliers window, the Home window Reports menu and the Reports pane.

Click   the **Suppliers icon** [Suppliers] to open the Suppliers window. The Reports menu in this window now lists only supplier reports. **Select** the **report** you want from this list to open the report options window.

Choose the **Reports menu** in the Home window, then **choose Payables** and **click** the **report** you want for the report options.

Click the **Reports list arrow** in the Reports pane to list the supplier reports:

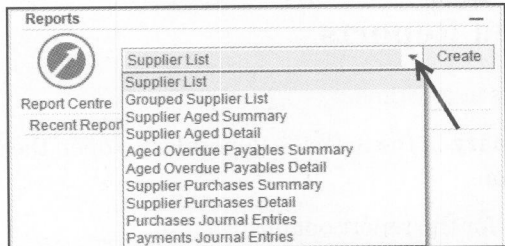

We will work from the Report Centre again so that we can include the report samples, descriptions and options.

Reporting from the Report Centre

Click the **Report Centre icon** in the Home window.

Click **Payables** in the Select A Report Type list to open the list of available supplier reports:

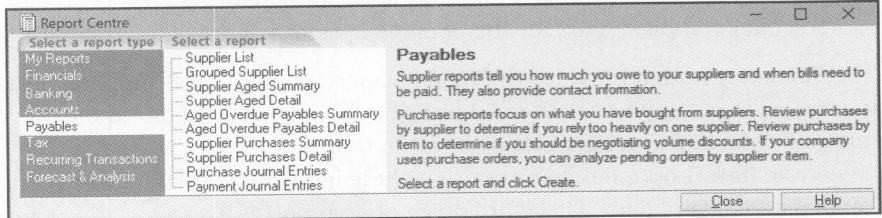

A general description of the Payables module reports with some suggestions of how the reports may assist with business decisions opens next.

Displaying Supplier Lists

Click **Supplier List** in the Select A Report list to open the sample report and description. **Click Modify This Report** for the report options:

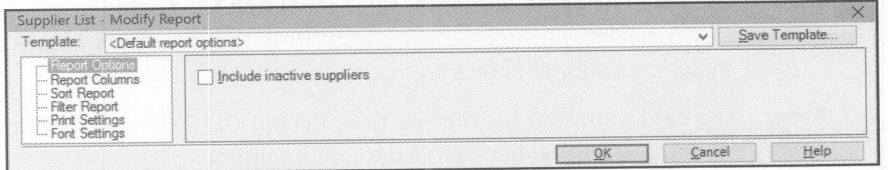

In any Home window, you can choose the Reports menu, then choose Lists and click Suppliers for the report options.

By default, the supplier address and balance owing are displayed. To include additional supplier details, you can choose the supplier record fields by customizing the Report Columns. You can include suppliers marked as inactive if you want.

Click **OK** to open the report.

Close the **display** when you have finished viewing the report.

You will return to the starting point for the report.

If you want to organize the list of suppliers, you can group them automatically by a number of criteria with the **Grouped Supplier List**. Organizing the list may be helpful for assigning suppliers to different staff for phone calls.

Click Grouped Supplier List and then click Modify This Report. Click the Grouped By list arrow for your options. Close the display when you have finished viewing the report.

Displaying Supplier Aged Reports

You can display Supplier Aged reports at any time.

Click **Supplier Aged Summary** in the Select A Report list to open the sample report and description.

Click **Modify This Report** for the report options:

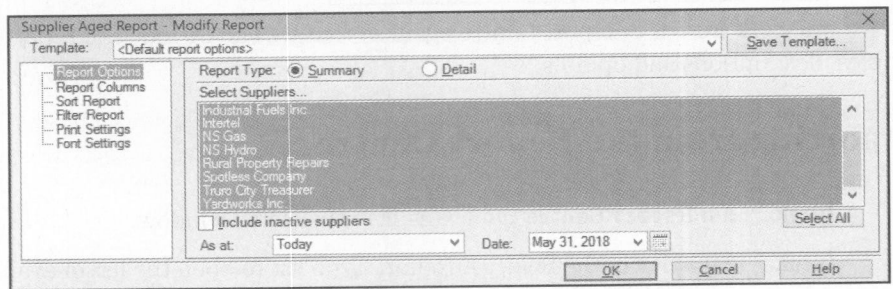

Or, from any Home window, choose the Reports menu, then choose Payables and click Supplier Aged for this report's options window.

The **Summary** option provides the total balance owing to each supplier. It displays an alphabetic list of suppliers with outstanding total balances organized into aged columns. By default, the program selects this option.

Select the **Detail** option if you want to include individual outstanding invoices and payments made to suppliers. This more descriptive report is also aged. Management can use it to make payment decisions. With the Detail option, you can also add supplier payment terms by clicking **Include Terms**.

You can sort and filter the reports by supplier name or balance owing (or by aging period for the Summary Report). You can select or omit any columns to customize reports.

Click **Detail** if you want the Detail Report.

Click the **name** or **press** and **hold** ⎡ctrl⎤ and **click** the **names** in the Suppliers List to select the suppliers you want in the report. **Click Select All** to include all suppliers or to remove all when all are selected.

Enter the **date** you want for the report or accept the session date given by default. After you have indicated all the options,

Click **OK** to open the report.

Close the **displayed report** when you have finished.

Displaying Aged Overdue Payables Reports

You can display Aged Overdue Payables reports at any time.

Click **Aged Overdue Payables Summary** in the Select A Report list to open the sample report and description.

Click **Modify This Report** for the report options:

NOTES
The Supplier Aged Summary and Detail reports are both available directly from the Report Centre.

NOTES
If you chose either One-Time Supplier or Continue for Anything on Paper, it will not be included by name in the list of suppliers for reports. Suppliers for whom you used Quick Add will be included.

NOTES
For the Detail Report, you can also choose the number of days worth of paid invoices to add to the report.

NOTES
From the Supplier Aged Detail Report, you can drill down to look up invoices and supplier ledgers. From the Summary Report, you can drill down to the Detail Report.

NOTES
You can drill down to look up invoices and to the Supplier Aged Report from the Aged Overdue Payables Report. From the Summary Report, you can drill down to the Detail Report.

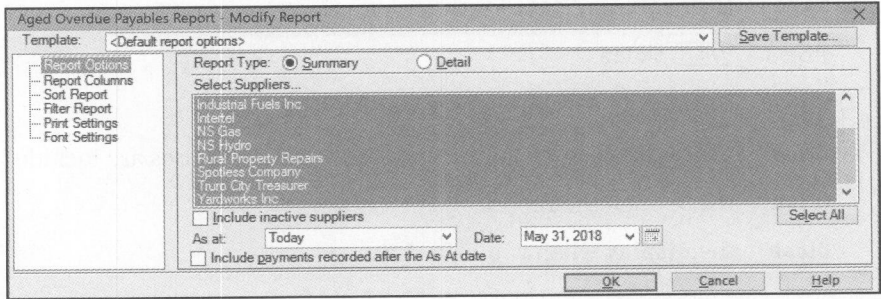

Or, from the Home window, choose the Reports menu, then choose Payables and click Aged Overdue Payables for the report options.

The Aged Overdue Payables Report includes the same information as the Supplier Aged Report but it adds a column for the invoice amounts that are overdue. Supplier name and balance owing may be selected as the criteria for sorting and filtering. The **Summary Report** has totals for each supplier while the **Detail Report** includes details for each invoice.

When you **Include Payments Recorded After The As At Date**, invoices for which you have remitted postdated cheques will be omitted from the report.

You can sort and filter the reports by supplier name or by the balance owing. You can select or omit any of the columns to customize the report.

Choose	**Summary** or **Detail**.
Press	and **hold** `ctrl` and then **click** the **names** in the Suppliers List to select the suppliers that you want in the report. **Click Select All** to include all suppliers or to remove all when all are selected.
Enter	the **date** you want for the report, or accept the session date given by default. After you have indicated all the options,
Click	**OK** to open the report. One invoice from Rural Property Repairs and the balance on the first invoice from Data Savers are overdue.
Close	the **displayed report** when you have finished.

Displaying the Purchases Journal Report

Click	**Purchase Journal Entries** in the Select A Report list to open the sample report and description.
Click	**Modify This Report** for the report options:

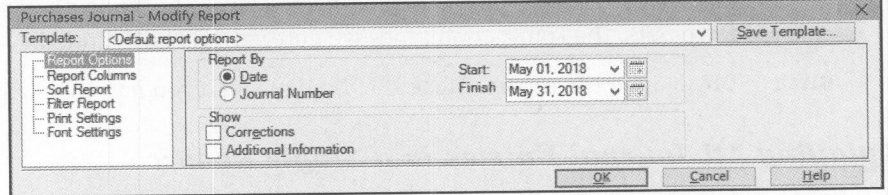

Or, choose the Reports menu, then choose Journal Entries and click Purchases.

Entries for the Purchases Journal can be selected by posting date or by journal entry number. By default, the Date option is selected, and the first transaction date and session date are the default dates for the report. All journal reports may be sorted and filtered by date, journal number, source or comment. You can choose the account name and number, and debits and credits columns to customize the report column settings. Correcting or adjusting entries may be included or omitted from the report.

NOTES
Postdated payments may be omitted because these invoices are deemed to be paid.

CLASSIC VIEW
From the Home window, right-click the Purchases icon

to select it. Click (the Select A Report tool on the tool bar).

If no icons are selected in the Home window, Purchases and Payments Journal reports are available from the Select Report list when you click the Select A Report tool.

NOTES
The dates May 1 and May 31 are available from drop-down lists for both date fields.

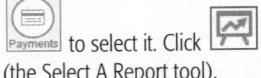

CLASSIC VIEW

From the Home window, right-click the Payments icon 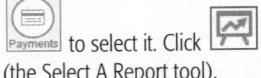 to select it. Click (the Select A Report tool).

NOTES

You can drill down to the Supplier Aged Report and to the General Ledger Report from the Purchases Journal or the Payments Journal Report. You can also look up the original journal transaction.

NOTES

Including the types of transactions for which you have no entries does not result in an error message and will not change the report.

Payroll remittances are covered in Chapter 8.

Type	the **beginning date** for the transactions you want.
Press	⌨ tab ⌨ **twice**.
Type	the **ending date** for your transaction period.
Click	**Corrections** so that adjusting and reversing entries are included.
Click	**OK** to open the report.
Close	the **display** when you have finished.

Displaying the Payments Journal Report

Click	**Payment Journal Entries** in the Select A Report list to open the sample report and description.
Click	**Modify This Report** for the report options:

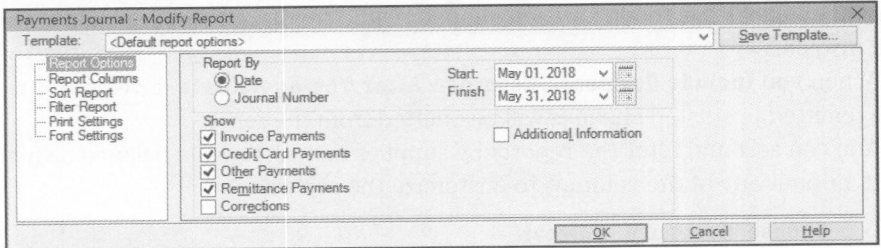

Or, choose the Reports menu, then choose Journal Entries and click Payments for the report options.

For the Payments Journal, like other journal reports, you can select the transactions by posting date — the default setting — or by journal entry number. In addition, you can choose the type of payment for the report — invoice payments, credit card payments, other payments (cash purchases) and payroll remittance payments. All types are selected initially, and clicking any one will remove it from the report. Corrections or adjustments may be included or omitted. Clicking will change your selections.

Type	the **beginning date** for the transactions you want.
Press	⌨ tab ⌨ **twice**.
Type	the **ending date** for your transaction period.
Click	**Corrections**.
Click	**Credit Card Payments** and **Remittance Payments** because we did not use these transaction types. Only Invoice Payments and Other Payments, the transaction types we entered, will be included.
Click	**OK** to open the report. **Close** the **display** when you have finished.

Displaying All Journal Entries in a Single Report

To view the entries for all journals in a single report from a Home window, choose the Reports menu, then choose Journal Entries and click All.

From the Report Centre, click Financials in the Select A Report Type list and then click All Journal Entries in the Select A Report list. Click Display or choose Modify This Report if you want to change the default options.

Displaying Cheque Log Reports

If you regularly print cheques through Sage 50 from the Payables journals or the Payroll journals, you can display and print a summary of these printed cheques in the Cheque Log Report.

Click   **Banking** in the Select A Report Type list to open the general description of banking reports and the list of available reports:

Click   **Cheque Log** in the Select A Report list to open the sample report and description.

Click   **Modify This Report** for the report options:

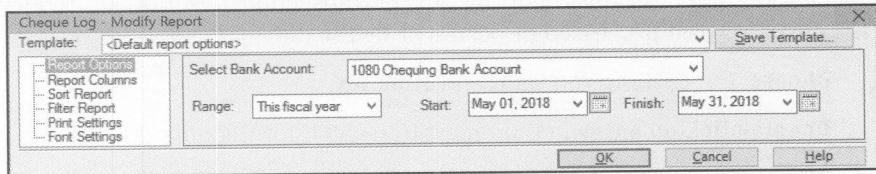

Or, from any Home window, choose the Reports menu, then choose Banking and click Cheque Log to open the report options window.

The report will include details for all cheques that you entered, including whether or not the journal entry was posted and the number of times the cheque was printed. If you do not print cheques through the program, these payments are listed with a 0 (zero) for the number of times printed. Adjusted cheques are identified as Reversed.

To customize the report, you can choose any of the column headings to sort or filter the report and you can choose to include or omit any of these columns.

Choose   the **bank account** from the Select Bank Account drop-down list.

Enter   the **Start** and **Finish dates** for the report.

Click   **OK** to open the report.

Close   the **display** when you have finished.

Recurring Transactions Report

If you have stored transactions, you can generate a report of these transactions.

Click   **Recurring Transactions** in the Select A Report Type list to open the general description of the report type and the list of available reports:

The list now includes the different types of transactions that can be stored.

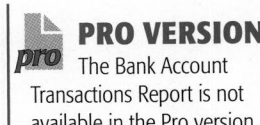

PRO VERSION

The Bank Account Transactions Report is not available in the Pro version.

NOTES

No drill-down reports are available from the Cheque Log Report, but you can sort or filter by any of the information in the report.

NOTES

Journals for hidden modules are not listed. When you use them and they allow recurring entries, they will be added to this list.

Click   **All Transactions** in the Select A Report list to open the sample report and description.

Click   **Modify This Report** for the report options:

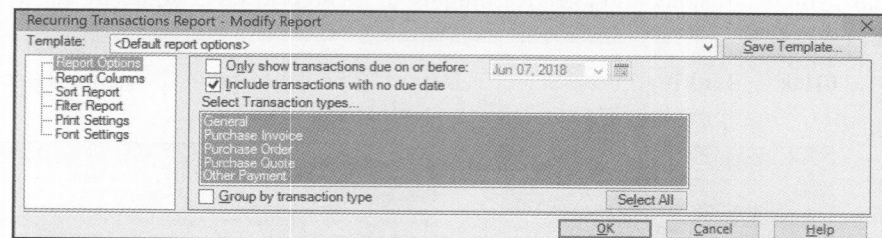

Again, the list includes the different types of transactions that can be stored, and all are selected initially. Transactions without due dates are also included by default. You can restrict the report to include only those entries that are due within a specific time period by selecting **Only Show Transactions Due On Or Before** and entering a date. The default date for this option is one week past the session date, but you can enter any date you want. You can **Group** the report **By Transaction Type**, or accept the default to show entries in order by the due date.

You can sort and filter this report by type of transaction, description, frequency, the date the entry was last processed or posted or by the due date.

Choose   the **options** you want and **click OK**.

Double-click   an **entry** in the report to recall it for the next due date.

Close   the **Report Centre** when you have finished.

Printing Supplier Reports

Before printing supplier reports, make sure that you set the print options.

Display   the **report** you want to print.

Click   the **Change Print Settings tool** 📇 to open the Reports & Forms Settings screen. Check that you have the correct printer and form files selected for your report. **Close** the **Settings screen**.

Click   the **Print tool** 🖨 or **choose** the **File menu** and **click Print**.

Printing Mailing Labels

To print labels, you should first make sure that the print options have been set correctly and that your printer is turned on and has the correct labels paper. To set the program to use your printing labels,

Choose the Setup menu in the Home window and click Reports & Forms.
Click Labels in the list under Reports. Choose your printer.
Enter the appropriate margins, label size and number of labels across the page for your labels.
Click OK to return to the Home window.

Choose   the **Reports menu** in the Home window, then **choose Mailing Labels** and **click Suppliers**:

NOTES
When you choose Random as the frequency for recurring transactions, they do not include a due date.

WARNING!
When you click the Print tool, printing will begin immediately with your current settings. Choosing Print from the File menu in the report will open the Print options screen and you can check and modify your printer selection and settings.

WARNING!
You cannot display labels, so you should check the printer settings first.

NOTES
For practice, you can print the labels on plain paper.

Press   and **hold** ⌨ctrl⌨ and then **click** the **names** of the suppliers for whom you want labels, or **click Select All** to include all suppliers.

Click   **OK** to print the labels. Printing will begin immediately.

Printing T4A and T5018 Slips

You can also print T4A and T5018 slips if you have suppliers with these options checked in the ledger records on the T4A & T5018 tab screen.

Choose   the **Reports menu** in the Home window, then **choose Payables** and **click Print T4A Slips** or **Print T5018 Slips**. **Select** the **suppliers** you want for the report.

Close   the **data file** to finish your Sage 50 session.

R E V I E W

The Student DVD with Data Files includes Review Questions and Supplementary Cases for this chapter.

Phoebe's Photo Studio

OBJECTIVES

After completing this chapter, you should be able to

- **enter** transactions in the General, Payables and Receivables journals
- **enter** and **post** cash, credit card and account sale transactions
- **enter** and **post** customer payment transactions
- **customize** journals and **preview** invoices
- **enter** transactions including GST and PST
- **store** and **recall** recurring entries
- **enter** customer discounts and partial payments
- **add** and **edit** customer accounts
- **reverse** receipts to enter NSF cheques from customers
- **edit** and **review** customer-related transactions
- **create** shortcuts for General and Payables journal transactions
- **display** and **print** customer reports
- **understand** linked accounts for the Receivables Ledger

COMPANY INFORMATION

Company Profile

NOTES
Phoebe's Photo Studio
100 Light St., Suite 202
Winnipeg, MB R2T 7G4
Tel 1: (204) 649-3358
Tel 2: (888) 649-3358
Fax: (204) 642-4967
Business No.: 296 654 590

Phoebe's Photo Studio has its main portrait studio in Winnipeg, Manitoba. Here Phoebe Maniwake takes individual and family portraits and develops and prints the black-and-white photographs. She also has a summer residence outside of Riverton, Manitoba, on Lake Winnipeg that allows her easier access to the northern parts of the province as well as the Hecla / Grindstone Provincial Park where she composes her nature photographs for sale in galleries across Canada.

After completing an art program at the Ontario College of Art, Maniwake opened her studio in Winnipeg, her home town, and has now had the studio for several years. In the summers she also accompanies Arctic cruises and other tours to photograph cruise passengers on location, as well as to take more of her own northern landscape photos. Revenue comes from these three sources: portraits (including students and weddings), photographing tour clients and art gallery

sales. Sometimes she brings in a student for the summer as an assistant/apprentice to accompany her on her personal photo tours.

Most regular customers — families, galleries, cruise lines — have accounts with Phoebe's Photo Studio and receive a 2 percent discount if they pay within 10 days. They are asked to settle their accounts in 30 days, paying by cash or by cheque. PST and GST apply to all work completed by Phoebe's Photo Studio.

Accounts have been set up with a local photographic supplies store, a camera sales and repair store and some other regular suppliers.

After remitting all taxes before the end of June 2018, Maniwake converted the accounts for Phoebe's Photo Studio using the following information:

- Chart of Accounts
- Post-Closing Trial Balance
- Supplier Information
- Customer Information
- Accounting Procedures

CHART OF POSTABLE ACCOUNTS

PHOEBE'S PHOTO STUDIO

ASSETS
1080	Chequing Account
1100	Credit Card Bank Account
1200	Accounts Receivable
1300	Darkroom Supplies
1310	Photo Paper
1320	Framing Supplies
1340	Other Supplies
1440	Computers and Software
1460	Developing Equipment
1480	Camera Accessories
1500	Digital SLR Cameras ▶
▶1550	Van
1580	Studios

LIABILITIES
2100	Bank Loan
2200	Accounts Payable
2640	PST Payable
2650	GST Charged on Services
2670	GST Paid on Purchases
2850	Mortgage Payable

EQUITY
3560	P. Maniwake, Capital ▶

▶3600	Net Income

REVENUE
4100	Revenue from Tours
4140	Revenue from Portraits
4180	Sales Discounts

EXPENSE
5100	Advertising & Promotion
5120	Bank Charges & Card Fees
5130	Interest Expense
5140	Hydro Expense
5150	Framing Supplies Used ▶

▶5160	Photo Supplies Used
5170	Other Supplies Used
5190	Postage Expenses
5200	Purchase Discounts
5220	Telephone Expenses
5240	Travel Expenses
5260	Vehicle Expenses
5300	Wages
5310	Payroll Service Charges

NOTES: The Chart of Accounts includes only postable accounts and the Net Income or Current Earnings account.

POST-CLOSING TRIAL BALANCE

PHOEBE'S PHOTO STUDIO

June 30, 2018		Debits	Credits
1080	Chequing Account	$ 48 486	
1100	Credit Card Bank Account	2 900	
1200	Accounts Receivable	7 989	
1300	Darkroom Supplies	420	
1310	Photo Paper	2 620	
1320	Framing Supplies	1 380	
1340	Other Supplies	240	
1440	Computers and Software	14 900	
1460	Developing Equipment	5 600	
1480	Camera Accessories	6 320	
1500	Digital SLR Cameras	7 370	
1550	Van	21 900	
1580	Studios	320 000	
2100	Bank Loan		$ 10 000
2200	Accounts Payable		5 840
2850	Mortgage Payable		180 000
3560	P. Maniwake, Capital		244 285
		$440 125	$440 125

SUPPLIER INFORMATION

PHOEBE'S PHOTO STUDIO

Supplier Name (Contact)	Address	Phone No. Fax No.	E-mail Web Site	Terms Tax ID
Calm Air (Arie Fliegel)	50 Jett Ave. Winnipeg, Manitoba R2P 1S7	Tel: (800) 839-2256 Fax: (204) 476-5110	af@calmair.com calmair.com	1/15, n/30 566 478 913
Lumber Shed (C. Woods)	91 Walnut St. Winnipeg, Manitoba R3P 8V3	Tel: (204) 382-7845 Fax: (204) 383-2489	cwoods@lumbershed.com lumbershed.com	1/5, n/30 571 277 631
Manitoba Hydro (Mannie Ergs)	1 Watts Rd. Winnipeg, Manitoba R6G 2C1	Tel: (204) 435-2633	m.ergs@mnhydro.man.ca mnhydro.man.ca	net 1
Manitoba Telephone (Chata Lot)	11 Vocal Channel Winnipeg, Manitoba R3E 6R4	Tel: (204) 488-8532	manitobatel.ca	net 1
Riverton Garage (Karl Fixe)	6 Ford St. Riverton, Manitoba R0C 2R0	Tel: (204) 378-1297 Fax: (204) 378-6388	Karl@rivercars.com rivercars.com	net 30 344 566 872
Starlight Photo Solutions (Star Lightman)	300 Aurora St. Winnipeg, Manitoba R3P 4D5	Tel: (204) 577-1369 Fax: (204) 577-2229	star@sps.com sps.com	2/10, n/30 610 728 365
UPS Delivery (Yvette Panier)	8 Carrier Ave. Winnipeg, Manitoba R2C 6A1	Tel 1: (204) 698-2357 Tel 2: (800) 477-1UPS Fax: (204) 698-6102	ups.com	net 1 498 458 561
Web Exposure (B. Online)	72 Memorial Cres. Brandon, Manitoba R7A 3G5	Tel: (204) 469-8080 Fax: (204) 469-4987	online@webexposure.com webexposure.com	net 15 385 416 822

OUTSTANDING SUPPLIER INVOICES

PHOEBE'S PHOTO STUDIO

Supplier Name	Terms	Date	Invoice No.	Amount	Total
Calm Air	1/15, n/30	Jun. 26/18	CA-224	$3 900	$3 900
Lumber Shed	1/5, n/30	Jun. 21/18	LS-894	$1 050	$1 050
Riverton Garage	net 30	Jun. 16/18	RG-1904	$890	$890
			Grand Total		$5 840

CUSTOMER INFORMATION

PHOEBE'S PHOTO STUDIO

Customer Name (Contact)	Address	Phone No. Fax No.	E-mail Web Site	Terms Credit Limit
Borealis Delights (J. Franklin)	4 Lighter Way Winnipeg, Manitoba R4A 1E1	Tel 1: (204) 476-4669	franklin@borealis.com borealis.com	2/10, n/30 $15 000
Brandon Art Gallery (Art North)	49 Viewer St. Brandon, Manitoba R7B 2T5	Tel 1: (204) 823-5100 Tel 2: (204) 826-1297 Fax: (204) 826-2196	AN@bag.com bag.com	2/10, n/30 $10 000
Geraldine Reuben (G. Reuben)	4 Chapel Lane Winnipeg, Manitoba R4A 1E1	Tel: (204) 476-4669	GReuben@yahoo.com weddings.com/GR	2/10, n/30 $10 000
Kandinski Party (Sophia Kandinski)	77 Memory Lane Winnipeg, Manitoba R3G 5D2	Tel: (204) 326-7528 Fax: (204) 326-7436	skandinski@gmail.com kandinskis.com	2/10, n/30 $5 000

▶

Customer Name (Contact)	Address	Phone No. Fax No.	E-mail Web Site	Terms Credit Limit
Polar Discoveries (Robert Peary)	4 Exploration Ave. Churchill, Manitoba R0B 0E0	Tel: (204) 624-7900 Fax: (204) 624-7556	peary@polartours.com polartours.com	2/10, n/30 $15 000
Young'uns Preschool (Ella Little)	588 Totts Cres. Winnipeg, Manitoba R3P 4C2	Tel: (204) 369-4545 Fax: (204) 369-8765	ella@YPS.com YPS.com	2/10, n/30 $8 000

OUTSTANDING CUSTOMER INVOICES

PHOEBE'S PHOTO STUDIO

Customer Name	Terms	Date	Inv/Chq No.	Amount	Total
Geraldine Reuben	1/10, n/30	Jun. 25/18	PS-377	$2 260	
		Jun. 25/18	Chq #266	1 460	
		Jun. 27/18	PS-381	1 695	
			Balance owing		$2 495
Young'uns Preschool	1/10, n/30	Jun. 28/18	PS-383	$4 294	
		Jun. 30/18	PS-387	1 200	
			Balance owing		$5 494
			Grand Total		$7 989

Accounting Procedures

Open-Invoice Accounting for Receivables

The open-invoice method of accounting for invoices issued by a business allows the business to keep track of each individual invoice and of any partial payments made against it. In contrast, other methods keep track only of the outstanding balance by combining all invoice balances owed by a customer. Sage 50 uses the open-invoice method. Fully paid invoices can be removed (cleared) periodically.

Discounts for Early Payments

Phoebe's Photo Studio offers discounts to regular customers if they pay their accounts within 10 days. Full payment is expected in 30 days. Customers who pay by credit card do not receive discounts. No discounts are allowed on partial payments.

Some suppliers with whom Phoebe's Photo Studio has accounts set up also offer discounts for early payments.

NSF Cheques

If a cheque is deposited from an account that does not have enough money to cover it, the bank may return it to the depositor as NSF (non-sufficient funds). The NSF cheque from a customer requires a reversing entry in the Receipts Journal. Sage 50 can complete these reversals automatically (refer to Keystrokes, page 175). In most companies, the accounting department notifies the customer who wrote the NSF cheque to explain that the debt remains unpaid. Many companies charge an additional fee to the customer to recover their bank charges for the NSF cheque. A separate sales invoice should be prepared for the additional charge. NSF cheques to suppliers are handled in the same way, through reversing entries in the Payments Journal.

NOTES

For a service business, the terms Revenues Journal and Client replace Sales Journal and Customer. These terms will be used interchangeably in this chapter.

Taxes (GST and PST)

Phoebe's Photo Studio is a service business using the regular method of calculating GST. GST, at the rate of 5 percent, charged and collected from customers will be recorded as a liability in *GST Charged on Services*. GST paid to suppliers will be recorded in *GST Paid on Purchases* as a decrease in tax liability. The balance owing, the difference between the GST charged and GST paid, or the request for a refund will be remitted to the Receiver General for Canada quarterly.

Phoebe's Photo Studio charges customers 8 percent PST on all sales and pays PST on some goods. The Studio is exempt from PST for purchases of items used in preparing photos, such as framing supplies, photo paper and developing chemicals because the customer pays PST on the products that use these components.

Cash and Credit Card Sales of Services

Cash and credit card transactions are a normal occurrence in most businesses. Sage 50 has payment options to handle these transactions. When you make the correct Payment Method or Paid By selection, the program will debit *Chequing Account* or *Credit Card Bank Account* instead of the *Accounts Receivable* control account (refer to Keystrokes, page 168 and page 180).

NOTES
Manitoba increased the PST rate from 7 percent to 8 percent in 2013.

INSTRUCTIONS

1. **Record entries for the source documents** in Sage 50 using all the information provided for Phoebe's Photo Studio. The procedures for entering each new type of transaction in this application are outlined step by step in the Keystrokes section with the source documents. These transactions are indicated with a ✓ in the upper part of the completion check box beside the source document. Source document numbers are included below or in the lower part of the check box.

2. **Print** the **reports** indicated on the following printing form after you have finished making your entries. Instructions for reports begin on page 190.

REPORTS

Accounts
- [ ] Chart of Accounts
- [ ] Account List
- [ ] General Journal Entries

Financials
- [✓] Balance Sheet: July 31
- [✓] Income Statement from July 1 to July 31
- [✓] Trial Balance date: July 31
- [✓] All Journal Entries: July 1 to July 31
- [✓] General Ledger accounts: 1300 4100 4140 from July 1 to July 31
- [ ] Statement of Cash Flows

- [✓] Cash Flow Projection Detail Report for account 1080 for 30 days

Taxes
- [✓] GST Report July 31
- [✓] PST Report July 31

Banking
- [ ] Cheque Log Report

Payables
- [ ] Supplier List
- [ ] Supplier Aged
- [ ] Aged Overdue Payables
- [ ] Purchases Journal Entries
- [ ] Payments Journal Entries

Receivables
- [ ] Client List
- [✓] Client Aged Detail for all customers
- [ ] Aged Overdue Receivables
- [✓] Revenues Journal Entries: July 1 to July 31
- [✓] Receipts Journal Entries: July 1 to July 31
- [ ] Client Statements

Mailing Labels
- [ ] Labels

KEYSTROKES

Opening Data Files

Open the data file **SageData16\PHOTO\PHOTO** to access the data files for Phoebe's Photo Studio.

Type July 8 2018 to enter the first session date.

Click **OK** to display a Sage 50 warning about the date:

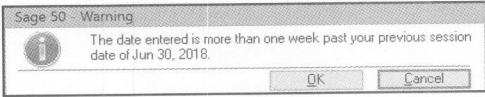

This warning appears whenever you advance the session date by more than one week. Normally a business would update its accounting records more frequently. If you have entered the correct date,

Click **OK** to accept the date entered and display the Home window.

The Payroll, Inventory and Project ledger names do not appear in the Modules pane list. These ledgers are hidden because they are not set up.

Accounting for Sales

Sales are entered in the Revenues Journal, accessed from the Client Invoices icon in the Receivables module Home window:

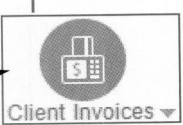

You can enter sales from the Client Invoices icon in the Receivables window. The Client Invoices label is used for service companies. For other company types, the label for this icon may be Sales, Invoices, Sales Invoices, Customer Invoices, Bills, Statements or Charges. The icon itself does not change.

Customer balances are given as of the date of the latest transaction.

Sales Invoice #PS-391   **Dated July 1/18**

To Brandon Art Gallery, $4 200 plus $210 GST and $336 PST for sale of three framed original photographic prints. Invoice total $4 746. Terms: 2/10, n/30. Create new Group account 4120 Revenue from Gallery Sales. Customize the sales invoice by removing the columns not used by Phoebe's Photo Studio.

NOTES
If you are using backup files, restore SageData16\PHOTO1.CAB or PHOTO1 to SageData16\PHOTO\PHOTO. Refer to the instructions for restoring data files in Chapter 1, page 24, if you need assistance.

PRO VERSION

pro Icon labels are the same for all company types.

Click the Sales Invoices icon

to open the Sales Journal. In the Pro version Classic view, this icon is labelled Sales.

WARNING!

Do not include PS- in the sales invoice number in the journal. The numeric portion will then be correctly updated by the program.

If you want to include PS- in the journal entries, you must update the invoice number manually for each invoice.

Click the **Client Invoices icon** to open the Revenues Journal input form:

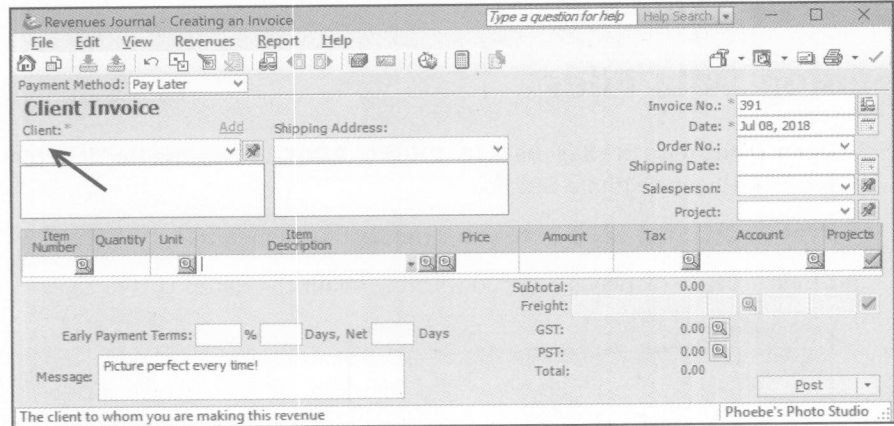

Most tool bar buttons in the Revenues Journal are familiar from other journals — Home window, Daily Business Manager, Store, Recall, Undo, Customize Journal, Calculator and Allocate. Print and E-mail buttons allow you to print or e-mail the invoice before posting to provide a customer or store copy of the sales invoice. You can also use tool buttons to preview an invoice, change print settings and adjust or reverse a posted invoice. The tools for Invoice Lookup, Additional Information, Track Shipments and Add Time Slip Activities will be explained in later applications.

Pay Later is correctly selected as the payment option for this regular sale.

Click the **Client field list arrow** to obtain the list of customers:

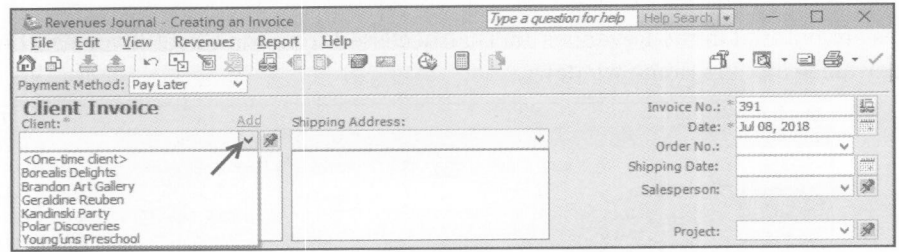

Click **Brandon Art Gallery**, the customer in the first source document, to select and enter it.

The customer's name and address have been added to your input form. If you have made an error in your selection, click the client list arrow and start again. By default, the Client and the Shipping Address fields are completed from the customer's ledger record. You can edit the shipping address if necessary. If the information is correct, you can skip over the shipping information.

The invoice number, 391, the numeric portion, is entered and correct. It is updated automatically by the program. The payment terms and tax code for the customer have also been entered. The default revenue account for the Receivables module is entered as the default. We need to change it — and create a new account — for this customer.

The session date is the default transaction date, so you need to change it as well. Enter the date on which the transaction took place: July 1, 2018.

Click the **Date field Calendar icon**.

Click **1**.

If you want, you can enter a quantity (three for the number of prints) and $1 400 as the price per unit in the Price field and let the program calculate the amount by multiplying the two together. You can use this method if you are selling more than one item that is not an inventory item.

Click   the **Item Description field** on the first line. The Item Description field is used to enter a description or comment concerning the sale.

Type   three framed original photo prints

Press   ⌨tab. The cursor is now in the Price field.

The Price field refers to unit prices; it is not needed for this sale.

Press   ⌨tab.

The cursor should now be positioned in the Amount field, where you will enter the amount for this invoice before taxes.

Type   4200 **Press** ⌨tab.

The cursor advances to the Tax field. The default tax code for the customer, GP, is entered from the customer record details in the data files and is correct. Customers pay both GST and PST on services. The invoice subtotal and total have been updated.

Press   ⌨enter to list the tax code descriptions set up for Phoebe's Photo Studio:

The tax code options are charge **No Tax** on the sale; code **G**, charge GST only; code **GP**, charge both GST and PST; and code **IN**, both GST and PST are charged and included in the price. PST is described as non-refundable.

You can select a different tax code from this list if the default is incorrect. Click the correct code and then click Select. You will return to the Revenues Journal with the cursor in the Account field.

Click   **Cancel** to return to the journal.

Press   ⌨tab to advance to the Account field.

The Account field in a sales invoice refers to the credit portion of the journal entry, usually a revenue account. Again, you cannot access *Accounts Receivable*, the linked account, directly. The software will automatically debit the *Accounts Receivable* control account in the General Ledger when you enter positive amounts.

You may set up a default revenue account for customers, just as you set up default expense accounts for suppliers. For Phoebe's Photo Studio customers, more than one revenue account applies. We have entered 4100 as the default account for the module, but it is not correct for this sale. In the Account field, you can choose an account from the list of accounts or create a new account, just as you can in any other account field. We need to create a new revenue account for this sale.

Type   4120 **Press** ⌨enter.

Press   ⌨enter to open the Add An Account wizard (Add An Account is selected).

Press   ⌨tab.

Type   Revenue from Gallery Sales as the **account name** and **accept** the remaining **defaults**. **Click Finish** to return to the journal.

The new account number is added to the journal.

Press   ⌨tab to advance the cursor to line 2 in the Item field, ready for additional sale items if necessary.

The Message field can be used in two ways: you can set up a default comment for the business that appears on all invoices, or you can enter a comment at the time of the sale. You can add to or change a default comment if you want. The default comment is entered for Phoebe's Photo Studio.

The payment terms have been set up as defaults for customers as 2 percent discount in 10 days with net payment due in 30 days. You can change terms for individual customers or sales invoices.

Click the **List icon beside the GST** or the **PST amount field** to provide the detailed summary of taxes included in the sale:

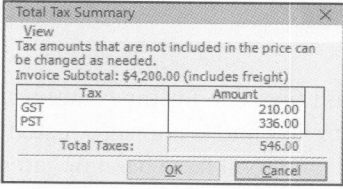

Close the **Tax Summary window** to return to the completed invoice:

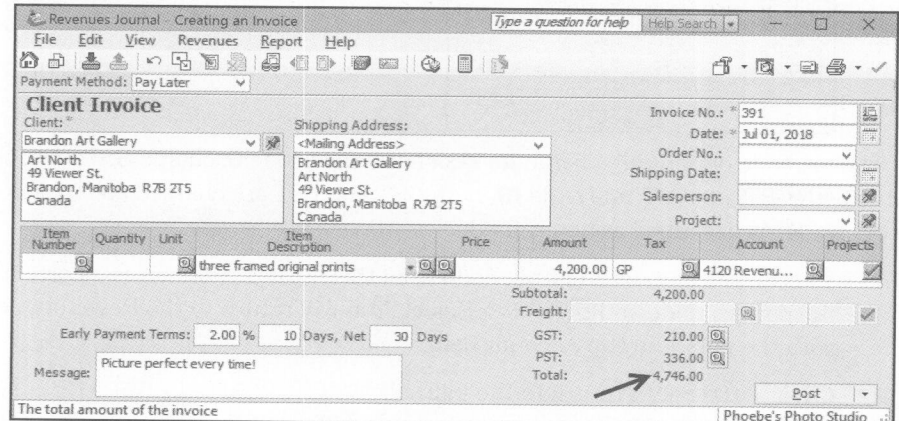

Before storing, printing or posting a Revenues Journal entry, review it carefully.

Reviewing the Revenues Journal Entry

Choose the **Report menu** and **click Display Revenues Journal Entry** or **press** `ctrl` + **J** to display the transaction:

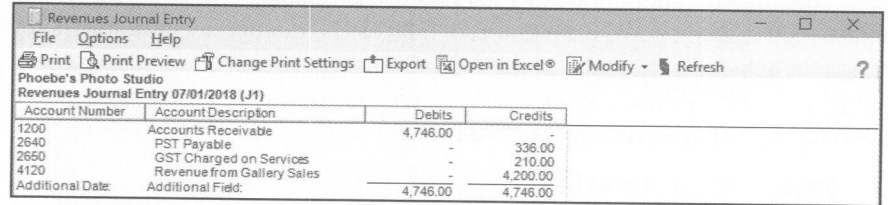

Review the **journal entry** to check for mistakes.

The display informs you that *Accounts Receivable*, the **control account**, has been updated automatically by Sage 50 because the Receivables and General ledgers are fully integrated. All credit sales are debited to *Accounts Receivable*, the default linked account for the Receivables Ledger. *GST Charged on Services* has also been updated correctly because of the tax code you entered and because *GST Charged on Services* was defined as the GST linked account for sales. Similarly, *PST Payable* is defined as the linked account for PST collected from customers, and it too is updated correctly because of the tax code. You did not need to enter any of these accounts or amounts directly in

---

NOTES
Payment terms can be modified for individual customers in the client ledger record. You can also edit the terms for individual sales in the Revenues Journal.

NOTES
If necessary, such as for rounding errors or to separate tax amounts that are combined, you can edit the tax amounts on the Tax Summary screen.

PRO VERSION
pro Choose the Report menu and click Display Sales Journal Entry.

NOTES
Using the Revenues Journal for sales instead of the General Journal is recommended because the accounts, tax codes and payment terms can be set up automatically for the business or linked to individual customers. Preset linked accounts ensure that tax amounts are calculated and updated correctly. Outstanding amounts are directly connected with the correct customer and ledger records are updated. The total Accounts Receivable amount is also updated.

Furthermore, you are unlikely to reverse debit and credit amounts in error.

the Revenues Journal. The balance owing by this customer is also directly updated as a result of the linked *Accounts Receivable* account and journal entry.

Close   the **display** to return to the Revenues Journal input screen.

CORRECTING THE REVENUES JOURNAL ENTRY BEFORE POSTING

Move to the field that has the error. **Press** (tab) to move forward through the fields or **press** (shift) and (tab) together to move back to a previous field. This will highlight the field information so you can change it. **Type** the **correct information** and **press** (tab) to enter it.

You can also use the mouse to **point** to a field and **drag through** the **incorrect information** to highlight it. **Type** the **correct information** and **press** (tab) to enter it.

If the customer is incorrect, **reselect** from the **Client** list by **clicking** the **Client list arrow. Click** the name of the **correct client.** Verify that the tax code, terms and default account are correct.

Click an **incorrect amount** or description to highlight it. Then **type** the **correct information** and **press** (tab) to enter the change.

To correct an account number or tax code, **click** the **Account List icon** to display the selection list. **Click** the **correct entry** to highlight it, then **click Select** and **press** (tab) to enter the change.

To insert a line or remove a line, **click** the **line** that you need to move. **Choose** the **Edit menu** and **click Insert Line** and **type** the new line or **click Remove Line** to delete a line.

To discard the entry and begin again, **click** ⊠ (Close) to close the journal or **click** ↰ (Undo) on the tool bar to open a blank journal window. When Sage 50 asks whether you want to discard the entry, **click Yes** to confirm your decision.

Customizing the Sales Invoice

The sales invoice includes a number of fields/columns that we do not need. Before saving the invoice, we will customize it to remove the unnecessary columns.

Click   the **Customize Journal tool** ▦ or **choose** the **View menu** and **click Customize Journal** to open the Settings options for Client Invoices:

We can modify the selection of columns and the order in which the tab key advances you from one part of the invoice to another. For the Client Invoices (Sales Invoices), we will modify the column selections. For Receipts, we will modify the tabbing order.

Click   **Columns** to open the column selection window:

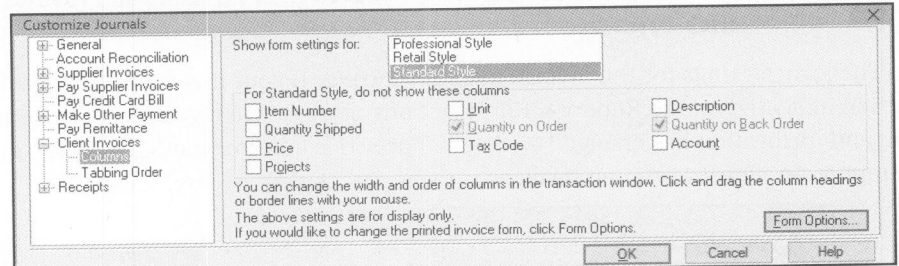

The Premium version has three predefined invoice styles for different business types. Each style displays a different set of columns. The Standard Style, the default, includes all columns. The Standard and Retail styles include columns for inventory and orders, while the Professional Style does not. The Tax Code, Account, Description and Projects columns are common to all styles.

NOTES
Other Receivables Ledger linked accounts will be used and explained later. These are the Receivables bank account, Freight Revenue account and Sales Discount account.

NOTES
To correct Revenues Journal entries after posting, refer to page 182 and Appendix C.

NOTES
When Orders and Quotes are used (Company Settings, Features), they will appear on the list as well. You can customize orders and quotes differently from invoices in the Premium version.

PRO VERSION
pro   Different invoice styles are not available in the Pro version. The Standard Style is the only one used. Form Options for printed invoices cannot be accessed from this window.
    You cannot customize orders and quotes separately from invoices.
    The term Purchase Invoices replaces Supplier Invoices and Sales Invoices replaces Client Invoices.

We can remove or hide most of the fields to match the Professional Style (refer to sidebar Warning). The columns we can remove are listed under the **For Standard Style, Do Not Show These Columns** heading. We can remove additional columns by clicking check boxes to add ✓s. The **Form Options** button accesses printer setup options for the forms. Modifying printed forms is covered in Appendix F on the Student DVD.

Click the **check boxes** for **Item Number**, **Quantity Shipped**, **Price**, **Unit** and **Projects**.

Click **OK** to return to the modified journal:

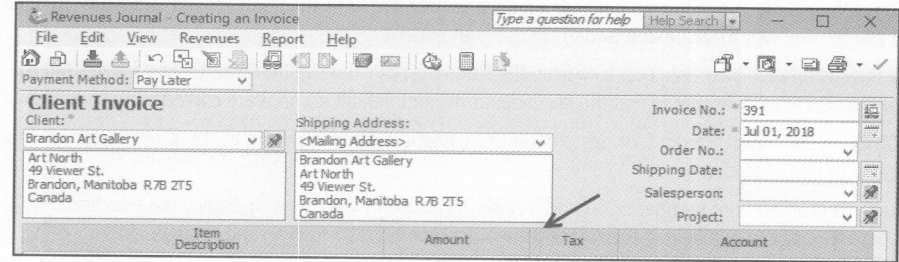

You can adjust the column spacing by dragging the column headings to change the size of columns and display all the information in all fields. We have resized the columns for this screenshot.

 NOTES
You can customize journals by dragging the column headings to rearrange or remove columns or to change column size.

Point to the column heading margin. When the arrow changes to ↔ (a double-headed arrow), drag the margin to its new location or size. Dragging the right column margin to the left until it overlaps the next column will remove that column. You can restore missing columns from the Customize Journal window.

Now when we press the ⌨tab key for the invoice details, the cursor will advance to the next field, and it will be one we use for the sale.

Previewing Invoices

Before printing and posting the invoice, you can preview it from the Preview tool 🖼. You can preview the invoice or, if you have the packing slip details, you can preview the packing slip (an invoice with shipping and item details, but without prices).

Click the **list arrow** ▼ beside the Preview tool 🖼 to list preview options:

Click **Print Preview For Invoice** or **choose** the **File menu** and **Invoices** and **click** **Print Preview**.

The form settings for the invoice must be correct. If your invoice form is not in the location indicated on the Report & Form Options page — when you have a customized form and its location has changed — Sage 50 provides an error message when you attempt to preview or print an invoice:

Click OK to open the Report & Form Options window:

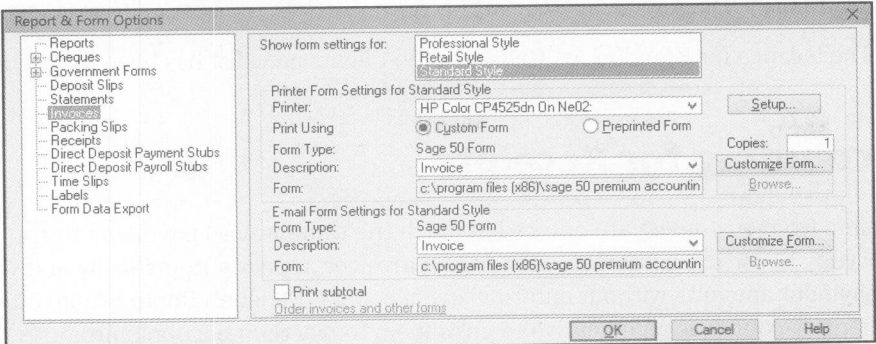

In the journal window, you can click 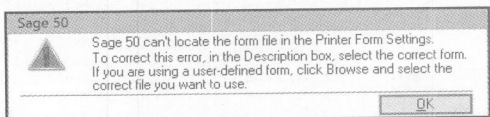, the Change The Default Printer Settings tool, any time to open the Forms settings screen for customer invoices. If a user-defined form location is incorrect, Sage 50 provides another warning:

NOTES
This screenshot has the form settings you need to preview the invoice — Custom Form as the Print Using selection and Invoice as the Description entry for both printed and e-mail copies.

> Sage 50 can't locate the form file in the Printer Form Settings.
> To correct this error, in the Description box, select the correct form.
> If you are using a user-defined form, click Browse and select the correct file you want to use.
>
> OK

Click OK. Choose Custom Form as the Print Using option and a valid file. Click OK. You should now be able to preview the invoice. Click the Print Preview For Invoice tool to display a copy of your invoice:

NOTES
A Sage 50 error message referring to the location of the default form in the Forms folder opens when the folder is missing or has moved.

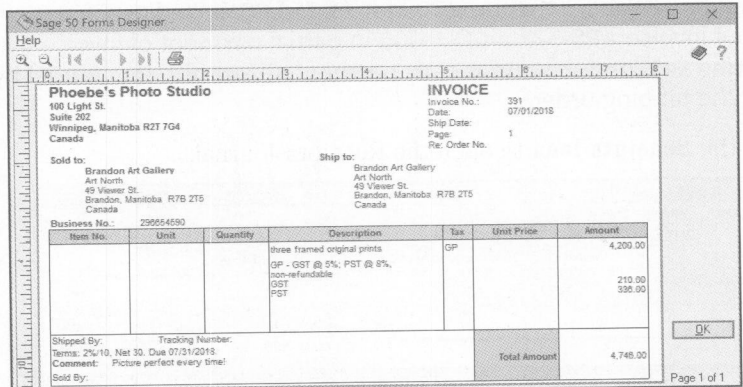

NOTES
Customizing the journal does not change the printed invoice. Refer to Appendix F on the Student DVD to learn how to customize printed invoices and other forms.

You can now print the invoice if you want by clicking the Print tool 🖨 in the Preview window. Or, click OK, return to the Invoice, choose the File menu and click Print or click the Print tool in the journal window.

Posting

When you are certain that you have entered the transaction correctly, you must post it. The Revenues Journal Post button has a list arrow with two options:

> Post ▾
> ✓ Post
> Print & Post

If you regularly print invoices when you enter them, as for point-of-sale transactions, you can click Print & Post on this button (add a ✓). Print and Post becomes the default selection and the button label changes to reflect this choice:

> Print & Post ▾

Previewing invoices is always recommended before printing. Because we do not want to print all invoices, we will accept the initial default setting to Post.

Click the **Post button** Post ▾ . **Click OK** to confirm successful posting.

A new blank Revenues Journal form appears on the screen.

NOTES
Printing begins immediately when you start from the Print tool. If you need to check or change your printer settings, you should start printing from the File menu in the journal.

NOTES
If invoices are printed as a batch or when you are learning the program, you should use Post as the default selection.
Batch printing of invoices and other forms is covered in Chapter 14.

NOTES
You can also choose the Revenues menu and click Post or press alt + P to save your transaction.

Close the **Revenues Journal** because the next transaction is a receipt.

The balance for Brandon Art Gallery in the Clients pane list has been updated.

Accounting for Receipts

> **NOTES**
> A discount of 2 percent for paying within 10 days is comparable to an interest penalty of 36 percent per year — it costs the customer 2 percent to borrow the money for the extra 20 days.
> Client balance amounts in the Clients list pane have been updated.

Receipts from customers are entered in much the same way as payments to suppliers. After you choose the customer, outstanding invoices appear automatically and you enter the payment amounts without entering any accounts. Phoebe's Photo Studio offers early payment discounts as an incentive to customers to pay their accounts promptly.

Receipts are entered in the Receipts Journal accessed from the Receipts icon in the Tasks pane:

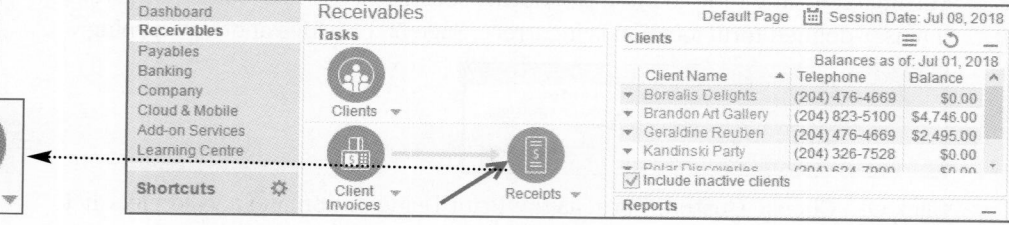

> **CLASSIC VIEW**
> The Receipts icon is located below the Revenues icon. It has no shortcuts list arrow.

> **PRO VERSION**
> The Refresh tools do not appear in the Pro version.

| ✓ | **Receipt #41** | **Dated July 2/18** |
| 2 | | |

From Geraldine Reuben, cheque #302 for $1 754.80, including $754.80 in full payment of invoice #PS-377 and $1 000 in partial payment of invoice #PS-381, and allowing $45.20 discount for early payment. Customize the journal by changing the tabbing order.

Click the **Receipts icon** to open the Receipts Journal:

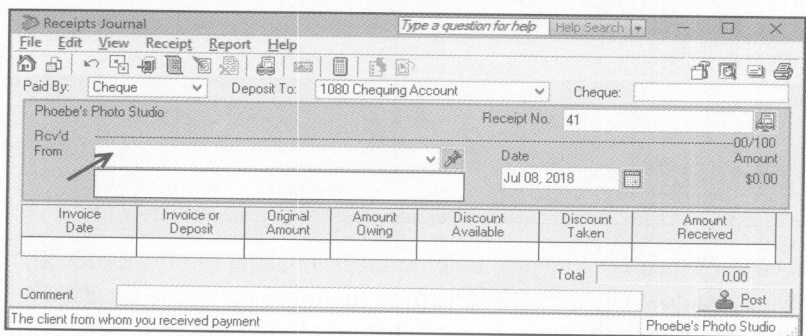

> **NOTES**
> Two tools, 🖾 and 🖾, will refresh the journal with changes made by other users, such as the addition of new invoices. The list of outstanding invoices and the invoices themselves can be updated.
> These tools are used when the option to refresh lists automatically is not selected — a User Preference setting (refer to page 80).

As with the Sales Invoice, you can customize the journal by removing fields and changing the tabbing order.

Click the **Customize Journal tool** 🖾 or **choose** the **View menu** and **click** **Customize Journal**:

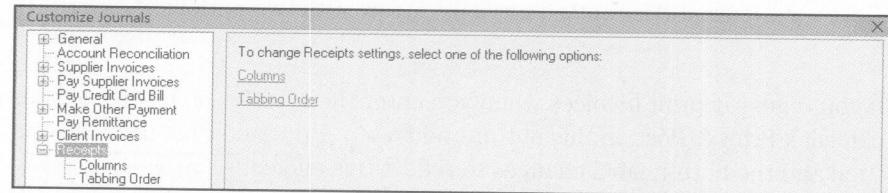

Click **Columns** to open the customization options for columns.

When they are not needed, you can remove the Invoice Date and the two Discount columns. Phoebe's Photo Studio offers customer discounts, so we must include these columns.

Click   **Tabbing Order** in the list under Receipts to continue:

You can choose the default tabbing order or you can change the order.

Click   **Custom Tabbing Order** to continue:

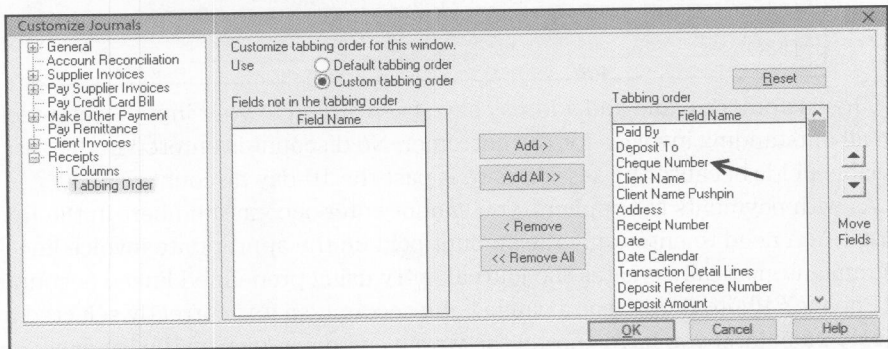

We will change the order so that after choosing the customer, the cursor will move to the cheque number field. This field is in the upper right-hand corner. With the default tabbing order, the cursor reaches this field last, making it easy to forget to enter the number. The cheque number is not a required field, so the program does not warn you if you omit the number.

Cheque Number appears before Client Name. However, when you open the Receipts Journal, the cursor starts in the Client Name field, so the Cheque Number field is last. We want the second field to be the Cheque Number.

To move a field, select it and then click the Move Fields Up and Down arrows beside the list until you have the order you want.

Click   **Cheque Number**.

Click   the **Move Fields Down button** [▼] beside the Tabbing Order list. This will place Cheque Number after the Client Name.

Click   **Address** in the Tabbing Order column. **Click Remove** to skip all the address field lines when you press (tab).

Removing fields from the tabbing order does not remove them from the journal, just from the tabbing sequence.

Click   **OK** to return to the form. You can now enter the receipt.

Click   the **From field list arrow** to display the Client list:

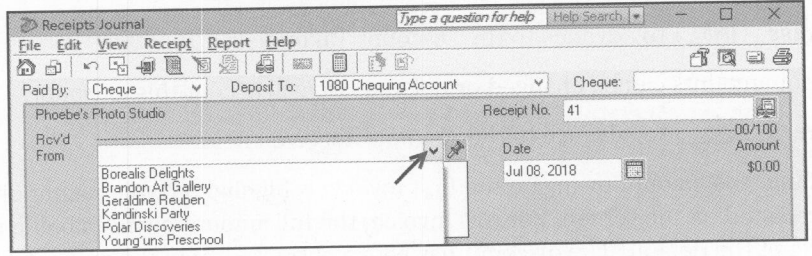

The From (Client) field has the Same Client tool [📌] we saw earlier, to use for recording several receipts from the same client.

NOTES
You can customize the order further by making the Date field follow the Cheque Number and so on.

You can also choose to remove other fields that are not used, such as Invoice Date and Original Amount. To access a skipped field after you remove it from the tabbing order, you can click the field.

Click   **Geraldine Reuben** to choose this customer:

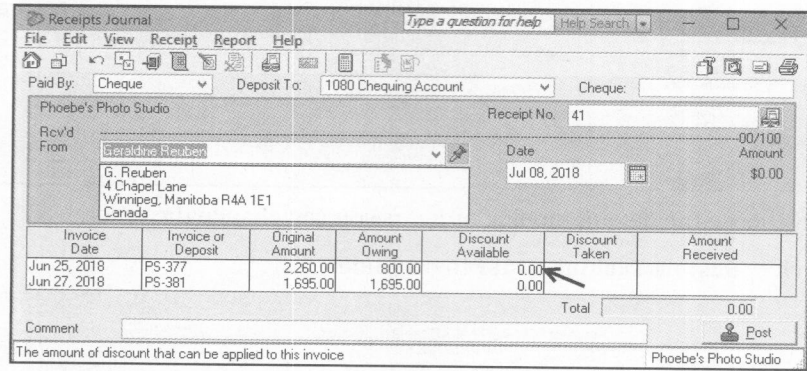

The customer's name and address have been added to your input form, together with all outstanding invoices for the customer. No discount is entered in the Discount Available fields because the session date is past the 10-day discount period.

As with payments to suppliers, you cannot enter account numbers in the Receipts Journal. You need to enter only the amount paid on the appropriate invoice line. The program automatically creates the journal entry using predefined linked accounts.

Phoebe's Photo Studio has a single bank account, so it is correctly selected in the **Deposit To** field. If you have chosen the wrong customer, display the list again and click the correct customer. If you have selected correctly,

> **Press**   (tab)   to move to the **Cheque field**.

> **Type**   302

The Receipt No. field records the receipt number, which increases automatically.

From the Lookup icon beside the Receipt No. field ⌨️ , you can look up previously posted receipts.

We need to replace the session date with the date for this transaction.

> **Choose** **July 2** from the Date field pop-up calendar. **Press** (tab) to move the cursor to the Invoice Date field. The discounts are now available:

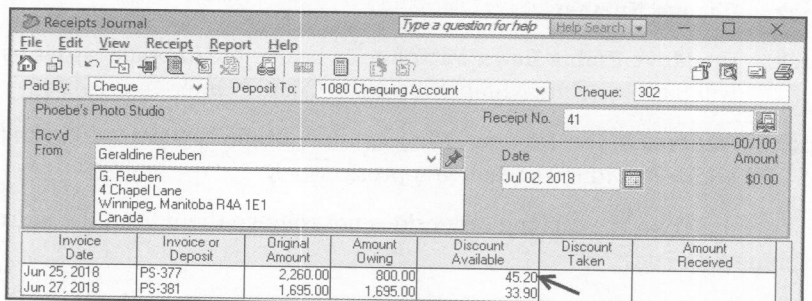

The discount is 2 percent of the original amount, not the amount owing. Until the discount period has passed, the full discount remains available.

> **Press**   (tab)   to advance to the Discount Taken field.

Discount amounts can be changed or deleted. We will accept this discount.

> **Press**   (tab)   to advance to the Amount Received field.

By default, the amount owing on the first invoice is highlighted. All outstanding invoices are listed on the screen. For this invoice, the full amount owing is being paid, so you can accept the default. The discount has been subtracted from the amount owing automatically.

> **Press**   (tab)   to accept the discounted amount in the Amount Received field.

NOTES

Sage 50 allows you to set up more than one bank account. When more than one bank account is set up, choose the account from the Deposit To drop-down list.

NOTES

You can use the Lookup button beside the Receipt No. field to review a receipt (refer to page 176).

NOTES

The year is added correctly in the Receipts Journal when you type the month and day.

NOTES

For other company types, the Invoice Date column may be labelled Statement Date, Bill Date and so on.

NOTES

You can accept a highlighted amount or type an exact amount for a partial payment.

The cursor will advance to the Discount Taken field for the next invoice:

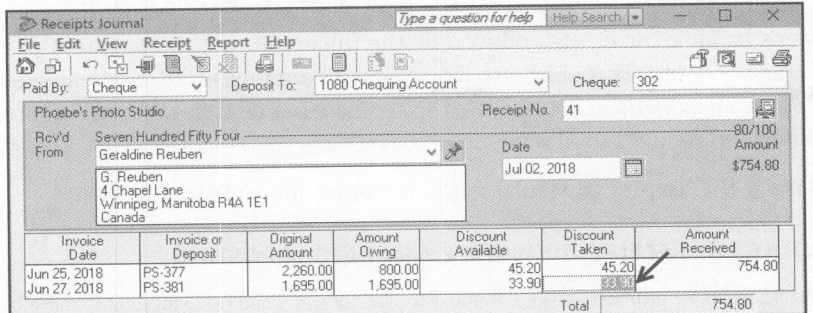

Because the payment for invoice PS-381 is only a partial payment, we need to remove the discount.

Press ⬚del⬚ to remove the discount for the second invoice.

Press ⬚tab⬚ to advance to the Amount Received field.

This time the full invoice amount is entered because the discount has been changed to zero. However, the full amount is not being paid, so we must edit the amount. To replace the highlighted default amount,

Type 1000

Press ⬚tab⬚ to enter the new amount and complete the invoice:

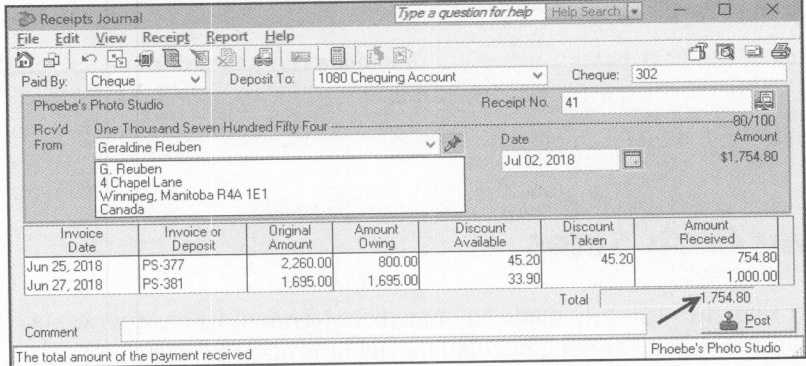

The upper cheque portion of the form has also been completed. In making Receipts Journal entries, you do not need to enter any accounts because Sage 50 chooses the linked bank and receivable accounts defined for the Receivables Ledger to create the journal entry.

You have made all the entries for this transaction, so you are ready to review before posting your transaction.

Reviewing the Receipts Journal Entry

Choose the **Report menu** and **click Display Receipts Journal Entry**:

Account Number	Account Description	Debits	Credits
1080	Chequing Account	1,754.80	-
4180	Sales Discounts	45.20	-
1200	Accounts Receivable	-	1,800.00
Additional Date:	Additional Field:	1,800.00	1,800.00

The related journal entry has been created for the Receipts Journal transaction. Sage 50 updates the General Ledger *Accounts Receivable* **control account** and *Chequing Account* because the Receivables and General ledgers are fully integrated.

NOTES
The direct link between sales and payments for a customer provides another reason for using the Receivables Ledger for sales entries instead of the General Ledger. In addition, discounts are calculated automatically when the dates are correct; you cannot select incorrect accounts, and total Accounts Receivable amounts are updated directly.

Furthermore, you are unlikely to reverse debit and credit amounts in error.

Phoebe's Photo Studio uses *Chequing Account* as its single default linked bank account for the Receivables Ledger as well as for the Payables Ledger. *Accounts Receivable* and the customer's balance owing are reduced by the full amount of the payment plus the amount of the discount taken ($1 800). The discount amount is automatically debited to the linked *Sales Discounts* account. *Sales Discounts* is a **contra-revenue account**. It has a debit balance and reduces total revenue.

Close   the **display** to return to the Receipts Journal input screen.

CORRECTING THE RECEIPTS JOURNAL ENTRY BEFORE POSTING

Move to the field with the error. **Press** `tab` to move forward or `shift` and `tab` together to move back to a previous field. This will highlight the field contents. **Type** the **correct information** and **press** `tab` to enter it.

You can also use the mouse to **point** to a field and **drag through** the **incorrect information** to highlight it. **Type** the **correct information** and **press** `tab` to enter it.

If the customer is incorrect, **reselect** from the **Client** list by **clicking** the **Client list arrow**. **Click** the name of the correct **client**. To confirm that you want to discard the current transaction, **click Yes** to display the outstanding invoices for the correct customer. **Type** the **correct** receipt **information**.

You can also discard the entry and begin again. **Click** ⊠ or �っ and then **click Yes** to confirm.

Posting

When you are certain that you have entered all the information correctly, you must post the transaction to save it.

Click   the **Post button** 🖳 Post or **choose** the **Receipt menu** and **click Post** to save your transaction. **Click OK**.

Close   the **Receipts Journal**.

Entering Cash Sales

For the next sale, the customer made an immediate payment by cheque. We use the term cash sale for all sales when immediate payment is made by cash or cheque.

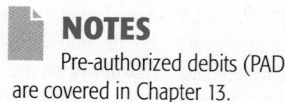
> ✓
> ───
> 3

Cash Sales Invoice #PS-392   **Dated July 3/18**

To Kandinski Party, $1 800 plus $90 GST and $144 PST for family portrait photo package before wedding. Terms: 2 percent discount ($40.68) with cash received on completion of work. Received cheque #569 for $1 993.32 in full payment.

Click   the **Client Invoices icon** 🖳 Client Invoices to open the Revenues Journal — the invoice number has been updated to 392.

Click   the **Payment Method list arrow** for the payment options — Pay Later, Cash, Cheque, Pre-Authorized Debit and Credit Card:

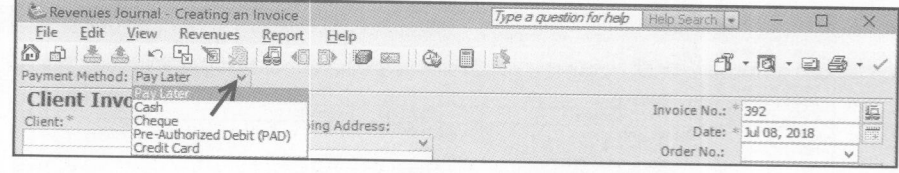

Click   **Cheque** as the method of payment to modify the invoice screen.

> **NOTES**
> When you choose Cash or Credit Card as the payment method, the Cheque No. field is not included. For Pre-Authorized Debits, the Cheque No. field becomes the PAD No. field.

When you choose Cheque as the method of payment, a cheque number field is added in the upper right-hand corner of the invoice so that you can add the customer's cheque number. This is a required field in the Revenues Journal. The Deposit To bank account field is also added. In the payment terms section, the Net Days field has been removed and a Cheque Amount field has been added.

Press   `tab` **twice** to advance to the Cheque No. field.

Type   569 **Press** `tab` to advance to the Client field.

Type   K

Kandinski Party is added to the Client field because it is the first customer entry beginning with K. The rest of the name is still highlighted in case you want to continue typing another name.

Enter   **July 3** in the Date field as the transaction date.

Enter   a **description**. **Press** `tab` to advance to the Amount field.

Type   1800

Double-click the **Account field**.

The cheque amount below the terms has been updated to include the discount applied for the immediate payment, based on the customer's terms.

Click   **Suggested Accounts** below the account list to modify the list:

> **NOTES**
> When you open the Purchases Journal, only the expense accounts will be listed. You will need to choose All Accounts to include asset accounts in the list.

The list of suggested accounts now includes only revenue accounts because we are in the Revenues Journal. This shorter list makes it easier to select the correct account. For purchases, only expense accounts will be listed. You can switch back to the complete account list at any time by selecting **All Accounts**. When we close the journal, the Suggested Accounts button remains selected until we change the selection again.

In this case, however, the default account for the customer is correct and may still be selected.

Click   **4140 Revenue from Portraits**. **Press** `enter`.

Click the **Message field**. **Type** Thank you to complete the sales entry:

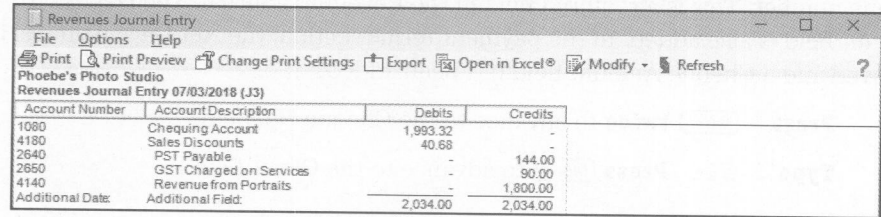

As usual, you should review the entry.

Choose the **Report menu** and **click Display Revenues Journal Entry**:

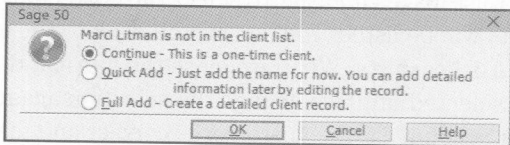

Chequing Account is debited automatically instead of *Accounts Receivable* because we selected Cheque as the method of payment.

Close the **display** when you have finished. **Make corrections** if necessary.

Click Post to save the entry. **Click OK**. Leave the journal open.

Adding a New Client

The next sale is to a new customer who should be added to your files. We will add the customer directly from the Revenues Journal.

NOTES

Marci Litman
(contact Marci)
36 Runway Alley, Apt. 201
Oakbank, MB R0E 1J0
Tel: (204) 538-2436
Mobile: (204) 638-2436
E-mail: marci@hotmail.com
Web: marci.com
Terms: 2/10, n/30
Revenue account: 4140
Tax code: GP
Credit limit: $3 000

Sales Invoice #PS-393 **Dated July 3/18**

To Marci Litman (use Full Add for the new customer), $2 100 plus $105 GST and $168 PST for modelling portfolio. Invoice total $2 373. Terms: 2/10, n/30.

Click the **Payment Method field** and **choose Pay Later**. The date is correct.

Click the **Client field**.

Type Marci Litman

Press (tab) to display the notice that you have typed a name that is not on the list. This notice provides the option to add a ledger record:

The options are the same as for new suppliers. If you typed an incorrect name, click **Cancel** to return to the journal and start again. If you typed the name correctly, you can choose to add the customer's name only — **Quick Add** — or to add a full customer

record with the **Full Add** option. If you need to change any defaults, you must choose Full Add. You can still skip customer fields that you do not need. The remaining option, **Continue**, will add the customer's name to the journal entry but will not create a ledger record for the customer or add the customer to the other Receivables Ledger reports.

Click   **Full Add**.

Click   **OK** to open the customer's Address information screen:

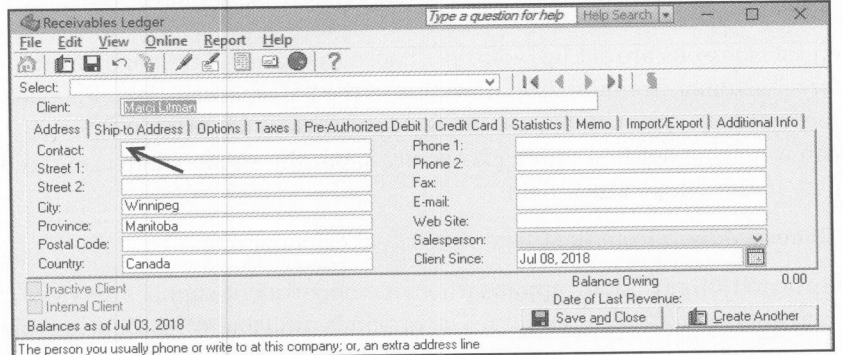

Clicking Add above the Client field in the journal opens this ledger form directly from the journal at the Address tab screen.

You are ready to enter your new customer. The Client field is completed with the new name highlighted for editing if necessary. The Client name is the only **required field** for new customer records. Because it is already entered, the * reminder symbol for required fields has been removed and the Save tool icon is available (not dimmed).

The field we need next is the Contact field. Enter the name of the individual Phoebe's Photo Studio normally deals with.

Click   the **Contact field** or **press** (tab).

Type   Marci

Press   (tab) to move the cursor to the Street 1 field.

Type   36 Runway Alley **Press** (tab).

Type   Apt. 201 **Press** (tab) to move to and select the City field.

The city, province and country in which Phoebe's Photo Studio is located have been entered by default from the Address Settings. The province is correct, but you must change the city.

Type   Oakbank

Click   the **Postal Code field**.

You do not need to use capital letters or to leave a space within Canadian postal codes. The program will make these adjustments automatically.

Type   r0e1j0

Click   the **Phone 1 field**. The postal code format is corrected automatically.

You do not need to add spaces, dashes or brackets for telephone numbers. Telephone and fax numbers may be entered with or without the area code.

Type   2045382436 **Press** (tab). Enter the mobile number as Phone 2.

Type   2046382436 **Press** (tab) to move to the Fax field.

Press   (tab) to skip the fax field and advance to the E-mail field.

PRO VERSION

pro Remember that the term Customer replaces Client. The Internal Client option and the Refresh tool do not apply to the Pro version.

The format for the telephone numbers has also been corrected automatically.

E-mail and Web addresses are typed exactly as you would type them in your regular Internet and e-mail programs. You can also add these details later when you actually want to use them. When you click the Web or E-mail tools, you will be prompted to enter the addresses if they are not part of the customer's record already.

Type   marci@hotmail.com   **Press** (tab).

Type   marci.com

When salespersons are set up, you can choose the name of the regular sales contact person for a customer from the drop-down list in the **Salesperson** field. Phoebe's Photo Studio does not have salespersons set up. Salespersons are covered in Chapter 9.

Litman is making her first purchase on July 3, but the session date is entered as the default date in the **Client Since** field.

Choose   **July 3** from the Client Since field calendar icon.

The **Internal Client** option applies when one department supplies services to another and charges for these services. The option is available when time and billing is used. If the customer no longer buys from the company, but you still want to keep the record on file, mark the customer as **Inactive**. The **Balance Owing** and **Date Of Last Sale** will be entered automatically by the program based on the customer's transactions.

Click   the **Ship-To Address tab**.

Click   the **Address Name list arrow** to list the predefined names:

You can enter multiple customer addresses and apply your own labels for these addresses. For example, you may have separate summer and winter addresses for residential customers or different store locations for wholesale customers. The billing address may be different from the location where a service is provided or products are delivered. The Shipping Address field in the journal has a list arrow for selecting one of the addresses you have defined. The mailing address is provided as the default ship-to address, as indicated by the ✓ for Default Ship-To Address and its entry in the Address Name field. The address information is dimmed because you cannot remove the mailing address on this screen. You can enter complete address and contact information for the shipping address, add new address labels and information for them, edit the labels and remove address names and labels that are not needed.

Click   **Ship-To Address** (or another address name) in the drop-down list.

This will remove ✓ for the Default Ship-To Address and open the address fields for editing:

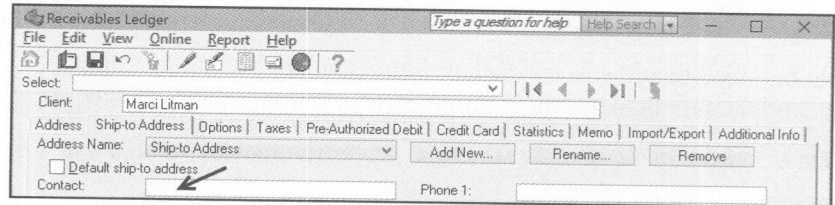

All the fields are now open for editing. You can make any address the Default Ship-To Address by clicking the check box when this label's information is displayed.

PRO VERSION

The Pro version does not have an Internal Client option.

NOTES

Inactive clients may be included in or omitted from reports.

PRO VERSION

The Pro version allows only one additional address – the shipping address. You cannot edit the name of this second address. If the mailing address is different from the shipping address, click the Same As Mailing Address check box to remove the ✓ and then enter or edit the address fields.

PRO VERSION

The Shipping Address fields are available immediately.

The shipping address is the same as the mailing address for this customer, so we can remove the ship-to address name for this customer.

Click **Remove** — Sage 50 requests confirmation:

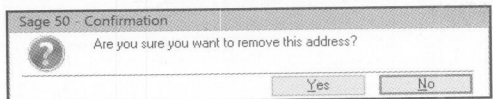

Click **Yes** to confirm the removal.

Click **Add New** to open the name field to add a new address:

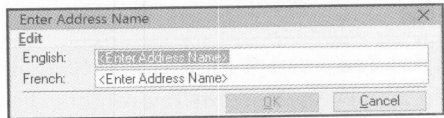

Type a new name and then click OK to have the new name appear in the Address Name field drop-down list. Then you can select it to add the address details.

Click **Cancel** to return to the Ship-To Address tab screen.

Click the **Options tab**:

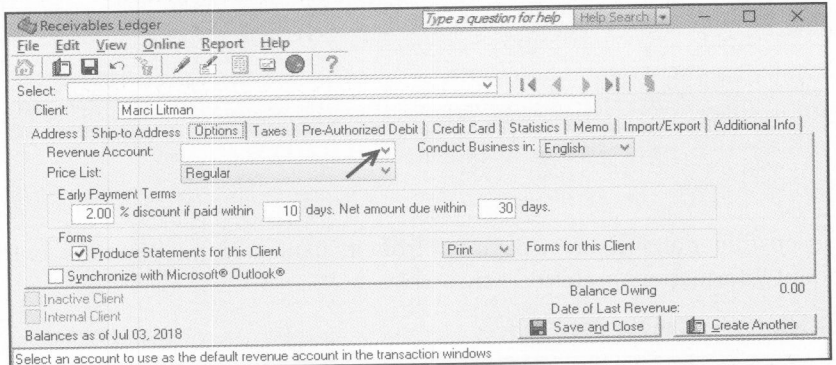

The first option is to add a default revenue account for the customer.

Click the **Revenue Account list arrow**.

Click **4140**.

The Options tab screen contains the details of the payment terms. The default terms are entered from the ledger settings. The **Price List** — Regular, Preferred or Web Price — refers to the prices customers pay for inventory items and will be introduced in Chapter 10. For Phoebe's Photo Studio, all customers pay Regular prices. You can select French or English as the customer's preferred **language for conducting business**. Sales invoices and other forms you prepare for customers will be printed in the language you select here. Your own program screens will not change.

The payment terms for Marci Litman are the same as those for other customers and are entered by default.

You may also choose to **Produce Statements For This Client**, and you may print or e-mail invoices and quotes — selecting the option from the drop-down list. From the journal, you can change the print/e-mail selection. You should use the correct forms, but you can also print statements on ordinary printer paper.

If you use **Microsoft Outlook** to organize your contacts, you can synchronize the address list in Sage 50 with Outlook.

You can change the Options tab settings at any time.

Click the **Taxes tab**:

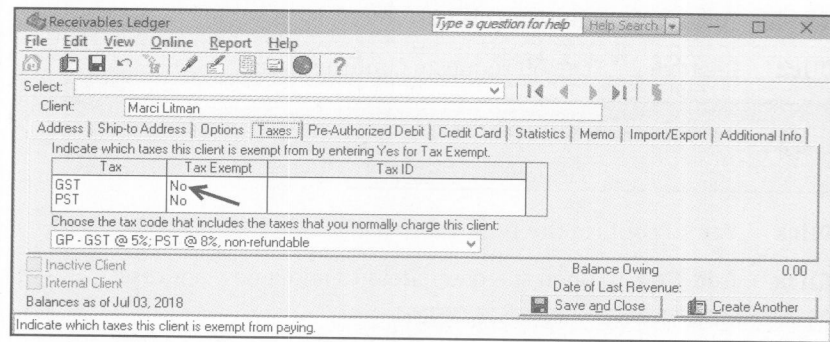

The customer is correctly described as **not Tax Exempt** for PST and GST, allowing accurate tax calculations for sales transactions to be included in Tax reports. The default tax code taken from the ledger settings is also correct.

Click **GP - GST @ 5%; PST @ 8%, non-refundable** to list the codes available. Do not change the tax code for this customer.

Click the **Pre-Authorized Debit tab**:

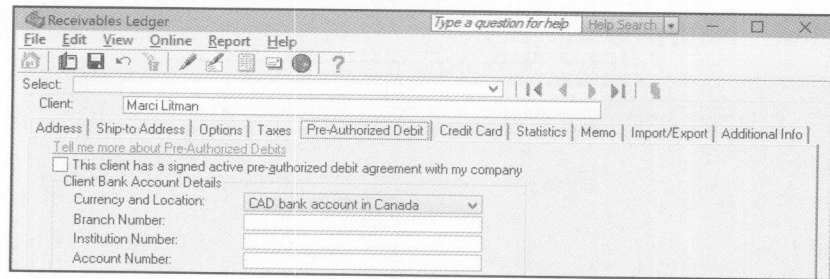

If your customer allows direct payment from its bank account, you must enter the bank account information on this screen.

Click the **Credit Card tab**:

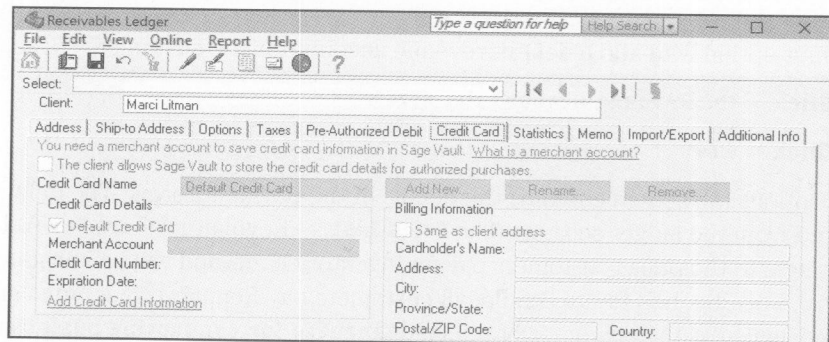

If you have a merchant credit card account and your customer allows automatic credit card payments, you must enter the information on this screen.

Click the **Statistics tab** to open the next screen we need:

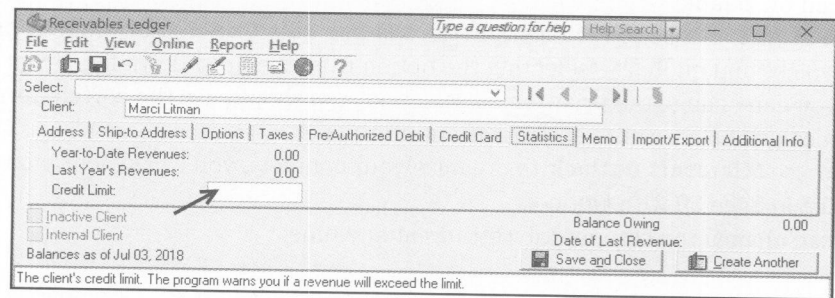

The Statistics screen has a summary of the sales to the customer for the current year and the previous year. These fields are updated from sales transactions.

In the **Credit Limit** field, you can enter the customer's credit limit to help minimize bad debts. When a customer exceeds the credit limit, the program will warn you with this message before you can post the sale:

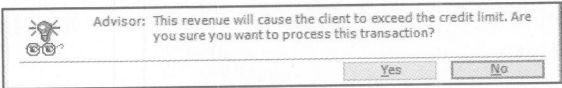

You can click Yes to accept the over-the-limit sale, or No to return to the invoice and ask for a deposit to avoid exceeding the credit limit. Customers who have previously defaulted on making their payments can be placed on a cash-only basis by setting their credit limits to zero. Phoebe's Photo Studio is analyzing customer payment trends at present and will set Litman's limit at $3 000 on a trial basis.

> **Click**   the **Credit Limit field** to position the cursor and **type** 3000

Saving a New Customer Account

The remaining tab screens are not required. They serve the same purpose as they do for suppliers. When you are certain that all the information is correct, you must save the newly created customer account and add it to the current list.

> **Click**   **Save And Close** Save and Close to save the new customer information.

You will return to the journal. Notice that the tax code, revenue account and payment terms are added. Any of these fields can be edited for an individual invoice.

> **Enter**   the **sale** (page 170) for Litman by following the procedures outlined earlier.
>
> **Review** the **journal entry**. **Close** the **display** and **make corrections**.
>
> **Click**   Post ▼ . **Click OK** and then **close** the **Revenues Journal**.

Reversing a Receipt (NSF Cheques)

When a cheque is returned by the bank as NSF, you need to record the fact that the invoice is still outstanding. You can do this in the Receipts Journal by reversing the cheque.

> ✓ / 5

Bank Debit Memo #14321   **Dated July 4/18**

From Red River Credit Union, cheque #302 for $1 754.80 from Geraldine Reuben has been returned because of non-sufficient funds. Reverse the payment and notify the customer of the outstanding charges.

> **Click**   the **Receipts icon** Receipts ▼ **shortcuts list arrow**:

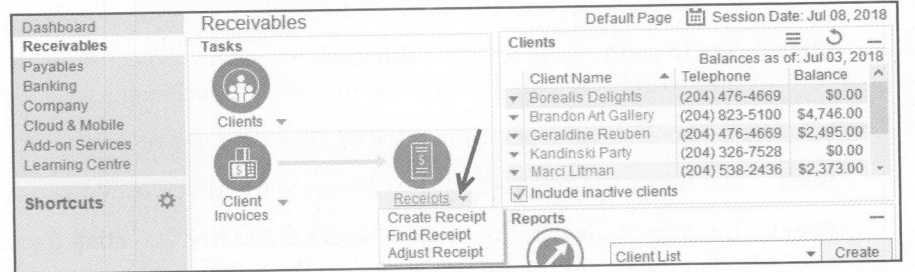

NOTES
Sage 50 adds the total amount from the current sale to the balance owing to assess whether the customer has exceeded the credit limit.

NOTES
Customers should be notified of credit policy changes.

NOTES
Remember to select Pay Later as the Payment Method for the sale to Litman.

NOTES
The Home window Clients list pane has the balances as at July 3, the latest transaction date, and not at the session date. This selection is a user preference.

NOTES

The Lookup and Adjust tools both open the Search window. The Reverse tool and menu option are available from the journal windows provided by both.

From Lookup and Find Receipt, the search parameters will have Receipt Lookup as the heading and Select A Receipt in the window that lists the receipts.

NOTES

If you recorded a receipt incorrectly and do not need to reverse it, you can choose the Adjust Receipt tool to access the posted receipt and make the correction, just as you do for sales (page 182) or for payments (page 137).

NOTES

In Chapter 15, you will learn that you cannot reverse the receipt if the cheque is not deposited directly to the bank account when you enter the receipt (that is, the bank deposit is recorded later as a separate transaction). Instead, you must enter a negative receipt.

NOTES

If you started from the Lookup window, the window title will be Receipt Lookup. You can click the Adjust Receipt tool if you need to open the fields for editing.

Depending on your starting point, the first invoice line may or may not be highlighted or selected.

NOTES

If you change the customer when adjusting a receipt, the program will reverse the original receipt when you click Yes to confirm this action.

CLASSIC VIEW

From the Home window, right-click the Receipts icon

. Click , the Select A Report tool, to open the Receipts Journal report options.

Click   Adjust Receipt or **click** Find Receipt.

Or, with the Receipts Journal open,

Click   the **Adjust Receipt tool** , or **press** ctrl + **A**, or **choose** the **Receipt menu** and **click Adjust Receipt**.

Or **click** the **Lookup tool** , or **press** ctrl + **L**, or **choose** the **Receipt menu** and **click Look Up Receipt**.

The familiar Search screen opens with Receipts as the search area:

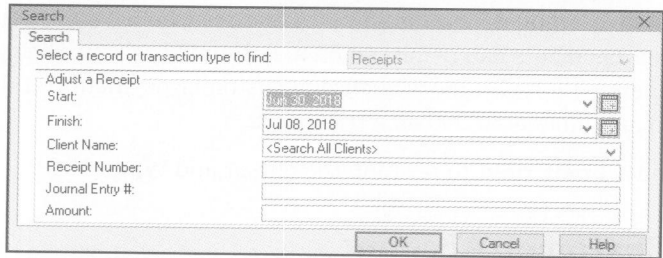

Click   **OK** to list all the receipts we have entered:

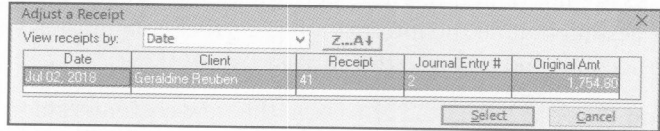

The single cheque we entered is selected — the one from Geraldine Reuben.

Press   enter or **click Select** to open the cheque we entered:

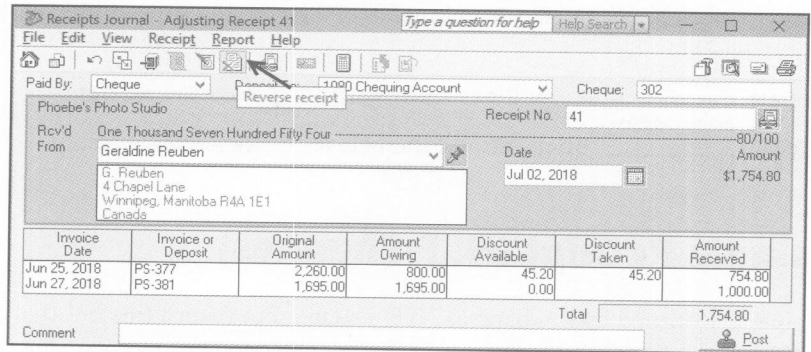

At this stage you can adjust the cheque by editing incorrectly entered information, just as you can edit a purchase invoice or payment cheque.

We need to reverse the cheque because it has been returned as NSF.

Click   the **Reverse Receipt tool** or **choose** the **Receipt menu** and **click Reverse Receipt**. Sage 50 requires your confirmation to proceed:

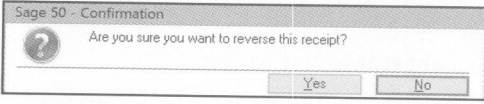

Click   **Yes** to confirm the reversal. **Click OK** when Sage 50 confirms the successful reversal. A blank Receipts Journal form opens.

We will review the Journal Report generated by reversing this receipt.

Click   the **Home window tool** to return to the Home window.

Choose the **Reports menu**, then **choose Journal Entries** and **click Receipts** to open the report options window:

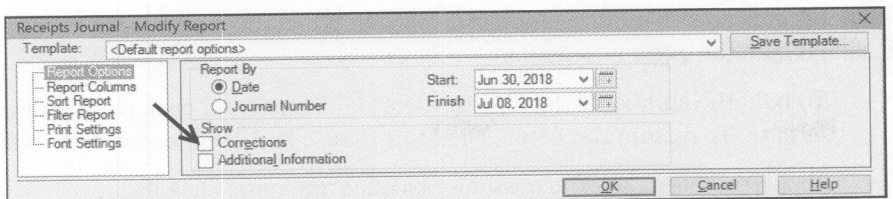

NOTES
You can also click the Report Centre icon. Then click Receivables, Receipts Journal Entries and Modify This Report to open the report options.

By default, corrections are not included in the report — we must include them in order to add adjusting and reversing entries. The remaining defaults are correct.

Click   Corrections under the Show heading. **Click OK**:

```
Receipts Journal Display                                          —  □  ×
File    Options    Help
🖶 Print  🔍 Print Preview  🖶 Change Print Settings  📤 Export  📊 Open in Excel®  📝 Modify ▾  🔄 Refresh        ?
Phoebe's Photo Studio
Receipts Journal 06/30/2018 to 07/08/2018
                    Account Number    Account Description          Debits        Credits
07/02/2018    J2    41, Geraldine Reuben
                    1080              Chequing Account          1,754.80              -
                    4180              Sales Discounts              45.20              -
                    1200              Accounts Receivable              -        1,800.00
07/02/2018    J5    ADJ41, Geraldine Reuben: Rev. of J2. Corr. is J5.
                    1200              Accounts Receivable       1,800.00              -
                    1080              Chequing Account                 -        1,754.80
                    4180              Sales Discounts                  -           45.20
                                                                3,600.00        3,600.00
```

The report confirms that the two entries cancel each other — all amounts were reversed, including the discount. The original debits to *Chequing Account* and *Sales Discounts* were entered as credits in the reversing entry, and the credit to *Accounts Receivable* was entered as a debit. Sage 50 created the reversing entry automatically when we reversed the receipt, adding ADJ to the receipt number to link the two transactions.

When you adjust a receipt and post the corrected entry, Sage 50 will create the intermediate reversing entry automatically. Three entries result — the original incorrect one, the reversing entry and the final corrected version, just as they do when you make adjustments in the General, Purchases and Payments journals. By including Corrections in the Journal Reports, you can provide the complete audit trail.

Close   the **display** when you have finished.

Restore the **Receipts Journal**.

Choose Geraldine Reuben from the Client list.

Both invoices have been fully restored. When the replacement payment is received, you can enter it in the usual way.

Close   the **Receipts Journal** without entering a payment.

Editing Client Information

You can change customer information and you can change the way the Home window displays Clients pane details, just as you can modify the Suppliers pane.

Clicking the ▤ button at the top of the Clients pane lists the items that can be removed from this pane: the telephone number and balance owing.

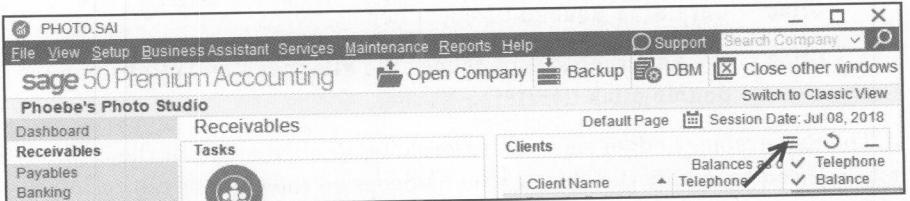

WARNING!
If you display the Journal Report from the Home window Reports pane list of reports, you will use the default settings, which do not show corrections. The message will state that there are no data to report because there are no other Receipts Journal entries.

NOTES
To restore the Receipts Journal, point to the Sage 50 icon or name on the Windows task bar. You should have pop-ups for both the Home window and the Receipts Journal. Click the Receipts Journal pop-up. (Refer to the screenshot on page 14.)

The ✓ indicates that information is displayed. When the computer is in a public area, you should hide the extra information.

To hide the additional details, click the ▤ button and click the detail you want to hide. To restore the detail, click this button and click an option to add the ✓.

To refresh or update the customer balance amounts, click ↺.

Click ▭ if you want to hide the entire customer list and ❐ to restore the list.

✓	**Memo #1**	**Dated July 5/18**
6		

From Owner: Edit the ledger record for Geraldine Reuben to change the payment terms to net 1. Certified cheques will be requested in the future. Set her credit limit to zero.

Edit the customer names as well — the last name should be first to keep the records in correct alphabetic order. Edit the records for Geraldine Reuben, Marci Litman and Borealis Delights. Change these customer names to Reuben, Geraldine; Litman, Marci; and Borealis Mysteries.

Most fields in the customer record can be changed at any time. Only the current balance owing, which is updated from sales and payment transactions, cannot be changed.

Click the **Clients icon shortcuts list arrow**:

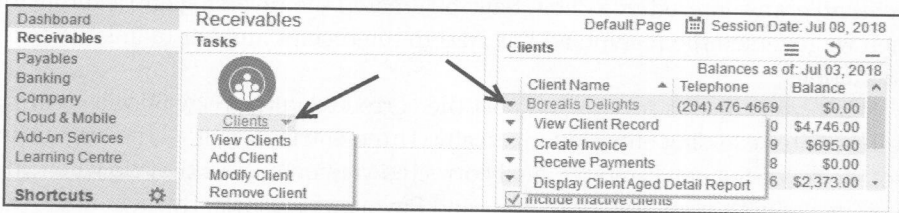

From the Clients shortcuts list, you can choose Modify Client. When the Search screen opens, you can select the customer.

You can click the customer's name in the right-hand Clients pane, or you can click the list arrow beside the customer's name and click View Client Record to open a record for a customer directly.

We will use a third option — to work from the Clients window.

Click the **Clients icon** to open the Clients window:

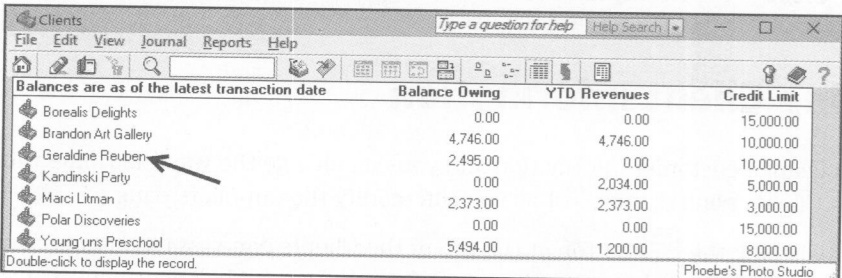

Click **Geraldine Reuben** to select her.

Click the **Edit tool** 🖉 or **choose** the **File menu** and **click Open** or **double-click Geraldine Reuben**.

The Receivables Ledger record for Geraldine Reuben opens at the Address screen. First, we need to modify the Terms, which appear on the Options tab.

Click the **Options tab** to access the payment terms information:

NOTES
From the Clients list pane shortcuts you can also enter transactions for the client or view that client's Aged Receivables Report.

PRO VERSION
Click the Customers icon shortcuts list arrow.
Click the Customers icon to open the Customers window.

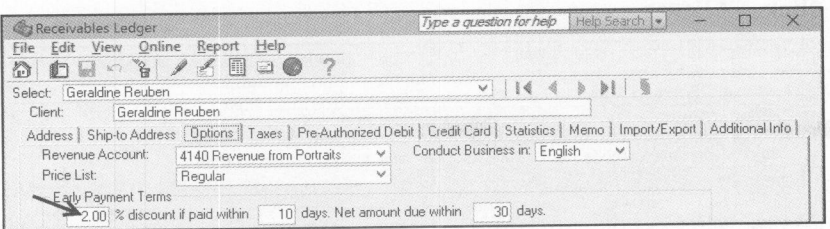

Click   **2.00** in the % Discount field of the Early Payment Terms section.

Press   ⌈del⌉ to remove the entry. **Press** ⌈tab⌉ to advance to the Days field.

Press   ⌈del⌉. **Press** ⌈tab⌉ to advance to the Net Days field. **Type** 1

Click   the **Statistics tab**:

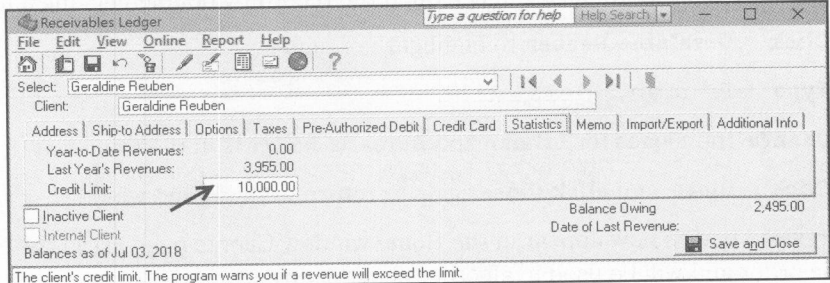

Click the **Credit Limit field** and **type** 0

To modify other customer records, click Next ▶ or Previous ◀ to move to a different record or choose the customer you need from the Select drop-down list. Your previous tab screen will remain selected.

Close   the **Receivables Ledger** and **close** the **Clients window**.

Editing Records from the Setup Guide

Some customer information can be edited for all customers from a single location — the Setup Guide, just as we edited account information in Chapter 4.

Click   the **Home window Setup menu** and **click Setup Guide**:

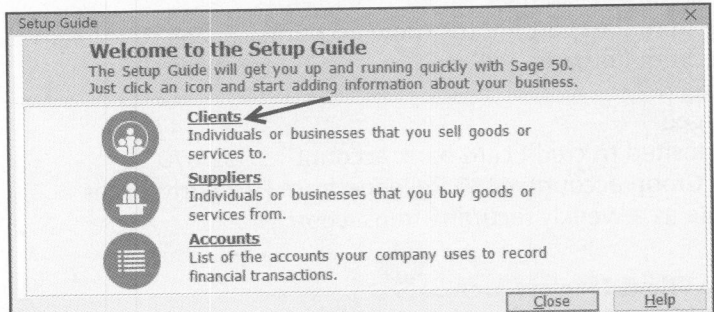

Information for clients, suppliers, accounts and employees (when the Payroll module is used) can be accessed from this guide.

NOTES
Typing zero (0) in the Net Days field will leave the field blank in the ledger and the journal.

NOTES

Similarly, address tab details may be modified for suppliers and employees.

You must open the record to modify other record details — by double-clicking the name, or from the Home window, as we described in the previous section.

NOTES

When you open the Setup Guide Client list again, the edited names will be in the correct alphabetic order.

NOTES

The transaction fee varies from one card company to another, as well as from one retail customer to another, and usually ranges from 2 to 4 percent. Stores that have a larger volume of credit card sales usually pay lower transaction fees.

NOTES

When you recall the entry, you can edit amounts and, if necessary, the accounts. Refer to page 185.

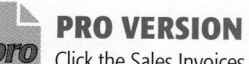

NOTES

Close the message about credit card processing if it opens. Credit card processing is covered in Chapter 13.

Click   **Clients**:

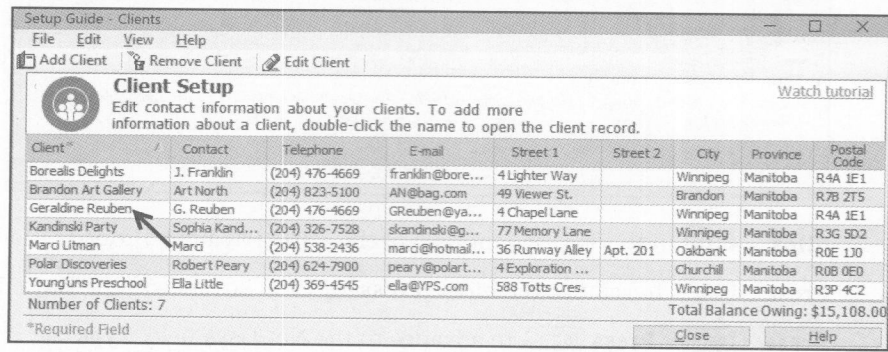

Only information on the Address tab screens for the clients may be edited here. If you need to change other details, you can open the record by double-clicking a name.

Click   **Geraldine Reuben** to highlight her name.

Type   Reuben, Geraldine

Change the **names** for **Litman** and **Borealis Delights** in the same way.

Click   **Close** and **click Close** again to return to the Home window.

The revised names now appear in the Home window Clients pane list in the correct alphabetic order and will be used in all other client listings.

Entering Credit Card Sales

Most businesses accept credit cards from customers in lieu of cash and cheques. Customers expect this convenience, and although businesses benefit by avoiding NSF cheques, they do incur a cost for this service. Credit card companies charge the business a transaction fee: a percentage of each sale is withheld by the card company.

Credit card sales are entered like other sales, by selecting the correct payment method and then entering the invoice details.

✓	**Credit Card Sales Invoice #PS-394**	**Dated July 5/18**
7		

Sales Summary

To various one-time customers

Revenue from Passport Photos (new account)	$ 240.00
Revenue from Portraits	1 600.00
GST charged	92.00
PST charged	147.20
Total deposited to credit card bank account	$2 079.20

Create new Group account: 4160 Revenue from Passport Photos
Store the sale as a weekly recurring transaction.

Click   the **Client Invoices icon** .

Click   the **Payment Method list arrow** and **click Credit Card** to modify the invoice.

As for cash sales, the Net Days field for early payment discounts is removed and a Credit Card Amount field is added. There is no cheque number field for credit cards.

Choose **One-Time Client** from the Client drop-down list.

Type   Sales Summary in the Address text box.

Enter   **July 5** as the transaction date.

Click   the **Item Description field** and **type** the **description** for the first sale item.

Press   ⌊tab⌋ and **type** 240

Press   ⌊tab⌋ **twice** and **type** 4160 as the account. **Press** ⌊tab⌋ to start the Add An Account wizard. **Enter** the **account name** and finish adding the account.

Enter   the **second invoice line details** for the portrait revenue work. **Change** the **default account**. This step will complete the invoice:

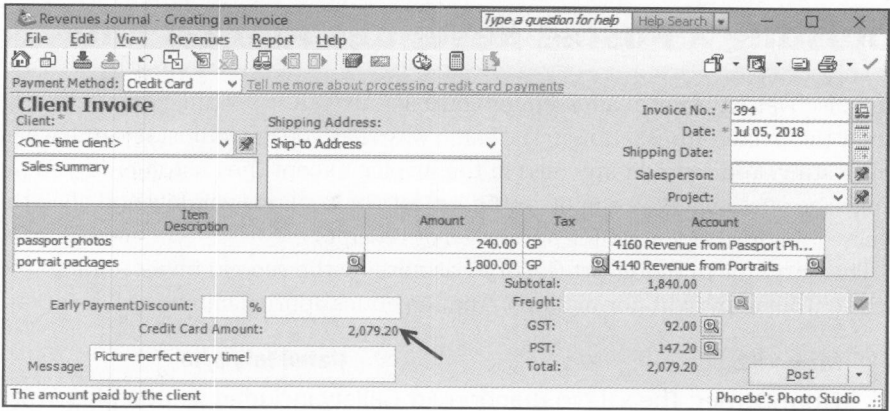

As usual, we will review the journal entry before posting.

Choose   the **Report menu** and **click Display Revenues Journal Entry**:

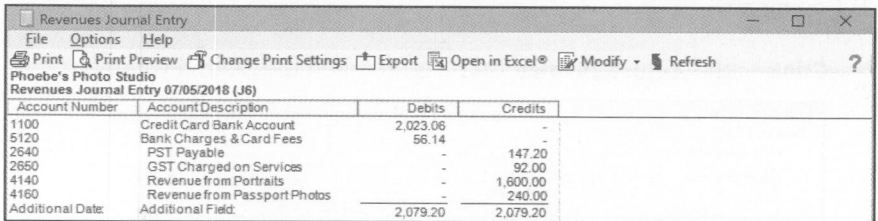

This entry differs from the standard cash sale entry. Instead of *Chequing Account*, the linked *Credit Card Bank Account* is debited for the amount of the deposit, but this is less than the total amount of the sale. The deposit is reduced by the credit card company's transaction fee that is charged to the linked expense account *Bank Charges & Card Fees*. In this case, the credit card company withholds 2.7 percent of each transaction as the fee for using the card. This fee includes the cost to the credit card company for collecting from customers and assuming the risk of non-payment.

Close   the **display** and **make corrections** to the invoice if necessary.

Before posting the transaction, we will store it so that we will not need to re-enter all the details the next time we enter the sales summary transaction.

Storing a Recurring Sales Entry

Completing and storing a recurring entry in the Revenues Journal is similar to storing a General or Purchases Journal entry.

Click   the **Store tool** 🖳 or **choose** the **Sales menu** and **click Store**.

The familiar Store Recurring Transaction window appears with the customer name as the entry name and the default frequency, Monthly, selected. If you want, you can change the entry name to Sales Summary.

> **Click**   **Monthly** to display the frequency options. **Click Weekly** as the frequency.

> **Click**   **OK** to save the entry and return to the Revenues Journal. The Recall button will be available.

> **Click**   Post ▾   to save the journal entry. **Click OK**.

<table>
<tr><td>**NOTES**</td></tr>
</table>

NOTES
If you get a message about credit card processing with Sage Payment Solutions, click Do Not Show This Message Again to close the window. This message may appear when you post the entry or when you close the journal. Credit card processing is covered in Chapter 13.

Adjusting a Posted Revenues Journal Entry

If you discover an error in a Revenues Journal entry after posting it, you can adjust or correct the posted transaction in the same way that you can adjust a purchase invoice after posting. You can edit any field in the invoice except the customer. If you need to change the customer, you can open the Adjust (or Lookup) window and click the Reverse tool, just as you do for purchases or receipts.

The entry for Brandon Art Gallery was missing the second invoice line to record the revenue from copyright permissions. The Revenues Journal should still be open.

✓	**Memo #2**	**Dated July 5/18**
8		

From Owner: The sale to Brandon Art Gallery included $2 000 plus $100 GST and $160 PST for copyright permissions to display artwork on the gallery Web site. The revised and correct invoice total is $7 006. Adjust the posted entry (reference invoice #PS-391). Create new Group revenue account: 4170 Revenue from Copyrights.

> **Click**   the **Adjust Invoice tool** 🗐 to open the Search window:

NOTES
Just as you can choose a specific supplier for purchase invoice adjustments, you can choose a specific customer and click OK to reduce the list of invoices to the selected customer. You can also enter a specific invoice number, journal entry number or amount and click OK to access the invoice directly.

NOTES
If the invoice has already been paid, the program will ask if you want to create a credit note for the customer — a negative invoice. The default source for this invoice will be CN plus the original invoice number, e.g., CN-391, but you can enter a different reference number if you want.

This credit amount can be applied (paid) to other outstanding invoices for the customer.

We demonstrate credit notes in Chapter 10.

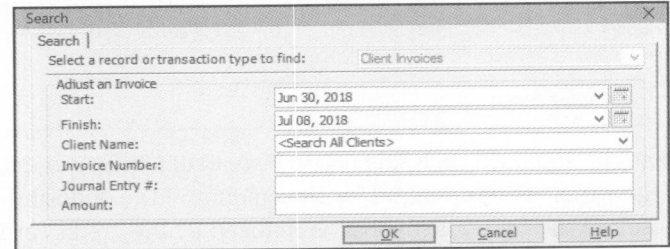

The default date and customer selections will include all invoices.

> **Click**   **OK** to open the Select Entry To Adjust screen:

Date	Client	Invoice #	Journal Entry #	Original Amt
Jul 05, 2018	<One-time client>	394	6	2,079.20
Jul 03, 2018	Marci Litman	393	4	2,373.00
Jul 03, 2018	Kandinski Party	392	3	2,034.00
Jul 01, 2018	Brandon Art Gallery	391	1	4,746.00

All Revenues Journal entries for the selected customers and within the selected date range are listed. You can **view** the list of transactions in order by date, the default selection, or by customer, invoice number, journal entry number or amount. For each view, you can switch between descending and ascending order with the Z...A↑ button. Journal Entry #1 for Brandon Art Gallery is the one we need to edit.

> **Click**   **Brandon Art Gallery**.

To choose an invoice for adjusting, you can click on any part of the line for that invoice to highlight it then click Select, or you can double-click the entry to open the journal immediately.

Click   **Select** to open the invoice. It is ready for editing:

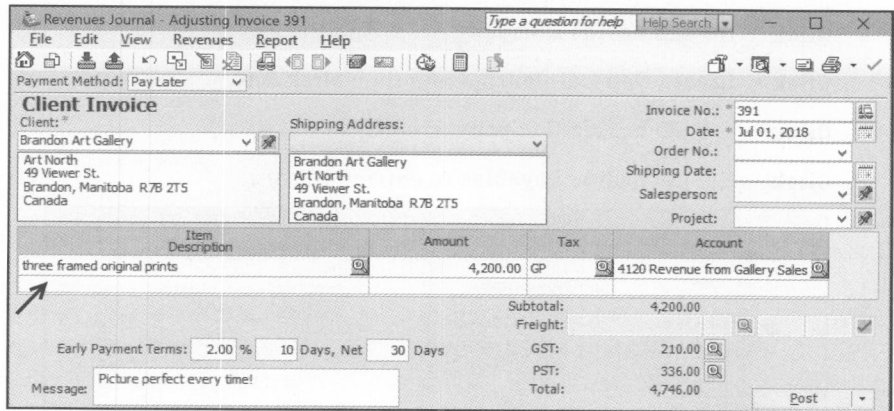

Click   the **Item Description field** on the second line, below the first description.

Type   copyright permissions **Press** (tab) to advance to the Amount field.

Type   2000 **Press** (tab).

The default tax code and revenue account should be entered. You can select or change them if needed. Click the Tax field List icon to open the Tax Code screen and change the selection. We need to change the account.

Click   the **Account field**. **Type**   4170

Press   (tab). **Create** the **new revenue account** when prompted.

Click   the **Message field** and **type**   Revised invoice

As with other adjustments in other journals, this adjustment creates a reversing entry (J7) in addition to the corrected journal entry (J8). You will have all three transactions in the journal reports when you include corrections. You can preview the invoice to ensure that you made the changes correctly.

If you change the customer for an invoice, Sage 50 warns that the name will be changed, but the remaining information (terms, tax codes and so on) will not. If you need to change the customer for a posted invoice, you should reverse the original entry and then create a new invoice for the correct customer. This ensures that the correct customer's settings will apply to the sale.

Review the **entry**. **Close** the **display**. **Make corrections** if necessary.

Post   the **transaction** and then **close** the **Revenues Journal**.

Adding Shortcuts for Other Transactions

Just as we added a shortcut for General Journal entries in Chapter 5, we can add shortcuts for the Payables journals and tasks we will use for Phoebe's Photo Studio. Refer to page 132 if you need help.

NOTES
You can change the invoice number if you want to make the audit trail clearer. For example, you can enter 391-R as the invoice number to identify it as a revised invoice.
If you change the date, only the corrected entry will have the revised date. Remember that changing the date will affect the discount period as well, so change the date only if it is incorrect.

NOTES
To reverse a sale, open the Adjusting Client Invoice (Sale) window and click the Reverse tool. Click Yes to confirm that you want to reverse the sale.

NOTES
Refer to page 162 and Appendix F on the Student DVD for more detail on previewing and printing invoices.

NOTES
The transaction confirmation message tells you that two entries were posted for the adjustment.

PRO VERSION
Add shortcuts for Create General Journal, Create Purchase Invoice, Pay Purchase Invoices, Pay Expenses, View Vendors and View Accounts.

NOTES
Collapsing a list after finishing with it makes it easier to advance to the next ledger heading. Alternatively, you can scroll down the list.

NOTES
You can add more shortcuts if you want. The maximum number is 10 for each user.

NOTES
The View Accounts icon opens the Accounts window.

NOTES
PST paid on purchases is included with the expense or asset part of the purchase because this tax is not refundable. Therefore it is not recorded separately.

| ✓ | **Memo #3** | **Dated July 5/18** |
| 9 | | |

Create shortcuts for tasks and transactions in other modules.

Click   the **Shortcuts tool** ⚙ beside **Shortcuts** in the Shortcuts pane in the Home window.

Click   the ⊞ **beside Company** to expand the list.

Click   **Create General Journal** and then **click Add**.

Click   the ⊟ **beside Company** to collapse this list.

Click   the ⊞ **beside Payables** to expand this list:

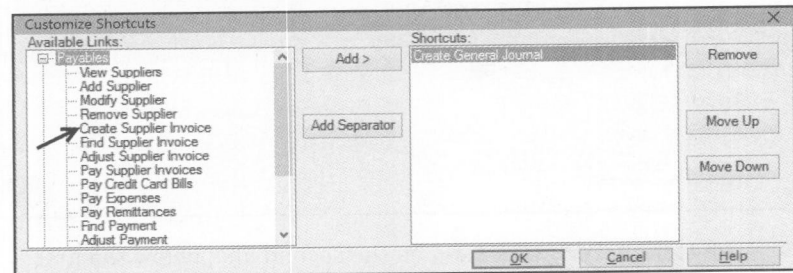

All transactions that are available from the Invoices, Payments and Suppliers drop-down lists can be added as Home window shortcuts. We will add shortcuts for the types of Payables transactions we use most frequently: creating and paying invoices and making other cash purchases (expenses). We will also add a shortcut to View Suppliers so that we can edit supplier records.

Click   **Create Supplier Invoice** and then **click Add**.

Click   **Pay Supplier Invoices** and then **click Add**.

Click   **Pay Expenses** and then **click Add**.

Click   **View Suppliers** and then **click Add**.

Click   the ⊞ **beside Banking** to expand the list.

Click   **View Accounts** and then **click Add**.

Click   **OK** to return to the Home window with your shortcuts added:

These six tasks/windows are now available from any module Home window by clicking the shortcut.

Enter   the **transactions** until the sales summary on July 12.

| | **Payment Cheque #451** | **Dated July 6/18** |
| 10 | | |

To Calm Air, $3 861 in payment of account, including $39 discount for early payment. Reference invoice #CA-224.

| | **Purchase Invoice #RG-3160** | **Dated July 6/18** |
| 11 | | |

From Riverton Garage, $80 for gasoline for van, including taxes (use tax code IN). Terms: net 30.

| | **Purchase Invoice #CA-392** | **Dated July 6/18** |
| 12 | | |

From Calm Air, $1 215 plus $60.75 GST. Invoice total $1 275.75 for return flight to Churchill. Terms: 1/15, n/30. Store as a bi-weekly recurring transaction.

13

Sales Invoice #PS-395   Dated July 7/18

To Polar Discoveries, $2 270 plus $113.50 GST and $181.60 PST for tour customer photographs. Invoice total $2 565.10. Terms: 2/10, n/30.

14

Payment Cheque #452   Dated July 7/18

To Lumber Shed, $1 050 in payment of account. Reference invoice #LS-894. The discount period has expired.

15

Payment Cheque #453   Dated July 7/18

To Riverton Garage, $890 in payment of account. Reference invoice #RG-1904.

16

Purchase Invoice #SPS-4668   Dated July 8/18

From Starlight Photo Solutions, $1 820 plus $91 GST for rolls of large photo paper for gallery prints. Invoice total $1 911. Terms: 2/10, n/30.

17

Sales Invoice #PS-396   Dated July 8/18

To Calm Air (use Full Add for the new customer), $1 900 plus $95 GST and $152 PST for permission to use photographs on Web site. Invoice total $2 147. Terms: 2/10, n/30.

SESSION DATE — JULY 15, 2018

18

Receipt #42   Dated July 9/18

From Litman, Marci, cheque #29 for $2 325.54, including $47.46 discount for early payment of invoice #PS-393.

19

Sales Invoice #PS-397   Dated July 9/18

To Kandinski Party, $4 600 plus $230 GST and $368 PST for wedding photo package with DVD. Invoice total $5 198. Terms: 2/10, n/30. Create new revenue account: 4150 Revenue from Weddings. Allow the customer to exceed the credit limit.

20

Receipt #43   Dated July 10/18

From Brandon Art Gallery, cheque #28874 for $6 865.88 in full payment of invoice #PS-391 with $140.12 discount for early payment.

21

Receipt #44   Dated July 11/18

From Reuben, Geraldine, certified cheque #302 for $2 495 in full payment of account to replace NSF cheque. Reference invoices #PS-377 and #PS-381.

Recalling a Stored Sales Entry

The procedures for recalling and changing a stored entry are the same for all journals.

22 ✓

Credit Card Sales Invoice #PS-398   Dated July 12/18

Sales Summary
To various one-time customers

Passport photos	$ 130.00
Portraits	1 200.00
GST charged	66.50
PST charged	106.40
Total deposited to credit card bank account	$1 502.90

Recall the stored transaction.

NOTES

Calm Air
(contact Arie Fliegel)
50 Jett Ave.
Winnipeg, MB R2P 1S7
Tel: (800) 839-2256
Fax: (204) 476-5110
E-mail: af@calmair.com
Web site: calmair.com
Revenue account: 4170
Terms: 2/10, n/30
Tax code: GP
Credit limit: $8 000

NOTES

Remember to change the amounts when you recall the sales summary.

NOTES

You can store the changed sales summary if you want. In this case, you should confirm that you are replacing the previous stored transaction.

Click	the **Client Invoices** (Sales or Sales Invoices) **icon** [Client Invoices ▾] to open the Revenues Journal.	

Click the **Recall tool** [icon] or **choose** the **Revenues menu** and **click Recall** to display the Recall Recurring Transaction window.

Click the **transaction** you want to use. **Click Select** to display a copy of the entry previously posted.

Edit the **amounts** as needed.

The default date is entered according to the frequency selected. The payment method is still selected as Credit Card. The invoice number is updated automatically, so the entry is complete.

Review the **entry** to be certain that it is correct. **Click** [Post ▾] to save it.

When you make changes to a stored entry, Sage 50 warns that posting the entry may affect the next due date. This warning appears if you have made any changes to the entry before posting, although the message mentions only the date.

Click **Yes** to accept the change and post. **Click OK** to confirm posting.

Enter the **remaining transactions** for July.

---

[23] **Bank Debit Memo #29321** **Dated July 15/18**

From Red River Credit Union, cheque #29 for $2 325.54 from Litman has been returned because of non-sufficient funds. Reverse the payment and notify the customer of the outstanding charges. Edit the customer's terms to net 1 and change her credit limit to zero.

---

[24] **Cash Purchase Invoice #UPS-6101** **Dated July 15/18**

From UPS Delivery, $380 for courier delivery of photographs to clients plus $19 GST. Invoice total $399. Issued cheque #454 in full payment.

---

[25] **Purchase Invoice #CA-487** **Dated July 15/18**

From Calm Air, $1 215 plus $60.75 GST. Invoice total $1 275.75 for return flight to Churchill. Terms: 1/15, n/30. Recall the stored entry, edit the date and then store it as a weekly recurring transaction. Replace the previous stored transaction.

SESSION DATE — JULY 22, 2018

[26] **Payment Cheque #455** **Dated July 17/18**

To Starlight Photo Solutions, $1 872.78 in payment of account, including $38.22 discount for early payment. Reference invoice #SPS-4668.

---

[27] **Purchase Invoice #WE-56691** **Dated July 18/18**

From Web Exposure, $3 100 plus $155 GST and $248 PST for redesigning Web site with updated text and photos. Invoice total $3 503. Terms: net 15.

---

[28] **Cash Purchase Invoice #SBD-4821** **Dated July 19/18**

From Staples Business Depot (use Full Add for the new supplier), $60 plus $3.00 GST and $4.80 PST for stationery and office supplies. Invoice total $67.80. Paid by cheque #456.

---

[29] **Payment Cheque #457** **Dated July 19/18**

To Calm Air, $1 262.99 in payment of account, including $12.76 discount for early payment. Reference invoice #CA-392.

30

Phoebe's Photo Studio
phoebephoto.com

100 Light Street, Suite 202
Winnipeg, MB R2T 7G4
Phone: (204) 649-3358   Toll free: (888) 649-3358   Fax: (204) 642-4967

Invoice:	PS-399
Date:	July 19, 2018
Sold to:	Borealis Mysteries
	(J. Franklin)
	4 Lighter Way
	Winnipeg, MB R4A 1E1

Description	Tax Code	Amount
Photographs of tour customers	GP	1 140.00

bi-weekly recurring sale:

Picture perfect every time!

Payment Terms: 2/10, net 30	Customer Initials	GST	57.00
		PST	91.20
GST #296 654 590	*JF*	TOTAL	1 288.20

31

Phoebe's Photo Studio
phoebestudio.com

100 Light Street, Suite 202
Winnipeg, MB R2T 7G4
Phone: (204) 649-3358   Toll free: (888) 649-3358   Fax: (204) 642-4967

Invoice:	PS-400
Date:	July 19, 2018
Sold to:	Sales Summary

Description	Tax Code	Amount
Passport photos	GP	180.00
Portrait packages	GP	1 400.00

Deposited to credit card bank account
July 19/18

Picture perfect every time!

Payment Terms: Credit Card	Customer Initials	GST	79.00
		PST	126.40
Business No.: 296 654 590		TOTAL	1 785.40

NOTES
Remember to change the amounts when you recall the sales summary.

Sales Invoice #PS-401   **Dated July 21/18**

32

To Polar Discoveries, $2 270 plus $113.50 GST and $181.60 PST for tour customer photographs. Invoice total $2 565.10. Terms: 2/10, n/30.

Purchase Invoice #CA-598   **Dated July 22/18**

33

From Calm Air, $1 215 plus $60.75 GST. Invoice total $1 275.75 for return flight to Churchill. Terms: 1/15, n/30. Recall the stored entry.

Purchase Invoice #RG-5619   **Dated July 22/18**

34

From Riverton Garage, $85 including taxes for gasoline. Terms: net 30.

35

Borealis Mysteries
4 Lighter Way
Winnipeg, MB R4A 1E1

No: 18963

Date 2018 07 22
     Y Y Y Y M M D D

Pay to the order of   Phoebe's Photo Studio $ 1262.44

—— One thousand two hundred sixty-two dollars ——————— 44/100 Dollars

RR Red River Credit Union
389 Prairie Blvd.
Winnipeg MB R2P 1B6

                                                    Signature

⑈⑈—— 92999⑈⑈ 16883 18963

Re: pay invoice #PS-399 $1262.44   No: 18963
     includes $25.76 discount (receipt #45)   July 22, 2018

SESSION DATE – JULY 31, 2018

Purchase Invoice #SPS-5936   **Dated July 25/18**

36

From Starlight Photo Solutions, $310 plus $15.50 GST for developing solutions and $420 plus $21 GST and $33.60 PST for camera repairs. Invoice total $800.10. Terms: 2/10, n/30. Create new Group expense account: 5180 Repair Expenses.

NOTES
Change the default account to 1300 for the developing solutions and apply tax code GP for the repair expenses.

37

Calm Air
50 Jett Ave.
Winnipeg, MB R2P 1S7
Tel: (800) 839-2256

RR Red River Credit Union
389 Prairie Blvd.
Winnipeg MN R2P 1B6

No: 2910

Date 2018 07 26
     Y Y Y Y M M D D

Pay —— Two thousand one hundred forty-seven dollars —— 00 —— $ 2,147.00

TO THE ORDER OF   Phoebe's Photo Studio
100 Light St. Suite 202
Winnipeg, MB R2T 7G4

PER Ariel F lugel

⑈⑈—— 92999⑈⑈ 46771 2910

Re: pay invoice #PS-396 $2,147   No: 2910
     (receipt #46)   July 26, 2018

38 | **Payment Cheque #458** | **Dated July 26/18**

To Starlight Photo Solutions, $400 in partial payment of account. No discount is allowed on the partial payment. Reference invoice #SPS-5936.

39 | **Cash Purchase Invoice #MT-421576** | **Dated July 26/18**

From Manitoba Telephone, $190 plus $9.50 GST and $15.20 PST for telephone and Internet service. Invoice total $214.70. Paid by cheque #459.

40 | **Cash Purchase Invoice #MH-66832** | **Dated July 26/18**

From Manitoba Hydro, $180 plus $9 GST for hydro for two studios. Invoice total $189. Paid by cheque #460.

41 | **Credit Card Sales Invoice #PS-402** | **Dated July 26/18**

Sales Summary
To various one-time customers

Passport photos	$ 130.00
Portraits	1 200.00
GST charged	66.50
PST charged	106.40
Total deposited to credit card bank account	$1 502.90

Recall the stored transaction.

NOTES
Remember to change the amounts when you recall the sales summary.

42 | **Purchase Invoice #CA-622** | **Dated July 29/18**

From Calm Air, $1 215 plus $60.75 GST. Invoice total $1 275.75 for return flight to Churchill. Terms: 1/15, n/30. Recall the stored entry.

43 | **Receipt #47** | **Dated July 29/18**

From Polar Discoveries, cheque #43692 for $1 200 in partial payment of invoice #PS-395.

44 | **Sales Invoice #PS-403** | **Dated July 30/18**

To Borealis Mysteries, $1 800 plus $90 GST and $144 PST for tour customer photographs. Invoice total $2 034. Terms: 2/10, n/30. Recall the stored entry and edit the date and amount. Store the revised entry.

45 | **Bank Credit Memo #55131** | **Dated July 30/18**

From Red River Credit Union, $4 000 six-month loan at 7% interest for new dichroic enlarger approved and deposited to bank account.

46 | **Bank Debit Memo #61821** | **Dated July 30/18**

From Red River Credit Union, pre-authorized monthly payroll for assistant.

Wages and payroll expenses	$3 000.00
Payroll services fee	30.00
GST paid on payroll service	1.50
Total withdrawal	$3 031.50

47 | **Memo #4** | **Dated July 31/18**

From Owner: Create new Group expense account for supplies used during the month: 5145 Darkroom Supplies Used. Enter adjustments for supplies used:

Framing supplies	$510
Photo paper & supplies	480
Darkroom supplies	290
Office & other supplies	140

Bank Debit Memo #62002   **Dated July 31/18**

From Red River Credit Union, pre-authorized withdrawals for service charges, mortgage and loan payments.

Bank charges, including NSF cheques	$ 135
Interest expense	1 120
Loan principal repayment	1 040
Mortgage principal repayment	920

Displaying Client/Customer Reports

Client (or customer) reports can be accessed at any time from the Home or the Clients window, or from the Report Centre.

Click the Clients icon to open the Clients window.

The Clients window Reports menu now contains only client reports. Select the report you want from this list and follow the instructions below to choose report options. You can also obtain all client (customer) reports from the Home window **Reports menu**.

In the Receivables module Home window, the **Reports pane** includes all the customer reports in the drop-down list. Opening the reports from this list will display them immediately with the default settings. Clicking Client List expands the report list:

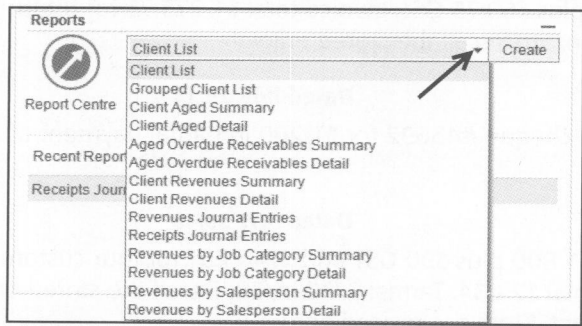

We will continue to work from the Report Centre so that we include the sample reports, descriptions and report options on the screen.

Click   the **Report Centre icon** ▢ in the Home window.

The Receivables reports are listed because we started from the Receivables window. The sample and description for Client List, the first report, are displayed:

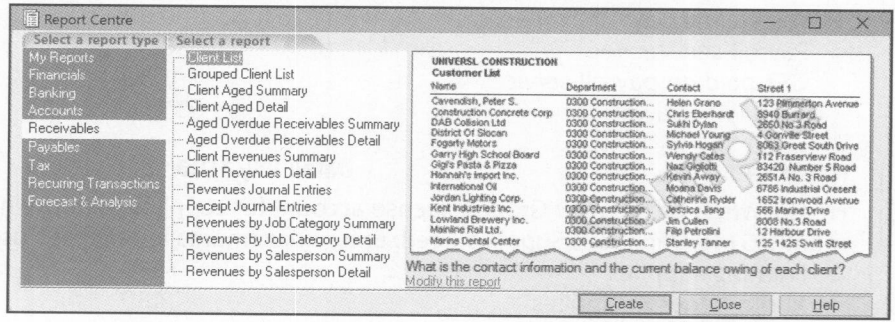

If you click Receivables in the Select A Report Type list, you will display the general description for Receivables reports.

*Sidebar notes:*

Displaying Client/Customer Lists

Click   **Client List** in the Select A Report list to open the sample report and its description.

Click   **Modify This Report** to open the report options:

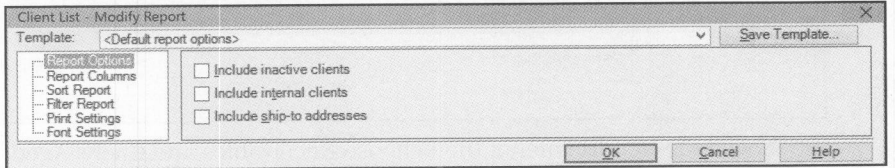

Or, choose the Reports menu, then choose Lists and Clients.

You can include or omit inactive and internal customers, and shipping addresses. You can sort and filter Client Lists by any of the fields selected for the report. You can select customer record fields by customizing the Report Columns. You can also sort the columns directly in the report. For example, if you want to list customers in order according to the amount they owe, with the largest balance reported first, click the Balance column heading to sort the report by balance. Then click the heading again to reverse the order.

Click   **OK. Close** the **display** when you have finished viewing it.

Displaying Grouped Client Lists

The Grouped Client List organizes clients by a specific criterion. You could use this list to prepare customer contact lists for salespersons in different regions.

Click   **Grouped Client List** in the Select A Report list to open the sample report and its description.

Click   **Modify This Report** to open the report options.

Click   the **list arrow for the Group By field**:

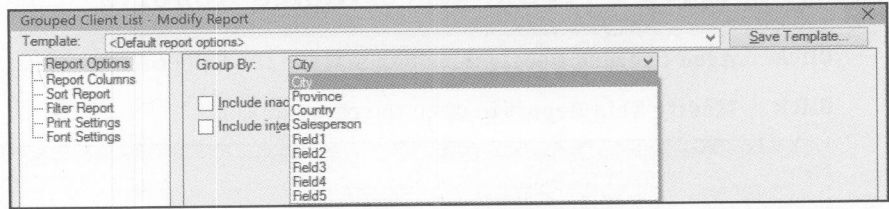

The criteria you can use to group the customers are displayed.

Choose the **grouping criterion** you want. **Click OK** to display the report.

Close   the **display** when you have finished viewing it.

Displaying Client Aged Reports

Click   **Client Aged Summary** in the Select A Report list to open the sample report and its description.

CLASSIC VIEW
From the Home window, right-click the Clients icon. Click , the Select A Report tool.

NOTES
You can drill down to the Client Aged Report from the Client List.

PRO VERSION
The options to Include Ship-to Address and Internal Clients are not available.

NOTES
Field1, Field2 and so on are extra fields you define for the company that appear on the Additional Information tab screens of customer records.

NOTES
You can drill down to look up invoices and to the Client Ledger from the Client Aged Detail Report. From the Summary Report you can drill down to the Detail Report.

Click   Modify This Report to open the report options:

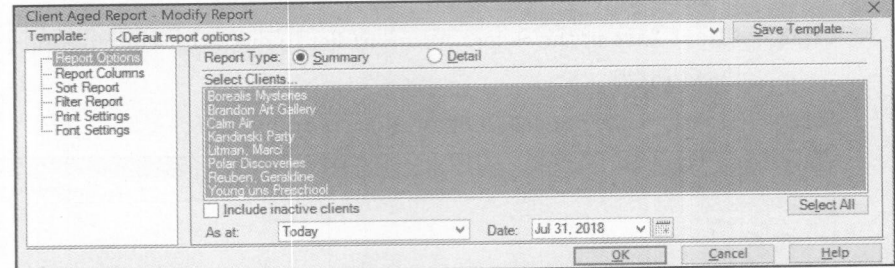

Or, choose the Reports menu, then choose Receivables and Client Aged.

New customers you entered using Quick Add will appear on the list of customers in the report options windows. Sales for one-time customers and customers for whom you chose the Continue option will not appear because these cash transactions did not create a ledger record or an entry for *Accounts Receivable*.

The **Summary** option will display an alphabetic list of the selected customers with outstanding total balances owing, organized into the aging periods columns set up for the company. The **Detail** option will include all the invoices and payments made by customers for a period up to 999 days. The current balance owing and unpaid invoices are always included. This more descriptive report is also aged and can be used to make credit decisions. You can add payment terms to the Detail Report. You can choose any columns in the report and sort and filter by name and balance owing to customize the Client Aged Report.

NOTES
The Client Aged and Aged Overdue Detail Reports are also available directly from the Select A Report list for Receivables in the Report Centre.

Click   Detail to include details for individual transactions.

Enter   the **date** for the report or accept the default session date.

Press   and **hold** `ctrl` and **click** the **client names**. **Click Select All** to include all customers or remove them when they are all selected.

Click   OK to open the report. **Close** the **displayed report** when finished.

Displaying Aged Overdue Receivables Reports

Click   Aged Overdue Receivables Summary in the Select A Report list.

NOTES
You can drill down to look up invoices and to the Client Aged Report from the Aged Overdue Receivables Detail Report. From the Summary Report you can drill down to the Detail Report.

Click   Modify This Report to open the report options:

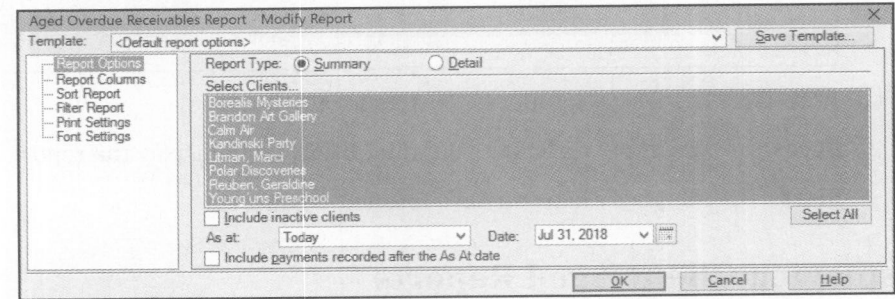

From the Home window, choose the Reports menu, then Receivables and then click Aged Overdue Receivables.

Enter   the **date** for the report, or accept the default session date.

NOTES
You can use name and balance owing as the criteria for sorting and filtering the Aged Overdue Receivables reports and you can choose any of the columns in the report.

The **Summary** option will display an alphabetic list of the selected customers with outstanding total balances owing, organized into aging periods, with an additional column for the overdue amount. Individual invoices, due dates, payments, overdue amounts and the balance owing for the selected customers are added when you choose

the **Detail** Report. Selecting **Include Payments Recorded After The As At Date** will add postdated receipts to the report and not count these clients as having overdue amounts.

Click	**Detail** if you want to include the invoice details.
Enter	the **date** for the report, or accept the default session date.
Press	and **hold** `ctrl` and **click** the appropriate **names** in the client list. **Click Select All** to include all customers or remove them all.
Click	**OK** to open the report. **Close** the **displayed report** when finished.

Displaying the Client Revenues Report

Click	**Client Revenues Summary** in the Select A Report list to open the sample report and its description.
Click	**Modify This Report** to open the report options:

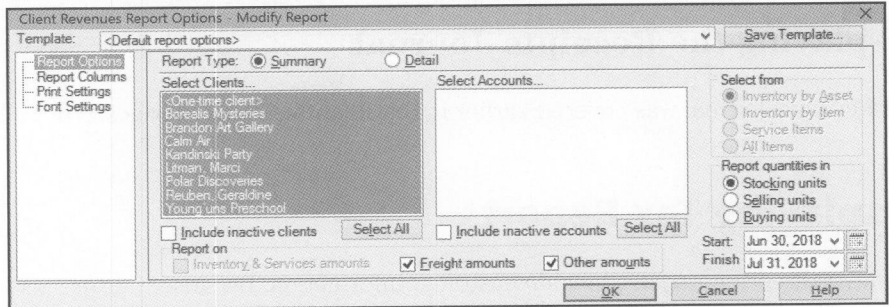

Or, choose the Reports menu and Receivables and click Client Revenues.

In this report, you can display the total number of transactions and the total sales for each customer (in the **Summary** Report) or the individual sales invoice amounts (in the **Detail** Report). The Detail Report also includes journal details (date, source, journal entry number and revenue amounts) for each transaction. Only the Other Amounts and Freight Amounts are available when the inventory module is not set up. When inventory items are set up, you can display the sales for these items as well. This report will be introduced again with inventory in Chapter 10. The earliest transaction and session date provide the default date range. You can select the customers to include.

Click	**Detail** if you want to include the invoice details.
Press	and **hold** `ctrl` and **click** the appropriate **names** in the customer list. **Click Select All** to include all customers or remove the entire selection.
Enter	the **Start** and **Finish dates** for the report.
Click	**OK** to open the report. **Close** the **displayed report** when finished.

Displaying the Revenues (Sales) Journal

Click	**Revenues Journal Entries** in the Select A Report list. **Click Modify This Report** to open the report options:

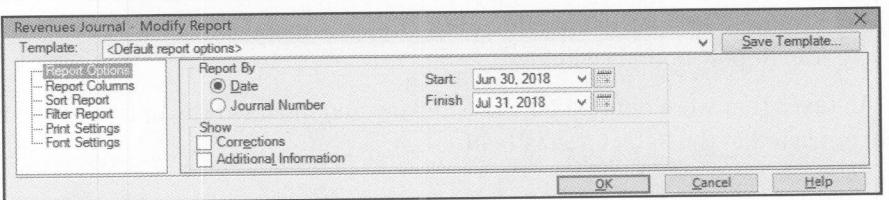

NOTES
Invoices with postdated receipts are deemed to be paid, and can, therefore, be omitted from the report.

PRO VERSION
Click Customer Sales Summary to open this report.

NOTES
You can drill down to the Journal Report and the Client Aged Report and look up the invoice from the Client Sales Detail Report. From the Summary Report you can drill down to the Detail Report.

NOTES
Each sales invoice line in the Detail Client Revenues Report is counted as one transaction for this report. For Brandon Art Gallery, four transactions are counted, the final two invoice lines, the original one we adjusted, and its reversing entry.

PRO VERSION
Click Sales Journal Entries to access the report.

CLASSIC VIEW

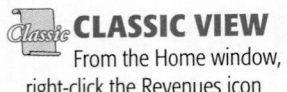

From the Home window, right-click the Revenues icon

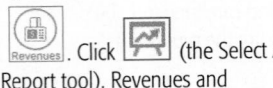

. Click (the Select A Report tool). Revenues and Receipts Journal reports are also available from the Select A Report list when you click the Select A Report tool button if no icon is selected in the Home window.

NOTES

You can drill down to an invoice, to the Client Aged Report and to the General Ledger Report from the Revenues and the Receipts Journal reports. You can also look up the original journal transaction window.

NOTES

To include all journal entries in a single report, choose the Reports menu, then choose Journals and click All. Enter June 30 and July 31 in the Start and Finish date fields if these are not the default entries.

From the Report Centre, you can choose Financials and then All Journal Entries to include all transactions in a single report.

PRO VERSION

The terms Sales and Purchases replace Revenues and Expenses.

NOTES

You can sort and filter tax reports by taxable amounts for purchases and sales including or excluding taxes, taxes paid/charged, other taxes paid/charged and total amounts including taxes.

No drill-down reports are available from tax reports.

From the Home window, choose the Reports menu, then choose Journal Entries and click Revenues (Sales) for the report options.

You can select Revenues Journal entries by posting date or by journal entry number. We use the default setting, By Date, for all reports in this workbook, so leave the selection unchanged. You can include **corrections** (adjusting and reversing entries) or omit them.

You can sort and filter journal reports by Date, Journal No., Source and Comment. You can choose account, description, debits and credits columns for the reports.

Enter the **beginning date** for the journal transactions you want. Or, choose a date from the list arrow selections.

Press ⌜tab⌝ **twice**. **Enter** the **ending date** for the transaction period.

Click **Corrections** to provide a complete audit trail.

Click **OK** to view the report. **Close** the **display** when you have finished.

Displaying the Receipts Journal

The Receipts Journal was covered earlier in this chapter. Refer to pages 176–177.

Displaying Tax Reports

The next three reports also include customer information. Because they are accessed from the Report Centre, they are included before the final customer reports that are accessed from the Home window Reports menu.

Tax reports provide the taxable purchases and sales with and without tax amounts included, the taxes paid or charged on each transaction and the totals.

Click **Tax** in the Select A Report Type list to open the list of tax reports:

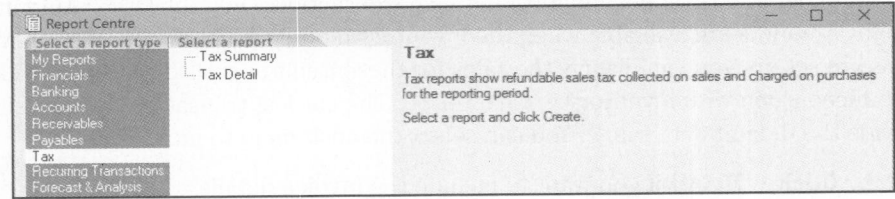

Click **Tax Summary** to display a sample report and description.

Click **Modify This Report** to display the Tax Report options window:

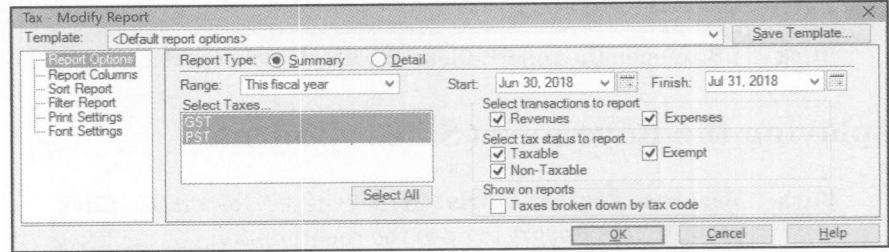

From the Home window, choose the Reports menu and click Tax to display the Tax Report options window.

All taxes that were defined for the company and included the option to report on them are listed in the **Select Taxes** field.

The earliest transaction and the session date are entered as the default date range for the report. You can include either transactions for revenues or expenses (sales or purchases) that include tax or for both. Both purchases and sales are reported by default for all taxes. In addition, the report can include taxable, exempt and non-taxable transactions. By default all are selected. You can also organize the report by **tax codes**.

The **Summary** Report has only the totals for each category selected while the **Detail** Report lists individual transactions for each category. You can include the total tax amounts for each tax code as well.

The reports include a column for **Other Taxes**. For the GST, this column has the PST related to the sale or purchase; for the PST, this column has the GST related to the sale or purchase.

Click   **Detail** to select the more detailed level for the report.

Enter   or **choose** the **dates** for which you want the report to start and finish.

Click   a **tax name** in the Select Tax list to change the selection.

Click   the **transactions** (Revenues or Expenses) to remove a ✓ or to add one if it is not there to include the transaction in the report.

Click   a **transaction tax status** (Taxable, Exempt or Non-Taxable) to remove a ✓ or to add one if it is not there.

Click   **Taxes Broken Down By Tax Code** to add this option to your report.

Once you have selected the options you want,

Click   **OK** to view the report. **Close** the **display** when you have finished.

Displaying Cash Flow Reports

Displaying the Statement of Cash Flows

The Statement of Cash Flows summarizes sources (income, investments, etc.) and uses (purchase of assets, etc.) of cash and changes in liabilities during the designated period.

Click   **Financials** in the Select A Report Type list to open the list of reports:

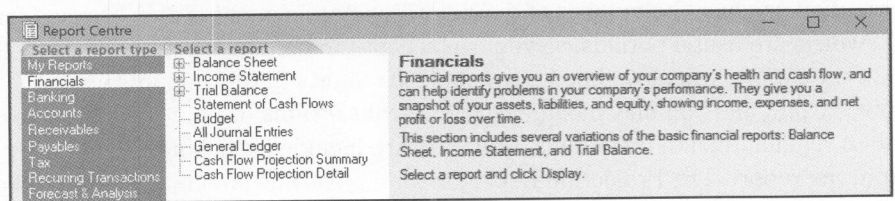

Click   **Statement Of Cash Flows** to display a sample report and description.

Click   **Modify This Report** to display the Modify Report window:

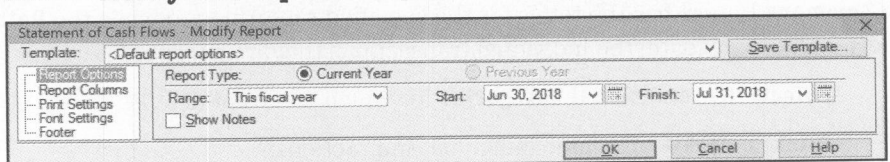

From the Home window, choose the Reports menu, then choose Financials and click Statement Of Cash Flows for the report options.

Enter   the **Start** and **Finish dates** for the report. The fiscal start and session dates are the defaults.

NOTES
You cannot sort or filter the Statement of Cash Flows or the Cash Flow Projection Report, but you can choose report columns.

NOTES
You can drill down to the General Ledger from the Statement of Cash Flows.

Click   **OK** to view the report.

By organizing the transactions involving cash, net changes in cash positions, as well as changes in liabilities, the statement allows the owner to judge how efficiently cash is being used for the business. The owner can also judge whether potential problems will result from increases in liabilities or decreases in the collection of receivables.

Close   the **display** when you have finished.

Displaying Cash Flow Projection Reports

Cash Flow Projection reports predict the flow of cash in and out of an account — usually a bank account — over a specific future period based on current information.

Click   **Cash Flow Projection Summary** to display a sample report and description. **Click Modify This Report** to display report options:

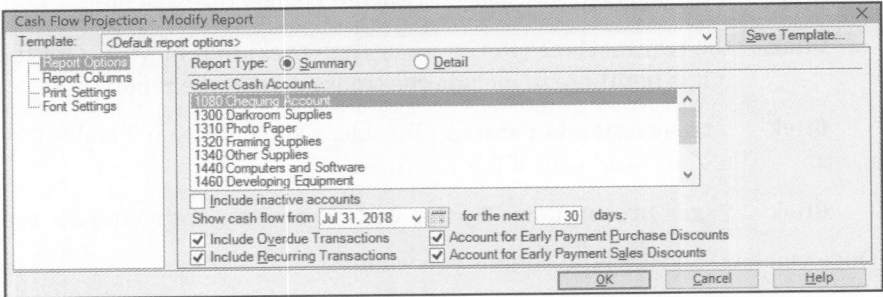

From the Home window, choose the Reports menu, then choose Financials and click Cash Flow Projection for the report options.

Click   **1080 Chequing Account** or the account for which you want the report.

Click   the **Date field**. **Type** the **date** at which you want the projection to start.

Press   tab **twice** to advance past the Calendar icon.

Enter   the **number of days** in the future for which the report should project the cash flow.

Usually, you will include only the number of days for which you have reasonable information, such as the number of days in which net payment is due. The session date and 30 days are useful periods, so you can accept the defaults.

In the report, you may choose to include **discounts** in the amounts you expect to receive or pay, and you may include **overdue transactions** or omit them if you expect them to remain unpaid. By default, all details are included. Clicking a detail will remove it from the report. The Projection Report assumes overdue amounts will be paid and all other amounts will be paid on the invoice due date.

The report projects the account balance based on receivables and payables due and **recurring transactions** coming due within the time frame specified, if you include these. The **Summary** Report has the totals for the specified report period while the **Detail** Report includes, by date, the individual transactions that are expected.

Select   the **additional categories** for which you want details.

Click   **Detail** to include individual transactions.

Click   **OK** to view the report.

Close   the **display**. **Close** the **Report Centre** to return to the Home window.

NOTES
You might want to compare projection reports prepared with and without some of these extra details.

Printing Client Reports

Display the **report** you want to print.

Click   the **Change Print Settings tool** 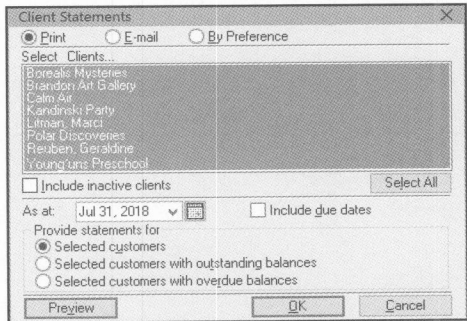 to check that you have the correct printer selected. **Click OK** to return to the report.

Click   the **Print tool** 🖨 or **choose** the **File menu** in the report window, and then **click Print**.

Close   the **display** when you have finished.

Printing Client Statements

You can e-mail all customer statements or print them, or you can choose e-mail and print on a customer-by-customer basis according to the setting (preference) in the customer's ledger record Options tab screen (refer to page 173). You can also choose to print statements only for those customers that have outstanding or overdue balances.

Choose the **Reports menu** in the Home window, then **choose Receivables** and **click Client Statements**.

The customer list with statement options opens:

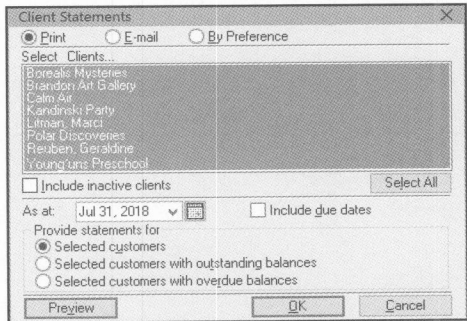

You can select some or all customers, only customers with outstanding balances or only customers with overdue amounts.

You should preview statements before printing them.

Press   and **hold** ⌈ctrl⌋ and **click** the **clients** for whom you want to print statements, or **click Select All** to include all clients.

Enter   the **date** for the statements.

Click   **Include Due Dates** if you want to add the payment due dates for invoices, and **click Preview**.

Click   **OK** to close the preview and return to the options screen.

Click   **OK** again to print the statements.

Printing Client Mailing Labels

You should turn on the printer, insert labels paper and set the program for printing labels before choosing the options for the labels, because printing begins immediately.

Choose the Setup menu in the Home window and click Reports & Forms. Click Labels. Enter the details for the labels. Click OK.

PRO VERSION
Your only options are to print mailing addresses or shipping addresses.

Choose the **Reports menu** in the Home window, then **choose Mailing Labels** and **click Clients** for the printing options:

You can print labels for business mailing addresses, for shipping addresses or for any address list you created.

Press and **hold** <kbd>ctrl</kbd> and **click** the **clients** for whom you want to print the labels, or **click Select All** to include all customers. **Click OK**.

R E V I E W

The Student DVD with Data Files includes Review Questions and Supplementary Cases for this chapter.

AirCare Services

OBJECTIVES

After completing this chapter, you should be able to

- **plan** and **design** an accounting system for a small business
- **prepare** procedures for converting from a manual system
- **understand** the objectives of a computerized system
- **create** company files
- **create** and **understand** linked accounts
- **set up** accounts in the General, Payables and Receivables ledgers
- **enter** historical information for suppliers and customers
- **correct** historical transactions after recording them
- **set up** credit cards for receipts and payments
- **set up** sales taxes and tax codes
- **leave** history in an unbalanced state
- **finish** entering history after entering journal transactions
- **enter** postdated transactions

COMPANY INFORMATION

Company Profile

NOTES
Air Care Services
100 Belair Avenue, Unit 25
Regina, SK S4T 4U2
Tel 1: (306) 456-1299
Tel 2: (888) 455-7194
Fax: (306) 456-3188
Business No.: 533 766 455

Air Care Services, located in sunny Regina, Saskatchewan, has been operating successfully for the past 15 years under the ownership and management of Simon Arturro. After his mechanical engineering education and several years' experience with heating installations, he became a certified installer of solar electrical panels. As more consumers are eager to rely less on fossil fuels as their source of power, the demand for solar energy is steadily increasing. Arturro has two assistants: a certified electrician and an assistant installer.

Revenue comes from four sources: installation of new units, repairs, service contracts and subcontracting. Most jobs are new installations, either for individual customers or subcontracts for building projects. Small and medium-sized home roof installation jobs are usually finished in two to four days. Repair work, outside of the service contracts, may include removing and replacing the panels when customers

are replacing a roof. Arturro also offers annual service contracts that provide free labour for existing installations.

Some customers — homeowners, owners of office buildings and builders — have accounts with Air Care and receive a 1 percent discount if they pay within 10 days. They are asked to settle their accounts in 30 days, paying by cash or by cheque. PST and GST apply to all work completed by Air Care.

Accounts have been set up with a local hardware store, with suppliers of solar panels and inverters (units that convert the solar DC power to AC) and other regular suppliers.

After remitting all taxes before the end of March 2018, Arturro converted the accounts for Air Care using the following information:

- Business Information
- Chart of Accounts
- Income Statement
- Balance Sheet
- Trial Balance
- Supplier Information
- Customer Information
- Accounting Procedures

BUSINESS INFORMATION

AIR CARE SERVICES

COMPANY INFORMATION
Address: 100 Belair Avenue, Unit 25
                Regina, Saskatchewan S4T 4U2
Telephone 1: (306) 456-1299
Telephone 2: (888) 455-7194
Fax: (306) 456-3188
Business No.: 533 766 455 RT0001
Fiscal Start: January 1, 2018
Fiscal End: June 30, 2018
Earliest Transaction: March 31, 2018
Company Type: Construction/Contractor

REPORTS & FORMS
Choose settings for your printer and forms

USER PREFERENCES
Options
    Use Accounting Terms
    Automatically Save Changes to Records
    Show List Buttons
    Calculate Record Balances in Home Window
        by Session Date
    Automatic download of updates: off

View Settings
    Hide: Inventory & Services, Employees &
        Payroll, Job Sites, Time & Billing
    Daily Business Manager: turn off
    Checklists: turn off
    Show Session Date at Startup

Transaction Confirmation: turned on

Pop-Ups: your preferences

COMPANY SETTINGS
System
    Do not allow dates before March 31, 2018
    Allow Future Transactions,
        Warn If Transactions Are 7 Days In Future
    Warn If Accounts Are Not Balanced

Backup
    Backup Weekly; Display reminders
    Turn off scheduled backup

Features
    Do not use orders, quotes, packing slips &
        projects (job sites)
    Use both French and English

Credit Card Information
    Card Used: Visa
    Payable Account: 2160
    Expense Account: 5020

    Card Accepted: Visa
    Discount Fee: 2.9%
    Expense Account: 5020
    Asset Account: 1070

    Card Accepted: MasterCard
    Discount Fee: 2.7%
    Expense Account: 5020
    Asset Account: 1080

Sales Taxes
    Taxes: GST; PST
    Codes: G - GST @ 5%;
        GP - GST @ 5%, PST @ 5%,
        non-refundable

Forms Settings (Next Number)
    Sales Invoices   No. 710
    Receipts   No. 20

Date Format
    Short Date Format: MM dd yyyy
    On The Screen Use long Dates

Logo: SageData16\LOGOS\AIRCARE.BMP

GENERAL SETTINGS: No changes

PAYABLES SETTINGS
Address: Regina, Saskatchewan, Canada
Options
    Aging Periods: 10, 30, 60 days
    Discounts Before Tax: Yes

RECEIVABLES SETTINGS
Address: Regina, Saskatchewan, Canada
Options
    Aging Periods: 10, 30, 60 days
    Interest Charges: compound, 1.5% monthly
                        rate, after 1 day
    Statements: Include Invoices for 31 days
    New Customer Tax Code: GP

Discounts
    Payment Terms: 1/10, n/30 after tax
    Discounts Before Tax: No
    Line Discounts: No

Comments
    Sales Invoice: Interest @ 1.5% per month
        charged on accounts over 30 days

BANK ACCOUNTS: NEXT CHEQUE NO.
    Bank: Chequing   101

CHART OF ACCOUNTS

AIR CARE SERVICES

ASSETS

1000	CURRENT ASSETS [H]
1010	Test Balance Account
1060	Bank: Chequing [A]
1070	Bank: Visa [A]
1080	Bank: MasterCard [A]
1100	Net Bank [S]
1200	Accounts Receivable
1210	Prepaid Insurance
1300	Solar Panels
1310	Inverters
1320	Electrical Supplies
1340	Office Supplies
1390	TOTAL CURRENT ASSETS [T]
1400	SHOP & EQUIPMENT [H]
1440	Computer System
1460	Service Equipment
1480	Tools
1500	Van ▶

▶1550 Shop
1590 TOTAL SHOP & EQUIPMENT [T]

LIABILITIES

2000	CURRENT LIABILITIES [H]
2100	Bank Loan
2160	Credit Card Payable
2200	Accounts Payable
2640	PST Payable
2650	GST Charged on Sales [A]
2670	GST Paid on Purchases [A]
2750	GST Owing (Refund) [S]
2790	TOTAL CURRENT LIABILITIES [T]
2800	LONG TERM LIABILITIES [H]
2850	Mortgage Payable
2890	TOTAL LONG TERM LIABILITIES [T] ▶

▶EQUITY

3000	OWNER'S EQUITY [H]
3560	S. Arturro, Capital
3650	Net Income [X]
3690	UPDATED CAPITAL [T]

REVENUE

4000	GENERAL REVENUE [H]
4100	Installation Revenue
4140	Service Contract Revenue
4160	Subcontracting Revenue
4180	Sales Discounts
4200	Interest Revenue
4290	TOTAL REVENUE [T]

EXPENSE

5000	OPERATING EXPENSES [H]
5010	Bank Charges
5020	Credit Card Fees ▶

▶5040 Purchase Discounts

5060	Hydro Expense
5070	Maintenance Services
5110	Computer Supplies Used
5120	Office Supplies Used
5150	Solar Panels Used
5160	Inverters Used
5180	Insurance Expense
5190	Telephone Expense
5200	Loan Interest Expense
5210	Mortgage Interest Expense
5290	TOTAL OPERATING EXPENSES [T]
5300	PAYROLL EXPENSES [H]
5320	Wages
5340	Payroll Service Charges
5390	TOTAL PAYROLL EXPENSES [T]

NOTES: The Chart of Accounts includes all accounts. Account types are marked for all subgroup Accounts [A], Subgroup totals [S], Heading accounts [H], Total accounts [T] and the type X account. All other unmarked accounts are postable Group accounts.

INCOME STATEMENT

AIR CARE SERVICES

January 1 to March 31, 2018

Revenue

4000	GENERAL REVENUE	
4100	Installation Revenue	$ 82 500
4140	Service Contract Revenue	9 900
4160	Subcontracting Revenue	21 000
4180	Sales Discounts	−800
4200	Interest Revenue	525
4290	TOTAL REVENUE	$113 125
	TOTAL REVENUE	$113 125 ▶

▶ Expenses

5000	OPERATING EXPENSES	
5010	Bank Charges	$ 225
5020	Credit Card Fees	590
5040	Purchase Discounts	−300
5060	Hydro Expense	750
5070	Maintenance Services	1 365
5110	Computer Supplies Used	1 200
5120	Office Supplies Used	1 150
5150	Solar Panels Used	36 000
5160	Inverters Used	16 000
5180	Insurance Expense	3 600
5190	Telephone Expense	400
5200	Loan Interest Expense	625
5210	Mortgage Interest Expense	2 400
5290	TOTAL OPERATING EXPENSES	$64 005
5300	PAYROLL EXPENSES [H]	
5320	Wages	12 000
5340	Payroll Service Charges	330
5390	TOTAL PAYROLL EXPENSES	$12 330
	TOTAL EXPENSE	$76 335
	NET INCOME (LOSS)	$36 790

BALANCE SHEET

AIR CARE SERVICES

March 31, 2018

Assets			
1000	CURRENT ASSETS		
1060	Bank: Chequing	$ 34 660	
1070	Bank: Visa	1 950	
1080	Bank: MasterCard	1 060	
1100	Net Bank		$ 37 670
1200	Accounts Receivable		24 200
1210	Prepaid Insurance		3 800
1300	Solar Panels		28 280
1310	Inverters		33 420
1320	Electrical Supplies		6 100
1340	Office Supplies		400
1390	TOTAL CURRENT ASSETS		$ 133 870
1400	OFFICE & EQUIPMENT		
1440	Computer System		10 500
1460	Service Equipment		10 000
1480	Tools		3 000
1500	Van		31 000
1550	Shop		110 000
1590	TOTAL SHOP & EQUIPMENT		$164 500
	TOTAL ASSETS		$298 370 ▶

Liabilities			
2000	CURRENT LIABILITIES		
2100	Bank Loan		$ 25 000
2160	Credit Card Payable		1 010
2200	Accounts Payable		20 100
2640	PST Payable		1 530
2650	GST Charged on Sales	$1 530	
2670	GST Paid on Purchases	−840	
2750	GST Owing (Refund)		690
2790	TOTAL CURRENT LIABILITIES		$ 48 330
2800	LONG TERM LIABILITIES		
2850	Mortgage Payable		80 000
2890	TOTAL LONG TERM LIABILITIES		$ 80 000
	TOTAL LIABILITIES		$ 128 330
Equity			
3000	OWNER'S EQUITY		
3560	S. Arturro, Capital		$ 133 250
3650	Net Income		36 790
3690	UPDATED CAPITAL		$ 170 040
	TOTAL EQUITY		$ 170 040
	LIABILITIES AND EQUITY		$298 370

TRIAL BALANCE

AIR CARE SERVICES

March 31, 2018

		Debit	Credit			Debit	Credit
1060	Bank: Chequing	$ 34 660		3560	S. Arturro, Capital		$133 250
1070	Bank: Visa	1 950		4100	Installation Revenue		82 500
1080	Bank: MasterCard	1 060		4140	Service Contract Revenue		9 900
1200	Accounts Receivable	24 200		4160	Subcontracting Revenue		21 000
1210	Prepaid Insurance	3 800		4180	Sales Discounts	$ 800	
1300	Solar Panels	28 280		4200	Interest Revenue		525
1310	Inverters	33 420		5010	Bank Charges	225	
1320	Electrical Supplies	6 100		5020	Credit Card Fees	590	
1340	Office Supplies	400		5040	Purchase Discounts		300
1440	Computer System	10 500		5060	Hydro Expense	750	
1460	Service Equipment	10 000		5070	Maintenance Services	1 365	
1480	Tools	3 000		5110	Computer Supplies Used	1 200	
1500	Van	31 000		5120	Office Supplies Used	1 150	
1550	Shop	110 000		5150	Solar Panels Used	36 000	
2100	Bank Loan		$ 25 000	5160	Inverters Used	16 000	
2160	Credit Card Payable		1 010	5180	Insurance Expense	3 600	
2200	Accounts Payable		20 100	5190	Telephone Expense	400	
2640	PST Payable		1 530	5200	Loan Interest Expense	625	
2650	GST Charged on Sales		1 530	5210	Mortgage Interest Expense	2 400	
2670	GST Paid on Purchases	840		5320	Wages	12 000	
2850	Mortgage Payable		80 000 ▶	5340	Payroll Service Charges	330	
						$376 645	$376 645

SUPPLIER INFORMATION

AIR CARE SERVICES

Supplier Name (Contact)	Address	Phone No. Fax No.	E-mail Web Site Tax ID	Terms Account	YTD Purchases (Pre- & Post-Tax Payments) Tax Code
Beausejour Electrical Products (Janine Beausejour)	50 Shockley Rd., Unit 18 Regina, Saskatchewan S4F 2T2	Tel 1: (306) 476-5282 Tel 2: (306) 476-3997 Fax: (306) 476-5110	jb@beausejour.com beausejour.com 444 276 534	1/10, n/30 (before tax) 1320	$2 100 ($2 000 & $2 100) G
Green Earth Products Inc. (Ezra Green)	2 Greening St. Regina, Saskatchewan S4F 9J9	Tel: (306) 475-6432 Fax: (306) 475-8600	egreen@greenearth.com greenearth.com 177 235 441	1/10, n/30 (before tax) 1310	G
Killarney Solar Equipment (Kieper Warme)	91 Radiation St. Regina, Saskatchewan S4B 4F4	Tel: (306) 363-0210 Fax: (306) 363-2000	kw@heatexchange.com heatexchange.com 571 277 631	1/5, n/30 (before tax) 1300	G
Receiver General for Canada	Sudbury Tax Services Office PO Box 20004 Sudbury, Ontario P3A 6B4	Tel 1: (800) 561-7761 Tel 2: (800) 959-2221	cra-arc.gc.ca	net 1	($790) No tax
Saskatchewan Energy Corp. (Kira Strong)	50 Watts Rd. Regina, Saskatchewan S4G 5K8	Tel 1: (306) 755-6000 Tel 2: (306) 755-3997 Fax: (306) 754-7201	accounts@seg.ca seg.ca 459 021 643	net 10 5060	$840 ($800 & $840) G
Saskatel (Sotto Voce)	4 Speakers Corners Regina, Saskatchewan S4L 4G2	Tel: (306) 361-3255	accounts@saskatel.ca saskatel.ca 492 304 590	net 10 5190	$660 ($600 & $660) GP
Starbuck Advertising Agency (Pam Fletts)	300 Flyer St. Suite 800 Regina, Saskatchewan S4B 1C6	Tel: (306) 361-1727 Fax: (306) 361-8229	pfletts@saa.com saa.com 610 728 365	net 10	$1 100 ($1 000 & $1 100) GP
Wheatfields Hardware (Nutley Bolter)	72 Hammer St. Regina, Saskatchewan S4P 1B8	Tel 1: (306) 369-0808 Tel 2: (306) 369-6222	nbolter@yahoo.com 385 416 822	net 15 1480	$990 ($900 & $990) GP
Willow Garage (Axel Rodd)	699 Willow St. Regina, Saskatchewan S4P 1B3	Tel 1: (306) 368-6444 Tel 2: (306) 368-6000	axel@wefixcars.com wefixcars.com 129 732 010	net 30	$440 ($400 & $440) GP

OUTSTANDING SUPPLIER INVOICES

AIR CARE SERVICES

Supplier Name	Terms	Date	Inv/Chq No.	Amount	Tax	Total
Beausejour Electrical Products	1/10, n/30 (before tax)	Mar. 26/18 Mar. 26/18	B-894 Chq 94	$10 000	$500	$10 500 4 500
	1/10, n/30 (before tax)	Mar. 28/18	B-921 Balance owing	2 000	100	2 100 $ 8 100
Killarney Solar Equipment	1/5, n/30 (before tax)	Mar. 25/18 Mar. 28/18 Mar. 31/18	KS-1031 Chq 96 Chq 98 Balance owing	$20 000	1 000	$21 000 5 200 9 900 $ 5 900
			Grand Total			$14 000

CUSTOMER INFORMATION

CUSTOMER INFORMATION

AIR CARE SERVICES

Customer Name (Contact)	Address	Phone No. Fax No.	E-mail Web Site	Terms Revenue Acct Tax Code	YTD Sales (Credit Limit) Customer Since
Grande Pointe Towers (Sophie Grande)	77 LaPointe Cr. White City Saskatchewan S0G 5B0	Tel: (306) 322-7500 Fax: (306) 322-7436	sgrande@GPTowers.com GPTowers.com	1/10, n/30 (after tax) 4100 GP	$11 000 ($20 000) Jan. 1/18
Midwest Funeral Home (N. Mourning)	8 Quiet St. Regina, Saskatchewan S4B 1E1	Tel: (306) 763-WAKE or (306) 763-9253 Fax: (306) 762-9301	nm@midwestfh.com midwestfh.com	1/10, n/30 (after tax) 4140 GP	($10 000) Aug. 1/15
Oak Bluff Banquet Hall (Ann Oakley)	4 Celebration Ave. Regina, Saskatchewan S4V 3H7	Tel: (306) 622-7391 Fax: (306) 622-7900	annie@OBBH.com OBBH.com	1/10, n/30 (after tax) 4160 GP	($20 000) Mar. 1/18
Passions Dept Store (Mann E. Kinn)	44 Highlife Ave. Regina, Saskatchewan S4L 2K0	Tel: (306) 762-8662 Fax: (306) 763-9115	passions.com	1/10, n/30 (after tax) 4100 GP	$6 300 ($15 000) Jan. 1/12
Regina School Board (Ed Ducate)	49 Trainer St. Regina, Saskatchewan S4C 4B6	Tel 1: (306) 466-5000 Tel 2: (306) 466-1123 Fax: (306) 466-2000	edd@rdsb.ca rdsb.ca	1/10, n/30 (after tax) 4100 GP	$8 400 ($15 000) Mar. 1/18
Selkirk Community Centre (Elsa Peeples)	588 Populous St. Regina, Saskatchewan S4T 8N1	Tel: (306) 368-4575 Fax: (306) 368-2198	elsa@selkirk.com selkirk.com	1/10, n/30 (after tax) 4100 GP	($20 000) Jul. 1/14

OUTSTANDING CUSTOMER INVOICES

AIR CARE SERVICES

Customer Name	Terms	Date	Inv/Chq No.	Amount	Total
Grande Pointe Towers	1/10, n/30 (after tax)	Mar. 24/18	699	$4 400	
		Mar. 28/18	Chq 4896	2 400	
	1/10, n/30 (after tax)	Mar. 28/18	703	2 200	
			Balance owing		$4 200
Regina School Board	1/10, n/30 (after tax)	Mar. 28/18	701	$22 000	
		Mar. 28/18	Chq 10367	2 000	
			Balance owing		$20 000
				Grand Total	$24 200

Accounting Procedures

Open-Invoice Accounting for Payables and Receivables

The open-invoice method of accounting for invoices allows the business to keep track of each individual invoice and any partial payments made against it. This method is in contrast to methods that keep track of only the outstanding balance by combining all invoice balances owed to a supplier or by a customer. Sage 50 uses the open-invoice method. When invoices are fully paid, they should be removed periodically after statements are received from the supplier or sent to the customers.

GST and PST

Air Care Services is a contractor business using the regular method of calculating GST. GST, at the rate of 5 percent, charged and collected from customers will be recorded as a liability in *GST Charged on Sales*. GST paid to suppliers will be recorded in *GST Paid on Purchases* as a decrease in tax liability. The balance owing, the difference between the GST charged and GST paid, or the request for a refund will be remitted to the Receiver General for Canada quarterly.

Air Care charges customers 5 percent PST on all sales and pays PST on some goods. Air Care is exempt from PST for purchases of items that are sold or used in the installation work because the customer pays PST on the sales using these products.

Sales of Services

Accounts are set up for several customers. Other customers pay for their purchases immediately by cash, cheque or credit card. Separate bank accounts are set up for credit card deposits. You can enter transactions for cash and credit card customers by choosing One-Time Customer and typing the name of the customer in the Address field or by typing the customer's name in the Name field and choosing the Quick Add or Continue option.

For cash sales, the program will debit *Bank: Chequing* (or *Bank: Visa* or *MasterCard* for credit card payments) instead of the *Accounts Receivable* control account.

Purchases

Most regular suppliers have given Air Care credit terms, including some discounts for early payment. Some purchases are accompanied by immediate payment, usually by cheque or credit card. Cheque payments are preferred because the cancelled cheques become part of the business records. Enter the cash transaction for purchases from new suppliers in the Payments Journal as an Other Payment or in the Purchases Journal. Choose the appropriate Payment Method; choose One-Time Supplier from the Supplier list and type the supplier's name in the Address field. You can also type the name in the Supplier field and choose Quick Add or Continue.

For cash purchases paid by cash or cheque, the program will credit *Bank: Chequing* instead of the *Accounts Payable* control account. For credit card purchases, *Credit Card Payable* is credited. All other accounts for this transaction will be appropriately debited and credited.

Discounts

Air Care Services offers a 1 percent discount to account customers if they settle their accounts within 10 days. Full payment is requested within 30 days. These payment terms are set up as defaults. When the receipt is entered, if the discount is still available, the program will display the amount of the discount and the net amount owing automatically. Discounts are not allowed on partial payments or on cash purchases paid by cheque or credit card. All customer sales discounts are calculated on after-tax amounts.

Some suppliers also offer discounts, calculated on the amounts before taxes, for early settlement of accounts. Again, when the terms are entered for the supplier and full payment is made before the discount period expires, the program will display the pretax discount as available and automatically calculate a net balance owing. Payment terms vary from supplier to supplier.

INSTRUCTIONS

NOTES

Source documents begin on page 251 after the setup instructions.

1. **Set up** the **company accounts** using the Business Information, Chart of Accounts, Balance Sheet, Income Statement, Trial Balance and Supplier and Customer Information provided for March 31, 2018. Detailed instructions follow to assist you in setting up the company accounts follow.

   When you are ready to enter transactions (page 251), the Payables Ledger will be unbalanced. This is intentional to demonstrate working with an unfinished history and entering historical transactions after entering current transactions.

2. **Enter** the **transactions** beginning on page 251 in Sage 50 using the Chart of Accounts, Supplier Information, Customer Information and Accounting Procedures.

3. **Print** the **reports** checked on the printing form after completing your entries:

REPORTS

Accounts
- [ ] Chart of Accounts
- [ ] Account List
- [ ] General Journal Entries

Financials
- [✓] Comparative Balance Sheet: April 1 and May 1, difference in percentage
- [✓] Income Statement: January 1 to May 1
- [✓] Trial Balance: May 1
- [✓] All Journal Entries: April 1 to June 11
- [✓] General Ledger accounts: 1060 4100 4120 from April 1 to May 1

- [✓] Cash Flow Projection Detail Report for account 1060 for 30 days
- [ ] Statement of Cash Flows

Tax
- [✓] GST Report April 1 to May 1

Banking
- [ ] Cheque Log Report

Payables
- [ ] Supplier List
- [ ] Supplier Aged
- [✓] Aged Overdue Payables: May 1
- [ ] Expenses Journal Entries
- [ ] Payments Journal Entries

Receivables
- [ ] Customer List
- [ ] Customer Aged
- [✓] Aged Overdue Receivables: May 1
- [ ] Sales Journal Entries
- [ ] Receipts Journal Entries
- [ ] Customer Statements

Mailing Labels
- [ ] Labels

KEYSTROKES FOR SETUP

Creating Company Files

For Air Care Services, we will create the company files from scratch rather than use one of the starter files. Once we create the files and define the defaults, we will add the accounts; define linked accounts for the General, Payables and Receivables ledgers; and create supplier and customer records.

Start the **Sage 50 program**.

You should open the familiar Sage 50, Welcome and Select Company window:

PRO VERSION

The program name is Sage 50 Pro Accounting.

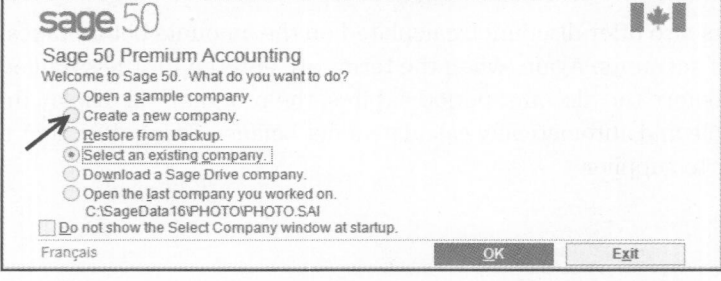

Click   **Create A New Company**. **Click OK**.

You will start with the New Company Setup wizard introduction screen:

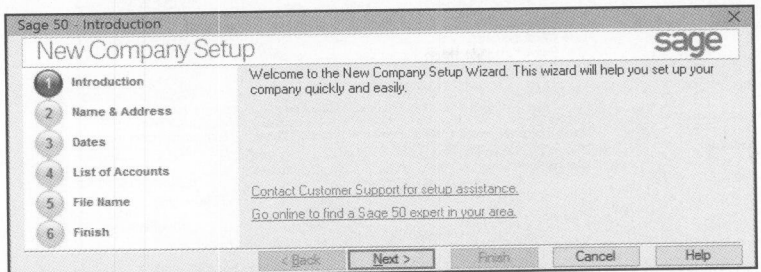

This screen introduces the Setup wizard and some support options.

Click   **Next** to continue:

You must now enter company information for the business. The cursor is in the Name field. Alberta and its two-letter abbreviation — the first entry in the province list — are entered as defaults. Use the Business Information on page 200 to enter the company name and address details.

Type   Air Care Services **Press** ⌷tab⌷ to enter the name.

Type   100 Belair Avenue **Press** ⌷tab⌷ to enter the street address.

Type   Unit 25 **Press** ⌷tab⌷ to complete the address.

Type   Regina **Press** ⌷tab⌷ and **Type** S

Click   the **Postal Code field**. SK and Saskatchewan are entered automatically as this is the only province name beginning with S.

Type   s4t4u2 **Press** ⌷tab⌷ to enter the postal code.

Type   Canada **Press** ⌷tab⌷ to enter the country.

Type   3064561299 **Press** ⌷tab⌷ to enter the phone number.

Type   8884557194 to enter the alternate number in the Phone 2 field and move to the Fax field.

Type   3064563188

Click **Next** to open the company fiscal dates screen:

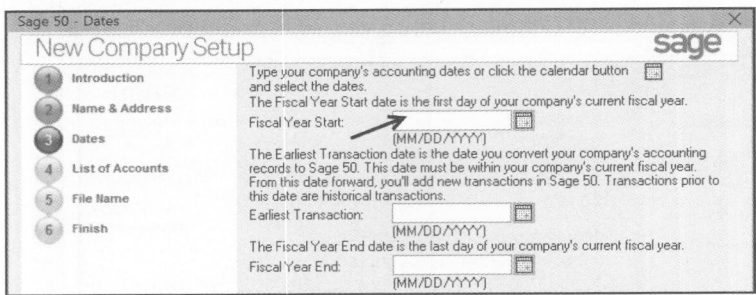

These company fiscal dates are like the ones you entered for Love It Again (Chapter 4) as part of the Company Information setup. The cursor is in the Fiscal Year Start field. This is the date on which the business begins its fiscal year. For Air Care Services, the fiscal start date is the beginning of the calendar year.

Type jan 1 2018 **Press** ⟨tab⟩ to advance to the calendar.

Initially the program enters the fiscal start as the **earliest transaction date**. You need to enter the date on which the business is starting to use Sage 50 as its computerized accounting system — the earliest date for posting journal entries and the latest date for historical information. Air Care is converting its records on March 31.

Press ⟨tab⟩ to advance to the Earliest Transaction date field.

Type mar 31 2018

Press ⟨tab⟩ **twice** to advance to the Fiscal Year End field — the date Air Care Services ends its fiscal period. The end of the year is the default fiscal end date. Air Care Services' fiscal period is six months.

Type jun 30 2018 **Click Next** to continue:

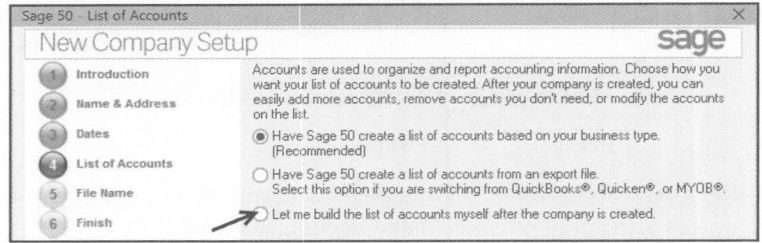

You can let Sage 50 create a set of accounts that are suitable for the business type you select, start from scratch to create the accounts or copy data exported from another program. The set of accounts created by the program will include many accounts not required for Air Care Services. Because our setup is relatively small and we want to demonstrate all the stages of the setup, we will create the accounts ourselves. This approach allows us to present all the options available for each stage.

Click **Let Me Build The List Of Accounts Myself After The Company Is Created**. **Click Next**:

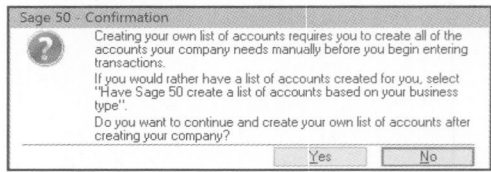

This message confirms your selection to create all the accounts on your own.

Click **Yes** to continue to the industry type selection list:

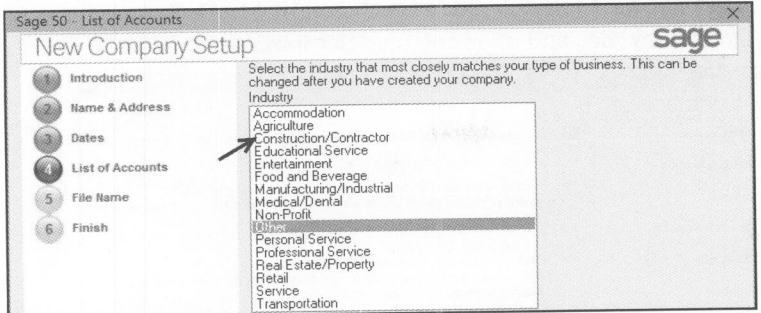

PRO VERSION
Remember that icon labels are the same for all company types — Customer and Vendor are the terms used throughout the Receivables and Payables modules, respectively.

At this stage you should choose the type of business that best describes your company. This selection will determine some of the default settings and icon labels. Air Care Services is a construction/contractor business.

> **Click**   **Construction/Contractor** as the Industry type.

> **Click**   **Next** to open the File Name screen:

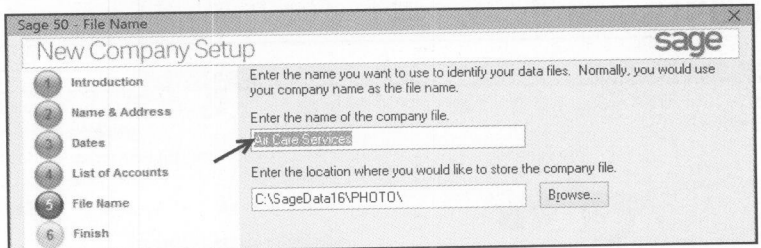

NOTES
Sage 50 will automatically add the correct file extension. You do not need to type it when you are creating a new data set.
You may type the new names in upper or lower case. For consistency we use upper-case letters for names.

Now you must choose a file name and folder to store the new data set. The company name is entered as the default name for the data file, and it is selected.

> **Type**   AIRCARE **Press** ⌨ tab ⌨ to advance to the location field.

The last folder you used will be the default selection — that is, PHOTO, if you last worked with the Phoebe's Photo Studio data set. Change folders if necessary to access the one with your other data files. If you have already created the folder you want to use,

> **Click**   **Browse** to open the Browse For Folder screen to select a folder. Otherwise,

> **Drag through PHOTO** in the folder name or the last folder in the location field.

> **Type**   AIRCARE to replace PHOTO\ or the last folder in the location field.

> **Click**   **Next** — Sage 50 requests confirmation:

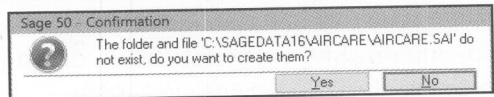

Sage 50 asks if you want to create the new folder.

> **Click**   **Yes** to create the new folder and file:

This screen reminds you that you can change this information from the Setup menu.

NOTES

If you get a message about the payroll plan or any other Advisor messages, you can close them.

The Getting Started window may be hidden by the Home window initially. Click the Sage 50 icon in the task bar and then click the window you want to display.

Click   **Finish**. **Wait** for Sage 50 to finish creating the database for your new company files and open the final Setup screen:

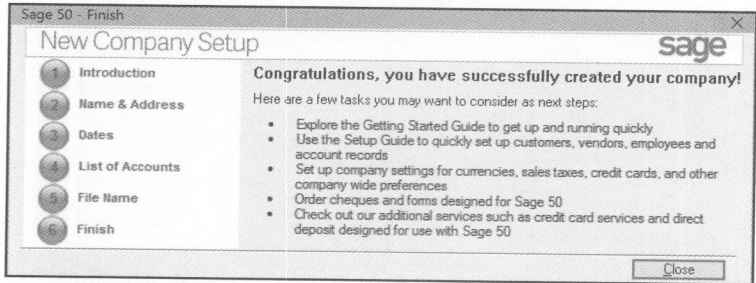

Click   **Close** to complete the file creation stage. The Getting Started and Home window will be open.

Click   **Show This Window On Startup** to remove the ✓ in the Getting Started Guide window so that it will not open each time you start the program.

Click   **Close** to display the Receivables module Home window:

NOTES

The session date you have initially will depend on the date settings in your own computer system. You may have the day, month or year first, and the year may have two or four digits.

PRO VERSION

pro Pro replaces Premium as the program name.

The Sales Invoices icon replaces Bills, and Job Sites are named Projects. You will not have icons for Estimates, Contracts and Time Slips.

In the Modules pane, the labels Vendors & Purchases and Projects are used.

NOTES

The list of equivalent accounting and non-accounting terms is provided in Appendix B.

NOTES

Update your backup copy frequently as you work through the setup. Until you change the backup settings (page 212), the file will be backed up automatically when you close the program.

NOTES

You may want to refer to the keystrokes in Chapter 4 to assist you in completing the setup and to the keystrokes in other chapters to assist you with the transactions for this application.

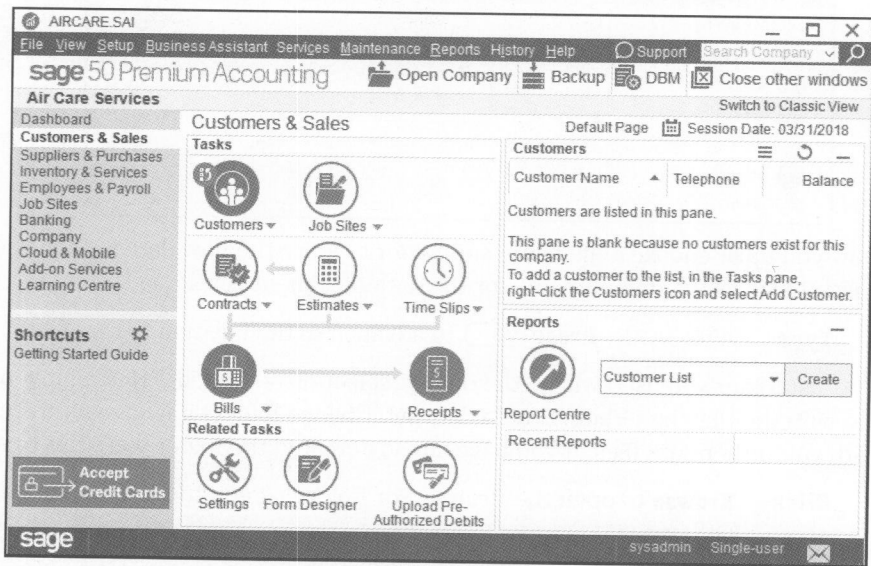

The Home window is now open with the name AIRCARE in the title bar. One shortcut, for the Getting Started Guide, is added by default. However, non-accounting terms are selected, so the module names are different from the ones in previous applications. Customers & Sales replaces Receivables, and Suppliers & Purchases replaces Payables. We will change these terms as part of the setup.

Because the ledgers are still open for entering historical information, , the open history symbol, is still on the Customers ledger icon. No ledgers are hidden.

Display the **Chart of Accounts** for the Current Year.

The only account provided by default is the type X account, the General Ledger linked account, *Current Earnings*.

Close   the **Chart of Accounts**.

Preparing the System

The next step is to enter the company information that customizes the files for Air Care Services. You begin by preparing the system and changing the defaults. Use the Business Information on page 200 to enter defaults for Air Care Services.

You should change the user preference and reports and forms defaults to suit your own work environment. The ones we provide will match the screens we provide.

Changing User Preferences

Choose the **Setup menu**, then **click User Preferences**.

If you are working in multi-user mode, decide whether you want to refresh lists automatically so that changes other users make affect your file immediately. The option to Show List Buttons is already selected. Automatic download of updates must be turned off.

Choose **Use Accounting Terms** so that your on-screen terms will match the ones used in this workbook.

Choose **Automatically Save Changes To Supplier, Customer And Other Records**.

Choose **Calculate Record Balances In The Home Window By Session Date**, instead of the default — balances based on the latest transactions.

Verify that there is **no** ✓ beside **Automatically Download Product Updates**.

Click **View**.

Click **Inventory & Services**, **Employees & Payroll** and **Time & Billing** to hide the unused modules and features. You can hide Job Sites if you want, but you do not need to.

Click **After Changing Session Date** for **Daily Business Manager** and **Checklists** to remove the two ✓s.

Choose **Show Change Session Date At Startup**.

Click **Transaction Confirmation**. **Confirm** that the **Confirmation Message Box** is checked to activate this option.

Click **Pop-ups**. Choose the messages you want to display and hide.

Click **OK** to save the preference changes and return to the Home window.

You will now have the familiar accounting term labels for the modules. At this stage the hidden modules have been removed from the Home window:

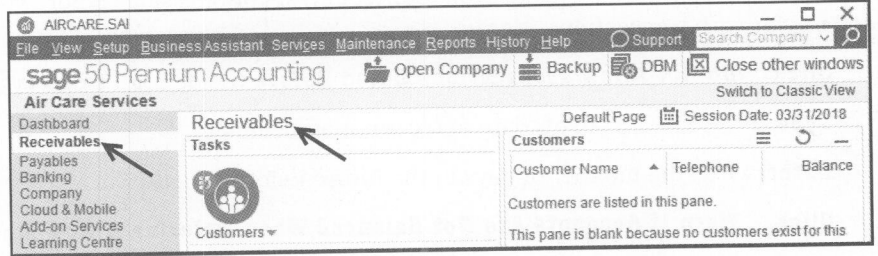

Changing Company Default Settings

Many of the next steps for setting up company defaults and entering General Ledger accounts can be completed directly from the Company module Home window. We will start from that point.

Click **Company** in the Modules list to change the Home window.

The company window is the same as the one we used for Muriel's Murals and Love It Again. You can now open the Company Settings screen from the Settings icon, and you are able to create ledger accounts by clicking on the Chart of Accounts icon.

If you need help entering company settings, refer to page 73.

Changing Company Information

Click   the **Settings icon** ⚒ Settings in the Related Tasks pane.

Click   **Information** to display the Company Information screen.

From any Home window, you can also choose the Setup menu, then click Settings, Company and Information.

Most of the fields on this screen are already filled in based on the information we entered when we created the company files. You can edit the information if you made a mistake. We still need to add the business number.

Notice that the earliest transaction date appears as the session date on the Company Information screen. If there are any postdated transactions in the file, the Latest Transaction Date will be later than the session date.

You can return to the Company Information screen at any time to make changes. The program will set up defaults for the session date based on this information.

Click   the **Business Number field**.

Type   533 766 455 RT0001

Changing System Defaults

Click   **System** in the list of company options on the left.

Most of the default System Settings are correct. Air Care uses the accrual basis of accounting, so Use Cash-Basis Accounting should remain unchecked. The option to Use Cheque No. as the source code can remain selected. This setting will include the cheque number in reports.

Initially, we will not allow any transactions before March 31, the earliest transaction date. We want to allow posting to future transactions but receive a warning if the dates are more than seven days in the future. Since you can enter transactions before completing the history, you should activate the warning about unbalanced accounts to prevent mistakes. The warning makes you aware of errors or omissions before you proceed too far with transactions.

Click   **Do Not Allow Transactions Dated Before** to add a ✓. **Press** (tab).

Type   3-31-18   (This date entry is not ambiguous.)

Enter   **7** as the number of days in the future before you are warned.

Click   **Warn If Accounts Are Not Balanced When Entering A New Month**.

Changing the Backup Options

We will back up the files on a weekly basis and leave on the reminder to back up each time we close the data file.

Click   **Backup** in the list on the left. **Choose Weekly** as the frequency for Backup Reminders.

Click   **Automatically Back Up This File** to remove the ✓.

CLASSIC VIEW

The Settings tool ⚙ is available. Clicking it when a ledger icon is selected will display the settings for that ledger.

If you click the Settings tool when no ledger or journal icon is selected, you must select a ledger from the list.

NOTES

The RT extension for the business number indicates the area of the business for reporting to the Canada Revenue Agency. For example, registered charity and payroll GST reports have different extensions than income tax.

NOTES

If you click the calendar for the prior transactions field, you cannot access any month before March. Entering a date prior to March 31 will generate an error with the advice that the date must be between March 31 (the earliest transaction date) and June 30 (the fiscal end date).

NOTES

If you choose to back up your file automatically, leave the option checked and choose the backup frequency, the backup file location and the number of backup files you want to keep.

Changing the Features Selections

Customizing the icons and features that appear can simplify journal entries.

> **Click**   **Features**   in the list on the left.

> **Click**   **each feature** and the **language setting** to change the status.

This removes the unused features and makes bilingual data entry and forms available.

Since we need to choose linked accounts when we set up credit cards and sales taxes, we will create accounts before entering these settings. Since Air Care does not use other currencies, we can skip this setup screen.

Changing Forms Default Settings

> **Click**   **Forms** to display the Settings for Forms:

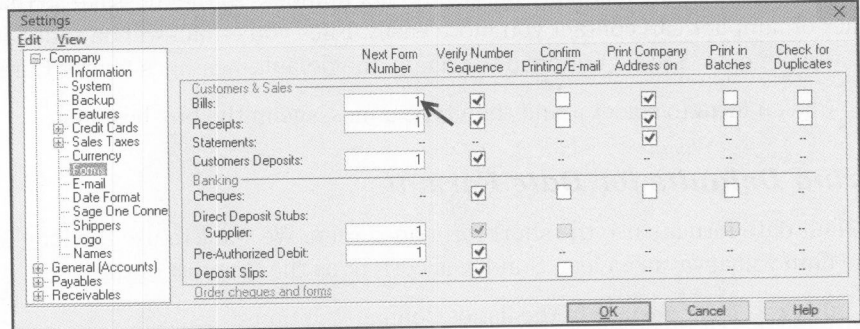

The Forms screen allows us to set up the automatic numbering sequences for business forms and to include warnings if the number you entered is a duplicate or out of sequence. You can set up the numbering sequence for all business forms that are generated internally or within the company.

We can skip the forms that Air Care does not use — for customer deposits, direct payments and pre-authorized debits. Cheque and bank deposit sequence numbers are added separately in the reports and forms settings for each bank account (refer to page 219).

> **Click**   the **Bills Next Form Number field**. **Type** 710

> **Click**   the **Receipts Next Form Number field**. **Type** 20

The five column checklists on the Forms Settings screen allow you to **verify number sequences** and add reminders if you print bills or invoices, quotes, purchase orders and so forth. Verifying sequence numbers will warn you if you skip or duplicate a number and give you a chance to make a correction if necessary before posting. Choosing to **confirm** will set up the program to remind you to print or e-mail the form if you try to post before printing since posting removes the form from the screen. You should add the confirmation if you print or e-mail these forms regularly.

The third column allows you to add the **company address** to various forms. If you use preprinted forms that already include the address, remove the checkmarks to avoid double printing this information. If you have generic blank forms, leave the checkmarks so that the address is included. The next column refers to **batch printing**. If you want to print the forms on the list in batches (for example, print all the invoices for the day at the end of each day) you should check this option. The final column allows the program to check for **duplicate** bill and receipt numbers. We should check for these duplicates.

> **Click**   the **check box for Bills** and the **check box for Receipts** in the Check For Duplicates column.

Click to add a ✓ to any check box and click again to remove a ✓ .

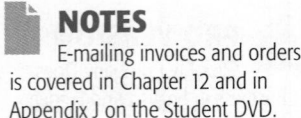
Entering Default Comments for E-mail

The next step is to add a default message to e-mail communications.

Click **E-mail** in the list of Company options to open the next Settings screen:

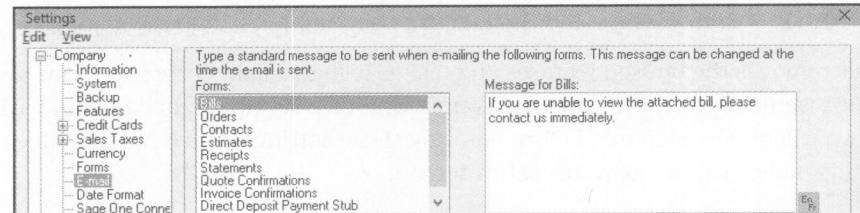

The left-hand list box contains the forms that you can e-mail to suppliers or customers. The right-hand box contains the message that will be added to the selected e-mail. You could add the company phone and fax numbers to the message so that the customer or supplier can contact you more easily. Files you e-mail will be sent with PDF format attachments. You do not need to change the default messages for Air Care.

Click a form to select it and then type a message in the box beside it.

Entering Defaults for Date Formats

The default date formats use the short form on-screen. We want to use the long form so that the date will always be clear. Sunday is correct as the first day of the week.

Click **Date Format** in the list of Company options:

Choose MM dd yyyy from the Short Date Format drop-down list. **Click Long Dates** beside On The Screen, Use to change the selection.

Adding a Company Logo

We will add the company logo next. The logo is located in the SageData16\LOGOS folder (or the folder you chose) where you installed the other data files.

Click **Logo** in the list on the left:

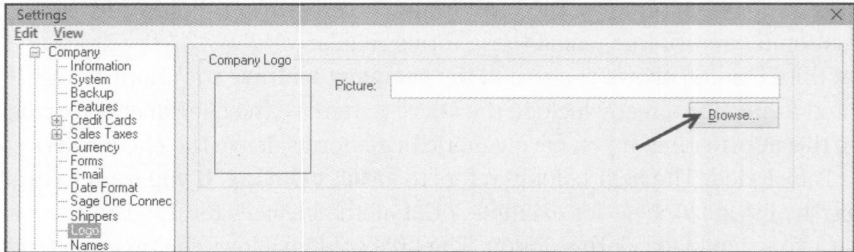

Click **Browse. Click This PC** (or **Computer**) in the left-hand pane. **Double-click C:, SageData16, LOGOS** and then **click AIRCARE**.

Click the **Open button** to add the image and file name:

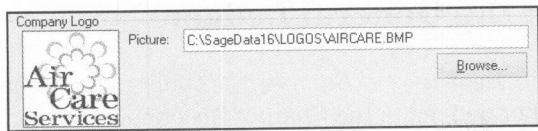

Check   the **information** you have just entered and **make** any necessary **corrections**, including corrections to the fiscal dates.

Click   **OK** to save the new information and return to the Home window.

Changing the Printer Defaults

Choose   the **Setup menu** and **click Reports & Forms**.

The printer setting options for reports are given. Notice that the defaults include adding the computer system (calendar) date to reports and information about whether the report is filtered. You can check whether the report fits on the page to improve the appearance of your printed reports, and you can change Reports & Forms settings any time. When the settings are correct,

Click   **OK** to save the new information, or **click Cancel** if you have not made any changes, and return to the Home window.

Preparing the Ledgers

Before entering the remaining settings, we should create the Chart of Accounts because many of the settings require default or linked accounts.

The next stage in setting up an accounting system involves preparing each ledger, beginning with the General Ledger. This stage involves the following steps:

1. organizing all accounting reports and records (this step has been completed)
2. modifying the *Current Earnings* account
3. creating new accounts
4. setting up credit cards, taxes and other features
5. defining linked accounts for the ledgers
6. entering supplier and customer information
7. adding historical account balances, invoices and payments

Preparing the General Ledger

Accounts are organized by section, including Assets, Liabilities, Equity, Revenue and Expense. **Account type** — such as **Heading** (H), **Subgroup total** (S), **Total** (T), **subgroup Account** (A), **Group account** (G) and **Current Earnings** (X) — is a method of classifying and organizing accounts within a section or subsection of a report.

The accounts follow the same pattern described previously:

- 1000–1999   Assets
- 2000–2999   Liabilities
- 3000–3999   Equity
- 4000–4999   Revenue
- 5000–5999   Expense

Use the Chart of Accounts, Income Statement and Balance Sheet on pages 201–202 to enter all the accounts you need to create. Remember to include all group headings, totals and subgroup totals in addition to the postable group and subgroup accounts.

NOTES
The Forms folder in the Sage 50 Program folder is the default location for the logo when you click Browse.
   If you are showing file extensions, the picture file will be named AIRCARE.BMP.

WARNING!
Verify that the Form locations for the forms are valid for your program setup. If they are not, you will get an error message when you try to close the Reports & Forms window. The default folder is Sage 50 Premium Accounting Version 2016\Forms.

NOTES
Refer to Appendix E on the Student DVD for more information about printing options and customizing reports.

NOTES
Although you can create new accounts as you need them in any Account field, creating them all at the beginning allows you to check them more easily for accuracy and type. In the same way, it is safer to add all the opening balances at once rather than one at a time to check that the Trial Balance is correct.

NOTES
If necessary, refer to the Love It Again application, pages 85–87, for a review of the financial statement formats, the organization of accounts and the Current Earnings account.

NOTES
We are not using expanded account numbering so that the instructions will be the same for Premium and Pro version users in all chapters in Part Two.

Modifying Accounts in the General Ledger

The following keystrokes will modify the *Current Earnings* account in the General Ledger to match the account number defined in the Chart of Accounts.

In the Home window,

Click   the **Chart Of Accounts icon** in the Accountants' Tasks pane to open the Accounts window.

The accounts should be displayed in Type view — in numerical order, with names, account types and balances. There is only one predefined account.

Double-click   3600 Current Earnings to display its ledger record.

You can also open the ledger by clicking the account to select it. Then click the Edit tool button or choose the File menu and click Open.

Press *tab* to select the Account number field.

Type   3650 **Press** *tab* and **type** Net Income

The account types are dimmed because the *Current Earnings* account type must remain as type X. Only the account number and account name can be edited. You cannot enter a balance because the program automatically calculates the amount as the net difference between the total revenue and expense account balances for the fiscal period.

Click   Save And Close

Close the Accounts window to return to the Home window unless you want to continue to the next step, which also involves working in the General Ledger.

Creating New Accounts in the General Ledger

We will enter account balances later as a separate step so that you can enter all balances in a single session. This may help you avoid leaving the data file with an incorrect Trial Balance.

Open   the **Accounts window** or any **account ledger window**, if necessary.

Click   the **Create tool** in the Accounts window or **choose** the **File menu** and **click Create**.

Enter   account information for all accounts from the Chart of Accounts on page 201. Remember, you cannot use duplicate account numbers.

Type   the **account number** and **press** *tab* .

Type   the **account name** or title.

Click   the **account Type** for the account.

If this is a postable account, indicate whether you want to omit the account from financial statements if its balance is zero. You do not need to change the default setting for Allow Project Allocations. The option will be checked when you enter 4000- and 5000-level accounts.

Skip   the **Opening Balance field** for now. We will enter all account balances in the next stage.

When all the information is entered correctly, you must save your account.

Click   Create Another to save the new account and advance to a new blank ledger account window.

Create   the **remaining accounts** from the Chart of Accounts.

Click   ⊞ Save and Close   to close the General Ledger account window after entering the last account.

Display or **print** your updated **Chart of Accounts** to check for account type errors as well as incorrect numbers and misspelled names. **Make corrections**.

Click   the **Check The Validity Of Accounts tool** ☑ for descriptions of errors in account type. **Make** the **corrections** required.

Check   the **validity** again and repeat the process until you receive the message that the accounts are in logical order.

Entering Opening Account Balances

The opening historical balances for Air Care Services can be found in the Trial Balance dated March 31, 2018, on page 202. Headings, totals and subgroup totals — the non-postable accounts — have no balances and the Balance field is removed.

Use the *Test Balance Account* for any adjustments that would leave the Trial Balance in a forced balance position before you are finished or if one of the remaining balances is incorrect.

If you want to use the Retained Earnings linked account to enter these adjustments, do not enter opening balances until you have added the linked accounts for the General (Accounts) Ledger (pages 225–226). Using this approach, you should verify that this account has the correct opening balance.

The Accounts window should be open.

Open   the **General Ledger** account information window for the first account that has a balance, **1060 Bank: Chequing**.

Click   the **Opening Balance field** to highlight its contents.

Type   34660

Balances for accounts that decrease the total in a group or section (i.e., *GST Paid on Purchases*, *Sales Discounts* and *Purchase Discounts*) must be entered as negative numbers. The balances for these accounts have a (–) minus sign in the Balance Sheet or Income Statement. Balances for Drawings accounts would also be entered as negative amounts.

Correct the **information** if necessary by repeating the above steps.

Click   the **Next button** ▷ in the Ledger window to advance to the next account ledger record.

Enter   the **remaining account balances** in the Trial Balance by repeating the above procedures.

Close   the **General Ledger window** to return to the Accounts window. You can check your work from the Trial Balance.

Choose the **Reports menu** and **click Trial Balance** to display the Trial Balance. **Print** the **report** and **close** the **display**.

Correct the account **balances** if necessary. Open the ledger window, click the amount and type the correction.

Close   the **Accounts window** if you want to finish your session.

⚠ WARNING!
Remember that Net Bank and GST Owing (Refund) are subgroup totals, following the subgroup bank and GST accounts, respectively.

📄 NOTES
After entering all balances, the Test Balance Account should have a zero balance, and you can remove it.

To remove the Test Balance Account, click its icon or name in the Accounts window and click the Remove tool, or choose the File menu and click Remove. Check that you have selected the right account. Click Yes to confirm that you want to remove the account.

If the Test Balance Account balance is not zero, you cannot remove the account.

Entering the Account Class: Bank Accounts

NOTES

You can also change the account class in the Setup Guide for Accounts by selecting the correct class from the drop-down list in the Class column.

The initial class for expense accounts is Expense when you create the account in the Guide.

Before setting up the Payables and Receivables ledgers, we must change the account class for bank accounts and some other accounts. **Account class** is another way of organizing accounts into related groups. Each section may be divided into various classes. For example, assets may be subdivided into bank accounts, credit card accounts, receivables, inventory and so on. When you create a new account, the program assigns a default class (Asset, Liability, Equity, Operating Revenue or Cost of Goods Sold) according to the first digit of the account number. For most accounts, you can accept this setting and the program will prompt you to change the class for special purpose accounts as needed. Bank accounts are not automatically reassigned by the program. You should also change the class for expense accounts by choosing either Expense or Operating Expense as the account class. Air Care does not sell merchandise and has no Cost of Goods Sold accounts.

NOTES

The available account classes vary for different account sections. For example, you cannot assign the Bank class to an expense account. You can assign the Bank class to liability accounts. This allows you to set up a line of credit as an account that you can choose to pay for purchases and update cheque numbers automatically. In Chapter 11, we define and use the Line of Credit liability account as a Bank class account.

Chequing bank accounts have additional information that must be entered in the ledger and therefore require that you change the class. You cannot select bank accounts for payments and receipts unless the **Bank** or **Cash class** is assigned. Bank class accounts must also be defined as such before you can select them as the default linked accounts for the Payables, Receivables and Payroll ledgers. The chequing account *Bank: Chequing* must be defined as a Bank class account.

Click the **Chart Of Accounts icon** if you closed the Accounts window.

Double-click **1060 Bank: Chequing** to open its ledger window.

Click the **Class Options tab** — the current class setting is Asset:

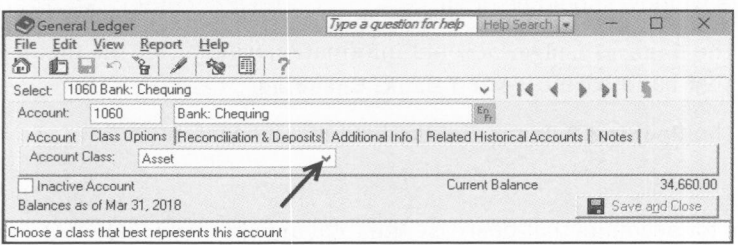

Click the **Account Class list arrow** to display the asset account class options.

Click **Bank** from the list to open the bank-related fields:

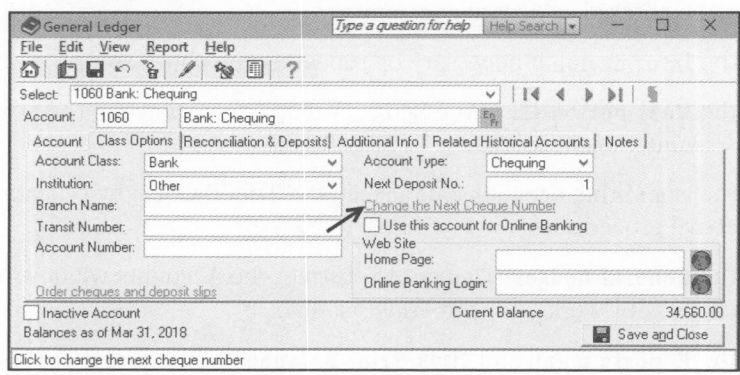

NOTES

Deposit slips are used in Chapter 15 together with account reconciliation. Online banking is introduced in Appendix I on the Student DVD.

This screen allows you to define the type of bank account, and Chequing, the default, is correct. You can also enter a starting number for the deposit slip sequence and identify the bank for online banking access. We are not using deposit slips in this exercise, so you can skip this field. When different currencies are used, the currency for the bank account is also identified on the Class Options tab screen.

Click   Change The Next Cheque Number to open the cheque Form settings:

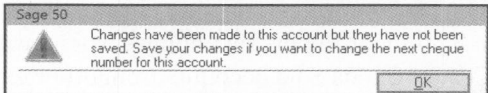

Before entering the cheque number, we need to save the account class change.

Click   OK to return to the ledger window.

Click   the Save tool 🖫 or **choose** the **File menu** and **click Save**.

Click   Change The Next Cheque Number again to open the Form settings:

We need to enter only the cheque number. You do not need to change the printer settings for the cheques.

Click   the Next Cheque No. field near the bottom of the form. **Type** 101

Click   OK to return to the account ledger window at the Class Options tab.

Defining the Class for Credit Card Accounts

Although credit card accounts are bank accounts, they are used as credit card linked accounts and are assigned the Credit Card class. Before setting up the cards with their linked accounts, we must change the account class for the accounts we need. We will change the linked asset accounts to the Credit Card Receivable class and the payable account to the Credit Card Payable class. If you also write cheques from or deposit customer cash or cheques to these accounts, you should use the Bank class so they will be available in the bank account fields in the journals.

Click   the Next button ▶ to advance to account 1070 Bank: Visa.

Choose Credit Card Receivable from the Account Class list to change the class.

Click   the Next button ▶ to open the ledger for 1080 Bank: MasterCard.

Choose Credit Card Receivable from the Account Class list.

Click   the Select field list arrow to open the list of accounts.

Click   2160 Credit Card Payable to open this account ledger.

Choose Credit Card Payable from the Account Class list.

Defining the Class for Expense Accounts

Expense accounts are defined as Cost of Goods Sold by default when you create them from the General Ledger new account window. These account classes should be changed unless they refer to inventory cost accounts. The default class is Operating Expense

NOTES
Until you have saved the record or closed the ledger, the account class change has not been recorded. The cheque numbering fields for the account will not be available.

WARNING!
To avoid an error message, the Form fields must contain valid file locations. The forms you need are in the Forms folder inside the Sage 50 Premium Accounting Version 2016 program folder.

NOTES
The Class options available for 2160 — a liability account — are different from those for the asset accounts.

NOTES
You can assign the Payroll Expense class to the two payroll accounts.

when you create expense accounts from an Account field using the Add An Account wizard and Expense from the Setup Guide, so you will not need to change these.

To create the Gross Margin Income Statement Report that applies when inventory is sold, you must correctly separate the Cost of Goods Sold accounts from other expenses.

Choose account **5010** from the Select Account list to open the ledger.

Choose **Operating Expense** (or **Expense**) from the Account Class list.

Click the **Next button** ▶. **Change** the **class** for all Group expense accounts.

Click **Save And Close** to close the Ledger window.

Close the **Accounts window** to return to the Home window.

Setting Up Credit Cards

Now that all the ledger accounts have been created, we can enter the remaining company and ledger settings.

Since Air Care accepts credit card payments from customers and uses credit cards in payment for purchases, we must set up the credit cards by naming them and identifying the linked accounts for deposits, payments and fees associated with the cards.

Air Care accepts Visa and MasterCard for sales, and uses Visa for credit card payments. You should be in the Company module Home window.

Entering the Credit Cards

Click the **Settings icon** to open the Company Settings options list.

Click **Credit Cards** (**click Company** first if necessary):

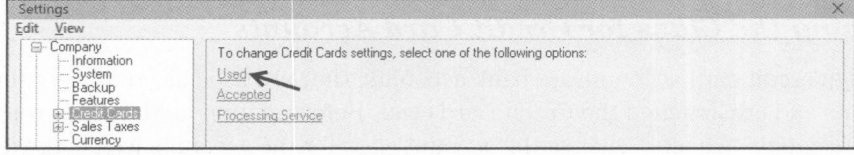

NOTES
You may get a message about credit card processing services, a fee-based service offered by Sage. Read and then close this message.
Information about this online service is also available from the Sales Journal when you choose a credit card for payment.

You can set up **Credit Cards Used** to make purchases from suppliers and **Credit Cards Accepted** to enter receipts from customers.

Click **Used** to open the screen for the cards that the business uses:

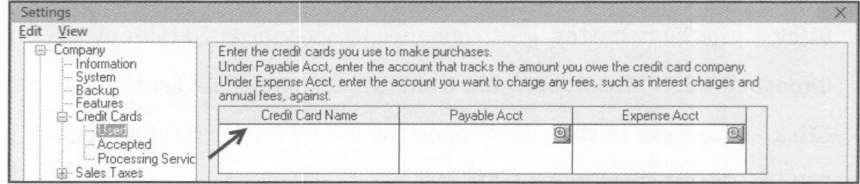

NOTES
The setup and use of credit card processing services are introduced in Chapter 13.

Each card named on this screen will appear in the Purchases and Payments journals in the Payment Method list. There is no discount fee associated with individual purchases, although there may be an annual or monthly fee attached to the card. Each card is listed on a separate line with its associated linked accounts.

Click the **Credit Card Name field** or **press** tab.

Type Visa **Press** tab.

The cursor moves to the **Payable Acct** field. This account is the liability account that records the balance owing to the card company.

Click the **Account List icon** to access the list of available accounts.

Click **2160**, the liability account for the card.

Click **Select** to add the account and move to the Expense Acct field.

The **Expense Account** records any monthly or annual fees paid to the card company for the privilege of using the card and interest charges on cash advances or overdue amounts. Not all cards have user fees, but all cards charge interest on cash advances and balances not paid by the due date. These additional fees are added to this linked expense account for credit card payment transactions in the Payments Journal (refer to Chapter 12). Air Care uses one expense account for all credit card–related expenses.

Click the **Account List icon** to access the account list.

Double-click **5020**.

Cards accepted in payment from customers are set up in the same way. The business may use and accept the same cards or different cards.

Click **Accepted** in the Company list under Credit Cards.

If you did not change the account class correctly, Sage 50 provides a warning about incorrect account classes:

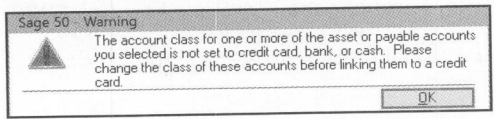

Click OK. Click Cancel to close the Credit Card Information window. Make the necessary account class changes and re-enter the credit card details.

The cards customers can use to make payments are entered on this screen:

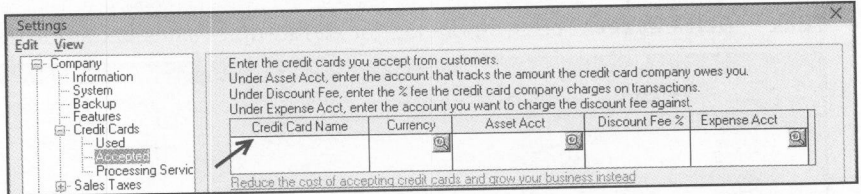

All the cards you name here will appear in the Payment Method list for Sales Invoices. Each card accepted should be listed on a separate line.

Click the **Credit Card Name field** or **press** (tab).

Type Visa **Press** (tab). The cursor advances to the **Currency** field.

Click the **List icon** for the options:

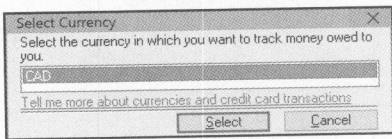

You can choose the currency of this credit card. Air Care has only Canadian customers, so CAD is preselected. Credit cards in other currencies must be connected to Credit Card Receivable or Bank class accounts with those currencies.

Click **Select** or **press** (enter) to continue. **Press** (tab).

The cursor is in the **Asset Acct** field, the linked account for deposits from the card company. Normally a bank account is set up for credit card deposits.

Click the **Account List icon** to display the accounts available for linking.

Click **1070 Bank: Visa** to choose the account.

⚠ WARNING!
You must choose a Bank, Cash or Credit Card Payable class account as the linked Payable account for credit cards used.

📝 NOTES
You can add a new account at this stage if necessary. Type the new account number and press (tab). Click Add to start the Add An Account wizard. Remember to choose the correct Account Class – Credit Card Payable – (on the fifth wizard screen) when using the wizard. Additional screens related to bank account settings are added to the wizard when you select the correct Account Class. You do not need to enter information on these screens.

📝 NOTES
Return to the section Defining the Class for Credit Card Accounts (page 219) if you need assistance with changing the account class.

🔷 PRO VERSION
The Currency option for credit cards is not available in the Pro version. You will advance to the Asset Account field after the Name.

⚠ WARNING!
You must choose either a Credit Card, Cash or Bank class account as the linked asset account for cards accepted. Although other accounts are displayed, choosing them will give you a warning error message like the one on this page.

Click **Select** to add the account and advance to the next field.

The cursor advances to the **Discount Fee %** field. The discount fee is the amount that the card company withholds as a merchant transaction fee for use of the card. This expense is withheld from the total invoice amount that the card company deposits to the business bank account for each sale. Fees vary from one credit card company to another and also for the type of business. For example, high-volume businesses pay a lower percentage than businesses with a smaller volume of sales.

Type 2.9 **Press** tab .

The cursor advances to the **Expense Acct** field. This is the linked account that will be debited automatically for the discount fee for a credit card sale. The expense amount or fee is the total invoice amount times the discount fee percentage.

Click the **Account List icon** 🔍 to display the accounts available for linking.

Click **5020** to choose the account.

Click **Select** to add the account to the Card Information screen.

Enter **MasterCard** in the Name field. **Choose** Asset Account **1080**, **enter 2.7** in the Discount Fee % field and **choose** Expense Account **5020**.

You can enter information for additional credit cards the same way.

Setting Up Sales Taxes

Setting up sales taxes before entering supplier and customer records will allow us to choose default tax codes for customers and suppliers for automatic entry in journals.

Click **Sales Taxes**. The components for the setup of sales tax are listed:

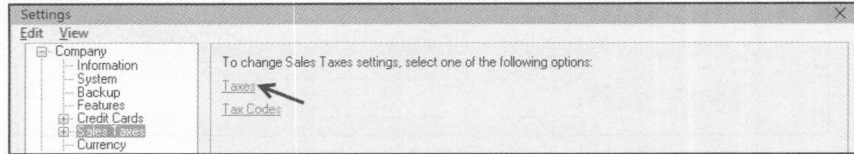

To set up sales taxes, we must identify the taxes that are charged and paid, and then define the codes that will be displayed in the journals.

Click **Taxes**:

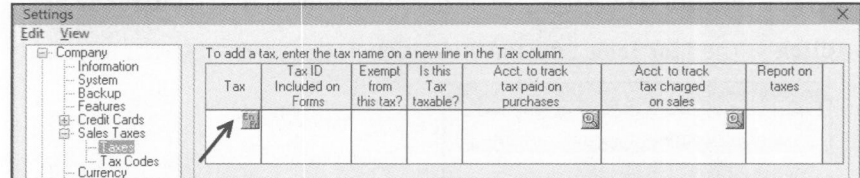

Sage 50 has no preset tax information. You can customize the taxes to suit any business by entering the taxes applied and paid by a business and by creating the tax codes needed to account for the combinations of taxes. Taxes can be added later or edited if needed. Air Care has two taxes, GST and PST, and reports on both. Because PST is not refundable, PST paid is not tracked in a separate account.

Click the **Tax field** or **press** tab so you can enter the name of the tax.

Type GST and **press** tab to advance to the Tax ID field.

The tax number should be included on invoices, so you should enter it in this field. For GST, this is the business number. For PST, it is the provincial registration number that

indicates the supplier is licensed to charge PST. GST numbers are normally included on forms because GST is refundable. PST numbers are not normally included on invoices.

Type   533 766 455 RT0001 **Press** (tab).

The cursor moves to the **Exempt From This Tax?** column. Choose Yes only if your business — Air Care in this case — does not pay the tax. Air Care Services pays GST, so the default selection No is correct. The next field, **Is This Tax Taxable?** asks if another tax includes this tax in its base calculation. Currently no provinces apply this method of tax calculation. For Saskatchewan, where Air Care is located, the correct answer is No.

The next two fields define the linked accounts that **track the taxes paid** and the **taxes charged**. The taxes paid account records the total of the amounts entered in the GST field in the Purchases Journal whenever a purchase is made. Although you may choose an asset or a liability account, we use liability accounts because there is normally a balance owing to the Receiver General. If the tax is not refundable, such as PST paid, you should leave the account field for tracking taxes paid blank.

Click   the **List icon for Acct. To Track Tax Paid On Purchases**.

Double-click 2670 GST Paid on Purchases.

The cursor advances to the field for the Account To Track Tax Charged On Sales. This account records the total of the amounts entered in the GST field in the Sales Journal whenever a sale is made. You may use an asset or a liability account.

Choose 2650 GST Charged on Sales from the List icon list of accounts.

The cursor advances to the **Report On Taxes** field. To generate tax reports from Sage 50, you should choose Yes. The Yes and No entries on the tax screens act as toggle switches. Clicking will change the entry from one to the other, and you can change these entries at any time.

Click   **No** to change the default entry to Yes.

Press   (tab) to advance to the next line and **type** PST

Click   the **List icon for Acct. To Track Tax Charged On Sales**.

Choose 2640 PST Charged on Sales. Press (tab).

Click   **No** to change the default entry to Yes for reporting.

Click   **Tax Codes**. The Tax Codes Settings screen opens:

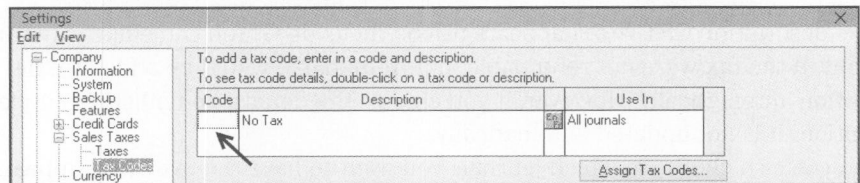

On this screen, you can create the tax codes required for all the different rates and combinations of taxes that apply to a business. No codes are entered initially, so the only entry is the blank code used when **No Tax** is applied. If you want to change or assign tax codes for all suppliers and customers, use the **Assign Tax Codes** feature.

Click   the **Code column** below the blank on the first line.

Type   G **Press** (tab) to move to the Description field.

NOTES
PST registration is required for businesses that charge PST on sales and do not pay PST on purchases of merchandise that they sell to customers (only the final customer pays PST).

NOTES
Sales tax amounts entered in the General Journal are also tracked in these linked accounts.

NOTES
By using liability accounts for both taxes paid and taxes charged, we can display the subtotal (GST Owing) on the Balance Sheet. Normally a business owes GST because sales are larger than expenses.

NOTES
If you do not enter an account for the taxes charged, you must confirm that you will not be able to track the tax by clicking Yes.

NOTES
After creating all tax codes and all supplier and customer records, you can update all tax information from the Assign Tax Codes window. We use this approach in Chapter 16.

NOTES
If at any time the tax regulations change, you can return to this screen and change the settings. For example, in 2013, BC replaced the HST with separate GST and PST, Prince Edward Island implemented the HST to replace the separate GST and PST, Nova Scotia changed the HST rate and Manitoba increased the PST rate. To make these changes in the data files, just edit the Rate in the Tax Code Details screen and the Description in the Tax Code screen. The description is not automatically updated when you change the tax rate. New tax codes may be needed as well.

Press (enter) or **double-click** to open the Tax Code Details screen:

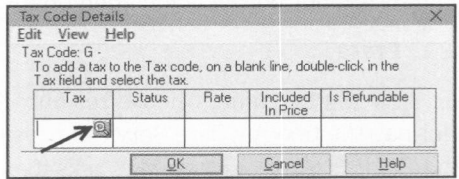

On this screen, you define how the tax is calculated and reported.

Click   the **Tax field List icon** 🔍 to open the list of taxes entered:

Both taxes we named are listed here. At this stage, you are asked to choose the taxes that should be applied (charged or paid) when this code is used in a journal entry.

Click   **Select**, because GST is already selected, and return to the Details.

Defaults are entered for the remaining fields. The tax **Status** is Taxable, and this is correct — tax is calculated and charged. Other status options and their explanations can be viewed by clicking the List icon 🔍. The Non-Taxable Status is used when items are not taxed but their amounts are included in reports to the Receiver General. Similarly, the Exempt Status is used for items that are exempt from the tax but the amounts are included in the tax reports filed. For example, although food is zero rated (no tax is charged), suppliers may still claim a GST refund and must report their sales amounts.

The remaining fields are straightforward. **Rate** is the percentage rate for the tax. Taxes may be **included** in the sales and purchase prices or not included. If some suppliers include the tax and others do not, create two separate tax codes. And finally, is the tax **refundable** — that is, are the taxes paid on purchases refunded? GST is not included for any of Air Care's suppliers' or customers' prices and GST is refundable. Non-refundable taxes, like PST for which you do not enter an account to track taxes paid on expenses, are automatically added to the asset or expense amount for the purchase.

Click   the **Rate field**. **Type** 5

Click   **No** in the Is Refundable column to change the entry to Yes.

Click   **OK** to return to the Tax Codes screen for additional codes.

The description GST @ 5% appears beside the code G. You can edit the description if you want. If the tax were not refundable, non-refundable would be added to the description automatically. However, if you change the details, you must also update the description. It is not updated automatically.

You can also choose in which journals you want to have the tax codes appear. The default is to have the codes available in all journals, which is usually the correct choice.

Click   **All Journals** and then **click** the **List icon** 🔍:

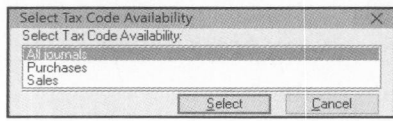

You can choose to have the tax codes available for all revenues, all expenses, or for all transactions (Purchases Journal, Sales Journal and General Journal). The default selection, All Journals, is correct for Air Care.

Click   **Cancel** or **Select** to return to the Tax Codes screen.

Click   the **Code field below G**. **Type** GP **Press** (tab) and then **press** (enter).

Select   **GST** as the first tax for this code. **Click** the **Rate field**. **Type** 5

Click   **No** in the Is Refundable column to change the entry to Yes.

Press   (tab). **Select** or **type PST** as the second tax for this code.

Click   the **Rate field**. **Type** 5 **Click OK** to return to the Settings screen. (PST is not refundable, so the default selection, No, is correct.)

Click   the ▣ **beside Company** to reduce the Settings list.

Linked Accounts

Linked accounts are accounts in the General Ledger that are affected by entries in journals for the other ledgers. We have seen some of these linked accounts at work in journal entries in previous chapters. For example, an entry to record a credit sale in the Sales Journal will cause automatic changes in several General Ledger accounts. In the General Ledger, the *Accounts Receivable* [+], *Revenue from Sales* [+], *GST Charged on Services* [+] and *PST Payable* [+] accounts will all be affected by the sale. The type of change, increase [+] or decrease [–], is indicated in the brackets. The program must know which account numbers to use for posting journal entries in any of the journals. Often you do not enter account numbers for linked accounts in the journals. It is this interconnection of accounts between ledgers that makes Sage 50 fully integrated.

Since only *Current Earnings*, the General linked account for Current Earnings, is defined, we must identify the remaining linked accounts for the General, Payables and Receivables ledgers. Air Care does not use the Payroll or Inventory ledgers, so you do not need to define linked accounts for them. Linked accounts are entered from the Settings screens for the ledgers, so we will enter them with other default ledger settings.

Changing Ledger Settings and Linked Accounts

Changing General Ledger Settings and Linked Accounts

Click   **General (Accounts)** in the list on the left:

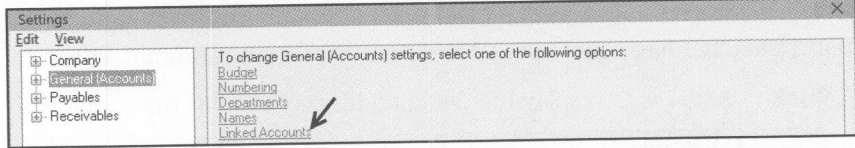

The General Ledger settings are correct for Air Care Services. The budget feature, departmental accounting and expanded account numbers are not used.

We need to add linked accounts.

Defining the General Linked Accounts

Click   **Linked Accounts** to display the General Linked Accounts window:

Press   (tab) to place the cursor in the Retained Earnings field.

The Retained Earnings account is the capital (equity) account to which expense and revenue accounts are closed at the end of the fiscal period. You must choose a capital (3000-range) account.

> **Click**   the **list arrow** beside the field. All postable capital accounts are listed.
>
> **Click**   **3560 S. Arturro, Capital**.

You can also type account numbers directly in the linked account fields. Then press (tab) to complete the entry and advance to the next field. If you type a new account number, you can create the new account.

The Current Earnings account is predefined — the single type X account is always used. This linked setup cannot be changed, although you can modify the account number and account name.

The final option, to **Record Opening Balances In My Retained Earnings Account**, will automatically use the Retained Earnings linked account for amounts that will balance the Trial Balance when you close the ledger. With this option, instead of showing the select account window from which we selected *Test Balance Account*, as on page 94, Sage 50 confirms the change to the linked account when you have a discrepancy:

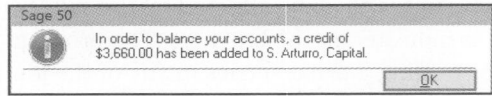

To use this option, you must define the Retained Earnings linked account before adding historical account opening balances. We have already added the opening balances. Click OK to confirm and to update the Retained Earnings opening balance.

Payables Default Settings

> **Click**   **Payables** in the list on the left to expand the options list:

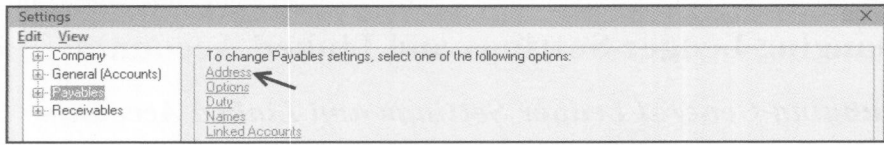

The Payables Ledger has Address settings, general Options, settings for imports (Duty), Names for icons and additional ledger fields, and Linked Accounts. Air Care does not import items that have duty applied and does not use the additional fields.

> **Click**   **Address** to display the default address fields for the suppliers:

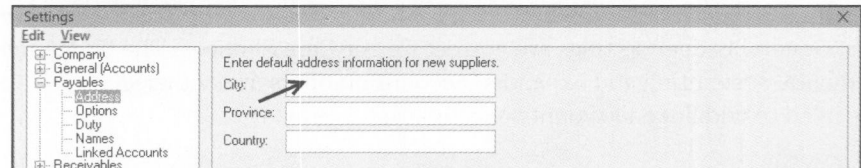

The information you enter here will be used in the ledger records as the defaults when you add suppliers. If most suppliers are in the same location, entering these locations here will save data entry time later. Most of the suppliers for Air Care are located in Regina, Saskatchewan.

> **Click**   the **City field**.
>
> **Type**   Regina **Press** (tab) to advance to the Province field.
>
> **Type**   Saskatchewan **Press** (tab) to advance to the Country field.
>
> **Type**   Canada

Click   **Options** to display the default settings for the Payables Ledger:

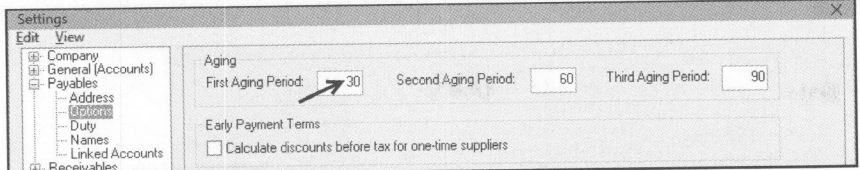

The option for the **aging** of accounts in the Payables Ledger is preset at 30, 60 and 90 days. We will change these options for Air Care to reflect the payment and discount terms most commonly used by Air Care's suppliers.

Press   〔tab〕 or **double-click 30** in the First Aging Period field.

Type   10 **Press** 〔tab〕 to advance to the Second Aging Period field.

Type   30 **Press** 〔tab〕 to advance to the Third Aging Period field.

Type   60

The second option determines how discounts are calculated. If the discount is taken only on pretax subtotals, the discount is calculated before taxes. If the discount is applied to the entire invoice amount, including taxes, the discount is not calculated before taxes. Air Care's suppliers calculate discounts before taxes, so you must change the setting.

Click   **Calculate Discounts Before Tax For One-Time Suppliers**.

Changing Payables Terminology

Sage 50 has a set of default terms that it uses based on the type of company you define. These are the terms that changed for different company types in previous chapters. If you want, you can modify the default selections.

Click   **Names** under Payables to display the Names and Terminology window:

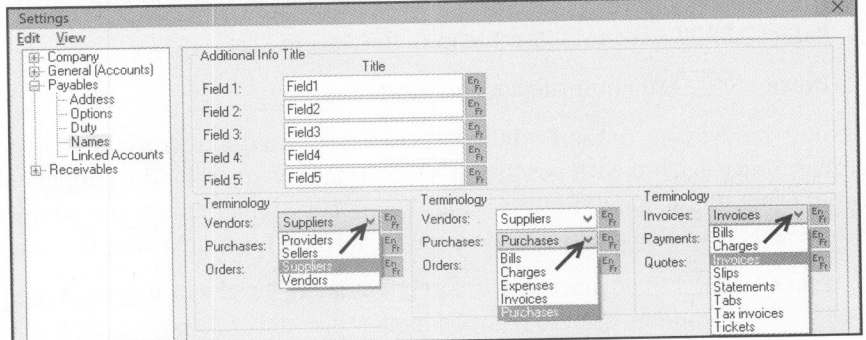

The Names window includes fields for five **Additional Information** names for the Payables Ledger. These will be used on the Additional Information tab screen for ledger records, and you have the option to include them in journal windows.

The second part of the screen has the terms used for icons and fields throughout the program. The names you can change — for Vendors, Purchases and Invoices — are available in their drop-down lists. You cannot modify the Payments label — it has no list arrow. The names you select will apply to icons, fields and reports.

If you want to use different names, click the field for the name you want and select a different name from the drop-down list.

Defining the Payables Linked Accounts

We will enter the Payables Ledger linked accounts next.

NOTES

The decision to calculate discounts before or after tax may also be affected by tax regulations.

NOTES

Usually, clicking a number in a field will select the entire number. Sometimes, however, depending on exactly where you click, only part of the number is selected or an insertion point is added. Double-clicking will always select the entire number in the field so that you can edit it.

NOTES

We will add discount terms to individual supplier records when we set up the Payables Ledger.

PRO VERSION

The Names screen includes only the Additional Information fields. You cannot change the terminology in the Pro version.

Click   **Linked Accounts** under Payables to display the Linked Accounts window:

 CLASSIC VIEW
In the Home window, you can right-click the Purchases Journal or Payments Journal icon,

 or ___ . Click the

Settings tool ___ to open the Payables Linked Accounts screen.

NOTES
The total owed to all suppliers is the sum of the individual outstanding historical balances in the Supplier Ledger records.

NOTES
The linked account for prepayments is also a required linked account. Because we are not using the feature, we can enter Accounts Payable.

NOTES
Credit card and tax accounts are also linked accounts and the accounts must be removed from the relevant Settings before you can remove the account.

We need to identify the default General Ledger bank account used to make payments to suppliers. This is an essential linked account — it is required before you can finish the history for the company data file. Cash transactions in the Payments Journal will be posted to the bank account you select in the journal window. All Bank and Cash class accounts are available in the journals, and the **principal bank account** defined here will be selected as the default.

Clicking the drop-down list arrow for any linked account field will open the list of accounts available for linking. Only Bank class (or Cash) accounts may be used in the bank fields. That is why we needed to define the Bank class accounts first.

When additional currencies are used, fields will be available for linked bank accounts for those currencies as well. Because we have not set up foreign currencies, their linked bank account fields are omitted. The chequing account is Air Care's principal bank account for supplier transactions.

Click   the **Principal Bank Account field list arrow**. Only the single Bank class account is available for selection.

Click   **1060 Bank: Chequing** and **press** (tab).

The cursor advances to the **Accounts Payable** field. This control account is also required and is used to record the amounts owing to suppliers whenever a credit (Pay Later) Purchases Journal entry or invoice payment is completed. The balance in this account reflects the total owing to all suppliers, which must match the opening General Ledger balance for *Accounts Payable*. You must use a liability account in this field.

Select   **2200 Accounts Payable** from the Account list.

Press   (tab) to enter the account number.

The cursor advances to the **Freight Expense** field, used to record the delivery or freight charges associated with purchases. Only freight charged by the supplier should be entered using this account. Since Air Care's suppliers do not charge for delivery, you should leave this field blank. You can add a linked account for freight later if you need it.

Press   (tab) to advance to the **Early Payment Purchase Discount** field. This account is used to record supplier discounts taken for early payments.

Choose   **5040 Purchase Discounts** from the drop-down list.

Press   (tab) to advance to the **Prepayments And Prepaid Orders** field.

Air Care's suppliers do not request prepayments at this time, but you cannot leave this field blank.

Choose   **2200 Accounts Payable** from the drop-down list.

Check the linked accounts carefully. To **delete a linked account**, click it to highlight it and press (del). You must complete this step of deleting the account from any linked accounts screen before you can remove the account in the General Ledger from the Accounts window.

To select a different account, highlight the one that is incorrect and type the correct number, or select an account from the drop-down list.

Receivables Default Settings

Click **Receivables** to display the Receivables Ledger choices:

The Receivables Ledger has Address, general Options, Discount and Comments settings, Names for icons and additional ledger fields, and Linked Accounts.

Click **Address** to display the default address fields for customers:

The information you enter here will be used in the ledger records as the defaults when you add customers. Most of Air Care's customers are located in Regina.

Click the **City field. Type** Regina **Press** (tab).

Type Saskatchewan in the Province field.

Press (tab) to advance to the Country field. **Type** Canada

Click **Options** to display the default settings for the Receivables Ledger:

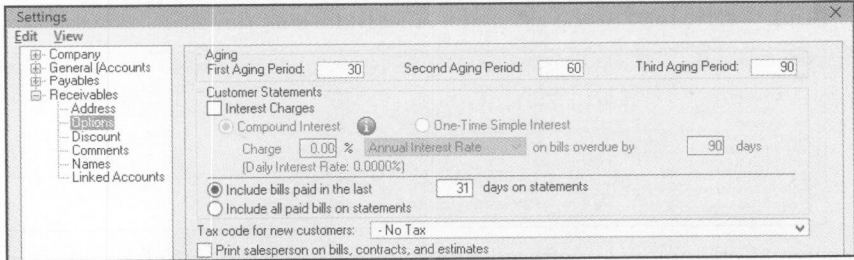

Air Care Services offers a 1 percent discount if customers pay within 10 days and expects full payment within 30 days. After 30 days, customers are charged 1.5 percent interest per month on the overdue accounts. Therefore, the **aging periods** 10, 30 and 60 days will be used, and we must change the default settings.

Press (tab), or **double-click 30** in the First Aging Period field.

Type 10 **Press** (tab) to advance to the Second Aging Period field.

Type 30 **Press** (tab) to advance to the Third Aging Period field. **Type** 60

Click **Interest Charges** to add a ✓ and select this feature.

Point to the 🛈 **button** to open a pop-up balloon with more information about how interest is calculated:

When interest is charged on overdue invoices, Sage 50 calculates interest amounts and prints them on the customer statements. However, the program does not create an invoice for the interest. You must create a separate entry for the interest amount.

The default selection, **Compound Interest**, is correct.

Press   ⌜tab⌝ to advance to and select the contents of the Interest Rate field.

Type   1.5 **Press** ⌜tab⌝ to advance to the Annual Interest Rate entry.

Click   the **list arrow** and **choose Monthly Interest Rate** to change the basis of calculation.

Press   ⌜tab⌝ to advance to the Days field.

Type   1   Interest charges begin immediately after the net amount is due.

The next option relates to printing historical information on invoices. The maximum setting is 999 days. Air Care Services sends customer statements monthly, so the period should be 31 days. Invoices paid in the past 31 days will be included and you can include all paid bills. Unpaid invoices are always included. The default setting is correct.

If all or most customers use the same sales tax code, you can choose a **default tax code** that will be entered when you create new customers or when you choose One-Time Customer or Quick Add in a sales invoice.

Click   the **Tax Code For New Customers list arrow**.

Click   **GP - GST @ 5%; PST @ 5%** to use this as the default tax code.

When salespersons are set up, you can **print** the name of the **salesperson** on invoices, orders and quotes. Air Care does not have sales staff.

Entering Discount Settings

Next we must enter the payment terms for account customers.

Click   **Discount** in the list under Receivables on the left:

All account customers are offered a discount of 1 percent if they pay the full account balance in the first 10 days, and net payment is due in 30 days. All customer discounts are calculated on after-tax amounts, so the **Calculate Early Payment Discounts Before Tax** selection is correctly turned off.

Click   the **% field** in the first Early Payment Terms field to advance the cursor.

Type   1.0 **Press** ⌜tab⌝ to advance to the Days field.

Type   10 **Press** ⌜tab⌝ to advance to the Net Days field and **type** 30

Sage 50 adds the payment terms you just entered as a default for all customers. Individual customer records or invoices can still be modified if needed.

Air Care does not use the remaining discount option — to apply discounts to individual lines on an invoice. A % Discount column will be added to the invoice form when you use this feature.

Click   **Calculate Line Item Discounts On Bills, Contracts And Estimates** to remove the ✓. Sage 50 requires you to confirm the selection:

NOTES
We will use the line discount feature in Chapter 19.

PRO VERSION
pro Line discounts are not available in the Pro version, so you will skip this step and the confirmation message.

Click   Yes to confirm the removal of line discounts.

If you later change the default customer payment terms, you will be asked whether you want to update all customer terms to match the new terms.

Entering Default Comments

Sage 50 allows you to add a default comment to the Message field on all customer forms. You can change the default message any time you want, and you can edit it for a particular form when you are completing the invoice, quote or order confirmation.

Click   Comments under Receivables to open the screen for default comments:

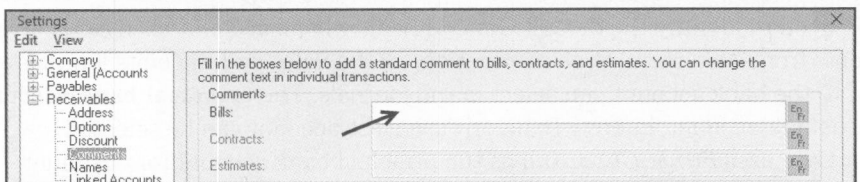

We want to add a comment that will appear on every customer invoice. The comment may include payment terms, company motto, notice of an upcoming sale or a warning about interest charges.

Click   the Bills (Invoices) field to move the cursor.

Type   Interest @ 1.5% per month charged on accounts over 30 days.

You can enter the same comment for all sales forms (invoices, orders and quotes), or you can add a unique comment for each. The comment fields for quotes and orders are dimmed because Air Care does not use these features.

Changing Receivables Terminology

The terms for the Receivables Ledger can also be customized.

Click   Names under Receivables to display the Names and Terminology window:

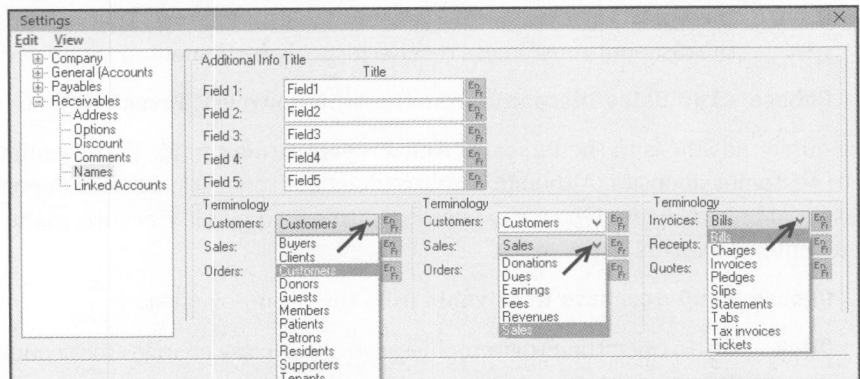

For Receivables, you can also name five additional fields to appear in ledger records and, if you choose, in journal windows.

The second part of the screen has the industry-specific terms used. The names you can change — for Customers, Sales and Bills (Invoices) — are available in the drop-down lists for each field. You cannot modify the Receipts label. The names you select will apply to icons, fields and reports.

If you want to use different names, click the field for the name you want and select a different name from the drop-down list.

 CLASSIC VIEW
In the Home window, you can right-click the Sales Journal or Receipts Journal icon,

 or 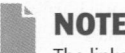. Click the Settings tool to open the Receivables Linked Accounts screen.

NOTES
The linked accounts for Principal Bank, Accounts Receivable and Deposits are all essential linked accounts.

NOTES
Only the single bank class account is available on the drop-down list.

When additional currencies are used, fields will be available for linked bank accounts for them as well. You can choose a separate linked account for each currency, or you can use the Canadian dollar account for more than one currency. Because we have not set up foreign currencies, their linked bank account fields are omitted.

WARNING!
You may prefer to leave the Default Revenue Account field blank. If you enter 4100 Installation Revenue as the default revenue account, you must remember to change the account for journal entries that require a different revenue account.

NOTES
You must choose Yes to confirm the account class changes and continue. If you choose No, you will return to the Linked Accounts screen.

Defining the Receivables Linked Accounts

The Receivables Ledger linked accounts parallel those for the Payables Ledger.

> **Click**   **Linked Accounts** under Receivables:

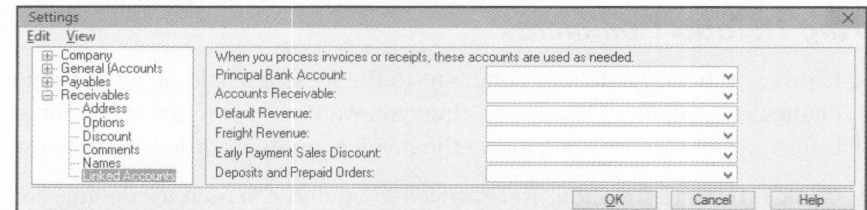

We need to identify the default General Ledger bank account used to receive payments from customers. Cash transactions in the Sales and Receipts journals will be posted to the bank account you select in the journals. The **principal bank account** will be the default account, but any Bank or Cash class account can be selected.

Air Care uses *Bank: Chequing* as the principal bank account for customer transactions. Although most linked accounts may be used only once, one bank account can be linked to the Payables, Receivables and Payroll ledgers.

> **Click**   the **Principal Bank Account field list arrow**.

> **Click**   **1060 Bank: Chequing** and **press** [tab].

The cursor advances to the **Accounts Receivable** field. This control account records the amounts owed to Air Care by customers whenever a credit (Pay Later) Sales Journal invoice or receipt is entered. The General Ledger balance for *Accounts Receivable* reflects and must match the total owed by all customers (from the ledger records). You must use an asset account in this field.

> **Select**   **1200 Accounts Receivable** from the drop-down list. **Press** [tab].

> **Click**   the **Default Revenue list arrow** and **choose 4100 Installation Revenue**.

Air Care does not charge for deliveries. Leave the Freight Revenue field blank.

> **Click**   the **Early Payment Sales Discount field list arrow**. This account records the discounts customers receive for early settlement of their accounts.

> **Choose 4180 Sales Discounts** from the drop-down list. **Press** [tab].

The cursor advances to the **Deposits And Prepaid Orders** field. This account is linked to customer deposits. Although Air Care does not request customer deposits, this is an essential linked account, so we cannot leave this field blank. Because we do not use it, we can enter *Accounts Receivable*.

> **Choose 1200 Accounts Receivable** from the drop-down list.

> **Click**   **OK** to open the program's message about class changes for account 3560:

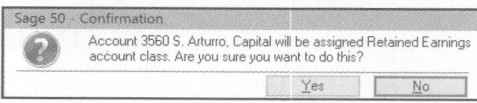

Many linked accounts must have a specific account class to be used as linked accounts. Normally, you can allow the program to assign and change the account class. The exceptions are the Credit Card and Bank class accounts, which you must define before you can use them as linked bank accounts.

> **Click**   **Yes** to accept the change and save the linked account setting. Sage 50 displays a second confirmation message for account 2200:

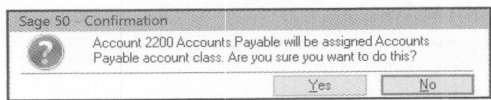

Click   Yes to accept the class change and save the linked accounts. The final message about the account class change for account 1200 opens:

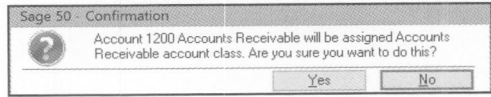

Click   Yes to accept the change and return to the Home window.

This may be a good time to take a break.

Entering Suppliers in the Payables Ledger

Use the Supplier Information for Air Care Services on page 203 to enter supplier details and historical invoices. The following keystrokes will enter the information for Beausejour Electrical Products, the first supplier on Air Care Services' list.

You can enter new supplier records from the Setup Guide for Suppliers, but you can enter only some of the details on the Address tab screen. Because we need to add other details, we will work from the ledgers. You can open the ledger screen from the Payables module window Suppliers icon or from its shortcuts list. First we must open the Payables module window.

Click   Payables in the Modules pane to open the window we need.

Click   the Suppliers shortcuts list arrow and **choose View Suppliers**:

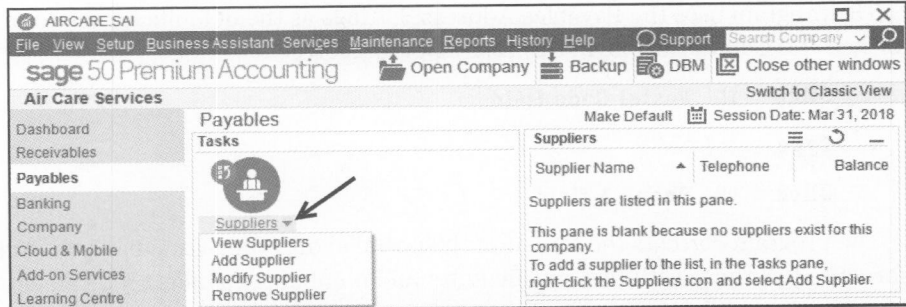

Or, **click** the **Suppliers icon** 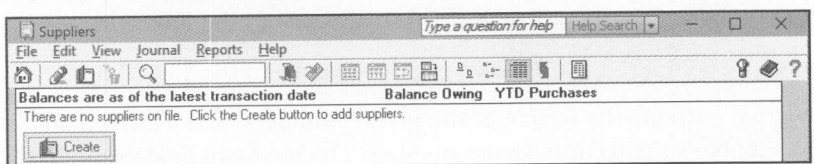 in the Payables Home window:

The Suppliers window is empty because no suppliers are on file. Once we add the supplier accounts, this window will contain a listing for each supplier that you can use to access the supplier's ledger record. The suppliers may be displayed in icon form or by name with balances and year-to-date amounts. The default is the listing by name.

Click   the Create button ⬛ Create or the **Create tool** 🗔 in the Suppliers window.

NOTES
If you click Add Supplier on the shortcuts list, you will open the New Supplier Ledger window immediately.

pro PRO VERSION
Click the Vendors icon to open the Vendors window. The term Vendor replaces Supplier in the Suppliers window and in all ledger windows.

NOTES
If you prefer to list the suppliers by icon in the Suppliers window, choose the View menu and click Icon or click the Display By Icon tool. New suppliers will be added at the end of the display, but you can drag icons to any position you want so that frequently used icons appear together at the top of the window.
If you display the suppliers by icon, you can restore the alphabetic order for the icons by choosing the View menu and clicking Re-sort Icons.

NOTES
Pressing ⌨ctrl + N in the Suppliers window or in a ledger record window will also open a new Supplier Ledger record form.

Or, **choose** the **File menu** and **click Create**:

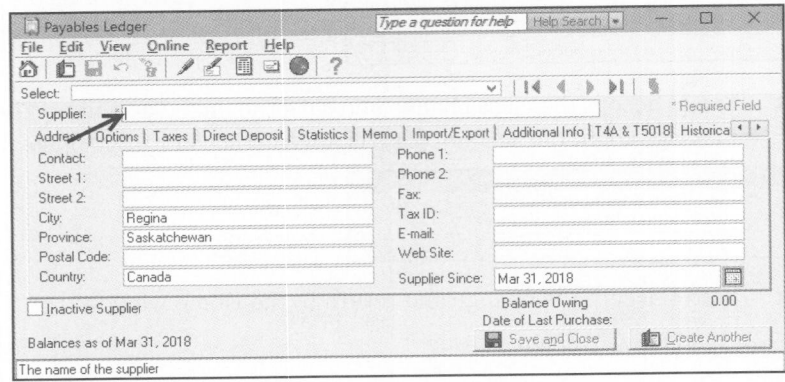

The supplier Address tab screen opens. Most of the supplier input screens should be familiar from entering records for new suppliers in previous chapters. The cursor is in the Supplier name field, the only required field for the record.

Type Beausejour Electrical Products **Press** ⟨tab⟩.

The cursor advances to the Contact field. Here you should enter the name of the person (or department) at Beausejour Electrical Products with whom Air Care Services will be dealing. This information enables a company to make professional and effective inquiries. For a small business, the owner's name may appear in this field.

Type Janine Beausejour **Press** ⟨tab⟩ to advance to the Street 1 field.

Type 50 Shockley Rd. **Press** ⟨tab⟩ to move to the Street 2 field.

Type Unit 18

The program uses the Payables Address Settings as the defaults for the City, Province and Country fields. In this case, they are correct.

Click the **Postal Code field**.

Type s4f2t2

Click the **Phone 1 field**.

The program corrects the format of the postal code. (Only Canadian postal codes are reformatted — those with the specific letter and number sequence.) You can enter phone and fax numbers with or without the area code.

Type 3064765282 **Press** ⟨tab⟩ to advance to the Phone 2 field.

Type 3064763997 **Press** ⟨tab⟩ to advance to the Fax field.

Type 3064765110 **Press** ⟨tab⟩ to advance to the Tax ID field.

The program corrects the format of the phone numbers. The Tax ID field allows you to enter the supplier's tax ID or business number. The next two fields contain the e-mail and Web site addresses for the supplier. Enter them just as you would type them in your e-mail and Internet programs.

Type 444 276 534 **Press** ⟨tab⟩.

Type jb@beausejour.com **Press** ⟨tab⟩.

Type beausejour.com **Press** ⟨tab⟩.

The cursor moves to the Supplier Since field. The program has entered the session date as the default, but we should change it to reflect the company's actual transaction history. All suppliers have been used by Air Care since January 1, 2012.

NOTES
If you choose to skip the Suppliers icon window from the Home window Setup menu (User Preferences, View), you will open this Payables Ledger (supplier) Address tab window immediately when you click the Suppliers icon.

NOTES
As soon as you start typing in the supplier name, the * and Required Field * notations disappear. The Save And Close and Create Another buttons are also no longer dimmed.

NOTES
You may skip any of the address tab fields, except the name, if the information is missing for the supplier. To move the cursor, just click the next field for which you have information. To edit any field, drag to highlight the contents and type the correct information.

NOTES
Remember that the postal code sequence for Canada is letter, number, letter, number, letter and number.

Type   Jan 1 2012

The supplier's account balance appears at the bottom of the ledger. A supplier may be marked as **Inactive**, also at the bottom of the ledger, if there are currently no transactions. You have the option to include or omit inactive suppliers from reports. All Air Care's suppliers are active.

The remaining supplier details are entered from the other tab screens.

Click   the **Options tab** to open the next screen:

The supplier's name appears on each tab screen for reference. We want to enter the default expense account so that it will automatically appear in journal entries.

Click   the **Expense Account list arrow**. All postable accounts are listed.

Click   **1320 Electrical Supplies**.

When you use multiple currencies, they can also be linked to suppliers on the Options tab screen. The **Usually Store Item In** field refers to inventory locations. When multiple locations are used for storage, you can link the supplier to one of these locations. Air Care does not sell inventory and has only one location.

Regardless of the language you use to work in Sage 50, you can choose a language for the supplier so that all Sage 50 forms you send to this supplier will be in the language selected on the Options tab screen.

If the supplier offers a discount for early payment or has a term for the net amount, enter these details in this screen. The terms with Beausejour are 1/10, net 30.

Click   the **% Discount field** (the first Early Payment Terms field).

Type   1   **Press** `tab` to advance to the If Paid In ___ Days field.

Type   10   **Press** `tab` to advance to the Net Due In ___ Days field.

Type   30

Click   the **Calculate Discounts Before Tax check box** to select this option.

Do not turn on the option to **Print Contact On Cheques** because the Contact field does not contain address information.

If you e-mail purchase orders to a supplier, choose this option from the drop-down list to replace the default option to print purchase orders. Click **E-mail Confirmation** if you e-mail purchase orders to be certain that the order is sent. Even if you choose Print as the default, you can still e-mail the order from the Purchases Journal.

Synchronizing with Microsoft Outlook will add this supplier to your Outlook contact list.

NOTES
If you have not yet created the account you want to use as the default account, type the new account number in the Expense Account field and press `tab` to start the Add An Account wizard. Choose Add when asked if you want to create the account.

PRO VERSION
pro You will not have the Usually Store Item In Location field or the options to Include The Supplier When Filing T5018 Slips and Synchronize With Microsoft Outlook.

NOTES
Multiple inventory locations are used in Chapter 18.

NOTES
Remember that all supplier discounts are calculated on before-tax amounts.

NOTES
For suppliers who request payment on receipt, enter 1 in the Net Days field. When you enter zero in the Net Days field, the Terms fields remain blank and invoices will be counted as overdue. Payment terms may be changed in the journal for individual invoices.

NOTES
When PST applies, businesses that sell inventory or other products do not pay PST on the products they purchase for sale or use to make the products they sell. Thus they are exempt from paying PST. If, however, the supplier provides other items that are subject to PST charges, you must choose No in the Exempt column for PST so that taxes can be calculated correctly for those items.

Click the **Taxes tab** to access the next input screen:

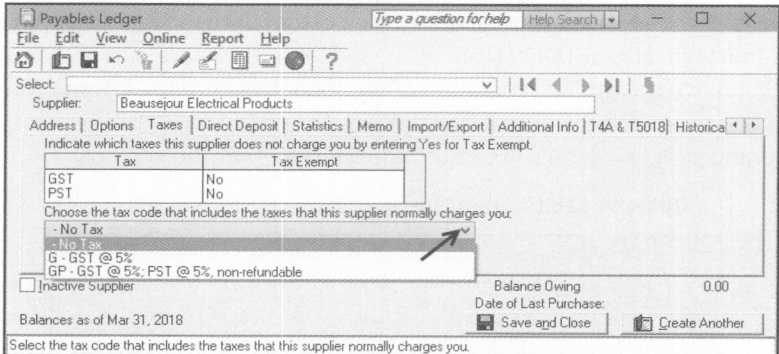

This screen allows you to indicate which taxes the supplier normally charges and the default tax code for journal entries. The codes are available from the drop-down list.

All suppliers for Air Care Services, except the Receiver General, charge GST, so the correct entry for the Tax Exempt column is No. Some suppliers also charge PST. Suppliers such as the Receiver General for Canada, who do not supply goods or services eligible for input tax credits, should have Yes in the Tax Exempt column. If you choose Yes, the tax will not be calculated in the Purchases Journal for that supplier, even if you choose a tax code that applies the tax.

Leave all **Tax Exempt** entry settings at **No** to make all tax codes available for purchases. Clicking No changes the entry to Yes.

Click the **list arrow beside No Tax** to choose a default tax code.

Click **G - GST @ 5%** to select the code.

Click the **Direct Deposit tab** to open the next information screen:

NOTES
Direct Deposit is covered in Chapter 13.

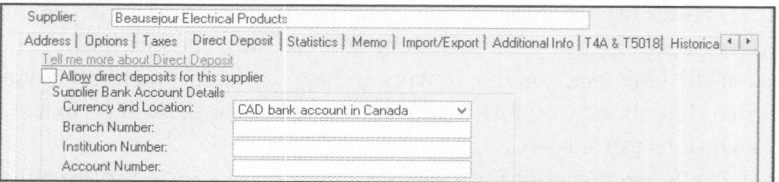

The Direct Deposit fields record your bank account details for automatic withdrawals you allow this supplier to make.

Click the **Statistics tab** to open the next information screen:

NOTES
When the supplier uses a foreign currency, the statistics summary information is presented for both currencies.

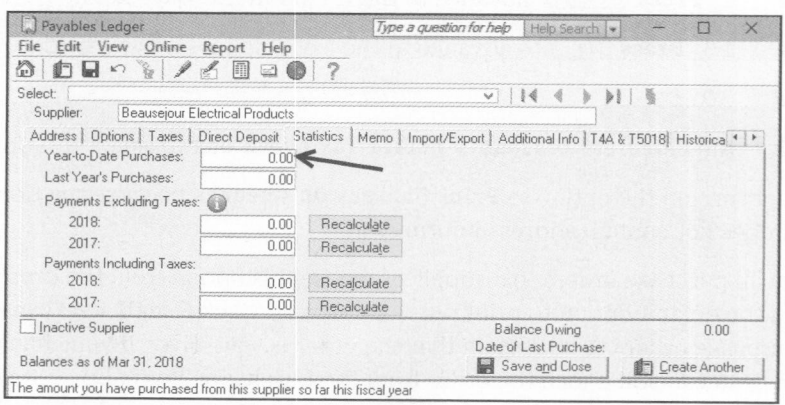

Point to the ℹ️ button for more information about amounts without taxes:

The Statistics fields record the historical purchase and payment totals for two years and are updated automatically from journal entries. You can enter amounts with and without taxes.

Click   the **Year-To-Date Purchases field**.

Type   2100

Click   the **Payments Excluding Taxes for 2018 field**. **Type**   2000

Click   the **Payments Including Taxes for 2018 field**. **Type**   2100

Click   the **Memo tab** to advance to the next screen:

Supplier:	Beausejour Electrical Products	

Address | Options | Taxes | Direct Deposit | Statistics | Memo | Import/Export | Additional Info | T4A & T5018 | Historica ◄ | ►

Memo: _____

To-Do Date: _____ 📅   🔖 Clear Memo

☐ Display this memo in the Daily Business Manager

The Memo tab screen allows you to enter a message and date related to the supplier that may be added to the Daily Business Manager lists, the automatic reminder system.

Click   the **Import/Export tab** to open the next information screen:

Supplier:	Beausejour Electrical Products	

Address | Options | Taxes | Direct Deposit | Statistics | Memo | Import/Export | Additional Info | T4A & T5018 | Historica ◄ | ►

☐ This supplier has Sage 50 and can import orders
☐ This supplier uses my item numbers on invoices and quotes
Match the supplier's item number to my item number or an account number for importing invoices & quotes:

Supplier's Item No.	My Item No.	My Account
	🔍	🔍

The Import/Export screen refers to orders and quotes. If the supplier also uses Sage 50, you can match the supplier's inventory item codes to your own for electronic transfers of information.

Click   the **Additional Info tab**:

Supplier:	Beausejour Electrical Products	

Address | Options | Taxes | Direct Deposit | Statistics | Memo | Import/Export | Additional Info | T4A & T5018 | Historica ◄ | ►

Display this information when
the supplier is selected in a
transaction

Field1 : _____   ☐
Field2 : _____   ☐
Field3 : _____   ☐
Field4 : _____   ☐
Field5 : _____   ☐

You can customize the records for any ledger by adding up to five fields. The customized names you added from the Names Settings option for the ledger will appear on this Additional Info screen. This additional information can be included in journal transaction windows and in Supplier List reports. Air Care Services does not use any additional fields.

Click   the **T4A & T5018 tab**:

Supplier:	Beausejour Electrical Products	

Address | Options | Taxes | Direct Deposit | Statistics | Memo | Import/Export | Additional Info | T4A & T5018 | Historica ◄ | ►

Forms
☐ Include this Supplier When Filing
  ◉ T4A
  ○ T5018
Click the Statistics tab to view payment amounts.

T4A Filing
Select the box in which you want to report the
payment amount on the T4A form.
Box: 20 - Self-employed commissions

If the business pays subcontractors who require these forms for income tax purposes, enter the information here. Purchases from these suppliers will be used to prepare the forms. Air Care does not have subcontractors or contract employees, so we are now ready to enter the supplier's historical transactions.

Correct any **errors** by returning to the field with the mistake. **Highlight** the **errors** and **enter** the **correct information**.

NOTES
The message in the memo may be up to 255 characters in length.
The Daily Business Manager is used in Chapter 11.
The Import/Export feature is described in Appendix J on the Student DVD.

NOTES
When you and your supplier use the same item numbers, and you check this option, the matching part of the screen is no longer needed and is removed.
Importing orders is covered in Appendix J on the Student DVD.

NOTES
The field names on this tab screen are taken from the Names settings for the ledger (refer to page 227).
We will customize Payroll Ledger records by adding fields in Chapter 9.

NOTES
If you prepare T4A slips for the supplier, you can select the box on the form that is used for the amount paid.

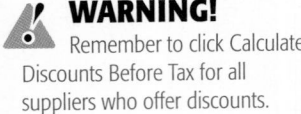

WARNING!
Remember to click Calculate Discounts Before Tax for all suppliers who offer discounts.

NOTES
If you have already created and saved the record, the Save Now option will be removed from the Historical Transactions tab screen. Instead, you will open the next screen asking you to choose Invoices or Payments.

WARNING!
Enter invoice details carefully. To correct a historical invoice amount, you must pay the invoice and clear the paid transactions (Maintenance menu); then reset the historical payments for the year to zero (Payables Ledger, Statistics tab screen) and re-enter the year-to-date amounts and the outstanding invoices. Refer to page 249.

If there are **no historical invoices**, proceed to the final step of saving the supplier record. Click Create Another and then click the Address tab to prepare for entering the next supplier.

For all suppliers, the date for **Supplier Since** is **January 1, 2012**.

Entering Historical Supplier Information

You can enter all the historical invoices and payments for the fiscal year to date, but you must enter all outstanding invoices and partial payments toward them. Beausejour Electrical Products has outstanding invoices, so we must enter historical transaction details. The following keystrokes will enter the historical information from page 203 for Beausejour Electrical Products.

You can also enter and save other ledger details for all suppliers and then open the ledger to add historical information by clicking the Historical Transactions tab. In this case, the Save Now button will be removed. Open the ledger for any supplier by double-clicking the supplier's name in the Suppliers window.

Click   the **Historical Transactions tab**:

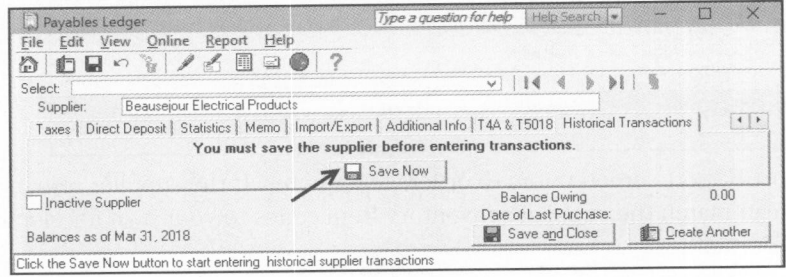

You must save or create the supplier record before adding historical invoices.

Click   the **Save Now button** to modify the ledger screen:

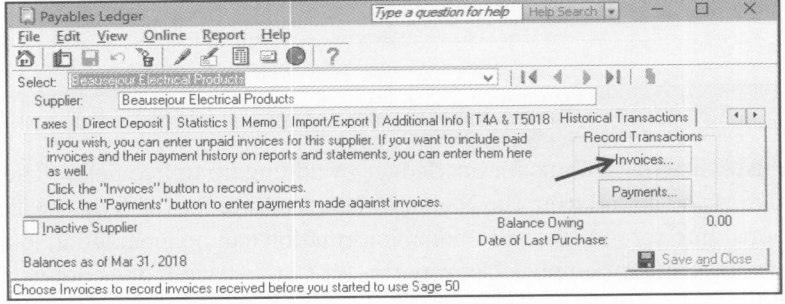

The Create Another button has been removed and the Save And Close button is dimmed again. The screen now has two new buttons: Invoices and Payments. You should select **Invoices** to record outstanding invoices and **Payments** to record prior payments that you want to keep on record after entering invoices.

Click   the **Invoices button** to open the input screen:

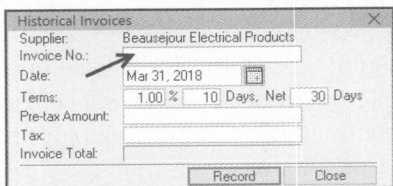

The cursor is in the Invoice No. field so you can enter the first invoice number.

Type   B-894 **Press** [tab] to advance to the Date field.

Enter the invoice date to replace the default earliest transaction date. The invoice date must not be later than the earliest transaction date — the date allowed for the first journal transaction after the historical data in the setup.

Type   03-26-18

The Terms are entered from the Supplier record and are correct, although they can be edited if necessary. You should enter the amount for the first invoice. The amount is divided into pretax and tax amounts so that Sage 50 can correctly calculate the discount on the before-tax amount. When the option to calculate discounts before tax is not selected, a single amount field appears on the invoice for the full amount of the invoice with taxes included — as on page 244 for customers.

Click   the **Pre-tax Amount field** to advance the cursor.

Type   10000 **Press** (tab) to advance to the Tax amount field.

Type   500 **Press** (tab) to update the Invoice Total.

The total of all outstanding invoice and payment amounts must match the opening balance in the *Accounts Payable* control account in the General Ledger.

Correct any **errors**. **Press** (tab) to return to the field with the error and **highlight** the **error**. Then **enter** the **correct information**.

Be sure that all the information is entered correctly before you save your supplier invoice. If you save incorrect invoice information and you want to change it, refer to page 249 for assistance.

Click   **Record** to save the invoice and to display a blank invoice for the supplier.

Enter   **invoice B-921** (not the payment, Chq #94) for Beausejour Electrical Products by repeating the steps above. **Click Record**.

When you have recorded all outstanding invoices for a supplier,

Click   **Close** to return to the ledger.

The two invoices have been added to the Balance Owing field at the bottom of the ledger screen. Now you can enter historical payment information for this supplier.

Click   the **Payments button** to display the payments form:

Invoice	Amount	Disc. Available	Disc. Taken	Amount paid
B-894	10,500.00	100.00		
B-921	2,100.00	20.00		
			Total:	

All outstanding invoices that you entered are displayed. Notice that the discount amounts are 1 percent of the pretax amounts. Entering historical payments is very much like entering current payments in the Payments Journal. You should make separate payment entries for each cheque.

Click the Number field if necessary to place the cursor in the cheque Number field.

Type   94 **Press** (tab) to advance to the Date field.

Enter the cheque date for the first payment toward invoice #B-894 to replace the default earliest transaction date.

Type   3-26

WARNING!
You must choose Record to save each invoice and payment and then Close the invoice form. If you close the input screen before selecting Record, the information is not saved.

NOTES
The View menu has the option to refresh the invoices from information added by other users. It applies only to the multi-user mode and is not available in the Pro version.

NOTES
The discount amounts based on pretax amounts are $100 (1 percent of $10 000) and $20 (1 percent of $2 000).

Click   the **Amount Paid column** on the line for Invoice #B-894.

Because the full amount is not being paid, the discount does not apply. The full amount of the discount will remain available until the 10 days have passed. If the balance is paid within that time, the full discount will be taken.

The full invoice amount, displayed as the default, is highlighted so you can edit it.

Type   4500 **Press** tab . **Press** del to delete the Disc. Taken amount.

Check   the **information** carefully and **make corrections** before you proceed.

Click   **Record** to save the information and display another payment form for this supplier in case there are additional payments to record.

The amount owing for invoice #B-894 has been updated to include the payment you entered, but the full discount amount remains available.

Repeat these procedures to enter any other payments to this supplier.

When you have recorded all outstanding payments to a supplier,

Click   **Close** to return to the supplier information form.

On the Statistics tab screen, the invoices and payment you entered have been included to increase the totals for 2018.

Click   the **Create tool** or **press** ctrl + N to enter the next supplier.

Click   the **Address tab** to prepare for entering the next supplier record.

Sage 50 has created a Supplier icon and listing for Beausejour Electrical Products in the Suppliers window. The default view for suppliers is to list them alphabetically by name with the balance owing and year-to-date purchases. The Create button has been removed, although the Create tool is still available.

Enter   the **remaining suppliers** and historical transactions on page 203.

Click   **Save And Close** to close the Supplier Ledger after entering the last supplier record (it has no historical transactions).

Display or **print** your **Supplier List** to check the address details from the Reports menu in the Suppliers window.

Display or **print** a **Supplier Aged Detail Report**. Include terms and historical differences. Your report should include a historical difference.

Close the **Suppliers window** to return to the Home window.

Entering Customers in the Receivables Ledger

Use the Customer Information chart for Air Care Services on page 204 to complete this step. The following keystrokes will enter the information for Grande Pointe Towers, the first customer on the list for Air Care Services. You should open the Receivables window.

Click   **Receivables** in the Modules pane list to open the window we need.

Click   the **Customers icon** to display the Customers window. The Customers window is empty because there are no customers on file yet.

Click   the **Create button** or **tool** in the Customers window, or **choose** the **File menu** and **click Create**.

You will open the Receivables Ledger new customer Address tab screen:

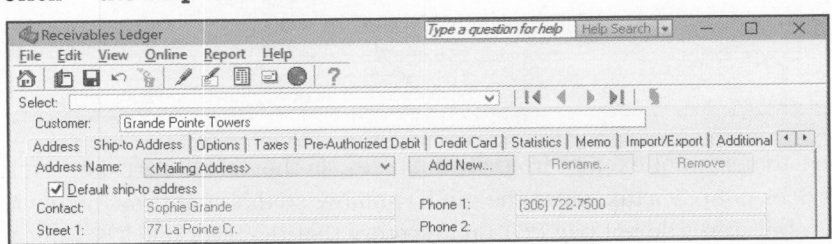

The customer information screen opens at the Address tab screen. The cursor is in the Customer field, the only required field. The default Province and Country entered from the module's Address settings are correct, but we need to change the city name.

Type   Grande Pointe Towers **Press** (tab).

You may skip any address tab fields if information is missing. Just click the next field for which you have information to move the cursor.

Air Care's primary contact about a sale should be entered in the Contact field.

Type   Sophie Grande **Press** (tab) to advance to the Street 1 field.

Type   77 LaPointe Cr. **Press** (tab) to move to the Street 2 field.

Press   (tab) to advance to the City field. We need to replace the default entry.

Type   White City

Click   the **Postal Code field**. **Type** s0g5b0

Click   the **Phone 1 field**. The postal code format is corrected.

Type   3067227500 **Press** (tab). The format is corrected automatically.

Click   the **Fax field**.

Type   3063227436 **Press** (tab) to advance to the E-mail field.

Type   sgrande@GPTowers.com **Press** (tab).

Type   GPTowers.com to enter the Web site.

Press   (tab) **twice** to move to the Customer Since date field.

Type   Jan 1 18

The current balance is included at the bottom of the Ledger window. Like suppliers and accounts, customers may be marked as inactive and omitted from reports if they have not bought merchandise or services for some time.

Click   the **Ship-To Address tab**:

NOTES
As soon as you choose another address in the Address Name field, the address fields will open. Refer to Chapter 6 for more information on shipping addresses.

NOTES
The option to calculate discounts before or after tax is selected for the Receivables Ledger as a whole (refer to page 230). You cannot change the setting for individual customers.

PRO VERSION
You will not have the options for inventory location (Usually Ship Item From), Synchronize With Microsoft Outlook or Internal Customer.

NOTES
Multiple inventory locations are used in Chapter 18.

NOTES
If you do not add a default revenue account for a customer, the default linked revenue account for the ledger (page 232) will be entered in the journal.

NOTES
The PST Tax ID number identifies retailers that can collect PST from their customers and are exempted from paying the tax on purchases of the items they sell.

NOTES
You can change the default tax code for individual customers if necessary by choosing a different code from the Tax Code list. You can also change the code for individual invoices or amounts on the invoice.

The Ship-To Address screen allows you to enter multiple addresses for customers who want merchandise to be shipped to different addresses. You can apply labels to each address. The default setting is to use the mailing address as the shipping address.

Click the **Options tab** to access the customer's payment and invoice options:

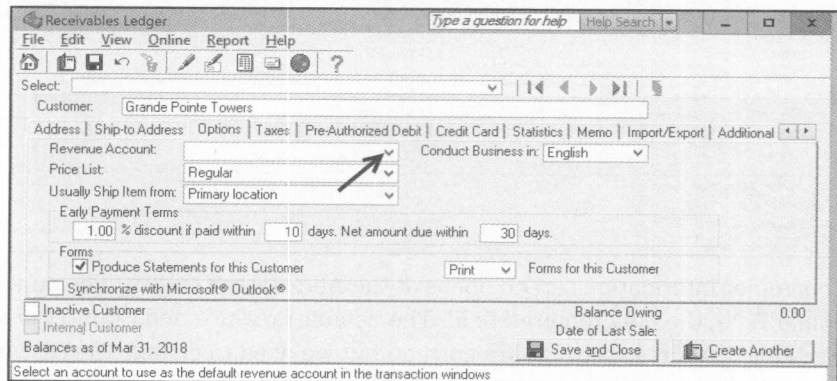

Most of the options are taken from the settings for the Receivables Ledger, and all the default settings are correct. You can select English or French as the customer's language — all forms you send to the customer will be prepared in the selected language. The **Price List** field applies to inventory and services prices that can be set at different rates for different customers. Air Care supplies customized services and does not use the Inventory module. The payment terms are entered automatically from the Receivables Settings. Terms can be edited if necessary for individual customers and invoices in the Sales Journal. Air Care charges interest on overdue accounts, so we need to be able to **produce statements**.

When a business sells inventory from more than one location, you can link a customer to one of these locations with the entry in the **Usually Ship Item From** location field. Air Care has only one location. The customer's currency is also defined on the Options tab screen when a business uses more than one currency.

You need to add only a default revenue account for the customer. Although there are three revenue accounts that apply to customers, most customers use Air Care's installation services, so we can choose this as the default. Remember that you can choose a different account in the Sales Journal for any invoice. You may prefer to omit the default revenue account to avoid using an incorrect revenue account for sales.

Click the **Revenue Account field list arrow**.

Click **4100 Installation Revenue**.

Click the **Taxes tab**:

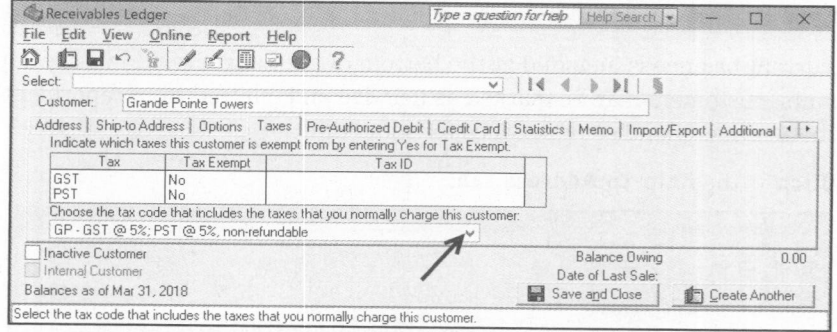

The customer is not exempt from paying taxes, so the defaults are correct. If the customer does not pay a tax, enter the tax ID number so that it appears on invoices. For example, retail stores do not pay PST on inventory that they will sell. They must register and have a tax number to permit the exemption. Some customers are also exempt from

GST payments. Taxes will be calculated only if the customer is marked as not tax exempt. The default tax code, GP - GST @ 5%, PST @ 5%, non-refundable, should be entered.

The **Pre-Authorized Debit** and **Credit Card** screens hold the customer's bank and credit card information when you are authorized to make automatic withdrawals.

> **Click** the **Statistics tab** to view the next set of customer details:

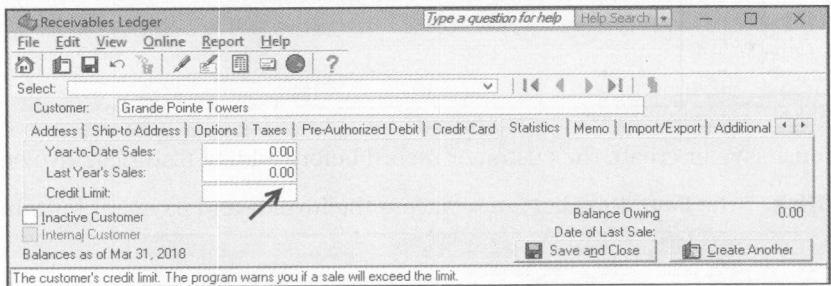

NOTES
Pre-authorized debit and automatic credit card charges are covered in Chapter 13. These tab screens are also illustrated in Chapter 6, page 174.

Balances will be included automatically once you provide the outstanding invoice information. **Year-To-Date Sales** are updated from journal entries, but you can add a historical balance as well. When you have two years of data, there will be an amount for last year's sales too. Records for foreign customers will have sales summary amounts and balances in both currencies.

The **Credit Limit** is the amount that the customer can purchase on account before payments are required. If the customer goes beyond this credit limit, the program will issue a warning when you attempt to post the invoice. You can accept the sale or revise it.

> **Click** the **Year-To-Date Sales field**.
>
> **Type**   11000 **Press** (tab) **twice** to advance to the Credit Limit field.
>
> **Type**   20000

The **Memo tab** screen for customers is just like the Memo tab screen for suppliers. It allows you to enter messages related to the customer. If you enter a reminder date, the program can display the message in the Daily Business Manager on the date you provide. If the customer also uses Sage 50, you can match the customer's inventory codes to your own on the **Import/Export tab** screen to allow for electronic data transfers. The **Additional Info tab** screen allows you to enter details for the custom-defined fields you created for customers, similar to the Additional Info tab fields for suppliers.

NOTES
The Daily Business Manager is covered in Chapter 11.
The Additional Information field labels are defined on the Receivables Names Settings screen (refer to page 231).

> **Correct** errors by returning to the field with the error. **Click** the appropriate tab, **highlight** the **error** and **enter** the **correct information**. You can correct address and options details any time.
>
> If there are no historical invoices, proceed to the final step of saving the customer record (page 246). Click Create Another [Create Another] and then click the Address tab to prepare for entering the next customer. Sage 50 has created a listing for the customer in the Customers window.

Entering Historical Customer Information

As for suppliers, you can enter all historical invoices and payments for the year to date, but you must enter outstanding invoice amounts. The following keystrokes will enter historical information for Grande Pointe Towers from page 204.

> **Click** the **right scroll arrow** [▶] on the tab heading line to access the tab for Historical Transactions.

NOTES
If you have already saved (created) the record, the Save Now option on the Historical Transactions tab screen will be removed. Instead, you will open the next screen asking you to choose Bills or Payments.

Click the **Historical Transactions tab**:

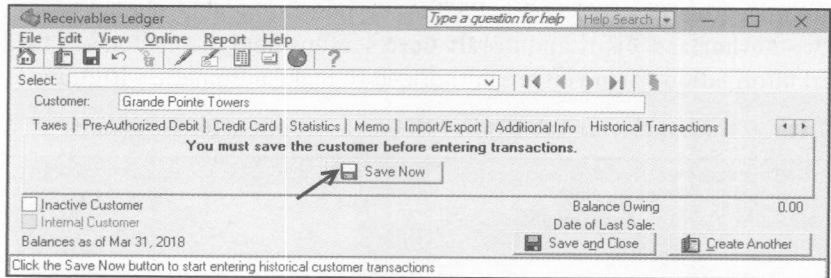

You must save or create the customer record before adding historical invoices.

Click the **Save Now button** to access the invoice and payment buttons:

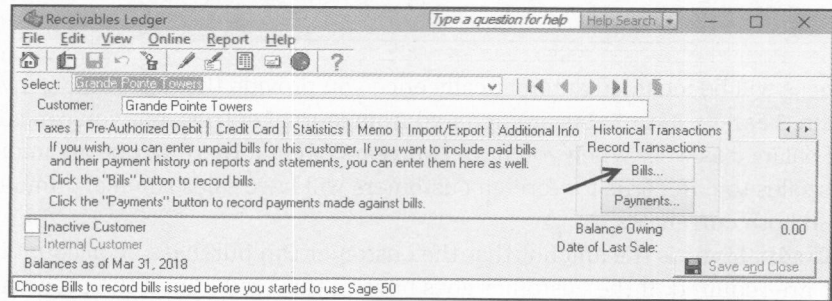

PRO VERSION
pro Invoices replaces Bills on the Historical Transactions tab screen and the Historical Bills screen on the next page.

Again, the Create Another button has been removed and the Save And Close button is dimmed because you have already saved the record.

If you prefer, you can enter address, options and credit limit details for all customers before adding historical bills and payments. Open a customer ledger record by double-clicking the customer's name in the Customers window. Then click the Historical Transactions tab to access the Bills and Payments buttons.

Just as in the Payables Ledger, you enter invoices and payments separately. You can use the Payments option to record any payments against previous invoices that you want to keep on record. The totals of all outstanding invoices, after payments, must match the opening balance in the *Accounts Receivable* control account in the General Ledger.

WARNING!
Enter invoice details carefully. To correct a historical invoice amount, you must pay the invoice and then clear paid transactions (Maintenance menu); then re-enter the outstanding invoices. Refer to page 249.

Click the **Bills button** to display the input form:

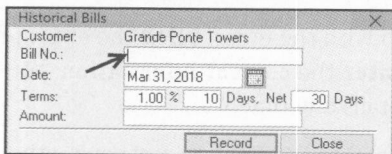

There is a single Amount field because customer discounts are calculated on after-tax amounts. When discounts are calculated before tax, there is an additional input field so that the sale and the tax amounts can be entered separately, as we saw in the Payables Historical Invoices screen. The earliest transaction date is the default invoice date. The cursor is in the Bill No. field so you can enter the first invoice number.

Type 699 **Press** (tab) to advance to the Date field.

Type mar 24

Because the payment terms are correctly entered, we can skip them. Discounts are calculated after taxes, so only the single after-tax amount is needed.

NOTES
This invoice amount will be added to the Year-To-Date Sales amount on the Statistics tab screen.

Click the **Amount field**. **Type** 4400

Correct **errors** by returning to the field with the error, **highlighting** the **error** and **entering** the **correct information**.

Check the **information** carefully before saving the invoice.

Incorrect invoices can be changed only by paying the outstanding invoices, clearing paid transactions (Home window, Maintenance menu, Clear Data, Clear Paid Transactions, Clear Paid Customer Transactions) and then re-entering the statistics and invoices (refer to page 249).

Click **Record** to save the invoice and to display a new blank invoice form for this customer.

Repeat these **procedures** to record the second invoice for this customer.

Click **Close** to return to the Historical Transactions window after entering all invoices for a customer.

The program has added the customer's balance to the ledger window. You are now ready to record the payment made by Grande Pointe Towers against the first invoice.

Click the **Payments button** to display the customer Historical Payments form:

WARNING!
You must click Record for each invoice you enter to save it. Clicking Close will discard the entry.

All outstanding invoices that you entered are displayed. Entering historical customer payments is much like entering current receipts in the Receipts Journal. As usual, the earliest transaction date is the default. The default March 31 transaction date is less than 10 days after the invoice dates, so the discounts are still available. The first discount amount — $44.00— is 1 percent of the total after-tax invoice amount.

Click the Number field to place the cursor in the cheque number field if necessary.

Type 4896 **Press** ⌨tab⌨ to advance to the Date field.

Type 03-28

Discounts can be taken only when the full payment is made before the due date, so we must skip the Discount fields. The full discount remains available until the discount period has ended.

Click the **Amount Paid column** on the line for invoice #699.

The full invoice amount is displayed as the default and highlighted so you can edit it.

Type 2400 **Press** ⌨tab⌨. **Press** ⌨del⌨ to remove the second discount amount.

Check your **information** carefully before you proceed and **make corrections** if necessary.

Click **Record** to save the information and to display another payment form for this customer in case there are additional payments to record.

WARNING!
If an amount appears in the Disc. Taken field, delete it before recording the payment. If you do not, you cannot finish the history because the ledgers will not be balanced.

The full discount remains available after the payment — its amount is not reduced, although the balance owing has been reduced.

Repeat these steps to enter other payments by this customer if there are any.

When you have recorded all outstanding payments by a customer,

Click **Close** to return to the customer information form.

In the ledger, the balance owing has been updated to $4 200 to include the payment entry just completed.

Click   the **Address tab** to prepare for entering the next customer.

Click   the **Create tool** to open another new customer input screen.

Saving a Customer Record without Historical Information

When all the information is entered correctly, you must save the customer information. If you have not added historical information,

Click   **Create Another** ![Create Another] to save the information and advance to the next new customer input screen.

Click   the **Address tab** to prepare for entering the next customer.

Repeat   these **procedures** to enter the remaining customers and historical transactions on page 204. After entering the last customer,

Click   **Save And Close** ![Save and Close] to close the Customer Ledger window.

Display or **print** the **Customer List** from the Customers window Reports menu to check the accuracy of your address information.

Display or **print** a **Customer Aged Detail Report**, including terms and historical differences, to check the historical information. Your report should have no historical differences for customers.

Close   the **Customers icon window** to return to the Home window.

Preparing for Journal Entries

The last stage in setting up the accounting system involves closing the historical entries. This step indicates that all historical data have been entered and cannot be changed. You can proceed with journalizing before finishing the history, but you must finish the history before beginning a new fiscal period. Finishing the history involves changing the status of each ledger from an open to a finished history state. In the open history state the ledgers are not integrated, so you can add or change historical information in one ledger without affecting any other ledger. It is easier to correct mistakes.

Making a Backup of the Company Files

To make a backup of the not-finished files, you can use Save A Copy from the File menu or use the Backup command. Both methods allow you to keep working in your original working data file.

Choose the **File menu** and **click Backup** or **click** the **Backup tool** ![Backup tool] :

On this backup screen, you should enter the name and location of the new backup.

Click Browse:

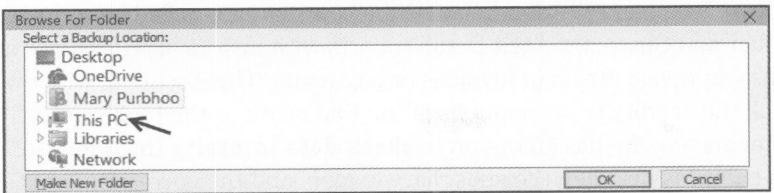

Click   **This PC** or **Computer** and **C:**. **Scroll down** and **click SageData16** to locate and select the SageData16 folder with your other data files.

Click   the **Make New Folder button** and **type** NF-AIR to replace New Folder — the selected name. **Click OK** to return to the Backup screen.

Double-click **Backup** in the File Name field. **Type** NF-AIRCARE

Click   **OK** to begin backing up the data file.

The "NF" designates files as not finished (the history is still open) to distinguish them from the ones you will work with to enter journal transactions. Continue by following the backup instructions on-screen. You can use another name and location for your backup if you want. This will create a backup copy of the files for Air Care Services.

Click   **OK** when the backup is complete.

Working with Unfinished History

Sage 50 allows you to enter current journal transactions before the history is finished and balanced. In this way, you can keep the journal records current and enter the historical details later when there is time available to do so, or the setup may be completed later by a different individual.

There are, however, a number of elements that you must complete before you can make journal entries. You must define the essential linked accounts before you can use the journals, so you must create General Ledger accounts for them. You must enter historical customer and supplier invoices before you can enter payments for them, and invoices must have the correct payment terms and dates. Automatic payroll tax calculations are also unavailable until the history is finished.

You do not need to enter General Ledger opening account balances. These balances may be added later in the Opening Balance field on the Account tab screen. The General Ledger also has the current balance, which changes as you post new journal entries. However, without the opening balances, the current balance is not correct and you cannot generate accurate reports. The Trial Balance and the Accounts window display only current balances, making it more difficult to trace the correct historical amounts.

Some errors may be corrected at any time. For example, after entering journal transactions and after finishing the history, you can correct account, supplier and customer names and address details, but you cannot change historical amounts because their dates precede the earliest transaction date.

From a control point of view, it is preferable to enter all historical information first so that you do not confuse the historical and current data or work with accounts that are not correct in some way. You cannot change account numbers after the accounts are used in journal entries, so some corrections may be difficult to make later. After you start journalizing, the balances for *Accounts Receivable* and *Accounts Payable* reflect all the entries made to date. There may be mistakes in current journal entries as well as in the history, making it more difficult to find the historical errors later.

There are a number of checks that you can perform to increase the accuracy of your work. You should compare your reports carefully with the financial reports for your company — the charts given at the beginning of this application — and make

NOTES
Substitute the appropriate drive and folders for the location of your files.

WARNING!
Read this section carefully before proceeding.

NOTES
You can create new accounts "on the fly" while making journal entries by using the Add An Account wizard. You will also be prompted to add the essential linked accounts when you try to open the journals. Some linked accounts, such as Sales Discounts, are not essential and you can access the journals without them. However, the journal entry will not be correct without the linked account, so there are some accounts that you must create before you can use the journals.

WARNING!
Make sure that the Test Account balance is zero. An error in this amount will not prevent you from finishing the history.

corrections. Pay particular attention to correct account numbers and historical invoices. Printing Supplier and Customer Aged Detail reports with historical differences and payment terms can reveal errors in invoices or payments. The Accounts window has an option to check the validity of accounts from the File menu or the tool button. The Home window Maintenance menu has an option to **check data integrity** that looks for differences in balances between the subsidiary ledgers and the corresponding General Ledger control accounts. All these checks help point to mistakes that should be corrected before proceeding.

Choose the **Maintenance menu** and **click Check Data Integrity**:

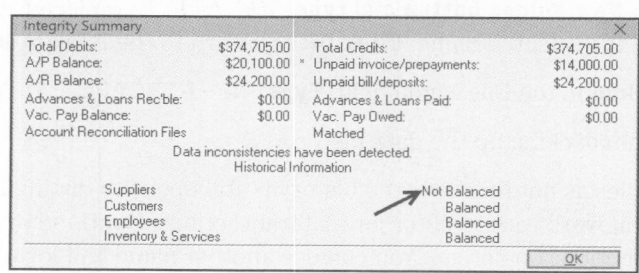

Click   OK to return to the Home window.

Both the data integrity check and the error summary (on this page) that opens when we attempt to finish the history inform us that the supplier history is not correct — the A/P Balance does not match the Unpaid Invoices amount. This error will prevent us from finishing the history. (Remember that this imbalance was intentional, the Accounts Payable discrepancy amount at this stage is $6 100.)

Choose the **History menu** and **click Finish Entering History**:

When all your essential linked accounts are defined and all historical amounts balance, you will be warned that this step cannot be reversed, as in Chapter 4, page 95. Otherwise, Sage 50 warns about errors that prevent you from finishing the history. For example, the accounts may be out of order if a subgroup total is missing after a set of subgroup accounts, or the Receivables Ledger balances may not equal the *Accounts Receivable* control account balance. If you have omitted an essential linked account, that information will also be included on this screen.

In this case, we learn that the Suppliers or Accounts Payable history is not balanced, the same information we had in the data integrity check. Because we know that the Trial Balance is correct, we may be missing a historical Payables Ledger invoice.

Click   Print to print the message for reference to help you correct mistakes.

Click   OK to return to the Home window.

We can proceed with entering the source documents. When the missing invoice surfaces, we can enter it and finish the history. You can proceed with journal entries until you start the next fiscal period. At that point, you must finish the history.

Correcting Historical Invoices

In reviewing all the records for the year to date, Air Care discovered part of the discrepancy between the *Accounts Payable* balance and the Supplier Ledger balances. Invoice #B-921 from Beausejour Electrical Products was incorrectly entered. The correct amount was $4 000 plus $200 tax, and the amount for cheque #94 was $3 800. We will correct these errors before making journal entries. The first step is to pay the invoices already entered.

Click   **Payables** in the Home window Modules pane list.

Click   **Beausejour Electrical Products** in the Suppliers list pane to open the ledger.

Click   the **Historical Transactions tab**.

Click   **Payments** to open the Historical Payments form:

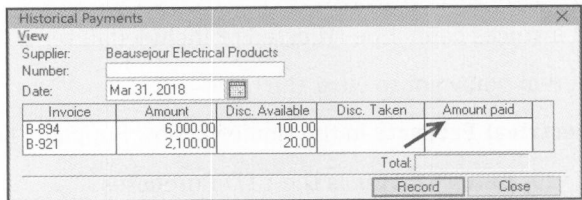

Type   95 in the Number field.

Type   3-28 in the Date field.

Click   the **Amount Paid column for Invoice B-894** to enter the full amount owing and avoid including the discount amount.

Click   the **Amount Paid column for Invoice B-921** and **press** (tab) to enter the amount and update the total.

Click   **Record** and then **click Close**.

Click   the **Statistics tab**.

Delete   the **year-to-date** expense and payment **amounts** to restore the balance amounts to zero. **Close** the **Supplier Ledger record**.

Next we must clear the paid transactions for Beausejour. This step will remove invoices and payments from the records, allow us to reuse the invoice numbers and provide accurate reports.

Choose   the **Maintenance menu** and then **choose Clear Data** and **Clear Paid Transactions**. **Click Clear Paid Supplier Transactions**:

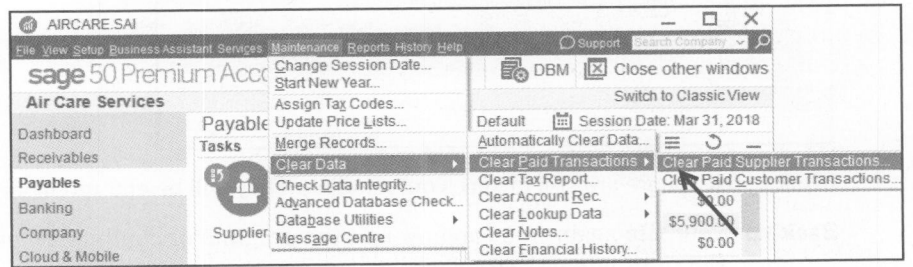

NOTES
You must pay the invoices before you can clear them. You also cannot use the same invoice numbers if you have not cleared the incorrect entries.

WARNING!
Be certain that the Discount Taken amounts are not selected and included in the amounts paid.

PRO VERSION
 Choose Clear Paid Vendor Transactions.

NOTES
If you do not clear the transactions, they will be stored for the supplier and will be included in the Aged Detail Report. By clearing them, you can also use the original invoice and cheque numbers. Duplicate numbers are not allowed, but if they are cleared the numbers are not stored.

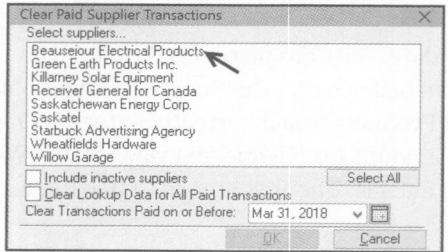

NOTES

You must pay and clear all invoices for the supplier and then re-enter all invoices. Otherwise, the errors will be included in the aged reports and the historical amounts on the Statistics tab screen will be incorrect.

You will open the list of suppliers:

Click   **Beausejour Electrical Products** to select the supplier.

Accept the **default date** and the other **settings** and **click OK**:

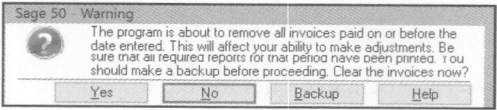

Sage 50 warns that cleared invoices cannot be adjusted or included in reports.

Click   **Yes** to confirm that you want to clear the data.

Click   **Beausejour Electrical Products** in the Home window Suppliers list pane.

Click   the **Statistics tab**. **Enter $2 100** as the YTD Purchases.

Enter   **$2 000** as the Payments for 2018 Excluding Taxes and **$2 100** as the Payments Including Taxes.

Click   the **Historical Transactions tab**.

Enter   the **correct invoices** and **payments** in the following chart:

Supplier Name	Terms	Date	Inv/Chq No.	Amount	Tax	Total
Beausejour Electrical Products	1/10, n/30 (before tax)	Mar. 26/18	B-894	$10 000	$500	$10 500
		Mar. 26/18	Chq 94			3 800
	1/10, n/30 (before tax)	Mar. 28/18	B-921	4 000	200	4 200
			Balance owing			$ 10 900

Close   the **Supplier Ledger record**.

Advance the **session date** to **April 7** to prepare for the journal entries.

When we change the session date to April 7, Sage 50 reminds us of the imbalance because we are entering a new month and we turned on the warning (page 212):

NOTES

Sage 50 will provide this same reminder when you advance the session date to May 1. The Accounts Payable discrepancy has been reduced to $3 300.

Click   **OK**. There are still invoices outstanding. They will be entered in Memo #8.

Back up your **file** again. You can now exit the program or continue by entering the transactions that follow.

SOURCE DOCUMENTS

SESSION DATE – APRIL 7, 2018

1 | **Memo #1**   **Dated April 1/18**

Create shortcuts for General Journal entries, purchase invoices, pay expenses (other payments) and pay invoices, the journals used in this chapter.

2 | **Sales Invoice #710**   **Dated April 1/18**

To Selkirk Community Centre, $1 800 plus $90 GST and $90 PST for removing and reapplying solar panels for roof replacement. Invoice total $1 980. Terms: 1/10, n/30. Create new Group account 4120 Repairs Revenue.

3 | **Receipt #20**   **Dated April 2/18**

From Grande Pointe Towers, cheque #5033 for $2 456, including $1 956 in full payment of invoice #699 and $500 in partial payment of invoice #703, and allowing $44 discount for early payment. Customize the journal by changing the tabbing order so that the cheque number follows the customer number.

4 | **Purchase Invoice #WH-42001**   **Dated April 3/18**

From Wheatfields Hardware, $1 500 plus $75 GST and $75 PST for new ladders and other tools. Invoice total $1 650. Terms: net 15.

5 | **Payment Cheque #101**   **Dated April 4/18**

To Beausejour Electrical Products, $10 760 in payment of account, including $140 discount for early payment. Reference invoices #B-894 and #B-921.

6 | **Payment Cheque #102**   **Dated April 5/18**

To Killarney Solar Equipment, $5 900 in payment of invoice #KS-1031.

7 | **Sales Invoice #711**   **Dated April 5/18**

To Selkirk Community Centre, $18 000 plus $900 GST and $900 PST for installing additional solar panels. Invoice total $19 800. Terms: 1/10, n/30.

8 | **Memo #2**   **Dated April 6/18**

Create new tax code IN using taxes GST at the rate of 5% and PST at the rate of 5%. GST is included and refundable; PST is included and not refundable. The description is not included so you must add it.

9 | **Memo #3**   **Dated April 6/18**

Edit the supplier record for Willow Garage. Change the default tax code to IN and create 5220 Vehicle Expenses, a new Group expense account as the default expense account for the supplier.

10 | **Purchase Invoice #W-1993**   **Dated April 6/18**

From Willow Garage, $120 including taxes (tax code IN) for gasoline for van. Store the transaction as a bi-weekly recurring entry. Terms: net 30.

11 | **Receipt #21**   **Dated April 7/18**

From Regina School Board, cheque #12488 for $19 780 including $220 discount for early payment. Reference invoice #701.

12 | **Sales Invoice #712**   **Dated April 7/18**

To Hazel Estates (use Full Add for the new customer), $1 200 plus $60 GST and $60 PST for a one-year service contract. Invoice total $1 320. Terms: 1/10, n/30.

⚠ WARNING!
Be sure to select the correct revenue account for sales. You may need to change the default selection.

▤ NOTES
You can also add shortcuts for View Suppliers and View Accounts (Banking module). Refer to pages 132 and 183 if you need assistance with creating shortcuts.

⚠ WARNING!
A screen with the Opening Balance field will be added when you create new accounts because the history is not finished. Leave this field blank.

▤ NOTES
You can customize the sales invoice by removing the columns that are not used by Air Care Services — Item Number, Quantity, Unit, Price and Job Sites — and the purchase invoice by removing the columns that are not used by Air Care Services — Item Number, Quantity, Unit, Price and Job Sites.

▤ NOTES
Allow Selkirk Community Centre to exceed the credit limit.

▤ NOTES
Add the description GST @ 5% included; PST @ 5% included, non-refundable.

▤ NOTES
Hazel Estates
(contact Joelle Beausoleil)
488 Sunshine St., Ste 1200
Moose Jaw, SK S4G 5H3
Tel 1: (306) 367-7711
Tel 2: (877) 367-9770
Fax: (306) 369-2791
E-mail: JB@hazelestates.com
Web: hazelestates.com
Terms: 1/10, n/30
Revenue account: 4140
Tax code: GP
Credit limit: $10 000

| 13 | **Visa Sales Invoice #713** | **Dated April 7/18** |

Sales Summary
To various one-time customers

Repairs revenue	$3 600
Service contract revenue	2 800
GST charged	320
PST charged	320
Total deposited to Visa bank account	$7 040

SESSION DATE — APRIL 14, 2018

| 14 | **Bank Debit Memo #14321** | **Dated April 8/18** |

From Flatlands Credit Union, cheque #5033 for $2 456 from Grande Pointe Towers has been returned because of non-sufficient funds. Reverse the payment and notify the customer of the outstanding charges.

| 15 | **Memo #4** | **Dated April 8/18** |

From Owner: Change the payment terms for Grande Pointe Towers to net 1. Certified cheques will be requested in the future. Set the credit limit to zero.

| 16 | **Memo #5** | **Dated April 8/18** |

From Owner: The work done for Hazel Estates included $1 600 plus $80 GST and $80 PST for replacement of damaged microinverters. The revised and correct invoice total is $3 080. Adjust invoice #712 to add the extra amount.

| 17 | **MasterCard Sales Invoice #714** | **Dated April 9/18** |

To Vinod Residence (use Full Add for the new customer), $600 plus $30 GST and $30 PST for repairs. Invoice total $660 paid in full by MasterCard.

| 18 | **Receipt #22** | **Dated April 10/18** |

From Selkirk Community Centre, cheque #533 for $7 960.20, including $1 960.20 in full payment of invoice #710 with $19.80 discount for early payment, and $6 000 in partial payment of invoice #711.

| 19 | **Purchase Invoice #GE-2579** | **Dated April 10/18** |

From Green Earth Products Inc., $14 000 plus $700 GST for microinverters. Invoice total $14 700. Terms: 1/10, n/30. Store as a bi-weekly recurring entry.

| 20 | **Cash Purchase Invoice #WI-6913** | **Dated April 11/18** |

From Westrock Insurance (use Quick Add), $185 per month for a one-year car insurance policy with $2 000 000 liability coverage and $4 000 deductible. Terms: first month payable in advance on acceptance of quote followed by monthly instalments at the end of each month. Pay first month's premium of $185 in advance. Issue cheque #103. Store as a recurring monthly transaction.

| 21 | **Memo #6** | **Dated April 11/18** |

Recall the stored entry for car insurance from Westrock Insurance to enter a postdated payment for next month's premium of $185. Issue cheque #104 postdated for May 11. After posting, recall the entry again and make a postdated payment for the premium due June 11 with cheque #105.

| 22 | **Payment Cheque #106** | **Dated April 14/18** |

To Green Earth Products Inc., $14 560 in payment of account, including $140 discount for early payment. Reference invoice #GE-2579.

NOTES

Vinod Residence
(contact Viran Vinod)
56 House St.
Regina, SK S4P 8K1
Tel: (306) 761-8114
E-mail: v.vinod@interlog.com
Terms: net 1
Revenue account: 4120
Tax code: GP
Credit limit: $2 000

NOTES

Use Full Add for the new supplier if you want to add the default expense account (Insurance Expense). GST is not charged on insurance, so you must delete the tax code.

NOTES

Add B and C to the original purchase invoice numbers for the postdated payment entries.

NOTES

If you used the Payments Journal for the cash purchases, remember to reset the date for the invoice payment.

| 23 | **Receipt #23** | **Dated April 14/18** |

From Selkirk Community Centre, cheque #586 for $13 602 in payment of account, including $198 discount for early payment. Reference invoice #711.

SESSION DATE — APRIL 21, 2018

| 24 | **Bank Debit Memo #35589** | **Dated April 15/18** |

From Flatlands Credit Union, cheque #12488 for $19 780 from Regina School Board has been returned because of non-sufficient funds. Reverse the payment and notify the customer of the outstanding charges.

| 25 | **Cash Purchase Invoice #SAA-1098** | **Dated April 15/18** |

From Starbuck Advertising Agency, $1 100 plus $55 GST and $55 PST for flyers on clean energy alternatives. Create new Group expense account: 5230 Promotion Expenses. Invoice total $1 210. Paid by cheque #107.

| 26 | **Receipt #24** | **Dated April 15/18** |

From Hazel Estates, cheque #230 for $3 049.20 in full payment of account, including $30.80 discount for early payment. Reference invoice #712.

| 27 | **Cash Purchase Invoice #FX-3467** | **Dated April 16/18** |

From FedEx (use Quick Add for the new supplier), $120 for special delivery of solar panels plus $6 GST. Invoice total $126. Issued cheque #108 in full payment. Create new Group account 5240 Delivery Expenses.

| 28 | **Payment Cheque #109** | **Dated April 16/18** |

To Wheatfields Hardware, $1 650 in payment of account. Reference invoice #WH-42001.

| 29 | **Cash Purchase Invoice #SEC-44371** | **Dated April 19/18** |

From Saskatchewan Energy Corp., $200 plus $10 GST for two months of hydro service. Invoice total $210. Paid by cheque #110.

| 30 | **Cash Purchase Invoice #SKT-36128** | **Dated April 19/18** |

From Saskatel, $330 plus $16.50 GST and $16.50 PST for telephone, cellular and Internet service. Invoice total $363. Paid by cheque #111.

NOTES
Remember to change the default revenue account for invoices as required.

NOTES
Change the tax code to G for the purchase from FedEx.

31

AirCare Services

clean energy for a better future

www.aircare.com

100 Belair Avenue, Unit 25
Regina, SK S4T 4U2
Phone: (306) 456-1299   Toll free: (888) 455-7194   Fax: (306) 456-3188

Invoice:	715
Date:	April 19, 2018
Sold to:	Oak Bluff Banquet Hall (Ann Oakley) 4 Celebration Ave. Regina, SK S4V 3H7

Description	Tax Code	Amount
Installation of additional solar panels	GP	20 000.00
Adjustments to older solar panels	GP	2 000.00

Authorization to exceed credit limit: _Simon Antunes_

Interest at 1.5% charged on accounts over 30 days.	**Payment Terms:** 1/10, net 30	**Customer Initials**	**GST**	1 100.00
			PST	1 100.00
	GST #533 766 455	*AO*	**TOTAL**	24 200.00

32

AirCare Services

clean energy for a better future

www.aircare.com

100 Belair Avenue, Unit 25
Regina, SK S4T 4U2
Phone: (306) 456-1299   Toll free: (888) 455-7194   Fax: (306) 456-3188

Invoice:	716
Date:	April 21, 2018
Sold to:	Sales Summary

Description	Tax Code	Amount
Installation upgrades	GP	6 000.00
Service contracts	GP	900.00

Deposited to Visa bank account
April 21/18 _Simon Antunes_

Thank you.	**Payment Terms:** Visa Credit Card	**Customer Initials**	**GST**	345.00
			PST	345.00
	Business No.: 533 766 455		**TOTAL**	7 590.00

SESSION DATE — APRIL 30, 2018

33 | **Purchase Invoice #W-3466** | **Dated April 22/18**

From Willow Garage, $120 including taxes (use tax code IN) for gasoline for van. Terms: net 30. Recall stored entry and edit the date.

34 | **Purchase Invoice #GE-4906** | **Dated April 24/18**

From Green Earth Products Inc., $14 000 plus $700 GST for microinverters. Invoice total $14 700. Terms: 1/10, n/30. Recall stored entry.

35 | **Purchase Invoice #KE-1679** | **Dated April 25/18**

From Killarney Solar Equipment, $30 000 plus $1 500 GST for solar panels. Invoice total $31 500. Terms: 1/5, n/30.

36 | **Sales Invoice #717** | **Dated April 25/18**

To Grande Pointe Towers, $24 000 for new subcontracting job, plus $1 200 GST and $1 200 PST. Invoice total $26 400. Terms: net 1.

NOTES
Close the Advisor message for Grande Pointe Towers about the customer often paying late.

37

Grande Pointe Towers 77 LaPointe Cr. White City, SK S0G 5B0 Tel: (306) 322-7500	*F* **Flatlands Credit Union** 389 Prairie Blvd. Regina, SK S4P 1B6 **No: 6114**

Date 2 0 1 8 0 4 2 7
Y Y Y Y M M D D

Pay ——— Thirty thousand six hundred dollars ——— 00 $ 30,600—

TO THE ORDER OF
Air Care Services
100 Belair Ave. Unit 25
Regina, SK S4T 4U2

PER *Sophie Grande*

⑈⑈——92999·⑈46771 6114

Re: certified cheque pays invoices $30,600.00   **No: 6114**
    #699, 703, 717 (receipt #25)   April 27, 2018

38 | **Bank Debit Memo #55131** | **Dated April 30/18**

From Flatlands Credit Union, pre-authorized monthly payroll for employees.

Wages and payroll expenses	$7 000
Payroll services fee	100
GST paid on payroll service	5
Total withdrawal	$7 105

39 | **Bank Debit Memo #56159** | **Dated April 30/18**

From Flatlands Credit Union, pre-authorized withdrawals for service charges, mortgage and loan payments.

Bank charges, including NSF cheques	$ 120
Loan interest	125
Mortgage interest	775
Loan principal repayment	1 000
Mortgage principal repayment	800

40

AirCare
Services

www.aircare.com
clean energy for a better future
125 Belair Ave., Unit 25, Regina, SK S4T 4U2

MEMO #7

Tel: (306) 456-1299   (888) 455-7194   Fax: (306) 456-3188

```
Date:   April 30, 2018
From:   Simon Arturro
Re:     End of month adjustments needed

Supplies used in April: Solar Panels          $29 000
                        Inverters              24 200
                        Electrical Supplies     2 550
                        Office Supplies           150

New expense account required: 5170 Electrical Parts Used.

Authorization   SA April 30/18
```

NOTES
When you enter May 1 as the session date, Sage 50 reminds you that the Payables Ledger history is not balanced. There is still a difference of $3 300 – refer to page 250.

WARNING!
You must enter these outstanding invoices as historical invoices and the payments as current payments or you will be unable to finish the history.

NOTES
Refer to page 238 if you need help with adding historical invoices.

SESSION DATE – MAY 1, 2018

Memo #8   **Dated May 1/18**

41

From Owner: Received monthly statements showing missing historical information. The statement from Wheatfields Hardware included an overdue amount of $1 100 from invoice #WH-20001 dated March 24, 2018. The statement from Starbuck Advertising Agency included an overdue amount of $2 200 from invoice #SAA-987 dated March 14, 2018.

Add the historical invoices for these two transactions in the Supplier Ledger records as historical transactions. You can open the Payables module window or use the View Suppliers shortcut to access the records for these suppliers.

Pay these two invoices in the Payments Journal as current transactions dated May 1 using cheques #112 and #113.

Memo #9   **Dated May 1/18**

42

Check the data integrity (Maintenance menu) after entering the historical invoices. Make a backup copy of the data files and finish entering the history. Choose the History menu in the Home window and click Finish Entering History.

Memo #10   **Dated May 1/18**

43

From Owner: Print or preview customer statements. One invoice for Regina School Board is overdue. Complete sales invoice #718 for Regina School Board for $29.39, the interest charges on the overdue amount. Terms: net 15 days. Use the No Tax code for the interest charges and choose Interest Revenue as the account. Remember to remove the early payment discount.

REVIEW

The Student DVD with Data Files includes Review Questions and Supplementary Cases for this chapter.

HELENA'S ACADEMY

OBJECTIVES

After completing this chapter, you should be able to

- **open** the Payroll Journal
- **enter** employee-related payroll transactions
- **understand** automatic payroll deductions
- **understand** Payroll Ledger linked accounts
- **edit** and **review** payroll transactions
- **adjust** Payroll Journal invoices after posting
- **enter** employee benefits and entitlements
- **complete** payroll runs for a group of employees
- **release** vacation pay to employees
- **remit** payroll taxes
- **enter** payroll transactions in a future year
- **display** and **print** payroll reports
- **prepare** Record of Employment and T4 slips

COMPANY INFORMATION

Company Profile

NOTES
Helena's Academy
250 Satchel Lane
Edmonton, AB T7F 3B2
Tel: (780) 633-8201
Fax: (780) 633-8396
Business No.: 189 245 053

Helena's Academy was opened in Edmonton, Alberta, in 2002 by Helena Teutor as a small private junior elementary school. The school has maintained its small size in order to offer individualized programming with high academic standards for students with artistic interests and abilities. Helena works as principal and also teaches the upper grades. Two other teachers handle the kindergarten and junior primary grades. Although all teachers have a background in fine arts and are trained music teachers, an additional half-time art and music specialist rotates among all the classes. A full-time office administrator, caretaker and classroom assistant make up the rest of the staff. The classroom assistant also runs the after-school program.

Parents pay tuition fees in two instalments, one before the start of the school year in August and the second at the beginning of January. They pay additional

fees to participate in the after-school programs. Three teachers offer private half-hour weekly music lessons that parents also pay for separately.

All classes are split-grade classes, an arrangement required by the small school enrolment, but desired because of the opportunities for students to help each other. Older students in each class, even in kindergarten, are expected to help their younger classmates. All parents are also required to volunteer in the classroom and library, and the kindergarten parents provide the healthy daily snacks for the kindergarten classes. The volunteer expectations are viewed favourably by the families at the school because they enable parents to understand and reinforce the learning philosophy of the school.

The school closes for the month of July each year, but all teachers and staff return to work in August to plan their programs for the coming year. The caretaker uses this month before students return to catch up on repairs and maintenance.

Individual client accounts are not set up for this exercise, and tuition fees for the first semester have been paid. Fees for the after-school program and private lessons are paid on the first of each month. No taxes are charged on any of the school's fees, and as an educational institution providing only tax-exempt services, the Academy is not eligible for GST refunds on the taxes it pays. The school has accounts set up with a few regular suppliers, and some of these offer discounts.

On October 1, 2018, Helena's Academy converted its accounts using the following information:

- Chart of Accounts
- Trial Balance
- Supplier Information
- Client Information
- Employee Profiles and Information Sheet
- Accounting Procedures

CHART OF POSTABLE ACCOUNTS

HELENA'S ACADEMY

ASSETS
- 1080 Bank: Chequing Account
- 1090 Bank: Savings Account
- 1100 Investments: Restricted Use Funds
- 1200 Fees Receivable
- 1240 Advances & Loans Receivable
- 1260 Prepaid Taxes
- 1280 Office Supplies
- 1300 Art Supplies
- 1320 Library Material
- 1340 Textbooks
- 1520 Classroom Computers
- 1540 Office Equipment
- 1560 Furniture
- 1580 Vehicle
- 1620 School Premises ▶

▶LIABILITIES
- 2100 Bank Loan
- 2200 Accounts Payable
- 2300 Vacation Payable
- 2310 EI Payable
- 2320 CPP Payable
- 2330 Income Tax Payable
- 2400 RRSP Payable
- 2410 Family Support Payable
- 2430 Medical Payable - Employee
- 2440 Medical Payable - Employer
- 2460 WCB Payable
- 2920 Mortgage Payable

EQUITY
- 3560 Academy, Invested Capital
- 3580 Retained Surplus
- 3600 Net Income ▶

▶REVENUE
- 4020 Revenue from School Fees
- 4040 Revenue from Lessons
- 4060 Revenue from Programs
- 4100 Revenue from Interest

EXPENSE
- 5020 Purchase Discounts
- 5040 Bank Charges
- 5060 Hydro Expenses
- 5080 Insurance Expense
- 5100 Office Supplies Used
- 5110 Textbook Expenses
- 5120 Art Supplies Used
- 5140 Interest Expense
- 5180 Promotional Expenses
- 5190 Property Taxes
- 5200 Telephone Expenses ▶

- ▶5210 Vehicle Expenses
- 5250 Wages: Teaching Staff
- 5260 Wages: Support Staff
- 5280 Wages: Music Lessons
- 5310 EI Expense
- 5320 CPP Expense
- 5330 WCB Expense
- 5380 Tuition Fees Expense
- 5400 Medical Premium Expense

NOTES: The Chart of Accounts includes only postable accounts and Net Income.

TRIAL BALANCE

HELENA'S ACADEMY

October 1, 2018

Acct	Account	Debits	Credits
1080	Bank: Chequing Account	$ 220 010.00	
1090	Bank: Savings Account	160 000.00	
1100	Investments: Restricted Use Funds	540 000.00	
1260	Prepaid Taxes	2 700.00	
1280	Office Supplies	4 100.00	
1300	Art Supplies	3 850.00	
1320	Library Material	14 500.00	
1340	Textbooks	5 300.00	
1520	Classroom Computers	6 800.00	
1540	Office Equipment	4 900.00	
1560	Furniture	16 000.00	
1580	Vehicle	23 000.00	
1620	School Premises	640 000.00	
2100	Bank Loan		$ 65 000.00
2200	Accounts Payable		1 880.00
2300	Vacation Payable		3 841.68
2310	EI Payable		1 241.00
2320	CPP Payable		2 979.66
2330	Income Tax Payable		5 453.81
2400	RRSP Payable		300.00
2410	Family Support Payable		1 000.00
2430	Medical Payable - Employee		484.00
2440	Medical Payable - Employer		484.00
2460	WCB Payable		392.30
2920	Mortgage Payable		420 000.00 ▶

Acct	Account	Debits	Credits
▶ 3560	Academy, Invested Capital		$ 685 000.00
3580	Retained Surplus		57 665.79
4020	Revenue from School Fees		480 000.00
4040	Revenue from Lessons		500.00
4060	Revenue from Programs		3 000.00
4100	Revenue from Interest		2 150.00
5040	Bank Charges	$ 66.00	
5060	Hydro Expenses	1 220.00	
5080	Insurance Expense	3 680.00	
5100	Office Supplies Used	240.00	
5110	Textbook Expenses	800.00	
5120	Art Supplies Used	280.00	
5140	Interest Expense	4 600.00	
5180	Promotional Expenses	2 800.00	
5190	Property Taxes	1 800.00	
5200	Telephone Expenses	350.00	
5210	Vehicle Expenses	600.00	
5250	Wages: Teaching Staff	35 956.40	
5260	Wages: Support Staff	29 370.48	
5280	Wages: Music Lessons	1 680.00	
5310	EI Expense	1 443.02	
5320	CPP Expense	2 979.66	
5330	WCB Expense	762.68	
5380	Tuition Fees Expense	660.00	
5400	Medical Premium Expense	924.00	
		$1 731 372.24	$1 731 372.24

SUPPLIER INFORMATION

HELENA'S ACADEMY

Supplier Name (Contact)	Address	Phone No. / Fax No.	E-mail / Web Site	Terms / Tax ID
Alberta Workers' Compensation Board	55 Payout Cr. Edmonton, AB T5J 2S5	Tel: (780) 498-3999 Fax: (780) 498-7999	wcb.ab.ca	net 1
Aspen Life Financial (A.M. Weller)	280 Wellness Blvd. Edmonton, AB T6G 2B7	Tel: (780) 327-7164 Fax: (780) 327-8109	aspenlife.com	net 1
Energy Supply Services (N.U. Cleer)	690 Service Ave. Edmonton, AB T6T 4G4	Tel: (780) 456-3293 Fax: (780) 456-1229	nucleer@ess.ca ess.ca	net 1
Loomis Art Supplies (Dee Ziner)	64 Canvas St. Edmonton, AB T5Z 2S4	Tel: (780) 462-1706 Fax: (780) 452-1700	dz@loomis.com loomis.com	1/10, n/30 186 519 184
Maintenance Enforcement Program (Al I. Mony)	43 Brownlee St. Edmonton, AB T5J 3W7	Tel: (780) 422-5555 Fax: (780) 401-7575	alberta.mep@gov.ab.ca justice.gov.ab.ca/mep	net 1
Receiver General for Canada	56 Heron Rd. Ottawa, Ontario K3A 6B4	Tel 1: (800) 561-7761 Tel 2: (800) 959-2221	cra-arc.gc.ca	net 1
Rocky Mountain Trust (Rocky)	59 High St. Edmonton, AB T4P 1M3	Tel: (780) 388-1825 Fax: (780) 388-2663	rockymtntrust.ca	net 1
Telus Alberta (Toks Lotts)	499 Cellular Rd. Edmonton, AB T8F 2B5	Tel: (780) 348-5999	telus.com	net 1

OUTSTANDING SUPPLIER INVOICES

HELENA'S ACADEMY

Supplier Name	Terms	Date	Invoice No.	Amount	Total
Loomis Art Supplies	1/10, n/30	Sep. 29/18	LA-438	$1 880	$1 880

CLIENT INFORMATION

HELENA'S ACADEMY

Client Name	Address
Parents of Students (individual client records are not set up for this application)	Edmonton

EMPLOYEE INFORMATION SHEET

HELENA'S ACADEMY

	Helena Teutor	Marina Booker	Lars Teicher	Arte Tiste	Neela Nerture	Morty Filer	Jerome Handie
Position	Principal	Teacher	Teacher	Specialist	Assistant	Office Admin	Caretaker
Social Insurance No.	699 344 578	277 639 118	403 401 599	513 288 191	129 495 768	374 588 127	813 402 302
Address	21 Socratic Blvd. Edmonton, AB T5H 2L2	49 Dewey Pl. Edmonton, AB T6K 4K2	15 Practicum St. Edmonton, AB T5B 4C1	2 Creative Way Edmonton, AB T6H 1X3	93 Formula Cr. Edmonton, AB T5E 2L2	10 Basics Lane Edmonton, AB T5A 4K2	4 Repairal Cr. Edmonton, AB T5B 4C1
Telephone	(780) 466-7736	(780) 436-9015	(780) 463-4870	(780) 429-5656	(780) 488-8554	(780) 440-3301	(780) 461-1328
Date of Birth (mm-dd-yy)	7-28-75	9-14-87	10-5-87	7-18-85	5-19-83	4-3-80	3-3-77
Federal (Alberta) Tax Exemption – TD1							
Basic Personal	$11 474 (18 451)	$11 474 (18 451)	$11 474 (18 451)	$11 474 (18 451)	$11 474 (18 451)	$11 474 (18 451)	$11 474 (18 451)
Other Indexed	–	$13 595 (18 451)	–	$18 262 (29 131)	$11 474 (18 451)	$11 474 (18 451)	–
Other Non-indexed	–	$3 200 (3 500)	–	–	–	$6 260 (6 860)	–
Total Exemptions	$11 474 (18 451)	$28 269 (40 402)	$11 474 (18 451)	$29 736 (47 582)	$22 948 (36 902)	$29 208 (43 762)	$11 474 (18 451)
Employee Earnings							
Regular Wage Rate	–	–	–	$40.00	$26.00	$28.00	$28.00
Overtime Wage Rate	–	–	–	–	$39.00	$42.00	$42.00
Regular Salary	$5 500	$4 600	$4 200	–	–	–	–
Pay Period	monthly	monthly	monthly	semi-monthly	semi-monthly	semi-monthly	semi-monthly
Hours per Period	160	160	160	44	82.5	82.5	82.5
Lessons (#/Period)	–	$30.00 (16)	$30.00 (12)	$30.00 (22)	–	–	–
Vacation	4 weeks	4 weeks	4 weeks	6% retained	6% retained	6% retained	6% retained
Vacation Pay Owed	–	–	–	$2 179.20	$533.52	$564.48	$564.48
WCB Rate	0.89	0.89	0.89	0.89	1.15	0.89	2.44
Employee Deductions							
Medical	$44.00	$88.00	$44.00	$44.00	$44.00	$44.00	$22.00
RRSP	$100.00	$50.00	$50.00	–	$25.00	–	$25.00
Family Support	–	–	$500.00	–	–	–	$250.00
Additional Tax				$200.00			
EI, CPP & Income Tax Calculations are built into Sage 50.							
Direct Deposit	No	Yes	Yes	No	Yes	No	Yes

NOTES: Medical premiums are deducted every pay period. The amounts are adjusted for the monthly rates.

Employee Profiles and TD1 Information

Employee Benefits and Entitlements   All employees are entitled to 10 days per year as sick leave. If the days are not needed, employees can carry these days forward to a new year, to a maximum of 90 days. Currently, all employees have some unused sick leave days accrued from previous years. Most employees take their vacations in July when the school is closed, with salaried employees receiving their regular salary and the full-time hourly workers receiving the retained vacation pay at the end of June with their regular paycheque. Vacation pay cannot be accumulated or carried forward beyond the calendar year. Tiste has not yet collected any vacation pay this year.

In keeping with the educational goals, the Academy encourages all employees to continue their education by paying part of their tuition fees for college or university programs. Booker and Filer are currently taking courses and receiving the tuition fee benefit. A second benefit applies to all employees — the Academy pays 50 percent of the medical premiums for an extended health care insurance plan. Both benefits are taxable income for the employee and expenses for Helena's Academy.

Music Lessons   Booker, Teicher and Tiste give private music lessons at lunchtime and after school. Parents pay the school $35 per half-hour lesson and the school pays the teachers. These fees are set up on a "piece rate" basis at $30 per lesson for teachers and added to each paycheque.

Employer Expenses   In addition to the expenses for the tuition fees and medical premium benefits, Helena's Academy pays the compulsory CPP, EI and WCB.

Helena Teutor   As the principal and founder of the school, Teutor frequently speaks to parent groups in order to promote the school. She also teaches the senior class of grade 4, 5 and 6 students and hires new staff when needed. She is married and has no children. Since her husband is also fully employed, she uses the single federal and provincial tax claim and medical premium amounts. At the end of each month, she receives her salary of $5 500 per month by cheque. She makes monthly contributions to her RRSP plan as well.

Marina Booker   is the regular teacher for the primary class of grade 1, 2 and 3 students. She supplements her monthly salary of $4 600 with income from private music lessons offered through the school. For each half-hour lesson taught in the previous month, she earns $30. Booker is married with one child and claims the basic, spousal and child amounts for income tax purposes. She also has a claim for her RRSP contributions and her tuition fees of $2 640 for a four-month university course and the $140 per month federal ($215 provincial) education deduction for the part-time course. She pays medical premiums at the family rate. Her pay is deposited directly to her bank account every month.

Lars Teicher   teaches the two junior and senior kindergarten classes. He too supplements his monthly salary of $4 200 with income from private music lessons at $30 per lesson. Teicher is separated from his wife and is required to make family support payments. For this, $500 is deducted from each paycheque. As a single employee, he claims only the basic federal and provincial amounts for income tax purposes, but he does have an additional deduction for his RRSP contributions. He also pays the single rate toward the provincial medical plan. He too has his paycheque deposited directly to his bank account.

Arte Tiste   is the half-time art teacher who works four hours in the school every afternoon, dividing his time among the three classes but concentrating on the senior class. He spends the mornings painting in his home art studio. Although he is single, he can claim the spousal equivalent plus caregiver amounts because he looks after his

NOTES
In January 2009, the province of Alberta eliminated the provincial medical plan premiums. Private health care plans usually cover the costs of services not included in the provincial plan, such as prescription drugs, dental care or semi-private hospital rooms.

NOTES
The Academy pays Booker's tuition fees at the rate of $130 per pay period until the full amount is paid.

The federal child claim is allowed only for infirm children.

infirm brother. These claims significantly reduce the income tax he pays on his wages of $40 per hour. He teaches music lessons after school at the per-lesson rate of $30. His medical premium is deducted from his semi-monthly paycheque at the family rate to cover himself and his brother. His 6 percent vacation pay is retained. Instead of receiving his vacation pay in June like the other hourly workers, Tiste takes his vacation pay sometime in the fall to pay for his December travels. Because Tiste has additional income from the sale of his paintings, he has elected to pay additional federal taxes in each pay period instead of making extra quarterly tax remittances on this extra income. Tiste is paid by cheque twice each month.

Neela Nerture works full-time in the school as a classroom assistant and also runs the after-school program for children who require daycare. She divides her time among the three classes as needed by the teachers and program schedules. Nerture is married and fully supports her child and her husband while he is finishing his studies. Therefore, she pays the family medical premiums and has the basic and spousal claim amounts for income taxes. She is paid twice a month at the hourly rate of $26 per hour. When she works more than 7.5 hours in a day, she earns $39 per hour for the extra time. Overtime is often required for extended daycare and can be charged back to the parents. This extra charge encourages parents to pick up their children on time. On top of her pay, she earns 6 percent vacation pay that is retained until the end of June. Nerture has her paycheques deposited directly to her bank account.

Morty Filer runs the school office, handling the routine phone calls to and from parents, arranging lessons, scheduling parent volunteers, collecting fees and doing the bookkeeping. For these duties he earns $28 per hour for the first 7.5 hours each day in each half-month pay period and is paid by cheque. For additional hours, he earns $42 per hour. The 6 percent vacation pay he earns on his regular and overtime wages is retained until the end of June. Filer supports his wife and claims both the basic and spousal federal and provincial amounts for tax purposes. His medical premium is at the family rate. He has an additional claim for his university tuition of $5 140 and the $140 per month federal education deduction ($215 provincial) for the eight-month school year.

Jerome Handie is the caretaker for the school and grounds. He works year-round, except for his vacation time in July, cleaning the school's rooms and providing general maintenance. During August, he paints the classrooms and steam-cleans all carpets. From each semi-monthly paycheque that is deposited to his bank account, $250 is withheld to support his ex-wife and two children. He claims only the basic federal and provincial amounts for tax purposes and the single medical premium. He also makes contributions to his RRSP program with regular payroll deductions. His hourly pay rate is $28 for the first 7.5 hours per day and $42 per hour for any additional time. His vacation pay is calculated and retained at the rate of 6 percent.

Accounting Procedures

Taxes: GST and PST

As an educational institution that offers only tax-exempt services, Helena's Academy is not eligible for any refunds on the GST it pays for products and services. Therefore, no sales taxes are set up in this application — taxes are not tracked — and the prices in the source documents include all taxes. Provincial sales tax is not charged in Alberta.

Discounts

Some suppliers offer discounts on after-tax purchase amounts. These discount terms are set up in the supplier records so that Sage 50 will automatically calculate the discount

NOTES
Because full-time hourly employees are paid twice a month, the hours worked in the pay period vary. The number of regular hours may be either 75 (10 days) or 82.5 hours (11 days), based on working 7.5 hours per day. Occasionally a half-month period has 12 working days for a total of 90 regular hours.

NOTES
Nerture's child is not eligible for the federal claim amount.

NOTES
The Academy pays Filer's tuition at the rate of $135 per pay period until the full amount is paid.

NOTES
The sales tax amounts are included with the asset or expense portion of the purchase.

NOTES
For an educational service company, the Customers icon is labelled Clients, Sales Invoices are labelled as Statements and Sales or Revenues are renamed Fees.

when full payment is made within the discount period. No discounts are offered on school fees.

Direct Payroll Deposits

The Academy allows employees to have their regular pay deposited directly to their bank accounts or to be paid by cheque. Four employees have selected direct payroll deposits.

Payroll Remittances

Some suppliers are identified as payroll authorities with the following remittances: EI, CPP and income tax are remitted to the Receiver General for Canada; medical premiums are remitted to Aspen Life Financial; Workers' Compensation Board (WCB) premiums are remitted to Alberta Workers' Compensation Board; RRSP contributions are remitted to Rocky Mountain Trust; family support payments are remitted to the Maintenance Enforcement Program. All payments are remitted monthly for the pay period ending the previous month.

Tuition fees are reimbursed directly to the employee on their regular payroll cheques.

PRO VERSION

In the Pro version, Customer replaces the term Client, Vendor replaces the term Supplier, Sales Invoices replaces the icon label Statements and Sales Journal replaces the term Fees Journal.

INSTRUCTIONS

1. **Enter** the **transactions** in Sage 50 using the Chart of Accounts and Supplier, Client and Employee Information. The procedures for entering new transactions for this application are outlined step by step in the Keystrokes section with the source documents.

2. **Print** the **reports** marked on the following printing form after you have finished making your entries:

REPORTS

Accounts
- ☐ Chart of Accounts
- ☐ Account List
- ☐ General Journal Entries

Financials
- ☑ Balance Sheet: Dec. 31
- ☑ Income Statement: Aug. 1 to Dec. 31
- ☑ Trial Balance date: Dec. 31
- ☑ All Journal Entries: Oct. 1 to Dec. 31
- ☑ General Ledger accounts: Oct. 1 to Dec. 31
  5250 5260 5280
- ☐ Statement of Cash Flows
- ☑ Cash Flow Projection Detail Report:
  for 1080 for next 30 days

Banking
- ☐ Cheque Log Report

Payables
- ☐ Supplier List
- ☐ Supplier Aged
- ☐ Aged Overdue Payables
- ☐ Purchases Journal Entries
- ☐ Payments Journal Entries

Receivables
- ☐ Client List
- ☐ Client Aged
- ☐ Aged Overdue Receivables
- ☐ Fees Journal Entries
- ☐ Receipts Journal Entries
- ☐ Client Statements

Employees & Payroll
- ☐ Employee List
- ☑ Summary for all employees
- ☐ Deductions & Expenses
- ☑ Remittances Summary Report:
  for all payroll authorities Dec. 31
- ☑ Payroll Journal Entries: Oct. 1, 2018, to
  Jan. 15, 2019
- ☑ T4 Slip for Tiste
- ☑ Record of Employment for Tiste
- ☑ Year End Review (PIER) for all employees

Mailing Labels
- ☐ Labels

KEYSTROKES

Open   **SageData16\HELENA\HELENA.SAI** for Helena's Academy. **Enter October 15** as the session date.

NOTES

If you are using the backup files, restore HELENA1.CAB or HELENA1 to SageData16\ HELENA\HELENA.

PRO VERSION
The shortcuts will be named Create Sales Invoices and Pay Purchase Invoices.

NOTES
The option to confirm successful posting of transactions is turned on, so you should click OK each time this message appears.

NOTES
Global Liability Inc.
Terms: net 1
Expense account: 5080

NOTES
Remember that you must have a valid and active Payroll ID code from Sage to use the payroll features if you are not using the Student version.
Choose the Services menu in the Home window and click Payroll And Support for more information.

The Employees & Payroll module window opens. This is the default Home window for Helena's Academy.

Create shortcuts for **Create General Journal** (Company), **Create Statement** (Receivables) and **Pay Expenses** or **Pay Invoices** (Payables).

If you choose not to create shortcuts, you can change modules each time you need to access a journal in a different module.

Enter the **cash sale** and the **cash purchase** and **payment transactions**.

Transaction confirmation is turned on, so you should click OK after posting each transaction. We will not repeat this instruction.

Cash Sales Invoice #1036   **Dated Oct. 1/18**
To parents of students, $3 200 total monthly fees for after-school programs and $2 130 total monthly fees for individual music lessons. Deposited $5 330 to chequing account. You can customize the journal by removing the columns not needed, including the Tax Code column.

Cash Purchase Invoice #GL-38827   **Dated Oct. 2/18**
From Global Liability Inc. (use Full Add for new supplier), $1 800 for monthly premium on a one-year insurance policy for school and staff. Paid by cheque #211. Store as a recurring monthly entry.

Payment Cheque #212   **Dated Oct. 5/18**
To Loomis Art Supplies, $1 861.20 in payment of account, including $18.80 discount for early payment. Reference invoice #LT-438.

Entering Payroll Transactions

Payroll transactions may be entered in the Payroll Journal or in the Payroll Run Journal. We will provide instructions for both methods. If you are preparing paycheques for more than one employee, the Payroll Run Journal is usually faster.

Individual paycheques are entered in the Payroll Journal that you open from the Paycheques icon:

Click   the **Paycheques icon** to open and display the Payroll Journal:

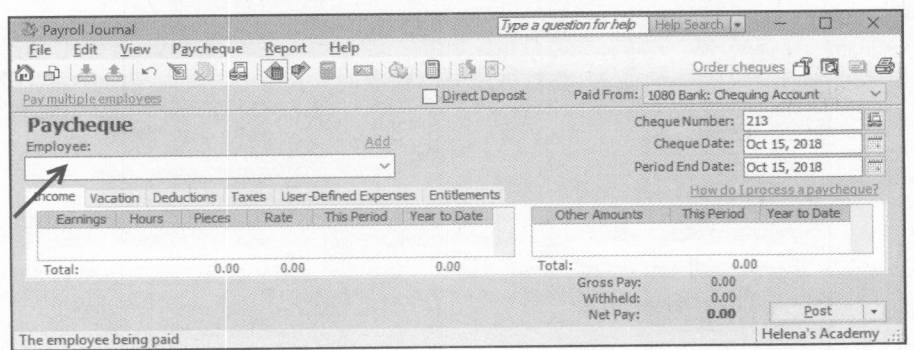

PRO VERSION

The Refresh and Time Slips tools do not appear in the Pro version.

NOTES

The Payroll Journal has a link below the tool bar to switch to the Payroll Run Journal to Pay Multiple Employees. The Payroll Run Journal is introduced on page 283.

The Calculate Taxes Automatically, [icon], Enter Taxes Manually [icon] and Recalculate Taxes [icon] tools apply specifically to the Payroll Journal. Automatic calculation is selected.

The Time Slips tool is dimmed — it is used to add information from time slips for the employee and will be covered in Chapter 18. The remaining tools — Home window, Daily Business Manager, Store, Recall, Undo, Adjust Paycheque, Reverse Paycheque, Look Up Paycheque, Enter Additional Information, Windows Calculator and Refresh — serve the same purpose as they do in other journals. You can also change report form options and preview and e-mail the paycheque before printing. Adjust, Reverse and Look Up Paycheque are the Payroll equivalent of these tools in other Journals.

Four hourly paid employees are paid on the first payroll date. Filer is first.

| ✓ 4 | **Employee Time Summary Sheet #19**   **Dated Oct. 15/18** |

For the pay period ending October 15, 2018

Name of Employee	Regular Hours	Overtime Hours	Lessons	Tuition	Advance (Repaid)	Loan (Repaid)	Sick Days	Direct Deposit
Filer, Morty	82.5	4	–	$135	$200	–	–	No
Handie, Jerome	82.5	2	–	–	–	–	1	Yes
Nerture, Neela	82.5	–	–	–	–	–	–	Yes
Tiste, Arte	44.0	–	24	–	–	–	–	No

a. Using Employee Time Summary Sheet #19 and the Employee Information Sheet, complete payroll for hourly paid employees. Handie has taken one sick day.
b. Issue $200 advance to Morty Filer and recover $50 from each of the following four paycheques.
c. Issue cheques #213 and #214 and Direct Deposit (DD) slips #55 and #56.

NOTES

The pay period for hourly paid employees included 11 days and 7.5 hours per day.

NOTES

Use the bookmark attached to the back cover to mark the page with the source document.

The cursor is in the Employee field.

Click   the **Employee field list arrow** to open the employee list:

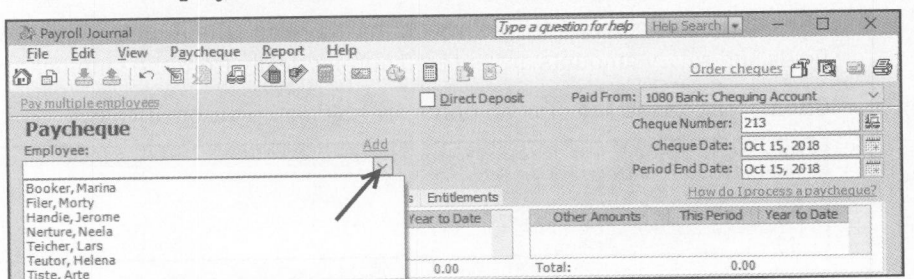

Click   **Filer, Morty** to select this employee and add his name to the form. If you have not chosen correctly, return to the employee list and select again.

NOTES

You can add new employees from the Payroll Journal. Type the new name in the Name field. Press *tab* and click Add. Or, click the Add link above the Employee field. You will open the Employee Ledger window. There is no Quick Add option for employees because additional details are required for income tax purposes.

NOTES
Year To Date amounts in payroll are always based on the calendar year, not on the fiscal year as in other modules.

NOTES
Helena's Academy uses a single chequing account for Payables and Payroll cheques, so there is a single sequence of cheque numbers.

NOTES
The period end date is usually earlier than the cheque date for hourly paid employees who must complete the hours and have this summary submitted to the payroll department before a cheque is prepared.

NOTES
You can define 20 different sources of income in addition to the predefined ones.
If sales commissions are paid to employees, they must be calculated separately and added manually.

Press `tab` to add the payroll details for the selected employee:

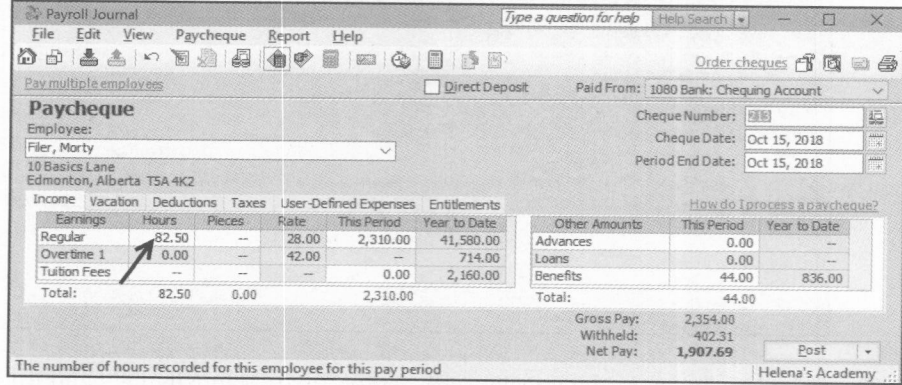

Most of the payroll form is completed automatically based on the ledger details for the employee. The cursor is now in the Cheque Number field. The employee's address has been added. The cheque number, 213, should be correct because we have set up automatic numbering. If the number is incorrect, you can change it.

There are two date fields. In the **Cheque Date** field, you should enter the date of payment. As usual, the session date, October 15, has been entered by default. Since this session date is correct, you should accept it. The **Period End Date** field refers to the last day of the pay period for the employee. It may be later or earlier than the cheque date. In this case, the session date is also the same as the pay period ending date, so you can accept the default date again.

The Payroll Journal has several tabs. The **Income** tab screen has all the sources of income for the employee divided into two categories: Earnings and Other Amounts. **Earnings** include the regular income sources such as Regular and Overtime wages for the hourly paid employees and tuition fees repaid. Employee records are set up so that only their own sources of income appear on the form. The **Other Amounts** pane has all the other sources of income, including payroll advances, loans and taxable benefits. Year-to-date amounts based on the calendar year are added for all fields.

The **Regular Hours** field contains the number of hours an employee has worked for the regular pay rate during the pay period. You can edit the default entry. The **Overtime** field contains the number of overtime hours an employee has worked during the pay period. No default number of overtime hours is entered because the time varies. If there are different overtime rates, you can set up a second overtime field and rate or create additional incomes. For example, employees may be paid more for overtime work on Sundays or holidays than in the evenings.

The **Gross Pay** amount (the pay rate times hours worked plus other income and earnings amounts) is calculated and added to the bottom portion of the journal window. The total amount **Withheld** for taxes and other deductions and the **Net Pay** also appear at the bottom of the journal.

For salaried employees, the Salary field will replace the Regular and Overtime fields and salary amounts are entered automatically from the employee record.

Click the **Taxes tab**. Tax amounts are calculated automatically:

Income	Vacation	Deductions	Taxes	User-Defined Expenses	Entitlements	How do I process a paycheque?

Tax	This Period	Year to Date
CPP	109.30	2,152.19
EI	43.43	829.69
Tax	205.58	4,377.64
Total:	358.31	

Because we have chosen to let the program complete the tax calculations, the tax fields are not available for editing. If you need to edit the tax amounts,

Click the **Enter Taxes Manually tool** to open tax fields for editing amounts.

Click   the **Income tab** to continue with the payroll entry. This pay period included eleven 7.5 hour days, so the number of regular hours is correct.

Click   the **Overtime 1 Hours field**.

Type   4   **Press** ⟨tab⟩ to advance to the **Tuition Fees This Period** field.

The Gross Pay is updated to include the additional overtime pay. Vacation pay and all year-to-date amounts are also updated continually as you add information.

If amounts are not updated, click the **Calculate Taxes Automatically tool** 🏢 on the tool bar. The option to enter taxes manually may be selected, an option that allows you to edit tax amounts but will not update these amounts automatically.

Helena's Academy pays a portion of eligible tuition fees, and the amount refunded to employees — a taxable benefit — is entered in this income field. Because the amount is paid directly to the employee, and it is taxable, it is set up as an income amount. Filer is currently receiving $135 per pay period as the refund for his tuition until the entire amount has been repaid.

Type   135 **Press** ⟨tab⟩ to add the tuition fees amount to gross pay.

The cursor now highlights the amount for Benefits in the Other Amounts pane. The **Benefits** field under Other Amounts is used to enter the total amount of taxable benefits a business offers to its employees, such as health insurance or dental plans when the payments are made to a third party. Half of Filer's medical premium is paid by Helena's Academy. Benefit amounts are included in the gross income to arrive at the amount of income tax and then subtracted again to determine the net pay amount.

An advance of $200 for Morty Filer has been approved by management for a personal emergency, so we need to enter this amount. The **Advances This Period** field is used to enter amounts advanced to an employee in addition to his or her normal pay from wages or salary. An advance offered to an employee is displayed as a positive amount. An advance recovered is indicated as a negative amount in this same field. Advanced amounts are taxable in the period received. Advance amounts owing will appear in the Year To Date column for Advances.

Click   the **Advances This Period field**.

Type   200 **Press** ⟨tab⟩.

Click   the **Vacation tab**:

Income	Vacation	Deductions	Taxes	User-Defined Expenses	Entitlements		How do I process a paycheque?
			This Period		Year to Date		
	Type		Hours	Amount	Hours	Amount	
Balance Forward (as of Jan 01, 2018)			--	--	--	--	
Vacation Earned			--	160.68	--	2,559.72	
Vacation Paid *			0.00	0.00	--	1,834.56	* These hours are recorded as EI Insurable Hours
Vacation Owed			--	--	--	725.16	

The **Vacation tab screen** has the employee amounts for this period based on the income and the year-to-date amounts. Sage 50 automatically calculates an amount in the **Vacation Earned This Period Amount** field and displays it as a default. Filer's default amount, calculated at the vacation pay rate of 6 percent, will be retained by the business — accrued in the *Vacation Payable* account — until he takes a vacation in July or leaves the employ of the Academy. Therefore, the Vacation Paid amount on this cheque is zero. (Refer to the Employee Information Sheet on page 260 for each employee's vacation pay rate.) The Vacation Paid amount in the Year To Date column has the amount of vacation pay paid to the employee already this calendar year.

The total accumulated vacation pay owing (withheld since vacation pay was last paid and including this pay) is entered in the Year To Date amount field for the Vacation Earned. This amount appears in the **Vacation Paid This Period** field as a default when you turn off the option to retain vacation in the Employee Ledger (refer to page 276).

NOTES
To verify that tax amounts have changed, click the Taxes tab. Click the Income tab again to continue with the payroll entry, and click the Tuition Fees This Period field to position the cursor.

NOTES
The tuition fee benefit could also be set up in the Employee Ledger so that it is added automatically. When the entire amount has been paid, you would remove it from the ledger. Instead, we will edit the amount in the journal.

NOTES
By dividing the tuition fee benefit among several pay periods, the income tax burden will also be spread out over several paycheques.

NOTES
Advances not repaid before the end of the year are converted to payroll loans automatically by Sage 50. Preferred interest rate amounts are taxable benefits.

NOTES
Benefits are not paid in cash to the employee. They are added to gross pay to determine income tax and then subtracted again to determine the net pay.
Deleting the amount and then re-entering it will provide the changes in gross pay and amounts withheld that demonstrate the tax implications of benefits.
Premiums paid to private health care providers are not usually taxable benefits for employees, but we want to show the tax effect of benefits.

NOTES
Salaried employees receive their regular pay during their vacations instead of receiving vacation pay. They receive vacation days as an entitlement.

NOTES
If the amount of a deduction or user-defined expense is incorrect, and it is not a one-time change, you should edit the Employee Ledger record. The next time you open the Payroll Journal for the employee, the edited amount will be entered.

Click the **Deductions tab**:

Income	Vacation	Deductions	Taxes	User-Defined Expenses	Entitlements	How do I process a paycheque?
	Deduction		This Period	Year to Date		
	Med-Employee		44.00	836.00		
	Total:		44.00			

The **Deductions tab screen** has the employee medical deduction entered automatically from the amounts stored in the ledger record. For other employees, the RRSP contributions and/or family support payments also appear on this screen. These amounts can be edited in the journal if necessary.

Click the **User-Defined Expenses tab**:

Income	Vacation	Deductions	Taxes	User-Defined Expenses	Entitlements	How do I process a paycheque?
Employer-paid payroll expenses						
	Expense		This Period	Year to Date		
	Med-employer		44.00	836.00		
	Total:		44.00			

NOTES
If the User-Defined Expenses amount is omitted from the record, it can be entered in the Payroll Journal as needed.

The employer contribution to medical premiums (an employer expense) is also set up as an automatic entry that appears on the User-Defined Expenses tab screen.

We will use the Entitlements tab screen for Handie's payroll entry.

Click the **Income tab** to continue:

NOTES
The Post button has a list arrow that provides the option to select Print & Post as the default setting. With this selection, you will automatically print the paycheque when you post the entry.

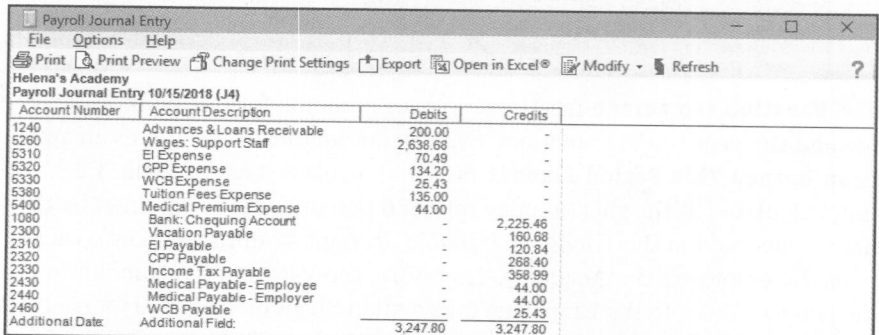

You have now entered all the information for Filer, so you should review the completed transaction before posting.

Reviewing the Payroll Journal Transaction

Choose the **Report menu** and **click Display Payroll Journal Entry**. The transaction you have just completed opens:

NOTES
If you are using a version of the Sage 50 program later than Release 2016.2, your tax amounts and total amount withheld may be different from those we have because different tax tables are used. Your Gross Pay and Vacation amounts should always be the same as ours.

The tax tables for version Release 2016.2 cover the period from July 1, 2015, to June 30, 2016, as indicated in the confirmation note on page 270. The rates in later 2016 tax tables may be different.

Helena's Academy
Payroll Journal Entry 10/15/2018 (J4)

Account Number	Account Description	Debits	Credits
1240	Advances & Loans Receivable	200.00	-
5260	Wages: Support Staff	2,638.68	-
5310	EI Expense	70.49	-
5320	CPP Expense	134.20	-
5330	WCB Expense	25.43	-
5380	Tuition Fees Expense	135.00	-
5400	Medical Premium Expense	44.00	-
1080	Bank: Chequing Account	-	2,225.46
2300	Vacation Payable	-	160.68
2310	EI Payable	-	120.84
2320	CPP Payable	-	268.40
2330	Income Tax Payable	-	358.99
2430	Medical Payable - Employee	-	44.00
2440	Medical Payable - Employer	-	44.00
2460	WCB Payable	-	25.43
Additional Date:	Additional Field:	3,247.80	3,247.80

All the relevant wage expense accounts have been debited. The hourly wages and tuition fee benefit are tracked in separate wage expense accounts. The expense for vacation pay is added to the wages expense account. In addition, all the wage-related liability accounts and *Bank: Chequing Account* have been updated automatically because the Payroll Ledger is linked to the General Ledger. All accounts in the journal entry have

been defined as linked accounts for the Payroll Ledger, so you do not enter any account numbers directly.

Sage 50 uses the Canada Revenue Agency tax formulas to calculate the deduction amounts for CPP, EI and income tax. These formulas are updated every six months. The remaining deductions are determined from Employee Ledger entries that can be modified for individual employees.

Payroll expense accounts reflect the employer's share of payroll tax obligations. The liabilities reflect the amounts that the owner must remit to the appropriate agencies and include both the employer's share of these tax liabilities and the employee's share (deductions withheld). For example, CPP contributions by the employee are matched by the employer. Therefore, the *CPP Expense* (employer's share) is one-half of the *CPP Payable* amount (employee plus employer's share). WCB is paid entirely by the employer, so the expense amount is the same as the liability amount. Medical contributions by employer and employee are equal, but they are represented in different accounts — the employer's share is included in expense and payable accounts, *Medical Premium Expense* and *Medical Payable - Employer*, while the employee's share appears only in the payable account, *Medical Payable - Employee*. For EI, the employer's share (*EI Expense*) is 1.4 times the employee's share. Vacation pay is part of the wages expense. The tuition benefit is entered as a debit to *Tuition Fees Expense*.

Close the **display** to return to the Payroll Journal input screen.

CORRECTING THE PAYROLL JOURNAL ENTRY BEFORE POSTING

Move the cursor to the field that contains the error. If you need to change screens to access the field you want, **click** the appropriate **tab**. **Press** (tab) to move forward through the fields or **press** (shift) and (tab) together to move back to a previous field. This will highlight the field information so that you can change it. **Type** the **correct information** and **press** (tab) to enter it.

You can also use the mouse to **point** to a field and **drag through** the **incorrect information** to highlight it. You can highlight a single number or letter or the entire field. **Type** the **correct information** and **press** (tab) to enter it.

Click an **incorrect amount** to highlight it. **Type** the **correct amount** and **press** (tab).

You can discard the entry by **clicking** ☒ (**Close**) or ↺ (**Undo**) or by returning to the Employee list and **clicking** a **different employee** name. **Click** the name of the **correct employee** and **press** (tab). When prompted, confirm that you want to discard the incorrect entry. **Click Yes**, and start again.

You can preview the paycheque before printing it. You can also modify the reports and forms settings from the journal. Tool buttons are included for both these functions. You must have selected Custom Forms in the Reports and Forms settings screen to preview the cheque. The default form locations (file name references) should be correct (refer to margin Notes). However, they may refer to incorrect file locations because these settings are saved with the data file that was created with different default settings.

Click the **Print Preview tool** �8 (read the margin Notes). Sage 50 requests a confirmation because of the effect of advances on tax calculations:

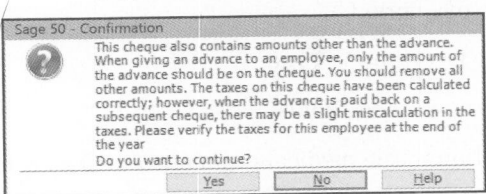

The warning advises that payroll advances are usually issued in a separate cheque to allow for correct payroll tax calculation. Advances are taxable amounts; advances repaid later will reduce the tax for that period. We included the advanced amount with the cheque to familiarize you with Sage 50 warning messages.

NOTES
Both the employer's and the employee's share of the medical premiums are payable to Aspen Life Financial.
The province of Alberta has eliminated the personal medical premiums for the provincial health plan.

NOTES
Correcting Payroll Journal entries after posting is covered on page 273.

NOTES
If you get an error message about a missing file or form when you preview the cheque, click OK. The Reports & Forms window should open immediately. Or, in the Journal, click the Change The Default Printer Settings tool 🖩 to access the form settings. Choose Custom Forms. In the Description fields, choose the generic forms Payment Cheque for payments and Payroll Cheque With YTD Totals for paycheques. These selections should automatically enter the forms you need in the Forms folder in the Sage 50 Premium Accounting Version 2016 folder. Click OK.
You should now be able to preview the payment.

NOTES
A real business should work only with the current payroll tax tables. Sage provides regular payroll updates when you sign up for the payroll service. We cannot change the source dates in the text after publishing, and using fixed dates and program (tax table) versions ensures that you can obtain the same results we do.
You cannot update payroll tax tables in the Student version.

NOTES
Payroll Journal entries may be stored as recurring entries before posting. Follow the same steps as you do for recurring sales or purchases.

NOTES
Refer to the Employee Time Summary Sheet on page 265 for Handie's payroll details.
Uploading direct deposits is covered in Chapter 13.

Click **Yes** to continue. You must confirm that your dates do not match the payroll formula dates:

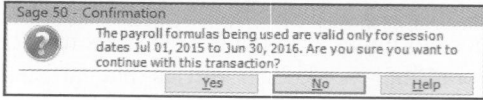

The caution is displayed whenever the dates of the transaction are different from the dates of the tax tables in your Sage 50 program.

Click **Yes** to continue to the preview. At this point, you have not yet posted the transaction, so you can still make changes if needed.

The preview includes the cheque and cheque stub with payroll summary details for the current period and the year to date.

Click **OK** to close the preview when finished to return to the journal.

Posting

When all the information in your journal entry is correct,

Click **Post** [Post ▾]. The Post button includes the option to print and post, which may be selected as the default setting from the list arrow. A blank Payroll Journal input screen appears.

Entering Payroll Entitlements

Choose **Handie, Jerome** from the Employee list. **Press** (tab):

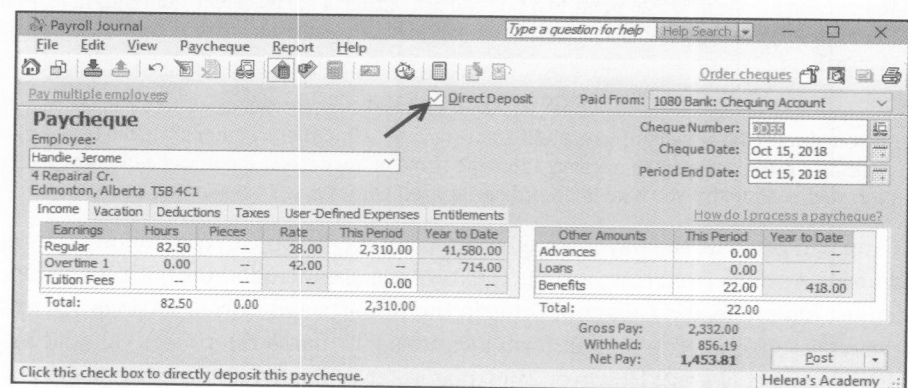

Handie's payroll details are added to the form. Instead of a cheque number, the entry DD55 appears on the form because the check box for **Direct Deposit** is selected. Handie has chosen to have his pay deposited directly to his bank account. The bank account deposit details are added to the employee's ledger record.

Handie has overtime hours for this pay period.

Click the **Hours field** beside Overtime 1. **Type** 2

Click the **Deductions tab** to open these fields.

Handie has two deductions in addition to the medical premium: one for his RRSP contribution and one for his family support payment.

Jerome Handie has taken a sick leave day during the two-week period. We add this information on the Entitlements tab screen.

Click the **Entitlements tab** to open these fields:

Income	Vacation	Deductions	Taxes	User-Defined Expenses	Entitlements		How do I process a paycheque?
Hours worked this period:		82.50					
Entitlement	Days Earned	Days Taken	Net Days Accrued				
Vacation	0.00	0.00	0.00				
Sick Leave	0.55	0.00	21.55				

Two entitlements are defined for Helena's Academy: vacation days (only for salaried employees) and sick leave days for all full-time employees. The amounts entered in the Days Earned fields are the number of days earned only for this pay period — two weeks. Sick leave is accrued at the rate of 5 percent per hour worked. The total number of days accrued from prior work periods is recorded and updated in the ledger record and on the employee's cheque stub. If the number of days taken exceeds the number of days accrued, you will be asked if you want to allow a negative balance.

The entry 82.5 in the Hours Worked This Period field is based on 11 days, the default we entered as a setting in the employee's ledger record. If the number of hours is different for a single pay period, you can change the number of hours.

Handie has taken one day of sick leave in this pay period.

Click the **Days Taken column beside Sick Leave**.

Type 1 **Press** (tab) to update the Net Days Accrued:

Income	Vacation	Deductions	Taxes	User-Defined Expenses	Entitlements		How do I process a paycheque?
Hours worked this period:		82.50					
Entitlement	Days Earned	Days Taken	Net Days Accrued				
Vacation	0.00	0.00	0.00				
Sick Leave	0.55	1.00	20.55				

Gross Pay: 2,416.00
Withheld: 887.54
Net Pay: **1,506.46**
Post ▾

The number of Sick Leave the employee has accrued   Helena's Academy

Entitlements do not affect gross pay, net pay or taxes, so you can review the entry.

Choose the **Report menu** and **click Display Payroll Journal Entry**:

Helena's Academy
Payroll Journal Entry 10/15/2018 (J5)

Account Number	Account Description	Debits	Credits
5260	Wages: Support Staff	2,537.64	-
5310	EI Expense	63.01	-
5320	CPP Expense	112.37	-
5330	WCB Expense	58.95	-
5400	Medical Premium Expense	22.00	-
1080	Bank: Chequing Account	-	1,506.46
2300	Vacation Payable	-	143.64
2310	EI Payable	-	108.02
2320	CPP Payable	-	224.74
2330	Income Tax Payable	-	433.16
2400	RRSP Payable	-	250.00
2410	Family Support Payable	-	26.00
2430	Medical Payable - Employee	-	22.00
2440	Medical Payable - Employer	-	22.00
2460	WCB Payable	-	58.95
Additional Date:	Additional Field:	2,793.97	2,793.97

This entry is similar to the previous one, with the additional payable entries for RRSP and family support. Entitlements taken do not appear in the payroll journal entry, but the days accrued are recorded on the cheque stub and in the employee's ledger record.

Close the **journal entry display** to return to the journal.

Make **corrections** to the journal entry if necessary.

Click [Post ▾] to save your work.

Click **Yes** to bypass the warning about payroll dates. **Click** the **Income tab**.

Select **Nerture, Neela** for the next payroll transaction. **Press** (tab).

All the default entries are correct for Nerture. No changes are required.

Click [Post ▾]. **Click Yes** to bypass the warning about payroll dates.

Select **Tiste, Arte** for the next payroll transaction.

NOTES
For every 20 days of work, the employee is entitled to one day of sick leave (the rate is 5 percent).

For some entitlements, employers may require the employee to work a minimum number of months before taking any time off.

The total number of days accrued also appears in the journal and is printed on the cheque stub.

NOTES
To preview a direct deposit stub, click the Preview tool 🔲. The deposit stub has the message "non-negotiable" added.

If you get an error message about missing forms, click OK. The Reports & Forms window should open immediately. Or, in the Journal, click the Change The Default Printer Settings tool 🖨️ to access the form settings. Choose Custom Forms. In the Description fields, choose the generic form Direct Payroll Deposit Stubs as the description. These selections should automatically enter the files you need in the Forms folder in the Sage 50 Premium Accounting Version 2016 folder. Click OK.

You should now be able to preview the payment.

Press (tab) to add his default payroll amounts:

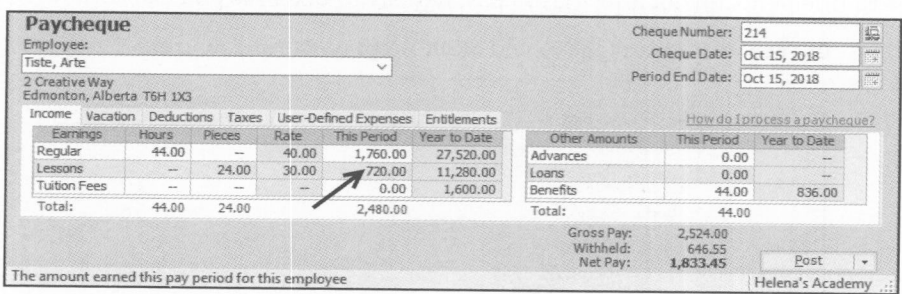

Tiste has 44 entered as the regular number of hours per period. Because this half month has 11 days and he works 4 hours per day, the default entry is correct. Tiste does not receive overtime pay.

Lesson rates and a default number of lessons per period are also entered in each teacher's ledger record. Sage 50 calculates the total dollar amount by multiplying the per lesson piece rate times the number of lessons. You can define a different rate for each employee. Tiste has given 24 individual lessons in the past two weeks, so we need to change the default entry from 22 to 24.

> **NOTES**
> If different rates are paid for different kinds of work, you can define additional piece rate fields.

Click **22.0** in the Pieces field for Lessons.

Type 2 4 **Press** (tab) to enter the number of Lessons for This Period, update all amounts and complete the entry:

Press (ctrl) + **J** to open the journal entry display:

> **NOTES**
> Tiste has $200 in additional federal taxes deducted from each paycheque. This amount is not separated from other income tax amounts in the journal or in the report. It is combined with regular income tax as a single entry for Income Tax Payable.

Helena's Academy
Payroll Journal Entry 10/15/2018 (J7)

Account Number	Account Description	Debits	Credits
5250	Wages: Teaching Staff	2,628.80	-
5310	EI Expense	65.27	-
5320	CPP Expense	117.72	-
5330	WCB Expense	22.46	-
5400	Medical Premium Expense	44.00	-
1080	Bank: Chequing Account	-	1,833.45
2300	Vacation Payable	-	148.80
2310	EI Payable	-	111.89
2320	CPP Payable	-	235.44
2330	Income Tax Payable	-	438.21
2430	Medical Payable - Employee	-	44.00
2440	Medical Payable - Employer	-	44.00
2460	WCB Payable	-	22.46
Additional Date:	Additional Field:	2,878.25	2,878.25

Again, we have a similar journal entry. For each employee, you can choose one account for all sources of income, or you can choose the separate default linked accounts for each income. For Tiste, a teacher, we have linked his hourly wages to *Wages: Teaching Staff* rather than to the *Wages: Support Staff* account used for other hourly employees. Therefore, his wages for lessons are included with the expense for teaching wages. For salaried teachers, lesson wages are linked to a separate expense account.

Close the **display** when finished and **make corrections** if necessary.

Post the **entry** and **click Yes** to bypass the warning about payroll formulas.

Close the **Payroll Journal window** to return to the Home window.

Advance the **session date** to October 31 and **back up** your **data file**.

Adjusting Payroll Entries

The memo on October 17 explains the need for a paycheque correction.

☑
5

Memo #1   **Dated Oct. 17/18**

From Manager: Morty Filer returned his paycheque for adjustment. He worked 6 hours of overtime during the week but was paid for only 4 hours. He has also taken one day of sick leave that was not recorded. Adjust his paycheque and re-issue cheque #213 to make the correction.

Sage 50 does not require reversing and correcting entries for these situations. Instead, you can complete a paycheque adjustment in the Payroll Journal, as you do in the other journals. You can access the Adjust Paycheque screen in different ways.

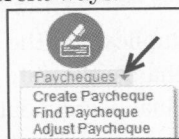

Click   the **Paycheques icon shortcuts list arrow** and **click Adjust Paycheque**. Or,

Click   the **Paycheques icon** [icon]. **Click** the **Adjust Paycheque tool** [icon] or **choose** the **Paycheque menu** and **click Adjust Paycheque**.

These methods will open the familiar Search window:

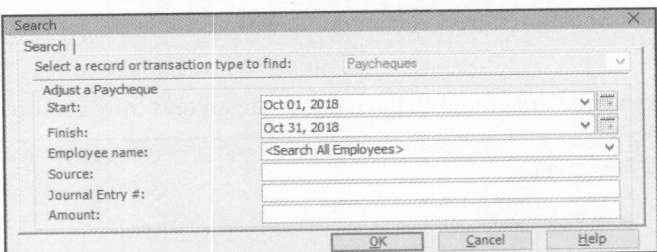

Paycheques is selected as the search area because of our starting point.

You can select beginning and ending dates to create the list. You can also enter the source (cheque or direct deposit number), journal entry number or amount and click OK to access the paycheque immediately.

The default dates are the earliest transaction date and the session date for the data file. We can accept the default dates to have all payroll transactions listed.

Click   **OK** to access the list of posted payroll entries:

Journal Entry #	Date	Source	Employee	Amount
7	Oct 15, 2018	214	Tiste, Arte	1,833.45
6	Oct 15, 2018	DD56	Nerture, Neela	1,717.97
5	Oct 15, 2018	DD55	Handie, Jerome	1,506.46
4	Oct 15, 2018	213	Filer, Morty	2,225.46

Click   **Journal Entry #4 Filer, Morty** to select Filer's journal entry.

Click   **Select** to display the entry that was posted.

First, Sage 50 reminds you about recalculating taxes:

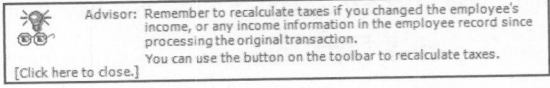

Advisor: Remember to recalculate taxes if you changed the employee's income, or any income information in the employee record since processing the original transaction.
You can use the button on the toolbar to recalculate taxes.
[Click here to close.]

NOTES
You can look up Payroll Journal entries in the same way you can look up transactions in other journals.

NOTES
In the Payroll Journal, pressing *ctrl* + A also opens the Adjust entry search screen, as it does in the other journals.

NOTES
Your journal entry numbers may be different if you have made other correcting or adjusting entries.

Sage 50 advises you that tax recalculation will not be automatic if you change any amount on the payroll entry. The Recalculate Taxes button is no longer dimmed.

Click   the **Advisor icon** to close the warning and display the journal:

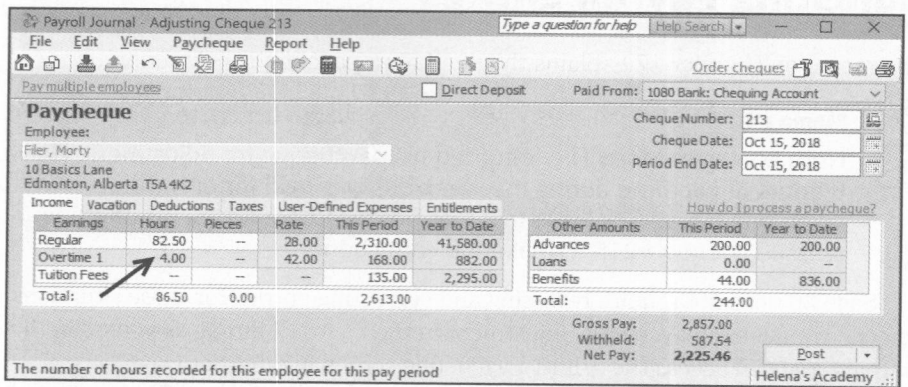

This is a duplicate of the payroll entry. All fields can be edited except the employee name. If you change the date for the new cheque to October 17, the reversing entry will retain the original posting date. Normally you would prepare a new cheque. However, Filer has returned the cheque so we can use the same number. We need to change the number of overtime hours.

Click   **4.00** in the **Hours column for Overtime 1** to select the current entry.

Type   6 **Press** (tab) to enter the change and update the gross pay.

The Vacation Pay and Withheld amounts have not been updated for the new amount of gross pay. Compare your Vacation tab screen amounts with those in the journal screen display on page 267.

Click   the **Taxes tab**. Tax amounts have not changed and they can be edited:

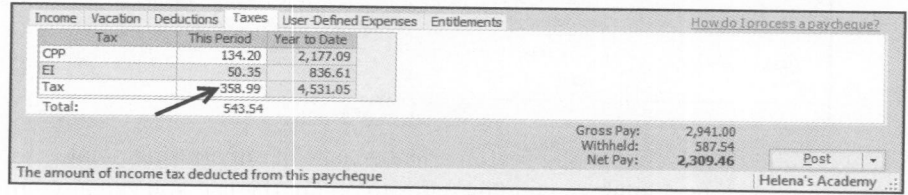

Click   the **Recalculate Taxes button** on the Payroll Journal tool bar or **choose** the **Paycheque menu** and **click Recalculate Taxes**:

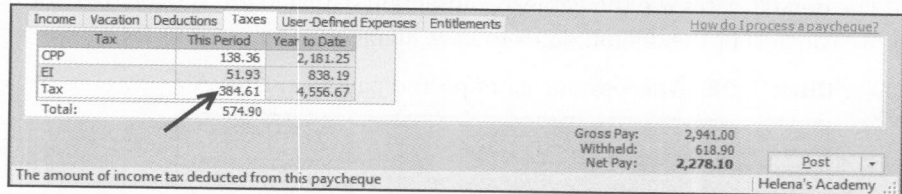

All the tax deduction and vacation pay amounts are updated for the extra hours.

Click   the **Vacation tab** to verify that the Vacation amount has increased from $160.68 to $165.72.

Click   the **Entitlements tab**.

Type   1 in the Days Taken field for Sick Leave and **press** (tab).

Review the Payroll Journal **entry**. **Close** the **display** when you have finished.

Make   **corrections** if necessary. **Click** [Post |▼] to save the adjustment.

NOTES
Dates should be changed only if they are incorrect.

NOTES
If you need to change the employee or cancel a paycheque for other reasons, you can reverse the payroll transaction. Refer to page 275.

NOTES
Until you recalculate the taxes, the total amount withheld from gross pay is still $587.54 and the Vacation Accrued amount is still $160.68.

WARNING!
Do not confuse the Recalculate Taxes tool with the Windows Calculator tool. The Calculator tool is the last one on the left-hand side of the tool bar before the Refresh tools.

NOTES
The adjusted entry you display is J9. The reversing entry in the background is J8.

Sage 50 displays a warning when you do not recalculate the taxes:

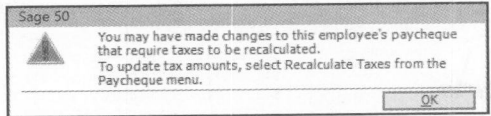

Sage 50 displays another warning when you do not change the cheque number:

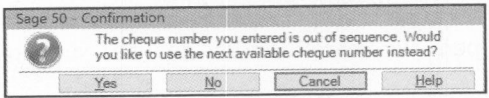

Read the question in the warning carefully. To change the cheque number to the next number in the automatic sequence, click Yes. In this case, you can use the duplicate cheque number because Filer returned the original cheque.

Click **No** to continue. **Click OK** to confirm posting the two journal entries.

Close the **Payroll Journal** to return to the Home window.

When you display the Payroll Journal and include corrections, you will have three journal entries for Filer: the original entry (J4), the reversing adjusting entry (J8) and the final correct entry (J9).

All three journal entries are posted with the original date, unless you changed it.

Reversing a Paycheque

You should reverse an entry to correct it when you have selected the wrong employee or if you need to delete it. The Reverse tool performs this in a single step.

Open the Payroll Journal.

Click the Adjust Paycheque tool 🖳 or press ⌨ctrl⌨ + A.

Define your search parameters and click OK to access the list of posted entries.

Double-click the entry you want to reverse to open the journal entry.

Click the Reverse Paycheque tool 🖳 or choose the Paycheque menu and click Reverse Paycheque.

Click Yes to confirm that the entry will be reversed.

Sage 50 saves both the original and the reversing entry. When you show corrections for journal reports, you have a complete audit trail.

Releasing Vacation Pay

Tiste needs to receive his retained vacation amount to pay for his booked vacation.

✓	**Memo #2**	**Dated Oct. 17/18**
6	Tiste has booked his vacation and will receive his retained vacation pay to pay for the holiday. Release the accrued retained vacation pay for Arte Tiste and issue cheque #215.	

Before releasing the vacation pay, we will view the setting in the employee ledger that controls whether vacation pay is retained or released with each paycheque. There are several ways to open the employee record.

From the Home window, you can access the employee record from the Employees icon shortcuts list or from the Employees pane. The Employees pane also has a drop-down list for creating an employee paycheque or report. (Refer to page 276.)

(Refer to page 276.)

NOTES
The program provides a warning about the cheque sequence because we selected to verify number sequences in the Forms Settings window (refer to page 213).

NOTES
The procedure for reversing a transaction is the same in all journals when the option is available.
You can also click 🖳, the Lookup tool, to view a payroll transaction and then click the Reverse tool 🖳.

CLASSIC VIEW
Click the Employees icon 👤 Employees to open the Employees window. Then double-click the entry for Tiste to open his record. Or, click Tiste to select the employee and then click the Edit tool or choose the File menu and click Open to open his ledger record.

NOTES

From the Employees pane shortcuts list arrow you can complete other tasks directly for the selected employee — create a paycheque or display the Detail Report.

You can hide the year-to-date details for employees from the Employees list pane, just as you can hide details for vendors and customers.

Click the ▤ tool for the list of details you can hide. Refer to page 284.

NOTES

In the Employees window, if Tiste is selected, you can click the

Payroll Journal icon 🖳 or choose the Journal menu and click Payroll Journal to access the journal with Tiste already selected.

NOTES

If the Use column has a ✓, the item will appear in the journal for this employee. There is no ✓ for Overtime 1, so Overtime does not appear in the journal's Earnings column for Tiste (refer to the Payroll Journal screen for Tiste on page 272).

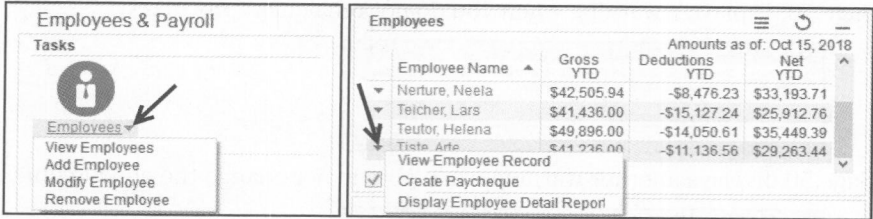

The **Modify Employees** shortcut opens the Search window and you can choose from the list of employees.

The **Employees icon** ⓘ or the **View Employees** shortcut will open the Employees window:

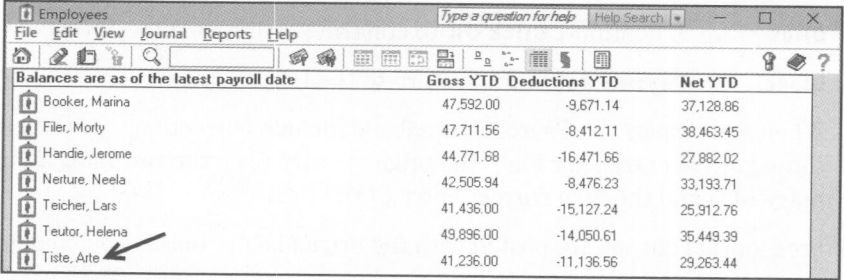

Double-click **Tiste** to view his ledger record. Or, in the Employees pane,

Click **Tiste** or **click** the **shortcuts list arrow** beside his name and **choose View Employee Record**. The record opens with the Personal tab screen.

Click the **Income tab** to access the vacation pay settings:

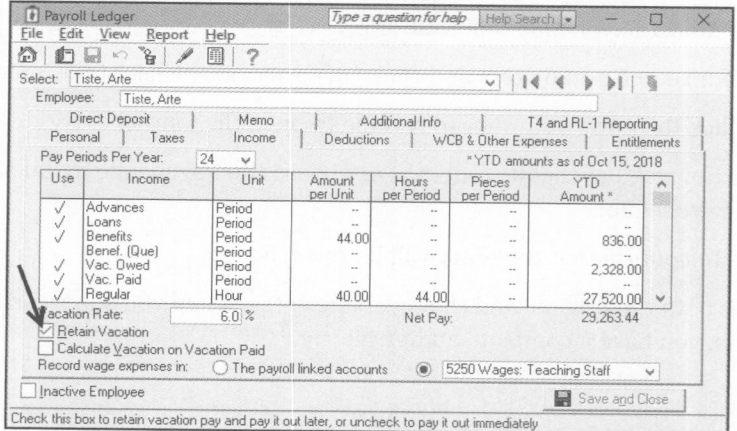

The checkmark for **Retain Vacation** indicates that vacation pay for Tiste is withheld. It can be released when Tiste receives his retained pay. If the vacation pay is paid out with each paycheque, the Retain Vacation checkbox should not be marked.

We do not need to make any changes to the ledger — we can pay out his retained vacation pay directly from the journal.

Close the **Ledger window** to return to your starting point. Close the Employees window if it is open.

Click the **Paycheques icon** 🖳 .

Choose **Tiste** from the employee list and **press** ⌨️ tab to continue. **Click** the **Vacation tab**:

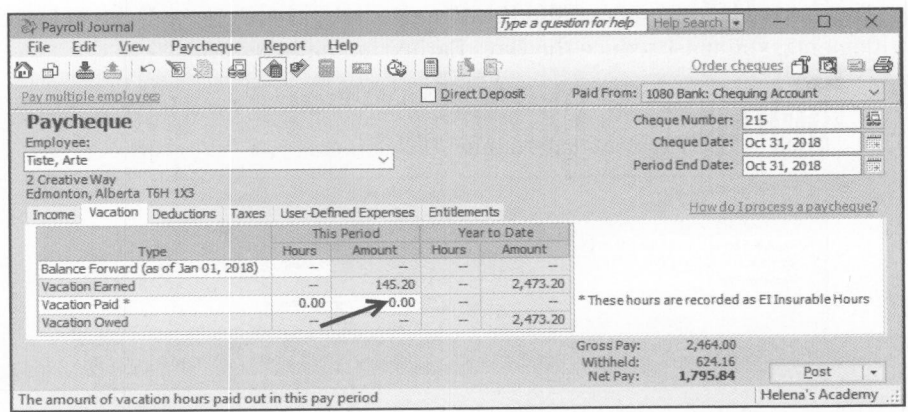

NOTES

The Vacation Earned Amount ($145.20) is the vacation pay on the wages for this pay period and is included in the Vacation Paid Amount.

When you remove the regular hours and number of lessons, the earned amount is reduced to zero and the vacation pay owed is also reduced by $145.20.

Employers should always check whether provincial regulations require them to add Insurable Hours for vacation paid.

This is a normal journal entry with default amounts and retained vacation pay. Tiste has already received his paycheque so, in this case, vacation pay should be issued as a separate cheque. To do this, we must remove all the regular amounts. No regular hours should be included and benefits and optional deductions do not apply to vacation pay.

Click   the **Income tab**:

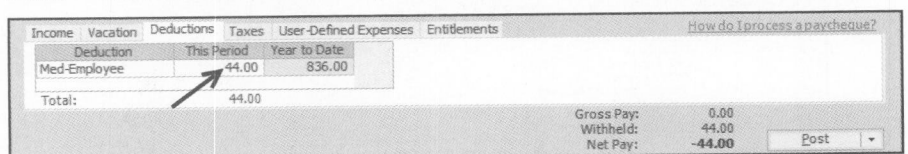

Click   **44.00** in the Regular Hours field. (Double-click if the entire amount is not selected.)

Press   del . **Press** tab to select the entry for number of lessons (Pieces).

Press   del to remove the entry and update the amounts again.

Click   **44.00** in the Benefits This Period field. **Press** del .

Press   tab . The Vacation tab screen opens — the vacation earned amount is now zero, but we still need to delete other amounts.

Tiste's medical premium amount should also be deleted before recording the entry. This is a one-time change, and it should be made directly in the journal.

Click   the **Deductions tab** to open this screen:

NOTES

Although the benefit, deduction and user-defined expense amounts do not change the vacation pay amount, they should not be charged to the employee or the employer. The amounts for this period were already included on the original paycheque for regular hours.

Click   **44** in the Med-Employee This Period field and **press** del .

Click   the **User-Defined Expenses tab**:

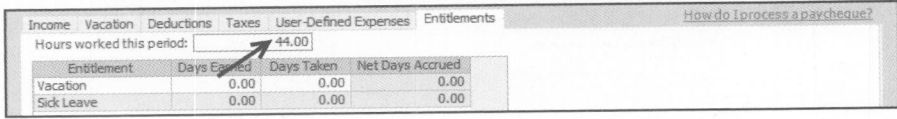

Click   **44** in the Med-employer This Period field and **press** del . **Press** tab :

The journal is updated and the Entitlements tab screen opens. For employees with entitlements, you must reduce the Days Earned amounts to zero:

Click   **44.00** in the Hours Worked field. **Press** (del) to remove the entry.

Click   the **Vacation tab** to open this screen:

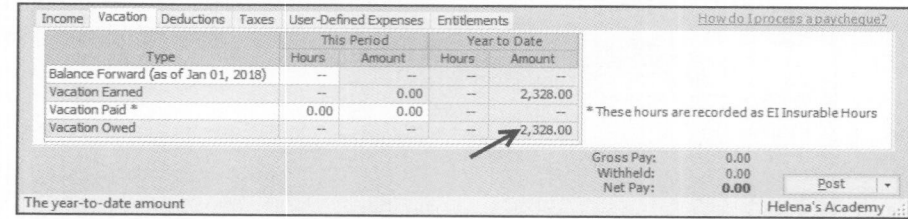

The Amount This Period entry has been removed. The Gross Pay, Withheld and Net Pay amounts are all reduced to zero.

The vacation pay amount that has accrued since the last time it was paid out is the Vacation Owed Amount, $2 328. This is the amount that will be paid now by entering it in the Vacation Paid Amount field.

Click   **0.00** in the Vacation Paid Amount field.

Type   2328 **Press** (tab) to update the net pay. The Deductions tab screen opens.

Click   the **Vacation tab**:

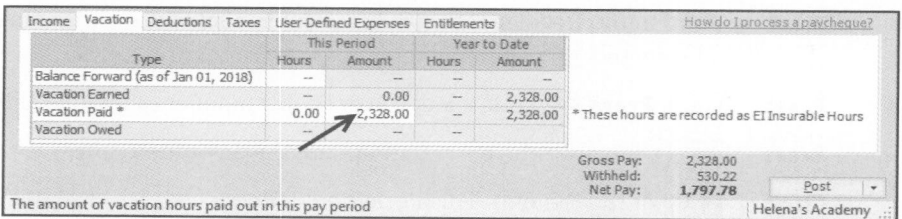

The Gross Pay amount now matches the vacation paid amount and taxes have been updated. We still need to change the dates for the paycheque.

Enter   **Oct 17** as the cheque date and **Oct 15** as the Period Ending date.

Choose   the **Report menu** and **click Display Payroll Journal Entry**:

Helena's Academy
Payroll Journal Entry 10/17/2018 (J10)

Account Number	Account Description	Debits	Credits
2300	Vacation Payable	2,328.00	-
5310	EI Expense	61.28	-
5320	CPP Expense	108.02	-
5330	WCB Expense	20.72	-
1080	Bank: Chequing Account	-	1,797.78
2310	EI Payable	-	105.05
2320	CPP Payable	-	216.04
2330	Income Tax Payable	-	378.43
2460	WCB Payable	-	20.72
Additional Date:	Additional Field:	2,518.02	2,518.02

The released vacation pay is entered as a debit (decrease) to *Vacation Payable*. Payroll taxes are charged on the vacation pay, as they are on other wages, because taxes were not paid on the retained vacation pay. The employer's expense for vacation pay, a debit to the linked wages expense account, was recognized when the original paycheque was prepared. At that time *Vacation Payable* was credited to create the liability.

Close   the **display** to return to the journal and **make corrections** if necessary.

Click   [Post ▼]. Sage 50 wants confirmation before proceeding:

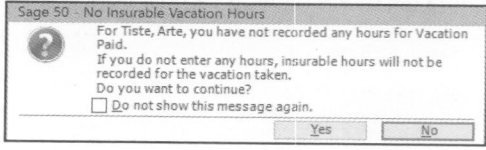

If the employee is taking regular time off for vacation, you should enter the number of hours in the Hours field beside Vacation Paid.

Click   **Yes** to continue and then **click Yes** again to bypass the payroll dates warning. **Close** the **Payroll Journal**.

Making Payroll Tax Remittances

Sage 50 tracks payroll liabilities and remittances when the suppliers are linked to payroll taxes. Helena's Academy has five suppliers for whom remittances are due.

✓	**Memo #3**	**Dated Oct. 17/18**
7		

Make payroll remittances for the pay period ending October 1.
  Receiver General for Canada: EI, CPP and income tax
  Aspen Life Financial: Medical premiums from employee and employer
  Alberta Workers' Compensation Board: WCB
  Rocky Mountain Trust: RRSP
  Maintenance Enforcement Program: Family support payments
Issue cheques #216 to #220.

Taxes are remitted from the Payments Journal. You can open this journal from the Payables module Payments Journal or its Home window shortcuts list, or from the Employees & Payroll module.

We will demonstrate the access from the Payroll window first.

NOTES
The Pay Remittance shortcuts list includes the options to Find and Adjust remittances.

Click   the **Pay Remittance icon** to open the Payments Journal form we need.

Click   the **To The Order Of list arrow** for the remittance suppliers set up:

CLASSIC VIEW
Click the Payments icon

to open the Payments Journal. Then select Pay Remittance from the Pay transaction list to open the journal form we need (refer to page 283).

The five suppliers who collect payroll deductions and taxes are listed. The first remittance will be to the Receiver General for EI, CPP and income tax.

Click   **Receiver General for Canada** to select the supplier.

NOTES
Accept the default amounts in your data file, unless you know that you have made an error in the paycheque. In that case, you should correct the paycheque first.

The Payments Journal is updated with the taxes collected for this supplier:

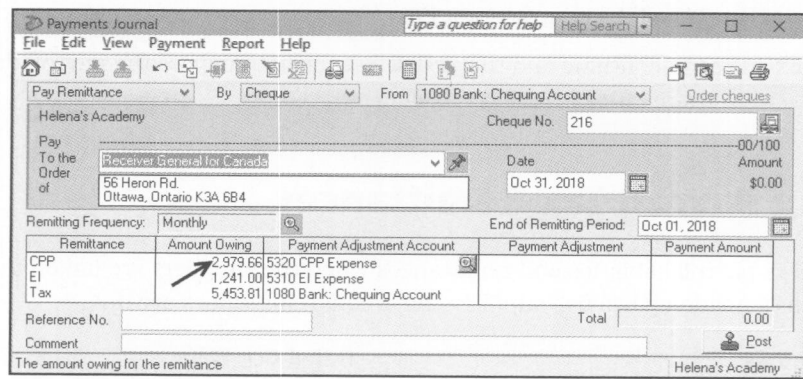

Three taxes are remitted to the Receiver General for Canada. The balances are the amounts in the General Ledger linked accounts as at the remittance period end date, October 1. For Helena's Academy, taxes were not remitted immediately before the files were converted to Sage 50 and the payroll tax liability accounts had outstanding balances. These balances match the amounts in the Trial Balance for October 1 on page 259. The remitting period and the next payment due date are entered as Payroll Ledger settings.

The Remittance Journal has two date fields: one for the date of the cheque and a second below the cheque section for the payroll period covered by the remittance. The session date is the default cheque date. The **End Of Remitting Period date** is entered as a Payroll setting. When you change the End Of Remitting Period date, the amounts will be updated to the General Ledger amounts at that date. Remittances are usually due one month after the pay period they cover, so we are paying the taxes that were withheld to the end of September. The period end date is updated according to the frequency of payment entered as a Payroll Remittance setting.

The **Payment Adjustment** field should be used for any tax expenses that are not already included in the payable account balances. Separate linked accounts may be used for these adjustments. A positive entry will increase the tax expense and the total amount submitted. Negative adjustment amounts will decrease the tax expense amount and the total amount submitted.

The full amount is being paid for each tax.

Click   the **Payment Amount column for CPP** to enter the amount owing as the payment amount.

Press   ⬇ to enter the payment amount for EI.

Press   ⬇ to enter the payment amount for Tax.

Press   ⬇tab⬇ to accept the final payment, update the cheque amount and advance to the Reference No. field.

Type   Memo 3A **Press** ⬇tab⬇ to advance to the Comment field.

Type   Payroll tax remittance for September

NOTES
In Chapter 9, we explain how to enter the Payroll Ledger settings.

NOTES
Because the earliest transaction date allowed is October 1, we cannot enter September 30 as the date for the end of the remitting period. The amounts for October 1 are the same as the amounts for September 30.

If any employees were paid on October 1, you must enter September 30 as the pay period ending date. In this case, September 30 would also be the earliest transaction date.

NOTES
The Reference No. is added for the Remittance Journal report, so you do not need to repeat it in the Comment as we did for Other Payment entries in this journal.

Enter   **Oct 17** as the cheque Date to complete the form:

We can now review the journal entry.

Choose the **Report menu** and **click Display Payments Journal Entry**:

Helena's Academy Payments Journal Entry					
	Account Number	Account Description	Debits	Credits	
10/01/2018 (J11)		Memo 3A, Receiver General for Canada : Payroll tax remittance for September			
	2310	EI Payable	1,241.00	-	
	2320	CPP Payable	2,979.66	-	
	2330	Income Tax Payable	5,453.81	-	
	2200	Accounts Payable	-	9,674.47	
10/17/2018 (J12)		216, Receiver General for Canada : Payroll tax remittance for September			
	2200	Accounts Payable	9,674.47		
	1080	Bank: Chequing Account	-	9,674.47	
Additional Date: Additional Field:			19,348.94	19,348.94	

The remittance creates two journal entries. The three payroll liability accounts have been debited to reduce the liability, and *Accounts Payable* is credited with October 1 as the effective date to reflect the liability to the Canada Revenue Agency. If you had entered adjustments, those amounts would be debited (for positive adjustments) to the corresponding linked account. The second entry recognizes the payment on the cheque date, October 17 — it clears the *Accounts Payable* liability with a credit entry to the Bank account.

Close   the **display** when finished.

CORRECTING THE PAYROLL REMITTANCE

Move the cursor to the field that contains the error. **Double-click** or **drag through** the **incorrect information** to highlight it. **Type** the **correct information** and **press** ⌨tab to enter it. **Enter** a different **remittance end period date**, if this is appropriate, to enter the amounts owing for that date.

You can discard the entry by **clicking** ✖ (**Close**) or ↶ (**Undo**) or by returning to the Supplier list and **clicking** a **different supplier** name. **Click** the name of the **correct remittance supplier** and **press** ⌨tab. When prompted, confirm that you want to discard the incorrect entry. **Click Yes** and start again.

You can adjust a remittance **after posting** as you can other payments. **Choose Adjust Remittance** from the Pay Remittances icon shortcuts list. Or, open the Pay Remittance journal and **click** the **Adjust Remittance tool** or **choose** the **Payment menu** and **choose Adjust Remittance. Enter** the search **criteria** you want to determine the list of payments. Only remittances appear on this list. **Select** the **remittance** that requires correction and **make** the **changes** you need. **Post** the revised correction after reviewing it.

From the journal's Report menu you can also display the Remittance Report, the same report that you get from the Home window Reports menu or Report Centre. If you display this report before posting the payment, the payment amounts will still be zero. First, we must make corrections and post the payment.

Make   **corrections** if necessary and then **post** the **payment**.

Choose the **Report menu** and **click Display Remittance Report**:

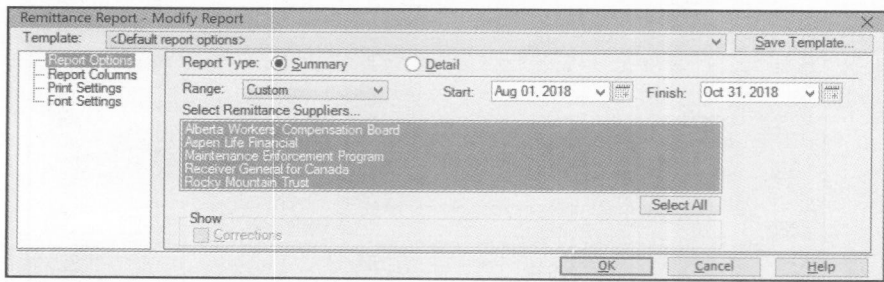

You can display a **Summary Report** with total amounts for each tax or a **Detail Report** with a line entry for each tax for each payroll transaction in the report period. You can prepare the report for one or more payroll authorities, and you can choose a remittance period for the report. We can accept the default dates — we want the report for October. Only one remittance was posted, so we will view the Summary Report for the Receiver General to display the remittance we just completed.

NOTES

The Amount column entries in the report reflect only the amounts from Payroll Journal entries for the four paycheques on October 15 and Tiste's vacation pay. They do not include the opening balance forward amounts.

The note reminds us that the report accounts only for transactions completed with the Pay Remittance feature.

NOTES

When you choose Receiver General for Canada again as the supplier, the remitting period date has been advanced by one month and the current account balances are displayed.

NOTES

The Medical liability has two entries, one for the employee's share and one for the employer's share.

Click   **Receiver General For Canada** and then **click OK** to open the report:

Range: Custom	Start: Aug 01, 2018	Finish: Oct 31, 2018			

Helena's Academy
Remittances Summary 08/01/2018 to 10/31/2018

Payable	Amount	Payment Adjustments	Payments	Balance	No. Of Employees
Receiver General for Canada					
CPP	1,155.22	0.00	-2,979.66	1,155.22	4
EI	546.38	0.00	-1,241.00	546.38	4
Tax*	1,850.97	0.00	-5,453.81	1,850.97	4
Total - Receiv...	3,552.57	0.00	-9,674.47	3,552.57	4
* The gross (taxable) payroll amount for all employees for this period is $12,398.00					
Grand Total	3,552.57	0.00	-9,674.47	3,552.57	4
Amounts in the Payment Adjustments and Payments columns are payment adjustments and payments made through the remittance journal.					

The report includes the total of Payroll Journal entry amounts for all tax, adjustments, payments and final balances. The new balances are the total amounts for the October paycheques for the four employees and the vacation pay for Tiste.

Close   the **report** when finished to return to the Payments Journal.

Choose **Aspen Life Financial** as the supplier for the next remittance.

Pay   the **two Medical premium amounts**. The dates October 1 and October 17 should be correct from the previous remittance.

Enter   **Memo 3B** in the Reference field and **enter** an appropriate **comment**.

Review and then **post** the **payment**.

Choose **Alberta Workers' Compensation Board** as the supplier.

Pay   the **WCB amount**.

Enter   **Memo 3C** in the Reference field and **enter** an appropriate **comment**.

Review and then **post** the **payment**.

Choose **Rocky Mountain Trust** as the supplier for the next remittance.

Pay   the **RRSP contributions** withheld.

Enter   **Memo 3D** in the Reference field and **enter** an appropriate **comment**.

Review and then **post** the **payment**.

Choose **Maintenance Enforcement Program** as the supplier.

Pay   the **Family Support payments** withheld.

Enter   **Memo 3E** in the Reference field and **enter** an appropriate **comment**.

Review and then **post** the **payment**. **Close** the **Payments Journal**.

Entering Remittances from the Payables Module Window

Click Payables in the Modules pane list to open the Payables Home window. Click the Payments icon shortcuts list arrow:

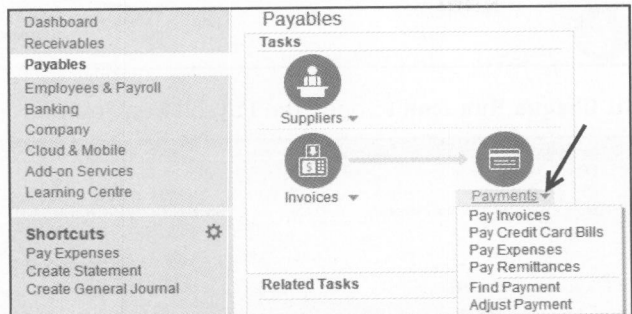

PRO VERSION
Remember that you will see Vendors as the icon label instead of Suppliers. Pay Purchase Invoices replaces Pay Invoices in the shortcuts drop-down list.

The shortcuts include Pay Remittances. Click Pay Remittances to modify the Payments Journal.

You can also click the Payments icon to open the Payments Journal. Once the journal is open, click Pay Invoices to access the payment types:

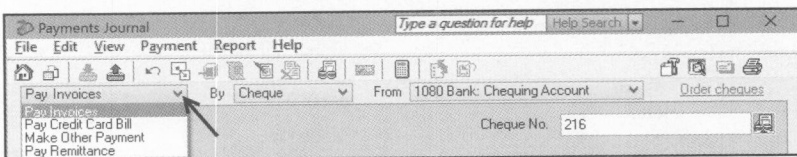

Click Pay Remittance to modify the Payments Journal. Choose the remittance supplier and continue with the remittance entry as outlined above.

Enter the **next two cash purchase transactions** and then close the journal.

8 | **Cash Purchase Invoice #ESS-4689**   **Dated Oct. 18/18**
From Energy Supply Services, $810 including taxes for heat and hydro on equal monthly billing plan. Store as a recurring monthly entry. Paid by cheque #221.

9 | **Cash Purchase #TA-113368**   **Dated Oct. 20/18**
From Telus Alberta, $220 including all taxes for one month of telephone services. Invoice total paid in full with cheque #222.

Completing a Payroll Cheque Run

When several employees are paid at the same time, you can complete a payroll cheque run to prepare all the cheques and journal entries in a single transaction.

Click **Employees & Payroll** in the Modules list to return to the default page.

The Payroll Run Journal is used to pay multiple employees:

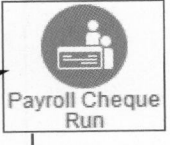

NOTES
The Payroll Cheque Run icon does not have a shortcuts list. Employee list balances are at the latest transaction date, October 20.

All the amounts in the Home window Employees list have been updated.

NOTES
You can update the amounts in the Employees pane by clicking ↻, the Refresh tool above the list.

PRO VERSION
pro The Refresh and Reset tools apply to multi-user operation of the program. They do not apply or appear in the single-user Pro version. The Time Slips tool also does not appear in the Pro version.

NOTES
The Payroll Run Journal has a link below the tool bar to switch to the Payroll Journal if you want to Pay One Employee.
You must use the Payroll Journal to edit tax amounts or previous payroll entries.

NOTES
You cannot adjust or reverse paycheques from the Payroll Run Journal — Adjust and Reverse entry tools are not included in the tool bar. However, paycheques prepared here can be adjusted in the Payroll Journal. Refer to page 293.
Taxes cannot be changed in the Payroll Run Journal — the Manually Calculate Taxes tool is omitted from the tool bar.
The Store and Recall tools are also missing.

As you can for suppliers and customers, you can hide the year-to-date details for employees from the Employees pane List tool ☰:

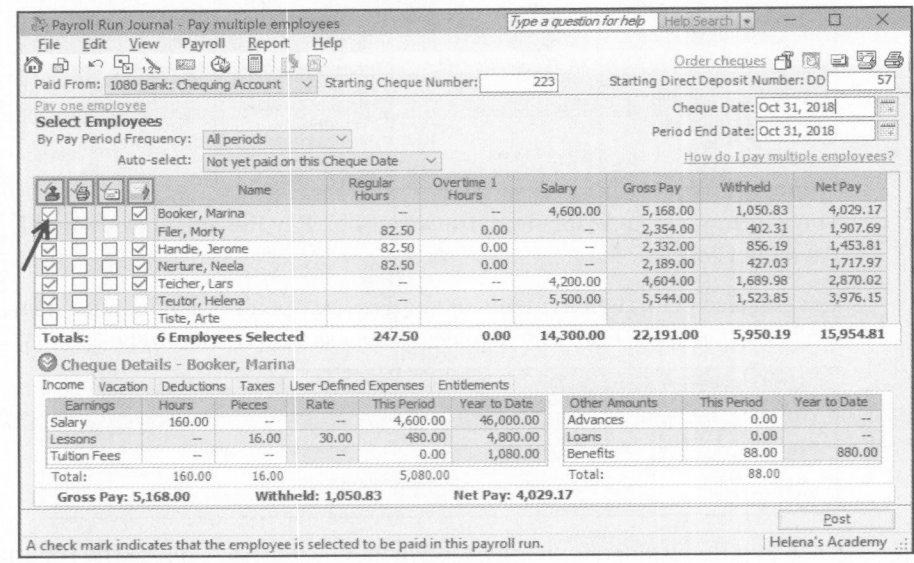

Click   the **Payroll Cheque Run icon** to open the Payroll Run Journal:

From this screen you can pay all employees, and you can enter or edit any details that you can enter or edit in the Payroll Journal. Employees are listed in alphabetic order, and checkmarks indicate who will be paid in this payroll run. If there is no checkmark in the Post column 🗜, you cannot create a paycheque for that employee.

The form also includes deposit information in the **Direct Deposit column** 🗜. A ✓ in this column indicates that the pay will be deposited to the employee's bank account. Both the next Cheque and Direct Deposit Numbers are on the form.

For direct deposit employees, you can check the **E-mail column** 📧 if you e-mail the cheque stubs to them. This check box is dimmed for employees paid by cheque.

By adding ✓s to the **Print column** 🖨, you can print cheques and deposit stubs directly from the summary.

The upper journal pane lists all active employees, with summary information for each. You can **edit** three details directly in the **summary pane** without opening the cheque details — the number of regular and overtime hours for hourly paid employees and salary amounts for salaried employees. This offers a quick way to complete simple payroll runs.

You cannot change the Gross Pay, Net Pay or Withheld amounts. Sage 50 calculates these from the details you enter.

The lower pane has the cheque details for the selected employee with tabs that mirror the tabs in the Payroll Journal. Because Booker is selected, her cheque details are provided initially. To change details that are not in the summary pane — the other details that are available in the Payroll Journal — you can access fields by selecting an employee and the appropriate tab screen.

In the summary on the following page, all employees are being paid on October 31.

✓
10

Employee Time Summary Sheet #20   **Dated Oct. 31/18**

For the pay period ending October 31, 2018

Name of Employee	Regular Hours	Overtime Hours	Lessons	Tuition	Advance (Repaid)	Loan (Repaid)	Sick Days	Direct Deposit
Filer, Morty	90.0	2	–	$135.00	($50)	–	–	No
Handie, Jerome	90.0	2	–	–	–	–	–	Yes
Nerture, Neela	90.0	–	–	–	–	–	–	Yes
Tiste, Arte	48.0	–	24	–	–	$100	–	No
Booker, Marina	160	–	16	$130.00	–	–	1	Yes
Teicher, Lars	160	–	12	–	–	–	–	Yes
Teutor, Helena	160	–	–	–	–	–	–	No

a. Using Employee Time Summary Sheet #20 and the Employee Information Sheet, complete payroll for all employees.
b. Recover $50 advanced to Morty Filer.
c. Issue $100 loan to Tiste and recover $25 from each of the next four paycheques.
d. Issue cheques #223, #224 and #225 and DD slips #57, #58, #59 and #60.

The program selects all employees for inclusion if their pay cycle has ended because All Periods is entered as the **By Pay Period Frequency**. You can select any single pay frequency from the list or all of them. If you select 24 periods, only the four hourly employees will be marked with a ✓.

Initially, all employees have a ✓ in the **Post column** except Tiste. From the Auto-Select options you can decide how to select the employees to be paid. Because the initial selection is **Not Yet Paid On This Cheque Date**, Tiste is excluded — he received his vacation pay after October 15.

Click   the **Auto-Select list arrow**:

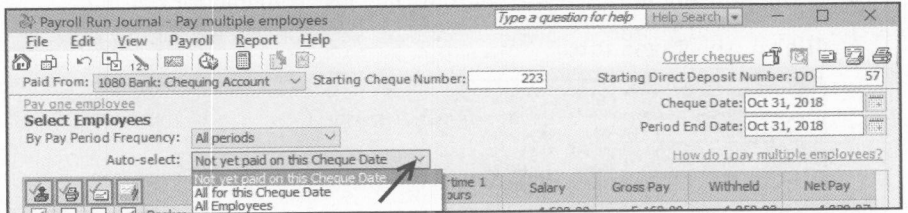

You can select all employees, all employees who should be paid on this date or all employees not yet paid for this cheque date.

Click   **All For This Cheque Date**. Tiste is now marked for payment, too.

The cheque date, pay period end date and initial cheque and deposit numbers can all be edited if necessary.

You can remove an employee from the payroll run by clicking the ✓ in the Post column to remove it. You can change the direct deposit status for an employee by clicking the ✓ in the Direct Deposit column to remove it. A cheque will then be created instead.

Click   **Filer** to select this employee with his income details on the screen:

Cheque Details - Filer, Morty								
Income	Vacation	Deductions	Taxes	User-Defined Expenses	Entitlements			
Earnings	Hours	Pieces	Rate	This Period	Year to Date	Other Amounts	This Period	Year to Date
Regular	82.50	--	28.00	2,310.00	43,890.00	Advances	0.00	200.00
Overtime 1	0.00	--	42.00	--	966.00	Loans	0.00	--
Tuition Fees	--	--	--	0.00	2,295.00	Benefits	44.00	880.00
Total:	82.50	0.00		2,310.00		Total:	44.00	
Gross Pay: 2,354.00		Withheld: 402.41		Net Pay: 1,907.69				Post

The number of hours recorded for this employee for this pay period   Helena's Academy

This screen is just like Filer's Income tab screen in the Payroll Journal on page 266, and we can enter or edit all amounts in the same way as in that journal. For Filer, we need to change the number of regular hours and add the overtime hours, the tuition fee amount and the advances repayment. All these details are entered in the Income tab screen.

Click **82.5** in the **Hours column beside Regular**. **Type** 90

Press ⎡tab⎤ to select the Overtime 1 Hours. **Type** 2

Press ⎡tab⎤ to select the Tuition Fees amount. **Type** 135 **Press** ⎡tab⎤.

By default, –200.00, the entire amount owing, is entered as the Advances Amount for This Period. Filer is repaying $50 each pay period, so we must change the amount.

Type –50

Click the **Vacation tab**:

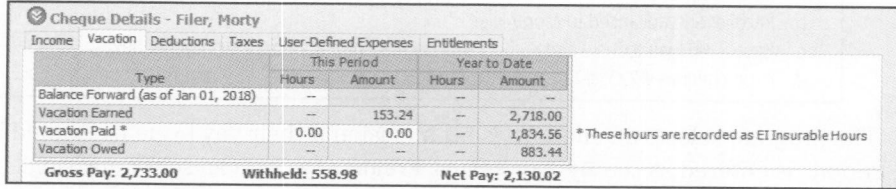

Vacation amounts are calculated and updated automatically.

Click the **Deductions tab**:

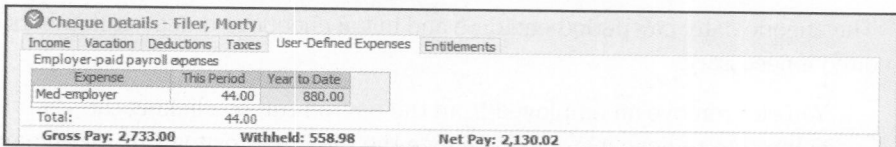

The deduction amounts are correct, but they are available for editing.

Click the **Taxes tab**:

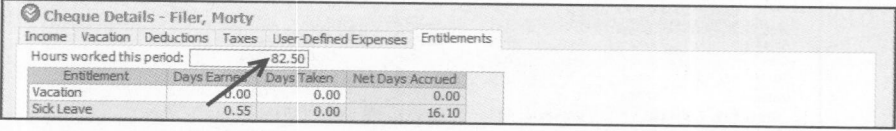

Taxes cannot be edited in the Payroll Run Journal. To change tax amounts you must use the Payroll Journal and choose to calculate taxes manually.

Click the **User-Defined Expenses tab**:

The employer's expense for the medical premium is included here and can be edited if required. Entitlements can also be edited — for Filer, we need to change the number of hours worked on the Entitlements screen.

Click the **Entitlements tab**:

Once again, the fields are the same as those in the Payroll Journal Entitlements tab screen (refer to page 271).

WARNING! Remember to enter a negative number for advances that are repaid.

NOTES Vacation may be paid in the same way as in the Payroll Journal. Enter the Vacation Owed Amount in the Vacation Paid Amount field.

NOTES Remember that the entry for Days Earned reflects only the amount earned for this pay period based on the number of hours worked in this pay period.

Type   90   as the number of hours worked in this period.

Click   **Handie** to select him and prepare for entering his additional details.

As soon as you select another employee, you will open a warning about partial payments of advances:

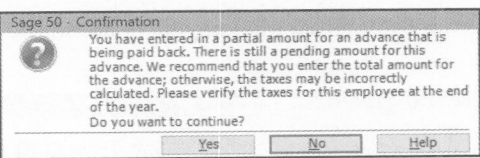

The warning advises that the entire amount of an advance should be repaid at one time to facilitate the correct calculation of taxes.

Click   **Yes** to continue. The Entitlements tab screen details open for Handie.

We need to update the number of overtime hours for Handie. We can change this in the upper summary pane. Handie is already selected.

Press   (tab) to highlight his number of Regular Hours in the upper summary pane.

Type   90 **Press** (tab) to select the Overtime Hours entry for Handie.

Type   2 to enter the Overtime hours. **Press** (tab) to update all amounts.

Click   **82.5** in the Entitlements details section. **Type**   90   as the number of hours worked.

For Nerture's pay, we need to change the number of regular hours worked and the entitlement hours. The Entitlements tab is still selected.

Click   **Nerture** to select her. **Press** (tab) to highlight her number of Regular Hours and **type**   90   in the Summary pane.

Click   **82.5** in the Entitlements tab Hours field. **Type**   90

For Tiste, we need to include the loan and change the regular hours worked. We need to work in the Cheque Details pane to access the loan amount field.

Click   **Tiste** and **press** (tab). **Type**   48   as the number of Regular Hours.

Click   the **Income tab** to open the Cheque Details pane and access the Loan fields.

Click   **22.00** in the Pieces column for Lessons. **Type**   24

Click   **0.00 beside Loans** in the column for This Period.

Type   100 **Press** (tab) to update all amounts.

Click   **Booker** to prepare for entering the additional details for her.

The Income tab should still be open. The screenshot on page 284 has the income details for Booker.

Booker is a salaried employee who also teaches music lessons after school. The default entry from the ledger record is correct. Her regular salary is also entered as a default, but both amounts can be edited if necessary in the Cheque Details pane. The salary amount can be edited in the summary pane as well.

We need to add her tuition fees benefit and enter one day of sick leave.

Click   **0.00** in the column for Tuition Fees This Period.

Type   130 **Press** (tab) to update all amounts.

NOTES
Each time you enter a partial repayment for an advance, Sage 50 will provide this warning. Click Yes.
    Taxes for partial repayments of advances may not add up to the same amount as those for the total advance because different tax brackets may apply.
    We chose the partial repayment method to include the various warning and confirmation messages in Sage 50.

NOTES
You do not need to delete the entitlement hours. They do not apply to Tiste, who does not receive these entitlements.

Click the **Entitlements tab** to open the entitlements fields.

Click the **Days Taken field beside Sick Leave**.

Type 1 **Press** (tab) to update the form, reducing the number of Net Days Accrued to 18.07.

No changes are required for Teicher or Teutor's salaried paycheques, so the transaction is complete:

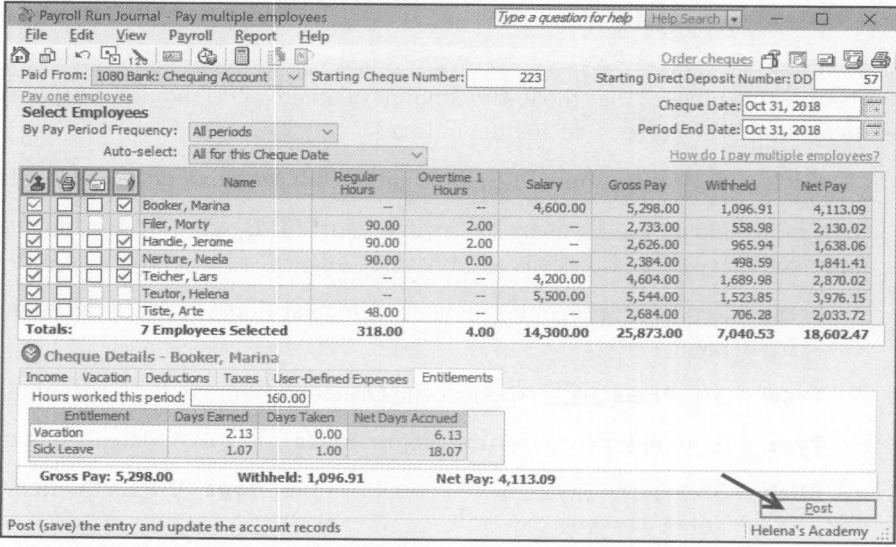

You are now ready to review the journal entry.

Choose the **Report menu** and **click Display Payroll Journal Entry** to review the journal entry. There are seven journal entries, one for each employee in the payroll run.

Close the **display** when finished.

You can print paycheques from the Payroll Run Journal, but you cannot preview them. You can modify the reports and forms setting from the journal from the tool button.

Turn on your **printer**.

Choose the **Report menu** and **click Print Payroll Cheque Run Summary** to provide a printed record of the payroll run transactions paid by cheque or **click Print Direct Deposit Stub Summary** to provide a printed record of the payroll run transactions paid by direct deposit. You cannot display these summaries.

Click **Post** [Post] to save the transaction. **Click Yes** to bypass the warning about payroll formula dates.

The confirmation message advises that seven journal entries were posted. The Payroll Run Journal remains open with the direct deposit and cheque numbers updated after the payroll run cheques and direct deposits. All employees are still selected with pay amounts because of the Auto-Select entry.

Choose Not Yet Paid On This Cheque Date from the Auto-Select list.

NOTES

To print from the Payroll Run Journal, click the Print check box in the second column beside the employee's name. Then click the Print tool, press (ctrl) + P or choose the File menu and click Print Payroll Cheques.

To print direct deposit stubs, choose the File menu and click Print Direct Deposit Stubs.

Or, you can use the respective tool buttons.

You will print the requested forms for all employees selected for printing.

The Post button in the Payroll Run Journal does not include the Print & Post option that is available in the Payroll Journal.

The updated form is displayed:

Now, no employees are selected because they have all been paid. There are no ✓s in the Post column. The Starting Cheque and Direct Deposit numbers have been updated.

Close the **Journal** to return to the Home window.

Enter the following **source documents** for October 31 and November 15.

11

Bank Debit Memo #277581　　　　**Dated Oct. 31/18**

From Scholar Heights Bank, $4 255 was withdrawn from chequing account for the following pre-authorized transactions:

Bank charges	$ 55
Interest on bank loan	320
Reduction of principal on bank loan	880
Interest on mortgage	2 500
Reduction of principal on mortgage	500

Store as a recurring monthly entry.

12

Bank Credit Memo #467116　　　　**Dated Oct. 31/18**

From Scholar Heights Bank, $1 800 interest on investments and bank account was deposited to chequing account. Store as a recurring monthly entry.

13

Memo #4　　　　**Dated Oct. 31/18**

Complete end-of-month adjusting entries for the following:

Office supplies used	$180
Art supplies used	335
Textbooks damaged	385
Prepaid property taxes	900

You can store this as a recurring monthly entry if you want.

NOTES
Remember that when you store adjusting entries, you must edit the source and amounts when you recall the transaction.

SESSION DATE – NOVEMBER 15, 2018

14

Cash Sales Invoice #1037　　　　**Dated Nov. 1/18**

To parents of students, $3 200 total monthly fees for after-school programs, and $2 280 total monthly fees for individual music lessons. Deposited $5 480 to chequing account.

15

Cash Purchase Invoice #GL-38827-B　　　　**Dated Nov. 2/18**

To Global Liability Inc., $1 800 for monthly insurance premium as stated on policy #GL-38827. Paid by cheque #226. Recall stored entry.

16

Cash Purchase Invoice #ES-1446　　　　**Dated Nov. 15/18**

From Engine Services (use Quick Add), $440 including taxes for gasoline, tire repairs, oil change and lubrication on vehicle. Invoice total paid in full with cheque #227.

NOTES

This pay period included 11 days at 7.5 hours each for hourly employees.

NOTES

Type –50 in the Advances This Period field for Filer and –25 in the Loans This Period field for Tiste to recover these amounts.

The warning about the partial repayment of Filer's advance amount will open again.

17

HELENA'S ACADEMY

Aim higher!

Employee Time Summary Sheet
Business No.: 189 245 053 RP 0001

#21
Cheque Date: November 15, 2018   Last day of pay period: November 15, 2018

Employee SIN	M. Filer 374 588 127	J. Handie 813 402 302	N. Nerture 129 495 768	A. Tiste 513 288 191	H. Teutor 699 344 578	M. Booker 277 639 118	L. Teicher 403 401 599
Nov 1-2	15.0	17.0	15.0	12			
Nov 5-9	37.5	39.5	37.5	20			
Nov 12-15	30.0	30.0	30.0	12			
Reg. hrs	82.5	82.5	82.5	44			
Overtime	--	4	--	--			
Lessons	--	--	--	22			
Tuition	135.00	--	--	--			
Loan	--	--	--	-25.00			
Advance	-50.00	--	--	--			
Sick leave	--	--	1	--			
Chq/DD #	Chq 228	DD61	DD62	Chq 229			

Payroll Prepared by: Morty Filer Nov 15/18

When you first open the Payroll Run Journal for the November 15 pay period, the four hourly paid employees will be selected:

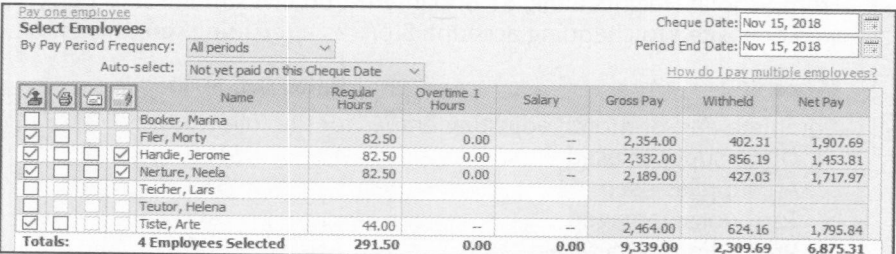

The salaried employees are not due to be paid until November 30 and are not selected.

Complete the **November 15 payroll run** for the four employees.

Advance the **session date** to **November 30**; **make** a **backup**. **Continue** entering **transactions** up to the payroll adjustment for December 17.

18

Memo #5   **Dated Nov. 17/18**

Make payroll remittances for the pay period ending October 31.
   Receiver General for Canada: CPP, EI and income tax
   Aspen Life Financial: Medical premiums from employee and employer
   Alberta Workers' Compensation Board: WCB
   Rocky Mountain Trust: RRSP
   Maintenance Enforcement Program: Family support payments
Issue cheques #230 to #234. (Read margin Notes and Warning.)

19

Cash Purchase Invoice #ESS-5568   **Dated Nov. 18/18**

From Energy Supply Services, $810 including taxes for heat and hydro on equal monthly billing plan. Recall the stored entry. Paid by cheque #235.

WARNING!

If any employees were paid on November 1, you must enter October 31 as the end of the remitting period.

NOTES

The default date entry for the End Of Remitting Period is November 1, one month past the previous October 1 remittance. If you enter October 31 instead, a message opens about the date preceding the current period, which may affect prior period earnings (because October 31 is in the previous month). You can click Yes to confirm that this is correct or you can accept November 1 as the remittance period ending date.

20

Cash Purchase #TA-193245   **Dated Nov. 20/18**

From Telus Alberta, $165 including all taxes for one month of telephone services. Invoice total paid in full with cheque #236.

21

Aim higher!

Employee Time Summary Sheet
Business No.: 189 245 053 RP 0001

#22
Cheque Date: November 30, 2018   Last day of pay period: November 30, 2018

Employee SIN	M. Filer 374 588 127	J. Handie 813 402 302	N. Nerture 129 495 768	A. Tiste 513 288 191	H. Teutor 699 344 578	M. Booker 277 639 118	L. Teicher 403 401 599
Nov 1-2	pd	pd	pd	pd	➤➤	➤➤	➤➤
Nov 5-9	pd	pd	pd	pd	➤➤	➤➤	➤➤
Nov 12-16	7.5	9.5	9.5	4	➤➤	➤➤	➤➤
Nov 19-23	37.5	37.5	39.5	20	➤➤	➤➤	➤➤
Nov 26-30	37.5	37.5	39.5	20	➤➤	➤➤	➤➤
Reg. hrs	82.5	82.5	82.5	44	160	160	160
Overtime	--	2	6	--	--	--	--
Lessons	--	--	--	22	--	16	12
Tuition	135.00	--	--	--	--	130.00	--
Advance	-50.00	--	--	--	--	--	--
Loan	--	--	--	-25.00	--	--	--
Sick leave	--	--	1	--	--	--	--
Chq/DD #	Chq 237	DD64	DD65	Chq 239	Chq 238	DD63	DD66

Payroll Prepared by: Morty Filer Nov 30/18

NOTES

Type –50 in the Advances This Period field for Filer and –25 in the Loans This Period field for Tiste to recover these amounts.

The November 30 pay period included 11 days for hourly workers.

22

Bank Debit Memo #422344   **Dated Nov. 30/18**

From Scholar Heights Bank, $4 255 was withdrawn from chequing account for the following pre-authorized transactions. Recall the stored entry.

Bank charges	$ 55
Interest on bank loan	320
Reduction of principal on bank loan	880
Interest on mortgage	2 500
Reduction of principal on mortgage	500

23

Bank Credit Memo #64567   **Dated Nov. 30/18**

From Scholar Heights Bank, $1 800 interest on investments and bank account was deposited to chequing account. Recall the stored entry.

24

Memo #6   **Dated Nov. 30/18**

Complete end-of-month adjusting entries for the following:

Office supplies used	$175
Art supplies used	420
Textbooks damaged	405
Prepaid property taxes	900

SESSION DATE – DECEMBER 15, 2018

When you approach the end of a calendar year, the year-end advisor message opens, similar to the year-end advisor messages we saw earlier.

NOTES

The CRA usually posts the new TD1 claim amounts on its Web site at the beginning of December for the following year.

The message includes information about renewing the payroll plan and updating TD1 claim amounts for employees:

> Advisor: Now is a good time to prepare for your company's year end. Refer to the Help for more information.
> [Click here to close.]
> Reminder! Payroll users, check your Sage Business Care renewal date! Sage Business Care provides access to payroll tax updates whenever a new tax table is released.
> To subscribe to this service, call our Customer Sales Department at 1-888-261-9610. Enroll early to ensure prompt delivery.

Payroll taxes are updated every six months, and these updates should be downloaded regularly in an active business.

---

25 **Cash Sales Invoice #1038** **Dated Dec. 1/18**

To parents of students, $2 400 total monthly fees for after-school programs, and $1 580 total monthly fees for individual music lessons. Deposited $3 980 to chequing account.

---

26 **Cash Purchase Invoice #GL-38827-C** **Dated Dec. 2/18**

To Global Liability Inc., $1 800 for monthly insurance premium as stated on policy #GL-38827. Paid by cheque #240. Recall the stored entry.

27

HELENA'S ACADEMY

Aim higher!

Employee Time Summary Sheet
Business No.: 189 245 053 RP 0001

#23
Cheque Date: December 15, 2018   Last day of pay period: December 15, 2018

Employee SIN	M. Filer 374 588 127	J. Handie 813 402 302	N. Nerture 129 495 768	A. Tiste 513 288 191	H. Teutor 699 344 578	M. Booker 277 639 118	L. Teicher 403 401 599
Dec 3-7	37.5	38.5	38.5	20			
Dec 10-14	37.5	38.5	41.5	20			
- - - -							
- - - -							
Reg. hrs	75.0	75.0	75.0	40			
Overtime	--	2	5	--			
Lessons	--	--	--	22			
Tuition	135.00	--	--	--			
Loan	--	--	--	-25.00			
Advance	-50.00	--	--	--			
Sick leave	--	--	--	--			
Chq/DD #	Chq 241	DD67	DD68	Chq 242			

Payroll Prepared by: Morty Filer Dec 15/18

NOTES

Type −50 in the Advances This Period field for Filer and −25 in the Loans This Period for Tiste to recover these amounts.

The December 15 pay period includes 10 days for hourly paid employees. Enter 75 as the number of regular hours for Filer, Handie and Nerture. Enter 40 as the number of regular hours for Tiste.

NOTES

Sage 50 no longer gives the warning about advances for Filer because the full balance is being repaid.

SESSION DATE – DECEMBER 31, 2018

28 **Memo #7** **Dated Dec. 17/18**

Make payroll remittances for the pay period ending November 30.
   Receiver General for Canada: CPP, EI and income tax
   Aspen Life Financial: Medical premiums from employee and employer
   Alberta Workers' Compensation Board: WCB
   Rocky Mountain Trust: RRSP
   Maintenance Enforcement Program: Family support payments
Issue cheques #243 to #247.

Adjusting a Payroll Cheque Run Entry

We can adjust a Payroll Run Journal entry from the Payroll Journal, just as we edited the transaction for Filer. Tiste has handed in his resignation and should repay the remainder of his loan. As described in Memo #8, Tiste should also receive his final vacation pay.

29

Aim higher!

MEMO #8

From the desk of Morty Filer
Dated: Dec. 17, 2018

RE: Payroll Adjustment required for Arte Tiste
          and vacation pay

          Adjust the Dec. 15 paycheque for Tiste —
          Tiste is leaving the Academy and should receive his total accrued vacation pay.
          In addition, he should have the full loan amount recovered from his paycheque.
          The original cheque #242 has been voided. Issue cheque #248 and increase
          the loan recovered to $50.
          Include the vacation pay owing to him in the revised paycheque.

Paycheque (cheque #248) released *Dec 17 Morty Filer*

Click   the **Paycheques icon** .

Click   the **Adjust Paycheque tool** 🔲 or **press** ⌨ctrl + **A**.

Click   **OK** to access the list of posted payroll entries. All the entries from both
               payroll journals are included.

Double-click the **Dec. 15 entry for Tiste**.

Click   the **Advisor icon** to close the warning about recalculating taxes and
               display the paycheque:

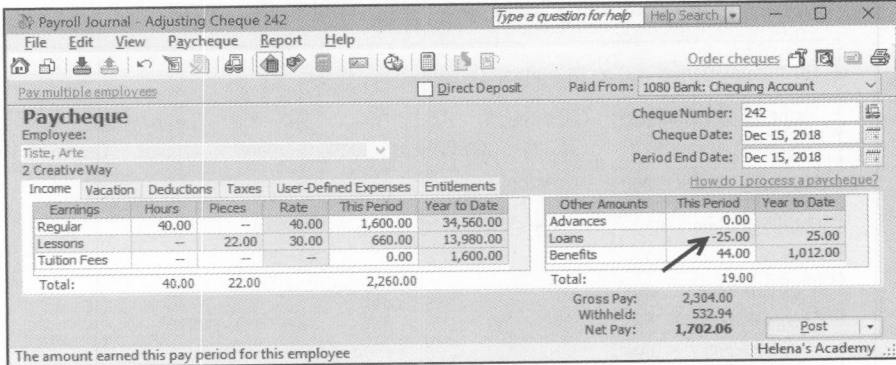

Click   **-25** in the **This Period field for Loans** to select the current entry.

Type   −50 **Press** ⌨tab to enter the change and update the gross pay. The
               Year To Date amount for Loans is reduced to zero.

Click   the **Vacation tab**.

Amounts are entered in the Vacation Earned and Vacation Owed fields:

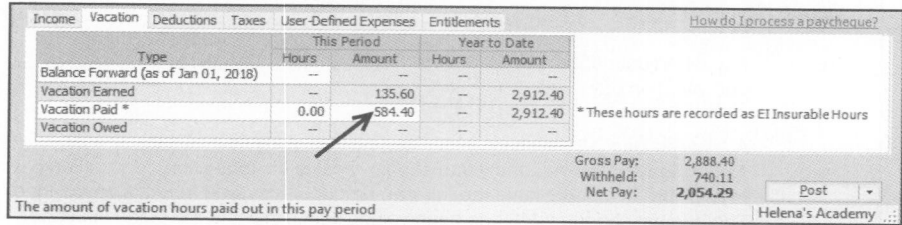

The vacation owed amount, $584.40, includes the amount for this paycheque (Vacation Earned) and amounts withheld since vacation was last paid.

Click the **Vacation Paid Amount field** and **type** 584.40

Press (tab) and **click** the **Vacation tab** again.

Click the **Recalculate Taxes tool** 🔲 on the Payroll Journal tool bar or **choose** the **Paycheque menu** and **click Recalculate Taxes**:

		This Period		Year to Date	
Type		Hours	Amount	Hours	Amount
Balance Forward (as of Jan 01, 2018)		--	--	--	--
Vacation Earned		--	135.60	--	2,912.40
Vacation Paid *		0.00	584.40	--	2,912.40
Vacation Owed		--	--	--	--

* These hours are recorded as EI Insurable Hours

Gross Pay: 2,888.40
Withheld: 740.11
Net Pay: **2,054.29**

The amount of vacation hours paid out in this pay period

Helena's Academy

Review the Payroll Journal **entry**. **Close** the **display** when you have finished. **Make corrections** if necessary.

Click Post ▾ to save the adjustment.

Click **Yes** to bypass the message about hours and **click Yes** again to **accept** the next cheque number (#248).

Close the **Payroll Journal**. **Enter** the **next group of transactions**.

30

Cash Purchase Invoice #ESS-7889   **Dated Dec. 18/18**

From Energy Supply Services, $810 including taxes for heat and hydro on equal monthly billing plan. Recall the stored entry. Paid by cheque #249.

31

Cash Purchase #TA-266778   **Dated Dec. 20/18**

From Telus Alberta, $170 including all taxes for one month of telephone services. Invoice total paid in full with cheque #250.

32

Employee Time Summary Sheet #24   **Dated Dec. 31/18**

For the pay period ending December 31, 2018

Name of Employee	Regular Hours	Overtime Hours	Lessons	Tuition	Advance (Repaid)	Loan (Repaid)	Sick Days	Direct Deposit
Filer, Morty	82.5	–	–	$135.00	–	–	–	No
Handie, Jerome	82.5	4	–	–	–	–	–	Yes
Nerture, Neela	82.5	–	–	–	–	–	1	Yes
Booker, Marina	160	–	10	$130.00	–	–	–	Yes
Teicher, Lars	160	–	8	–	–	$200	–	Yes
Teutor, Helena	160	–	–	–	–	–	–	No

a. Using Employee Time Summary Sheet #24 and the Employee Information Sheet, complete payroll for all employees. Hourly paid employees are paid for their regular hours during the Christmas holiday break.

b. Issue $200 loan to Teicher and recover $50 from each of the next four paycheques.

c. Issue cheques #251 and #252 and DD slips #69, #70, #71 and #72.

NOTES
Remember to remove Tiste from the list of employees paid in this pay period.

NOTES
Holidays are counted as regular days worked, so the pay period for hourly paid employees is 11 days.

33 **Bank Credit Memo #69886**   **Dated Dec. 31/18**

From Scholar Heights Bank, $1 800 interest on investments and bank account was deposited to chequing account. Recall the stored entry.

34 **Bank Debit Memo #532281**   **Dated Dec. 31/18**

From Scholar Heights Bank, $4 265 was withdrawn from chequing account for the following pre-authorized transactions. Recall the stored entry and edit the bank charges amount. Store the revised entry.

Bank charges	$ 65
Interest on bank loan	320
Reduction of principal on bank loan	880
Interest on mortgage	2 500
Reduction of principal on mortgage	500

35 **Memo #9**   **Dated Dec. 31/18**

Complete end-of-month adjusting entries for the following:

Office supplies used	$230
Art supplies used	250
Textbooks damaged	350
Prepaid property taxes	900

36 **Cash Sales Invoice #1039**   **Dated Dec. 31/18**

Received $300 000 payment for school fees for the next semester. Total cash deposited to bank account.

NOTES
Enter the fees payment as revenue.

Entering Paycheques in a Future Year

Sometimes you will need to prepare payroll transactions in advance, such as when the payroll preparation date falls during a holiday period. When that date also falls in a future calendar year, you need to separate the year-to-date amounts for the two years for income tax reporting purposes. Sage 50 allows you to enter payroll entries for a later year and tracks these amounts separately. Current year reports are not affected.

PRO VERSION
pro This feature is not available in the Pro version. Instead, you can start a new calendar year (refer to page 307). Then complete the payroll run.

37 **Employee Time Summary Sheet #25**   **Dated Jan. 15/19**

For the pay period ending January 15, 2019

Name of Employee	Regular Hours	Overtime Hours	Lessons	Tuition	Advance (Repaid)	Loan (Repaid)	Sick Days	Direct Deposit
Filer, Morty	82.5	–	–	$135	–	–	–	No
Handie, Jerome	82.5	–	–	–	–	–	–	Yes
Nerture, Neela	82.5	–	–	–	–	–	–	Yes

a. Using Employee Time Summary Sheet #25 and the Employee Information Sheet, complete payroll for hourly paid employees. (Adjustments for overtime hours worked will be made on the following paycheque.)
b. Issue cheque #253 and Direct Deposit (DD) slips #73 and #74.

PRO VERSION
pro To complete this payroll entry in the Pro version, you must first start the new calendar year (advance the session date to January 1, 2019).

Permission to complete these entries is controlled from the Company Settings :

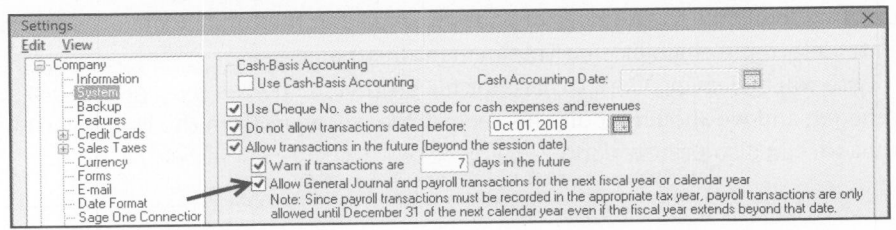

NOTES
The option to post transactions to the next fiscal or calendar year applies only to Payroll and General Journal entries.

Because the beginning of term is a very busy period, Filer may not have time to complete the first payroll entry in January. He can create these cheques in December.

> **Open** the **Payroll Run Journal**. **Enter Jan 15, 2019** as the **Cheque Date** and as the **Period End Date**. The journal form is revised:

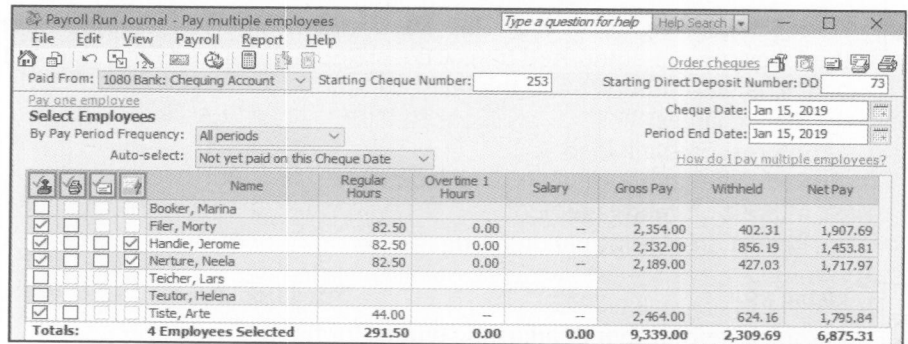

All hourly paid employees are selected. Tiste should not be paid — he has resigned.

> **Click** the **Post column** 🖲 for **Tiste** so that he will not be paid in January.

The number of hours is correct for this period.

> **Click** **Filer's name** and **type** 135 as his tuition amount for this period to complete the entry.

> **Review** your **entry** and **make corrections** if needed.

> **Click** **Post** for another confirmation warning:

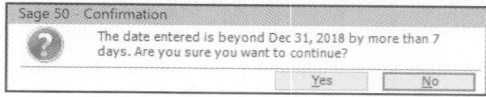

Our Company System Settings allow future dates but warn if these are more than seven days in the future (refer to the screenshot on page 295).

> **Click** **Yes** to continue to the next confirmation warning about using a date in a future calendar year:

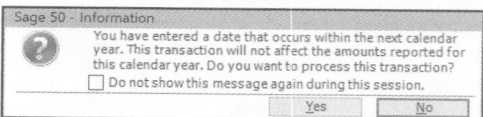

Read the message carefully — it advises that prior year amounts (those for 2018) will not be affected by this entry.

> **Click** **Yes** to continue and save the payroll entry. **Close** the **journal**.

Terminating an Employee

When an employee leaves the company, his or her ledger record should be updated with the date of termination and the reason for leaving. Then a record of employment can be issued that indicates the number of hours worked and the total income. This form is used to determine eligibility for Employment Insurance.

Tiste will be leaving work to care for his brother, so he has received his last paycheque and we should modify his record. We will work from the Employees window so that we can also print reports.

Memo #10   **Dated Dec. 31/18**

38

Prepare a Record of Employment and T4 slip for Tiste.

Click   the **Employees icon** 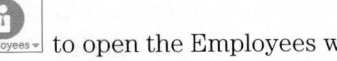 to open the Employees window.

Double-click   **Tiste, Arte** to open his ledger record at the Personal tab screen:

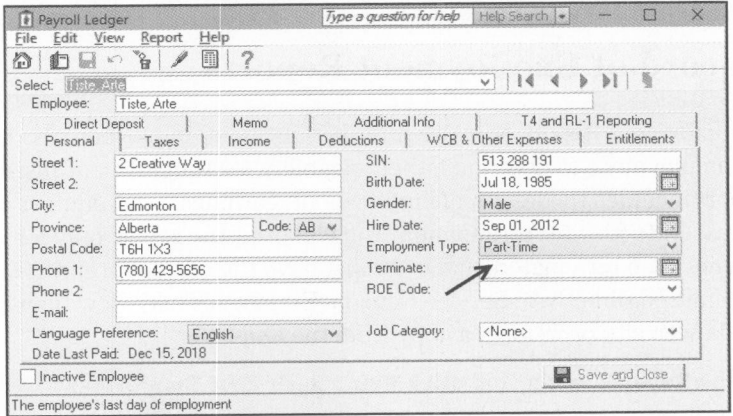

NOTES

You can also open the ledger record for Tiste by clicking his name in the Home window Employees pane list. Then, you can view reports from the Home window Reports menu.

We need to enter the Terminate date and the ROE (Record of Employment) Code.

Click   the **Terminate field. Type** 12 15

Click   the **ROE Code list arrow** to access the codes available:

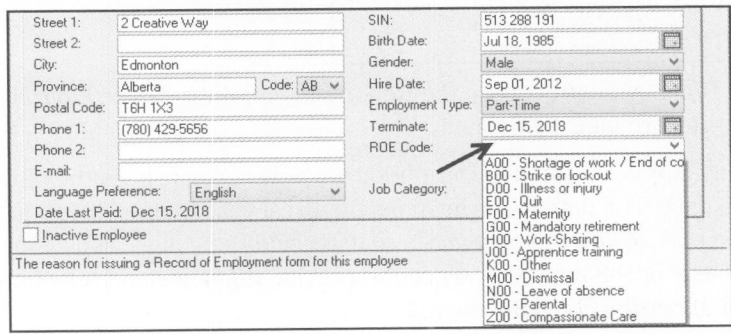

Click   **Z00 - Compassionate Care**.

Click   **Save And Close** to open the following confirmation message:

Normally, an employee's status is changed to inactive when he or she has left the company. In this way, the employee's name will no longer appear in employee lists for journals or reports. Data for the inactive employees can still be included in any reports by choosing to include inactive employees.

Click   **Yes** to change Tiste's status to inactive.

Click the T4 and RL-1 Reporting tab to get the total EI Insurable Earnings amount for the year. We provide the screenshot for this tab screen on page 299.

Close   the **ledger record**.

We will now be able to print a Record of Employment for Tiste. We will print this report from the Employees window.

Printing Payroll Reports

You can access payroll reports from the Reports menu in the Employees window and from the Home window. In addition, most payroll reports can also be accessed from the Report Centre. Some payroll reports cannot be displayed; they are printed directly.

    The Employees window should be open.

Printing Record of Employment Reports

NOTES

You cannot access the Record of Employment from the Report Centre.

Submitting ROE reports to Service Canada electronically from Sage 50 is covered in Appendix K.

Service Canada is the branch of the federal government that deals with Employment Insurance and pensions.

The Record of Employment Report provides information about employees who have terminated their employment to determine their eligibility for Employment Insurance benefits. The report includes the length of employment, earnings, total number of hours worked and the reason (code) for termination. You can print the report only for employees who have been terminated, and you must have the correct preprinted forms.

    Reports are remitted directly to Service Canada. Employees may view their ROE on the Service Canada Web site or request a copy from the employer.

    Choose the **Reports menu**, and **click Print Record Of Employment**:

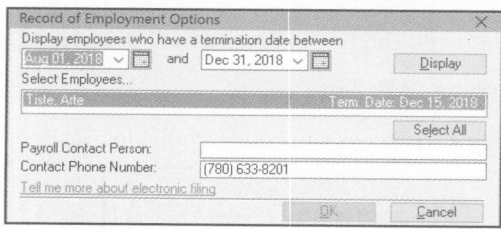

NOTES

The Record Of Employment Options screen includes a link to information about electronic filing. To use the link, you must be connected to the Internet.

From the Home window, choose the Reports menu, then choose Payroll and click Print Record Of Employment.

    Tiste is the only employee listed in this option window because he is the only one with a termination date. The date range includes the fiscal year to date. If you have data for a different time period, you can change these dates and then click Display to update the list of employees. For this report, you need to provide the name and telephone number to contact about the company payroll.

    Click   **Tiste, Arte** to select the employee for the report.

If there are more employees with termination dates, you can click Select All to create reports for all the listed employees.

    Click   the **Payroll Contact Person field**. **Type** Morty Filer

    Click   **OK** to continue:

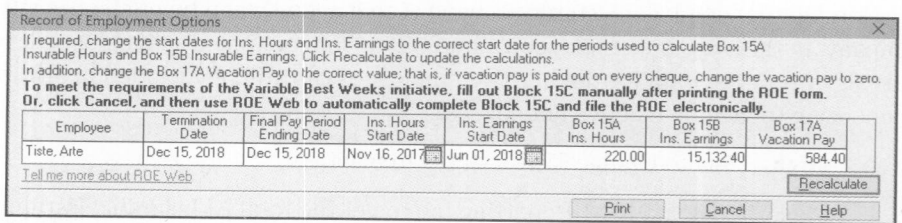

You now have the summary details for the selected employee. They include only the amounts entered in the payroll journals; they do not include the year-to-date opening balance amounts. You can edit the fields in this window. If you have payroll data for a longer period, you can enter those dates and recalculate the amounts. However, only the three months of payroll data we entered in Sage 50 are tracked in this form, so we must update the details.

The year-to-date insurable earnings amount is tracked in the Employee Ledger on the T4 and RL-1 Reporting tab screen:

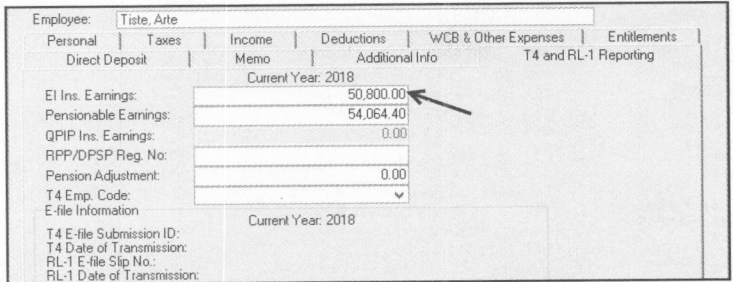

NOTES
You cannot view the employee's ledger record while the Record of Employment report or its options window is open.

According to the ledger record, Tiste has $50 800 in EI insurable earnings this year (the maximum amount for 2016). He has also worked additional hours before October. His total number of hours is 1 040 (52 weeks **x** 20 hours per week). And finally, he has received all his vacation pay, so this amount should be changed to zero. You can also edit the start dates for EI insurable hours and earnings.

NOTES
Because our tax tables apply to 2016, the 2016 maximum amounts for EI Insurable Earnings and Pensionable Earnings will apply. These are $50 800 and $54 900 respectively.
Once an employee earns the maximum amounts, no further pay amounts are added and no further EI or CPP (respectively) will be deducted.

Enter   **Jan 1** in the Ins. Hours Start Date field and also in the Ins. Earnings Start Date field.

Click   **220.00** in the Box 15A Ins. Hours field.

Type   1040

Press   (tab) to select the Ins. Earnings amount.

Type   50800

Press   (tab) to select the Vacation Pay amount.

Press   (del). Check your entries.

Click   **Print**. Sage 50 provides an additional warning:

NOTES
For practice, you can print the ROE on plain paper, but you will not have any labels for the details on the report.

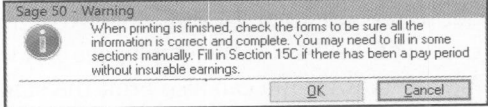

NOTES
When you submit the forms electronically, you have a chance to review and edit all the details before submitting.

You may need to add missing details on the form manually if the final printed form is not complete.

Click   **OK** to begin printing. **Close** the **Employees window**.

Printing T4s

T4 slips and Relevé 1 slips are also not available for display, but they can be printed. Relevé 1 slips are used only in Quebec, and the Print Relevé 1 Slips Report options screen will list only employees for whom Quebec is the province of taxation. Relevé 1 options are similar to those for T4 slips. You can print T4 slips, which are compulsory for employees filing income tax returns, using either the tax statement forms from the Canada Revenue Agency (CRA) or plain paper. You should retain payroll information for employees who leave during the year so that you can prepare T4 slips to mail to them.

Before printing T4s, you should check your printer and forms selections.

NOTES
You cannot access T4 Slips from the Report Centre.
Submitting T4s electronically to the Canada Revenue Agency is covered in Appendix K.

Choose the **Setup menu**, then **choose Reports & Forms** and **click Government Forms** and **click Federal Payroll** to display the options:

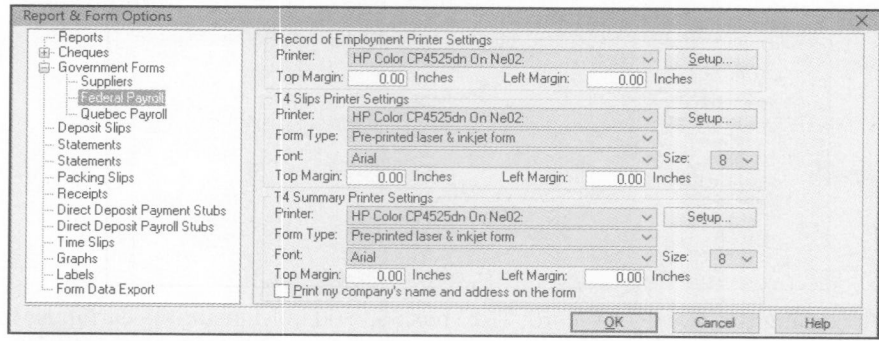

Select   **Plain Paper** as the Form Type for T4 Slips and T4 Summary.

Click   **OK** to save the selections and return to the Home window.

Choose the **Reports menu**, then **choose Payroll** and **click Print T4 Slips And Summary** (or Print Relevé 1 Slips) to display the options:

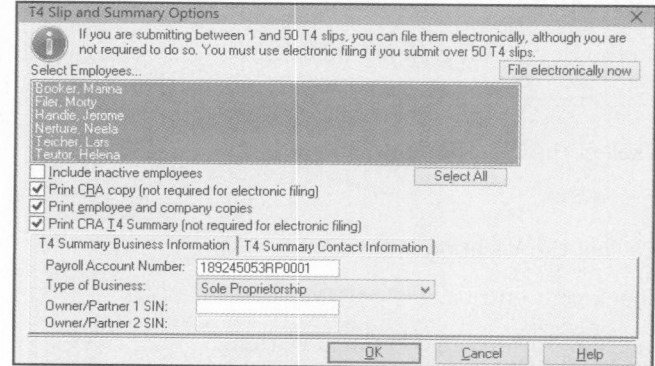

You need to select employees in order to prepare their T4 slips. Inactive employees are not listed by default. You can print copies of the T4s for the employees and the company and for the Canada Revenue Agency (CRA). You can also print the summary for the CRA. All are selected as the default.

To submit the report, you must include the type of business, business payroll account number (the business number with an RP code extension), the social insurance numbers (SIN) of the owners/partners, the name of the person who can be contacted about the form and the phone number and position of that individual. The Payroll Account Number should be entered from the Company Settings Information window.

Click   **Include Inactive Employees** to add Tiste to the list.

Click   **Tiste, Arte**.

Press and hold (ctrl) and click the names of the employees for whom you want the report printed or click Select All to prepare T4s for all employees.

Select   the **Type Of Business**. **Click** the **Type** that applies: sole proprietorship, partnership or private company.

Enter   **189245053RP0001** (without spaces) in the Payroll Account Number field if it is not entered automatically.

Enter   the **social insurance number** of the owners or partners. You can enter Teutor's social insurance number (from page 260) as the owner's SIN.

On the second tab screen, you must enter the contact details for the person completing the forms.

Click　the **T4 Summary Contact Information tab** to open the contact fields:

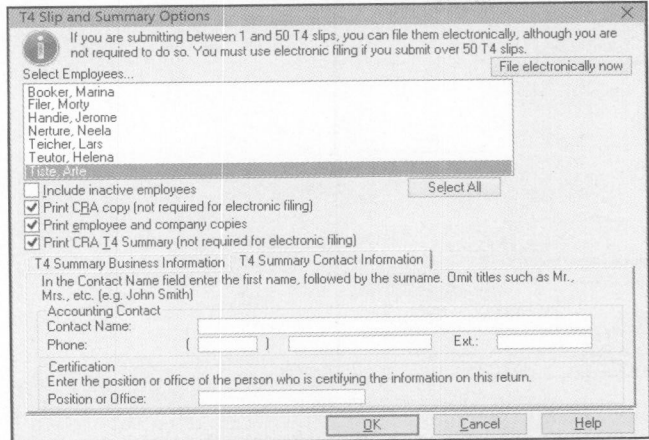

Enter　the **contact details** for the person completing the forms: name, phone number and position in the company. You can use Morty Filer's name with the school phone number (refer to page 257). You must enter a first and last name.

Click　**OK** to open the warning:

The warning appears when you do not select all employees because the remittance amounts apply to all employees. Thus, reported amounts for employer contributions may be incorrect.

Click　**OK** to open the T4 Box Options screen:

Each box on the T4 slip is numbered and can be designated for a specific deduction or income. You can choose a form box number for these amounts if they are related to income tax and should be included on the T4s. Each item has a list of box numbers that you can select. Income and tax items that are standard for T4s are not listed because their boxes are already assigned. If you do not change the box selections, the income amounts on this screen are all combined and the deductions listed are not reported. You can check with the CRA to learn what each box number is used for. The **Help** button also provides information about the numbers that should be used for different types of income and deductions.

Choose　appropriate **box numbers** for the items that should appear on the T4.

Click　**OK** to begin printing.

NOTES
The T4 Options screen includes a link for filing T4 slips electronically.

NOTES
Morty Filer is the office manager. His work phone number is (780) 633-8201.

NOTES
The printed T4 slips will also include descriptions of the purpose of each box on the form. This information is used by the employee to complete his or her income tax return and can serve as a guide for employers preparing the T4s.

NOTES
Total income includes vacation pay paid and benefits.

Employee year-to-date historical amounts are entered in the ledger record when you set up the Payroll module, and they are included in the T4 Summary. However, year-to-date employer amounts are not included as part of the setup, so these amounts may be incomplete.

If you entered all payroll transactions for the year, the amounts on the summary should be correct.

You can edit the employer payment amounts for CPP and EI.

After the T4s are printed, the T4 Summary report is displayed:

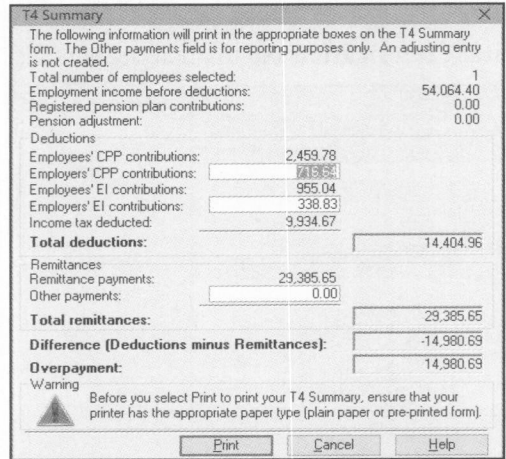

The contribution amounts are only those for Tiste because he was the only employee selected. The remittance amounts are those for all employees for three months. The employee contribution amounts are the year-to-date totals for the individual, and the employer contribution amounts are those related to this employee for three months. The employer contribution and remittance year-to-date totals are not included in the payroll history when you do not set up the program at the start of the calendar year. You should edit the amounts.

Click**Print** to continue when the amounts are correct.

After printing, you should have a summary of the items printed:

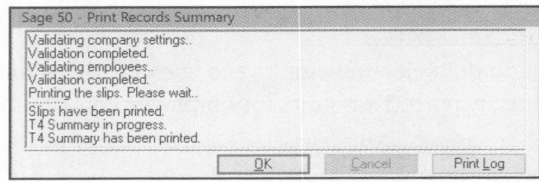

Click**Print Log** to print this summary or **click OK** to close the summary.

Printing Employee Mailing Labels

NOTES
You cannot display mailing labels.

You can include or omit inactive employees.

We will continue with the payroll reports that are not available from the Report Centre. You can print labels for employees (like labels for suppliers and clients).

Set up the **printer** for printing labels (Setup menu, Reports & Forms, Labels) before starting.

Choose the **Reports menu**, then **choose Mailing Labels** and **click Employees**.

NOTES
Remember to check that you have selected the correct printer for your setup. If you click the Print tool, printing will start immediately and you cannot change the selected printer.

You will display the list of employee names:

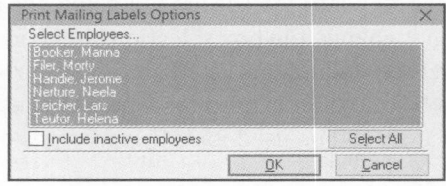

Press and **hold** (ctrl) and **click** the **employees' names** you want to print labels for, or **click Select All** to include all employees. **Click OK** to start printing.

To print other reports, **display** the **report** you want to print as instructed below. **Choose** the **File menu** from the report window and **click Print. Choose** your printer. **Click OK. Close** the **display** when finished.

Displaying Payroll Reports

Most payroll reports can be accessed from the Employees window Reports menu, the Home window Reports menu, the Reports drop-down list in the Reports pane or the Report Centre.

In the Reports pane, click the list arrow in the Reports field to open the list of reports:

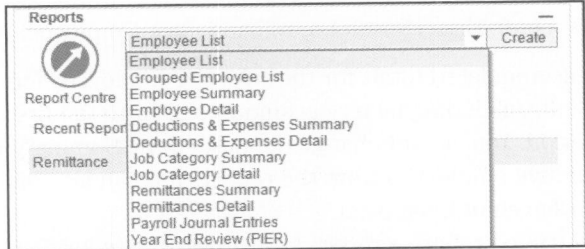

As usual, we will work from the Report Centre to include sample reports and the report description and purpose.

Click the **Report Centre icon** in the Reports pane.

Click **Employees & Payroll** in the Select A Report Type list for the general description of payroll reports:

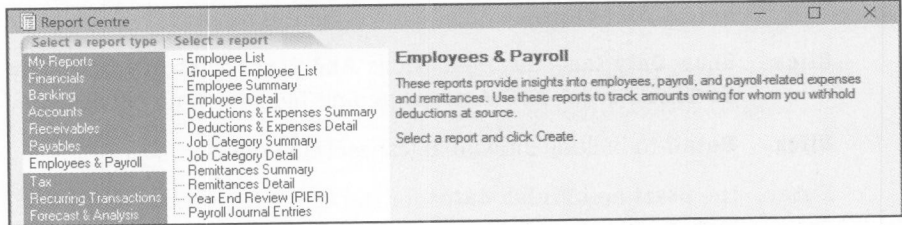

Displaying Employee Lists

Lists of employees are available, just like lists for other ledgers.

Click **Employee List** in the Select A Report list.

Click **Modify This Report** for the report options:

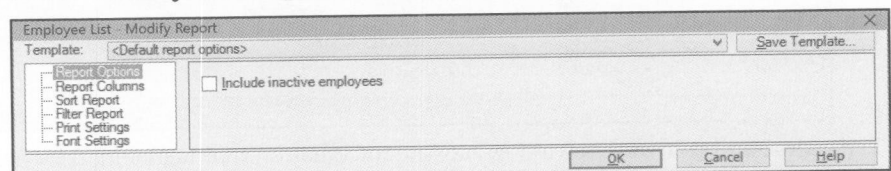

To select employee fields, you can customize the Report Columns. Choose Custom Report Column Settings and select the ones you want.

The report will display a list of all current employees, together with data for all the details you chose. The default report has the address, phone number and date of hire.

Close the **display** when you have finished.

Displaying Employee Reports

Click   **Employee Summary** in the Select A Report list.

Click   **Modify This Report** for the report options:

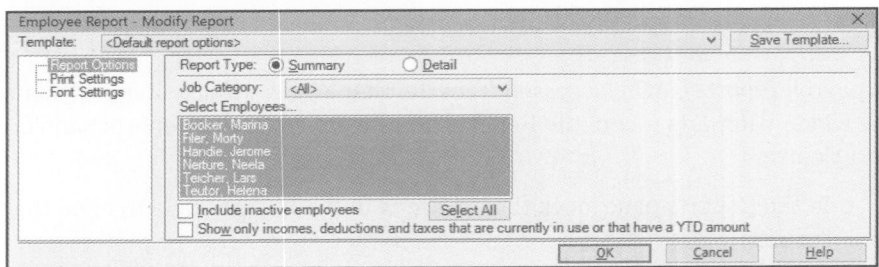

Or, choose the Reports menu, then choose Payroll and click Employee.

The **Summary Report** has accumulated totals for the selected employees for all incomes, deductions and payments, including historical amounts prior to the first Sage 50 entry; it is updated each pay period. You cannot change the date of the Summary Report.

You can include or omit inactive employees from the report. You can also omit details that have no amounts or have not been used.

If you use job categories, you can prepare a report for a specific category by choosing it from the drop-down list of categories.

You cannot customize the Employee Summary Report. You can use the **Detail Report** to include individual amounts for each paycheque. To prepare a report for specific deductions or payments, you can customize the column selection for the Detail Report.

Click   **Include Inactive Employees** if you want to report on them as well.

Press   and **hold** <u>ctrl</u> and **click** the **employees** you want in the report, or **click Select All** to include all employees in the report.

Click   **Show Only Incomes, Deductions And Taxes That Are Currently In Use Or That Have A YTD Amount** to omit fields with no entries.

Click   **Detail** to include individual transaction details.

Enter   the **Start** and **Finish dates** for the Detail Report.

Click   **Report Columns** in the left-hand pane. **Click Custom Report Column Settings**:

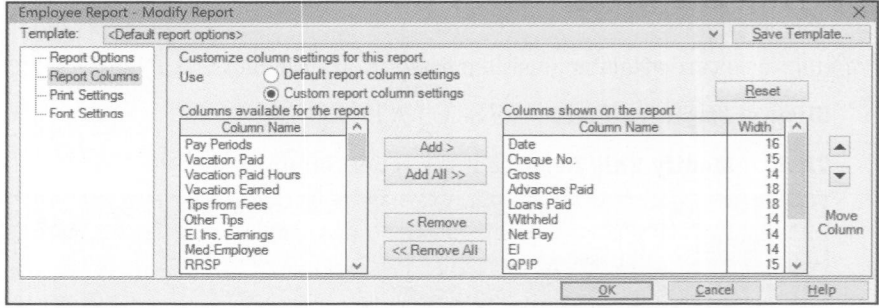

The right-hand side of this window has the information that is included by default, and the left side has the details that you can add to the report. The amount for each detail you choose will be listed for each payroll period in the selected date range for the selected employees, together with the totals for the period selected. The calendar year provides the default dates for the Detail Report.

Select   the **columns** you want to include or remove.

NOTES

The Summary Report also has the tax claim amounts and rates of pay for each employee.

NOTES

Sorting, filtering and column selection are not available for the Employee Summary Report.

You can drill down to the Detail Report from the Summary Report. From the Detail Report you can look up the Payroll Journal entry and open the Employee Ledger.

Click   **OK** to open the report. **Close** the **display** when you have finished.

Displaying Deductions and Expenses Reports

Click   **Deductions & Expenses Summary** in the Select A Report list.

Click   **Modify This Report** for the report options:

From the Home window, choose the Reports menu, then choose Payroll and click Deductions & Expenses.

This report provides details for all payable amounts resulting from deductions and expenses. Only amounts entered in the Payroll journals in Sage 50 will be included in this report. Prior historical balance amounts for the year to date from the employee records will not be included. The **Summary Report** has the total amounts and the number of employees the deduction or expense applied to for each payroll item in the selected date range. The **Detail Report** includes individual entries for each selected item, with the date, cheque or deposit number, employee, job category, amount, period totals and number of employees.

You can customize the report by selecting the columns you want to include.

Select the details you want in the report and the date range for the report. The earliest transaction and session dates are the default selections.

Press   and **hold** $\boxed{ctrl}$ and **click** the **deductions** and **expenses** you want in the report, or **click Select All** to include all details in the report.

Enter   the **Start** and **Finish dates** for the report.

Click   **OK** to open the report. **Close** the **display** when you have finished.

Displaying Payroll Remittance Reports

The Payroll Remittance Report is described on page 281. To access this report from the Report Centre,

Click Remittances Summary in the Select A Report list. Click Modify This Report for the report options and click OK to display the report.

The Payroll Remittance Journal Entries are included with the Payments Journal Entries Report (refer to the Payments Journal Modify Report screen on page 148). To access this journal report from the Report Centre,

Click Payables in the Select A Report Type list. Click Payment Journal Entries and Modify This Report for the options. Remittance Payments should have a ✓ in the check box as the default selection. Click OK to display the report.

NOTES
From the Summary Deductions and Expenses Report you can drill down to the Detail Report. From the Detail Report you can drill down to the Employee Detail Report and look up the paycheque.

NOTES
From the Remittance Summary Report, you can drill down to the Detail Report. From the Detail Report, you can drill down to the Supplier Ledger, the Employee Detail Report, the journal entry and look up the entry in the Payroll Journal.

Displaying Year End Review (PIER) Reports

The PIER (Pensionable and Insurable Earnings Review) report provides the total amounts contributed for the year to date for EI and CPP. Based on the Insurable Earnings amount for each employee (also in the report), the program determines whether the employee has contributed the correct amounts and displays the amount of under- or overcontributions.

NOTES

You cannot sort or filter the PIER report.

You can modify this report by selecting the report columns, removing any of the default information or adding the amounts for expected EI and CPP deductions and the number of paycheques and pay periods.

NOTES

The PIER report for Helena's Academy informs us that three employees have undercontributed to CPP.

CLASSIC VIEW

From the Home window, right-click either the Paycheques or the Payroll Cheque Run icon,

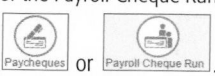

Then click , the Select A Report tool, to open the Modify Report window for the Payroll Journal Report.

NOTES

January 15, the latest transaction date, will be included in the drop-down lists in the date fields.

NOTES

You can drill down to the Employee Detail Report and the General Ledger Report from the Payroll Journal.

Click   Year End Review (PIER) in the Select A Report list.

Click   Modify This Report for the report options:

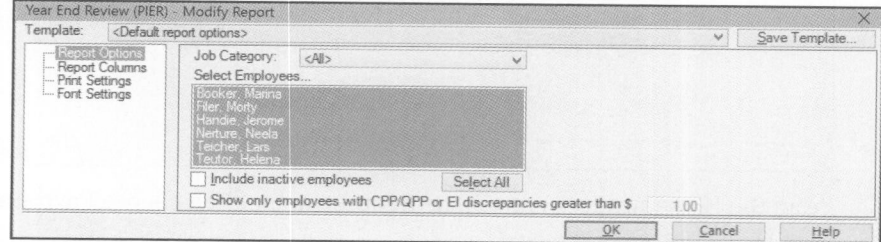

From the Home window, choose the Reports menu, then choose Payroll and click Year End Review (PIER) to display the report options.

You can define the minimum discrepancy that should be included and then prepare the report only for those employees who have a discrepancy of this amount or more. The default amount is $1.00.

Click   Include Inactive Employees to add these employees to the list.

Click   the name of the employee you want the report for, **press** and **hold** ⌈ctrl⌉ and **click additional names** or **click Select All** to include all employees in the report.

Click   OK to display the report. **Close** the **display** when you have finished.

Displaying the Payroll Journal

The Payroll Journal Report includes all transactions from the Payroll Journal and the Payroll Run Journal.

Click   Payroll Journal Entries in the Select A Report list.

Click   Modify This Report for the report options:

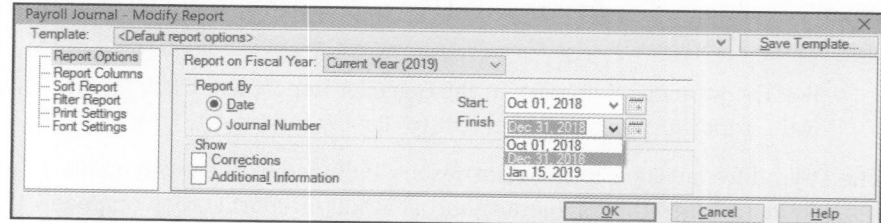

Or, choose the Reports menu, then choose Journal Entries and click Payroll to display the Options window.

The usual sort and filter journal options are available for the Payroll Journal Report, and the Date option we use for selecting transactions is the default. Your earliest transaction and session dates appear as the default Start and Finish dates.

Type   the beginning and **ending dates** for the report.

Click   **Corrections** to include the original and reversing entries for the paycheques you adjusted or reversed.

Click   **OK**. **Close** the **display** when you have finished.

Printing All Journal Entries

Remember that you can include the journal entries for all journals in a single report.

From the Report Centre, choose the Financials list of reports and then click All Journal Entries to open the report options window.

From the Home window, choose the Reports menu, then choose Journal Entries and click All to open the report options window.

Click Corrections to include the reversed and adjusted entries.

Starting a New Calendar Year

When you are ready to advance to the next session date at the end of December, you must start a new year.

Close   **all other windows** except the Home window. You can click 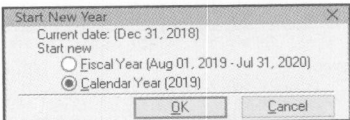 (the Close Other Windows tool).

Choose   the **Maintenance menu** and **click Start New Year**:

Because the fiscal period ends July 31, 2019, the new calendar year comes first and this will be the default option.

Click   **OK** to continue to the next information screen:

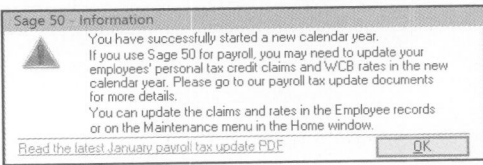

This message advises you about the changes that Sage 50 will make when you start the new year. Because this step is not reversible, you should have an end-of-year backup. This is the default selection.

Click   **OK** to proceed with the backup.

After the backup has been completed, Sage 50 will provide the confirmation message that the date has been changed and the reminder to update TD1 amounts.

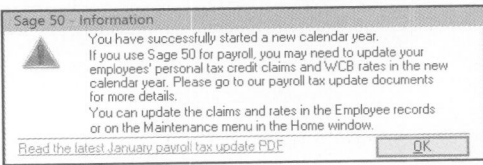

Click **OK** to proceed to the locking date screen:

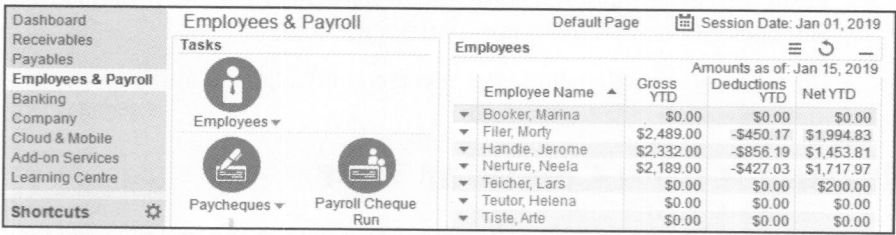

Enter **Jan 1 2019** as the new date on this screen.

Click **OK** to return to the Home window.

Click the **Refresh tool** above the Employees list pane to update the amounts to include the latest transaction entries:

The new year-to-date amounts are the balances as at January 15 for the hourly paid employees. Teicher's loan amount, carried forward from his December 31 paycheque, is also included.

If you have not entered any payroll transactions yet when you start the new calendar year, the amounts in the Employees list pane will be zero except for Teicher's loan amount.

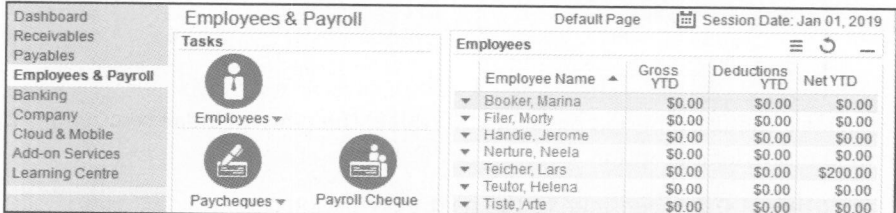

R E V I E W

The Student DVD with Data Files includes Review Questions and Supplementary Cases for this chapter.

NORTHERN Lights

OBJECTIVES

After completing this chapter, you should be able to

- *add* the Payroll Ledger to a company data file
- *enter* Payroll Ledger settings
- *enter* Payroll Ledger linked accounts
- *create* Employee Ledger records
- *enter* employee historical information
- *set up* payroll remittances with remittance suppliers
- *set up* taxes for income, benefits and deductions
- *create* job categories
- *assign* employees to job categories
- *enter* salespersons on invoices
- *display* and *print* job category and salesperson reports

COMPANY INFORMATION

Company Profile

NOTES
Northern Lights
25 Snowy Court
Whitehorse, YT Y1A 2B2
Tel: (867) 873-8201
Fax: (867) 873-8396
Business No.: 324 732 911

Northern Lights, owned by M. Promtou, opened with its first play in Whitehorse, Yukon, in 1999. Now Northern Lights, a theatre with a seating capacity of 350, regularly runs two plays each month, five nights a week. Afternoons are used for rehearsals. Two actors, a director, a box office and a stand concession employee, an usher and a sound and light engineer make up the full-time staff. For plays requiring more players, actors are hired from an agency as needed, and the director and owner also step into roles occasionally. The actors volunteer one morning each week to run drama workshops in schools. The owner is involved primarily in promoting the theatre, and usually the theatre is nearly filled.

Northern Lights has established favourable account terms with regular suppliers, including some discounts for early payment. All discounts are calculated on after-tax amounts. Most tickets are sold to season's subscribers and individual customers. A few organizations — tour companies that offer a theatre night as part of the tour package, charities using theatre nights as a fundraiser, local book groups

and a community theatre school— regularly buy blocks of tickets. Discount terms for these account customers also encourage timely payment of accounts.

Tickets, food and beverages sold by Northern Lights are subject to 5 percent GST. Northern Lights pays the 5 percent GST on all purchases except for food.

On May 31, 2018, Promtou closed his books so he could begin using the payroll feature in Sage 50. The following information summarizes his data:

- Chart of Accounts
- Post-Closing Trial Balance
- Supplier Information
- Customer Information
- Employee Profiles and Information Sheet
- Accounting Procedures

PRO VERSION

The term Vendor will replace Supplier. Purchases replaces the term Expenses in the program for journals and reports.

CHART OF POSTABLE ACCOUNTS

NORTHERN LIGHTS

ASSETS
1080	Bank: Chequing
1100	Bank: Credit Card
1200	Accounts Receivable
1240	Loans Receivable
1260	Prepaid Insurance
1280	Office Supplies
1300	Cleaning Supplies
1320	Food & Beverage Inventory
1520	Computer System
1540	Concession Appliances
1560	Van
1580	Sound & Light Equipment
1600	Theatre Seats & Furnishings
1620	Theatre Building
1620	Theatre Property ▶

▶LIABILITIES
2100	Bank Loan
2200	Accounts Payable
2250	Accrued Wages
2300	Vacation Payable
2310	EI Payable
2320	CPP Payable
2330	Income Tax Payable
2400	EHC Payable - Employee
2410	VRSP Payable
2420	Tuition Fees Payable
2440	EHC Payable - Employer
2450	Players' Guild Payable
2460	WCB Payable
2650	GST Charged on Services
2670	GST Paid on Purchases
2920	Mortgage Payable ▶

▶EQUITY
3560	M. Promtou, Capital
3600	Current Earnings

REVENUE
4020	Revenue: Ticket Sales
4040	Revenue: Concession Sales
4060	Revenue: Movies
4140	Sales Discounts

EXPENSE
5010	Purchase Discounts
5020	Advertising Expenses
5040	Bank Charges
5050	Credit Card Fees
5060	Hydro Expenses
5080	Insurance Expense ▶

▶5100	Cleaning Supplies Used
5140	Food & Beverages Sold
5160	Telephone Expenses
5180	Maintenance and Repairs
5200	Van Expenses
5410	Salaries: Performance Staff
5420	Wages: Support Staff
5430	Vacation Earned
5440	Commissions
5450	Sales Bonuses
5510	EI Expense
5520	CPP Expense
5530	WCB Expense
5560	Travel Allowances
5570	Tuition Fees Expense
5580	EHC Premium Expense

NOTES: The Chart of Accounts includes only postable accounts and Current Earnings.

POST-CLOSING TRIAL BALANCE

NORTHERN LIGHTS

June 1, 2018

		Debits	Credits				Debits	Credits
1080	Bank: Chequing	$ 53 040.30		▶	2200	Accounts Payable		$ 9 960.00
1100	Bank: Credit Card	5 525.00			2250	Accrued Wages		1 150.00
1200	Accounts Receivable	12 600.00			2300	Vacation Payable		4 143.16
1240	Loans Receivable	350.00			2310	EI Payable		1 227.23
1260	Prepaid Insurance	2 200.00			2320	CPP Payable		2 625.00
1280	Office Supplies	1 240.00			2330	Income Tax Payable		3 661.61
1300	Cleaning Supplies	780.00			2400	EHC Payable - Employee		948.48
1320	Food & Beverage Inventory	2 000.00			2410	VRSP Payable		250.00
1520	Computer System	7 200.00			2420	Tuition Fees Payable	$ 4 000.00	
1540	Concession Appliances	4 950.00			2440	EHC Payable - Employer		948.48
1560	Van	24 800.00			2450	Players' Guild Payable		90.59
1580	Sound & Light Equipment	160 000.00			2460	WCB Payable		541.72
1600	Theatre Seats & Furnishings	140 000.00			2650	GST Charged on Services		8 860.00
1600	Theatre Building	250 000.00			2670	GST Paid on Purchases	3 250.00	
1620	Theatre Property	120 000.00			2920	Mortgage Payable		260 000.00
2100	Bank Loan		$45 000.00 ▶		3560	M. Promtou, Capital		452 529.03
							$791 935.30	$791 935.30

SUPPLIER INFORMATION

NORTHERN LIGHTS

Supplier Name (Contact)	Address	Phone No. / Fax No.	E-mail / Web Site	Terms / Tax ID
Class Acts (Tempe Handler)	78 Extra St. Whitehorse, YT Y1A 3V2	Tel: (867) 667-3601 Fax: (867) 667-1577	tempe@classacts.com classacts.com	1/10, n/30 (after tax) 366 455 281
Manulife Financial (M.T. Handed)	7 Fiscal Way Whitehorse, YT Y1A 2K4	Tel: (867) 993-3488 Fax: (867) 993-8109	manulife.com	net 1
Midnight Sun Bakery (D. Lishus)	43 Danish Ave. Whitehorse, YT Y1A 2S6	Tel: (867) 633-3929 Fax: (867) 633-3935	lishus@midnightsun.ca midnightsun.ca	1/10, n/30 (after tax) 445 668 714
Otto's Autos (Otto Sparks)	64 Mechanic St. Whitehorse, YT Y1A 2S4	Tel: (867) 689-7106 Fax: (867) 689-7188	sparks@ottos.com ottos.com	net 1 672 910 186
Receiver General for Canada		Tel: (800) 561-7761	cra-arc.gc.ca	net 1
Stage Stagers (A. Carpenter)	244 Woods Rd. Whitehorse, YT Y1A 4A1	Tel: (867) 666-8877 Fax: (867) 666-9100		2/15, n/30 (after tax) 458 459 766
Thirst Quenchers (Thurston Wade)	555 Water St. Whitehorse, YT Y1A 1N6	Tel: (867) 634-1618 Fax: (867) 634-5127	tw@tq.com tq.com	net 30 129 554 377
YT Energy (Sol R. Heater)	33 Windmill Rd. Whitehorse, YT Y1A 3C3	Tel: (867) 841-1298	srh@yteg.ca yteg.ca	net 10
Yukon Telephone (Kommue Nicate)	91 Cellular Way Whitehorse, YT Y1A 8B5	Tel: (867) 665-2355	yttel.ca	net 10
Yukon Workers' Compensation Board (I.T. Herts)	55 Accidental Cr. Whitehorse, YT Y1A 3X6	Tel: (867) 668-7199	ytwcb.com	net 1

OUTSTANDING SUPPLIER INVOICES

NORTHERN LIGHTS

Supplier Name	Terms	Date	Invoice No.	Amount	Total
Stage Stagers	2/15, n/30	May 27/18	SS-4011	$6 510	$6 510
Thirst Quenchers	net 30	May 3/18	TQ-644	$3 450	$3 450
			Grand Total		$9 960

CUSTOMER INFORMATION

NORTHERN LIGHTS

Customer Name (Contact)	Address	Phone No. / Fax No.	E-mail / Web Site	Terms / Credit Limit
Literati Borealis (Lotta Reads)	3 Volumis Cr. Whitehorse, YT Y1A 5D3	Tel 1: (867) 668-2563	lreads@literati.com literati.com	1/15, n/30 (after tax) $7 000
Polar Discoveries (Robert Peary)	4 Exploration Ave. Churchill, MN R5P 4C2	Tel: (204) 369 4545 Fax: (866) 369-4545	rp@polardiscoveries.com polardiscoveries.com	1/15, n/30 (after tax) $15 000
SAD (Seasonal Affective Disorder) Foundation	56 Sliepers Rd. Whitehorse, YT Y1A 6F3	Tel 1: (867) 664-7155 Tel 2: (800) 664-9175	SAD.com/yt	1/15, n/30 (after tax) $10 000
Subscribers				net 1
Whitehorse Little Theatre (B. Little)	5 Performance Ct. Whitehorse, YT Y1A 2W2	Tel: (867) 536-7188 Fax: (867) 536-7528	little@wlt.com wlt.com	1/15, n/30 (after tax) $10 000

OUTSTANDING CUSTOMER INVOICES

NORTHERN LIGHTS

Customer Name	Terms	Date	Invoice No.	Amount	Total
Literati Borealis	1/15, n/30	May 28/18	344	$4 200	$4 200
Polar Discoveries	1/15, n/30	May 30/18	348	$8 400	$8 400
				Grand Total	$12 600

EMPLOYEE INFORMATION SHEET

NORTHERN LIGHTS

	Taika Tikett	Kay Kabanza	Ayla Usher	Bev Ridges	Jiane Apsimak	Francine Player	Pawluk Staige
Gender	Male	Female	Female	Female	Female	Female	Male
Position	Box Office Staff	Engineer	Usher	Concession Staff	Director	Actor	Actor
	Support	Support	Support	Support	Performance	Performance	Performance
	Full Time	Full Time	Full Time	Full Time	Full Time	Full Time	Full Time
Social Insurance No.	218 738 631	638 912 634	931 771 620	552 846 826	422 946 541	726 911 134	822 546 859
Address	29 Stubbs Rd.	2 Aural Rd.	63 Walker Blvd.	34 Stratford Ln.	410 Revue Ave.	11 Asides Cres.	122 Spotlight Ct.
	Whitehorse, YT	Whitehorse, YT	Whitehorse, YT	Whitehorse, YT	Whitehorse, YT	Whitehorse, YT	Whitehorse, YT
	Y1A 4K2	Y1A 6D2	Y1A 5M8	Y1A 4C1	Y1A 1X3	Y1A 2L2	Y1A 8B3
Telephone	(867) 689-7595	(867) 356-7995	(867) 668-2291	(867) 634-8138	(867) 536-6353	(867) 667-6291	(867) 456-2238
Date of Birth (mm-dd-yy)	8-10-86	8-8-76	3-31-90	11-3-88	5-21-78	7-31-80	11-3-83
Date of Hire (mm-dd-yy)	11-6-16	2-7-11	12-4-15	4-6-11	1-1-09	8-5-14	6-6-09
Federal (YT) Tax Exemption – TD1							
Basic Personal	$11 474 (11 474)	$11 474 (11 474)	$11 474 (11 474)	$11 474 (11 474)	$11 474 (11 474)	$11 474 (11 474)	$11 474 (11 474)
Other Indexed	$11 474 (11 474)	$26 263 (26 263)	–	–	$11 474 (11 474)	–	$11 474 (11 474)
Non-Indexed	$2 095 (2 095)	–	$12 120 (12 120)	–	–	–	–
Total Exemptions	$25 043 (25 043)	$37 737 (37 737)	$23 594 (23 594)	$11 474 (11 474)	$22 948 (22 948)	$11 474 (11 474)	$22 948 (22 948)
Additional Fed Taxes	$50	$100		–	–	–	–
Employee Taxes							
Historical Income Tax	$1 120.30	$3 610.30	$571.74	$1 919.40	$3 628.10	$3 517.20	$2 626.80
Historical EI	$308.91	$468.10	$162.24	$271.64	$472.80	$408.90	$408.90
Historical CPP	$765.03	$1 186.50	$442.13	$655.99	$1 195.60	$1 015.60	$1 026.70
Deduct EI; EI Rate	Yes; 1.4	Yes; 1.4	Yes; 1.4	Yes; 1.4	Yes; 1.4	Yes; 1.4	Yes; 1.4
Deduct CPP, Tax	Yes	Yes	Yes	Yes	Yes	Yes	Yes
Employee Income							
Pay Periods	26 (bi-weekly)	26 (bi-weekly)	52 (weekly)	52 (weekly)	12 (monthly)	12 (monthly)	12 (monthly)
Vacation Rate	6% retained	8% retained	6% retained	6% retained	0% (3 weeks)	0% (3 weeks)	0% (3 weeks)
Record Wage Exp in	Linked Accts	Linked Accts	Linked Accts	Linked Accts	Linked Accts	Linked Accts	Linked Accts
Loans: Hist Amt	$100.00	$150.00	$100.00	(use) ✓	(use) ✓	(use) ✓	(use) ✓
Benefits per Period	$41.54	$41.54	$10.38	$10.38	$90.00	$45.00	$90.00
Benefits: Hist Amt	$1 015.40	$415.40	$1 897.98	$217.98	$450.00	$225.00	$450.00
Vacation Pay Owed	$939.00	$1 992.00	$345.28	$866.88	–	–	–
Vacation Paid	$610.00	$458.00	–	–	–	–	–
Regular Wage Rate	$18.00	$30.00	$16.00	$16.00	(do not use)	(do not use)	(do not use)
(Hours per Period)	(80 hours)	(80 hours)	(40 hours)	(40 hours)	–	–	–
Reg. Wages: Hist Amt	$14 400.00	$24 000.00	$8 320.00	$13 440.00	–	–	–
Overtime 1 Rate	$27.00	$45.00	$24.00	$24.00	(do not use)	(do not use)	(do not use)
Overtime 1: Hist Amt	$810.00	$900.00	$312.00	$504.00	–	–	–
No. Sold/Number	$0.10	(do not use)	(do not use)	$0.10	(do not use)	(do not use)	(do not use)
No. Sold: Hist Amt	$440.00	–	–	$504.00	–	–	–

▶

EMPLOYEE INFORMATION SHEET CONTINUED

	Taika Tikett	Kay Kabanza	Ayla Usher	Bev Ridges	Jiane Apsimak	Francine Player	Pawluk Staige
Employee Income Continued							
Salary	(do not use)	(do not use)	(do not use)	(do not use)	$4 900.00	$4 350.00	$4 350.00
(Hours per Period)	–	–	–	–	(160 hours)	(160 hours)	(160 hours)
Salary: Hist Amt	–	–	–	–	$24 500.00	$21 750.00	$21 750.00
Commission	(do not use)	(do not use)	(do not use)	(do not use)	1% ticket sales	(do not use)	(do not use)
Commission: Hist Amt	–	–	–	–	$1 650.00	–	–
Travel Allow	–	–	–	–	–	$50.00	$50.00
Travel Allow: Hist Amt	–	–	–	–	–	$250.00	$250.00
Employee Deductions							
VRSP	2.5%	5.0%	(use) ✓	(use) ✓	5.0%	5.0%	2.5%
VRSP: Hist Amt	$400.00	$1 300.00	–	–	$1 250.00	$1 100.00	$650.00
EHC-Employee	$41.54	$41.54	$10.38	$10.38	$90.00	$45.00	$90.00
EHC-Employee Hist Amt	$415.40	$415.40	$217.98	$217.98	$450.00	$225.00	$450.00
Players' Guild Fees	(do not use)	(do not use)	(do not use)	(do not use)	(do not use)	1.01%	1.01%
Guild Fees: Hist Amt	–	–	–	–	–	$221.95	$224.20
WCB and Other Expenses							
WCB Rate	1.55	3.38	1.75	1.55	1.55	1.55	1.55
Tuition Fee	$60.00	–	$80.00	–	–	–	–
Tuition Fee: Hist Amt	$600.00	–	$1 680.00	–	–	–	–
EHC-Employer	$41.54	$41.54	$10.38	$10.38	$90.00	$45.00	$90.00
EHC-Employer: Hist Amt	$415.40	$415.40	$217.98	$217.98	$450.00	$225.00	$450.00
Entitlements: Rate, Maximum Days, Clear? (Historical Amount)							
Vacation: Rate, Max	–	–	–	–	8%, 25 days	8%, 25 days	8%, 25 days
Clear? (Days Accrued)	–	–	–	–	No (20 days)	No (10 days)	No (25 days)
Sick Leave: Rate, Max	5%, 20 days	5%, 20 days	5%, 20 days	5%, 20 days	5%, 20 days	5%, 20 days	5%, 20 days
Clear? (Days Accrued)	No (16 days)	No (14 days)	No (10 days)	No (18 days)	No (16 days)	No (16 days)	No (18 days)
Personal Days: Rate, Max	2.5%, 10 days	2.5%, 10 days	2.5%, 10 days	2.5%, 10 days	2.5%, 10 days	2.5%, 10 days	2.5%, 10 days
Clear? (Days Accrued)	No (4 days)	No (6 days)	No (8 days)	No (3 days)	No (6 days)	No (4 days)	No (6 days)
Direct Deposit							
Yes/No	Yes	Yes	No	No	Yes	No	Yes
Branch No., Institution No.	06722, 180	49921, 300	–	–	30099, 103	–	12084, 285
Account No.	4556221	2883912	–	–	2009123	–	2399012
Percent	100%	100%	–	–	100%	–	100%
Additional Information							
Emergency Contact	Kierin Tikett	Marie Kabanza	Alex Usher	Petra Blackstone	Dene Uniak	Sima Player	Marina Staige
Contact Number	(867) 689-1892	(867) 356-1469	(867) 668-4573	(867) 634-6353	(867) 536-2197	(867) 667-7995	(867) 456-5602
T4 and RL-1 Reporting							
EI Insurable Earnings	$16 300.00	$24 900.00	$8 632.00	$14 448.00	$26 150.00	$21 750.00	$21 750.00
Pensionable Earnings	$17 315.40	$25 773.40	$10 529.98	$14 665.98	$26 600.00	$21 975.00	$22 200.00
Withheld	$3 009.64	$6 980.30	$1 394.09	$3 065.01	$6 996.50	$6 488.65	$5 386.60
Net Pay	$13 390.56	$18 527.70	$7 337.91	$11 382.99	$19 153.50	$15 511.35	$16 613.40

NOTES: Travel Allowances are reimbursement income.

Medical (EHC) premiums are deducted every pay period. The amounts are adjusted for the monthly rates.

EI, CPP and income tax are calculated automatically by the program.

Vacation pay at the rate of 6 percent is approximately equal to three weeks' vacation and 8 percent is equal to approximately four weeks.

Employee Profiles and TD1 Information

Employee Benefits and Entitlements   All employees work full time and are entitled to 10 days per year as sick leave and five days' leave for personal reasons. If the days are not needed, employees can carry these days forward to a new year, to a maximum of 20 and 10 days, respectively. Currently, all employees have some unused sick leave and personal leave days accrued from the previous year. Salaried employees are allowed to carry forward two of their three weeks' vacation entitlement. That is, they are allowed to accumulate a maximum of 25 unused vacation days at any one time. Northern Lights also set up a voluntary retirement savings program (VRSP) with Manulife that allows employees to deduct a percentage of their paycheques to pay directly to their plans.

To encourage personal development, Northern Lights pays 50 percent of the tuition fees for any employee enrolled in college or university programs. Currently, Usher and Tikett are receiving the tuition fee benefit. This taxable benefit is considered an expense for Northern Lights. A second benefit applies to all employees — Northern Lights pays 50 percent of the premiums for an extended health care plan (EHC).

Sales Bonuses   Northern Lights records the number of tickets and beverages sold in excess of a base number each week and pays Tikett and Ridges, respectively, a piece rate bonus of 10 cents per unit; this bonus is added to each paycheque.

Employer Expenses   Northern Lights currently has two employer payroll expenses beyond the compulsory CPP, EI and WCB: 50 percent of the employees' EHC premiums and 50 percent of eligible tuition fees. In addition, Player and Staige receive a travel allowance as compensation for using their cars to volunteer at community schools.

Jiane Apsimak   As the artistic and managing director of the theatre, Apsimak oversees the production of each play, schedules work, hires new staff and discusses problems with the owner, who does not participate in the day-to-day affairs of the business. She is married and has no children. Since her husband is not employed, she uses the basic and spousal federal and provincial tax claim amounts and pays the family health care premium. At the end of each month, her salary of $4 900 per month plus a commission of 1 percent of revenue from ticket sales, net of taxes, is deposited to her account. She is recorded as salesperson for all these sales for the purpose of calculating her commission. She makes monthly contributions to her VRSP as well. In lieu of vacation pay, she is entitled to take three weeks of paid vacation each year.

Kay Kabanza   As the sound and lighting engineer, Kabanza controls all the electronic equipment. She has several years of experience with Northern Lights. Her regular pay of $30 per hour is supplemented by overtime wages at the rate of $45 per hour when she works more than 40 hours per week. In addition, she receives vacation pay at the rate of 8 percent of her total wages, but this amount is retained until she chooses to take a vacation. She has already received some of the vacation pay owing to her this year. Although she is single, she supports an infirm and dependent sister, so she claims the spousal and disability amounts for income tax purposes. She also pays EHC premiums at the family rate and deducts 5 percent of her pay as VRSP contributions. To offset the tax from additional income, she chooses to have an additional $100 in taxes withheld each pay period. She has received a loan of $150, which she will repay over the next three pay periods. Her bi-weekly pay is deposited directly to her bank account.

Ayla Usher   the usher, earns $16 per hour, $24 per hour overtime when she works more than 40 hours in a week. She worked part time while a full-time student and is now a full-time employee while studying part time. Thus her $7 840 tuition fees plus the education deduction are added to the basic claim amount for income tax purposes. She is also entitled to the tuition benefit — fifty percent of her tuition is paid by Northern Lights at the rate of $80 per pay. Usher's weekly pay by cheque is supplemented by

6 percent vacation pay, which is retained, and she pays single EHC premiums.

Bev Ridges   handles all concession sales. Ridges is single, so she claims the basic TD1 amount and pays the single EHC premium from her wages of $16 per hour and $24 for overtime hours. Her weekly pay, paid by cheque, includes a piece rate bonus of $0.10 per beverage over a base amount. The 6 percent vacation pay is retained.

Taika Tikett   manages the box office and telephone sales. He is married with no dependants, so he pays family EHC premiums and has the basic and spousal TD1 claim amounts. Because he studies business part time at the local community college, he has additional claims for his tuition of $1 535 and education amounts ($140 per month federal and provincial). From his weekly deposited pay, he contributes 2.5 percent to a VRSP program. His pay is $18 per hour and $27 for overtime hours with 6 percent vacation pay; he also has a piece rate bonus added of $0.10 per ticket above a base number sold. Northern Lights pays half of his tuition. This taxable benefit, entered on Tikett's paycheque at the rate of $30 per week, has already been paid for five months, and Tikett has also taken some vacation time with pay.

Francine Player   is one of two actors with Northern Lights. Because she is single, Player claims the basic single TD1 amount and pays the single EHC premium. Player earns a base salary of $4 350 per month by cheque, contributes 5.0 percent of this to her VRSP and can take three weeks of vacation yearly. One morning per week she teaches and performs at community schools and is reimbursed for her travel expenses.

Pawluk Staige   is the second actor with Northern Lights. As a single parent who supports one child, he pays the family EHC premium. For income tax purposes, he claims the spousal amount. At the end of each month, Staige has his monthly salary of $4 350 deposited to his bank account. He also contributes 2.5 percent of his pay to his VRSP program with regular payroll deductions. As a salaried employee, he is entitled to take three weeks of paid vacation per year. Like Player, Staige volunteers in community schools teaching acting and improvisation and is reimbursed for his travel costs.

Accounting Procedures

Taxes: GST and PST

GST at the rate of 5 percent applies to sales and purchases in Yukon. All sales and all purchases — other than food and some beverages — have GST applied. Northern Lights uses the regular method for remitting the GST. It records the GST collected from customers as a liability in *GST Charged on Services*. GST paid to suppliers is recorded in *GST Paid on Purchases* as a decrease in the liability to the Canada Revenue Agency. The GST refund or remittance is calculated automatically in the *GST Owing (Refund)* subgroup total account. Northern Lights files for a refund or remits the balance owing to the Receiver General for Canada by the last day of the month for the previous quarter.

     Tax codes are set up in the defaults for the company so that Sage 50 can automatically calculate the tax when it applies.

Discounts

All customers are offered a discount of 1 percent on the after-tax amount of the sale if they pay their accounts in full within 15 days. Full payment is requested in 30 days. Discount terms are set up as the default in the customer records. Some suppliers also offer discounts on after-tax purchase amounts. These discount terms are set up in the supplier records so that Sage 50 will automatically calculate the discount when full payment is made within the discount period.

NOTES
PST is not applied in Yukon. Purchases of food and some beverages are zero rated.

Direct Payroll Deposits

Promtou allows employees to have their regular pay deposited directly to their bank accounts or to be paid by cheque. Four employees have selected direct payroll deposits.

Payroll Remittances

Four suppliers are identified as payroll authorities with the following remittances: EI, CPP and income tax are remitted to the Receiver General for Canada; EHC and VRSP premiums are remitted to Manulife; Workers' Compensation Board premiums are remitted to the Yukon Workers' Compensation Board and Players' Guild fees are paid to the Canadian Actors' Guild.

INSTRUCTIONS

1. **Set up** the **Payroll Ledger** using the employee information, employee profiles and TD1 information. Detailed keystroke instructions for setting up payroll follow.

2. **Enter** the **transactions** in Sage 50 using the Chart of Accounts and Supplier, Customer and Employee Information. The first source document is on page 341.

3. **Print** the following **reports** after you have finished making your entries:

REPORTS

Accounts
- ☐ Chart of Accounts
- ☐ Account List
- ☐ General Journal Entries

Financials
- ☑ Comparative Balance Sheet: June 1 and June 30 with difference in percentage
- ☑ Income Statement: June 1 to June 30
- ☑ Trial Balance date: June 30
- ☑ All Journal Entries: June 1 to June 30
- ☑ General Ledger accounts: June 1 to June 30: 4020 5410 5420
- ☐ Statement of Cash Flows
- ☑ Cash Flow Projection Detail Report: for 1080 for next 30 days

Tax
- ☐ GST Report

Banking
- ☐ Cheque Log Report

Payables
- ☐ Supplier List
- ☐ Supplier Aged
- ☐ Aged Overdue Payables
- ☐ Expenses Journal Entries
- ☐ Payments Journal Entries

Receivables
- ☐ Customer List
- ☐ Customer Aged
- ☐ Aged Overdue Receivables
- ☐ Sales Journal Entries
- ☐ Receipts Journal Entries

- ☑ Sales by Salesperson June 1 to June 30
- ☐ Sales by Job Category
- ☐ Customer Statements

Employees & Payroll
- ☐ Employee List
- ☑ Summary for all employees
- ☐ Deductions & Expense
- ☐ Job Category
- ☐ Remittances
- ☑ Payroll Journal Entries: June 1 to June 30
- ☐ T4 Slips
- ☐ Record of Employment
- ☐ Year End Review (PIER)

Mailing Labels
- ☐ Labels

PAYROLL SETUP KEYSTROKES

Adding the Payroll Module

Open   `SageData16\NORTHERN\NORTHERN` to access the data file for **Northern Lights**. **Accept** June 1 as the **session date**.

The Payroll module is hidden because it was not used. Before we can set it up, we need to unhide it. We will then work from this module to enter settings and employees.

NOTES
Remember that you must have a valid and active Payroll ID code from Sage in order to use the payroll features for non-Student versions of the program.
Choose the Services menu and click Payroll And Support for more information.

Choose the **Setup menu** and **click User Preferences** to open the Options screen.

Click **View** to access the screen we need:

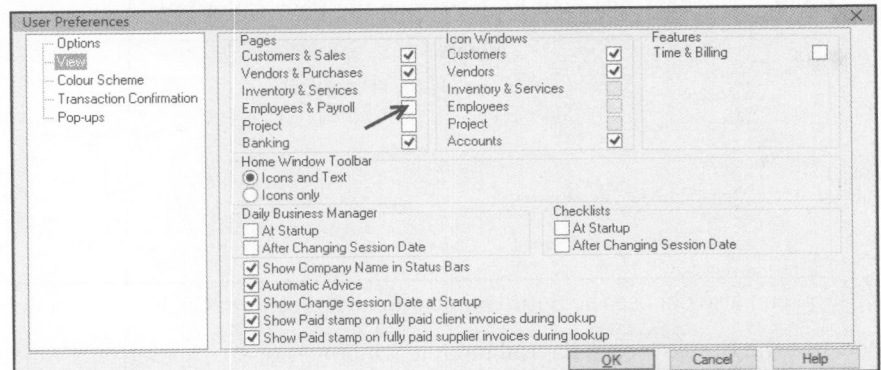

Click the **Pages check box for Employees & Payroll** to add ✓s for Pages and Icon Windows.

Click **OK** to save the settings and return to the Home window.

Click **Employees & Payroll** in the Modules pane list:

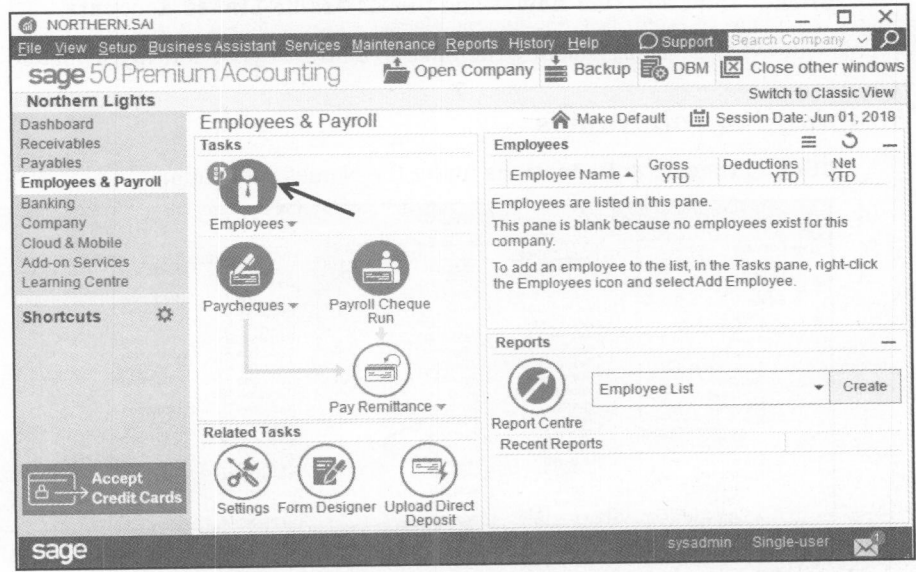

All Payroll module icons have been added. The not-finished symbol 🔁 on the Employees icon indicates that the module history is open or unfinished. If you try to finish the Payroll history now, Sage 50 will generate an error message about several missing linked accounts.

From the Employees & Payroll window we can enter ledger settings and records.

Setting Up the Payroll Ledger

Before you can enter Payroll Journal transactions, you must set up the payroll module. This involves the same steps as setting up other ledgers:

1. Change the settings for the ledger.
2. Create Employee Ledger records.
3. Add historical employee data.
4. Back up the data file and finish the history.

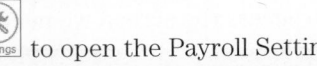
CLASSIC VIEW
From the Home window, right-click the Employees icon

. Then click , the Settings tool. You can also click the Settings tool and select Employees from the drop-down list.

Changing Payroll Ledger Settings

Click   the **Settings icon** to open the Payroll Settings screen:

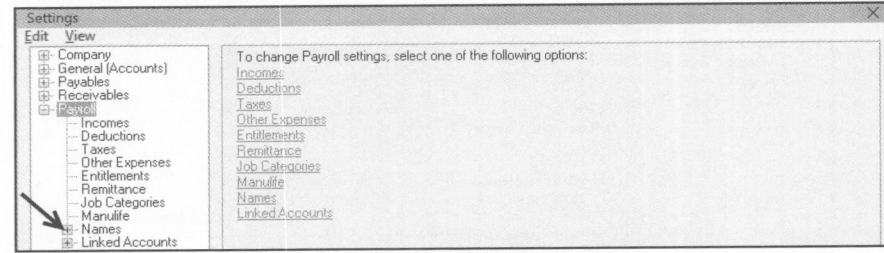

You can also choose the Setup menu and click Settings. Click Payroll if necessary.

> **NOTES**
> In any module window, click the Settings icon and then click Payroll to open the Payroll Settings screen.

Because the Employees & Payroll module window is open, the Settings window opens with the Payroll Settings list. For payroll, we need to define the types of income paid to employees, the payroll deductions, payroll taxes, employee entitlements, remittances, job categories, names for income, deductions and additional fields and linked accounts for all these functions. We will begin by entering names and deleting the ones we do not need. The reduced list will be easier to work with.

Click   the ⊞ beside **Names** and the ⊞ beside **Linked Accounts**.

This will expand the list, making the links to all the Payroll settings available.

> **NOTES**
> By modifying the names first, only the ones we need to set up will appear on later screens.

Changing Payroll Names

Click   **Income & Deductions** under the Names subheading:

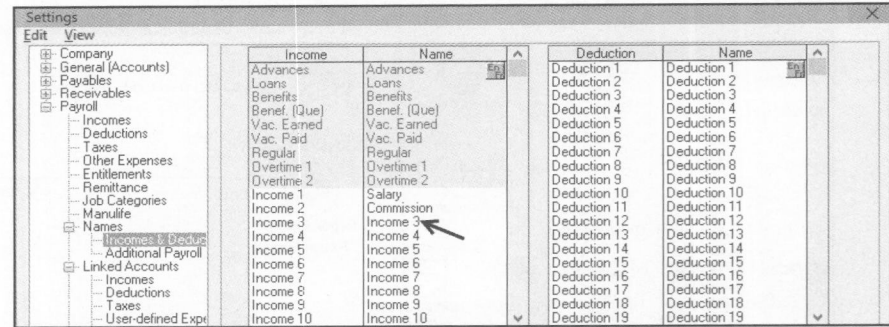

> **PRO VERSION**
> The Expense Groups entry under Linked Accounts is not included in the Pro version.

The first screen we need to modify has all the names for incomes and deductions used. Many of the standard income types are mandatory and cannot be changed. These fields are on a shaded background. Some of the other default names are also correct, so you do not need to redefine them. You can leave Income 1 and Income 2, labelled "Salary" and "Commission," unchanged because Northern Lights has salaried employees and pays a sales commission to Apsimak. There is allowance for 20 different kinds of income in addition to the compulsory fields and 20 different payroll deductions. Each income and deduction label may have up to 12 characters.

> **NOTES**
> You can enter names for any of these fields later if you need to add more incomes or deductions.

Northern Lights uses an additional income field for the piece rate bonus that is based on the number of tickets or beverages sold. The travel allowance for Player and Staige is also set up as an income. The remaining income fields are not used.

Northern Lights also has three payroll deductions at this time: VRSP, the Registered Retirement Savings Plan; the employee share of extended health care plan premiums (EHC-Employee); and the actors' guild fees. The remaining deduction fields are not used.

> **NOTES**
> Northern Lights does not use Expense Groups (under Linked Accounts).

Click   **Income 3 in the Name column** to highlight the contents.

Type   No. Sold **Press** (tab) to advance to the Income 4 field.

Click the **En/Fr language icon** to open the extra fields if you want to enter labels or names in both French and English.

Type `Travel Allow` **Press** (tab) to advance to the Income 5 field.

Press (del). **Press** (tab) to advance to the Income 6 field.

Press (del). **Press** (tab) to advance to the Income 7 field.

Press (del) to remove the entry. **Press** (tab) to select the next field.

Delete the **remaining Income names** until they are all removed.

Press (tab) after deleting Income 20 to select Deduction 1 in the Name column. **Press** (tab) again if you are in the Deduction column.

Type `VRSP` **Press** (tab) to advance to the second deduction Name field.

Type `EHC-Employee` **Press** (tab) to highlight the next field.

Type `Guild Fees` **Press** (tab) to highlight the next field.

Delete the **remaining deductions** because Northern Lights does not use them.

Click **Additional Payroll** under the Names subheading:

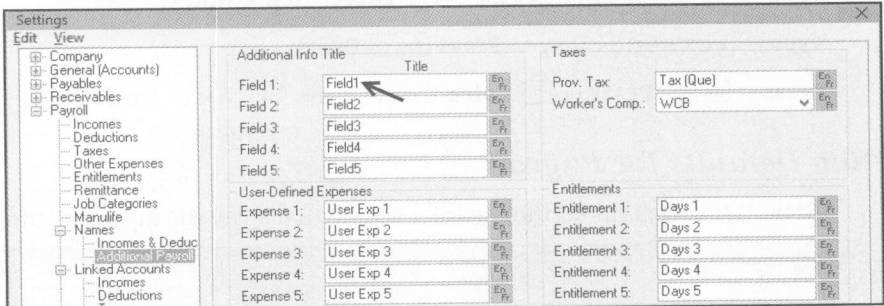

The Prov. Tax field is used for additional payroll taxes applied by the province. You can change the tax name. Since we will not enter linked accounts for provincial payroll taxes, the program will automatically skip the related payroll fields. WCB (Workers' Compensation Board) is entered as the name for Workers' Compensation because we selected Yukon as the business province.

We can also name the additional ledger fields, the additional payroll expenses for Northern Lights and the entitlements for employees. Northern Lights pays 50 percent of the employees' health care plan medical premiums and eligible tuition fees and a travel allowance to Player and Staige. It provides sick leave and personal leave days for all employees, as well as vacation days for salaried employees as entitlements. First, we will name the additional ledger fields. These fields will store the name and phone number of each employee's emergency contact.

Double-click **Field1** or **press** (tab).

Type `Emergency Contact`

Press (tab) **twice** to skip the language label icon and highlight the next field.

Type `Contact Number`

Press (tab) **twice**. **Press** (del) to delete the name for Field3.

Delete the **names** for Field4 and Field5.

Benefits and expenses can be handled in different ways. The medical premium payment is a taxable benefit for employees. It is also entered as a user-defined expense because the premiums are paid to a third party rather than to the employee. Tuition, the

NOTES
We are setting up travel allowances as income — it will be added to the paycheque as non-taxable income. When it is paid separately to the employees, it is entered as an other expense.

NOTES
If clicking does not highlight the field contents, drag through an entry to select it. Double-clicking will open the English/French names screen.

WARNING!
If you later change the province in the Company Information screen, the WCB name entered for Worker's Comp. will not change automatically. You must enter the correction manually by choosing from the drop-down list.

NOTES
The Worker's Comp. drop-down list has several other employer expenses that may apply to all employees.
You may use up to 20 characters to name the additional fields and 12 characters for user-defined expenses.

NOTES
When you are not using both French and English (Company Settings, Features options) you will press (tab) once after each entry.

NOTES
For Northern Lights, we use the generic Benefits field to enter all employee benefits.

NOTES
You can use up to 12 characters, including spaces, for user-defined expense and entitlement names — that is why we omitted the space for the Personal Days entitlement name.

NOTES
The incomes with shaded background are defined by the program and cannot be changed — System is entered in the Type column.

NOTES
When you close and re-open the Payroll Settings screen, the hidden and resized columns will be restored — the column changes you made are not saved.
QHSF is the provincial health services plan for Quebec.
QPIP (Quebec Parental Insurance Plan) provides parental leave benefits to EI insurable employees. Both employers and employees pay into the plan.
EHT (Employer Health Tax) applies only in Ontario.

NOTES
VRSP refers to voluntary registered pension plans that the company sets up for employees. They are managed by Manulife for Sage.

other taxable benefit and user-defined expense, is also paid to a third party — the educational institution. Benefits paid directly to the employee on the payroll cheque should be set up as income. Reimbursements for expenses may be entered as non-taxable income or as user-defined expenses. Because we repay the expenses on the payroll cheque, we define them as reimbursements — an income type that is not taxable — and link them to an expense account. If we entered them as user-defined expenses, we would create both a linked payable and expense account and issue a separate payment to the employee.

Drag through **User Exp 1**, the Expense 1 field, to highlight the contents.

Type `Tuition Fees` **Press** `tab` **twice**.

Type `EHC-Employer` **Press** `tab` **twice**.

Press `del`. **Press** `tab` **twice** to select Expense 4. **Press** `del`.

Press `tab` **twice** to select Expense 5. **Press** `del`.

Drag through **Days 1**, the Entitlement 1 field, to highlight the contents.

Type `Vacation` **Press** `tab` **twice** to select the next entitlement name.

Type `Sick Leave` **Press** `tab` **twice**.

Type `PersonalDays` **Press** `tab` **twice**.

Press `del`. **Press** `tab` **twice** to select the final name. **Press** `del`.

Setting Defaults for Payroll

Click **Incomes** under the Payroll heading to display the income setup:

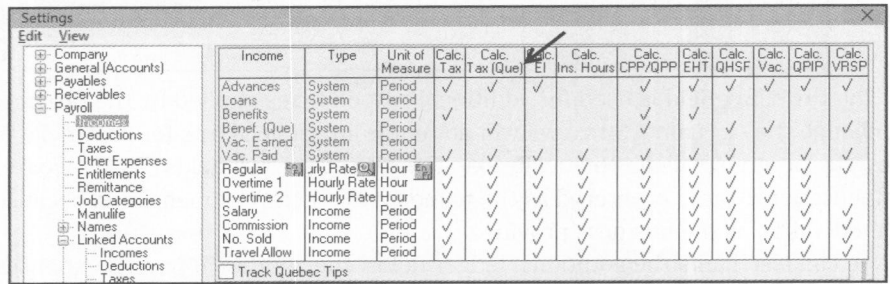

At this stage, we will change the tax settings for Incomes and Deductions.

We will first modify this screen by hiding the columns that do not apply to Yukon so that only the columns we need are on-screen at the same time.

Point to the **right-hand column heading margin for Calc. Tax (Que.)** until the pointer changes to a two-sided arrow ⟷.

Drag the **margin to the left** until the column is hidden.

Point to the **right-hand column heading margin for Calc. EHT** until the pointer changes to a two-sided arrow. **Drag** the **margin to the left**.

Remove the **columns for Calc. QHSF** and **Calc. QPIP** in the same way.

Only the income names you did not delete (page 318) appear on this screen. For each type of income you must indicate what taxes are applied and whether vacation pay is calculated on the income. Most of the information is correct. Regular and overtime hours are paid on an hourly basis, while salary and commissions are paid at designated income amounts per period. All taxes apply to these types of income in Yukon, so these default settings are correct. Vacation pay, however, is paid only to the hourly paid employees, so some checkmarks should be removed. In addition, we should designate

the type of income for No. Sold and Travel Allow, the incomes we added, and the taxes that apply. Choosing the type of income will change the defaults that are applied, so we make this change first.

Click   **No. Sold** to place the cursor on the correct line.

Press   `tab` to move to the Type column. A List icon is added.

Click   the **List icon** to access the list of income types we can select:

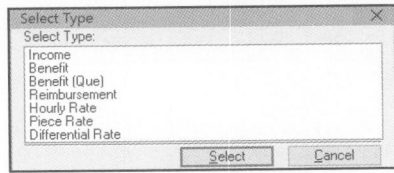

By default, all new income entries are assigned to the **Income** type. This assignment is correct for Salary. Taxable benefits paid to a third party should be classified as **Benefits** (read the Warning note). The benefit amount is added to income to determine taxes and then subtracted again to calculate the net pay amount. Taxable benefits paid directly to the employee instead of a third party should also be classified as Income. If a benefit is added to net pay, it should be classified as Income. Tuition is not paid to the employee, so it is a benefit.

Reimbursements are not taxable — the employee is being repaid for company-related expenditures. The **Piece Rate** type calculates pay based on the number of units. **Differential Rates** apply to different hourly rates paid at different times and are not used by Northern Lights.

Click   **Piece Rate** to select this type for No. Sold.

Click   **Select** to add the Type to the Settings screen. **Press** `tab`.

The cursor advances to the Unit of Measure field and the entry has changed to Item. The amount paid to employees is based on the number of tickets or beverages sold.

Type   `Number`

The checkmark for Insurable Hours was removed as soon as we changed the type.

Click   **Travel Allow** and **press** `tab`.

Click   the **List icon** and **click Reimbursement**.

All checkmarks are removed because this type of income is not taxable.

We need to modify the other Insurable Hours settings. The number of hours worked determines eligibility for Employment Insurance benefits. Regular, overtime and salary paid hours are included but commissions are not — no time can be reasonably attached to commissions, so they are not counted. The checkmark for it should be removed. The ✓ for No. Sold was automatically removed when we changed the income type.

Click   **Commission** to select this income line.

Press   `tab` **repeatedly** until the cursor is in the **Calc. Ins. Hours field**.

Click   to remove the ✓, or **press** the **space bar**.

We also need to modify the entries for vacation pay. In Yukon, vacation pay is calculated on all performance-based wages. This includes the regular wages, overtime wages and piece rate pay. We need to remove the remaining ✓s. Salaried workers receive paid time off rather than a percentage of their wages as vacation pay. We do not need to remove the ✓ for Overtime 2. If it is used later, vacation pay will be calculated on it as well. The settings for VRSP are correct — all incomes included in gross pay are selected by default.

NOTES
Vacation pay is also paid for statutory holidays. Northern Lights pays workers their regular pay for these days, as if they had worked. For occasional workers, this pay may be calculated as a percentage of wages.
In Quebec, vacation pay is also paid on benefits.

Click   **Salary** in the Income column.

Press   tab **repeatedly** to get to the **Calc. Vac. column**.

Click   to remove the ✓, or **press** the **space bar**.

Press   ⬇ to place the cursor in the **Calc. Vac. field for Commission**.

Click   to remove the ✓, or **press** the **space bar** and complete the Settings:

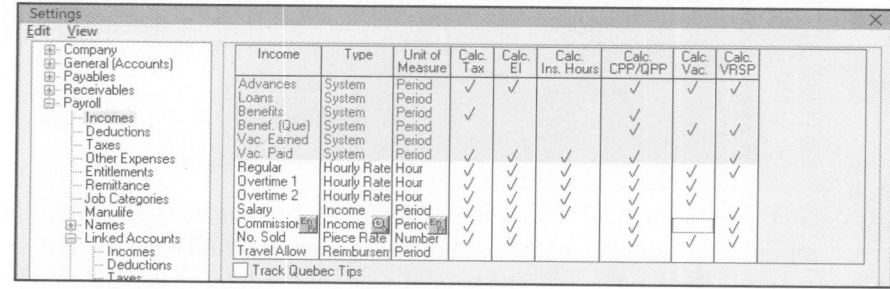

Click   **Deductions** under the Payroll heading:

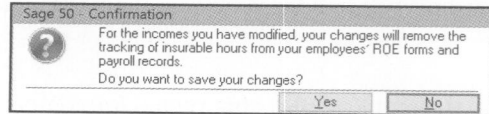

You are warned that the changes will affect the insurable earnings amounts reported on the Record of Employment. The changes are correct, so you should continue.

Click   **Yes** to continue to the Deductions settings:

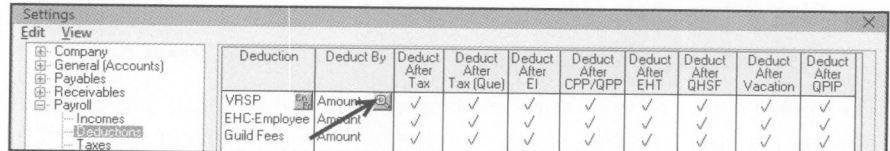

Only the deduction names you entered earlier appear on this screen. You can calculate deductions as a percentage of the gross pay or as a fixed amount. The default is to deduct by amount. This is the correct selection for EHC-Employee. The other two deductions are taken as a percentage.

Click   the **List icon** 🔍 in the Deduct By column beside VRSP:

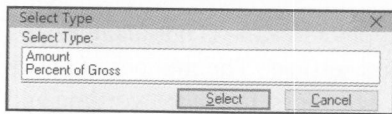

Click   **Percentage of Gross** and then **click Select**.

Select   **Percentage of Gross** for Guild Fees in the same way.

All deductions are set by default to be calculated after all taxes (Deduct After Tax is checked). For EHC-Employee, this is correct — it is subtracted from income after income tax and other payroll taxes have been deducted. However, VRSP contributions qualify as tax deductions and will be subtracted from gross income before income tax is calculated, but not before EI, CPP and so on, so you must change only this setting.

Click   the **Deduct After Tax column** for VRSP to remove only the one ✓ and change the setting to before tax.

The remaining settings are correct. VRSP is deducted after the other payroll taxes and vacation pay because these deductions are based on gross wages.

Click   **Taxes** under the Payroll heading:

NOTES
Although checkmarks will remain for the columns we hid, the fields for them will be skipped in ledger screens and journals because we will not enter linked accounts for them.

NOTES
You can modify the Deductions screen as you modified the Incomes Settings screen so that only the columns you need are on-screen. You can remove the Deduct After Tax (Que.), EHT, QHSF and QPIP columns.

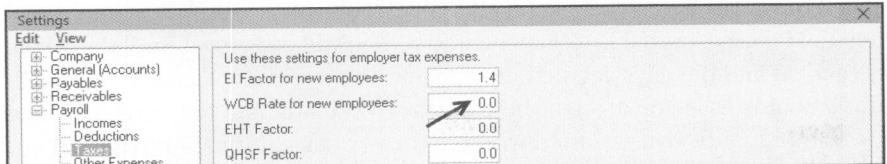

This next group of fields refers to the rate at which employer tax obligations are calculated. The factor for Employment Insurance (**EI Factor**) is correct at 1.4 — the employer's contribution is set at 1.4 times the employee's contribution. In the next field, you can set the employer's rate for **WCB** (Workers' Compensation Board) premiums. On this screen, you can enter 1.55, the rate that applies to most Northern Lights employees. We will modify the rates for Kabanza and Usher in their ledger records.

The next field, **EHT Factor**, is the percentage of payroll costs that the employer contributes to the provincial health plan in Ontario. The rate is based on the total payroll costs per year. It does not apply to employees in other provinces.

The **QHSF Factor** (Quebec Health Services Fund) applies to payroll in Quebec, so we do not need to enter it. QHSF is similar to EHT.

> **Click**   the **WCB Rate field**.

> **Type**   1.55

The Quebec tax fields will not be available for employees because we will not enter linked accounts for them. They do not apply to employees in Yukon.

> **Click**   **Other Expenses** under the Payroll heading:

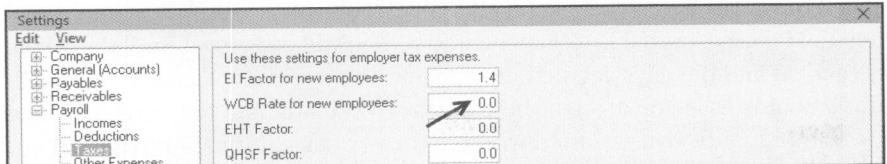

The default settings for employer expenses are correct — both expenses are calculated by amount.

> **Click**   **Entitlements** under the Payroll heading:

On this screen you can enter the rules for entitlements that apply to all or most employees. When we enter the rules here, they will be added to each employee's record. You can change entitlement amounts for individual employees in their ledger records.

Entitlements may be given directly or may be linked to the number of hours worked. For example, usually employees are not entitled to take vacation time or sick leave until they have worked for a certain period of time. You can use the **Track Using % Hours Worked** to determine how quickly vacation or sick days accumulate. For example, one day per month equals about 5 percent of hours worked. Thus, you would enter 5 percent if the employee is entitled to 12 days of leave per year. You can also indicate the **Maximum** number of **Days** per year that an employee can take or accumulate. And finally, you must indicate whether the unused days are **cleared at the end of a year** or can be carried forward. If the days earned but not used at the end of a year are carried forward, then the Maximum will still place a limit on the number of days available. When the maximum

NOTES

The WCB rate is based on the injury history and risk factors for the job and for the industry. Kabanza and Usher have different rates than the others because their jobs are in different rate classes.

If WCB does not apply, you can select a different expense name from the drop-down list and then enter rates for this expense.

NOTES

EHT applies to payroll in Ontario. The factor or rate ranges from 0.98 to 1.95 depending on the total payroll amount.

QHSF is used for Village Galleries in Chapter 14.

NOTES

Northern Lights does not contribute to the VRSP, so this is not entered as a user-defined expense.

NOTES

You can also apply entitlements as a fixed amount per year by omitting the tracking percentage, entering a maximum and then entering the balance for the employee in the ledger.

NOTES

The number of hours per working day is set at 8 by default, but you can change this. For Helena's Academy, we changed it to 7.5. You can also change the entry for individual employees in their ledger records.

NOTES
Three weeks' vacation is equivalent to about 6 percent when paid as a percentage of wages. When tracked as a percentage of hours worked, 8 percent will yield about four weeks of time off.

number of days has been reached, no additional days will accrue — the entry in the Days Earned field on the journal Entitlements tab screen will be zero — until the employee takes time off and the days accrued drops below the maximum again. The number of days of entitlement is based on an eight-hour day as the default, but this can be changed.

Northern Lights gives salaried workers three weeks of vacation (tracked at 8 percent) and allows a maximum of 25 days. Sick leave at 10 days per year is earned at the rate of 5 percent to a maximum of 20 days. Personal leave days (5 days) accrue at the rate of 2.5 percent to a maximum of 10 days. None are cleared at year-end.

Northern Lights allows two weeks of vacation time and sick leave and one week of personal days to be carried over to the following year.

Click   the **Track Using % Hours Worked field for Vacation**.

Type   8 **Press** (tab) to advance to the Maximum Days field.

Type   25 **Press** (tab).

Click   the **Track Using % Hours Worked field for Sick Leave**.

Type   5 **Press** (tab) to advance to the Maximum Days field.

Type   20 **Press** (tab).

Click   the **Track Using % Hours Worked field for PersonalDays**.

Type   2.5 **Press** (tab) to advance to the Maximum Days field.

Type   10 **Press** (tab).

Until we identify linked accounts we cannot set up Remittances. To set up Job Categories, we must first create employee records. Therefore, we will add Payroll Remittance and Job Category settings later.

Click   **Manulife** under the Payroll heading:

NOTES
Clicking the first underlined link (Identify Which...) will open the Income Settings screen on page 320.
Clicking the Learn How... link opens Help information with more information about these plans.

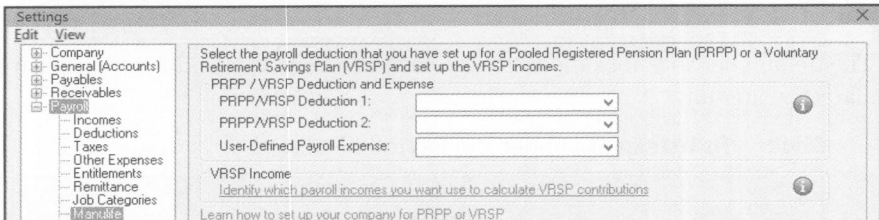

Here we enter the name of the deduction that is set up for the voluntary retirement savings plan. No employer contribution is added by Northern Lights, so there is no user-defined expense associated with the plan. Pointing to the information buttons provides additional information about entering the required information:

CLASSIC VIEW
You can access the Payroll Ledger linked accounts by right-clicking the Paycheques or the Payroll Cheque Run icon,
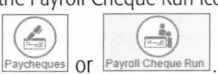
Then click , the Settings tool, or choose the Setup menu; then click Settings, Payroll, Linked Accounts and Income.
If no Home window icon is selected, you can use the Settings tool pop-up list, choose Payroll and click Select.

Click   the **list arrow for PRPP/VRSP Deduction 1**. The three deductions names we entered earlier are listed.

Click   **VRSP**.

Identifying the Payroll Linked Accounts

There are many linked accounts for payroll because each type of income, tax, deduction and expense that is used must be linked to a General Ledger account. You do not need to

create any of these accounts; they are already in the Chart of Accounts. The following **linked accounts** are used by Northern Lights for the Payroll Ledger:

```
PAYROLL LINKED ACCOUNTS

Income
 Principal Bank      1080  Bank: Chequing
 Vacation Owed       2300  Vacation Payable        Advances & Loans  1240  Loans Receivable

   Vac. Earned       5430  Vacation Earned         Salary       5410  Salaries: Performance Staff
   Regular           5420  Wages: Support Staff    Commission   5440  Commissions
   Overtime 1        5420  Wages: Support Staff    No. Sold     5450  Sales Bonuses
   Travel Allow      5560  Travel Allowances       Overtime 2: Not used

Deductions          Deduction Payable Account     Payment Adjustment
 VRSP:               2410  VRSP Payable            2410  VRSP Payable
 EHC-Employee:       2400  EHC Payable - Employee  2400  EHC Payable - Employee
 Guild Fees:         2450  Players' Guild Payable  2450  Players' Guild Payable

Taxes
 Payables                      Expenses                  Payment Adjustment
  EI    2310  EI Payable        5510  EI Expense           5510  EI Expense
  CPP   2320  CPP Payable       5520 CPP Expense           5520  CPP Expense
  Tax   2330  Income Tax Payable                           1080  Bank: Chequing
  WCB   2460  WCB Payable       5530 WCB Expense           5530  WCB Expense
  EHT, Tax (Que.), QPP, QHSF, QPIP: Not used

User-Defined Expenses
 Payables                                Expenses and Payment Adjustments
  Tuition Fees       2420  Tuition Fees Payable   5570  Tuition Fees Expense
  EHC-Employer       2440  EHC Payable - Employer 5580  EHC Premium Expense
```

Click   Incomes under the Linked Accounts subheading:

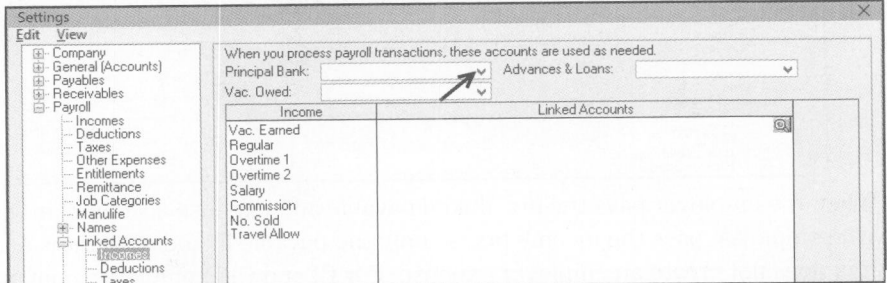

The linked accounts for all types of income appear together on this first screen. You must identify a wage account for each type of employee payment used by the company, even if the same account is used for all of them. Once the Payroll bank account is identified as the same one used for Payables, the program will apply a single sequence of cheque numbers for all cheques prepared from the Payables and Payroll journals.

Accounts you can use for more than one link will be available in the drop-down list. Otherwise, once an account is selected as a linked account, it is removed from the list.

To enter accounts, you can **type** the **account number** or **select** the **account** from the drop-down list and **press** (tab) to advance to the next linked account field.

Choose 1080 Bank: Chequing for the Principal Bank field.

Choose 2300 Vacation Payable for the Vacation Owed field.

Choose 1240 Loans Receivable for the Advances & Loans field.

Choose 5430 Vacation Earned for Vac. Earned.

Choose 5420 Wages: Support Staff for Regular and Overtime 1. Do not enter an account for Overtime 2.

NOTES
You can also access the Payroll Linked Accounts screens from the Setup menu (and from the Payroll Journal at this stage). Choose Settings and click Payroll and Linked Accounts or open the journal and click OK in response to the warning about missing essential linked accounts.

NOTES
All the accounts you will need for this stage are already in the Chart of Accounts.
However, you can add accounts from the Linked Accounts windows. Type a new number, press (enter) and choose to add the account.

NOTES
The deleted income and deduction names do not appear on the screens for linked accounts. Deleting the unused names also simplifies the data entry for linked accounts.

NOTES
Only the single bank class account is available on the Principal Bank drop-down selection list.

WARNING!
Do not enter linked accounts for Overtime 2 and other unused incomes. In this way, the program will skip these fields in the employee records.

Choose 5410 Salaries: Performance Staff for Salary.

Choose 5440 Commissions for Commission.

Choose 5450 Sales Bonuses for No. Sold.

Choose 5560 Travel Allowances for Travel Allow.

Click Deductions under Linked Accounts for the next set of accounts:

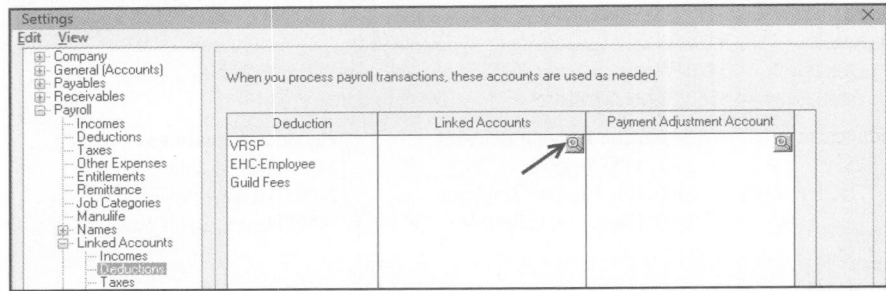

The names here are the ones you entered in the Names: Incomes & Deductions screen. If you deleted a name, it will not appear here.

Enter the Deductions and Payment Adjustment linked accounts for VRSP, EHC-Employee and Guild Fees from the chart on page 325.

Click Taxes under Linked Accounts to access the next set of linked accounts:

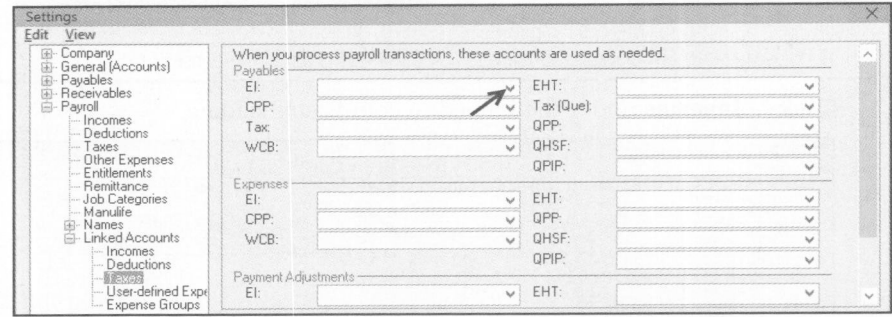

When the employer pays the tax, linked payable and expense accounts are needed. Only the employee pays the income tax, so only the payable linked account is needed. This tax does not create an employer expense. For EI and CPP, employee contributions are added to those of the employer to calculate the total amount payable.

Enter the linked Payables accounts for EI, CPP, Tax and WCB in the Payables section. **Enter** the linked accounts for EI, CPP and WCB in the Expenses section and for the related Payment Adjustments accounts from the chart on page 325.

Click User-Defined Expenses under the Linked Accounts subheading to open the screen for the final Payroll accounts:

NOTES

Payment Adjustment accounts are not essential. You may omit them until you need to use them. If you enter an adjustment amount, Sage 50 will prompt you to enter the linked account.

WARNING!

Do not enter linked accounts for the unused taxes. In this way, the program will skip these fields in the employee records.

Enter   the **linked Payable accounts**, the **linked Expenses accounts** and the **linked Payment Adjustments accounts** for **Tuition Fees** and **EHC-Employer**. Refer to the chart on page 325.

Check   the **linked** payroll **accounts** against the chart on page 325 before proceeding. Click each heading under Linked Accounts to open the different screens.

Changing Payroll Form Settings

Before closing the Settings screens, we still need to enter the form number to set up the automatic numbering of direct deposit slips. This number is entered with the other automatic numbering sequences as part of the Company Settings.

Click   **Company** and then **click Forms** to open the number setup screen:

PRO VERSION
The entry for Packing Slips is not included.

Click   the **Direct Deposit Stubs Next Form Number field** for **Employees**.

Type   242

Click   **OK** to save the Settings changes:

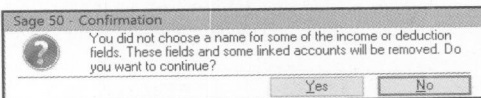

Because we deleted some income and deduction names, we are being warned that any accounts linked to these deleted fields will also be removed. We can proceed.

Click   **Yes** to open a second confirmation message:

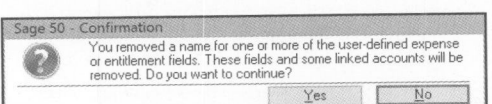

Again, we are warned because of the other field names we deleted.

Click   **Yes** to continue and return to the Payroll Home window.

NOTES
You are still unable to finish the Payroll history (History menu). Although we have entered linked accounts, the ledger is unbalanced because the Loans Receivable and Vacation Payable ledger account balances do not match these amounts in the employee records.

Entering Employee Ledger Records

Use the Northern Lights Employee Information Sheet and Employee Profiles on pages 312–315 to create the employee records and add historical information. We will enter the information for Northern Lights employee Taika Tikett.

Click   the **Employees icon** in the Home window.

The Employees icon window is blank because no employees are on file at this stage.

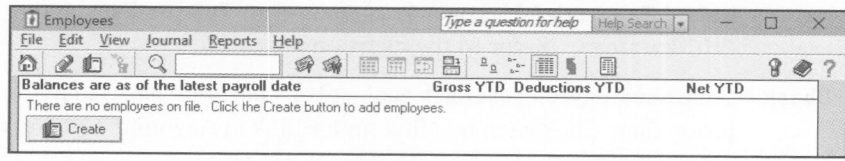

Click   the **Create button** [Create] or **choose** the **File menu** and **click Create**.

Or, to bypass the Employees window and open the Payroll Ledger employee window,

Click   the **Employees icon shortcuts list** and **choose Add Employee**:

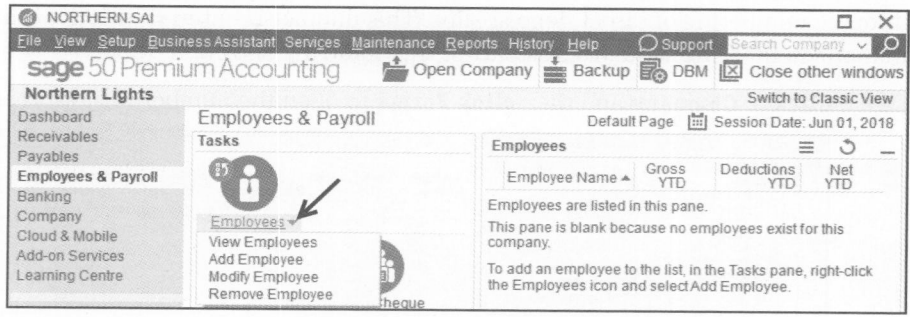

Entering Personal Details

The Payroll Ledger new employee information form will open so you can begin to enter the employee record. There are several required fields in the Employee Ledger records because this information links to government income tax tables and rules.

The opening Personal information page holds the personal details for the employee:

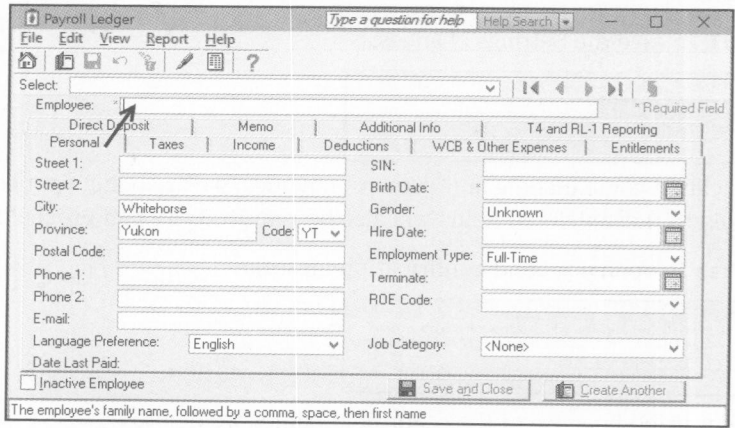

The Payroll Ledger has a large number of tabs for the different kinds of payroll information and many required fields — those marked with *. The default city, province and province code, those for the business, are entered and are correct. The cursor is in the Employee field. If you enter the surname first, employee lists will be in correct alphabetic order. You can change the Address tab screen information at any time.

Type   Tikett, Taika **Press** `tab`.

The cursor advances to the Street 1 field.

Type   29 Stubbs Rd.

Click   the **Postal Code field**.

Type   y1a4k2 **Press** `tab`.

NOTES

If you hide the Employees icon window (Setup menu, User Preferences, View screen), the Payroll Ledger window opens immediately when you click the Employees icon.

You will also skip the Employees window if you use the Add Employee shortcut.

NOTES

The Set Field Names tool in the ledger window will open the Payroll Settings Additional Names screen where we added emergency contact field names.

NOTES

As in other ledgers, required fields that you cannot leave blank are marked with *.

On the Personal tab screen, the employee name and the date of birth are essential. All other fields on this screen can be completed later.

The program corrects the postal code format and advances the cursor to the Phone 1 field.

Type   8676897595 **Press** (tab) to correct the phone number format.

The default **Language Preference** is correctly set as English.

Click   the **Social Insurance Number (SIN) field**. You must use a valid SIN.

Type   218738631 **Press** (tab) to advance to the Birth Date field.

Enter the month, day and year using any accepted date format.

Type   8-10-86 **Press** (tab) **twice** to advance to the Gender field.

Choose Male from the drop-down list. **Press** (tab).

The cursor moves to the Hire Date field, which should contain the date when the employee began working for Northern Lights.

Type   11 6 16 **Press** (tab). **Full-Time** as the employment type is correct.

The next two fields will be used when the employee leaves the job — the date of termination and the reason for leaving that you can select from the drop-down list. The final option designates employees as active or inactive. All employees at Northern Lights are active, so the default selection is correct.

Job Categories are used to identify salespersons who can be linked to specific sales so that their sales revenue is tracked and used to calculate commissions. The employee's Job Category can be selected here from the drop-down list if categories are already set up, or you can place employees in categories later from the Payroll Settings screen. We will create categories later and assign employees to them at that stage.

When you use Sage 50 to pay employees, the Date Last Paid will be entered automatically by the program.

The remaining details for the employee are entered on the other tab screens.

Entering Tax Information

Click   the **Taxes tab** to advance to the next set of employee details:

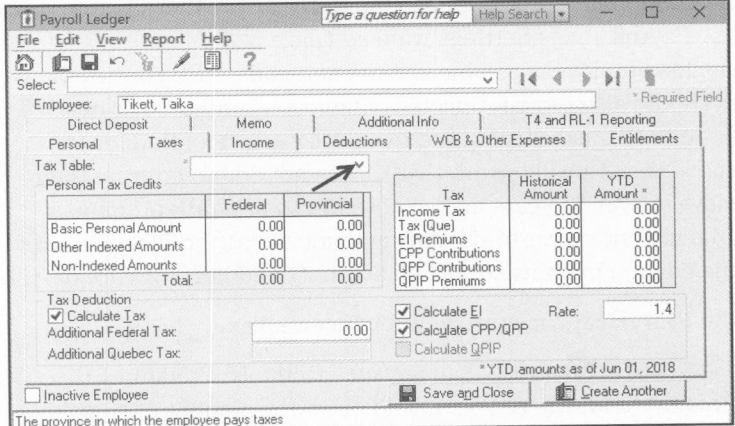

This screen allows you to enter income tax–related information. **Personal Tax Credits** are divided between **federal** and **provincial** and then again among the **basic** amount, the total of all other amounts that are **indexed** and the total of amounts that are **non-indexed**. Provincial personal income taxes are not linked to the rates for federal income taxes, so separate claim amounts are needed. Sage 50 will enter the total claim amount. The total is used to calculate income taxes for each paycheque. Historical tax amounts for the year to date are also entered on this screen.

NOTES
The program will allow you to omit the social insurance number, but you must enter the employee's date of birth. The SIN can be added later and is required for the Record of Employment. The date of birth is required because it determines whether CPP deductions are mandatory.

NOTES
The termination date and reason for leaving a job will determine the employee's eligibility to collect Employment Insurance. Refer to page 297.

NOTES
You should drag the column margins so that all amounts and headings are on-screen. The YTD column may be hidden initially.

NOTES
The Tax Table (Province) is the only required field on this screen. Taxes will be based on the minimum basic claim amounts if no claim amounts are entered. Tax Table is a required field because different provinces have different income tax rates.

| Click | the **Tax Table list arrow**. A list of provinces and territories appears on the screen. This is a required field. |

Click   **Yukon**, the province of taxation for Northern Lights for income tax purposes.

Press   ⌨tab to advance to the Basic Personal Amount label.

Press   ⌨tab again for the Federal amounts field, which holds the basic claim amount.

Type   11474 **Press** ⌨tab to advance to the field for the Provincial Basic Personal Amount.

Type   11474 **Press** ⌨tab to advance to the field for Other Federal Indexed Amounts.

Type   11474 **Press** ⌨tab to advance to the field for Other Provincial Indexed Amounts.

Type   11474 **Press** ⌨tab to advance to the Federal Non-Indexed Amounts.

Type   2095 **Press** ⌨tab to advance to the Provincial Non-Indexed Amounts.

Type   2095

Usher is the only other employee who has non-indexed amounts.

Press   ⌨tab to update the totals. **Click** the **Additional Federal Tax** field.

When an employee has chosen to have additional federal income tax deducted from each paycheque, enter the amount of the deduction in the **Additional Federal Tax** field. Employees might make this choice if they receive regular additional income from which no tax is deducted. By making this choice, they avoid paying a large amount of tax at the end of the year and possible interest penalties.

Type   50

For **Kabanza** enter **100** in the Additional Federal Tax field.

If an employee is insurable by EI, you must leave the box for **Deduct EI** checked. The default EI contribution factor, 1.4, for all employees at Northern Lights is correct. We entered it in the Payroll Taxes Settings window (page 323).

All Northern Lights employees pay income tax and make CPP contributions, so these check boxes should also remain selected. Employees under 18 or over 70 years of age do not contribute to CPP, so clicking the **Deduct CPP/QPP** option for these employees (to remove the ✓) will ensure that CPP is not deducted from their paycheques. Employees over 65 years may choose not to pay CPP premiums.

We will enter the historical year-to-date tax amounts next (for five months of pay). You should drag the column margins so that all amounts and headings are on-screen.

Click   the **Historical Amount field** for **Income Tax**.

Type   1120.30 **Press** ⌨tab to advance to the EI Premiums Historical Amount field, where you should enter the amount of EI paid to date.

Type   308.91 **Press** ⌨tab to move to the CPP Contributions Historical Amount field.

Type   765.03

NOTES
When you subscribe to the payroll services plan, you can update the tax claim amounts with the aid of a tax wizard. Only the indexed amounts will be updated.

NOTES
Deduction amounts for tuition and education are not subject to indexing.

NOTES
All employees between 18 and 65 must pay CPP premiums if they are employed. They may collect CPP as early as 60 years, with a reduction for taking the pension early, or after 65 with increased payouts for the delay in collecting.
If an employee does not pay a tax, click the Calculate Taxes check box for it.

WARNING!
Enter employee historical payroll details carefully. You will be unable to edit these fields after finishing the history.
These historical details are needed because there are yearly maximum amounts for CPP and EI contributions. Totals for optional deductions are retained in the employee record. They must also be correct because they are used to create T4s for tax reporting.

NOTES
The program skips the Quebec tax fields because no linked account was entered for the extra provincial tax.

Entering Income Amounts

We defined all the types of income for Northern Lights when we set up Names (refer to page 318). All the details you need to complete the Income tab chart are on pages 312–313. The following list summarizes the types of income used by each employee. Not all will be used on all paycheques.

- Loans and Benefits: all employees (read margin Notes)
- Vac. Owed and Vac. Paid: all hourly paid employees (read margin Notes)
- Regular: four hourly paid employees — Tikett, Kabanza, Usher, Ridges
- Overtime 1: four hourly paid employees — Tikett, Kabanza, Usher, Ridges
- No. Sold: two hourly paid employees — Tikett, Ridges
- Salary: three salaried employees — Apsimak, Player, Staige
- Travel Allow: two actors — Player, Staige
- Commission: Apsimak

Click the **Income tab** to open the next screen of employee details:

On the Income chart you can indicate the types of income that each employee receives (the **Use** column), the usual rate of pay for that type of income (**Amount Per Unit**), the usual number of hours worked (**Hours Per Period**), the usual number of units for a piece rate pay base (**Pieces Per Period**) and the amounts received this calendar year before entering the first paycheque in Sage 50 (**Historical Amount**). The **Year-To-Date (YTD) Amount** is added automatically by the program based on the historical amounts you enter and the paycheques entered in the program.

Checkmarks must be entered in the Use column to make the fields available in the Payroll journals, even if they will not be used on all paycheques.

We need to add the historical loans, benefits and vacation amounts for Tikett. Tikett has $100 in loans not yet repaid, and he has not received all the vacation pay earned last year. The total of the advances/loans and vacation owed amounts for all employees must match the opening General Ledger balances for the corresponding linked accounts.

Two employees have received some of their vacation pay this year. We enter that amount in the **Vac. Paid Historical Amount** field. Vacation pay not yet received is entered in the **Vac. Owed Historical Amount** field. Any loans paid to the employees and not yet repaid are recorded in the **Loans Historical Amount** field. There is no record of loan amounts recovered.

Pay Periods Per Year refers to the number of times the employee is paid, or the pay cycle. This is a required field. Tikett is paid every two weeks, 26 times per year.

NOTES
The incomes that are used by an employee are marked with a ✓ in the chart on pages 312–313 or have an amount in the employee's column.

NOTES
Checkmarks are added by default for all incomes, deductions and expenses that have linked accounts entered for them.
The checkmarks for Advances, Loans, Benefits, Vacation Owed and Vacation Paid cannot be removed.

NOTES
Because advances are taxable, Northern Lights issues short-term loans to employees instead.

NOTES
If calculating vacation on vacation paid is required by legislation, you should click the check box for this option.

⚠ **WARNING!**
The totals for all employees for advances and loans paid and vacation pay owing must match the corresponding General Ledger linked account balances before you can finish entering the history. These are the two control accounts for the Payroll Ledger.

Click   the **list arrow** beside the field for **Pay Periods Per Year**:

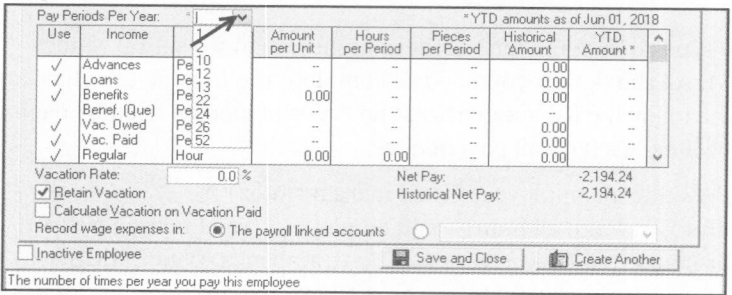

Click   **26**.

Click   the **Historical Amount column beside Loans** to move the cursor.

Type   100 **Press** `tab` to move to the Benefits Amount Per Unit column.

The medical premiums paid by the employer are employee benefits.

Type   41.54 **Press** `tab` to move to the Historical Amount for Benefits.

Type   1015.40 **Press** `tab` to advance to the Vac. Owed Historical Amount.

Type   939 **Press** `tab` to advance to the Historical Vac. Paid Amount.

Type   610 **Press** `tab` again to advance to the **Use column for Regular**.

Press   `tab` to advance to the Amount Per Unit field where we need to enter the regular hourly wage rate for Tikett.

Type   18 **Press** `tab` to advance to the Hours Per Period field.

Bi-weekly paid employees usually work 80 hours per period. Salaried workers normally work 160 hours each month. You can change the number of hours and the rate in the Payroll journals.

Type   80 **Press** `tab` to advance to the Historical Amount field.

Historical income and deduction amounts for the year to date are necessary so that taxes and deductions can be calculated correctly and T4 statements will be accurate.

Type   14400 **Press** `tab`.

This amount is entered automatically in the YTD column and the cursor advances to the Use column for Overtime 1.

Press   `tab` so you can enter the overtime hourly rate.

Type   27

Press   `tab` **twice** to advance to the Historical Amount field. There is no regular number of overtime hours.

Type   810 **Press** `tab` to advance to the Overtime 2 Use column.

Some income types do not apply to Tikett, so they should not be checked. The next income that applies is No. Sold, the piece rate method of pay. We need to enter the rate or amount per unit (number) and the historical amount. There is no fixed number of pieces per period.

If no linked account is entered for an income, the Use column will be blank, as for Overtime 2.

Click   the **Use column beside Salary** to remove the ✓.

Click   the **Use column beside Commission** to remove the ✓.

Click   the **Use column beside Travel Allow** to remove the ✓.

Click   **No. Sold** in the Income column to select the line. Do not click the Use column. **Press** `tab` .

Type   0.10   to enter the amount received for each set. **Press** `tab` **twice**.

Type   440   to enter the historical amount.

For **Player** and **Staige**, click the Use column for Regular, Overtime 1, Commission and No. Sold to remove the ✓s. Enter the monthly **Salary** and press `tab` . Enter **160** as the number of hours worked in the pay period for them. Press `tab` and enter the historical amount. You cannot remove the ✓s for Vac. Owed and Vac. Paid, even if they are not used. Enter the amount per period and the year-to-date amounts for **Travel Allow**.

For **Apsimak**, remove the ✓s for the Regular, Overtime 1 and No. Sold, enter the **Salary** per period, the number of hours and the year-to-date amounts. Leave **Commission** checked and enter **1650** as the historical amount. There is no regular amount for each pay period.

   Retaining Vacation pay is normal for full-time hourly paid employees. Part-time and casual workers often receive their vacation pay with each paycheque because their work schedule is irregular. You will turn the option to retain vacation off for these employees — their vacation pay will then be added to each paycheque. If the employee is salaried and does not receive vacation pay, the option should also be turned off. For employees who receive vacation pay, leave the option to Retain Vacation checked and type the vacation pay rate in the % field.

Double-click   the **% field beside Vacation Rate**.

Type   6

For **Apsimak**, **Player** and **Staige**, click Retain Vacation to remove the ✓.

   Employee wages may be linked to their separate default expense accounts or they can all be linked to the single expense account that you select from the drop-down list. Wage expenses for all Northern Lights employees are linked to the default accounts entered on pages 325–326, so the default selection is correct.

Entering Payroll Deduction Amounts

The next step is to enter current and historical details for deductions, just as we did for income. You must indicate which deductions apply to the employee (Use column), the amount or percentage normally deducted and the historical amount — the amount deducted to date this year.

Click   the **Deductions tab** to open the screen for payroll deductions:

Employee:	Tikett, Taika					
Direct Deposit		Memo		Additional Info	T4 and RL-1 Reporting	
Personal	Taxes	Income	Deductions	WCB & Other Expenses	Entitlements	
Use	Deduction	Amount per Pay Period	Percentage per Pay Period	Historical Amount	YTD Amount *	
✓	VRSP	--	0.0000	0.00	--	
✓	EHC-Employee	0.00	--	0.00	--	
✓	Guild Fees	--	0.0000	0.00	--	

*YTD amounts as of Jun 01, 2018

☐ Inactive Employee   💾 Save and Close   📋 Create Another

The deduction percentage per pay period

All deductions are selected in the Use column (a ✓ is entered).

   By entering deduction amounts or percentages here, they will be included automatically on the Payroll Journal input forms. Otherwise, you must enter them

manually in the journal for each pay period. Not all employees make VRSP contributions at this time, but they may do so later, so we will leave this field available. When you enter the amounts or percentages here, the deductions are automatically added in the journal, but changes can still be made in the journals. You should make permanent changes by editing the Employee Ledger record. Tikett has VRSP contributions withheld from his pay.

When deductions are made as a percentage, as for VRSP and Guild Fees, the Percentage Per Pay Period field is available.

> **Click**   **VRSP** in the Deduction column to select the line. **Press** `tab`.

The cursor advances to the Percentage Per Period field. You should enter the percentage of gross pay that is withheld in each pay period.

> **Type**   2.5 **Press** `tab` to advance to the Historical Amount field.
>
> **Type**   400 **Press** `tab` to update the YTD Amount.
>
> **Press**   `tab` to advance to the Use column for EHC-Employee.
>
> **Press**   `tab` to advance to the Amount Per Pay Period Field.
>
> **Type**   41.54 **Press** `tab` to advance to the Historical Amount field.
>
> **Type**   415.40 **Press** `tab` to update the YTD Amount.
>
> **Click**   the **Use column for Guild Fees** to remove the ✓.

For **Player** and **Staige**, enter the percentage per period and year-to-date amounts for **Guild Fees**. The remaining deductions are not used by Northern Lights. The names were deleted, so they do not appear on our chart or in the ledger.

Entering WCB and Other Expenses

In other provinces, the tab label will be changed to match the name used for WCB in that province. Ontario uses the name WSIB — Workplace Safety and Insurance Board — instead of WCB, so the tab label will be WSIB & Other Expenses.

> **Click**   the **WCB & Other Expenses tab**:

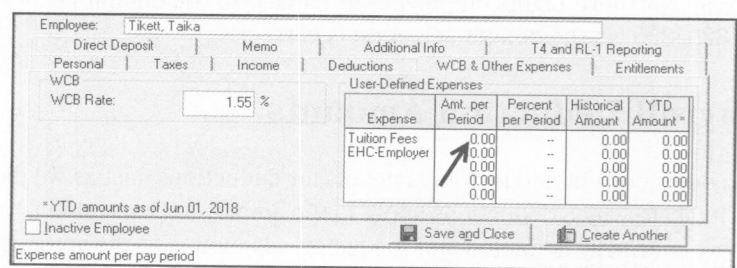

The user-defined expenses we created in the Additional Payroll Names screen (page 319) and the default WCB rate (page 323) are entered on this screen. The default WCB rate is entered from our setup information, but you can enter a different rate for an individual employee in this field. The rate is correct for Tikett.

For **Kabanza**, enter **3.38** as the WCB rate. For **Usher**, enter **1.75**.

Other user-defined expenses are also added on this screen. Northern Lights has two user-defined expenses, and both apply to Tikett. The remaining expenses are not used by Northern Lights at this time.

> **Click**   the **Tuition Fees Amt. Per Period**. Enter the amount that the employer contributes in each pay period.
>
> **Type**   60 **Press** `tab` to advance to the Historical Amount field.

Type   600

Click   the **EHC-Employer Amt. Per Period**. **Type**   41.54

Press   ⟨tab⟩ to advance to the Historical Amount field. **Type**   415.40

For **Usher**, enter **80** as the Tuition Fees Amt. Per Period and **1680** as the Historical Amount.

Entering Entitlements

Click   the **Entitlements tab**:

We entered the default rates and amounts for entitlements as Payroll Settings (page 323), but they can be modified in the ledger records for individual employees.

We must also enter the historical information for entitlements. The number of **Historical Days** will include any days carried forward from previous periods. The number of days accrued cannot be greater than the maximum number of days defined for the entitlement for an employee. The number of **Net Days Accrued**, the amount unused and available for carrying forward, is updated automatically from the historical information and current Payroll Journal entries.

You cannot enter information directly in the Net Days Accrued field.

Tikett receives vacation pay instead of paid time off, so the vacation entitlements details should be removed. The defaults for sick leave and personal days are correct.

Click   the **Track Using % Hours Worked field for Vacation**.

Press   ⟨del⟩ to remove the entry 8.00.

Press   ⟨tab⟩ to advance to the Maximum Days field. **Press** ⟨del⟩.

Click   the **Historical Days field for Sick Leave**. **Type**   16

Press   ⟨↓⟩ to advance to the Historical Days field for PersonalDays. The number of days is added to the Net Days Accrued.

Type   4 **Click** the **Net Days Accrued** field to enter the amount.

For Apsimak, Player and Staige, the default entries for tracking and maximum days are correct, but you must enter the Historical Days for each entitlement.

Entering Direct Deposit Information

Four employees have elected to have their entire paycheques deposited directly to their bank accounts. On this screen, we need to enter the bank account details. For each employee who has selected the Direct Deposit option, you must turn on the selection in the **Direct Deposit Paycheques For This Employee** check box. Then you must add the five-digit Transit or **Branch Number**, the three-digit Bank or **Institution Number**, the bank **Account Number** and finally the amount that is deposited, or the percentage of the cheque. Refer to the bank account deposit details on page 313.

NOTES
You should drag the column margins so you can include all the columns and amounts on-screen.

NOTES
If employees take days before the sufficient number of hours worked have been accrued, the program will warn you. Then you can allow the entry for entitlements or not. This permission is similar to allowing customers to exceed their credit limits.

NOTES
Third parties, such as Beanstream, provide the service of transferring the payroll deposits to the employees' bank accounts.
Direct deposits are covered in Chapter 13.

NOTES

All banks in Canada are assigned a three-digit bank or institution number, and each branch has a unique five-digit transit number. You must enter the correct number of digits for these.

Account numbers may vary from five to twelve digits.

NOTES

The paycheque deposit may be split among more than one bank account by entering different percentages for the accounts or by entering an amount for each bank account.

To delete bank account details, click the employee's Direct Deposit tab. Click Active in the Status column to change the entry to Inactive and then delete the bank information. Click the check box for Direct Deposit Paycheques to remove the ✓. Click Active to reset the status.

For individual paycheques, you can click the Direct Deposit check box in the journal to remove the ✓ and pay the employee by cheque.

NOTES

The Daily Business Manager is covered in Chapter 11.

NOTES

Additional information for other ledgers may also be displayed or hidden in journal transactions.

In the Manulife section, you can indicate the plan type (pooled – PRPP – or Voluntary – VRSP) and enter the employee's Manulife plan number.

WARNING!

The Contact Number field is not predefined as a telephone number, so the format will not be corrected automatically by the program.

Click   the **Direct Deposit tab**:

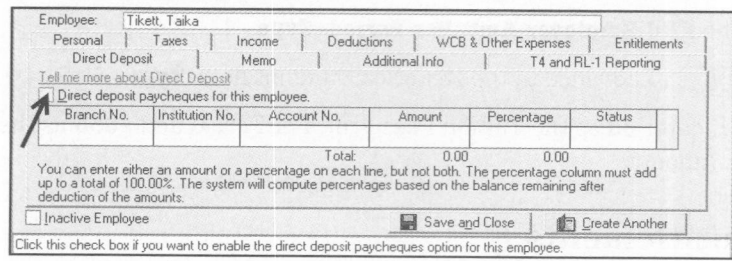

Click   the **Direct Deposit Paycheques For This Employee check box** to add a ✓.

Click   the **Branch No. field**.

Type   06722 **Press** [tab] to advance to the Institution No. field.

Type   180 **Press** [tab] to advance to the Account No. field.

Type   4556221 **Press** [tab] **twice** to advance to the Percentage field.

Type   100

Click   the **Memo tab**:

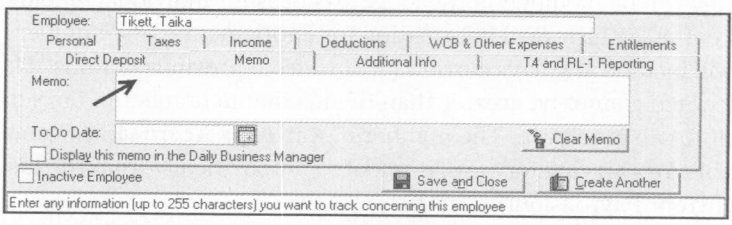

The Memo tab will not be used at this time. You could enter a note with a reminder date to appear in the Daily Business Manager; for example, a reminder to issue vacation paycheques on a specific date, to recover advances and loans or to celebrate a birthday.

Entering Additional Information

Northern Lights enters emergency contacts for each employee.

Click   the **Additional Info tab** to access the additional fields:

You can indicate whether you want to display any of the additional information when the employee is selected in a transaction. We do not need to display the contact information in the Payroll Journal. Enter the contact information from page 313.

Click   the **Emergency Contact field**.

Type   Kierin Tikett **Press** [tab] **twice**.

Type   (867) 689-1892 to enter the contact's phone number.

Entering T4 and RL-1 Reporting Amounts

The next information screen allows you to enter the year-to-date EI insurable and pensionable earnings. By adding the historical amounts, the T4 slips prepared for income taxes at the end of the year and the Record of Employment termination reports will also be correct. Refer to the T4 historical information on page 313.

Click   the **T4 and RL-1 Reporting tab** to open the final screen:

In the **Historical Amounts field for EI Ins. Earnings**, you should enter the total earned income received to date that is EI insurable. The program will update this total every time you make payroll entries until the maximum salary on which EI is calculated has been reached. At that time, no further EI premiums will be deducted.

Pensionable Earnings — the total of all income plus benefits — are also tracked by the program. This amount determines the total income that is eligible for the Canada Pension Plan. Again, when the maximum is reached, no further CPP deductions are made. The **Pension Adjustment** amount is used when the employee has a workplace pension program that will affect the allowable contributions for personal registered pension plans and will be linked with the Canada Pension Plan. Workplace pension income is reduced when the employee also has income from the Canada Pension Plan. Since Northern Lights has no company pension plan, the Pension Adjustment amount is zero and no pension plan registration number is needed.

The T4 Employee Code applies to a small number of job types that have special income tax rules.

> **Double-click** the **Historical Amounts field for EI Ins. Earnings**.
>
> **Type**   16300
>
> **Double-click** the **Historical Amounts field for Pensionable Earnings**.
>
> **Type**   17315.40

Correct any employee information **errors** by returning to the field with the error. **Highlight** the **error** and **enter** the **correct information**. **Click each tab** in turn so that you can check all the information.

When all the information is entered correctly, you must save the employee record.

> **Click**   **Create Another** [Create Another] . Changes are saved automatically.

A new blank employee information form opens.

> **Click**   the **Personal tab** so that you can enter address information.
>
> **Repeat**   these procedures to **enter** other employee **records** using the information on pages 312–315.
>
> **Click**   [Save and Close] after entering the last record to save it and close the Payroll Ledger. Sage 50 may prompt you to finish the history now.

NOTES
The EI Insurable amount is the total of gross wages, including overtime wages and vacation pay. If EI is calculated on the income, the income is added to EI Insurable Earnings.
For pensionable earnings, benefits are added to EI insurable amounts.

NOTES
The T4 Employee Code is required only for the types of employment in the drop-down list for the field. No employees with Northern Lights are in these positions.

WARNING!
Do not finish the history until you have printed your reports to check all the historical setup information and made a backup.
When you close the Employee Ledger after entering the last hourly employee, or after all employees, you may get the message that the payroll history is balanced, asking if you want to finish the history now. Choose No.

NOTES
If you started from the Add Employee shortcut, you will return directly to the Payroll Home window.

Click   **No** in response to the message about finishing the history:

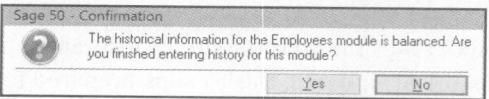

Only the *Advances & Loans Receivable* and *Vacation Payable* amounts must match before you can finish the history. Other amounts that are not verified may be incorrect and you will be unable to change them after finishing the history.

Close   the **Employees window** to return to the Home window.

Display or **print** the **Employee List** and the **Employee Summary Report** to check the accuracy of your work.

Setting Up Payroll Remittances

Because we have entered all other payroll settings and records, we can modify the final settings — for payroll remittances and job categories. Supplier records are also required for this step, but they had already been entered. Entering remittance settings involves two steps: linking the suppliers who receive payroll remittance amounts to the taxes or deductions they receive and entering payment frequency and next remittance dates.

Linking Remittances to Suppliers

The chart below identifies remittance suppliers, the liability linked to each supplier, the remitting period frequency and the ending payroll date for the next remittance period.

PAYROLL SUPPLIERS

Supplier	Payroll Liability	Remitting Frequency	Next Remittance Period End Date
Receiver General for Canada	EI	Monthly	June 30, 2018
	CPP	Monthly	June 30, 2018
	Tax	Monthly	June 30, 2018
Manulife Financial	EHC-Employee	Monthly	June 30, 2018
	EHC-Employer	Monthly	June 30, 2018
Yukon Workers' Compensation Board	WCB	Monthly	June 30, 2018
Manulife Financial	VRSP	Monthly	June 30, 2018

Click   the **Settings icon** [Settings] to open the Payroll Settings screen.

Click   **Payroll** and then **click Remittance** to open the screen we need:

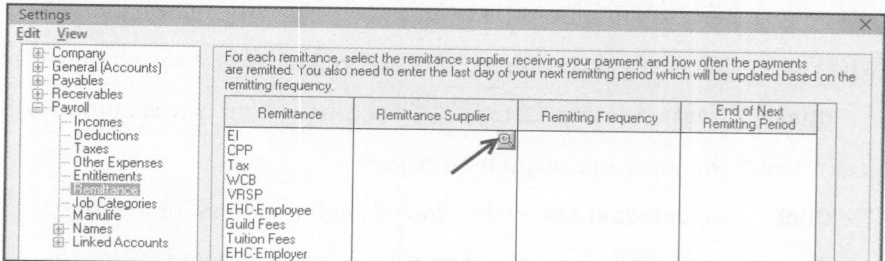

All the payroll items that are linked to liability (remittance) accounts are listed: taxes, deductions and user-defined expenses. For each liability, we can select a supplier and payment frequency from lists and then enter the last date of the pay period covered by the next remittance payment.

Click   the **List icon** 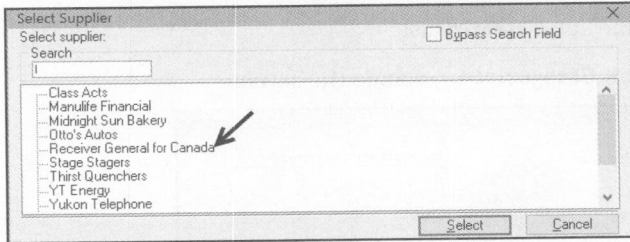 in the Remittance Supplier column on the line for EI. The selection list opens with all suppliers included:

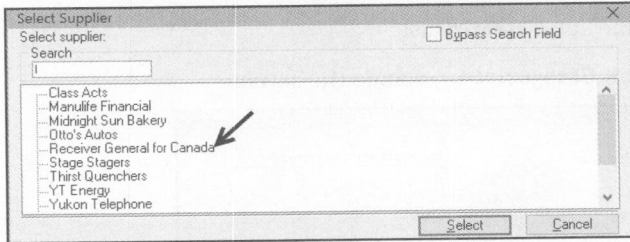

Click   **Receiver General for Canada**.

Click   **Select** or **press** (enter) to return to the Remittance Settings screen.

The cursor advances to the Remittance Frequency field for EI. The frequency for all remittances is Monthly. The next remittance for all liabilities will be made on June 30.

Click   the **List icon** in the Remitting Frequency field. **Double-click Monthly**. **Press** (tab) to advance to the End Of Next Remitting Period field.

Type   6 30 **Press** (tab).

Enter   the remaining **suppliers**, **periods** and **dates** from the chart on page 338.

Entering Job Categories

Job categories can be used to identify salespersons and to organize reports.

Click   **Job Categories**:

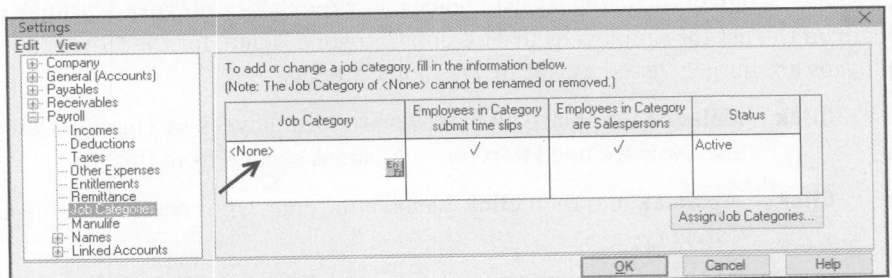

On the Job Categories screen, you enter the names of the categories and indicate whether the employees in each category submit time slips and whether they are salespersons. Categories may be active or inactive. We need a new category called Sales.

If you do not create categories, all employees can be selected in the Sales Journal and can submit time slips. Employees in the category <None> are salespersons, allowing them to be selected in the journal when no categories are set up or assigned.

Click   the **Job Category field below <None>**.

Type   Sales **Press** (tab) to add checkmarks to the next two columns and set the status to Active.

Click   the **Job Category field below Sales**.

Type   Other **Press** (tab) to add the checkmarks.

The Other category does not apply to sales or time slips, so we need to change the settings. Employees in the Other category should not appear in the Salesperson field on sales invoices. We will remove the ✓s for them.

NOTES
You can also double-click the supplier's name to add it to the Settings screen.

If you type the first few letters of the name and then press (tab), the Select Supplier list will have the supplier you need selected. Press (enter) to add the name to the Settings screen.

When you choose Receiver General for CPP and Income Tax, the frequency and date will be entered automatically from the one for EI. When you choose Manulife for EHC-Employee and EHC-Employer, the entries from VRSP will be added automatically. You can change these if they should be different.

PRO VERSION
pro The column for Submit Time Slips is not available in the Pro version. It applies to Time & Billing, a Premium feature.

Click	the ✓ in the column Employees In Category Submit Time Slips.
Click	the ✓ in the column Employees In Category Are Salespersons.
Click	**Sales** in the Job Category list.
Click	**Assign Job Categories** to change the screen:

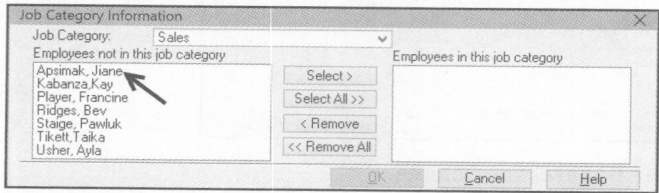

The screen is updated with employee names. Initially all are Employees Not In This Job Category.

You can add employee names to the category by choosing an employee and clicking **Select** or by choosing **Select All**. Once employees are in a category (the column on the right), you can remove them by selecting an employee and clicking **Remove** or clicking **Remove All** to move all names at the same time. Apsimak is the only person responsible for soliciting ticket sales from subscribers and groups.

Click	**Apsimak** and then **click Select** to place her in the Sales category.
Click	the **Job Category drop-down list** and **click Other**:

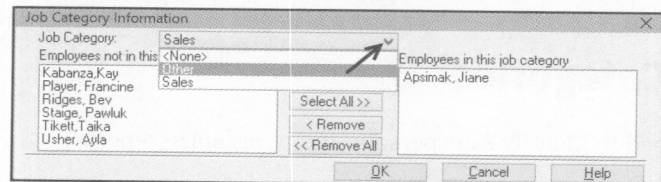

<None> is one of the category list choices. For the Sales Category, Apsimak now appears on the list for Employees In This Job Category. Again, for the Other category, all employees are initially listed as Not In This Job Category.

Click	**Select All** to place all names on the Employees In This Job Category list. Now we need to remove Apsimak's name from this list.
Click	**Apsimak** and then **click Remove** to remove her name from the Other category.
Click	**OK** to save the information and return to the Settings screen. **Click OK** to save the settings and close the Settings screen.

Finishing Payroll History

Once the setup is complete, we can back up the data file and finish the payroll history. Like the other modules, you can use the Payroll journals before finishing the history. However, the automatic payroll calculation feature will be turned off and you cannot use the Payroll Run Journal. Therefore, we should finish the history first. We can also check the data integrity as we did for Air Care to check if there are any data inconsistencies that we need to correct.

Choose the **Maintenance menu** and **click Check Data Integrity**.

Two control accounts are used for the Payroll Ledger — *Advances & Loans Receivable* and *Vacation Payable*. The General Ledger account balance for these must

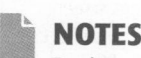

NOTES

Employees may be in more than one job category.

WARNING!

If the payroll history is not finished, you must calculate and enter taxes manually. You will also be unable to use the Payroll Run Journal.

NOTES

These two payroll control accounts are like Accounts Payable and Accounts Receivable in that historical amounts must match the General Ledger account balances.

equal the total advances and loans paid and the total vacation owed to all employees. The Historical Information entry for **Employees** should be **Balanced**.

Click   **OK** to close the Data Integrity window.

Compare your amounts with the ones on pages 312–313, and if corrections are necessary, modify the Employee Ledger records.

Once we finish the history we cannot change any historical amounts. Therefore, we should prepare a backup first.

Back up the **data file**. Refer to page 246 if necessary.

Choose the **History menu** and **click Enter Historical Information** and **Payroll**:

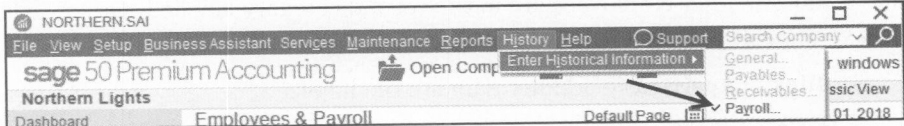

When we added the Payroll module, the History menu became available again, but only for this module — the other modules are dimmed and have the ✓ removed because the history for them is finished. When you finish the Payroll history, the Home window has all modules in the finished history state — the not-finished icon will be removed from the Employees icon and the History menu will be removed from the Home window. You are now ready to enter transactions.

Click   **Proceed** in response to the Sage 50 warning about finishing the history.

Adding Salespersons to Sales Invoices

The first transaction adds the salesperson to an invoice, applying the job category we set up to track sales for commissions.

When employees receive sales commissions, you can add the salesperson's name to the sales invoice. You can then use the Sales By Salesperson Report to determine the sales revenue amount for calculating the commission. After creating job categories, we indicated for each category whether its employees were salespersons and then identified the employees in the category.

Advance the session date to **June 7**.

Click   **Receivables** in the Modules pane list and **make** this your **default page** again if you made Employees & Payroll your default Home page.

Cash Sales Invoice #351   **Dated June 1/18**

From Subscribers, $64 000 plus $3 200 GST for advanced ticket sales. Sales total amount $67 200 deposited to chequing account. Enter Apsimak as the salesperson. Store as a monthly recurring transaction.

Click   the **Sales Invoices icon** to open the Sales Journal.

Choose **Subscribers** as the customer.

Enter   **June 1, 2018** as the invoice date.

Choose **Cash** as the method of payment.

Enter   a **description** for the sale.

Enter   **64000** as the invoice amount.

NOTES
Enter Apsimak as the salesperson for all ticket sales, either in the journal or by adding her to the customer records (as explained on pages 342–343).

Click   the **Salesperson list arrow** to open the list of salespersons:

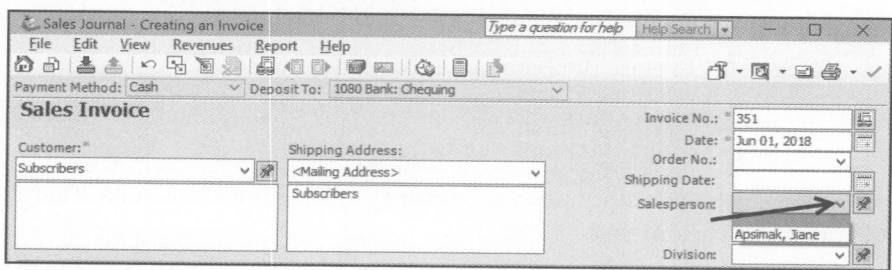

Apsimak is the only employee responsible for sales at Northern Lights, so she is the only employee we placed in the Sales job category. Therefore, Apsimak is also the only name listed. All other employees are in the second category labelled "Other," which does not have any salespersons.

Click   **Apsimak** to add her name to the invoice.

Click   the **Use The Same Salesperson pin icon** .

This will lock in the salesperson's name on the invoice Salesperson: Apsimak, Jiane until we close the journal.

The pin has changed — it now looks like it has been pushed in.

If you leave the journal open in the background, the salesperson remains selected. If you close the journal, you must reselect the salesperson for each invoice. You must close the journal before advancing the session date.

Review   the **journal display**. The salesperson is not added to the journal report.

Close   the **display** when finished.

Check   your **work** and **make corrections** if necessary.

Store   the **transaction** to recur **monthly**. Apsimak will be entered as the salesperson in the stored transaction.

Post   the **invoice** and **minimize** (or close) the **Sales Journal**.

Adding Salespersons to Customer Records

Because Apsimak is the only salesperson, we can add her name to all customer records. By changing the ledger records, Apsimak will be entered in the Sales Journal automatically for these customers. For new customers, you can create a record (full or incomplete) and add the salesperson, or you can add the name in the journal.

Click   **Subscribers** in the Customers pane list to open the ledger. **Click** the **Salesperson field list arrow**:

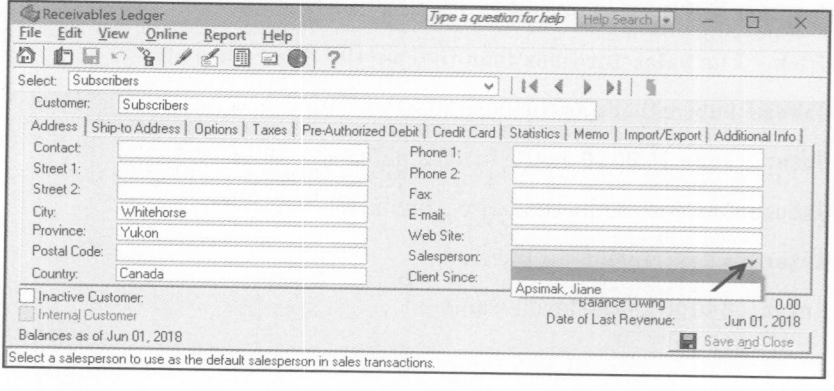

NOTES
The Use The Same Salesperson pin icon is the same as the Use The Same Customer Next Time tool, and it works the same way.

If Job Categories are not set up, all employees are on the Salesperson field drop-down list. By default, they are in the category <None>, and employees in this category are salespersons (refer to the screenshot on page 339).

NOTES
You can still select a different salesperson in the journal if the default selection is incorrect for an individual sale.

Click   **Apsimak** to add her name. **Click** the **Next Record tool** 🔲 or the
Previous Record tool 🔲 to open another record.

Choose   **Apsimak** for all the remaining customers. **Click Save And Close** to
return to the Home window.

When you open the sales journal and choose any customer on record, Apsimak will
be entered automatically in the Salesperson field.

Continue with the **transactions** for June.

Memo #20   **Dated June 1/18**
2
Add shortcuts for entries in other journals.

Memo #21   **Dated June 2/18**
3
Complete an adjusting entry to reverse the year-end accrued wages entry for
$1 150. (Debit 2250 Accrued Wages and credit 5420 Wages: Support Staff.)

Cash Purchase Invoice #OA-2378   **Dated June 2/18**
4
From Otto's Autos, $420 plus $21 GST for maintenance service and repairs to
delivery truck. Invoice total $441. Paid by cheque #841. Change the default tax
code to G for this transaction.

Payment Cheque #842   **Dated June 2/18**
5
To Thirst Quenchers, $3 450 in payment of account. Reference invoice #TQ-644.

Purchase Invoice #TQ-845   **Dated June 3/18**
6
From Thirst Quenchers, $580 plus $29 GST for taxable beverages and $310 for tax
exempt beverages. Invoice total $919. Terms: net 30. Store as a bi-weekly
recurring entry.

Purchase Invoice #MSB-12990   **Dated June 5/18**
7
From Midnight Sun Bakery, $1 150 for tax exempt freshly baked goods delivered
daily and invoiced weekly. Terms: 1/10, n/30. Store as a weekly recurring entry.

Purchase Invoice #SS-4556   **Dated June 5/18**
8
From Stage Stagers, $680 plus $34 GST for costumes and wigs. Invoice total
$714. Terms: 2/15, n/30. Create a new Group asset account: 1340 Costumes.

Sales Invoice #352   **Dated June 5/18**
9
To Literati Borealis, $1 200 plus $60 GST for group ticket sales. Invoice total
$1 260. Terms: 1/15, n/30. Enter Apsimak as the salesperson. Store as a
recurring bi-weekly transaction.

Receipt #465   **Dated June 6/18**
10
From Literati Borealis, cheque #612 for $4 158 in payment of account, including
$42 discount for early payment. Reference invoice #344.

Cash Purchase Invoice #GN-2991   **Dated June 6/18**
11
From Grey Eyes Narwal (use Quick Add), $6 500 plus $325 GST for copyright
permission to perform his play. Invoice total $6 825 paid in full with cheque
#843. Create a new Group expense account: 5120 Copyright Expenses.

NOTES
You will need shortcuts for Create General Journal (Company), Create Supplier Invoice and Pay Supplier Invoices (Payables), View Employees, Payroll Cheque Run and Create Paycheque (Employees & Payroll).
You can Pay Remittances and Make Other Payments from the Pay Supplier Invoices transaction drop-down list. You can adjust paycheques from the Payroll Journal.

PRO VERSION
pro Purchase will replace Supplier for the shortcut labels.

NOTES
Enter the purchase from Thirst Quenchers on two separate invoice lines so that you can apply the correct tax codes.

WARNING!
Remember not to include the discount for the second invoice in payments and receipts.

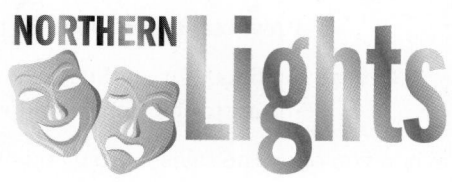

12

Northern Lights Theatre
Employee Time Summary Sheet #21

Cheque Date: June 7, 2018   Pay period end: June 7, 2018

Employee SIN	A. Usher 931 771 620	B. Ridges 552 846 826	T. Tikett 218 738 631	K. Kabanza 638 912 634	F. Player 726 911 134	P. Staige 822 546 859	J. Apsimak 422 946 541
Week 1	40	40					
Regular hrs	40	40					
Overtime hrs	2	—					
Number sold	—	530					
Benefits	90.38	10.38					
Loan	-25.00*	—					
Sick leave days	—	—					
Personal days	—	1**					
Chq/DD #	Chq 845	Chq 844					

* $100 loan being repaid at $25 per paycheque
** personal day to enroll in university course

Completed by: *Tikett 6/7/18*

SESSION DATE – JUNE 14, 2018

13

Memo #22   **Dated June 8/18**

Ridges returned her paycheque because the overtime hours were not included. Adjust her paycheque to add 4 hours of overtime. Post this entry with cheque #846 (use the next cheque number when prompted).

14

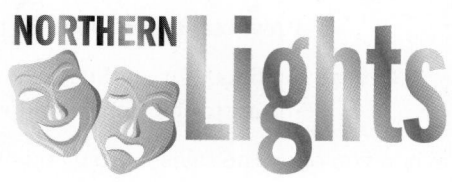

Memo #23
From Owner's Desk

Dated June 9/18

Apsimak received her income tax assessment and must pay additional taxes for the previous year. She has Canada Revenue Agency approval to pay at the rate of $100 per month for the rest of the year.
Modify the Payroll Settings to add Tax Arrears as Deduction4 (Names, Deductions) with the linked payable account (2470 Tax Arrears Payable).
Add the Receiver General as the Remittance supplier linked to this deduction with monthly remittances starting June 30.
Add the $100 deduction to Apsimak's ledger record (Deductions Tab).

M. Promtou

15

Payment Cheque #847   Dated June 9/18

To Stage Stagers, $6 379.80 in payment of account, including $130.20 discount for early payment. Reference invoice #SS-4011.

16

Receipt #466   Dated June 10/18

From Polar Discoveries, cheque #3774 for $8 316 in payment of account, including $84 discount for early payment. Reference invoice #348.

17

Sales Invoice #353   Dated June 11/18

To Whitehorse Little Theatre, $3 200 plus $160 GST for group ticket sales. Invoice total $3 360. Terms: 1/15, n/30. Enter Apsimak as the salesperson. Store as a recurring bi-weekly transaction.

18

Purchase Invoice #MSB-13428   Dated June 12/18

From Midnight Sun Bakery, $1 150 for tax exempt freshly baked goods delivered daily and invoiced weekly. Terms: 1/10, n/30. Recall stored transaction.

19

Sales Invoice #354   Dated June 12/18

To SAD Foundation, $6 000 plus $300 GST for theatre fundraising event. Invoice total $6 300. Terms: 1/15, n/30. Enter Apsimak as the salesperson.

20

Sales Invoice #355   Dated June 13/18

To Polar Discoveries, $4 000 plus $200 GST for group ticket sales. Invoice total $4 200. Terms: 1/15, n/30. Enter Apsimak as the salesperson. Store as a recurring bi-weekly transaction.

21

Payment Cheque #848   Dated June 13/18

To Midnight Sun Bakery, $1 138.50 in payment of account, including $11.50 discount for early payment. Reference invoice #MSB-12990.

22

NORTHERN Lights

Northern Lights Theatre
Employee Time Summary Sheet #22

Cheque Date: June 14, 2018   Pay period end: June 14, 2018

Employee SIN	A. Usher 931 771 620	B. Ridges 552 846 826	T. Tikett 218 738 631	K. Kabanza 638 912 634	F. Player 726 911 134	P. Staige 822 546 859	J. Apsimak 422 946 541
Week 1	pd	pd	40	40			
Week 2	40	40	40	42			
Regular hrs	40	40	80	80			
Overtime hrs	—	—	—	2			
Number sold	—	470	990	—			
Benefits	90.38	10.38	101.54	41.54			
Loan	-25.00	200.00*	-50.00	-50.00			
Sick leave days	—	—	—	—			
Personal days	1	—	—	—			
Chq/DD #	Chq 850	Chq 849	DD243	DD242			

* new loan to be repaid at $50 per paycheque

Completed by: *Tikett 6/14/18*

NOTES

Type –25 in the Loans This Period field for Usher and –50 for Tikett to recover the loans. Type 200 in the Loans This Period for Ridges to add the new loan.

Type 90.38 in the Benefits This Period field for Usher and 101.54 for Tikett.

Cash Purchase Invoice #YTE-78522   Dated June 14/18

23

From YT Energy, $600 plus $30 GST for one month of hydro services. Invoice total $630 due within 10 days to avoid interest penalty. Paid in full with cheque #851.

Cash Purchase #YTT-11229   Dated June 14/18

24

From Yukon Telephone, $360 plus $18 GST for one month of telephone services. Invoice total $378. Paid in full with cheque #852.

SESSION DATE – JUNE 21, 2018

Purchase Invoice #TQ-1285   Dated June 17/18

25

From Thirst Quenchers, $580 plus $29 GST for taxable beverages and $310 for tax exempt beverages. Invoice total $919. Terms: net 30. Recall stored entry.

Purchase Invoice #SS-8256   Dated June 18/18

26

From Stage Stagers, $5 050 plus $252.50 GST for building stage set. Invoice total $5 302.50. Terms: 2/15, n/30. Create a new Group expense account: 5250 Set Building Expenses.

Sales Invoice #356   Dated June 19/18

27

To Literati Borealis, $1 200 plus $60 GST for group ticket sales. Invoice total $1 260. Terms: 1/15, n/30. Enter Apsimak as the salesperson. Recall stored entry.

Purchase Invoice #MSB-14102   Dated June 19/18

28

From Midnight Sun Bakery, $1 150 for tax exempt freshly baked goods delivered daily and invoiced weekly. Terms: 1/10, n/30. Recall stored entry.

Payment Cheque #853   Dated June 19/18

29

To Stage Stagers, cheque #853 for $5 896.17 in payment of invoices #SS-4556 and SS-8256 and including $120.33 discount for early payment.

30

> # NORTHERN Lights
>
> Memo #24
> From Owner's Desk
>
> Dated June 20/18
> Tikett will receive an increase in his hourly wage because he will
> have more responsiblity for administration for Northern Lights.
> He is taking over some of the tasks formerly completed by Apsimak.
> Modify Tikett's ledger record. His new wage rate will be $20
> per regular hour and $30 for each hour of overtime work.
>
> *M. Promton*

Receipt #467   Dated June 20/18

31

From Polar Discoveries, cheque #5120 for $4 158 in payment of account, including $42 discount for early payment. Reference invoice #355.

NOTES

Apsimak will be entered as the salesperson in the stored transaction.

NOTES

Employee income is entered on the Income tab screen. Refer to page 331.

Receipt #468   **Dated June 20/18**

`32`

From Literati Borealis, cheque #2692 for $1 247.40 in payment of account, including $12.60 discount for early payment. Reference invoice #352.

Receipt #469   **Dated June 20/18**

`33`

From SAD Foundation, cheque #4439 for $3 237 in partial payment of account. Reference invoice #354.

Cash Purchase Invoice #BE-6998   **Dated June 21/18**

`34`

From Blackfoot Equipment (use Quick Add), $540 plus $27 GST to repair sound equipment. Invoice total $567 paid by cheque #854.

Employee Time Summary Sheet #23   **Dated June 21/18**

`35`

For the pay period ending June 21, 2018

Name of Employee	Regular Hours	Overtime Hours	Number Sold	Benefits	Loan (Repaid)	Sick Days	Personal Days	Direct Deposit
Usher, Ayla	40	2	–	$90.38	–$25	1	–	No
Ridges, Bev	40	2	520	$10.38	–$50	–	–	No

a. Using Employee Time Summary Sheet #23 and the Employee Information Sheet, complete payroll for the weekly paid employees. Use the Payroll Journal or the Payroll Run Journal.
b. Recover $25 loaned to Usher and recover $50 loaned to Ridges.
c. Issue cheques #855 and #856.

NOTES

Type –25 in the Loans This Period field for Usher and –50 for Ridges to recover these amounts.

Type 90.38 in the Benefits This Period field for Usher.

SESSION DATE – JUNE 30, 2018

Payment Cheque #857   **Dated June 22/18**

`36`

To Midnight Sun Bakery, cheque #857 for $1 138.50 in payment of invoice #MSB-13428, including $11.50 discount for early payment.

Sales Invoice #357   **Dated June 25/18**

`37`

To Whitehorse Little Theatre, $3 200 plus $160 GST for group ticket sales. Invoice total $3 360. Terms: 1/15, n/30. Enter Apsimak as the salesperson. Recall stored transaction.

Purchase Invoice #MSB-15029   **Dated June 26/18**

`38`

From Midnight Sun Bakery, $1 150 for tax exempt freshly baked goods delivered daily and invoiced weekly. Terms: 1/10, n/30. Recall stored transaction.

Memo #25   **Dated June 26/18**

`39`

From Manager: Receipt #469 from SAD Foundation for $3 237 was entered incorrectly. On June 20, cheque #4439 for $6 237 was received from SAD Foundation in full payment of invoice #354, including $63 for early payment. Adjust or reverse the original receipt and enter the correct receipt amount.

Sales Invoice #358   **Dated June 27/18**

`40`

To Polar Discoveries, $4 000 plus $200 GST for group ticket sales. Invoice total $4 200. Terms: 1/15, n/30. Enter Apsimak as the salesperson. Recall stored transaction.

NOTES

If you use the Adjust Receipt tool to correct the receipt, Sage 50 will automatically make the reversing entry. Delete the original Payment Amount. You will need to enter the amount of discount taken manually. It may be easier to reverse the receipt (refer to page 175) and then enter the customer's payment correctly.

When you reverse the receipt, the new receipt number will be updated to 470.

Bank Debit Memo #532281   **Dated June 28/18**

41

From NorthWest Bank, $2 045 was withdrawn from the chequing account for the following pre-authorized transactions:

Bank charges	$ 45
Interest on bank loan	120
Reduction of principal on bank loan	880
Interest on mortgage	750
Reduction of principal on mortgage	250

Create new Group account: 5110 Interest Expense

Employee Time Summary Sheet #24   **Dated June 28/18**

42

For the pay period ending June 28, 2018

Name of Employee	Regular Hours	Overtime Hours	Number Sold	Benefits	Loan (Repaid)	Sick Days	Personal Days	Direct Deposit
Usher Ayla	40	–	–	$90.38	–$25	–	–	No
Ridges, Bev	40	2	510	$10.38	–$50	–	–	No
Tikett, Taika	80	2	1 030	$101.54	–$50	–	–	Yes
Kabanza, Kay	80	–	–	$41.54	–$50	1	–	Yes

a. Using Employee Time Summary Sheet #24 and the Employee Information Sheet, complete payroll for all employees. Use the Payroll Journal or the Payroll Run Journal.
b. Recover $25 loaned to Usher, $50 from Ridges, $50 from Tikett and $50 from Kabanza.
c. Issue cheques #858 and #859, and DD #244 and #245.

Visa Sales Invoice #359   **Dated June 30/18**

43

To one-time customers, $6 000 plus $300 GST for single ticket purchases during June. Invoice total $6 300 paid by Visa and deposited to Bank: Credit Card. Enter Apsimak as the salesperson.

Cash Sales Invoice #360   **Dated June 30/18**

44

To one-time customers, $8 600 plus $430 GST for concession sales and $9 600 plus $480 GST for movie ticket sales during June. Sales total $19 110 deposited to chequing account.

Memo #26   **Dated June 30/18**

45

Complete an adjusting entry for one month of prepaid insurance expired. The one-year insurance policy was purchased on December 31, 2017, for $2 400.

Memo #27   **Dated June 30/18**

46

Pay Apsimak, Player and Staige their monthly salary. Issue cheque #860 and deposit slips #246 and #247. Jiane Apsimak earned a sales commission of $818 for the month of June and took five days' vacation.

Memo #28   **Dated June 30/18**

47

Complete month-end adjusting entries for supplies used in June. Create a new Group expense account: 5130 Office Supplies Used.

Food inventory sold	$1 680
Beverage inventory sold	1 050
Cleaning supplies used	220
Office supplies used	120

Memo #29   **Dated June 30/18**

48

Bev Ridges is taking one week of vacation time. Release her retained vacation pay and issue cheque #861. Enter 40 as the number of hours for this paycheque because this replaces her regular work days during this week.

NOTES
Type –25 in the Loans This Period field for Usher and –50 for Ridges, Tikett and Kabanza to recover the loans.
Type 90.38 in the Benefits This Period field for Usher and 101.54 for Tikett.

NOTES
Do not enter Apsimak as the salesperson for the non-ticket sales, and be sure to choose the correct revenue account.

NOTES
The travel allowance for Player and Staige is set up in their ledger record so that the amount is included automatically as a non-taxable income.
Use the Vacation Days Taken field on the Entitlements tab screen to enter the vacation days.

NOTES
Refer to page 275 if you need help preparing the vacation paycheque.

Displaying Salesperson Reports

Click the **Report Centre icon** in the Home window.

Click **Receivables** to open the list of customer reports. Two additional reports are available when we add salespersons to journal entries.

✓ **Memo #30**   **Dated June 30/18**
49 Adjust the paycheque for Apsimak. She has returned her deposit pay stub because her earned commission was incorrect. Use the Sales By Salesperson Report to verify that the correct amount was $928, not $818. Prepare direct deposit #248 to replace the incorrect payment.

NOTES
Use the next available direct deposit number for the payroll adjustment.

Displaying the Sales by Salesperson Report

Click **Sales By Salesperson Summary** in the Select A Report list.

Click **Modify This Report** to open the report options:

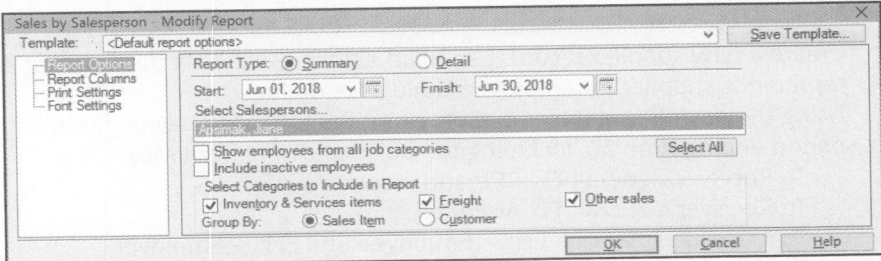

NOTES
You can also choose the Reports menu, then choose Receivables and click Sales By Salesperson to open the report options screen.

Apsimak is the only employee designated as a salesperson, so only her name appears on the list, and she is already selected. You have the option to include all employees, but we do not need them all — we want Apsimak's June sales data. The default dates for Start and Finish cover the period we want. You can group the sales information by customer or by sales item. You can also include information for freight and other non-inventory sales. For Northern Lights, we need to include only the Other Sales because inventory and freight do not apply. You can prepare this report as a **Detail Report** with a line item for each sale, or as a **Summary Report** with totals only for each item or customer.

> You can exclude amounts that do not apply. Click Freight and Inventory & Services Items to remove the ✓s.

NOTES
You can also access the Sales by Salesperson Report from the Reports menu under Services Reports. The Services Reports entry will be renamed to match the industry type for other companies. Thus, this report may be named Business Reports, Retail Reports, Construction Reports and so on in the Reports menu.

Click **OK** to open the report. The total sales revenue for May was $92 800, so Apsimak's commission amount (1 percent) should be changed to $928.

Close the displayed **report**.

Adjust the **payroll entry** to increase the commission amount. Remember to **recalculate taxes**. **Post** the revised **entry**.

Displaying the Sales by Job Category Report

This next report is similar except that it combines the information for all employees in each category. Because we have only one person in the Sales category, reporting by this category should give us the same information as the Sales By Salesperson Report.

Open the **Report Centre**.

Click **Sales By Job Category Summary** in the Select A Report list.

NOTES
You can also choose the Reports menu, then choose Receivables and click Sales By Job Categories to open the report options screen.

NOTES

Because employees in the <None> category are salespersons, this category is included in the report options.

NOTES

For both the Sales by Salesperson and Job Category reports, you can drill down to the Detail Report from the Summary Report. From the Detail Report you can drill down to look up the sales invoices.

NOTES

Create a new supplier record for Canadian Actors' Guild.

Tax Code: No tax

Terms: net 1.

You cannot add the remittance supplier when the journal is open.

Refer to page 338 for help with adding a remittance supplier.

WARNING!

When you choose Receiver General for the second remittance (Tax Arrears), you must reset the End Of Remitting Period date to June 30. The date automatically advances after the tax remittance. When prompted, save the new remittance period dates.

Repeat this procedure for VRSP, the second remittance to Manulife.

Click   Modify This Report to open the report options:

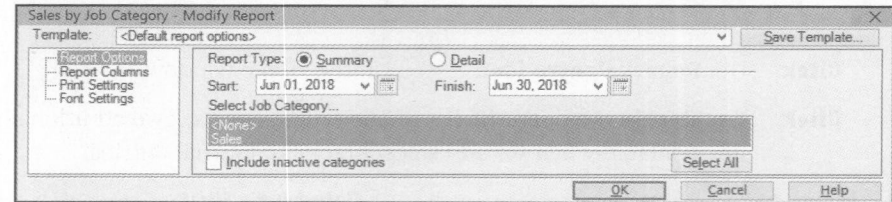

Again the default dates give us the report for the month we need. Categories that do not have salespersons in them are not included in this report. You can create a **Detail Report** with a listing for each individual invoice or a **Summary Report** that provides the total for each selected category.

Click   Sales to select only this category. **Click OK** to display the total sales for all persons in the Sales category.

Close   the report when finished. **Close** the **Report Centre**.

Enter   the remittances for June 30 to complete the application.

Memo #31   **Dated June 30/18**

50

Create a new supplier record: Canadian Actors' Guild. Link this supplier as the remittance supplier for employee Guild Fees deductions.

Using the payroll remittance option, remit the following payroll taxes for the pay period ending June 30, including the balance owing from May:

    To Receiver General: EI , CPP and Income Tax

    To Receiver General: Tax Arrears

    To Manulife Financial: EHC - Employee and EHC - Employer

    To Manulife Financial: VRSP

    To Yukon Workers' Compensation Board: WCB

    To Canadian Actors' Guild: Guild Fees

Issue cheques #862 through #867 in payment.

REVIEW

The Student DVD with Data Files includes Review Questions and Supplementary Cases for this chapter.

OBJECTIVES

After completing this chapter, you should be able to

- **enter** inventory-related purchase transactions
- **enter** inventory-related sale transactions of goods and services
- **make** inventory adjustments
- **assemble** new inventory items from other inventory
- **enter** returns on sales and purchases
- **create** credit notes
- **enter** sales to preferred customers
- **enter** freight on purchases
- **understand** the integration of the Inventory Ledger with the Payables, Receivables and General ledgers
- **create** new inventory items
- **display** and **print** inventory reports

COMPANY INFORMATION

Company Profile

NOTES

Flabuless Fitness
199 Warmup Rd., Unit 500
Winnipeg, MB R8T 3B7
Tel 1: (204) 642-2348 (B-FIT)
Tel 2: (800) 448-2348 (B-FIT)
Fax: (204) 642-9100
Business No.: 245 138 121

Flabuless Fitness, in Winnipeg, Manitoba, sells a wide range of fitness equipment and accessories for home and light commercial use. Stephen Reeves, the owner, opened his business a few years ago after retiring from his career as a professional athlete, gaining business experience with another store and completing some business courses. Reeves has two employees to assist with the work in the store. Reeves works mostly outside the store, promoting the business.

Several of the equipment suppliers offer discounts to the store for early payment. Accounts are also set up for other supplies and services that are provided locally. The store uses a credit card for some of these purchases.

Most customers are located in the Winnipeg region, but Reeves has contacted some colleges and hotels in nearby US cities as potential customers.

All account customers are given discounts for early payment, and some preferred customers receive additional discounts. Individual customers who pay by cash, debit or credit card do not receive any discounts and pay for delivery.

NOTES

RST, Retail Sales Tax, is the name of the provincial sales tax in Manitoba.

All items and services sold by the store are set up as inventory so that sales can be monitored. GST is charged on all sales and services. RST (Retail Sales Tax) is charged on sales of inventory items and equipment assembly, but not on books or on other services. The store pays GST and RST on all taxable purchases, but inventory purchased for resale in the store is exempt from RST.

Reeves' assistant used the following information to convert the accounting records to Sage 50 on February 1, 2018:

- Chart of Accounts
- Post-Closing Trial Balance
- Supplier Information
- Customer Information
- Employee Information
- Inventory Information
- Accounting Procedures

CHART OF POSTABLE ACCOUNTS

FLABULESS FITNESS

ASSETS
Current Assets
1060 Bank Account: Chequing
1080 Bank Account: MasterCard
1090 Bank Account: Visa
1100 Investments
1200 Accounts Receivable
1260 Office Supplies
1265 Linen Supplies
1280 Prepaid Insurance

Inventory Assets
1520 Accessories
1540 Fitness Equipment
1550 Home Gym Equipment
1560 Books

Centre & Equipment
1640 Computer Equipment
1670 Furniture & Fixtures
1700 Retail Premises
1730 Van ▶

▶LIABILITIES
Current Liabilities
2100 Bank Loan
2200 Accounts Payable
2250 Credit Card Payable
2310 EI Payable
2320 CPP Payable
2330 Income Tax Payable
2410 Group Insurance - Employer
2420 Group Insurance - Employee
2460 WCB Payable
2640 RST Payable
2650 GST Charged on Sales
2670 GST Paid on Purchases

Long Term Liabilities
2820 Mortgage Payable

EQUITY
3560 Share Capital
3600 Current Earnings ▶

▶REVENUE
General Revenue
4020 Revenue from Sales
4040 Revenue from Services
4060 Sales Discounts
4150 Interest Revenue
4200 Freight Revenue

EXPENSE
Operating Expenses
5010 Advertising and Promotion
5020 Bank Charges
5030 Credit Card Fees
5035 Promotional Package Services
5040 Damaged Inventory
5060 Cost of Goods Sold
5065 Cost of Services
5070 Cost Variance
5080 Freight Expense
5090 Purchase Discounts ▶

▶5100 Purchases Returns
5130 Depreciation
5190 Delivery Expense
5200 Hydro Expense
5210 Insurance Expense
5220 Interest Expenses
5240 Maintenance of Premises
5250 Supplies Used
5280 Telephone Expenses
5285 Van Maintenance & Operating Expense

Payroll Expenses
5300 Salaries
5310 Commissions
5330 EI Expense
5340 CPP Expense
5350 WCB Expense
5370 Gp Insurance Expense

POST-CLOSING TRIAL BALANCE

FLABULESS FITNESS

Feb. 1, 2018		Debits	Credits				Debits	Credits
1060	Bank Account: Chequing	$ 77 988.00		▶	2100	Bank Loan		$ 50 000.00
1080	Bank Account: MasterCard	9 350.00			2200	Accounts Payable		16 800.00
1090	Bank Account: Visa	8 635.00			2250	Credit Card Payable		255.00
1100	Investments	108 250.00			2310	EI Payable		363.00
1200	Accounts Receivable	14 690.00			2320	CPP Payable		765.00
1260	Office Supplies	300.00			2330	Income Tax Payable		1 692.00
1265	Linen Supplies	450.00			2410	Group Insurance - Employer		48.00
1280	Prepaid Insurance	4 800.00			2420	Group Insurance - Employee		48.00
1520	Accessories	7 010.00			2460	WCB Payable		284.00
1540	Fitness Equipment	58 500.00			2640	RST Payable		2 400.00
1550	Home Gym Equipment	15 120.00			2650	GST Charged on Sales		3 430.00
1560	Books	5 200.00			2670	GST Paid on Purchases	$ 1 495.00	
1640	Computer Equipment	8 000.00			2820	Mortgage Payable		180 000.00
1670	Furniture & Fixtures	2 000.00			3560	Share Capital		295 703.00
1700	Retail Premises	200 000.00					$551 788.00	$551 788.00
1730	Van	30 000.00		▶				

SUPPLIER INFORMATION

FLABULESS FITNESS

Supplier Name (Contact)	Address	Phone No. Fax No.	E-mail Web Site	Terms Tax ID
Feelyte Gym Accessories (Stretch Theraband)	7 Onondaga Dr. Vancouver, BC V4G 4S5	Tel: (604) 588-3846 Fax: (604) 588-7126	stretch@feelyte.com feelyte.com	2/10, n/30 (before tax) 466 254 108
Footlink Corporation (Onna Treadmill)	39 Treadwell St. Winnipeg, MB R6M 3K9	Tel: (204) 777-8133 Fax: (204) 777-8109	onna@footlink.com footlink.com	1/15, n/30 (before tax) 274 309 481
Grand Life Insurance			net 1	
Manitoba Bell (Annie Heard)	82 Wireless Alley Winnipeg, MB R3B 5R9	Tel: (204) 781-2355 bell.ca	heard@bell.ca	net 7
Manitoba Energy (Manny Watts)	91 NacNab St. Winnipeg, MB R3R 2L9	Tel: (204) 463-2664 mbenergy.ca	watts@mbenergy.ca	net 7
Prohealth Exercisers Inc. (C. Glider)	1500 Redmond Rd., Suite 100 Red River, MB R4S 1T4	Tel 1: (204) 597-4756 Tel 2: (888) 597-4756	glider@prohealth.ex.com prohealth.ex.com	2/10, n/30 (before tax) 344 566 799
Receiver General for Canada		Tel: (800) 561-7761	cra-arc.gc.ca	net 1
Riverview Sunoco (Mick Annick)	101 Niska Dr. Winnipeg, MB R3R 2H3	Tel: (204) 622-6181 goodforcars.com	mick@goodforcars.com	net 21
Trufit Depot (Varry Shapely)	43 Paling Ave. Hamilton, ON L8H 5J5	Tel: (905) 529-7235 Fax: (905) 529-2995	shapely@trufitdepot.ca trufitdepot.ca	2/5, n/20 (before tax) 244 573 650
Workers' Compensation Board			net 1	

OUTSTANDING SUPPLIER INVOICES

Supplier Name	Terms	Date	Inv/Chq No.	Amount	Tax	Total
Footlink Corporation	1/15, n/30 (before tax)	Jan. 20/18	FC-618	$16 000	$800	$16 800

CUSTOMER INFORMATION

FLABULESS FITNESS

Customer Name (Contact)	Address	Phone No. Fax No.	E-mail Web Site	Terms Credit Limit
Ariandanos Residence (Arianne Ariandanos)	29 Spinning Blvd. Winnipeg, MB R2P 2M2	Tel: (204) 762-8664	arianne@radiantway.com radiantway.com	2/5, n/15 $5 000
Botelli & Giroux, Lawyers (Gina Botelli)	30 Court St. Winnipeg, MB R3R 1C7	Tel: (204) 699-2911 Fax: (204) 697-2735	gina@botelli.giroux.com botelli.giroux.com	2/5, n/15 $10 000
*Brandon University (Outov Shape)	Kinesiology Dept. Brandon University Brandon, MB R7A 6A9	Tel 1: (204) 529-3000 Tel 2: (204) 529-3198 Fax: (204) 529-3477	oshape@brandonu.ca brandonu.ca	2/15, n/30 $10 000
Lavendar Estates (Katherine Harris)	9 Lavender Ct. Winnipeg, MB R2X 3J6	Tel: (204) 782-7300 Fax: (204) 782-8190	harris@lavender.com lavender.com	2/5, n/15 $5 000
*Red River College (Phat Nomore)	Physical Education Dept. Red River College Winnipeg, MB R3H 0J9	Tel 1: (204) 622-9250 Tel 2: (204) 622-9238 Fax: (204) 622-9729	nomore@rcc.ca rcc.ca	2/15, n/30 $10 000
*The Forks Film Corporation (Francine Despardieu)	6 Gilroy St. Winnipeg, MB R3C 2M2	Tel: (204) 787-1226	fdes@forksfilm.com forksfilm.com	2/15, n/30 $10 000

NOTES: The * indicates preferred price list customers. A record is also set up for Cash & Credit Card Sales Customers.

OUTSTANDING CUSTOMER INVOICES

Customer Name	Terms	Date	Inv/Chq No.	Amount	Total
Brandon University	2/10, n/30 (after tax)	Jan. 29/18	2199	$9 040	$9 040
Red River College	2/10, n/30 (after tax)	Jan. 25/18	2194	$5 650	$5 650
				Grand Total	$14 690

EMPLOYEE INFORMATION SHEET

FLABULESS FITNESS

Employee	George Prekor	Asumpta Kisangel
Address	55 Track Rd.	300 Meditation Circle
	Winnipeg, MB R8B 2V7	Winnipeg, MB R4G 4K8
Telephone	(204) 426-1817	(204) 688-5778
Social Insurance No.	532 548 625	488 655 333
Date of Birth (mm-dd-yy)	09/18/74	05/24/80
Federal (Manitoba) Tax Exemption - TD1		
Basic Personal	$11 474 (9 134)	$11 474 (9 134)
Employee Earnings		
Salary (Hours per Period)	$4 000.00 (150 Hours)	$4 000.00 (150 Hours)
Commission	2% of sales (less returns)	2% of sales (less returns)
Employee Deductions		
Group Insurance	$24	$24
EI, CPP & Income Tax	Calculations are built into Sage 50.	

Employee Profiles and TD1 Information

Asumpta Kisangel and **George Prekor** both assist with sales in the store, provide the personal training services to customers and assemble the equipment for customers. Kisangel also does the accounting and teaches yoga classes. Both are salaried employees who receive their $4 000 monthly pay by cheque and contribute $24 each period to a group insurance plan. This amount is matched by the employer — a benefit for the employees. Kisangel and Prekor are single and self-supporting with no dependants and no other deductions, so they have the basic claim amounts for income tax. Instead of vacation pay, they take three weeks of vacation with regular pay each year. Neither has received any payroll advances or loans.

Both employees are listed as salespersons. They receive a sales commission of 2 percent of their net sales (sales less returns) with each paycheque. Their names are entered as salespersons on invoices so that the commissions can be tracked for the Sales by Salesperson Report.

INVENTORY INFORMATION

FLABULESS FITNESS

Code	Description	Min Stock	Prices Reg	(Pref)	Unit	Qty on Hand	Total (Cost)	Taxes
Accessories: Total asset value $7 010 (Linked Accounts: Asset 1520, Revenue 4020, COGS 5050, Variance 5070)								
A010	Body Fat Scale	2	$ 150	(130)	unit	20	$1 400	GP
A020	Yoga/Pilates Mat	5	40	(35)	each	60	1 200	GP
A030	Dumbbells	25	2.50	(2.20)	kg	600	540	GP
A040	Jump Rope: Weighted	10	40	(35)	each	20	420	GP
A050	Heart Rate Monitor	4	90	(80)	unit	20	800	GP
A060	Power Blocks	3	300	(250)	set	5	750	GP
A070	Stability Ball	5	12	(10)	each	30	180	GP
A080	Weight/Workout Bench	2	175	(150)	each	10	840	GP
A090	Workout Gloves: all sizes	25	15	(13)	pair	35	280	GP
A100	Aerobic Stepper w/ Risers	5	70	(60)	each	15	600	GP
Fitness Equipment: Total asset value $58 500 (Linked Accounts: Asset 1540, Revenue 4020, COGS 5060, Variance 5070)								
E010	Elliptical Exerciser: AE-200	2	2 100	(1 900)	unit	6	6 600	GP
E020	Elliptical Exerciser: LE-400	2	2 600	(2 300)	unit	6	8 400	GP
E030	Bicycle: Dual Action Calorie Counter	2	850	(720)	unit	12	5 400	GP
E040	Bicycle: Recumbent R-80	2	1 100	(960)	unit	12	7 200	GP
E050	Step Master: Adjustable SC-A60	2	1 900	(1 700)	unit	6	5 700	GP
E060	Treadmill: Basic T-800B	3	1 400	(1 220)	unit	12	9 000	GP
E070	Treadmill: Deluxe T-1100D	3	2 800	(2 500)	unit	12	16 200	GP
Home Gyms Total asset value $15 120 (Linked Accounts: Asset 1550, Revenue 4020, COGS 5060, Variance 5070)								
E080	Home Gym: Basic HG-1400	2	1 600	(1 380)	set	6	$5 520	GP
E090	Home Gym: Deluxe Multi HG-1402	2	2 950	(2 700)	set	6	9 600	GP
Books Total asset value $5 200 (Linked Accounts: Asset 1560, Revenue 4020, COGS 5060, Variance 5070)								
B010	Books: Fitness Guide	15	40	(35)	each	208	5 200	G (RST Exempt)
Services (Linked Accounts: Revenue 4040, COGS 5065)								
S010	Personal Trainer: 1 hour		80	(70)	hour			G (RST Exempt)
S020	Personal Trainer: 1/2 day		200	(190)	1/2 day			G (RST Exempt)
S030	Personal Trainer: full day		400	(380)	day			G (RST Exempt)
S040	Yoga Instructor: 1 hour		100	(95)	hour			G (RST Exempt)
S050	Yoga Instructor: 1/2 day		200	(190)	1/2 day			G (RST Exempt)
S060	Equipment Assembly/Demonstration		75	(60)	job			GP (not exempt for RST)

NOTES: Buying units, selling units and stocking units are the same for all items. Inventory is not oversold.

Accounting Procedures

The Goods and Services Tax (GST): Remittances

Flabuless Fitness uses the regular method for remittance of the Goods and Services Tax. GST collected is recorded as a liability in *GST Charged on Sales*. GST paid, recorded in *GST Paid on Purchases*, decreases the liability. The store files its return with the Canada Revenue Agency (CRA) quarterly, either requesting a refund or remitting the balance owing.

NOTES
RST is not usually charged on personal services, but it is charged on services that are applied to items that RST is applied to.

Books and children's clothing are normally exempt from RST.

Retail (Provincial) Sales Tax (RST)

Retail Sales Tax of 8 percent is applied to all cash and credit sales of goods in Manitoba. Customers do not pay RST on the services provided by Flabuless Fitness, except for equipment assembly. RST on goods is remitted quarterly to the Minister of Finance.

RST at the rate of 8 percent is also paid on purchases that are not inventory items for resale. Because RST paid is not refundable, it is charged to the asset or expense account associated with the purchase, not to a separate account.

Sales Invoices

Flabuless Fitness allows customers to pay on account or by cash, cheque or credit card. The keystrokes for cash and credit card inventory transactions are similar to those for account sales, except for the method of payment. The program will automatically debit the appropriate bank account instead of *Accounts Receivable*.

Source documents for cash and credit card sales are presented as summaries to avoid a large number of small revenue transactions. A record for Cash & Credit Card Sales is set up to track these sales.

You can print and e-mail sales invoices through the program. Before posting the Sales Journal transaction, preview the invoice. Then click the Print button or the E-mail button.

Credit Card Sales and Purchases

Flabuless Fitness has set up its accounts for credit card sales and purchases.

Freight Expenses and Charges

When a business purchases inventory items, the cost of any freight that cannot be directly allocated to a specific item must be charged to *Freight Expense*. This amount is regarded as an expense rather than a charge to an inventory asset account. Freight or delivery charges to customers are allocated to *Freight Revenue*.

Discounts

To encourage customers to settle their accounts early, Flabuless Fitness offers its account customers a 2 percent discount on before-tax amounts if they pay their accounts within five days. Discounts are calculated automatically when the payment terms are set up and the customer is eligible for the discount. These new terms begin on February 1. There are no discounts on cash or credit card sales.

In addition, some customers have preferred price list status that entitles them to reduced prices. Regular and preferred prices are set up in the Inventory Ledger, so the prices are entered automatically. For preferred customers, the discount period is extended to 15 days with net payment due in 30 days.

Promotional Packages

Each February, Flabuless Fitness offers special promotional packages that include a variety of accessories, one exercise bicycle and either yoga training or personal trainer time. Assembly of these packages incurs additional costs for the training service.

Returns

Returned goods are a normal part of retail businesses. Flabuless Fitness provides full refunds on unused items returned within 14 days. Some items such as gloves cannot be returned for hygienic reasons. Returned items are debited to the contra-revenue account *Sales Returns* so that the returns can be tracked. Refer to page 380.

Returns on purchases also occur regularly. Refer to page 382.

INSTRUCTIONS

1. **Record entries** for the source documents in Sage 50 using the Chart of Accounts, Trial Balance, and Supplier, Customer, Employee and Inventory Information provided. The procedures for entering each new type of transaction are outlined step by step in the Keystrokes section with the source documents.

2. **Print** the **reports** indicated on the following printing forms after finishing your entries. Instructions for inventory reports begin on page 388.

REPORTS

Accounts
- [ ] Chart of Accounts
- [ ] Account List
- [ ] General Journal Entries

Financial
- [✓] Balance Sheet date: Feb. 28
- [✓] Income Statement: Feb. 1 to Feb. 28
- [✓] Trial Balance date: Feb. 28
- [✓] All Journal Entries: Feb. 1 to Feb. 28
- [✓] General Ledger accounts: 1520 1540 1550 4020 4040 from Feb. 1 to Feb. 28
- [ ] Statement of Cash Flows
- [ ] Cash Flow Projection Detail Report
- [✓] Gross Margin Income Statement: Feb. 1 to Feb. 28

Tax
- [ ] Report on

Banking
- [ ] Cheque Log Report

Payables
- [ ] Supplier List

- [ ] Supplier Aged
- [ ] Aged Overdue Payables
- [ ] Purchases Journal Entries
- [ ] Payments Journal Entries
- [ ] Supplier Purchases

Receivables
- [ ] Customer List
- [ ] Customer Aged
- [ ] Aged Overdue Receivables
- [ ] Sales Journal Entries
- [ ] Receipts Journal Entries
- [ ] Customer Sales
- [✓] Sales by Salesperson: Feb. 1 to Feb. 28
- [ ] Customer Statements

Payroll & Employees
- [ ] Employee List
- [✓] Summary: All employees
- [ ] Deductions & Expenses
- [ ] Remittances
- [ ] Payroll Journal Entries
- [ ] T4 Slips
- [ ] Record of Employment

- [ ] Year End Review (PIER)

Inventory & Services
- [ ] Inventory & Services List
- [✓] Summary
- [ ] Quantity
- [ ] Inventory Statistics
- [✓] Sales Summary for all Services: from Feb. 1 to Feb. 28
- [✓] Transaction Summary for A020 Yoga/Pilates Mat, all journals: Feb. 1 to Feb. 28
- [ ] Price Lists
- [✓] Item Assembly Journal Entries: Feb. 1 to Feb. 28
- [✓] Adjustments Journal Entries: Feb. 1 to Feb. 28

Mailing Labels
- [ ] Labels

Forecast & Analysis
- [ ] Forecast
- [ ] Customer Analysis
- [ ] Product Analysis
- [✓] Sales Analysis Report: Feb. 1 to Feb. 28

KEYSTROKES

Accounting for Inventory Sales

Open **SageData16\FLABULESS\FLABULESS** to access the data files for Flabuless Fitness.

Type 2 7 18 or **choose Feb. 7** from the calendar and **click OK**.

This will enter the session date February 7, 2018. The familiar Receivables module window appears. Inventory & Services has been added to the Modules pane list. Inventory sales are entered in the Sales Journal.

NOTES
If you are working from backups, restore the backup file SageData16\FLABULESS1.CAB or FLABULESS1 to SageData16\FLABULESS\FLABULESS.
Refer to the instructions in Chapter 1, page 24, if you need assistance with restoring files from backups.

The first transaction involves the sale of inventory items. Many of the steps are identical to those you used for sales in previous applications. You will be using the inventory database and all the Sales Invoice fields to complete this transaction.

Sales Invoice #3000   **Dated February 1, 2018**

Sold by Kisangel to Botelli & Giroux, Lawyers,

3	A050	Heart Rate Monitor	$ 90 /unit
40	A030	Dumbbells	2.50 /kg
1	E010	Elliptical Exerciser: AE-200	2 100 /unit
1	E020	Elliptical Exerciser: LE-400	2 600 /unit
2	E060	Treadmill: Basic T-800B	1 400 /unit
5	B010	Books: Fitness Guide (tax code G)	40 each
6	S040	Yoga Instructor: 1 hour (tax code G)	100 /hour
		Delivery (tax code G)	50
		GST	5%
		RST	8%

Terms: 2/5, n/15.

Click the **Sales Invoices icon** to open the familiar Sales Journal:

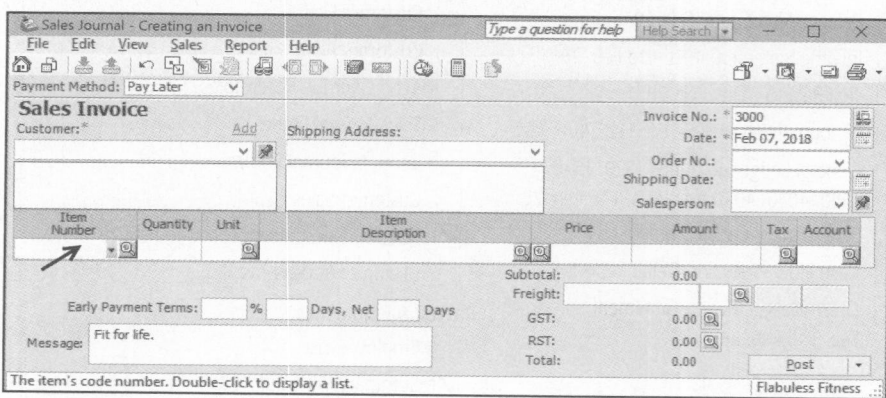

The Sales Journal looks the same as in earlier data files, except for the Sales Journal we customized for Phoebe's Photo Studio in Chapter 6. All the invoice fields are used when we sell inventory. Pay Later is correctly selected as the payment method.

Click the **Customer field list arrow** to display the list of customers.

Click **Botelli & Giroux, Lawyers** to enter the customer's name and address on the form.

The Shipping Address fields, Invoice number, payment terms and tax code defaults are all correct. If necessary, you can edit them. The Order No. is not used for invoices.

Click the **Date field Calendar icon** to advance the cursor. The default session date is incorrect.

Click **1** on the February calendar.

Click the **Salesperson field** and **choose Kisangel** as the salesperson.

One line is used for each inventory item or service sold by the business. A separate line would also be used for non-inventory sales and to enter returns or allowances.

Click the **Item Number field List icon**, or **click** the **field** and **press** _enter_ or **double-click** to access the inventory list:

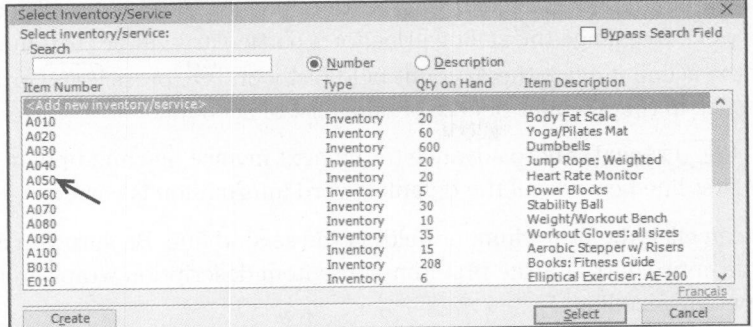

You can add new inventory items from the Select Inventory/Service screen, just as you can add accounts from the Select Account screen. Items are listed in order by number or code, and, for inventory items, available quantities are included for reference.

The cursor is in the Search field. We will bypass the Search field so that future references to this list will place the cursor in the list rather than in the Search field.

Click   Bypass Search Field so that the next time the cursor will start in the item list.

Click in the list and type the first letter of a code if you want to advance the list to the codes beginning with that letter.

Click   A050 Heart Rate Monitor from the list.

Click   Select to add the inventory item to your form. If you have made an incorrect selection, return to the Item Number field and reselect from the inventory list.

You can also type the code number in the Item Number field and press (tab), but you must match the case of the code number in the ledger.

The cursor moves to the Quantity field. The program adds information in each field automatically, based on the inventory record information. All the information except quantity and amount is added by default as soon as you enter the inventory item number. If you select a preferred customer, the default price is the preferred customer price instead of the regular selling price (refer to the screens on pages 379 and 380).

You should enter the number of units of this item sold in the Quantity field.

Type   3 Press (tab) .

If your company settings do not allow inventory levels to go below zero, the program prevents you from continuing when you enter a quantity greater than the available stock, more than 20 in this case, with this warning:

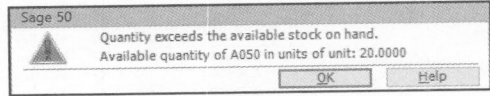

Click OK to return to the journal so you can reduce the quantity.

Since the remaining default information is correct, you do not need to change it. The default tax code — GP — is the code entered for the customer because the customer pays both GST at 5 percent and RST at 8 percent. Services have been set up in the Inventory Ledger so that by default RST is not applied.

The program automatically calculates an amount based on the selling price per unit. This figure appears in the Amount field.

The default revenue account for the item is entered, but it can be accepted or changed. You would change the account for returns and allowances or exceptional entries. Accept the default revenue account for this sale.

NOTES

If you want to search for items by description, you can type a letter in the Item Description field — the list will have all items that include the letter you typed and it will be sorted alphabetically by description.

To have all items sorted by description instead of by item number, click the List icon in the Description field.

The option to sort items by number or description in the Inventory Settings (page 662) applies only to lists in the Adjustments and Item Assembly journals.

NOTES

Inventory codes are case sensitive — you must type A050 in the journal (match the upper case A in the item code) to enter the item directly in the journal. To use the list of items, you can type a lower case letter to advance to a later part of the list.

NOTES

Inventory items can be oversold, but you must change the Inventory Ledger settings to allow the quantity on hand to go below zero. This setting is used in Chapter 13 and the setup for it is explained in Chapter 16.

No quantities for services are in the list because they are not held in stock.

NOTES

If your company settings allow, you may want to oversell the items if the customer is purchasing backordered inventory stock.

NOTES
If you have entered a default revenue account for the customer that is different from the one for the item, the account for the item replaces the customer's revenue account.

WARNING!
If you click the second line and it is used for part of the description for the first item, you may select and replace the first item instead.

NOTES
If you type the entire code in lower case letters (or upper case letters), the Item field drop-down list will include the single item. You can click it and press (tab) to advance to the Quantity field.

NOTES
The quantity for A050 has not yet been reduced because the sale has not been completed.

WARNING!
The cursor does not advance to the Quantity field when you select from the drop-down lists, so if you type the quantity before pressing (tab), you will enter an incorrect code.

NOTES
The inventory list is also available when you type in the Item Description field, but it is sorted by description instead of by item number.

NOTES
If you want to type in the item codes instead of using the selection list for each item, turn on Caps Lock for your keyboard. This will speed up your data entry and ensure that you are using the correct case. Type the item code and then press (tab) to advance to the Quantity column.

You can select another tax code from the Tax Code list if necessary. You can also edit the price to change the selling price for a particular item or customer. To change the account, click the Account field List icon, press (enter) or double-click in the Account field to obtain a list of accounts.

Press   (tab) **repeatedly** to advance to the next invoice line and update the first line because all the default record information is correct.

Or, you can click the Item Number field on the second line. Be sure you click below the entire entry for the first item if the item description wraps around to the second invoice line.

Type   a

The Item Number field now provides a drop-down item list. Click to select an item from this list. When you type the first letter or number of the code (in this case, the letter a) the drop-down list has the items starting with A. Eight items can be displayed at one time, but you can scroll down to access more items. You can also create a new inventory item from this drop-down list.

Click   **A030** and **press** (tab) to advance to the Quantity field. **Type**   40

Enter   the **remaining sale items** using the steps above.

As you complete each line and advance to the next, the totals and tax amounts at the bottom of the form are updated to include the last item entered. A new invoice line opens automatically.

GP — the customer's tax code — is entered as the tax code for the books and service items, but only GST is added to the invoice total — the RST amount does not increase when you add these items. We will confirm this when we review the journal entry.

To include more invoice lines on your screen, drag the lower frame of the Sales Journal window down or maximize the window.

At this stage, before adding delivery (freight) charges, the inventory portion of invoice is complete:

Click   the **first Freight field**, the amount field, below the Subtotal.

Type   50   **Press** (tab).

The customer's tax code, GP, is entered as the default, so you must change it. Freight is not automatically connected with a tax code.

Type   G or **press** (enter) to open the familiar list of tax codes. **Click G** and then **click Select**.

Press   (tab) to complete the journal entry:

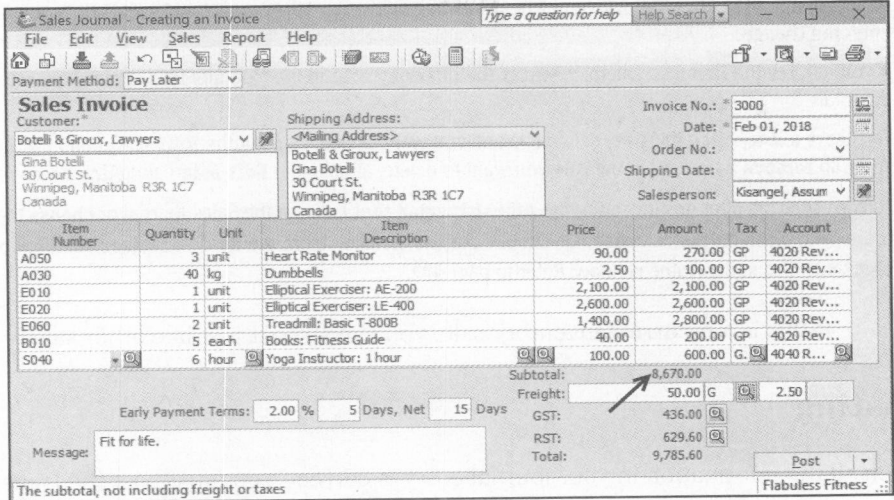

You should review the journal entry before posting it.

Reviewing the Inventory Sales Journal Transaction

Choose the **Report menu** and **click Display Sales Journal Entry**:

Account Number	Account Description	Debits	Credits
1200	Accounts Receivable	9,785.60	-
5060	Cost of Goods Sold	4,281.00	
1520	Accessories	-	156.00
1540	Fitness Equipment	-	4,000.00
1560	Books	-	125.00
2640	RST Payable	-	629.60
2650	GST Charged on Sales	-	436.00
4020	Revenue from Sales	-	8,070.00
4040	Revenue from Services	-	600.00
4200	Freight Revenue	-	50.00
Additional Date:	Additional Field:	14,066.60	14,066.60

Flabuless Fitness
Sales Journal Entry 02/01/2018 (J1)

RST and GST tax amounts are separated. RST is not charged on the sale of books or services — 8% × $7 870 = $629.60 — while GST is charged on sales and services plus freight — 5% × $8 720 = $436. Both taxes are calculated correctly because of the tax codes and exemptions assigned in the Inventory Ledger records. Books and services are marked as exempt for RST.

All relevant accounts have been updated automatically because the Inventory and Receivables ledgers are linked to the General Ledger. Therefore, the linked asset, revenue and expense accounts defined for each inventory item have been debited or credited as required. In addition, the linked receivables accounts we saw earlier are used — *RST Payable, GST Charged on Sales* and *Accounts Receivable*. The inventory database and customer record are also updated. Linked inventory accounts are available only for inventory-related transactions — they are not available on account selection lists in journal account fields.

Flabuless Fitness uses the average cost method to determine the cost of goods sold. If the stock for an inventory item was purchased at different times and prices, the average of these prices would be used as the cost of goods sold.

Close   the **display** to return to the journal input screen.

NOTES
Pressing (ctrl) + J will also open the journal display.

WARNING!
You should always check that the taxes are correct. If you are unsure, you can change the tax code for the books and service items to G. This extra step is required in Chapters 16, 17 and 18.

NOTES
Flabuless Fitness uses a single cost of goods sold account for all inventory items.
In the Premium version you can choose the first-in, first-out (FIFO) method of costing.

NOTES
For corrections of other, non-inventory invoice details, refer to page 161.

WARNING!
If you adjust a posted invoice to correct for selecting the wrong customer, the customer options, such as payment terms, price list or tax codes, are not updated and may be incorrect. For these errors, you should reverse the entry.

NOTES
Transaction confirmation is turned on, so you should click OK when you post or record each transaction. We will not continue the reminder for this step.

NOTES
You can also add shortcuts for Pay Expenses and View Accounts if you want.

CORRECTING THE INVENTORY SALES ENTRY

To **correct** an **item** on the inventory line, **click** the **incorrect field** to move the cursor and highlight the field contents. Press *enter* to display the list of inventory items, tax codes or accounts. **Click** the **correct selection** to highlight it, then **click Select**, or for the remaining fields, **type** the **correct information**. **Press** *tab* to enter the change.

If you **change** the **inventory** item, re-enter the **quantity sold** in the Quantity field. Press *tab* to update the totals.

To **insert a line, click** the **line below** the one you want to add. Choose the **Edit menu and click Insert Line**. To **remove a line, click** the **line** you want to delete; **choose** the **Edit menu and click Remove Line**.

To correct errors after posting, **click** the **Adjust Invoice tool** 🖅 in the Sales Journal or **choose** the **Sales menu** and **click Adjust Invoice**. Or **choose Adjust Invoice** from the **Sales Invoices icon drop-down shortcuts list** in the Home window. Refer to page 182.

If this is a recurring inventory sale, you can store it just like other sales.

Posting

When all the information in your journal entry is correct, you must post the transaction.

Click Post ▾ to save the transaction. **Click OK**.

Close the **Sales Journal** to exit to the Home window.

Create **shortcuts** as described in the following memo.

> **Memo #1** **Dated February 1, 2018**
>
> **2** Create shortcuts for transactions in other modules (Create Purchase Invoice, Pay Purchase Invoices, Create General Journal and Payroll Cheque Run).

Accounting for Inventory Purchases

The third transaction involves the purchase of inventory items. Inventory purchases are entered in the Purchases Journal, and many of the steps are the same as those for other credit purchases. Now the inventory database will provide the additional information.

> **Purchase Invoice #PE-364** **Dated February 2, 2018**
>
> **3** From Prohealth Exercisers Inc.
>
> | | | | |
> |---|---|---|---|
> | 4 | E010 | Elliptical Exerciser: AE-200 | $ 4 600.00 |
> | 4 | E020 | Elliptical Exerciser: LE-400 | 5 600.00 |
> | | | Freight | 100.00 |
> | | | GST | 515.00 |
> | | | Total | $10 815.00 |
>
> Terms: 2/10, n/30.

Click Create Purchase Invoice in the Shortcuts pane to display the familiar Purchases Journal input form window:

CLASSIC VIEW
Click the Purchases icon

to open the journal.

NOTES
If you did not create shortcuts, click Payables in the Modules pane list to open the Payables window. Then click the Purchase Invoices icon to open the journal.

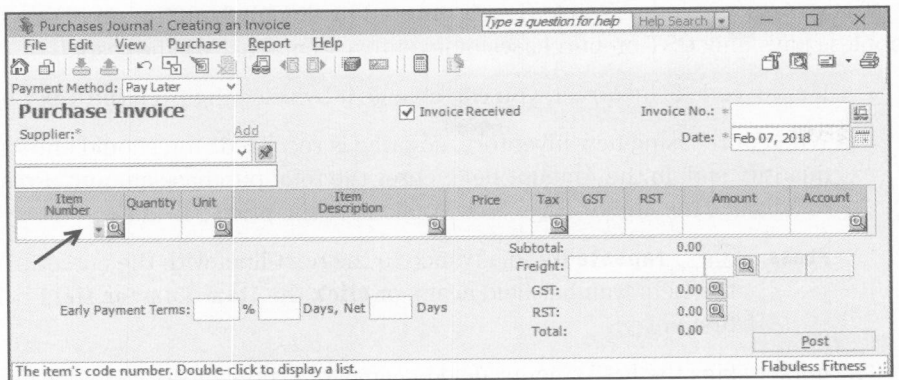

Pay Later is correctly selected as the method of payment.

Click   the **Supplier field list arrow** to display the list of suppliers.

Click   **Prohealth Exercisers Inc.** from the list to add it to your input form.

Check your selection. If you chose an incorrect supplier, select again from the supplier list. If you selected correctly, proceed by entering the invoice number.

Click   the **Invoice No. field**.

Type   PE-364 **Press** (tab) twice.

The cursor advances to the Date field, where you should enter the invoice date.

Type   Feb 2

Click   the **Item Number field**.

Press   (enter) or **click** the **List icon** to open the list of inventory items.

You can add new inventory from the Select Inventory/Service window here as well.

Scroll down   and **click E010 Elliptical Exerciser: AE-200** from the list to highlight it.

Press   (enter). If you have made an incorrect selection, return to the Item Number field and select again.

You can also click the list arrow to access the entire inventory item list, or a partial list if you type the first letter of the item code, just as you did in the Sales Journal. The first eight items will be displayed, and you can scroll down to access more items. Press (tab) to move to the next field.

The cursor advances to the Quantity field. The Item Description field should now have the name of the item, Elliptical Exerciser: AE-200. The default price is the most recent purchase price. Now enter the quantity for this item.

Type   4 **Press** (tab).

The cursor advances to the Unit field. The Unit and Description are correct based on Inventory Ledger records.

The Price field records the most recent unit price paid for the purchase of the inventory items. This amount should not include any GST paid that can be used as an input tax credit. The price has changed since the previous purchase, so it is now incorrect. We will update the price by changing the total amount.

Click   **4,400.00**, the Amount entered as the default.

Type   4600 **Press** (tab) to update the unit Price to $1 150.

PRO VERSION
pro The term Vendor will replace Supplier.

NOTES
If you want to search for items by description, you can type the first letter in the Item Description field to provide a list of all items that include the letter you typed. The list will be sorted alphabetically by description.

NOTES
Remember that you can customize the tabbing order.

NOTES
The next time you purchase this item, the new price, $1 150, will be entered as the default.

The correct tax code — code G — is entered by default from the supplier record. Flabuless pays only GST on purchases of inventory items that will be resold.

If a tax code is incorrect, you can change it by selecting from the Tax Code list.

When purchasing new inventory, no price is recorded. You should enter the quantity and, in the Amount field, enter the total purchase amount. Press (tab) to advance the cursor. Sage 50 will calculate the price per unit.

Press (tab) **repeatedly** to advance to the next line, with the cursor blinking in the Item Number field again, or **click** the **Item Number field** below the first entry.

The cursor skips the RST amount field because the supplier tax code does not include RST. The Account field was also skipped over because you cannot change the entry for inventory purchases. The account number is dimmed and the Account field is not available. The Asset account for the inventory purchase is defined in the Inventory Ledger as the linked account for purchases and sales. To change the account in the journal, you must edit the Inventory Ledger record. The default account for the supplier does not apply to the inventory purchase.

Enter the **second item** from the source document, using the same steps that you used to record the first item. The default price and amount are correct.

The inventory details of the invoice are completed and you are ready to enter the freight charge:

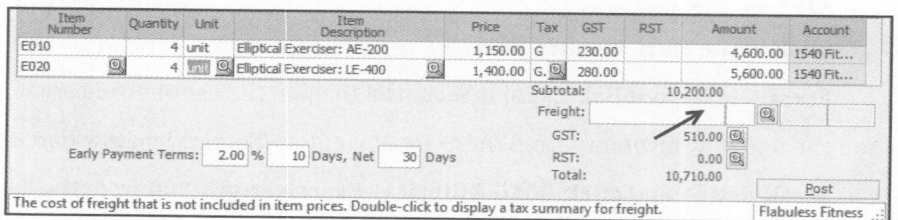

The Freight fields are used to enter any freight charges that cannot be allocated to the purchase of a specific item and to enter the taxes paid on the freight charges. There are four Freight fields: the base amount of the freight charge, tax code, GST amount and, finally, the RST amount. Because GST is paid on freight you must enter a tax code if the supplier charges freight.

Click the **first Freight field**, the amount field, below the Subtotal.

Type 100 **Press** (tab).

The tax code for the supplier, code G, should be entered by default.

If the tax code for freight is not entered automatically, press (enter) to open the familiar list of tax codes. Click G and then click Select.

You do not need to enter amounts for the taxes on freight; they are calculated as soon as you enter the amount of freight charged and the tax code.

Sage 50 calculates the amount of GST (and RST if it is paid) and updates all the totals.

Your input form is now complete:

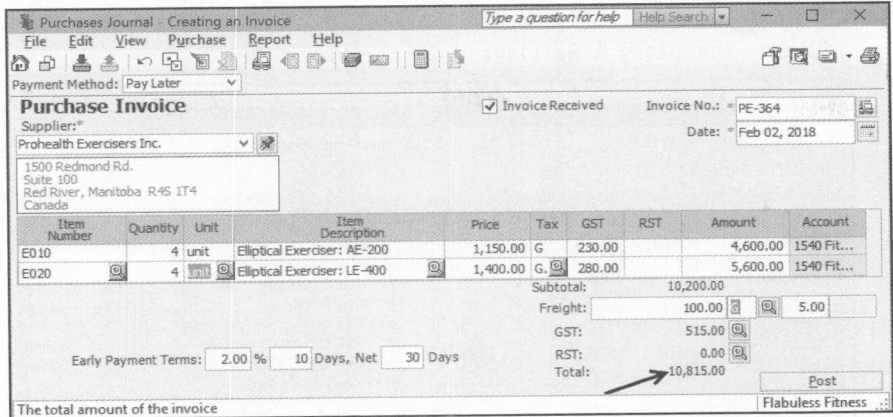

The Subtotal includes all items purchased but does not include freight or taxes.

Reviewing the Inventory Purchase Transaction

As usual, we will review the journal entry before posting it.

Choose the **Report menu** and **click Display Purchases Journal Entry**:

Account Number	Account Description	Debits	Credits
Flabuless Fitness			
Purchases Journal Entry 02/02/2018 (J2)			
1540	Fitness Equipment	10,200.00	-
2670	GST Paid on Purchases	515.00	-
5080	Freight Expense	100.00	-
2200	Accounts Payable	-	10,815.00
Additional Date:	Additional Field:	10,815.00	10,815.00

The program has automatically updated all accounts relevant to this transaction. The appropriate inventory asset account (*Fitness Equipment*), *Accounts Payable, GST Paid on Purchases* and *Freight Expense* have been updated as required because the ledgers are linked — the inventory purchase uses only predefined linked accounts. The inventory database and the supplier record are also updated.

Close the **display** to return to the Purchases Journal input screen.

CORRECTING THE INVENTORY PURCHASES JOURNAL ENTRY

If the inventory item is incorrect, **reselect** from the **inventory** list by **pressing** (enter) while in this field. **Click Select** to add the item to your form. **Type** the **quantity** purchased and **press** (tab) to update the totals.

Account numbers cannot be changed for inventory items on the purchase invoice. They must be edited in the Inventory Ledger.

To **insert** a new **line**, if you have forgotten a complete line of the invoice, **click** the **line** that should come after the line you forgot. **Choose** the **Edit menu** and **click Insert Line** to add a blank invoice line to your form. To **remove** a complete **line**, **click** the **line** you want to delete, **choose** the **Edit menu** and **click Remove Line**.

For assistance with correcting other invoice details, refer to page 114.

To correct an inventory purchase after posting, use the **Adjust Invoice tool** or **choose** the **Purchase Menu** and **click Adjust Invoice**. Refer to page 127. If you selected the wrong supplier, you should reverse the purchase transaction (refer to page 139).

Posting

When all the information in your journal entry is correct, you must post the transaction.

Click . **Close** the **Purchases Journal**.

NOTES
Pressing (ctrl) + J will also open the journal display.

NOTES
If this is a recurring purchase, you can store it, just like other recurring purchases.

WARNING!
If you adjust a posted invoice to correct for selecting the wrong supplier, the supplier options, such as payment terms and tax codes, are not updated and may be incorrect. For these errors, you should reverse the entry.

The Inventory Module

Click **Inventory & Services** in the Modules pane list:

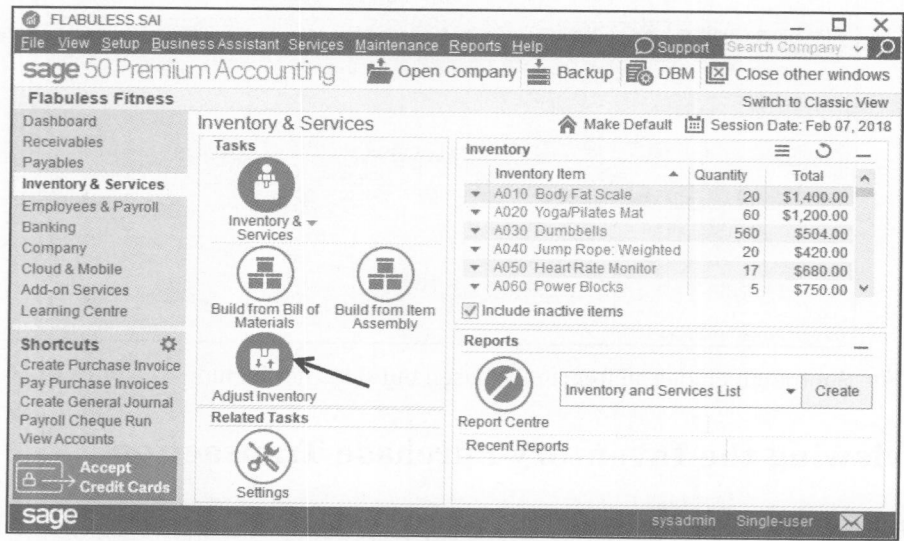

The Inventory module has icons for the ledger records, journal entries and settings. Records are listed in the Inventory Item list pane as they are for other modules so you can access them directly. The Reports pane includes all inventory reports in the Reports list, updated for the recent sale and purchase quantities.

Making Inventory Adjustments

Sometimes inventory is lost, stolen or damaged and adjusting entries are required to reflect the expenses. These inventory adjustments are made in the Inventory Adjustments Journal in the Inventory & Services window. This journal is also used to record lost inventory that is recovered and inventory that is used by the business instead of being sold to customers.

| ✓ | **Memo #2** | **Dated February 2, 2018** |
| 4 | From Owner: Adjust inventory records for Stability Balls, item A070. Three balls were punctured and are unusable. Charge losses to Damaged Inventory. | |

Click the **Adjust Inventory icon** [Adjust Inventory] to open the blank Adjustments Journal:

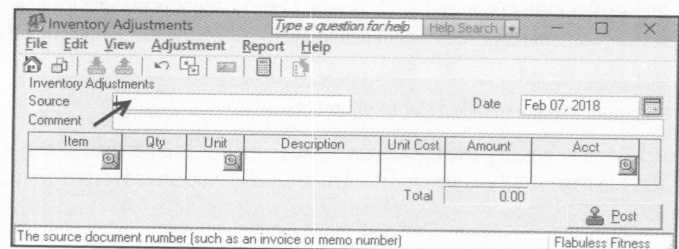

The cursor is in the Source field. The source for an adjustment will normally be a memo from a manager or owner.

Type Memo 2 **Press** (tab).

The cursor is in the Date field, with the session date entered and highlighted.

Type 02-02 **Press** (tab) **twice** to place the cursor in the Comment field to add a brief explanation for this transaction.

Type `Stability balls punctured` **Press** (tab). The cursor advances to the Item field.

Press (enter) or **click** 🔍 to display the familiar inventory list.

The quantities on this list have also been updated to include the previous sale and purchase. Services are not included in the list because they have no quantities in stock and cannot be lost or damaged.

Double-click A070 Stability Ball from the list to select and enter it on the form.

The item description, Stability Ball, the unit, unit cost and account have been added automatically. The cursor advances to the Quantity (Qty) field. You need to indicate that the inventory has been reduced because of the damaged item. You do this by typing a **negative** number in the field. Remember always to enter a negative quantity when there is an inventory loss. If lost inventory is recovered later, enter the adjustment with a positive quantity.

Type -3 **Press** (tab).

The cursor advances to the Unit field. The rest of the journal line is completed automatically. In the Amount field, a negative amount, reflecting the inventory loss, automatically appears as a default based on the average cost. In the Account field, *Damaged Inventory*, the default linked account for inventory losses, appears for this entry. This is the correct account.

If you need to choose another account, press (enter) to display the list of accounts and select the account as usual. You can also edit the unit cost or amount if you know that the price of the unit was different from the default price, the average of all inventory in stock. You can store and recall Adjustments Journal entries just as you do entries in other journals, but you cannot look up or adjust them after posting.

Your entry is complete and you are ready to review it:

Reviewing the Adjustments Journal Entry

Choose the **Report menu** and **click Display Inventory Adjustments Journal Entry** to display the transaction you have entered:

Sage 50 has automatically updated the relevant accounts for this transaction. The appropriate inventory asset defined for this inventory item, *Accessories*, and the

> **NOTES**
> Stores that sell inventory frequently use some inventory stock in the store. Use the Adjustments Journal to record these transfers by choosing the appropriate asset or expense account to replace the default inventory adjustments linked account for inventory losses. Enter negative quantities because the inventory stock is reduced. Because the store has become the final customer — it has bought the items from itself — it is responsible for reporting the purchase and paying RST on the cost price of these internal sales.

> **NOTES**
> Pressing (ctrl) + J will also open the journal display.

> **NOTES**
> The second Inventory Ledger linked account is used for item assembly costs in the Item Assembly Journal. Item assembly is introduced in the next transaction.

inventory database have been reduced to reflect the loss at the average cost price. *Damaged Inventory*, the Inventory linked expense account that was defined for inventory losses or adjustments, has been debited or increased.

Close   the **display** to return to the Adjustments Journal input screen.

CORRECTING THE ADJUSTMENTS JOURNAL ENTRY

Move to the field that has the error. **Press** (tab) to move forward or **press** (shift) and (tab) together to move back to a previous field. This will highlight the field information so you can change it. **Type** the **correct information** and **press** (tab) to enter it.

You can also use the mouse to **point** to a field and **drag** through the **incorrect information** to highlight it. **Type** the **correct information** and **press** (tab) to enter it.

If the inventory item is incorrect, **reselect** from the **inventory** list by **pressing** (enter) while in this field. **Click Select** to add it to the form. **Type** the **quantity** and **press** (tab). After changing any information on an inventory item line, **press** (tab) to update the totals.

You can insert and remove lines by selecting these options from the Edit menu.

To start over, **click** ✕ or ↶ (or **choose** the **Edit menu** and **click Undo Entry**). **Click Yes** when asked to confirm that you want to discard the transaction.

⚠ **WARNING!**
You cannot adjust or look up an inventory adjustment after posting, so check the entry carefully before posting.

Posting

When all the information in your journal entry is correct, you must save the transaction.

Click   the **Post button** ⬛ Post .

Close   the **Adjustments Journal** to return to the Inventory window. The next keystroke transaction creates and assembles new inventory items.

Adding a New Inventory Item

Before entering the item assembly transaction, we will create the necessary new inventory items. Memo #3 has the inventory item details.

📄 **NOTES**
The image files YP01.BMP and TP01.BMP (or YP01 and TP01) were copied to the SageData16\LOGOS folder when you installed your other data files.

✓ **Memo #3**   **Dated February 2, 2018**
5   Create two new inventory items for winter promotions. Create a new Group asset account, 1570 Promotional Offers, to use as the linked account for the new items.

Number Description	Unit	Min Level	Regular Price	Preferred Price	Linked Accounts Asset	Revenue	COGS	Tax
P010 Yoga Training Package	pkg	1	$1 400	(1 250)	1570	4020	5060	GP
P020 Training Workout Package	pkg	1	$1 600	(1 400)	1570	4020	5060	GP
Variance account not required								

Inventory items can be added from any inventory item field in a journal, from the Inventory & Services icon (that opens the Inventory & Services window) or from the icon's Add Inventory & Service shortcut:

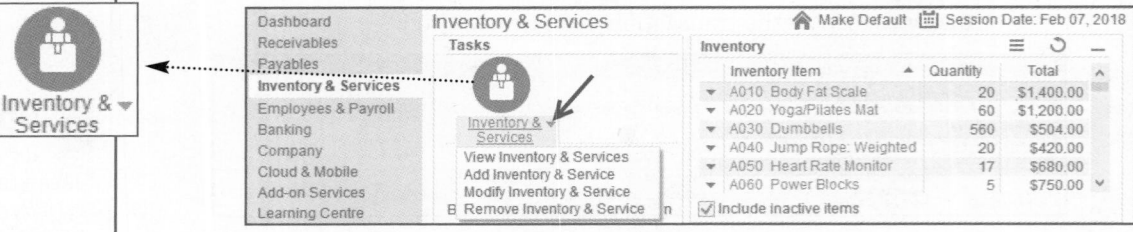

Click   the **Inventory & Services icon** to open the Inventory & Services window:

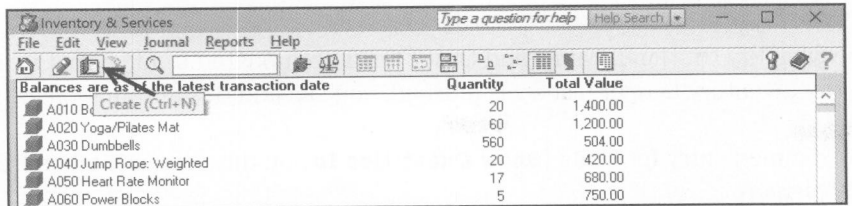

This window is like the Accounts, Suppliers, Customers and Employees windows in other modules, and it lists all inventory items and services. If you choose the Add Inventory shortcut, you will open a new ledger record directly and skip this Inventory & Services window.

Click   the **Create tool** 🖻, **choose** the **File menu** and **click Create** or **press** ⌨ `ctrl` + **N.**

Each of these methods opens the Inventory & Services Ledger:

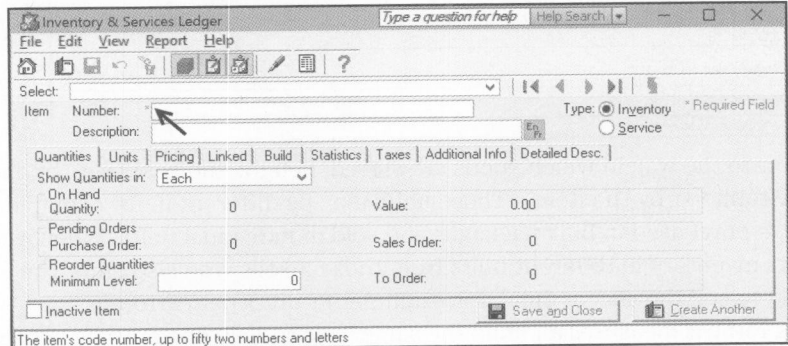

The Inventory & Services Ledger record has many of the tools that are available in other ledgers, including the Refresh tool. The **Show** tool icons allow you to limit the Select field list to inventory items, services or activities (for time and billing). If all three tools are selected, the list includes all three kinds of items. All Show tools are selected for Flabuless Fitness, so all records are included in the Select list.

You can enter both inventory and service items in the Inventory Ledger. You can designate a service as an activity with time and billing information attached. Activities are available for the time and billing features and for selection as internal services — services that are provided by one department to another within the company and can be tracked as expenses. The Time & Billing function will be covered in Chapter 18.

The packages are inventory, so as a result the type selection is correct and the fields we need are included. The Quantities tab information is displayed because it is the first tab screen. As usual, **required fields** are marked with *.

The setup option we selected for inventory sorts the items by code or number. Therefore, the Item Number field is the first item field. When you choose to sort by description, the longer Description field will come first. (Refer to Chapter 16, page 662.)

From the source document information, you must enter the item code and description. The first Item field contains the code or number of the inventory item — the only required field on this screen; the second Item field contains the description or item name.

Click   the **Item Number field**.

Type   P010 **Press** `tab` to advance to the Item Description field.

Type   Yoga Training Package

Click   the **Minimum Level field** in the Reorder Quantities section.

Here you must enter the stock level at which you want to reorder the item in question, or in this case, assemble more packages.

NOTES
You can add inventory items from any journal inventory field when the selection list is available, that is, in the Sales, Purchases, Adjustments and Item Assembly journals. Click the List icon in the Item field to open the selection list. Click Add New Inventory/Service and press `enter` or click the Create button to open the Inventory Ledger window. (Refer to the screenshot on page 359.)

PRO VERSION
The Pro version does not have the Build tab. It applies to the Build From Bill Of Materials option in the Bill of Materials & Item Assembly Journal. This feature is not available in the Pro version.

NOTES
As in other ledgers and journals, the Refresh tool applies when you work in multi-user mode. Clicking the tool will update the record with changes made by other users who are accessing the data file at the same time.

PRO VERSION
The Time & Billing function is not available in the Pro version. The Pro version has only two Show tools — one for inventory items and one for service items. The Refresh tool is also not on the Pro version tool bar.

NOTES
When you print inventory reports, items that have fallen below the minimum level will be flagged.

Type   1

The Quantity On Hand, Value, and Order fields are updated from journal entries. Before the Inventory Ledger history is finished, you can add this information as historical data.

The dimmed entry for Units (**Show Quantities In**) on this screen is taken from the Units tab screen.

Click   the **Units tab**:

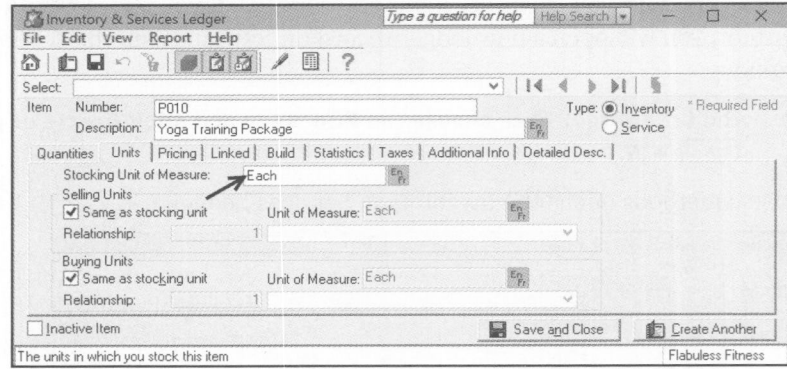

Units refer to the way in which goods are stored, bought and sold (e.g., by the dozen, by the tonne or by the item). These units may be different if, for example, merchandise is purchased in bulk packages and sold in individual units. When a store buys or stocks inventory in different units from those it sells, you also enter the relationship between the sets of units, for example, 12 units per carton.

Flabuless Fitness measures all units the same way, so only one entry is needed.

Double-click   **Each** in the Stocking Unit Of Measure field. **Type**   pkg

Click   the **Pricing tab**:

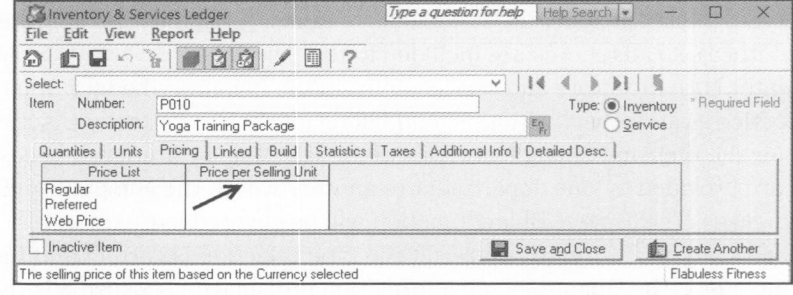

A business may have different price lists. Each item may be assigned a regular price, a selling price for preferred customers and a Web price. Flabuless Fitness has three customers with preferred customer status, marked with the * in the Customer Information list on page 353. Regular, preferred and Web selling prices can also be entered in foreign currencies when other currencies are used.

Click   the **Price Per Selling Unit column** beside Regular.

Type   1400

Press   ⌷tab⌷ to advance to the Price Per Selling Unit field for preferred prices.

The regular price is entered as the default Preferred and Web Price.

Type   1250 to replace the default preferred price entry.

Click   the **Linked tab** to access the linked accounts for the inventory item:

NOTES

You can select the price list in the Sales Journal from the Price field select list icon. By adding it to the customer's record, the correct price is selected automatically in the journal.

NOTES

The Premium version allows you to create additional price lists. The Pro version does not include this feature. When you create additional price lists (Inventory Ledger Settings), they will be added to this screen, and you can enter prices for them.

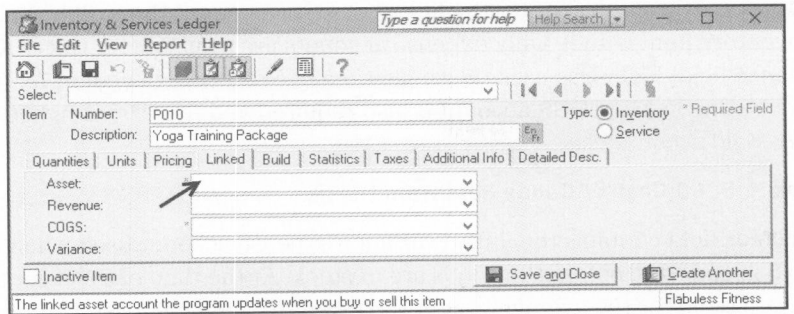

NOTES
For other ledgers, the linked accounts are defined for the entire ledger. For example, there is only one Accounts Receivable account.

There are two sets of linked accounts for inventory: those that apply to the entire ledger — the default accounts for inventory adjustments and item assembly costs — and those that apply to specific inventory items. The ones in the ledger are item specific and are used as the default accounts whenever inventory items are sold or purchased. By defining linked accounts for each item in the Inventory Ledger, each inventory item can be related to separate asset, revenue, expense and variance accounts. Two of these four **linked accounts** are **required**: the linked asset account and COGS (Cost of Goods Sold). You cannot choose or change the asset account in the Purchases Journal, and it is not available on the account selection list in any journal. You also cannot change or select the Cost of Goods Sold account for Sales. Sage 50 automatically enters it in the background — there is no field for it on-screen.

In the **Asset** field, you must enter the number of the linked asset account affected by purchases and sales of this item. A list of accounts is available from the drop-down list arrow in the Asset field. Only asset accounts are available in the list for the Asset field. Because the account we need does not exist yet, we cannot choose it from the account list for the field. We can create it here.

> **Click**   the **Asset field**.
>
> **Type**   1570 Promotional Offers **Press** (tab).

The next screen allows you to create the new account:

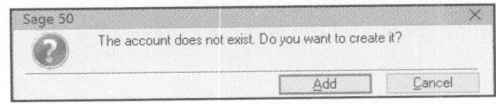

NOTES
When you type the account name in the field at the same time and then press (tab), the wizard will add both the number and the name for the account. Some account fields with list arrows allow you to enter both the number and name for new accounts; those with List icons do not.

> **Click**   **Add** to proceed to the Add An Account wizard. **Click Next** to continue.
>
> **Accept** the **remaining** account **settings** and **finish** creating the account.

After you click Finish, you will generate another message advising you of an account class change for the linked account:

NOTES
If necessary, you can create new linked revenue and expense accounts in the same way you created the new asset account.

> **Click**   **Yes** to accept the change. Clicking No will return you to the Linked Accounts screen so you can select a different account.

In the **Revenue** field, you must enter the linked revenue account that will be credited when this inventory item is sold. You can type the account number or select from the list. Only revenue accounts are available for the Revenue field.

> **Click**   the **Revenue field list arrow** to list the revenue accounts available.
>
> **Click**   **4020 Revenue from Sales** to enter it on your form.
>
> **Click**   the **COGS field list arrow** (Cost of Goods Sold expense) to list the expense accounts available.

NOTES
The linked revenue account is not a required account — you can choose an account in the Sales Journal when you sell inventory. This allows you to use a different account in the journal, such as for returns. The linked asset and COGS accounts are required. You do not enter COGS accounts when entering inventory sales — the program adds it automatically.

In the **COGS** field, you must enter the linked expense account that will be debited when this inventory item is sold. Only expense accounts are available for the COGS field and the Variance field. Flabuless uses the single *Cost of Goods Sold* account for all inventory items. The linked COGS account is also required and must be assigned the Cost of Goods Sold account class.

Click   **5060 Cost of Goods Sold** from the list.

The **Variance** field contains the linked variance expense account used when the inventory sold is on order, before the goods are in stock. At the time of the sale, *Cost of Goods Sold* is debited for the average cost of the inventory on hand, based on previous purchases. When the goods are received, the actual purchase price may be different from this historical average cost. The price difference is charged to the variance account. Flabuless Fitness does not allow inventory to be oversold, so you can leave the Variance account field blank.

Click   the **Build tab**:

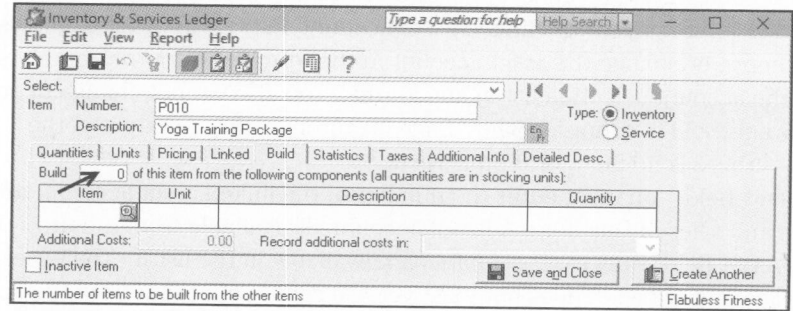

On the Build tab screen, you enter the inventory components needed to make the item. You identify the number of items you are building and the component items required to build this number. This process is similar to the one found in the Components section of the Item Assembly Journal (refer to page 375). When it is time to build the item (in the Bill of Materials & Item Assembly Journal), you indicate how many items you are building — the Assembled Items section of the Item Assembly — and the rest of the details are taken from the Build screen of the ledger record. We will use the Build feature in Chapter 18.

Click   the **Statistics tab**:

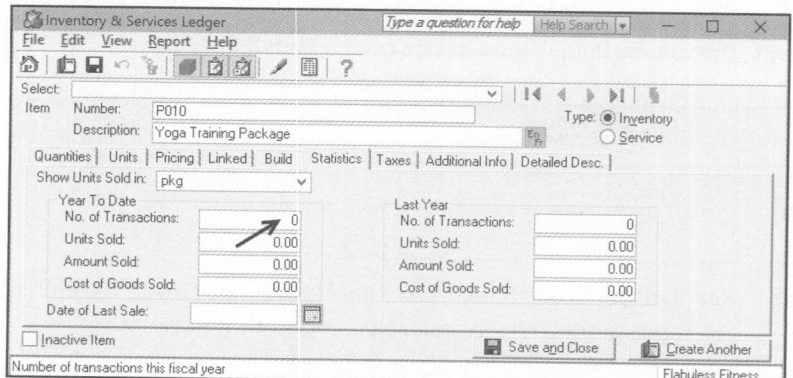

This screen applies to historical data. Since this is a new inventory item, there are no previous sales, and you should leave all entries at zero. The **Date Of Last Sale** is the most recent date that this item was sold. The **Year To Date** section refers to historical information for the current fiscal period, and the **Last Year** fields apply to the previous year. Inventory Statistics are added to inventory tracking reports.

The **No.** (number) **Of Transactions** refers to the total number of times the item was sold. For example, if one customer bought the item on three separate dates, there would

be three transactions. If four customers bought the item on one day, there would be four transactions. If one customer bought four of the same item at one time, there would be one transaction. The **Units Sold** counts the total number of items that were sold on all occasions to all customers in the relevant period. The **Amount Sold** field holds the total sale price of all items sold in the period, and the **Cost Of Goods Sold** field records the total purchase price of all items sold.

If you have historical data for the item, you can add it. Sage 50 continually updates the Statistics tab fields from journal entries.

Click   the **Taxes tab**:

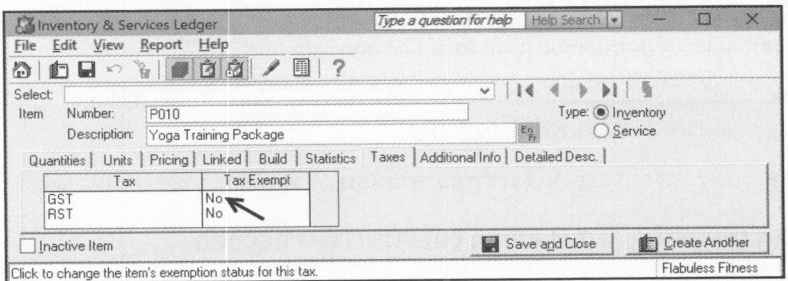

All taxes set up for the company will appear on this screen. RST and GST may be charged or omitted by default. Because most goods have these taxes applied to the sale, the default is to charge them — No is entered in the Tax Exempt column. The **Tax Exempt** entry is a toggle switch. Clicking the current entry changes it. The default settings are correct — both taxes are charged. Books and services provided by Flabuless Fitness were designated as tax exempt for RST.

When inventory items are imported and duty is charged, you can enter the duty rate on this screen as well.

The **Additional Info** tab allows for custom-defined information fields relating to the item, just like the Additional Info tabs in other ledgers. It is not used by Flabuless Fitness.

Click   the **Detailed Desc. tab**:

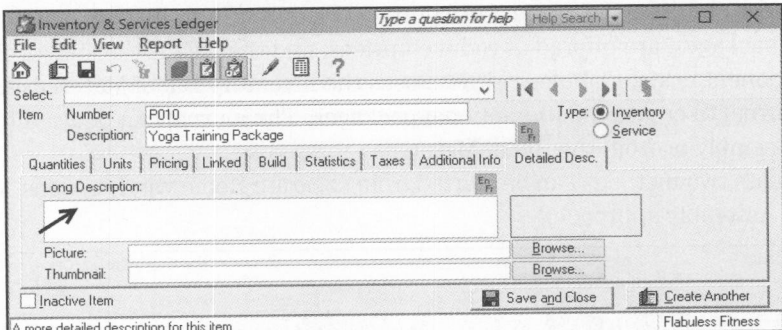

On this screen you can enter a detailed description of the inventory item and the name of a file and location where an image of the item is stored. The bitmap (.BMP) file for this item was copied to the SageData16\LOGOS folder with your other data files.

Click   **Browse** beside the Picture field to open the file location window.

Locate   and **open** the **SageData16 folder**. **Double-click C:**, **SageData16** and **LOGOS** to open this folder. **Double-click YP01** (or **YP01.BMP**) to add the image and file name:

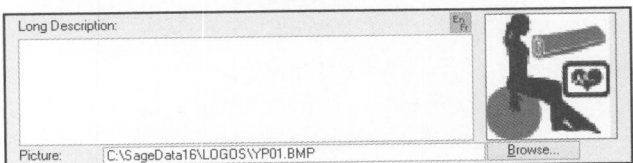

NOTES
The tax exemption in the ledger record will ensure that a tax is not applied. Books and service items were marked as tax exempt for RST on this screen so that RST does not apply to their sales. The default tax code in the journal is taken from the customer's ledger record.

NOTES
You could enter the list of components in the Description field.

NOTES
Because we do not know your initial default location, we continue to use C:\SageData16 as the location for all the files for this text. This allows us to give clear file path instructions.

CORRECTING THE INVENTORY ITEM BEFORE CREATING THE RECORD

Correct the information if necessary by **clicking** the field that contains the **error**. **Click** the appropriate **tab** to change information screens if necessary. **Highlight** the **error** and **type** the **correct information**. **Press** `tab` to enter the correction.

When all the information is correct, you must save your information.

Click   **Create Another** [Create Another] to save the new record. The ledger remains open so you can add the second new item.

Click   the **Quantities tab**.

Enter   all the details for item **P020** from page 368.

Click   [Save and Close] to save the new record. Both items are added to your ledger list of inventory items.

Close   the **Inventory & Services window** to return to the Home window.

EDITING AN INVENTORY ITEM AFTER CREATING THE RECORD

You cannot edit an Inventory Ledger record while you are using the item in a journal. You must first **delete** the **journal line containing the item**. **Click** the **journal line, choose** the **Edit menu** and **click Remove Line**. Then **click** the journal's **Home window tool** [icon] to return to the Home window. **Click Inventory & Services** in the Modules pane list. **Click** the name of the **inventory item** that you need to change in the Inventory pane Item list to open the item's record. **Click** the **tab** you need. **Highlight** the **information** that is incorrect, and then **type** the **correct information**. **Close** the **Ledger window**. **Click** the **Home window journal icon you need** (or the task bar icon/button for the journal) to return to the journal.

Assembling Inventory Items

Inventory item assembly can be used to build new inventory from other inventory items, to create package offers of two or more regular items for sale at a special price or to reserve inventory for a special project or contract. Flabuless' new inventory items, the promotional packages, are offered at reduced prices, and the cost is the sum of the original component costs. Flabuless Fitness uses the inventory Bill of Materials & Item Assembly Journal to create the promotional packages. The journal can be used to build from Item Assembly or from the Bill of Materials.

The journal's two methods can be started from separate Home window icons. We will use the Item Assembly approach:

Build from Item Assembly

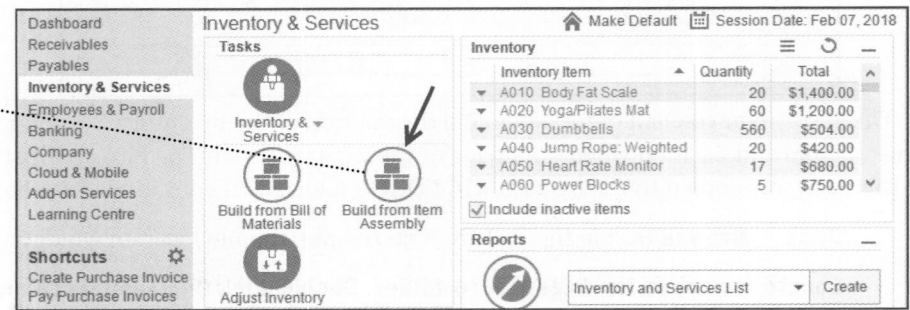

PRO VERSION
In the Pro version, only the Item Assembly approach is available.

CLASSIC VIEW
Click the Bill of Materials & Item Assembly icon to open the journal.

Click   the **Build From Item Assembly icon** to open the Journal:

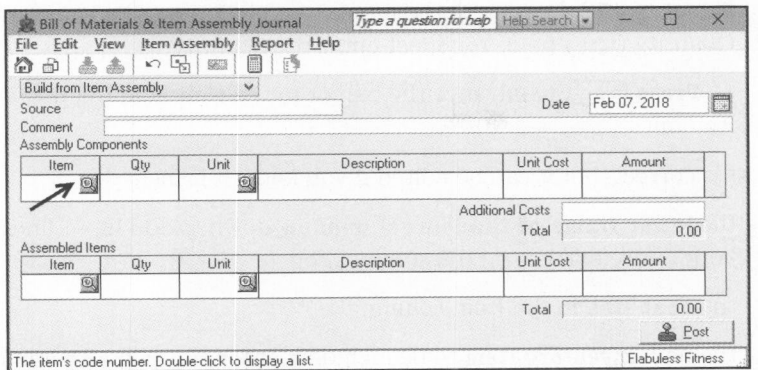

There are two ways to assemble items in the Premium version of Sage 50: Item Assembly or Build From Bill Of Materials as defined in the ledger on the Build tab screen (refer to page 372). When you build items from the bill of materials, the journal has only the assembled items part — the components information is drawn from the ledger record. The bill of materials method will be covered in Chapter 18. We will use the item assembly method now. You can access both methods from the Build drop-down list in the journal:

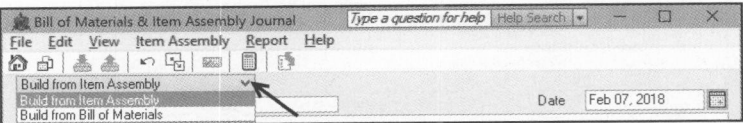

We are using the item assembly method, so you do not need to modify the journal.

<table>
<tr><td>✓</td><td colspan="2">**Item Assembly #IA-01**</td><td>**Dated February 3, 2018**</td></tr>
<tr><td>6</td><td colspan="3">Create five (5) Yoga Training Packages. Transfer 5 of each component item as follows:</td></tr>
</table>

5	A020	Yoga/Pilates Mat	$ 20 each
5	A050	Heart Rate Monitor	40 /unit
5	A070	Stability Ball	6 each
5	A080	Workout/Weight Bench	84 each
5	E040	Bicycle: Recumbent R-80	600 /unit

Additional Costs (for Yoga Instructor: $1/2$ day)   450

Assembled Items
  5   P010   Yoga Training Package $840 /pkg

Click   the **Source field**, where you should enter the reference or form number.

Type   IA-01 **Press** (tab) to advance to the Date field. Enter the date of the transfer.

Type   02-03 **Press** (tab) **twice** to advance to the Comment field.

Type   Assemble yoga training packages

Press   (tab) to advance to the first line in the Item field.

You are in the **Assembly Components** section. This first section refers to the items that are being removed from inventory, the "from" part of the transfer or assembly. Together, these items will form the gift package.

Press   (enter) or **click** the **List icon** to display the familiar inventory selection list.

If needed, you can add new inventory items from the Select Inventory list in the Item Assembly Journal. Services are not on this list because they cannot be assembled.

Click   **A020 Yoga/Pilates Mat** to select the first item needed.

NOTES
We will use the Item Assembly Journal to refer to the Bill of Materials & Item Assembly Journal.

PRO VERSION
pro The drop-down list is not available. The cursor will be in the Source field.

CLASSIC VIEW
Classic Click Build From Item Assembly in the Build drop-down list if necessary to open the journal form we need.

NOTES
You could also add the new inventory items, the packages, and the new asset account, 1570 Promotional Offers, directly from the journal while creating the new item.

NOTES
Services have no quantities or purchase costs, so you cannot choose them for item assemblies.

NOTES
The unit cost may be different when the cost of transferred items is lower than the default because older stock is being transferred and it was purchased at a lower price. If you change the unit cost, press (tab) to update the amount.

Click   **Select** to add the item to the item assembly form and advance to the Quantity (Qty) field. You must enter the quantity.

Type   5 **Press** (tab) to advance the cursor to the Unit field to update the Amount.

The unit cost is correct, but it can be edited if you know it is incorrect.

Drag   the **lower frame of the journal window** down to add input lines so that your entire entry is on the screen at once.

Click   the **next line** in the Item column.

Select   the next **inventory item** to be included, **enter** the **quantity** and then continue to **enter** the **remaining components** for the package.

At this stage, the Assembly Components portion is complete:

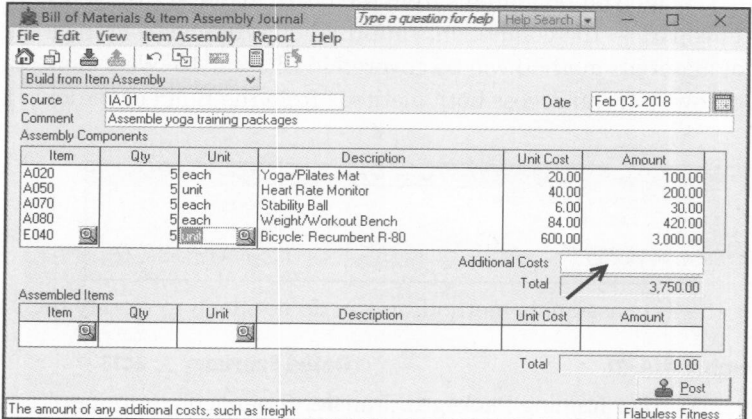

The middle part of the item assembly form contains two fields: Additional Costs and Total. **Additional costs** may come from shipping or packaging involved with assembling, moving or transferring the inventory. Services involved in the package may also be entered as additional costs. The extra costs for all items transferred should be entered into the Additional Costs field. The **Total** is calculated automatically by Sage 50 to include the individual costs of all items transferred — the assembly components — plus any additional costs. Flabuless Fitness has additional costs of $450 ($90 per package) for personal yoga training.

Click   the **Additional Costs field**.

Type   450 **Press** (tab) to update the total.

The cursor advances to the first line in the Item column of the **Assembled Items** section. This section refers to the new or reserved inventory, the item being assembled or the "to" part of the transfer.

Press   (enter) or **click** the **List icon** to display the familiar inventory selection list.

Click   **P010 Yoga Training Package** to select the item we created.

Click   **Select** or **press** (enter) to add the item to the item assembly form and advance to the Quantity (Qty) field.

Type   5

The Unit Cost and Amount fields are blank because the cost of the new item is still unknown. The unit cost of the assembled items is the total cost of all assembly components, plus additional costs, divided by the quantity or number of units assembled.

When a single type of item is assembled and the quantity is greater than one, it is simpler to enter the quantity and amount (the Total in the assembly components portion in the top half of the form) and let the program calculate the unit cost. You can also enter the individual item cost in the Unit Cost field and allow the program to calculate the Amount (Qty × Unit Cost). We will enter the total from the upper portion of the journal.

> **Click**   the **Amount field**.
>
> **Type**   4200 **Press** (tab) to enter the cost and update the unit cost and total.

The totals in the two parts of the assembly form should now be the same. If they are not, you will be unable to post the entry.

Your item assembly form is now completed:

Bill of Materials & Item Assembly Journal						
File Edit View Item Assembly Report Help						
Build from Item Assembly						
Source	IA-01				Date	Feb 03, 2018
Comment	Assemble yoga training packages					
Assembly Components						
Item	Qty	Unit	Description	Unit Cost	Amount	
A020	5	each	Yoga/Pilates Mat	20.00	100.00	
A050	5	unit	Heart Rate Monitor	40.00	200.00	
A070	5	each	Stability Ball	6.00	30.00	
A080	5	each	Weight/Workout Bench	84.00	420.00	
E040	5	unit	Bicycle: Recumbent R-80	600.00	3,000.00	
				Additional Costs	450.00	
				Total	4,200.00	
Assembled Items						
Item	Qty	Unit	Description	Unit Cost	Amount	
P010	5	pkg	Yoga Training Package	840.00	4,200.00	
				Total	4,200.00	
					Post	
The total value of items being assembled					Flabuless Fitness	

> **NOTES**
> Because the two totals must be the same, entering the total cost and allowing the program to determine the unit cost ensures this balance.
> Of course, this method will work only when you are assembling one item at a time.

Reviewing the Item Assembly Journal Entry

> **Choose** the **Report menu**, then **click Display Bill Of Materials & Item Assembly Journal Entry** to display the transaction you have entered:

Bill of Materials & Item Assembly Journal Entry			
File Options Help			
Print Print Preview Change Print Settings Export Open in Excel® Modify ▾ Refresh			?
Flabuless Fitness			
Bill of Materials & Item Assembly Journal Entry 02/03/2018 (J4)			
Account Number	Account Description	Debits	Credits
1570	Promotional Offers	4,200.00	
1520	Accessories	-	750.00
1540	Fitness Equipment	-	3,000.00
5035	Promotional Package Services	-	450.00
Additional Date:	Additional Field:	4,200.00	4,200.00

> **PRO VERSION**
> *pro* In the Pro version, you will choose the Report menu and then click Display Item Assembly Journal Entry to place the transaction on-screen.

Sage 50 has moved the inventory items from their original asset accounts (credit entries to *Accessories* and *Fitness Equipment*) to the newly created inventory account (debit entry to *Promotional Offers*). The quantities for all items involved have been updated in inventory selection lists or quantity reports. The necessary items are taken out of their regular individual item inventory account and transferred to the new account. Thus the quantities of the original items are reduced because they have been transferred to the new item. Additional Costs are assigned to *Promotional Package Services*, the linked account defined for these costs. This is a contra-expense account — the credit entry for the expense account is added (debit amount) to the inventory value of the assembled inventory asset.

> **NOTES**
> Pressing (ctrl) + J will also open the journal display.

> **Close**   the **display** to return to the Item Assembly Journal input screen.

Because the item assembly is a complex transaction, it is very easy to make a mistake, so check your work carefully. You may also want to store the original entry. If you discover later that you have made an error, you can recall the entry and add a minus sign to each quantity and to the Additional Costs amount to create a reversing entry.

But first you should make corrections.

CORRECTING THE ITEM ASSEMBLY JOURNAL ENTRY

Move to the field that has the error. **Press** ⌨tab to move forward through the fields or **press** ⌨shift and ⌨tab together to move back to a previous field. This will highlight the field information so you can change it. **Type** the **correct information** and **press** ⌨tab to enter it. You must advance the cursor to the next field to enter a change.

You can also use the mouse to **point** to a field and **drag** through the **incorrect information** to highlight it. **Type** the **correct information** and **press** ⌨tab to enter it.

If an inventory item is incorrect, **press** ⌨enter while the cursor is in the Item field to **display** the appropriate list. **Double-click** the **correct inventory item**. **Re-enter** the **quantity** and **press** ⌨tab to update the totals.

Click the **Store button** 📥 to display the familiar Store Recurring Transaction screen:

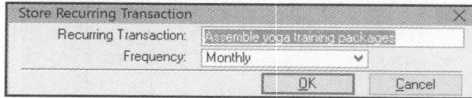

Because this is not a regular recurring transaction, we will use the **Random** frequency. Choosing the Random frequency for recurring entries uses the session date as the default transaction date when you recall the journal entry. You can then change the transaction date as needed.

Click **Monthly** to display the Frequency options.

Click **Random** to select this frequency.

Click **OK** to save the entry and return to the Item Assembly Journal — the Recall button is now active.

Posting

Click the **Post button** [🔖 Post] when you are certain that all the information is correct.

Enter the next **assembly transaction**.

7	

Item Assembly #IA-02   **Dated February 3, 2018**

Create five (5) Training Workout Packages. Transfer 5 of each component item as follows:

5	A020	Yoga/Pilates Mat	$ 20 each
5	A040	Jump Rope	21 each
5	A050	Heart Rate Monitor	40 /unit
5	A060	Power Blocks	150 /set
5	A070	Stability Ball	6 each
5	A080	Workout/Weight Bench	84 each
5	A090	Workout Gloves: all sizes	8 /pair
5	A100	Aerobic Stepper w/ Risers	40 each
5	E030	Bicycle: Dual Action Calorie Counter	450 /unit

Additional Costs (for Personal Trainer: 1/2 day)   450

Assembled Items

5	P020	Training Workout Packages $909 /pkg

Store the assembly as a recurring transaction with random frequency.

When you post the second assembly entry, you will open a low inventory message:

Read the **Advisor message** about low inventory and then **click** to close it.

Close the **Journal** to return to the Inventory & Services module window.

Click **Receivables** in the Modules pane list to restore this window.

Add shortcuts for **Item Assembly** and **Inventory Adjustments** from the Inventory & Services list in the Customize Shortcuts window.

Selling to Preferred Customers

Sage 50 allows you to record multiple inventory prices and to identify customers by the prices they will pay (preferred, regular, Web or a user-defined price). Sales for each group of customers are entered the same way since the program automatically enters the correct price depending on the customer selected and the price option in their ledger record.

> ✓ 8
>
> **Sales Invoice #3001**   **Dated February 3, 2018**
>
> Sold by Prekor to Red River College (preferred customer)
>
> | 80 | A030 | Dumbbells | $ 2.20 /kg |
> |---|---|---|---|
> | 3 | E040 | Bicycle: Recumbent R-80 | 960 /unit |
> | 3 | E080 | Home Gym: Basic HG-1400 | 1 380 /set |
> | | GST | | 5% |
> | | RST | | 8% |
>
> Terms: 2/15, n/30. Free delivery. Allow customer to exceed credit limit.

Red River College is a preferred customer — Preferred is entered as the Price List on the customer's Options tab screen.

Click Red River College in the Customers pane to open the ledger record. Click the Options tab. Preferred is entered in the Price List field. Close the ledger record.

Click the **Sales Invoices icon** ⬚ Sales Invoices ▾ to open the Sales Journal.

Pay Later is the correct selection for this sale to Red River College. The Invoice number is also correct by default.

Choose Red River College from the Customer list.

Type Feb 3 in the Date field and **choose Prekor** as the salesperson.

Type a in the **Item Number field** and **click A030 Dumbbells** to add it. **Press** (tab) to advance to the Quantity field.

Type 80 **Press** (tab) to add the first item at the preferred customer price of $2.20 instead of $2.50, the regular price.

Click the **Price field List icon** ⬚ to open the Select Price list:

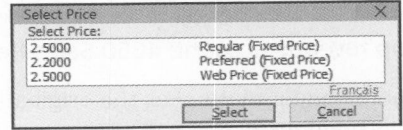

You can also select the item price you need from this screen.

Click the price you want and then click Select to use it in the journal.

Click **Cancel** because the correct price has already been entered.

Enter the **remaining items** sold to this customer to complete the entry:

Choose the **Report menu** and **click Display Sales Journal Entry** to review:

Flabuless Fitness				
Sales Journal Entry 02/03/2018 (J6)				
Account Number	Account Description	Debits	Credits	
1200	Accounts Receivable	8,131.48	-	
5060	Cost of Goods Sold	4,632.00	-	
1520	Accessories	-	72.00	
1540	Fitness Equipment	-	1,800.00	
1550	Home Gym Equipment	-	2,760.00	
2640	RST Payable	-	575.68	
2650	GST Charged on Sales	-	359.80	
4020	Revenue from Sales	-	7,196.00	
Additional Date:	Additional Field:	12,763.48	12,763.48	

This entry looks the same as a regular non-discounted sale. Revenue is reduced because of the change in selling price, but this change is not recorded as a discount.

Close the **display** when finished. **Make corrections**. **Post** the **entry**. **Click Yes** to allow the customer to exceed the credit limit.

Entering Sales Returns

Customers may return purchases for many different reasons. For example, the size, colour or quality may have been other than expected. Stores have different policies with respect to accepting and refunding returns. Most stores place reasonable time limits on the period in which they will give refunds. Some stores offer credit only, and some charge a handling fee on goods returned. Flabuless Fitness will provide full refunds for purchases within two weeks of the sale if the items have not been used or opened. Sales returns are entered in the Sales Journal and are similar to sales, but the quantity is entered with a minus sign — a negative quantity is sold. Different accounts may be used.

<table>
<tr><td>✔</td><td>Sales Return #3000-R</td><td>Dated February 3, 2018</td></tr>
<tr><td>9</td><td colspan="2">Returned from Feb. 1 sale to Kisangel by Botelli & Giroux, Lawyers:</td></tr>
</table>

   −1 E060   Treadmill: Basic T-800B $1 400 /unit
        GST   5%
        RST   8%
Terms: 2/5, net 15. Create new Subgroup revenue account: 4050 Sales Returns.

The return must use the same customer and payment method as the original sale. Pay Later is correctly selected. The Sales Journal should still be open.

Choose Botelli & Giroux, Lawyers from the Customer list.

You should use a different invoice number so that the return can be differentiated from a normal sale.

Click the **Invoice No. field** and **type** 3000-R

NOTES
Using the same terms for the return as for the sale will prorate the discount for the amount of the return. For this situation, you also need to enter the same dates for both transactions. In this way, we enter the return as if we are adjusting the original sale.

NOTES
Most stores have separate forms for returns with their own number sequences.

Enter   **Feb. 1** in the Date field to match the date of the original sale.

Enter   **Kisangel** as the salesperson.

Click   the **Item Number field** and **type** e to open the inventory list.

Click   **E060 Treadmill: Basic T-800B** to enter it and **press** (tab) to move the cursor to the Quantity field.

This adds the first item returned by the customer at the regular price.

Type   −1 **Press** (tab).

A positive amount appears in the Price field and a negative amount is added to the Amount field — a positive price times the negative quantity. The tax amounts are also negative.

We should change the default account so that returns can be tracked separately.

Click   the **Account field List icon** 🔍 and **type** 4050

Press   (tab) and **add Sales Returns**, the new account. Do not forget to change the account type to **Subgroup** (the account balance is included in a Subtotal).

Enter additional items returned, if there are any, in the same way.

Your journal entry is complete:

> **NOTES**
> The salesperson should be entered for sales returns because commissions are calculated on total sales less returns.

> ⚠️ **WARNING!**
> If you do not change the account type to Subgroup, your accounts will not be in logical order and you will be unable to generate reports. In this case, you must edit the account type.

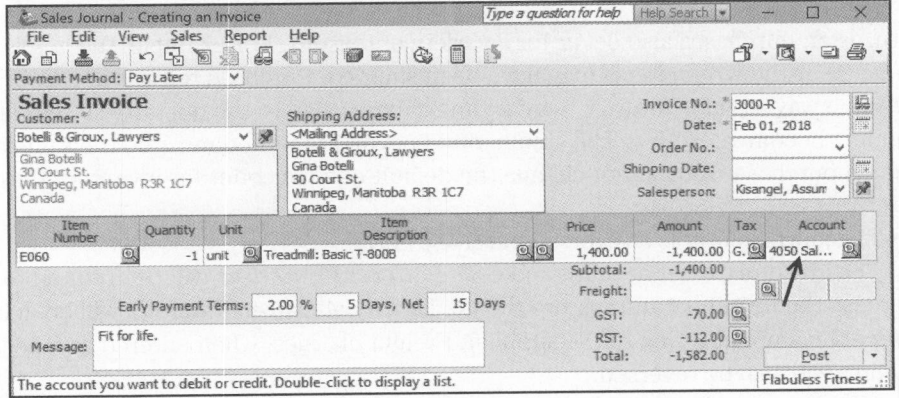

> **NOTES**
> In the Comment field, you could add the reason for the return.

Choose the **Report menu** and **click Display Sales Journal Entry** to review it:

Flabuless Fitness
Sales Journal Entry 02/01/2018 (J7)

Account Number	Account Description	Debits	Credits
1540	Fitness Equipment	750.00	-
2640	RST Payable	112.00	-
2650	GST Charged on Sales	70.00	-
4050	Sales Returns	1,400.00	-
1200	Accounts Receivable	-	1,582.00
5060	Cost of Goods Sold	-	750.00
Additional Date:	Additional Field:	2,332.00	2,332.00

The entry is the reversal of a regular sale. The inventory asset account has been debited because inventory is added back. *Sales Returns* — a contra-revenue account — is debited, reducing revenue, and *Accounts Receivable* is credited because money has been returned to the customer's account to reduce the balance owing. Similarly, *RST Payable* and *GST Charged on Sales* are debited because the tax liabilities have decreased, and finally the expense account *Cost of Goods Sold* is credited because this expense has been reversed.

For credit card sales, the return entry will also reverse credit card fees expenses.

Close   the **display** when finished. **Make corrections** if necessary.

Post   the **entry**. **Close** the **Sales Journal**.

In the Receipts Journal for this customer, a negative amount has been entered for the return:

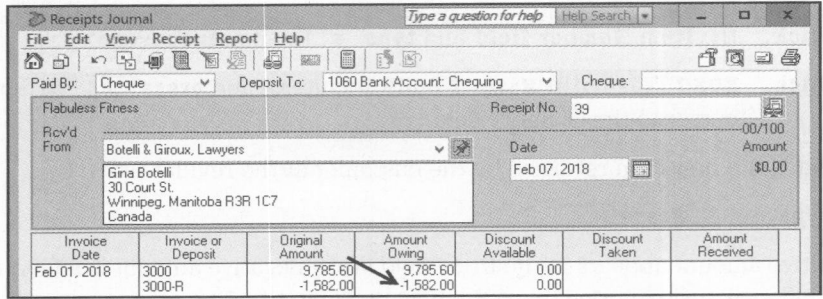

When the customer makes the final payment, accept the Amount Received field for the return to subtract the amount of the return from the original invoice.

Enter the **payment to Prohealth Exercisers**.

> **10** **Payment Cheque #251** **Dated February 3, 2018**
> To Prohealth Exercisers Inc., $10 609 in payment of account including $206 discount for early payment. Reference invoice #PE-364.

Entering Purchase Adjustments and Credit Notes

Returns on purchases also occur for a variety of reasons. For example, the goods may be damaged or the wrong items may have been shipped. Purchase returns are entered in the same way as sales returns — by adding a minus sign to the quantity so that all the amounts become negative. The supplier and payment method must be the same as the original purchase. You cannot change the default asset account for inventory purchases or returns.

The journal entry is a reversed purchase entry.

The inventory asset account and *GST Paid on Purchases* will be credited to decrease the inventory and restore the tax liability. *Accounts Payable* will be debited to reduce the amount owing to the supplier. Freight charges, when entered as a negative amount, will also be reversed.

Adjustments for purchases of inventory are made in the same way as other purchase adjustments. However, differences occur when the invoice has already been paid.

> **11** **Adjust Purchase Invoice #PE-364-R** **Dated February 4, 2018**
> From Prohealth Exercisers, Credit Note
>
> | | | | |
> |---|---|---|---|
> | 3 | E010 | Elliptical Exerciser: AE-200 | $3 450.00 |
> | 3 | E020 | Elliptical Exerciser: LE-400 | 4 200.00 |
> | | | Freight | 100.00 |
> | | | GST Paid | 387.50 |
> | | | Total Invoice | $8 137.50 |
> | | | Total Credit amount | $2 471.50 |
>
> Terms: net 60 days.

Open the **Purchases Journal**. **Click** the **Adjust Invoice tool** and **select** invoice **PE-364** from **Prohealth Exercisers Inc.**

Type PE-364-R as the invoice number.

Click **4**, the Quantity for E010 Elliptical Exerciser: AE-200 and **type** 3

Click **4**, the Quantity for E020 Elliptical Exerciser: LE-400 and **type** 3

Change the **payment terms** to **net 60** to complete the entry:

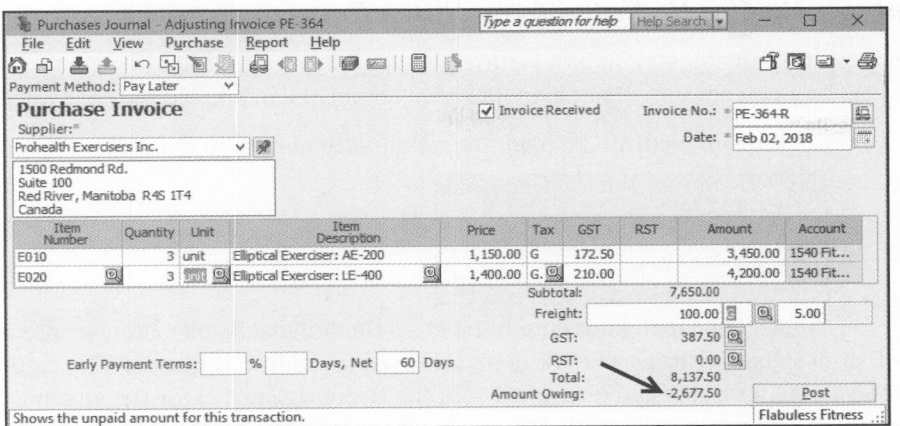

The amount owing appears as a negative amount on the invoice, but unlike the sales return, all other amounts are still positive.

Review the **journal entry** — it looks like a normal purchase entry.

Close the **display**. **Make corrections** if needed.

Click **Post**.

Creating Automatic Credit Notes from Returns

When you reverse or adjust an invoice after an account has been paid, and the original purchase was a "pay later" transaction, as in this example, Sage 50 can automatically create a credit note for the adjustment or reversing entry.

First, you may see a confirmation that payments have already been applied:

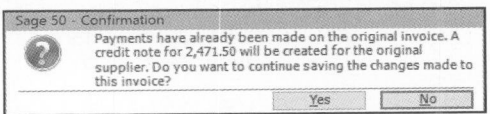

Click Yes to continue if you see this message.

An additional message about the credit note will open (read the margin Notes):

You can accept or change the default note number — the original invoice number preceded by CN that designates this as a credit note.

Click **OK** to continue.

In the Payments Journal, the credit note is entered as an invoice with a negative amount that you can accept to reduce the amount you pay for future purchases:

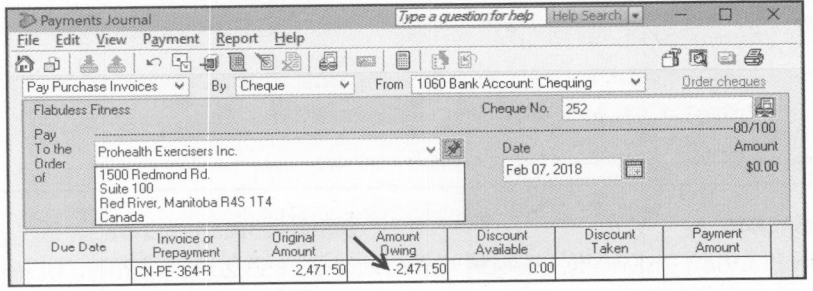

NOTES
The amount owing in the journal is different from the credit note amount by the amount of the discount on the original payment.

NOTES
The credit note amount is calculated as follows:
$10 609 was paid toward the original invoice;
$8 137.50 is the amount on the adjusted invoice;
$2 471.50 is the difference between these amounts.
The calculation of the credit amount is complicated by the discount that was already taken. The discount taken should be prorated to reduce the credit. The preferred method of entering this transaction is as a return. If the same terms are applied to the returned items, the credit amount will also be reduced by the discount and it will be correctly adjusted.

NOTES
The return creates three journal entries: the reversal or cancellation of the discount, the reversing entry and the final correct purchase entry. The net result in the journal's Amount Owing column is a credit balance of $2 471.50, not $2 677.50.

NOTES
The purchase return and credit note do not have a due date in the Payments Journal.

Automatic Credit Notes from Sales Returns

When posting an adjustment or a return for a sales invoice that has been paid, you may first get a notice advising that payments have already been applied to the invoice.

Click Yes to confirm. Instead, the credit note may open immediately:

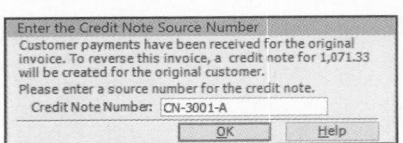

Enter the Credit Note Source Number
Customer payments have been received for the original invoice. To reverse this invoice, a credit note for 1,071.33 will be created for the original customer.
Please enter a source number for the credit note.
Credit Note Number: CN-3001-A

OK   Help

You can accept the default note number — the original invoice number preceded by CN that designates this as a credit note. Click OK to confirm the entry. The credit note for the customer is a negative invoice — in the Receipts Journal for the customer, it appears as a negative amount that you can accept with the next customer payment to reduce the amount owing by the customer.

Enter the **remaining transactions** for February.

12

Payment Cheque #252   **Dated February 4, 2018**

To Footlink Corporation, $16 640 in payment of account including $160 discount for early payment. Reference invoice #FC-618.

13

Receipt #39   **Dated February 4, 2018**

From Red River College, cheque #4782 for $5 537 in payment of account including $113 discount for early payment. Reference invoice #2194.

14

To:
Customer: **Flabuless Fitness**
Address: 199 Warmup Ave., #500
            Winnipeg, MB R8T 3B7
            Reg # 245138121

Feelyte Gym Accessories
7 Onandaga Dr., Vancouver, BC V4G 4S5
Tel: (604) 588-3846 Fax: (604) 588-7126
www.feelyte.com

Invoice #: FG-4100
GST # 466 254 108

Feb. 6, 2018

qty	code	item		total
5	A050	Heart rate monitor @ $40		200.00
10	A060	Power blocks @ $150		1,500.00
10	A080	Weight/workout bench @ $84		840.00
5	A100	Aerobic stepper w/risers @ 40		200.00
			Freight	100.00
			GST	142.00
			Invoice Total	2,982.00

Terms: 2/10, n/30 *ST*

15

Receipt #40   **Dated February 7, 2018**

From Brandon University, cheque #14701 for $8 859.20 in payment of account including $180.80 discount for early payment. Reference invoice #2199.

16

INVOICE # 3002
Flabuless Fitness
199 Warmup Ave., Suite 500
Winnipeg, MB R8T 3B7
#245138121

Salesperson: Kisangel

Sold to: Lavendar Estates
Address: 9 Lavender Ct.
              Winnipeg, MB R2X 3J6
ATTN: Katherine Harris

Date: Feb. 7/18

QTY	CODE	DESCRIPTION	PRICE/UNIT	TAX CODE	TOTAL
4	A070	Stability ball	12 /each	1	48.00
1	B010	Books: fitness guide	40/each	2	40.00
1	E020	Elliptical exerciser: LE-400	2600/unit	1	2,600.00
1	E060	Treadmill: basic T-800B	1400/unit	1	1,400.00
4	S040	Yoga instructor: 1 hour	100/hour	2	400.00
1	P020	Training workout pkg	1600/pkg	1	1,600.00
			Delivery	2	50.00

Authorization to exceed credit limit *GP 2/7/18*

Terms: 2/5, n/15	**GST** 5%	306.90
	RST 8%	451.84
	Invoice Total	**6,896.74**

Tel 1: (204) 642-B-FIT   or (800) 448-B-FIT   Fax: (204) 642-9100
www.flabulessfitness.com
fit for life

NOTES
Remember to change the tax code for delivery (freight).

SESSION DATE – FEBRUARY 14, 2018

17

Purchase Invoice #TD-6891   **Dated February 9, 2018**

From Trufit Depot

2	E080	Home Gym: Basic HG-1400	$2 100.00
2	E090	Home Gym: Deluxe Multi HG-1402	3 200.00
	Freight		100.00
	GST		270.00
	Total		$5 670.00

Terms: 2/5, n/20.

NOTES
The price for E080 has changed.

18

Memo #4   **Dated February 9, 2018**

Edit the selling price to reflect the increase in the purchase price for item E080 Home Gym: Basic HG-1400. The new regular and Web price will be $1 750 and the preferred price will be $1 600.

19

Cash Purchase Invoice #WD-114   **Dated February 9, 2018**

From Winnipeg Daily (use Quick Add for new vendor), $1 200 plus $60 GST and $96 RST for ads to run for 12 weeks. Purchase invoice total $1 356 paid in full by cheque #253. Create new Group account: 1290 Prepaid Advertising.

20

Purchase Invoice #RS-6112   **Dated February 12, 2018**

From Riverview Sunoco, $130 including GST and RST for gasoline purchase for delivery vehicle. Terms: net 21. Store as a recurring bi-weekly entry.

21

INVOICE # 3003
Flabuless Fitness
199 Warmup Ave., Suite 500
Winnipeg, MB R8T 3B7
#245138121

Sold to: The Forks Film Corp.
Address: 6 Gilroy St.
          Winnipeg, MB R3C 2M2
ATTN: Francine Despardieu

Salesperson: Prekor

Date: Feb. 14/18

QTY	CODE	DESCRIPTION	PRICE/UNIT	TAX CODE	TOTAL
2	A010	Body fat scale	130/unit**	1	260.00
80	A030	Dumbbells	2.20/kg	1	176.00
3	A060	Power blocks	250/set	1	750.00
8	A070	Stability ball	10 /each	1	80.00
2	A080	Weight/workout bench	150/each	1	300.00
2	A100	Aerobic stepper w/risers	60 /each	1	120.00
2	E060	Treadmill: basic T-800B	1220/unit	1	2,440.00
1	E080	Home gym: basic HG-1400	1600/set	1	1,600.00

* preferred customer discounts & free delivery GP 2/14/18

Terms: 2/15, n/30		
	GST 5%	286.30
	RST 8%	458.08
	Invoice Total	**6,470.38**

Tel 1: (204) 642-B-FIT   or (800) 448-B-FIT   Fax: (204) 642-9100
www.flabulessfitness.com
fit for life

SESSION DATE – FEBRUARY 21, 2018

22

Sales Invoice #3004   **Dated February 17, 2018**

Sold by Prekor to Brandon University

2	A010	Body Fat Scale	$ 130 /unit
100	A030	Dumbbells	2.20 /kg
2	A040	Jump Rope: Weighted	35 each
4	A080	Weight/Workout Bench	150 each
10	B010	Books: Fitness Guide	35 each
2	E020	Elliptical Exerciser: LE-400	2 300 /unit
2	E030	Bicycle: Dual Action Calorie Counter	720 /unit
2	E060	Treadmill: Basic T-800B	1 220 /unit
2	E080	Home Gym: Basic HG-1400	1 600 /set
	GST		5%
	RST		8%

Terms: 2/15, n/30. Allow customer to exceed credit limit.

23

Receipt #41   **Dated February 17, 2018**

From Brandon University, cheque #19664 for $5 000 in partial payment of invoice #3004.

24

Cash Purchase Invoice #MB-59113   **Dated February 19, 2018**

From Manitoba Bell, $140 plus $7.00 GST paid and $11.20 RST for phone service. Purchase invoice total $158.20 paid by cheque #254 in full payment.

25

Cash Purchase Invoice #ME-34910   **Dated February 19, 2018**

From Manitoba Energy, $210 plus $10.50 GST paid for hydro service. Purchase invoice total $220.50 paid by cheque #255.

26

Receipt #42   **Dated February 20, 2018**

From Lavender Estates, cheque #584 for $6 896.74 in payment of invoice #3002.

27

Sales Invoice #3005   **Dated February 21, 2018**

Sold by Kisangel to Ariandanos Residence

2	A070	Stability Ball	$ 12	each
1	A080	Weight/Workout Bench	175	each
2	A090	Workout Gloves	15	/pair
1	B010	Books: Fitness Guide	40	each
1	E080	Home Gym: Basic HG-1400	1 750	/set
1	P020	Training Workout Package	1 600	/pkg
		GST	5%	
		RST	8%	

Terms: 2/5, n/15. Includes complimentary delivery.

28

Receipt #43   **Dated February 21, 2018**

From Red River College, cheque #5961 for $4 000 in partial payment of invoice #3001.

SESSION DATE – FEBRUARY 28, 2018

29

Sales Invoice #3006   **Dated February 23, 2018**

Sold by Kisangel to Red River College

4	A060	Power Blocks	$ 250	/set
2	A080	Weight/Workout Bench	150	each
3	E040	Bicycle: Recumbent R-80	960	/unit
		GST	5%	
		RST	8%	

Terms: 2/15, n/30.

30

Memo #5   **Dated February 25, 2018**

Create new inventory item:

Number	Description	Unit	Min Level	Regular Price	Preferred Price	Linked Accounts Asset	Revenue	COGS
E100	Home Gym: Free Weight HG-1403	set	1	$3 200	(2 900)	1550	4020	5060

31

Purchase Invoice #TD-9133   **Dated February 25, 2018**

From Trufit Depot, new inventory item purchase

2	E100	Home Gym: Free Weight HG-1403	$3 000.00
		GST	150.00
		Invoice total	$3 150.00

Terms: 2/5, n/20. Free delivery.

32

Purchase Invoice #RS-7533   **Dated February 26, 2018**

From Riverview Sunoco, $130 including GST and RST for gasoline. Terms: net 21. Recall the stored entry.

33

Bank Debit Memo #91431   **Dated February 28, 2018**

From Red River Credit Union, authorized withdrawals were made from the chequing account on our behalf for the following:

Bank service charges	$ 65
Mortgage interest payment	1 880
Mortgage principal reduction	220
Bank loan interest payment	420
Bank loan principal reduction	480

> **NOTES**
> This is a new inventory item, so there is no historical cost and the amount field is blank. You will need to enter an amount.

Choose Cash & Credit Card Sales for the Visa and MasterCard sales summaries.

34

Flabuless Fitness

INVOICE # 3007
Flabuless Fitness
199 Warmup Ave., Suite 500
Winnipeg, MB R8T 3B7
245138121

Sold to: Visa Sales Summary
Address: Cash Customers

Salesperson: Kisangel   **Date:**   Feb. 28/18

QTY	CODE	DESCRIPTION	PRICE/UNIT	TAX CODE	TOTAL
3	A010	Body fat scale	150/unit	1	450.00
15	A020	Yoga/pilates mat	40/each	1	600.00
40	A030	Dumbbells	2.50/kg	1	100.00
5	A050	Heart rate monitor	90/unit	1	450.00
10	A090	Workout gloves: all sizes	15/pair	1	150.00
3	P020	Training workout package	1600/pkg	1	4,800.00
10	S010	Personal trainer: 1 hour	80/hour	2	800.00
4	S060	Equipment assembly/instruction	75/job	1	300.00
10	B010	Books: fitness guide	40/each	2	400.00

Direct deposit to Visa account   AK

Terms: Visa

GST 5%	402.50
RST 8%	548.00
Total	9,000.50

Tel 1: (204) 642-B-FIT   or   (800) 448-B-FIT   Fax: (204) 642-9100
www.flabulessfitness.com
fit for life

35

MasterCard Sales Invoice #3008   **Dated February 28, 2018**

Sold by Prekor to Cash & Credit Card Sales (sales summary)

2	A010	Body Fat Scale	$150 /unit	$ 300.00
5	A020	Yoga/Pilates Mat	40 each	200.00
4	A040	Jump Rope: Weighted	40 each	160.00
3	A060	Power Blocks	300 /set	900.00
6	A090	Workout Gloves: all sizes	15 /pair	90.00
8	B010	Books: Fitness Guide	40 each	320.00
8	S020	Personal Trainer: 1/2 day	200 /1/2 day	1 600.00
4	S030	Personal Trainer: full day	400 /day	1 600.00
8	S050	Yoga Instructor: 1/2 day	200 /1/2 day	1 600.00
	GST		5%	338.50
	RST		8%	132.00
	Total paid by MasterCard			$7 240.50

Use the Sales by Salesperson Summary Report (by Sales Item) to find the net sales for each employee. Do not include freight or other sales in the report.

The report by customer does not allow you to omit freight and other amounts.

36

Memo #6   **Dated February 28, 2018**

Prepare the payroll for the two salaried employees, Prekor and Kisangel. Add 2 percent of revenue from sales and services for February as a commission to their salaries. Issue payroll cheques #256 and #257.

Displaying Inventory Reports

Most inventory reports can be displayed from the Reports menu in the Inventory & Services window, from the Home window Reports menu, from the Inventory & Services module window Reports pane drop-down list and from the Report Centre. We will access the reports from the Report Centre.

Click the **Report Centre icon** in any window.

Click **Inventory & Services** to open the list of inventory reports:

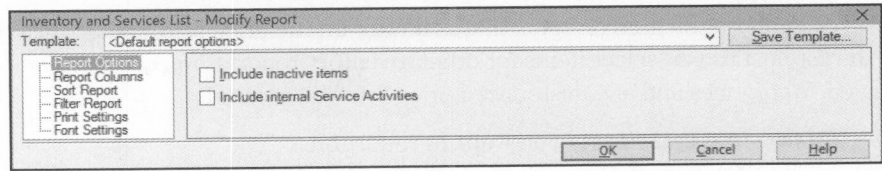

Displaying Inventory Lists

Click **Inventory And Services List**. **Click Modify This Report**:

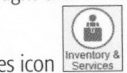

Or, you can choose the Reports menu and choose Lists, then click Inventory & Services for the report options.

The default report has the item number, description, type, quantity, total value and average cost. To select the fields for the report, choose Report Columns.

Click **OK** to produce the list. **Close** the **display** when you have finished.

Displaying Grouped Inventory Lists

Click **Grouped Inventory And Services List**. **Click Modify This Report**.

Click **Type** in the Group By field:

From this list, choose the way you want to sort the list. You can organize by Type (inventory and services are separated) or by any of the additional information fields you created for the ledger. To select the fields for the report, choose Report Columns.

Click **OK** to open the list. **Close** the **display** when you have finished.

Displaying Inventory Price Lists

The different inventory prices — regular, preferred, Web and customized prices — are not available in the other inventory reports, but you can place all of these prices together on the Price Lists Report.

PRO VERSION
The Pro version Select Items list does not include Activities.

NOTES
If you have created other price lists or use additional currencies, they will be listed in the Modify Report screen and you can include them in the report.
If you use other currencies, you can also add the price lists in these currencies and then group your lists by currency or by price list.

NOTES
You can customize Summary reports by selecting any of the columns usually included in the report. You can sort and filter by item or description.

NOTES
Select All acts as a toggle switch. When all items are selected, clicking Select All will remove all selections. When one or a few items are selected, clicking Select All will select all the entries on the list.

Click   Price Lists from the Select A Report list. **Click Modify This Report**:

You can also choose the Reports menu, then choose Inventory & Services and click Price Lists to display the report options.

You can choose the item or items that you want on the price list by selecting them from the list, just as you select items for other inventory reports. You can include Regular, Preferred, Web prices and any customized price lists you created.

Click   the **Price Lists** you want to report on.

Click   **OK** to open the price lists and **close** the **display** when you have finished.

Displaying Inventory Summary Reports

The Inventory Summary Report provides detailed quantity and cost information for the inventory you have in stock.

Click   **Summary** from the Select A Report list to open the sample report.

Click   **Modify This Report** to open the report options window:

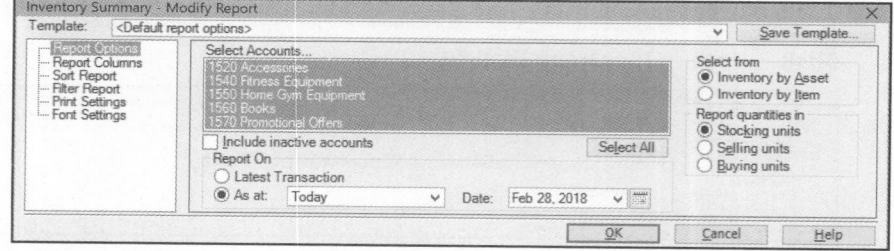

You can also choose the Reports menu, then choose Inventory & Services and click Summary to display the report options.

Selecting **Inventory By Asset** will provide information for all inventory items in the asset group(s) chosen. The **Inventory By Item** option will provide information for all the items selected. When you click Inventory By Item, the Select Accounts box lists all inventory items. Services are not included because there is no quantity or cost information for them.

Click a single asset or item to change selections or provide a report for that item only. To select multiple items, press and hold ⌐ctrl⌐ and then click the items you want in the report. To obtain information for all items, choose Select All.

The **Summary Report** lists the quantity on hand, the unit cost of the inventory and the total value or cost of inventory on hand for the items requested. The total value of the inventory in an asset group is also provided when you select one asset group. You

can create the Summary Report for the Latest Transaction Date or for another date that you enter in the **As At** Date field.

You can create the report with quantities in any of the units you use for the item if these are different, that is, the stocking, buying or selling units (refer to page 370).

Choose the **options** you need for your report.

Press and **hold** ⌘ctrl⌘ and **click** the **items** or **assets** you want included.

Click **OK**. **Close** the **display** when you have finished.

Displaying Inventory Quantity Reports

The Inventory Quantity Report provides current information about the quantity on hand, the minimum stock levels and outstanding purchase and sales orders. The report also displays the order quantity needed to restore the minimum level when an item has fallen below the minimum level.

Click **Quantity** from the Select A Report list. **Click Modify This Report**:

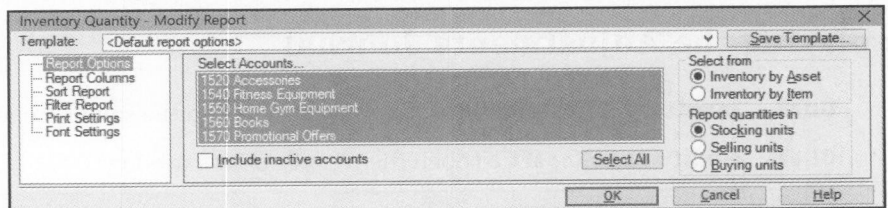

Or, choose the Reports menu, then choose Inventory & Services and click Quantity to display the report options.

You can select the items for the report in the same way you did for the Inventory Summary Report. Selecting **Inventory By Asset** will provide information for all inventory items in the asset group(s) chosen. The **Inventory By Item** option will provide information for all the items selected. When you click Inventory By Item, the Select Accounts box lists all inventory items. Services are not included in the Quantity Report because there is no quantity or cost information for them.

Click a single asset or item to change selections or provide a report for that item only. To select multiple items, press and hold ⌘ctrl⌘ and then click the items you want in the report. To obtain information for all items, choose Select All.

You can prepare the report with quantities in any of the units you use for the item if they are different, that is, the stocking, buying or selling units (refer to page 370).

Choose the **options** you need for your report.

Press and **hold** ⌘ctrl⌘ and **click** the **names** of all the items or asset groups you want to include in the report.

Click **OK** and **close** the **display** when you have finished.

Displaying the Item Assembly Journal

Click **Bill Of Materials & Item Assembly Journal Entries** to open the report sample and description.

NOTES
When you display the report with the Latest Transaction option, it includes the profit for each item — either the markup or margin, as selected in the Inventory Ledger Settings.

NOTES
You can drill down to the Inventory Transaction Detail Report from the Inventory Summary or Quantity reports.

NOTES
You can customize Quantity Reports by selecting any of the columns usually included in the report. You can sort and filter by most of the columns usually included in the report.

Classic **CLASSIC VIEW**
Right-click the Bill Of Materials & Item Assembly icon
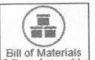
. Click the Select A
Report tool [icon] to open the Modify Report window.

PRO VERSION

In the Report Centre list, click Item Assembly Journal Entries. Or, choose the Reports menu, then choose Journal Entries and click Item Assembly.

NOTES
Additional Information for journal entries is covered in Chapter 11.

Click **Modify This Report** to open the report options window:

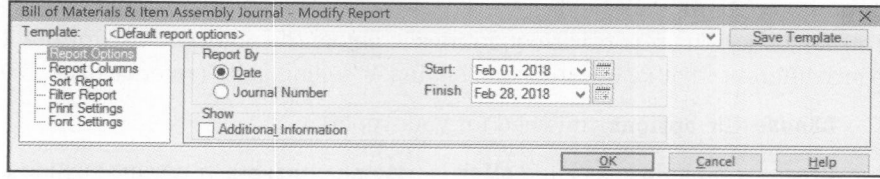

Or, choose the Reports menu, then choose Journal Entries and click Bill Of Materials & Item Assembly.

As usual, the earliest transaction date, session date and Report By Date options are provided by default. The sorting, filtering and column options are the same for all journal reports. There is no option to show corrections because these entries cannot be adjusted or reversed automatically.

Enter the **Start** and **Finish dates** you want for the report.

Click **OK**. **Close** the **display** when you have finished.

Displaying the Adjustments Journal

CLASSIC VIEW
Right-click the Inventory
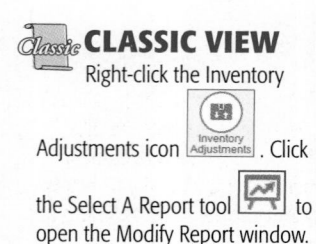
Adjustments icon . Click the Select A Report tool to open the Modify Report window.

NOTES
You can drill down to the General Ledger reports from the Item Assembly Journal and from the Adjustments Journal.

Click **Inventory Adjustment Journal Entries** to open the sample report.

Click **Modify This Report** to open the report options window:

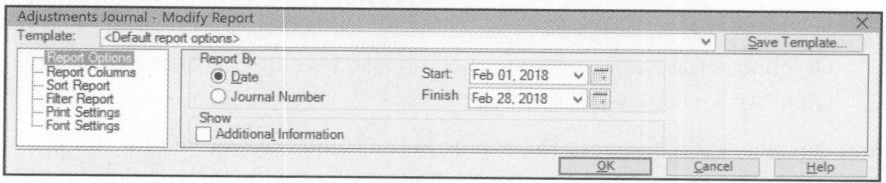

Or, you can choose the Reports menu, then choose Journal Entries and click Inventory Adjustments.

As usual, the earliest transaction date, session date and Report By Date options are provided by default. Showing corrections is not an option because these journal entries cannot be adjusted.

Enter the **Start** and **Finish dates** you want for the report.

Click **OK**. **Close** the **display** when you have finished.

Displaying Inventory Tracking Reports

Several reports provide information about the turnover of inventory products. These reports can let you know whether items are selling well and are profitable and how the sales are distributed over time and customers.

Inventory Statistics Reports

NOTES
For Inventory Statistics Reports, you can sort and filter by most of the columns usually included in the report.
You can customize Statistics Reports by selecting any of the columns usually included in the report.

Click **Statistics** from the Select A Report list. **Click Modify This Report** to open the report options window:

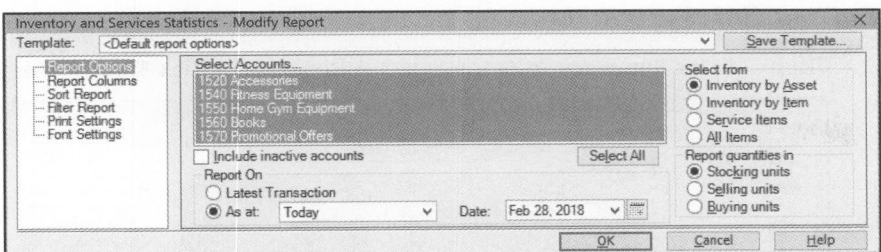

Or, choose the Reports menu, then choose Inventory & Services and click Statistics to display the report options.

The Statistics Report summarizes transactions for the year to date and the previous year, the same historical information that is contained in the Inventory Ledger record (refer to pages 372–373). For example, the report can let you know whether a large volume of sales resulted from a single sale for a large quantity or from a large number of smaller sales. Comparing the Statistics Report with the Statistics tab content in a ledger record for the same item will make the similarities apparent.

You can prepare the report for the session date (**Latest Transaction**) or for another date (**As At Date**). When you choose As At, the Date field is available. The report will include the statistics you request as at the date you enter.

The report has the **Number Of Transactions** (the number of separate sales invoices that included the inventory item), **Units Sold** (the total number of individual items of a kind that were sold in the period), the **Amount Sold** (the total revenue from all items sold) and the **Cost Of Goods Sold** (the total purchase cost of all the items that were sold). The average cost method is used to calculate the cost of goods sold for Flabuless Fitness. The cost method is selected as a ledger setting.

Press and hold (ctrl) and click one or more asset groups to include them in the report, or click Select All to include all asset groups in the report. Selecting an asset group will include all the inventory items in that group in the report. To select multiple assets or items, press (ctrl) and then click the items you want. The default selection — By Asset — will not include services in the report.

Click **Inventory By Item** to list individual inventory items. Select one or more items for the report, or click Select All to include all inventory items. Click **Service Items** to list individual services. Press (ctrl) and hold and click services to include them, or click Select All to include all services. Click **All Items** to include both individual inventory items and individual services in the report. Press (ctrl) and hold and click the items and services to include them in the report, or click Select All to include all items and services.

The list of items will expand according to your selection, and you can choose single or multiple items for inclusion. **Quantities** can be reported in any of the units on record — the units for stocking the inventory, for buying and for selling — if these are different.

Choose the **items** you want in the report.

Choose the **date** for the report (Latest Transaction or As At Date). **Enter** a **date** in the Date field if you chose the As At option.

Click **OK** to display the report. **Close** the **display** when you have finished.

NOTES
You can drill down to the Inventory Sales Detail Report from the Inventory Statistics Report.

NOTES
When you display the report with the Latest Transaction option, it includes the statistics for the previous year as well.

NOTES
You can also choose the FIFO (first-in, first-out) method of determining inventory costs. You make this choice in the Inventory Settings screen. This method is not available for the Pro version.

NOTES
Remember that Select All acts as a toggle switch — when all items are already selected, clicking Select All clears the selection. Clicking Select All when no items are selected, or when one or more items (but not all items) are selected, will select all items.

NOTES
You cannot sort or filter the Sales Report, but you can customize the report by selecting the columns you want to include.

NOTES
For the Inventory Sales Summary Report on Services, you must click Select From Service Items or choose All Items. Inventory By Item and Inventory By Asset – the default selection – include only inventory items.

NOTES
You can drill down to the Inventory Sales Detail Report from the Inventory Sales Summary Report. You can display the Customer Aged, Inventory Ledger and Journal Report. You can view Sales Invoices from the Inventory Sales Detail Report.

PRO VERSION
Item Assembly is the journal name in the Pro version instead of Bill of Materials & Item Assembly, and Adjustments replaces Adjustments and Transfers.

NOTES
You can drill down to the Transaction Detail Report from the Transaction Summary Report. You can display the Inventory Ledger and Journal Report from the Transaction Detail Report. You can also view invoices from the Detail Report.

Inventory Sales Reports

Click **Sales Summary** from the Select A Report list. **Click Modify This Report**:

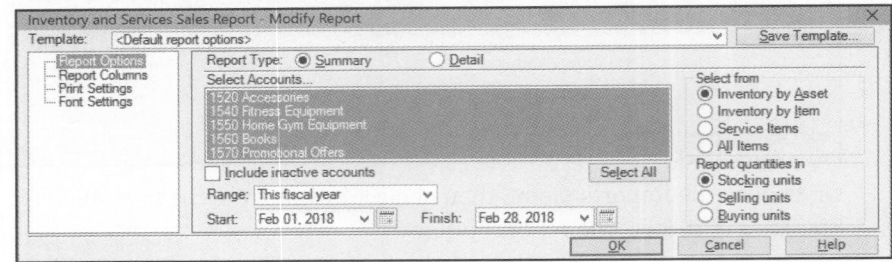

Or, choose the Reports menu, then choose Inventory & Services and click Sales.

The reports include the number of transactions (Summary option), the quantity of items sold, the revenue per item, the cost of goods sold and the profit for each item. Non-inventory sales are not included. The **Summary** option, selected by default, has the total for each detail for the selected inventory items organized by item. The **Detail** option provides the same information listed by individual journal entries, including the source document numbers and journal entry numbers. Click Detail to add these details.

As usual, you can choose to report on inventory items, services or both. To report only on all services, click **Service Items** and then Select All. Click **All Items** to include both inventory and services. The list of items will expand accordingly, and you can choose single or multiple items for inclusion. Select All at this stage will provide a report on all inventory and service items.

Again, **quantities** may be reported in stocking, buying or selling units.

Enter the **Start** and **Finish dates** you want for the report, or choose from the Range drop-down list.

Choose the **items** to include in the report.

Choose the **Summary** or **Detail** option.

Click **OK**. **Close** the **display** when you have finished.

Inventory Transaction Reports

The Transaction Report summarizes inventory activity according to the journal used to record the transaction.

Click **Transaction Summary**. **Click Modify This Report**:

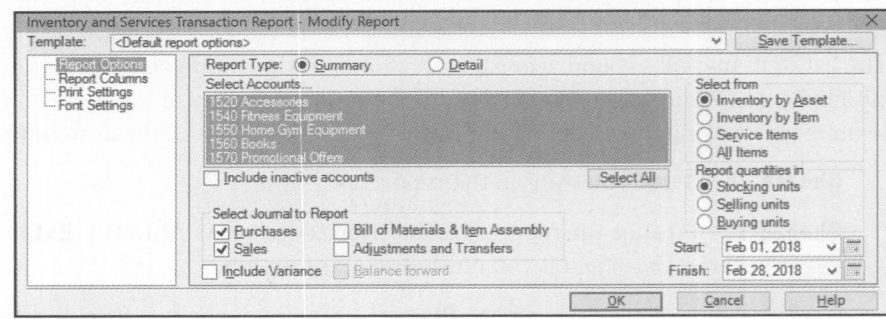

Or, choose the Reports menu, then choose Inventory & Services and click Transaction to display the report options.

The report includes details on the number of transactions (Summary option only), the **Quantity In** (increases to inventory from purchases, sales returns, recovery of lost items or assembled items) and **Out** (decreases in inventory from sales, purchase returns,

losses and adjustments or assembly components used) and the **Amount In** and **Out** (cost price) for each item chosen in each of the selected journals.

The **Summary** option, the default, includes totals for the selected inventory items organized by item. The **Detail** option provides the same information listed by individual journal entries, including the source document numbers and journal entry numbers.

As in the Sales Report, you can prepare a report for one or more asset groups, inventory items or service items, or a combination of services and items (All Items). Click the appropriate entry in the Select From list to expand the selection list accordingly.

Quantities may be reported in stocking, buying or selling units. Variances can also be added to the report when they are used.

You can choose to add the Balance Forward and include opening balances or to Include Variance and add cost variances for each item.

Click   **Detail** to include individual transaction details.

Enter   the **Start** and **Finish dates** you want for the report. By default, the earliest transaction and session date appear.

Click   the **journals** to include in the report.

Click   **OK**. **Close** the **display** when you have finished.

Supplier Purchases Reports

The next two reports combine inventory information with supplier or customer details to let you know how purchases are spread among suppliers and how sales are divided among customers. The Supplier Purchases and Customer Sales reports also allow you to include information for non-inventory purchases or sales.

Click   **Payables** in the Select A Report Type list.

Click   **Supplier Purchases Summary**. **Click Modify This Report**:

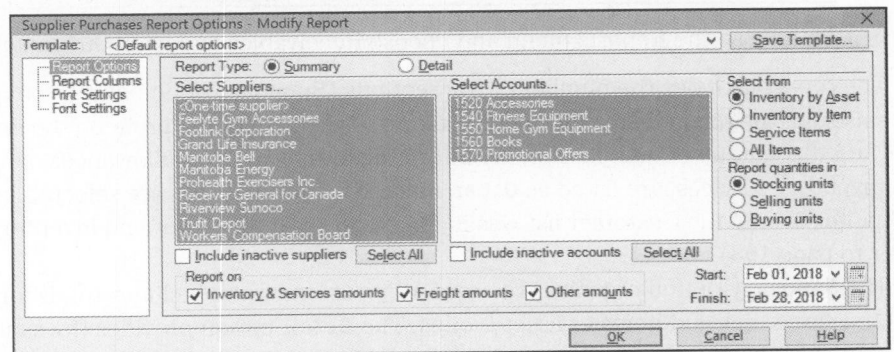

Or, choose the Reports menu and choose Payables and click Supplier Purchases.

The Supplier Purchases Report includes details on the number of transactions (Summary option only), the quantity purchased, the unit cost and the total cost of the purchase. Non-inventory purchases, such as telephone services, are listed as **Other**.

The **Summary** option organizes the report by supplier and includes totals for the selected categories and items or asset groups. The **Detail** option provides the same information by individual journal entries, including the source document numbers and journal entry numbers. Click Detail to choose the Detail option.

When other currencies are used, amounts for foreign suppliers may be displayed in either the home currency or the foreign currency.

The selection of inventory, services or asset groups is the same as for the other inventory reports. Reports can be prepared for either stocking, buying or selling units if these are different.

PRO VERSION
Choose Vendor Purchases Summary. This report is named the Vendor Purchases Report.

NOTES
You cannot sort or filter the Supplier Purchases Report, but you can select the columns you want in the report.

NOTES
You can drill down to the Inventory Purchases Detail Report from the Purchases Summary Report. You can look up invoices or drill down to the Supplier Aged and Purchases Journal Report from the Purchases Detail Report.

NOTES
To select multiple items, press and hold *ctrl* and then click the items or suppliers you want to add to the report.

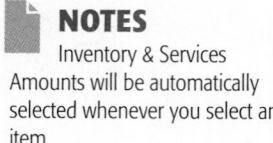
All items, categories and suppliers are selected initially.

> **Click** a **supplier name** or item to begin a new selection.
>
> **Enter** the **starting** and **ending dates** for the report in the Start and Finish fields.

All types of purchases are selected initially. Click a category — Inventory & Services, non-inventory (Other Amounts) and Freight Amounts — to remove the ✓ and deselect it for the selected supplier and item transactions. Click it again to select it.

> **Click** **OK**. **Close** the **display** when you have finished.

Customer Sales Reports

The Customer Sales Report provides the same details as the Inventory Sales Report but organizes the details by customer as well as by item. Customer Sales reports also have the option to include non-inventory sales.

> **Click** **Receivables** in the Select A Report Type list.
>
> **Click** **Customer Sales Summary**. **Click Modify This Report**:

Or, choose the Reports menu and choose Receivables and click Customer Sales.

The report includes the number of transactions (Summary option only), the quantity of items sold, the total revenue per item, the cost of goods sold, the profit on the item's sales and the markup or margin. Non-inventory sales, such as sales allowances or non-inventory services, are listed as **Other Amounts**. All categories are selected initially. In Chapter 6, only the Customer list was included because there were no inventory items (refer to page 193).

The **Summary** option organizes the report by customer and includes totals for the selected categories and items or asset groups. The **Detail** option provides the same information listed by individual journal entries, including the source document numbers and journal entry numbers. Click Detail to choose the Detail option. Reports can be prepared for stocking, buying or selling units if these are different. All customers and items are selected initially.

> **Select** **assets**, **inventory** or **services**, **customers**, **dates** and **categories** as you do for Supplier Purchases reports.
>
> **Click** **OK**. **Close** the **display** when you have finished.

Gross Margin Income Statement

This financial report becomes relevant when a business sells inventory. The report shows the income after inventory costs have been deducted from revenue and before operating expenses are included. This report is available from the Financials report type list.

Click   **Financials** in the Select A Report Type list.

Click   the ⊞ beside **Income Statement** to expand the list.

Click   **Gross Margin - Standard (under Income Statement)**.

Click   **Modify This Report** to open the report options window:

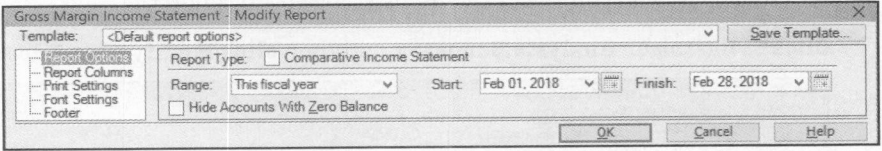

Or, choose the Reports menu, then choose Financials and click Gross Margin Income Statement to display the report options.

The report will include different income amounts: gross margin (revenue minus cost of goods sold, before taking into account the other operating expenses), income from operations (operating expenses are deducted from the gross margin) and net income (non-operating revenue and other expenses are entered).

The options for this Income Statement are the same as for regular Income Statements, including the option to generate a Comparative Income Statement.

Enter   the **Start** and **Finish dates** you want for the report.

Click   **OK**. **Close** the **display** when you have finished.

Displaying Forecast & Analysis Reports

This group of reports provides more detailed information about performance and trends.

Click   **Forecast & Analysis** in the Select A Report Type list:

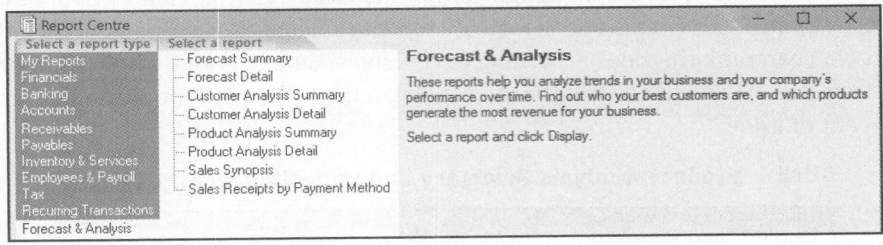

Displaying the Forecast Report

The report will provide monthly forecasts for revenues and expenses based on the same month in the previous year. The Forecast Report requires data for more than one year, so you will be unable to create this report with the data for Flabuless Fitness.

Click   **Forecast Summary** and then **click Modify This Report**:

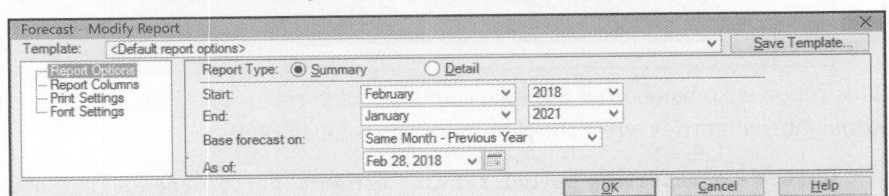

Choose the **months** for which you want the forecast and the date for the report.

Click   **OK**. **Close** the **display** when you have finished.

NOTES
Refer to page 58 for details on the Comparative Income Statement.

PRO VERSION
pro   Forecast & Analysis Reports and Retail Reports (in the Reports menu) are not available in the Pro version.

NOTES
From the Home window Reports menu, you can choose Retail Reports (or the <industry type> Reports) and click either Customer Analysis – Top 20% By Profit, or Customer Analysis – Bottom 30% By Profit for the report options.
The options screen will have the selections named in the menu report title (e.g., top 20%), but you can change the selections as you do in any report options window.

NOTES
You can drill down to the Detail Report from the Customer Analysis Summary Report. From the Detail Report, you can drill down to the Customer Sales Detail Report.

NOTES
From the Home window Reports menu, you can choose Retail Reports (or the <industry type> Reports) and click either Product Analysis – Top 20% Of Active Sales By ROI, or Product Analysis – Bottom 30% Of Sales Including Zero Sales By ROI for the report options.
The options screen will have the selections named in the menu report title (e.g., top 30%), but you can change the selections as you do in any report options window.
In the Product Analysis Report, ROI (return on investment) is measured as the profit divided by the average inventory value.

NOTES
You can drill down to the Detail Report from the Product Analysis Summary Report. From the Detail Report, you can drill down to the Inventory & Services Sales Detail Report.

Displaying the Customer Analysis Report

From this report, you can observe the customer sales for the fiscal year to date to learn which customers account for the most sales. You can include the customers in the top or bottom x percent; rank them according to revenue, profit, quantity or return on investment (ROI); and you can select the items you want to report on.

Click   Customer Analysis Summary and then **click Modify This Report**:

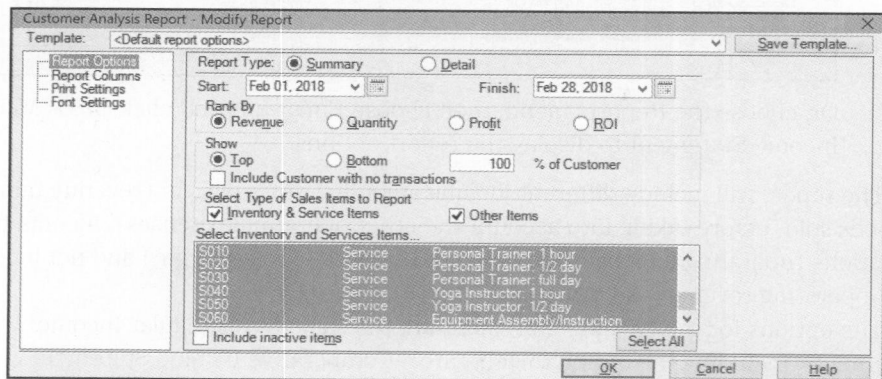

The Detail Report has individual journal entries while the Summary Report has total amounts.

Choose the **reporting period**, **ranking criteria**, **percentage** and **items**.

Click   OK. **Close** the **display** when you have finished.

Displaying the Product Analysis Report

The Product Analysis Report is similar to the Customer Analysis Report but organized primarily by product (items and services). You can select the customers to include. Again, you can rank the sales according to revenues, quantity sold, profit and return on investment. You can choose whether to report on the top x percent or the bottom x percent of items.

Click   Product Analysis Summary and then **click Modify This Report**:

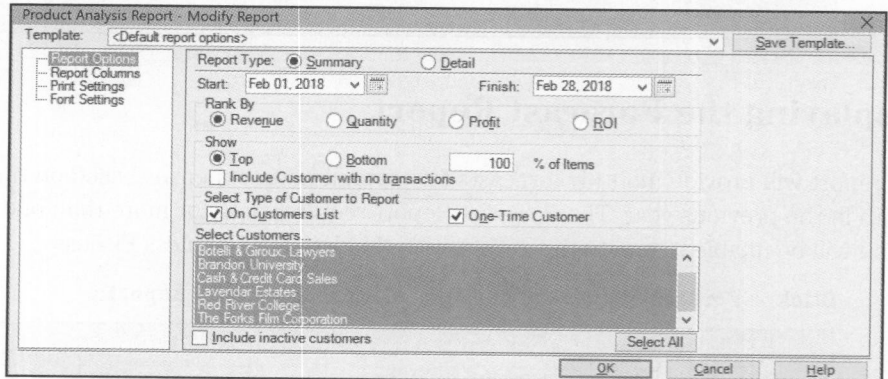

This report also has both a Summary and Detail version. The Detail Report has individual journal entries while the Summary has total amounts.

Choose the **reporting period**, **ranking criteria**, **percentage** and **customers**.

Click   OK. **Close** the **display** when you have finished.

Displaying the Sales Synopsis Report

The Sales Synopsis Report summarizes sales and receipts. The report includes the items sold (quantity and number of transactions) and the gross sales per item.

Click   Sales Synopsis and then **click Modify This Report**:

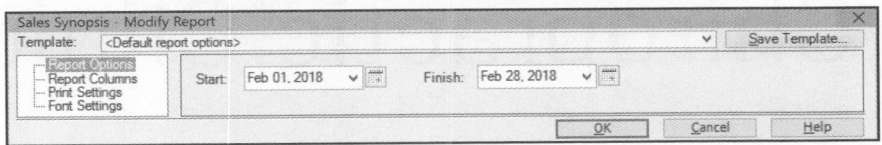

Choose the **reporting period**. Customize the report columns if you want to select details.

Click   OK. Close the **display** when you have finished.

Displaying Sales Receipts by Payment Method Reports

The final Forecast & Analysis Report summarizes the sales according to the customer payment methods, that is, by cash, by credit card or on account (pay later).

Click   Sales Receipts by Payment Method and then **click Modify This Report**:

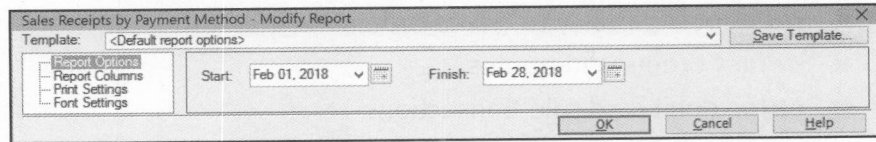

Choose the **reporting period**. Customize the report columns if you want to select details.

Click   OK. Close the **display** when you have finished. **Close** the **Report Centre**.

Printing Inventory Reports

Display the **report** you want to print.

Click   the Reports & Forms Settings tool to check your printer settings.

Choose the **File menu** and **click Print** or **click** the **Print tool. Close** the **display** when finished.

R E V I E W

The Student DVD with Data Files includes Review Questions and Supplementary Cases for this chapter.

NOTES
From the Home window Reports menu, choose Retail Reports and click Daily Sales Summary for the report options window.
You can drill down to the Inventory & Services Transaction Report from the Sales Synopsis Report.

NOTES
From the Home window Reports menu, choose Retail Reports and click Daily Sales Receipts for the report options window.

Andersson Chiropractic Clinic

OBJECTIVES

- **enter** receipts and payments with discounts
- **track** additional information for receipts, sales and purchases
- **understand** linked accounts for discounts
- **place** and **fill** purchase orders and quotes
- **enter** and **fill** sales quotes and orders
- **convert** sales and purchase quotes to orders
- **fill** quotes partially to create orders
- **adjust** orders and quotes
- **enter** debit card sale transactions
- **make** payments and deposits using multiple bank accounts and a line of credit
- **enter** deposits from customers and prepayments to vendors
- **delete** a stored transaction
- **remove** quotes

After completing this chapter, you should be able to

COMPANY INFORMATION

Company Profile

NOTES
Andersson Chiropractic Clinic
4500 Rae St.
Regina, SK S4S 3B4
Tel 1: (306) 577-1900
Tel 2: (306) 577-2199
Fax: (306) 577-1925
Business No.: 459 556 291

Andersson Chiropractic Clinic is a private clinic owned by Maria Andersson, who practises her profession in Regina, Saskatchewan. This is her second year in private practice after graduating with D.C. (Doctor of Chiropractic) and D.Ac. (Doctor of Acupuncture) degrees. She used some bank loans and her line of credit to consolidate her student loans and set up the clinic.

Andersson specializes in sports injuries and has some sports teams as clients. To treat patients, she uses chiropractic treatments and adjustments for back pain, and physiotherapy, massage, ultrasound, laser treatments, electrical stimulation and acupuncture for other joint and soft tissue injuries. Individual regular patients usually come two or three times per week, although some come daily. These patients settle their accounts bi-weekly. Sports teams have contracts and are billed

monthly. Contract customers are offered a discount if they settle their accounts within 10 days. Cash, cheques and debit cards are accepted in payment.

A single assistant in the clinic divides her time between reception, administration and some basic treatments such as laser and ultrasound under the chiropractor's supervision. Andersson designates the precise area to be treated and the time and intensity settings for the equipment.

The office space that Andersson rents has a reception area and four treatment rooms with tables. The monthly rent includes heat but not hydro or telephone. One of the four treatment rooms doubles as Andersson's office and another room has the potential to accommodate a whirlpool. She is considering adding a whirlpool for hydrotherapy and deep water massage treatments because some sports injuries respond well to hydrotherapy.

For new sports team contracts, Andersson prepares sales quotes. When they accept a contract, they pay a deposit that is applied to the first month's payment.

Andersson has two bank accounts and a line of credit she uses to pay her bills. The limit on her line of credit is $50 000, and she has already borrowed $15 000 against it. A third bank account is used exclusively for debit card transactions.

Accounts for regular suppliers of treatment equipment, linens, laundry services, office maintenance and so on are set up. Some of these suppliers also offer discounts for early payments and some require Andersson to make prepayments with purchase orders.

No taxes are charged for medical treatments and supplies. Because GST is not charged to customers, the business is not eligible for a GST refund. Therefore tax amounts are not tracked — they are included with the expense or asset amounts. Andersson pays both PST and GST for other goods and services.

To convert her accounting records to Sage 50 on October 1, 2018, she used the following information:

- Chart of Accounts
- Trial Balance
- Supplier Information
- Patient/Customer Information
- Accounting Procedures

CHART OF POSTABLE ACCOUNTS

ANDERSSON CHIROPRACTIC CLINIC

ASSETS
1060 Bank: Regina Chequing
1080 Bank: Eastside Chequing
1100 Bank: Interac
1200 Accounts Receivable
1220 Prepaid Insurance
1240 Prepaid Subscriptions
1280 Purchase Prepayments
1300 Linen Supplies
1320 Office Supplies
1340 Other Supplies
1420 Computer Equipment
1430 Accum Deprec: Computers
1450 Treatment Equipment
1460 Accum Deprec: Equipment
1520 Office Furniture ▶

▶ 1530 Accum Deprec: Furniture
1550 Treatment Tables
1560 Accum Deprec: Tables
1580 Vehicle
1590 Accum Deprec: Vehicle

LIABILITIES
2100 Loans Payable
2200 Accounts Payable
2250 Prepaid Sales and Deposits
2300 Line of Credit Payable

EQUITY
3400 M.A. Capital
3450 M.A. Drawings
3600 Net Income ▶

▶**REVENUE**
4100 Revenue from Services
4150 Sales Discounts
4200 Interest Income

EXPENSE
5010 Bank Charges and Interac Fees
5030 Purchase Discounts
5050 Office Supplies Used
5060 Other Supplies Used
5080 Subscriptions and Books
5090 Insurance Expense
5100 Interest Expense
5110 Freight Expense
5120 Clinic Maintenance ▶

▶ 5140 Laundry Services
5150 Professional Dues
5180 Depreciation Expenses
5200 Hydro Expense
5240 Telephone Expense
5260 Rent
5300 Vehicle Expenses
5500 Wages Expense
5520 Payroll Services

NOTES: The Chart of Accounts includes only postable accounts and the Net Income or Current Earnings account.

TRIAL BALANCE

ANDERSSON CHIROPRACTIC CLINIC

September 30, 2018		Debits	Credits				Debits	Credits
1060	Bank: Regina Chequing	$33 530		▶ 3450	M.A. Drawings		$ 18 000	
1080	Bank: Eastside Chequing	19 100		4100	Revenue from Services			$114 000
1100	Bank: Interac	3 430		4150	Sales Discounts		140	
1200	Accounts Receivable	12 500		4200	Interest Income			160
1220	Prepaid Insurance	1 600		5010	Bank Charges and Interac Fees		390	
1240	Prepaid Subscriptions	480		5030	Purchase Discounts			210
1300	Linen Supplies	1 300		5050	Office Supplies Used		350	
1320	Office Supplies	270		5060	Other Supplies Used		1 130	
1340	Other Supplies	530		5080	Subscriptions and Books		2 400	
1420	Computer Equipment	4 200		5090	Insurance Expense		8 000	
1430	Accum Deprec: Computers		$ 1 050	5100	Interest Expense		2 500	
1450	Treatment Equipment	12 600		5110	Freight Expense		120	
1460	Accum Deprec: Equipment		2 100	5120	Clinic Maintenance		2 100	
1520	Office Furniture	9 600		5140	Laundry Services		1 800	
1530	Accum Deprec: Furniture		800	5150	Professional Dues		1 495	
1550	Treatment Tables	8 400		5180	Depreciation Expenses		10 850	
1560	Accum Deprec: Tables		1 400	5200	Hydro Expense		1 200	
1580	Vehicle	22 000		5240	Telephone Expense		1 100	
1590	Accum Deprec: Vehicle		5 500	5260	Rent		23 000	
2100	Loans Payable		45 000	5300	Vehicle Expenses		3 300	
2200	Accounts Payable		7 290	5500	Wages Expense		21 000	
2300	Line of Credit Payable		15 000	5520	Payroll Services		450	
3400	M.A. Capital		36 355 ▶				$228 865	$228 865

SUPPLIER INFORMATION

ANDERSSON CHIROPRACTIC CLINIC

Supplier Name (Contact)	Address	Phone No. Fax No.	E-mail Web Site	Terms
Canadian Chiropractic Association (O. Fisshal)	33 Backer Road Toronto, Ontario M4T 5B2	Tel 1: (416) 488-3713 Tel 2: (888) 488-3713	cca.ca	net 10
Cleanol and Laundry Services (Bessie Sweeps)	19 Duster Road Regina, Saskatchewan S4R 4L4	Tel: (306) 398-0908 Fax: (306) 398-8211	bsweeps@cls.com cls.com	net 30
Grasslands Fuel				net 1 (cash)
Medical Linen Supplies (Oll Whyte)	500 Agar St. Saskatoon, Saskatchewan S7L 6B9	Tel: (306) 662-6192 Fax: (306) 662-4399	owhyte@medsupplies.com medsupplies.com	2/10, n/30
OnLine Books			onlinebooks.com	net 1 (cheque)
Prairie Power Corp. (M. Jouls)	48 Powers Bay Regina, Saskatchewan S4X 1N2	Tel: (306) 395-1125	prairiepower.ca	net 1
Pro Suites Inc. (Kendra Walls)	19 Tenant Cr. Regina, Saskatchewan S4N 2B1	Tel: (306) 396-6646 Fax: (306) 396-5397	walls@prosuites.com prosuites.com	net 1 (first of month)
Sonartek Ltd. (T. Waver)	390 Retallack St. Regina, Saskatchewan S4R 3N3	Tel: (306) 579-7923 Fax: (306) 579-8003	twaver@sonartek.com sonartek.com	2/15, n/30
The Papery				net 15
Thera-Tables Inc. (Li Flatte)	60 Flatlands Cr. Saskatoon, Saskatchewan S7K 5B1	Tel: (306) 662-6486 Fax: (306) 662-7910	theratables.com	2/5, n/30
Western Communications (V. Du Parler)	99 Listener St. Regina, Saskatchewan S4R 5C9	Tel: (306) 395-5533	westcom.ca	net 1

OUTSTANDING SUPPLIER INVOICES

ANDERSSON CHIROPRACTIC CLINIC

Supplier Name	Terms	Date	Invoice No.	Amount	Total
Cleanol and Laundry Services	net 30	Sep. 14/18	CLS-2419	$90	
	net 30	Sep. 28/18	CLS-2683	90	
			Balance owing		$180
Medical Linen Supplies	2/10, n/30	Sep. 26/18	MLS-102		$690
Sonartek Ltd.	2/15, n/30	Sep. 22/18	SL-3456		$6 420
			Grand Total		$7 290

PATIENT INFORMATION

ANDERSSON CHIROPRACTIC CLINIC

Patient Name (Contact)	Address	Phone No. Fax No.	E-mail Web Site	Terms Credit Limit
Albert Blackfoot	16 Prairie Bay Regina, Saskatchewan S4N 6V3	Tel: (306) 582-1919	ablackfoot@shaw.ca	net 15 $500
Canadian Royals (K. Player)	1910 Buckingham St. Regina, Saskatchewan S4S 2P3	Tel: (306) 578-4567 Fax: (306) 578-7382	kplayer@canroyals.com canroyals.com	1/10, n/30 $5 000
Interplay Ballet School (S. Lightly)	2755 Flamenco St. Regina, Saskatchewan S4V 8C1	Tel: (306) 396-6190 Fax: (306) 396-8186	lightly@lighterthanair.com lighterthanair.com	1/10, n/30 $5 000
Roughrider Argos (B. Ball)	2935 Fowler St. Regina, Saskatchewan S4V 1N5	Tel: (306) 399-8000 Fax: (306) 399-8115	proball.com/ra	1/10, n/30 $5 000
Suzanne Lejeune	301 Pasqua St. Regina, Saskatchewan S4R 4M8	Tel: (306) 573-6296	slejeune@hotmail.com	net 15 $500

OUTSTANDING PATIENT INVOICES

ANDERSSON CHIROPRACTIC CLINIC

Patient Name	Terms	Date	Invoice No.	Amount	Total
Canadian Royals	1/10, n/30	Sep. 28/18	#638	$4 500	$4 500
Interplay Ballet School	1/10, n/30	Sep. 26/18	#632	$3 100	$3 100
Roughrider Argos	1/10, n/30	Sep. 29/18	#639	$4 900	$4 900
			Grand Total		$12 500

Accounting Procedures

Taxes

Since medical services are not taxable, patients do not pay GST on the treatments and GST paid is not refundable. Therefore, no taxes have been set up in the data files, and no tax options are available in the journal tax fields. Andersson pays provincial tax at the rate of 5 percent and GST at 5 percent on normal purchases — medical equipment is not taxed. All prices are stated with taxes included, but taxes are not recorded separately — they are included with the expense or asset part of purchases.

NOTES
The terms Patient and Customer will be used interchangeably in this chapter. Sage 50 applies the label Patient for Customer for medical companies. For sports teams, we will use the term Customer unless the program displays the term Patient on the screen.

Cash and Debit Card Sales

Andersson's individual patients frequently pay by Interac or debit card. Sales invoice amounts are deposited directly to the linked bank account. For this service, Andersson pays a small fee to the bank for each transaction, as well as a monthly rental fee for the terminal. These fees are deducted from the account periodically and are not deducted from deposits for individual transactions. Debit card transactions are summarized and recorded every two weeks.

Payroll

Andersson's assistant is paid a monthly salary through arrangements with the bank. In lieu of a salary, Andersson draws $2 500 per month from her net income.

Discounts

NOTES
All discounts are calculated on the full invoice amounts. For purchases, these amounts include taxes.

Customers (sports teams) who have contracts with Andersson are offered a 1 percent discount if they pay their accounts in full within 10 days. Full payment is requested within 30 days. Individual patients are asked to pay their accounts every two weeks. Some suppliers also offer discounts for early payments.

All discount terms are set up in the customer and supplier records.

Deposits

When sports team managers sign new contracts for regular monthly billing for treating the team members, they pay a deposit to Andersson. Similarly, some suppliers ask for a deposit or prepayment when Andersson places a large order.

Revenue and Expense Accounts

The customer records for Andersson Chiropractic Clinic are set up with *Revenue from Services* as the default account. For suppliers, the account most often associated with purchases from a supplier has been entered as the default for that supplier.

Bank Accounts and Line of Credit

NOTES
The line of credit is set up as a liability account (the money is owed to the bank), but the Bank class is applied so that the account can be selected in journals to write cheques and deposit receipts. The amount of credit available does not appear on the Balance Sheet or Trial Balance. It is usually added as a Note to the financial statements.

Andersson has two chequing accounts for deposits and payments. A third bank account is used for all Interac or debit card payments.

Andersson also uses her line of credit to make payments by cheque. At the end of each month, Andersson makes a payment for the interest owing on the line of credit used. When she has the funds, she also pays down the principal owing.

All cheque numbers are updated automatically when the correct account is selected.

INSTRUCTIONS

1. **Record entries for the source documents** in Sage 50 using the Chart of Accounts, Supplier Information, Patient Information and Accounting Procedures for Andersson Chiropractic Clinic. The procedures for entering each new type of transaction in this application are outlined step by step in the Keystrokes section with the source documents.

2. **Print** the **reports** indicated on the following printing form after you have finished making your entries:

REPORTS

Accounts
- [ ] Chart of Accounts
- [ ] Account List
- [ ] General Journal Entries

Financials
- [x] Comparative Balance Sheet: amounts only for Oct. 31, 2018, and Nov. 30, 2018
- [x] Income Statement from Dec. 1, 2017, to Nov. 30, 2018
- [x] Comparative Trial Balance: amounts only for Nov. 30 and Dec. 1, 2018
- [x] All Journal Entries: Oct. 1 to Nov. 30
- [ ] General Ledger

- [x] Statement of Cash Flows from Oct. 1 to Nov. 30
- [x] Cash Flow Projection Detail Report for accounts 1060 and 1080 for 30 days

Taxes
- [ ] Tax

Banking
- [ ] Cheque Log Report

Payables
- [ ] Supplier List
- [x] Supplier Aged Detail for all suppliers
- [ ] Aged Overdue Payables
- [ ] Expenses Journal Entries
- [ ] Payments Journal Entries
- [x] Pending Supplier Orders as at Jan. 15, 2019

Receivables
- [ ] Patient List
- [x] Patient Aged Detail for all customers
- [ ] Aged Overdue Receivables
- [ ] Patient Statements
- [ ] Fees Journal Entries
- [ ] Receipts Journal Entries
- [x] Pending Patient Orders as at Jan. 15, 2019

Mailing Labels
- [ ] Labels

KEYSTROKES

Opening Data Files

Open SageData16\ANDERSSON\ANDERSSON to access the data files for Andersson. **Enter Oct 7, 2018** as the session date.

Entering a Purchase Quote

On October 1, Andersson received two quotes for a treatment table that will be delivered later in the month. A quote usually provides a guaranteed price for some work or products. The offer is often limited to a stated time period. If the business chooses to accept the offer, the quote may be filled as a purchase for immediate delivery or converted to a purchase order for future delivery. When the goods are received, or the work is completed, the quote is filled and the purchase is completed. Supplier quotes are entered and filled in the Expenses or Purchases Journal.

☑ 1 **Purchase Quote #TT-44**   **Dated October 1, 2018**
Delivery date October 10, 2018
From Thera-Tables Inc., $4 000 including taxes for custom-built adjustable height treatment table with drop ends. Terms: 2/5, n/30. Deposit of 10 percent required on accepting quote.

Click **Payables** in the Modules pane list. Icons are added for quotes and orders.

NOTES
From the backup file, restore SageData16\ANDERSSON1.CAB or ANDERSSON1 to SageData16\ANDERSSON\ANDERSSON to open the data files for Andersson. Refer to Chapter 1, page 24, if you need assistance.

NOTES
The Payroll, Inventory and Project modules are not included in the Modules pane — they are hidden because these ledgers are not used and are not set up.

CLASSIC VIEW
Click the Expenses, Orders & Quotes icon to open the journal. Choose Quote from the journal's Transaction drop-down list.

Click the **Supplier Quotes icon**:

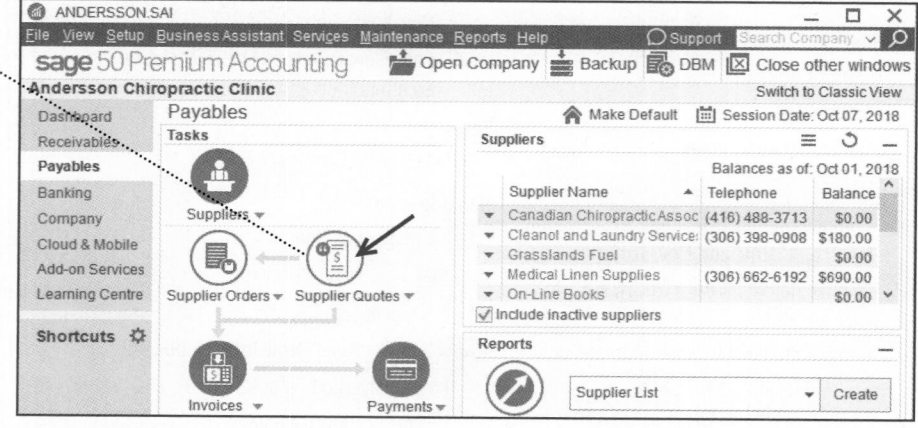

The Expenses Journal – Creating A Quote window opens:

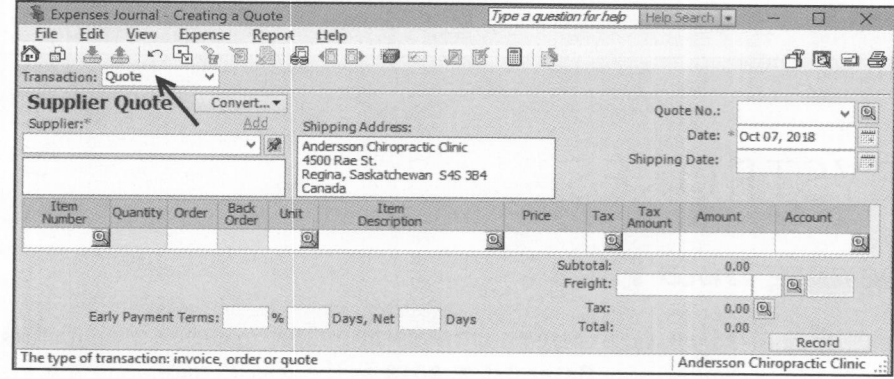

Quote is selected in the Transaction field.

Click the **Supplier field** and **select Thera-Tables Inc.**

Click the **Quote No.** field to advance the cursor and skip the address fields.

Type TT-44

Press (tab) **twice** to advance to the Date field.

Type 10-1-18

Press (tab) **twice** to advance to the Shipping Date field.

This is the date on which the order is to be received or the work is to be completed. Sometimes, instead of Shipping Date, we use the term Delivery Date for services or Starting Date for a contract because these terms are more appropriate for quotes and orders for services.

Type 10-10

The Item Number field refers to the code for inventory items. The Quantity (quantity received with this purchase) field will remain blank because this is not a purchase and no goods are received. However, you must enter the number of units that are ordered. You cannot leave the Order field blank. One table is being ordered.

Click the **Order field**. **Type** 1

Press (tab) to advance to the Unit field that also applies to inventory.

Press (tab) to advance to the Item Description field.

Type custom-built treatment table

Press (tab) to advance to the Price field. This field refers to the unit price of the items. You must enter a price in order to fill the order later.

Type 4000

Press (tab) to advance to the Tax field.

Because taxes are not used in this data set, we can skip the tax fields. The amount is entered automatically as the quantity on order times the unit price.

The account is also entered automatically from the supplier's ledger record, so the quote is complete:

NOTES
If you want, you can customize the journal by removing the columns that are not required. Refer to page 161.
You can remove (do not show) the Item Number, Unit, Tax Code and Tax Amount fields because they are not needed.

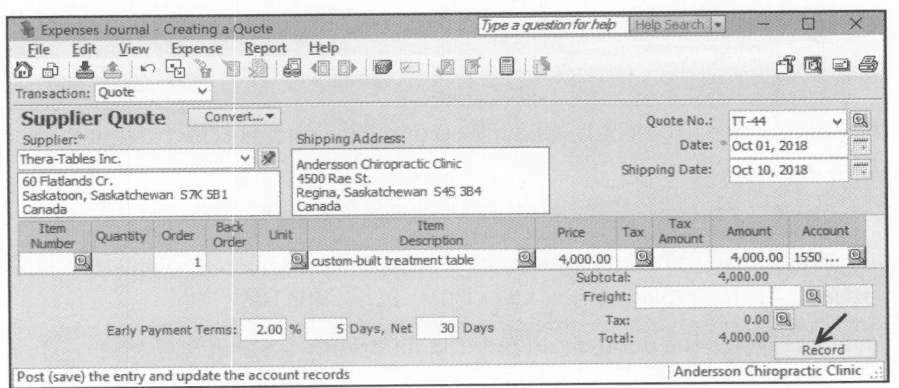

NOTES
Refer to page 114 if you need help correcting the entry.

Check your **work** carefully and **make** any **corrections** necessary, just as you do for Purchases Journal entries.

If you try to display the journal entry, you will find that there is no journal entry associated with the quote. The Record button replaces Post for quotes (and orders). The related journal entry will be completed when the quote is filled and the purchase is completed. When you are sure that the entry is correct, you should record it.

NOTES
The Record button label replaces Post for quotes and orders because no journal entry is posted.

Click the **Record button** [Record] or **choose** the **Expense menu** and **click Record** to save your transaction. **Click OK** to confirm successful recording. No journal entry number is included with the confirmation.

If you forgot to enter the quantity ordered, Sage 50 will warn you of this error:

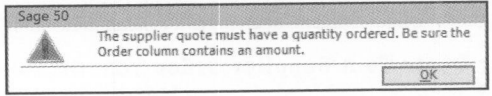

Click OK. Enter the quantity in the Order field and try again to record.

Enter the **second purchase quote** from a new supplier. Remember to add the account number and payment terms to the quote.

NOTES
Continue is not an option when you add a new supplier for a quote.

> **Purchase Quote #MT-511**   **Dated October 1, 2018**
>
> **2** Delivery date October 20, 2018
> From Medi-Tables (use Quick Add for the new supplier), $4 550 including all taxes for custom-built treatment table. Terms: net 20. Deposit of 20 percent required on accepting quote.

Placing a Purchase Order from a Quote

NOTES
We will use the terms purchase order and supplier order interchangeably, unless the term appears in the Sage 50 screen.

Sometimes purchase orders are entered without a quote and sometimes they are converted from a purchase quote. Entering a purchase order directly, without the quote, is the same as entering a purchase quote except that you choose Order as the type of transaction instead of Quote.

The purchase order to Thera-Tables Inc. is a quote converted to an order. The Expenses Journal should still be open with Quote selected as the Transaction type.

✓	**Purchase Order #TT-44**	**Dated October 2, 2018**

3

Delivery date October 10, 2018
To Thera-Tables Inc., $4 000 including taxes for custom-built treatment table. Terms: 2/5, n/30. Convert quote #TT-44 to purchase order #TT-44.

> **Click**   the **Quote No. field list arrow**:

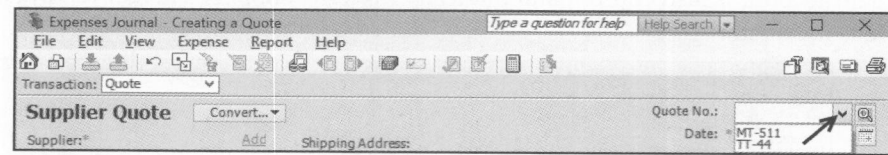

The drop-down list includes all unfilled purchase quotes. The two quotes entered above are listed.

> **Click**   **TT-44** to select it.

> **Press**   ⟨*tab*⟩ to select the quote and place it on-screen. Looking Up Quote TT-44 has replaced Creating A Quote in the title bar.

You can change the quote to an order in different ways.

> **Click**   the **Convert list arrow** to display conversion options:

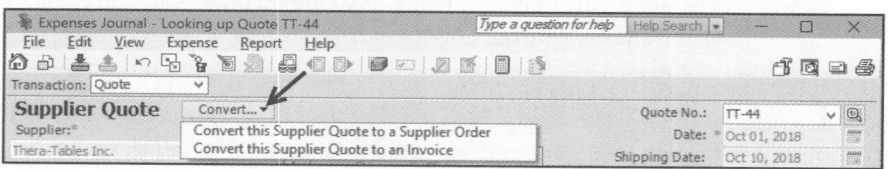

You can convert the quote to an order or directly to an invoice from this menu. Or,

> **Click**   the **Transaction list arrow** to display the transaction types:

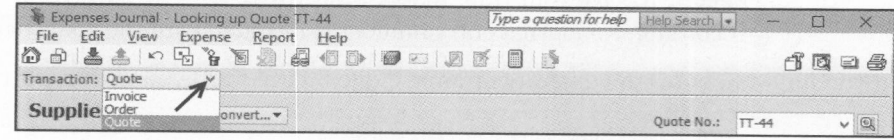

> **Click**   **Convert This Supplier Quote To A Supplier Order** from the Convert drop-down list, or

> **Click**   **Order** in the Transaction type drop-down list.

The quote screen changes to an order. Order No. replaces Quote No. as the field label:

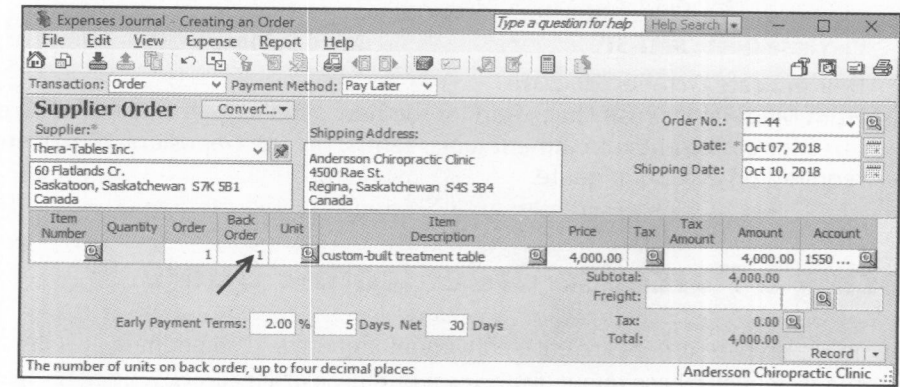

Order is now the transaction type and a Payment Method field is added. You can enter prepayments with the order. We explain this method of entering prepayments on page 419.

We explain this method of entering prepayments on page 419.

NOTES
When you select Order (or Invoice) as the type of transaction, the Order No. (or Order/Quote No.) field will list both unfilled quotes and unfilled orders.

PRO VERSION
pro Click Convert This Purchase Quote To A Purchase Order from the Convert drop-down list.

NOTES
The Project/Division module is hidden for Andersson because it is not needed, but when used, the term Partner will replace Division or Project for medical companies.

NOTES
The Record button replaces Post because the order does not generate a journal entry.

The Order quantity has been copied to the Back Order field. Creating An Order replaces Looking Up Quote in the title bar.

The session date is entered on the revised form, so we need to change it. If you try to change the quote number, you must confirm this is correct (read the margin Notes):

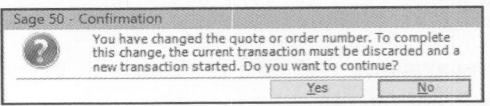

Click No to restore the original quote number.

Click   the **Date field Calendar icon** 🔲. **Choose October 2**. **Press** (tab).

Click   the **Record button** [Record | ▾].

The Record button now includes the option to print on its drop-down list. You can select Print & Record as the default, just as you can choose the Print & Post option for cash purchases and sales.

The program displays the warning message:

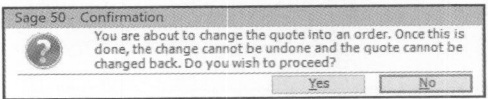

Since we want to convert the quote to an order, we can proceed. The order will replace the quote.

Click   **Yes** and **OK** to confirm recording. No journal entry number appears in the confirmation message.

Purchase order numbers are updated automatically by the program, just like sales invoice and cheque numbers. (Alphanumeric numbers are not updated.) If the number for the quote that you are converting is larger than the next purchase order sequence number, a second warning will appear when you record the order because the number is out of sequence. Sage 50 will ask if you want to update your sequence starting number:

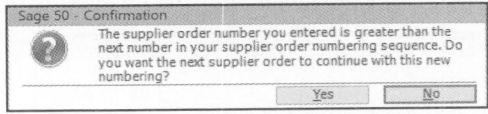

This does not apply to the alphanumeric number we used.

Click Yes if you want to reset the numbering sequence for future purchase orders. Click No to avoid resetting the automatic sequence to the higher number. When you choose No, the higher purchase order number will still be recorded, and later skipped, but the automatic counter will not be changed.

Close   the **Supplier Order window**.

Making a Prepayment to a Supplier

Businesses frequently request a deposit — down payment or prepayment — when an order is placed, especially for customized orders. Deposits may be refundable or not. A deposit may be used to pay for materials that are ordered specifically for a project, it may ensure that the purchaser will follow through with the order or it may provide the supplier with some revenue if the order is cancelled and part of the deposit is not refundable.

Prepayments can be made in the Payments Journal or in the Supplier Order Journal window. If the prepayment accompanies the order, you should enter it on the Order form. This prepayment is made later, so we will enter it in the Payments Journal.

NOTES
To change the number of a purchase order to match the number sequence on preprinted forms, you should
• recall the quote
• choose the Adjust Quote tool (adjust purchase quotes in the same way as sales quotes — refer to page 415)
• change the quote number
• record the revised quote
• recall the quote
• convert the quote to an order by choosing Order from the Transaction drop-down list or by choosing Convert to an Order from the Convert drop-down list
• record the purchase order
• confirm the conversion
• check that the order sequence number is correct and update the next order number if necessary

NOTES
We will not continue the instruction to confirm successful posting or recording.

WARNING!
The order will be posted whether you choose Yes or No in the message about updating the order number.

NOTES
If you choose not to reset the number sequence, the higher order number will be skipped in the automatic numbering sequence when you reach it.

NOTES
For entering a prepayment on the Supplier Order form, refer to page 419.

<table>
<tr><td>✓
4</td><td>**Payment Cheque #567**</td><td>**Dated October 3, 2018**</td></tr>
</table>

To Thera-Tables Inc., $400 from Regina Chequing account as prepayment in acceptance of quote #TT-44 and to confirm order #TT-44.

Click the **Payments icon** [Payments▾] to open the Payments Journal.

Click the **Enter Supplier Prepayments tool** 🖳 or **choose** the **Payment menu** and **click Enter Prepayments**.

This tool button/menu option acts as a switch that opens the fields for deposits:

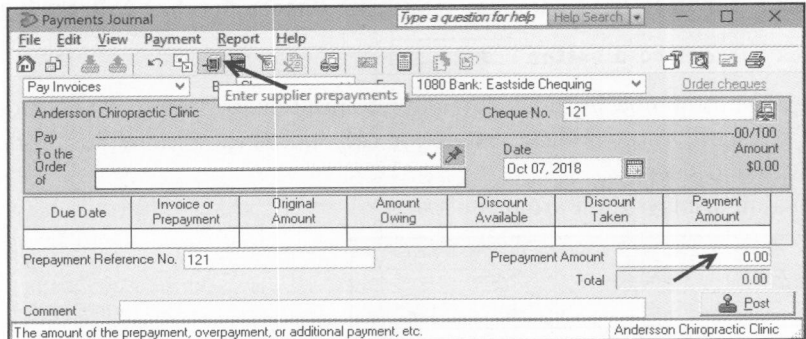

You can leave this tool selected so that the optional fields will always be available.

Two new fields are added to the journal: one for the **Prepayment Reference Number** and one for the **Amount**. The default reference number is the next cheque number in sequence for the selected bank account, and it is updated automatically by the program. The rest of the journal is the same as before, but the invoice payment lines are not used. If there are any outstanding invoices, they will be included in the journal.

When the payment is made by cheque, the **From** field has the list of bank accounts you can choose. The default bank account and cheque number for this payment are not correct. We must change them.

Click the **From field list arrow** to list the available bank accounts:

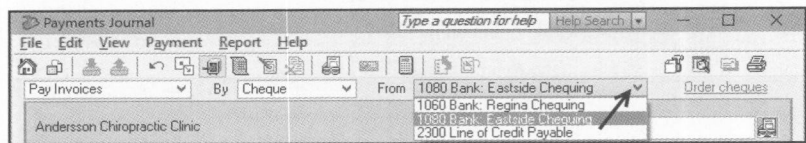

Click **Bank: Regina Chequing**. The cheque number changes.

When you choose a different bank account, the cheque and reference numbers are updated for the selected account. Each bank account has its own cheque number sequence, and these numbers are updated as you make payments from each account.

Choose Thera-Tables Inc. as the supplier from the drop-down list.

Enter October 3 as the date of the cheque.

Click the **Prepayment Amount field**.

Type 400

Click the **Comment field**. Advancing the cursor updates the Total.

Type Prepayment for order #TT-44

If an outstanding invoice is paid with the same cheque, enter the invoice payment in the usual way in addition to the deposit amount.

The entry is now complete:

PRO VERSION
Click the Enter Vendor Prepayments tool. Pay Purchase Invoice is entered as the type of transaction.

NOTES
You can change the Prepayment Reference Number and this will not affect the automatic cheque numbering sequence.

WARNING!
Two bank accounts and the line of credit are available for receipts and payments. Before posting a transaction, check carefully that you have selected the right account.

NOTES
Processing the advance in this way ensures that the advance will appear in the correct supplier account in the Payables Ledger. The manual approach, a General Journal entry that credits the bank account and debits Prepaid Expenses, an asset account, does not show this link with the supplier – the supplier's ledger must be updated separately.

This link provides another reason for using the Payables journals instead of the General Journal for supplier transactions.

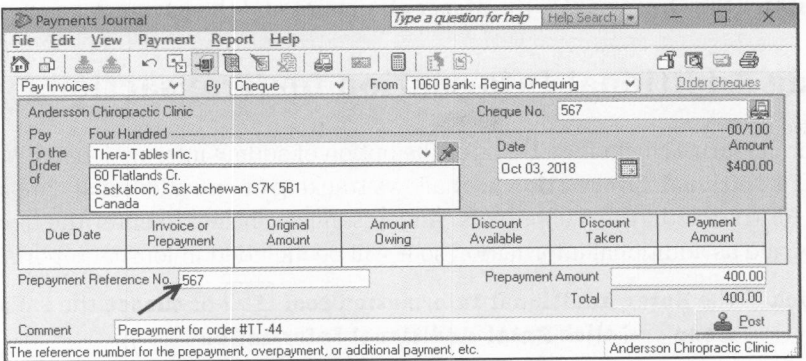

NOTES
You can also use the Prepayment Amount field if you are paying more than the full amount owing for an invoice. You cannot enter an amount in the Payment Amount field greater than the amount owing, but you can record this excess amount as a prepayment.

You are ready to review the journal entry.

Choose the **Report menu** and **click Display Payments Journal Entry**:

Andersson Chiropractic Clinic			
Payments Journal Entry 10/03/2018 (J1)			
Account Number	Account Description	Debits	Credits
1280	Purchase Prepayments	400.00	-
1060	Bank: Regina Chequing	-	400.00
Additional Date:	Additional Field:	400.00	400.00

NOTES
The journal entry number (J1) has not increased because of the quotes and order.

As for other payments, the bank account is credited. However, the prepayment creates an asset until the order is filled, so *Purchase Prepayments*, the linked asset account, is debited — the supplier owes something to us. If there is no previous balance owing to the supplier, the prepayment creates a debit balance for the account. After the purchase, when you pay the supplier, the prepayment will be displayed in red under the heading "Prepayments" and you "pay" it by accepting the amount, just as you do to pay the invoice itself.

Close   the **display** when you have finished and **make corrections** to the journal entry if necessary.

Click   [Post] to save the transaction.

Click the Enter Supplier Prepayments tool [image] again to close the prepayment fields if you want to close these optional fields.

NOTES
For corrections to deposits or prepayments after posting, use the Adjust tool or refer to Appendix C. They can also be reversed, just like receipts. (Refer to page 175.)

Entering Payments from a Line of Credit

Choose Sonartek from the Supplier list to prepare for the next payment.

> ✓
> **5**
>
> **Payment Cheque #103**   **Dated October 3, 2018**
> To Sonartek Ltd., $6 291.60 from the line of credit in payment of account including $128.40 discount for early payment. Reference invoice #SL-3456.

This payment is made from Andersson's line of credit. However, *Bank: Regina Chequing* is still selected as the bank account in the From field.

Click   the **From list arrow** to select a different account:

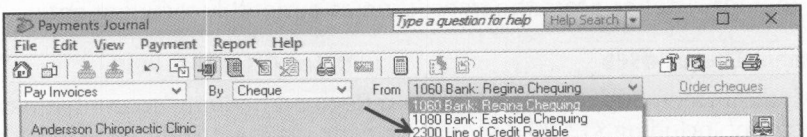

NOTES
The Credit Card account class is assigned to Bank: Interac, so it does not appear with the list of banks.
The Bank account class is available for all Balance Sheet accounts from the Options tab in the General Ledger. Account classes were introduced in Chapter 7, page 218.

The line of credit is a liability account — it has a credit balance — but it operates like a bank account. By defining it as a Bank class account, it can be used to write cheques in the Payments Journal, as it would be in an ongoing business.

Choose Line of Credit Payable to select this account and to update the cheque number for the new account.

Enter the cheque **date**, the **discount** amount and the **payment amount**.

Entering Additional Information for Transactions

The tool bar in journals includes a for the option of adding information to a journal report. This **Additional Information tool** allows tracking of one additional date and one other field for transactions in all journals. Andersson has chosen to enter the number of the invoice paid as additional information so it will be included in journal reports.

Click the **Enter Additional Information tool** or **choose** the **Payment menu** and **click Enter Additional Information**:

Additional Information	✕
Additional Date	
Additional Field	
	OK Cancel

You can enter one additional date for the transaction and additional text. Both will be available for journal reports when you show the Additional Information (page 450). You can rename these fields as part of the company setup (refer to pages 639–640).

Click the **Additional Field** text box.

Type Ref: inv #SL-3456

Click **OK** to return to the journal.

Adding the extra details does not change the appearance of the journal. You are ready to review the transaction before posting it.

Press ctrl + **J** to open the journal display:

Andersson Chiropractic Clinic
Payments Journal Entry 10/03/2018 (J2)

Account Number	Account Description	Debits	Credits
2200	Accounts Payable	6,420.00	
2300	Line of Credit Payable	-	6,291.60
5030	Purchase Discounts	-	128.40
Additional Date:	Additional Field: Ref: inv #SL-3456	6,420.00	6,420.00

One difference between this and earlier payment entries is the credit to a liability instead of an asset bank account for the payment. This increases the business liability — more money has been borrowed against the line of credit available.

In addition to the usual debit and credit details, the invoice number entered as additional information is included in the display so that you can check it as well.

Close the **journal display**. **Check** your transaction **details** carefully.

Post the **payment** when you are certain the details are correct.

Enter the **next two transactions**. Remember to change bank accounts as needed.

Cash Purchase #R-2018-10   **Dated October 3, 2018**

6   To Pro Suites Inc., cheque #121 for $2 300 from Eastside Chequing account to pay rent for October. Store the transaction as a monthly recurring entry.

Payment Cheque #568   **Dated October 4, 2018**

7   To Medical Linen Supplies, $676.20 from Regina Chequing account in payment of account including $13.80 discount for early payment. Reference invoice #MLS-102.

Close the **Payments Journal**.

Click **Receivables** in the Modules pane. **Enter** the next **receipt** and then **close** the **journal**.

NOTES
You can click the Invoice Or Prepayment field and press tab to accept the discount and payment amounts.

NOTES
You can name the additional fields in the Company Settings Names window.

WARNING!
Because the additional information is optional, although it does appear in the journal display, the program does not warn you if you forget to enter it. Therefore, you should make reviewing the journal entry routine practice.

NOTES
Details you enter in the Comment field are also added to the journal report, but the comment is not included in the journal display.

8

Receipt #58   **Dated October 4, 2018**

From Interplay Ballet, cheque #447 for $3 069 in payment of account including $31 discount for early payment. Reference invoice #632. Deposited to Eastside Chequing account. Add the invoice number as additional information.

NOTES
You can modify the tabbing order by placing the cheque number after the customer.

Entering a Sales (Patient) Quote

Sales quotes are like purchase quotes. Your business offers a customer a guaranteed price for a limited time for merchandise or for work to be completed. The customer may choose to accept or reject the offer.

Quotes are entered from the Patient Quotes icon in the Enhanced view Receivables window:

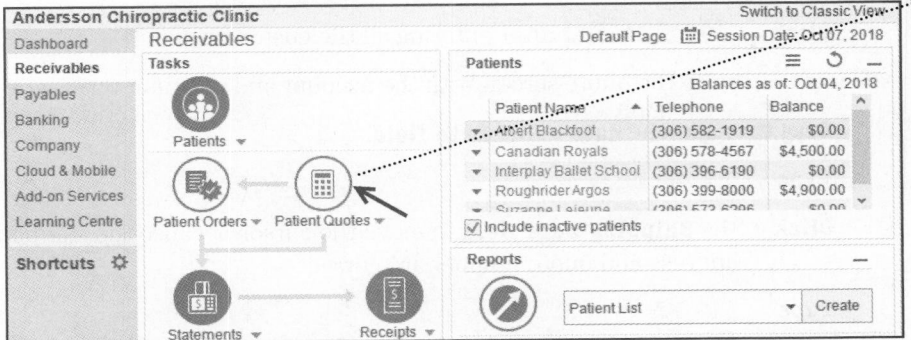

Separate icons are added for orders and quotes, just as they are for the suppliers.

PRO VERSION
Sales Quotes, Sales Orders and Sales Invoices will replace the icon labels Patient Quotes, Patient Orders and Statements. The term Customer replaces Patient.
Click the Sales Quotes icon to open the form you need.

✓
9

Sales Quote #51   **Dated October 4, 2018**

Starting date October 15, 2018
To Giant Raptors (use Full Add for the new customer), a local basketball team, $3 500 per month for unlimited chiropractic services during the regular six-month training and playing season. Andersson will attend or be on call for all home games. If the team enters the playoffs, the contract may be extended for $1 200 per week. Terms: 1/10, n/30. A deposit of $2 000 will be required on acceptance of the contract. Enter 6 as the number ordered. Each month, the sales invoice for Giant Raptors will be entered as partially filling the order.

NOTES
For services such as those provided by Andersson, the term Shipping Date is not appropriate. In the source documents, we use Starting Date instead.

CLASSIC VIEW
Click the Fees, Orders & Quotes icon to open the journal, and choose Quote from the journal's Transaction drop-down list.

Click the **Patient Quotes icon** to open the Fees Journal.

The invoice screen changes to the form for a patient quote:

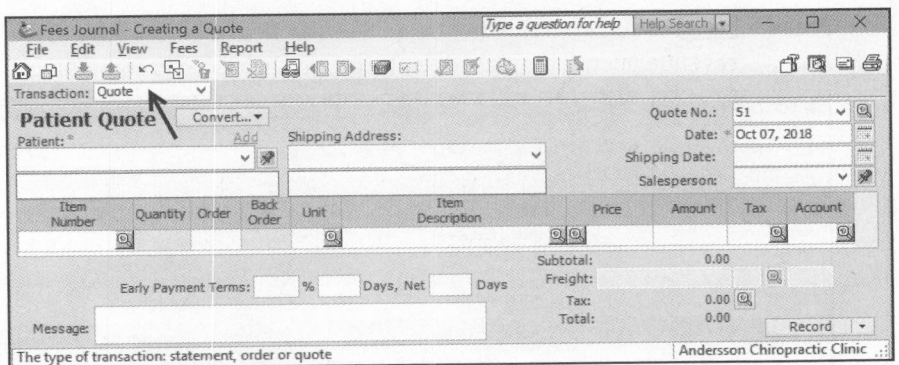

The quote is completed in much the same way as the sales invoice. However, you must enter a quantity in the Order field, just as you did for purchase quotes and orders. The quote number is entered and updated automatically from the defaults for the Company Forms settings. As for purchase quotes, the Record button replaces Post.

PRO VERSION
Sales Journal – Creating A Quote will appear in the journal's title bar instead of Fees Journal – Creating A Quote. Sales replaces Fees in the Menu bar.

NOTES
Statement replaces the term Invoice for a medical company. Fees Journal replaces Sales Journal.

Additional fields are not available for quotes and orders. The tool is dimmed.

Click the **Patient field**.

Type `Giant Raptors` **Click** the **Add link** above the Patient field to open the ledger directly. **Enter** the following new **patient details**:

Patient Name (Contact)	Address	Phone No. Fax No.	E-mail Web Site	Revenue Account	Terms Credit Limit
Giant Raptors (Rex Saurus)	550 Tyrannus Dr. Regina, Saskatchewan S4R 5T1	Tel 1: (306) 398-8753 Tel 2: (306) 398-5338 Fax: (306) 398-5339	rex@raptors.com raptors.com	4100	1/10, n/30 (change default terms) $5 000

When you type the new name and press $\boxed{tab}$, Continue is not an option for a quote. You must create at least a partial ledger record.

Click 🖫 Save and Close after entering all the customer details.

You will return to the quote screen with the account and payment terms added.

Drag through the **date** in the **Date field**.

Type `10 4 18`

Click the **Shipping Date field** to move the cursor because the shipping address and quote number are correct.

Type `10 15`

Click the **Order field**. You must enter an order quantity.

Instead of entering the quote as the monthly rate and filling it in the first month, we will enter it as a six-month contract with monthly unit prices. After each month of service, the quote will be partially filled with one month of service.

Type `6`

Click the **Item Description field**.

Type `monthly fee for treatment`

Press $\boxed{tab}$ to move to the Price field. You must complete the Price field.

Type `3500`

Press $\boxed{tab}$ to advance to the Amount field. The program enters the amount correctly as the quantity times the price.

Press $\boxed{tab}$ to move to the Tax field. The Tax field is not used and the correct revenue account is already entered, so the quote is complete:

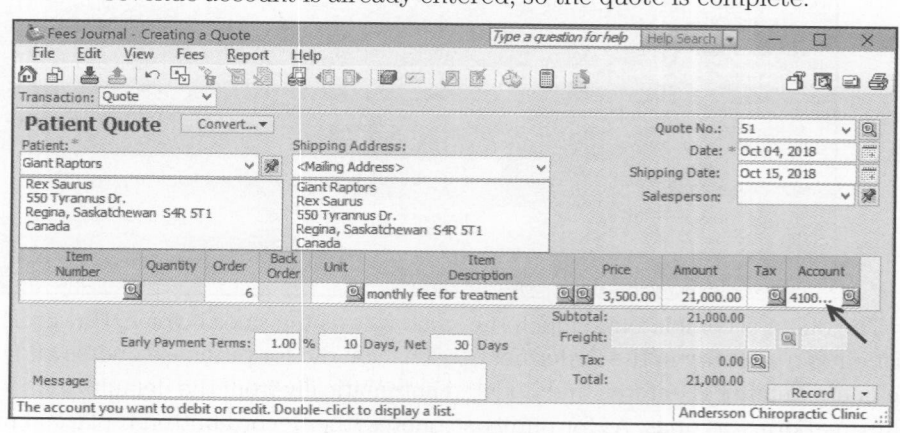

Check   the **quote** carefully and **correct mistakes**, just as you do for sales invoices. Refer to page 161 for assistance if needed.

There is no journal entry to display. When a quote is filled by making a sale, the journal entry will be created.

Click   **Record** [Record ▼] to save the quote. No journal entry results from the quote.

Leave   the **Fees Journal open** to adjust the quote.

Adjusting a Sales Quote

Sometimes a quote contains an error or must be changed if prices are renegotiated. You can adjust sales and purchase quotes and orders after recording them, just as you can adjust sales and purchase invoices after posting.

Memo #1   **Dated October 5, 2018**

☑ **10**

After some negotiations with the Giant Raptors, Andersson agreed to reduce the contract price to $3 300 per month for the playing season. Playoff games will be billed at $1 100 per week. Adjust the sales quote to change the price.

The Fees Journal – Creating A Quote screen should still be open.

Click   the **Quote No. field list arrow** to open the list of quotes on file.

Click   **51** to select the quote you just entered.

Press   (tab) to add the quote to the screen:

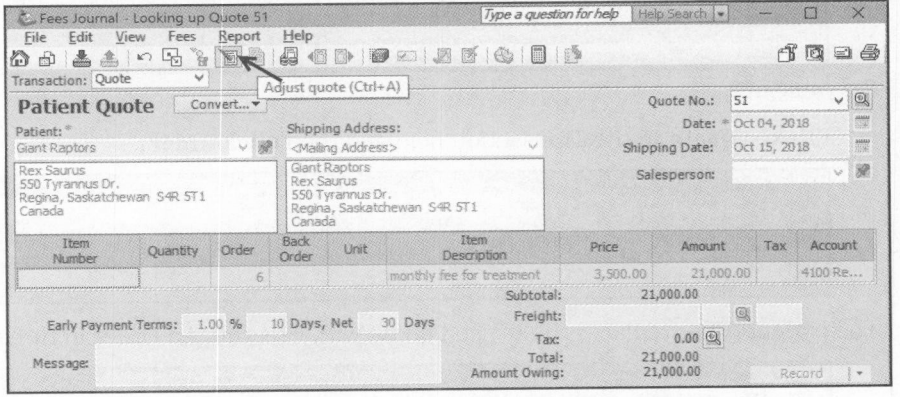

The List icon 🔍 beside the Quote No. field opens the Search window for all quotes. By entering search criteria, it may be easier to find a quote on the resulting list.

At this stage, you cannot edit the quote. All fields are dimmed.

Click   the **Adjust Quote tool** 🔲 or **choose** the **Fees menu** and **click Adjust Quote** to open the fields for editing.

Adjusting Quote 51 replaces Looking Up Quote 51 in the title bar.

Click   **3,500.00** in the Price field.

Type   3300 **Press** (tab) to update the subtotal and total amount to $19 800.

Drag through   the **date in the Date field**.

Type   10-5 to enter the date for the revised quote.

Click   the **Message field** and **type** Revised quote

NOTES
You can choose Print & Record or Record as the default action for the quote by selecting your preference from the Record button drop-down list.
You can also preview quotes.

WARNING!
If Quote is not selected as the Transaction type, you will convert the quote to a sales order or fill the quote when you bring the quote on to the screen.

NOTES
To view and adjust orders and quotes, you do not need to use the lookup or search features we used to adjust purchase and sales invoices after posting. Orders and quotes are available directly from the Order/Quote No. field.

PRO VERSION
pro Choose the Sales Journal and click Adjust Quote or use the Adjust Quote tool.

NOTES
Pressing (ctrl) + A will open the quote fields for editing. In other journals, pressing (ctrl) + A opens the Adjust/Search window.

NOTES
All fields in a quote can be edited, except name and address details. To change the name, you must remove the quote and re-enter it for the correct customer. However, you cannot use the same quote number twice.

Check your **work** carefully.

Click [Record ▾] to save the revised quote. Keep the journal open.

Converting a Sales Quote to a Sales Order

Sales quotes can be converted to orders just as purchase quotes can be converted to purchase orders.

> ✓
> 11
>
> **Sales Order #51**   **Dated October 5, 2018**
> Starting date October 15, 2018
> The Giant Raptors have accepted the modified sales quote #51. Convert the quote to a sales order. All terms and dates are unchanged from the revised quote for $3 300 per month.

The Fees Journal should be open with Quote selected as the Transaction type.

Click the **Quote No.** field drop-down list.

Click **51**, the quote number we want, and **press** (tab) to recall the quote.

There are different ways to convert the quote to an order, as there were for supplier quotes.

Click **Convert This Patient Quote To A Patient Order** from the Convert drop-down list.

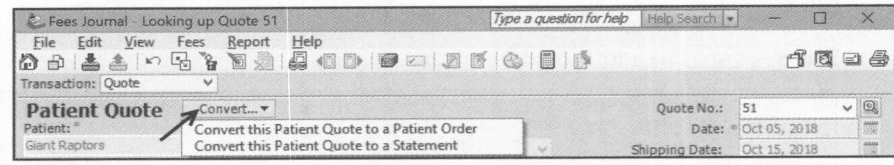

Or, you can

Click **Quote** in the Transaction field and then **click Order**:

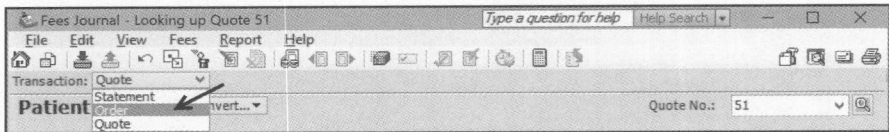

The patient order replaces the revised quote with Creating An Order in the title bar:

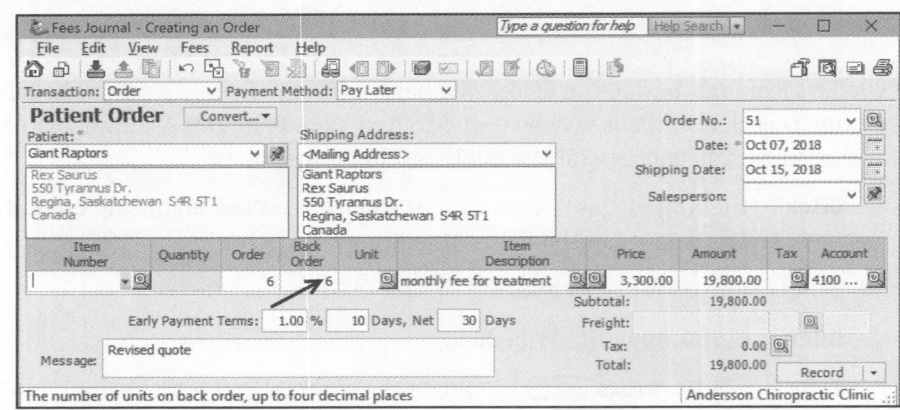

You can also choose Order from the Transaction list first, or click the Home window Patient Orders icon, then choose #51 from the Order No. drop-down list. Press (tab) to place the quote on-screen as an order.

The order quantity — 6 — has been added to the Back Order field.

Enter **Oct 5** as the order date to replace the session date.

Check all the **details** carefully because there is no journal entry to review.

All other details should be correct for the order because they have not changed. The order can be edited at this stage if needed. We will revise the comment.

Click the **Message field**. **Type** Order based on revised quote

Click Record 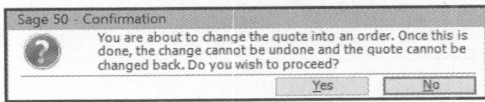 to save the sales order. Sage 50 asks for confirmation:

> Sage 50 - Confirmation
>
> You are about to change the quote into an order. Once this is done, the change cannot be undone and the quote cannot be changed back. Do you wish to proceed?
>
> Yes   No

Since we want to change the quote to an order, we should proceed.

Click **Yes**.

Close the **Fees Journal** so that you can enter the customer's deposit.

Entering Customer Deposits

Andersson also requests deposits from new customers when they place orders. Deposits can be entered in the Receipts Journal in the same way as supplier prepayments are entered in the Payments Journal. The customer deposit tool opens fields for a reference number and an amount.

> ✓ 12

Receipt #59   **Dated October 6, 2018**

From the Giant Raptors, cheque #838 for $2 000 as deposit #14 to confirm sales order #51. Deposited to Regina Chequing account.

Click the **Receipts icon** to open the Receipts Journal.

Click the **Enter Patient Deposits tool** or **choose** the **Receipt menu** and **click Enter Deposits**.

This tool button/menu option acts as a switch that opens the fields for deposits:

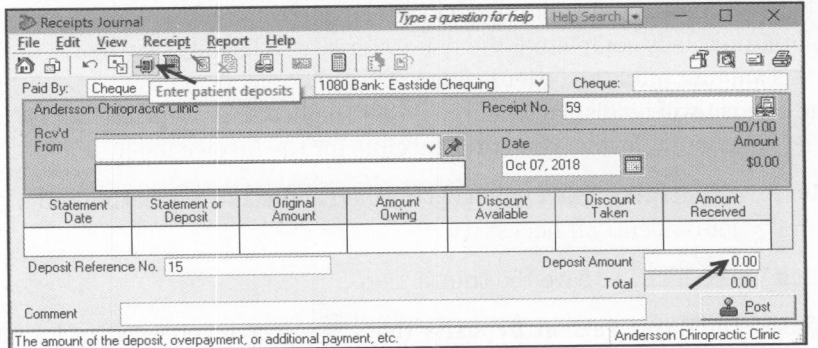

The two new fields added to the journal for the **Deposit Reference Number** and for the **Deposit Amount** serve the same purpose as they do for supplier prepayments. The reference number is the deposit number, and it is updated automatically by the program. The deposit number is different from and updated separately from the receipt number. Both are entered as Company Forms Settings. The invoice lines are not used for the deposit. Outstanding invoices, if there are any, will be included in the journal. If they are being paid with the same customer cheque, enter the receipt in the usual way in addition to the deposit amount.

The receipt number is updated and correct, but we need to change the bank account.

NOTES
You can make Print & Record the default action for the Record button by choosing this from the button's drop-down list, and you can preview the order.

NOTES
We will enter the next customer deposit directly with the sales order (refer to page 426).

PRO VERSION
Click the Enter Customer Deposits tool – Customer replaces the term Patient in the Pro version.

NOTES
If you modified the tabbing order, pressing tab after selecting the customer will place the cursor in the Cheque field.

NOTES
The Credit Card account class is assigned to Bank: Interac; it does not appear with the list of banks.
Line of Credit Payable has been defined as a Bank class account. Therefore, it appears on the list of bank accounts.
Cash class accounts will also appear on this list. We will use the Cash class in Chapter 15.

NOTES
If a customer overpays an invoice, you can enter the overpayment – the difference between the amount owing and the cheque amount – in the Deposit Amount field to create the required credit balance.

NOTES
Processing the advance in this way ensures that the advance will appear in the correct customer account in the Receivables Ledger. The manual approach, a General Journal entry that debits the bank account and credits Unearned Revenue, does not show this link with the customer directly – the customer's ledger is updated separately. This link gives us another reason for using the Receivables journals instead of the General Journal for customer transactions.

NOTES
Closing or hiding the deposit fields is not required.

NOTES
Remember to change the selected bank account when necessary.

Choose **Giant Raptors** in the patient From drop-down list.

Click the **Cheque field**. **Type** 838

Enter **October 6** as the date of the cheque.

Click the **Deposit To list arrow** to access the list of bank accounts:

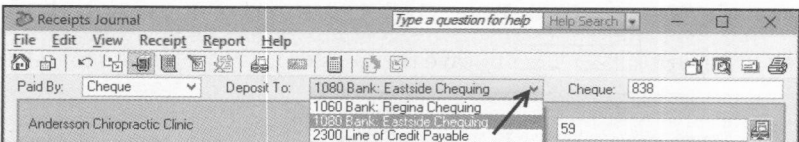

Just as we can pay from any of the accounts that we identify as Bank class accounts, we can deposit to any bank account, including the line of credit.

Choose **Bank: Regina Chequing** to change the account selection.

Click the **Deposit Amount field** at the bottom of the journal.

Type 2000 **Press** (tab) .

Click the **Enter Additional Information tool** , or **choose** the **Receipt menu** and **click Enter Additional Information**:

This data entry screen is the same for all journals.

Click the **Additional Field** text box. **Type** Deposit for SO #51

Click **OK** to return to the journal so you can review the transaction.

Choose the **Report menu** and **click Display Receipts Journal Entry**:

Andersson Chiropractic Clinic
Receipts Journal Entry 10/06/2018 (J6)

Account Number	Account Description	Debits	Credits
1060	Bank: Regina Chequing	2,000.00	-
2250	Prepaid Sales and Deposits	-	2,000.00
Additional Date:	Additional Field: Deposit for SO #51	2,000.00	2,000.00

As for other receipts, the bank account is debited. The account credited is *Prepaid Sales and Deposits*, a liability account linked to the customer deposits field. If the customer has no previous outstanding balance, the deposit creates a credit entry for the account. Until the sale is completed, the deposit creates a liability — we owe the customer this amount until the order is filled. After the sale, when the customer pays the invoice, the deposit will be displayed in red under the heading "Deposits" and it is "paid" by accepting its amount, just as you enter receipts for the invoice itself.

Close the **display** when you have finished and **make corrections** to the journal entry if necessary.

Click **Post** to save the transaction.

Click the **Enter Patient Deposits tool** again if you want to close the deposit fields.

Close the **Receipts Journal** to return to the Receivables module window.

Change the **session date** to **October 14** and **make** a **backup**. **Enter** the **next two receipts** and then **close** the **journal**.

Receipt #60   **Dated October 8, 2018**

13 From Roughrider Argos, cheque #1122 for $4 851 in payment of account including $49 discount for early payment. Reference sales invoice #639. Deposited to Eastside Chequing account.

Receipt #61   **Dated October 8, 2018**

14

From Canadian Royals, cheque #3822 for $4 455 in payment of account including $45 discount for early payment. Reference sales invoice #638. Deposited to Regina Chequing account.

Placing a Purchase Order with Prepayment

Placing a purchase order directly without the quote is similar to entering a purchase quote. For this order, a prepayment is included, so we will enter it on the order.

✓

15

Purchase Order #44 and Cheque #104   **Dated October 9, 2018**

Delivery date October 19, 2018
From Sonartek Ltd., $6 000 including taxes for ultrasound machine with multiple frequencies and interchangeable wands. Terms: 2/15, n/30. Deposit of $1 500 paid with cheque #104 from Line of Credit Payable account to confirm order.

Close   the **Receipts Journal**.

Click   **Payables** in the Modules pane list to open the Payables window.

Click   the **Supplier Orders icon** to open the Expenses Journal with Order selected as the Transaction type.

The Order No. is entered automatically (Forms Settings), and it will be incremented automatically because purchase orders are generated within your business.

Choose **Sonartek Ltd.** from the supplier list.

Enter   **Oct 9 18** as the order date and **Oct 19 18** as the shipping date.

Click   the **Order field**. You must enter a quantity in the Order field.

Type   1 **Press** `tab` .

The program automatically completes the Back Order field with the quantity on order. The entire order quantity is considered as backordered.

Click   the **Item Description field**.

Type   ultrasound machine **Press** `tab` to move to the Price field.

Type   6000 **Press** `tab` .

If the account number is not entered by default, or if it is incorrect for this order, choose the correct account from the Account field selection list.

We will now enter the prepayment details.

Click   the **Payment Method field list arrow** for the payment options:

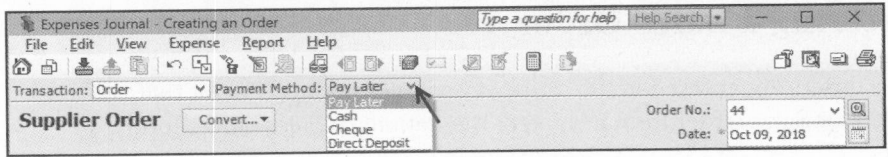

The options are the same as they are for other payments and purchases.

Click   **Cheque** to open the Paid From bank account field. *Bank: Eastside Chequing*, the default bank account, is entered.

CLASSIC VIEW

Click the Expenses, Orders & Quotes icon to open the journal, and choose Order from the journal's Transaction drop-down list.

PRO VERSION

Click the Purchase Orders icon to open the Purchases Journal with Order selected as the Transaction type.

NOTES

You must choose the type of transaction before selecting the supplier or customer. If you do not, the supplier or customer field will be cleared when you select a different type of transaction.

Click the **Paid From list arrow** to open the familiar list of Bank class accounts:

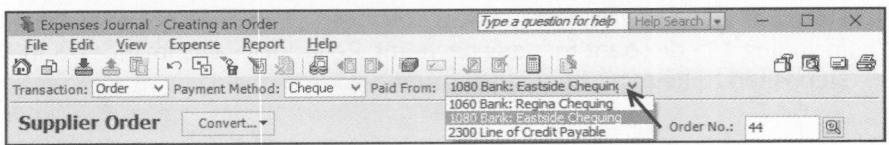

Choose Line of Credit Payable to open the cheque number field with the next cheque number for this account.

A **Prepayment Applied** field has also been added below the invoice lines on the order form. By default the entire order amount is entered, so we need to change it; $1 500 is being paid at this time.

Double-click the **Prepayment Applied field** to select the default amount.

Type 1500 **Press** tab to complete the order form:

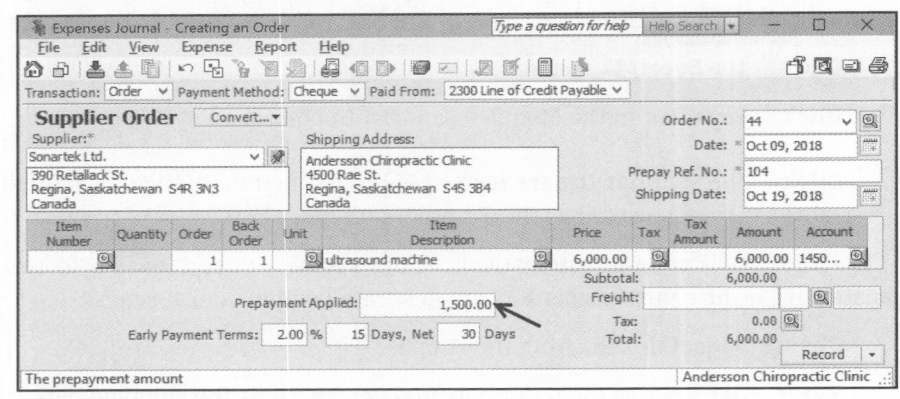

Check the **order** details carefully.

Because we have now actually entered a transaction that affects our account balances, there is a journal entry to review for the order.

Choose the **Report menu** and **click Display Expenses Journal Entry**:

Andersson Chiropractic Clinic			
Expenses Journal Entry 10/09/2018 (J9)			
Account Number	Account Description	Debits	Credits
1280	Purchase Prepayments	1,500.00	-
2300	Line of Credit Payable	-	1,500.00
Additional Date:	Additional Field:	1,500.00	1,500.00

This prepayment journal entry is the same as the one we made earlier from the Payments Journal (page 411). Only the bank account used is different.

Close the **journal display** to return to the order.

Make **corrections** if necessary. **Click Record** to save the order. Leave the journal open for the next transaction.

Entering a Sales Order

Sales orders are entered in the same way as sales quotes, except that you start with the Patient or Sales Order form instead of the Patient or Sales Quote form.

Click Receivables in the Modules pane and click the Patient Orders icon. Then choose the customer and complete the order details. The Order field cannot be left blank. Sales order numbers are usually generated by the customer, but they can also be entered and updated by the program, with the initial number entered in the Company Forms Settings window.

NOTES
The cheque number is entered as the Prepay Ref. No. (the prepayment reference number).

PRO VERSION

Choose Display Purchases Journal Entry from the Report menu.

NOTES
You can choose Print & Record as the default action for the supplier order by making this selection from the Record button's drop-down list. Previewing the order and cheque is also an option.

CLASSIC VIEW
Click the Fees, Orders & Quotes icon to open the journal, and choose Order from the journal's Transaction drop-down list.

Filling a Purchase Order

When an ordered item is received or work is completed you must complete a purchase invoice entry to record the transaction. Andersson will record the purchase order number in the Additional Field for the journal reports.

> ☑ **Purchase Invoice #TT-4599**   **Dated October 10, 2018**
> 16 From Thera-Tables Inc., to fill purchase order #TT-44 for $4 000 including taxes for custom-built treatment table. Terms: 2/5, n/30.

The Expenses Journal should still be open with Order selected as the Transaction type. Again, there are different ways to turn the order into an invoice.

Choose **TT-44** from the Order No. field drop-down list. **Press** (tab) to recall the order.

Choose **Convert This Supplier Order To An Invoice** from the Convert drop-down list. This is the only conversion option available now:

Instead, you can **click** the **Transaction drop-down list** and **choose Invoice**:

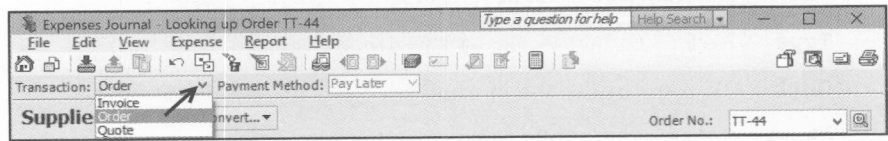

Or, choose Invoice from the Transaction list and then choose TT-44 from the Order/Quote No. drop-down list and press (tab).

The purchase order details from October 2 will be entered on the invoice:

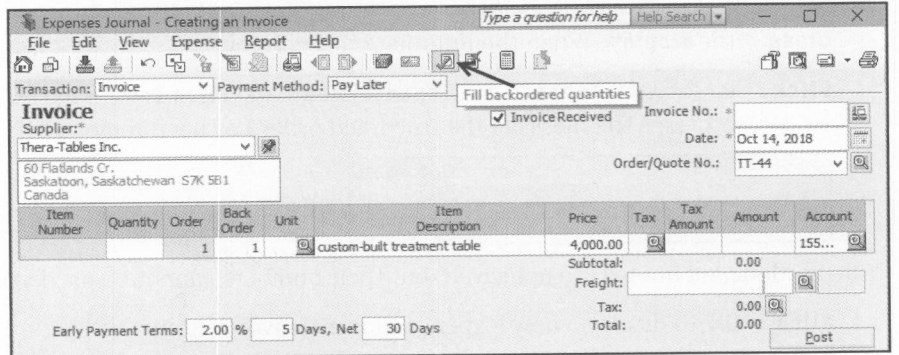

Pay Later, the default selection in the Payment Method field, is correct because this is a credit purchase. Creating An Invoice now appears in the title bar.

Click   the **Invoice field**. **Type** TT-4599

Press   (tab) **twice** to advance to the Date field.

Type   10-10

The invoice is still incomplete because the quantity displays as backordered and the invoice amount is zero. We need to "fill" the order.

Click   the **Fill Backordered Quantities tool** (refer to the previous screen) or **choose** the **Expense menu** and **click Fill Supplier Order**.

---

pro **PRO VERSION**
The Purchases Journal opens with Order as the Transaction type. Purchases Journal – Creating An Order appears in the journal's title bar.
Choose Invoice as the Transaction type or choose Convert This Purchase Order To A Purchase Invoice.

NOTES
After you choose the purchase order number, the order does not appear until after you press (tab) or advance to the next field.

NOTES
On the Order form, the Order No. field list has all unfilled quotes and orders because you can convert and fill quotes.
On the Invoice form, this field label changes to Order/Quote No. and will also include all unfilled quotes and orders because both can be converted to invoices.

NOTES
The Project/Division module is hidden for Andersson because it is not needed, but when used, the term Partner will replace Division or Project for medical companies.

pro **PRO VERSION**
Choose the Purchase menu and click Fill Purchase Order.

If you did not enter the price for the order, you cannot fill it — you must first edit the invoice to add the missing details.

The amount has been added to the invoice:

NOTES
If the order is partially filled, the backordered quantity will be reduced, as in the sales order on page 424.

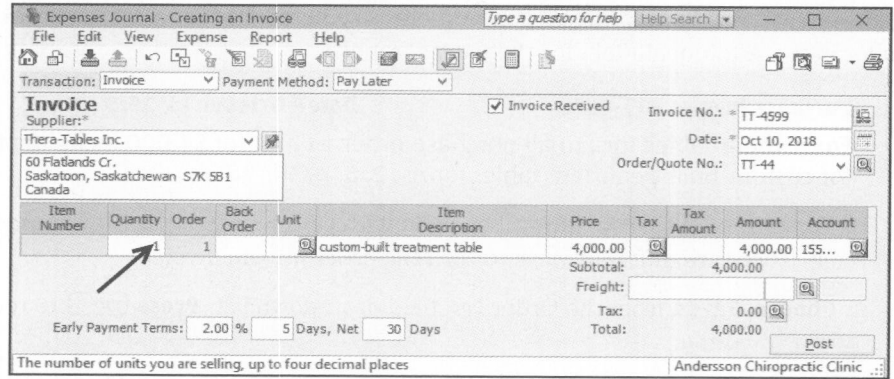

The Back Order quantity has been added to the Quantity column to reflect the completion of the order. The prepayment made in the Payments Journal does not appear on the invoice and the full amount is invoiced. When the prepayment is added to the order form, it is also entered on the invoice form (page 430).

PRO VERSION
pro Choose the Purchase menu and click Enter Additional Information.

Click the **Enter Additional Information tool** ☑ or **choose** the **Expense menu** and **click Enter Additional Information**.

Click the **Additional Field** text box.

Type `Ref: fill P.O. #TT-44`

Click **OK** to return to the journal.

Check the **entry** carefully to be sure that it is correct.

Choose the **Report menu** and **click Display Expenses Journal Entry**.

This is a normal journal entry with the order number as additional information. Prepayment amounts are not included.

Close the **display**. When the information is correct,

Click Post or **choose** the **Expense menu** and **click Post**. Sage 50 provides the message that the filled order has been removed:

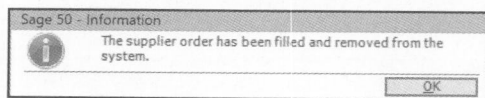

Filled orders and quotes are not saved, but their numbers cannot be used again.

Click **OK** to display a new Expenses Journal invoice form.

Close the **Expenses Journal**.

Filling a Purchase Quote

NOTES
To fill the quote, you can start with the quote on-screen. Then choose Invoice from the Transaction drop-down list or Convert This Supplier/Purchase Quote To An Invoice from the Convert drop-down list. Refer to the screenshots on page 408.

Filling a purchase quote is similar to filling an order. Choose Invoice, select the quote number and press (tab) to place the quote on-screen as an invoice. The Order quantity automatically moves to the Quantity column and the total Amount is added. You do not need to choose Fill Backordered Quantities for quotes. Again, you can record the quote number as an additional field for the journal.

Filling a Sales Order

Filling a sales order is similar to filling a purchase order, and there are different ways to do this.

✓	**Sales Invoice #649** **Dated October 10, 2018**
17	To Giant Raptors, to fill the first month of the contract on sales order #51 for $3 300. Terms: 1/10, n/30.

Click   **Receivables** in the Modules pane list to open the Receivables window for the next group of transactions.

Click   the **Patient Orders icon** to open the Fees Journal.

Click   the **Order No. list arrow** to display the available orders.

Click   **51**. **Press** (tab) to display the original sales order on the screen.

Click   **Convert This Patient Order To A Statement** from the Convert drop-down list. This is the only conversion option for orders:

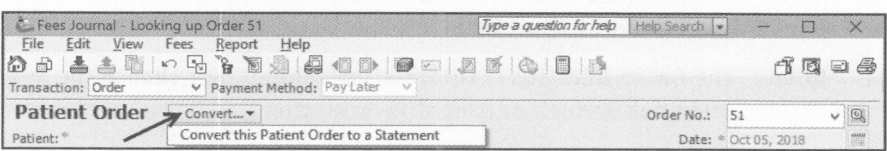

Or, **click** the **Transaction drop-down** list and **choose** **Statement**:

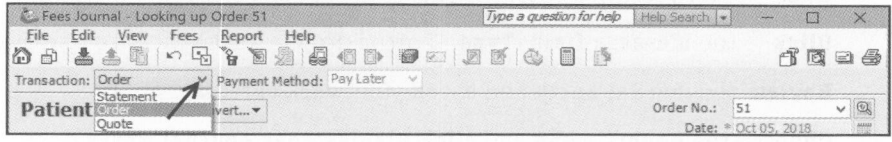

Or, choose the Statements icon from the Receivables module Home window. Then choose #51 from the Order/Quote field drop-down list and press (tab).

Each of these three approaches will replace the order with an invoice:

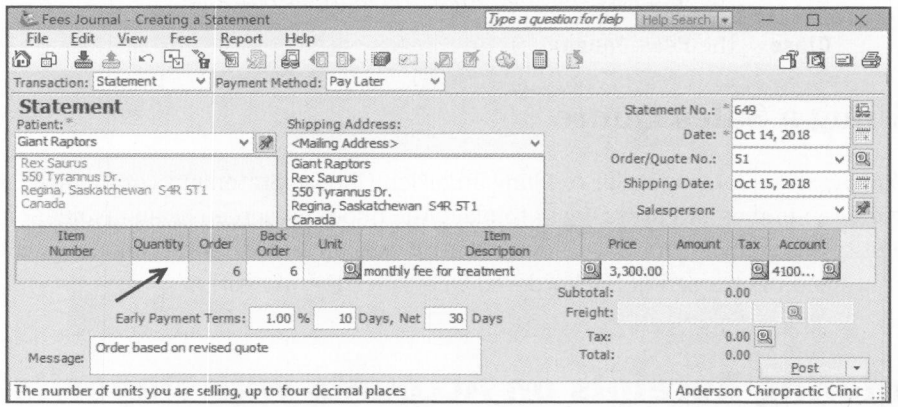

Sometimes only part of the order is received and the order is not completely filled at once, as in this case.

Pay Later should be selected as the Payment Method for the Statement transaction.

Enter   **October 10** as the transaction date.

Click   the **Quantity field**. Only one month is being billed at this time.

PRO VERSION

pro Click the Sales Orders icon to open the Sales Journal. Choose Order #51 and press *(tab)*. Sales Journal – Looking Up Order 51 appears in the journal's title bar.

Choose Convert This Sales Order To A Sales Invoice from the Convert drop-down list or choose Invoice from the Transaction list.

NOTES

Only one conversion option is possible from the order screen, that is, changing the order to an invoice.

The list in the Order No. field will include both unfilled quotes and unfilled orders.

NOTES

Statement replaces Invoice for medical companies.

NOTES

If you customized the columns for the Quote form, they will be restored for the Order. In the Premium version, Quote, Order and Invoice forms are customized separately.

PRO VERSION

pro If you customized the columns for the Quote form, the same changes will be applied on the Order and Invoice forms. You cannot customize them differently.

Type 1 **Press** (tab) to update the invoice:

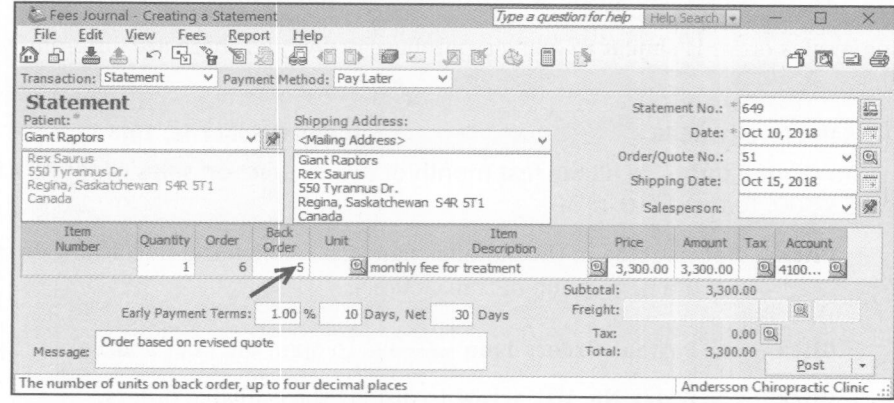

The Amount entered is the fee for one month of service, and the Back Order quantity is reduced to five. When the sixth and final month is completed, the order will be filled and removed.

To fill the sales order for all 6 months at the same time, you would choose to Fill Backordered Quantities, using the tool button or the Fees menu option.

Click the **Enter Additional Information tool** or **choose** the **Fees menu** and **click Enter Additional Information**.

Click the **Additional Field** text box. **Type** Ref: S.O. #51

Click OK to return to the journal. We should also modify the comment.

Click the **Message field**. **Type** Invoice based on revised quote

Review the **journal entry** and **check** your **work** carefully.

Choose the **Report menu** and **click Display Fees Journal Entry**.

Close the **display** to return to the invoice. **Make corrections** if necessary.

Click Post to record the invoice. The order is not filled, so you do not get the message that the order will be removed.

Close the **Fees Journal**.

Filling a Sales Quote

Filling a sales quote is similar to filling an order. Choose Statement (or Invoice), select the quote number and press (tab) to place the quote on-screen as an invoice. The order quantity automatically moves to the Quantity column and the total Amount is added. You do not need to choose Fill Backordered Quantities for quotes.

Entering Receipts on Accounts with Deposits

The next receipt pays the balance of an account for a customer who has made a deposit.

Receipt #62 **Dated October 13, 2018**

From the Giant Raptors, cheque #939 for $1 267 in full payment of account including $33 discount for early payment. Reference sales invoice #649 and deposit #14. Deposited to Eastside Chequing account.

Click the **Receipts icon** to open the Receipts Journal.

Choose Giant Raptors from the customer drop-down list:

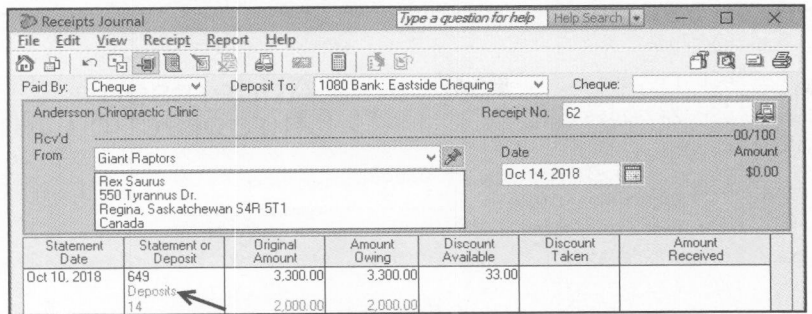

NOTES

If necessary, drag the lower frame of the journal to include the deposit on the screen, or maximize the window.

Customer deposits are displayed in red below the outstanding invoices. The colour indicates that they are negative invoices that reduce the balance owing. The invoice line has the full amount owing and the full discount amount available.

Enter   **939** as the Cheque number and **enter Oct 13** in the Date field.

Click   the **Discount Taken field** for invoice #649 to accept the discount.

Press   ⌨tab to accept the Amount Received and add the Deposit amount.

Press   ⌨tab to accept the Deposit amount and update the receipt.

Enter   the **invoice** and **deposit numbers** as additional information.

The discount and deposit are subtracted from the full invoice amount so that the total amount now matches the cheque amount in the completed receipt:

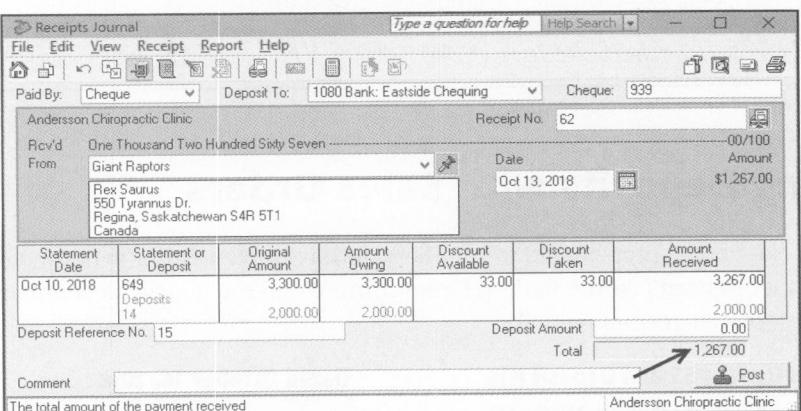

Choose the **Report menu** and **click Display Receipts Journal Entry**:

Andersson Chiropractic Clinic
Receipts Journal Entry 10/13/2018 (J12)

Account Number	Account Description	Debits	Credits
1080	Bank: Eastside Chequing	1,267.00	-
2250	Prepaid Sales and Deposits	2,000.00	-
4150	Sales Discounts	33.00	-
1200	Accounts Receivable	-	3,300.00
Additional Date:	Additional Field: Ref: inv #649 & d...	3,300.00	3,300.00

Accounts Receivable has been credited for the full invoice amount as in regular receipts. The *Sales Discounts* contra-revenue account has been debited to record the reduction to sales revenue. The *Prepaid Sales and Deposits* liability account has been debited for the full deposit amount to clear its credit balance, and the bank account is debited for the amount of the cheque.

The initial deposit creates a liability — the customer has paid us and we have not provided anything yet. When the order is filled, the liability is removed, so the *Accounts Receivable* balance debit is offset by the initial liability. When the customer pays the invoice for the balance owing, the initial credit entry must be removed from the record.

Close   the **journal display window**. **Make corrections** if necessary. **Post** the **receipt** and then **close** the **Receipts Journal**.

NOTES
Use Full Add for the new customer.

   Email: vkain@dancestudio.ca
   Revenue account: 4100
   Credit limit: $4 000
   Use the source document for the remaining customer details.
   Remember to change the default payment terms.
   Enter 1 as the Order quantity.

Enter   sales quote #52 for a new customer.

19

Quote:	52	
Date:	Oct 13, 2018	
Starting date:	Oct 25, 2018	
Customer:	Veronica Kain	
	Veronica Kain School of Dance	
	35 Lady Slipper Rd.	
Address:	Regina, SK S3V 4H7	
Phone No:	(306) 376-3218	

Andersson Chiropractic Clinic
www.betterbacks.com

4500 Rae St.
Regina, SK S4S 3B4
Tel 1: (306) 577-1900
Tel 2: (306) 577-2199   Fax: (306) 577-1925

QUOTE

Treatment description	Amount
Chiropractic services for the school year (Sep-Jun)	
Monthly contract rate	
$1 000 deposit when contract accepted	2 500.00
Contract may be extended for summer months	

Terms: 1/10, n/30
Signed: *Maria Andersson* | Customer Initials: *VK* | TOTAL | 2 500.00

Entering Deposits with Sales Orders

Just as you can enter prepayments to suppliers in the Supplier Order window, you can enter customer deposits on the Patient Order form. When the deposit accompanies the order, this method is recommended.

✓
20

Sales Order #52 and Deposit #15   **Dated October 14, 2018**

Starting date October 25, 2018
From Veronica Kain School of Dance, acceptance of quote #52. Convert the quote to a sales order leaving all terms and amounts unchanged. Received cheque #865 for $1 000 as deposit #15 to confirm sales order #52. Deposited to Eastside Chequing account.

The Fees Journal should still be open with Quote selected as the Transaction type.

Choose 52 from the Quote No. field list and **press** (tab).

Choose Order as the Transaction type or **choose Convert This Patient Quote To A Patient Order** from the Convert list to convert the quote to an order.

Click   the **Payment Method list arrow** for the payment options:

PRO VERSION
Choose Order from the Transaction list in the Sales Journal, or choose Convert This Sales Quote To A Sales Order from the Convert drop-down list.

PRO VERSION
Sales Journal – Creating An Order will be the title for the journal.

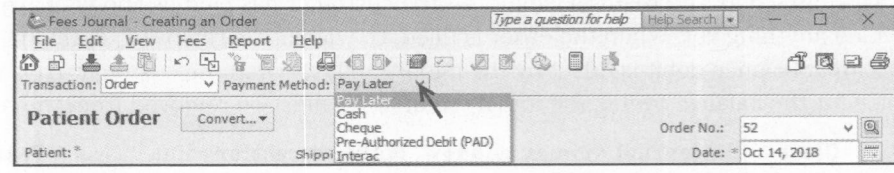

The same customer payment types are available here as in the Receipts Journal.

Click **Cheque** in the Payment Method list to open the extra payment fields:

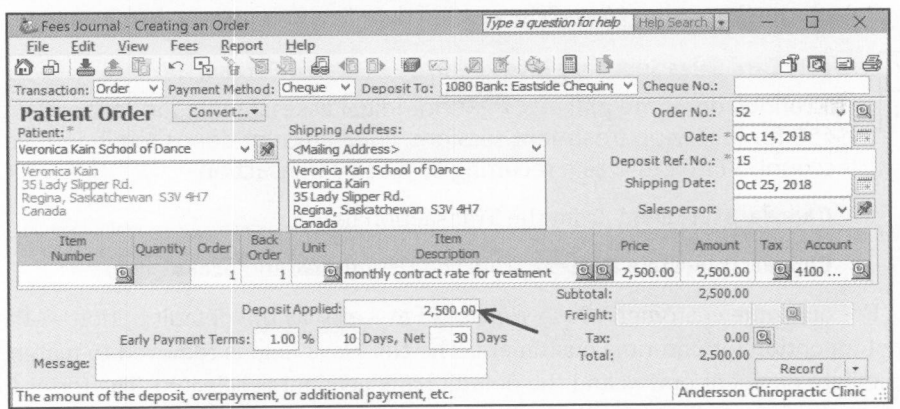

The default bank account is selected for the Deposit To field at the top of the order form. A Cheque No. field and a **Deposit Reference No.** field with the next deposit number have been added to the top of the form. A **Deposit Applied** amount field has been added to the bottom of the order form, as for purchase orders with prepayments.

The session date and bank account are correct, so we can add the payment details.

Click the **Cheque No. field**.

Type 865

Double-click the **Deposit Applied field**. The full amount of the order is entered as the default amount and we need to change it.

Type 1000

Press (tab) to update and complete the form.

Choose the **Report menu** and **click Display Fees Journal Entry**:

Andersson Chiropractic Clinic			
Fees Journal Entry 10/14/2018 (J13)			
Account Number	Account Description	Debits	Credits
1080	Bank: Eastside Chequing	1,000.00	-
2250	Prepaid Sales and Deposits	-	1,000.00
Additional Date:	Additional Field:	1,000.00	1,000.00

Except for the amounts, this journal entry is identical to the journal entry for deposits entered in the Receipts Journal (page 418). Only the bank account is different. The prepayment or deposit with the sales order creates a journal entry, although the sales order itself does not.

Close the **display** and **click** 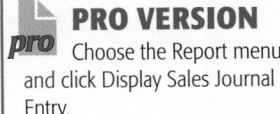 to save the transaction.

Click **Yes** to confirm that you are changing the quote to an order.

Entering Debit Card Sale Transactions

Customers pay for purchases using cash, cheques, credit cards or debit cards. Debit and credit card purchases are similar for a store — the payment is deposited immediately to the linked bank account. The difference is that debit card transactions withdraw the money from the customer's bank account immediately while credit cards advance a loan that the customer repays on receipt of the credit card bill. The store pays a percentage discount or transaction fee to the credit card company for the service. For debit card transactions, the store pays a flat fee for each transaction. Both involve a setup fee and a monthly rental charge for the terminal that communicates electronically with the card-issuing company. Andersson uses the name Interac for all debit card transactions.

NOTES
You cannot enter additional information for quotes and orders, even if the payment accompanies the order.

PRO VERSION
pro Choose the Report menu and click Display Sales Journal Entry.

NOTES
Fees for debit cards can be lower than credit card fees because the risk of non-payment is eliminated. Debit card payments require the customer's bank balance to cover the amount before the payments are approved.

For Andersson, we set up the debit card as a credit card with a 0.0% transaction fee.

The Fees Journal should be open from the previous transaction. If it is not, open it by clicking the Statements icon. The session date is correct as the invoice date.

✓ **Debit Card Sales Summary Invoice #650**   **Dated October 14, 2018**
21 To various one-time patients, $260 for initial assessments for new patients and $450 for follow-up treatment sessions. Total amount deposited in Interac bank account, $710. Store as a recurring bi-weekly transaction.

Choose **Statement** from the Transaction list.

Choose **One-Time Patient** from the Patient list and **press** (tab).

For one-time customers, **Cash** replaces Pay Later as the default option — Pay Later is not an option for one-time customers. The Net Days field is removed to match the immediate payment option and the default bank account is selected. The terms for new customers offer no discount, so the discount fields are blank.

Click the **Payment Method list arrow** for the payment options:

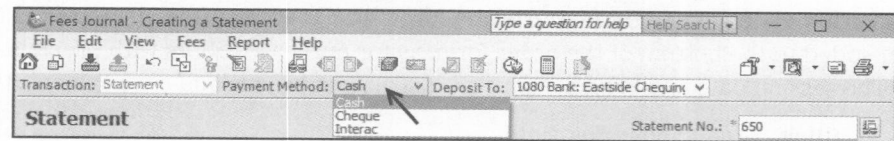

Click **Interac** as the method of payment to modify the invoice.

There is no Deposit To bank account field or Cheque Number field as there is when the payment is made by cheque. Interac is linked automatically to a dedicated bank account as part of the company file setup, just like credit cards. Interac Amount replaces Cash Amount as the label for the amount received.

Type `Debit Card Sales Summary` (in the Address field).

Complete the rest of the **invoice** in the same way as credit card or cash sales.

Click the **Item Description field** and **type** `initial assessments`

Click the **Amount field** and **type** `260`

The account is added automatically because we entered it as the default linked revenue account for the Receivables Ledger.

Click the **Item Description field** on the second line of the invoice.

Type `follow-up treatments`

Click the **Amount field** and **type** `450`

Press (tab) to complete the invoice:

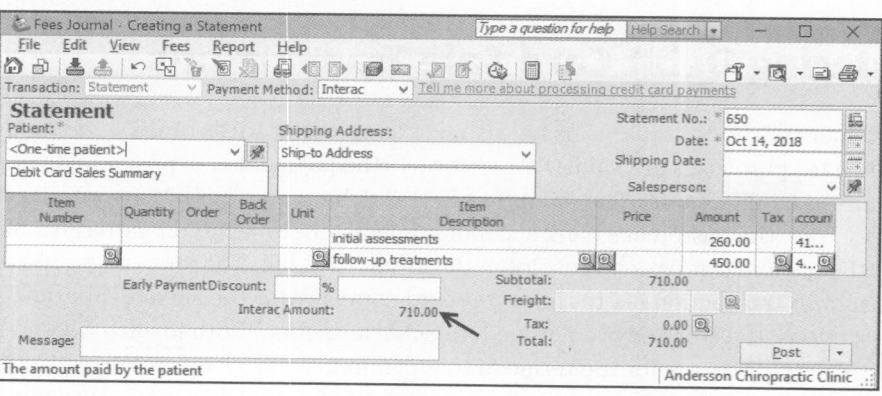

Choose the **Report menu** and **click Display Fees Journal Entry** to review the entry before posting:

Andersson Chiropractic Clinic			
Fees Journal Entry 10/14/2018 (J14)			
Account Number	Account Description	Debits	Credits
1100	Bank: Interac	710.00	-
4100	Revenue from Services	-	710.00
Additional Date:	Additional Field:	710.00	710.00

A new linked account is used for this transaction. The debit card account — *Bank: Interac* — replaces the usual bank account for other cash sales and *Accounts Receivable* for account sales. Unlike credit card sales, no additional fees are withheld.

Close the **display** to return to the Fees Journal input screen.

Make **corrections** if necessary, referring to page 161 for assistance.

We can store the entry and use it to enter the debit card summaries every second week. When you recall the transaction, you can edit the amounts. You will not need to save the changes and store the transaction again.

Click the **Store tool** to save the transaction for repeated entries.

Choose **Biweekly** as the frequency and **click OK** to save the stored entry.

Click Post .

Close the **Fees Journal**. **Click Payables** in the Modules pane list.

Enter the **next three transactions** for October 14.

Payment Cheque #122   **Dated October 14, 2018**

22 To Cleanol and Laundry Services, $90 from Eastside Chequing account in payment of account. Reference invoice #CLS-2419.

Payment Cheque #123   **Dated October 14, 2018**

23 To Thera-Tables Inc., $3 520 from Eastside Chequing account in full payment of account including $80 discount for early payment. Reference invoice #TT-4599 and cheque #567. Remember to "pay" the prepayment.

Purchase Invoice #CLS-3926   **Dated October 14, 2018**

24 From Cleanol and Laundry Services, $120 for contracted twice-weekly laundry service. Terms: net 30. Store the transaction as a bi-weekly recurring entry.

Filling Purchase Orders with Prepayments

When a prepayment is added directly to the purchase order, the payment details remain on the invoice when you fill the order.

Advance the **session date** to **October 21, 2018** and **back up** your **data**.

Purchase Invoice #SL-4622   **Dated October 17, 2018**

25 From Sonartek Ltd., to fill purchase order #44, $6 000 including taxes for multi-frequency ultrasound machine. Terms: 2/15, n/30.

Open the **Payables Module** and **click** the **Supplier Orders icon** to open the Expenses Journal.

Choose **order #44** from the Order No. field drop-down list and **press** tab .

Choose **Convert This Supplier Order To An Invoice**, or **choose Invoice** from the Transaction drop-down list.

PRO VERSION Choose the Report menu and click Display Sales Journal Entry.

NOTES The third-party provider that processes the Interac transactions does charge fees, but these would be entered at the time of account reconciliation when the statement is received and the account is reconciled. Close the message about credit card processing if it pops up — click Do Not Show This Message Again.

NOTES You may need to scroll down to include the line for the prepayment amount.

PRO VERSION Click the Purchase Orders icon to open the journal. Choose Invoice from the Transaction list.

CLASSIC VIEW Click the Expenses, Orders & Quotes icon. Choose Order from the Transaction drop-down list.

This will add the order details to the invoice form:

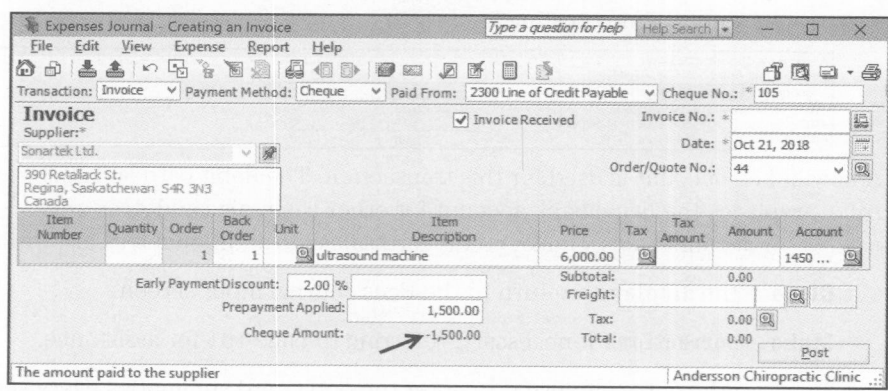

Cheque is still selected as the Payment Method. The prepayment information from the order is entered as the amount in the **Prepayment Applied** field. The cheque amount is negative because no invoice amount has been added yet.

Click the `Fill Backordered Quantities tool` in the tool bar or **choose** the `Expense menu` and **click** `Fill Supplier Order`.

Now the cheque amount is $4 380.00 — the total invoice amount minus the prepayment and 2 percent discount. This is not a cash purchase, so we need to change the payment method.

Choose `Pay Later` from the Payment Method drop-down list.

The form is updated — the Paid From, Cheque Number and Cheque Amount fields have been removed. The amount owing (near the bottom of the invoice) changes to $4 500 ($6 000 minus the $1 500 prepayment).

Add the **invoice number** and **purchase date** to the form:

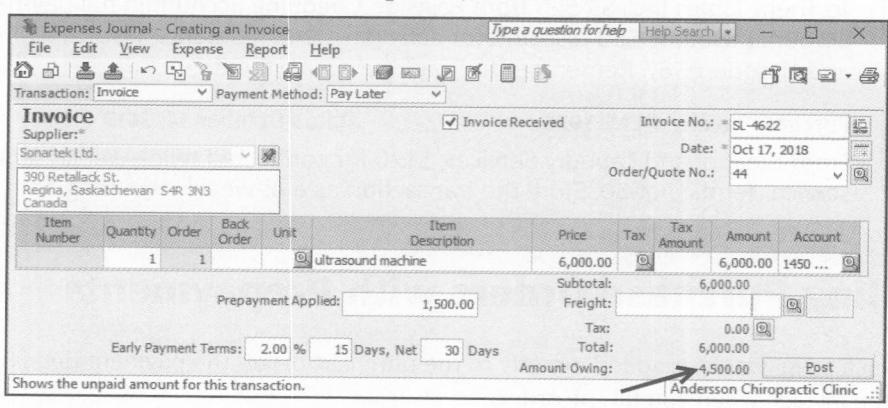

Click the `Additional Information tool` . **Click** the `Additional Information field`.

Type `Ref: fill PO #44` **Click** `OK` to return to the journal.

Press `ctrl` + **J** to open the journal display:

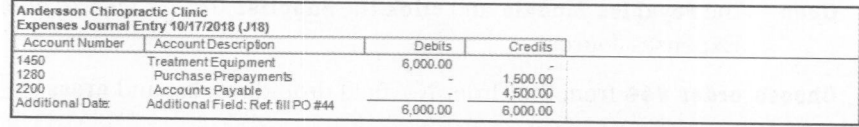

The entry differs from the standard purchase entry because the amount for *Purchase Prepayments* has been added. Because the purchase is complete, the credit with the supplier is removed and the prepayment is treated like a partial payment

toward the invoice. Thus, *Purchase Prepayments* has been credited to reduce this account's balance to zero for the supplier. *Treatment Equipment* is debited for the full purchase invoice amount and *Accounts Payable* is credited for the balance owing after the prepayment is subtracted.

When you enter a prepayment in the Payments Journal, the program does not know which purchase it is related to, so the prepayment is added in the Payments Journal for that supplier. It can be applied to any purchase. Entering the prepayment on the order establishes a link to this purchase. When the prepayment is made at the same time as the order, it should be entered on the order. When it is made at a different time, either prior to or later than the order, it should be entered in the Payments Journal.

> **Close** the **Journal display**.
>
> **Make** corrections to the invoice if necessary and then **post** the **purchase**.
>
> **Click** **OK** to confirm that the order has been filled.
>
> **Enter** the **next four transactions**. **Change** modules as needed.

NOTES
If the deposit is made after the order is entered, you can edit (adjust) the order to add the prepayment using the cheque date for the revised order.

---

26 | **Cash Purchase #GF-2641** | **Dated October 18, 2018**

From Grasslands Fuel, $124 for gasoline for business vehicle. Invoice total $124 paid in full by cheque #569 from Regina Chequing account. Store as a bi-weekly recurring entry.

---

27 | **Cash Sales Invoice #651** | **Dated October 20, 2018**

To Albert Blackfoot, $315 for seven treatment sessions. Invoice total paid in full by cheque #426 and deposited to Eastside Chequing account. Store as a monthly recurring entry.

---

28 | **Purchase Quote #SU-5532** | **Dated October 21, 2018**

Starting date December 1, 2018
From Space Unlimited (use Quick Add), $2 250 per month for rent of office space for the next 12 months. (Enter 12 as the order quantity.) Rent does not include heat or hydro. Terms: security deposit of one month's rent required with postdated cheques for one year dated on the first of each month.

NOTES
Enter 12 in the Order column for the two rent quotes so that we can partially fill the quote.

---

29 | **Purchase Quote #45** | **Dated October 21, 2018**

Starting date December 1, 2018
From Pro Suites Inc., $2 350 per month for rent of office space for the next 12 months. (Enter 12 as the order quantity.) Rent includes heat and hydro. Rent payment is due on the first of each month with a series of postdated cheques.

Filling Sales Orders with Deposits

> **Change** the **session date** to October 31 and **back up** your **data**.

When you advance the session date to October 31, you will open an Advisor message:

> Advisor: Now is a good time to prepare for your company's year end. Refer to the Help for more information.
>
> [Click here to close.]

> **Click** to close the message about year-end preparation.

---

30 | **Sales Invoice #652** | **Dated October 25, 2018**

To Veronica Kain School of Dance, to fill sales order #52, $2 500 for contracted services for one month. Terms: 1/10, n/30. Store as a recurring monthly entry.

PRO VERSION
Click the Sales Invoices icon to open the Sales Journal. Invoice will be selected as the Transaction type.

Click   the **Statements Icon** to open the **Fees Journal**. Statement should be selected as the Transaction type.

Select   **Sales Order #52** from the Order/Quote No. list and **press** $\boxed{tab}$ to recall the order as a statement or invoice:

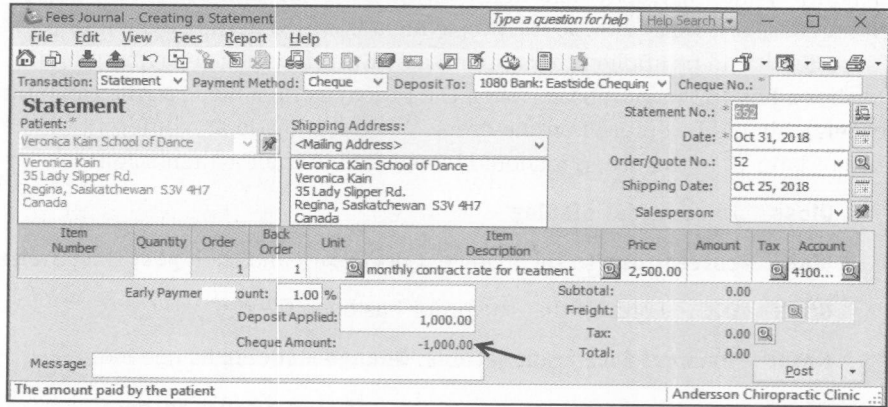

Or, click the Patient Orders icon to open the Order form of the journal. Choose #52 from the Order No. drop-down list and press $\boxed{tab}$ to recall the order. Then choose Convert This Patient Order To A Statement from the Convert drop-down list, or choose Statement from the Transaction drop-down list to change the order to a statement.

Information about the deposit is included on the invoice. Because the deposit was paid by cheque, this is also the default payment method for the invoice, and we need to change it.

Click   the **Payment Method list arrow** and **choose Pay Later**.

In the modified form the Bank and Cheque Number fields have been removed. The Deposit Applied amount field is not available for entering an amount.

NOTES
When the deposit for a sales order is entered as a receipt separately from the sales order, the deposit amount does not appear in the Sales Journal when you fill the order.

PRO VERSION
Choose the Sales menu and click Fill Sales Order.

Click   the **Fill Backordered Quantities tool** 🗔 in the tool bar or **choose** the **Fees menu** and **click Fill Patient Order**.

With this step, you will update the amounts and fill the order:

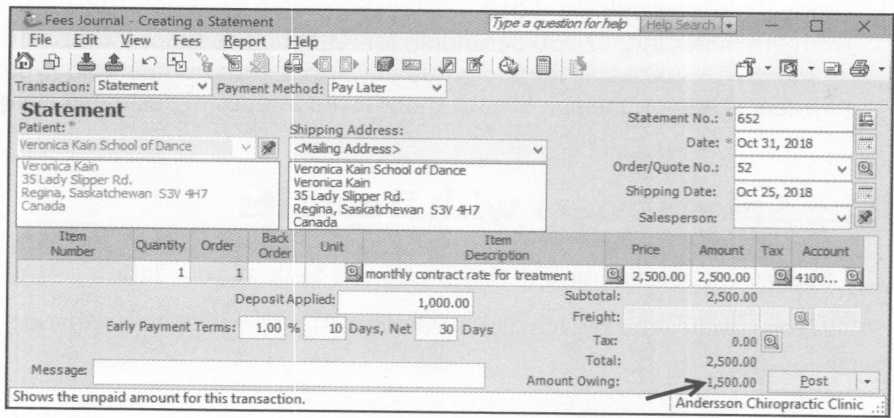

The Cheque Amount field has been removed, but the Deposit Applied details remain. The Amount Owing is reduced by the $1 000 deposit.

Enter   **Oct 25** as the date for the sale.

Click   the **Enter Additional Information tool** ☑ or **choose** the **Fees menu** and **click Enter Additional Information**.

Type   Ref SO #52 & deposit #15 as the Additional Information.

PRO VERSION
Choose the Sales menu and click Enter Additional Information.

Click   **OK** to return to the journal.

Choose   the **Report menu** and **click Display Fees Journal Entry**:

Andersson Chiropractic Clinic Fees Journal Entry 10/25/2018 (J21)			
Account Number	Account Description	Debits	Credits
1200	Accounts Receivable	1,500.00	-
2250	Prepaid Sales and Deposits	1,000.00	-
4100	Revenue from Services	-	2,500.00
Additional Date:	Additional Field: Ref: SO #52 & de...	2,500.00	2,500.00

The entry is similar to the Expenses Journal entry on page 430. Because the sale is complete, the liability is removed and the prepayment is treated like a partial payment toward the invoice. Thus, *Prepaid Sales and Deposits* has been debited to reduce this account's balance to zero for the customer, *Revenue from Services* is credited for the full sales invoice amount and *Accounts Receivable* is debited for the balance owing after subtracting the deposit.

Close   the **display**. **Store** the **entry** as a monthly recurring transaction.

Click   **Post** to save the invoice. **Click OK** to confirm the removal of the order.

Enter   the **next group of transactions** up to Receipt #64. **Change modules** as needed, or **create shortcuts**.

NOTES
When the deposit for a sales order is entered as a receipt separately from the sales order, the deposit amount does not appear in the journal entry for the sale that fills the order.

Sales Invoice #653   **Dated October 25, 2018**

31   To Interplay Ballet School, $2 500 for contracted services for one month. Terms: 1/10, n/30. Store transaction as a recurring monthly entry.

Purchase Invoice #CLS-4723   **Dated October 28, 2018**

32   From Cleanol and Laundry Services, $120 for contracted laundry service. Terms: net 30. Recall stored transaction.

33

Sales Invoice:	654

Date: Oct 28, 2018

Customer: Debit card sales summary

Address:

Phone No:

Andersson Chiropractic Clinic
www.betterbacks.com
4500 Rae St.
Regina, SK S4S 3B4
Tel 1: (306) 577-1900
Tel 2: (306) 577-2199   Fax: (306) 577-1925

NOTES
Recall the stored transaction but do not store the changed transaction. When you post the transaction, you will be advised that the transaction has changed and the next due date will be updated. Click Yes to continue. Refer to page 185.

Treatment description	Amount
Initial assessments	130.00
Follow-up treatments	630.00

Terms: paid by Interac

Direct deposit to Interac account

Signed: *Maria Andersson* | Customer Initials: | **INVOICE TOTAL** | 760.00 |

34

Cash Purchase Invoice #WC-83825   **Dated October 28, 2018**

From Western Communications, $125 including taxes for one month of telephone and Internet service. Invoice total paid by cheque #124 from Eastside Chequing account. Store as a monthly recurring entry.

35

Sales Invoice #655   **Dated October 28, 2018**

To Canadian Royals, $4 500 for contracted services for one month. Terms: 1/10, n/30. Store transaction as a recurring monthly entry.

36

Sales Invoice #656   **Dated October 28, 2018**

To Roughrider Argos, $4 900 for contracted services for one month. Terms: 1/10, n/30. Store transaction as a recurring monthly entry.

37

Receipt #63   **Dated October 29, 2018**

From Interplay Ballet School, cheque #501 for $2 475 in payment of account including $25 discount for early payment. Reference sales invoice #653. Deposited to Regina Chequing account.

38

Payment Cheque #570   **Dated October 29, 2018**

To Cleanol and Laundry Services, $210 from Regina Chequing account in payment of account. Reference invoices #CLS-2683 and #CLS-3926.

39

Bank Debit Memo #477211   **Dated October 29, 2018**

From Eastside Trust, $2 700 for monthly payroll and $45 payroll service fee withdrawn from chequing account. Store payroll transaction as a monthly recurring entry. Use the General Journal for this payroll transaction.

Entering Receipts for Sales with Deposits on Orders

When a customer makes the final payment toward an invoice that had a deposit with the sales order, the journal entry is different from an entry with a separate deposit.

> **Open**   the **Receivables module window**.

✓
40

Receipt #64   **Dated October 29, 2018**

From Veronica Kain School of Dance, cheque #878 for $1 475 in payment of account including $25 discount for early payment. Reference sales invoice #652 and deposit #15. Deposited to Eastside Chequing account.

> **Open**   the **Receipts Journal** and **select Veronica Kain School of Dance**:

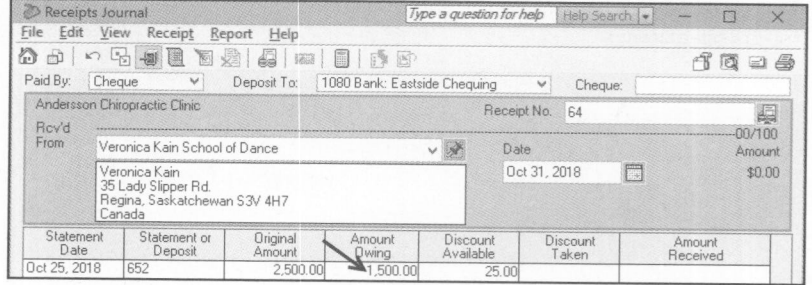

Because the prepayment was cleared at the time of the sale, it does not appear in the Receipts Journal. Instead, the Amount Owing has been reduced, so this is a standard receipt entry. The discount is based on the full invoice amount, or 1 percent of $2 500.

> **Enter**   the **remaining transaction details** to complete the entry. **Review** the transaction and then **post** it.

> **Enter**   the **remaining transactions** for the October 31 session date.

Purchase Quote #FS-644   **Dated October 29, 2018**

41

Starting date November 1, 2018
From Fresh Spaces (use Quick Add for the new supplier), $125 per week for daily laundry service. Terms: net 30.

42

PURCHASE QUOTE #46

Cleanol
and
Laundry Services

19 Duster Road
Regina, SK S4R 4L4
(306) 398-0908

Date:	Oct 29, 2018
Starting date:	Nov 1, 2018
For:	Andersson Chiropractic Clinic
Address:	4500 Rae St.
	Regina, SK S4S 3B4
Phone No:	(306) 577-1900
Fax No:	(306) 577-1925
Contact:	Maria Andersson

Order description	Amount
Contract for daily laundry service bi-weekly rate including GST terms: net 30 days	210.00

Quote Total	210.00
Deposit	——
Total Amount	210.00

Authorization: *Bessie Sweeps*

Purchase Order #46   **Dated October 29, 2018**

43

Starting date November 1, 2018
Convert quote #46 from Cleanol and Laundry Services to an order. The order confirms the price at $210 every two weeks for daily service. Terms: net 30.

Memo #2   **Dated October 31, 2018**

44

Transfer $1 060 from the Regina Chequing account to pay down the line of credit. This amount includes $60 for one month of interest on the amount of credit used. Store as a monthly recurring entry. (Use the General Journal.)

Advance the **session date** to November 7. **Back up** your **data file**.

Working from the Daily Business Manager

Sage 50 helps a business monitor its performance and cash flow by generating several of the reports covered in previous chapters. It also keeps track of recurring transactions, payments and receipts with the Daily Business Manager lists. These lists offer an additional method of internal control.

You should be in the Home window after changing the session date to November 7. You can enter many transactions directly from the Daily Business Manager.

You can open the Daily Business Manager from the Company window Daily Business Manager icon, the Business Assistant menu or the Daily Business Manager (DBM) tool.

These alternatives are combined in the following screenshot:

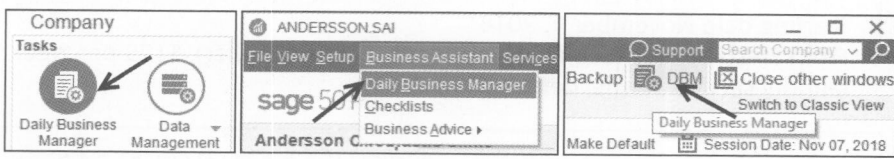

Click   the **Daily Business Manager icon** in the Company module window or **choose** the **Business Assistant menu** and **click Daily Business Manager** or **click** the **DBM tool**:

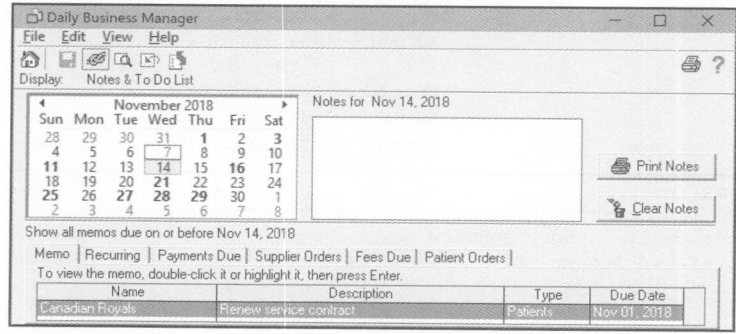

In any journal, you can access the Daily Business Manager from the tool icon or from the View menu Daily Business Manager option.

You can show Daily Business Manager lists automatically each time you advance the session date, each time you start the program or both. Choose the Setup menu, then choose User Preferences and click View (refer to page 81). Click At Startup and After Changing Session Date below Daily Business Manager to select these options. Menu and tool bar access to the lists are always available.

By default, Sage 50 chooses a date that is one week past the current session date for its Daily Business Manager. The date can be changed by clicking a new date on the calendar. Lists will be updated to reflect the change in date.

Each tab screen includes instructions for accessing journals or selecting an entry.

You can also type notes for a date directly into the Notes box. They will remain on-screen for that date until you choose Clear Notes. You can print these notes and clear them when they are no longer needed.

The Memo tab screen opens with a reminder to renew a customer contract. This memo was entered in the customer's ledger Memo tab screen with a due date and the option to display it in the Daily Business Manager.

| ✓ | **Memo #3** | **Dated November 1, 2018** |

45   Review and update memos and enter the next transactions from the Daily Business Manager. The annual contract for Canadian Royals has been renewed.

Double-click Canadian Royals to open the memo in the customer's ledger:

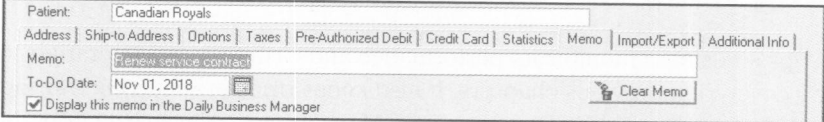

The customer's record opens at the Memo tab screen. You now have the option to edit the memo, remove it if it no longer applies (**Clear Memo**) or change the date that it will appear in the Daily Business Manager. We have checked the option to display the memo in the Daily Business Manager.

Change the **date** in the To-Do Date field to **Nov. 1, 2019**.

Click   in the ledger record to return to the Daily Business Manager. The memo has been removed from the list.

Payments Due

The first journal entry for November is a cheque issued for an outstanding invoice. To be certain that all outstanding invoices are paid in a timely fashion, we can enter payments from the Daily Business Manager.

> ☑ 46
>
> **Payment Cheque #571**   **Dated November 1, 2018**
>
> To Sonartek Ltd., $4 380 from Regina Chequing account in full payment of account including $120 discount for early payment. Reference purchase invoice #SL-4622 and cheque #104 (prepayment).

Click   the **Payments Due tab**:

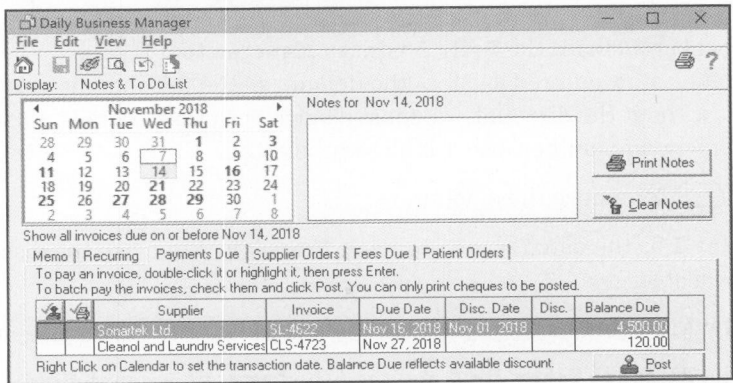

The list includes payments due and any applicable discounts. To add the payments due in a longer period, and to be sure that all discounts available will be included, you can select a later date on the calendar. You might use this list to plan a payment schedule. We want to take advantage of purchase discounts.

The list includes the Supplier name, Invoice number, payment Due Date, Discount Date, Discount availability and the Balance Due (owing). The Discount Date informs you when the discount period ends. You can pay the invoices directly from this screen when no changes are needed. You can also open the Payments Journal by double-clicking an invoice line or by clicking an invoice and pressing (enter).

If you pay from the Daily Business Manager, the session date is the default, so the discount is no longer available. To change the cheque date, right-click the date you want in the calendar.

Right-click Nov 1 on the calendar. The discount for Sonartek is now available.

In the calendar section, November 1 now has an open box framing it to indicate it will be the transaction posting date. The Disc. column now has a ✓ and the Balance Due for invoice #SL-4622 has been updated to include the discount:

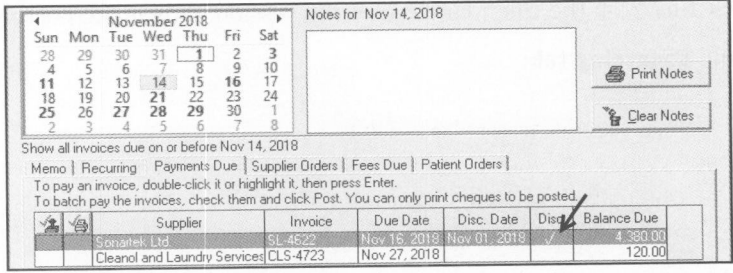

If we post from the Daily Business Manager now, the date and discount will be correct, but the bank account will not. The default amount and bank account (Bank: Eastside Chequing) will be entered when you pay from the Daily Business Manager, and you cannot change these fields. Therefore, we must open the journal to pay the invoice.

Double-click the **entry for Sonartek** to open the Payments Journal:

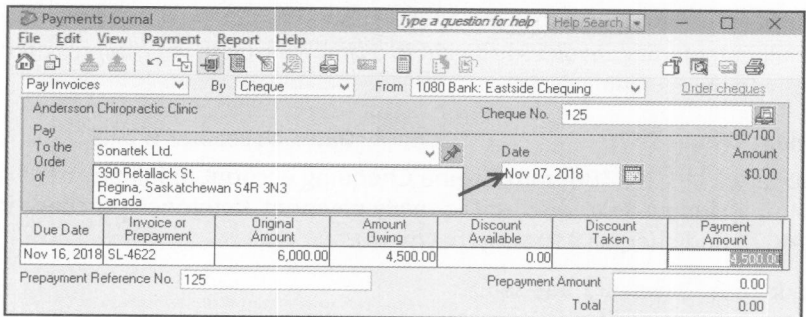

The journal tool bar includes the **Daily Business Manager tool** .

The session date is now entered again as the default, so the full amount owing is entered by default without the discount. We must change both these details. First we will delete the payment amount because it is already selected.

Press (del) to remove the amount.

Enter **Nov 1** as the date for the payment. **Press** (tab) to make the discount available.

Choose **Bank: Regina Chequing** in the From field to update the cheque number.

Click the **Discount Taken field** and then the **Payment Amount field.**

Press (tab). **Enter** the **Invoice Number** as Additional Information to complete the payment. **Check** your **entry**.

Click [Post] to save the entry when you are certain it is correct.

Close the **Payments Journal** to return to the Daily Business Manager.

The Sonartek Ltd. entry has been removed from the list.

Click the **Refresh** tool if necessary to update the list immediately.

Recurring Transactions Due

The next transaction is a recurring cash purchase.

Another advantage to using the Daily Business Manager is that the recurring entries for all journals are listed together. You can open a journal and recall a stored transaction in a single step. You can also post and print sales invoices, individually or in batches, directly from this screen, but you cannot preview them.

Right-click Nov 7 on the calendar to reset the session date as the posting date.

Click the **Recurring tab**:

NOTES
The prepayment was entered on the order and cleared when we filled the order, so it does not appear in the Payments Journal.

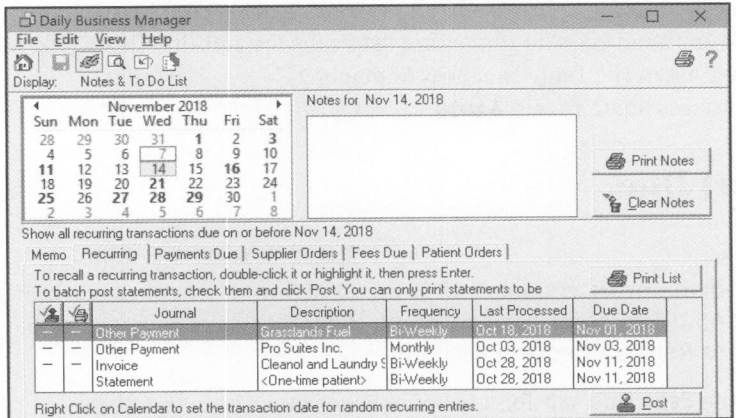

All recurring entries due on or before November 14 (the transaction display date marked on the calendar) should be listed, together with the journal used for the original entry, the entry name (Description) and its recurring Frequency. The most recent posting date (Last Processed) and the Due Date are also included. The entries are listed according to the Due Date, with the earliest date at the top of the list.

✓ 47

Cash Purchase Invoice #GF-3677   **Dated November 1, 2018**

From Grasslands Fuel, $124 for gasoline for business vehicle. Invoice total paid in full from Regina Chequing account by cheque #572. Recall stored entry.

The first recurring entry — the fuel purchase from Grasslands Fuel — is due Nov. 1. Recurring purchases require an invoice number as additional information, so we need to open the journal first. This payment does not use the default bank account selection.

Double-click   Grasslands Fuel, the cash purchase entry, to open the journal with this transaction on-screen. (**Click 30** in the November calendar if all the transactions are not listed.)

Bank: Regina Chequing is preselected as the bank account in the From field because we stored the transaction with this selection. This is another advantage to storing a transaction.

Enter   GF-3677 in the Invoice/Ref. field. If you are using the Make Other Payment approach, you should update the Comment as well.

Post   the **transaction** when you are sure it is correct.

Close   the **journal** to return to the Daily Business Manager. The Grasslands Fuel entry has been removed.

If necessary, click the Refresh tool to update the Daily Business Manager immediately.

✓ 48

Cash Purchase #R-2018-11   **Dated November 3, 2018**

To Pro Suites Inc., cheque #125 for $2 300 from Eastside Chequing account to pay rent for November. Recall stored entry.

Double-click   Pro Suites, the next cash purchase entry, to open the journal.

Enter   R-2018-11 in the Invoice/Ref. field. Copy this number to the Comment line as well if you are using the Make Other Payment method.

Post   the **transaction** after making certain it is correct.

Close   the **Payments Journal**.

The Recurring Transactions list has been updated again — the Pro Suites transaction has been removed. The remaining list items are not due this week, so we can proceed to another list in the Daily Business Manager.

We want to process some receipts next.

Fees (Sales) Due

✓
49

Receipt #65   **Dated November 5, 2018**

From Canadian Royals, cheque #4011 for $4 455 in payment of account including $45 discount for early payment. Reference sales invoice #655. Deposited to Regina Chequing account.

PRO VERSION

Click the Sales Due tab. Customer, Invoice and Invoice Date replace Patient, Statement and Statement Date as the column headings.

Click   the **Fees Due tab** for a list of Invoices due within the week:

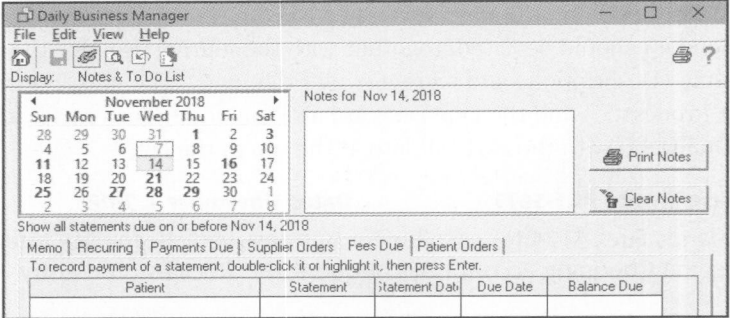

The Fees Due list is easy to use as well. It can be used to locate customers with outstanding debts. The display includes the Patient's name, Statement number and Date, payment Due Date and Balance Due (owing) on the due date without the discount. Invoices displayed can be matched against receipts on hand, and you can open the Receipts Journal directly from this window. No invoices are listed because they are not due in the next week. However, most of Andersson's customers take advantage of sales discounts, so we should look at sales due over a longer span than one week. Payments were received from Canadian Royals and Roughrider Argos. These payments are not due until late November, but the customers are paying early to take the discounts.

We cannot post receipts from the Daily Business Manager because customer cheque numbers should be added. We also need to change the bank account for the deposit when it is different from the default.

Click   **30** (left-click) on the November calendar to include all sales invoices due on or before November 30:

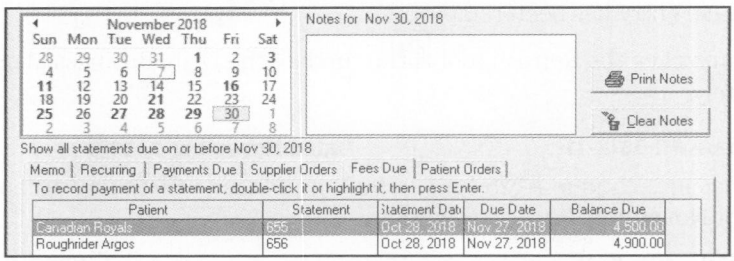

The invoices we need now appear on the list, so we can enter receipts for them.

To open the journal, you can double-click any part of the line for the entry you want or click the line and press (enter) .

Double-click   the **Canadian Royals** (Statement #655) to open the Receipts Journal for the selected customer.

Press (tab) to accept the discount and amount for the first invoice. The amount should appear in the Total field and the upper cheque portion.

Choose **Bank: Regina Chequing** as the bank account in the Deposit To field.

Add the customer's **cheque number** (#4011) in the Cheque field.

Enter **Nov 5** as the date. **Add** the **invoice number** as additional information.

Display the **journal entry** to review your work. **Close** the **display** and **make corrections** if necessary.

Click Post ▾ to record the transaction.

Enter the next **receipt** from the Receipts Journal because it is already open.

Receipt #66   **Dated November 7, 2018**

50

From Roughrider Argos, cheque #1636 for $4 851 in payment of account including $49 discount for early payment. Reference sales invoice #656. Deposited to Regina Chequing account.

Close the **Receipts Journal**. Both Sales Due entries have been removed. **Close** the **Daily Business Manager window** and **enter** the following **Purchase Order** from a new supplier:

51

PO#:	47
Date:	Nov 7, 2018
Shipping date:	Dec 28, 2018

Andersson Chiropractic Clinic
www.betterbacks.com

Ordered from:	Get Better Whirlpools
Address:	35 Eddy Circle
	Saskatoon, SK S7K 6E3
Phone No:	(306) 665-7210 or
	(877) 699-1270
Fax No:	(306) 663-6281
Contact:	Ira Spinner

4500 Rae St.
Regina, SK S4S 3B4
Tel 1: (306) 577-1900
Tel 2: (306) 577-2199   Fax: (306) 577-1925

PURCHASE ORDER

Order description	Amount
therapeutic whirlpool (Model WP-299X) including GST and PST terms: net 20 days	24 000.00
Deposit: $2 000 paid by cheque #573 (Regina Chequing Account)	

Order Total	24 000.00
Deposit	2 000.00
Balance Owing	22 000.00

Authorization: *Maria Andersson*

WARNING!

If the discount had expired by November 7, the session date, you would delete the default amount and change the date first, as we did for the payment entry. Then re-enter the discount taken and payment amount.

NOTES

If you return to the Daily Business Manager, the default date is correct for the receipt from Roughrider Argos, but you must change the bank account because the default account is incorrect. If you remain in the Receipts Journal, you must change the date.

NOTES

Use Full Add for the new supplier:
Web: gbw.com
Expense account: 1480 Whirlpool (create new account)
Use the source document for the remaining supplier details.

Patient (Sales) Orders Due

Two more Daily Business Manager lists are available: Supplier Orders and Patient Orders. To list outstanding items, click the corresponding tab. Lists for orders display unfilled orders due within the next week. You can access the journal windows for items

on these lists, just as you did for payments and fees due. We can enter the sale from order #51 on November 9 from the Daily Business Manager.

Advance the **session date** to November 14 and **back up** your data.

✓	**Sales Invoice #657** **Dated November 9, 2018**
52	To Giant Raptors, to fill one month of the contract in sales order #51 for $3 300. Terms: 1/10, n/30.

Open   the **Daily Business Manager window**.

Click   the **Patient Orders tab**:

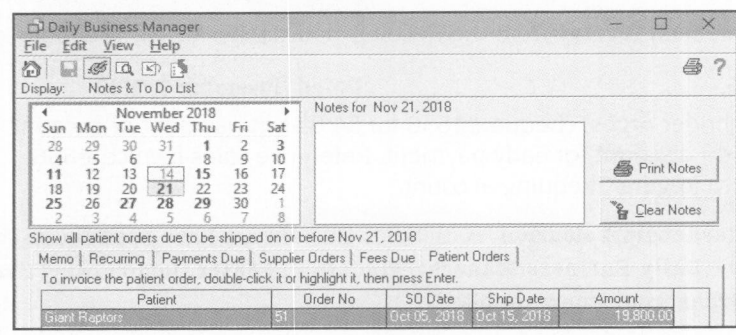

PRO VERSION
pro Click the Sales Orders tab. Customer replaces Patient as the column heading.

The list displays the Patient, Order Number, order date (SO Date), Shipping Date and Amount. Sales quotes are not displayed.

The order we want is listed. You can turn the order into an invoice directly from the Daily Business Manager. As usual, double-clicking will open the transaction window we need — the invoice will open as an unfilled order.

Double-click   **Giant Raptors** (Order #51).

The Fees Journal opens with the order converted to a statement or invoice. The backordered amount is 5. One month of the contract has already been completed.

Enter   **Nov 9** in the Date field.

Click   the **Quantity field** and **type** 1

Press   (tab) to update the amount. The backordered amount changes to 4.

Check   your **entry**, and when it is correct **click Post**.

Close   the **Fees Journal** to return to the Daily Business Manager.

The order remains on the list because it has not been completely filled and because the initial shipping date precedes the session date.

Purchase Orders Due

NOTES
Advance the calendar date selection in the Daily Business Manager if the recurring transaction is not listed.

The next transaction fills the order from Cleanol and Laundry Services.

✓	**Purchase Invoice #CLS-6543** **Dated November 11, 2018**
53	From Cleanol and Laundry Services, to fill purchase order #46, $210 for contracted daily laundry service. Terms: net 30. Store as a bi-weekly recurring entry. Remove the old stored entry then store the new one.

Click   the **Supplier Orders tab**:

PRO VERSION
pro Click the Purchase Orders tab. Vendor replaces Supplier as the column heading.

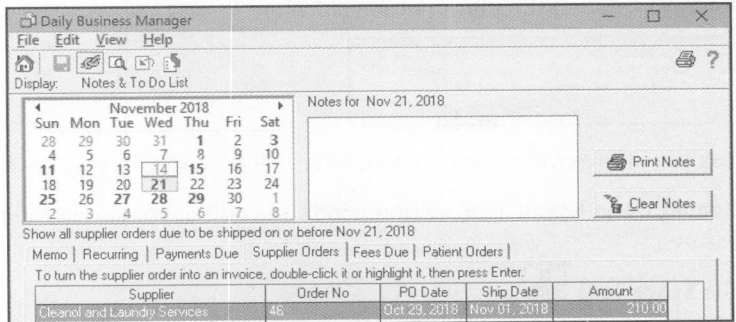

The list displays the supplier, order number, order date, shipping date and amount, making it easy to find orders that you need to track or follow up with the supplier.

We can turn the order from Cleanol and Laundry Services into an invoice from the Daily Business Manager — the journal opens with the invoice as an unfilled order.

Press (enter) to open the journal entry — Cleanol and Laundry Services is already selected.

Enter **CLS-6543** as the invoice number.

Enter **Nov 11** as the invoice date.

Click the **Fill Backordered Quantities tool**.

Enter the **order number** as Additional Information.

Do not post the **transaction** yet because we want to store it.

Removing Recurring Transactions

Sometimes a recurring transaction is no longer required, or it needs to be replaced. If you try to store the new purchase invoice from Cleanol and Laundry Services before removing the old entry, the program will not allow you to continue because the name duplicates the entry on file.

Click the **Store tool**. **Choose Bi-Weekly** as the frequency for the transaction and **click OK**.

You will be warned that the duplicate entry is not permitted. The name and frequency are already stored from a different source transaction:

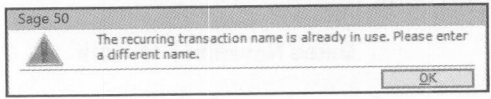

Click **OK** to return to the Store Recurring Transaction screen.

Click **Cancel** to return to the journal. We need to remove the old stored transaction first.

Click the **Recall tool** to open the Recall Recurring Transaction list:

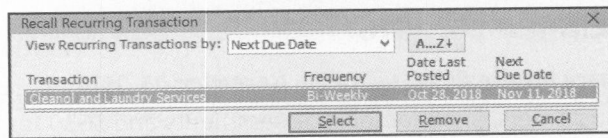

Cleanol and Laundry Services should be selected. If you entered the transactions for Pro Suites and Grasslands Fuel in the Purchases Journal instead of the Payments Journal, they will be listed in this window as well. The entry for Cleanol should still be selected because it is the next entry that is due. If it is not selected, click to select it.

Click   **Remove** to open the confirmation warning:

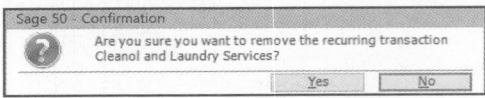

Click   **Yes** to confirm the removal if you have selected the correct entry.

Click   **Cancel** if the Recall Transaction window is still open. (Read the margin Notes.)

Click   the **Store tool** 🖫 .

Choose   **Bi-Weekly** as the frequency for the new recurring invoice. **Click OK**.

Post   the **purchase transaction**.

Click   **OK** to confirm that the filled order has been removed.

Close   the **Expenses Journal** to return to the Daily Business Manager. The order is no longer listed.

NOTES
If you have only one recurring transaction, the window closes after you remove it. If there are more transactions, the window stays open and you must click Cancel to close it.

---

54 **Debit Card Sales Summary Invoice #658   Dated November 11, 2018**

To various one-time patients, $260 for initial assessments and $450 for follow-up treatment sessions. Total amount deposited in Interac bank account, $710. Enter the stored transaction from the Daily Business Manager.

Close   the **Daily Business Manager**.

Enter   the **next of group of transactions**, including the **recurring purchase from Cleanol and Laundry Services** on November 25.

---

55 **Cash Purchase Invoice #TP-1188   Dated November 12, 2018**

From The Papery, $230 for paper supplies for treatment rooms and $50 for office supplies. Invoice total $280 paid in full from Eastside Chequing account by cheque #126.

SESSION DATE – NOVEMBER 21, 2018

56 **Receipt #67   Dated November 18, 2018**

From the Giant Raptors, cheque #1334 for $3 267 in full payment of account including $33 discount for early payment. Reference sales invoice #657. Deposited to Eastside Chequing account.

NOTES
HydraTub Care
550 Splash St.
Regina, SK S4T 7H5
Tel: (306) 578-2996
Terms: net 20
Expense account: 5220
(Create a new Group account: 5220 Whirlpool Maintenance)

57 **Purchase Order #48   Dated November 19, 2018**

Starting date January 1, 2019
From HydraTub Care (use Full Add for new supplier), $200 per month including taxes for one-year service contract. The contract includes weekly maintenance of whirlpool and repairs. Parts required for repairs will be billed separately. Terms: net 20. Remember to enter 2019 as the year for the starting date.

WARNING!
You must enter the year for order #48. If you do not, the program will enter Jan 1, 2018, as the default, and this date is not allowed.

SESSION DATE – NOVEMBER 28, 2018

58 **Debit Card Sales Summary Invoice #659   Dated November 25, 2018**

To various one-time customers, $260 for initial assessments and $630 for follow-up treatment sessions. Total amount deposited in Interac bank account, $890. Recall the stored transaction and edit the amounts.

NOTES
The year-end Advisor appears when you advance the session date. Read the message and close the Advisor.

59 | **Purchase Invoice #CLS-8210**   **Dated November 25, 2018**

From Cleanol and Laundry Services, $210 for contracted laundry service. Terms: net 30. Recall the stored transaction. (Read the margin Notes.)

Posting Directly from the Daily Business Manager

All the Daily Business Manager transactions so far have been posted after opening the journals. Cheques (payments) and recurring sales invoices can also be posted directly from the Daily Business Manager if you can accept the default information, that is, the bank account used.

Posting Sales Directly

Although you can post several sales invoices at the same time, you should open the journal and review each entry to verify it is correct. However, to demonstrate the method we will post one sale without opening the journal.

✓
60 | **Sales Invoice #660**   **Dated November 25, 2018**

Enter the recurring sale to Interplay Ballet School, $2 500 for contracted services for one month, directly from the Daily Business Manager. Terms: 1/10, n/30.

> **Open**   the **Daily Business Manager**. **Click** the **Recurring tab** if necessary.

If you need to print the invoices, click the Print column beside the invoice.

We will post the next recurring sale directly without opening the journal. It is due on November 25, so we must change the date. The calendar displays the week ending December 5. We must choose the posting (sale) date on the November, not the December, calendar.

> **Click**   the **left arrow** ◀ at the top of the December calendar to access the November calendar.

The date will be entered from the recurring transaction information.

> **Click**   (left-click) **28** to reset the session date. (When you first returned to the November calendar, November 1 was the session date and the recurring entries were removed.)

> **Click**   the **Post column** 🖳 (the first column) **beside** the sale for **Interplay Ballet** to add a ✓.

> **Click**   the **Post button** 🖳 Post in the Daily Business Manager window.

Sage 50 asks if there is additional information to enter before posting:

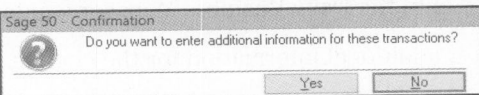

If you want to add details, click Yes to open the Additional Information screen. This screen will not open the journal itself for any other changes — this is the only change you can make. There are no details to add to the Sales Journal entry. We can continue.

> **Click**   **No**. A Sage 50 message names the invoices that are currently being processed and the confirmation:

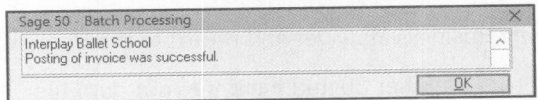

NOTES
If you recall the recurring transactions from the Daily Business Manager, advance the calendar date selection in the Daily Business Manager if the recurring transaction is not listed. If the next due date is incorrect, you can edit the date when you recall the entry. Store it again to reset the next due date.

⚠ WARNING!
When you post directly from the Daily Business Manager, you cannot review the journal entry or make other changes.
Opening the journal entry before posting allows you to review the entry and correct errors, if there are any.
If you want to post directly from the Daily Business Manager, back up your data file first and check the journal entries to be sure that they are correct.

NOTES
You can also right-click to set a posting date. In this case, if you have set the dates correctly, November 25 on the calendar (the posting date) should have an open box framing it and November 28 (the date for showing transactions) should appear in a solid, shaded and coloured box.

All the invoices that were processed will be listed.

Click   **OK** to return to the list of recurring entries. The sale we posted has been removed.

If the entry did not post successfully, Sage 50 will provide that information. Check the journal report for the transaction. If it is not included, open the Fees (Sales) Journal to enter the transaction.

Close   the **Daily Business Manager**. **Enter** the next **four recurring transactions**. If you enter these from the Daily Business Manager, open the journals and review each journal entry to be certain they will be posted correctly.

61

Sales Invoice #661   **Dated November 25, 2018**

To Veronica Kain School of Dance, $2 500 for contracted services for one month. Terms: 1/10, n/30. Recall the stored transaction.

62

Sales Invoice #662   **Dated November 28, 2018**

To Canadian Royals, $4 500 for contracted services for one month. Terms: 1/10, n/30. Recall the stored transaction.

63

Sales Invoice #663   **Dated November 28, 2018**

To Roughrider Argos, $4 900 for contracted services for one month. Terms: 1/10, n/30. Recall the stored transaction.

64

Cash Purchase Invoice #WC-122022   **Dated November 28, 2018**

From Western Communications, $125 including taxes for telephone and Internet service. Invoice total paid from Eastside Chequing account by cheque #127. Recall the stored transaction.

Posting Payments Directly

The payment to Cleanol can be posted directly without opening the journal because it uses the default account. The cheque is posted on the session date.

✓
65

Payment Cheque #128   **Dated November 28, 2018**

To Cleanol and Laundry Services, $330 from Eastside Chequing account in payment of account. Reference invoices #CLS-4723 and CLS-6543.

Open   the **Daily Business Manager** if necessary. **Click** the **Payments Due tab**.

Click   the **Post column** 🔲 beside **Inv #CLS-4723 and CLS-6543 (Cleanol and Laundry Services)** to add two ✓s.

Click   the **Post button** 🔲 **Post** in the Daily Business Manager window.

You will be asked if you want to enter additional information for the cheque.

Click   **Yes** to open the Additional Information window or **click No** to continue.

After a brief period, Sage 50 will confirm the successful posting:

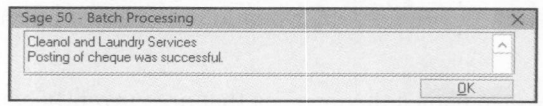

Click   **OK**.

Click   🔲 to close the Daily Business Manager and return to the Home window.

Advance the **session date** to November 30 and **back up** your data file.

NOTES
Advance the Daily Business Manager date to December 31 if necessary to include all recurring transactions.

NOTES
Check that the payment method for Sales Invoice #661 is Pay Later if you use the Daily Business Manager to recall the recurring entries.

WARNING!
Remember that when you pay from the Daily Business Manager, the default amount and bank account are selected. You cannot change them.
Opening the journal entry before posting allows you to review the entry and correct errors, if there are any.

NOTES
Choosing to enter additional information will not open the journal, so you will not be able to make other changes.

Enter   the **remaining transactions** for November 30, including memo #8.

66 | **Receipt #68** — **Dated November 29, 2018**

From Interplay Ballet, cheque #553 for $2 475 in payment of account including $25 discount for early payment. Reference invoice #660. Deposited to Eastside Chequing account.

67 | **Bank Debit Memo #747721** — **Dated November 29, 2018**

From Eastside Trust, $3 000 for monthly payroll and $45 payroll service fee withdrawn from chequing account 1080. Recall, edit and store the transaction.

NOTES
After editing the wage amount, store the changed entry to replace the previous one because this will be the new monthly salary.

68 | **Bank Debit Memo #120022** — **Dated November 29, 2018**

From Regina Trust, $75 withdrawn from account for service charges.

69 | **Memo #4** — **Dated November 29, 2018**

Transfer $1 060 from the Regina Chequing account to pay down the line of credit. This amount includes $60 for one month of interest on the amount of credit used. Recall the stored transaction and change the date.

70 | **Bank Debit Memo #747937** — **Dated November 29, 2018**

From Eastside Trust, pre-authorized withdrawals from chequing account:
    For bi-monthly loan repayment, $1 370 principal and $230 interest
    For bank service charges and debit card fees, $108

71 | **Cash Purchase Invoice #PPC-76511** — **Dated November 30, 2018**

From Prairie Power Corp., $380 including taxes for two months of hydro service. Invoice total paid from Regina Chequing account by cheque #574.

72 | **Memo #5** — **Dated November 30, 2018**

From Manager: Record the adjusting entries for supplies used in the previous two months:

Office Supplies	$105
Paper and Other Supplies	260

73 | **Memo #6** — **Dated November 30, 2018**

From Manager: Record the accumulated depreciation for the two-month period for all fixed assets as follows:

Computer Equipment	$ 230
Treatment Equipment	420
Office Furniture	160
Treatment Tables	280
Vehicle	1 100

74 | **Payment Cheque #129 & Memo #7** — **Dated November 30, 2018**

To M. Andersson (use Quick Add), $5 000 from Eastside Chequing account for drawings to cover personal expenses.

NOTES
Enter the drawings cheque in the Expenses (Purchases) Journal or as an Other Payment in the Payments Journal. You can add a memo number as the source if you want.

75 | **Memo #8** — **Dated November 30, 2018**

From Manager: Close out the M.A. Drawings account by transferring the balance to M.A. Capital.

NOTES
To close the Drawings account, credit Drawings and debit Capital. You can find the amount in the Trial Balance, Balance Sheet or General Ledger.

Partially Filling a Quote

Andersson has accepted the rent quote from Pro Suites Inc. and will fill the quote with an invoice for the first month's rent.

PRO VERSION
Click the Purchases icon or click the Create Purchase Invoice shortcut if you created shortcuts.

> ✓ 76

Cash Purchase Invoice #R-2018-12   **Dated November 30, 2018**

From Pro Suites Inc., $2 350 for one month rent of office space. Fill quote #45 for one month and convert the remainder of the quote to an order. Invoice total paid from Regina Chequing account by cheque #575.

Click   the **Invoices icon** in the Payables module window or **click** the **Create Invoice shortcut** if you added one to open the Expenses Journal.

Choose   quote **#45** and **press** tab to place the quote on-screen as an invoice.

The entire quote for 12 months has been entered as the default for the invoice.

Click   **12** in the Quantity field and **type**   1

Press   tab to update the invoice and fill it for one month of rent.

Click   **Post** to record the invoice and open another confirmation message:

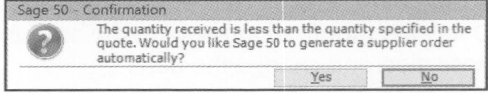

Sage advises you that the entire quote is not being filled and asks if you would like the program to convert the remainder of the quote to an order for 11 months of rent. This order can then be partially filled for one month at a time like any other order.

Click   **Yes** to continue and accept the conversion. Do not click No as this will delete the remainder of the quote.

If you look up Order #45 now, the backordered quantity will be 11.

Removing Quotes and Orders

Quotes and orders that will not be filled should be removed so that they are not confused with active quotes and orders.

> ✓ 77

Memo #9   **Dated November 30, 2018**

From Manager: Three purchase quotes that are on file are no longer valid. Remove quote #MT-511 from Medi-Tables, quote #FS-644 from Fresh Spaces and quote #SU-5532 from Space Unlimited.
Remove the recurring transactions for Grasslands Fuel (cash purchase) and Albert Blackfoot (sale) because they will no longer be used.

Choose **Quote** from the Transaction list.

Choose   quote **#MT-511** and **press** tab to place the quote on-screen.

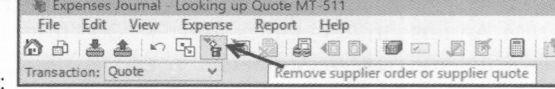

Click   the **Remove tool**:

Or, **choose** the **Expense menu** and **click Remove Supplier Order Or Supplier Quote**. As usual, you must confirm this action:

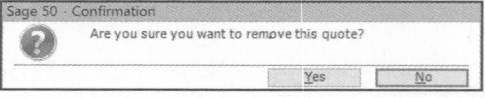

Click   **Yes** to confirm.

To remove purchase orders, open the Expenses (Purchases) Journal. Choose Supplier Order from the Transaction list. Choose the order number and press

WARNING!
If you do not convert the unfilled part of the quote to an order, you will delete the balance, that is, remove the quote.

NOTES
If you click the Adjust tool, the Remove tool and option will not be available.

NOTES
Instead of using the Remove tool, you can choose the Expense menu in the Expenses (Purchases) Journal and click Remove Supplier Quote Or Supplier Order, or the Fees menu in the Fees (Sales) Journal and click Remove Patient Quote Or Patient Order.

(tab) to put the order on-screen. Click ⬛ (the Remove Supplier Order tool). Click Yes to confirm the deletion.

To remove sales quotes or sales orders, open the Fees (Sales) Journal. Choose Quote (or Patient Order) as the transaction and then select the Quote or Order No. from the list. Press (tab) to bring the quote or order onto the screen. Click ⬛ (the Remove Patient Quote or Patient Order tool). Click Yes to confirm.

Remove the **other two quotes** and the recurring entries that are not needed.

Close the **journal** and then **enter Memo #10**.

Memo #10   **Dated November 30, 2018**

> 78

From Manager: Print all financial reports. Back up the data files and start a new fiscal period on December 1, 2018.

Displaying Reports

Displaying Pending Supplier (Purchase) Orders

Any purchase orders that are not yet filled can be displayed in a report. You can also use this report to check for orders that are delayed or should be removed.

Open the **Report Centre**. **Click Payables** in the Select A Report list.

Click **Pending Supplier Orders Summary By Supplier**.

Click **Modify This Report**:

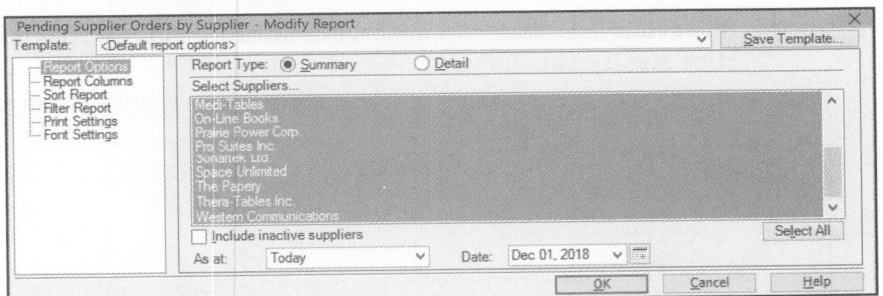

Press and **hold** (ctrl) and **click** the appropriate **names** in the Supplier list.

Enter Dec. 31, 2018 as the date for the report. **Click OK** to view the report.

All orders due in the next month should be included in the report. The purchase order with HydraTub Care is not included because its starting date is January 1.

Double-click an order to display it on-screen as an invoice. At this stage you can fill the order.

Click the **Modify Report tool** ▦ and **enter January 15, 2019**, as the report date, or **type** this **date** in the Date field at the top of the report.

Display the **report** again to include all three outstanding orders. **Close** the **display** when you have finished.

Displaying Pending Patient (Sales) Orders

Any sales orders that are not yet filled can be displayed in the Pending Sales Orders Report. You can also use this report to check for orders that should be removed.

NOTES
Refer to page 101 for assistance with starting a new fiscal period if needed.

NOTES
The Home window Reports menu has an entry for Medical/Dental Reports. This replaces the entry for Service or Retail Reports used in previous chapters for those industry types.

PRO VERSION
pro Choose Pending Purchase Orders Summary By Vendor.

NOTES
From the Home window Reports menu, choose Payables and Pending Supplier Orders and click By Supplier to access the report options.

NOTES
The Pending Supplier/Patient Orders reports can be sorted and filtered by Order No., Order Date, Ship Date and Amount.

NOTES
From the Pending Orders reports, you can drill down to the Supplier/Patient Aged Report and to the order form.
If you drill down to the order, you can fill the order directly by choosing Invoice as the type of transaction and then filling the order as usual. Confirm your intention to change the order to an invoice.

Click   Receivables in the Select A Report list.

Click   **Pending Patient Orders Summary By Patient** to open the sample.

Click   **Modify This Report** to open the report options window:

Press   and **hold** (ctrl) and **click** the appropriate **names** in the Patient list.

Enter   **Dec. 31, 2018** as the report date to display orders for the next month.

Click   **OK** to view the report. One sales order is listed, the partially filled order for the Giant Raptors' contract.

Double-click the order to open it as an invoice ready to be filled.

Close   the **display** when finished.

Displaying Additional Information in Journal Reports

When you choose to include additional fields in the journal entries, you can include these details in the journal reports.

Click   **Financials** in the Select A Report list. **Click All Journal Entries** and **click Modify This Report**:

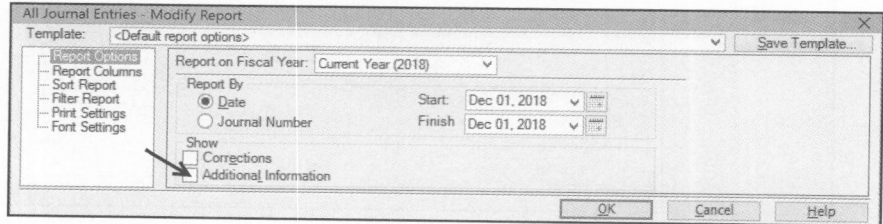

Click   **Additional Information** to add a ✓. **Click Corrections**.

Enter   the **Start** and **Finish dates** for the report. You must change the Start date because there are no transactions for December 1.

Click   **OK**.

Close   the **display** when you have finished.

Close the **Report Centre**.

REVIEW

The Student DVD with Data Files includes Review
Questions and Supplementary Cases for this chapter.

OBJECTIVES

- **make** payments toward credit card accounts
- **make** GST, HST and PST remittances
- **apply** sales taxes to interprovincial sales
- **enter** sales and receipts for foreign customers
- **enter** purchases and payments for foreign suppliers
- **access** supplier or customer Web sites
- **e-mail** invoices to customers
- **look up** invoices after posting them
- **track** shipments to customers
- **transfer** funds between different currency bank accounts
- **monitor** business routines with checklists
- **create** an Accountant's Copy of data for year-end adjustments
- **import** Accountant's Copy journal entries

After completing this chapter, you should be able to

COMPANY INFORMATION

Company Profile

Maple Leaf Rags Inc. is a privately held corporation operated by Jaz Bands. After a few years on the East coast, he missed the mountains and moved his small home office from Summerside, Prince Edward Island, to Nanaimo, British Columbia. Bands first considered starting his own business while studying fine arts at Concordia University and business administration at Queen's University. During these years he worked part time in local music stores, dealing with customers who were sometimes frustrated that they had to look in every department to find a variety of types of music by Canadians. With his knowledge and contacts in the music industry and after doing some careful business research, he was ready to establish Maple Leaf Rags Inc., a store specializing in Canadian recording artists. He also sells the book that he wrote and published — *A Guide to Canadian Music*.

NOTES
Maple Leaf Rags Inc.
2642 Coldstream Avenue
Nanaimo, BC V9T 2X2
Tel 1: (250) 63M-USIC
Tel 2: (888) 63M-USIC
Fax: (250) 633-4888
Business No.: 128 488 632
Rag is a style of music set in ragtime. Many of Scott Joplin's tunes, including "Maple Leaf Rag," are examples of ragtime music.

NOTES

It was not possible to keep the exchange rates in this chapter current because they were changing so rapidly at the time of writing.

Maple Leaf Rags Inc. sells CDs by Canadian artists over the Internet to individuals. It also sells to music stores throughout Canada and the United States, usually to American stores that serve a large Canadian resident and tourist clientele. These stores rely on Bands as a convenient source of Canadian artists' recordings, including native and ethnic music produced by A.B. Original Sounds, which is Bands' recording company. Bands hopes to expand the business to other countries where pockets of Canadian populations can be found, such as countries with Canadian Armed Forces bases. His recent book has also been popular with these customers.

Bands is fortunate to be able to rely on the advice of his friend Dave Manga, whose Outset Media boardgame business distributes its products in a similar way to Maple Leaf Rags. His friend also shares information about suppliers who might be able to provide some of Bands' supplies.

Maple Leaf Rags has expanded rapidly, though Bands is still able to operate out of his own home because the demands for inventory storage space are small. He pays himself rent for use of his home office space.

Bands buys CDs from various recording studios. He buys CD masters from A.B. Original Sounds, and suppliers across Canada copy and package the CDs for his company at competitive prices. He has accounts set up for all his regular suppliers, many of whom offer discounts for early payments. Bands has also set up accounts for his wholesale customers with discounts for early payment.

At the end of each fiscal year, Bands creates a copy of the data files for the accountant, who checks the accuracy of the accounting records and adds the outstanding adjusting entries.

Bands converted his accounting records to Sage 50 after working carefully through a comprehensive Sage 50 textbook by Purbhoo. The following company information summarizes the conversion after the first nine months of the current fiscal period:

- Chart of Accounts
- Trial Balance
- Supplier Information
- Customer Information
- Accounting Procedures

CHART OF POSTABLE ACCOUNTS

MAPLE LEAF RAGS INC.

ASSETS
1020 Bank: Savings Account
1040 Bank: Chequing Account
1060 Bank: Visa
1080 Bank: MasterCard
1140 Bank: USD
1200 Accounts Receivable
1240 Purchase Prepayments
1280 Office Supplies
1300 CD Inventory
1340 Book Inventory
1380 Prepaid Expenses
1410 Computers
1420 Accum Deprec: Computers
1450 Furniture & Equipment
1480 Accum Deprec: Furn & Equip ▶

▶1500 Automobile
1520 Accum Deprec: Automobile

LIABILITIES
2100 Bank Loan
2180 Prepaid Sales and Deposits
2200 Accounts Payable
2250 Amex Payable
2260 Visa Payable
2460 PST Payable
2650 GST Charged on Sales
2660 HST Charged on Sales
2670 GST Paid on Purchases
2680 HST Paid on Purchases
2850 Long Term Loan ▶

▶**EQUITY**
3560 Common Stock
3600 Retained Earnings
3800 Current Earnings

REVENUE
4100 Revenue from CD Sales
4140 Revenue from Book Sales
4180 Sales Discounts
4200 Freight Revenue
4250 Interest Revenue
4280 Sales Tax Compensation
4300 Exchange Rate Differences

EXPENSE
5100 Advertising & Publicity
5150 Bank Charges & Card Fees ▶

▶5200 Depreciation Expense
5220 Freight & Shipping Expenses
5260 Purchase Discounts
5280 Interest Expense
5300 Internet & Web Site Expenses
5320 Storage Expense
5340 Cost of Books Sold
5360 Materials and Assembly Costs
5380 Cost of CDs Sold
5400 Office Rent
5500 Office Supplies Used
5520 Research Expenses
5560 Telephone Expenses
5580 Travel Expenses

NOTES: The Chart of Accounts includes only postable accounts and the Net Income or Current Earnings account.

TRIAL BALANCE

MAPLE LEAF RAGS INC.

June 30, 2018		Debits	Credits				Debits	Credits
1020	Bank: Savings Account	$ 76 675		▶	2850	Long Term Loan		$ 60 000
1040	Bank: Chequing Account	41 000			3560	Common Stock		160 000
1060	Bank: Visa	1 800			3600	Retained Earnings		29 261
1080	Bank: MasterCard	2 350			4100	Revenue from CD Sales		389 000
1140	Bank: USD ($690 USD)	860			4140	Revenue from Book Sales		61 000
1200	Accounts Receivable	71 680			4180	Sales Discounts	$ 6 840	
1280	Office Supplies	600			4200	Freight Revenue		5 460
1300	CD Inventory	180 350			4250	Interest Revenue		2 150
1340	Book Inventory	44 840			4280	Sales Tax Compensation		45
1380	Prepaid Expenses	5 900			5100	Advertising & Publicity	18 800	
1410	Computers	8 200			5150	Bank Charges & Card Fees	1 980	
1420	Accum Deprec: Computers		$ 1 100		5220	Freight & Shipping Expenses	4 810	
1450	Furniture & Equipment	9 100			5260	Purchase Discounts		850
1480	Accum Deprec: Furn & Equip		1 500		5280	Interest Expense	3 960	
1500	Automobile	16 800			5300	Internet & Web Site Expenses	2 540	
1520	Accum Deprec: Automobile		9 800		5340	Cost of Books Sold	32 400	
2100	Bank Loan		12 000		5360	Materials and Assembly Costs	1 800	
2200	Accounts Payable		1 540		5380	Cost of CDs Sold	194 250	
2250	Amex Payable		390		5400	Office Rent	7 200	
2260	Visa Payable		860		5500	Office Supplies Used	800	
2460	PST Payable		450		5520	Research Expenses	1 100	
2650	GST Charged on Sales		1 450		5560	Telephone Expenses	905	
2660	HST Charged on Sales		3 634		5580	Travel Expenses	1 950	
2670	GST Paid on Purchases	800					$740 490	$740 490
2680	HST Paid on Purchases	200		▶				

SUPPLIER INFORMATION

MAPLE LEAF RAGS INC.

Supplier Name (Contact)	Address	Phone No. Fax No.	E-mail Web Site	Terms Tax ID
A.B. Original Sounds (Marie Raven)	380 Abbey Rd. Vancouver, BC V3P 5N6	Tel: (778) 882-6252 Fax: (778) 882-1100		1/10, n/30 (before tax) 129 646 733
Federal Express (DayLee Runner)	59 Effex Road Nanaimo, BC V9R 6X2	Tel: (800) 488-9000 Fax: (250) 488-1230	fedex.com	n/1
Grandeur Graphics (Kathy Grandeur)	26 Drawing Way Victoria, BC V8C 3D1	Tel: (250) 665-3998 Fax: (250) 665-3900	wedesignit.com	2/20, n/30 (before tax) 459 112 341
Let 'm Know (Jabber Jaws Lowder)	599 Broadcast Rd. Nanaimo, BC V9S 7J8	Tel: (250) 604-6040 Fax: (250) 604-4660	wetellit.com	2/20, n/30 (before tax) 453 925 376
Miles 'R on Us (N. Gins)	522 Drivers St. Saskatoon, SK S7F 5E3	Tel: (800) 592-5239 Fax: (306) 591-4929		n/1
Minister of Finance			gov.bc.ca/fin	n/1
Purolator (Speedy Carriere)	46 Shipping Mews Nanaimo, BC V9S 6S2	Tel: (800) 355-7447 Fax: (250) 355-7000	purolator.com	n/1
Receiver General for Canada	Summerside Tax Centre Summerside, PE C1N 6L2	Tel: (902) 821-8186	cra-arc.gc.ca	n/1
Western Tel (Manny Voyses)	45 Nexus Ave. Nanaimo, BC V9R 3D1	Tel: (250) 679-1011 Fax: (250) 679-1000	westerntel.ca	n/7
Wrap It (Able Boxer)	80 Cubit Road Richmond Hill, ON L5R 6B2	Tel: (905) 881-7739 Fax: (905) 881-7000		1/5, n/30 (before tax) 634 529 125

OUTSTANDING SUPPLIER INVOICES

MAPLE LEAF RAGS INC.

Supplier Name	Terms	Date	Invoice No.	Amount	Tax	Total
Grandeur Graphics	2/20, n/30 (before tax)	6/28/18	GG-1304	$ 400	$ 20	$ 420
Let 'm Know	2/20, n/30 (before tax)	6/30/18	LK-692	$1 000	$120	$1 120
			Grand Total			$1 540

CUSTOMER INFORMATION

MAPLE LEAF RAGS INC.

Customer Name (Contact)	Address	Phone No. Fax No.	E-mail Web Site	Terms Credit Limit
Canadian Sounds (X. Pats)	46 Ontario St. Tampa, Florida 33607 USA	Tel: (813) 930-4589 Fax: (813) 930-7330	XPats@cansounds.com cansounds.com	3/30, n/60 (before tax) $20 000 USD
CDN Music (Michelle Strings)	230 Nightingale Pl. Vancouver, BC V4R 9K4	Tel: (778) 288-6189 Fax: (778) 288-6000	mstrings@upbeat.com cdn.music.ca	3/30, n/60 (before tax) $20 000
Entertainment House (Rob Blinde)	101 Booker St. Toronto, ON M4F 3J8	Tel: (647) 484-9123 Fax: (647) 488-8182	ent.house.com	3/30, n/60 (before tax) $150 000
It's All Canadian (Leaf Mapleston)	39 Federation Ave. Victoria, BC V8W 7T7	Tel: (250) 598-1123 Fax: (250) 598-1000	canstuff.com	3/30, n/60 (before tax) $20 000
Music Music Music (M. Porter)	10 Red Rock Canyon Sedona, Arizona 86336 USA	Tel: (520) 678-4523 Fax: (520) 678-4500	mporter@music3.com music3.com	3/30, n/60 (before tax) $10 000 USD
Total Music (Goode Sounds)	93 Waterside Rd. Fredericton, NB E3B 4F4	Tel: (506) 455-7746 Fax: (506) 455-7000	goode@totalmusic.com totalmusic.com	3/30, n/60 (before tax) $50 000
Treble & Bass (Bea Flatte)	399 Chord Blvd. Nanaimo, BC V9R 5T6	Tel: (250) 557-5438 Fax: (250) 557-5550	bflatte@t&b.com t&b.com	3/30, n/60 (before tax) $30 000
Web Store Customers				Prepaid by Credit Card

OUTSTANDING CUSTOMER INVOICES

MAPLE LEAF RAGS INC.

Customer Name	Terms	Date	Invoice No.	Amount	Tax	Total
CDN Music	3/30, n/60 (before tax)	6/25/18	591	$ 4 500	$ 225	$ 4 725
Entertainment House	3/30, n/60 (before tax)	1/4/18	233	$56 000	$7 280	$63 280
It's All Canadian	3/30, n/60 (before tax)	6/6/18	589	$ 3 500	$ 175	$ 3 675
			Grand Total			$71 680

Accounting Procedures

GST and HST

Maple Leaf Rags Inc. uses the regular method of calculating GST. The GST charged and collected from customers is recorded as a liability in *GST Charged on Sales*. Customers in New Brunswick, Newfoundland and Labrador and Ontario pay HST at the rate of 13 percent instead of GST; Nova Scotia customers pay HST at 15 percent; and Prince Edward Island customers pay HST at 14 percent. These HST amounts are recorded in *HST Charged on Sales*. Customers in British Columbia pay GST at 5 percent and PST at 7 percent. In the remaining provinces and territories, customers pay the 5 percent GST on all their purchases. Bands has set up both GST and HST as taxes with appropriate codes. GST (or HST) paid to suppliers is recorded in *GST Paid on Purchases* (or *HST Paid on Purchases*) as a decrease in tax liability. The balance owing is the difference between the GST plus HST charged and GST plus HST paid. Customers who buy books pay only GST at the rate of 5 percent on their purchases — books are exempt from PST and HST in all provinces.

Cash Sales of Services

Cash transactions for Maple Leaf Rags are limited to credit card sales since most of its business is with wholesale customers who have accounts. Bands has merchant Visa and MasterCard arrangements with two financial institutions. Maple Leaf Rags pays a percentage of each sale directly to the credit card companies (the fee is withheld from the sale amount). To simplify the transaction entries, we provide summaries of these credit card sales as if they were to a single customer called Web Store Customers.

Bands uses a Visa gold card and an American Express card for some business purchases and pays annual user fees for these cards.

Discounts

Discounts are calculated automatically by the program when the discount terms are entered as part of the invoices. If the payments are made before the discount term has expired, the discount appears in the Payments and Receipts journals automatically. All discounts are calculated on before-tax amounts. Bands offers a 3 percent discount to wholesale customers to encourage them to pay their accounts on time. Customers who purchase from the Web store and pay by credit card do not receive discounts.

Some suppliers offer before-tax discounts to Maple Leaf Rags as well. These discount terms are set up in the supplier and customer records.

PST

PST, also called Revenue Tax, is charged at the rate of 7 percent on the base price of goods in British Columbia. Wholesale customers do not pay PST on merchandise they buy for resale. Thus, when Bands sells directly to stores, he charges only GST; he does not charge PST to stores because they are not the final consumers of the product. Individual retail customers in British Columbia pay GST and PST on the purchase of CDs but only GST on books. Customers in other provinces pay GST at 5 percent or HST at the rate for their province. When Maple Leaf Rags makes the PST remittance, it reduces the amount of the remittance by 6.6 percent, the rate of sales tax compensation, when the PST collected amount is greater than $333.33 for the reporting period.

Freight

Customers who order through the Internet pay a shipping rate of $5 for the first CD or book and $2 for each additional item. Wholesale customers pay the actual shipping costs.

NOTES
In 2013, British Columbia reverted to collecting and charging PST and GST separately.
Because Maple Leaf Rags is not registered for HST, it is not required to pay HST on purchases from suppliers in provinces that charge HST. For these purchases it pays GST, unless the goods or services are used or "consumed" in that province.

NOTES
The sales tax rules for discounts are complex and may vary from province to province. Rules for federal taxes may also be different from those for provincial taxes. Sage 50 calculates sales discounts as before or after tax but applies the same formula to GST and retail sales taxes. Adjusting General Journal entries may be required to adjust the amount of tax owing and calculate the tax remittance. We have omitted the tax adjustments for sales discounts.

NOTES
Wholesale customers in HST provinces do pay HST on all purchases from Maple Leaf Rags except books.

GST is charged on freight in British Columbia. Bands has accounts set up with three regular shippers so that he can track shipments online. Their Web site addresses are included in the shipping setup data.

Sales Orders and Deposits

When a customer places a sales order, Bands requests a deposit as confirmation of the order. Deposits are entered on the Sales Order form (refer to page 426) or in the Receipts Journal (refer to page 417).

Foreign Customers and Suppliers

Customers outside Canada do not pay GST, HST or PST on goods imported from Canada. Therefore, sales outside the country do not have taxes applied to them. These customers also do not pay any taxes on their shipping charges.

Purchases from suppliers outside of Canada are subject to GST when the goods are used in Canada.

INSTRUCTIONS

NOTES
For Maple Leaf Rags' retail business type, the terms Customer and Supplier are used. Sales and Purchases are used as icon labels in journal names and in reports.

PRO VERSION
Vendors will replace Suppliers for icon, field and report names.

1. **Record entries for the source documents** in Sage 50 using the Chart of Accounts, Supplier Information, Customer Information and Accounting Procedures for Maple Leaf Rags. The procedures for entering each new type of transaction in this application are outlined step by step in the Keystrokes section with the source documents.

   Change module windows as needed, or create shortcuts for journals in other modules.

2. **Print** the **reports for the end of the fiscal period** suggested by the Sage 50 checklists after you have finished making your entries. Refer to the Keystrokes section, pages 488–489. If you have started a new fiscal period, choose **Previous Year** to display the reports you need.

KEYSTROKES

Opening Data Files

PRO VERSION
Restore the backup file SageData16\MAPLE1.CAB or MAPLE1 to SageData16\MAPLE\ MAPLE. Refer to Chapter 1, page 24, if you need assistance with restoring backup files.

NOTES
Payroll, Inventory and Project are hidden from the Modules pane list because these ledgers are not set up.

    Open   **SageData16\MAPLE\MAPLE** to access the data files.

    Enter   **July 15, 2018** as the first session date for this application.

    Click   **OK** and then **click OK** again to bypass the session date warning.

Session dates are advanced semi-monthly for Maple Leaf Rags, and the backup frequency is set at two-week intervals. The Receivables Home window opens.

Interprovincial Sales and Tracking Shipments

Businesses that ship goods to customers in other provinces usually have accounts set up with shipping companies so they can track shipments. First we enter the sale.

✓	**Visa Credit Card Sales Invoice #593**	**Dated July 2/18**

1

To various Web Store Customers, for sales during previous three months:

CD sales to BC customers	$ 800 plus 5% GST and 7% PST
CD sales to PEI customers	200 plus 14% HST
CD sales to NS customers	300 plus 15% HST
CD sales to other HST customers	2 280 plus 13% HST
CD sales to other GST customers	900 plus 5% GST
Book sales	3 000 plus 5% GST
Shipping	680 plus 5% GST

(Shipped by Purolator #PCU773XT)
Invoice total $8 854.40. Paid by Visa.

Click the **Sales Invoices icon** ![Sales Invoices] to open the Sales Journal.

Choose Web Store Customers from the Customer list. Invoice is correct as the transaction type. Web Store purchases are usually paid by credit card.

Click the **Payment Method list arrow**:

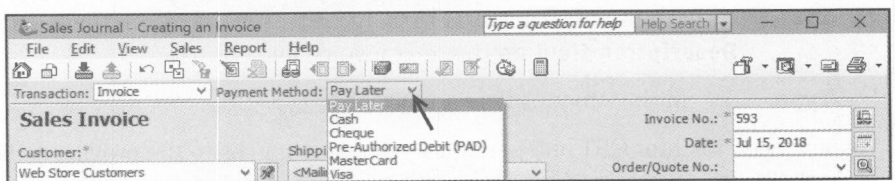

Internet customers have been set up without discounts, so the discount fields are blank. Two credit cards are accepted as methods of payment.

Click **Visa** as the method of payment.

Type July 2 (as the transaction date).

Click the **Item Description field** and **type** CD sales - BC

Click the **Amount field** and **type** 800

Press (tab) to advance to the Tax field and **press** (enter) to list the tax codes:

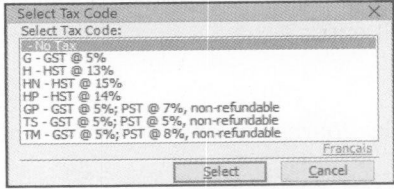

No default tax code has been entered for Internet sales because multiple codes are required. We have created tax codes to accommodate interprovincial sales to customers who pay HST (**code H**, or **HN** for NS, or **HP** for PEI customers) and to customers in other provinces who pay only GST (**code G**). For the first sale, to BC customers, the **code GP** is used (GST rate at 5 percent and PST rate at 7 percent).

Click **GP - GST @ 5%, PST @ 7%, non-refundable**.

Click **Select** to return to the sales invoice and advance to the Account field. Account 4100 is correctly entered as the default revenue account.

Click the **Item Description field** on the second invoice line.

NOTES
The shipper has been added to this transaction for illustration purposes only.

NOTES
Usually the same tax code would apply for all invoice lines for a single customer and it can be entered from the customer's record.

NOTES
We have used the tax name PST for provincial sales tax. Three codes apply only to purchases — TS for Saskatchewan (GST @ 5%, PST @ 5%), Q for Quebec (GST @ 5%, QST @ 9.975%) and TM for Manitoba (GST @ 5%, PST @ 8%).
    Goods and services consumed in a province are subject to the PST for that province. Goods shipped to other provinces are exempt from the PST, but not from HST or GST.

NOTES
Remember that you can change the width of a column by dragging its border in the title line of the column. You can customize the journal by removing the Item and Unit columns.

Type CD sales - PEI **Enter 200** in the Amount field. **Press** (tab).

Customers in PEI pay 14 percent HST, for which we created the tax code HP.

Press (enter) or **click** the **List icon** 🔍 to open the Tax Code list.

Double-click HP - HST @ 14% to add the code and the account.

Click the **Item Description field** on the next invoice line.

Type CD sales - NS

Click the **Amount field**. **Type** 300 **Press** (tab).

The HST rate at 15 percent applies to sales to customers in Nova Scotia — code HN.

Press (enter) or **click** the **List icon** 🔍 to open the Tax Code list.

Double-click HN - HST @ 15% to add the code and move to the Account field.

Click the **Item Description field** on the next invoice line.

Type CD sales to other provinces - HST

Click the **Amount field** and **type** 2280 **Press** (tab).

NOTES
You can also type the tax codes in the Tax field. For example, you can type G (or g) for GST @ 5%, or HP (or hp) for HST @ 14%.

The HST rate at 13 percent applies to these sales — tax code H.

Choose H - HST @ 13% as the code.

Type CD sales to other provinces - GST in the **Item Description field** on the next invoice line.

Type 900 in the Amount field and **press** (tab).

We now need to enter GST at 5 percent — this rate applies to the provinces that do not apply HST.

Open the **Tax Code list** and **double-click G - GST @ 5%** to add the code and advance to the Account field.

Click the **Item Description field** on the next line. **Type** Book sales

Click the **Amount field** and **type** 3000 **Press** (tab).

Tax code G is also applied to the sale of books in all provinces.

Open the **Tax Code** list and **double-click G - GST @ 5%**.

The cursor advances to the Account field. Book sales are recorded in a separate revenue account, so we must change the default entry.

Type 4140

There are two freight entry fields in the Sales Journal, below the subtotal amount:

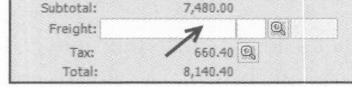

The first field is for the freight amount and the second is for the tax code. Because taxes are paid on freight you must enter a tax code if the customer pays freight. In British Columbia, only GST applies to freight.

Click the **first Freight field**.

Type 680 **Press** (tab) to advance to the tax code field for Freight.

Click the **List icon** 🔍 to display the Tax Code list and **select Code G**.

The tax amount is calculated and added as soon as you enter the amount of freight charged and the tax code. This amount is added to the Tax total.

We will now enter the shipping information so that the shipments can be traced if they are not delivered within the expected time. To track a shipment, you must have the tracking number for the package. To arrange for tracking shipments online, most businesses have an account with the shipper and a PIN (personal identification number) to access the account. When an invoice for these shipments is received from the shipper, it will be entered as a purchase to record the expense to Maple Leaf Rags.

Shippers used regularly can be entered in the Company Settings under Shippers after activating the Track Shipments option:

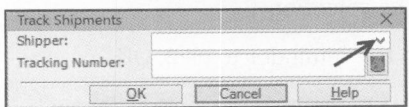
NOTES
The tracking number alone is usually sufficient for tracking the shipment.

Settings

Shipper	Tracking Site	Shipper	Tracking Site
Federal Express	www.fedex.com		
Purolator	www.purolator.com		
Canada Post	www.canadapost.ca		

☑ Track Shipments
Names and Web Sites of Shipping Services:

Company: Information, System, Backup, Features, Credit Cards, Sales Taxes, Currency, Forms, E-mail, Date Format, Sage One Connection, Shippers, Logo

Click the **Track Shipments tool** 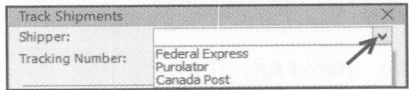 or **choose** the **Sales menu** and **click Track Shipments** to open the shipping data entry window:

Track Shipments
Shipper:
Tracking Number:
OK   Cancel   Help

Click the **Shipper field list arrow** to open the list of shippers:

Track Shipments
Shipper:
Tracking Number:
Federal Express
Purolator
Canada Post

Click **Purolator**. **Press** tab to advance to the Tracking Number field.

Type PCU773XT **Click OK** to return to the completed invoice. Tracking details do not appear on the invoice form.

All taxes are combined on the invoice as a single entry in the Tax field below Freight. For the breakdown of individual taxes paid by the customer,

Click the **List icon** beside the Tax field to display the tax details:

Total Tax Summary
View
Tax amounts that are not included in the price can be changed as needed.
Invoice Subtotal: $8,160.00 (includes freight)

Tax	Amount
HST	369.40
PST	56.00
GST	269.00
Total Taxes:	694.40

OK   Cancel

Individual amounts are listed for the three taxes applied to the sale. You can edit these tax amounts if they are incorrect.

Click **OK** to return to the Sales Journal so that you can review it.

Choose the **Report menu** and **click Display Sales Journal Entry**:

Maple Leaf Rags Inc.
Sales Journal Entry 07/02/2018 (J1)

Account Number	Account Description	Debits	Credits
1060	Bank: Visa	8,544.50	-
5150	Bank Charges & Card Fees	309.90	-
2460	PST Payable	-	56.00
2650	GST Charged on Sales	-	269.00
2660	HST Charged on Sales	-	369.40
4100	Revenue from CD Sales	-	4,480.00
4140	Revenue from Book Sales	-	3,000.00
4200	Freight Revenue	-	680.00
Additional Date:	Additional Field:	8,854.40	8,854.40

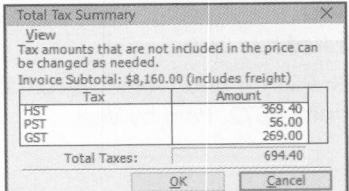
NOTES
You can access the settings for Shippers when the Sales Journal is open and enter additional shippers, but the check box for Track Shipments and the shippers already entered will be dimmed.

NOTES
Pressing ctrl + K will also open the Track Shipments screen from the journal.

NOTES
Tax amounts may be incorrect because rounded off amounts are added together. If tax is calculated for each line, the total may be different from the tax calculated on a single subtotal amount.

Several linked accounts are used for this transaction. The credit card account — *Bank: Visa* — is debited for the total invoice amount minus the transaction discount fees withheld by the credit card company. These fees are debited to the linked fees expense account — *Bank Charges & Card Fees*. Both the *GST* and *HST Charged on Sales* accounts are credited because they increase the tax liability to the Receiver General. PST collected from customers is credited to the *PST Payable* account to reflect the increased liability to the Minister of Finance for British Columbia. Freight charged to customers is credited automatically to the linked *Freight Revenue* account.

Close the **display** to return to the Sales Journal input screen. **Make corrections** if necessary, referring to page 161 for assistance.

Click **Store** 🔽 and **choose Random** as the frequency.

Add **Visa** to the description to identify this recurring sale.

The next transaction is also a summary sale to Web Store Customers. We can choose to use the same customer next time so that the customer is selected automatically.

Click the **Use The Same Customer Next Time tool** 📌 beside the customer name.

The Use The Same Customer Next Time tool 📌 has changed shape to indicate it is selected. Clicking the tool again will turn off the selection.

Click Post 🔽 . We will not repeat the reminder to click OK.

Create **shortcuts** to enter purchases, payments and General Journal transactions or **change modules** as needed.

Enter the second credit card **sale** and the Visa car rental **purchase**.

NOTES When you recall the Visa sales summary, you need to change only the amounts. You will not need to re-enter the descriptions, accounts and tax codes.

NOTES When you close the Sales Journal, the Use The Same Customer Next Time tool is automatically turned off or deselected. You can also recall the stored Visa sale to enter the MasterCard sales summary. Change the method of payment and the amounts. Store this entry by adding MC to the description.

NOTES If a message about credit card processing opens, you can click Do Not Show This Message Again.

NOTES Remember to select the correct credit card name. You do not need to enter shipping information for the remaining Web Store sales.

NOTES Because the car rental is purchased and used in Saskatchewan, the Saskatchewan Provincial Sales Tax rate applies. Use tax code TS (GST plus Saskatchewan PST) – the default code for the supplier.

NOTES If you changed modules for the previous transaction, the Payables window will be open. If you created and used the shortcut, you will need to change the module window.

2 **MasterCard Credit Card Sales Invoice #594**   **Dated July 2/18**
To various Web Store Customers, for sales during previous three months:

CD sales to BC customers	$ 700 plus 5% GST and 7% PST
CD sales to PEI customers	200 plus 14% HST
CD sales to NS customers	340 plus 15% HST
CD sales to other HST customers	1 840 plus 13% HST
CD sales to other GST customers	920 plus 5% GST
Book sales	2 700 plus 5% GST
Shipping	630 plus 5% GST

Invoice total $7 944.70. Paid by MasterCard.

3 **Visa Purchase Invoice #MR-1699**   **Dated July 2/18**
To Miles 'R on Us, $520 plus 5% GST and 5% PST for two-week car rental while attending trade show in Saskatoon. Invoice total $572. Paid by Visa.

Entering Credit Card Bill Payments

Click **Payables** in the Modules pane to open this Home window, if necessary.

4 **Visa Payment: Cheque #761**   **Dated July 2/18**
To Visa, $723.50 in payment of credit card account, including $609 for purchases charged from May 16 to June 15, $105 for annual renewal fee and $9.50 in interest charges on the unpaid balance from a previous statement.

Credit card payments are entered in the Payments Journal. You can access the bill payment window from the Pay Credit Card Bills shortcut with the Payments icon:

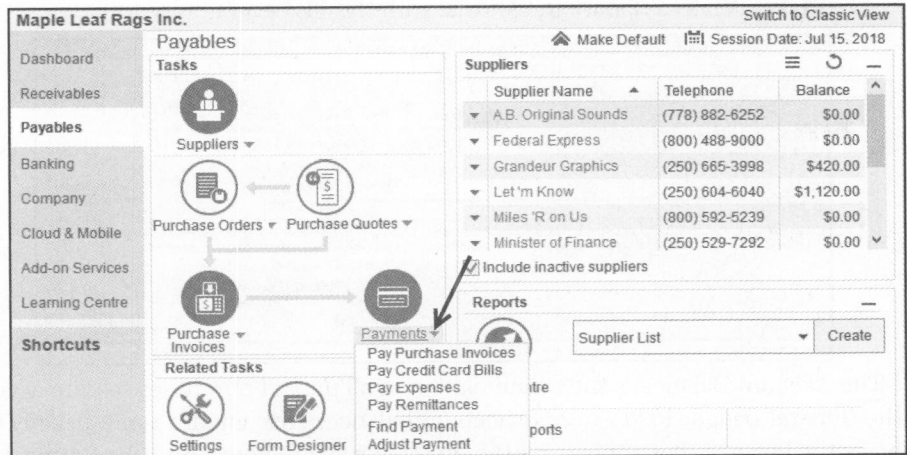

Click   **Pay Credit Card Bills** in the Payments icon shortcuts list:

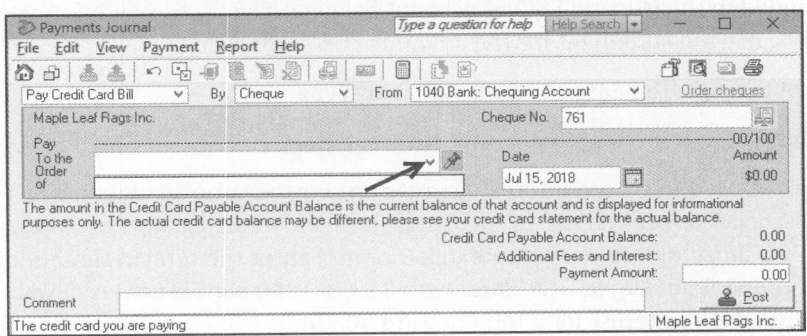

Pay Credit Card Bill is selected as the transaction type in the Pay field. The Pay list in the journal allows you to choose between paying suppliers, paying credit card bills, making cash purchases (other payments) and making payroll remittances. You have the same choices from the Pay field drop-down list as from the Home window.

To access the form you need, you can also click the Payments icon and select Pay Credit Card Bill from the transaction (Pay) drop-down list:

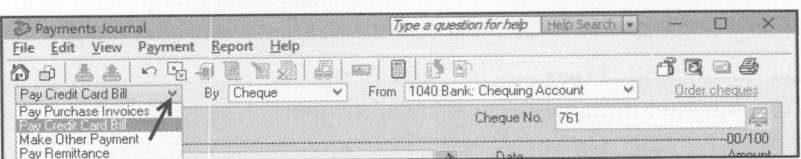

The **By** field (method of payment) has the same options as other journals — payment by cash, cheque or any of the credit cards set up. The **From** field allows you to select a bank account from which to pay because more than one bank account is defined as a Bank class account. The default payment is by cheque. The From list has three bank accounts. The bank account and the cheque number — the next one in the sequence for this account — are correct.

Click   the **To The Order Of field list arrow** to access the list of credit cards Maple Leaf Rags has set up for purchases:

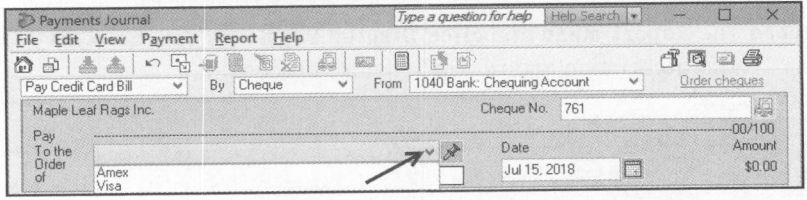

Credit card accounts are set up for Visa and Amex (American Express).

NOTES
Credit card companies charge interest on cash advances and on statement balances that are unpaid by the due date.

NOTES
When a partial payment is made to a credit card bill, the payment is applied first to interest and additional fees before reducing the outstanding balance from current purchases.

Click **Visa** to update the journal with the Visa account information:

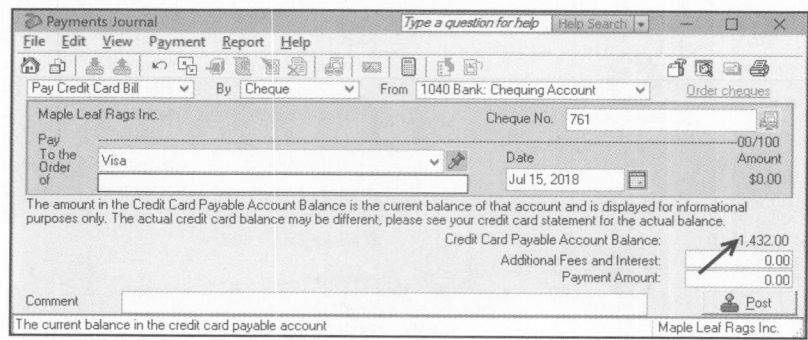

The Account Balance is the accumulation of all unpaid purchases to date according to the General Ledger *Visa Payable* account balance. This amount is not usually the same as the balance that appears on the credit card statement. Purchases after the statement date will not appear on the statement, and interest charges or renewal fees are not included in the General Ledger account balance. The on-screen information also directs you to use the statement for the amounts currently owing.

Drag through the **date in the Date field**. **Type** Jul 2

Click the **Additional Fees And Interest field**.

This field is used to record interest charges on previous unpaid amounts as well as other fees associated with the use of the card. These amounts usually appear on the statement. You must add these amounts together and enter the total in the Additional Fees And Interest field. Maple Leaf Rags owes $105 for the annual card renewal fee and $9.50 in accumulated interest for a total of $114.50.

Type 114.50 **Press** (tab) to advance to the Payment Amount field.

In the **Payment Amount** field you should enter the total amount of the cheque that is written in payment, including interest, fees and purchases. This will match the balance owing on the statement if the full amount is being paid, or some other amount if this is a partial payment. The remaining balance in the General Ledger *Visa Payable* account reflects current charges or purchases made after the statement date that will be included in the balance owing on the next statement and paid at that time.

Type 723.50 **Press** (tab) to update the journal and complete the cheque amount in the upper portion of the journal:

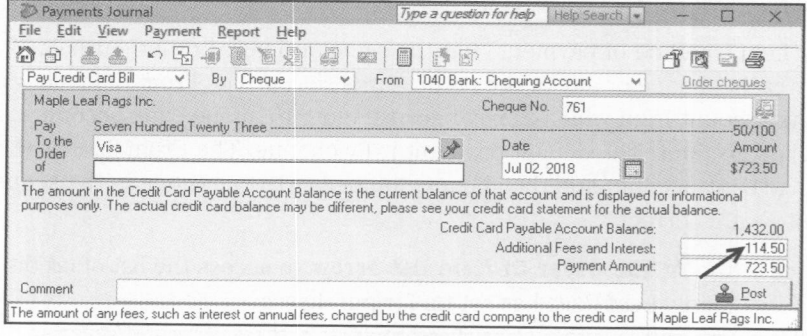

Choose the **Report menu** and **click Display Payments Journal Entry** to display the transaction and review it before proceeding:

Maple Leaf Rags Inc.			
Payments Journal Entry 07/02/2018 (J4)			
Account Number	Account Description	Debits	Credits
2260	Visa Payable	609.00	-
5150	Bank Charges & Card Fees	114.50	-
1040	Bank: Chequing Account	-	723.50
Additional Date:	Additional Field:	723.50	723.50

The linked Payables bank account is credited for the full amount of the payment. The payment amount is divided between the debit to *Visa Payable* to reduce the liability for prior purchases and the debit to *Bank Charges & Card Fees*, the linked expense account for additional credit card expenses.

Close   the **display** when you have finished reviewing it to return to the Payments Journal.

Enter   an appropriate **comment** in the Comment field.

Make   **corrections** by reselecting from a drop-down list or by highlighting an incorrect entry and typing the correct amount. Press (tab) after changing an amount to update the totals.

Click   [🖱 Post] . A message appears about the cheque number:

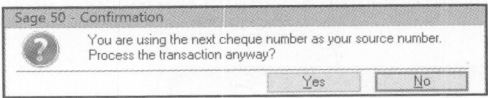

Sage 50 - Confirmation
❓ You are using the next cheque number as your source number. Process the transaction anyway?
[Yes]   [No]

Click   **Yes** to continue processing the payment.

Close   the **Payments Journal** to return to the Payables window.

Accessing a Supplier's Web Site

Before making the GST remittance, we will search the Canada Revenue Agency Web site in case there are any recent tax changes that affect this business.

✓ **Memo #43**   **Dated July 3/18**
5   From J. Bands: Access the Web site for the Canada Revenue Agency to learn whether any recent announcements about GST affect the business.

There are a number of ways to access a supplier record. Because the principles for finding records are the same in all ledgers, we will illustrate different methods.

Click   **Receiver General** in the Suppliers pane list in the Payables module window to open the record directly. **Close** the **ledger record**.

You can type text in the Search field or use the Search tool .

Click   the **Search field** in the upper-right section of the Home window.

Type   rec and **press** (enter):

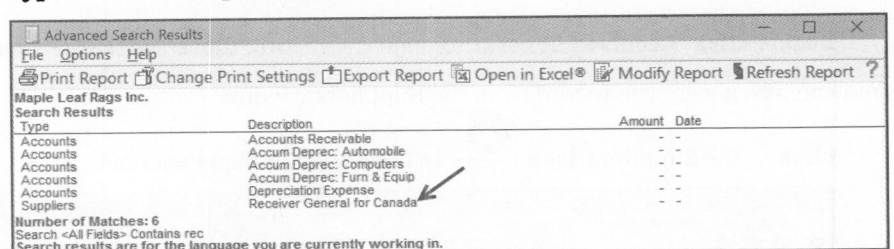

Several account names as well as the supplier record we want include this text.

Double-click   the supplier **Receiver General for Canada** to open the record.

Close   the **ledger record** and **Search window**.

NOTES
This message appears only for credit card bill payments, and only for the first credit card bill payment.

NOTES
If you choose Visa in the journal after posting the payment, the balance will match the General Ledger account balance.

PRO VERSION
pro Remember that the term Vendor will replace Supplier.

NOTES
The Search field is not case sensitive, so the results from the Search field entry will display all uses of the text you entered in the data file (both Rec and rec). The Search tool allows you to choose the search area, either records or transactions.

PRO VERSION

pro The Advanced Search tab and option are not available in the Pro version.

NOTES

If the last window you had open was a Supplier Ledger, the initial search area will be Suppliers. It would be Payments if you last used the Payments Journal.

You can type a letter in the Search field to advance the list if you have many suppliers.

The Advanced Search feature allows you to define additional search parameters.

NOTES

If you click the Search tool after entering a transaction, you will open the search for a transaction screen. If you click the Search tool after viewing a ledger record, you will list the records for that module.

The Search field is not case sensitive.

NOTES

When you begin a search from another lookup or find location (Home window icon drop-down lists or journal windows), the Select A Record Or Transaction Type field will be dimmed — you will be able to search only for the type you started from.

NOTES

Choosing View Suppliers from the Suppliers icon list also opens the Suppliers window.

Click the **Search tool** :

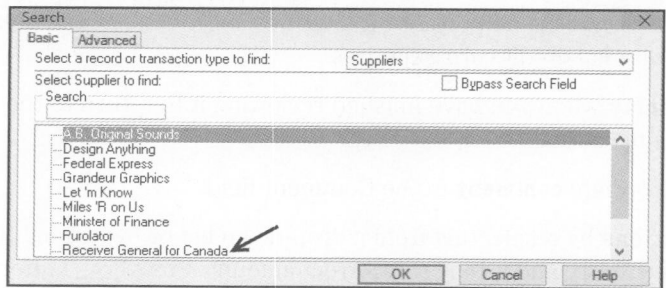

The Search window opens. The default list depends on your previous transaction. We opened a supplier record, so Suppliers is the starting point. When you start from the Home window Search tool, you can select the search area from the Select A Record Or Transaction Type To Find drop-down list in any Search window:

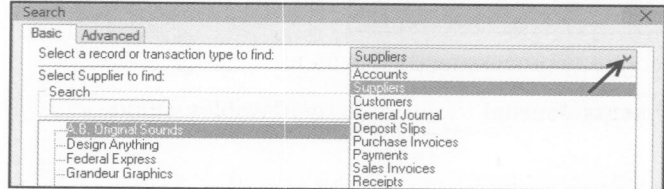

Clicking Suppliers will display the list of suppliers. Click the Search field and type r to advance to that part of the list. Receiver General for Canada will be selected because it is the first record beginning with r.

Double-click Receiver General to open the record. **Close** the **ledger record**.

Another option is to start from the Suppliers icon shortcuts list.

Choose Modify Supplier from the Suppliers (Payables window) drop-down shortcuts list to open the Search window:

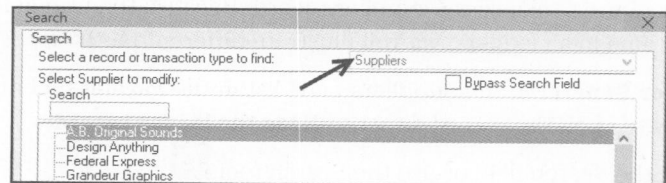

This Search screen looks the same, but **Supplier**, the entry for Select Record Or Transaction To Find, is dimmed. Select Supplier To Modify replaces Select Supplier To Find.

Double-click Receiver General to open the record. **Close** the **ledger record**.

You can also access the record from the Suppliers window.

Click the **Suppliers icon** to open the Suppliers window:

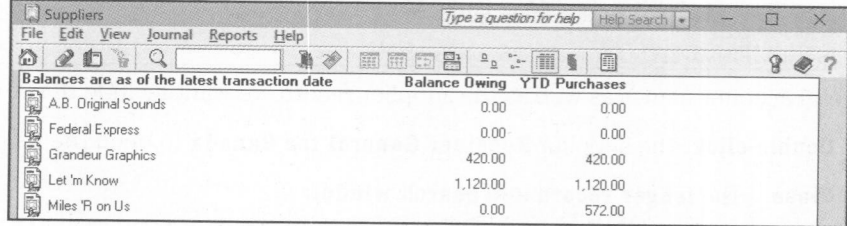

All suppliers are listed with their balances and total year-to-date purchases.

Start your **Internet connection**.

Double-click Receiver General for Canada to open the supplier's ledger:

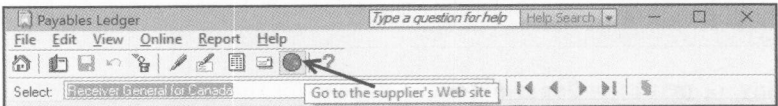

You can access the Web site directly from this Supplier Ledger page. The Web address must be included on the Address tab screen.

With most Internet connection setups you will access the Web site directly. Follow your usual procedure for starting your Internet connection because your setup may be different from ours.

Click   the **Web tool** or **choose** the **Online menu** and **click Web Site**:

This action should open the home page for the Canada Revenue Agency.

Choose your language preference.

Click   the **Find A Form Or Publication** option in the left-hand side pane under **I Want To...**

Click   the **Forms And Publications Listed By Document Type** option.

Type   HST and BC in the Search field to find information about recent tax changes in this province.

Close   your **Internet browser** when you have found the information you need or when you have finished. You will return to the supplier's ledger.

Close   the **Ledger window**. **Close** the **Suppliers window** if it is open.

Tax Remittances

Tax remittances are entered in the Purchases Journal as non-taxable purchase invoices with payment by cheque or as Other Payments in the Payments Journal. There are two parts to a GST/HST remittance — accounting for the GST (and HST) collected from customers and accounting for the GST (and HST) paid for purchases. The first is owed to the Receiver General while the second part — the input tax credit — is refunded or used to reduce the amount owing. Refer to Chapter 2 for further details. The GST/HST Report can be used to help prepare the return, but the ledger account balances for the date of the filing period should be used as a final check in case there are opening balance amounts that were not entered in the journals. For Maple Leaf Rags, the opening or historical balances are needed. These amounts were not entered through journal transactions so we cannot use built-in tax reports.

PST remittances also have two parts — accounting for the PST collected from customers and reducing the tax remitted by the sales tax compensation for filing the return on time.

Display or **print** the **General Ledger Report** for the tax accounts for June 30, 2018. This report has the amounts you must enter. (Refer to page 59.)

The General Ledger balances you need are the GST, HST and PST amounts in the Trial Balance on page 453. You can also display or print the Trial Balance or Balance Sheet for June 30 to get the amounts for the following tax accounts:

- 2460 PST Payable
- 2650 GST Charged on Sales
- 2660 HST Charged on Sales
- 2670 GST Paid on Purchases
- 2680 HST Paid on Purchases

Making GST Remittances

Choose **Pay Expenses** from the Payments icon shortcuts list.

Memo #44   **Dated July 5/18**

From J. Bands: Refer to June 30 General Ledger balances to remit GST and HST to the Receiver General. Issue cheque #762 for $4 084 from Chequing Account.

Choose **Receiver General for Canada** as the supplier.

Choose **July 5** from the pop-up calendar as the transaction date.

Click the **Account field List icon** to display the account list.

Choose **2650 GST Charged on Sales** to advance to the Description field.

Type Debiting GST Charged on Sales

Press (tab) to advance to the Amount field. **Type** 1450

No Tax should be entered as the default tax code. If it is not, select the correct code from the Tax field list icon.

Click the **Account field List icon** on the next journal line.

Choose **2660 HST Charged on Sales** and advance to the Description field.

Type Debiting HST Charged on Sales

Press (tab) to advance to the Amount field. **Type** 3634

Click the **Account field List icon** on the next journal line.

Choose **2670 GST Paid on Purchases**. In the Description field,

Type Crediting GST Paid

Press (tab) to advance to the Amount field.

Type −800 (Use a **minus sign** or hyphen. The minus sign is necessary to enter a negative amount that credits the liability account.)

Click the **Account field List icon** on the next journal line.

Choose **2680 HST Paid on Purchases**. In the Description field,

Type Crediting HST Paid **Press** (tab).

NOTES Electronic filing of GST/HST returns is covered in Appendix K.

NOTES If the Payments Journal is already open, choose Make Other Payment from the Pay transactions drop-down list.

CLASSIC VIEW Click the Payments icon to open the journal and select Make Other Payment from the Pay drop-down list.

NOTES No default account was entered for the Receiver General because four different accounts are required.

Type   −200 This entry also reduces the amount remitted.

Click   the **Invoice/Ref. field**. **Type** Memo 44 **Press** (tab).

Type   Memo 44, GST/HST remittance for June in the Comment field to complete your entry:

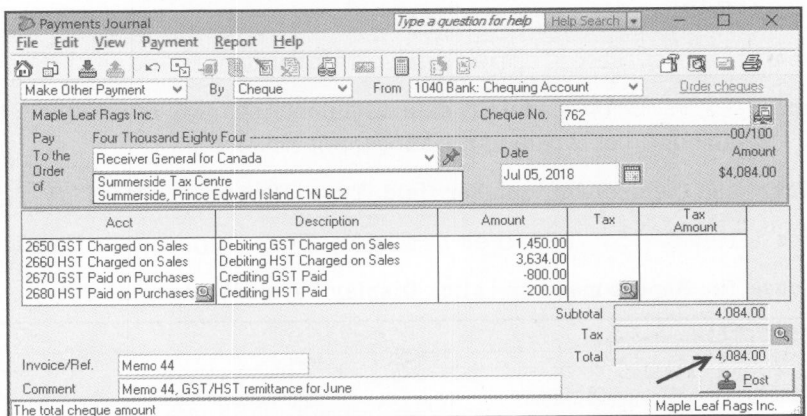

A review of the journal entry will help to clarify the transaction.

Choose the **Report menu** and **click Display Payments Journal Entry**:

Maple Leaf Rags Inc.
Payments Journal Entry 07/05/2018 (J5)

Account Number	Account Description	Debits	Credits
2650	GST Charged on Sales	1,450.00	-
2660	HST Charged on Sales	3,634.00	-
1040	Bank: Chequing Account	-	4,084.00
2670	GST Paid on Purchases	-	800.00
2680	HST Paid on Purchases	-	200.00
Additional Date:	Additional Field:	5,084.00	5,084.00

NOTES
GST paid and HST paid are input tax credits that reduce the amount of the remittance.

Normally, a positive amount will create a debit entry in the Payments Journal for an expense or an asset purchase. *GST/HST Charged on Sales* are GST payable accounts with a credit balance. Therefore, entering a positive amount will reduce the GST payable balance by debiting the accounts, as we do when we pay suppliers. The negative entries or credits for the refundable *GST Paid on Purchases* and *HST Paid on Purchase*s will offset the debit balance in the ledger for these contra-liability accounts and will reduce the total amount that is paid to the Receiver General. The net cheque amount is credited to the bank account.

Close   the **display** when finished. **Make corrections** if necessary.

Click   [Post]. You are now ready to make the PST remittance.

Making PST Remittances

You should still be in the Payments Journal with Make Other Payment selected as the type of transaction.

> **Memo #45**   **Dated July 5/18**
>
> From J. Bands: Refer to the June 30 General Ledger balance to remit PST Payable to the Minister of Finance. Reduce the payment amount by the sales tax compensation of 6.6%. Issue cheque #763 for $420.30 from Chequing Account.

Choose Minister of Finance as the supplier. Accept the default bank account.

Accept July 5 as the date and **accept** the default **account**, *2460 PST Payable*.

Click   the **Description field**.

Type   Debiting for PST collected

Press   (tab) to move the cursor to the Amount field. **Type** 450

You are now ready to enter the revenue from sales tax compensation, 6.6 percent of the *PST Payable* amount.

Click the **Account field List icon** on the second journal line.

Choose **4280 Sales Tax Compensation**. The cursor advances to the Description field.

Type Sales Tax Compensation **Press** (tab).

Type -29.70 (Use a **minus sign**. The minus sign will reduce the total amount that is paid to the Minister of Finance.)

Click the **Invoice/Ref. number field. Type** Memo 45 **Press** (tab).

Type Memo 45, PST remittance for June in the Comment field.

Choose the **Report menu** and **click Display Payments Journal Entry**:

The full *PST Payable* amount is debited to reduce the entire liability. Credit entries to the bank account for the amount of the cheque and the *Sales Tax Compensation* revenue account for the amount of the tax reduction balance the transaction.

Close the **display** when you have finished. **Make corrections** if needed.

Click Post . **Close** the **Payments Journal**.

Entering Sales to Foreign Customers

Click **Receivables** in the Modules pane list to open the Receivables window.

Click the **Sales Invoices icon** to open the Sales Journal. Invoice and Pay Later, the default selections, are correct.

Sales Invoice #595   **Dated July 5/18**

To Canadian Sounds, $2 190 USD for CDs and $300 USD for books. Shipped by Federal Express (#F19YTR563) for $140. Invoice total $2 630 USD. Terms: 3/30, n/60. The exchange rate is 1.260.

Choose Canadian Sounds from the Customer drop-down list:

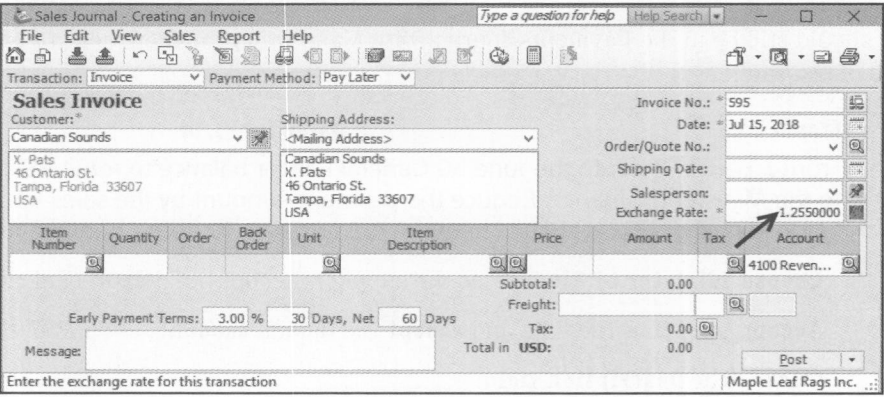

The invoice is modified for the foreign customer. A field for the exchange rate has been added, and the Total is expressed in USD (United States dollars) rather than in

Canadian dollars. An exchange rate button 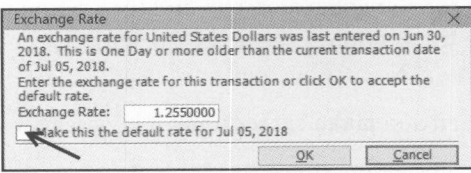 provides a list of exchange rates already entered for various dates. There is no rate for July 5.

Choose July 5 from the Date field calendar.

The Exchange Rate screen opens because the exchange rate on record is more than one day old and no rate has been recorded for this date:

Exchange Rate

An exchange rate for United States Dollars was last entered on Jun 30, 2018. This is One Day or more older than the current transaction date of Jul 05, 2018.
Enter the exchange rate for this transaction or click OK to accept the default rate.

Exchange Rate: 1.2550000

☐ Make this the default rate for Jul 05, 2018

OK   Cancel

The Exchange Rate setting for the company file warns when the exchange rate on record is more than one day old so that an incorrect old rate is not accepted in error. The most recent exchange rate is entered and selected for editing. You can also edit the exchange rate directly in the journal screen, just as you enter information in other fields.

Type   1.260

Click   **Make This The Default Rate For Jul 05, 2018. Press** ⟨enter⟩ **or click OK** to return to the Sales Journal.

Click   the **Item Description field. Type** CDs

Click   the **Amount field. Type** 2190 The default revenue account is correct.

Click   the **Item Description field** on the next invoice line. **Type** books

Click   the **Amount field. Type** 300

Click   the **Account field List icon** 🔍 and **select** account **4140**.

Exported goods are not taxable because they are "consumed" outside of Canada. The No Tax code (blank) is entered as the default and it is correct.

Click   the **Freight field. Type** 140 **Press** ⟨tab⟩ to update the amounts. Maple does not charge taxes on freight for exported goods.

Click   the **Track Shipments tool** 📦.

Choose Federal Express as the shipper from the Shipped By list.

Press   ⟨tab⟩ to advance to the Tracking Number field.

Type   F19YTR563 **Click OK** to return to the completed journal entry:

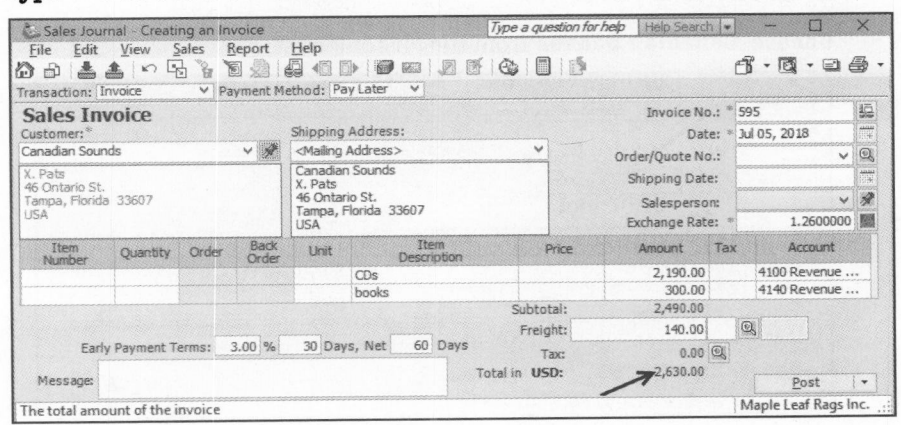

WARNING!
Always check that the date on the Exchange Rate screen matches the transaction date.

Choose the **Report menu** and **click Display Sales Journal Entry**:

Maple Leaf Rags Inc.				
Sales Journal Entry 07/05/2018 (J7)				
Account Number	Account Description	Foreign A...	Debits	Credits
1200	Accounts Receivable	US$2,630.00	3,313.80	-
4100	Revenue from CD Sales	US$2,190.00	-	2,759.40
4140	Revenue from Book Sales	US$300.00	-	378.00
4200	Freight Revenue	US$140.00	-	176.40
1 United States Dollars equals 1.2600000 Canadian Dollars			3,313.80	3,313.80

Although the journal itself looks the same as for regular invoices — with amounts in US dollars — the journal entry has both the Canadian amounts and the US amounts as well as the exchange rate applied to the transaction. Otherwise, the entry is the same as it would be for sales to Canadian customers. No new accounts are used.

Close the **display** when finished and **make corrections** if necessary.

Click Post ▾ to save the transaction. **Close** the **Sales Journal**.

Enter the **next three transactions**.

> **NOTES**
> You can use the Additional Field for the invoice number.
> Use the default bank account 1040 for receipts from Canadian customers.

> 9

Receipt #125   Dated July 5/18

From It's All Canadian, cheque #884 for $3 570 in payment of account including $105 discount taken for early payment. Reference invoice #589.

> **NOTES**
> Wholesale customers who will be selling the product to their own customers do not pay PST.
> Remember to change the revenue account for book sales.

> 10

Sales Order #24 & Deposit #14   Dated July 5/18

Shipping date July 10/18
From Treble & Bass, $10 300 for CDs and $900 for books plus 5% GST. Enter one (1) as the order quantity for each invoice line. Shipping by Purolator for $120 plus GST. Invoice total $11 886. Terms: 3/30, n/60. Received cheque #911 for $2 000 as deposit #14 to confirm the order. Refer to page 426.

> ⚠ **WARNING!**
> Remember to change the payment method to Pay Later for invoice #596. Cheque remains selected from the sales order. Refer to page 431. The balance owing is $9 886.

> 11

Sales Invoice #596   Dated July 10/18

To Treble & Bass, to fill sales order #24, $10 300 for CDs and $900 for books plus 5% GST. Shipped by Purolator (#PCU899XT) for $120 plus GST. Invoice total $11 886. Terms: 3/30, n/60. Enter the shipper so you can track the shipment.

Entering Foreign Customer Receipts

Click the **Receipts icon** [Receipts ▾] to open the Receipts Journal.

> ✓
> 12

Receipt #126   Dated July 15/18

From Canadian Sounds, cheque #2397 for $2 551.10 USD in payment of account less $78.90 discount for early payment. Reference invoice #595. The exchange rate for July 15 is 1.270.

Choose Canadian Sounds from the customer list:

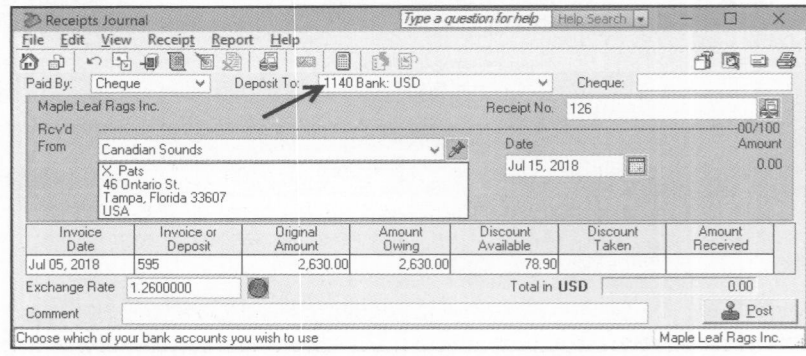

The journal is modified for the foreign customer. The outstanding invoice appears on the screen and the currency is marked as USD. An Exchange Rate field also becomes available with the most recent exchange rate entered.

Deposits from US customers are made to the USD bank account. This account is set up and entered as the default bank account for foreign currency transactions.

Click the **Cheque field**. **Type** 2397

Click the **Date field**. The session date is correct as the transaction date.

Click **15** and **press** (tab) to open the Exchange Rate screen.

If the rate has not changed, you can accept it by clicking Make This The Default Rate For Jul 15, 2018 and clicking OK.

Again, because the last exchange rate we entered was for July 5, the rate is out of date, and we must enter a new one. The previous rate is highlighted.

Type 1.270

Click **Make This The Default Rate For Jul 15, 2018**.

Click **OK** to return to the Receipts Journal. The cursor is on the calendar icon.

Click the **Discount Taken field**.

Press (tab) to accept the discount because the full invoice is being paid. The cursor advances to the Amount Received field.

Press (tab) to accept the amount and update the cheque portion of the form.

Click the **Enter Additional Information tool** ✔.

Click the **Additional Field text box** to move the cursor.

Type Ref: inv #595

Click **OK** to return to the completed journal entry:

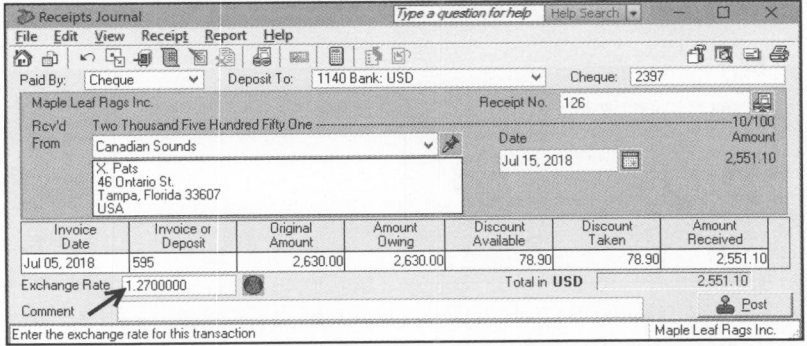

Choose the **Report menu** and **click Display Receipts Journal Entry** to review the entry:

Maple Leaf Rags Inc.				
Receipts Journal Entry 07/15/2018 (J11)				
Account Number	Account Description	Foreign A...	Debits	Credits
1140	Bank: USD	US$2,551.10	3,239.90	-
4180	Sales Discounts	US$78.90	100.20	-
1200	Accounts Receivable	US$2,630.00	-	3,313.80
4300	Exchange Rate Differences		-	26.30
1 United States Dollars equals 1.2700000 Canadian Dollars			3,340.10	3,340.10
Additional Date:	Additional Field: Ref inv #595			

In addition to the usual linked accounts for receipts, an entry for *Exchange Rate Differences* appears. Because the exchange rate was lower on the day of the sale, the date the revenue was recorded, than on the day of the receipt, there has been a credit to the account. Maple Leaf Rags has gained money on the delay in payment — more Canadian dollars are received for the same US dollar amount when the exchange rate is higher. When the rate decreases, there is a loss. As for foreign customer sales, amounts are given in both currencies along with the exchange rate.

Close the **display** to return to the journal and **make corrections** if necessary.

NOTES
If the correct bank account is not selected by default, you can choose it from the Deposit To drop-down list of bank accounts.

NOTES
The Exchange Rate screen does not open until you "touch" the date field in some way. If the Exchange Rate screen does not open when you enter a date, you can type the exchange rate directly in the Exchange Rate field.

NOTES
The gain/loss situation is reversed for payments to foreign suppliers. When the rate increases, the purchased goods cost more and money is lost. A decrease in exchange rate creates a gain.

Click 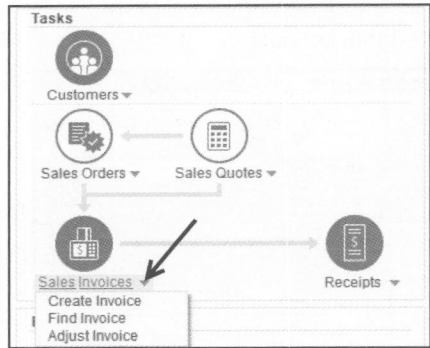 to save the transaction.

Close the **Receipts Journal** and **enter** the next **sales transaction**.

13	**Sales Invoice #597** **Dated July 15/18**

To Music Music Music, $1 630 USD for CDs plus $450 USD for books. Shipped by Federal Express (#F27CGB786) for $110. Invoice total $2 190 USD. Terms: 3/30, n/60. The exchange rate is 1.270.

Looking Up Invoices to Track Shipments

Lookup provides an exact copy of the posted invoice that you can store, print or e-mail if you have forgotten to do so before posting. This feature can be useful if a customer has an inquiry about a purchase or needs a copy of the invoice. Once a sales or purchase invoice is posted with details about the shipping company, you can look up the invoice to track the shipment to learn when delivery is expected. You can use the Find Invoice approach or the Search feature (read the margin Notes).

✓ **14**	**Memo #46** **Dated July 16/18**

From J. Bands: Treble & Bass called to inform you that they have not received their shipment of CDs and books. Look up invoice #596, e-mail a copy of the invoice to the customer and check the delivery status.

Advance the **session date** to **July 31**. **Back up** your data set.

Click the **Sales Invoices shortcuts list** and **choose Find Invoice**:

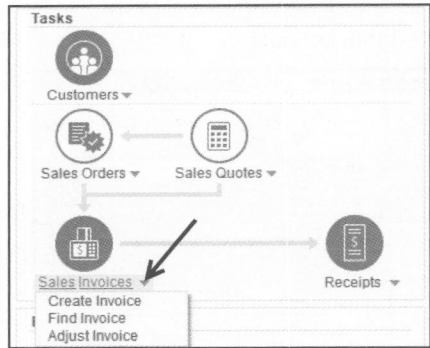

You will open the familiar Search dialogue window:

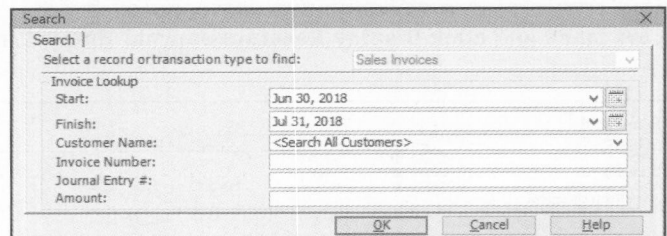

If the Sales Journal is open, you can click the **Look Up An Invoice tool** 🖳 on the tool bar or beside the Invoice field, or choose the Sales menu and click Look Up Invoice to open this Search window.

The Search screen options for Look Up are like those for adjusting an invoice. You can search through all invoices for the fiscal year to date (or for the previous year if you have not cleared the transactions and lookup data) or enter a narrower range of dates; you can search through invoices for all customers or for a specific customer; or you can

search for a specific invoice, journal entry number or amount. Your search strategy will depend on how much information you have before you begin the search and how many invoices there are altogether.

The default Start and Finish dates will include all transactions. You can change these dates to narrow the search, just as you would edit any other date fields, or you can choose dates from the drop-down list or calendar. We want to include all invoices in the search, so we can accept the default range of dates.

The Customer Name option allows you to Search All Customers, the default setting, or a specific customer's invoices. You can also look up the invoices for one-time customers.

> To display the list of customers, click the Customer Name field or its drop-down list arrow and click the name you need to select a specific customer.

> If you know the Invoice Number or the Journal Entry number, you can enter that detail in the related field and click OK. You can also search for a specific Amount.

In this case we will look at all invoices, choosing the default to Search All Customers.

Click   **OK** to display the list of invoices that meet the search conditions of date and customers:

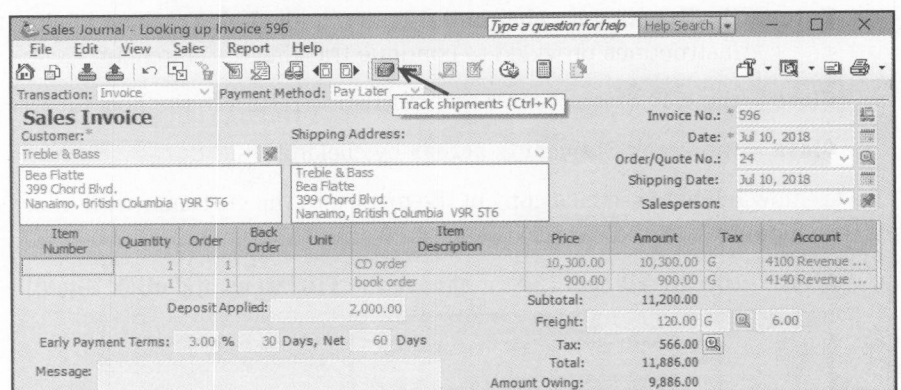

You can sort the list by order of posting date, customer, journal entry number, invoice number or amount. You can also reverse the order of the entries in the list by clicking the Z...A+ button.

Click   **Treble & Bass, Invoice Number 596** for $11 886.00 to select it. Click anywhere on the line.

Click   **Select** to display the requested invoice:

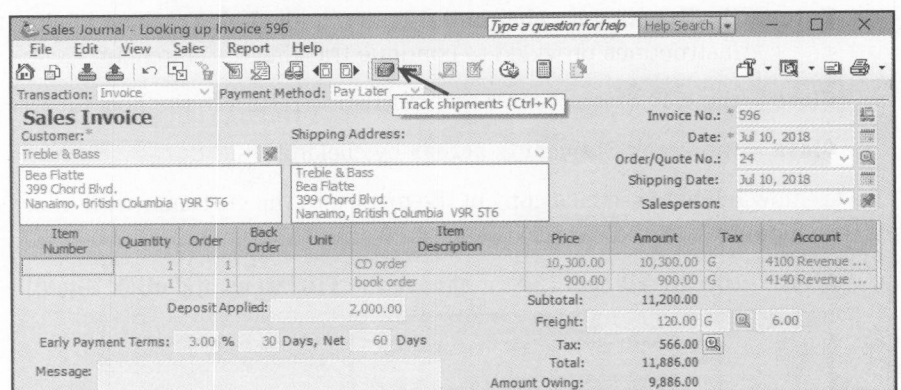

This is an exact copy of the original invoice, except that you cannot edit or post it — there is no Post button. All fields are dimmed, but several familiar tool options are available. You can store, preview, e-mail or print the invoice. Although you cannot adjust an invoice from the Lookup window directly, the Adjust Invoice tool is available. When you click the Adjust Invoice tool, the journal screen changes and the fields become available for editing and posting. You can use the Lookup method to locate the invoice you need to adjust. You can also reverse a transaction directly from the Lookup screen.

If you have selected the wrong invoice, or if you want to view other invoices, you can access them with any Lookup window as your starting point. If there are no invoices in one or both directions, the corresponding tools will be dimmed.

Click **Look Up Next Invoice** or **Look Up Previous Invoice** . Or, choose Previous or Next Invoice from the Sales menu to display other invoices. You can browse through the invoices in this way until you find the one you need. You should practise viewing other invoices by clicking the Look Up Next and Previous Invoice tools.

Click   the **Track Shipments tool** or **choose** the **Sales menu** and **click Track Shipments** to obtain the shipping details for the sale.

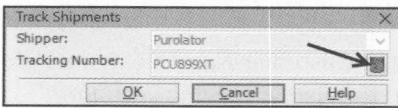

If you need to add or edit the shipping information, click Cancel to close the tracking details window. Click the Adjust Invoice tool in the journal and then the Track Shipments tool.

Click   the Web icon to close the shipping details screen and continue:

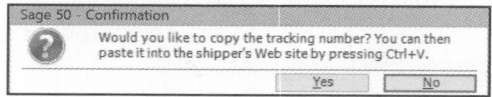

If you have actually shipped an item and have entered the tracking number provided by the shipper, you can choose Yes and save the number for entering on the Web site tracking page. However, we do not have an actual tracking number or account with Purolator.

Click   **No** to continue to the Internet connection.

Your screen at this stage will depend on your Internet setup — you may connect and access the Web site directly, or you may need to enter your account and password first.

Continue as you would for your **usual Internet connection**.

You will access the Web site for Purolator.

Enter   the **Tracking Number** in the Track field, **click Track** and follow the instructions provided to continue tracking the shipment.

Close   the **Web Site screen** when finished to return to the Lookup screen.

Close   the **Track Shipments screen** by clicking OK.

We are now ready to e-mail a copy of the invoice to the customer with information about the shipping date and carrier. (Read the Warning margin note.)

Click   the **E-mail tool** or **choose** the **File menu** and **click E-mail**.

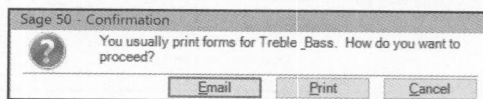

Since printing invoices is the default setting in the customer's ledger record, you are asked if you want to continue, just in case you clicked the wrong button.

Click   **E-mail** to continue to the E-mail Information screen:

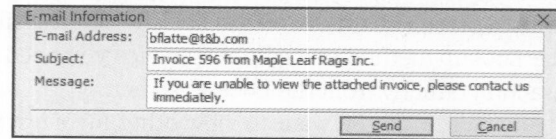

If the e-mail address is missing, you can enter it here. You should replace the address with your own e-mail address if you want to test the e-mail feature.

Type   (Type your own e-mail address in this field, or that of a classmate.)

You can add a message in the Message field about the shipment tracking details to inform the customer of the expected delivery date.

Click   Send.

Another advisory screen asks whether you want to update the e-mail address in the ledger record.

Click   Yes to update the ledger record and proceed.

At this stage, your screens will depend on your e-mail, Internet and security program setups. You should be connected to your Internet provider. You may get a message requesting permission to send a message:

Click   Allow Access For and then **click** the **Allow button**. Your screen may include a progress bar as the message is transmitted.

Click   Allow again if necessary. **Close** your **e-mail** and **Internet connections** to return to the Sales Journal – Invoice Lookup window.

Close   the Lookup window to return to the Receivables window.

Your Outlook program will have an e-mail message indicating the attached invoice document Invoice_596.PDF:

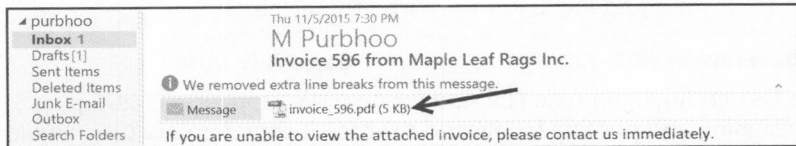

If you have another e-mail program as your default, the single PDF invoice page may be included directly on-screen in your message along with the attached PDF document, or you can click Invoice_596.PDF to preview the invoice:

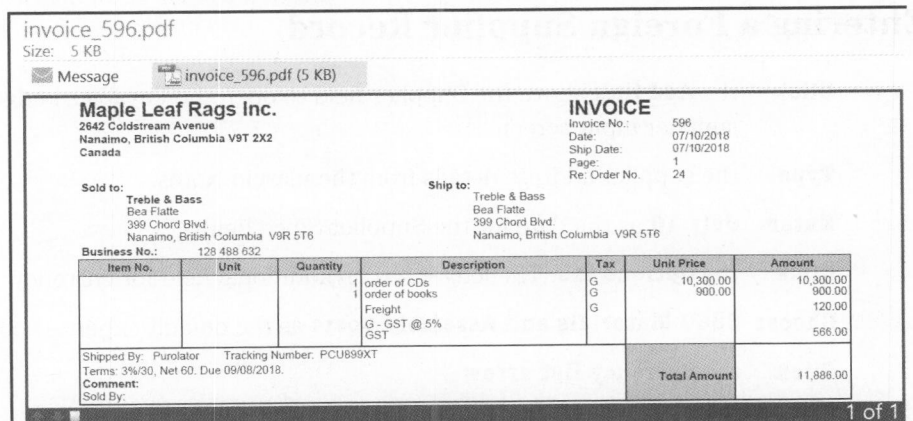

Double-clicking Invoice_596.PDF will open the attached invoice with Adobe Acrobat. The invoice has the date of the invoice as well as shipping and tracking details.

NOTES

The Sage 50 E-mail feature expects a Microsoft Outlook account and profile set up as your default e-mail program.

If you are using a program other than Outlook as your default e-mail program, you will need to enter additional settings before you can e-mail the invoice.

Start your Outlook program before starting the e-mail process if the e-mail is not sent.

NOTES

If a permission screen opens with the Yes and No buttons replacing Allow and Deny, you should click Yes.

NOTES

You may have to enter your ID and password before your e-mail program starts.

If necessary, click Allow again when the progress bar has finished to send the message.

NOTES

You can also click Invoice_596.PDF to preview the file in the Outlook mail message. From there, you can print it.

Looking Up and Tracking Purchases

You can look up purchase invoices in the same way you look up sales invoices. You can look up purchase invoices from the Purchases Journal and from the Payments Journal.

Open the Purchases or Payments Journal, click Look Up An Invoice , decide whether you want to restrict the search dates or suppliers and click OK. Choose an invoice from the displayed list and click Select. If you know the invoice number, journal entry number or amount, you can enter it directly and click OK to display the requested invoice.

From the Payments Journal, choose Make Other Payment then click (Look Up An Invoice) to find cash invoices posted in the Payments Journal.

Once you look up a purchase invoice, you can track shipments and look up other invoices in the same way as you do for sales. You can also adjust the invoice. Tracking is not available for cash purchases entered as Other Payments in the Payments Journal.

Entering Purchases from Foreign Suppliers

Purchases from foreign suppliers are entered in much the same way as purchases from other suppliers. Once you choose a supplier who uses a different currency, the Purchases Journal changes to add the appropriate fields.

Open   the **Payables module window**.

Click   the **Purchase Invoices icon** to open the Purchases Journal. Invoice and Pay Later are correctly selected.

NOTES
Use Full Add so you can enter the correct currency.
Design Anything
(contact Joy Pikchur)
900 Park St., Unit 5
Seattle, Washington 98195
USA
Tel: (800) 639-8710
Fax: (206) 755-8852
Currency: USD
Terms: net 30
Expense account: 5360
Tax code: G

WARNING!
You must choose Full Add for new foreign currency suppliers so that you can choose USD as the currency.

✓ **15** | **Purchase Invoice #DA-722**   **Dated July 16/18**

From Design Anything (use Full Add for new US supplier), $3 200 plus 5% GST for designing and printing labels and CD case inserts for new CDs. Invoice total $3 360 USD. Terms: net 30. The exchange rate is 1.255.

Click   the **Supplier field**. **Type** Design Anything

Entering a Foreign Supplier Record

Click   the **Add link** above the Supplier field to open the Payables Ledger supplier input screen.

Type   the supplier address details from the margin Notes.

Enter   **July 16** as the date for the Supplier Since field.

Click   the **Options tab**. The ledger has an additional field for currency.

Choose **5360 Materials and Assembly Costs** as the default expense account.

Click   the **Currency list arrow**:

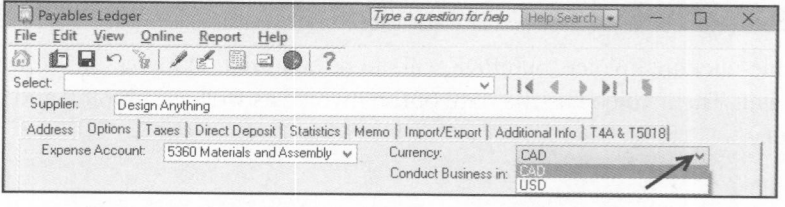

Choose USD. A Balance Owing In USD amount is added to the record.

Enter   **net 30 days** as the payment terms.

Click   the **Taxes tab** that has the default settings.

Click   the **Tax Code list arrow** for the options:

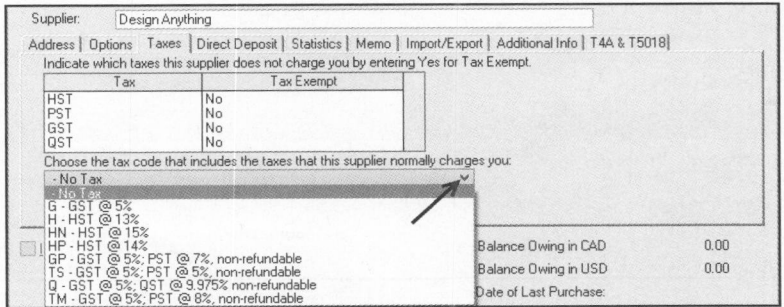

Maple Leaf Rags is not exempt from paying taxes on purchases from Design Anything, and that is the default selection. All tax codes will be available. Most purchases from US suppliers are subject to GST, so we should choose G - GST @ 5% as the default tax code. Maple pays GST on imported goods.

Click   **Code G - GST @ 5%.**

Click   [Save and Close] to return to the modified invoice:

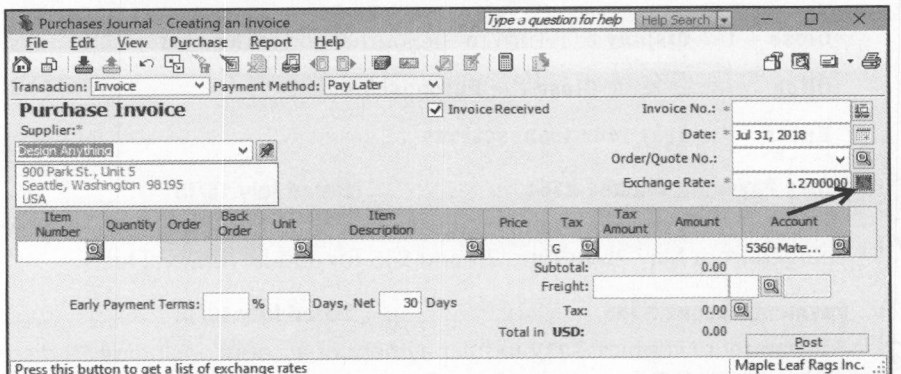

USD is now selected as the currency for the invoice and an Exchange Rate field has been added. The default terms, expense account and tax code are also on the invoice.

Enter   the **Invoice number** and **Date. Do not press** (tab). If the Exchange Rate update screen opens, click Cancel.

Click   the **Exchange Rate tool** 🔲 beside the Exchange Rate field to open the list of rates we have already used so that we can choose from this list:

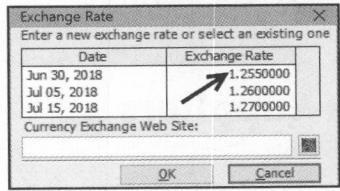

Click   **1.255**, the rate for June 30. **Click OK** to return to the journal.

NOTES

The additional tax code, Q, is available for purchases in Quebec. Provincial taxes on purchases are added to the expense or asset part of the purchase, just like other PST paid amounts. Tax code Q is not in the Sales Journal tax list because no linked account was entered for taxes charged on sales.

⚠ WARNING!

Leave all Tax Exempt settings at No in case other tax codes are required for taxes on other purchases or on freight.

NOTES

GST or HST is paid directly to the Receiver General at the time the goods arrive in Canada. The foreign supplier does not collect these taxes.

To simplify the exercises, we omit this aspect of the tax collection and instead include the GST on foreign purchases with the invoices.

Enter the **Amount** and **Description** to complete the invoice:

Choose the **Report menu** and **click Display Purchases Journal Entry** to review the entry:

The only difference between this and other purchase entries is the addition of the USD currency amounts and exchange rate.

Close the **display** to return to the journal and **make corrections** if necessary.

Click [Post]. **Close** the **Purchases Journal**.

Enter the **next four transactions**.

16 **Amex Payment: Cheque #764**   **Dated July 16/18**

To Amex, $335 in payment of credit card account, including $290 for purchases charged from May 25 to June 25 and $45 for annual renewal fee.

17 **Payment Cheque #765**   **Dated July 18/18**

To Grandeur Graphics, $412 in full payment of account, including $8 discount for early payment. Reference invoice #GG-1304.

18 **Payment Cheque #766**   **Dated July 18/18**

To Let 'm Know, $1 100 in full payment of account, including $20 discount for early payment. Reference invoice #LK-692.

19 **Receipt #127**   **Dated July 20/18**

From CDN Music, cheque #28563 for $4 590 in payment of account including $135 discount taken for early payment. Reference invoice #591.

Entering Payments to Foreign Suppliers

Click the **Payments icon** [Payments] or use the shortcut to open the Payments Journal.

20 **Payment Cheque #284**   **Dated July 30/18**

To Design Anything, $3 360 USD in full payment of account. Reference invoice #DA-722. The exchange rate is 1.258.

Choose **Design Anything** from the Supplier list to modify the journal:

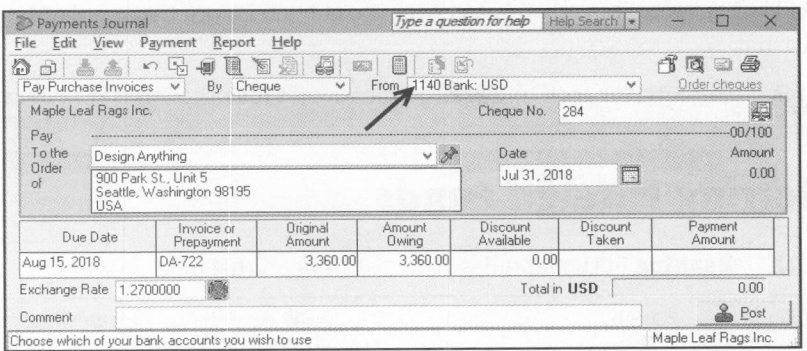

NOTES
The exchange rate we selected for July 16 from the list for June 30 was not entered as the most recent rate used because we did not save it as the default rate for July 16.

The outstanding invoice appears on the screen and the currency is marked as USD. An Exchange Rate field also becomes available.

Payments to US suppliers are made from the USD bank account. This account is set up as the default bank account for foreign currency transactions. The cheque number is the next in sequence for this account.

Click   the **Calendar icon** 📅 and **choose July 30** as the transaction date.

The Exchange Rate screen should open automatically — the rate is out of date.

Type   1.258 **Click Make This The Default Rate For Jul 30, 2018**.

Press   (enter) to return to the journal. The cursor is on the calendar icon.

Click   the **Payment Amount field**. There is no discount.

Press   (tab) to accept the amount and complete the entry:

NOTES
If the Exchange Rate screen stays open after you click OK with the session date replacing the transaction date, you may enter an incorrect rate. Click Cancel to close the screen and select the correct exchange rate from the Exchange Rate select list.
Click the Exchange Rate tool 💲 beside the field to open the list of rates. You can also type the rate directly in the Exchange Rate field.

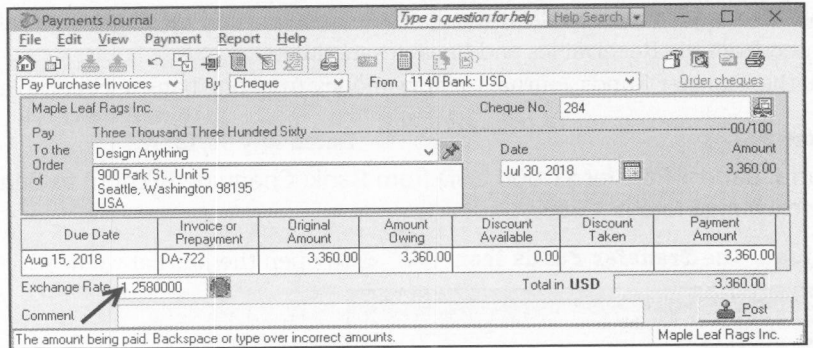

Press   (ctrl) + **J** so you can review the journal entry:

Maple Leaf Rags Inc.				
Payments Journal Entry 07/30/2018 (J18)				
Account Number	Account Description	Foreign A...	Debits	Credits
2200	Accounts Payable	US$3,360.00	4,216.80	-
4300	Exchange Rate Differences		10.08	-
1140	Bank: USD	US$3,360.00	-	4,226.88
1 United States Dollars equals 1.2580000 Canadian Dollars			4,226.88	4,226.88

NOTES
The Accounts Payable amount is $4 216.80 CAD and the amount paid is $4 228.88. The difference ($10.08) is caused by the exchange rate change.

Exchange Rate Differences has a debit entry because the exchange rate was lower on the day of the purchase (the date the purchase was recorded) than on the day of the payment. However, because this is a payment, Maple Leaf Rags has lost on the payment delay, as indicated by the debit entry for a revenue account — more Canadian dollars are needed to pay the same US dollar amount. As for other foreign currency transactions, amounts are given in both currencies and the exchange rate is included.

Close   the **display** to return to the journal. **Make corrections** if necessary and

click   💾 Post to display the advisor message:

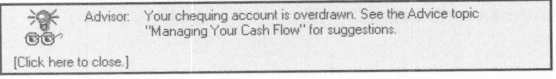

The advisor informs us that our chequing account is overdrawn. We will transfer funds to the USD account immediately to cover the cheque before the supplier has a chance to cash it.

Click the **Advisor icon** to close the message. **Close** the **Payments Journal**.

Transferring Foreign Funds

Click **Banking** in the Modules pane list to open this module window:

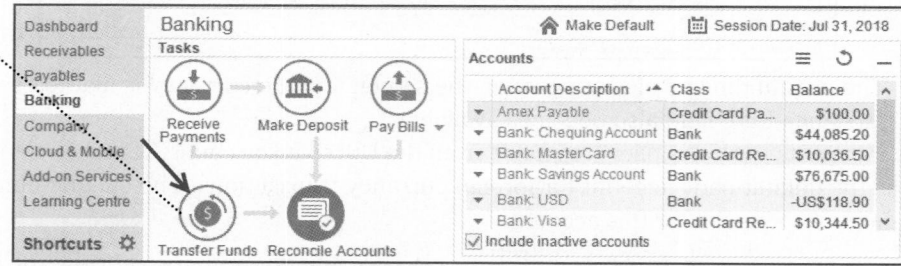

Clicking the **Refresh icon** ⟳ in the Accounts pane will update the account balances.

The Accounts pane list also informs us that *Bank USD* is overdrawn — it has a negative balance amount. The Banking module window has no ledger icons, although it does allow direct access to the ledger records for all accounts involved in making or receiving payments (Cash, Bank and Credit Card class accounts). Three journal icons — Make Deposit, Transfer Funds, Reconcile Accounts — are for bank account transactions. The Receive Payments and Pay Bills icons open the Receipts and Payments journals and are duplicated from the Receivables and Payables modules.

We use the Transfer Funds Journal to move money from one bank account to another.

✓ 21 | **Memo #47** | **Dated July 30/18**

From J. Bands: Transfer $1 000 USD from Bank: Chequing Account to Bank: USD. The exchange rate is 1.258.

Click the **Transfer Funds icon** to open the journal we need:

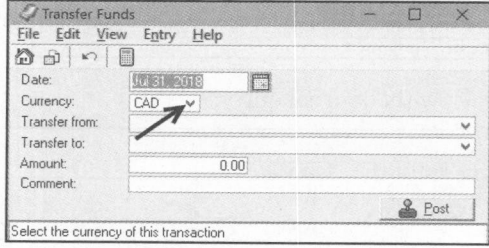

Type July 30 (as the Date).

Click the **Currency list arrow** for the currency options:

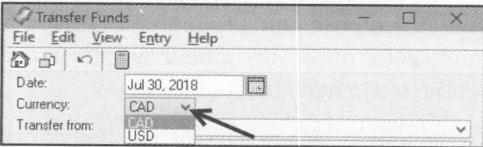

Both currencies are available for Transfer Funds transactions.

Click **USD**. The exchange rate is entered correctly for this date.

NOTES
Access to the Payments and Receipts journals from the Banking module allows all bank-related activities to be completed from this screen.

Account reconciliation and deposits are covered in Chapter 15.

Make Other Payment (Pay Expenses) is the default type of transaction from the Pay Bills icon.

CLASSIC VIEW
The Transfer Funds Journal is not available in the Classic view, so you must use the General Journal instead.

WARNING!
You must choose USD as the currency for the transfer of funds. The CAD bank account will be available for the foreign currency transaction. If you choose CAD as the currency, you cannot access the USD bank account.

NOTES
The Exchange Rate window does not open because we have already entered a rate for July 30. You can still change the rate if needed by editing the amount in the Exchange Rate field.

Click   the **Transfer From list arrow** for the list of available accounts:

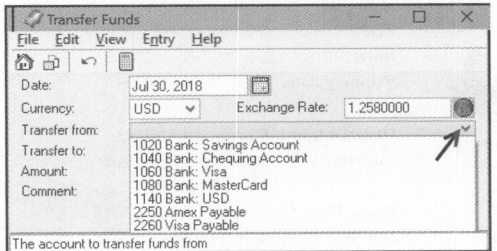

Choose   **1040 Bank: Chequing Account** in the Account field. **Press** $\boxed{tab}$.

Click   the **Transfer To list arrow**; the same list of available accounts opens.

Choose   **1140 Bank: USD** and **press** $\boxed{tab}$ to advance to the Amount field.

Type   1000 **Press** $\boxed{tab}$ to advance to the Comment field.

Type   Memo 47: Transfer funds to cover cheque

Adding the comment will complete the entry:

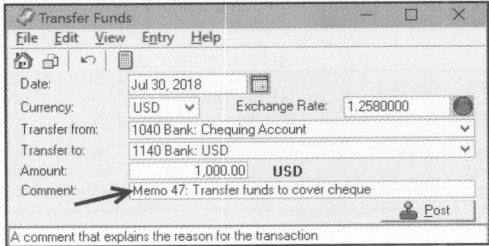

Check your transaction carefully. You cannot display the journal entry before posting. To make corrections after posting, adjust or reverse the transfer in the General Journal.

When you display the Journal Entries Report, the transfer is included as a typical debit and credit entry, with the amounts given in both currencies, as for other foreign currency transactions, and the exchange rate that was applied.

Click   to save the transaction.

Close   the **Transfer Funds Journal**. The Banking Home window balances are updated.

Enter   the **remaining transactions** up to memo #58 on September 30.

Purchase Order #204 & Cheque #767   **Dated July 31/18**

22

Shipping date Aug. 15/18
To A.B. Original Sounds, $50 000 plus 5% GST for master copies of new CDs.
Invoice total $52 500. Enter 1 as the order quantity. Terms: 1/10, n/30. Use Materials and Assembly Costs account.
Paid $10 000 as prepayment on order with cheque #767.

Purchase Order #205 & Cheque #768   **Dated July 31/18**

23

Shipping date Aug. 15/18
To Super Dupers (use Full Add for the new supplier), $15 000 to duplicate CDs and books plus 5% GST. Invoice total $15 750. Terms: 1/10, n/30.
Paid $4 000 as prepayment on order with cheque #768.

24

Maple Leaf Rags

www.mapleleafrags.com

2642 Coldstream Avenue
Nanaimo, BC V9T 2X2
Tel 1: (250) 63M-USIC
Tel 2: (888) 63M-USIC   Fax: (250) 633-4888

PO#:	206
Date:	July 31, 2018
Shipping date:	Aug 15, 2018

Ordered from:	Wrap It
Address:	80 Cubit Road
	Richmond Hill, ON L5R 6B2
Phone No:	(905) 881-7739
Fax No:	(905) 881-7000
Contact:	Able Boxer

PURCHASE ORDER

Order description	Amount
Provide CD cases add labels and inserts terms: 1/5, n/30	6 300.00

Freight (Canada Post)	120.00
GST	321.00
HST	--
Order Total	6 741.00
Deposit	2 000.00
Balance Owing	4 741.00

Deposit: chq #769 for $2 000

Approved by: *Jaz Bands*

NOTES
Change the default account to Prepaid Expenses for the invoice from Let 'm Know.

25

Purchase Invoice #LK-2303   **Dated July 31/18**

From Let 'm Know, $1 500 plus 5% GST and 7% PST for series of ads to run for the next five months (prepaid expense). Invoice total $1 680. Terms: 2/20, n/30.

26

Cash Purchase Invoice #WT-6632   **Dated July 31/18**

From Western Tel, $205 plus 5% GST and 7% PST for telephone services for two months. Invoice total $229.60. Terms: payment on receipt of invoice. Paid by cheque #770.

27

Cash Purchase Invoice #PE-49006   **Dated July 31/18**

From Purolator, $1 400 plus 5% GST for shipping services used from May 25 to July 25. Invoice total $1 470. Terms: payment on receipt of invoice. Paid by cheque #771.

NOTES
Use Quick Add for the new supplier. Include gasoline costs with Travel Expenses. Use tax code G – GST @ 5%. The remaining provincial and federal taxes are not refundable and are already included in the price.

28

Visa Purchase Invoice #PC-34992   **Dated July 31/18**

From Petro-Canada (use Quick Add), $120 plus 5% GST for gasoline for business use. Invoice total $126 paid by Visa.

SESSION DATE — AUGUST 15, 2018

29

Visa Payment: Cheque #772   **Dated Aug. 2/18**

To Visa, $823 in payment of balance shown on Visa account statement for purchases before July 15, 2018.

30

Receipt #128   **Dated Aug. 7/18**

From Music Music Music, cheque #8531 for $2 124.30 USD in payment of account less $65.70 discount for early payment. Reference invoice #597. The exchange rate for August 7 is 1.262. Deposit to Bank: USD account.

31 | **Payment Cheque #773**   **Dated Aug. 8/18**

To Let 'm Know, $1 650 in full payment of account, including $30 discount for early payment. Reference invoice #LK-2303.

32 | **Receipt #129**   **Dated Aug. 9/18**

From Treble & Bass, cheque #1144 for $9 546.40 in payment of account, including $339.60 discount taken for early payment. Reference invoice #596 and deposit #14. Deposit to Bank: Chequing Account.

33 | **Sales Order #25**   **Dated Aug. 9/18**

Shipping date Aug. 22/18
From Total Music, $28 000 plus HST for CDs and $9 000 for books plus 5% GST — items purchased by major music store chains. Shipping charges $200 plus GST. Invoice total $41 300. Terms: 3/30, n/60.

34 |

Maple Leaf Rags

No: 774

2642 Coldstream Avenue
Nanaimo, BC V9T 2X2

Date [2][0][1][8][0][8][1][0]
     Y Y Y Y M M D D

Pay to the order of   Amex $ 100.00

———— One hundred dollars ————   00 /100 **Dollars**

GT **GulfstreamTrust**
3598 Oceans Avenue
Nanaimo, BC V9T 1K1

Jaz Bands

⑆ 029 17643 ⑆ 988652 774

- -

Re: pay Amex bill for June 26-July 25 purchases $100.00 **No: 774**
                                                             Aug. 10, 2018

---

35 | **Receipt #130**   **Dated Aug. 11/18**

From Total Music, cheque #502 for $5 000 as down payment, deposit #15, to confirm sales order #25.

36 | **Purchase Invoice #CA-7998**   **Dated Aug. 12/18**

From Cars for All (use Quick Add for new supplier), $20 000 plus 5% GST and 7% PST for new automobile less $5 000 plus GST and PST as a trade-in allowance on old car. Invoice total $16 800. The entry to write off the old car will be made by the accountant at year-end.

37 | **Purchase Invoice #ABO-8823**   **Dated Aug. 12/18**

From A.B. Original Sounds, to fill purchase order #204, $50 000 plus 5% GST for CD masters. Invoice total $52 500. Terms: 1/10, n/30. (Balance is $42 500.)

SESSION DATE — AUGUST 31, 2018

38 | **Purchase Invoice #SD-9124**   **Dated Aug. 18/18**

From Super Dupers, to fill purchase order #205, $15 000 to duplicate CDs and books plus 5% GST. Invoice total $15 750. Terms: 1/10, n/30. (Balance owing is $11 750.)

⚠️ **WARNING!**
Remember to change the payment method to Pay Later for invoices that fill purchase orders with prepayments.

📄 **NOTES**
When you advance the session date to August 31, an Advisor message informs you that it is time to prepare for year-end. Read and then close the advice statement to proceed.

39
Purchase Invoice #WI-3719   **Dated Aug. 18/18**

From Wrap It, to fill purchase order #206, $6 300 plus 5% GST to prepare CDs for sale. Shipped by Canada Post (#75 553 789 249) for $120 plus 5% GST. Invoice total $6 741. Terms: 1/5, n/30. (Balance owing is $4 741.)

40
Memo #48   **Dated Aug. 20/18**

From J. Bands: Owner invests $50 000 personal capital to finance production of new inventory. Amount deposited to Bank: Savings Account and credited to Common Stock.

41
Sales Invoice #598   **Dated Aug. 21/18**

To Total Music, to fill sales order #25, $28 000 plus HST for CDs and $9 000 plus 5% GST for books. Shipping charges $200 plus GST. Invoice total $41 300. Terms: 3/30, n/60.

42
Payment Cheque #775   **Dated Aug. 21/18**

To A.B. Original Sounds, $42 000 in full payment of account, including $500 discount for early payment. Reference invoice #ABO-8823 and prepayment by cheque #767.

43
Payment Cheque #776   **Dated Aug. 23/18**

To Wrap It, $4 676.80 in full payment of account, including $64.20 discount for early payment. Reference invoice #WI-3719 and prepayment by cheque #769.

44
Payment Cheque #777   **Dated Aug. 23/18**

To Super Dupers, $11 600 in full payment of account, with the $150 discount for early payment. Reference invoice #SD-9124 and prepayment by cheque #768.

45
Memo #49   **Dated Aug. 23/18**

From J. Bands: Transfer $60 000 CAD from Bank: Savings Account to Bank: Chequing Account to cover cheques because the chequing account is overdrawn.

46
Purchase Invoice #JH-0875   **Dated Aug. 25/18**

To J. Henry & Associates (use Quick Add), $1 500 plus $75 GST for legal fees to recover money owed by Entertainment House. Invoice total $1 575. Terms: net 30. Create new Group account 5240 Legal Fees.

47
Visa Purchase Invoice #PC-49986   **Dated Aug. 28/18**

From Petro-Canada, $128 plus 5% GST for gasoline for business use. Invoice total $134.40 paid by Visa.

SESSION DATE — SEPTEMBER 15, 2018

48
Memo #50   **Dated Sep. 2/18**

When his Visa bill arrived, Bands realized that he had entered the purchase from Cars for All as a Pay Later invoice instead of a Visa payment. Adjust invoice #CA-7998 from Cars for All. Change the method of payment to Visa.

49
Visa Payment: Cheque #778   **Dated Sep. 2/18**

To Visa, $16 926 in payment of account for purchases from July 16 to August 15, 2018.

50
Sales Invoice #599   **Dated Sep. 5/18**

To Canadian Sounds, $4 500 USD for CDs and $750 for books. Shipped by Federal Express (#F36FYT863) for $170. Invoice total $5 420 USD. Terms: 3/30, n/60. The exchange rate is 1.268.

51

Maple Leaf Rags

www.mapleleafrags.com

2642 Coldstream Avenue
Nanaimo, BC V9T 2X2
Tel 1: (250) 63M-USIC
Tel 2: (888) 63M-USIC   Fax: (250) 633-4888
GST # 128 488 632

I N V O I C E

Sales Invoice:	#600
Date:	September 10, 2018
Customer:	Music Music Music
Address:	10 Red Rock Canyon
	Sedona, Arizona 86336 USA
Phone No:	(520) 678-4523
Fax No:	
Contact:	M. Porter

Item description	Amount
150 CDs	1 500.00 USD
25 Books	750.00 USD
Freight	140.00 USD
GST	—
PST	—
HST	—
Invoice Total	2 390.00 USD

Shipped by: Federal Express #F49XDT563

Payment: 3/30, n/60
Exchange rate for Sep 10 was 1.281 — *JB*

Sold by: *Jaz Bands*

SESSION DATE — SEPTEMBER 29, 2018

52
Receipt #131   Dated Sep. 18/18
From Total Music, cheque #574 for $35 184 in payment of account including $1 116 discount taken for early payment. Reference invoice #598 and deposit #15. Deposit to Bank: Chequing Account.

53
Cash Purchase Invoice #WT-9810   Dated Sep. 29/18
From Western Tel, $245 plus 5% GST and 7% PST for telephone services for two months. Invoice total $274.40. Terms: payment on receipt of invoice. Paid by cheque #779.

54
Cash Purchase Invoice #PE-62331   Dated Sep. 29/18
From Purolator, $1 200 plus 5% GST for shipping services. Invoice total $1 260. Terms: payment on receipt of invoice. Paid by cheque #780.

55
MasterCard Credit Card Sales Invoice #601   Dated Sep. 29/18
To various Web Store Customers, for sales during previous three months:

CD sales to BC customers	$1 740 plus 5% GST and 7% PST
CD sales to PEI customers	150 plus 14% HST
CD sales to NS customers	280 plus 15% HST
CD sales to other HST customers	2 100 plus 13% HST
CD sales to other GST customers	1 020 plus 5% GST
Book sales	2 800 plus 5% GST
Shipping	650 plus 5% GST

Invoice total $9 508.30. Paid by MasterCard.

NOTES
When you advance the session date to September 29, the Advisor message about the year-end adjustments required should open. Read and then close the advisory statement to proceed.

56

Cash Purchase Invoice #FE-46678   **Dated Sep. 29/18**

From Federal Express, $2 100 plus 5% GST for shipping services. Invoice total
$2 205. Terms: payment on receipt of invoice. Paid by cheque #781.

57

Maple Leaf Rags

www.mapleleafrags.com

2642 Coldstream Avenue
Nanaimo, BC V9T 2X2
Tel 1: (250) 63M-USIC
Tel 2: (888) 63M-USIC   Fax: (250) 633-4888
GST # 128 488 632

Sales Invoice: #602
Date: September 29, 2018

Customer: Web Store Customers
Address:

Phone No:
Fax No:
Contact:

INVOICE

Description	Amount
Sales summary for 3 months	
CDs sold to BC customers (add GST and PST)	1 800.00
CDs sold to PEI customers (add 14% HST)	100.00
CDs sold to NS customers (add 15% HST)	120.00
CDs sold to customers in other HST provinces (add 13% HST)	1 500.00
CDs sold to customers in other GST provinces (add 5% GST)	1 050.00
Books sold in all provinces (add 5% GST)	2 500.00

Freight (add GST)	690.00
GST	302.00
PST	126.00
HST	227.00
Invoice Total	8 415.00

Shipped by: Purolator

Payment: Visa
Direct deposit to Visa bank account *JB*

SESSION DATE — SEPTEMBER 30, 2018

58

Memo #51   **Dated Sep. 30/18**

From J. Bands: Refer to the Sep. 30 General Ledger balance to remit PST Payable
to the Minister of Finance. Reduce the $352.80 payment by $23.28, the sales tax
compensation of 6.6% of the balance owing. Issue cheque #782 for $329.52
from Bank: Chequing Account.

59

Memo #52   **Dated Sep. 30/18**

From J. Bands: Prepare for closing the books by completing adjusting entries for
prepaid expenses and supplies used.
    Office Supplies $ 280
    Prepaid Internet Expenses (3 months)   165
    Prepaid Rent (3 months of 6)   2 400
    Prepaid Advertising (2 months of 5)   663

60

Memo #53   **Dated Sep. 30/18**

From J. Bands: Complete an adjusting entry for goods sold during the quarter.
    CDs $36 500   (Debit Cost of CDs Sold and credit CD Inventory)
    Books $12 600   (Debit Cost of Books Sold and credit Book Inventory)

61

Memo #54   **Dated Sep. 30/18**

From J. Bands: Complete an adjusting entry to transfer $77 116 in completed
inventory. Transfer $68 316 to CD Inventory and $8 800 to Book Inventory. Debit
the inventory asset accounts and credit Materials and Assembly Costs.

| 62 | **Memo #55** | **Dated Sep. 30/18** |

From J. Bands: Received debit memo from Gulfstream Trust regarding pre-authorized withdrawals from Bank: Chequing Account for quarterly interest payments on loans. Complete adjusting entries for quarterly interest paid.

| On bank loan | $ 200 |
| On long term loan | 1 100 |

> **NOTES**
> Bands pays only interest on the loans. Both amounts are deducted from the Bank: Chequing Account.

| 63 | **Memo #56** | **Dated Sep. 30/18** |

From J. Bands: The following transfers of funds were completed:
$15 000 from Bank: Chequing Account to Bank: Savings Account
$12 000 from Bank: Visa to Bank: Savings Account
$12 000 from Bank: MasterCard to Bank: Savings Account

> **NOTES**
> To use the Transfer Funds Journal for the transfer, you must enter the transfer for each account as a separate transaction. To complete the funds transfer entry as a single journal entry, you must use the General Journal.

| 64 | **Memo #57** | **Dated Sep. 30/18** |

From J. Bands: Record Interest Revenue as follows:

| Bank: Savings Account | $200 |
| Bank: Chequing Account | 10 |

Creating an Accountant's Copy

Many businesses rely on professional accountants to assist them with their accounting. The accountants will check the data entered by the business for errors and make corrections. They also may add the adjusting entries required at the end of a fiscal period to bring the books up to date and to prepare for filing tax returns. The business then begins the new year with a complete and accurate data file.

Sage 50 allows a data file to be saved as an Accountant's Copy. This backup data file can only be restored and opened in the Accountant Edition of Sage 50. The accountant makes journal entries in the file that can be added back to the original business data file. The business may continue with day-to-day journal entries and even start a new fiscal period while the accountant is preparing the additional entries.

| ✓ 65 | **Memo #58** | **Dated Sep. 30/18** |

From J. Bands: Create an Accountant's Copy of the data files so the accountant can review the accounting entries and add the final adjustments for depreciation and the trade-in on the automobiles.

You can create an Accountant's Copy from the File menu or from the Company window Accountant's Tasks pane Accountant's Copy icon shortcuts.

Click   **Company** in the Modules pane list to open that module window.

Choose the **File menu**, then **choose Accountant's Copy** and **click Create Accountant's Copy** or **choose Create Accountant's Copy** from the Accountant's Copy icon shortcuts drop-down list:

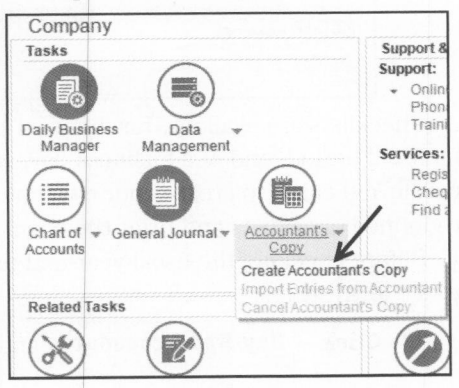

> **PRO VERSION**
> The Pro version File menu does not have the options to Switch To Multi-User Mode or Consolidate Company.

You will be asked to choose a location for the new backup file:

The default name for the file adds Accountant's_Copy_ to the original name so it will not be confused with your other backup files. The default location is a new folder inside the Sage 50 program folder. You must choose a different folder.

> **Click**   **Browse** and **choose** the **folder** you want to use. Enter a different name for the file if you want.

> **Click**   **OK** to begin making the specialized backup.

When the copy is complete, Sage 50 provides a warning:

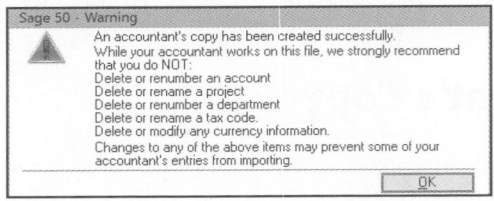

Read this message carefully as it warns what changes you cannot make to your working file while the accountant is working with the Accountant's Copy of your file.

> **Click**   **OK** to return to your data file.

Monitoring Routine Activities

The end of September is the end of Bands' fiscal year. There are a number of steps to complete before beginning the new year. Sage 50 provides assistance with these steps in its checklists.

 Memo #59   **Dated Sep. 30/18**

66 From J. Bands: Review the year-end checklists. Print all reports for the fiscal period ended. Back up the data files. Check data integrity. Advance the session date to October 1, the first day of the next fiscal period.

> **Choose** the **Business Assistant menu** and **click Checklists**:

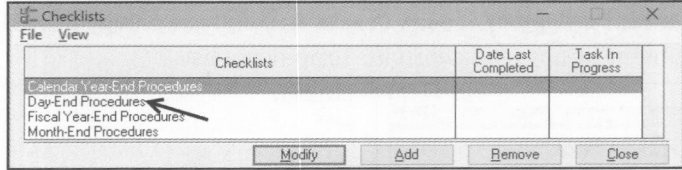

Checklists are available for different periods that are important for a business — end of a fiscal period, end of a business day, end of a month and end of a calendar year for payroll. You can also create your own checklists, add procedures to one of the predefined checklists and print the checklists for reference.

Before checking the fiscal year-end procedures, we will add a reminder to the daily tasks checklist.

> **Click**   **Day-End Procedures** and then **click Modify** to open the list:

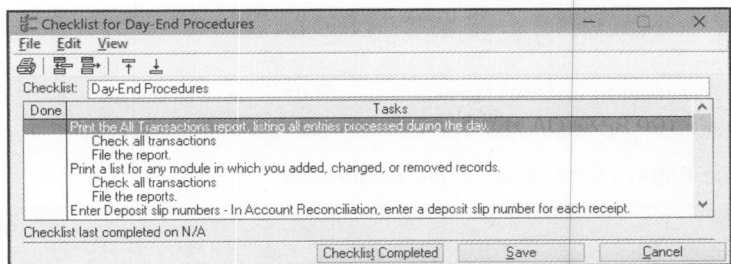

Each checklist can be customized for a company by using the tool buttons or the Edit menu options to insert tasks, delete them or rearrange them.

Click   the **Insert Item tool** or **choose** the **Edit menu** and **click Insert** to add a blank line at the top of the task list.

Press   (tab) to advance to the Tasks field.

Type   `Check bank balances for possible overdrafts`

Click   **Save** to return to the Checklists window.

Double-click **Fiscal Year-End Procedures** for the checklist we need:

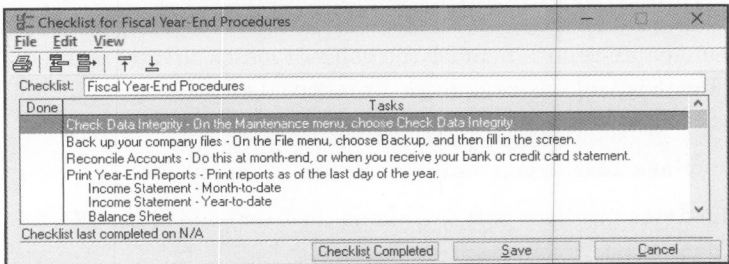

Maple Leaf Rags does not use the budgeting or account reconciliation features of the program, so we can remove these tasks from the checklist.

Scroll down and **click Print Budget Reports**.

Click   the **Remove Item tool** or **choose** the **Edit menu** and **click Remove**.

Click   **Yes** to confirm that you want to continue with the deletion.

Click   the **Print tool** to print the checklist for reference.

Back up the **data files** and **print reports**. These are the most important elements on this list. There are no reports for Payroll, Inventory or Projects. You can remove these reports from the list if you want.

Click   the **Done column** after completing a task — a ✓ will be added to the Done column.

Click Save if you want to leave the list and return later. A ✓ will appear in the Task In Progress column on the Checklists screen.

Complete   all the **tasks** listed, except printing the reports for the modules that are not used. After finishing all the tasks,

Click   **Checklist Completed**. The session date will be added to the Date Last Completed column on the Checklists screen.

Open the remaining checklists to learn which tasks to complete at the end of each month and at the end of a calendar year. Print these lists for reference.

Click   **Close** to leave the Checklists window when you have finished.

Start   the **new fiscal year** on October 1, 2018.

NOTES
You cannot modify (edit) checklists in multi-user mode.

PRO VERSION
pro The Pro version does not include the View menu.

NOTES
Reconciling accounts will be explained in Chapter 15, and budgeting is covered in Chapter 14.

NOTES
In Chapter 15, we describe how to clear data from company files.

NOTES
If you need to check or change your printer settings, you should print from the File menu.

NOTES
Refer to page 101 for assistance with starting a new fiscal period.

Displaying Exchange Rate Reports

When a business has foreign currency transactions, Sage 50 will generate reports related to exchange rate gains and losses.

Open   the **Report Centre** and **click Financials**:

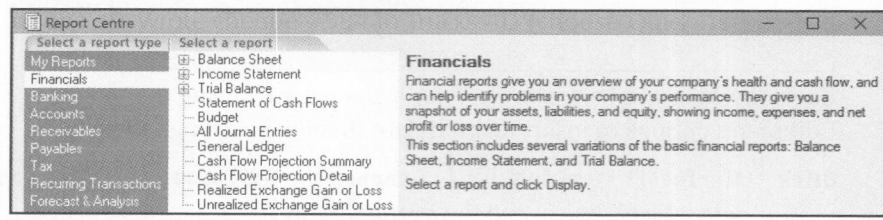

Click   **Realized Exchange Gain Or Loss**.

Click   **Modify This Report**:

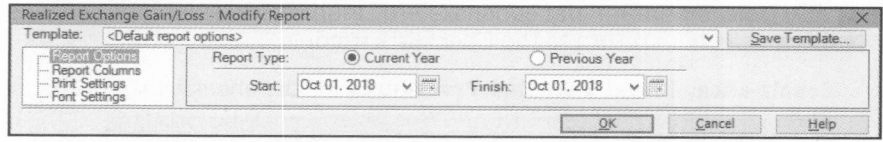

This first exchange rate report includes the gains or losses already realized or recorded because the payment has been made or received and the exchange rate difference is known.

Click   **Previous Year** to generate reports for this application.

Enter   the **dates** for the report (including the year) and **click OK**.

Close   the **display** when finished.

To access the second exchange rate report,

Click   **Unrealized Exchange Gain Or Loss** in the Select A Report list.

Click   **Modify This Report**:

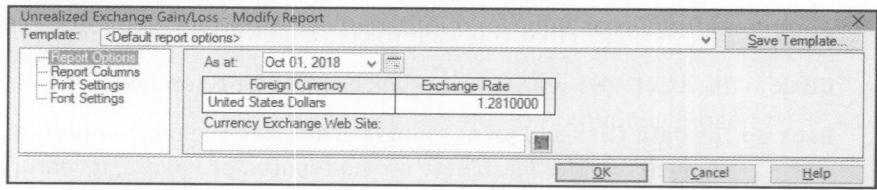

The second report includes the gains or losses that have not yet been realized or recorded — the payment has not been made but the exchange rate is known to have changed since the purchase or sale. When the payment is made or received, the actual gain may be different if the rate has changed again.

The report also revalues existing account balances and previous payments and receipts for the new exchange rate.

Enter   the **date** for the report (including the year) and an **Exchange Rate** for that date. **Click OK**.

Close   the **display** when finished. **Close** the **Report Centre**.

NOTES

From the Home window, choose the Reports menu, then choose Financials and click Realized Exchange Gain/Loss to access the report options.

NOTES

You cannot sort or filter the Exchange Rate reports. You can choose the columns for these reports.

NOTES

From the Home window, choose the Reports menu, then choose Financials and click Unrealized Exchange Gain/Loss to display the report options.

The Accountant Works with Your Data

When the accountant opens the file you sent, it will be restored in the same version of Sage 50 that you used — Pro, Premium and so on. Only the General Journal, the one used for adjusting entries, is available to the accountant. The following two screenshots represent your data file as it will open for the accountant using the special Accountant Edition version of Sage 50. The next two screens will not be available in your own program; we include them for reference only.

The accountant who opens your data file, will have restrictions:

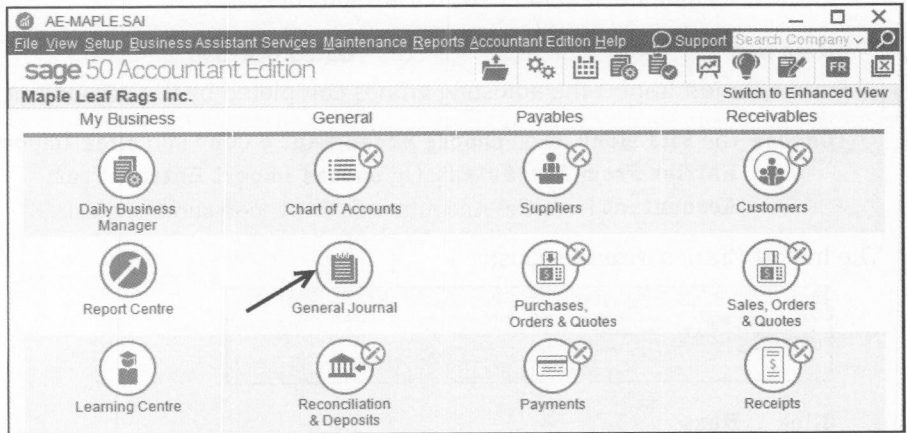

The **No Edit** symbol ⊗ appears with all the ledger and journal icons except for the General Journal. The accountant can view, but not change, the information in the other journals and ledgers.

After adding the required adjustments, the accountant exports the new journal entries to a text file. This option is available from the Accountant Edition menu by choosing Accountant's Copy and then Export Entries For Client:

The exported text file of journal entries is sent back to you, the client.

Importing the Accountant's Journal Entries

Restore the data file **SageData16\ACCOUNTANT\AE-MAPLE1.CAB** for this step.

More menu options are available in the data file now:

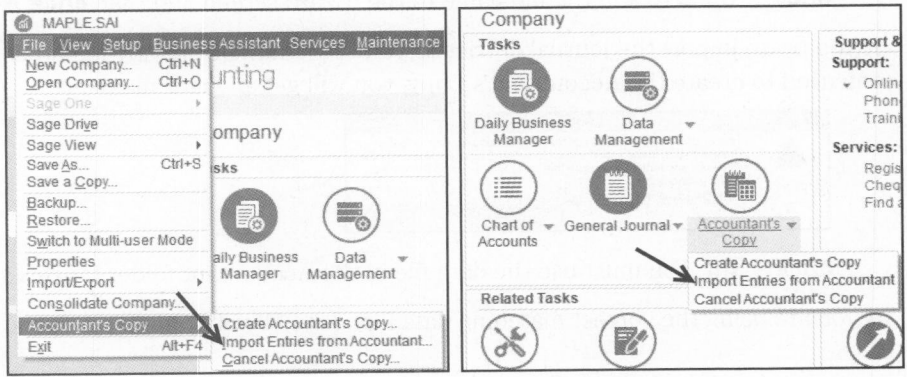

NOTES

The accountant works with a special version of the program — the Accountant Edition. This program must be used to restore the Accountant's Copy backup file you created.

The Accountant Edition allows full access to regular data files created in any version: Pro, Premium and Quantum. The Accountant's Copy data file restricts access to the General Journal in all versions but can access all accounts, including linked accounts not available in the other versions.

NOTES

On the Classic view Home window the restrictions are immediately apparent (the No Edit symbols).

NOTES

Year-end adjusting entries are typically General Journal entries.

WARNING!

Do not use your own data file for this section.

You must use the special file we created for this part of the exercise because it matches the imported entries.

You must use the same file for creating the Accountant's Copy and importing the accountant's entries. You will not be able to import the accountant's entries to your own working file.

Both the File menu options and the shortcuts list for Accountant's Tasks in the Company module window have changed. Once you create an Accountant's Copy, the program stores the information that there is an outstanding Accountant's Copy for the file so you can import journal entries later. This option remains available until the entries have been imported. You cannot create another Accountant's Copy while there is one outstanding. If you discover an error after you create the Accountant's Copy, you can choose **Cancel Accountant's Copy** to cancel that version and then create a new Accountant's Copy. After cancelling, the option to create becomes available again.

When you receive the file from the accountant, you must import the journal entries created by the accountant to add them to your working file.

✓	**Memo #60**	**Dated Oct. 1/18**
67	From J. Bands: Import the adjusting entries completed by the accountant.	

Choose the **File menu**, then **choose Accountant's Copy** and **click Import Entries From Accountant**. Or, **choose Import Entries From Accountant** from the Accountant's Copy icon shortcuts list.

The Import Entries wizard begins:

Click   Next:

You are asked to make a backup before proceeding. Since the step of importing entries cannot be reversed, you should back up the data file first.

Click   Backup and follow the backup wizard steps. **Click Next** to continue:

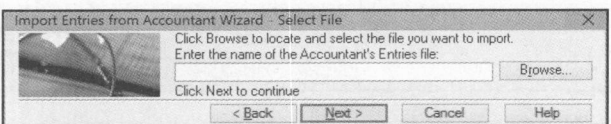

Now you must locate the file the accountant sent. We have added the file you need to the SageData16\ACCOUNTANT folder where the AE-MAPLE backup is stored.

Click   Browse.

Locate   SageData16\ACCOUNTANT\Accountant's_Entries_AE-MAPLE.TXT and **click** to select it.

Click   Open to add the file name to the wizard screen and then **click Next**.

If you try to import the journal entries to your own data file, or any file other than the one used to create the Accountant's Copy, you will get an error message:

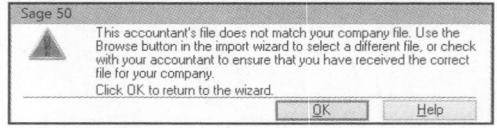

Click   OK. You must use the data file in the Accountant folder for this step.

If you are using the correct matching data file, Sage 50 will require confirmation:

NOTES
The accountant cannot create new accounts in your data file, so we added the account 5600 Loss on Trade-in for the additional data file AE-maple.

NOTES
The procedure for importing entries from the accountant is similar to importing other General Journal entries. Refer to Appendix J.

WARNING!
The file you need to import is Accountant's_Entries_ AE-MAPLE.TXT. It is located in the SageData16\ACCOUNTANT folder.

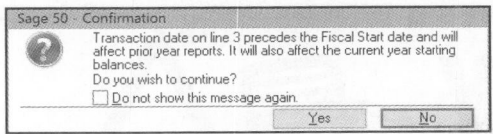

This warning appears because the entries are dated in the previous fiscal year. We want to accept the dates the accountant used because they are correct and the entries should be added to the financial reports for the previous year. We have already changed the settings for this file to allow transactions dated before October 1. Sage 50 still provides this warning whenever you are posting to a previous month. We need to allow all these entries and do not want the message to appear for each separate transaction.

Click   Do Not Show This Message Again.

Click   Yes to display the summary of entries added to your data file:

Click   OK:

Click   Finish. The process is now complete.

The General Journal Report for September 30 will include the accountant's entries:

Maple Leaf Rags Inc.
General Journal 06/30/2018 to 09/30/2018

		Account Number	Account Description	Debits	Credits
09/30/2018	J1***		AE-Deprec, Year-end depreciation adjustments		
		5200	Depreciation Expense	1,520.00	-
			depreciation on furniture & fixtures		
		5200	Depreciation Expense	3,900.00	-
			depreciation on computers		
		5200	Depreciation Expense	4,280.00	-
			depreciation on automobile		
		1480	Accum Deprec: Furn & Equip	-	1,520.00
		1420	Accum Deprec: Computers	-	3,900.00
		1520	Accum Deprec: Automobile	-	4,280.00
09/30/2018	J2***		AE-Adjust Car, Adjustment for disposal of old car		
		1520	Accum Deprec: Automobile	9,800.00	-
			clear prior accum deprec amt		
		1520	Accum Deprec: Automobile	1,050.00	-
			clear current year deprec amt		
		5600	Loss on Trade-in	950.00	-
		1500	Automobile	-	11,800.00
			remove old car from asset (origi...		
*** Imported accountant's entry					

The journal entry numbers are marked *** with a note that they were created outside the regular file by the accountant.

R E V I E W

The Student DVD with Data Files includes Review Questions and Supplementary Cases for this chapter, including a case with stock transactions that can be completed in the General Journal.

NOTES
If your system settings do not allow transactions in the previous year, you must first change this setting. Refer to page 104.

NOTES
For this report, we selected the journal options Previous Year and Include Only Entries Posted After Year End.

NOTES
The journal report has journal entry numbers 1 and 2. The AE-MAPLE file you are using has no other journal entries. It is provided only to demonstrate the step of importing the accountant's entries.
When you import entries to your working file, the journal entry numbers may be out of sequence if you have added transactions while the accountant was working with the file. The numbers will be the ones immediately following the last entry in the file you sent to the accountant.

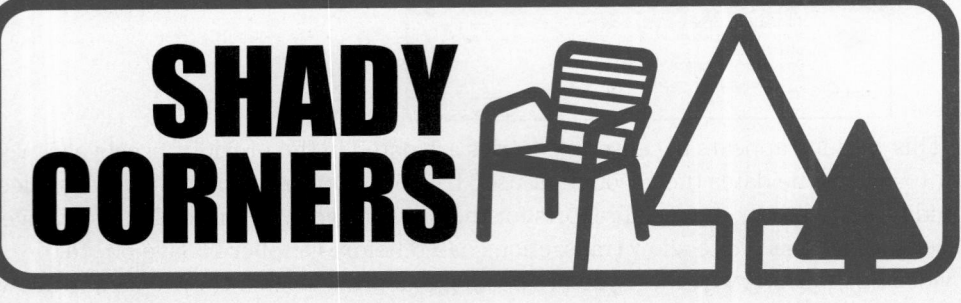

OBJECTIVES

After completing this chapter, you should be able to

- **enter** transactions in all journals
- **create** new divisions
- **change** the Division Ledger name
- **enter** import duty on purchases from foreign suppliers
- **allocate** revenues and expenses in the General, Sales, Purchases, Payroll and Inventory journals
- **make** import duty remittances
- **enter** purchases with cost variances
- **process** regular and pre-authorized credit card sales transactions
- **set up** records for direct payments and pre-authorized debits
- **enter**, **upload** and **review** pre-authorized debits and direct deposits and payments
- **display** and **print** transactions with division details
- **display** and **print** division reports

COMPANY INFORMATION

Company Profile

NOTES
Shady Corners
599 Ivy Lane
Halifax, NS B3J 2N3
Tel 1: (902) 289-3904
Tel 2: (888) 289-3904
Fax: (902) 285-7532
Business No.: 230 192 821

Shady Corners, located in Halifax, Nova Scotia, owned and operated by Julie and Jules Jardin, is a brother-and-sister partnership. Both majored in science at university; Jules went on to complete a master's degree in landscape architecture while Julie earned a business degree.

The store carries a range of shade-tolerant plants and shrubs as well as a variety of high-end garden and patio furniture. Most of the plants are grown locally, many in the nursery Julie and Jules operate as a separate company. The modern-style, moulded plastic, teak and cast aluminum patio furniture pieces are imported from Denmark, while the hammocks and umbrellas are Canadian made.

Most customers are from the local Halifax region and buy for their city or nearby cottage properties. Delivery (shipping or freight) is charged on most orders. In addition, new development projects or office complexes place large

orders for landscaping services, furniture and plants. Charges for services are based on hourly rates. Some homeowners complete their own work and pay only for the designs.

The business has six employees: planting and soil preparation are completed by two gardeners, designs are prepared by another employee and assistant or by Jules, a fifth employee works in and manages the store and the sixth delivers plants and furniture.

Preferred price list customers do not pay for delivery, and they receive discounted inventory prices. All account customers are entitled to a before-tax 2 percent discount if they settle their accounts within 15 days. After 30 days, interest charges accrue at the rate of 1.5 percent per month. Customer deposits from 20 to 25 percent of the total sale are required on all orders. Customers may pay by cheque, cash or credit card.

Some suppliers with whom Shady Corners has accounts require deposits to accompany purchase orders, and some suppliers offer after-tax purchase discounts for early payment. The store has a business credit card account with Visa.

The currency for all foreign transactions is the Danish krone (DKK). Foreign prices for inventory are calculated from the exchange rate at the time of sale, so foreign prices are not entered in the Inventory Ledger. There are currently no foreign customers. Shady Corners pays import duties on the imported wood, plastic and metal furniture items.

Julie Jardin used the following to set up the accounting files in Sage 50:

- Chart of Accounts
- Post-Closing Trial Balance
- Supplier Information
- Customer Information
- Employee Information
- Employee Profiles and TD1 Information
- Inventory Information
- Division Information
- Accounting Procedures

pro PRO VERSION
The term Vendors will be used instead of Suppliers throughout the program.

CHART OF ACCOUNTS

SHADY CORNERS

ASSETS

Current Assets
1050 Bank: Chequing CAD
1060 Bank Account: DKK
1070 Bank: Visa and Interac
1080 Bank: MasterCard
1200 Accounts Receivable
1220 Purchase Prepayments
1230 Advances & Loans
      Receivable
1240 Plant Care Supplies
1260 Office Supplies

Inventory Assets
1340 Books
1360 Plants and Soil
1380 Shrubs
1400 Patio Furniture

Fixed Assets
1650 Cash Register & Computers
1670 Tools & Equipment ▶

▶1680 Store Fixtures
1700 Delivery Vehicles
1720 Store

LIABILITIES

Current Liabilities
2100 Bank Loan
2150 Prepaid Sales and Deposits
2200 Accounts Payable
2220 Import Duty Payable
2250 Credit Card Payable
2300 Vacation Payable
2310 EI Payable
2320 CPP Payable
2330 Income Tax Payable
2400 RRSP Payable
2410 Professional Dues Payable
2420 Union Dues Payable
2460 WCB Payable
2650 GST/HST Charged on Sales
2670 GST/HST Paid on Purchases
          ▶

▶Long Term Liabilities
2850 Mortgage Payable

EQUITY
3560 Jardins, Capital
3580 Jardins, Drawings
3600 Current Earnings

REVENUE
4020 Revenue from Store Sales
4040 Revenue from Services
4100 Revenue from Delivery
4150 Sales Discounts

EXPENSE
Operating Expenses
5060 Assembly Costs
5070 Cost of Goods Sold
5080 Variance Costs
5090 Cost of Services
5100 Freight Expense
5110 Inventory Losses ▶

▶5120 Exchange Rate Differences
5160 Credit Card Fees
5200 Advertising & Promotion
5230 Interest Expenses
5250 Truck Rentals
5260 Garden Supplies Used
5270 Purchase Discounts
5280 Repairs & Maintenance
5290 Utilities Expenses

Payroll Expenses
5450 Vacation Pay Expense
5460 Salaries
5470 General Wages
5480 Piece Rate Wage Expense
5490 Commissions and Bonuses
5500 Tuition Expense
5510 EI Expense
5520 CPP Expense
5530 WCB Expense

NOTES: The Chart of Accounts includes only postable accounts and the Net Income or Current Earnings account.

POST-CLOSING TRIAL BALANCE

SHADY CORNERS

May 31, 2018

		Debits	Credits				Debits	Credits
1050	Bank: Chequing CAD	$ 40 675.00		▶	2100	Bank Loan		$ 40 000.00
1060	Bank Account: DKK (Dkr 21.580,00)	4 100.00			2200	Accounts Payable		4 890.00
1070	Bank: Visa and Interac	6 450.00			2220	Import Duty Payable		320.00
1080	Bank: MasterCard	3 980.00			2250	Credit Card Payable		630.00
1200	Accounts Receivable	4 140.00			2300	Vacation Payable		2 588.40
1240	Plant Care Supplies	3 980.00			2310	EI Payable		960.08
1260	Office Supplies	640.00			2320	CPP Payable		1 733.26
1340	Books	500.00			2330	Income Tax Payable		3 022.01
1360	Plants and Soil	1 648.00			2400	RRSP Payable		550.00
1380	Shrubs	1 370.00			2410	Professional Dues Payable		60.00
1400	Patio Furniture	22 465.00			2420	Union Dues Payable		94.06
1650	Cash Register & Computers	10 800.00			2460	WCB Payable		1 017.72
1670	Tools & Equipment	9 400.00			2650	GST/HST Charged on Sales		11 900.00
1680	Store Fixtures	12 000.00			2670	GST/HST Paid on Purchases	$ 8 700.00	
1700	Delivery Vehicles	43 000.00			2850	Mortgage Payable		160 000.00
1720	Store	230 000.00		▶	3560	Jardins, Capital		184 082.47
					3580	Jardins, Drawings	8 000.00	
							$411 848.00	$411 848.00

SUPPLIER INFORMATION

SHADY CORNERS

Supplier Name (Contact)	Address	Phone No. Fax No.	E-mail Web Site	Terms Tax ID
Bell Canada (I. Hurd)	1234 Listener Rd. Halifax, Nova Scotia B3R 2K8	Tel: (902) 310-2355	bell.ca	n/10
Canadian Agricultural Workers' Union (Membership Office)	Toronto, Ontario	Tel: (416) 699-2019		n/15
Capital Trust				n/1
Home Energy (Serge Powers)	880 Gardenia Blvd. Halifax, Nova Scotia B3J 4B6	Tel: (902) 288-9988	home.energy.com	n/10 557 882 991
Groen Fields (Arjen Groen)	RR #2 Truro, Nova Scotia B2N 5B1	Tel: (902) 454-6111 Fax: (902) 454-6900		n/60
Jorgensen Mobler (J. Jorgensen)	Gronladsvej 7640 7422 Harlev, Denmark	Tel: 011 45 7822 3402 Fax: 011 45 7822 9300	JMobler.dk	2/30, n/60
Mobler Dansk (Karl Nyberg)	Gronlandsdage 48 5000 Odense, Denmark	Tel: 011 45 2887 4334 Fax: 011 45 2887 8201	nyberg@moblerdansk.dk moblerdansk.dk	2/15, n/30
Office Plus	55 Industry Ave. Truro, Nova Scotia B2N 2L1	Tel: (902) 455-7231	officeplus.com	1/15, n/30
Professional Landscapers' Association (Membership Office)	Toronto, Ontario	Tel: (416) 783-4990		n/15
Receiver General for Canada	333 Laurier Avenue West Ottawa, Ontario K1A 0L9	Tel: (613) 238-7125	cra-arc.gc.ca	n/1
Workers' Compensation Board				n/1

OUTSTANDING SUPPLIER INVOICES

SHADY CORNERS

Supplier Name	Terms	Date	Invoice No.	Amount CAD	Amount DKK
Groen Fields	net 60	May 27/18	GF-1142	$ 900	
Jorgensen Mobler	2/30, n/60	April 26/18	JM-842	$2 380	Dkr 12.400,00
Mobler Dansk	2/15, n/30	May 10/18	MD-724	$1 610	Dkr 8.450,00
			Grand Total	$4 890	

CUSTOMER INFORMATION

SHADY CORNERS

Customer Name (Contact)	Address	Phone No. Fax No.	E-mail Web Site	Terms Credit Limit
*Acadian Towers (Jardine LePlante)	88 Maple Ave. Halifax, Nova Scotia B3B 4B4	Tel: (902) 486-7298 Fax: (902) 486-6911	acadiantowers.ca	2/15, n/30 $15 000
*Eastrose Hotel (Janine Bouquet)	455 Rosehill Drive Halifax, Nova Scotia B3T 1N2	Tel 1: (902) 277-8614 Tel 2: (888) 277-8614 Fax: (902) 277-2388	jbouquet@eastrose.com eastrose.com	2/15, n/30 $15 000
*Hopewell College (Holly Greene)	4500 Spruce Ave. Halifax, Nova Scotia B3F 7G9	Tel 1: (902) 782-5611 Tel 2: (902) 775-8014	h.greene@hopewell.edu hopewell.edu	2/15, n/30 $15 000
Rockcliff Manor (Aidel Weiss)	400 Rocky Ridge Rise Halifax, Nova Scotia B3B 5V8	Tel 1: (902) 972-7181 Tel 2: (902) 972-3939	aidel.weiss@gmail.com	2/15, n/30 $8 000

NOTES: Preferred price list customers are marked with an asterisk (*) beside their names. All discounts are after tax.

OUTSTANDING CUSTOMER INVOICES

SHADY CORNERS

Customer Name	Terms	Date	Invoice No.	Amount	Tax	Total
Acadian Towers	2/15, n/30	May 24/18	155	$1 200	$180	$1 380
Hopewell College	2/15, n/30	May 26/18	159	$1 500	$225	$1 725
Rockcliff Manor	2/15, n/30	May 29/18	163	$ 900	$135	$1 035
				Grand Total		$4 140

Employee Profiles and TD1 Information

General Information   All employees are allowed 10 days per year for illness and five for personal reasons. All employees have their paycheques deposited directly into their bank accounts. Eligible tuition fees are partially reimbursed on successful completion of courses. All payroll remittances are due at the end of each month.

Three employees (Anthemum, Pine and Iola) receive a commission in addition to their regular pay, and three employees (Phlox, Aster and Fineum) receive a piece rate bonus based on the number of plantings they complete. Phlox, Aster and Fineum are union members and pay union dues; Anthemum and Pine pay professional association fees. The 6 percent vacation pay for hourly paid workers is retained.

Chris Anthemum is the senior landscape designer at Shady Corners. Her salary of $3 900 per month is supplemented by a commission of 2 percent of all revenue from services. She is paid at the end of each month and is allowed four weeks of vacation with pay. Anthemum is married with one eligible child under 12 and claims the basic, spousal and child (federal only) tax claim amounts. She has $200 deducted from each paycheque to invest in her RRSP and pays professional association dues.

Lou Pine is the assistant designer who helps Anthemum with all her design work and also manages the accounting records for the business. He is paid a monthly salary of $3 400 plus a commission of 1 percent of service revenue and is allowed three weeks of vacation with pay. He has only the basic tax claim amount because he is single and self-supporting. He invests $100 of each paycheque in his RRSP and also pays monthly professional association fees.

Glad Iola works in the store as the salesperson for an hourly rate of $22 (plus $33 per overtime hour and a commission on store sales). She is single and pays $50 from each paycheque toward the purchase of RRSP investments from her bi-weekly pay.

Rose Aster also invests in her RRSP through payroll deductions and pays union dues. She works as the gardener, planting shrubs and other plants for customers and assisting in the store for the hourly rate of $20 and $30 per overtime hour plus the piece rate bonus. As a recent graduate, she has tuition and education amounts to increase her basic single tax claim amount and is reimbursed for her tuition at the rate of $100 per bi-weekly pay.

Dell Fineum also does gardening work and assists in the store for the hourly rate of $20 ($30 per overtime hour) plus the piece rate bonus for planting. He is single so has the basic claim amounts. Dell has deductions for his RRSP and for his union dues from his bi-weekly pay.

Daisy Phlox is married, so she has the basic and spousal tax claim amounts. She does not invest in her RRSP through payroll but does have deductions for union dues from her bi-weekly salary of $1 650. Instead of vacation pay, Phlox takes three weeks of vacation each year. Her primary responsibility is delivery, but she also assists with gardening on job sites and is allowed the piece rate bonus for this work.

NOTES

Iola's commission is calculated at the rate of about 0.5 percent of sales revenue. We provide commission amounts for Iola in the source documents. This amount is included for the calculation of vacation pay because her commission is based on performance.

Salaried employees do not receive vacation pay on commissions because their vacation rate is 0 percent.

EMPLOYEE INFORMATION SHEET

SHADY CORNERS

	Chris Anthemum	Lou Pine	Glad Iola	Rose Aster	Dell Fineum	Daisy Phlox
Position	Designer	Asst Designer	Sales	Gardener	Gardener	Delivery
Social Insurance No.	618 524 664	821 887 114	398 577 619	572 351 559	404 535 601	464 375 286
Address	98 Arbutus Ave. Halifax, Nova Scotia B3J 2A5	44 Lilac Lane Halifax, Nova Scotia B3C 3E5	36 Locust Ave. Halifax, Nova Scotia B3V 4S3	8 Magnolia Cres. Halifax, Nova Scotia B3J 1Y7	18 Forsythia Cres. Halifax, Nova Scotia B3G 4K1	59 Cherry Rd. Halifax, Nova Scotia B3Z 3X3
Telephone	(902) 641-6773	(902) 648-1916	(902) 784-7195	(902) 738-5188	(902) 788-2826	(902) 645-6238
Date of Birth (mm-dd-yy)	05-28-81	08-08-83	05-21-85	02-03-86	08-19-87	09-28-74
Federal (Ontario) Tax Exemption - TD1						
Basic Personal	$11 474 (8 481)	$11 474 (8 481)	$11 474 (8 481)	$11 474 (8 481)	$11 474 (8 481)	$11 474 (8 481)
Other Indexed	$13 595 (8 481)	–	–	–	–	$11 474 (8 481)
Other Non-indexed	–	–	–	$10 930 (8 810)	–	–
Total Exemptions	$25 069 (16 962)	$11 474 (8 481)	$11 474 (8 481)	$22 404 (17 291)	$11 474 (8 481)	$22 948 (16 962)

▶

EMPLOYEE INFORMATION SHEET CONTINUED

SHADY CORNERS

	Chris Anthemum	Lou Pine	Glad Iola	Rose Aster	Dell Fineum	Daisy Phlox
Employee Earnings						
Regular Wage Rate	–	–	$22.00	$20.00	$20.00	–
Overtime Wage Rate	–	–	$33.00	$30.00	$30.00	–
Regular Salary	$3 900/mo	$3 400/mo	–	–	–	$1 650/2 weeks
Pay Period	monthly	monthly	bi-weekly	bi-weekly	bi-weekly	bi-weekly
Hours per Period	150	150	75	75	75	75
Piece Rate	–	–	–	$0.50/shrub	$0.50/shrub	$0.50/shrub
Tuition	–	–	–	$100	–	–
Commission	2% (services)	1% (services)	based on sales	–	–	–
Vacation	4 weeks	3 weeks	6% retained	6% retained	6% retained	3 weeks
Vacation Pay Owed	–	–	$942.40	$818.50	$827.50	–
WCB Rate	4.93	4.93	2.48	4.93	4.93	6.72
Employee Deductions						
RRSP	$200	$100	$50	$50	$25	–
Professional Dues	$30	$30	–	–	–	–
Union Dues	–	–	–	0.78%	0.78%	1.2%
EI, CPP & Income Tax	Calculations built into Sage 50 program.					

INVENTORY INFORMATION

SHADY CORNERS

Code	Description	Unit	Min Qty	Selling Price Reg	(Pref)	Qty on Hand	Total (Cost)	Taxes Rate	Duty
Books: Total asset value $500 (Linked accounts: Asset 1340; Revenue 4020; COGS 5070; Variance 5080)									
BK01	Gardening in the Shade	book	10	$45	$38	20	$500	GST	n/a
Plants and Ground Covers: Total asset value $1 648 (Linked accounts: Asset 1360; Revenue 4020; COGS 5070; Variance 5080)									
PL01	Plant/ground cover: 5 litre	each	8	18	16	24	240	HST	n/a
PL02	Plant/ground cover: 10 litre	each	8	29	25	24	384	HST	n/a
PL03	Plant/ground cover starters	4-pack	8	8	6	40	160	HST	n/a
PL04	Plant: perennial specialty	each	6	49	42	16	400	HST	n/a
PL05	Plant: annual 10 cm	each	8	9	8	24	120	HST	n/a
PL06	Plant: annual 15 cm	each	6	16	13	24	216	HST	n/a
PS10	Topsoil: 50 litre bag	bag	20	6	4.50	32	128	HST	n/a
PS11	Topsoil: cubic metre	cu m	0	125	105	0	0	HST	n/a
Shrubs: Total asset value $1 370 (Linked accounts: Asset 1380; Revenue 4020; COGS 5070; Variance 5080)									
SH01	Shrubs: 50 cm	each	10	13	11	30	$180	HST	n/a
SH02	Shrubs: 1 metre	each	8	29	25	20	320	HST	n/a
SH03	Shrubs: 3 metre	each	6	55	48	10	320	HST	n/a
SH04	Shrubs: 1 metre specialty	each	6	89	80	10	550	HST	n/a
Patio & Garden Furniture: Total asset value $22 465 (Linked accounts: Asset 1400; Revenue 4020; COGS 5060; Variance 5070)									
FA01	Patio set: Cast Aluminum round table 1.5 m	7-pc set	1	1 340	1 090	2	$1 400	HST	8.0%
FA02	Patio set: Cast Aluminum rect. table 2 m	7-pc set	1	1 340	1 150	2	1 400	HST	8.0%
FA03	Patio table: Cast Aluminum round 2 m	each	1	795	690	4	1 600	HST	8.0%
FA04	Arm chair: Cast Aluminum	each	4	95	85	12	660	HST	8.0%
FA05	Ottoman: Cast Aluminum	each	2	55	50	5	125	HST	8.0%
FA06	End table: Cast Aluminum	each	2	105	95	5	300	HST	8.0%
FA07	Bench: Cast Aluminum	each	2	245	185	4	640	HST	8.0%

▶

INVENTORY INFORMATION CONTINUED

SHADY CORNERS

Code	Description	Unit	Min Qty	Selling Price Reg	(Pref)	Qty on Hand	Total (Cost)	Taxes Rate	Duty
FP21	Patio table: Moulded Plastic 2 m	each	2	590	535	4	$ 1 240	HST	9.5%
FP22	Arm chair: Moulded Plastic	each	8	75	65	10	410	HST	9.5%
FP23	Folding chair: Moulded Plastic	each	12	55	48	10	300	HST	9.5%
FP24	Chaise longue: Moulded Plastic	each	3	165	140	4	360	HST	9.5%
FT31	Patio table: Teak round 1.5 m	each	2	925	750	2	1 040	HST	9.5%
FT32	Patio table: Teak rect. 2 m	each	2	1 180	950	2	1 160	HST	9.5%
FT33	Arm chair: Teak	each	8	725	615	8	3 040	HST	9.5%
FT34	Chaise longue: Teak	each	2	980	810	4	1 960	HST	9.5%
FT35	End table: Teak	each	2	245	210	5	700	HST	9.5%
FT36	Ottoman: Teak	each	4	105	95	4	220	HST	9.5%
FT37	Bench: Teak	each	2	1 125	980	4	2 320	HST	9.5%
FX41	Hammock w/stand	each	3	175	155	8	760	HST	n/a
FX42	Umbrella w/stand	each	6	225	200	10	1 100	HST	n/a
FX43	Cushion: deep seating chair	each	12	45	40	30	600	HST	n/a
FX44	Cushion: deep seating lounge	each	4	105	95	8	480	HST	n/a
FX45	Cushion: deep seating set	5-pc set	3	245	205	5	650	HST	n/a
Total Inventory Value							$25 983		

Services: (Linked Revenue account: 4040; COGS account: 5090)

SC01	Consultation/Design	hour		110	90			HST	
SC02	Report	report		200	160			HST	
SC03	Planting & Soil Preparation	hour		50	40			HST	

Division Information

Shady Corners uses three divisions — one for store sales, one for planting work and one for design work. Pine will set up these divisions at the beginning of June and keep track of the percentage of time each employee works in each division. Because these times vary from one job to another, the percentage allocation is included with each source document. Allocation details for other expenses and revenues are also included with the source documents. Amounts for asset, liability and equity accounts are not allocated.

Accounting Procedures

Taxes: HST

Shady Corners pays 15 percent HST on all goods and services that it buys, including the imported products, and charges HST on the sales and services it provides, except for books. It uses the regular method for remittance of the Harmonized Sales Tax. HST collected from customers is recorded as a liability in *GST/HST Charged on Sales*. HST paid to suppliers is recorded in *GST/HST Paid on Purchases* as a decrease in liability to the Canada Revenue Agency. The report is filed with the Receiver General for Canada by the last day of the month for the previous quarter, either including the balance owing or requesting a refund.

Some items, such as books, are exempt from HST and have only GST at the rate of 5 percent charged. A separate tax code has been created for this tax rate.

In Nova Scotia, PST is harmonized with GST. The provincial portion of HST is 10 percent.

NOTES
When PST only is charged — as for insurance — it is included with the expense or asset part of the journal entry because it is not refundable.

NSF Cheques

When a bank returns a customer's cheque because there were insufficient funds in the customer's bank account to cover the cheque, the payment must be reversed. If the payment was processed through the Receipts Journal, the reversal should also be processed through the Receipts Journal (refer to page 175). If the sale was a cash sale to a one-time customer, the reversal must be processed through the Sales Journal. Create a customer record and process a credit (Pay Later) sale for the full amount of the NSF cheque without tax (taxes for the sale were recorded at the time of the original sale). Enter the amount as a **positive** amount in the Amount field and enter *Bank: Chequing CAD* in the Account field. On a separate invoice line, enter the amount of the handling charge for the NSF cheque in the Amount field with *Other Revenue* in the Account field. Again, the handling charge is non-taxable.

Returns

When customers return merchandise, they are charged a 20 percent handling charge unless the merchandise is defective. In the Sales Journal, enter the quantity returned with a **minus** sign at the regular sale price, add the tax code and enter *Sales Returns & Allowances* in the Account field. The amounts will automatically be negative because of the minus sign in the quantity field, so *Accounts Receivable* will be credited automatically as well. On a separate invoice line, enter the amount withheld — the handling charge — as a positive amount and credit *Other Revenue*. *Accounts Receivable* will be debited automatically for the amount of the handling charge.

If the original sale was a credit sale and the account is not yet paid, the return should also be entered as a credit sale so that *Accounts Receivable* will be credited. If the original sale was paid in cash or by credit card or the account has been paid, the return should be entered as a cash sale or credit card sale so that the appropriate bank account will be credited. (Refer to page 380.)

Reserved Inventory for Divisions

When customers sign a contract, the inventory items needed to complete the work are set aside or reserved by transferring them through the Item Assembly Journal to a designated account. (Refer to page 374.) In this way, these items cannot be sold to other customers because the inventory quantities available are already reduced. The minimum stock level for reserved inventory will be zero.

Cash, Credit and Debit Card, and Pre-Authorized Debit (PAD) Sales

Most types of businesses accept these different methods of payment. The program handles these transactions automatically through the Sales Journal when you choose the appropriate method of payment. For cash and debit and credit card sales, if this is not a regular customer, choose One-Time Customer from the Customer list, or type the new customer's name and choose Continue or Quick Add. For payments by cheque, a Cheque Number field opens. Shady Corners accepts Visa, MasterCard and Interac debit cards from customers for store sales. Instructions for setting up and processing credit card sales, pre-authorized credit card sales and pre-authorized debits are provided in this chapter (refer to pages 514–524).

The program will debit the related bank account instead of the *Accounts Receivable* control account and all other accounts will be appropriately debited or credited.

Cash Purchases and Direct Payments

Choose the supplier from the Supplier list or add the supplier using Quick Add and then choose the correct method of payment. Cash purchases may be entered in the

NOTES The Sales Journal entry will credit Bank: Chequing CAD for the full amount of the sale including taxes and debit Accounts Receivable for the customer.

NOTES If you created a customer record by using Quick Add or used an existing record (e.g., Cash Customers), you can adjust the sales invoice by changing the method of payment from Cheque to Pay Later. You cannot choose Pay Later as the payment method for one-time customers.

NOTES If the refund is paid in cash, choose Cash as the payment method instead of Pay Later.

NOTES We use the term Cash Sales and Purchases for cash and cheque transactions.
When you choose Continue, the name is added to the journal report without creating a customer record.

PRO VERSION

pro Remember that the term Vendors replaces the term Suppliers.

NOTES

After completing the entry as usual in Sage 50, the payments are uploaded and the funds transferred through an account with a third-party supplier.

NOTES

To preview, print or e-mail invoices, you must have the correct forms selected for invoices in the Reports & Forms Settings. You can access these settings from the journal tool bar.

NOTES

The transactions in this exercise provide a comprehensive practice set. If you want to use it only for review, you can complete the transactions without setting up divisions and entering allocations.

Payments Journal as Other Payments or in the Purchases Journal. For cheque payments, a Cheque Number field opens with the next cheque number entered. Complete the remainder of the cash transaction in the same way you would enter other transactions. Instructions for setting up direct payments are provided (refer to page 528).

The program will credit *Bank: Chequing CAD* instead of *Accounts Payable*, the control account. All other accounts for the transaction will be appropriately debited or credited.

Electronic Funds Transfers (EFT)

Pre-authorized debits, direct payments and direct deposits use electronic transfers. Money is taken directly from the customer bank account and deposited to the business bank account, or taken from the business bank account and deposited to supplier and employee bank accounts. Shady Corners has an account set up with a third-party supplier to upload these bank account transfers from the program.

Freight Expense

When a business purchases inventory items, the cost of any freight that cannot be directly allocated to a specific item must be charged to *Freight Expense*. This amount will be regarded as an expense rather than charged to an inventory asset account.

Printing Invoices, Orders and Quotes

To print the invoices, purchase orders or sales quotes through the program, complete the journal transaction as you would otherwise. Before posting the transaction, preview the invoice. If the invoice is correct, you can print it from the preview window or directly from the invoice by choosing the File menu and then Print or by clicking the Print tool on the tool bar for the invoice form. Printing will begin immediately, so be sure you have the correct forms for your printer before you begin. If you and the customer or supplier have e-mail, click the E-mail tool to send the invoice or order.

Foreign Purchases

Shady Corners imports some inventory items from companies in Denmark. The currency for these transactions is the Danish krone (DKK) and the currency symbol is Dkr. Amounts in kroner are written as Dkr 10.500,50 (ten thousand, five hundred Danish kroner and fifty cents) — the period (.) separates the thousands and the comma (,) is the decimal point separator.

Shady Corners pays HST and import duties on these purchases. Duty rates are set up in the Inventory Ledger for the individual items and the amounts are calculated automatically by the program.

INSTRUCTIONS

1. **Record entries** for the source documents for June 2018 in Sage 50 using the Chart of Accounts, Trial Balance and other information. The procedures for entering each new type of transaction are outlined step by step in the Keystrokes section with the source documents.

2. **Print** the **reports** indicated on the following printing form after you have finished making your entries:

REPORTS

Accounts
- [ ] Chart of Accounts
- [ ] Account List
- [ ] General Journal Entries

Financials
- [✓] Comparative Balance Sheet: June 1 and June 30, difference in percentage
- [✓] Income Statement from June 1 to June 30
- [✓] Trial Balance date: June 30
- [✓] All Journal Entries: June 1 to June 30 with division allocations, foreign amounts and corrections
- [✓] General Ledger accounts: 1400 4020 4040 from June 1 to June 30
- [ ] Statement of Cash Flows
- [✓] Cash Flow Projection Detail Report for account 1050 for 30 days
- [✓] Gross Margin Income Statement from June 1 to June 30

Tax
- [✓] Report on HST from June 1 to June 30

Banking
- [ ] Cheque Log Report

Payables
- [ ] Supplier List
- [ ] Supplier Aged
- [ ] Aged Overdue Payables
- [ ] Purchases Journal Entries
- [ ] Payments Journal Entries
- [ ] Supplier Purchases

Receivables
- [ ] Customer List
- [ ] Customer Aged
- [ ] Aged Overdue Receivables
- [ ] Sales Journal Entries
- [ ] Receipts Journal Entries
- [ ] Customer Sales
- [ ] Sales by Salesperson
- [ ] Customer Statements

Payroll
- [ ] Employee List
- [✓] Employee Summary for all employees
- [ ] Deductions & Expenses
- [ ] Remittance
- [ ] Payroll Journal Entries
- [✓] T4 Slips for all employees

- [ ] Record of Employment
- [✓] Year End Review (PIER)

Inventory & Services
- [ ] Inventory & Services List
- [ ] Inventory Summary
- [ ] Inventory Quantity
- [ ] Inventory Statistics
- [✓] Inventory Sales Summary for Plants and Soil from June 1 to June 30
- [✓] Inventory Transaction Summary for Shrubs, all journals from June 1 to June 30
- [ ] Item Assembly Journal Entries
- [ ] Adjustment Journal Entries
- [ ] Inventory Price Lists

Division
- [ ] Division List
- [✓] Division Income Summary: all divisions, all accounts from June 1 to June 30
- [ ] Division Allocation Report

Mailing Labels
- [ ] Labels

KEYSTROKES

Creating New Divisions

Sage 50 allows allocations for all accounts. Each account ledger record has a check box to allow division allocations for the account (refer to page 91). If this box is checked, the allocation option is available for that account in any journal entry. If it is not checked, you cannot allocate an amount for that account. If you are unable to allocate an amount, check the ledger record for the account you are using to be sure that the option to **Allow Division Allocations** is selected. Shady Corners will allocate amounts for all revenue and expense accounts. This is the default setting for new income statement accounts. The option to allow allocations is already turned on for all these accounts in your data file.

Open   SageData16\SHADE\SHADE. **Enter June 7, 2018** as the session date.

Click   **OK** to enter the session date. The Receivables Home window appears.

Before entering any transactions with allocations, you should create the divisions as instructed in memo #1.

> [✓ 1] Based on memo #1 from Owner on June 1, create three new divisions: Store Sales, Planting and Design. All divisions begin June 1, 2018, and are active. Allocations will be made by percentage.

NOTES
If you are working with backups, you should restore SageData16\SHADE1.CAB or SHADE1 to SageData16\SHADE\SHADE.

PRO VERSION
pro The ledger record option is to Allow Project Allocations.

NOTES
For Shady Corners, the option to allow allocations is not selected in the ledger records for Balance Sheet accounts.

NOTES
We have used a straight text format for source documents in this chapter.

Divisions ▾

Click   **Divisions** in the Modules pane list to change the Home window:

Click   **Make Default** to keep this as the Home window.

The Divisions module window has access to the Divisions Ledger records, as well as to four journals that most often have allocated amounts. Divisions are created from the Divisions icon that opens the Division window. The Division window can also be accessed from the Company, Receivables, Payables and Employees & Payroll modules:

These four modules include the Divisions icon in the Tasks panes. These modules have journals that use allocations.

Click   the **Divisions icon** to open the Division window:

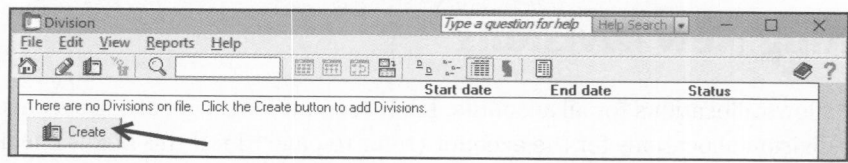

Click   **Create** to open a new Division Ledger screen:

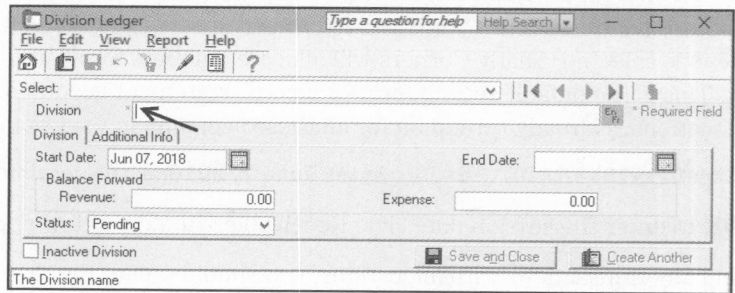

The cursor is in the Division name field, the only required field for the new record. You must enter the name of the first division.

Type   Store Sales   **Press** (tab) **twice** to skip the language button.

The cursor moves to the Start Date field. Enter the date on which you want to begin recording division information, June 1, 2018, to replace the default session date.

Type   6-01

You can enter an **Ending Date** for the division if this is appropriate. The ledger also has a **Balance Forward** field for **Revenue** and **Expense**. These fields can be used to enter historical information — the amount of revenue and expense generated by the division before the records were converted to Sage 50 or before the Division Ledger was used. The balances are zero for Shady Corners because a new fiscal period is beginning.

In the next field you must choose the Status for the division.

Click   the **Status field** or its list arrow for the status options:

The division may be Pending (not yet started), In Progress or ongoing, Cancelled or Completed. All divisions at Shady Corners are In Progress or active.

Click   **In Progress** from the Status drop-down list.

Click   Create Another to save the new division.

Create   the **Planting** division and the **Design** division using the steps described above for Store Sales; **use June 1, 2018** as the starting date and **select In Progress** as the Status.

Click   Save and Close to save the third division.

You will return to the Division window. Sage 50 has created a listing for each division including the name, starting and ending dates and status.

Close   the **Division window** to return to the module window. The **three** divisions are added to the Divisions pane in the module window.

Changing Division Settings

Click   the **Settings icon** ⚒ to display the Settings window:

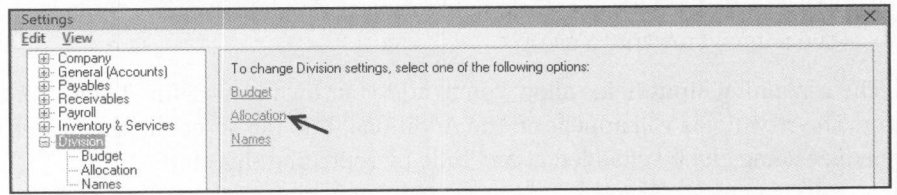

Or, choose the Setup menu, then choose Settings. If the Divisions module window is open, the Division Settings screen should open directly.

The Division Ledger has settings for budgeting, allocation and names. Budgeting is covered in Chapter 14. We need to view the settings for allocations.

Click   **Allocation** either in the list under Division or in the list on the right:

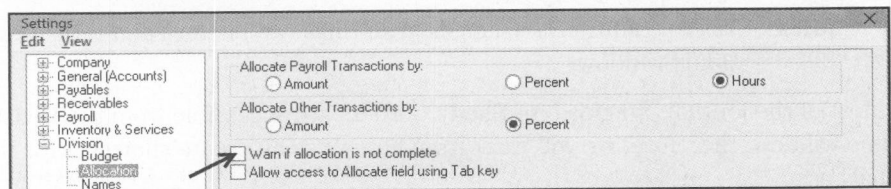

You can enter the allocation in different ways — by Amount, by Percent or by Hours (payroll only). The option to Allocate By Amount requires you to enter the exact dollar

NOTES
Project Ending Dates might be used for construction or other projects that have an expected or definite term.

NOTES
You can list divisions by icon in the Divisions window by choosing the View menu and icon.
You can re-sort the division icons if they are out of order by choosing the View menu and Re-sort Icons.

Classic **CLASSIC VIEW**
Right-click the Divisions icon

and click the Settings tool. If the Divisions icon is not selected, choose Division from the Select Setup drop-down list and click Select.

PRO VERSION
pro Project will replace Division in the list of modules.

NOTES
You cannot change Division settings in multi-user mode.

amount for each division. Division work for payroll purposes is often recorded by time worked for the division, the default option for payroll allocations.

Sage 50 includes a warning for incomplete allocations. It is easy to miss an allocation because you must complete the allocation procedure even if 100 percent of the costs are allocated to a single division, and you must allocate each account line in the journals. You can choose to be warned if you try to post an entry that has not been fully allocated. If you are using divisions, you should always leave the warning turned on.

Click   Percent as the method of allocating payroll amounts.

Click   Warn If Allocation Is Not Complete.

You can also choose to access Allocate fields in journals with the (tab) key. Without this option, you must click the Divisions field to access it or click the Allocate tool to open the Allocation window. Using the (tab) key allows you to use the keyboard to enter the transaction and allocation. You can still click the field to move the cursor if you want.

Click   Allow Access To Allocate Field Using Tab Key.

Changing Division Names

In any version, you can change the name of the ledger to Project, Department, Profit Centre, Cost Centre or something that is more appropriate for a business. The new name will replace Division in all windows and reports. Division is an appropriate ledger name for Shady Corners.

Pro version users should change the name from Project to Division.

Click   Names under the Division heading:

Double-click the Project Title field to select the default name. Type Division (or the name you want to use).

The remaining input fields allow you to add your own user-defined fields for the ledger. The new fields will appear on the Additional Info tab screen in the ledger record. The ledger name can be changed at any time by repeating this step.

Click   OK to save the Division settings and display a confirmation message:

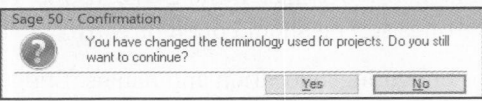

When you change the name, you must confirm that you want the name changed — all labels for the ledger icons, field names and report names will be changed.

Click   Yes to confirm the changes in settings (and name) and return to the Home window.

Most of the journals we need for Shady Corners are accessible from the Divisions module window; therefore, we will work from here. We can create shortcuts for the other journals used.

NOTES
If you are not using the allocation feature, do not select the option to Allow Access To Allocate Field Using Tab Key so that the cursor will skip the unused Divisions column.

PRO VERSION
These steps are included so that Pro version users will have the same names as the Premium version users.

NOTES
We are not renaming Divisions as Departments because Sage 50 has a departmental accounting feature that is different from division allocation (refer to Chapter 19).

NOTES
Once the project is renamed by changing the Names setting, the new name will apply for all industry types. You must change the name on the Settings screen again if you want to use a different term.

Create **shortcuts** for **Pay Purchase Invoices** (Payables), **Create Receipt** (Receivables), **Transfer Funds** and **View Accounts** (Banking), **Item Assembly** and **Inventory Adjustments** (Inventory & Services) and **Payroll Cheque Run** (Employees & Payroll).

Entering Cost Allocations

Costs (or expenses) and revenues are allocated after the regular journal details are added but before the entry is posted. In a journal entry, whenever you use an account for which you have allowed division allocations in the General Ledger, the allocation option is available. For Shady Corners, all revenue and expense accounts allow division allocations.

Click   the **Purchase Invoices icon** [Purchase Invoices] to open the Purchases Journal and prepare for entering the first transaction.

> ☑ 2
>
> On June 1, received invoice #HE-4441 for store heat and hydro from Home Energy for $280 plus $42 HST for a total of $322. Terms: net 10 days. Charged 70% of the expenses to Store Sales, 20% to Planting and 10% to Design. The store is on an equal billing plan, so store this as a monthly recurring entry.

The journal has not changed with the setup of allocations, and we enter the purchase details the same way.

The first transaction does not involve the purchase of inventory items, so you will not use the inventory database to complete this transaction. Invoice is correct as the transaction type, and Pay Later is the correct payment method.

From the list of suppliers,

Click   **Home Energy**.

Click   the **Invoice No. field**. **Type** HE-4441

Type jun 1 in the Date field to replace the default session date.

The tax code H and the account number 5290 should be added as the default. If they are not, you can add them or edit them as needed.

Enter   a **description**.

Click   the **Amount field** or press ⟨tab⟩ repeatedly to advance the cursor.

Type 280

Press   ⟨tab⟩ **twice** to enter the amount of the invoice and the tax amounts and advance to the Divisions column.

The journal still looks like a regular completed purchase transaction:

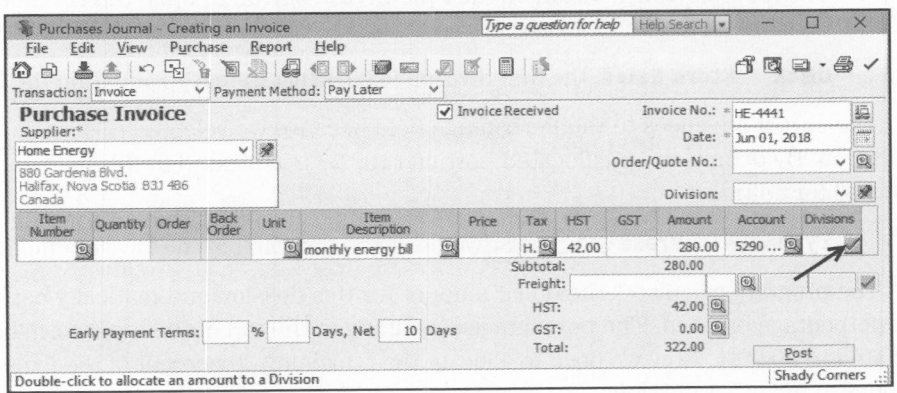

NOTES
All transactions can be completed from these shortcuts and journal windows. For example, other payments and payroll remittances are completed from the Payments Journal. Orders and Quotes are entered from the Sales Invoices or Purchase Invoices windows by selecting from the transactions drop-down list in the journal.
Alternatively, you can change module windows.

NOTES
You can allow allocations for Balance Sheet accounts, but we have not done so for Shady Corners.

To access the Division Allocation window, the cursor must be on an invoice line with an account that allows allocation. If the account does not allow allocation or if the cursor has advanced to an invoice line without an account, the Allocate tool and menu option will be unavailable.

Click the invoice line for the amount you want to allocate to activate the Allocate option. Only accounts for which you have selected the option to Allow Division Allocations will activate the Allocate tool.

Click   the **Allocate tool** ☑ in the tool bar or in the Divisions column, **double-click** the **Divisions column** beside the account, or **choose** the **Purchase menu** and **click Allocate**.

NOTES
You can also press ⌃ctrl +
⇧shift + A to open the Division
Allocation window.

You will open the Division Allocation window for the Purchases Journal:

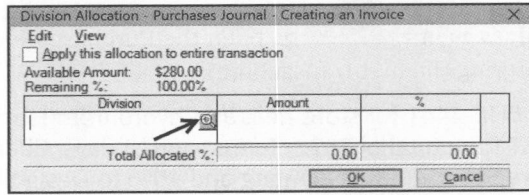

The cursor is in the Division field. The full amount to be allocated, $280 (the base expense amount), is provided at the top for reference together with the proportion remaining to be allocated, 100.00%. Amounts can be allocated by percentage or by actual amount. This choice is made in the Division Settings window (refer to page 505). (Choose the Setup menu, click Settings and then click Division and Allocation.) The setting can be changed as needed. Shady Corners uses the Percentage allocation method as indicated in the Division Information.

NOTES
When you change the ledger name, the new name you entered will appear in the screen and column headings in the allocation windows instead of Division.

You must complete the allocation process even if 100 percent of the revenue or expense is assigned to a single division. You must complete the allocation process for each account or invoice line on your input form.

Click   the **Division List icon** 🔍 to display the Divisions in alphabetic order:

NOTES
The HST amount is not allocated because it is not part of the expense.

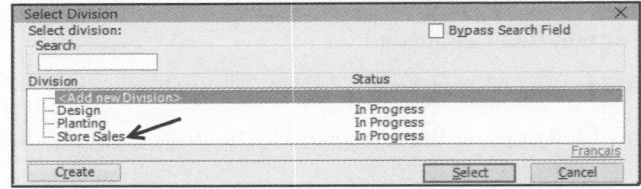

According to the source document information, the first division is Store Sales, which incurs 70 percent of the total energy expense. You can add a new division from the Select Division window.

Choose Add New Division or click the Create button to open the Division Ledger if you need to create a new division.

Click   **Store Sales**, the first division used. **Click Select** to add it on the form.

The cursor advances to the Percentage field because we selected this method of allocation. By default the unallocated portion (100%) is indicated in this field and selected for editing.

Type   70   **Press** ⊨tab⊨ to advance to the next line in the Division field.

The program calculates the dollar amount for this division automatically based on the percentage entered. The percentage remaining at the top of the input form has been updated to 30.00%. Now we need to allocate the remaining 30 percent of the expense amount to the other divisions.

Press   (enter) to open the Select Division window.

Double-click Planting to add the division.

The cursor is in the Percentage field again, with 30.00 as the default because this was the unallocated percentage remaining.

Type   20 **Press** (tab) to enter it and update the unallocated amount to 10%.

Press   (enter) to open the Select Division window.

Double-click Design to add the division with 10.00 as the default entry.

Press   (tab) to accept this amount because it is correct and completes the allocation:

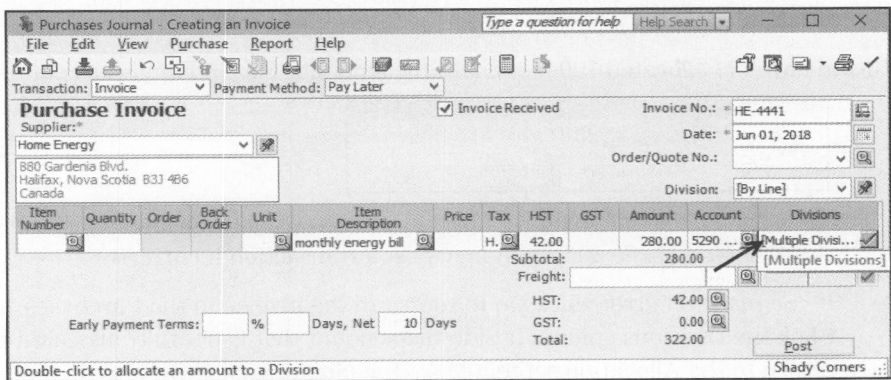

Click   OK to return to the completed Purchases Journal entry:

The journal appears unchanged, except for the entry in the Divisions column indicating that the amount has been allocated. Usually, the Division name is entered, but because more than one division was used, the entry is Multiple Divisions. The [By Line] entry in the Division field above the invoice lines also indicates that more than one division has been applied to the purchase.

Reviewing the Purchases Journal Allocation

Choose the **Report menu** and **click Display Purchases Journal Entry**:

Shady Corners
Purchases Journal Entry 06/01/2018 (J1)

Account Number	Account Description	Division	Debits	Credits	Division Amt
2670	GST/HST Paid on Purchases		42.00	-	
5290	Utilities Expenses		280.00	-	
		- Store Sales			196.00
		- Planting			56.00
		- Design			28.00
2200	Accounts Payable		-	322.00	
Additional Date:	Additional Field:		322.00	322.00	

Sage 50 has automatically updated the *Accounts Payable* control account because the Payables and General ledgers are fully integrated. The utilities expense has been allocated to the three divisions according to the proportions we entered for them. Only the amount for the expense account *Utilities Expenses* is allocated because the other accounts are Balance Sheet accounts that are not set up to allow allocations.

Close the **display** to return to the Purchases Journal input screen.

NOTES
When PST is paid separately from GST, it will be included with the expense amount and fully allocated with it.

CORRECTING THE PURCHASES JOURNAL ENTRY ALLOCATION

Correct the Purchases Journal part of the entry as you would correct any other purchase invoice. Refer to page 114 if you need assistance.

If you have made an error in the allocation, **click** the **Allocate tool** ☑ to return to the Allocation window. **Click** the **line** for the amount being allocated to activate the Allocate tool if necessary. **Click** an **incorrect division** to highlight it. **Press** ⌐enter⌐ to access the Division list. **Click** the **correct division** and **click Select** to enter the change. **Click** an **incorrect percentage** and **type** the **correct information. Press** ⌐tab⌐ to save the correction. **Click OK** to return to the Journal window.

Click   the **Store tool** 🖫. Accept the supplier **name** and **Monthly** as the frequency. **Click OK** to return to the journal.

When you store a transaction with allocations, allocation information is also stored.

To review or edit the allocation, click the Allocate tool ☑ when the cursor is on the relevant line or click the ✓ in the Divisions column.

Posting

When you are certain that you have entered all the information correctly,

Click   ⌐ Post ⌐ to save the entry. **Click OK** to confirm posting.

If you have not allocated 100 percent of the amounts, Sage 50 requests confirmation:

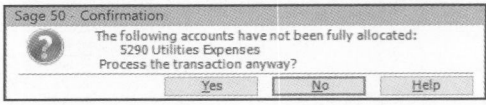

This message appears if you have not fully allocated a journal amount. If the warning option is not selected (page 505), you may post a transaction incorrectly.

If you made an error, click No to return to the invoice in the Purchases Journal. Click the Divisions column beside the account that is not fully allocated to return to the Allocation screen. Make the changes, click OK and then post.

If you do not want to allocate the full amount, or if the account was one for which you cannot access the allocation procedure, such as *Variance Costs* (refer to the screenshots on page 525), you should click Yes to continue.

Close   the **Purchases Journal**. The Divisions list pane total expense amounts have been updated with amounts from this transaction. Click the list pane refresh tool 🔄 if necessary to update division amounts.

If the option to allow allocations is not activated for the account in the ledger record, Sage 50 will block this action when you click the Allocation tool:

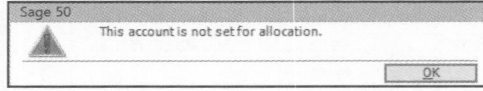

Open the ledger record for the account and click the Allow Division Allocations.

Enter   the next **two payments** and the **receipt transaction**.

3 Sent cheque #581 for $900 to Groen Fields on June 1 to pay invoice #GF-1142 in full.

4 On June 2, sent cheque #375 for Dkr 8.450,00 to Mobler Dansk to pay invoice #MD-724. The exchange rate for June 2 was 0.191.

5 Received cheque #4887 for $1 356 on June 2 from Acadian Towers. Receipt #420 was applied to invoice #155 with early payment discount of $24.

Entering Import Duties

Governments may apply import duties that raise the price of imported goods to encourage the local economy. Duty rates or tariffs vary for different kinds of items and for different countries. The duty is collected by the Canada Revenue Agency when the goods first enter Canada, before they are released to the buyer.

In Sage 50, before you can enter duty amounts with the purchase, you must change the Payables settings to charge and track import duties (refer to page 651). You must also indicate in the foreign supplier's record (Options tab screen) that duty is applied to purchases from that supplier (refer to page 664). In the Inventory Ledger records (Taxes tab screen), you can enter the duty applied as a percentage (refer to pages 682–683), or you can enter the rates in the Purchases Journal. For non-inventory purchases, you must enter the rate directly in the Purchases Journal.

The purchase invoice from Mobler Dansk has import duties applied.

6 Recorded invoice #MD-916 from Mobler Dansk on June 2/18. Terms: 2/15, net 30. The exchange rate on June 2 was 0.191. Total import duty charged was Dkr 937,60 (CAD $179.08). The freight expense was allocated entirely to Store Sales. Create new asset account for fabrics: 1320 Upholstery Fabrics.

items purchased			amount	duty rate
	Upholstery fabrics		Dkr 6.000,00	4%
4	FA04	Arm chair: Cast Aluminum	1.120,00	8%
2	FA01	Patio set: Cast Aluminum round table 1.5 m	7.600,00	8%
	Freight		1.200,00	
	HST Paid		2.388,00	
Invoice Total			Dkr 18.308,00	

Open the **Purchases Journal. Choose Mobler Dansk. Press** tab :

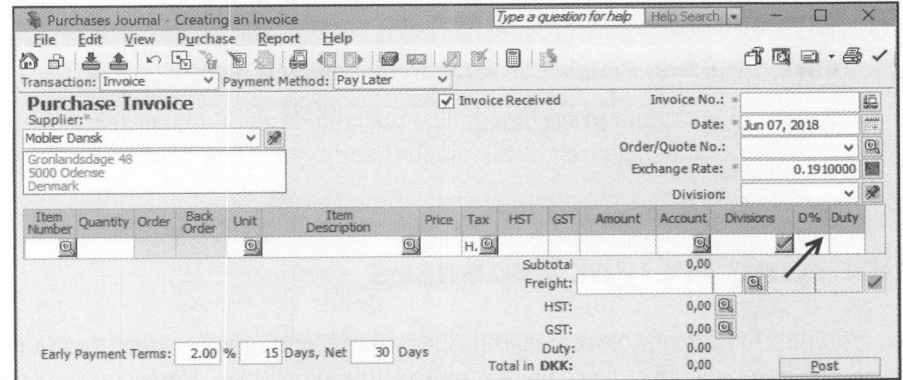

> **NOTES**
> Edit the purchase amounts. HST is charged on freight expenses.
> Amounts for Balance Sheet accounts are not allocated so, except for the freight amount, there is no allocation for inventory purchases.

The company settings and the Supplier and Inventory Ledger records for Shady Corners are set up to apply duty.

In addition to the Exchange Rate field and the indication that Danish kroner (DKK) is the currency for this supplier, the duty fields are added because we selected a supplier for whom duty applies. The extra fields are used for the duty percentage and for the duty amount. Duty is charged on all items purchased from Mobler Dansk.

Click the **Invoice No. field** and **type** MD-916

Type Jun 2 in the Date field and **press** tab . The exchange rate is correct from the rate entered for the payment made on this date.

> **NOTES**
> If you need to update exchange rates in the Purchases Journal, the Exchange Rate screen may stay open after you click OK with the session date replacing the transaction date. Click Cancel to close the screen and select the correct exchange rate from the Exchange Rate select list. Click the Exchange Rate tool 💲 beside the field to open the list.

Click   the **Allocate tool button** ✓ to the right of the Freight fields.

The Division Allocation screen opens. It is the same as the one we saw earlier. The Freight amount, Dkr 1.200,00, is entered as the amount to be allocated.

Choose Store Sales and **accept** the **amount** and percentage allocation.

Click   **OK** to return to the journal. The journal has not changed in appearance.

Choose the **Report menu** and **click Display Purchases Journal Entry**:

Account Number	Account Description	Division	Foreign A...	Division Frgn Amt	Debits	Credits	Division Amt
1320	Upholstery Fabrics		Dkr6.240,00		1,191.84	-	
1400	Patio Furniture		Dkr9.417,59		1,798.76	-	
2670	GST/HST Paid on Purchases		Dkr2.388,00		456.11	-	
5100	Freight Expense		Dkr1.200,00		229.20	-	
		- Store Sales		Dkr1.200,00			229.20
2200	Accounts Payable		Dkr18.308,00		-	3,496.83	
2220	Import Duty Payable		Dkr937,60		-	179.08	
1 Danish Kroners equals 0.1910000 Canadian Dollars					3,675.91	3,675.91	

Shady Corners — Purchases Journal Entry 06/02/2018 (J5)

Only the Freight Expense amount — the only Income Statement amount and the only amount allocated for the transaction — has a division allocation in the journal entry.

Close   the **Journal Entry** to return to the journal.

To correct the freight expense allocation, click the Allocate button ✓ beside the field to open the Division Allocation screen and make the needed changes.

Click   Post   to save the entry.

If you have not allocated the freight amount, Sage 50 generates the warning on page 510 about incomplete allocations.

Enter   the following **purchase transaction** from Jorgensen Mobler.

7 Recorded invoice #JM-876 from Jorgensen Mobler for furniture on June 2, 2018, at the exchange rate of 0.191. Terms: 2/30, net 60 days. Total import duty assessed was Dkr 695,40 (CAD $132.82). Freight was charged to Store Sales.

items purchased			amount	duty rate
4	FP21	Patio table: Moulded Plastic 2 m	Dkr 6.400,00	9.5%
2	FP24	Chaise longue: Moulded Plastic	920,00	9.5%
	Freight		800,00	
	HST Paid		1.218,00	
Invoice Total			Dkr 9.338,00	

Close   the **Purchases Journal**. The next transaction is a credit card sale.

Allocating in the Sales Journal

8 ✓ Sale #166 to Efren Barrato was made on June 4/18. Barrato paid by Visa. 100% of revenue and expenses for inventory items and delivery was allocated to Store Sales, and the service item (SC03) was allocated to Planting. Create a new record for Barrato. Set up the data files to process credit card transactions before entering the sale.

items sold			amount	total
1	FT31	Patio table: Teak round 1.5 m	$ 925 each	$ 925.00
4	FT33	Arm chair: Teak	725 each	2 900.00
1	FT37	Bench: Teak	1 125 each	1 125.00
10	SH03	Shrubs: 3 metre	55 each	550.00
3	SC03	Planting & Soil Preparation	50 /hour	150.00
		Delivery		100.00
	Harmonized Sales Tax		15%	862.50
Total paid by Visa #4111 1111 1111 1111				$6 612.50

NOTES
The Import Duty Payable credit entry is matched by the total increase for the two asset accounts — the debit entries for Upholstery Fabrics and Patio Furniture — over their purchase costs.

NOTES
You can allocate freight revenue amounts in the same way. Simply click the Allocate tool beside the Freight fields.

NOTES
Efren Barrato (contact Efren Barrato) 35 Birchmount Rd. Halifax, NS B3T 1G7 Terms: net 1

NOTES
No discount applies to cash, credit card or debit card sales (Visa, MasterCard and Interac).

Amounts for revenue accounts in the Sales Journal are allocated in the same way as amounts for expense accounts in the Purchases Journal. Each revenue amount in the journal must be allocated completely, but you can assign the same allocation percentages to all accounts in the journal rather than repeating the allocation entry for each invoice line. We will demonstrate this method with the steps involved in the Visa sale to Barrato on June 4.

Because this is a credit card sale, we will first set up the data files to allow credit card processing. You cannot enter the credit card processing settings when the Sales Journal is open, so we must complete this step first.

If you do not have an Internet connection, you can skip this section and proceed to the Allocating the Revenue Amounts section (page 515). You will also skip the steps for processing the transaction after entering the sales details.

Setting Up Credit Card Processing

If you do not want to process credit card transactions, do not complete the credit card setup section. Just enter the transaction in the usual way.

When credit card processing details are added to the Company Credit Card Settings, the credit card transaction can be processed directly. You must have a merchant account with the processing company. Sage 50 links with Sage Exchange, and all kinds of credit cards are processed through this single company. Merchants pay a fee for this service that is separate from the transaction fees charged by the credit card company. The advantage is that the transaction is processed directly as a bank transfer to the merchant.

You must have the Sage Exchange program installed and running on your computer to complete this next step. You can download this program from the Company Credit Card Settings screen.

> **Click** the **Settings icon**, then click **Company**, **Credit Cards** and **Processing Service** to open the Settings screen you need:

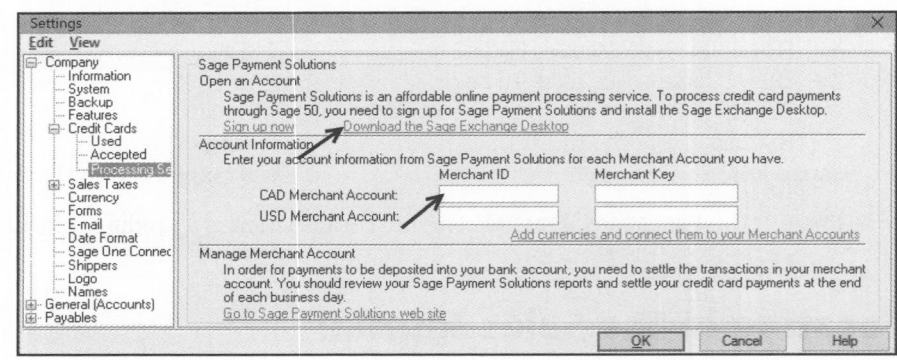

> **Start** your **Internet connection**.

> **Click** the **Download The Sage Exchange Desktop link** on the Settings screen. Follow the instructions to complete the installation.

You must add the Merchant ID number and Key (password) provided for this text by Sage Payment Solutions to activate the feature.

> **Click** the **Merchant ID field**. This is the number provided by Sage.

> **Type** 651259884634

> **Press** ⌐tab⌐ to advance to the Merchant Key field. This field holds the password for your account.

> **Type** B8B904S6E2K2 As you type, the characters are replaced by *.

Click   **OK** to close the Settings screen.

Start   the **Sage Exchange program**. It will be running in the background.

You are now ready to enter the sales transaction for Barrato.

Allocating the Revenue Amounts

Click   the **Sales Invoices icon** to open the Sales Journal.

Type   Efren Barrato in the Customer field. **Click Add** and **enter** the customer's **address** and **terms** to the ledger record. **Click Save And Close**.

Choose   **Visa** as the method in the Payment Method field.

Enter   **Jun 4 18** as the invoice date.

Choose   **FT31** from the inventory selection list as the first item for the sale. The cursor advances to the Quantity field.

Type   1 **Press** (tab) repeatedly to advance to the Divisions column.

Double-click the **Divisions column** or **click** ☑ in the Divisions column to open the Division Allocation window.

As long as the cursor is anywhere on the invoice line you are allocating the allocate function is available. Click the Allocate tool button in the tool bar or choose the Sales menu and click Allocate to open the Division Allocation screen.

Choose **Store Sales** for 100% of the revenue amount. **Press** (tab).

The allocation screen has a check box for the option Apply This Allocation To Entire Transaction:

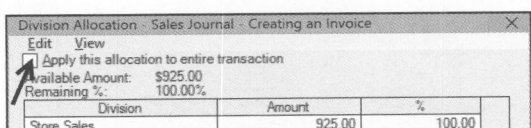

This option allows you to enter the allocation for one amount and have the program automatically apply the same percentages for all other amounts, including freight. Otherwise you need to repeat the allocation procedure for each account in the journal.

Click   **Apply This Allocation To Entire Transaction** to open the message about this selection:

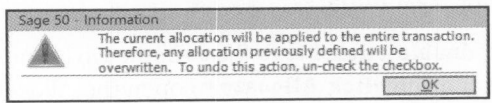

Read   the **message** and then **click OK** to return to the allocation screen.

If you do not want to continue with this selection, click the check box again.

The Division Allocation screen has changed:

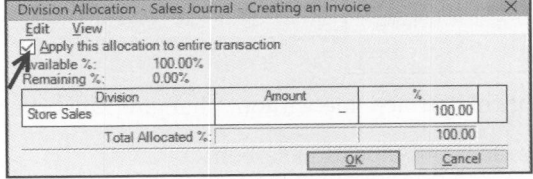

⚠ WARNING!
If the Sage Exchange program does not start properly, your firewall may be blocking it. You may need to temporarily disable your firewall program to install Sage Exchange. You may also need to change the firewall settings to "allow" Sage Exchange. After this, you can start the program normally.

NOTES
You can also press (ctrl) + (shift) + A to open the Division Allocation window whenever the cursor is on a line with an account that allows allocation.

No amounts are entered now because the same percentages will be applied and the amounts will be different for each account.

Click   **OK** to save the allocation and return to the journal.

Enter   the **remaining inventory** and **service items** and the **delivery charge** for the sale.

The division name is added to the Divisions column for each line automatically as you complete the invoice:

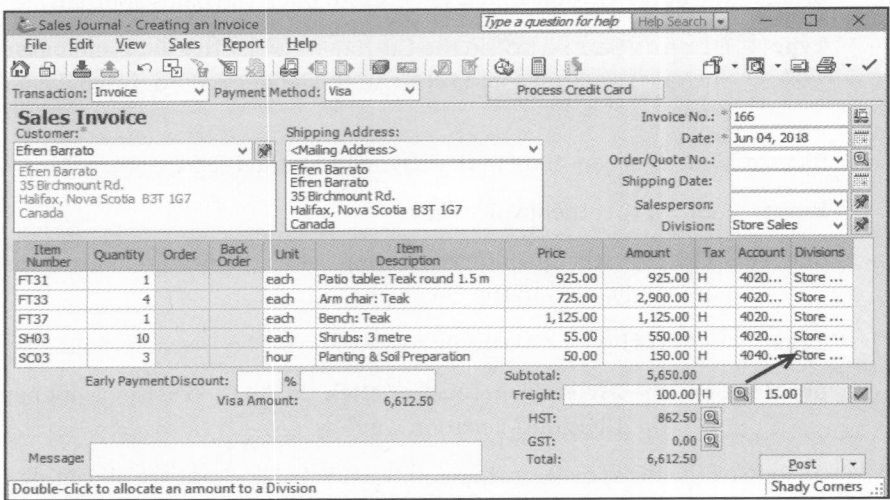

The invoice has been completely allocated, but the allocation is not correct, as you learn from reviewing the journal entry for the transaction.

Press   ⌃ctrl⌃ **+ J** to open the journal display:

Account Number	Account Description	Division	Debits	Credits	Division Amt.
Shady Corners					
Sales Journal Entry 06/04/2018 (J7)					
1070	Bank: Visa and Interac		6,427.35	-	
5070	Cost of Goods Sold		2,940.00	-	
		- Store Sales			2,940.00
5160	Credit Card Fees		185.15		
		- Store Sales			185.16
1380	Shrubs		-	320.00	
1400	Patio Furniture		-	2,620.00	
2650	GST/HST Charged on Sales		-	862.50	
4020	Revenue from Store Sales		-	5,500.00	
		- Store Sales			5,500.00
4040	Revenue from Services		-	150.00	
		- Store Sales			150.00
4100	Revenue from Delivery		-	100.00	
		- Store Sales			100.00
Additional Date:	Additional Field:		9,552.50	9,552.50	

All amounts, including delivery, are allocated to the Store Sales division. However, the service revenue should be allocated to the Planting division, so we must change it.

Close   the displayed **report** to return to the journal.

Click   anywhere on the line for **item SC03**.

Click   the **Allocate tool** 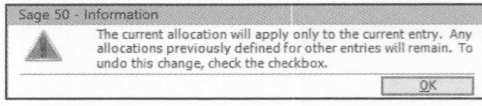, **double-click Store Sales** in the Divisions column or **choose** the **Sales menu** and **click Allocate** to open the Allocation screen.

Click   **Apply This Allocation To Entire Transaction** to remove the ✓.

Sage 50 displays a message about the effects of changing the allocation selection:

> **Sage 50 - Information**
> ⚠ The current allocation will apply only to the current entry. Any allocations previously defined for other entries will remain. To undo this change, check the checkbox.
> [OK]

We can change the allocation for this invoice line without changing any other line.

Click   **OK** to return to the Division Allocation screen.

Click   the **List icon** 🔍 in the Division field to open the list of divisions.

NOTES
You can also press ⌃ctrl⌃ + ⌃shift⌃ + A for the selected item to open the Division Allocation screen.

NOTES
This message appears only for the first allocation you change. You can now change the allocation for additional amounts without displaying the message again.

Double-click **Planting** to add it to the Division Allocation screen.

Click   **OK** to save the change. Planting has been entered in the journal.

Choose the **Report menu** and **click Display Sales Journal Entry**:

Shady Corners Sales Journal Entry 06/04/2018 (J7)					
Account Number	Account Description	Division	Debits	Credits	Division Amt.
1070	Bank: Visa and Interac		6,427.35	-	
5070	Cost of Goods Sold		2,940.00	-	
5160		- Store Sales			2,940.00
	Credit Card Fees		185.15	-	
		- Store Sales			180.33
		- Planting			4.83
1380	Shrubs		-	320.00	
1400	Patio Furniture		-	2,620.00	
2650	GST/HST Charged on Sales		-	862.50	
4020	Revenue from Store Sales		-	5,500.00	
		- Store Sales			5,500.00
4040	Revenue from Services		-	150.00	
		- Planting			150.00
4100	Revenue from Delivery		-	100.00	
		- Store Sales			100.00
Additional Date:	Additional Field:		9,552.50	9,552.50	

The allocation is now correct. The allocation for *Credit Card Fees* is automatically split in the correct proportion. *Cost of Goods Sold* is also allocated.

Close   the **Journal Entry** to return to the journal.

The Division field in the journal (above the invoice lines) has By Line as the entry. SC03 has Planting in the invoice line Division field while the other lines still have Store Sales. You can now change allocations for other amounts individually if needed.

Processing a Credit Card Transaction

Once we are certain that the sales invoice is correct, we can process the credit card.

The Process Credit Card button beside the Visa Payment Method selection replaces the link Tell Me More About Processing Credit Card Payments — refer to page 181.

Start   your **Internet connection** if you have not already done so.

Click   the **Windows Start button** . **Type** `Sage Exch` in the Search field. The Sage Exchange program you need will be in the pop-up list:

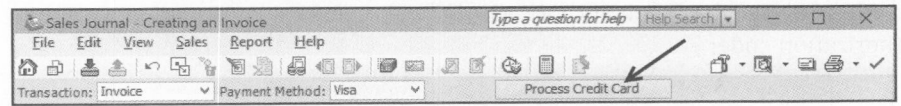

Click   **Sage Exchange Desktop App** to run this program. Click the Sage 50 task bar icons to return to your Sage 50 data file and the Sales Journal.

Click   the **Process Credit Card button** in the Sales Journal:

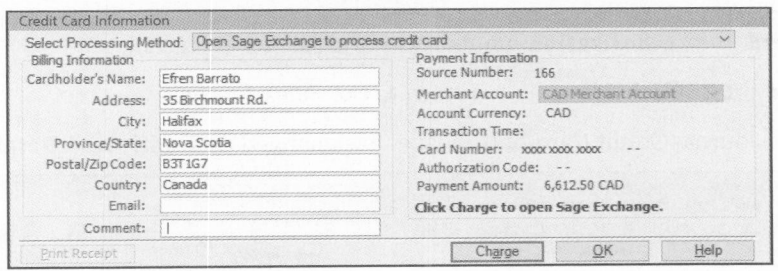

The cardholder information screen opens:

> **NOTES**
> After you change the setting to Apply This Allocation To Entire Transaction, you can change allocations for other amounts individually without affecting the remaining allocations.

> **NOTES**
> The program you need has the Sage Exchange logo [SE] beside it — it appeared as the best match when we performed these steps. The remaining list items allow you to search for them on the Internet.

> **NOTES**
> If the Sage Exchange program does not start, check that your firewall is not blocking the program.

> **NOTES**
> If you did not complete the address fields in the customer's record, you must add the details here. Information from the Contact field in the ledger is entered in the Cardholder's Name field.

The first screen holds the customer information. If you select a customer for whom you have a complete ledger record, the address information will be added from the record. The entry from the Contact field will appear in the Name field. You must fill in the name and address fields to continue.

> **Enter**   the **cardholder's name** and **address** details.
>
> **Click**   the **Select Processing Method list arrow**:

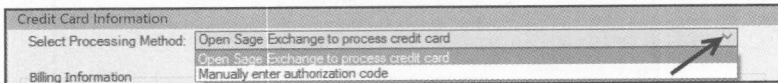

Card information may be processed/authorized manually or automatically. If you have an account set up with Sage, you can complete the processing automatically. You should have the Sage Exchange program and your Internet connection running.

> **Click**   the **Charge button** in the lower right-hand corner of the Payment Information pane to connect to the Sage Exchange Payment site (refer to the screenshot on the previous page):

You are now connected to a secure site so that you can provide the credit card information. All Sage Exchange connections are timed — the connection will be broken after the time has elapsed. The cursor is in the Card Number field.

> **Type**   4111111111111111   the 16-digit credit card number.
>
> **Select**   the **month** and **year** for the Expiration Date from the drop-down lists. The date must be later than the current calendar date on your computer system — the card must not be expired.

Entering the CVV code (the code located on the back of the credit card) is optional.

> **Click**   **Next** to review the information and to add the customer's telephone number or e-mail address. Make corrections by clicking the Back button to return to previous screens.
>
> **Click**   **Submit** to begin the processing. If there is any delay, your screen may include the Processing message progress bar.

After the sale has been authorized, you will receive a confirmation with the authorization code:

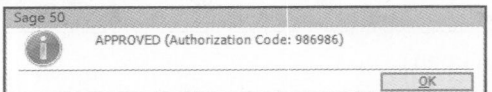

> **Record**   the **authorization** number with the sale for reference.
>
> **Click**   **OK**. **Click OK** again to return to the Sales Journal.

The Sales Journal Credit Card button label has changed to **Credit Card Details**:

NOTES
The name on the credit card may be different from the customer account name, so you should verify that it is correct.

NOTES
The system date from your computer will be entered as the date below the Thank You message and as the starting point for the card expiry date.

NOTES
This is the only Visa number that will be accepted in the test account for processing.

NOTES
If you omit any essential information, the program will warn you and prevent you from continuing until you provide the missing details.

NOTES
When you return to the Credit Card Information screen after authorizing the transaction, the option to Void the transaction replaces the Charge button. Clicking this will immediately reverse the charge to the customer's credit card.

You can click the Credit Card Details button to review the details.

Click   Post ▾   to save the entry. An Advisor message informs you that some inventory items have fallen below the reorder point. **Click** the **message** to continue.

NOTES
If you need to change credit card details after processing, you should reverse the sale. You may need to do this manually in order to reverse the credit card charges. Before posting, closing the journal will automatically void the credit card amount.

If you change the method of payment after processing the credit card, you must confirm that the credit card payment will be voided:

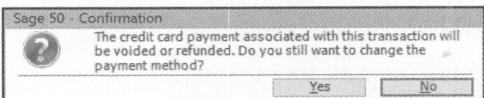

Or, if you do not post the transaction after processing the credit card, that is, you discard the transaction, you must also confirm that the payment will be voided:

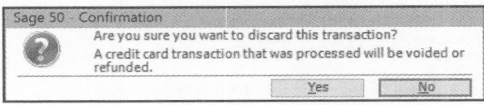

Click   **Yes** to continue and void or reverse the charges.

Processing Credit Card Transactions Manually

If you do not have a direct Internet connection, you can process the credit card transaction manually. On the Credit Card Information screen,

Select Manually Enter Authorization Code as the processing method from the drop-down list:

NOTES
If you did not add the address details in the customer's record, you can enter them here — or use your own address for practice.

The Card Number field and the Authorization Code fields will become available.

Click the Card Number field. Enter the last four digits of the card number.

Type 1111

Click the Authorization Code field. This code can be obtained by telephone or may be given automatically when the card is swiped on a terminal.

Type 488922

Click OK to return to the Sales Journal. Post the transaction.

Pre-Authorized Credit Card Processing with Sage Vault

If a customer has authorized automatic credit card payments, you can set these up in the customer's ledger record. This is similar to setting up pre-authorized payments from a bank account (refer to page 522).

We will process the next sales transaction for a new customer with Sage Vault.

Iola completed MasterCard sale #167 to Leanne McGill on June 4, 2018, and allocated 100% of revenue to Store Sales. McGill has authorized Shady Corners to withdraw the amounts automatically from her credit card. Create a new complete customer record and add her credit card details.

Complete the MasterCard sales transaction. The following items were sold:

items sold			amount	total
6	FT33	Arm chair: Teak	$725 each	$4 350.00
1	FT34	Chaise longue: Teak	980 each	980.00
		Delivery		100.00
		Harmonized Sales Tax	15%	814.50
Total paid by MasterCard #5499 7400 0000 0057				$6 244.50

Open   the **Sales Journal** and **click** the **Customer field**.

Type   Leanne McGill **Click** the **Add link** to open the ledger.

Enter   the **address details** and **payment terms** (Options tab).

Click   the **Credit Card tab**:

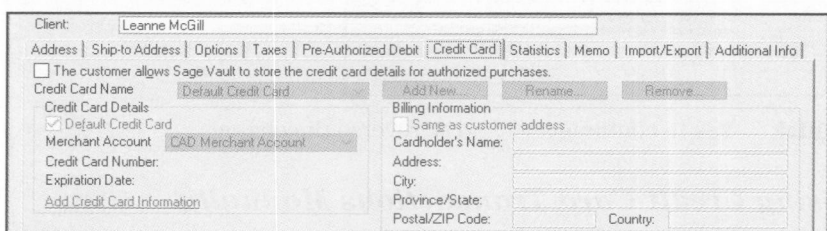

Click   **The Customer Allows Sage Vault To Store The Credit Card Details....**

This will open the remaining fields for entering the required details.

Click   **Same As Customer Address** under Billing Information to have the required address details added to these fields automatically.

Click   the **Add Credit Card Information** link so we can add the card details:

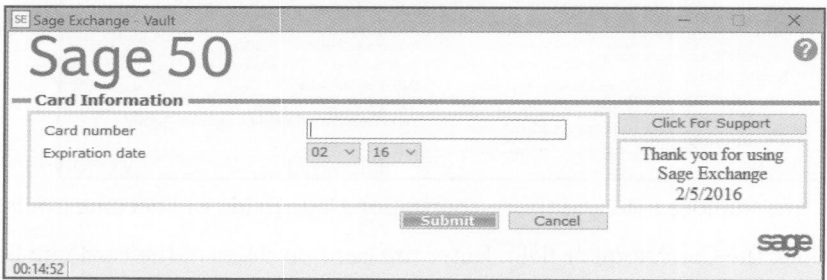

At this stage, you are connected to the Sage Exchange - Vault secure site. On this screen, you must add the card number and its expiry date.

Click   the **Card Number field** and **type** 5499740000000057

Choose **month** and **year** dates from the Expiration Date drop-down lists.

Click   **Submit**. **Save** the **new record** to return to the Sales Journal.

Choose **MasterCard** from the Payment Method drop-down list.

Enter **Jun 4** as the date for the sale.

Enter the first **inventory item** and **quantity**. **Press** ⌞tab⌟ to update the amount.

Entering Allocations from the Journal Division Field

Both the Sales Journal and the Purchases Journal have a Division field above the invoice lines with a drop-down list of divisions. By using this selection list, you can quickly apply the same division to all invoice lines and freight.

When you enter allocations with the methods we used earlier, this field has the entry [By Line] because we entered different or multiple allocations for one or more individual lines on the invoice, as in the Purchase Invoice on page 509. The Sales Invoice on page 516 has Store Sales as the entry in this field because, at that stage, we had allocated the entire transaction to that division.

When the entire transaction is allocated to one division, you can select the division from the Division field drop-down list. We will use this method for the sale to McGill.

> **Click**   the **Division field list arrow** to list all divisions available for selection:

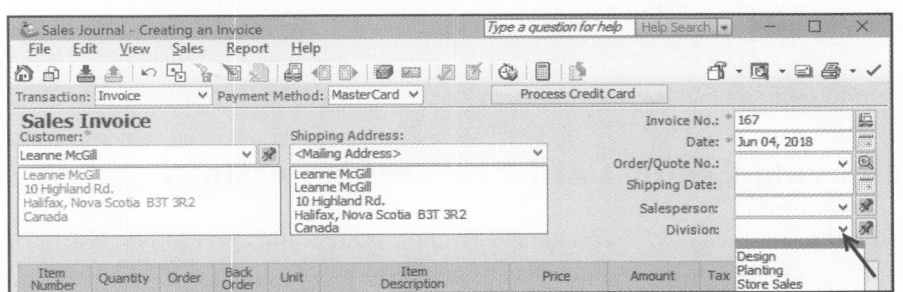

> **Click**   **Store Sales**. **Press** `tab`. This division is added to the first invoice line.
>
> **Enter**   the **second item** and **quantity**. Store Sales is added automatically.
>
> **Enter**   the **delivery amount** to complete the transaction. Store Sales is added automatically for this charge as well.

When you open the Division Allocation window from either line on the invoice, a ✓ informs you that the same allocation applies to the entire transaction:

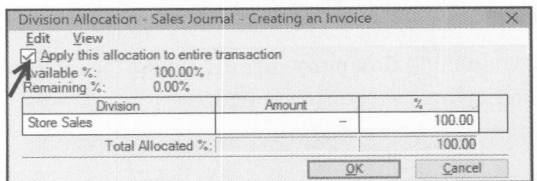

If you need to change the allocation for individual line amounts, you can do so from this window, as we did for the previous sale. Click OK to close this window.

> **Review** your **journal entry** display and **make corrections** if necessary.
>
> **Click**   the **Process Credit Card button** in the Sales Journal. The Credit Card Information screen opens:

The first screen holds the customer information. If you select a customer for whom you have a complete record, the address information will be added from the record with the Contact field entry in the Name field. You must enter the name and address.

> **Click**   the **Select Processing Method list arrow**:

NOTES
You can use the journal's Division field list to allocate freight amounts as well. In the Purchases Journal for inventory purchases, the allocation entry will apply only to freight.

NOTES
The Advisor message about low inventory will appear several times. Shady Corners allows inventory levels to go below zero. You should close the message each time it appears.
If inventory levels have fallen below zero, they will trigger a cost variance entry when the item is purchased (refer to page 525).

NOTES
If you get a message that the credit card fees are not fully allocated, you must accept the incomplete allocation to continue.

Once the ledger record has a customer's card information, the selection list changes. Processing with Sage Vault is now the default and it is correct for this sale. You can still process the transaction with Sage Exchange, as we did for the previous sale, or manually.

Click   **Charge**. **Click OK**. Sage 50 provides the Authorization number for recording.

Click   **OK** again to return to the Sales Journal and **post** the **entry**.

Close   the **Advisor message** about low inventory to continue and then **close** the **Sales Journal**.

The stock for item FT33 now is –2 — oversold by two units. This is the quantity in the updated Inventory List that opens from the Sales Journal Item Number field.

Removing Credit Card Processing Settings

When entering a sale while you have account information in your credit card processing settings, you must process the transaction before you can post the sale. If you try to post the sale without the processing step, you will be blocked with this message:

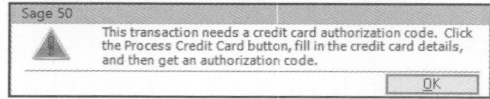

Click   **OK**. **Close** the **Sales Journal**. You cannot access the merchant account settings while the journal is open.

You need to remove the credit card processing account information, unless you want to process all credit card sales and generate authorization codes.

Click   the **Settings icon**, then click **Company**, **Credit Cards** and **Processing Service** to open the Settings screen you need:

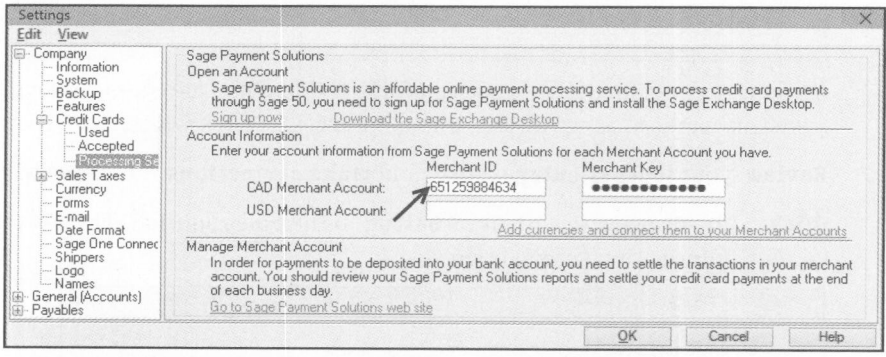

Double-click the **Merchant ID number** and **press** (del).

Double-click the **Merchant Key password** and **press** (del).

Click   **Yes** to confirm the changes you are making.

Click   **OK** to save the changed settings.

Pre-Authorized Payments and Deposits

Businesses may have bills paid directly from their bank accounts by allowing suppliers to make automatic withdrawals. Customers may also permit automatic withdrawals for bill payments, and many businesses arrange for paycheques to be deposited directly to employee bank accounts. For these transactions, funds are transferred electronically,

directly from one bank account to another. Funds may be transferred between different banks and branches.

Third-party solution providers manage these electronic funds transfers (EFTs). PayPal and Beanstream are two of the providers whose services can be linked with features in Sage 50 for these transfers. We have a test account set up with Beanstream to illustrate the processes involved.

Pre-Authorized Debits (PAD)

When customers allow a business to withdraw funds directly to pay their accounts, usually for recurring bills, their method of payment is Pre-Authorized Debit. This arrangement removes concerns about lost cheques and overdue bills.

 Received memo #2 from Owner: Two customers have authorized automatic debit payments. Set up the permission in the customer records and enter bank account details as follows:

customer	branch number	institution (bank) number	account number
Hopewell College	67320	001	6557777
Rockcliff Manor	78129	003	9928821

Setting Up Pre-Authorized Debits

Before entering a pre-authorized debit sale or receipt, the customer's ledger must be updated to authorize the transactions and to add the customer's bank account details.

Click   **Receivables** in the Modules pane to switch to this window.

Click   **Hopewell College** in the Customers List pane to open this record.

Click   the **Pre-Authorized Debit tab** to access the screen we need:

All the fields on this screen are required. The customer must complete and sign a form or agreement including the bank account details and authorizing the withdrawals. Often a blank void cheque accompanies the form to provide the bank account information. Withdrawals may be made in Canadian or US dollars from bank accounts in Canada or the United States. The **Currency And Location** drop-down list allows you to make this selection.

Click   **This Customer Has A Signed Active Pre-Authorized Debit Agreement With My Company** to add a ✓.

Click   the **Branch Number field. Type** 67320

Press   ⌶tab⌶ to advance to the Institution (bank) Number field.

Type   001 **Press** ⌶tab⌶ to advance to the Account Number field.

Type   6557777

Click   the **Select list arrow** and **click Rockcliff Manor** to open the ledger.

NOTES
The customer is still responsible for ensuring that the bank account has sufficient funds to pay the bill to avoid overdraft or NSF charges.

NOTES
As soon as you click the check box, a note is added to the tab screen to remind you that the data file does not have user passwords. Strong passwords are essential when bank details are included in your data files. For practice exercises, we have omitted passwords. Adding passwords is covered in Chapter 16.

NOTES
The bank account information is similar to that entered for employees who have paycheques deposited directly to their bank accounts (refer to page 336).
Each bank has a unique three-digit bank or institution number, with unique five-digit branch numbers for their different branch locations. The account number is unique for the account holder and varies in length from bank to bank.

Click the **authorized agreement check box** and **enter** the **bank account details** for Rockcliff Manor.

Click .

Entering Pre-Authorized Debits

Pre-authorized debit is available as a method of payment for both receipts and sales invoices from the Paid By/Method Of Payment drop-down lists, respectively. Receipts and sales are entered in the same way as regular receipts and sales. Only the method of payment selection differs.

✓ 11 Entered pre-authorized payment from Hopewell College on June 6 for $1 695 including $30 discount. Receipt #421 was applied to invoice #159. CP20 will be entered as the cheque number.

Open the **Receipts Journal**.

Choose **Hopewell College** as the customer.

Enter **Jun 6** as the transaction date.

Click the **Paid By list arrow** for the options:

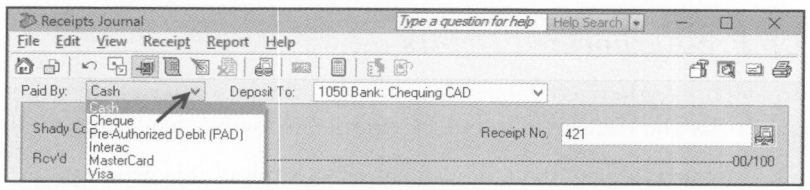

Click **Pre-Authorized Debit (PAD)**.

PAD number replaces the Cheque number field and CP20 (customer payment #20) is entered in this field as the reference number.

If you have omitted any of the information in the customer's ledger record, either the authorization check box or the bank details, Sage 50 blocks the action when you select the Pre-Authorized Debit method of payment:

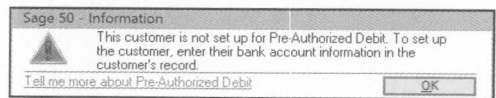

Click **OK**. Complete the ledger record before continuing.

Accept the **Discount** and **Amount** to complete the receipt.

Press ⌘ ctrl + **J** to review the transaction.

It looks like a normal receipt — the bank account is debited for the amount received because EFT transactions transfer the money directly from the customer's account. *Sales Discounts* and *Accounts Receivable* are credited as usual.

Close the **journal entry** and **post** the receipt. Enter the next PAD receipt.

✓ 12 Entered pre-authorized payment (CP21) from Rockcliff Manor on June 6 for $1 017 including $18 discount. Receipt #422 was applied to invoice #163.

Close the **Receipts Journal**.

Click **Divisions** in the Modules pane so you can enter the next purchase.

Creating Cost Variances

If items are sold to a customer when the inventory stock is too low to fill the sale completely, the levels in inventory fall below zero and the outstanding items are backordered. The estimated cost of goods for the sale is based on the average cost for the items in stock at the time of the sale. When the items are received later the price may have changed, and the items that fill the rest of the customer's order will have a different cost price from the one recorded for the sale. The difference is the cost variance and is assigned to the linked variance account for the inventory item. The amount of the variance is added to the journal entry for the purchase. Thus two conditions are required for a variance to occur: the inventory is oversold and the cost has changed.

You do not have to do anything to record a cost variance other than allowing inventory levels to go below zero. The program makes the calculations automatically and assigns the amount to the linked variance account for the inventory item.

Enter   **purchase invoice #MD-1018** from Mobler Dansk.

 Recorded purchase invoice #MD-1018 on June 6, 2018, from Mobler Dansk for teak patio furniture. Terms: 2/15, net 30. The exchange rate on June 6 was 0.200. Total import duty charged was Dkr 13.300,00 (CAD $2 660). The freight expense was allocated entirely to Store Sales.

items purchased			amount	duty rate
15	FT31	Patio table: Teak round 1.5 m	Dkr 40.500,00	9.5%
48	FT33	Arm chair: Teak	96.000,00	9.5%
5	FT35	End table: Teak	3.500,00	9.5%
		Freight	2.000,00	
		HST Paid	21.300,00	
Invoice Total			Dkr 163.300,00	

Display the **journal entry** with the variance amount included:

There was insufficient stock left for item FT33 on June 4 when sale #167 was recorded, so the average historic cost for six chairs, $2 280, was credited to *Cost of Goods Sold*. Only four chairs were in stock at the time of the sale, with an average cost of $380 per chair ($760 for two chairs). When the purchase of item FT33 was recorded, the total cost for 48 chairs was $19 200, or $800 for two chairs, plus duty at 9.5%, for a total of $876. The difference, $116, between the new cost and the cost in the sales transaction for the two out-of-stock chairs is the cost variance.

When you post the transaction, Sage 50 requests confirmation:

Variance costs cannot be allocated, so you must accept the incomplete allocation.

Click   **Yes** to continue posting the purchase. Close the Purchases Journal.

Open   the **Sales Journal** so you can enter the sale to Hopewell College.

WARNING!
If you have not entered a cost variance linked account in the item's ledger record, you will be prompted to select one when a purchase creates a variance, but you cannot create a new account from this selection list.
If the company settings for inventory do not allow inventory levels to go below zero, you must reduce the quantity to continue with the sale.

NOTES
If you have made corrections to journal entries, your variance cost amount may be different.

NOTES
The calculated price for the chairs includes the import duty at the rate of 9.5%.
The 48 chairs cost Dkr 96.000,00 plus 0.095% duty for a total cost of Dkr 105.120,00. This amount is multiplied by the exchange rate of 0.200 for a cost of CAD $21 024.

NOTES
When a purchase entry creates a variance and you have not set up the linked account for variances, you will be prompted to select a variance account.

NOTES
You may also generate incomplete allocations that you must accept for rounding errors for currency conversions or credit card fees.

Entering Sales with Pre-Authorized Debits

  Sale #168 to Hopewell College was recorded by Iola on June 7. The preferred customer has pre-authorized debits and is entitled to free delivery and the 2% discount for immediate payment. All revenue was allocated to Store Sales.

items sold			amount	
6	FT31	Patio table: Teak round 1.5 m	$750	each
30	FT33	Arm chair: Teak	615	each
10	FX42	Umbrella w/stand	200	each
30	FX43	Cushion: deep seating chair	40	each
		Harmonized Sales Tax	15%	

$29 549.50 was uploaded to our bank account (reference number CP22).

Choose   **Hopewell College** as the customer for the sale.

Enter   **Jun 7** as the transaction date.

Click   the **Payment Method drop-down list**. The options are the same as those in the Receipts Journal.

Click   **Pre-Authorized Debit (PAD)** to update the form with a PAD number; CP22 is entered automatically.

Enter   the **remaining details** for the sale, including the division allocations.

Review   the **journal entry** — it looks like a regular sale paid by cash or cheque. The bank account is debited for the full amount (minus the 2 percent discount) instead of *Accounts Receivable*.

Close   the **journal entry** and **post** the invoice.

Close   the **Sales Journal**.

Uploading Pre-Authorized Debits

After the pre-authorized debit transactions are entered in Sage 50, they must be uploaded to the company that manages the transfer of funds. For our example, the author has a test account set up courtesy of Beanstream.

  Received memo #3 from Owner: Upload three pre-authorized customer receipts.

Click   **Receivables** in the Modules pane. There are two methods you can use to upload pre-authorized transactions.

Click   the **Upload Pre-Authorized Debits icon** in the Related Tasks pane:

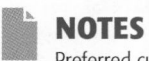
NOTES
Preferred customers do not pay for delivery.

If you are not working in the Receivables module window, you can upload the transactions from the File menu in any Home window.

Choose the **File menu** and **Import/Export**, then **click Upload Direct Payments** and **Pre-Authorized Debits**:

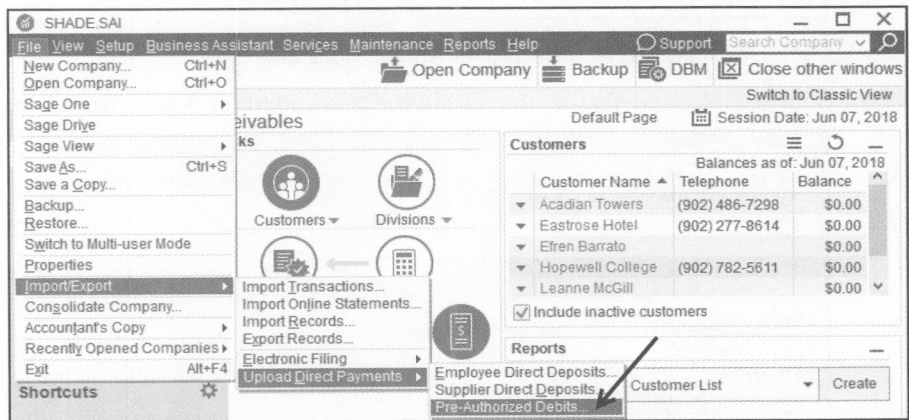

PRO VERSION

pro The Pro version does not have the File menu options to Switch To Multi-User Mode or to Consolidate Company.

The Upload Transactions window opens, listing the pre-authorized debits entered:

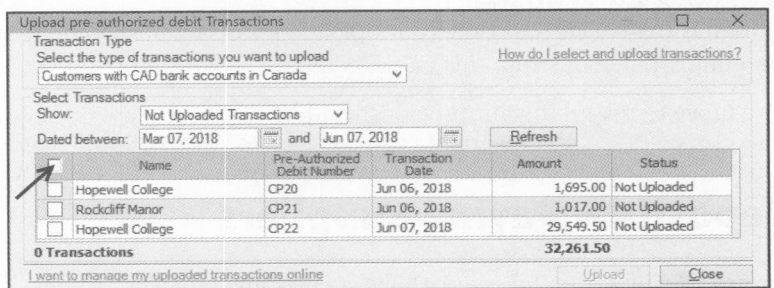

NOTES

You can view transactions for the previous three months.

In this window, you can **Select Transactions** to display from the drop-down list for the **Show** field. The default setting is for **Not Uploaded Transactions**, and the receipts we entered are listed. You can also list only transactions already uploaded (refer to the next page) or all transactions — those uploaded and not yet uploaded.

Each transaction has a check box for selection.

You can select payments individually by clicking the box beside a transaction or select all of them by clicking the check box in the column heading (marked with the arrow in the previous screen).

Click the **column heading check box** to add checkmarks for all receipts. The Upload button is no longer dimmed.

Click the **Upload button** to open the authorization screen:

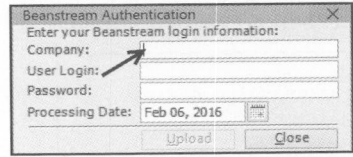

NOTES

Because of the way this account is set up, you will not be able to follow through with uploading any direct payments.

To cancel the uploading process, click Close to return to the Upload Transactions screen and then click Close to return to your starting point.

The screens we include for the rest of the process are for illustration purposes only. You will require a Beanstream (or other direct payment) account to continue.

Enter your Beanstream Company name, User Login and Password. Choose the date you want these payments to be processed — the current calendar date and two days later are the defaults for the deposit (refer to page 535).

Click Upload to begin processing.

After the transfer is completed, you will receive a message that the transactions have been uploaded successfully:

Click OK to return to the Upload Transactions screen.

Choose Uploaded Transactions from the Show field for Select Transactions:

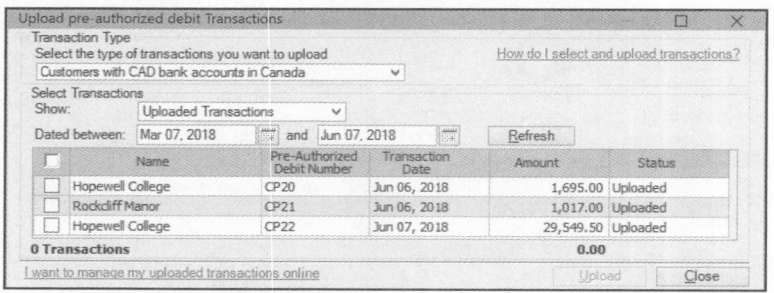

The status of the three receipts has changed to Uploaded. You can view these transactions and their status at any time.

Another option is to manage and view your uploaded transactions online from your Beanstream account. We demonstrate this on page 535.

Click   Close to return to your previous window.

Direct Deposits — Paying Suppliers

Direct deposits are usually set up for regular bills such as insurance or utilities. The process for suppliers is similar to the one for customers. You need to modify the supplier record (authorize the withdrawal of funds from your bank account and enter your bank account details), choose Direct Deposit as the method of payment for the transactions, enter and post the transactions and upload the payments.

Memo # 4 requests that we modify two supplier records to set up direct deposits.

Memo #4 from Owner: Authorized direct payments and set up of bank account details for Capital Trust for insurance and Bell Canada for telephone services:

branch number	institution (bank) number	account number
38930	012	298899

Open   the **Payables module window**.

Click   **Capital Trust** in the Suppliers list pane to open the ledger.

Click   the **Direct Deposit tab** to access the screen we need to edit:

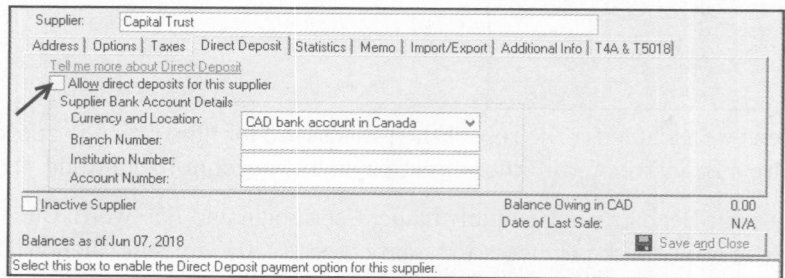

Click   Allow Direct Deposits For This Supplier.

Enter   the **Branch**, **Institution** and **Account numbers**.

Choose `Bell Canada` from the Select field list of suppliers and **make** the **same changes** for this supplier record. **Click Save And Close**.

You are now ready to enter the insurance bill for which we set up direct deposits.

<table>
<tr><td>☑
17</td><td>Capital Trust notified us that the monthly insurance premium for $330 including PST for invoice #CT-36698 was withdrawn from our bank account on June 7 as direct deposit (number VP35). Create new expense account 5210 Insurance Expense. The expense was allocated as follows: Store Sales — 60%; Planting — 20%; Design — 20%. Store the payment as a monthly recurring entry.</td></tr>
</table>

Open the **Purchases Journal** (or the Payments Journal with Make Other Payment as the transaction type). **Choose Capital Trust** as the supplier.

Choose `Direct Deposit` from the Payment Method field to modify the journal:

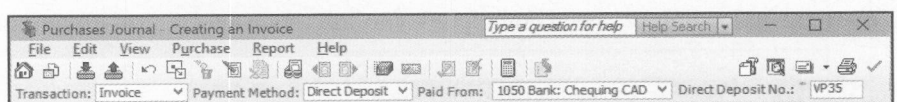

The bank account is entered in the Paid From field and the Cheque No. field label has been replaced by Direct Deposit No. with VP35 (vendor payment #35) entered as the reference.

Enter the **remaining invoice details**, including allocations, in the usual way.

The transaction you review looks like a regular cash or cheque purchase — the bank account has been credited for the total invoice amount.

Post the **entry**. **Enter** the next **direct deposit invoice** and **close** the **journal**.

<table>
<tr><td>18</td><td>Invoice #BC-64261 marked as PAID was received on June 7 from Bell Canada for $350 plus $52.50 HST for store telephones, staff mobile phones and Internet services. $402.50 was withdrawn from our chequing account (VP36). The expense was allocated to Store Sales — 40%, Planting — 30% and Design — 30%.</td></tr>
</table>

<table>
<tr><td>☑
19</td><td>Memo #5 from Owner: Upload the two direct payments made to Capital Trust (VP35) and Bell Canada (VP36).</td></tr>
</table>

Choose the **File menu** and **Import/Export** in the Home window and then **click Upload Direct Payments** and **Supplier Direct Deposits**. Or,

Click the **Upload Direct Deposit icon** in the Related Tasks pane of the Payables module window:

These two methods start the process of uploading the payments:

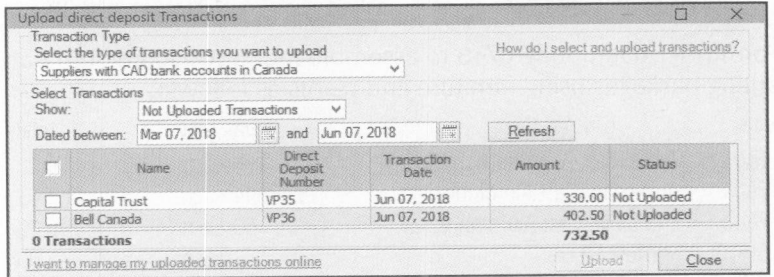

The two payment transactions are entered. As for receipts, we can show Not Uploaded Transactions (the default), Uploaded Transactions or All Transactions — both

NOTES
The PST on insurance is not refundable and is included as part of the expense. HST is not charged on insurance.

NOTES
Until you choose a supplier for whom you have set up direct deposit, the Direct Deposit Number field does not open.

NOTES
Double-click the Allo column to open the Allocation screen.

NOTES
You can edit the starting reference number for direct payments on the Forms screen of Company Settings.

those uploaded and those not yet uploaded. The selection of payments is the same as for receipts. You can select all transactions or individual ones.

Click   the **Select check box** in the column heading to choose both payments.

Click   the **Upload button** to open the Beanstream authorization window:

Enter your Beanstream account Company name, User Login and Password and choose the date you want the payments to be processed. Click Upload.

After the uploading has been completed, you will receive a confirmation message:

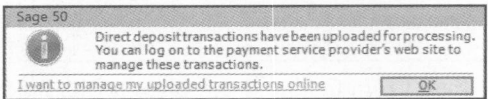

Click OK to return to the Upload Transactions window. Choose All Transactions from the Show drop-down list:

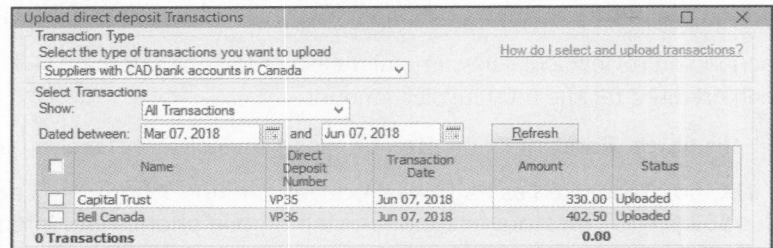

The change in status to Uploaded confirms that we uploaded both deposits.

Click   **Close** to return to your previous window.

SESSION DATE – JUNE 14, 2018

20 Received memo #6 from Owner. Created two new inventory records for summer garden specials, both including furniture, plants, one hour of consultation and one hour of planting service. A new asset Group account was used for the packages: 1420 Summer Garden Packages. The other linked accounts used were Revenue from Sales (account 4020) and Cost of Goods Sold (account 5070). Both items are taxed for HST. Import duty does not apply.

new item	description	min amt	regular (preferred) selling price/unit
SU01	Aluminum patio set/planting	0	$1 250 ($1 000) /pkg
SU02	Teak patio set/planting	0	$3 800 ($3 500) /pkg

21 Used Form ITA-1 dated June 8/18 to assemble four SU01 Aluminum patio set/planting packages using furniture and plants as follows:

components				unit cost	total
4	FA03	Table: Cast Aluminum round 2 m	$ 400 each		$1 600.00
16	FA04	Arm chair: Cast Aluminum	55.6894 each		891.03
4	FA06	End table: Cast Aluminum	60 each		240.00
8	SH01	Shrubs: 50 cm	6 each		48.00
4	BK01	Gardening in the Shade	25 each		100.00
Additional Costs (for services)					240.00

assembled items (package)			unit cost	total
4	SU01	Aluminum patio set/planting	$779.7575 each	$3 119.03

22

Used Form ITA-2 dated June 8/18 to assemble four SU02 Teak patio set/planting packages using furniture and plants as follows:

components			unit cost	total
4	FT31	Patio table: Teak round 1.5 m	$586.844 each	$ 2 347.38
16	FT33	Arm chair: Teak	438 each	7 008.00
4	FT35	End table: Teak	145.55 each	586.60
8	SH04	Shrubs: 1 metre specialty	55 each	440.00
4	BK01	Gardening in the Shade	25 each	100.00
	Additional Costs			240.00

assembled items (package)			unit cost	total
4	SU02	Teak patio set/planting	$2 680.495 each	$10 721.98

23

Merchandise requested from Groen Fields was received on June 9 with invoice #GF-1299. Payment is due in 60 days.

items purchased			amount
20	PL01	Plant/ground cover: 5 litre	$ 200
20	PL02	Plant/ground cover: 10 litre	320
100	PL03	Plant/ground cover starters	4 000
30	PL04	Plant: perennial specialty	750
30	PL05	Plant: annual 10 cm	150
20	SH03	Shrubs: 3 metre	640
3	PS11	Topsoil: cubic metre	180
	HST Paid		936
Invoice Total			$7 176

24

Sale #169 to Marjorie Blackhorn was completed on June 10. Blackhorn paid for the consultation with Visa. 100% of revenue was allocated to Design.

items sold			amount	total
8	SC01	Consultation/Design	$110 /hour	$ 880
	HST Paid			132
Invoice total paid by Visa				$1 012

25

Invoice #GC-6821 from Garden Crafts (use full add for new Canadian supplier) was received with the shipment of furniture on June 10. Terms for the new supplier are net 30. Allocate 100% of the freight expense to Store Sales.

items purchased			amount
10	FX42	Umbrella w/stand	$1 100
20	FX43	Cushion: deep seating chair	400
4	FX44	Cushion: deep seating lounge	240
4	FX45	Cushion: deep seating set	520
	Freight		100
	HST Paid		354
Invoice Total			$2 714

26

Recorded purchase order #140 from Mobler Dansk on June 10 at the exchange rate of 0.197. Terms: 2/15, n/30 days after delivery on June 13.

items purchased			amount
2	FA02	Patio set: Cast Aluminum rect. table 2 m	Dkr 7.200,00
4	FA03	Table: Cast Aluminum round 2 m	8.000,00
8	FA04	Arm chair: Cast Aluminum	2.240,00
4	FA06	End table: Cast Aluminum	1.200,00
	Freight		1.200,00
	HST		2.976,00
Invoice Total			Dkr 22.816,00

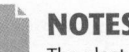 **WARNING!**

The unit costs change continually as new inventory is purchased at different prices.

Accept your default prices for assembly components and copy the total to the assembled items total. The totals for assembly components (including additional costs) and assembled items must be exactly the same.

 NOTES

The plant starters have different buying and selling units. They are purchased in flats of ten 4-pack units and sold as individual 4-pack items.

NOTES

For cash, credit card or debit card sales, you can type the new customer name and choose Continue or choose One-Time Customer and use the Additional Field for the customer name. No discounts apply to these sales.

NOTES

Garden Crafts
(contact Jon Quill)
290 Daffodil Lane
Richmond Hill, ON L3T 1P1
Terms: net 30
Tax code: H

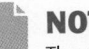 **NOTES**

The duty rate does not appear on purchase orders or quotes.

27 Recorded purchase order #141 from Jorgensen Mobler on June 10 at the exchange rate of 0.197. Terms: 2/30, n/60 days after delivery on June 13.

items purchased		amount
4 FT32	Patio table: Teak rect 2 m	Dkr 11.600,00
6 FT33	Arm chair: Teak	12.000,00
3 FT34	Chaise longue: Teak	7.350,00
	Freight	1.000,00
	HST Paid	4.792,50
Invoice Total		Dkr 36.742,50

NOTES
Remember to change the currency setting to DKK for the bank transfer.

28 Memo #7 from Owner, dated June 12, authorized bank transfer. Dkr 30.000,00 was taken from Bank: Visa and Interac account and deposited to Bank: DKK for upcoming payments. The exchange rate was 0.200.

29 Sale #170 to Acadian Towers was completed on June 12. Terms for the sale were 2/15, n/30. 100% of revenue and expenses for inventory items was allocated to Store Sales; 100% of revenue from consultation was allocated to Design; and 100% of revenue from planting was allocated to Planting.

items sold		amount
4 PL01	Plant/ground cover: 5 litre	$ 16 each
4 PL02	Plant/ground cover: 10 litre	25 each
200 PL03	Plant/ground cover starters	6 /4-pack
10 PL04	Plant: perennial specialty	42 each
20 PL06	Plant: annual 15 cm	13 each
3 PS11	Topsoil: cubic metre	105 /cu m
5 SH01	Shrubs: 50 cm	11 each
5 SH02	Shrubs: 1 metre	25 each
24 SC01	Consultation/Design	90 /hour
20 SC03	Planting & Soil Preparation	40 /hour
	Harmonized Sales Tax	15%

30 Entered 0.200 as the exchange rate on June 12. Paid invoice #JM-842 from Jorgensen Mobler with cheque #376 for Dkr 12.400,00 and paid cheque #377 to Mobler Dansk for Dkr 17.941,84 including Dkr 366,16 discount for early payment for invoice #MD-916.

NOTES
Credit card fees are not fully allocated because amounts are rounded off.

31 Violet Birch paid for her purchase on June 13 with her MasterCard, entered as cash sale #171. 100% of revenue from plant sales was allocated to Store Sales and 100% of consultation and report revenue was allocated to Design.

items sold		amount	total
30 PL03	Plant/ground cover starters	$ 8 each	$ 240.00
8 SC01	Consultation/Design	110 /hour	880.00
1 SC02	Report	200 /report	200.00
	HST Paid		198.00
Invoice total paid by MasterCard			$1 518.00

NOTES
Remember to change the payment method back to Pay Later.

32 Sale #172 to Acadian Towers was completed on June 13. Terms for the sale were 2/15, n/30. 100% of revenue and expenses was allocated to Store Sales.

items sold		amount
1 FA01	Patio set: Cast Aluminum round table 1.5 m	$1 090 each
2 FA05	Ottoman: Cast Aluminum	50 each
2 FA06	End table: Cast Aluminum	95 each
2 FA07	Bench: Cast Aluminum	185 each
6 FX43	Cushion: deep seating chair	40 each
	Harmonized Sales Tax	15%

 33 Received all items ordered from Mobler Dansk on purchase order #140 on June 13 with invoice #MD-1241 with payment terms of 2/15, net 30. Used the exchange rate of 0.199. Total import duty charged was Dkr 1.491,20 (CAD $296.74). The freight expense was allocated entirely to Store Sales.

items purchased			amount	duty rate
2	FA02	Patio set: Cast Aluminum rect. table 2 m	Dkr 7.200,00	8.0%
4	FA03	Table: Cast Aluminum round 2 m	8.000,00	8.0%
8	FA04	Arm chair: Cast Aluminum	2.240,00	8.0%
4	FA06	End table: Cast Aluminum	1.200,00	8.0%
		Freight	1.200,00	
		HST	2.976,00	
Invoice Total			Dkr 22.816,00	

 WARNING!
The exchange rate from the order will be the default and you will need to change it.

NOTES
If the duty fields are omitted when you convert the order, close and re-open the journal. They should now be included. You can add the rates manually if needed.
Variance costs will not be allocated.

 34 On June 13, all items ordered from Jorgensen Mobler on purchase order #141 arrived. Invoice #JM-1088 confirmed payment terms of 2/30, net 60. Used the exchange rate of 0.199 for the invoice. Total import duty charged was Dkr 2.940,25 (CAD $585.11). The freight expense was allocated to Store Sales.

items purchased			amount	duty rate
4	FT32	Patio table: Teak rect 2 m	Dkr 11.600,00	9.5%
6	FT33	Arm chair: Teak	12.000,00	9.5%
3	FT34	Chaise longue: Teak	7.350,00	9.5%
		Freight	1.000,00	
		HST Paid	4.792,50	
Invoice Total			Dkr 36.742,50	

✓ **35** Completed a payroll cheque run for the bi-weekly paid employees using Time Summary Sheet #51. The pay period ending date is June 14/18. Issue deposit slips #66 to #69.

EMPLOYEE TIME SUMMARY SHEET #51   DATED JUNE 14/18

Name of Employee	Regular Hours	Overtime Hours	No. of Plantings	Sick Days	Personal Days	Sales Commission	Allocations
Aster	75	0	100	1	–	–	90% Planting, 10% Store Sales
Fineum	75	2	120	–	1	–	80% Planting, 20% Store Sales
Iola	75	2	–	–	–	$106	100% Store Sales
Phlox	$1 650 Salary		40	–	–	–	10% Planting, 90% Store Sales

Allocating in the Payroll and Other Journals

The same principles outlined above to allocate revenues and expenses also apply to the General Journal and Adjustments Journal, and the same Division Settings apply. Payroll allocations have their own setting: by amount, percentage or hours (refer to page 505). We chose percentage for Shady Corners.

Once you have entered the journal information for an account that allows allocation, the Allocate tool ✓ will be available. You can use it to enter the allocation information.

In the **Paycheques Journal**, click the Allocate tool ✓ to begin the allocation.

In the **Payroll Run Journal**, use the Divisions column for a selected employee. **Click** the **employee's name** and **double-click** the **Divisions column**.

In both Payroll journals, you can **choose** the **Paycheque/Payroll menu** and **click Allocate To Division** to begin the allocation for a single employee (after first selecting an employee in the Payroll Run Journal).

NOTES
Instead of clicking the Division column ✓ beside an employee's name in the Payroll Run Journal, you can click the employee name and then click the Allocate tool button.

If the amounts for all employees should be allocated in the same proportions, you can apply the same allocation to the entire transaction by clicking **Apply This Allocation To Entire Transaction** as we did for sales.

To correct allocations, click ☑ to re-open the allocation screen.

In the Payroll journals, all payroll expenses for an employee are allocated by the same percentages (or amounts or hours). This includes the wage and vacation expenses as well as employer contributions such as EI, CPP and WCB. In the journal entry you review, all the payroll-related expenses are divided among the divisions according to the percentages you entered. They are provided under the Division column. You may have to scroll to include all the information.

NOTES
All the amounts for an employee will be allocated the same way.

Uploading Payroll Direct Deposits

All employees have direct deposit set up in their ledger records, so we can upload the payroll cheques for deposit to their accounts.

✓
36

Memo #8 from Owner: Upload the payroll deposits.

Again, the same two methods are available for uploading payroll deposits.

Click the **Upload Direct Deposit icon** 🖼️ in the Related Tasks pane of the Employees & Payroll module window. Or,

Choose the **File menu** and **Import/Export** in the Home window and then **click Upload Direct Payments** and **Employee Direct Deposits**:

NOTES
The Upload button becomes available as soon as you select an employee.

NOTES
Our test account with Beanstream will not permit you to follow through with uploading and reviewing transactions.

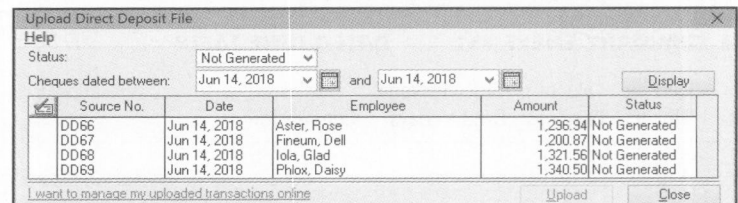

The four employees we paid are listed. **All** is entered as the Status selection with the range of dates for the cheques we are uploading. All deposits are not generated yet.

NOTES
Remember that unless you have a valid account with Beanstream (or another provider), you cannot follow through with uploading the deposits.
To cancel the uploading process, click Close to return to the Upload Transactions screen and then click Close to return to your starting point.

Click 🖼️, the **Select check box** in the column heading, to add ✓s for all employees.

Click the **Upload button** to open the Beanstream authorization window.

Enter your Beanstream account Company name, User Login and Password and choose the date you want the payments to be processed. Click Upload.

After the uploading has been completed, you will receive a confirmation message:

Click OK. Choose Generated from the drop-down list for Status. Click Display:

NOTES
The Status drop-down list options are to list Generated deposits, Not Generated deposits or All deposits.

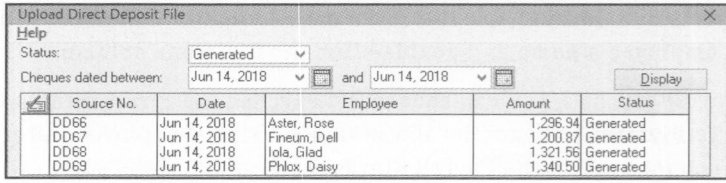

All transactions now have Generated as their status.

Click Close to finish your uploading session.

Reviewing the Uploaded Transactions

At any time you can review your uploaded transactions online.

To review your transactions, click **I Want To Manage My Uploaded Transactions Online** in any upload window. You will be connected to the Beanstream login page. Enter your Beanstream account Company name, User Login and Password. Click Processing and Employee Direct Deposit to list your employee transactions:

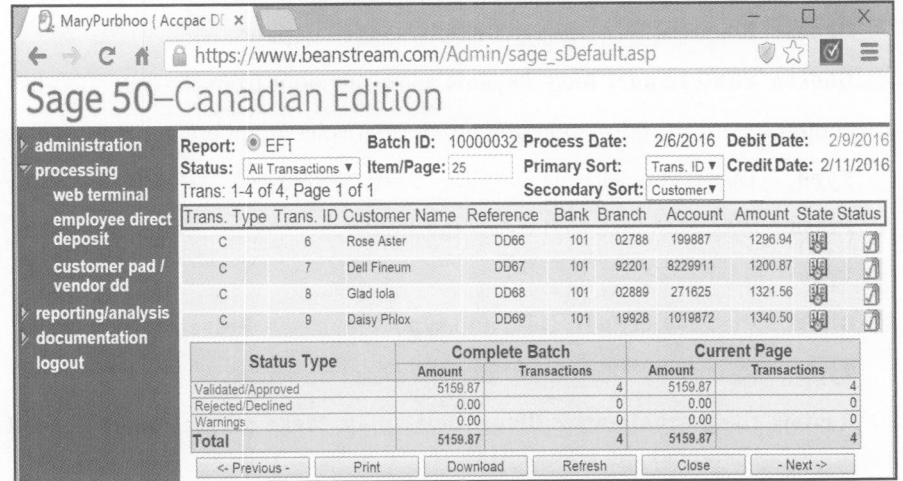

Click Customer PAD/Vendor DD and any line in the summary to provide details:

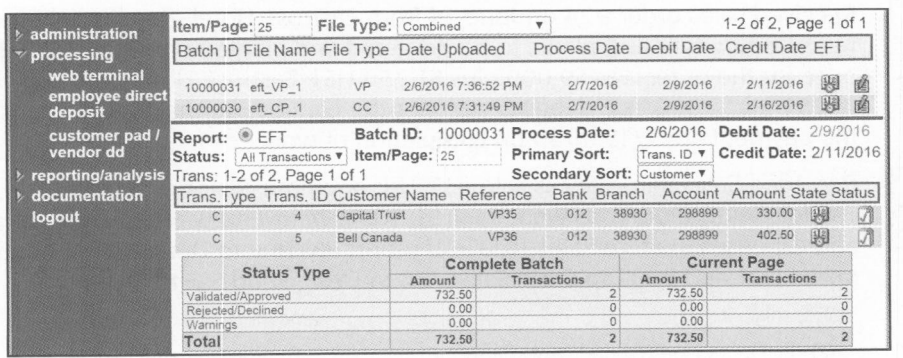

From your account, you can edit the transactions you have uploaded.

Click the Edit tool in a Summary line of the review page, that is, eft_CP_1, eft_VP_1 and so on, to open the options for editing:

You can change the processing date or delete the batch of all items you uploaded at the same time. If you choose Delete, you will be asked to confirm your decision:

Click OK to continue. Click Logout when finished to end the session safely.

Making Import Duty Remittances

Paying the import duty owing on imported merchandise is like paying other taxes. Normally, duty must be paid before the package is released by Customs.

✓ 37   June 14 memo #9 from Owner requested payment to the Receiver General for import duty charged on purchases to date. Wrote cheque #582 for $4 173.75 to pay duty on invoices #MD-916, MD-1018, MD-1241, JM-876 and JM-1088.

> **Open** the **Payments Journal**. The cheque number, bank account and date are correct.
>
> **Choose Make Other Payment**.
>
> **Choose Receiver General for Canada** as the supplier.
>
> **Choose 2220 Import Duty Payable** as the account from the Selection list.

You should record the corresponding purchase invoice numbers in the journal as well.

> **Type** `Duty re MD-916, MD-1018, MD-1241, JM-876 & JM-1088`
>
> **Press** (tab) to move to the Amount field.
>
> **Type** `4173.75`
>
> **Click** the **Invoice/Ref. field** and **type** Memo 9 **Press** (tab).
>
> **Type** `Memo 9, Import duty remittance`
>
> **Review** the **journal entry**. **Close** the **display**. **Make corrections** if needed and then **post** the **transaction**.
>
> **Enter** the remaining **transactions** for June.

38   Received sales order #24 on June 14 from Eastrose Hotel. The special order requires furniture and plants to be delivered and planted on June 21/18. The price for the order was $9 000 plus $1 350 HST. Eastrose Hotel provided cheque #9754 for $2 500 as a deposit (#81) for the contract. Terms for the balance of the payment are 2/15, n/30 on completion of work.

39   Recorded Sales Summary as sale #173 for one-time customers on June 14, 2018. The following allocations were applied: 100% of inventory and delivery revenue and expenses to Store Sales; 100% of report revenue to Design; 90% of revenue from SU01 and SU02 to Store Sales, 5% to Design and 5% to Planting.

items sold			amount	total
100	PL03	Plant/ground cover starters	$ 8 /4-pack	$ 800.00
10	PL05	Plant: annual 10 cm	9 each	90.00
10	PL06	Plant: annual 15 cm	16 each	160.00
20	PS10	Topsoil: 50 litre bag	6 /bag	120.00
2	SC02	Report	200 /report	400.00
2	SU01	Aluminum patio set/planting	1 250 /pkg	2 500.00
2	SU02	Teak patio set/planting	3 800 /pkg	7 600.00
5	BK01	Gardening in the Shade (GST @ 5%)	45 /book	225.00
		Delivery		400.00
		Goods and Services Tax	5%	11.25
		Harmonized Sales Tax	15%	1 810.50
		Total cash deposited to chequing account		$14 116.75

NOTES You can also enter the remittance in the Purchases Journal by choosing Cheque as the method of payment.

NOTES This is a non-inventory sales order. Credit Revenue from Store Sales.

NOTES If the Divisions column is not included in the journal after recording the sales order, close and then re-open the journal.

WARNING! You must change the tax code for BK01 to G.

SESSION DATE – JUNE 21, 2018

40

On June 16, invoice #JM-1134 from Jorgensen Mobler arrived with merchandise and payment terms of 2/30, net 60. The exchange rate was 0.201 on June 16. Total import duty charged was Dkr 1.786,00 (CAD $358.99). The freight expense was allocated to Store Sales.

items purchased			amount	duty rate
8	FP21	Patio table: Moulded Plastic 2 m	Dkr 12.800,00	9.5%
30	FP22	Arm chair: Moulded Plastic	6.000,00	9.5%
		Freight	1.200,00	
		HST Paid	3.000,00	
		Invoice Total	Dkr 23.000,00	

41

Used Form ITA-3 dated June 16/18 to assemble eight plastic patio sets using furniture items on hand. Created new inventory item FP25 for assembled item.

new item	description		min amt	regular (preferred) selling price/unit
FP25	Patio set: Moulded Plastic		1	$820 (750) /5-pce set

linked accounts: Asset 1400; Revenue 4020; COGS 5070

assembly components			unit cost	total
8	FP21	Patio table: Moulded Plastic 2 m	$337.2344 each	$2 697.88
32	FP22	Arm chair: Moulded Plastic	43.2643 each	1 384.46

assembled item (5-pce set)			unit cost	total
8	FP25	Patio set: Moulded Plastic	$510.2925 /5-pce set	$4 082.34

42

Recorded Visa sale #174 for Holly Yew on June 17, 2018. The following allocations were applied: 100% of report revenue to Design; 100% of revenue from book to Store Sales.

items sold			amount	total
1	SC02	Report	$200 /report	$200.00
1	BK01	Gardening in the Shade (GST @ 5%)	45 each	45.00
		Goods and Services Tax	5%	2.25
		Harmonized Sales Tax	15%	30.00
		Total amount paid by Visa		$ 277.25

43

Used Form RIF-1001 dated June 18/18 to reserve contract items for Eastrose Hotel. Free delivery included. All items entered at average cost prices. New inventory record was created for the contract using a new linked inventory asset Group account 1450 Reserved Inventory and existing accounts 4020 and 5070 for linked Revenue and COGS. HST is charged on the sale and duty does not apply.

new item	description	min amt	regular selling price
EH01	Eastrose Hotel Inventory	0	$9 000 /job

reserved (assembly) components		unit cost	total
100 PL03	Plant/ground cover starters	$ 4.00 /4-pack	$ 400.00
10 PL05	Plant: annual 10 cm	5.00 each	50.00
10 SH02	Shrubs: 1 metre	16.00 each	160.00
5 SH03	Shrubs: 3 metre	32.00 each	160.00
3 FX42	Umbrella w/stand	110.00 each	330.00
6 FP25	Patio set: Moulded Plastic	510.2925 /5-pce set	3 061.76
Additional Costs			$1 000.00

job (assembled) item		unit cost	total
1 EH01	Eastrose Hotel Inventory	$5 161.76 each	$5 161.76

WARNING!
The unit costs change continually as new inventory is purchased at different prices or adjusting entries are made.
Accept your default prices for assembly components and copy the total to the assembled items total. The totals for assembly components (including additional costs) and assembled items must be exactly the same.

NOTES
No journal entry results from the assembly because the same asset account is used for assembly components and the assembled item.

WARNING!
You must change the tax code for BK01 to G.

WARNING!
Accept your default prices for assembly components and copy the total to the assembled items total. The totals for assembly components (including additional costs) and assembled items must be exactly the same.

NOTES

Refer to page 415 for assistance with editing the sales order. Editing orders is like editing quotes. Choose Sales Order as the transaction type before choosing the order to adjust. Do not edit the prepayment amount.

44 June 19 memo #10 requested that sales order #24 from Eastrose Hotel be edited. Changed the order by entering EH01 as the item number. The quantity ordered (one), price and terms are unchanged.

45 Purchased new rototiller from Yardworks Inc. (use Quick Add) on June 19 for $600 plus $90 HST. Paid $690 for this purchase on invoice #YI-499 with cheque #583.

46 On June 19, wrote cheque #584 to Trucks 4U (choose Quick Add) for $161 for truck rental needed for extra deliveries. Invoice #T4U-48221 amounted to $140 plus $21 HST. 90% of the expense was allocated to Store Sales and 10% to Planting.

47 Plant care supplies were purchased from Yardworks Inc. on June 19 and paid for with cheque #585 for $241.50. Invoice #YI-584 provided the details of the sale: the cost of the supplies was $210 plus $31.50 HST.

48 Owner authorized bank transfer of Dkr 165.000,00 on memo #11, dated June 21, to cover cheques. Money was taken from Bank: Chequing account and deposited to Bank: DKK account. The exchange rate for the transfer was 0.198.

49 Entered 0.198 as the exchange rate on June 21 to pay invoice #MD-1018 from Mobler Dansk with cheque #378 for Dkr 160.034,00 including the discount of Dkr 3.266,00. Also paid invoice #JM-876 from Jorgensen Mobler with cheque #379 for Dkr 9.151,24 including Dkr 186,76 discount.

SESSION DATE – JUNE 30, 2018

WARNING!

When filling the sales order, change the method of payment to Pay Later.

50 Sales order #24 for Eastrose Hotel was filled on June 22 as sale #175. Terms of sale were 2/15, n/30 with $7 850 as the balance owing. 20% of the revenue was allocated to Design, 25% to Planting and 55% to Store Sales.

items sold		amount
1 EH01	Eastrose Hotel Inventory	$9 000 /job
	Harmonized Sales Tax	15%

NOTES

Remember to enter the quantity returned with a minus sign and to change the default account.

Use the Inventory Adjustments Journal to write off the returned inventory.

51 Efren Barrato returned a shrub because it died shortly after planting. The returned item was recorded on form #R-166 on June 22 using account 4130 Sales Returns & Allowances, a new Group revenue account. The returned item was written off according to memo #12. All amounts were allocated to Store Sales. With the Owner's permission, the refund was paid in cash. (Choose Cash as the payment method for the return. Refer to Accounting Procedures.)

items returned		amount	total
−1 SH03	Shrubs: 3 metre	$55 each	−$55.00
	Harmonized Sales Tax	15%	-8.25
Total cash paid to customer			−$63.25

52 On June 25, invoice #MD-1982 from Mobler Dansk arrived with merchandise and payment terms of 2/15, net 30. The exchange rate was 0.205 on June 25. Total import duty charged was Dkr 883,20 (CAD $181.06). The freight expense was allocated to Store Sales.

items purchased		amount	duty rate
2 FA01	Patio set: Cast Aluminum round table 1.5 m	Dkr 7.600,00	8.0%
8 FA04	Arm chair: Cast Aluminum	2.240,00	8.0%
4 FA06	End table: Cast Aluminum	1.200,00	8.0%
	Freight	1.000,00	
	HST Paid	1.806,00	
Invoice Total		Dkr 13.846,00	

53 Memo #13 from the Owner on June 27 requested that the HST owing be remitted as of May 31, 2018. Issued cheque #586 for $3 200 in full payment. (Use Trial Balance amounts on page 496.)

54 Complete a payroll cheque run for the bi-weekly paid employees using Time Summary Sheet #52. The pay period ending date is June 28/18. Allocate the payroll expenses for employees as instructed below. Issue deposit slips #70 to #73.

EMPLOYEE TIME SUMMARY SHEET #52   DATED JUNE 28/18

Name of Employee	Regular Hours	Overtime Hours	No. of Plantings	Sick Days	Personal Days	Sales Commission	Allocations
Aster	75	2	140	–	–	–	90% Planting, 10% Store Sales
Fineum	75	2	150	–	–	–	90% Planting, 10% Store Sales
Iola	75	4	–	–	–	$60	100% Store Sales
Phlox	$1 650 Salary		50	–	–	–	10% Planting, 90% Store Sales

NOTES

If you have difficulty accessing the Divisions column in the Payroll Run Journal, you can click an employee name and then click the Allocate tool button.

55

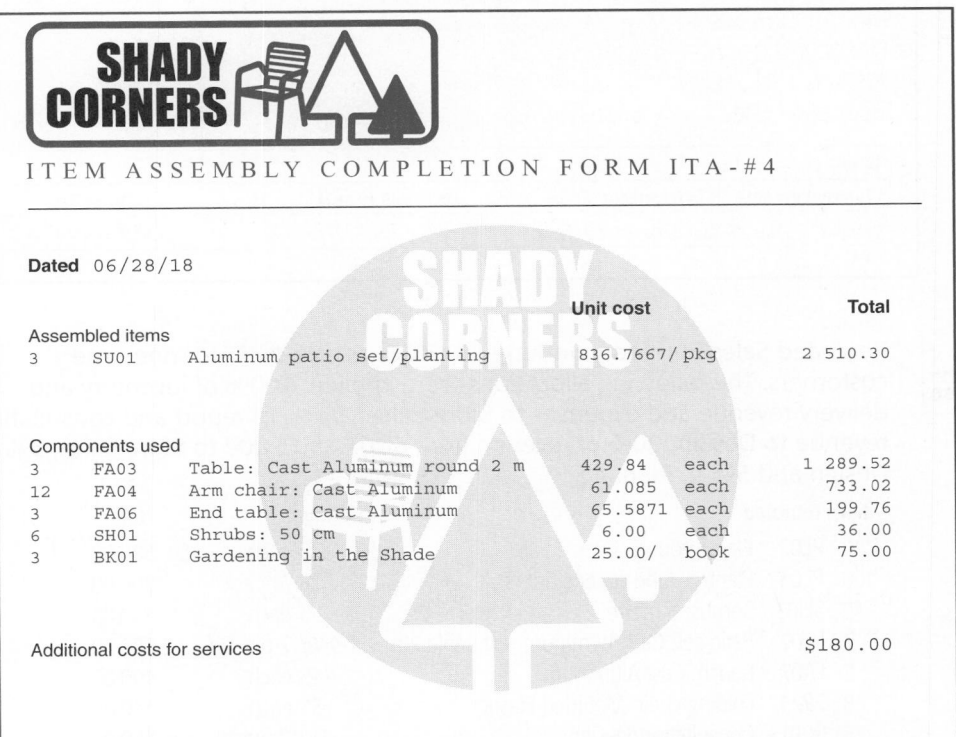

SHADY CORNERS

ITEM ASSEMBLY COMPLETION FORM ITA-#4

Dated 06/28/18

			Unit cost		Total
Assembled items					
3	SU01	Aluminum patio set/planting	836.7667/ pkg		2 510.30
Components used					
3	FA03	Table: Cast Aluminum round 2 m	429.84	each	1 289.52
12	FA04	Arm chair: Cast Aluminum	61.085	each	733.02
3	FA06	End table: Cast Aluminum	65.5871	each	199.76
6	SH01	Shrubs: 50 cm	6.00	each	36.00
3	BK01	Gardening in the Shade	25.00/	book	75.00
Additional costs for services					$180.00

WARNING!

The unit costs change continually as new inventory is purchased at different prices.

Accept your default prices for assembly components and copy the total to the assembled items total. The totals for assembly components (including additional costs) and assembled items must be exactly the same.

56 Pre-authorized withdrawals from the chequing account were recorded on June 28. Debit memo #92564 from Capital Trust itemized the transaction details. The mortgage payment of $900 included an interest amount of $690 and the loan payment of $1 000 included $200 for interest. The remaining amounts for these withdrawals were principal. Bank charges of $65 were also on this memo. Create a new expense account: 5010 Bank Charges. All expense amounts were shared as follows: Store Sales 50%, Planting 10% and Design 40%.

57

Shady Corners
599 Ivy Lane, Halifax, NS B3J 2N3
Tel: (902) 289-3904 or (902) 289-3904 Fax: (902) 285-7532

Date of sale: June 28/18

To: Rockcliff Manor
    400 Rocky Ridge Rise, Halifax, NS B3B 5V8

I N V O I C E   1 7 6

No.	Item		Price	Total	Division*
80	PL03	Plant/ground cover starters	8	640.00	1
10	SH01	Shrubs: 50 cm	13	130.00	1
10	SH03	Shrubs: 3 metre	55	550.00	1
2	FT37	Bench: Teak	1 125	2 250.00	1
2	FX41	Hammock w/stand	175	350.00	1
10	SC01	Consultation/Design	110	1 100.00	3
15	SC03	Planting & Soil Preparation	50	750.00	2
2	BK01	Gardening in the Shade (5% GST)	45	90.00	1
	GST 5%			4.50	

Division Code: 1 = Store Sales; 2 = Planting; 3 = Design

Terms: 2/15, net 30 days			
* Internal use only	Salesperson: Iola	HST# 230 192 821 15%	865.50
Total cash deposited to bank 6/28/18	*G Iola*		**6 730.00**

58

Recorded Sales Summary on June 28, 2018, as sale #177 for one-time customers. The following allocations were applied: 100% of inventory and delivery revenue and expenses to Store Sales; 100% of report and consultation revenue to Design; 90% of revenue from SU01 and SU02 to Store Sales, 5% to Design and 5% to Planting.

items returned			amount	total
20	PL02	Plant/ground cover: 10 litre	$ 29 each	$ 580.00
100	PL03	Plant/ground cover starters	8 /4-pack	800.00
10	SH03	Shrubs: 3 metre	55 each	550.00
2	FA02	Patio set: Cast Aluminum rect. table 2 m	1 340/ 7-pce set	2 680.00
2	FA07	Bench: Cast Aluminum	245 each	490.00
8	FP23	Folding chair: Moulded Plastic	55 each	440.00
5	SC01	Consultation/Design	110 /hour	550.00
1	SC02	Report	200 /report	200.00
1	SU01	Aluminum patio set/planting	1 250 /pkg	1 250.00
1	SU02	Teak patio set/planting	3 800 /pkg	3 800.00
5	BK01	Gardening in the Shade (GST @ 5%)	45 each	225.00
		Delivery		400.00
		Goods and Services Tax	5%	11.25
		Harmonized Sales Tax	15%	1 761.00
Total cash deposited to chequing account				$13 737.25

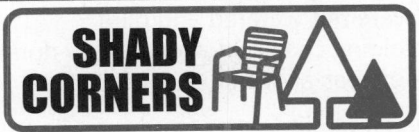

59

Shady Corners
599 Ivy Lane, Halifax, NS B3J 2N3
Tel: (902) 289-3904 or (902) 289-3904 Fax: (902) 285-7532

Date of sale: June 30/18

To: Luanne Bindweed
    One-time customer

INVOICE 178

No.	Item		Price	Total	Division*
1	FT32	Patio table: Teak rect. 2 m	1 180	1 180.00	1
4	FT33	Arm chair: Teak	725	2 900.00	1
1	FT34	Chaise longue: Teak	980	980.00	1
1	FT35	End table: Teak	245	245.00	1
2	FT36	Ottoman: Teak	105	210.00	1
1	FX45	Cushion: deep seating set	245	245.00	1
5	SC01	Consulting/Design	110	550.00	3
1	SC02	Report	200	200.00	3
		Upholstery fabric	300	300.00	1
		Delivery	100	100.00	1

Division Code: 1 = Store Sales; 2 = Planting; 3 = Design

Terms: Interac (8201 7827 4563 8900)				
* Internal use only	Salesperson: Iola	HST# 230 192 821 15%		1 036.50
Total deposited to Visa account 6/30/18 *G Iola*				7 946.50

NOTES
Use revenue account 4020 and tax code H for the upholstery fabrics.

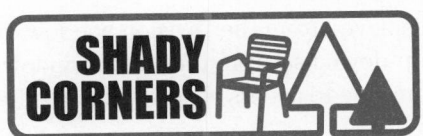

60

MEMO #14

Date   6/30/2018
From: Lou Pine
To: Owner

Paid import duty charged to Receiver General on all outstanding
purchases (#MD-1982 and JM-1134).

Wrote cheque #587 for $540.05 to pay balance in full.

Lou Pine

61

Memo #15 from the Owner on June 30 authorized the payment of monthly
salaries. Added 2 percent of service revenue for Anthemum and 1 percent of
service revenue for Pine to deposit slips #74 and #75 as their sales commissions.
Allocated 100% of Anthemum's and 80% of Pine's salary and commission to
Design. The remaining 20% of Pine's amounts are to be allocated to Store Sales.

62	Memo #16 on June 30 required us to record inventory losses as follows:

Memo #16 on June 30 required us to record inventory losses as follows:
  10 PL05 plants were not watered and died
   1 FP23 plastic folding chair had a leg broken during delivery
100% of the write-off was allocated to Store Sales.

63	

Memo #17 included a reminder to record payroll remittances for the pay period ending June 30. Entered Memo #17a, 17b, etc. as the reference. Cheques #588 to #592 were submitted in payment.
  Receiver General for Canada: EI, CPP and Income Tax
  Capital Trust: RRSP Payable
  Canadian Agricultural Workers' Union: Union Dues
  Workers' Compensation Board: WCB
  Professional Landscapers' Association: Professional Fees

64	

Received credit memo #65925 from Capital Trust on June 30. $40 interest was deposited to chequing account. This entry required a new Group account 4200 Revenue from Interest. 50% of the interest revenue was allocated to Store Sales, 30% to Design and 20% to Planting.

NOTES
The account 5115 should be assigned to the Cost of Goods Sold class so that it will be included correctly in the Gross Margin Income Statement.

65	

Memo #18 from Owner on June 30 reminded that adjusting entries were needed based on inventory counts. Allocated 90% of the plant and garden supplies to Store Sales and 10% to Planting. Allocated 100% of the fabrics to Store Sales. Allocated 80% of the Office Supplies to Store Sales, 10% to Planting and 10% to Design.

supplies used	amount	new account required
Plant and garden supplies	$1 900	
Upholstery fabrics	200	5115 Fabrics Sold
Office supplies	130	5180 Supplies Used: Office

Displaying Division Reports

Division reports can be displayed from the Division window, from the Division module window Reports pane drop-down list, from the Home window Reports menu or from the Report Centre. We will continue to access reports from the Report Centre.

PRO VERSION
Remember that if you have not changed the ledger name, Project will replace Division throughout the report menus and options.
  For other company types, Division may be replaced by a name that is appropriate for that type of company. Refer to Appendix B in this text.

Click the **Report Centre icon** [Report Centre] in the Home window.

Click **Division** to open the list of division reports:

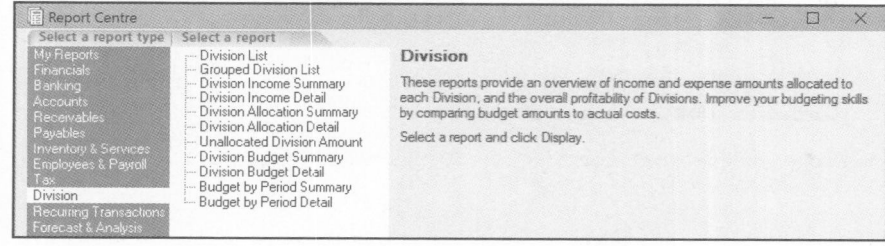

NOTES
The terms used for other types of industries will replace Division in all report titles and fields.

PRO VERSION
The Pro version does not have Forecast & Analysis reports, Grouped Division Lists or the Unallocated Division Amount Report.

Displaying the Division List

CLASSIC VIEW
Right-click the Divisions icon
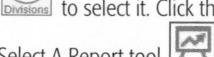 to select it. Click the
Select A Report tool [icon].

Click **Division List**. **Click Modify This Report** to open the report options:

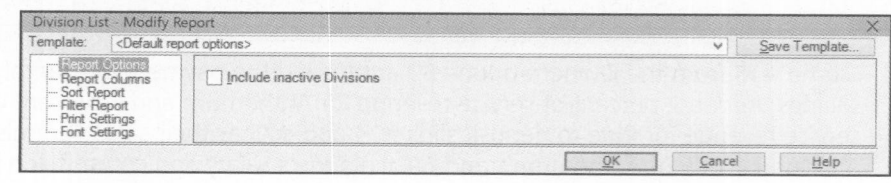

Or, choose the Reports menu, then choose Lists and click Division.

Click Report Columns to customize the fields included in the report.

Click   **OK**. **Close** the **display** when you have finished viewing the report.

Displaying the Grouped Division List

Click   **Grouped Division List**. **Click Modify This Report** for the options.

Click   the **Group By drop-down list arrow** for the ways you can organize the report:

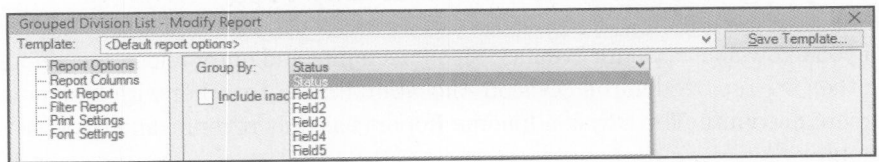

You can group the divisions by division status (e.g., pending, in progress and so on) or by any of the additional fields you added for the ledger.

Choose the **criterion** for grouping.

Click   **OK**. **Close** the **display** when you have finished viewing the report.

Displaying Division Income Reports

The Division Income Report provides an Income Statement with revenue and expense amounts and net income for each division you select for the report.

Click   **Division Income Summary**. **Click Modify This Report**:

Or, choose the Reports menu, then choose Division and click Income to display the Options window.

You can sort and filter Division Income Detail reports by date, comment, source, journal number or amount per transaction. As usual, the fiscal start and session dates are the defaults. All divisions and accounts are selected initially.

Enter   the **beginning** and **ending dates** for the report.

Click   a **division** to change the selection. **Press** and **hold** ⌨ctrl⌨ and **click** the **divisions** you want to include in the report. **Click Select All** to include all divisions in the report.

Leave the **Summary** option, the one selected by default, if you want your report to provide summary information (i.e., totals) for each account selected for each division. The **Detail** option provides complete journal information for each account for each

NOTES
You can display the Division Allocation Detail Report from the Division List.

NOTES
You can drill down to the Division Income Detail Report from the Division Income Summary Report. You can drill down to the Division Ledger, Journal Report, General Ledger, Customer or Supplier Aged or Employee Report or look up the transaction from the Division Income Detail Report.

NOTES
Remember that Select All works as a toggle switch. When no or some items are selected, clicking will select all items. When all are selected, clicking will remove all selections.

division selected, including the names of all customers, suppliers and employees, as well as the transaction's reference number, journal entry number and date. Both options provide a calculation for revenue minus expense.

Next you should select the revenue and expense accounts you want in the report.

Click   an **account** to change the selection. **Press** and **hold** ⌃ctrl⌃ and **click** the **accounts** you want to include in the report or **click Select All** to include them all.

Click   **OK** to display the report. **Close** the **display** when finished.

Displaying Division Allocation Reports

When you allow allocation for Balance Sheet accounts and enter allocation amounts for them, they are reported in the Division Allocation Report together with Income Statement accounts. The Division Income Report has only revenue and expense accounts.

Click   Division Allocation Summary. Click Modify This Report:

From any Home window, choose the Reports menu, then choose Division and click Allocation to display the Division Allocation Report Options window.

The Division Allocation Report tells you the breakdown of amounts for each division by account. It is similar to the Division Income Report, but the total revenue and expense and the net division income are replaced by a single total for all accounts for each division.

Although the report options look the same as for the Income Report, when you scroll up the list of accounts all reports for which you have allowed allocation will be included, including the Balance Sheet accounts.

Enter   the **Start** and **Finish dates** for the report.

Click   a **division** to change the selection. **Press** and **hold** ⌃ctrl⌃ and **click** the **divisions** you want to include in the report or **click Select All**.

Like the Income Report, the Summary option has totals and the Detail option provides complete journal information for each account for each division.

After you have indicated which options you want, choose the accounts.

Press   and **hold** ⌃ctrl⌃ and **click** the **accounts** you want or **click Select All**.

Click   **OK** to display the report. **Close** the **display** when you have finished.

Displaying the Unallocated Division Amounts Report

If you have any journal transactions with amounts that were not fully allocated, you can display all these transactions in the Unallocated Division Amounts Report. The

incomplete allocation may have occurred because you did not add the allocation details or because the program did not allow you to enter them (such as for cost variance amounts).

Click   **Unallocated Division Amount**. **Click Modify This Report**:

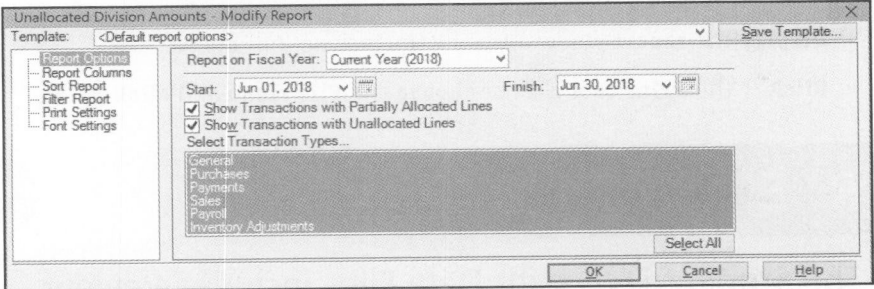

Or, choose the Reports menu, then choose Division and click Unallocated Amounts.

Amounts in the report are grouped by journal on separate detail lines that include the invoice or reference number, date, supplier or customer, account and amount. All journals that allow allocations may be selected for the report. You can choose to include transactions with amounts that were partially allocated, fully unallocated or both. Initially both types of incomplete allocations are selected for all journals with the dates ranging from the earliest transaction to the session date.

Choose   the **journals** you want included in the report. **Press** ⎡ctrl⎤ and **click** to select more than one journal.

Choose   the **types of incomplete allocations** you want — partial or full.

Enter   the **Start** and **Finish dates** for the report.

Click   **OK** to display the report. **Close** the **display** when finished.

Adding Division Details to Journal Reports

When you have entered division information in a journal, you can include the allocation details in any journal report.

Click   **Financials** in the Select A Report Type list.

Click   **All Journal Entries**. **Click Modify This Report**:

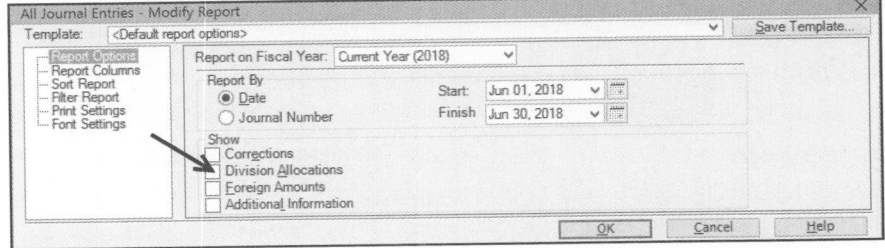

Or, choose the Reports menu, then choose Journal Entries and click All.

The Journal Report Options window includes a check box for Division Allocations under the Show heading. For a complete Journal Report, you should also show foreign amounts, corrections and additional information.

Click   **Division Allocations** to include division information in journal reports. By default, journal reports do not include division details.

NOTES
Credit card expense amounts may be included with the partially allocated accounts. Variance amounts will be included with the unallocated amounts.

NOTES
If you include all the details in the Journal Report, you should print the report in landscape orientation.

Choose the **other details** that you want to include in the report and **click OK**.

Close the **display** when finished. **Close** the **Report Centre**.

Printing Division Reports

Display the **report** you want using the instructions above.

Click the **Print tool** or **choose** the **File menu** and **click Print**.

R E V I E W

The Student DVD with Data Files includes Review Questions and Supplementary Cases for this chapter.

Village Galleries

OBJECTIVES

After completing this chapter, you should be able to

- **turn on** the budgeting feature in Sage 50
- **determine** and **enter** budgeting periods and amounts
- **allocate** budget amounts to revenue and expense accounts
- **enter** transactions involving Quebec Sales Tax
- **display** and **print** income statements with budget comparisons
- **analyze** budget reports
- **print** invoices in batches

COMPANY INFORMATION

Company Profile

> **NOTES**
> Village Galleries
> 509 Boul. Rouin
> Montreal, QC H3F 5G5
> Tel: (514) 529-6391
> Fax: (514) 529-7622
> Business No.: 236 412 540

Village Galleries, located in Outremont, an upscale area of Montreal, is owned and operated by Renée and Gilles Montand, a husband-and-wife partnership. The small family-run business recently hired one employee, who will earn a commission on sales. She works in the store several days a week, but the Montands maintain the regular operation of the business. Renée performs the accounting duties for the business. Other jobs are occasionally subcontracted.

The store, more like a furniture boutique, carries a limited range of high-quality inventory, selling to clients who are selective in their furniture and accessory preferences. Accessories and furniture for living rooms, bedrooms, dining rooms and kitchens compose the major inventory items in the boutique. The brass furniture pieces are imported from Italy, and some items are high-quality reproductions of antiques made in small Quebec furniture factories by respected artisans. Most of the furniture is made of wood or wood frames covered with fine fabrics. The choice of wood includes mahogany, oak, cherry, ash and, of course, maple and pine. Rich select woods of the highest quality are used to create solid wood pieces, but sometimes expensive veneers are used to complement the designs. In addition, the furniture boutique sells home accessories such as lamps, a small selection of handmade Persian and Oriental rugs made of wool and silk, mirrors and original framed numbered prints imported from Italy.

Most customers are local, but occasionally customers from abroad who visit Montreal ask for furniture to be shipped to them. Delivery (shipping or freight) is charged on most orders and exported items. Preferred price list customers do not pay for delivery, and they receive discounted inventory prices. All account customers are entitled to a before-tax 2 percent discount if they settle their accounts within 10 days. After 30 days, interest charges accrue at the rate of 1.5 percent per month. Customer deposits from 20 to 25 percent of the total sale are required on all orders. Customers may pay by cheque, cash or credit card.

Some suppliers with whom Village Galleries has accounts require deposits to accompany purchase orders, and some suppliers offer after-tax purchase discounts for early payments. The store has a business credit card account with American Express.

The currency for all foreign transactions, including the purchases from Italy and the sales to European customers, is the euro (€). Foreign prices for inventory are calculated from the exchange rate at the time of sale, so foreign prices are not entered in the Inventory Ledger. Village Galleries pays import duties on the imported furniture but not on original artwork such as the numbered prints.

Renée Montand used the following to set up the accounting files for Village Galleries in Sage 50:

- Chart of Accounts
- Post-Closing Trial Balance
- Supplier Information
- Customer Information
- Employee Information
- Inventory Information
- Accounting Procedures

CHART OF ACCOUNTS

VILLAGE GALLERIES

ASSETS

Current Assets
1060 Chequing Bank Account
1070 Visa Bank Account
1080 MasterCard Bank Account
1090 Bank Account - Euro
1100 Investment Portfolio
1150 Purchase Prepayments
1200 Accounts Receivable
1220 Office Supplies
1240 Furniture Supplies
1260 Prepaid Insurance

Inventory Assets
1320 Bedroom Furniture
1340 Home Accessories
1360 Kitchen & Dining Room Furniture
1380 Living Room Furniture ▶

Fixed Assets
▶1440 Computer Equipment
1460 Equipment & Tools
1480 Gallery Fixtures
1500 Gallery

LIABILITIES

Current Liabilities
2200 Accounts Payable
2220 Prepaid Sales and Deposits
2250 Credit Card Payable
2260 Import Duty Payable
2330 Income Tax Payable
2350 QPP Payable
2360 Quebec Income Tax Payable
2370 QHSF Payable
2460 CSST Payable
2650 GST Charged on Sales
2670 GST Paid on Purchases
2800 Refundable QST Paid
2810 QST Charged on Sales ▶

▶Long Term Liabilities
2950 Mortgage Payable - Gallery

EQUITY

Owner's Equity
3560 Montand, Capital
3580 Montand, Drawings
3600 Current Earnings

REVENUE
4020 Revenue from Sales
4040 Sales Discount
4060 Freight Revenue
4100 Investment Revenue
4120 Interest Revenue

EXPENSE

Operating Expenses
5020 Advertising & Promotion
5030 Exchange Rate Differences
5040 Bank Charges
5050 Credit Card Fees ▶

▶5060 Cost of Goods Sold
5070 Variance Costs
5080 Furniture Supplies Used
5100 Damaged Inventory
5120 Purchase Discounts
5130 Freight Expense
5140 Delivery Expense
5160 Hydro Expense
5180 Insurance Expense
5190 Mortgage Interest Expense
5200 Office Supplies Used
5220 Telephone Expenses

Payroll Expenses
5300 Commissions
5330 CSST Expense
5340 QPP Expense
5350 QHSF Expense
5380 Subcontractor Fees

NOTES: The Chart of Accounts includes only postable accounts and Current Earnings. QPP (Quebec Pension Plan) replaces CPP in Quebec. QHSF (Quebec Health Services Fund) is an employer-funded provincial health and services tax program.
Linked payable and expense accounts for EI, CPP and QPIP (Quebec Parental Insurance Plan) are also included because they are essential linked accounts, but they are not used in this example.

POST-CLOSING TRIAL BALANCE

VILLAGE GALLERIES

June 30, 2018

		Debits	Credits				Debits	Credits
1060	Chequing Bank Account	$ 51 792.25		▶ 1440	Computer Equipment	$ 3 800.00	
1070	Visa Bank Account	5 445.00		1460	Equipment & Tools	1 500.00	
1080	MasterCard Bank Account	3 555.00		1480	Gallery Fixtures	1 200.00	
1090	Bank Account - Euro (€ 1 560)	2 100.00		1500	Gallery	150 000.00	
1100	Investment Portfolio	50 000.00		2200	Accounts Payable		$ 11 395.00
1200	Accounts Receivable	5 748.75		2250	Credit Card Payable		240.00
1220	Office Supplies	400.00		2260	Import Duty Payable		240.00
1240	Furniture Supplies	600.00		2650	GST Charged on Sales		1 680.00
1260	Prepaid Insurance	250.00		2670	GST Paid on Purchases	980.00	
1320	Bedroom Furniture	38 720.00		2800	Refundable QST Paid	90.00	
1340	Home Accessories	34 020.00		2810	QST Charged on Sales		1 926.00
1360	Kitchen & Dining Room Furniture	27 510.00		2950	Mortgage Payable - Gallery		145 000.00
1380	Living Room Furniture	46 165.00 ▶		3560	Montand, Capital		263 395.00
						$423 876.00	$423 876.00

SUPPLIER INFORMATION

VILLAGE GALLERIES

Supplier Name (Contact)	Address	Phone No. Fax No.	E-mail Web Site	Terms Tax ID
Domo Carvaggio (Arturo Dessini)	8 Via Artistes Forli, 47100 Italy	Tel: (39-0543) 457 882 Fax: (39-0543) 457 113	domocarvaggio.com	net 30
Énergie Québec (Marie Nuclaire)	5010 Ave. Atomique Montreal, Quebec H2B 6C9	Tel: (514) 782-6101	energie.quebec.ca	net 7
L'Ascension Mobiliers (Suzie LaChaise)	RR #2 Jonquière, Quebec G7S 4L2	Tel: (450) 821-1029 Fax: (450) 822-1927	suzie@lascension.com lascension.com	1/5, n/30 (after tax) 322 749 610
Montreal Persia Emporium (Perse Moquette)	40 Rue de Tapis Longueuil, Quebec J4K 2L7	Tel: (450) 288-4334 Fax: (450) 288-8201	moquette@MPE.com MPE.com	2/5, n/30 (after tax) 473 540 911
Normandin Meubles (Normand Armoire)	RR #3 Nicolet, Quebec J3T 1H5	Tel: (450) 371-7273 Fax: (450) 371-7229	na@normand.meubles.com normand.meubles.com	2/10, n/30 (after tax) 136 492 446
Papineau Delivery (Martin Camion)	56 Papineau Ave. Outremont, Quebec H1M 3B3	Tel: (514) 690-2810 Fax: (514) 691-7283	martin@papineau.com papineau.com	net 10 288 344 566
Receiver General for Canada	Sudbury Tax Services Office PO Box 20004 Sudbury, Ontario P3A 6B4	Tel 1: (800) 561-7761 Tel 2: (800) 959-2221	cra-arc.gc.ca	net 1
Staples (Hélène Magazinier)	777 Ave. de Bureau Montreal, Quebec H4K 1V5	Tel: (514) 759-3488 Fax: (514) 758- 3910	staples.ca	net 15 128 634 772
Telébec (Robert Bavarde)	84 Rue Causerie Montreal, Quebec H3C 7S2	Tel: (514) 488-2355	bell.ca	net 1

NOTES: All supplier discounts are calculated on after-tax amounts.

OUTSTANDING SUPPLIER INVOICES

VILLAGE GALLERIES

Supplier Name	Terms	Date	Invoice	Amount CAD	Total
L'Ascension Mobiliers	1/5, n/30 (after tax)	June 29/18	LM-2114	$4 558.00	$4 558.00
Normandin Meubles	2/10, n/30 (after tax)	June 28/18	NM-192	$6 837.00	$6 837.00
				Grand Total	$11 395.00

CUSTOMER INFORMATION

VILLAGE GALLERIES

Customer Name (Contact)	Address	Phone No. Fax No.	E-mail Web Site	Terms Credit Limit
Caisse Metropolitain (Tomas Monaire)	50 Rue Berri Montreal, Quebec H1B 6F4	Tel: (514) 466-2991 Fax: (514) 468-1826	tmonaire@caissemetro.ca caissemetro.ca	2/10, n/30 $5 000
Cash Customers				cash or credit card
Deon Estates (Kaline Deon)	600 Rue St. Denis Montreal, Quebec H2K 7C9	Tel: (514) 729-8217 Fax: (514) 729-9283	kaline.deon@istar.com	2/10, n/30 $5 000
*St. Leonard's Homebuilders (Félice Charpentier)	31 Boul. St. Joseph Montreal, Quebec H4N 2M1	Tel: (514) 788-3645 Fax: (514) 787-7114	felice@stleonards.com stleonards.com	2/10, n/30 $10 000
*Westmount Primrose Condos (M.T. Sweets)	121 Rue Notre Dame Montreal, Quebec H3K 4G5	Tel: (514) 499-7117 Fax: (514) 498-2889	sweets@wpcondos.com wpcondos.com	2/10, n/30 $10 000

NOTES: All customer discounts are calculated on amounts before tax. Customers pay 1.5% interest per month on accounts over 30 days. Asterisk (*) indicates preferred price list customer.

OUTSTANDING CUSTOMER INVOICES

VILLAGE GALLERIES

Customer Name	Terms	Date	Invoice	Amount	Tax	Total
Deon Estates	2/10, n/30 (before tax)	June 24/18	168	$5 000	$748.75	$5 748.75

NOTES

As an employer, Village Galleries makes contributions to the Quebec Health Services Fund equal to 2.7 percent of the total payroll amount for the provincial health care plan. This amount is entered in the Payroll Settings.

CSST (La Commission de la Santé et de la Sécurité du Travail) is the workers' compensation agency in Quebec.

Employer and employee deductions for the Quebec Parental Insurance Plan are not required because Décor is not EI-insurable.

Employee Profile and TD1 Information

Lianne Décor started working for the boutique on July 1, 2018. Using her interior decorating and design skills, she visits homes for consultations to assess needs and suggest furniture from the store that matches the home's style and customer's taste. She is paid a commission of 20 percent of her monthly sales and takes four weeks of vacation each year. Décor is single and self-supporting. Her tax claim amounts are $17 474 federal and $17 225 provincial for basic amounts plus amounts for education. She works for the store part time and supplements her sales commission with her independent business as an interior design consultant.

Other employee details:

SIN:	566 811 014	Address:	45 Rue Collage
Date of birth:	August 26, 1982		Montreal, QC H2G 4R5
CSST (WCB) rate:	2.24	Tel:	(514) 639-9202

INVENTORY INFORMATION

VILLAGE GALLERIES

Code	Description	Unit	Min Qty	Selling Price Reg	(Pref)	Qty on Hand	Total (Cost)	Duty (Taxes)
Bedroom Furniture: Total asset value $38 720 (Linked accounts: Asset 1320; Revenue 4020; COGS 5060; Variance 5070)								
BF-01	Armoire: dark oak	1-pc	0	$3 420	$3 070	2	$4 840	9.5%
BF-02	Armoire: light ash	1-pc	0	3 310	2 970	2	4 400	9.5%
BF-03	Bed: 3 piece oak	set	0	2 200	1 980	2	2 640	9.5%
BF-04	Bed: 5 piece light ash/oak	set	0	3 310	2 970	2	3 960	9.5%
BF-05	Bed: brass/silver	1-pc	0	1 990	1 790	3	3 630	8.0%
BF-06	Chest: cherry	1-pc	0	1 100	990	3	1 980	9.5%
BF-07	Dresser: cashmere, burl-maple	1-pc	0	1 770	1 590	5	4 950	9.5%
BF-08	Dresser: highboy - dark oak	1-pc	0	2 090	1 880	5	6 050	9.5%
BF-09	Wardrobe: light ash	1-pc	0	3 090	2 780	2	3 960	9.5%
BF-10	Wardrobe: pine	1-pc	0	1 930	1 730	2	2 310	9.5%
Home Accessories: Total asset value $34 020 (Linked accounts: Asset 1340; Revenue 4020; COGS 5060; Variance 5070)								
HA-01	Framed Art: prints 45 x 60cm	each	0	230	200	40	4 400	0.0%
HA-02	Framed Art: prints 75 x 100cm	each	0	330	290	30	4 980	0.0%
HA-03	Lamp: floor solid brass	1-pc	0	450	400	10	2 420	8.0%
HA-04	Lamp: table solid brass	1-pc	0	660	590	10	3 850	8.0%
HA-05	Mirror: oval dark oak	1-pc	0	550	490	5	1 650	9.5%
HA-06	Mirror: square ash/mahogany	1-pc	0	610	540	5	2 090	9.5%
HA-07	Rugs: Persian Isfahan 185 x 275cm	each	0	1 650	1 480	10	6 600	n/a
HA-08	Rugs: Persian Kashan 185 x 275cm	each	0	1 310	1 200	10	4 950	n/a
HA-09	Rugs: Persian Tabriz 90 x 160cm	each	0	950	860	10	3 080	n/a
Kitchen & Dining Room Furniture: Total asset value $27 510 (Linked accounts: Asset 1360; Revenue 4020; COGS 5060; Variance 5070)								
KD-01	Buffet: oak	1-pc	0	1 930	1 730	2	2 200	9.5%
KD-02	Buffet: cherry	1-pc	0	2 480	2 230	2	2 420	9.5%
KD-03	Chairs: 4 piece cherry	set	0	1 210	1 080	5	3 300	9.5%
KD-04	Chairs: 4 piece oak	set	0	1 080	970	5	2 610	9.5%
KD-05	China Cabinet: walnut	1-pc	0	2 310	2 070	2	2 310	9.5%
KD-06	China Cabinet: cherry	1-pc	0	940	840	2	880	9.5%
KD-07	Credenza: maple	1-pc	0	1 850	1 660	2	2 150	9.5%
KD-08	Extension Table: oak	1-pc	0	2 010	1 800	2	2 260	9.5%
KD-09	Huntboard: white pine	1-pc	0	800	720	2	940	9.5%
KD-10	Server: fruitwood	1-pc	0	1 080	970	2	1 100	9.5%
KD-11	Sideboard: cherry	1-pc	0	1 790	1 610	2	2 040	9.5%
KD-12	Table: brass with glass	1-pc	0	1 960	1 760	4	3 860	8.0%
KD-13	Table: ivory lacquer/pine	1-pc	0	690	620	4	1 440	9.5%
Living Room Furniture: Total asset value $46 165 (Linked accounts: Asset 1380; Revenue 4020; COGS 5060; Variance 5070)								
LR-01	Bookcase: oak/walnut solid	1-pc	0	1 270	1 140	3	2 160	9.5%
LR-02	Chair: various patterns cotton	1-pc	0	580	520	10	3 030	9.5%
LR-03	Cocktail Table: cherry	1-pc	0	1 020	910	5	2 610	9.5%
LR-04	Console Table: oak	1-pc	0	1 050	940	5	2 750	9.5%
LR-05	Curio Cabinet: walnut/oak	1-pc	0	1 600	1 440	3	2 640	9.5%
LR-06	Desk: mahogany	1-pc	0	2 030	1 820	5	4 840	9.5%
LR-07	End Table: brass with glass	1-pc	0	680	610	5	1 540	8.0%
LR-08	Lamp Table: ash/oak solid	1-pc	0	910	810	5	2 900	9.5%
LR-09	Loveseat: chenille	1-pc	0	1 460	1 310	5	4 000	9.5%
LR-10	Ottoman & Slipcover: grey leather	2-pc	0	420	370	5	1 100	9.5%
LR-11	Recliner & Ottoman: brown leather	2-pc set	0	1 130	1 010	5	3 410	9.5%
LR-12	Sectional Sofa: charcoal linen	3-pc	0	2 530	2 270	3	4 620	9.5%
LR-17	Settee: light ash	1-pc	0	940	840	3	1 815	9.5%
LR-18	Sofa & Slipcover: celadon	2-pc	0	1 630	1 460	5	4 800	9.5%
LR-19	Swivel Chair & Slipcover: cotton	2-pc	0	710	630	5	2 150	9.5%
LR-20	Wing Chair: pastel	1-pc	0	640	570	5	1 800	9.5%
Total Inventory Value							$146 415	

Accounting Procedures

The Goods and Services Tax (GST) and Quebec Sales Tax (QST)

Village Galleries uses the regular method for remittance of sales taxes. GST collected from customers is recorded as a liability in *GST Charged on Sales*. GST paid to suppliers is recorded in *GST Paid on Purchases* as a decrease in the liability collected provincially for remittance to the Canada Revenue Agency.

Provincial sales tax (Quebec Sales Tax, or QST) of 9.975 percent is applied to all cash and credit sales of goods and services in the province of Quebec. QST collected from customers is recorded as a liability in *QST Charged on Sales*. QST paid to suppliers — recorded in *Refundable QST Paid* — decreases the liability to Revenu Québec.

GST is administered provincially in Quebec, so Montand files returns for both GST and QST with the ministre des Finances du Québec. Returns are remitted by the last day of the month for the previous quarter, either requesting a refund or remitting the balance — the difference between *QST Charged on Sales* and *Refundable QST Paid*.

Deposits on Custom Orders

When new customers place an order for furniture, they pay an advance of 20 to 25 percent of the price. The deposit may be entered in the Receipts Journal or on the Sales Order form. The Accounts Receivable Ledger for the selected customer will be credited for the advance and *Chequing Bank Account* will be debited. When the work is complete, fill the sales order to make a Sales Journal entry for the full amount of the contract, including relevant taxes. When the customer settles the account, accept both the invoice amount and the deposit (if you used the Receipts Journal) to indicate they are included and the full balance owing is paid. The balance in the Receipts Journal should then match the amount of the customer's cheque.

Partially filled quotes are automatically converted to orders for the backordered items by the Sage 50 program.

Freight Expenses

When a business purchases inventory items, the cost of freight that cannot be directly allocated to a specific item purchased must be charged to *Freight Expense*. This amount will be regarded as an expense and will not be part of the costs of any inventory asset account.

Printing Sales Invoices

If you want to print sales invoices through the program, complete the Sales Journal transaction as you would otherwise. Preview the transaction before posting it. You can print from the preview window or from the journal (click the Print tool button or choose the File menu and then Print). Before printing, check that you have selected the correct printer and forms. To e-mail an invoice, click the E-mail tool.

Foreign Purchases and Import Duty

Goods imported from Italy are subject to GST and QST and to import duties at various rates. These taxes are collected at the time the goods are received and are usually paid directly to the ministre des Finances. To simplify the transactions in Sage 50, we have set up the foreign supplier record so that the supplier collects GST, just like suppliers in Canada.

Import duties are handled separately in the program. Duty is calculated automatically because the rates are entered in the Inventory Ledger records. The

amount is credited to the linked *Import Duty Payable* account instead of *Accounts Payable*, so the duty is not added to the balance owing to the supplier. The linked asset account is debited.

On receiving the merchandise, the business writes a cheque to the Receiver General to pay the import duties on the purchase. This payment is just like any other tax remittance — enter the duty payable as a positive amount for a cash purchase from the Receiver General and choose *Import Duty Payable* as the account. The amount is the current General Ledger account balance.

INSTRUCTIONS

1. **Open** the data files and set up the **budget** for Village Galleries on July 1, 2018, using Sage 50. Detailed keystroke instructions to assist you follow these instructions.

2. **Enter** the **source documents** for July 2018 in Sage 50 using all the company information provided.

3. **Print** the following **reports**:

   - Balance Sheet as at July 31
   - Journal Entries for all journals from July 1 to July 31
   - Inventory Sales Detail Report for Bedroom Furniture
   - Inventory Quantity Report for all items to check reorder requirements

NOTES
Instructions for the Budget Report begin on page 558. Instructions for budget income reports begin on page 568.

KEYSTROKES

Setting Up Budgets

It is important for a business to gauge its performance against some standards. These standards can be provided through comparisons with other companies that are in the same line of business or by comparing the same company over several time periods. It is common for a business to set goals for the future based on past performance. For example, there may be an expectation that profits will increase by 10 percent over the previous year or that expenses will be reduced because of the introduction of new cost-reduction methods. If a business waits until the end of the year to assess its progress toward its goals, it may be too late to make necessary corrections if things are not proceeding according to plan. Budgets offer a realistic financial plan for the future that can be used to assess performance.

Before creating and analyzing budget reports, you must turn on the option and enter the budget amounts for the relevant accounts.

Turning On the Budgeting Feature

Open   **SageData16\VILLAGE\VILLAGE**. Do not advance the session date until you have finished the budget setup.

Click   the **Settings icon** .

NOTES
If you are working from backups, restore the backup file SageData16\VILLAGE1.CAB or VILLAGE1 to SageData16\ VILLAGE\VILLAGE.

PRO VERSION
Departments (for
departmental accounting) are not
available in the Pro version.

Click   **General (Accounts)** to open the General Settings list:

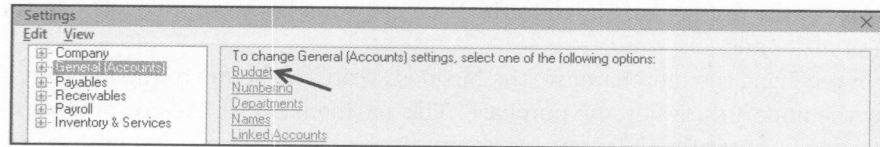

Click   **Budget** to open the budgeting options:

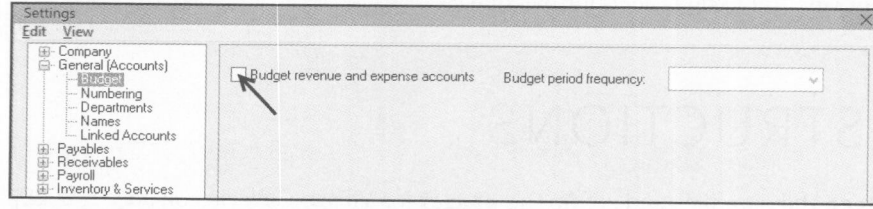

Click   **Budget Revenue And Expense Accounts** to turn on the budget feature.

NOTES
You cannot activate the
budget feature in multi-user
mode, but you can add and
change budget amounts.

The first decision after choosing the budgeting feature involves a budget period. Whether a business chooses to budget amounts on a yearly, quarterly or monthly basis depends on the needs and nature of the business. Monthly budget reports will be appropriate if the business cycle of buying and selling is short, but not appropriate for long-term projects. The period chosen must provide meaningful feedback about performance. If the periods are too short, there may be insufficient information to judge performance; if the periods are too long, there may be no opportunity to correct problems because they will not be detected soon enough. Village Galleries will use monthly budget periods initially because the Montands want frequent progress reports.

Click   the **Budget Period Frequency field** for the period options:

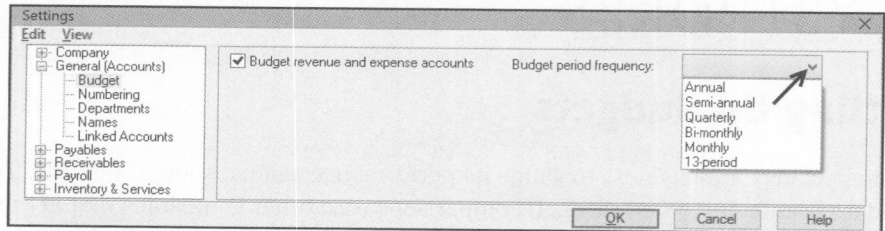

Click   **Monthly**.

Click   **OK** to return to the Home window and save the settings.

Setting a Budget

The next step is to enter the budget amounts for all expense and revenue accounts.

Budgets can be determined in several different ways. The most common methods are zero-based and incremental budgeting. With the zero-based method, a forecast is made for each revenue and expense account based on expectations about specific planned activities and expenditures. Each budget item must be justified. More commonly, last year's budgets and income statements are used as the starting point and a specific percentage change is applied. Thus, a company might expect to improve its performance over last year by 10 percent, either by increasing sales or by decreasing expenses. Planned special events such as annual month-long sales, new customer drives, and peak or slow periods can be built into the changes in budgeted amounts from one period to the next. Whatever method is used, it is important that the budget be realistic.

Renée Montand examined previous income statements and business practices to learn where improvements could be made and to get a realistic forecast. The business has been growing by about 10 percent per year. The corresponding expenses, sales discounts, cost of

goods sold and so on also increased by about the same amount. Sales are not divided evenly throughout the 12-month period. Most customers purchase new furniture in the spring and summer, the busiest home purchasing and moving seasons. Sales are slowest in the winter months, and store sales are planned for those months.

This pattern has led Montand to expect 12 percent of the year's sales to occur each month from April to August, 10 percent in January during the store annual sales event and 5 percent in each of the remaining months. The recent hiring of an interior design consultant should also boost sales over last year's results.

Renée Montand's detailed budget forecast is presented in the following item-by-item budget chart and rationale:

MONTHLY BUDGET FORECAST FOR 2018–2019

VILLAGE GALLERIES

Account	2018 Jul–Aug	2018 Sep–Dec	2019 Jan	2019 Feb–Mar	2019 Apr–Jun	2018–2019 Total for 12 months
REVENUE						
Revenue from Sales	$55 490	$23 125	$48 200	$23 125	$55 490	$464 400
Sales Discount	-554	-231	-482	-231	-554	–4 638
Freight Revenue	1 110	462	910	462	1 110	9 232
Investment Revenue	622	622	622	622	622	7 464
Interest Revenue	22	22	22	22	22	264
TOTAL REVENUE	$56 690	$24 000	$49 272	$24 000	$56 690	$476 722
EXPENSES						
Advertising & Promotion	$ 360	$ 126	$ 410	$ 126	$ 360	$ 2 966
Exchange Rate Differences	0	0	0	0	0	0
Bank Charges	48	32	65	32	48	497
Credit Card Fees	288	115	240	115	288	2 370
Cost of Goods Sold	32 250	13 440	26 880	13 440	32 250	268 770
Variance Costs	151	63	126	63	151	1 259
Furniture Supplies Used	56	56	56	56	56	672
Damaged Inventory	480	135	510	135	480	3 720
Purchase Discounts	-325	-135	-285	-135	-325	–2 720
Freight Expense	320	135	270	135	320	2 680
Delivery Expense	1 080	440	870	440	1 080	8 910
Hydro Expense	160	160	160	160	160	1 920
Insurance Expense	355	355	355	355	355	4 260
Mortgage Interest Expense	1 120	1 120	1 120	1 120	1 120	13 440
Office Supplies Used	64	64	64	64	64	768
Telephone Expenses	130	130	130	130	130	1 560
Commissions	3 150	1 310	2 625	1 310	3 150	26 235
CSST Expense	64	27	51	27	64	533
QPP Expense	131	54	108	54	131	1 087
QHSF Expense	151	63	126	63	151	1 259
Subcontractor Fees	630	265	525	265	630	5 265
TOTAL EXPENSES	$40 663	$17 955	$34 406	$17 955	$40 663	$345 451
NET INCOME	$16 027	$ 6 045	$ 14 866	$ 6 045	$ 16 027	$131 271

BUDGET RATIONALE FOR 2018–2019

VILLAGE GALLERIES

Estimates used to create budget forecasts

Revenue from Sales: increase by 10% over previous year. January, 10% of annual sales; February and March, 5% each; April, May, June, July and August, 12% each; September, October, November and December, 5% each

Sales Discount: expect about 1% of sales on average; most sales are not discounted

Freight Revenue: this has averaged around 2% of sales; most customers request delivery

Interest and Investment Revenue: constant monthly income; same as previous year

Cost of Goods Sold: 60% of net sales (based on markup)

Variance Costs: estimated from price variations in previous years

Damaged Inventory: 1% of Cost of Goods Sold

Purchase Discounts: average 1% of Cost of Goods Sold

Delivery: same amount as Freight Revenue

Freight Expense: average at about 1% of sales

Insurance and Mortgage Interest: same amount each month; small decrease from previous year

Furniture Supplies Used: for maintaining store inventory; constant amount each month

Commissions: estimate, will pay 20% of direct contributions to sales

EI, CPP and QPIP: these do not apply; do not choose Budget This Account

QPP, CSST (WCB) and QHSF: straight percentage of commissions (QPP replaces CPP for Quebec)

Subcontractors' Fees: estimated additional assistance needed for peak periods

Bank Charges & Credit Card Fees: increase over last year for increased credit card usage

Exchange Rate Differences: zero — these are expected to cancel each other over time

Other Expenses: constant each month; no change over last year

---

Entering Budget Amounts in the General Ledger

Click   **Company** in the Modules pane list to change windows.

Click   the **Chart of Accounts shortcuts list arrow** and **click Modify Account** to open the Search window. Accounts is selected as the record type:

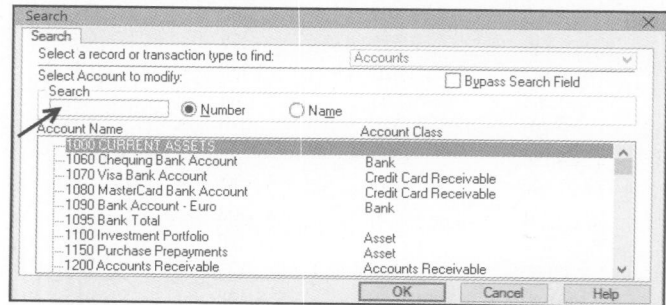

Click   the **Search field**.

Type   4 to advance the cursor to the beginning of the 4000-level Revenue accounts.

Click   **4020 Revenue from Sales** to highlight the first postable revenue account.

Click   **OK** to open the Account Ledger window:

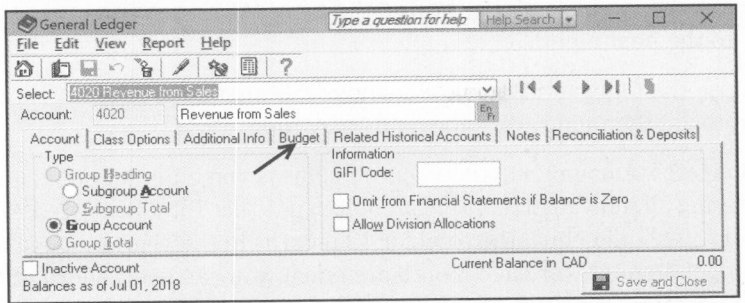

Because we turned on the Budgeting feature in the General Settings window, the Budget tab has been added. This tab will be added only for Income Statement — revenue and expense — accounts.

Click   the **Budget tab** to open the budget activation window:

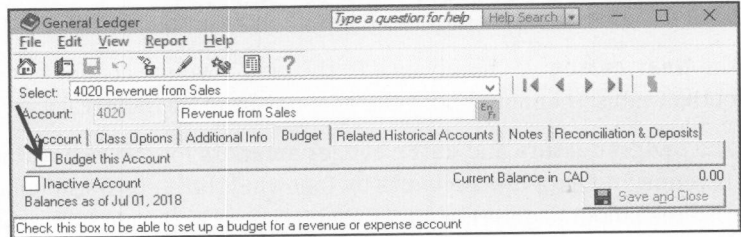

Click   **Budget This Account** to open the Budget amount fields:

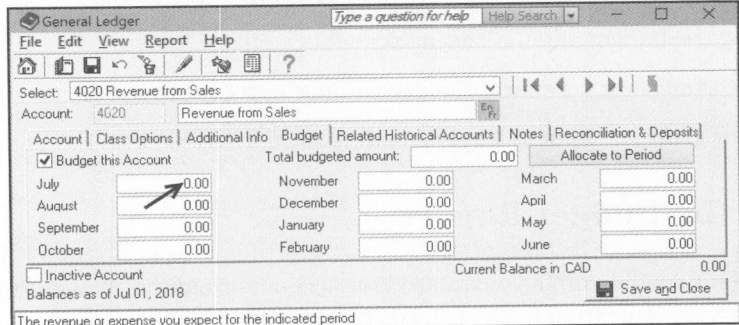

The budget periods displayed at this stage match the period frequency selected in the setup stage. Because we selected Monthly, a 12-month calendar is given, beginning with July, the first month of the fiscal year as entered in the Company Information window. If we had selected Quarterly, four input fields would be provided. You can enter the budget amounts for one period or for more, if the information is available. For Village Galleries, we will enter the amounts determined earlier for each month.

You can change the budget frequency at any time in the General Settings Budget option window. The program will reallocate the previously budgeted amounts proportionately for the new periods after warning you that this will be done and giving you a chance to confirm that you want to proceed.

Refer to the chart on page 555 for budget amounts.

For each revenue and expense, you can add or omit budget amounts. Including budget details for all accounts will, of course, provide the most meaningful budget reports.

Click   the **July field** to select the amount.

Type   55490 **Press** (tab).

The cursor advances to the August field and highlights the entry for editing.

PRO VERSION

The Refresh tool is not available in the Pro version.
   The term Project replaces Division.

NOTES

Budgeting applies only to the postable revenue and expense accounts on the Income Statement. Budget reports are Income Statement reports.

Enter the **amounts** for the **remaining 11 months** according to the budget forecast on page 555 by **typing** the **amount** and **pressing** (tab) to move to the next month.

You can use the **Copy** and **Paste** commands (Edit menu) to copy amounts from one field to another and save some data entry time.

The **Total Budgeted Amount** is updated continually as you enter amounts for each period. After entering all individual monthly amounts, use this Total Budgeted Amount to check your work. It should equal the total for 12 months in the chart on page 555.

When the budget amounts for each month are equal, you can use a shortcut to enter the amounts. For example, for *4100 Investment Revenue*, all amounts are equal.

Open the ledger for **4100 Investment Revenue**. **Click Budget This Account**.

Click the **Total Budgeted Amount field**.

Type 7464 **Click Allocate To Period** to divide the amount evenly among all budget periods (622 is entered for each month, that is, 7464/12).

Click the **Next button** [▶] to advance to the next revenue account in the budget tab screen, or choose the account from the Select list.

Turn on the **budget feature** and **enter budget amounts** for the **remaining** revenue and expense **accounts** by following the steps outlined above. Use the amounts determined for each account in the chart on page 555.

Remember to enter **negative** budget amounts for accounts that decrease the total in a group or section (e.g., *Sales Discount* and *Purchase Discounts*).

After entering the budget amounts for all accounts,

Close the **account's General Ledger window** to return to the Home window.

Display or **print** the **Budget Report** for July to June to check your amounts.

Displaying the Budget Report

You can check the budget amounts you entered for accounts from the Budget Report. Budget reports are available from the Financials report list in the Report Centre.

Open the **Report Centre** and **click Financials** in the Select A Report Type list.

Click **Budget** and then **click Modify This Report**:

Select the **accounts** you want in the report. To check your entries at this stage, you should accept the default to **Select All** accounts.

Choose **July** and **June** in the Start and Finish fields and **click OK**. The report will include only the accounts for which you entered budget amounts.

Close the **display** when you have finished.

Adding Budget Amounts to Divisions

If you are using division allocations, you can also enter budget amounts for each division. You must first turn on the budgeting feature and then choose a budget period or frequency. The following steps will illustrate this procedure.

Click the Settings icon and click Division to open the Division Settings:

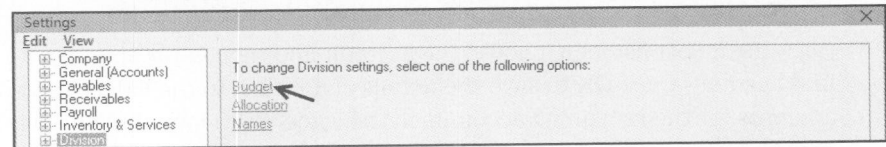

Click Budget to open the division budget activation screen with the familiar options:

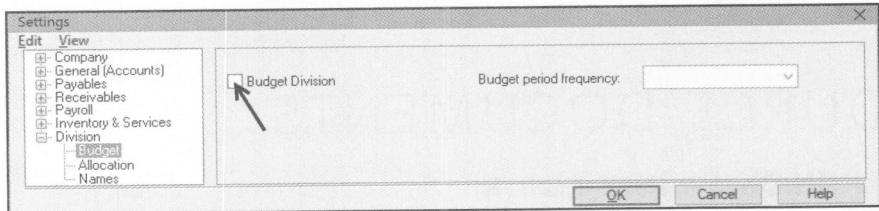

Click Budget Division. Choose a frequency from the Budget Period Frequency drop-down list. Click OK to save the settings.

Click the Divisions icon to open the Division window. Create the divisions if you have not already done so. Open the Division Ledger. A Budget tab has been added. Click the Budget tab to open the budget activation window:

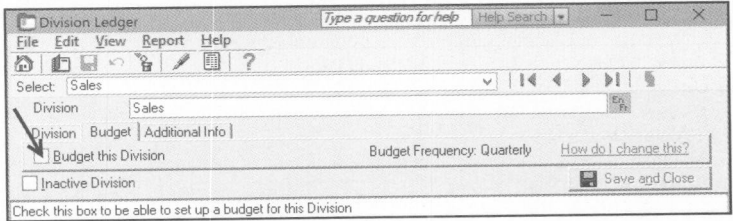

Click Budget This Division to open the budget amount fields. Quarterly periods have been selected for this illustration:

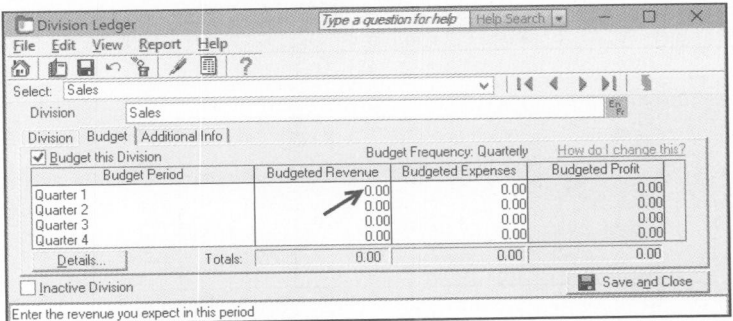

Enter the budgeted Revenue and Expense amounts for each period for this division. Click Details to enter division budget amounts for individual accounts:

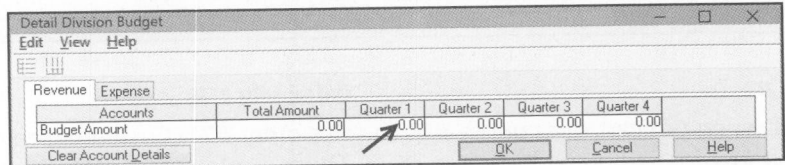

On the first line, enter the total revenue or expense amounts and the amounts for each period. The Select List icon will become available:

Detail Division Budget					
Edit View Help					

Accounts	Total Amount	Quarter 1	Quarter 2	Quarter 3	Quarter 4
Budget Amount	464,400.00	134,105.00	73,375.00	92,450.00	164,470.00

Clear Account Details   OK   Cancel   Help

Click the Select list icon, choose the account and then enter amounts for the first account. Click OK to save the details and return to the ledger record. Enter amounts for the remaining accounts in the same way. Open the ledger for the next division and enter the budget amounts.

Close the ledger when you have finished and enter the allocations as usual in the journals. Division budget reports will be available.

SOURCE DOCUMENTS

SESSION DATE – JULY 7, 2018

Memo #1   **Dated July 2/18**

1

From Owner: Pay import duties owing to the Receiver General on June 30. Issue cheque #125 for $240 in full payment of duty owing.

2

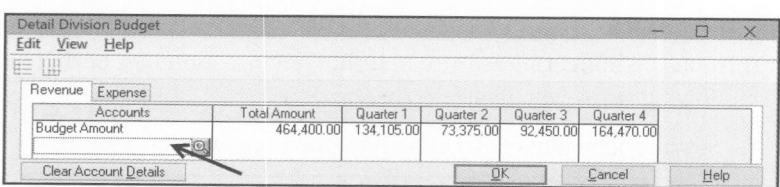

Village Galleries

509 Boul. Rouin
Montreal, Quebec
H3F 5G5

Telephone:
(514) 529-6391
Fax:
(514) 529-7622

Date: July 2/18
To be delivered: July 15/18
For: Caisse Metropolitain
                 (Tomas Monaire)
                 50 Rue Berri
                 Montreal, QC H1B 6F4

QUOTE #71

Description	Qty	Price	Total
HA-03 Lamp: floor solid brass	2	450	900.00
HA-09 Rugs: Persian Tabriz 90 x 160cm	2	950	1900.00
LR-01 Bookcase: oak/walnut solid	2	1270	2540.00
LR-12 Sectional Sofa: charcoal linen	2	2530	5060.00

Sale Terms: 2/10, n/30	Delivery	N/C
GST # 236 412 540	GST 5.0%	520.00
QST # 3344992	QST 9.975%	1037.42
Prices quoted will remain valid for 15 days	Total	11957.42

Memo #2   **Dated July 2/18**

3

From Owner: Convert sales quote #71 to sales order #71. Customer provided deposit #61 for $1 500 with cheque #933. Other quote details are unchanged.

Purchase Quote #224   Dated July 2/18

[4]

Policy start date July 5/18
From Quebecor Insurance Co. (use Quick Add), $4 260 for a one-year extension of business insurance policy. Terms: first two months' premium required as deposit on acceptance of quote. Balance is payable in 10 equal monthly payments. Enter 1 (one) as the quantity ordered and debit Prepaid Insurance.

NOTES
The tax on insurance is included. GST is not charged on insurance premiums.

Purchase Order #224 & Cheque #126   Dated July 2/18

[5]

Convert purchase quote #224 from Quebecor Insurance Co., $4 260 for a one-year extension of business insurance policy, to a purchase order. Issue cheque #126 for $710 as deposit to confirm the order.

Purchase Invoice #QI-7711   Dated July 3/18

[6]

From Quebecor Insurance Co., to fill purchase order #224, $4 260 for a one-year extension of business insurance policy. The premium balance is due in 10 equal monthly payments. Change the payment method to Pay Later.

Receipt #43   Dated July 3/18

[7]

From Deon Estates, cheque #118 for $5 648.75 in payment of account, including $100 discount for early payment. Reference invoice #168.

Payment Cheque #127   Dated July 3/18

[8]

To L'Ascension Mobiliers, $4 512.42 in payment of account, including $45.58 discount for early payment. Reference invoice #LM-2114. (Read margin Notes.)

NOTES
You may need to update the cheque number to 127 and then accept the new numbering.

Cash Sales Invoice #170   Dated July 4/18

[9]

To Vasco Cardigos (use Full Add for the new Portuguese customer)
    1   BF-02   Armoire: light ash   € 2 325.00
    1   HA-06   Mirror: square ash/mahogany   425.00
            Shipping   200.00
Received cheque #4322 for € 2 950 in full payment.
The exchange rate is 1.420.

NOTES
Edit the sales prices for invoice #170.
    Vasco Cardigos
    Rua Mariella 36
    1207 Lisbon, Portugal
    Tel: (351-21) 347 6273
    Terms: net 1
    Currency: EUR
    Tax code: no tax

Credit Card Purchase Invoice #A-1141   Dated July 4/18

[10]

From Antoine's Hardware Store (use Quick Add for the new supplier), $50.00 plus $2.50 GST and $4.99 QST for computer screen cleaning kit (office supplies). Purchase invoice total $57.49 paid in full by Amex credit card.

Credit Card Purchase Invoice #PD-211   Dated July 5/18

[11]

From Papineau Delivery, $280.00 plus $14.00 GST and $27.93 QST for contracted delivery of furniture. Purchase invoice total $321.93. Paid in full by Amex.

Debit Card Sales Invoice #171   Dated July 6/18

[12]

To Catherine Geneve (choose Continue or Quick Add)
    1   LR-04   Console Table: oak $1 050.00
    1   LR-05   Curio Cabinet: walnut/oak   1 600.00
            Delivery   100.00
            Goods and Services Tax   5.0%   137.50
            Quebec Sales Tax   9.975%   274.32
        Invoice total $3 161.82
Paid by debit card #7695 4559 0062 0103.

NOTES
You can choose Continue or Quick Add for new customers.

Payment Cheque #128   Dated July 7/18

[13]

To Normandin Meubles, $6 700.26 in payment of account including $136.74 discount for early payment. Reference invoice #NM-192.

SESSION DATE – JULY 14, 2018

14 | **Memo #3**   **Dated July 8/18**

From Owner: Adjust inventory for one HA-02 Framed Art Print dropped and damaged beyond repair. Charge to Damaged Inventory account.

15 | **Credit Card Purchase Invoice #QA-197**   **Dated July 10/18**

From Quik-Ads (use Quick Add), $200.00 plus $10.00 GST and $19.95 QST for promotional cards and flyers to advertise home design gallery. Purchase invoice total $229.95 paid in full by Amex credit card.

16 | **Cash Purchase Invoice #EQ-979764**   **Dated July 13/18**

From Énergie Québec, $140.00 plus $7.00 GST and $13.97 QST for hydro service for one month. Purchase invoice total $160.97 paid in full by cheque #129.

17 | **Cash Sales Invoice #172**   **Dated July 13/18**

To Marie Broussard

1	LR-18 Sofa & Slipcover: celadon		$1 630.00
	Goods and Services Tax	5.0%	81.50
	Quebec Sales Tax	9.975%	162.59
	Invoice total		$1 874.09

Received cheque #339 in full payment. Customer to arrange own delivery.

NOTES
Credit Freight Revenue for the delivery to Broussard.

18 | **Sales Invoice #173**   **Dated July 14/18**

To Marie Broussard (use Quick Add), $50.00 plus $2.50 GST and $4.99 QST for delivery of sofa. Sales invoice total $57.49. Terms: net 10.

19 | **Visa Sales Invoice #174**   **Dated July 14/18**

To Allysa Morel

1	KD-10 Server: fruitwood		$1 080.00
1	KD-12 Table: brass with glass		1 960.00
1	LR-09 Loveseat: chenille		1 460.00
	Goods and Services Tax	5.0%	225.00
	Quebec Sales Tax	9.975%	448.88
	Invoice total		$5 173.88

Paid by Visa #4185 4458 6712 8405.

20 | **Credit Card Purchase Invoice #QD-980**   **Dated July 14/18**

From Quickie Delivery Service (use Quick Add), $100.00 plus $5.00 GST and $9.98 QST for delivery of sofa to Marie Broussard. Purchase invoice total $114.98 paid in full by Amex. (Charge to Delivery Expense.)

21 | **Purchase Invoice #MPE-664**   **Dated July 14/18**

From Montreal Persia Emporium (create new inventory)

2	HA-10 Rugs: Mashad 170 x 240cm		$1 400.00
2	HA-11 Rugs: Qum silk 80 x 150cm		2 200.00
	Goods and Services Tax		180.00
	Quebec Sales Tax		359.10
	Invoice total		$4 139.10

Terms: 2/5, n/30.

New inventory items

Number	Description	Unit	Min	Reg.	(Pref.)
HA-10	Rugs: Mashad 170 x 240cm	1-pc	1	$1 200	($1 050)
HA-11	Rugs: Qum silk 80 x 150cm	1-pc	1	1 800	(1 650)

Linked Accounts: Asset 1340 **Revenue** 4020 **Cost of Goods Sold** 5060 **Variance** 5070
Taxes: GST exempt No **QST exempt** No **Duty Rate** Not applicable

SESSION DATE – JULY 21, 2018

22

Village Galleries

509 Boul. Rouin
Montreal, Quebec
H3F 5G5

Telephone:
(514) 529-6391
Fax:
(514) 529-7622

Date: July 15/18

To: Caisse Metropolitain
(Tomas Monaire)
50 Rue Berri
Montreal, QC H1B 6F4

I n v o i c e # 1 7 5

Description	Qty	Price	Total
HA-03 Lamp: floor solid brass	2	450	900.00
HA-09 Rugs: Persian Tabriz 90 x 160cm	2	950	1900.00
LR-01 Bookcase: oak/walnut solid	2	1270	2540.00
LR-12 Sectional Sofa: charcoal linen	2	2530	5060.00

Ref: quote/order #71 and deposit #61
Authorization to exceed credit limit

GM

Less deposit			(1500.00)

Sale Terms: 2/10, n/30	Delivery	N/C
GST # 236 412 540	GST 5.0%	520.00
QST # 3344992	QST 9.975%	1037.42
	Balance	10457.42

NOTES
Allow the customer to exceed the credit limit.

23

Memo #4   Dated July 17/18

From Owner: Adjust purchase invoice #MPE-664. Montreal Persia Emporium sent a revised invoice for MPE-664 that included a freight charge of $50.00 plus $2.50 GST and $4.99 QST. New purchase invoice total $4 196.59.

24

Payment Cheque #130   Dated July 19/18

To Montreal Persia Emporium, $4 112.66 in payment of account including $83.93 discount for early payment. Reference revised invoice #MPE-664.

25

MasterCard Sales Invoice #176   Dated July 20/18

To Jacques Altain

1	LR-06	Desk: mahogany	$2 030.00
1	LR-11	Recliner & Ottoman: brown leather	1 130.00
1	LR-20	Wing Chair: pastel	400.00
		Delivery	100.00
		Goods and Services Tax 5.0%	183.00
		Quebec Sales Tax 9.975%	365.09
		Invoice total	$4 208.09

Paid by MasterCard #5145 0559 0062 3612.
Edit the selling price of LR-20. The price was reduced because the chair legs were scratched.

26

Credit Card Bill #AM-07020   Dated July 20/18

From American Express (Amex), $964.35 for new purchases before the billing date, July 14, plus $10.50 monthly fee. Total payment required to avoid interest charges is $974.85. Issue cheque #131 for $974.85 to pay Amex balance in full.

27

Village Galleries

509 Boul. Rouin
Montreal, Quebec
H3F 5G5

Telephone:
(514) 529-6391
Fax:
(514) 529-7622

Date: July 20/18
To be delivered: July 21/18
From: St. Leonard's Homebuilders
(Félice Charpentier)
31 Boul. St. Joseph
Montreal, QC H4N 2M1

Q U O T E # 7 2

Description	Qty	Price	Total
BF-01 Armoire: dark oak	2	3070	6140.00
BF-05 Bed: brass/silver	2	1790	3580.00
HA-08 Rugs: Persian Kashan 185 x 275cm	2	1200	2400.00
LR-09 Loveseat: chenille	2	1310	2620.00

Telephone request for quote 7/20/18 *GM*

Sale Terms: 2/10, n/30			
GST # 236 412 540		Delivery	N/C
		GST 5.0%	737.00
QST # 3344992		QST 9.975%	1470.33
		Total	16947.33

NOTES

Choose Convert This Quote To An Invoice. The quote is automatically filled for the full order quantities. Enter 1 in the Quantity field for each item. When you post the sale, allow Sage 50 to generate the sales order automatically by clicking Yes. Refer to page 448.

28

Village Galleries

509 Boul. Rouin
Montreal, Quebec
H3F 5G5

Telephone:
(514) 529-6391
Fax:
(514) 529-7622

Date: July 21/18

To: St. Leonard's Homebuilders
(Félice Charpentier)
31 Boul. St. Joseph
Montreal, QC H4N 2M1

I n v o i c e # 1 7 7

Description	Qty	Price	Total
BF-01 Armoire: dark oak	1	3070	3070.00
BF-05 Bed: brass/silver	1	1790	1790.00
HA-08 Rugs: Persian Kashan 185 x 275cm	1	1200	1200.00
LR-09 Loveseat: chenille	1	1310	1310.00

Quote partially filled
Balance of quote converted to order #72

Ref: sales quote #72 *GM 7/21/18*

Sale Terms: 2/10, n/30			
GST # 236 412 540		Delivery	N/C
		GST 5.0%	368.50
QST # 3344992		QST 9.975%	735.15
		Total	8473.65

Cash Purchase Invoice #T-55612   Dated July 21/18

29

From Telébec, $175.00 plus $8.75 GST and $17.46 QST for store and mobile telephone service. Purchase invoice total $201.21 paid in full by cheque #132.

Receipt #44   Dated July 21/18

30

From Caisse Metropolitain, cheque #967 for $10 249.42 in payment of account including $208.00 discount for early payment. Reference invoice #175 and deposit #61.

SESSION DATE – JULY 31, 2018

Sales Invoice #178   Dated July 23/18

31

To Westmount Primrose Condos (free delivery for preferred customer)
1	KD-02	Buffet: cherry	$2 230
1	LR-12	Sectional Sofa: charcoal linen	2 270
2	LR-19	Swivel Chairs & Slipcovers: cotton	630 each
		Goods and Services Tax	5.0%
		Quebec Sales Tax	9.975%

Memo #5   Dated July 24/18

32

Adjust sales invoice #173 to Marie Broussard. The invoice was entered with the old rate for delivery. She was actually charged the correct amount of $100.00 plus $5.00 GST and $9.98 QST. Sales invoice total $114.98. Terms: net 10.

Receipt #45   Dated July 24/18

33

From Marie Broussard, cheque #357 for $114.98 in payment of account. Reference invoice #173.

MasterCard Sales Invoice #179   Dated July 28/18

34

To Pierre Binoche
1	KD-04	Chairs: 4 piece		$1 080.00
1	KD-08	Extension Table: oak		2 010.00
		Delivery		100.00
		Goods and Services Tax	5.0%	159.50
		Quebec Sales Tax	9.975%	318.21
		Invoice total		$3 667.71

Paid by MasterCard #5555 8445 5900 6236.

Credit Card Purchase Invoice #PD-304   Dated July 30/18

35

From Papineau Delivery, $580.00 plus $29.00 GST and $57.86 QST for contracted delivery of furniture. Purchase invoice total $666.86 paid in full by Amex.

Bank Debit Memo #643177   Dated July 30/18

36

From Bank of Montreal, $70 for bank service charges for one month and $1 700 for mortgage payment that included $1 120 interest and $580 principal.

Bank Credit Memo #46234   Dated July 30/18

37

From Bank of Montreal, $588 interest earned on investment securities deposited to chequing account.

Receipt #46   Dated July 30/18

38

From St. Leonard's Homebuilders, cheque #3199 for $8 326.25 in payment of account including $147.40 discount for early payment. Reference invoice #177.

Memo #6   **Dated July 31/18**

39

From Owner: Make adjusting entries for July.

Office supplies used	$ 75
Furniture supplies used	50
Prepaid insurance expired	355

Memo #7   **Dated July 31/18**

40

From Owner: Issue cheque #133 for $355 — the premium for one month — to Quebecor Insurance Co. in partial payment of invoice #QI-7711. Repeat the entry five times to make the remaining payments for 2018 with postdated cheques. Issue cheques #134 to 138, dated August 31, September 30, October 31, November 30 and December 31.

Memo #8   **Dated July 31/18**

41

From Owner: Lianne Décor earned $5 200 in commissions on her share of sales in July. Issue cheque #139 to pay Décor's commissions.

Updating Budgets

Changing Budget Amounts

Budget amounts can be updated if needed based on feedback from earlier budget reports. They should not, of course, be changed without good reason.

If you discover that your budget forecasts are incorrect, you can update the amounts for each account individually by repeating the process described above for entering initial budget amounts. Or you can globally update all amounts by a fixed percentage. At the end of July, we are asked to update all budget amounts by 10 percent.

✓   **Memo #9**   **Dated July 31/18**

42

From Owner: Decrease all revenue and expense budget amounts by 10%.

Choose the **Maintenance menu** in the Home window and **click Update Budget Amounts** to open the Update Budget window:

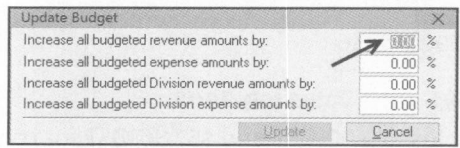

You can change the budgets for revenue and expense accounts separately. You can change division revenue and expense amounts by a different percentage. Use negative numbers to indicate a decrease in amounts and positive numbers for increases.

The entry for Increase All Budgeted Revenue Amounts By is selected.

Type −10 **Press** (tab) to advance to the field for expense amounts.

Type −10 **Click Update** to apply the change.

The next screen asks you to confirm that you want to update the budget:

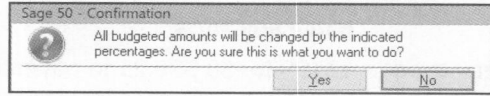

Click **Yes** to apply the changes and return to the Home window.

The account's budget information in the account ledger will have the changes applied. All budget amounts will be updated.

Changing Budget Frequencies

You can also change the budget frequency. This change is made in the General Ledger Settings screen.

For example, to change the period from monthly to quarterly,

> Choose the Setup menu, then click Settings. Click General (Accounts) and Budget. Then choose Quarterly from the Budget Period Frequency drop-down list and click OK.

When you have a quarterly budget with different amounts for each quarter and you change the frequency to monthly, each month will have the same budget amount — the total for the four quarters divided by 12. You must edit the amounts if they are incorrect.

For example, a quarterly budget of $1 000, $3 000, $2 000 and $6 000 for the four quarters becomes $1 000 each month if the frequency is changed to monthly ($12 000/12).

Before applying the new budget settings, Sage 50 generates a warning each time you change a budget frequency:

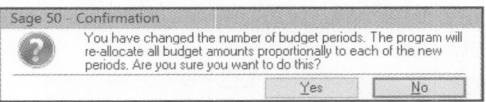
The statement warns that previous budget amounts will be reallocated evenly among the new number of periods. If you change a monthly budget to quarterly, each quarter will have the same budget amount. You can accept or cancel the change.

Printing in Batches

In addition to printing invoices, orders, quotes and cheques at the time of a transaction, you can print them in batches at the end of a period, such as the end of a business day. Batch printing makes it easier to share printers. Any forms that can be printed individually can be printed in batches.

Memo #10 asks us to print all sales invoices.

Memo #10   **Dated July 31/18**

From Owner: Print all sales invoices for July.

First you need to allow batch printing for the data file.

Choose the **Setup menu** and **click Settings**.

Click **Company** and then **click Forms** to open the Settings screen for Forms:

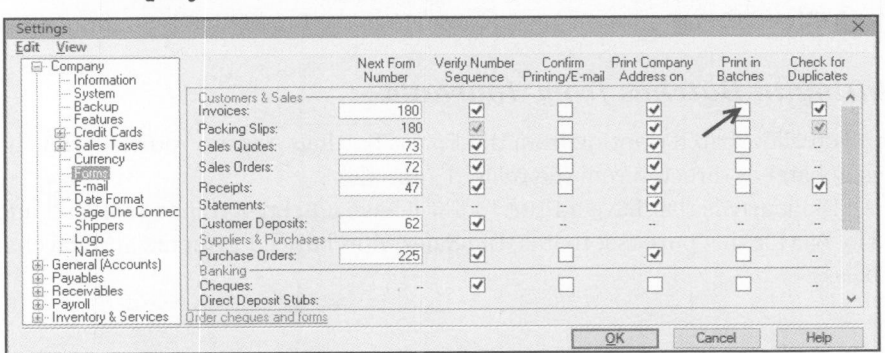

> **Click**   the **Print In Batches check box for Invoices**, the first form listed.
>
> **Click**   the **check box for the other forms** that you want to print in batches.
>
> **Click**   **OK** to save the changes.

Now, the Reports menu in the Home window has a Print Batches menu option.

> **Choose**   the **Reports menu** then **choose Print Batches** and **click Sales Invoices** for the printing options:

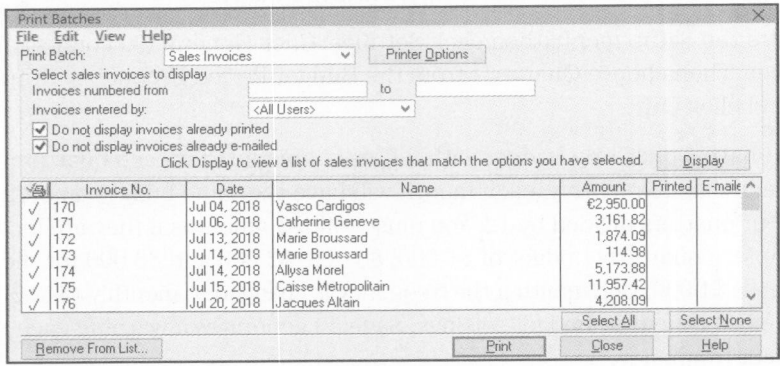

From this screen, you can choose other forms to print in batches. These are available from the **Print Batch** drop-down list:

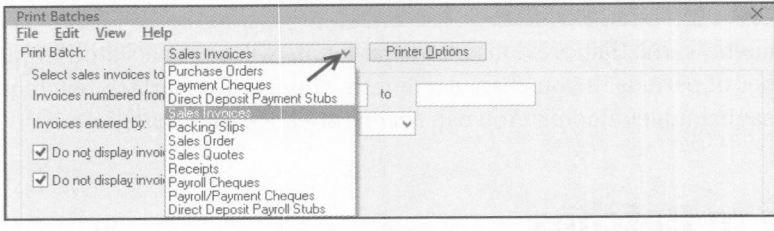

If some invoices have already been **Printed** or **E-mailed**, they will be displayed with a ✓ in the corresponding column. You can remove them from the display by clicking the appropriate check boxes. You can choose a **range of Invoice Numbers** or a specific **User** as selection criteria. After making these selections, click **Display** to include only the requested invoices.

Initially, the ✓s in the Print column indicate all invoices are selected for printing. Clicking **Select None** will remove all the ✓s, and clicking **Select All** will select all listed invoices. You can also select invoices individually by clicking Select None and then clicking the invoices you want to print.

> **Choose**   the **invoices** you want to print so that only those invoices have a ✓.
>
> **Click**   **Print**. Printing begins immediately, so be sure that you have loaded the forms you need (or use plain paper for practice).
>
> **Click**   **Close** or select another form from the Print Batch list to print other forms.

Printing in Batches from Journals

When you allow batch printing from the Forms Settings screen, you can print these forms in batches directly from the related journal.

All the journals that have a Print tool will have a **Print Batches tool** added to the tool bar for this purpose, that is, the Sales, Purchases, Payments and Paycheques journals.

PRO VERSION

pro The Pro version does not have packing slips.

NOTES

The list will include all the forms for which you selected Print In Batches.

NOTES

Remember that you can customize invoices before printing them. Refer to Appendix F on the Student DVD.

You cannot preview the invoices from the Print Batches window.

NOTES

To print the invoices, you must choose Custom Form in the Reports & Forms settings on the Invoices screen. Choose Invoice in the Description field for invoices and e-mail.

Budget Reports

Effective use of budget reports involves more than merely observing whether budgeted targets were met or not. Sometimes more information is gained when targets are not met, because the differences can lead to important questions:

- Were the targets realistic? What items were not on target and why?
- If performance exceeds the targets, how can we repeat the success?
- If performance did not meet the targets, were there factors that we failed to anticipate?
- Should we revise future budgets based on the new information?

The problem-solving cycle is set in motion. Even an Income Statement that is on target should be reviewed carefully. There may be room for improvement if the budget was a conservative estimate. Or you may want to include new information that will affect future performance and was unknown when the budget was drawn up.

Displaying Budget Income Statements

Reports used to analyze budget performance are Comparative Income Statements, comparing actual revenue and expense amounts with budgeted amounts.

Open   the **Report Centre** and **click Financials**.

Click   the ⊞ **beside Income Statement** to expand the list.

Click   **Comparative 2 Period** and then **click Modify This Report**:

Click   **Actual** in the **Second Period field** to open the budget-related option:

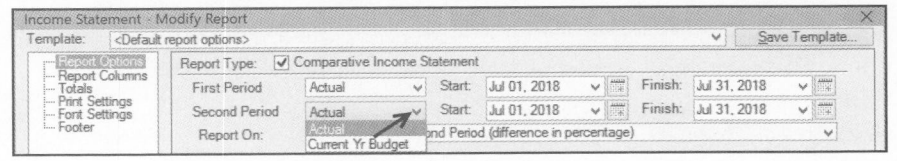

Click   **Current Yr Budget** to change the option.

Budget Income Statements compare budgeted to actual amounts.

The **Report On** options are the same as the options for regular Comparative Income Statements, but now you can choose budgeted amounts for the Second Period. Three types of reports are available. The first type, **First** (actual) **Period Vs. Second** (budget) **Period (Amounts Only)**, lists the amounts that were budgeted for the revenue and expense accounts for the period indicated and the revenues and expenses actually obtained for the same period. The second type, **First** (actual) **Period Vs. Second** (budget) **Period (Difference In Percentage)**, gives these two amounts as well as the percentage that the actual amount is above or below the budgeted amount. The third option, **First** (actual) **Period Vs. Second** (budget) **Period (Difference In Amounts)**, provides budget and actual as base amounts, plus the difference between them as a dollar amount.

NOTES
The Budget Report with budget amounts was described on page 558.

NOTES
You can also choose the Reports menu, then choose Financials and click Income Statement to display the Income Statement options. Click Comparative Income Statement as the Report Type.

NOTES
You can choose to display the budget amounts in either the first or the second period.

In our example, we have the budget data in the second period.

For the dollar difference and the percentage difference reports, a positive difference means that the budget was exceeded; a negative difference indicates that the results came in under budget. Remember that for revenues, a positive difference (first period amounts are greater than second period amounts) means results were better than expected, but for expenses a positive difference means that results were poorer than expected (expenses were higher than budgeted). Cost of goods sold will increase directly with sales, so positive differences can mean either improved sales or higher costs, or both.

> **Click** the type of comparative **budget report** you want to report on. **Close** the **display** when finished.

When you add budget details for divisions, you can also create **division budget reports**. Choose the Reports menu, then choose Division and click Budget. Choose the Report Type, dates and divisions and click OK.

Printing Budget Reports

> **Display** the **report** you want to print. **Click** the **Print button** or **choose** the **File menu** in the report window and **click Print**.

> **Close** the **displayed report** when you have finished. **Close** the **Report Centre**.

R E V I E W

The Student DVD with Data Files includes Review Questions and Supplementary Cases for this chapter.

Tesses Tresses

OBJECTIVES

- **prepare** bank deposit slips
- **print** Transaction Reports for bank accounts
- **compare** bank statements with Transaction Reports
- **turn on** the account reconciliation feature
- **create** new linked accounts for reconciliation
- **set up** the account reconciliation information
- **reconcile** the bank account statement with the General Ledger
- **reverse** receipts for NSF cheques manually
- **display** and **print** account reconciliation reports
- **clear** paid invoices and **remove** accounts

COMPANY INFORMATION

Company Profile

NOTES
Tesses Tresses
55 Salon Rd.
Charlottetown, PE C1A 6D3
Tel: (902) 729-6211
Fax: (902) 728-4821
Business No.: 136 422 374

Tesses Tresses, a hair salon in Charlottetown, Prince Edward Island, is a family business owned by Tess Dubois, her husband, Ian, and her daughter, Felicia. All three had both professional and business management training to prepare them for running the salon. Together they provide a full range of hair care services to clients, most of whom return regularly. Unlike many salons where the price depends on the stylist and client, Tesses Tresses charges one price for each service regardless of client gender or stylist. It also sells a limited range of high-quality hair care products.

The salon building they own includes two apartments that are rented to students. These tenants provided postdated cheques for three months at the beginning of January.

Instead of hiring a maintenance, cleaning and laundry company to take care of the premises, the Dubois family shares this responsibility to reduce expenses. Cleaning is required almost continually to meet hygiene standards for health and safety.

The salon's regular suppliers provide inventory products, including those used in the salon for client services; office supplies; cleaning supplies for the salon; linens such as towels, capes and gowns; and hairdressing equipment. Supplier records are set up for all of these suppliers as well as for utility service companies and government agencies to which Tesses Tresses remits taxes. The salon pays HST on all purchases.

Although most clients are one-time clients who pay by cash and credit card, some repeat clients have accounts and are entitled to a 2 percent discount if they pay within five days. Net payment is due in 15 days. The cash clients do not receive a discount. A record called Cash Customers is set up for the weekly summaries of cash and credit card sales. Clients pay HST at 14 percent on merchandise they buy from the salon and on all services. The tax rates and codes are entered into client and inventory records, so the program automatically calculates taxes.

Tesses Tresses also provides hair styling services to local theatre companies, cutting and styling hair for cast members before performances, re-styling throughout the show for cast character changes and styling wigs. These evening commitments do not conflict with the usual daytime salon business hours. The theatre companies pay preferred prices at about 20 percent off regular prices in addition to the discount for early payment.

At the beginning of February, some unfilled purchase orders will provide the inventory for the additional purchases anticipated for Valentine's Day.

The accounting records for Tesses Tresses were converted to Sage 50 at the beginning of January, and the transactions for January have been completed. The files are ready for January bank account transactions (deposits and account reconciliation) and February transactions. The current accounting records include the following:

- Chart of Accounts
- Trial Balance as at January 31, 2018
- Supplier Information
- Client Information
- Inventory Information
- Accounting Procedures

CHART OF ACCOUNTS

TESSES TRESSES

ASSETS
- 1030 Undeposited Cash and Cheques
- 1060 Bank: Chequing Account
- 1080 Bank: Credit Cards
- 1200 Accounts Receivable
- 1240 Prepaid Insurance
- 1260 Prepaid Subscriptions
- 1300 Towels and Capes
- 1320 Office Supplies
- 1340 Washroom & Cleaning Supplies
- 1360 Salon Supplies
- 1420 Hair Care Products ▶

- ▶1520 Computer and Cash Register
- 1540 Furniture and Fixtures
- 1560 Salon Equipment
- 1580 Salon and Building

LIABILITIES
- 2100 Bank Loan
- 2150 Credit Card Payable
- 2200 Accounts Payable
- 2750 HST Charged on Sales
- 2760 HST Paid on Purchases
- 2850 Mortgage Payable ▶

▶EQUITY
- 3100 TT Capital
- 3150 TT Drawings
- 3600 Net Income

REVENUE
- 4100 Revenue from Sales
- 4120 Revenue from Services
- 4140 Rental Income
- 4160 Sales Discounts
- 4220 Interest Revenue
- 4240 Other Revenue ▶

▶EXPENSE
- 5020 Advertising and Promotion
- 5040 Bank Charges
- 5060 Credit Card Fees
- 5080 Cost of Services
- 5180 Inventory Losses
- 5200 Cost of Goods Sold
- 5220 Purchase Discounts
- 5240 Insurance Expense
- 5260 Subscriptions Expense
- 5300 Supplies Used
- 5320 Utilities
- 5340 Interest Expense

NOTES: The Chart of Accounts includes only postable accounts and Net Income.

TRIAL BALANCE

TESSES TRESSES

January 31, 2018

		Debits	Credits
1030	Undeposited Cash and Cheques	$ 16 960.29	
1060	Bank: Chequing Account	34 158.35	
1080	Bank: Credit Cards	9 543.92	
1200	Accounts Receivable	29.64	
1240	Prepaid Insurance	750.00	
1260	Prepaid Subscriptions	270.00	
1300	Towels and Capes	530.00	
1320	Office Supplies	330.00	
1340	Washroom & Cleaning Supplies	365.00	
1360	Salon Supplies	807.00	
1420	Hair Care Products	2 435.00	
1520	Computer and Cash Register	4 200.00	
1540	Furniture and Fixtures	7 600.00	
1560	Salon Equipment	4 600.00	
1580	Salon and Building	220 000.00	
2100	Bank Loan		$ 23 510.00
2150	Credit Card Payable		79.80
2200	Accounts Payable		1 858.20 ▶
▶ 2750	HST Charged on Sales		$ 3 565.10
2760	HST Paid on Purchases	$ 798.98	
2850	Mortgage Payable		149 650.00
3100	TT Capital		104 799.00
4100	Revenue from Sales		5 618.00
4120	Revenue from Services		19 847.00
4140	Rental Income		1 005.00
4160	Sales Discounts	66.26	
5060	Credit Card Fees	370.28	
5200	Cost of Goods Sold	3 305.00	
5220	Purchase Discounts		102.62
5240	Insurance Expense	150.00	
5260	Subscriptions Expense	30.00	
5300	Supplies Used	1 140.00	
5320	Utilities	335.00	
5340	Interest Expense	1 260.00	
		$310 034.72	$310 034.72

SUPPLIER INFORMATION

TESSES TRESSES

Supplier Name (Contact)	Address	Phone No. Fax No.	E-mail Web Site	Terms Tax ID
Air Pro (Curly Locks)	390 Brows Lane Charlottetown, PE C1A 6M3	Tel: (902) 722-0217 Fax: (902) 723-8100	curly@airpro.com airpro.com	net 15 137 456 199
All U Need	Maypoint Plaza #64 Charlottetown, PE C1E 1E2	Tel: (902) 728-4314	alluneed.com	net 1 382 732 162
Atlantic Power Corp.	16 Lektrik Rd. Charlottetown, PE C1C 6G1	Tel: (902) 726-1615	apc.ca	net 1
Charlottetown City Treasurer	78 Fitzroy St. Charlottetown, PE C1A 1R5	Tel: (902) 725-9173	charlottetown.ca/fin	net 1
Eastern Tel (I.D. Caller)	36 Nassau St. Charlottetown, PE C1A 7V9	Tel: (902) 723-2355		net 1
Fine Brushes (Harry Bristle)	13 Ave. Costey Dorval, QC H9S 4C7	Tel: (514) 457-1826 Fax: (514) 457-1883	bristle@finebrushes.com finebrushes.com	net 20 188 462 457
Lookin' Good (N. Vayne)	18 Vivanle Cr. Summerside, PE C1N 6C4	Tel: (902) 829-4763 Fax: (902) 829-7392	vayne@lookingood.com lookingood.com	net 10 192 721 214
Pro-Line Inc. (Awl Fluff)	190 Rue Mutchmore Hull, QC J8Y 3S9	Tel: (819) 658-7227 Fax: (819) 658-7192	awl.fluff@proline.com proline.com	2/10, n/30 (after tax) 621 372 611
Receiver General for Canada	Summerside Tax Centre	Tel: (902) 821-8186		net 1
Seaside Papers (Fyne Pulp)	40 Harbour View Dr. Charlottetown, PE C1A 7A8	Tel: (902) 720-1623 Fax: (902) 720-1639	pulp@seasidepapers.com seasidepapers.com	net 1 810 721 011
Sharp Scissors (S. Cutter)	22 Bellevue Ave. Summerside, PE C1N 2C7	Tel: (902) 923-1995 Fax: (902) 923-1726	cutter@sharp.com sharp.com	net 10 138 221 100
Zines Inc. (Buetee Tipps)	344 Lepage Ave. Summerside, PE C1N 3E6	Tel: (902) 553-6291 Fax: (902) 553-7155	tipps@zines.com zines.com	net 10 205 602 301

SUPPLIER INVOICES

TESSES TRESSES

Supplier Name	Terms	Date	Inv/Chq No.	Amount	Discount	Total
Fine Brushes	net 20	Dec. 20/17	FB-4321	$330.00		$330.00
		Jan. 9/18	CHQ 411	330.00		330.00
	net 20	Jan. 17/18	FB-6219	946.20		946.20
			Balance owing			$946.20
Pro-Line Inc.	2/10, n/30	Dec. 28/17	PL-1002	$ 945.00		$ 945.00
		Jan. 4/18	CHQ 410	926.10	$18.90	945.00
	2/10, n/30	Jan. 4/18	PL-1012	4 186.08		4 186.08
		Jan. 14/18	CHQ 413	4 102.36	83.72	4 186.08
Sharp Scissors	net 10	Jan. 24/18	SS-432	$912.00		$912.00
					Grand Total	$1 858.20

NOTES: Cash and Credit Card Purchases are not included in the chart of supplier invoices.

CLIENT INFORMATION

TESSES TRESSES

Client Name (Contact)	Address	Phone No. Fax No.	E-mail Web Site	Terms Credit Limit
Atta Schule (tenant)		Tel: (902) 724-2996	atta.schule@undergrad.upei.ca	first of month
Brioche Bridal Party (Bonnie Brioche)	75 Marital Way Charlottetown, PE C1E 4A2	Tel: (902) 723-1194 Fax: (902) 726-1921	brioche@weddingbells.com	2/5, n/15 $1 000
Cash Customers				cash/credit card
Conn Seted	14 Hi Brow St. Charlottetown, PE C1E 3X1	Tel: (902) 723-0099	conn.seted@aol.com	net 15 $1 000
Irma Vannitee	77 Makeover Cr. Charlottetown, PE C1B 1J5	Tel: (902) 726-7715	irma.van@skindeep.com	2/5, n/15 $1 000
*On Stage Theatre Company (Marvelle Stage)	100 Marquee Blvd. Charlottetown, PE C1A 2M1	Tel: (902) 727-8201 Fax: (902) 727-0663	marvelle@onstage.com onstage.com	2/5, n/15 $2 000
Proud Family	98 Proud St. Charlottetown, PE C1B 3C1	Tel: (902) 721-1113	theprouds@shaw.ca	net 15 $1 000
Stu Dents (tenant)		Tel: (902) 724-7103	stu.dents@undergrad.upei.ca	first of month
*Twilight Theatre (Ona Roll)	55 Footlights Dr. Charlottetown, PE C1B 6V2	Tel: (902) 728-4661 Fax: (902) 724-1556	ona.roll@twilight.com twilight.com	2/5, n/15 $2 000

NOTES: All client discounts are calculated on after-tax amounts.
* Indicates preferred customer.

CLIENT INVOICES

TESSES TRESSES

Client Name	Terms	Date	Inv/Chq No.	Amount	Discount	Total
Atta Schule	rent payment	Jan. 2/18	CHQ 415			$420.00
	rent payment	Feb. 1/18	CHQ 416 (postdated rent payment)			420.00
	rent payment	Mar. 1/18	CHQ 417 (postdated rent payment)			420.00

CLIENT INVOICES CONTINUED

TESSES TRESSES

Client Name	Terms	Date	Inv/Chq No.	Amount	Discount	Total
Brioche Bridal Party	2/5, n/15	Jan. 9/18	468	$142.50		$142.50
		Jan. 14/18	CHQ 206	139.65	$2.85	142.50
Conn Seted	net 15	Jan. 24/18	477			$59.28
		Jan. 29/18	CHQ 238			$59.28
Irma Vannitee	2/5, n/15	Dec. 28/17	452	$120.00		$120.00
		Jan. 2/18	CHQ 46	117.60	$2.40	120.00
	2/5, n/15	Jan. 2/18	464	111.72		111.72
		Jan. 7/18	CHQ 918	109.49	2.23	111.72
	2/5, n/15	Jan. 7/18	467	158.46		158.46
		Jan. 17/18	CHQ CC-61	158.46		158.46
	2/5, n/15	Jan. 16/18	471	90.06		90.06
		Jan. 20/18	CHQ 74	88.26	1.80	90.06
	2/5, n/15	Jan. 27/18	478	29.64		29.64
			Balance owing			$29.64
On Stage Theatre Company	2/5, n/15	Dec. 29/17	455	$ 250.00		$ 250.00
		Jan. 3/18	CHQ 382	245.00	$ 5.00	250.00
	2/5, n/15	Jan. 20/18	474	1 194.72		1 194.72
		Jan. 24/18	CHQ 429	1 170.83	23.89	1 194.72
	2/5, n/15	Jan. 28/18	479	1 194.72		1 194.72
		Jan. 31/18	CHQ 498	1 170.83	23.89	1 194.72
Stu Dents	rent payment	Jan. 2/18	CHQ 161			$585.00
	rent payment	Feb. 1/18	CHQ 162 (postdated rent payment)			585.00
	rent payment	Mar. 1/18	CHQ 163 (postdated rent payment)			585.00
Twilight Theatre	2/5, n/15	Dec. 28/17	453	$210.00		$210.00
		Jan. 2/18	CHQ 5121	205.80	$4.20	210.00
			Grand Total			$29.64

INVENTORY ITEM INFORMATION

TESSES TRESSES

Item Code	Item Description	Unit	Min Qty	Selling Price Reg	(Pref)	Qty on Hand	Total (Cost)	Tax
Hair Products: Total asset value $2 435 (Asset account: 1420, Revenue account: 4100, Expense account: 5200)								
BRS1	Hair Brush: natural bristle	each	2	$32	(26)	17	$ 323.00	HST
BRS2	Hair Brush: styling	each	2	24	(20)	28	420.00	HST
CN1	Pro-Line Conditioner: 150 ml	bottle	3	34	(26)	7	126.00	HST
CN2	Pro-Line Hot Oil Treatment 75 ml	tube	3	35	(28)	24	456.00	HST
FRZ1	Pro-Line Defrizzer: cream 100 ml	jar	3	28	(22)	27	459.00	HST
GEL1	Pro-Line Spray Gel: shaper 150 ml	can	3	27	(22)	16	256.00	HST
SHM1	Pro-Line Shampoo: 225 ml	bottle	5	26	(21)	10	170.00	HST
SPR1	Pro-Line Hair Spray: gentle 150 ml	can	5	26	(21)	15	225.00	HST
							$2 435.00	
Salon Services (Revenue account: 4120, Expense account: 5080)								
SRV1	Colour	each		$ 55	($48)			HST
SRV2	Conditioning Treatment	each		24	(20)			HST
SRV3	Cut and Style	each		48	(42)			HST
SRV4	Highlights	each		110	(90)			HST
SRV5	Perm	each		88	(80)			HST
SRV6	Wash and Style	each		26	(21)			HST
SRV7	Wig Wash, Set and Style	each		32	(26)			HST

Accounting Procedures

Taxes

HST at 14 percent is charged on all goods and services sold by the salon. Tesses Tresses remits the HST owing — *HST Charged on Sales* less *HST Paid on Purchases* — to the Receiver General by the last day of each month for the previous month.

Sales Summaries

Most salon sales are to one-time clients who do not have accounts. These sales are summarized weekly according to the payment method — by cash or by credit card — and entered for the client named Cash Customers. By choosing Cash Customers as the client for these sales, the default tax codes and terms should be correct.

Receipts and Bank Deposits

Cash and cheques received in payment are held for weekly deposits in the temporary bank clearing account, *Undeposited Cash and Cheques*. Therefore, Tesses Tresses uses this account as the default Receivables linked bank account for all receipts.

NSF Cheques

If a cheque is deposited from an account that does not have enough money to cover it, the bank returns it to the depositor as NSF (non-sufficient funds). To record the NSF cheque, enter a negative receipt in the Receipts Journal. Select *Bank: Chequing Account* as the Deposit To account. Turn on the option to Include Fully Paid Invoices and enter a negative payment amount. Enter the bank debit number as the receipt and add NSF to the original cheque number in the Cheque field. If a discount was taken for early payment, reverse this amount as well. Then enter a Sales Journal invoice for the amount of the handling charge. Refer to pages 605 and A–23 if you need more help.

> You must enter a negative receipt for these NSF cheques. You cannot reverse the receipt because different accounts are involved. The original receipt was deposited to *Undeposited Cash and Cheques*, but the NSF cheque credits the *Bank: Chequing Account*, after the deposit was entered.

Cost of Supplies

Instead of buying separate salon supplies for regular client services, Tesses Tresses uses its inventory stock of shampoos, conditioners, gels and so on. Inventory Adjustment entries are completed to make these transfers at cost from the inventory asset account to the supplies account.

INSTRUCTIONS

1. **Enter** the **deposit slips** and **set up** and **complete** the **account reconciliation** for January using the Chart of Accounts, Trial Balance, Supplier, Client and Inventory information provided. Use the keystrokes with the source documents as a guide. The journal transactions for January have been completed for you.

2. **Enter** the **source documents** for February, including the account reconciliation.

3. **Print** the **reports** indicated on the following chart after completing your entries:

NOTES

In 2013, PEI modified its taxation rates and methods, adopting the single 14 percent HST to replace the separate 5 percent GST (on goods and services) and 10 percent PST on goods only. Before the change, the non-refundable PST was charged on the base price of goods plus GST – GST was taxable.

REPORTS

Accounts
- [ ] Chart of Accounts
- [ ] Account List
- [ ] General Journal Entries

Financials
- [✓] Comparative Balance Sheet dates: Feb. 1 and Feb. 28 with difference in percentage
- [✓] Income Statement from Jan. 1 to Feb. 28
- [✓] Trial Balance date: Feb. 28
- [✓] All Journal Entries: Feb. 1 to Feb. 28
- [✓] General Ledger: for accounts 1060 and 1080 from Jan. 1 to Feb. 28
- [ ] Statement of Cash Flows
- [✓] Cash Flow Projection Detail Report for account 1060 for 30 days
- [ ] Gross Margin Income Statement

Tax
- [ ] Tax

Banking
- [✓] Account Reconciliation Summary Report: for 1060 and 1080 from Jan. 1 to Feb. 28
- [ ] Bank Transaction Report
- [ ] Reconciliation Transaction Report
- [✓] Deposit Slip Detail Report for account 1060 from Jan. 1 to Feb. 28
- [✓] Account Reconciliation Journal Entries: Jan. 1 to Feb. 28
- [✓] Deposit Slip Journal Entries: Jan. 1 to Feb. 28
- [ ] Cheque Log Report

Payables
- [ ] Supplier List
- [ ] Supplier Aged
- [ ] Aged Overdue Payables
- [ ] Expenses Journal Entries
- [ ] Payments Journal Entries
- [ ] Supplier Expenses

Receivables
- [ ] Client List
- [ ] Client Aged
- [ ] Aged Overdue Receivables
- [ ] Revenues Journal Entries
- [ ] Receipts Journal Entries
- [ ] Client Revenues
- [ ] Client Statements

Inventory & Services
- [ ] Inventory & Services List
- [ ] Inventory Summary
- [ ] Inventory Quantity
- [✓] Inventory Statistics: all items and all details
- [ ] Inventory Sales Summary
- [ ] Inventory Transaction Summary
- [ ] Item Assembly Journal Entries
- [ ] Adjustment Journal Entries
- [ ] Inventory Price Lists

KEYSTROKES

Entering Bank Deposit Slips

Previously, we recorded receipts directly as deposits to the linked bank accounts. In this chapter, we explain the procedure for recording receipts and deposits separately. The deposits for the cash and cheques received in January have not yet been recorded.

Open   **SageData16\TESS\TESS**. **Accept January 31** as the session date.

Click   **Banking** in the Modules pane list.

Deposits are made using the Make Deposit icon:

NOTES
If you are using backup files, restore SageData16\TESS1.CAB or TESS1 to SageData16\TESS\TESS.

NOTES
Home window ledger record balances for Tesses Tresses are calculated as at March 1, the latest transaction date (for the postdated rent cheques).
Remember that Make Other Payment is the default type of transaction from the Pay Bills icon in the Banking module window.

The account order was reversed in the previous screenshot by clicking 🔼 beside the Account Description heading and changing it to 🔽.

The first memo requires us to record the deposits for January.

> ✓
> 1

Memo #7   **Dated Jan. 31/18**

Use the deposit information slips to prepare deposit slip #1. All amounts were deposited to Bank: Chequing Account.

✓ **DEPOSIT SLIP # 1**			**JANUARY 7, 2018**
Date	Cheque #	Client	Amount
Jan 2	46	Irma Vannitee	$ 117.60
Jan 2	5121	Twilight Theatre	205.80
Jan 2	161	Stu Dents	585.00
Jan 2	415	Atta Schule	420.00
Jan 3	382	On Stage Theatre Company	245.00
Jan 7	918	Irma Vannitee	109.49
		Total Cheques	$1 682.89
		Cash	$2 576.40
		(Consisting of 6 × $5; 19 × $10; 30 × $20; 13 × $50; 11 × $100; Coin $6.40)	
		Total Deposit	$4 259.29

Click   the **Make Deposit icon** [Make Deposit] to open the Reconciliation & Deposits Journal:

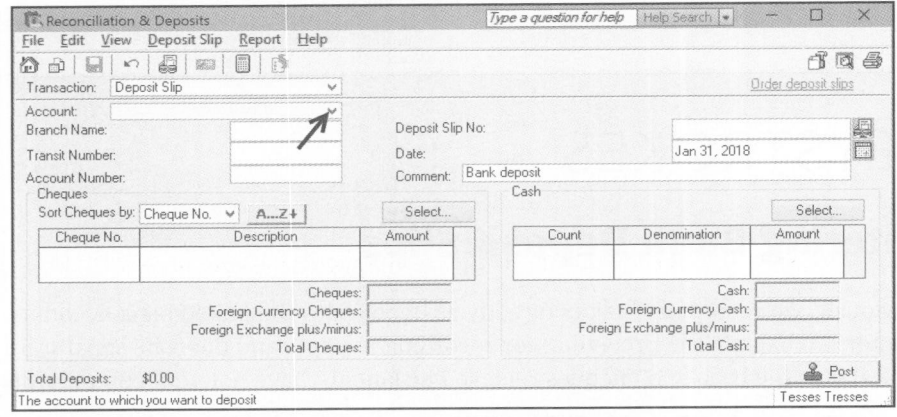

The journal is named Reconciliation & Deposits because both types of transactions are entered in this journal. You can choose from the **Transaction** drop-down list to change the type. Deposit Slip is selected in the Transaction field because we selected this Home window icon.

The deposit transaction has two parts: the Deposit To component that forms this main journal window and the Deposit From portion. All cash and cheques were debited to *Undeposited Cash and Cheques*, a Cash class **clearing account** that is the default account for all receipts. Now we need to transfer these receipts to the *Bank: Chequing Account* as deposits.

First, we choose the bank account receiving the deposit.

Click   the **Account list arrow**:

The following is the second screenshot showing the account dropdown with "1030 Undeposited Cash and Cheques" and "1060 Bank: Chequing Account".

Two accounts are listed: *Undeposited Cash and Cheques* (the default linked Receivables Cash class account) and the Bank class *Bank: Chequing Account*. We must select *Bank: Chequing Account*, the account that is receiving the deposit.

Click   **Bank: Chequing Account**.

The deposit slip number is entered and will be updated automatically, like the other forms in Sage 50.

Tesses Tresses makes weekly deposits to the bank account of all cash and cheques received during the week. We need to enter the date of the first deposit.

Enter   January 7, 2018 in the Date field for the first deposit.

Next, we must select the outstanding cheques and cash that will be deposited. The Deposit Slip has cheques on the left and cash on the right. There are separate **Select buttons** for these two types of currency. We will add the cheques first.

The Select button we need is in the centre of the journal, above the field for listing the cheques:

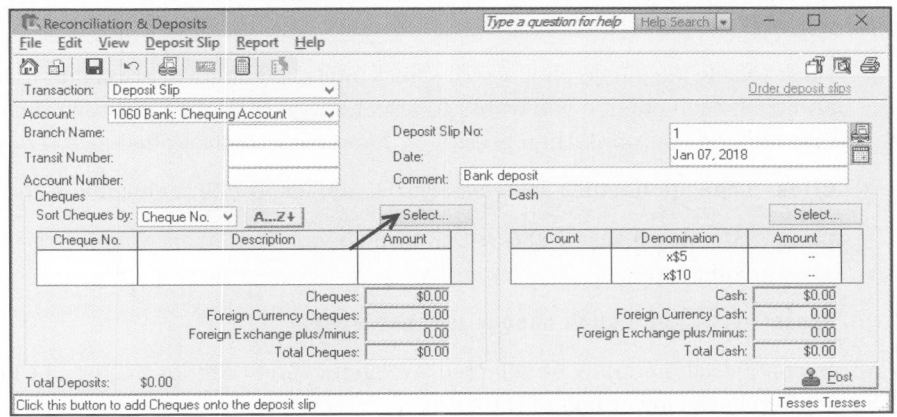

You can drag the column heading margins to change column sizes if all the information is not on-screen. Or you can maximize the journal.

Click   the **Select button for Cheques** to open the list of outstanding cheques:

The first banking account, *Undeposited Cash and Cheques*, is selected as the default **From Account**, and this is the one we want. Cheques are listed by date in ascending order, but you can choose a different order from the **Sort Cheques By** drop-down list. Cheques may be sorted by any of the column headings for the list of cheques (cheque number, currency, amount, description, foreign amount or foreign exchange amount). You can click the `A...Z↓` button — changing it to `Z...A↓` — to sort in descending order.

The session date, January 31, is entered in the **On Or After date** field, so only the cheques for January 31 and the postdated rent cheques are listed. We need to deposit all cheques that are dated on or after January 1, so this is the date we should enter. In this way, we will include all undeposited cheques.

Click   the **On Or After field Calendar icon** and **click Jan 1** as the date.

NOTES
You do not need to type the year in the Reconciliation & Deposits Journal date fields. It will be added correctly by the program.

NOTES
When the bank account is set up for online reconciliation, the branch, transit and account numbers are required information in the ledger record and will be added to the Deposit Slip Journal. Online banking is illustrated in Appendix I on the Student DVD.

NOTES
Once the list is in descending order, the order button label changes to `Z...A↓`. Clicking this button again restores the list to ascending order.

NOTES
You can also choose Jan 1 from the On Or After date field drop-down list. You can choose this date for all deposit slip transactions in this chapter if you want.

All the cheques received by the salon are now listed:

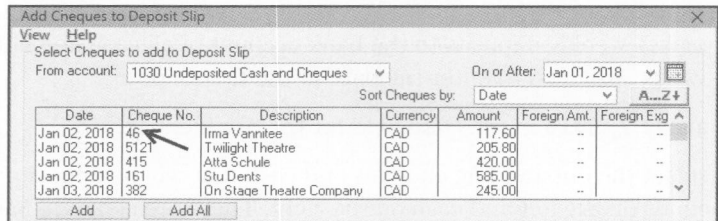

The next step is to select the cheques we want and add them to the deposit.

We should select the six cheques that are dated on or before January 7, cheques from Irma Vannitee, Twilight Theatre, Stu Dents, Atta Schule and On Stage Theatre Company.

Click to select a single cheque. To select multiple cheques, press and hold ⌈ctrl⌉ and click each cheque you want. To select several cheques in a row, click the first cheque you want, then press ⌈shift⌉ and click the last cheque you need.

Click   **cheque number 46 from Irma Vannitee**, the first cheque on the list.

Click   the **down scroll arrow** ⌄ until cheque #918 from Vannitee is included on-screen.

Press   ⌈shift⌉ and **click cheque number 918**.

All six cheques should now be selected. We should add them to the list of Cheques On Deposit Slip in the lower half of the form.

Click   the **Add button** to place the selected six cheques in the Cheques On Deposit Slip section:

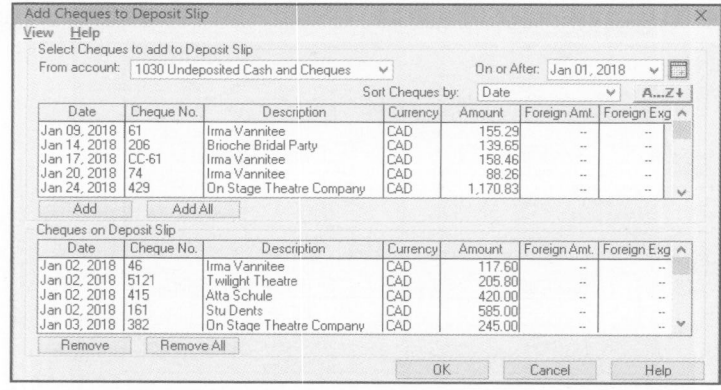

You can also add the cheques one at a time. Click a cheque and then click the Add button to move the cheque. Then click the next cheque and click Add. Repeat until all the cheques you want are in the Cheques On Deposit Slip list. If all cheques are deposited together, you can click Add All.

To **change a selection**, click a cheque in the Cheques On Deposit Slip list and click Remove. To start again, click Remove All to clear the list.

Click   **OK** to return to the updated Reconciliation & Deposits Journal:

NOTES
You may prefer to select cheques one at a time when the ones you are depositing are not in sequence.

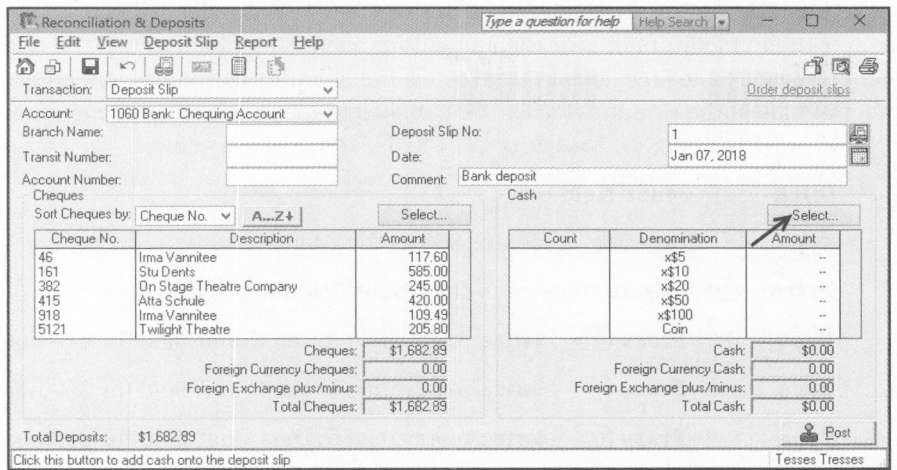

The selected six cheques are added and their total should match the amount on the Deposit Slip source document. If it does not, click the Select button again to correct the cheque selection. If a cheque amount is incorrect, close the journal without saving the changes and correct the original receipt transaction.

The next step is to add the cash portion of the deposit. Tesses Tresses has one cash sale summary amount to deposit, $2 576.40.

Click   the **Select button for Cash** to open the deposit form for cash:

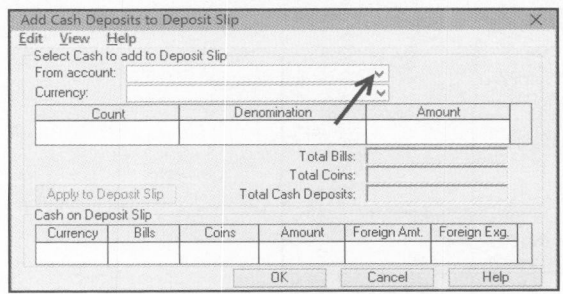

Cash receipts are not listed individually because they are usually combined in the store and held in the cash drawers or safe. When deposits are made, some cash is usually kept in the store to provide change for future clients. This balance may be transferred from *Undeposited Cash and Cheques* to a *Cash on Hand* account, recorded as a General Journal or Transfer Funds transaction. Similarly, the denominations of notes and coins that are received from clients may be different from the deposited ones. To simplify the exercise, we deposit the full amount of cash received each week.

Since no account is entered by default, we first need to select the account that we are depositing from.

Choose Undeposited Cash and Cheques from the From Account drop-down list to modify the deposit form:

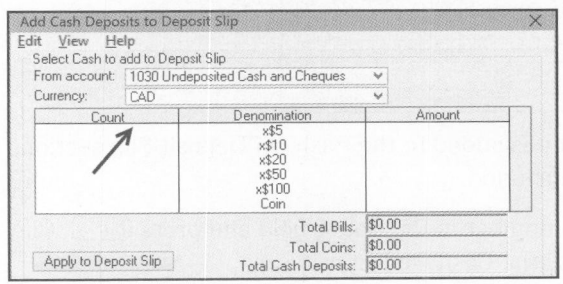

> **NOTES**
> The cheques on the deposit slip are sorted by cheque number. You can reverse the order (◄A...Z► button) or sort the cheques by description or amount by making the selection from the Sort Cheques By drop-down list.

> **NOTES**
> If you are unable to finish the deposit slip entry now, you can save it at any time and complete it later.

> **NOTES**
> The procedure for depositing partial amounts of cash is the same as the one we describe in this chapter — only the amount will be different.

> **NOTES**
> After selecting the From Account, the currency is added — the denomination of the notes will be known and added to the deposit form. Tesses Tresses uses only Canadian currency.

The Cash Deposit form is completed in the same way as a deposit slip at the bank. You enter the number of notes or the amount for each denomination and the total amount of coins. Sage 50 calculates and totals the amounts as soon as you enter the number of bills in the Count field. The $2 576.40 in deposited cash consists of 6 × $5; 19 × $10; 30 × $20; 13 × $50; 11 × $100; and $6.40 in coins.

Click   the **Count field beside** ×**$5**.

Type   6 **Press** (tab) to enter $30 as the Amount.

Press   (tab) **again** to move to the Count field for $10 notes.

Type   19 **Press** (tab) **twice** to advance to the Count field for $20 notes.

Type   30 **Press** (tab) **twice** to advance to the Count field for $50 notes.

Type   13 **Press** (tab) **twice** to advance to the Count field for $100 notes.

Type   11 **Press** (tab) **twice** to advance to the Count field for coins.

The amount for coins is entered as a total amount in the Amount field. You cannot type in the Count field for Coin.

Press   (tab) **again** to advance to the Amount field for coins.

Type   6.40 (You must enter the decimal for amounts less than one dollar.)

Press   (tab) to update the total:

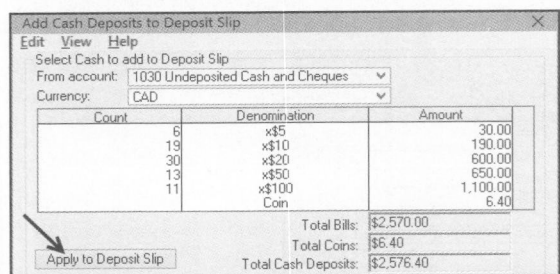

The total amounts for bills and coins remain separated, and the total for the cash deposit is calculated.

The next step is to apply the amount to the deposit slip.

Click   the **Apply To Deposit Slip button** to update the form:

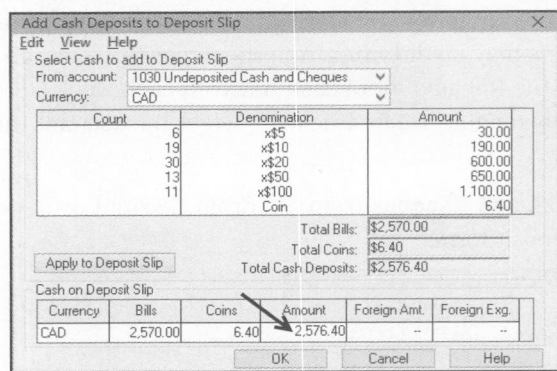

The total cash deposit amount is added to the Cash On Deposit Slip section. The currency for the amount is also included.

To make changes, edit a number in the Count field and press (tab). Click Apply To Deposit Slip to update the Cash On Deposit Slip.

Click   **OK** to add this cash deposit information to the journal form:

NOTES
Instead of pressing (tab) twice, you can press (↓) to move the cursor to the next Count line on the form.
Instead of entering the count for each denomination, you can enter the amount and Sage 50 will enter the corresponding count.

NOTES
If the coin amount is for a whole number, such as $6.00, you do not need to add the decimal and zeros. Instead, you can type 6, just as you do for amounts in other journals.

NOTES
Tesses Tresses does not have any foreign currency transactions.

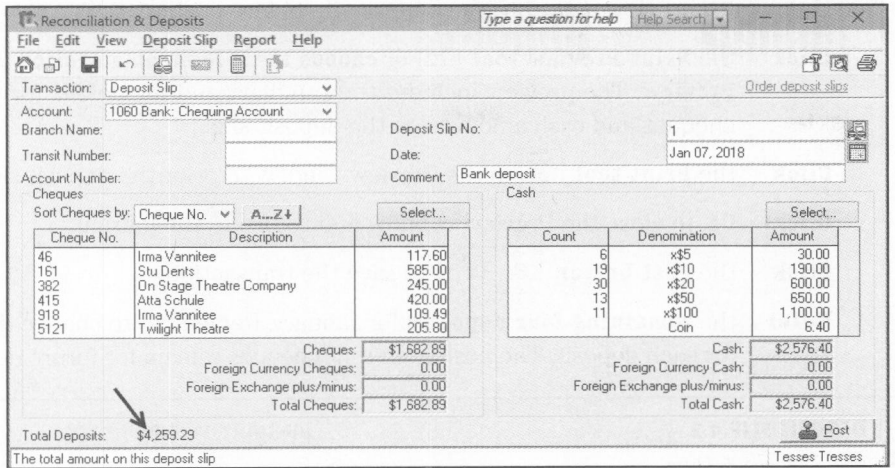

The form is complete. You can accept the default comment "Bank deposit" or change it. The comment will become part of the journal record.

Reviewing the Deposit Slip Entry

Before posting, we should review the journal entry created by the deposit.

Choose the **Report menu** and **click Display Deposit Slip Journal Entry**:

Deposit Slip Journal Entry

File   Options   Help

Print   Print Preview   Change Print Settings   Export   Open in Excel®   Modify ▾   Refresh   ?

Tesses Tresses
Deposit Slip Journal Entry 01/07/2018 (J53)

Account Number	Account Description	Debits	Credits
1060	Bank: Chequing Account Irma Vannitee	117.60	-
1060	Bank: Chequing Account Twilight Theatre	205.80	-
1060	Bank: Chequing Account Atta Schule	420.00	-
1060	Bank: Chequing Account Stu Dents	585.00	-
1060	Bank: Chequing Account On Stage Theatre Company	245.00	-
1060	Bank: Chequing Account Irma Vannitee	109.49	-
1060	Bank: Chequing Account CAD Cash Deposit From 1030	2,576.40	-
1030	Undeposited Cash and Cheques Irma Vannitee	-	117.60
1030	Undeposited Cash and Cheques Twilight Theatre	-	205.80
1030	Undeposited Cash and Cheques Atta Schule	-	420.00
1030	Undeposited Cash and Cheques Stu Dents	-	585.00
1030	Undeposited Cash and Cheques On Stage Theatre Company	-	245.00
1030	Undeposited Cash and Cheques Irma Vannitee	-	109.49
1030	Undeposited Cash and Cheques CAD Cash Deposit To 1060	-	2,576.40
Additional Date:	Additional Field:	4,259.29	4,259.29

In the journal entry, each cheque and cash amount is listed separately. The payer for each cheque is also included. Each deposit item is entered as a debit to *Bank: Chequing Account* and a credit to *Undeposited Cash and Cheques*. This detailed reporting makes it easier to find mistakes if any have been made.

Close the **Journal Entry Display** to return to the journal for corrections.

CORRECTING THE DEPOSIT SLIP JOURNAL ENTRY

To change the cheque part of the deposit, **click** the **Select button** for the **Cheque** part of the journal. To change a selection, **click** a **cheque** in the Cheques On Deposit Slip list and **click Remove**. To start again, **click Remove All** to clear the list. **Click Cancel** to close the Cheques Deposit form without saving changes.

If you need to make changes to the Cash part of the deposit, **click** the **Select button** on the **Cash** side of the Journal. **Click** the **incorrect amount** in the Count field and **type** the **correct amount. Press** _tab_ to update the total. **Click Apply To Deposit Slip** to update the deposit amount that will be recorded. **Click Cancel** to close the Cash Deposit form without saving changes.

NOTES

The deposit slip entry is J53. Journal entry numbers 1 to 52 are accounted for in the transactions for January.

The order of cheques in the journal report matches the date of receipt (refer to page 580). The default order in the Deposit Slip Journal is by cheque number.

⚠ WARNING!

You can look up deposit slips after posting them, but you cannot adjust them. You must make the correction with a General Journal entry. For example, you would reverse a deposit slip entry by debiting Undeposited Cash and Cheques and crediting Bank: Chequing Account. Then re-enter the individual cheques and cash amounts in the General Journal.

NOTES

If you get an error message about the form when you try to preview the deposit, click OK to open the Report & Form Settings. You must choose Deposit Slip in the Description field to preview the deposit slip, unless you are using your own customized forms.

You can also print the deposit slip from the journal's File menu, Print option.

NOTES

Click OK to confirm successful posting of transactions. We will not continue this reminder.

NOTES

For all deposits, choosing January 1 from the drop-down list in the On Or After field will include all cheques not yet deposited.

NOTES

At the end of January, the balance for Undeposited Cash and Cheques reflects the total of the four postdated rent cheques.

You should also preview and print the deposit slip before posting it.

Click the **Print Preview tool** or **choose** the **File menu** and **click Print Preview**. The preview includes the summary and the details for the cheques and cash amounts on the deposit slip.

Click the **Print tool** in the Preview window to print the deposit slip.

Click **OK** to close the Preview window and return to the journal.

Click the **Post button** to save the transaction.

Enter the **remaining four deposits** for January. Remember to change the date for each deposit. The postdated rent cheques remain for future deposits.

DEPOSIT SLIP # 2   **JANUARY 14, 2018**

2 Date   Cheque # Client   Amount

Jan 9   61   Irma Vannitee $155.29
Jan 14   206   Brioche Bridal Party   139.65
               Total Cheques $294.94
               Cash $2 177.40
               (Consisting of 23 × $5; 23 × $10; 24 × $20; 11 × $50; 8 × $100; Coin $2.40)
               Total Deposit $2 472.34

DEPOSIT SLIP # 3   **JANUARY 21, 2018**

3 Date   Cheque # Client   Amount

Jan 17   CC-61 Irma Vannitee $158.46
Jan 20   74   Irma Vannitee   88.26
                Total Cheques $246.72
                Cash $2 513.70
                (Consisting of 24 × $5; 23 × $10; 23 × $20; 16 × $50; 9 × $100; Coin $3.70)
                Total Deposit $2 760.42

DEPOSIT SLIP # 4   **JANUARY 28, 2018**

4 Date   Cheque # Client   Amount

Jan 24   429   On Stage Theatre Company $1 170.83
               Total Cheques $1 170.83
               Cash $2 228.70
               (Consisting of 27 × $5; 24 × $10; 20 × $20; 11 × $50; 9 × $100; Coin $3.70)
               Total Deposit $3 399.53

DEPOSIT SLIP # 5   **JANUARY 31, 2018**

5 Date   Cheque # Client   Amount

Jan 29   238   Conn Seted $ 59.28
Jan 31   498   On Stage Theatre Company   1 170.83
               Total Cheques $1 230.11
               Cash $2 838.60
               (Consisting of 9 × $5; 17 × $10; 21 × $20; 18 × $50; 13 × $100; Coin $3.60)
               Total Deposit $4 068.71

Close the **Reconciliation & Deposits Journal** and return to the Banking module window.

We are now ready to set up the bank accounts for reconciliation.

Account Reconciliation

For any bank account, the timing of monthly statements is usually not perfectly matched with the accounting entries of the corresponding transactions. Usually some of the cheques written do not appear on the statement, and interest amounts earned on the account or bank charges are not yet recorded because they may be unknown until receipt of the statement. Thus the balance of the bank statement usually does not match the General Ledger balance for the bank account. The process of identifying the differences to achieve a match is the process of account reconciliation.

In Sage 50 you can apply account reconciliation to any Balance Sheet account for which you have regular statements, including credit card payable accounts. For each account you want to reconcile, you must complete the setup procedure.

✓ 6 | **Memo #8** **Dated Jan. 31/18**
Set up account reconciliation for Bank: Chequing Account and Bank: Credit Cards.

Turning On the Account Reconciliation Feature

Before completing the reconciliation procedure, the General Ledger accounts that will be reconciled must be identified and modified. For the next stage, you will also need a report of all bank account transactions to compare with the bank statement. We will continue to work from the Banking module window to modify the account.

First, we will set up account reconciliation for *Bank: Chequing Account*.

Click **1060 Bank: Chequing Account** in the Banking module Home window Accounts list.

The ledger record for the bank account opens at the Account tab screen:

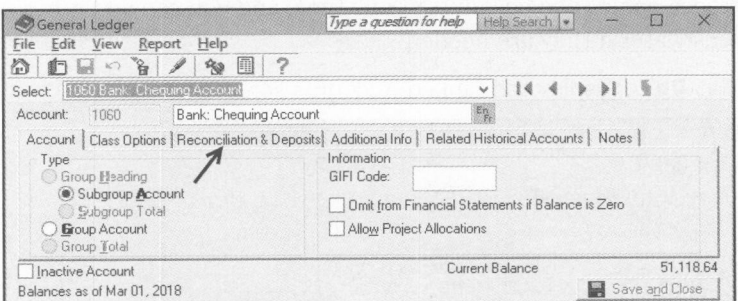

All postable Balance Sheet accounts have a Reconciliation & Deposits tab, but reconciliation is generally used for accounts with regular statements that summarize all transactions. Usually these are the bank accounts or credit card accounts.

Click the **Reconciliation & Deposits tab**:

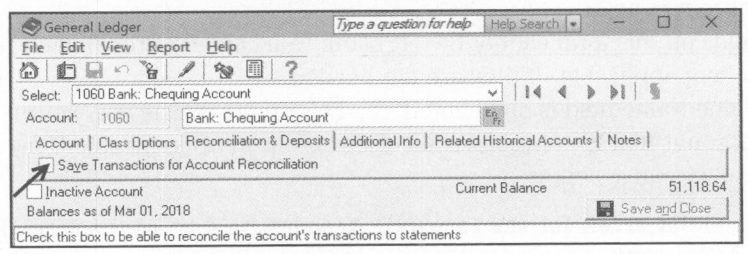

NOTES
Online bank reconciliation is explained in Appendix I on the Student DVD. The text enrichment Web site for this text is set up for online reconciliation so you can try this feature of the program.

Click   **Save Transactions For Account Reconciliation** to add the Set Up button to the ledger window:

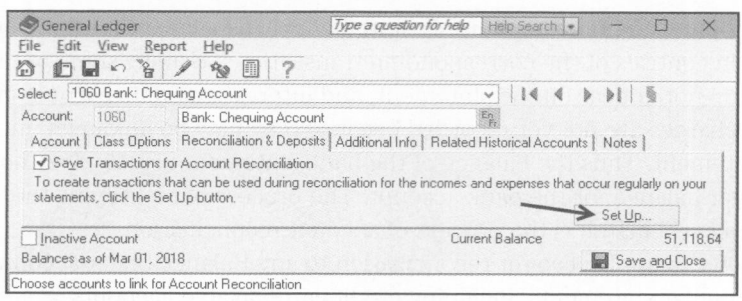

Naming and Linking Reconciliation Accounts

Most bank statements include monthly bank charges, loan or mortgage payments and interest on deposits. That is, there are usually some regular sources of income and expense. Normally the only source document for these bank account transactions is the bank statement. To use the account reconciliation feature in Sage 50, you should first create the accounts that link to these regular bank account transactions. In the January Bank Statement for Tesses Tresses on page 588, there is an interest deposit and a withdrawal for service charges. The salon already has accounts for both of these items.

The next step is to name bank statement–related transactions and identify the appropriate General Ledger accounts that link to these transactions. Tesses Tresses has income (interest received) from bank deposits and expenses associated with the bank account, such as bank charges or interest paid on bank loans. An additional account will be needed for adjustments — small discrepancies between the accounting entries and the bank statements, such as amounts entered incorrectly in journal transactions.

You can edit these names and accounts at any time, and you can add other sources of income or expense later if they are needed.

Click   **Set Up** to display the Linked Accounts screen:

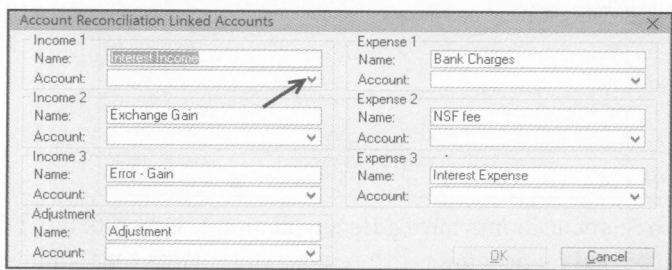

On this Account Reconciliation Linked Accounts form, you can identify up to three regular sources of income, three types of expenses and one adjustment account for each account you want to reconcile.

The name fields on this form cannot be left blank. You can leave the default names or enter "n/a" for "not applicable" if they are not needed.

The first Income Name field is highlighted, ready for editing. The only source of income for this account that is not recognized elsewhere is interest income. This name is already entered so we can accept it.

Click   the **list arrow for the Income 1 Account field** to list the revenue accounts that are available.

Click   **4220 Interest Revenue**. **Press** ⌞tab⌟ to advance to the second Income field.

This field and the third Income field are not needed, so we will indicate that they are not applicable.

Type   n/a

Press   (tab) **twice** to skip the Account field and advance to the third Income field. **Type** n/a to indicate that it too is not applicable.

Leave the default name for adjustments unchanged.

Click   the **Adjustment Account field list arrow**.

Either an expense or a revenue account can be used for adjustments. Tesses Tresses does not have an account for this purpose, so we will create a new expense account.

Type   5050 Reconciliation Adjustments

Press   (tab). **Click Add** to start the Add An Account wizard.

Accept   the **remaining defaults** and **click Finish** to add the account to the Linked Accounts form. **Press** (tab) to advance the cursor.

The Expense 1 Name field is highlighted. The salon has one automatic bank account–related expense, bank charges. NSF fee, the second expense, is also used but we do not expect this to be a regular expense. These names are already entered as the default, so we can accept them. Tesses Tresses uses the same account for both expenses.

Click   the **Account field list arrow** for **Expense 1** to display the list of expense accounts.

Select   **5040 Bank Charges** for this expense account.

Click   the **Account field list arrow** for **Expense 2**.

Select   **5040 Bank Charges** for this expense account.

Press   (tab) to advance to the third Expense field.

Type   n/a to indicate that it is not needed.

Check   your **work** carefully. When you are certain that all the names and accounts are correct,

Click   **OK** to save the new information. The Set Up button remains available because you can add and change linked accounts.

While the General Ledger is still open, we will set up the linked accounts for *Bank: Credit Cards*.

Click   the **Next Account button** ▶ to open the ledger we need.

Click   the **Reconciliation & Deposits tab** if necessary.

Click   **Save Transactions For Account Reconciliation**.

Click   **Set Up**.

Choose   **4220** as the linked account for Interest Income.

Choose   **5050** as the linked account for Adjustment. **Press** (tab) to advance to the Expense 1 Name field.

Type   Card Fees **Press** (tab).

Choose   **5060** as the linked account for Card Fees.

Click   **OK** to save the reconciliation accounts.

Close   the **Ledger window** to return to the Banking module window.

Reconciling the Bank Statement

Comparing the Bank Statement and Transactions Report

✓
7

Memo #9   **Dated Jan. 31/18**

Use the following bank statement to reconcile Bank: Chequing Account.

NOTES

The numbers in the Note column correspond to the explanation on pages 589–590.

1 Deposit recorded in December (outstanding prior transaction)

2 Deposit Slips: total amounts from deposit slips

3 Service charges

4 Interest received

5 Scheduled loan payments $2 100 (1 500 + 600)

SAVERS TRUST					
321 Queen St., Charlottetown, PE C1A 6D3					saverstrust.com

Tesses Tresses
55 Salon Road
Charlottetown, PE C1A 6D3

ACCOUNT STATEMENT
CHEQUING

Transit / Account No
02900   003 433 38-2

Statement period
Jan 1, 2018 to Jan 31, 2018

Date	Note #	Description	Deposits	Withdrawals	Balance
		Balance Fwd			37,238.00
2 Jan	1	Deposit	1,177.00		38,415.00
7 Jan		Cheque #410		926.10	37,488.90
7 Jan	2	Deposit	4,259.29		41,748.19
9 Jan		Cheque #411		330.00	41,418.19
14 Jan	2	Deposit	2,472.34		43,890.53
14 Jan		Cheque #412		239.40	43,651.13
14 Jan		Cheque #413		4,102.36	39,548.77
14 Jan		Transfer 0290 004 123 22-8	6,000.00		45,548.77
15 Jan		NSF Cheque #61		155.29	45,393.48
15 Jan	3	Service Charge – NSF cheque		40.00	45,353.48
17 Jan		Cheque #414		1,830.00	43,523.48
20 Jan		Cheque #415		142.50	43,380.98
21 Jan	2	Deposit	2,760.42		46,141.40
27 Jan		Cheque #416		431.00	45,710.40
27 Jan	5	Scheduled payment: loan		600.00	45,110.40
27 Jan	5	Scheduled payment: mortgage		1,500.00	43,610.40
28 Jan	2	Deposit	3,399.53		47,009.93
31 Jan	3	Service Charges		35.50	46,974.43
31 Jan	4	Interest	41.75		47,016.18
31 Jan		Closing balance			47,016.18

Total Deposits	#	7	$20,110.33
Total Withdrawals	#	12	$10,332.15

We need to compare this bank statement with the Bank Transaction Report provided by the program. Similar to the General Ledger Report, the Bank Account Transaction Report will include all transactions for the account.

Choose the **Reports menu**, then **choose Banking** and **click Bank Account Transactions Report**. The Modify Report window opens:

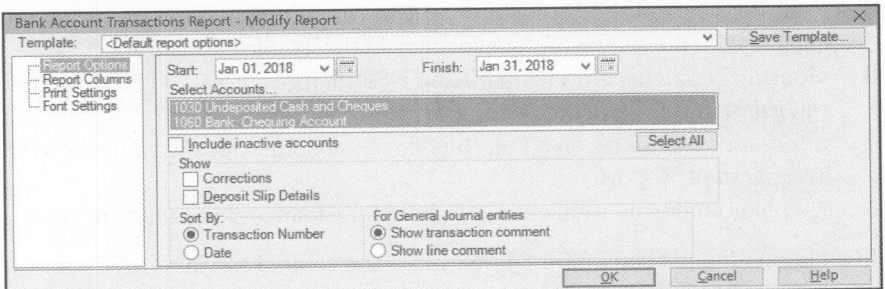

Only Bank and Cash class accounts are listed because the report is available only for bank accounts. The credit card bank account is not included because it is classified as a Credit Card Receivable account. In order to reconcile the credit card account, you can display or print the General Ledger Report for the period covering the bank statement.

For bank account reports, you can include corrections and deposit slip details or omit them. By default both items are omitted from the report. Since it is easier to work from a report that most closely matches the bank statement, you should omit corrections for this step. The deposit slip details do not appear on the bank statement, but they can be viewed or omitted in the Transactions Report. Because they can help us locate errors, we will include them at this stage. You may want to print the Transactions Report with and without deposit slip details to compare with the bank statement that has only the total deposit amounts.

You can report by date or transaction number and include transaction or line comments.

Click **1060 Bank: Chequing Account** to select the account.

The default report dates are correct. In an ongoing business, include the date of the oldest outstanding item from your previous bank statement up to the date of the most recent statement.

Click **Deposit Slip Details** to add the ✓. **Click** **OK** to view the report:

Tesses Tresses
Bank Account Transactions Report 01/01/2018 to 01/31/2018
Sorted by: Transaction Number

Date	Comment	Source #	JE#	Debits	Credits	Balance
1060	**Bank: Chequing Account**					38,415.00 Dr
01/04/2018	Pro-Line Inc.	410	J14	-	926.10	37,488.90 Dr
01/09/2018	Fine Brushes	411	J17	-	330.00	37,158.90 Dr
01/10/2018	Atlantic Power Corp.: AP-57321, hyd...	412	J22	-	239.40	36,919.50 Dr
01/14/2018	Pro-Line Inc.	413	J24	-	4,102.36	32,817.14 Dr
01/14/2018	Memo 1, Transfer funds	FundsTransfer	J25	6,000.00	-	38,817.14 Dr
01/14/2018	Receiver General for Canada: Memo...	414	J26	-	1,830.00	36,987.14 Dr
01/15/2018	Irma Vannitee	DM-61899	J27	-	155.29	36,831.85 Dr
01/18/2018	Eastern Tel: ET-4003, telephone ser...	415	J34	-	142.50	36,689.35 Dr
01/24/2018	Credit Card	416	J42	-	431.00	36,258.35 Dr
01/27/2018	Savers Trust - preauthorized withdra...	DM-792218	J44	-	2,100.00	34,275.95 Dr
01/07/2018	Bank deposit	1	J55	117.60	-	34,158.35 Dr
01/07/2018	Bank deposit	1	J55	205.80	-	34,481.75 Dr
01/07/2018	Bank deposit	1	J55	420.00	-	34,901.75 Dr
01/07/2018	Bank deposit	1	J55	585.00	-	35,486.75 Dr
01/07/2018	Bank deposit	1	J55	245.00	-	35,731.75 Dr
01/07/2018	Bank deposit	1	J55	109.49	-	35,841.24 Dr
01/07/2018	Bank deposit	1	J55	2,576.40	-	38,417.64 Dr
01/14/2018	Bank deposit	2	J56	155.29	-	38,572.93 Dr
01/14/2018	Bank deposit	2	J56	139.65	-	38,712.58 Dr
01/14/2018	Bank deposit	2	J56	2,177.40	-	40,889.98 Dr
01/21/2018	Bank deposit	3	J57	158.46	-	41,048.44 Dr
01/21/2018	Bank deposit	3	J57	88.26	-	41,136.70 Dr
01/21/2018	Bank deposit	3	J57	2,513.70	-	43,650.40 Dr
01/28/2018	Bank deposit	4	J58	1,170.83	-	44,821.23 Dr
01/28/2018	Bank deposit	4	J58	2,228.70	-	47,049.93 Dr
01/31/2018	Bank deposit	5	J59	59.28	-	47,109.21 Dr
01/31/2018	Bank deposit	5	J59	1,170.83	-	48,280.04 Dr
01/31/2018	Bank deposit	5	J59	2,838.60	-	51,118.64 Dr
				22,960.29	10,256.65	

Print the **report** with and without deposit slip details so that you can compare it with the statement. **Close** the displayed **report** when finished.

Comparing the reports reveals the differences outlined below. The numbers with them correspond to the numbers in the margin Notes and the Note # column in the bank statement above.

1 One deposit on January 2 appears on the bank statement and not in the Bank Transactions Report because the deposit was entered late in December.

2 Four deposits on the bank statement were multiple deposits entered on deposit slips and do not match any single entry in the Transactions Report.

3 Monthly bank charges of $35.50 and NSF charges of $40.00 have not been recorded in the Transactions Report.

4 Interest of $41.75 received on the deposit account does not appear in the Transactions Report.

5 A single General Journal entry combined the loan and mortgage payments.

In addition, deposit slip #5 for $4 068.71 — the total of the last three items in the report — is not listed on the bank statement, and the order of transactions is different. As a result of these differences, the total deposit and withdrawal amounts also differ.

All discrepancies must be accounted for in order to have the bank statement match the bank balance in the account's General Ledger or on the Balance Sheet.

Reconciling the Account

After entering the linked accounts, you can begin the reconciliation. The account reconciliation procedure consists of the following steps to update the General Ledger:

1. Record the opening and ending balances from the bank statement for the account.
2. Add outstanding transactions from prior periods that were not resolved in the previous bank statement (only for the first reconciliation).
3. Identify all the deposits and withdrawals that have been processed by the bank.
4. Complete journal entries for any transactions for which the bank statement is the source document.

The result should be a match between the bank balances in the two statements. If the amounts do not match, the difference will be assigned to the linked Adjustment account. All these steps are completed in the Account Reconciliation Journal.

Account record balances in the Home window are displayed at the latest transaction date, March 1, the date of the postdated rent cheques, as the Accounts pane informs us in the line above the accounts. The postdated cheques account for the *Undeposited Cash and Cheques* balance amount.

If you change User Preferences View Settings to view record balances as at the session date, the undeposited amount on January 31 will be zero:

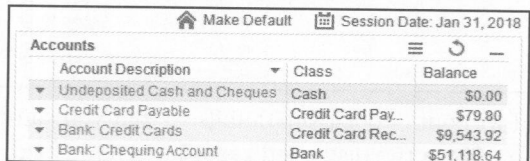

The additional information line (Balances As Of) above the accounts in the Accounts pane has been removed for this viewing option.

Click the **Reconcile Accounts icon** to open the Reconciliation Journal:

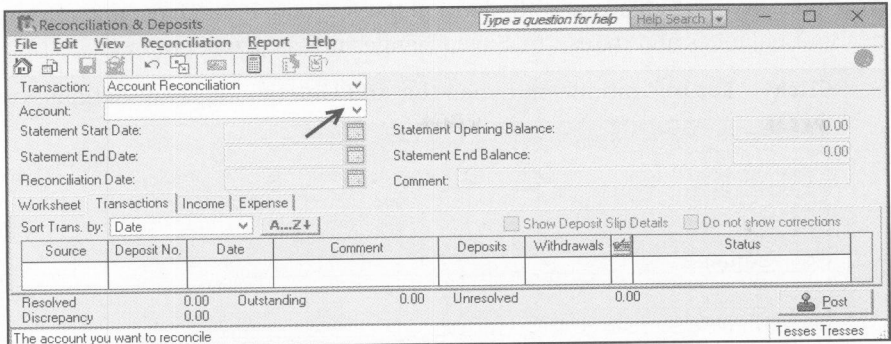

NOTES

There is no allocation option in the Account Reconciliation Journal but additional fields are available, as they are in the other journals.

Click   the **Account field list arrow**.

The list displays the bank and credit card accounts that we set up for account reconciliation. These are the only accounts available for reconciliation.

Select   1060 Bank: Chequing Account to start the reconciliation:

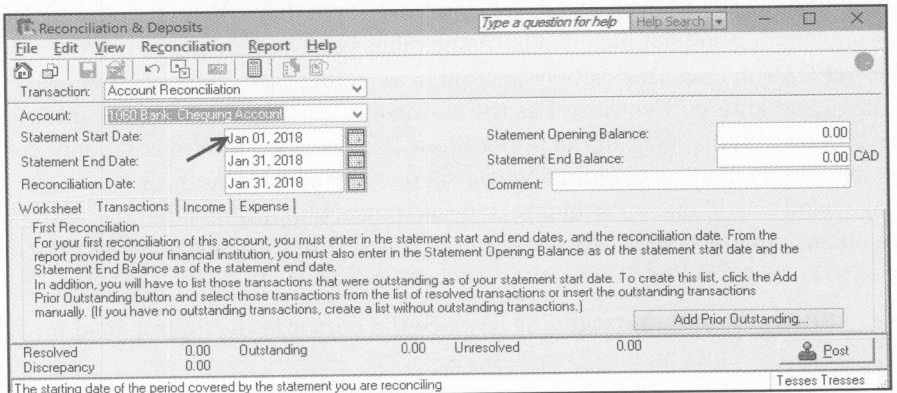

NOTES

Read the instructions on the screen about the first reconciliation before proceeding. It advises that you must go through the step of adding prior transactions.

The account is added to the Account field. The first day of the month is entered as the Statement Start Date, and the session date is entered automatically in the Statement End Date field and the Reconciliation Date field. These dates will advance by one month — or the length of the reconciliation period of 31 days in this case — when you have finished reconciling the bank account for the current month. The dates are correct, so do not change them.

We need to add the opening and closing bank statement balances from page 588.

Click   the **Statement Opening Balance field**.

Type   37238 **Press** (tab) to advance to the Statement End Balance field.

Type   47016.18 **Press** (tab) to advance to the Comment field.

Type   January Bank Reconciliation

For the first reconciliation, we need to add one outstanding transaction from the previous period. A deposit of $1 177 appears on the bank statement but not in the ledger report. The deposit was made at the end of December, too late to be included in the December bank statement, so we need to add it now. Adding prior transactions in the Account Reconciliation Journal does not create a journal entry and does not affect the ledger balance. The step is necessary only to create a match between the bank statement and the current ledger.

Click   Add Prior Outstanding. Sage 50 asks for confirmation:

You must save the changes to the journal to continue. If you have not yet entered the account balances and dates, the Save Changes message will not open.

Click   **Yes** to continue and open the Add Outstanding Transactions window:

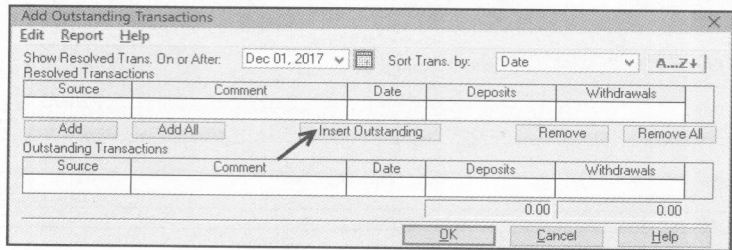

If there are no prior transactions that you need to insert, click OK at this stage to return to the journal.

If you have entered transactions in Sage 50 that precede the bank statement starting date, they will appear in the upper portion of the screen, in the Resolved Transactions section. If they have been resolved, you can leave them there. If, however, some of them were outstanding and not included in the previous bank statement, you can add them to the lower Outstanding Transactions section by selecting them and choosing Add.

If we had entered February 1 as the statement starting date, all the January transactions would appear in the upper Show Resolved Transactions section. We would then include them all as outstanding transactions by clicking Add All.

We need to add one outstanding deposit transaction. It preceded the first entry in Sage 50 on January 1, so it will not be in the transactions list. We must add these types of items to the Outstanding Transactions section.

Click   **Insert Outstanding** to place the cursor in the Source field for Outstanding Transactions.

Type   **5117** to enter the client's cheque number as the Source.

Press   (tab) to move to the Comment field. We will enter the client's name.

Type   Twilight Theatre **Press** (tab) to move to the Date field.

December 31, 2017, is entered as the default date, the last date before our statement start date. This date is correct, so you do not need to change it. You can enter a different date if necessary.

Press   (tab) to move to the Deposits column.

Type   1177 **Press** (tab).

If there are other outstanding prior transactions, enter them in the same way. For each additional outstanding transaction, you must click Insert Outstanding to move the cursor to the Source field on a new blank line for Outstanding Transactions.

If there are no prior transactions, click OK to return to the journal.

Click   **OK** to return to the journal window.

Marking Journal Entries as Cleared

You are now ready to begin processing individual journal entries to indicate whether they have been cleared in this bank statement. That is, you must indicate whether the bank has processed the items and the amounts have been withdrawn from or deposited to the account.

The journal window has been updated with outstanding transactions:

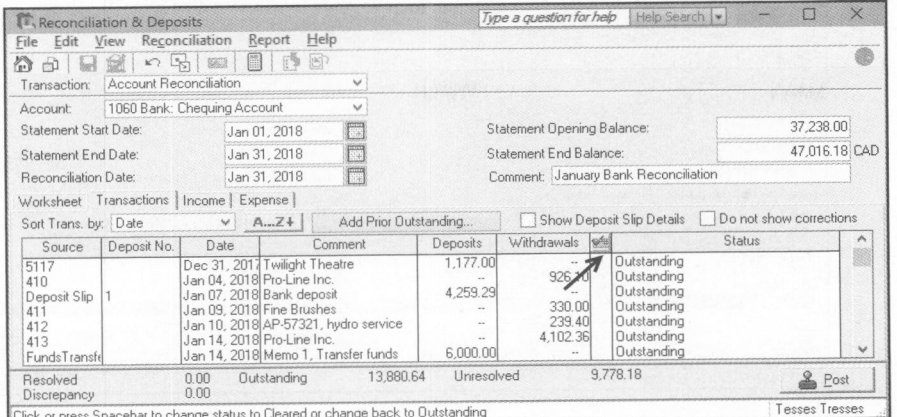

The Transactions tab is selected, and all January bank account transactions are now listed, including the one we just added. The bottom section of the screen contains a summary of the transactions. Our goal is to reduce the unresolved amount to zero with no discrepancy. At this stage, a discrepancy may indicate an incorrect account balance.

You can add or change the opening and end balances at this stage if necessary.

Showing Corrections

You can hide correcting journal entries in the list of transactions by clicking **Do Not Show Corrections**. Removing incorrect and reversing entries can make the reconciliation easier by increasing the match with the statement. When you hide the corrections and then clear transactions, Sage 50 automatically applies the Reversed status to the original incorrect entry and the Adjustment status to the reversing entry created by Sage 50 (refer to page 596).

Group Deposits

Sometimes several cheques are deposited as a group, as they were on the weekly deposit slips. Each of these group deposits can now be cleared as a group. If you have not used the Deposit Slip Journal to record deposits, you can define a group deposit by entering the deposit slip number for each item in the Deposit No. field beside the Source. When you clear one item in the group, the others will be cleared at the same time.

You may want to drag the lower frame of the journal window or maximize the journal window to include more transactions on your screen at the same time.

You are now ready to mark the transactions that have been cleared, that is, the ones that appear on the bank statement.

Click   the **Clear column** ☑ **for Cheque #5117** (click in the column), the first transaction on the list.

A checkmark appears in the Clear column ☑, the Status has changed from Outstanding to Cleared and the Resolved Amount has increased to $1 177. As you clear each item, the Resolved and Unresolved amounts are updated.

Clear   the **remaining journal entries** that appear on the bank statement on page 588 and scroll as necessary to display additional items.

Do not clear deposit slip #5 for $4 068.71.

NOTES
Transactions are sorted by date in ascending order. You can also arrange them by source, comment, deposit amount, withdrawal amount, the order of entry (journal entry number) or deposit number. For any of these, you can choose ascending or descending order with the ☐A...Z↓☐ button. Choosing a different order may make it easier to find a specific transaction.

NOTES
The option to add prior transactions remains available until you post the reconciliation, so you can make further additions and corrections as needed.

NOTES
Only the corrections made with the program's adjusting and reversing features will be hidden; manually reversed entries or corrections like the NSF cheque on page 605 will not be hidden.

NOTES
You can click the ☑ column heading to clear all entries on the transactions list. Then you can click an individual ✓ to restore the Outstanding status if needed.

NOTES
Remember to clear the withdrawal on Jan. 27 for $2 100 to match the two bank statement entries for $600 and $1 500.

NOTES
The Outstanding Amount at the bottom of the journal is the amount for the outstanding deposit (deposit #5).

Your transactions list has been updated:

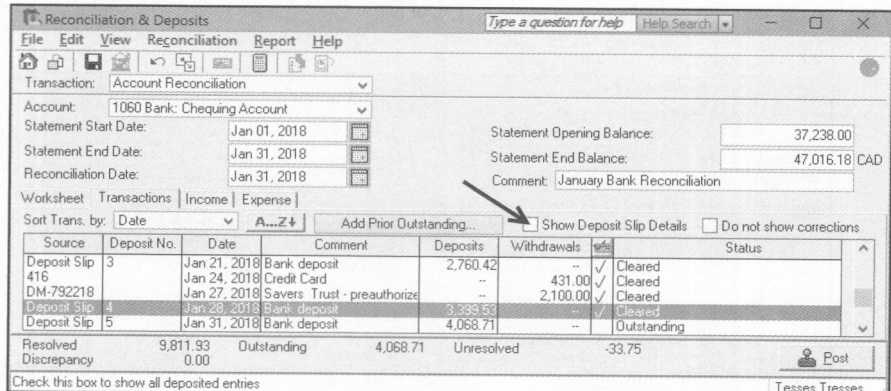

If you mark an item as Cleared by mistake, click the [icon] column again to return the status to Outstanding.

After clearing all transactions from the bank statement, the unresolved amount should be –33.75. This is the net difference for the three unmatched bank statement items: the NSF charge, the service charge and the interest. Journal entries for these items will be added later (page 596).

The next section describes the procedure for clearing transactions that are different in some way, like NSF cheques. By marking their status correctly, you will have a more accurate picture of your business transactions. Cheque #61 for $155.29 from Irma Vannitee was returned as NSF and should be marked as such. This cheque was included on deposit slip #2 (refer to page 584).

Showing Deposit Slip Details

The NSF cheque we need to mark was part of a group deposit, so it does not appear individually on the Transactions list. First we need to include the details of the deposit slips. For this, we use the **Show Deposit Slip Details** option above the Transactions list (refer to the screenshot at the top of this page). Its check box is a toggle switch; you can hide the details when they are not required or include them if you need to change the status of a single item in the deposit group.

Click **Show Deposit Slip Details** to add a ✓.

All individual amounts on the deposit slips are now part of the transactions list, and all are marked as cleared because we cleared the entire deposit slip.

Press the **down scroll arrow** [icon] until the items for deposit slip #2 are included on you screen:

NOTES
If you sort the transactions by Deposit Number, the deposit slip entries will appear together at the bottom of the list. If you sort by Source, they will appear together at the top of the list in our example because the deposit slip numbers (1 to 5) are smaller than all the cheque numbers.

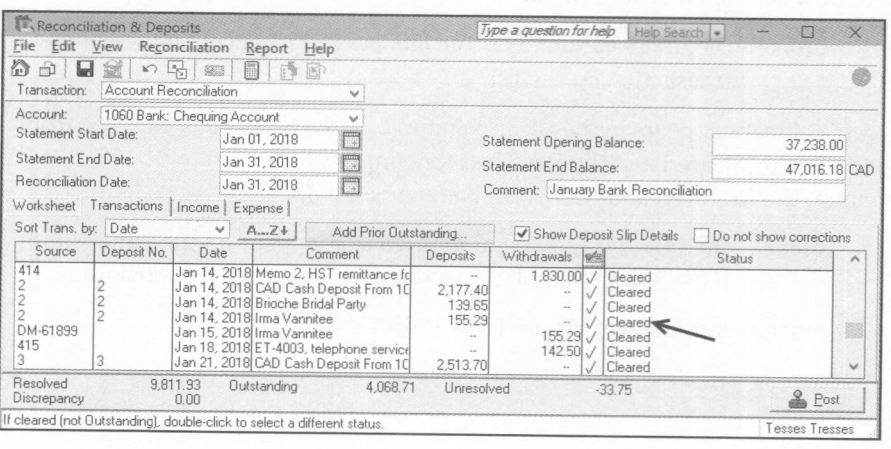

All three items on deposit slip #2, the two cheques and the cash amount, are marked as Cleared.

Marking NSF Cheques

For some items — for example, NSF cheques and their reversing entries — you should add further information because they have not cleared the account in the usual way.

To mark a cheque as NSF,

Click   **Cleared** in the Status column for Irma Vannitee's cheque for $155.29 in deposit slip #2, the NSF cheque.

Press   (enter) to display the alternatives for the Status of a journal entry:

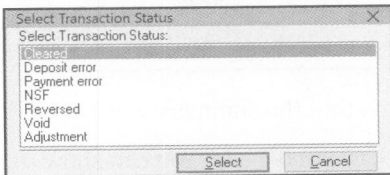

These status alternatives are explained in the Status Options chart that follows:

STATUS OPTIONS

Cleared	For deposits and cheques that have been processed correctly.
Deposit Error	For the adjusting journal entry that records the difference between the amount of a deposit that was recorded incorrectly and the bank statement amount for that deposit. Assign the Cleared status to the original entry for the deposit.
Payment Error	For the adjusting entry that records the difference between the amount of a cheque recorded incorrectly and the bank statement amount for that cheque. Assign the Cleared status to the original entry for the cheque.
NSF	For client cheques returned by the bank because there was not enough money in the client's account. Assign the Adjustment status to the adjusting entry that reverses the NSF cheque.
Reversed	For cheques that are cancelled by posting a reversing transaction entry to the bank account or the Sales or Purchases journals, that is, journal entries that are corrected. Assign the Adjustment status to the reversing entry that cancels the cheque.
Void	For cheques that are cancelled because of damage during printing. Assign the Adjustment status to the reversing entry that voids the cheque.
Adjustment	For the adjusting or reversing entries that are made to cancel NSF, void or reversed cheques. (Refer to the explanations for NSF, Void and Reversed above.)

Click   **NSF** to highlight this alternative.

Click   **Select** to enter it. The Cleared status changes to NSF for this item.

The final step is to change the status of the entry that reverses the payment or NSF cheque to Adjustment. The final certified cheque received in payment has been cleared normally, so its status as Cleared is already correct. Changing the status does not affect the resolved and unresolved amounts; the amounts are just cleared in different ways.

Double-click   **Cleared in the Status column for Bank Debit Memo #61899**, the reversing entry (155.29 in the Withdrawals column).

Double-click   **Adjustment** to select this as the status.

The unresolved, resolved and outstanding amounts have not changed.

> **NOTES**
> Void cheques are also used to set up automatic payments (direct deposit). Because these do not have amounts or journal entries associated with them, they will not appear in the Reconciliation Journal.

Your updated transactions list now has the revised status entries:

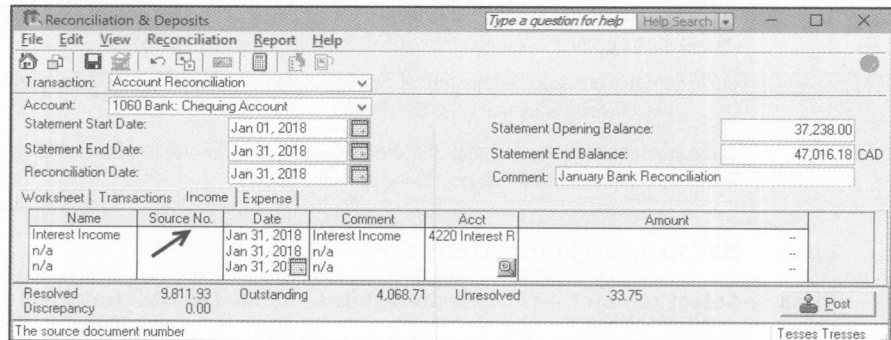

Click **Show Deposit Slip Details** to restore the summary version for deposits.

The status for deposit slip #2 has changed to Cleared again. You can show the details at any time again or if you need to make corrections by clicking the check box for it again.

The resolved, unresolved and outstanding amounts, the net of deposit and withdrawal amounts, are continually updated as you work through the reconciliation procedure. Your journal entry from the Report menu at this stage would have a credit to *Bank: Chequing Account* and a debit to the expense account *Reconciliation Adjustments* for $33.75, the unresolved amount at this stage — the net amount of interest and the two bank charges. The expense amount total is greater than the interest amount by $33.75. The journal entries for these items will reduce the unresolved amount to zero.

Adding Account Statement Journal Entries

Click the **Income tab**.

The Account Reconciliation Journal now includes journal entry fields:

The entry for Interest Income — the income source we named earlier — is partially completed with the correct default entries for date, comment and account. You can change any of these entries by editing the contents or selecting a different account.

Click the **Source No. field** beside Interest Income to advance the cursor.

Type Bk-Stmt

Click the **Amount field**.

Type 41.75 **Press** (tab). The unresolved amount — 75.50 — now matches the amount for the service fee plus the NSF charge.

You can edit these journal entries or transaction status entries at any time before posting. Choosing the **Save tool** will save the work you have completed so far, without posting, and still permit you to make changes later.

If there are other income categories, type the name, source, date, comment, account and amount on the second line. You can enter more than three sources of income on this form and you can choose any revenue account, although you can predefine only three linked accounts.

Click the **Expense tab** to open the input fields for expense transactions:

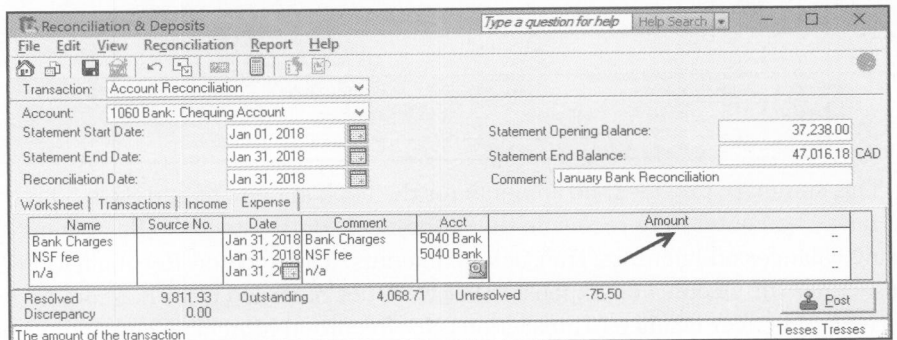

NOTES
Drag the column heading margins if necessary to include all the input columns.

The expense transactions are also partially completed. We need to add the Source No. and the Amount. For the NSF fee, we need to change the date as well.

You can combine regular service charges with charges for other one-time or unusual services such as stopping a payment on a cheque or NSF fees. We have created a separate category for the NSF charge in order to track this expense. The bank statement contains the amounts for the expenses.

Click the **Source No. field**. Duplicate source document codes are allowed in this journal.

Type Bk-Stmt

Click the **Amount field**.

Type 35.50 **Press** (tab) to advance to the next journal line.

NOTES
You can select a different expense account in the Reconciliation Journal for these predefined expenses if this is appropriate.

We can now enter the NSF service charges. You can use the same account for more than one journal entry, but you cannot choose the same expense or income category twice. The date for this charge was January 15, so we must also change the default date.

Click the **Source field**. We will enter the debit memo number as the source.

Type DM61899 **Press** (tab).

Type Jan 15

Click the **Amount field**. **Type** 40 **Press** (tab) to enter the amount.

If there are other expenses, enter the information in the same way. You can enter additional expenses and choose any expense account, although you can predefine only three linked accounts.

At this stage, your unresolved amount and discrepancy should be zero if everything is reconciled. We will look at the Worksheet — it summarizes the changes we made.

Click the **Worksheet tab**:

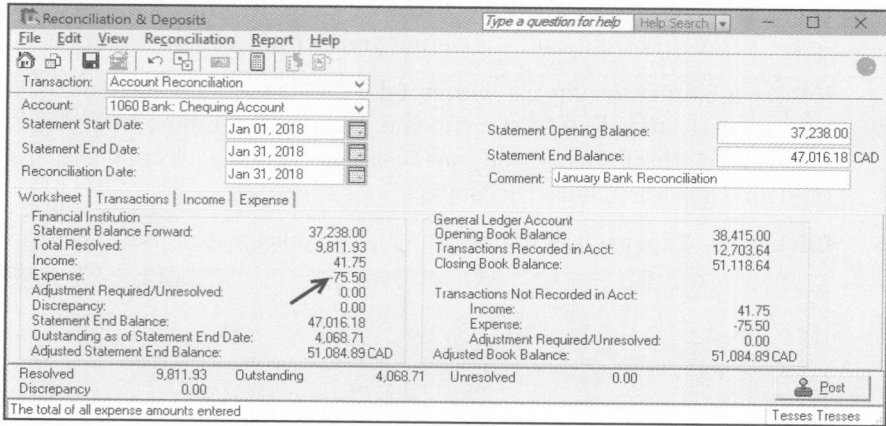

This summary provides the amounts for the bank statement and Sage 50 records that have been entered to reconcile the differences. Both lists have the opening and closing balances and net total transaction amounts. The Account Reconciliation Journal transactions for income and expenses that were not recorded elsewhere are added to the General Ledger balance (Transactions Not Recorded In Acct). Outstanding amounts that were in the General Ledger but not on the bank statement (Outstanding As Of Statement End Date) are added to the Bank Statement balance. The result is a match between the two adjusted balance amounts.

You should also review the Reconciliation Journal Entry before proceeding.

Press ctrl + **J**:

			Debits	Credits
01/31/2018	Bk-Stmt, Interest Income			
	1060	Bank: Chequing Account	41.75	-
	4220	Interest Revenue	-	41.75
01/31/2018	Bk-Stmt, Bank Charges			
	1060	Bank: Chequing Account	-	35.50
	5040	Bank Charges	35.50	-
01/15/2018	DM-61899, NSF fee			
	1060	Bank: Chequing Account	-	40.00
	5040	Bank Charges	40.00	-
Additional Date:	Additional Field:		117.25	117.25

The income and expense journal entries are listed. In addition, an adjustment entry will be displayed if there is any unresolved amount.

Close the **Report window** when you have finished.

If the unreconciled amount is not zero, you should check your journal entries to find whether you have made an error. Click each option and tab in the journal to review your work for the corresponding part of the reconciliation procedure. Make corrections if necessary. If you still have an unresolved amount, you can save the entry without posting and return later to try to determine whether you made a mistake or whether there was an error on the bank statement.

Any discrepancy or unresolved amount will be posted as an adjustment to the *Reconciliation Adjustments* expense account created earlier. This account should be used only for small amounts not significant enough to warrant a separate journal entry, such as differences from payroll tax rates in this text.

Click the **Save button** 🖫. **Click** ✕ to close the journal without posting.

Back up the **data file**. **Open** the **Account Reconciliation Journal**, **select 1060 Bank: Chequing Account** and resume your work.

Click 🖳 Post. You are ready to reconcile the next account.

Memo #10   **Dated Jan. 31/18**

Use the following bank statement to reconcile Bank: Credit Cards.
There is one outstanding item from the previous month:
Sale #457 for $230 to Cash Sales was deposited on Dec. 31, 2017.

SAVERS TRUST

321 Queen St., Charlottetown, PE C1A 6D3   saverstrust.com

Tesses Tresses
55 Salon Road
Charlottetown, PE C1A 6D3

ACCOUNT STATEMENT
CREDIT CARD

Transit / Account No
02900   004 123 22-8

Statement period
Jan 1, 2018 to Jan 31, 2018

Date	Description	Deposits	Withdrawals	Balance
	Balance Fwd			1,970.00
2 Jan	Deposit	230.00		2,200.00
2 Jan	Deposit	2,658.80		4,858.80
9 Jan	Deposit	2,935.00		7,793.80
14 Jan	Transfer to 0290 003 433 38-2		6,000.00	1,793.80
16 Jan	Deposit	2,740.88		4,534.68
23 Jan	Deposit	2,718.70		7,253.38
30 Jan	Deposit	2,290.54		9,543.92
31 Jan	Service Charges		22.50	9,521.42
31 Jan	Interest	6.50		9,527.92
31 Jan	Closing balance			9,527.92

Total Deposits   #   7 $13,580.42
Total Withdrawals #   2 $6,022.50

Choose account 1080.

Enter a **comment** and the **opening** and **closing bank statement balances**.

Enter the **prior outstanding transaction**.

Clear **transactions** to process the statement items.

Add **journal entries** for **service charges** and **interest**. **Review** your **work**, **make corrections** if necessary and then **post** the **transaction**.

Add **Shortcuts** for transactions in other modules, or change modules as needed.

Change the **session date** to **February 7** and then **enter** the **transactions for February** until the NSF cheque on Feb. 25.

Payment Cheque #417   **Dated Feb. 2/18**

To Sharp Scissors, $912.00 in payment of account. Reference invoice #SS-432.

Sales Invoice #482   **Dated Feb. 2/18**

To Irma Vannitee:

1	BRS1	Hair Brush: natural bristle	$32
1	CN2	Pro-Line Hot Oil Treatment 75 ml	35
1	SRV3	Cut and Style	48
1	SRV5	Perm	88
	HST		14%

Terms: 2/5, n/15.

NOTES

All these inventory items are purchased in units of dozens. Purchase orders were entered in January.

11

Purchase Invoice #PL-1988   **Dated Feb. 4/18**

From Pro-Line Inc., to fill purchase order #52:

2	CN1	Pro-Line Conditioner: 150 ml	$ 432.00
2	CN2	Pro-Line Hot Oil Treatment 75 ml	456.00
2	FRZ1	Pro-Line Defrizzer: cream 100 ml	408.00
2	GEL1	Pro-Line Spray Gel: shaper 150 ml	384.00
2	SHM1	Pro-Line Shampoo: 225 ml	408.00
2	SPR1	Pro-Line Hair Spray: gentle 150 ml	360.00
	HST	14%	342.72
	Invoice total		$2 790.72

Terms: 2/10, n/30.

12

Cash Purchase Invoice #CCT-18-2   **Dated Feb. 4/18**

From Charlottetown City Treasurer, $220 plus $30.80 HST for water and sewage treatment for three months. Purchase invoice total $250.80 paid by cheque #418 (Utilities account).

13

Sales Invoice #483   **Dated Feb. 4/18**

To Conn Seted:

1	FRZ1	Pro-Line Defrizzer: cream 100 ml	$28
1	GEL1	Pro-Line Spray Gel: shaper 150 ml	27
1	SRV1	Colour	55
1	SRV3	Cut and Style	48
	HST		14%

Terms: net 15.

NOTES

Sales Invoice #484 provides services for four theatre performances for six cast members. Do not fill the order. Enter the numbers in the Quantity field. The remainder of the order will be filled later.

14

Sales Invoice #484   **Dated Feb. 5/18**

To Twilight Theatre to partially fill sales order #102:

6	SRV3	Cut and Style	$42 each
18	SRV6	Wash and Style	21 each
	HST		14%

Terms: 2/5, n/15.

15

Cash Purchase Invoice #CCT-299392   **Dated Feb. 6/18**

From Charlottetown City Treasurer, $4 800 for annual property tax assessment, payable in three equal instalments of $1 600. First instalment is due on receipt of invoice. Remaining two instalments are due May 6 and August 6. Issue cheques #419, 420 and 421 dated February 6, May 6 and August 6 in payment of account. Create new Group account 5380 Property Taxes. Store as a quarterly recurring entry and recall the entry for the two postdated payments.

16

Credit Card Sales Invoice #485   **Dated Feb. 6/18**

Sales Summary for credit card sales (to Cash Customers):

4	BRS1	Hair Brush: natural bristle	$ 32 each	$ 128.00
4	CN1	Pro-Line Conditioner: 150 ml	34 /bottle	136.00
3	FRZ1	Pro-Line Defrizzer: cream 100 ml	28 /jar	84.00
3	GEL1	Pro-Line Spray Gel: shaper 150 ml	27 /can	81.00
8	SHM1	Pro-Line Shampoo: 225 ml	26 /bottle	208.00
26	SRV3	Cut and Style	48 each	1 248.00
5	SRV4	Highlights	110 each	550.00
6	SRV6	Wash and Style	26 each	156.00
	HST		14%	362.74
	Invoice total paid by credit cards			$2 953.74

Deposited to credit card bank account.

17 | **Credit Card Purchase Invoice #AUN-344**   **Dated Feb. 7/18**

From All U Need department store, $300 plus $42 HST for 100 white hand towels for use in the salon. Purchase invoice total $342 paid in full by credit card. Change the default account.

18 | **Cash Sales Invoice #486**   **Dated Feb. 7/18**

Sales Summary for cash sales (to Cash Customers):

6	BRS2	Hair Brush: styling	$24 each	$ 144.00
4	CN2	Pro-Line Hot Oil Treatment 75 ml	35 /tube	140.00
5	GEL1	Pro-Line Spray Gel: shaper 150 ml	27 /can	135.00
5	SPR1	Pro-Line Hair Spray: gentle 150 ml	26 /can	130.00
4	SRV1	Colour	55 each	220.00
24	SRV3	Cut and Style	48 each	1 152.00
	HST		14%	268.94

Invoice total paid by cash $2 189.94

Deposited to Undeposited Cash and Cheques.

19 |

DEPOSIT SLIP # 6			FEBRUARY 7, 2018	
Date	Cheque #	Client		Amount
Feb 1	416	Atta Schule		$ 420.00
Feb 1	162	Stu Dents		585.00
		Total Cheques		$1 005.00
		Cash		$2 189.94
		(Consisting of 17 × $5; 14 × $10; 18 × $20; 14 × $50; 9 × $100; Coin $4.94)		
		Total Deposit		$3 194.94

SESSION DATE – FEBRUARY 14, 2018

20 | **Cash Purchase Invoice #AP-63322**   **Dated Feb. 8/18**

From Atlantic Power Corp., $260 plus $36.40 HST for hydro services for one month. Purchase invoice total $296.40 paid by cheque #422.

21 | **Sales Invoice #487**   **Dated Feb. 9/18**

To Brioche Bridal Party to partially fill sales order #101:

3	SRV3	Cut and Style	$48 each
	HST		14%

Terms: 2/5, n/15.

22 | **Sales Invoice #488**   **Dated Feb. 9/18**

To Irma Vannitee:

1	SRV6	Wash and Style	$26
	HST		14%

Terms: 2/5, n/15. Store as a weekly recurring entry.

23 | **Purchase Invoice #Z-6775**   **Dated Feb. 10/18**

From Zines Inc., $130 plus $18.20 HST to renew subscriptions for one year to hair and fashion magazines (Prepaid Subscriptions account). Purchase invoice total $148.20. Terms: net 10.

24 | **Receipt #144**   **Dated Feb. 10/18**

From Irma Vannitee, cheque #93 for $261.06 in payment of account. Reference sales invoices #478 and 482.

NOTES

Ignore the message about late payments for Vannitee because her cheque is on hand.

25

Purchase Order #55   **Dated Feb. 10/18**

Delivery date Feb. 22/18
From Air Pro, $300 for two bonnet-style hair dryers and $50 for two handheld hair dryers plus $49 HST. Purchase order total $399. Terms: net 15.

26

Purchase Invoice #FB-27731   **Dated Feb. 10/18**

From Fine Brushes, to fill purchase order #53 (to stock up for anticipated Valentine's purchases):

30	BRS1	Hair Brush: natural bristle	$570.00
20	BRS2	Hair Brush: styling	300.00
	HST	14%	121.80
	Invoice total		$991.80

Terms: net 20.

27

Payment Cheque #423   **Dated Feb. 10/18**

To Pro-Line Inc., $2 734.91 in full payment of account including $55.81 discount for early payment. Reference invoice #PL-1988.

28

Sales Invoice #489   **Dated Feb. 11/18**

To Proud Family:

2	BRS1	Hair Brush: natural bristle	$ 32 each
2	BRS2	Hair Brush: styling	24 each
2	SHM1	Pro-Line Shampoo: 225 ml	26 each
4	SRV3	Cut and Style	48 each
1	SRV4	Highlights	110
1	SRV5	Perm	88
	HST		14%

Terms: net 15.

29

Credit Card Sales Invoice #490   **Dated Feb. 13/18**

Sales Summary for credit card sales (to Cash Customers):

8	BRS1	Hair Brush: natural bristle	$ 32 each	$ 256.00
6	BRS2	Hair Brush: styling	24 each	144.00
5	CN1	Pro-Line Conditioner: 150 ml	34 /bottle	170.00
8	SHM1	Pro-Line Shampoo: 225 ml	26 /bottle	208.00
30	SRV3	Cut and Style	48 each	1 440.00
7	SRV4	Highlights	110 each	770.00
3	SRV5	Perm	88 each	264.00
4	SRV6	Wash and Style	26 each	104.00
	HST		14%	469.84
	Invoice total paid by credit cards			$3 825.84

Deposited to credit card bank account.

30

Cash Sales Invoice #491   **Dated Feb. 14/18**

Sales Summary for cash sales (to Cash Customers):

6	BRS2	Hair Brush: styling	$ 24 each	$ 144.00
3	FRZ1	Pro-Line Defrizzer: cream 100 ml	28 /jar	84.00
8	GEL1	Pro-Line Spray Gel: shaper 150 ml	27 /can	216.00
7	SPR1	Pro-Line Hair Spray: gentle 150 ml	26 /can	182.00
6	SRV1	Colour	55 each	330.00
24	SRV3	Cut and Style	48 each	1 152.00
2	SRV4	Highlights	110 each	220.00
	HST		14%	325.92
	Invoice total paid by cash			$2 653.92

Deposited to Undeposited Cash and Cheques.

31 **Purchase Invoice #SS-555**   **Dated Feb. 14/18**

From Sharp Scissors, to fill purchase order #54, $600 plus $84 HST for professional high-grade stainless steel stylist scissors. Purchase invoice total $684. Terms: net 10.

32 **DEPOSIT SLIP # 7**   **FEBRUARY 14, 2018**

Date	Cheque #	Client	Amount
Feb 10	93	Irma Vannitee	$261.06
		Total Cheques	$261.06
		Cash	$2 653.92

(Consisting of 22 × $5; 25 × $10; 27 × $20; 17 × $50; 9 × $100; Coin $3.92)

Total Deposit $2 914.98

33 **Memo #11**   **Dated Feb. 14/18**

From Owners: Transfer $12 000 from credit card account to chequing account.

SESSION DATE – FEBRUARY 21, 2018

34 **Sales Invoice #492**   **Dated Feb. 16/18**

To Irma Vannitee:
    1   SRV6   Wash and Style $26
        HST   14%
Terms: 2/5, n/15. Recall stored transaction.

35 **Memo #12**   **Dated Feb. 17/18**

From Owners: Pay HST owing to the Receiver General for the period ending January 31, 2018. Issue cheque #424 in payment.

36 **Cash Purchase Invoice #ET-4588**   **Dated Feb. 17/18**

From Eastern Tel, $130 plus $18.20 HST for telephone service. Purchase invoice total $148.20 paid in full by cheque #425.

37 **Sales Quote #103**   **Dated Feb. 19/18**

First performance date Mar. 1/18
To On Stage Theatre Company (for 12 theatre performances for three cast members) at preferred customer prices:
    3   SRV3   Cut and Style $42 each
    36 SRV6   Wash and Style   21 each
    9   SRV7   Wig Wash, Set and Style   26 each
        HST   14%
Terms: 2/5, n/15.

38 **Receipt #145**   **Dated Feb. 19/18**

From Conn Seted, cheque #269 for $180.12 in payment of account. Reference invoice #483.

39 **Receipt #146**   **Dated Feb. 19/18**

From Twilight Theatre, cheque #5635 for $718.20 in payment of account. Reference invoice #484.

40 **Credit Card Purchase Invoice #SP-399**   **Dated Feb. 20/18**

From Seaside Papers, $200 plus $28 HST for office supplies for salon. Purchase invoice total $228 paid in full by credit card.

NOTES
You can use the Tax Report for HST for January to obtain the HST amounts for the remittance, or you can refer to the General Ledger Report for the two HST accounts.

41

Receipt #147   **Dated Feb. 20/18**

From Brioche Bridal Party, cheque #986 for $164.16 in payment of account.
Reference invoice #487.

42

Credit Card Sales Invoice #493   **Dated Feb. 20/18**

Sales Summary for credit card sales (to Cash Customers):

3	BRS1	Hair Brush: natural bristle	$32 each	$	96.00
2	CN2	Pro-Line Hot Oil Treatment 75 ml	35 /tube		70.00
2	FRZ1	Pro-Line Defrizzer: cream 100 ml	28 /jar		56.00
7	SPR1	Pro-Line Hair Spray: gentle 150 ml	26 /can		182.00
6	SRV1	Colour	55 each		330.00
26	SRV3	Cut and Style	48 each		1 248.00
	HST		14%		277.48
	Invoice total paid by credit cards				$2 259.48

Deposited to credit card bank account.

43

Cash Sales Invoice #494   **Dated Feb. 21/18**

Sales Summary for cash sales (to Cash Customers):

5	BRS2	Hair Brush: styling	$24 each	$	120.00
8	CN1	Pro-Line Conditioner: 150 ml	34 /bottle		272.00
6	GEL1	Pro-Line Spray Gel: shaper 150 ml	27 /can		162.00
4	SHM1	Pro-Line Shampoo: 225 ml	26 /bottle		104.00
3	SRV1	Colour	55 each		165.00
21	SRV3	Cut and Style	48 each		1 008.00
10	SRV6	Wash and Style	26 each		260.00
	HST		14%		292.74
	Invoice total paid by cash				$2 383.74

Deposited to Undeposited Cash and Cheques.

44

DEPOSIT SLIP #8   Date: Feb 21, 2018
Tesses Tresses
55 Salon Rd.
Charlottetown PE C1A 6D3

Account No: 02900 3433382

Cheques   Amount

269	Conn Seted	180.12	18	× 5	90	00	
5635	Twilight Theatre	718.20	31	× 10	310	00	
986	Brioche Bridal Party	164.16	34	× 20	680	00	
			14	× 50	700	00	
			6	× 100	600	00	
				coin	3	74	
			Total cash		2383	74	
			Total cheque		1062	48	
			Subtotal		3446	22	
			Cash received				
			Net Deposit		3446	22	

Signature *Tess Dubois*

02/21/18   PW

	Credit Card Purchase Invoice #AUN-478	**Dated Feb. 21/18**
45		

From All U Need department store, $90 plus $12.60 HST for cleaning supplies. Purchase invoice total $102.60 paid in full by credit card.

	Purchase Order #56	**Dated Feb. 21/18**
46		

Shipping date Mar. 3/18
From Lookin' Good, $400 plus $56 HST for 25 polyester and nylon water-resistant monogrammed capes for salon client use. Unit price is $16. Purchase invoice total $456. Terms: net 10.

	Payment Cheque #426	**Dated Feb. 21/18**
47		

To Sharp Scissors, $684 in payment of account. Reference invoice #SS-555.

SESSION DATE – FEBRUARY 28, 2018

	Purchase Invoice #AP-7111	**Dated Feb. 23/18**
48		

From Air Pro, to fill purchase order #55, $350 plus $49 HST for two bonnet-style hair dryers and two handheld hair dryers. Purchase invoice total $399. Terms: net 15.

	Sales Invoice #495	**Dated Feb. 23/18**
49		

To Irma Vannitee:

1	SRV6	Wash and Style	$26
	HST		14%

Terms: 2/5, n/15. Recall stored transaction.

	Sales Invoice #496	**Dated Feb. 23/18**
50		

To Brioche Bridal Party to fill remainder of sales order #101:

5	SRV6	Wash and Style	$26 each
	HST		14%

Terms: 2/5, n/15.

	Credit Card Bill Payment #2-18	**Dated Feb. 24/18**
51		

From credit card company, $421.80 for purchases made before Feb. 11 and $24 annual card fee. Total payment due to avoid interest penalty $445.80. Issued cheque #427 for $445.80 in full payment.

NOTES
You will be warned about using the next cheque number for the credit card payment.

Reversing NSF Cheques on Deposit Slips

In previous chapters, we reversed NSF cheques with the Reverse Receipt shortcut tool in the Adjusting receipt window of the Receipts Journal. In these cases, *Bank: Chequing Account* was the linked principal bank account for the Receivables module, so the cheque was recorded (deposited) directly to this account. The reversing procedure would select this same account. For Tesses Tresses, *Undeposited Cash and Cheques* is the principal linked bank account for deposits. The NSF cheque, however, is withdrawn from *Bank: Chequing Account* — until we deposit the cheque in the bank its validity is unknown. For this situation, we need to enter a negative receipt for the paid invoice that credits *Bank: Chequing Account*. The following steps describe the procedure for reversing the cheque from Brioche Bridal Party.

	Bank Debit Memo #983321	**Dated Feb. 25/18**
✓ **52**		

From Savers Trust Co., cheque #986 from Brioche Bridal Party was returned because of insufficient funds. The cheque amount, $164.16, was withdrawn from the chequing account.

WARNING!
Do not reverse the receipt to record this NSF cheque.

Open the **Receipts Journal**.

Choose **Brioche Bridal Party** as the client.

Choose **1060 Bank: Chequing Account** from the drop-down list in the Deposit To field.

Click the **Cheque field** so we can enter the client cheque number.

Type NSF-986

Click the **Receipt No. field**. We will enter the bank debit number here.

Type DM-983321 **Enter February 25** as the date for the transaction.

Click the **Include Fully Paid Invoices/Deposits tool** 🖹 or **choose** the **Receipt menu** and **click Include Fully Paid Invoices/Deposits**.

The two paid invoices (#468 and #487) are added to the form with the unpaid invoice. Invoice #487 was paid with the NSF cheque, so we need to select it.

Click **487** in the Invoice Or Deposit column.

Press (tab) until the cursor is in the Amount Received column for the line. We need to enter the full amount of the cheque as a negative number.

Type -164.16 **Press** (tab) to enter the amount.

The discount for the unpaid invoice is now selected and we need to remove it.

Press (del) to complete the entry.

Review the **journal entry**.

Accounts Receivable has been debited to restore the amount owing, and *Bank: Chequing Account* is credited to reverse the previous deposit. Verify that the discount for the unpaid invoice is not included.

Close the **journal display** and then **post** the **receipt**.

Click the **Include Fully Paid Invoices/Deposits tool** 🖹.

Choose Brioche Bridal Party again.

The invoice amount owing has been fully restored. When the payment is received, you will enter it in the usual way.

Close the **Receipts Journal** and **continue** with the **remaining transactions**.

Memo #13 **Dated Feb. 25/18**

53 Prepare sales invoice #497 for $30 to charge Brioche Bridal Party for the NSF fee. Credit Other Revenue. Terms: net 15. (Do not charge tax or allow discount.)

Receipt #148 **Dated Feb. 27/18**

54 From Brioche Bridal Party, certified cheque #RBC7333 for $194.16 in payment of account. Reference invoices #487 and #497 and bank debit memo #983321.

Sales Invoice #498 **Dated Feb. 27/18**

55 To Twilight Theatre to fill the remainder of sales order #102 (for four nights of theatre performances for four cast members) at preferred customer prices.

4	SRV3	Cut and Style	$42 each
16	SRV6	Wash and Style	21 each
4	SRV7	Wig Wash, Set and Style	26 each
	HST		14%

Terms: 2/5, n/15.

⚠ WARNING!
Remember to delete the selected discounts and amounts for any other invoices.

NOTES
If a discount has been included with the payment, you will need to reverse it as well. Enter the amount of the discount as a negative amount in the Discount Taken field and press (tab). The cheque amount may be automatically entered as the Amount Received, with the minus sign added. If it is not, enter it as a negative amount.
You should review the entry carefully before posting and then check the Receipts Journal again for the customer to ensure that the invoice has been fully restored.

NOTES
For Brioche, you may get an advisory message about the client often paying late.

56

Credit Card Sales Invoice #499   **Dated Feb. 27/18**

Sales Summary for credit card sales (to Cash Customers):

6	BRS2	Hair Brush: styling	$24 each	$ 144.00
4	CN1	Pro-Line Conditioner: 150 ml	34 /bottle	136.00
6	FRZ1	Pro-Line Defrizzer: cream 100 ml	28 /jar	168.00
8	SPR1	Pro-Line Hair Spray: gentle 150 ml	26 /can	208.00
3	SRV1	Colour	55 each	165.00
26	SRV3	Cut and Style	48 each	1 248.00
2	SRV5	Perm	88 each	176.00
2	SRV6	Wash and Style	26 each	52.00
	HST		14%	321.58
	Invoice total paid by credit cards			$2 618.58

Deposited to credit card bank account.

57

Cash Sales Invoice #500   **Dated Feb. 28/18**

Valentine's Day sales did not meet expectations, so all hair brushes were sold at discounted prices. Edit the selling price for BRS1 and BRS2.

Sales Summary for cash sales (to Cash Customers):

20	BRS1	Hair Brush: natural bristle	$22 each	$ 440.00
10	BRS2	Hair Brush: styling	16 each	160.00
28	SRV3	Cut and Style	48 each	1 344.00
4	SRV6	Wash and Style	26 each	104.00
	HST		14%	286.72
	Invoice total paid by cash			$2 334.72

Deposited to Undeposited Cash and Cheques.

58

DEPOSIT SLIP #9	Date: Feb 28, 2018
Tesses Tresses	
55 Salon Rd.	
Charlottetown PE C1A 6D3	

Account No: 02900 3433382

Cheques				Amount	
RBC7333 Brioche Bridal Party 194.16	12	× 5	60	00
	19	× 10	190	00
	14	× 20	280	00
	18	× 50	900	00
	9	× 100	900	00
		coin	4	72
	Total cash		2334	72
	Total cheque		194	16
	Subtotal		2528	88
	Cash received			
	Net Deposit		2528	88

Signature *Tess Dubois*

02/28/18   PW

59

Bank Debit Memo #100121   **Dated Feb. 28/18**

From Savers Trust Co. pre-authorized withdrawals for Mortgage: $1 500 ($1 140 interest & $360 principal) and for Loan: $600 ($105 interest & $495 principal).

60	

Memo #14   **Dated Feb. 28/18**

Convert sales quote #103 for On Stage Theatre Company to a sales order. All amounts, the service (shipping) date and the terms are unchanged.

61	

Memo #15   **Dated Feb. 28/18**

Enter the adjustments for expired prepaid expenses and supplies used:
Prepaid Insurance expired: $150
Prepaid Subscriptions expired: $40
Office Supplies used: $60
Salon Supplies used: $585
Washroom & Cleaning Supplies used: $75

62	

Memo #16   **Dated Feb. 28/18**

The following items were transferred from inventory at cost for salon use:
    8 CN1   Pro-Line Conditioner: 150 ml
    6 CN2   Pro-Line Hot Oil Treatment 75 ml
    8 GEL1 Pro-Line Spray Gel: shaper 150 ml
  11 SHM1 Pro-Line Shampoo: 225 ml
    9 SPR1 Pro-Line Hair Spray: gentle 150 ml

63	

Memo #17   **Dated Feb. 28/18**

Use the following statement to reconcile the Bank: Chequing Account for February.

> **NOTES**
> Use the Inventory Adjustments Journal to transfer the inventory to the supplies account. Enter **negative** quantities and change the default Inventory Losses account to Salon Supplies for all items. Refer to Accounting Procedures, page 576.

> **NOTES**
> Enter Feb. 28 as the Statement and Reconciliation dates to replace March 2 (31 days after the previous reconciliation).

> **NOTES**
> You do not need to add linked accounts or prior transactions. Enter the statement ending balance and then mark journal entries as cleared (keystrokes on page 592) to complete the reconciliation.
> There are four deposit slips for group deposits.
> The loan and mortgage payments were entered together: $1 500 + $600 = $2 100.
> Remember to change the status of the NSF cheque from Brioche Bridal Party for $164.16 (in deposit slip #8) to NSF and the status of its reversing entry to Adjustment.
> At the end of February, a cheque for $445.80 and one deposit for $2 528.88 are outstanding.

SAVERS TRUST					
321 Queen St., Charlottetown, PE C1A 6D3					saverstrust.com

Tesses Tresses
55 Salon Road
Charlottetown, PE C1A 6D3

ACCOUNT STATEMENT
CHEQUING

Transit / Account No
02900   003 433 38-2

Statement period
Feb 1, 2018 to Feb 28, 2018

Date	Deposit #	Description	Deposits	Withdrawals	Balance
		Balance Fwd			47,016.18
1 Feb	5	Deposit	4,068.71		51,084.89
5 Feb		Cheque #417		912.00	50,172.89
5 Feb		Cheque #418		250.80	49,922.09
7 Feb	6	Deposit	3,194.94		53,117.03
8 Feb		Cheque #419		1,600.00	51,517.03
10 Feb		Cheque #422		296.40	51,220.63
14 Feb	7	Deposit	2,914.98		54,135.61
16 Feb		Cheque #423		2,734.91	51,400.70
18 Feb		Transfer funds from 004 123 22-8	12,000.00		63,400.70
19 Feb		Cheque #425		148.20	63,252.50
21 Feb	8	Deposit	3,446.22		66,698.72
21 Feb		Cheque #424		2,766.12	63,932.60
25 Feb		NSF Cheque #986		164.16	63,768.44
25 Feb		Service Charge - NSF cheque		40.00	63,728.44
26 Feb		Cheque #426		684.00	63,044.44
28 Feb		Scheduled loan payment		600.00	62,444.44
28 Feb		Scheduled mortgage payment		1,500.00	60,944.44
28 Feb		Service Charges - chequing acct		35.50	60,908.94
28 Feb		Interest	44.25		60,953.19
28 Feb		Closing balance			60,953.19

Total Deposits	# 6	$25,669.10
Total Withdrawals	# 13	$11,732.09

<table>
<tr><td>64</td><td>**Memo #18**
Use the following statement to reconcile the Bank: Credit Cards Account.</td><td>**Dated Feb. 28/18**</td></tr>
</table>

SAVERS TRUST

321 Queen St., Charlottetown, PE C1A 6D3   saverstrust.com

Tesses Tresses
55 Salon Road
Charlottetown, PE C1A 6D3

ACCOUNT STATEMENT
CREDIT CARD

Transit / Account No
02900   004 123 22-8

Statement period
Feb 1, 2018 to Feb 28, 2018

Date	Deposit #	Description	Deposits	Withdrawals	Balance
		Balance Fwd			9,527.92
6 Feb		Deposit	2,873.99		12,401.91
13 Feb		Deposit	3,722.54		16,124.45
18 Feb		Transfer funds to 003 433 38-2		12,000.00	4,124.45
20 Feb		Deposit	2,198.47		6,322.92
28 Feb		Service charges		22.50	6,300.42
28 Feb		Interest	5.25		6,305.67
28 Feb		Closing balance			6,305.67

Total Deposits   #   4 $8,800.25
Total Withdrawals   #   2 $12,022.50

Displaying Banking Reports

Click   the **Report Centre icon** 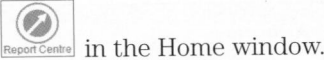 in the Home window.

Click   **Banking** to open the list of banking reports in the Report Centre:

Account Reconciliation Journal

Click   **Account Reconciliation Journal Entries**. **Click Modify This Report**:

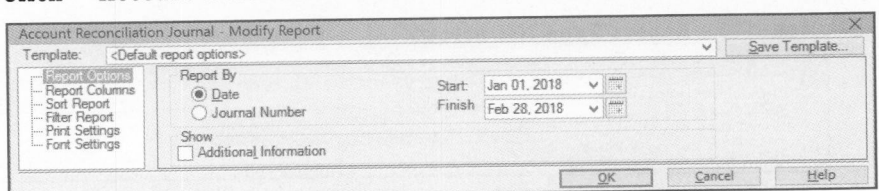

Or, choose the Reports menu, then choose Journal Entries and click Account Reconciliation to open the report options screen.

The journal can be prepared by selecting journal entry numbers or dates. By default, the report uses posting dates. The usual journal report customizing, sorting and filtering options are available. There is no option to show corrections.

NOTES
Enter Feb. 28 as the Statement and Reconciliation dates. There is one outstanding deposit at the end of February.

NOTES
The Reports pane list in the Banking module window has Account and Banking reports.

PRO VERSION
The Pro version does not have the Bank Account Transactions Report.

NOTES
The Cheque Log Report was covered in Chapter 5. Refer to page 149.
For the Bank Account Transactions Report, refer to pages 588–589.
The Direct Deposit Log is similar to the Cheque Log, but it reports on payroll direct deposits.

CLASSIC VIEW
Right-click the Reconciliation & Deposits icon to select the journal. Click the Select A Report tool to open the report options.

Enter   the **Start** and **Finish** dates or journal numbers for the report.

Click   **OK**. **Close** the **display** when you have finished.

Deposit Slip Journal

Click   **Deposit Slip Journal Entries** and **click Modify This Report**:

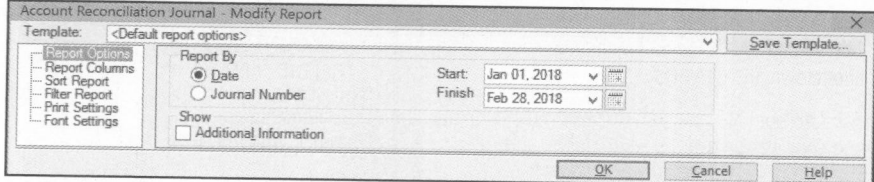

Or, from the Home window, choose the Reports menu, then choose Journal Entries and click Deposit Slip to open the report options screen.

The journal can be prepared by selecting journal entry numbers or dates. By default, the report uses posting dates. The usual journal report customizing, sorting and filtering options are available. There is no option to show corrections.

Enter   the **Start** and **Finish** dates or journal numbers for the report.

Click   **OK**. **Close** the **display** when you have finished.

Account Reconciliation Report

Click   **Account Reconciliation Summary** to display the report sample and **click Modify This Report** for the report options:

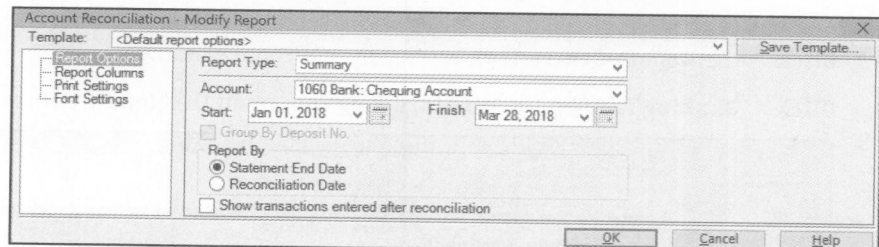

Or, from the Home window, choose the Reports menu, then choose Banking and click Account Reconciliation Report to display the options.

Accept   **1060** as the bank account or choose another account from the drop-down list for the Account field.

Enter   the **Start** and **Finish** dates. The default Finish date is one month past the latest reconciliation or bank statement date.

Click   the **Report Type list arrow**:

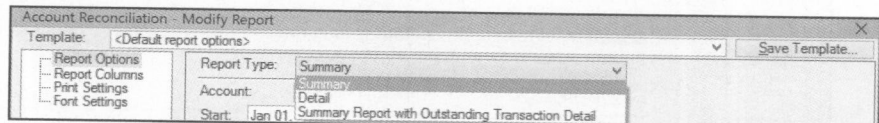

The Report Type drop-down list has three options. The **Summary** Report provides totals for deposits, withdrawals, income and expense categories for the bank statements and the General Ledger account, and outstanding amounts that will reconcile the two balances. Unresolved amounts and discrepancies are also reported, if there are any. The **Detail** Report lists all journal entries with their status, such as Cleared, NSF and so on. You can group the Detail Report by Deposit Number. Choose **Summary Report With**

Outstanding Transaction Detail to include only the total outstanding amounts and the adjusted bank and General Ledger balances. You can **report by** either the bank **Statement End Date** or the **Reconciliation Date** recorded in the journal for the report.

> **Choose** the **report type** and **date (Report By) options**.

> **Click**   OK. **Close** the **displayed report** when you have finished.

Reconciliation Transaction Report

> **Click**   **Reconciliation Transactions Detail** and **click Modify This Report** to open the report options window:

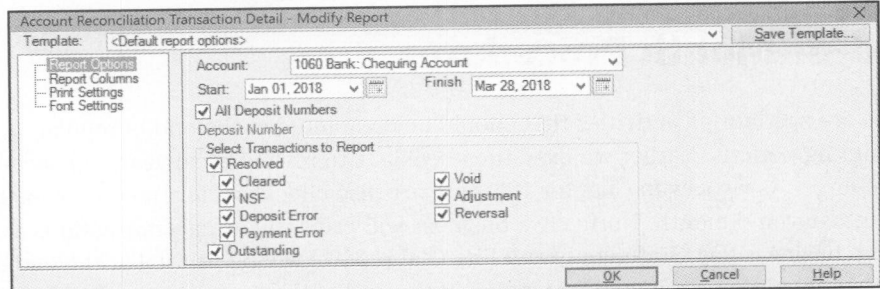

NOTES
You can drill down to Supplier or Client Aged or Employee reports (if applicable) and look up invoices from the Reconciliation Transaction Detail Report.

Or, from the Home window, choose the Reports menu, then choose Banking and click Account Reconciliation Transaction Report.

This detail report will list all the transactions with their reconciliation status for the selected bank account for all the status types you chose.

> **Choose** the **account** for the report from the drop-down list.

> **Enter**   **Start** and **Finish** dates for the report.

> **Choose** the **Status categories** to include in your reports. By default, all are included, so clicking a category will remove the ✓ from the check box and omit this category from your report.

> **Click**   OK. **Close** the **displayed report** when you have finished.

Deposit Slip Report

> **Click**   **Deposit Slip Summary** and **click Modify This Report**.

NOTES
You can customize the Reconciliation Transaction and Deposit Slip reports by selecting the columns to include, but you cannot sort or filter the reports.
You cannot drill down to other reports from the Deposit Slip Report.

Or, from the Home window, choose the Reports menu, then choose Banking and click Deposit Slip Report to display the options.

The Deposit Slip **Summary** Report has the total amounts for cash and cheques on each deposit slip, while the **Detail** Report lists all cheque, bill and coin amounts separately for each deposit.

> **Choose** the **account** for the report from the drop-down list.

You can display the report for a range of dates or deposit slip numbers.

Choose the **Summary** option to provide a list of totals for cash and cheques for each deposit slip. Choose **Detail** to include the individual items on each deposit slip and totals.

> **Enter** **Start** and **Finish** dates for the report.
>
> **Click** OK. **Close** the **displayed report** and the **Report Centre** when finished.

Printing Banking Reports

> **Display** the **report** you want to print. **Click** or **choose** the **File menu** and **click Print** to print the report. **Close** the **Report window** when finished.

End-of-Month Procedures

There are accounting activities that should be completed at the end of regular accounting periods. Earlier we used the checklists to review fiscal year-end accounting procedures. As we saw in Chapter 12, there are also checklists for the end of each business day and month. Normally a business will print all journal transactions at the end of each business day. Statements and financial reports will be printed at the end of each month, and all reports should be printed at the end of the fiscal period. T4s should be printed at the end of the calendar year.

Periodically, a business will clear old information from its accounting files. In the manual system, it might store the details in archives or with a secured offsite backup storage provider to keep the current files manageable. Computerized systems should be similarly maintained by making backups of the data files and then clearing information that is not required. These periodic procedures include clearing data and reports for prior periods, removing paid invoices from client and supplier records and removing suppliers and clients who no longer do business with the company. Checklists in Sage 50 can assist with these routine procedures.

> ✓ **Memo #19**   **Dated Feb. 28/18**
> 65   Back up the data files. Clear journal entries and paid transactions that are no longer needed using January 31 as the date for clearing. Do not clear data for February.

> **Choose** the **Business Assistant menu** in the Home window and **click Checklists**. Several lists are available (refer to page 488).
>
> **Click** **Month-End Procedures** to select it and then **click Modify**:

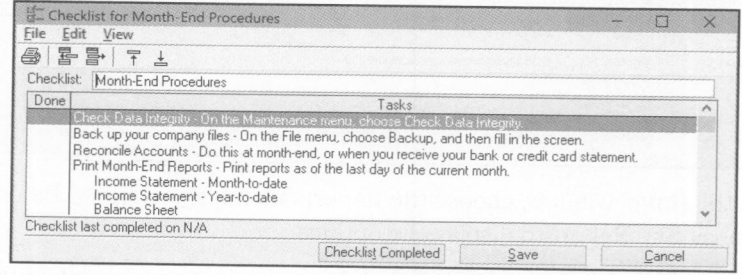

You will open the list of routines that should be completed at the end of a month.

Read the task list. You have already completed some tasks on this list.

> **Click** the **Done column** beside the two tasks that are completed — **Back Up** and **Reconcile Accounts**. We will complete the remaining tasks before marking them.

Click the **Home window** if part of it is visible or point to the Sage 50 button on the task bar and click the Home window pop-up.

Choose the **Maintenance menu** and **click Check Data Integrity**.

If you do not get the message "Data OK," make a note of any data inconsistencies and return to your most recent backup copy of the file.

Click **OK** to close the Integrity Summary window.

Click the **Done column** beside **Check Data Integrity**.

Click **Save** to return to the main checklists window. A ✓ appears in the Task In Progress column beside Month-End Procedures.

Click **Close** to leave the Checklist window and return to the Home window.

Clearing Paid Supplier and Client Transactions

Choose the **Maintenance menu**, then **choose Clear Data** and **Clear Paid Transactions** and **click Clear Paid Supplier Transactions** to open the list of suppliers:

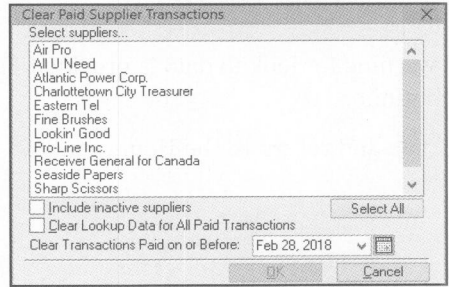

You can clear invoices for one or more suppliers at the same time. Unpaid invoices are always retained.

Enter **Jan 31** as the latest date for which you want to remove invoices.

Click **Select All**. (To select individual suppliers, **press** ⌃ctrl and **click** their names.) We also have stored lookup details that we no longer need.

Click **Clear Lookup Data For All Paid Transactions**.

Click **OK**. Sage 50 warns about the consequences of removing these details:

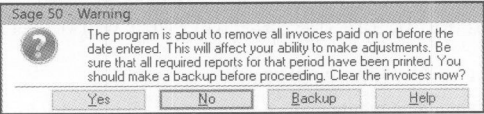

If you have selected correctly and are ready to proceed,

Click **Yes**. When you choose to clear lookup data another warning opens:

Click **Yes** if you are certain that you should continue.

You can clear client transactions in the same way.

Choose the **Maintenance menu**, then **choose Clear Data** and **Clear Paid Transactions** and **click Clear Paid Client Transactions**.

The list of clients and clearing options opens:

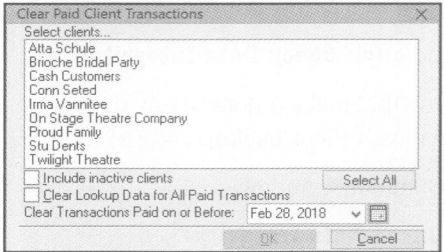

Enter   **Jan 31** as the last date for which you want to remove invoices.

Clearing client invoices is similar to clearing supplier invoices.

We will keep all transactions for February. We can clear the invoices and lookup data for Cash Customers and Atta Schule because these are not needed. You can clear paid invoices for all clients by clicking Select All.

Click   **Atta Schule**. **Press** ⌐ctrl⌐ and **click Cash Customers**.

Click   **Clear Lookup Data For All Paid Transactions**. **Click OK**.

The next warning is the same as the one we saw for removing supplier invoices. If you are ready, you should proceed.

Click   **Yes**. Again, the additional warning for lookup data is provided. If you are certain that you want to continue,

Click   **Yes** to remove the lookup data and return to the Home window.

Clearing Tax Reports

You should clear tax reports after filing the tax returns for the period covered by the return so that the next report will include only the current reporting period.

Choose   the **Maintenance menu**, then **choose Clear Data** and **click Clear Tax Report** to display the options:

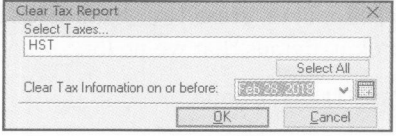

Select the tax or taxes for which you want to clear the reports or click Select All. Then enter the date. Entries on and before the date you enter will be removed.

Click   **OK**. Sage 50 provides the familiar warning:

We do not want to remove any tax data because we have not submitted the returns for February.

Click   **No** to cancel and return to the Home window.

Clearing Account Reconciliation Data

Choose   the **Maintenance menu**, then **choose Clear Data** and **Clear Account Rec.** and **click Clear Account Rec. Data** to display the options:

Select the account for which you want to remove the data. Then enter the date. Entries on and before the date you enter will be removed.

We do not want to remove the data at this time. If you choose to continue, Sage 50 will present the familiar warning before any information is removed.

Click   **Cancel** to return to the Home window.

Clearing Inventory Tracking Data

Choose   the **Maintenance menu**, then **choose Clear Data** and **click Clear Inventory Tracking Data** to display the clearing date dialogue box:

Enter   **Jan 31** as the date. Entries on and before January 31 will be removed.

Click   **OK**. Again, the warning is displayed before any data is removed.

If you are certain that you want to proceed,

Click   **Yes** to delete the requested information and return to the Home window.

Clearing Lookup Data

You can clear invoice lookup data for both purchase and sales invoices together in a single step or you can clear purchase and sales invoices in separate steps. You can also clear lookup data for remittances from this menu.

Choose   the **Maintenance menu**, then **choose Clear Data** and **Clear Invoice Lookup Data** and **click Clear Supplier Invoice & Client Invoice Lookup Data** to display the clearing options:

Enter   **Jan 31** as the date. Entries on and before January 31 will be removed.

Click   **OK**.

Once again, Sage 50 warns you before removing any data. If you are certain that you want to proceed,

Click   **Yes** to continue.

If you cleared the lookup data with the paid transactions, you will receive the message stating that there is no invoice data to clear. Click OK to continue.

The requested information is deleted and you will return to the Home window.

To clear only purchase invoice data, choose the Maintenance menu, Clear Data and Clear Invoice Lookup Data and click Clear Supplier Invoice Lookup Data. Choose suppliers for which you want to clear the invoices, enter the date and click OK to display the warning. Click Yes to continue with clearing the data.

NOTES
You can clear account reconciliation data for only one account at a time.

PRO VERSION
You will choose Clear Purchase Invoice Lookup Data to clear data for purchase invoices.
You will choose Clear Sales Invoice Lookup Data to clear data for sales invoices.

NOTES
If you choose to clear invoice lookup data for purchases or sales separately, you can choose to clear the data for one or more suppliers (or clients) or for all of them.

To remove only sales invoice data, choose the Maintenance menu, Clear Data and Clear Invoice Lookup Data and click Clear Client Invoice Lookup Data. Select clients for which you want to clear the invoices, enter the date and click OK. Click Yes to continue with clearing the data.

Clearing Deposit Slip Lookup Data

Choose the **Maintenance menu**, **Clear Data** and **Clear Lookup Data**. **Click Clear Lookup Data For Deposit Slips** to display the options:

Select the account for which you want to remove the data. Then enter the date. Entries on and before the date you enter will be removed.

We do not want to remove the data at this time. If you choose to continue, you will receive the familiar warning before any information is removed.

Click **Cancel** to return to the Home window.

Clearing Lookup Data for Other Payments

Lookup data for other payments are cleared separately from Purchases Journal invoices.

Choose the **Maintenance menu**, **Clear Data** and **Clear Lookup Data**. **Click Clear Lookup Data For Other Payments** to display the list of suppliers and the clearing options:

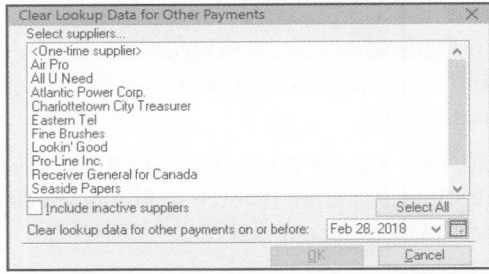

Enter **Jan 31** as the date for the data you want to remove.

Choose the **suppliers**. **Click Select All** to select all suppliers.

Click **OK**. Sage 50 will require confirmation before removing data. To proceed,

Click **Yes**.

The requested information is deleted, and you will return to the Home window.

From the Maintenance menu, Clear Data option, you can also clear lookup data for remittances, notes that you create in the Daily Business Manager, financial history and direct deposits. For each one, you can enter a date after which all data will be retained. You will be warned before any information is removed.

Automatically Clearing Data

You can also choose to clear data automatically when you start a new fiscal period.

Choose the **Maintenance menu**, then **choose Clear Data** and **click Automatically Clear Data** to view your options:

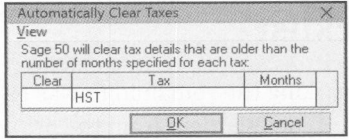

From this screen you can choose what data to clear and how many months of each type of data should be kept when the clearing occurs at the end of the fiscal period.

> **Click**   **Cancel** to return to the Home window.

Automatically Clearing Tax Data

Tax information can also be cleared automatically, but it has separate settings.

> **Choose** the **Maintenance menu**, then **choose Clear Data** and **click Automatically Clear Data**. **Click** the **Clear Taxes button**:

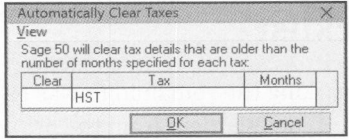

On this screen you can choose what taxes to clear. Data older than the number of months you enter will be removed when the clearing occurs at the end of the fiscal period.

> **Click**   the **Clear column** beside the tax to select it and then **enter** the number of **months**. The default is to keep the tax details for 12 months.

> **Click**   **Cancel** to return to the Automatically Clear Data screen and **click Cancel** again to return to the Home window.

Removing Supplier and Client Records

Sometimes you know that you will not be doing business with a client or supplier again. Removing their records reduces the length of the lists to scroll through for journal entries and saves on mailing costs. Suppliers are removed from the Suppliers window. Clients are removed from the Clients window. We will remove the client (tenant) Stu Dents because he will be moving out of his apartment after March, the date of his final cheque. First we must clear the paid transactions for this client.

> **Choose** the **Maintenance menu**, then **choose Clear Data** and **Clear Paid Transactions** and **click Clear Paid Client Transactions**.

> **Click**   **Stu Dents** on the client list. **Enter February 28, 2018** as the date. **Click OK**. When the warning is provided,

> **Click**   **Yes** to confirm. **Click Yes** to confirm removing lookup data if asked.

> **Click**   **Receivables** in the Modules pane list.

> **Click**   **Stu Dents** in the Home window Clients list to open the ledger record.

NOTES
Financial history can be stored for 100 years in the Premium version and 7 years in the Pro version.

PRO VERSION
pro The default entry for Clear Financial History Over is 6 Years.

NOTES
Refer to page 103 for the query about clearing old data. The periods you choose here will determine how much data will be cleared.

NOTES
When you click the Clear column for a tax, the default number of months, 12, is entered and you can change it.

NOTES
An alternative to removing records is to mark clients or suppliers as Inactive and not include them in reports. Inactive clients and suppliers are also not included in the drop-down lists in journals.
The record will be saved and you can restore it to active status at any time.

Click   the **Remove The Current Client tool** 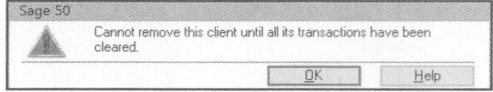 in the ledger window, or **choose** the **File menu** and **click Remove**. Sage 50 will block the action:

> Sage 50
> Cannot remove this client until all its transactions have been cleared.
>
> OK   Help

You can also choose Remove Client from the Clients icon shortcuts list in the Receivables window. The Search window opens with the Remove Client option selected. Click Stu Dents in the Search window to select the client and click OK.

We selected a client for whom all invoices have not been cleared. The program will not permit you to remove a client or supplier with uncleared transactions. Clients with unpaid transactions can never be removed.

Click   **OK** to return to the Receivables module window. Clear the details using March 1 as the date and then remove the client's record. If all transactions are cleared, you will get the familiar warning.

Check that you have selected the client you want before continuing.

Click   **Yes** if you have selected correctly.

Click Yes to confirm if you get the message about removing lookup data. If you get the message stating that there is no lookup data, click OK to continue.

Completing the Month-End Checklist

We will now return to the month-end checklist by marking the remaining tasks as done. The tasks relating to budgeting do not apply, so we can delete them from the list and customize the list for Tesses Tresses.

Choose   the **Business Assistant menu** and **click Checklists**.

Double-click   **Month-End Procedures** to open this list.

You can customize any checklist. Click on the list where you want to add a task, choose the Edit menu and click Insert. Then type the task description.

Scroll down   the **list** to the budget-related tasks.

Click   **Check Your Budget** to select this line.

Click   the **Remove Item tool** or **choose** the **Edit menu** and **click Remove**.

Click   **Yes** to confirm and select the next task. Remove it and the following one relating to budgets.

Click   the **Done column** for the remaining tasks.

Click   **Checklist Completed** to return to the opening Checklist window. The session date appears as the Date Last Completed beside Month-End Procedures. **Click Close** to return to the Home window.

R E V I E W

The Student DVD with Data Files includes Review Questions and Supplementary Cases for this chapter.

VeloCity

OBJECTIVES

After completing this chapter, you should be able to

- ■ *plan* and *design* an accounting system for a small business
- ■ *prepare* procedures for converting from a manual system
- ■ *understand* the objectives of a computerized system
- ■ *create* company files
- ■ *set up* company accounts, ledgers and records
- ■ *enter* settings for foreign currency transactions
- ■ *prepare* files for foreign currency transactions and importing goods
- ■ *identify* preferred customers for reduced prices
- ■ *enter* preferred customer prices and import duty rates for inventory
- ■ *enter* Inventory Ledger settings and records
- ■ *finish* entering the accounting history for all modules
- ■ *insert* new accounts, suppliers, customers and employees as required
- ■ *add* users, *create* passwords and *enter* access rights
- ■ *export* reports
- ■ *use* spreadsheets for analyzing, planning and decision making
- ■ *enter* end-of-accounting-period adjustments
- ■ *perform* end-of-accounting-period closing routines
- ■ *create*, *analyze* and *interpret* comparative reports

INTRODUCTION

This application provides a complete accounting cycle for a merchandising business. It is a comprehensive application covering a three-month fiscal period. You will use Sage 50 to convert a manual accounting system to a computerized accounting system and then enter transactions. The routines in this application are common to many small businesses, so they should be useful. The information in this chapter reflects the business realities in Ontario in April 2016.

You may substitute information relevant to other provinces or the latest payroll and tax regulations wherever it is appropriate to do so.

> **NOTES**
> If you change the province, remember that rules for the application of the Harmonized Sales Tax (HST), provincial sales taxes and payroll may vary from one province to another, and amounts in the source documents will change.

Because of the length of the setup, instructions for working with the source documents are presented with those documents on page 692.

COMPANY INFORMATION

Company Profile

VeloCity, in Niagara on the Lake, Ontario, sells a small range of bicycles and accessories. Steve Ryder, the owner, a regular participant in bicycle races and competitions, opened the shop in the popular tourist region because of the proximity to trails along the Niagara River and Peninsula. The flat terrain makes this area popular with casual bikers.

All the bicycles are high-quality, light-weight, 27-gear cycles with Shimano gears and derailleurs. The extras, such as the carriage and third-wheel attachments, have attracted touring families with young children, and the annual sell-off of all rental bikes appeals to budget-conscious residents and visitors.

Three employees assist with the work in the store that includes selling and servicing the bicycles, while Ryder spends more time promoting the rental services of the business with theatre and tourism businesses throughout the province.

Several suppliers offer discounts to the store for early payment, including two suppliers in the United States. Accounts are also set up for other supplies and services that are provided locally. The store uses a credit card for some of these purchases.

Most customers are situated in the Niagara region, but Ryder has contracts with some travel companies in New York State to include bicycle rentals with their tour packages. Prices in US dollars are entered in the ledger records so that all prices will be entered automatically in the correct amount and currency when the customer is selected. With the Canadian dollar valued below the US dollar, US dollar prices are currently about 25 percent below Canadian dollar prices.

All account customers are given discounts for early payment, and some preferred customers receive additional discounts. Individual customers usually pay by cash, debit or credit card and do not receive any discounts. Delivery is provided at a small charge and includes assembly and a brief demonstration on bicycle care.

All items and services sold by the store are set up as inventory so that sales can be monitored. HST is charged on all sales and services, except to foreign customers. The store pays HST on all taxable purchases, including inventory purchased for resale. The exception is books, for which the store pays 5 percent GST on purchases and customers pay 5 percent at the time of sale.

The owner decided to use Sage 50 for record keeping after a consultant prepared the report on pages 621 and 622. Ryder found an application in an older Sage 50 textbook by Purbhoo. It appeared similar in complexity and structure to VeloCity and even included complete instructions for creating the data files. Before converting the books for the store, he asked his assistant to work through this application for practice. Next she printed all the relevant business guide information and prepared the following reports to assist with the conversion on May 1, 2018:

- Income Statement
- Business Information
- Chart of Accounts
- Balance Sheet
- Post-Closing Trial Balance

- Supplier Information
- Customer Information
- Employee Information
- Inventory Information
- Accounting Procedures

NOTES

Because of the length of the application, group work is encouraged in setting up error-free company files and completing the transactions.

NOTES

VeloCity Inc.
27 Gearing Avenue
Niagara on the Lake
ON L0S 1J0
Tel 1: (905) 468-8356 (velo)
Tel 2: (888) 468-8356 (velo)
Fax: (905) 468-9100
Business No.: 335 677 822

NOTES

In this chapter, the terms Vendors and Suppliers will be used interchangeably, as will the terms Purchases and Expenses, and the terms Sales and Revenues.

NOTES

Foreign customers pay HST when they rent bicycles in Ontario because the services are "consumed" in Canada and not exported.

MANAGER'S REPORT ON SAGE 50

PREPARED FOR VELOCITY

1. Sage 50 allows a business to process all source documents in a secure and timely fashion. It can automatically prepare both single-period and comparative accounting reports for planning, decision making and controlling operations within the business.
2. The software eliminates some of the time-consuming manual clerical functions. It can automatically prepare invoices, cheques and statements; store and recall repeating transactions; and it can perform all the necessary mathematical calculations. Being freed from these chores, the accountant can extend her role to assume a much higher level of responsibility. For example, the accountant will have more time to spend analyzing reports with the owner and can work directly with the owner in making business decisions.
3. Sage 50 can easily export reports to spreadsheets for further analysis, or link with the Internet, with other software programs and with suppliers and customers for interactive data exchange. When combined with the account reconciliation and budgeting features, these reports permit the owner to analyze past trends and to make better predictions about the future behaviour of the business.
4. As the business grows, the manager can divide work more meaningfully among new accounting personnel. Since Sage 50 provides subsidiary ledgers that are linked to control accounts in the General Ledger, it automatically coordinates accounting work performed by different individuals. Customizable window backgrounds can even accommodate mood changes of the different users.
5. Sage 50 allows the owner to exercise business controls in a number of areas:

IN GENERAL

- Access to confidential accounting records and editing capability can be restricted to authorized personnel by using passwords.
- Mechanical errors can be virtually eliminated, since journal transactions with unequal debits and credits cannot be posted. Customer, supplier, employee, inventory and project names appear in full on the journal entry input forms, making errors less likely.
- The ability to customize and preview forms, store recurring entries and look up posted invoices makes it possible to avoid errors in repeated information and to double check invoices in response to customer and supplier inquiries.
- Errors in General, Sales, Receipts, Purchases, Payments and Payroll journal entries can be corrected as adjustments or reversed. The software automatically creates and posts the reversing entries.
- Sage 50 provides an audit trail for all journals.
- Bank account, customer, supplier and inventory records can be set up to calculate many foreign currency transactions automatically, including import duties. Payments may be transmitted electronically and securely.
- Daily Business Manager lists and checklists provide reminders of upcoming discounts, recurring entries and routine tasks.
- Business advice, management reports and built-in warnings all provide helpful information for running the business.
- Sage 50 provides a directory of customers, suppliers and employees and can create mailing labels for them.

GENERAL LEDGER

- Sage 50 provides a directory of accounts used by the business, including all linked accounts for the other ledgers.
- The information in these accounts can be used to prepare and analyze financial reports, such as the Balance Sheet and Income Statement.

RECEIVABLES LEDGER

- Credit limit entries for each customer should reduce the losses from non-payment of accounts. Customers with poor payment histories can have their credit limits reduced or their credit purchase privileges removed.
- Customers can be linked to price lists so that they automatically receive differential prices.
- Sales quotes and order entries result in automatic Sales Journal entries when the quotes or orders are filled.
- Tax codes, payment terms and accounts are added to the customer record and automatically entered for sales when the customer is selected.
- Accounts receivable can be aged, and each customer's payment behaviour can be analyzed. This feature allows for the accurate calculation of provisions for bad debts.

PAYABLES LEDGER

- The information from the review of transactions with suppliers and from the accounts payable aged analysis can be combined with detailed cash flow reports to make payment decisions. Sage 50 helps to predict short-term cash needs in order to establish priorities for making payments and to schedule payments to suppliers.
- The GST/HST remittance or refund is calculated automatically because of the linked GST/HST accounts in the Payables and Receivables ledgers.
- Sage 50 purchase quotes and order entries result in automatic Purchases Journal entries when quotes or orders are filled.
- The usual tax code, payment terms and expense account for a supplier can be entered in the supplier record so that they are entered automatically for purchases when the supplier is selected.

PAYROLL LEDGER

- Sage 50 maintains employee records with both personal and payment information for personnel files.
- Paycheques for several employees can be processed as a single payroll run entry with direct payroll deposit.
- Once records are set up, the program automatically withholds employee deductions, including income tax, CPP (Canada Pension Plan) and EI (Employment Insurance), and is therefore less prone to error. Sage provides updated tax tables with new releases every six months.

▶

PAYROLL LEDGER CONTINUED

- Payroll summaries permit easy analysis of compulsory and optional payroll expenses and benefits, employee contributions and entitlements.
- Different kinds of income can be linked to different expense accounts. In addition, the wages for different employees can be linked to different expense accounts, again permitting better tracking of payroll expenses.
- Sage 50 automatically links payroll with control accounts in the General Ledger. Remittance amounts are tracked and linked with the corresponding payroll authorities for monthly or quarterly remittance.

INVENTORY LEDGER

- The software provides an inventory summary or database of all inventory items.
- Services can be set up as inventory and tracked the same way as inventory items.
- Inventory reports flag items that need to be reordered, and the reports can be used to make purchase decisions.
- Import duty rates and different prices in home and foreign currencies can be set up in the ledger so they appear automatically in the journals. Additional price lists can be added.
- Inventory codes can be matched to the supplier and customer item codes so that common order forms are created automatically.
- The software calculates inventory variance costs when the items sold are out of stock and later purchased at different prices.
- Sage 50 automatically updates inventory records for multiple locations when inventory is purchased, sold, transferred, lost, recovered or returned. It warns when you try to oversell inventory.
- Different units for stocking, selling and buying items can be saved for inventory items so that prices are automatically entered correctly for both sales and purchases. Reports can be prepared for any of the units on record.
- Inventory tracking reports can monitor sales and purchase activity on individual inventory items to assess profitability and determine which ones are selling well and which are not. These reports can be used to determine optimum inventory buying patterns to reduce storage costs.

6. In summation, Sage 50 provides an integrated management accounting information system with extensive built-in controls.

INCOME STATEMENT

VELOCITY

February 1 to April 30, 2018

Revenue				▶	5160	Depreciation: Van	$ 190.00
4000	GENERAL REVENUE				5170	Depreciation: Retail Premises	2 740.00
4020	Revenue from Sales	$69 520.00			5180	Net Depreciation	$ 4 040.00
4040	Revenue from Services	28 430.00			5190	Delivery Expense	63.00
4060	Sales Discounts	−965.00			5200	Hydro Expense	828.00
4100	Net Sales		$96 985.00		5210	Insurance Expense	1 800.00
4120	Exchange Rate Differences		−12.00		5220	Interest on Loan	1 240.00
4150	Interest Revenue		980.00		5230	Interest on Mortgage	5 200.00
4200	Freight Revenue		245.00		5240	Maintenance of Premises	1 055.00
4390	TOTAL GENERAL REVENUE		$98 198.00		5250	Supplies Used	265.00
					5260	Property Taxes	2 700.00
TOTAL REVENUE			$98 198.00		5270	Uncollectable Accounts Expense	500.00
					5280	Telephone Expense	795.00
Expense					5285	Van Maintenance & Operating Expense	1 638.00
5000	OPERATING EXPENSES				5290	TOTAL OPERATING EXPENSES	$42 199.00
5010	Advertising and Promotion		$ 830.00				
5020	Bank Charges		169.00		5295	PAYROLL EXPENSES	
5030	Credit Card Fees		870.00		5300	Wages (including Vacation paid)	10 303.00
5040	Damaged Inventory	$ 210.00			5320	Salaries	23 400.00
5050	Cost of Goods Sold: Accessories	4 535.00			5330	Commissions & Bonuses	360.00
5060	Cost of Goods Sold: Bicycles	11 710.00			5410	EI Expense	790.00
5070	Cost of Goods Sold: Books	4 300.00			5420	CPP Expense	1 548.00
5080	Cost Variance	64.00			5430	WSIB Expense	403.00
5090	Freight Expense	432.00			5440	EHT Expense	332.00
5100	Purchase Discounts	−620.00			5450	Gp Insurance Expense	306.00
5110	Purchases Returns & Allowances	−425.00			5460	Employee Benefits	930.00
5120	Net Cost of Goods Sold		20 206.00		5490	TOTAL PAYROLL EXPENSES	$38 372.00
5130	Depreciation: Computer Equipment	910.00					
5140	Depreciation: Furniture & Fixtures	80.00			TOTAL EXPENSE		$80 571.00
5150	Depreciation: Service Tools	120.00	▶		NET INCOME		$17 627.00

BUSINESS INFORMATION

VELOCITY

USER PREFERENCES: Options
Use Accounting Terms
Automatically save changes to records
Calculate record balances by session date
Automatically refresh balances
Do not download updates

View Daily Business Manager and Checklists off
Show Company name, Advice, Session
date at startup, and Paid stamps

Pop-Ups Your own preferences

Transaction Confirmation Turned on

COMPANY SETTINGS: Information
Address   27 Gearing Avenue
Niagara on the Lake, ON L0S 1J0
Tel 1   (905) 468-8356 (VELO)
Tel 2   (888) 468-8356 (VELO)
Fax   (905) 468-9100
Industry   Retail
Business No. 335 677 829 RT0001
Fiscal Start May 1, 2018
Earliest Transaction May 1, 2018
Fiscal End   July 31, 2018

System Warn if accounts not balanced
No transactions before May 1, 2018

Backup Semi-monthly; Display reminder
Scheduled, automatic backup off

Features All used

Forms Settings (Next Number)
Sales Invoices No. 2470
Sales Orders No. 248
Sales Quotes No. 56
Receipts No. 812
Customer Deposits No. 21
Purchase Orders No. 38
Employee Direct Deposits No. 25
Check for duplicates
Print in batches

Date Format MM dd yyyy and Long Dates

Logo SageData16\LOGOS\VELO.BMP

Names Additional Field Ref. Number

Credit Card Information
Used: Visa
Payable 2250 Expense 5030

Accept:	Visa	Interac
Fee	2.5%	0%
Asset	1120	1120
Expense	5030	5030

Sales Taxes

Tax	ID on forms	Track:	Purch	Sales
HST	335 677 829		2670	2650
GST	335 677 829		2670	2650

	Exempt?	Taxable?	Report?
HST	No	No	Yes
GST	No	No	Yes

Tax Codes
H: HST, taxable, 13%, not included, refundable
G: GST, taxable, 5%, not included, refundable
IN: HST, taxable, 13%, included, refundable

Foreign Currency
USD   United States Dollars
Tracking Account   4120
Exchange Rate on 05/01/18   1.35

GENERAL SETTINGS No changes

PAYABLES SETTINGS
Address Niagara on the Lake, Ontario, Canada

Options: Aging periods 15, 30, 60 days
Discounts before tax Yes

Import Duty
Track import duty
Linked account 2220

RECEIVABLES SETTINGS
Address Niagara on the Lake, Ontario, Canada

Options: Aging periods 10, 30, 60 days
Interest charges 1.5% after 1 day overdue
(monthly rate)
Statements include invoices for 31 days
Use tax code H for new customers

Discount: Payment terms 2/10, n/30
Discounts before tax No
Line Discounts Not used

Comments
On Sales Invoice   Interest @ 1.5% per month
charged on accounts over 30 days.

PAYROLL SETTINGS
Names: Income and Deduction
Income 1   Salary
Income 2   Commission
Income 3   No. Clients
Income 4   Bonus
Income 5   Tuition
Income 6   Travel Exp
Deduction 1   VRSP
Deduction 2   Savings Plan
Deduction 3   Garnishee

Names: Additional Payroll
Field 1 Emergency Contact
Field 2 Contact Number
User Expense 1 Gp Insurance
Entitlement 1 Vacation
Entitlement 2 Sick Leave
Entitlement 3 PersonalDays

Incomes

Income	Type	Taxable	Vac. Pay
Regular	Hourly rate	Yes	Yes
Overtime 1	Hourly rate	Yes	Yes
Salary	Income	Yes	No
Bonus	Income	Yes	No
Commission	Income	Yes	No
No. Clients	Piece Rate	Yes	Yes
Tuition	Income	Yes	No
Travel Exp	Reimburse	No	No

Deductions all deductions are by amount
VRSP Before tax, after other deductions
Savings Plan After tax and other deductions
Garnishee After tax and other deductions

Taxes
EI factor 1.4
WSIB rate 1.29
EHT factor 0.98

Entitlements

Name	Track %	Max Days	Clear
Vacation	8.0%	25	No
Sick Leave	5.0%	15	No
PersonalDays	2.5%	5	No

Remittance

Payroll Liability	Remittance Supplier
EI, CPP, Income Tax	Receiver General
WSIB	Workplace Safety & Insurance Board
EHT	Minister of Finance
VRSP	Manulife Financial
Gp Insurance	Welland Insurance
Savings Plan	Escarpment Investments
Garnishee	Receiver General

End of next remitting period: May 1

Job Categories
Sales: employees are salespersons
All employees are in Sales category

INVENTORY SETTINGS
Profit evaluation by markup
Sort inventory by number
Foreign prices from inventory records
Allow inventory levels to go below zero

ACCOUNT CLASS SETTINGS
Bank
    1060 Bank: Niagara Trust Chequing (CAD)
        Next cheque no.   101
        Next deposit no.   18
    1080 Bank: Niagara Trust Savings (CAD)
    1140 Bank: USD Chequing (USD)
        Next cheque no.   346
Cash
    1030 Undeposited Cash and Cheques
Credit Card Receivable
    1120 Bank: Visa and Interac
Credit Card Payable
    2250 Credit Card Payable
Operating Expense Class
    All postable expense accounts except COGS
    subgroup (accounts 5040–5110)

LINKED ACCOUNTS FOR LEDGERS
Refer to pages 650–655, 660–661, 663

CHART OF ACCOUNTS

VELOCITY

ASSETS

1000	CURRENT ASSETS [H]
1010	Test Balance Account
1030	Undeposited Cash and Cheques [A]
1060	Bank: Niagara Trust Chequing [A]
1080	Bank: Niagara Trust Savings [A]
1120	Bank: Visa and Interac [A]
1140	Bank: USD Chequing [A]
1150	Net Bank [S]
1200	Accounts Receivable [A]
1210	Allowance for Doubtful Accounts [A]
1220	Advances & Loans Receivable [A]
1230	Interest Receivable [A]
1240	Net Receivables [S]
1250	Purchase Prepayments
1260	Prepaid Advertising
1270	Prepaid Insurance
1280	Office Supplies
1290	Bicycle Repair Parts
1300	Rental Bicycles
1400	TOTAL CURRENT ASSETS [T]
1500	INVENTORY ASSETS [H]
1520	Accessories
1540	Bicycles
1560	Books
1580	TOTAL INVENTORY ASSETS [T]
1600	CENTRE & EQUIPMENT [H]
1610	Computer Equipment [A]
1620	Accum Deprec: Computer Equipment [A]
1630	Net Computer Equipment [S]
1640	Furniture & Fixtures [A]
1650	Accum Deprec: Furniture & Fixtures [A]
1660	Net Furniture & Fixtures [S]
1670	Service Equipment & Tools [A]
1680	Accum Deprec: Service Tools [A]
1690	Net Service Tools [S]
1700	Van [A]
1710	Accum Deprec: Van [A]
1720	Net Van [S]
1730	Retail Premises [A]
1740	Accum Deprec: Retail Premises [A]
1750	Net Retail Premises [S]
1890	TOTAL CENTRE & EQUIPMENT [T] ▶

▶LIABILITIES

2000	CURRENT LIABILITIES [H]
2100	Bank Loan
2200	Accounts Payable
2210	Prepaid Sales and Deposits
2220	Import Duty Payable
2250	Credit Card Payable
2280	Accrued Wages
2300	Vacation Payable
2310	EI Payable [A]
2320	CPP Payable [A]
2330	Income Tax Payable [A]
2350	Receiver General Payable [S]
2380	EHT Payable
2400	VRSP Payable
2410	Savings Plan Payable
2420	Group Insurance Payable
2430	Garnisheed Wages Payable
2460	WSIB Payable
2500	Business Income Tax Payable
2650	GST/HST Charged on Sales [A]
2670	GST/HST Paid on Purchases [A]
2750	GST/HST Owing (Refund) [S]
2790	TOTAL CURRENT LIABILITIES [T]
2800	LONG TERM LIABILITIES [H]
2820	Mortgage Payable
2890	TOTAL LONG TERM LIABILITIES [T]

EQUITY

3000	OWNER'S EQUITY [H]
3560	S. Ryder, Capital
3600	Current Earnings [X]
3690	TOTAL OWNER'S EQUITY [T]

REVENUE

4000	GENERAL REVENUE [H]
4020	Revenue from Sales [A]
4040	Revenue from Services [A]
4060	Sales Discounts [A]
4100	Net Sales [S]
4120	Exchange Rate Differences
4150	Interest Revenue
4200	Freight Revenue
4390	TOTAL GENERAL REVENUE [T] ▶

▶EXPENSE

5000	OPERATING EXPENSES [H]
5010	Advertising and Promotion
5020	Bank Charges
5030	Credit Card Fees
5040	Damaged Inventory [A]
5045	Item Assembly Costs [A]
5050	Cost of Goods Sold: Accessories [A]
5060	Cost of Goods Sold: Bicycles [A]
5070	Cost of Goods Sold: Books [A]
5075	Cost of Services [A]
5080	Cost Variance [A]
5090	Freight Expense [A]
5100	Purchase Discounts [A]
5110	Purchases Returns & Allowances [A]
5120	Net Cost of Goods Sold [S]
5130	Depreciation: Computer Equipment [A]
5140	Depreciation: Furniture & Fixtures [A]
5150	Depreciation: Service Tools [A]
5160	Depreciation: Van [A]
5170	Depreciation: Retail Premises [A]
5180	Net Depreciation [S]
5190	Delivery Expense
5200	Hydro Expense
5210	Insurance Expense
5220	Interest on Loan
5230	Interest on Mortgage
5240	Maintenance of Premises
5250	Supplies Used
5260	Property Taxes
5270	Uncollectable Accounts Expense
5280	Telephone Expense
5285	Van Maintenance & Operating Expense
5290	TOTAL OPERATING EXPENSES [T]
5295	PAYROLL EXPENSES [H]
5300	Wages
5320	Salaries
5330	Commissions & Bonuses
5350	Travel Expenses
5410	EI Expense
5420	CPP Expense
5430	WSIB Expense
5440	EHT Expense
5450	Gp Insurance Expense
5460	Employee Benefits
5490	TOTAL PAYROLL EXPENSES [T]

NOTES: The Chart of Accounts includes all accounts and Current Earnings. Group account types are not marked. Other account types are marked as follows: [H] Heading, [A] subgroup Account, [S] Subgroup total, [T] Total, [X] Current Earnings.

BALANCE SHEET

VELOCITY

April 30, 2018

Assets

1000	CURRENT ASSETS		
1060	Bank: Niagara Trust Chequing	$ 52 744.00	
1080	Bank: Niagara Trust Savings	118 110.00	
1120	Bank: Visa and Interac	5 925.00	
1140	Bank: USD (7 120 USD)	9 500.00	
1150	Net Bank		$186 279.00
1200	Accounts Receivable	17 110.00	
1210	Allowance for Doubtful Accounts	−800.00	
1220	Advances & Loans Receivable	100.00	
1230	Interest Receivable	420.00	
1240	Net Receivables		16 830.00
1260	Prepaid Advertising		480.00
1270	Prepaid Insurance		4 800.00
1280	Office Supplies		300.00
1290	Bicycle Repair Parts		1 150.00
1300	Rental Bicycles		7 520.00
1400	TOTAL CURRENT ASSETS		$217 359.00
1500	INVENTORY ASSETS		
1520	Accessories	6 540.00	
1540	Bicycles	40 840.00	
1560	Books	5 000.00	
1580	TOTAL INVENTORY ASSETS		$ 52 380.00
1600	CENTRE & EQUIPMENT		
1610	Computer Equipment	7 000.00	
1620	Accum Deprec: Computer Equip	−3 000.00	
1630	Net Computer Equipment		4 000.00
1640	Furniture & Fixtures	2 000.00	
1650	Accum Deprec: Furn & Fixtures	−400.00	
1660	Net Furniture & Fixtures		1 600.00
1670	Service Equipment & Tools	3 000.00	
1680	Accum Deprec: Service Tools	−900.00	
1690	Net Service Tools		2 100.00
1700	Van	30 000.00	
1710	Accum Deprec: Van	−5 000.00	
1720	Net Van		25 000.00
1730	Retail Premises	200 000.00	
1740	Accum Deprec: Retail Premises	−5 000.00	
1750	Net Retail Premises		195 000.00
1890	TOTAL CENTRE & EQUIPMENT		$227 700.00
	TOTAL ASSETS		$497 439.00 ▶

Liabilities

▶ 2000	CURRENT LIABILITIES		
2100	Bank Loan		$ 50 000.00
2200	Accounts Payable		13 096.16
2250	Credit Card Payable		220.00
2280	Accrued Wages		760.00
2300	Vacation Payable		706.00
2310	EI Payable	$ 557.79	
2320	CPP Payable	1 168.48	
2330	Income Tax Payable	1 610.65	
2350	Receiver General Payable		3 336.92
2380	EHT Payable		331.00
2400	VRSP Payable		350.00
2410	Savings Plan Payable		350.00
2420	Group Insurance Payable		102.00
2430	Garnisheed Wages Payable		200.00
2460	WSIB Payable		403.00
2500	Business Income Tax Payable		3 600.00
2650	GST/HST Charged on Sales	6 860.00	
2670	GST/HST Paid on Purchases	−2 990.00	
2750	GST/HST Owing (Refund)		3 870.00
2790	TOTAL CURRENT LIABILITIES		$ 77 325.08
2800	LONG TERM LIABILITIES		
2820	Mortgage Payable		180 000.00
2890	TOTAL LONG TERM LIABILITIES		$180 000.00
	TOTAL LIABILITIES		$257 325.08

Equity

3000	OWNER'S EQUITY		
3560	S. Ryder, Capital		$222 486.92
3600	Current Earnings		17 627.00
3690	TOTAL OWNER'S EQUITY		$240 113.92
	TOTAL EQUITY		$240 113.92
	LIABILITIES AND EQUITY		$497 439.00

POST-CLOSING TRIAL BALANCE

VELOCITY

April 30, 2018

Acct	Name	Debits	Credits
1060	Bank: Niagara Trust Chequing	$ 52 744.00	
1080	Bank: Niagara Trust Savings	118 110.00	
1120	Bank: Visa and Interac	5 925.00	
1140	Bank: USD Chequing (7 120 USD)	9 500.00	
1200	Accounts Receivable	17 110.00	
1210	Allowance for Doubtful Accounts		$ 800.00
1220	Advances & Loans Receivable	100.00	
1230	Interest Receivable	420.00	
1260	Prepaid Advertising	480.00	
1270	Prepaid Insurance	4 800.00	
1280	Office Supplies	300.00	
1295	Bicycle Repair Parts	1 150.00	
1300	Rental Bicycles	7 520.00	
1520	Accessories	6 540.00	
1540	Bicycles	40 840.00	
1560	Books	5 000.00	
1610	Computer Equipment	7 000.00	
1620	Accum Deprec: Computer Equipment		3 000.00
1640	Furniture & Fixtures	2 000.00	
1650	Accum Deprec: Furniture & Fixtures		400.00
1670	Service Equipment & Tools	3 000.00	
1680	Accum Deprec: Service Tools		900.00
1700	Van	30 000.00	
1710	Accum Deprec: Van		$ 5 000.00
1730	Retail Premises	$200 000.00	
1740	Accum Deprec: Retail Premises		5 000.00
2100	Bank Loan		50 000.00
2200	Accounts Payable		13 096.16
2250	Credit Card Payable		220.00
2280	Accrued Wages		760.00
2300	Vacation Payable		706.00
2310	EI Payable		557.79
2320	CPP Payable		1 168.48
2330	Income Tax Payable		1 610.65
2380	EHT Payable		331.00
2400	VRSP Payable		350.00
2410	Savings Plan Payable		350.00
2420	Group Insurance Payable		102.00
2430	Garnisheed Wages Payable		200.00
2460	WSIB Payable		403.00
2500	Business Income Tax Payable		3 600.00
2650	GST/HST Charged on Sales		6 860.00
2670	GST/HST Paid on Purchases	2 990.00	
2820	Mortgage Payable		180 000.00
3560	S. Ryder, Capital		240 113.92
		$515 529.00	$515 529.00

SUPPLIER INFORMATION

VELOCITY

Supplier Name (Contact)	Address	Phone No. Fax No.	E-mail Web Site	Terms Tax ID	Expense Acct Tax Code
Complete Cycler Inc. (Strate Spokes) (USD supplier)	1500 Redmond Road Suite 100, Woodinville Washington 98072 USA	Tel: (425) 628-9163 Fax: (425) 629-7164	sspokes@cycler.com cycler.com	2/10, n/30 (before tax)	H
Energy Source (Manny Watts)	91 Power Rd. Niagara Falls, ON L2H 2L9	Tel: (905) 463-2664	watts@energysource.ca energysource.ca	net 1	5200 H
Escarpment Investments (P. Cuniary)	122 King St. W. Hamilton, ON L8P 4V2	Tel: (905) 462-3338 Fax: (905) 461-2116	pc@escarp.invest.ca escarp.invest.ca	net 1	2410 no tax (exempt)
Lakeshore Sunoco (Mick Annick)	101 Lakeshore Rd. Niagara on the Lake ON L0S 1J0	Tel: (905) 622-6181	mick@goodforcars.com goodforcars.com	net 1	5285 IN
Manulife Financial	PO Box 344, Stn A, Toronto ON M2W 1S1			net 1	no tax (exempt)
Minister of Finance (N.O. Money)	631 Queenston Rd. Hamilton, ON L8K 6R5	Tel: (905) 462-5555	gov.on.ca/fin	net 1	no tax (exempt)
Niagara Bell (Noel Coller)	100 Parkway Ave. Niagara Falls, ON L2E 2K5	Tel: (905) 525-2355	bell.ca	net 1	5280 H
Pro Cycles Inc. (C. Glider)	7 Trackway Dr. Waterloo, ON N2G 4S5	Tel: (519) 588-3846 Fax: (519) 588-7126	glider@procycles.com procycles.com	1/15, n/30 (before tax) 466 254 108	H
Receiver General for Canada		Tel: (800) 561-7761	cra-arc.gc.ca	net 1	no tax (exempt)
Welland Insurance (Feulle Cuvver)	718 Montgomery Dr. Welland, ON L3B 3H5	Tel: (905) 588-1773 Fax: (905) 588-1624	fc@welland.insur.ca welland.insur.ca	net 1	no tax (not exempt)

SUPPLIER INFORMATION CONTINUED

Supplier Name (Contact)	Address	Phone No. Fax No.	E-mail Web Site	Terms Tax ID	Expense Acct Tax Code
Wheel Deals (Onna Roller) (USD supplier)	4900 Tubular Circle El Cerrito, California 94533 USA	Tel 1: (510) 525-4327 Tel 2: (800) 567-9152 Fax: (510) 526-1135	onna@wheeldeals.com wheeldeals.com	2/10, n/30 (before tax)	H
Workplace Safety & Insurance Board (I.M. Hurt)	PO Box 2099 Oshawa, ON L1J 4C5	Tel: (800) 525-9100 Fax: (905) 523-1824	wsib.on.ca	net 1	2460 no tax (exempt)

OUTSTANDING SUPPLIER INVOICES

VELOCITY

Supplier Name	Terms	Date	Inv/Chq No.	Amount	Rate	Tax	Total
Complete Cycler Inc.	2/10, n/30 (before tax)	Apr. 28/18 Apr. 28/18	CC-918 Chq 344	$3 700 USD 2 000 USD	@1.36 @1.36	$481 USD	$5 686.16 CAD 2 000.00 USD $2 966.16 CAD
Pro Cycles Inc.	1/15, n/30 (before tax)	Apr. 20/18 Apr. 21/18	PC-618 Chq 96 Balance Owing	$8 000 3 000		$1 040	$9 040.00 3 000.00 $ 6 040.00
Wheel Deals	2/10, n/30 (before tax)	Apr. 30/18	WD-391	$2 670 USD		$347.10 USD	$ 4 090.00 CAD
					Grand Total		$13 096.16 CAD

CUSTOMER INFORMATION

VELOCITY

Customer Name (Contact)	Address	Phone No. Fax No.	E-mail Web Site	Terms Tax Code	Credit Limit
*Americas Vinelands Tours (B. Bacchus)	75 Graperie Ave. Buffalo, New York 14202 USA	Tel: (716) 367-7346 Fax: (716) 367-8258	bbacchus@avt.com avt.com Currency: USD	2/10, n/30 no tax	$15 000 ($15 000 USD)
*Backstage Tours (G. O. Rideout)	13 Wellspring Dr. Stratford, ON N5A 3B8	Tel: (519) 526-3344 Fax: (519) 525-1166	rideout@backstagetours.ca backstagetours.ca	2/10, n/30 H	$15 000
Festival Tours (Bea Player) 14301 USA	62 Ibsen Court Niagara Falls, New York	Tel: (716) 399-1489 Fax: (716) 399-2735 Currency: USD	bplayer@festivaltours.com festivaltours.com	2/10, n/30 no tax	$15 000 ($15 000 USD)
*Niagara Rapids Inn (Eddy Currents)	339 Picton St. Niagara on the Lake ON L0S 1J0	Tel 1: (905) 468-3000 Tel 2: (905) 468-3198 Fax: (905) 468-3477	currents@niagararapids.ca niagararapids.ca	2/10, n/30 H	$15 000
*Park 'N Ride Tours (G. O. Carless)	4900 Airport Rd. Toronto, ON M9P 7F2	Tel 1: (416) 622-9250 Tel 2: (416) 622-9238 Fax: (416) 622-9729	carless@parknride.ca parknride.ca	2/10, n/30 H	$15 000
Shavian B & B (G. B. Shaw)	93 Workout Rd. Niagara on the Lake ON L0S 1J0	Tel: (905) 468-1800 Fax: (905) 468-1278	gbshaw@shavianBB.com shavianBB.com	2/10, n/30 H	$15 000
Cash and Interac Customers	Terms: net 1	Tax code: H			
Visa Sales (for Visa customers)	Terms: net 1	Tax code: H			

NOTES: Preferred price list customers are marked with an asterisk (*). The ship-to address is the same as the mailing address for all customers.

OUTSTANDING CUSTOMER INVOICES

VELOCITY

Customer Name	Terms	Date	Inv/Chq No.	Amount	Total
Backstage Tours	2/10, n/30 (after tax)	Apr. 30/18	2199	$9 040	
		Apr. 30/18	Chq 488	2 100	
			Balance Owing		$6 940
Niagara Rapids Inn	2/10, n/30 (after tax)	Apr. 26/18	2194	$5 650	$5 650
Shavian B & B	2/10, n/30 (after tax)	Apr. 23/18	2191	$4 520	$4 520
				Grand Total	$17 110

EMPLOYEE INFORMATION SHEET

VELOCITY

Employee	Dunlop Mercier (Male)	Pedal Schwinn (Female)	Shimana Gearie (Female)
Position	Full-time Service/Sales	Full-time Sales/Tour Guide	Full-time Sales/Accounting
Address	55 Trailview Rd. Niagara on the Lake, ON L0S 1J0	2 Fallsview Drive Niagara Falls, ON L2J 4F8	300 Vineland Rd. Niagara on the Lake, ON L0S 1J0
Telephone	(905) 468-1817	(905) 489-4412	(905) 468-5778
Social Insurance No.	532 548 625	783 455 611	488 655 333
Date of Birth (mm-dd-yy)	09/18/85	03/15/82	05/24/85
Date of Hire (mm-dd-yy)	01/06/14	02/15/12	08/25/15
Federal (Ontario) Tax Exemption - TD1			
Basic Personal	$11 474 (10 011)	$11 474 (10 011)	$11 474 (10 011)
Other Indexed	–	–	$18 262 (13 219)
Other Non-Indexed	–	–	$4 070 (4 154)
Total Exemptions	$11 474 (10 011)	$11 474 (10 011)	$33 806 (27 384)
Additional Federal Tax	–	$50.00	–
Employee Taxes			
Historical Income Tax	$1 668.29	$3 022.96	$1 224.36
Historical EI	$232.97	$308.32	$284.78
Historical CPP	$547.31	$761.00	$760.39
Deduct EI; EI Factor	Yes; 1.4	Yes; 1.4	Yes; 1.4
Deduct CPP	Yes	Yes	Yes
Employee Income			
Loans: Historical Amount	$100.00	(use) ✓	(use) ✓
Benefits per Period	$16.00	$35.00	$35.00
Benefits: Historical Amount	$128.00	$140.00	$140.00
Vacation Pay Owed	$706.00	(do not use)	(do not use)
Vacation Paid	$386.00	(do not use)	(do not use)
Regular Wage Rate (Hours per Period)	$18.00/hr (80 hours)	(do not use)	(do not use)
Regular Wages: Historical Amount	$11 520.00	(do not use)	(do not use)
Overtime 1 Wage Rate	$27.00/hr	(do not use)	(do not use)
Overtime 1 Wages: Historical Amount	$486.00	(do not use)	(do not use)
Salary (Hours per Period)	(do not use)	$4 100.00 (150 hours)	$3 700.00 (150 hours)
Salary: Historical Amount	(do not use)	$16 400.00	$14 800.00
Commission	(do not use)	(do not use)	(use) ✓ 2% (service revenue)
Commissions: Historical Amount	(do not use)	(do not use)	$348.00
No. Clients (piece rate)	$10	$10	$10
Bonus:	(use) ✓	(use) ✓	(use) ✓

▶

EMPLOYEE INFORMATION CONTINUED			
Employee	Dunlop Mercier	Pedal Schwinn	Shimana Gearie
Employee Income continued			
Tuition: Per Period	(use) ✓	(use) ✓	$310
Tuition: Historical Amount	–	–	$1 240
Travel Exp.: Historical Amount	(use) ✓	$120.00	(use) ✓
Pay Periods	26	12	12
Vacation Rate	6% retained	0%, not retained	0%, not retained
Record Wage Expenses in	Linked Accounts	Linked Accounts	Linked Accounts
Deductions			
VRSP (Historical Amount)	$50.00 ($450.00)	$100.00 ($400.00)	$100.00 ($400.00)
Savings Plan (Historical Amount)	$50.00 ($450.00)	$100.00 ($400.00)	$100.00 ($400.00)
Garnishee (Historical Amount)	(do not use)	$200.00 ($800.00)	(do not use)
WSIB and Other Expenses			
WSIB Rate	1.29	1.29	1.02
Group Insurance (Historical Amount)	$16.00 ($128.00)	$35.00 ($140.00)	$35.00 ($140.00)
Entitlements: Rate, Maximum Days, Clear? (Historical Amount)			
Vacation	–	8%, 25 days, No (15)	8%, 25 days, No (15)
Sick Leave	5%, 15 days, No (12)	5%, 15 days, No (10)	5%, 15 days, No (8)
Personal Days	2.5%, 5 days, No (4)	2.5%, 5 days, No (2)	2.5%, 5 days, No (3)
Direct Deposit			
Yes/No	Yes	Yes	Yes
Branch, Institution, Account No.	89008, 102, 2998187	94008, 102, 3829110	89008, 102, 2309982
Percent	100%	100%	100%
Additional Information			
Emergency Contact & Number	Adrian Ingles (905) 548-0301	Alex Schwinn (905) 688-2973	Martha Gearie (905) 458-5778
T4 and RL-1 Reporting			
EI Insurable Earnings	$12 392.00	$16 400.00	$15 148.00
Pensionable Earnings	$12 520.00	$16 540.00	$16 528.00
Withheld	$3 348.57	$5 692.28	$3 069.53
Net Pay	$9 143.43	$10 827.72	$13 318.47

Employee Profiles and TD1 Information

All Employees VeloCity pays group insurance premiums for all employees. They also are reimbursed for tuition fees when they successfully complete a university or college course. These two benefits are taxable. In addition, when they use their personal vehicles for company business, they are reimbursed for car expenses.

All employees work full time and are entitled to three weeks' vacation, ten days' sick leave and five days of personal leave per year. All three employees have sick leave and personal days that they can carry forward from the previous year. The two salaried employees take three weeks' vacation as paid time, and the hourly employee receives 6 percent of his wages as vacation pay when he takes his vacation.

Starting in May, as an incentive to provide excellent customer service, all employees will receive a quarterly bonus of $10 for every completed satisfactory customer survey.

Dunlop Mercier is responsible for shipping, receiving, delivery and assembly for customers. He also does all the repair work in the store. As a single male, he uses only the basic tax claim amount. Every two weeks his pay, at the rate of $18 per hour, is deposited to his account. For the hours beyond 40 hours in a week, he receives an overtime rate of $27 per hour. He is owed four months of vacation pay. He contributes to

the investment savings plan through payroll deductions. He still owes $100 from a loan of $200 for which he will pay back $50 in each of the next two pay periods.

Pedal Schwinn is the store manager for VeloCity, and she assists with store sales. Her monthly salary of $4 100 is deposited directly into her bank account. Schwinn is married with one child, but uses the basic single claim amount because her husband is also employed and he uses the federal child tax claim amount. Her payroll deductions include additional federal income tax for other income, wages garnisheed to pay for prior taxes owing and regular contributions to her Registered Retirement Savings Plan and an investment savings plan.

Shimana Gearie does the accounting and manages the Payables, Receivables and Payroll in addition to sales in the store. Although she is single, she supports her infirm mother so she has the spousal equivalent claim and a caregiver amount in addition to the basic single claim and tuition amounts. A commission of 2 percent of revenue from services supplements her monthly salary of $3 700, which is deposited directly into her bank account. She has VRSP and investment savings plan contributions withheld from her paycheques.

> **NOTES**
> Wages may be garnisheed by any creditor, but the most common one is the Receiver General to pay back-taxes owing.

INVENTORY INFORMATION

VELOCITY

Code	Description	Min Stock	CAD Reg	Prices (Pref)	USD Reg	Prices (Pref)	Stock/Sell Unit	Buying Unit	Relationship	Qty on Hand	Total (Cost)
Accessories: Total asset value $6 540 (Linked Accounts: Asset 1520, Revenue 4020, COGS 5050, Variance 5080) Charge HST											
AC010	Bicycle Pump: standing model	5	$ 50	($ 45)	$ 37	($ 33)	unit	box	4/box	10	$ 300
AC020	Bicycle Pump: hand-held mini	5	80	(70)	60	(54)	unit	box	10/box	10	500
AC030	Helmet	15	120	(105)	90	(80)	helmet	carton	10/carton	40	2 400
AC040	Light: halogen	10	25	(22)	18	(16)	unit	box	10/box	20	200
AC050	Light: rear reflector	20	15	(12)	11	(10)	unit	box	10/box	30	210
AC060	Lock: kryptonite tube	10	70	(65)	52	(47)	lock	box	5/box	15	600
AC070	Pannier: front wicker clip-on	3	80	(75)	60	(54)	basket		same	6	300
AC080	Pannier: rear mesh	3	60	(55)	44	(40)	basket		same	10	380
AC090	Trailer: 2-child closed	1	620	(570)	445	(400)	unit		same	4	1 200
AC100	Trailer: third-wheel rider	1	260	(235)	190	(170)	unit		same	3	450
Books: Total asset value $5 000 (Linked Accounts: Asset 1560, Revenue 4020, COGS 5070, Variance 5080) HST exempt, charge GST only											
BK010	Books: Complete Bicycle Guide	10	40	(35)	30	(27)	book		same	110	2 200
BK020	Books: Endless Trails	10	40	(35)	30	(27)	book		same	140	2 800
Bicycles: Total asset value $40 840 (Linked Accounts: Asset 1540, Revenue 4020, COGS 5060, Variance 5080) Charge HST											
CY010	Bicycle: Commuter Steel frame CX10	3	640	(590)	475	(430)	bike		same	12	3 720
CY020	Bicycle: Commuter Alum frame CX90	3	960	(850)	715	(645)	bike		same	12	6 480
CY030	Bicycle: Racer Ultra lite RX480	1	3 100	(2 800)	2 300	(2 070)	bike		same	4	6 200
CY040	Bicycle: Trail Alum frame TX560	4	1 220	(1 090)	900	(810)	bike		same	16	9 920
CY050	Bicycle: Mountain Alum frame MX14	2	1 850	(1 650)	1 380	(1 240)	bike		same	6	5 580
CY060	Bicycle: Mountain Carbon frame MX34	1	2 950	(2 600)	2 175	(1 960)	bike		same	2	3 440
CY070	Bicycle: Youth YX660	4	460	(420)	340	(305)	bike		same	16	3 520
CY090	Stationary Converter	2	870	(800)	655	(590)	unit		same	6	1 980

NOTES: No duty is charged on items imported from the United States. The duty rate is 0%.
Stocking and selling units are the same for all items.
Buying units and the relationship to stocking units are entered only when these are different from the stocking/selling units.
"Same" is entered in the relationship column when the same unit is used for all measures.

▶

		CAD Prices		USD Prices			
Code	Description	Reg	(Pref)	(Reg)		Unit	Taxes

INVENTORY INFORMATION CONTINUED

Services (Linked Accounts: Revenue 4040, Expense 5075)

Code	Description	Reg	(Pref)	(Reg)		Unit	Taxes
S010	Boxing for shipping	$ 75	($70)	$57	($50)	job	HST (not exempt)
S020	Maintenance: annual contract	110	(100)	82	(75)	year	HST (not exempt)
S030	Maintenance: complete tune-up	70	(65)	53	(48)	job	HST (not exempt)
S040	Rental: 1 hour	10	(9)	7	(6)	hour	HST (not exempt)
S050	Rental: 1 day	30	(25)	22	(20)	day	HST (not exempt)
S060	Repairs	45	(40)	33	(30)	hour	HST (not exempt)

Accounting Procedures

Harmonized Sales Taxes: HST, GST and PST

HST at the rate of 13 percent is applied to all goods and services offered by VeloCity, except books. The Harmonized Sales Tax includes the provincial sales tax of 8 percent. Goods that are exempt for PST, such as books, have a different tax code applied (code G – GST @ 5%).

VeloCity uses the regular method for remittance of the Harmonized Sales Tax. HST and GST collected from customers are recorded as liabilities in *GST/HST Charged on Sales*. HST and GST paid to suppliers are recorded in *GST/HST Paid on Purchases* as a decrease in liability to the Canada Revenue Agency (CRA). These two postable accounts are added together in the subgroup total account *GST/HST Owing (Refund)* because a single return is remitted for both taxes. The balance of HST and GST to be remitted or the request for a refund is sent to the Receiver General for Canada by the last day of the current month for the previous month.

Tax calculations will be correct only for customers and suppliers for whom the tax exempt option was set as No. The GST and HST reports available from the Reports menu will include transactions completed in the Sales, Purchases and General journals, but the opening historical balances will not be included. Therefore, the amounts in the tax reports may differ from the balances in the General Ledger accounts. You should use the General Ledger accounts to verify the balance owing (or refund due) and make adjustments to the report manually as necessary.

After the report is filed, clear the HST and GST reports up to the last day of the previous month. Always back up your files before clearing the tax details.

The Employer Health Tax (EHT)

The Employer Health Tax (EHT) is paid by employers in Ontario to provide Ontario Health Insurance Plan (OHIP) coverage for all eligible Ontario residents. The EHT is based on the total annual remuneration paid to employees. Employers whose total payroll is less than $200 000 pay EHT at the rate of 0.98 percent. The EHT rate increases with total payroll to a maximum of 1.95 percent for payroll amounts of $400 000 and more. In this application, EHT will be remitted quarterly. *EHT Payable* is set up as a liability owing to the supplier, Minister of Finance. The Remittance Payments Journal will provide the balance owing to the Minister of Finance when the liability is linked to this supplier.

Aging of Accounts

VeloCity uses aging periods that reflect the payment terms it provides to customers and receives from suppliers. For customers, this will be 10, 30 and 60 days, and for suppliers,

NOTES
Because VeloCity also sells books that are exempt for HST but not GST, the name GST/HST is applied to accounts.

PRO VERSION
pro The term Vendors replaces Suppliers throughout the program.

NOTES
To clear the tax report, choose the Maintenance menu, then Clear Data. Click Clear Tax Report and select HST and GST.

15, 30 and 60 days. Interest at 1.5 percent per month is charged on customer accounts that are not paid within 30 days. Regular customer statements have the interest amounts, and invoices are then prepared to add the interest to the amount owing in the ledger record.

Discounts

VeloCity offers a 2 percent discount to regular account customers if they settle their accounts within 10 days. Full payment is requested within 30 days. These payment terms are set up as defaults. When the receipt is entered and the discount is still available, the program provides the amount of the discount and the net amount owing. No discounts are given on cash or credit card sales. Customer discounts are calculated on after-tax amounts.

Some customers receive preferred customer prices that are approximately 10 percent below the regular prices. These customers are identified in the ledger records and the preferred prices are set up in the Inventory Ledger records.

Some suppliers also offer discounts for early settlement of accounts. Again, when the terms are entered for the supplier and payment is made before the discount period expires, the program displays the discount as available and automatically calculates a net balance owing. Payment terms vary from supplier to supplier. Supplier discounts may be calculated on before-tax amounts or after-tax amounts.

Freight

When a business purchases inventory items, the cost of any freight that cannot be directly allocated to a specific item must be charged to *Freight Expense* — a general expense that is not charged to the costs of any inventory asset account. Customers also pay for delivery. HST is charged on freight for both sales and purchases (tax code H).

Bank Deposits

Deposit slips are prepared weekly when cash and cheques are received. Receipts are debited to *Undeposited Cash and Cheques* and transferred weekly to *Bank: Niagara Trust Chequing*.

Imported Inventory

Some inventory items are imported from the United States. The bank accounts, supplier records and inventory records are modified to accommodate the foreign currency transactions and import duties automatically.

Business Income Tax

VeloCity pays income tax in quarterly instalments to the Receiver General based on its previous year's net income.

Purchase Returns and Allowances

A business will sometimes return inventory items to suppliers because of damage, poor quality or shipment of the wrong items. Usually a business records these returns after it receives a credit note from a supplier. The return of inventory is entered in the Purchases Journal as an inventory purchase:

- Select the item in the Item field and enter the quantity returned as a **negative** amount in the Quantity field. The program will automatically calculate a negative amount as a default in the Amount field. You cannot change the account number.
- Accept the default amount and enter other items returned to the supplier.
- Enter the appropriate tax code for each item returned.

The program will create a negative invoice to reduce the balance owing to the supplier and will reduce the applicable inventory asset accounts, the freight accounts, *GST/HST Paid on Purchases* and the quantity of items in the Inventory Ledger database.

Purchase allowances for damaged merchandise that is not returned are entered as non-inventory negative purchase invoices. Enter the amount of the allowance as a **negative** amount in the Amount field and choose taxes included as the tax code. Enter *Purchases Returns & Allowances* in the Account field.

Sales Returns and Allowances

Sometimes customers will return inventory items. Usually, a business records the return after it has issued a credit note. The return is entered in the Sales Journal as a negative inventory sale, choosing the same customer and payment method as in the original sale:

- Select the appropriate item in the Item field.
- Enter the quantity returned with a **negative** number in the Quantity field.
- The price of the item appears as a positive number in the Price field, and the Amount field is calculated automatically as a negative amount.
- Enter the tax code for the sale and the account number for *Sales Returns & Allowances*.

The program will create a negative invoice to reduce the balance owing by the customer and to reduce *Cost of Goods Sold* and *GST/HST Charged on Sales*. The applicable inventory asset accounts and the quantity of items in the Inventory Ledger database will be increased.

Sales allowances are entered as non-inventory negative sales invoices with taxes included, creating a debit entry for *Sales Returns & Allowances* and a credit for *Accounts Receivable*. If the allowance is paid by cheque, enter the allowance in the Payments Journal as an Other Payment paid by cheque.

NSF Cheques

If a cheque is deposited from an account that does not have enough money to cover it, the bank returns it to the depositor as NSF (non-sufficient funds). If the cheque was in payment for a cash sale, you must process the NSF cheque through the Sales Journal because there was no Receipts Journal entry. Create a customer record if necessary and enter a positive amount for the amount of the cheque. Choose *Bank: Niagara Trust Chequing* as the account. Choose Pay Later as the method of payment. If the customer is expected to pay the bank charges, enter these on the second invoice line as a positive amount and select the appropriate revenue account.

If the NSF cheque in payment of an invoice was deposited to a different account than the one used in the Receipts Journal, create a negative receipt to reverse the cheque. Choose Include Fully Paid Invoices. Click the invoice line that this cheque was applied to. Enter the discount taken as a negative amount. Enter the Payment Amount as a negative amount. Choose the correct bank account from the Deposit To field. Refer to page 605 and Appendix C.

Adjustments for Bad Debt

Most businesses set up an allowance for doubtful accounts or bad debts, knowing that some customers will fail to pay. The amount entered for this will be a reasonable guess at how much of the *Accounts Receivable* amount will never be collected. When the allowance is set up, a bad debts or uncollectable accounts expense account is debited and the allowance is credited (effectively reducing the net receivables balance). When a business is certain that a customer will not pay its account, the debt should be written off by crediting *Accounts Receivable* and debiting *Allowance for Doubtful Accounts*. When taxes apply, an extra step is required. Part of the original sales invoice was entered

NOTES
Purchases Returns & Allowances is a contra-expense account with a credit balance. The return creates a credit entry that will reduce total expenses.

NOTES
The sales tax rules for credits, allowances and discounts are complex. They may be different for provincial and federal taxes and they may differ from one province to another. Adjusting General Journal entries may be required to adjust the amount of tax owing and calculate the tax remittance. We have chosen to leave out the tax component for transactions of this type. Refer to Chapter 2 for more information about sales taxes.

NOTES
Sales Returns & Allowances is a contra-revenue account with a debit balance. The sales return creates a debit entry that will reduce total revenue and Accounts Receivable.

NOTES
The Sales Journal entry for the NSF cheque will credit the bank account and debit Accounts Receivable for the allowance.

NOTES

Allowance for Doubtful Accounts is a contra-asset account that normally has a credit balance. Therefore, a debit entry from the negative amount will reduce this credit balance, reducing both the allowance and the Accounts Receivable balances.

as a credit (increase) to *GST/HST Charged on Sales*. By entering the full amount and the code IN for taxes included, the GST/HST payable amount will automatically be correctly reduced. In Sage 50, record the write-off of the debt in the Sales Journal:

- Select the customer whose debt will not be paid.
- Enter a source document number to identify the transaction (e.g., memo).
- Enter a **negative** amount for the total unpaid invoice in the Amount field.
- Enter *Allowance for Doubtful Accounts* in the Account field.
- Enter the tax code **IN** (taxes included).

Enter NSF charges, if any, on the next invoice line:

- Enter a **negative** amount for the total NSF charge in the Amount field.
- Enter *Allowance for Doubtful Accounts* in the Account field.
- Enter the tax code **No tax**.

Review the transaction. *Accounts Receivable* is credited (reduced) by the full amount of the invoice to remove the balance owing by this customer. *Allowance for Doubtful Accounts* has been debited (reduced) by the amount of the invoice minus taxes. *GST/HST Charged on Sales* has been debited for the tax portion of the invoice to reduce the tax liability.

After recording the write-off, "pay" both the original invoice and the write-off in the Receipts Journal. The balance will be zero and there will be no journal entry. This step removes the items from the Receipts Journal for the customer so that you can clear the paid transactions and later remove the customer's record.

Manually you would complete the entry as follows:

---

1. Set up the Allowance for Doubtful Account (bad debts).

Date	Particulars	Debit	Credit
04/01	5270 Uncollectable Accounts Expense	1 000.00	
	1210 Allowance for Doubtful Accounts		1 000.00

2. Customer G. Bell declares bankruptcy. Write off outstanding balance, $226, including HST.

Date	Particulars	Debit	Credit
04/30	1210 Allowance for Doubtful Accounts	200.00	
	2650 GST/HST Charged on Sales	26.00	
	1200 Accounts Receivable, G. Bell		226.00

Occasionally, a bad debt is recovered after it has been written off. When this occurs, the above procedure is reversed and the GST/HST liability must also be restored. The recovery is entered as a non-inventory sale in the Sales Journal as follows:

- Select the customer and enter the date and source document number.
- Type a comment such as "Debt recovered" in the Item Description field.
- Enter a **positive** amount for the total invoice amount in the Amount field.
- Enter the tax code **IN** (taxes included).
- Enter *Allowance for Doubtful Accounts* in the Account field.

NOTES

You would also follow these steps when only part of the bad debt amount is recovered.

Review the transaction — *Accounts Receivable* has been debited for the full amount of the invoice. *Allowance for Doubtful Accounts* has been credited for the amount of the invoice minus taxes. *GST/HST Charged on Sales* has been credited for the tax portion of the invoice to restore the tax liability.

As the final step, record the customer's payment in the Receipts Journal as you would record any other customer payment.

Remittances

For all remittances, the next payment is due in May for the pay period ending April 30. Because May 1 is the earliest transaction date, we cannot enter a date before this. Therefore, May 1 will be the first end of remitting period date for all remittances.

The Receiver General for Canada:
- Monthly EI, CPP and income tax deductions withheld from employees must be paid by the 15th of each month for the previous month.
- Monthly GST/HST owing or requests for refunds must be filed by the end of each month for the previous month.
- Business income tax is paid in quarterly instalments.
- Garnisheed wages are submitted by the 15th of each month for the previous month. A separate cheque is issued for this remittance.

The Minister of Finance:
- Quarterly Employer Health Tax (EHT) deductions must be paid by the 15th of May, July, October and January for the previous quarter.

The Workplace Safety and Insurance Board:
- Quarterly Workplace Safety and Insurance Board (WSIB) assessment for employees must be paid by the 15th of the month for the previous quarter.

Escarpment Investments:
- Monthly investment (Savings Plan) deductions withheld from employees must be paid by the 15th of the month for the previous month.

Welland Insurance:
- Group insurance contributions paid by the employer must be paid by the 15th of the month for the previous month.

Manulife Financial:
- Monthly Registered Retirement Savings Plan (VRSP) deductions withheld from employees must be paid by the 15th of the month for the previous month.

NOTES
In practice, a business would make these four federal tax remittances to different federal offices. Separate supplier accounts would be needed for each remittance. For this application, one supplier account and address has been used for the Receiver General to reduce the length of the supplier list.

INSTRUCTIONS FOR SETUP

Set up the **company accounts** in Sage 50 using the Business Information, Chart of Accounts, Balance Sheet, Income Statement, Post-Closing Trial Balance and Supplier, Customer, Employee and Inventory Information provided above for April 30, 2018. Instructions to assist you in setting up the company accounts follow. The setup of the Inventory Ledger is given in detail. Abbreviated instructions are included for the remaining steps. Refer to the Love It Again (Chapter 4), Air Care Services (Chapter 7) and Northern Lights (Chapter 9) applications if you need more detailed explanations for other ledgers. Page references for the coverage of these topics in earlier chapters are included in this chapter.

KEYSTROKES FOR SETUP

Creating Company Files

We will create the company files from scratch. Once we create the files and define the defaults, we will add the accounts; define linked accounts for all ledgers; set up additional features; create supplier, customer, employee and inventory records; and add historical data.

Start the **Sage 50 program**. The Select Company window should be open.

NOTES
Refer to page 206 for detailed instructions on creating company files.

NOTES
Save your work and update your backup file frequently as you complete the setup.

NOTES
You cannot complete the company setup in multi-user mode. Many of the settings options are dimmed and unavailable when you are working in multi-user mode.

NOTES
Add your own name to the company name to personalize your data files.

NOTES
Because we selected Ontario as the province, some defaults will be added to the data file. WCB will be renamed WSIB.

NOTES
If you later change the province, you may have to change some settings linked to the province selection.

NOTES
The default date format for new companies is determined by your own computer system settings and is displayed below the date fields. Day, month or year may be first.

NOTES
You can select another folder by clicking Browse to open the folder path screen and then clicking the folder you want to use. Click OK to return to the File Name screen.
If the folder you want does not yet exist, click the folder into which you want to place the new folder and click OK. Type VELOCITY\ at the end of the path in the Location field.

Click   **Create A New Company**.

Click   **OK** to open the Setup wizard welcome screen.

Click   **Next** to open the Company Name and Address screen. The cursor is in the Name field.

Type   VeloCity (and your own name)   **Press** (tab) to advance to the Street 1 address field.

Type   27 Gearing Ave. **Press** (tab). **Press** (tab) again.

Type   Niagara on the Lake **Press** (tab).

Type   o to enter the province code (ON) and province (Ontario).

Click   the **Postal Code field**.

Type   l0s1j0 **Press** (tab).

Type   Canada **Press** (tab).

Type   9054688356 **Press** (tab) to enter the first phone number.

Type   8884688356 **Press** (tab) to enter the second phone number.

Type   9054689100 to enter the fax number.

Click   **Next** to open the company Dates window.

The cursor is in the Fiscal Year Start field, the date on which the business begins its fiscal year. VeloCity closes its books quarterly and is beginning a new quarter in May. To be certain that you have the correct year, type the date in text style using four digits for the year. Until we change the date format, it is displayed in the short form.

Enter   the **fiscal dates** as follows:

- Fiscal Start: May 1, 2018
- Earliest Transaction Date: May 1, 2018
- Fiscal End: July 31, 2018

Remember that you can edit the company information and fiscal dates later from the Setup menu, Settings option (choose Company and Information).

Click   **Next**.

Click   **Let Me Build The List Of Accounts Myself....** **Click Next**.

Click   **Yes** to confirm your selection and continue to the industry type list.

Choose   **Retail** as the Industry for the business. **Click Next**.

Type   VELOCITY to replace the default entry for the file name.

Drag through Tess in the folder name field (or the folder you last worked with).

Type   VELOCITY\

If you are using an alternative location for your company files, substitute the appropriate path, folder or drive in the example.

Click Browse to locate the folder you want or type the complete path in the File Location field (e.g., type C:\SageData16\VELOCITY\).

Click   **Next**.

Click   **Yes** to confirm that you are creating a new folder.

Click   **Finish** to save the information. **Be patient**, and wait for Sage 50 to finish creating the data files.

Click   **Close** to close the Setup wizard screen.

Click   **Show This Window On Startup** in the Welcome/Getting Started window and **click Close** to close the Welcome window.

The Home window has the name VELOCITY in the title bar and non-accounting term labels for the modules in the Modules pane list. The program will automatically set up defaults based on the information you have just entered.

Preparing the System

The next step involves changing the defaults. Change the defaults to suit your own work environment, such as selecting your printer or choosing forms for cheques, invoices or statements. The keystroke instructions are given for computer-generated cheques, invoices and statements. Refer to the Business Information Chart on page 623 for the company default settings.

Changing the User Preference Settings

You should make the following changes to the User Preferences from the Setup menu. Refer to Chapter 4, page 80, for assistance if necessary.

Choose   the **Setup menu** and **click User Preferences** to open the Options.

Click   **Use Accounting Terms** and **Automatically Save Changes To Supplier....**

Verify   that **Automatically Download Updates** is **not selected**.

You can show Home window ledger record balances by the session date or the latest transaction date, and automatically recalculate these balances or refresh them manually when you want. Make the selections you prefer for your own use.

Click   **View**.

Click   **After Changing Session Date** for **Daily Business Manager** and for **Checklists** to turn off these features and remove the ✓s.

Click   **Show Change Session Date At Startup**.

Hiding the Division module and Time & Billing is optional. You can finish the history without this step because they have no linked accounts.

Click Division in the Pages column and Time & Billing in the Features column if you choose to hide them.

Transaction Confirmation should be selected by default.

Click   **Pop-ups** and **choose** the **messages** you want to display and hide.

Click   **OK** to save the settings and return to the Home window.

After changing these settings, modules have accounting term names. The user preference settings can be modified at any time by repeating these steps.

Changing Company Defaults

Correcting Company Information

The first steps in setting up the company data files apply to the Company module. We will work from that window.

Click OK at any time to save the settings and close the Settings window. To continue later, you can use the Settings icon to access Settings.

Click   **Company** in the Modules pane list to change the Home window.

Click   the **Settings icon** [icon], or **choose** the **Setup menu** and **click Settings**.

Click   **Information**.

Click   the **Business No. field**. **Type** 335 677 829 RT0001

Changing System Settings

Click   **System**. Use the following System settings:

- Use Cheque No. As The Source Code For Cash Purchases And Sales
- Do Not Allow Transactions Dated Before May 1, 2018
- Allow Transactions In The Future (Beyond The Session Date)
- Warn If Transactions Are More Than 7 Days In The Future
- Warn If Accounts Are Not Balanced When Entering A New Month

Changing Backup Settings

Click   **Backup**. Use the following Backup settings:

- Semi-monthly Backup Frequency
- Display A Backup Reminder When Closing This Company

Click   **Automatically Back Up This File** to **remove** the ✓. We do not want to schedule automatic backups for instructional files.

Changing Features Settings

VeloCity uses all features of the program except Divisions — orders, quotes and language options should be selected. Division and Packing Slips may be left unselected.

Click   **Features**.

Click   **each feature** to change its setting.

Changing Default Settings for Forms

Click   **Forms** to display the defaults.

Use the Forms options to set up the automatic numbering and printing of all cheques and invoices. They apply only to numerical invoices.

Typing the next number from the source documents allows automatic numbering to take over from the manual system. Using automatic numbering reduces the risk of typing and recording an incorrect invoice or cheque number even when you are not printing cheques and invoices through the program. For VeloCity, the next invoice is #2470.

Click   1 in the **Invoices Next Form Number field**. **Type** 2470

Click   the **Sales Quotes Next Form Number field**. **Type** 56

Click   the **Sales Orders Next Form Number field**. **Type** 248

Click   the **Receipts Next Form Number field**. **Type** 812

Click   the **Customer Deposits Next Form Number field**. **Type** 21

Click   the **Purchase Orders Next Form Number field**. **Type** 38

Click   the **Employee Direct Deposit Stubs Next Form Number field**.

Type 25

Leave selected the option to verify number sequences for all forms so that the program will warn you if you skip or duplicate a number.

Click a check box to add other features or to turn off an option once it is selected. The ✓ in the appropriate boxes indicates a feature is being used.

The option to Confirm Printing/E-mail will warn you to print before posting a transaction. When printing invoices, statements or cheques you should include the company address, unless it is already printed on your forms.

If you print or e-mail invoices and cheques through the computer, you should turn on the option to Confirm Printing/E-mail.

We want to allow batch printing, printing several forms at once after posting instead of one at a time while entering a transaction.

Click   the **Print In Batches check box** for each form to add a ✓ to each box.

We should also check for duplicate numbers. This control is not selected by default.

Click   the **Check For Duplicates check box** for Invoices and Receipts.

Changing Date Format Settings

Click   **Date Format**.

We want to use the long date form for all dates on the screen to verify that we are entering dates correctly. For the reports, you may use either the long or short form. MM (month) should be the first entry in the Short Date Format field.

Choose   **MM dd yyyy** from the Short Date drop-down list.

Click   **Long Dates** as the setting for On The Screen, Use.

Adding the Company Logo

Click   **Logo**. **Click Browse**. **Click Computer** in the folders and links pane on the left-hand side.

Double-click   **C:**. Then **double-click SageData16** to open this folder.

Double-click   the **LOGOS folder**.

Double-click   **VELO.BMP** or **VELO** to enter this file name. The picture and file name should be added to the Logo Settings screen.

Changing Default Names

VeloCity uses the additional information fields in journals. You can label these fields. However, you must use the same names for all journals. We will therefore enter a generic label for the Additional Information field.

NOTES
Many invoices include the alpha or letter portion of the invoice number on the preprinted invoice form. You could then enter the next number from the numeric portion in the Invoices Number field. Alphanumeric invoice numbers, such as VC-399, cannot be increased automatically by the computer.

NOTES
If you hide Time & Billing, the next number for time slips will not be included on the Forms screen. You can leave the field blank if you are not hiding the feature.

WARNING!
Check that the short date format begins with month (MM) so that your dates will match the ones we use for source documents.

Click   **Names**:

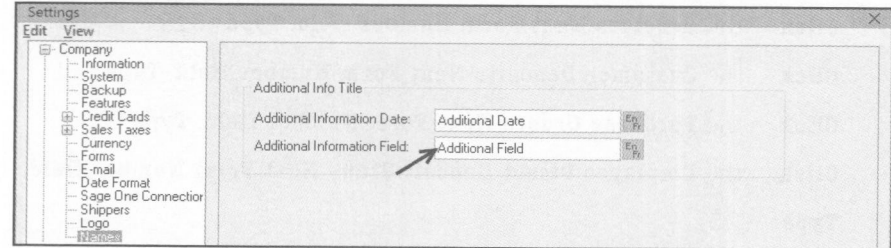

Drag through   **Additional Field** and **type**   Ref. Number

Click   **OK** to save the new information and return to the Home window.

Many of the other settings require linked accounts. Therefore, we will create all the General Ledger accounts before entering the remaining settings.

Preparing the General Ledger

The next stage in setting up an accounting system involves preparing the General Ledger for operation. This stage involves

1. organizing all accounting reports and records (this step has been completed)
2. creating new accounts and adding opening balances
3. printing reports to check the accuracy of your records

Creating New Accounts

The next step is to create the accounts, including the non-postable accounts. Remember to enter the correct type of account. For postable accounts, you should also indicate whether you want to omit accounts with zero balances from financial statements. You need to refer to the company Chart of Accounts on page 624 to complete this step. While creating the accounts, keep the Accounts window open in the background for reference.

Current Earnings is the only predefined account, and you do not need to edit it.

> Refer to The Format of Financial Statements (page 85) for a review of these topics, if needed. Refer to the instructions in the Love It Again application, pages 89–94, if you need help with creating accounts. You can use the Accounts window or the Setup Guide.

Click   the **Chart of Accounts icon** to open the Accounts window.

Click   ▢ to maximize the Accounts window.

If the accounts are not displayed by name or by type, you should change the view. Click the Display By Type tool or choose the View menu and click Type.

Click   the **Create tool** ▢ in the Accounts window tool bar or **choose** the **File menu** and **click Create**.

Drag the ledger window to a screen position so that both the list of accounts in the Accounts window and the ledger window are visible. This will make it easier to monitor your progress.

Type   the **account number**. **Press** tab and **type** the **account name**.

Click   the correct **account type**. Remember subgroup accounts (A) must be followed by a subgroup total (S).

Click   **Omit From Financial Statements If Balance Is Zero** to select this option.

Allow Division Allocations will be selected by default for all postable revenue and expense accounts, so you do not need to change this option, even if you use divisions. You will enter the account balances in the next stage.

When all the information is correct, you must save your account.

Click   [Create Another] to save the new account and advance to a blank ledger account window.

Create   the **other accounts** by repeating these procedures.

Close   the **General Ledger window** when you have entered all the accounts on page 624, or when you want to end your session.

After entering all the accounts, you should check for mistakes in account number, name, type and order.

Click   ✓ or **choose** the **File menu** and **click Check The Validity Of Accounts** to check for errors in account sequence such as missing subgroup totals, headings or totals. The first error will be reported.

Correct the **error** and **check** the **validity** again. Repeat this step until the accounts are in logical order.

Display or **print** your updated **Chart of Accounts** at this stage to check for accuracy of account names and numbers. **Choose** the **Reports menu** and **click Display Chart of Accounts**. Compare the report with the chart on page 624 and make corrections as needed.

Entering Historical Account Balances

The opening historical balances for VeloCity can be found in the Post-Closing Trial Balance dated April 30, 2018 (page 626). All Income Statement accounts have zero balances because the books were closed at the end of the first quarter. Headings, totals and subgroup totals (i.e., the non-postable accounts) do not have balances. Remember to put any forced balance amounts into the *Test Balance Account*.

Open   the account information window for **1060 Bank: Niagara Trust Chequing**, the first account requiring a balance.

Click   the **Opening Balance field**.

Type   the **balance**.

Correct the **information** if necessary by repeating the above steps.

Click   the **Next button** ▷ to advance to the next ledger account window.

Enter   **negative numbers for accounts that decrease the total** in a group or section (e.g., *Allowance for Doubtful Accounts*, *Accum Deprec*, *GST/HST Paid on Purchases*). These account balances are indicated with a minus sign (–) in the Balance Sheet on page 625.

Repeat these **procedures** to **enter** the **balances** for the remaining accounts in the Post-Closing Trial Balance on page 626. The *Test Balance Account* should have a zero balance.

Close   the **Ledger window**.

After entering all account balances, you should display the Trial Balance to check them against the amounts on page 626. You can do this from the Accounts window.

NOTES
If you use the Setup Guide to create accounts, you can accept the default settings for omitting zero balances and allowing allocations.

NOTES
We will change the account class for expense accounts when we change the class for other accounts that are used as linked accounts.

WARNING!
It is important to have the accounts in logical order at this stage. You will be unable to display some reports when the accounts are not in logical order, so you will not be able to check some of your work. You cannot finish the history if accounts are not in logical order.

NOTES
If you want to use the Retained Earnings linked account to enter account balance discrepancies, you must delay entering account balances until after you enter General Linked Accounts (refer to pages 225–226).

NOTES
For account 1140 Bank: USD Chequing, enter $9 500, the balance in Canadian dollars. The USD balance will be added after we set up currencies.

Choose the **Reports menu** and **click Trial Balance**. **Click** the **Print tool**.

Close the **display** when finished. Leave the Accounts window open.

Check all **accounts** and **amounts** and **make corrections** if necessary.

Defining Account Classes

Defining bank accounts involves changing the account class to Bank and indicating the currency for the accounts and the cheque and deposit number sequences. If you use online banking, you must also enter the bank name, account numbers and Web site. We must also change the class for *Undeposited Cash and Cheques* to either Bank or Cash to use it as the linked account for receipts. Cash is the appropriate selection. Remember that the bank account class changes must be saved before we can enter the next cheque numbers. Changes are saved automatically when we open the next ledger record.

In addition, we must define the account class for the credit card asset and the credit card payable accounts and change the account class for expense accounts. We will make all these changes before continuing the setup.

Double-click **1030 Undeposited Cash and Cheques** to open the ledger.

Click the **Class Options tab**.

Choose **Cash** from the drop-down list of account classes.

Click the **Next Account button** to open the ledger for account **1060**.

Choose **Bank** from the list of account classes.

Click the **Next Deposit Number field**. **Type** 18

Click the **Next Account button**.

Choose **Bank** as the account class for *1080 Bank: Niagara Trust Savings*.

Click **Chequing** (Account Type field). **Click Savings** from the list.

Click the **Next Account button** to **open** the ledger for **1120 Bank: Visa and Interac**.

Choose **Credit Card Receivable** as the account class.

Click the **Next Account button** to **open** the ledger for **1140 Bank: USD Chequing**.

Choose **Bank** as the account class.

Click the **Select account list arrow**.

Click **2250 Credit Card Payable** to open its ledger screen at the Class Options tab screen.

Choose **Credit Card Payable** as the account class. Credit Card Receivable is not available as a class option for the liability account.

Click the **Select account list arrow** again and **choose 5010 Advertising and Promotion**.

Select **Operating Expense** as the account class.

Click . **Select** the **Operating Expense** class for all postable expense accounts except the cost of goods subgroup accounts (#5040–5110).

Close the **General Ledger window** and the **Accounts window**.

NOTES
Refer to the chart on page 623 for bank information and to page 218 for a review of Bank class accounts.

NOTES
We must define 1030 Undeposited Cash and Cheques as a Bank or Cash class account in order to enter it as the linked bank account for Receivables. Cash is the most appropriate selection.
Both Bank and Cash class accounts are available in the Deposit To field for cash sales and receipts.

NOTES
To open the ledger for Credit Card Payable, you can click the Next Account button repeatedly or choose the account from the Select Account list arrow.

NOTES
Leave the account class for all accounts from 5040 to 5110 unchanged (set to Cost of Goods Sold class) so that you can create Gross Margin Income Statements.
If you used the Setup Guide, you must change the class for COGS accounts but not for other expense accounts.

Additional Company Default Settings

Adding a Foreign Currency

VeloCity purchases some inventory items from suppliers in the United States and must set up the company files to allow transactions in USD, United States dollars. We will set up the foreign currency now because we need this information for bank account and supplier and customer settings.

Click   the **Settings icon** and **Company**.

Click   **Currency** under Company to open the Currency Information window:

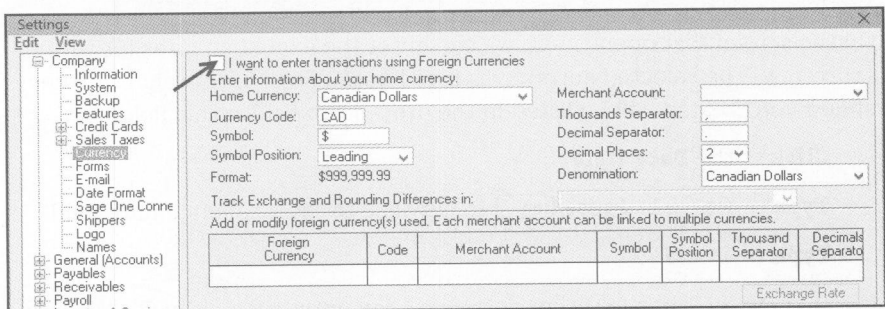

Canadian Dollars is the default in the Home Currency field, and its code, symbol, format and so on are added. You enter the other currencies in the columns in the lower half of the screen, but first you must turn on the option to use other currencies.

Click   **I Want To Enter Transactions Using Foreign Currencies**.

Exchange rates vary from day to day and even within the day. When purchases and payments are made at different times, they are subject to different exchange rates — as we demonstrated in the Maple Leaf Rags and Shady Corners applications (Chapters 12 and 13). Exchange rate differences may result in a gain — when the rate drops before a payment is made or when the rate increases before a payment is received from a customer — or a loss — when the rate increases before a payment is made or when the rate drops before a customer makes a payment. These differences are tracked in the linked account designated on this screen. Rounding differences may also result in gains and losses because the amounts are recorded with two decimal places and exchange rates usually have several significant digits. The account for these differences may be an expense account or a revenue account. VeloCity uses a revenue account.

Click   the **list arrow** for **Track Exchange And Rounding Differences In**.

Both revenue and expense accounts are available for linking.

Click   **4120 Exchange Rate Differences** to enter the linked account.

The next step is to identify the foreign currency or currencies.

Click   the **Foreign Currency field**. **Type** U

Click   the **List icon** for the field to open the list of currencies:

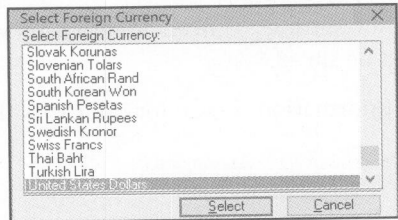

The list of currencies opens and United States Dollars should be selected.

> **Scroll down** if necessary, and **double-click United States Dollars** to add it to the Currency Information screen. The currency code, symbol and format are added for the selected currency. Accept the defaults.

> **Click**   the **Exchange Rate button**:

NOTES

If you have a Web site that you use for exchange rate information, you can enter it here as well. Then, with your Internet connection active, click the Web tool to access the Web site directly and obtain current rates. The Web tool appears on the Exchange Rate list screen that you access by clicking the Exchange Rate tool beside the Exchange Rate field in the journals.

On the screen that opens next, we can enter the exchange rates for various dates for each currency. The selected currency is listed in the Select A Foreign Currency field. All currencies you created will be listed in the drop-down list for this field.

> **Click**   the **Date field**.

> **Type**   05 01 **Press** (tab) to advance to the Exchange Rate field.

> **Type**   1.35

If you know the rates for other dates, you can enter them as well. Otherwise, you can enter current rates in the journals, as we did in the previous chapters. These rates will be added to the list on this screen.

To ensure that you do not use an old exchange rate that is no longer accurate, you should turn on the reminder that warns if the rate is out of date. A one-day period for updating should be sufficient.

> **Click**   **Display A Reminder If The Exchange Rate Is**.

> **Accept**   **One Day Old** as the time interval.

Now every time the transaction date is one day past the date of the rate previously used, the program will warn you and give you an opportunity to change the rate. If the rate has not changed, you can accept the old rate.

> **Click**   **OK** to return to the Currency Settings screen.

Setting Up Credit Cards

NOTES

Refer to the Business Information Chart on page 623 for credit card details. To review credit card setup, refer to page 220 for additional information.

VeloCity accepts Visa credit card payments from customers as well as debit cards (Interac). The store also uses a Visa card to pay for some purchases. Setting up credit cards includes naming them, identifying the linked accounts and entering fees associated with the cards.

> **Click**   **Credit Cards** for the next step. You will be asked for confirmation:

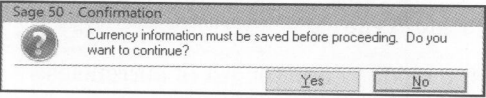

> **Click**   **Yes** to save the updated currency settings. Currencies are used with other settings so they must first be saved.

> **Click**   **Used** to open the Credit Card Information screen for the cards that the business uses.

> **Click**   the **Credit Card Name field**.

> **Type**   Visa **Press** (tab) to move to the Payable Account field.

Press (enter) for the list of available accounts.

Double-click 2250 to add the account and move to the Expense Account field.

Press (enter) to open the account list.

Double-click 5030.

Click Accepted under Credit Cards to open the Credit Card Information screen for the cards that the business accepts from customers.

Click the **Credit Card Name field**.

Type Visa **Press** (tab) to advance to the Currency field.

Click the **List icon** 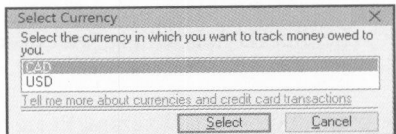 for the Currency field to open the list of currencies:

Sage 50 Premium version accepts credit cards in a foreign currency. You must use separate linked accounts for cards in different currencies.

Click Select to return to the Cards Accepted screen. **Press** (tab). The cursor advances to the Asset Account field.

Press (enter) to list the accounts available for linking.

Double-click 1120 to choose and add the credit card bank account. **Press** (tab).

Type 2.5 to enter the discount fee. **Press** (tab).

Press (enter) to list the accounts available for linking as the Expense Account.

Double-click 5030 to choose and enter the account.

Enter Interac as the name, **1120** as the Asset account, **0** as the %, and **5030** as the Expense Account to set up the debit card.

Click Processing Services only if you want to set up this service:

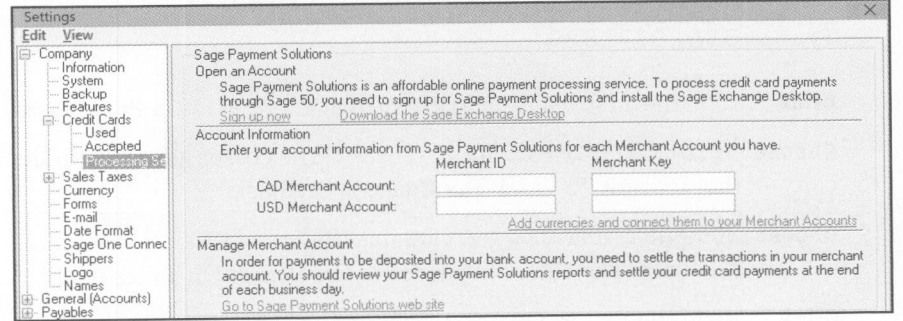

If you want to use the **credit card processing** service feature, you can use the merchant ID and key provided in Chapter 13 (read the margin Notes).

Click the Merchant ID field and enter your number. Press Tab. Type your Merchant Key in this field.

Setting Up Sales Taxes

VeloCity charges and pays GST on books and HST on all other purchases. We will set up codes for these two taxes. We want to generate reports on both taxes.

WARNING!
You must choose a Credit Card Payable or Bank class account as the Payable Account for cards used.
Although accounts in other classes appear on the Select Account list, selecting them will generate an error message when you try to save the entries.

PRO VERSION
The Pro version does not allow credit cards in foreign currencies. You will not have the currency list screen or the column to select the currency.

NOTES
You must choose a Credit Card Receivable or Bank class account as the Asset Account for cards accepted.

NOTES
You can enter these account details for processing credit cards:
Merchant ID: 651259884634
Merchant Key: B8B9O4S6E2K2
Remember that when you set up for processing credit cards, you must follow through with the processing for all Visa sales. And you must enter 4111111111111111 as the Visa number and leave your Internet connection on.
For Interac (debit card) sales, process the card transaction manually (refer to page 519).

NOTES
Refer to the Business Information Chart on page 623 for sales tax information. Refer to page 222 for a review of sales taxes.

Both taxes are linked to the GST/HST accounts because a single remittance to the Receiver General for Canada is made for both taxes; only the rates are different.

Click   **Sales Taxes** under Company. There are settings for tax names and codes.

Click   **Taxes** to access the Taxes information screen:

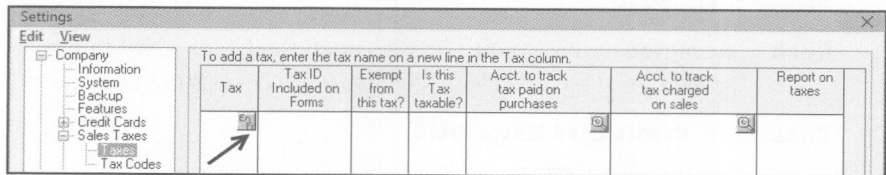

Press   (tab) to advance to the Tax field on the Taxes screen where you should enter the name of the tax. We will enter the HST first.

Type   HST **Press** (tab) to advance to the Tax ID field where we enter the business number.

Type   335 677 829 **Press** (tab) to advance to the **Exempt From This Tax?** column.

VeloCity is not tax exempt for HST, so the default, No, is correct. HST is also not taxable in Ontario (no other tax is charged on HST).

> **NOTES**
> PST is still charged separately on insurance in Ontario. Because this tax is not refundable, you do not need to track it or create a tax code for it. It will be included directly in the expense or asset component of the purchase.

Click   🔍, the **List icon for Acct. To Track Tax Paid On Purchases**.

Choose   **2670 GST/HST Paid on Purchases**. The cursor advances to the field for the Account To Track Tax Charged On Sales.

Choose   **2650 GST/HST Charged on Sales** from the List icon 🔍 list of accounts. The cursor advances to the Report On Taxes field.

Click   **No** to change the default entry to Yes.

Press   (tab) so you can enter the information for GST.

VeloCity is not exempt from GST. The ID number and linked accounts are the same as for HST. GST is not taxable and the tax is refundable.

Type   GST **Press** (tab) to advance to the Tax ID field.

Type   335 677 829

Click   🔍, the **List icon for Acct. To Track Tax Paid On Purchases**.

Choose   **2670 GST/HST Paid on Purchases**. The cursor advances to the field for the Account To Track Tax Charged On Sales.

Choose   **2650 GST/HST Charged on Sales** from the List icon 🔍 list of accounts. The cursor advances to the Report On Taxes field.

Click   **No** in the Report On Taxes column to change the entry to Yes.

Entering Tax Codes

Click   **Tax Codes** to open the next information screen:

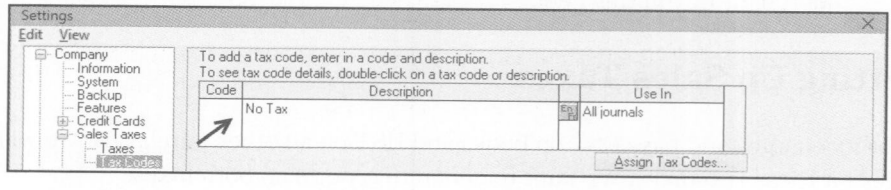

A single code, No Tax, is created as a default.

We need to create tax codes for sales and purchases when HST alone is charged and when only GST applies. There are also purchases with HST included, so we need a code for this situation as well (e.g., gasoline is priced with all taxes included).

Click   the **Code column** below the blank on the first line.

Type   H **Press** (tab) to move to the Description field.

Press   (enter) or **double-click** to open the Tax Code Details screen:

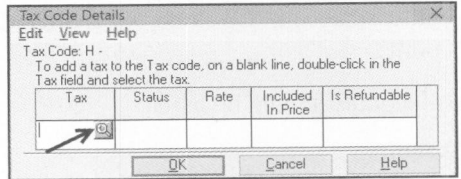

Click   the **Tax field List icon** to open the list of taxes entered.

Both taxes from the Taxes screen appear on the list.

Click   **Select** because HST is already selected. You will return to the Tax Code Details.

Defaults are entered for the remaining fields. The **Status** is **Taxable** and the tax is **not included** — these are correct — tax is calculated and charged and is not included in the price.

Click   the **Rate field. Type** 13

Click   **No** in the Is Refundable column to change the entry to Yes.

Click   **OK** to return to the Tax Codes screen for additional codes.

The description "HST @ 13%" appears beside the code H and the tax is used in all journals. You can edit the description if you want. If the tax were not refundable, non-refundable would be added to the description automatically. We are ready to enter the second code, to apply only GST.

Press   (tab) until you advance to the next line in the Code column.

Type   G **Press** (tab) to move to the Description field.

Press   (enter) to open the Tax Code Details screen.

Click   the **Tax field List icon** .

Select   **GST**. Taxable and not included are the correct selections.

Type   5 in the **Rate field**.

Click   **No** in the Is Refundable column to change the entry to Yes.

Click   **OK** to return to the Tax Codes screen. The description "GST @ 5%" has been added.

Press   (tab) until you advance to the next line in the Code column, below G.

Type   IN **Press** (tab) to move to the Description field.

Press   (enter) or **double-click** to open the Tax Code Details screen.

Enter   **HST** as the tax, and **13%** as the rate. Taxable as the status is correct.

Click   **No** in the Included In Price column to change the entry to Yes.

Click   **No** in the Is Refundable column to change the entry to Yes.

NOTES
If you need to remove a tax code detail line, click the line to be removed, choose the Edit menu and click Remove Line.

Click   **OK** to return to the Tax Codes screen. The description "HST @ 13%, included" appears beside the code IN. **Click OK** to close the Settings.

Updating Bank Account Settings

Adding Currency to a Bank Account

We need to complete more steps for bank accounts — identify the currency, and enter the next cheque number. By default, the home currency is selected. This is correct for the main chequing account and for the credit card account. We need to change the currency setting for the USD chequing account.

Click   the **Search tool** 🔍. The accounts should be listed.

Double-click   **1140 Bank: USD Chequing**.

Click   the **Class Options tab** — the current class setting is Bank.

Click   the **Currency list arrow**:

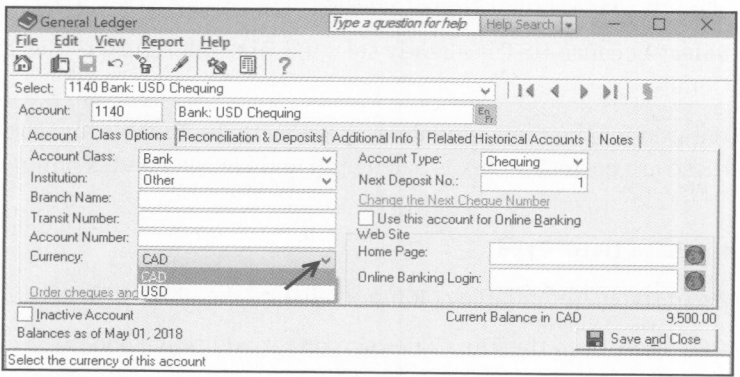

Once we identify an account as a bank account and allow foreign currency transactions, we identify the currency for the account on the Class Options tab screen.

Click   **USD**. Zero now appears as the balance amount for the USD currency.

Click   **Change The Next Cheque Number**. You will not be allowed to continue:

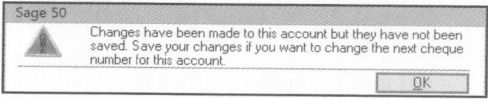

Click   **OK** to return to the ledger window; we must first save the changes.

Click   the **Save tool** 💾 or **choose** the **File menu** and **click Save**:

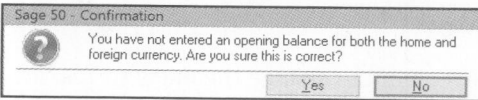

Because we have entered the balance in only the home currency, we are now asked to confirm that this is correct. It is not.

Click   **No** to return to the ledger window so we can add the USD balance.

Click   the **Account tab** to return to the Opening Balance fields. A second field has been added for the balance in USD.

Click   the **Opening Balance In USD field**. **Type**   7120

Click   the **Save tool** 💾.

You should now be able to add the next cheque number in the sequence.

Click   the **Class Options tab**.

Click   **Change The Next Cheque Number** to open the cheque Form settings:

The bank account we started from is selected, so the cheque number field is available.

Click   the **Next Cheque No. field. Type** 346

Click   **1060 Bank: Niagara Trust Chequing** in the left panel under Cheques.

Click   the **Next Cheque No. field. Type** 101

We will make additional printer setting changes before proceeding, while the Reports & Forms window is open.

Changing Other Printer Settings

Reports and forms settings apply only to the data file that you are using. They must be set for each data file separately, and the settings are saved with each file.

Click Reports or click the form for which you want to enter settings.

Choose the printer you will be using for reports. Change the margins if necessary. Choose fonts and type sizes for the report from the lists. Click Setup to choose other options for your printer, such as paper size, two-sided printing and so on.

Click OK to save your settings and return to the previous Printer setting screen.

Each type of form — cheques, invoices and so on — has its own setup.

Click   **Invoices** to open the settings for printing invoices.

Check   that the **file locations** for the forms are correct or dimmed.

For **E-mail** and **Printed Forms**, to avoid a file location error message, the location in the Form field should be the Forms folder in your Sage 50 Premium Accounting Version 2016 program folder.

As you did for reports, select the printer and set the margins, font and type size to match the forms you are using. Preprinted forms were included as part of the program installation and are located in the Forms folder in the main Sage 50 program folder. You should Print Subtotals In Invoices.

To preview invoices you must select **Custom Form**.

If you want to customize the invoice form choose Custom Form and click **Customize Form**.

WARNING!
The entries in the Form fields should be valid locations. The Form field references should be the Forms folder in your Sage 50 Premium Accounting Version 2016 program folder.

NOTES
You can change other printer settings at this stage if you want, or you can change them at any time as needed.

NOTES
From the Home window, choose the Setup menu and click Reports & Forms. The printer setting options for reports are given. More information about changing printer settings is available in Appendix E on the Student DVD.

NOTES
Refer to Appendix F on the Student DVD if you want to customize printed invoices.

NOTES
Choosing the generic form name in the Description field should automatically provide the correct form file locations.

To print labels, click Labels and enter the size of the labels and the number that are placed across the page.

To set the printer options for cheques or other forms, click the form you want and make the necessary changes.

Click   **OK** to save the information when all the settings are correct. You can change printer settings at any time.

Close   the **Ledger window** to continue entering the settings.

Entering Ledger Default Settings

General Ledger Settings

Most of the settings for the General Ledger are already correct. VeloCity is not setting up budgets or departments yet, and it does not use the additional ledger record fields. Using and showing numbers for accounts and four-digit account numbers, the default settings, are also correct for VeloCity. We need to add linked accounts.

> **Choose** the **Setup menu** and **click Settings** to continue entering the settings.

Defining Linked Accounts

Linked accounts are General Ledger accounts that are affected by entries in other journals. For example, recording an inventory purchase will update the Inventory Ledger, several General Ledger accounts and the balance owing to the supplier. Refer to page 225 for a review of linked accounts. Refer to page 87 for a review of the *Current Earnings* account. Linked accounts are also needed for other features.

Identifying General Linked Accounts

The *Current Earnings* capital account records the changes in net income resulting from sales and expenses. At the end of the fiscal period, the net income (the balance from *Current Earnings*) is transferred to the Retained Earnings capital account (*S. Ryder, Capital* is the Retained Earnings account for VeloCity) and income and expense accounts are reset to zero to prepare for the new fiscal period.

Click   **General (Accounts)**.

Click   **Linked Accounts under General (Accounts)**.

The General Ledger has two linked accounts. Both must be capital accounts.

GENERAL LINKED ACCOUNTS

Retained Earnings	3560 S. Ryder, Capital
Current Earnings	3600 Current Earnings

Type   the **account number** or **select** the **account** from the drop-down list.

Payables Ledger Settings

Click   **Payables** and then **click Address**.

Enter   **Niagara on the Lake**, **Ontario** and **Canada** as the default city, province and country for suppliers.

Click   **Options**.

CLASSIC VIEW
 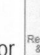

You can access the Linked Accounts screens for any ledger directly. Right-click a journal icon to select it for the ledger you want and then click the Settings tool.

For example, to access General Linked Accounts, right-click the General Journal or the Reconciliation & Deposits icon,

Click the Settings tool . The General Linked Accounts screen opens. If no icon is selected, click General in the Select drop-down list.

Follow the same steps for other ledgers. Start with the Sales or Receipts icon to open the linked accounts screen for the Receivables Ledger, and so on.

NOTES

Refer to page 225 to review General linked accounts.

NOTES

You can create new accounts from any Linked Accounts screen by typing a new account number in the Account field and pressing *tab* to start the Add An Account wizard.

NOTES

Refer to page 226 if you want to review Payables settings.

PRO VERSION

Remember that the term Vendors will replace Suppliers.

You should change the intervals for the aging of accounts. Some suppliers offer discounts for payment within 5, 10 or 15 days. Discounts from one-time suppliers are calculated on before-tax amounts.

Set   the **aging** intervals at **15**, **30** and **60** days.

Click   **Calculate Discounts Before Tax For One-Time Suppliers**.

Setting Up Import Duties

Although most goods imported from the United States are not subject to tariffs or import duties because of NAFTA (the North American Free Trade Agreement), you should know how to set up this feature. We will set up the program to charge duty but set the rate at zero so that no duty will be applied on purchases. You must activate the Duty option before creating supplier records so that you can indicate in the supplier records those suppliers that supply goods on which duty is charged. Without these two steps, the duty fields in the Purchases Journal will be unavailable.

Click   **Duty** to access the settings we need:

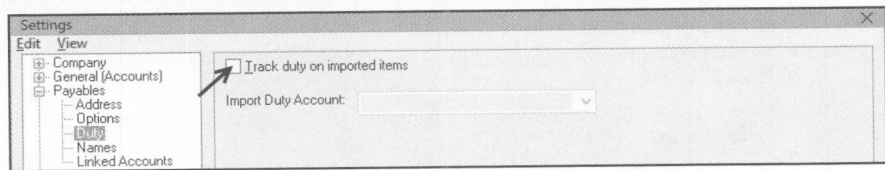

Click   **Track Duty On Imported Items** to use the feature and open the linked Account field.

A Payables Account is linked to import duties for the liability to the Receiver General.

Click   **2220 Import Duty Payable** from the Import Duty Account drop-down list.

Changing Payables Terminology

Sage 50 chooses a set of terms that is appropriate for the type of business. These terms can be modified by the user on the Names Settings screen. For the companies in this text, we have accepted the default terms Sage 50 applies for the industry. To change them,

Click   **Names** to open the settings:

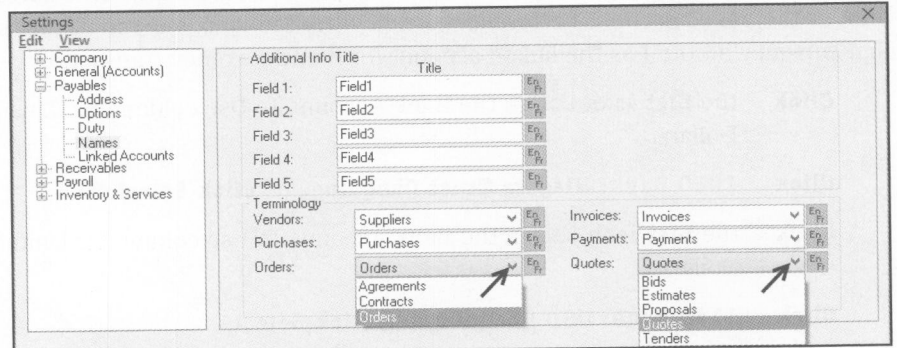

The upper part of the screen has five fields for the additional information you can add to the Payroll Ledger records. You can rename these fields if you want to use them.

The lower part of the screen has drop-down lists of terms for the various icons in the module. The names you select here will appear throughout the program as the names for icons, fields and reports. The drop-down lists for Orders and Quotes provide the options for naming these. For the terms you can choose for Vendors, Purchases and Invoices, refer to Chapter 7, page 227.

WARNING!

Sage 50 will not allow you to remove an account while it is being used as a linked account. When you try to remove an account, click OK in the Warning window to return to the Accounts window. First, turn the linking function off by deleting the account in the Linked Accounts window. Then delete the account balance and, finally, remove the account in the Accounts window. You cannot remove an account if it has a balance or if journal entries have been posted to it.

PRO VERSION

pro The Terminology part of the Names Settings screen is not included in the Pro version because you cannot change the terms used.

NOTES

You can change the terminology used for Vendors, Purchases, Invoices, Orders and Quotes from the Names Settings screen if you want.

NOTES

Refer to Appendix B, page A–16, for a list of the terms used for different types of industry.

To change the terms, click the term you want to change and choose a different term from the drop-down list.

Identifying the Payables Linked Accounts

VeloCity uses *Bank: Niagara Trust Chequing* as its principal linked bank account for all home currency cheque transactions in the subsidiary Payables and Payroll ledgers.

PAYABLES	
Bank Account to Use for Canadian Dollars	1060 Bank: Niagara Trust Chequing
Bank Account to Use for United States Dollars	1140 Bank: USD Chequing
Accounts Payable	2200 Accounts Payable
Freight Expense	5090 Freight Expense
Early Payment Purchase Discount	5100 Purchase Discounts
Prepayments and Prepaid Orders	1250 Purchase Prepayments

To enter the Payables Ledger linked accounts,

Click   **Linked Accounts** to display the Linked Accounts window:

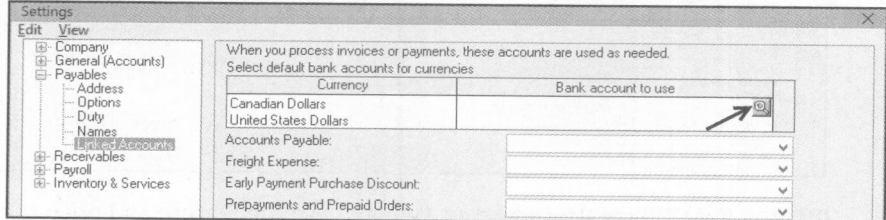

We need to identify the default General Ledger bank accounts used for payments to suppliers. Cash transactions in the Payments Journal will be posted to the bank account you select in the journal window. Bank and Cash class accounts are available in the journals, and the principal linked account defined here will be selected as the default.

You can list the accounts available for linking by clicking the drop-down list arrow for any linked account field. Only Bank and Cash class accounts may be used in the bank fields. That is why we needed to classify the bank accounts first.

VeloCity uses two bank accounts for payments. The chequing account is the principal bank account for Canadian currency transactions, and the USD chequing account is used for transactions in United States dollars.

You can choose a separate linked account for each currency, or you may use the Canadian dollar account for more than one currency. You can select a home currency account as the linked account for foreign currency transactions, but you cannot select a foreign currency account as the linked account for home currency transactions.

Click   the **List icon** 🔍 in the Bank Account To Use column for Canadian Dollars.

Click   **1060 Bank: Niagara Trust Chequing** and **click Select**.

Click   the **List icon** 🔍 in the Bank Account To Use column for United States Dollars.

Click   **1140 Bank: USD Chequing** and **click Select**.

Enter   the **remaining linked accounts** from the chart above. **Type** the **account number** or **select** the **account** from the drop-down list.

Check the linked accounts carefully. To delete a linked account, click it to highlight it and press (del). You must complete this step of deleting the linked account before you can remove the account in the General Ledger from the Accounts window.

CLASSIC VIEW
To add the Payables Ledger linked accounts from the Home window, right-click the Purchases or the Payments Journal icon in the Home window to select it.

Click the Settings tool ⚙. Or, choose the Setup menu, then choose Settings, Payables and Linked Accounts.

NOTES
The Linked Accounts screen for VeloCity is different from the one on page 228 for Air Care Services, which uses only one currency.

WARNING!
You cannot change the currency for an account when it is used as a linked account. You can choose a home currency account as the linked account to use with a foreign currency. If you had not yet changed the currency for 1140 Bank: USD Chequing, you could still choose it as the linked account. However, you would then be unable to change the currency to USD.

NOTES
The remaining Payables linked accounts were introduced in Chapter 7. Refer to page 228 if you need to review these accounts.

Receivables Ledger Settings

Click	**Receivables** and then **click Address**.
Enter	**Niagara on the Lake**, **Ontario** and **Canada** as the default address.
Click	**Options**.

VeloCity prints the salesperson's name on all customer forms for the customer's reference in case a follow-up is required. Most customers (and inventory items) use the tax code H, so we will use this as the default for new customers. The default tax code will be preselected when we enter the customer records.

VeloCity charges 1.5 percent interest per month on accounts after 30 days (one day overdue), includes paid invoices on customer statements for 31 days (an appropriate period for the monthly statements) and uses payment terms to set aging intervals.

Enter	**10**, **30** and **60** days as the **aging** periods.
Click	**Interest Charges** to add a ✓ and turn on the calculation.
Click	**Monthly Interest Rate** to enter the way interest is calculated.
Press	(tab) to advance to the % field for Interest Charges.
Type	1.5 **Press** (tab). **Type** 1
Click	the **Tax Code For New Customers field** for the list of tax codes.
Click	**H – HST @ 13%**.
Click	**Print Salesperson On Invoices, Orders And Quotes**.

Entering Discount Settings

VeloCity offers its account customers a 2 percent after-tax discount for 10 days; full payment is due in 30 days. VeloCity does not use the line discount feature.

Click	**Discount** to open the next Receivables settings screen.
Click	the **% field** of the **Early Payment Terms** section.
Type	2 **Press** (tab).
Type	10 **Press** (tab).
Type	30
Click	**Calculate Line Discounts On Invoices ...** to turn off the feature. Sage 50 advises that this action will remove the related columns from the Sales Journal:

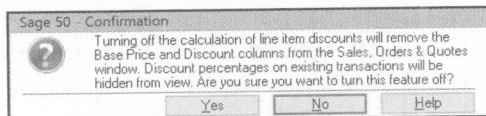

Click	**Yes** to confirm your selection.

Changing Default Comments

Click	**Comments** under Receivables.

You may add a comment or notice to all your invoices, quotes and order confirmations. You could use this feature to include payment terms, a company motto or notice of an upcoming sale. Remember that you can change the default message any

NOTES
Refer to page 229 if you need to review Receivables Ledger settings.

PRO VERSION
Line Discounts are not available in the Pro version.

time you want. You can also edit it for a particular sale or quote when you are completing the invoice. The cursor is in the Sales Invoices field.

Type `Interest @ 1.5% per month on accounts over 30 days.`

Repeat this procedure to enter comments for the other forms.

Changing Receivables Terminology

Click **Names** under Receivables:

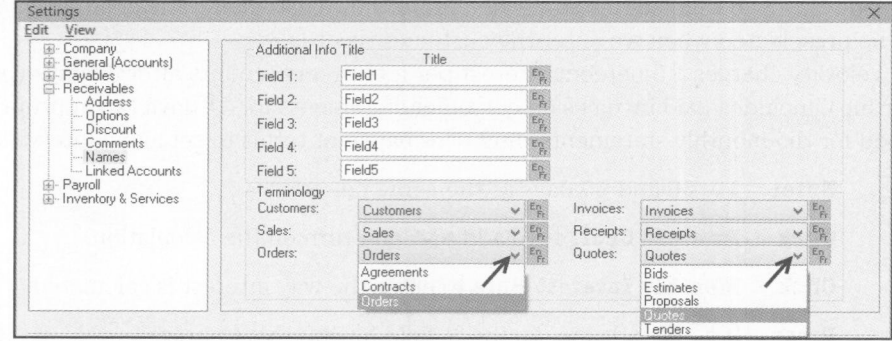

This screen has the same structure as the one for Payables additional information field names and ledger terminology.

The drop-down lists of terms for Orders and Quotes provide the options. The names you select here will appear throughout the program as the names for icons, fields and reports. For the terms you can choose for Customers, Sales and Invoices, refer to Chapter 7, page 231.

To change the terms, click the term you want to change and choose a different one from the drop-down list.

Defining the Receivables Linked Accounts

The Receivables Ledger linked accounts parallel those for the Payables Ledger.

Click **Linked Accounts** under Receivables:

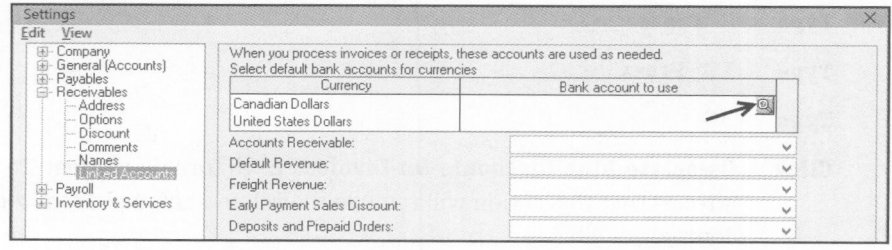

We need to identify the default General Ledger bank account used to receive payments from customers. Cash transactions in the Sales and Receipts journals will be posted to the bank account you select in the journals. The linked account will be the default, but any Bank or Cash class account may be selected in the journals.

VeloCity has several bank accounts. Cheques and cash receipts are held in the *Undeposited Cash and Cheques* clearing account and then deposited weekly to the *Bank: Niagara Trust Chequing* account. Therefore, the default Canadian bank account for receipts is *Undeposited Cash and Cheques. Bank: USD Chequing* is the default account for foreign currency customer transactions. Although most linked accounts may be used only once, one Canadian dollar bank account can be linked to the Payables, Receivables and Payroll ledgers and all currencies.

The following accounts are required as linked accounts for the Receivables Ledger:

PRO VERSION

The Terminology part of the Names Settings screen is not included in the Pro version because you cannot change the terms used.

NOTES

You can change the terminology used for Customers, Invoices, Sales, Orders and Quotes from the Names Settings screen if you want.

CLASSIC VIEW

To add the Receivables Ledger linked accounts from the Home window, right-click the Sales, Orders & Quotes or the Receipts Journal icon in the Home window to select it.

Click the Settings tool. Or, choose the Setup menu, then choose Settings, Receivables and Linked Accounts.

NOTES

The Linked Accounts screen has changed because of the second currency. You can compare it with the one on page 232 for Air Care Services.

NOTES

Any home currency Cash or Bank class account may also be linked to foreign currency receipts.

RECEIVABLES LINKED ACCOUNTS	
Bank Account to Use for Canadian Dollars	1030 Undeposited Cash and Cheques
Bank Account to Use for United States Dollars	1140 Bank: USD Chequing
Accounts Receivable	1200 Accounts Receivable
Default Revenue	do not use — leave blank
Freight Revenue	4200 Freight Revenue
Early Payment Sales Discount	4060 Sales Discounts
Deposits and Prepaid Orders	2210 Prepaid Sales and Deposits

NOTES
The linked Revenue account from the Inventory Ledger record will replace the Receivables Ledger Default Revenue account as the default for sale.

Click   the **List icon** 🔍 in the Bank Account To Use column for Canadian Dollars.

Click   **1030 Undeposited Cash and Cheques** and **click Select**.

Click   the **List icon** 🔍 in the Bank Account To Use column for United States Dollars.

Click   **1140 Bank: USD Chequing** and **click Select**.

Enter   the **remaining linked accounts** from the chart on this page. **Type** the **account number** or **select** the **account** from the drop-down list.

NOTES
The remaining linked accounts were introduced in Chapter 7. Refer to page 232 if you need to review these accounts.

Payroll Ledger Settings

At this stage, we will change the settings for Payroll Names, Income, Deductions, Taxes and Entitlements. After creating supplier and employee records, we can change the Remittance and Job Category settings.

Entering Payroll Names

Because the names we use will appear on the remaining payroll settings screens, we will define them first.

NOTES
Refer to pages 318–324 to review payroll settings if necessary.

Click   **Payroll** and then **click Names** in the list of Payroll options.

Click   **Incomes & Deductions** to access the first group of payroll names.

Many of the standard income types are mandatory and cannot be changed. These fields are on a shaded background. Some of the other default names are also correct, so you do not need to redefine them. You can leave Income 1 and Income 2, labelled "Salary" and "Commission," unchanged because VeloCity has two salaried employees and pays a sales commission to one employee. There is allowance for 20 different kinds of income in addition to the compulsory fields and 20 different payroll deductions. Each income and deduction label may have up to 12 characters.

VeloCity uses the additional income fields for bonuses, piece rate pay and taxable benefits (tuition fee payments) so that these incomes can be identified by name on the paycheque. The piece rate pay is based on completed favourable client surveys for the employees. Travel expenses repaid directly to employees are also entered as income, but they are reimbursements and will not be taxed.

VeloCity also has three payroll deductions at this time: VRSP — the Registered Retirement Savings Plan; Savings Plan — an investment plan; and Garnishee — the wages that are withheld and submitted to the Receiver General for prior years' taxes.

NOTES
Reimbursements are added to net pay (the amount of the paycheque), but are not included to calculate taxes.

Click   **Income 3 in the Name Column** to highlight the contents.

Type   No. Clients **Press** ⌨tab⌨ to advance to the Income 4 field.

Type   Bonus **Press** ⌨tab⌨ to advance to the Income 5 field.

NOTES
If clicking does not highlight the field contents, drag through an entry to select it. Double-clicking may open the language labels screen.

Type   Tuition **Press** (tab) to advance to the Income 6 field.

Type   Travel Exp. **Press** (tab) to advance to the Income 7 field.

Press   (del) to remove the entry. **Press** (tab) to select the next field.

Delete the **remaining Income names** until they are all removed.

Press   (tab) after deleting Income 20 to select Deduction 1 in the Deductions column.

Press   (tab) again if necessary to select Deduction 1 in the Name column.

Type   VRSP **Press** (tab) to advance to the second deduction Name field.

Type   Savings Plan **Press** (tab) to highlight the next field.

Type   Garnishee **Press** (tab) to highlight the next field.

Press   (del). VeloCity does not have other payroll deductions.

Press   (tab) to select the next field. **Delete** the **remaining deductions**.

Entering Additional Payroll Names

VeloCity keeps an emergency contact name and phone number for each employee as additional information in the personnel files. We will name these extra fields for the Payroll Ledger.

On this next screen, we also name the additional payroll expenses for VeloCity and the entitlements for employees. VeloCity has group insurance as a user-defined expense and offers sick leave and personal leave days for all employees as well as vacation days for salaried employees.

We will briefly review income, benefits and user-defined expenses.

Group insurance (Gp Insurance) is classified as a benefit for employees because the premiums are paid to a third party rather than to the employee. The employer's expense for the benefit is entered as a user-defined expense. Tuition is classified as an income because it is paid to the employee through regular paycheques. The employer's expense for this benefit is recorded in the expense account linked to the income, just like wage expenses. Reimbursements may also be entered as income or as user-defined expenses, depending on how the payment is made. If we entered travel expenses as a user-defined expense, we would create linked payable and expense accounts and then issue a separate cheque to the employee to provide the reimbursement. If we repay the expense on the payroll cheque, we define it as an income (with a linked expense account) — reimbursement — that is not taxable.

The Prov. Tax field is used for Quebec payroll taxes. Since we will not choose Quebec as the employees' province of taxation or enter linked accounts for them, the program will automatically skip the related payroll fields. WSIB is entered as the name for WCB (Workers' Compensation Board) because we selected Ontario as the business province. The field has a drop-down list of alternative names for WCB and other taxes you may use as an employer expense.

Click   **Additional Payroll**.

Double-click **Field1**. **Type** Emergency Contact

Press   (tab) **twice** to highlight the next field. (Read margin Notes.)

Type   Contact Number

Delete the **names for fields 3 to 5**.

Drag through **User Exp 1**, the Expense 1 field, to highlight the contents.

Type   Gp Insurance

Delete   the **remaining expenses**.

Drag through   **Days 1**, the Entitlement 1 field, to highlight the contents.

Type   Vacation   **Press** (tab) **twice** to highlight the next entitlement name.

Type   Sick Leave   **Press** (tab) **twice** to highlight the next name.

Type   PersonalDays

Delete   the **remaining entitlement names**.

Entering Settings for Incomes

Click   **Incomes** under Payroll.

This screen designates the types of income and the taxes that apply. By deleting the names we do not need this list becomes easier to work with. As we did for Northern Lights (Chapter 9), we can modify this screen by hiding the columns that apply to Quebec so that only the columns we need are on-screen at the same time.

Point to   the **right column heading margin for Calc. Tax (Que.)**.

When the pointer changes to a two-sided arrow ⟷, **drag** the **margin to the left** until the column is hidden.

Remove   the **column for Calc. QHSF** and **Calc. QPIP** in the same way.

For each type of income, you must indicate what taxes are applied and whether vacation pay is calculated on the income. Most of the information is correct. Regular and overtime hours are paid on an hourly basis, while salary and commissions are paid at designated income amounts per period. All taxes apply to these types of income at VeloCity, so these default settings are correct. Vacation pay and EI, however, are not calculated on all incomes, so some of these checkmarks should be removed. In addition, we should designate the type of income for the income names that we created and the taxes that apply to them. First, we should choose the type of income because that will change the defaults that are applied.

By default, all new incomes are assigned to the Income type. This assignment is correct for Bonus, the extra annual holiday payment. The tuition fee payment is a taxable benefit paid directly to the employee, so it is also classified as an Income. The generic Benefits field in journals is used for items that the employer pays directly to a third party on behalf of the employee. The monetary value of the premiums would be added as a benefit to the employee's gross wages to determine taxes and then subtracted again to determine the net pay. The employee does not receive the actual dollar amount. If a benefit is added to net pay, it should be classified as an Income. Therefore, in this example tuition is an Income.

Travel Expenses are **Reimbursements** and No. Clients is the name for the **Piece Rate** basis of paying bonuses. **Differential Rates** apply to different hourly rates paid at different times and are not used by VeloCity.

Click   **No. Clients** to place the cursor on the correct line.

Press   (tab) to move to the Type column. A List icon is added.

Click   the **List icon** to list the different income types.

Click   **Piece Rate** to select this type for No. Clients.

Click   **Select** to add the Type to the Settings screen. **Press** (tab) to advance to the Unit of Measure field — the entry here has changed to Item.

NOTES
You can use up to 12 characters for User-Defined Expense and Entitlement names including spaces — that is why we omitted the space for the Personal Days entitlement name.
You can use the language button to enter labels in the second language.

NOTES
If necessary, scroll to the right to include the column margin you need.

NOTES
When you close and re-open the Payroll Settings screen, the hidden and resized columns will be restored.
QPIP (Quebec Parental Insurance Plan) provides parental leave benefits to EI-insurable employees. Both employers and employees pay into the plan.

NOTES
Tuition is defined as a type of income because it is paid directly to the employee. It is not a reimbursement because it is taxable.
Using the generic Benefits requires a linked expense account and payable account (paid to the third party, as for Northern Lights in Chapter 9) while Income type and Reimbursements require only linked expense accounts (paid directly to the employee on the paycheque).
If you select the Benefit income type, the expense will not be included in the journal entry — it must be recorded separately as an adjustment.

The amount paid to employees is based on the number of completed surveys. The Insurable Hours checkmark was removed when we changed the type.

Type   Surveys

Click   **Travel Exp** to select this income line. **Press** (tab).

Click   the **List icon**. **Double-click Reimbursement** to enter this income type. All taxes are removed because this type of payment is not taxable.

Many of the changes are made automatically when we select the income type. We need to make more modifications. Insurable Hours, the number of work hours, is used to determine eligibility for Employment Insurance benefits. Regular, overtime and salary paid hours are counted, but commissions, bonuses and tuition are not; no time can be accurately attached to them, so they are not counted. EI is not calculated on benefits, so we also need to remove the Calc. EI ✓ for Tuition.

Click   **Commission** to select this income line.

Press   (tab) **repeatedly** until the cursor is in the **Calc. Ins. Hours field**.

Click   to remove the ✓, or **press** the **space bar**.

Press   ⬇ **twice** to place the cursor in the **Calc. Ins. Hours field for Bonus**.

Click   to remove the ✓, or **press** the **space bar**.

Press   ⬇ **again** to place the cursor in the **Calc. Ins. Hours field for Tuition**.

Click   to remove the ✓, or **press** the **space bar**.

Press   ⬅ to place the cursor in the **Calc. EI field for Tuition**.

Click   to remove the ✓, or **press** the **space bar**.

We still need to modify the entries for vacation pay. In Ontario, vacation pay is calculated on all performance-based wages. This includes the regular wages, overtime wages and piece rate pay. We need to remove the remaining ✓s. All ✓s for Travel Exp have been removed. Salaried workers receive paid time off rather than a percentage of their wages as vacation pay. We do not need to remove the ✓ for Overtime 2. If it is used later, vacation pay will be calculated on it as well. VRSP is deducted by amount, so the Calc column for it does not apply.

Click   **Salary** in the Income column.

Press   (tab) **repeatedly** until the cursor is in the **Calc. Vac. column**.

Click   to remove the ✓, or **press** the **space bar**.

Remove   the ✓ for **Calc. Vac.** for **Salary, Commission, Bonus** and **Tuition**

We do not need to change the settings for Quebec taxes or tracking of tips — they do not apply to Ontario employees — so the setup for Income Settings is complete:

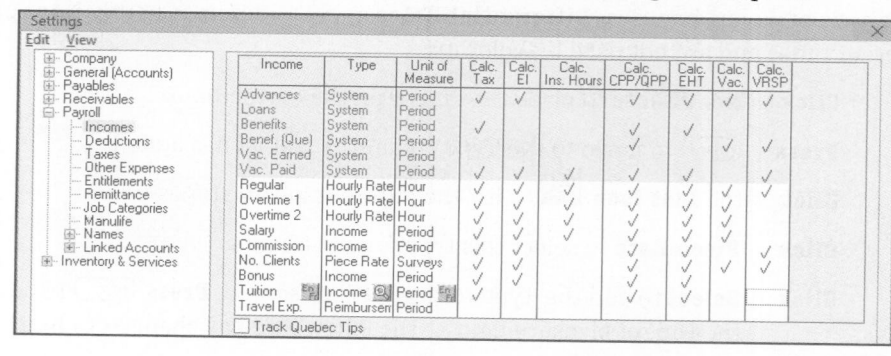

Entering Tax Settings for Deductions

> **Click**   **Deductions** under Payroll:

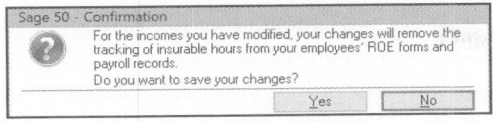

> **Click**   **Yes** when prompted to save the settings and confirm that ROE information connected to the deleted incomes will not be tracked.

Only the deduction names you entered earlier appear on this screen. You can calculate deductions as a percentage of the gross pay or as a fixed amount. Some deductions, like union dues, are usually calculated as a percentage of income. The Amount settings are correct for VeloCity.

All deductions are set by default to be calculated by amount after all taxes (Deduct After Tax is checked). For Savings Plan and Garnishee, this is correct — they are subtracted from income after income tax and other payroll taxes have been deducted. However, VRSP contributions qualify as tax deductions and will be subtracted from gross income before income tax is calculated, but not before EI, CPP and so on, so you must change its setting.

> **Click**   the **Deduct After Tax column** for VRSP to remove the ✓ and change the setting to Before Tax.

The remaining settings are correct. VRSP is deducted after the other payroll taxes and vacation pay because these deductions are based on gross wages.

Defining Default Tax Rates

> **Click**   **Taxes** under Payroll.

This group of fields refers to the rate at which employer tax obligations are calculated. The factor for Employment Insurance (**EI Factor**) is correct at 1.4 — the employer's contribution is set at 1.4 times the employee's contribution. In the next field, you can set the employer's rate for **WSIB** (Workplace Safety and Insurance Board) premiums. On this screen, you can enter 1.29, the rate that applies to the majority of employees. You can modify rates for individual employees in the ledger records.

The next field, **EHT Factor**, is the percentage of payroll costs that the employer contributes to the provincial health plan. The rate is based on the total payroll costs per year; the percentage for VeloCity is 0.98 because the total payroll is less than $200 000.

The **QHSF Factor** (Quebec Health Services Fund) applies only to Quebec employees, so we do not need to enter a rate for it. QHSF is similar to EHT.

> **Click**   the **WSIB Rate field. Type** `1.29`
>
> **Press**   `tab` to advance to the EHT Factor field.
>
> **Type**   `.98`

Defining Other Expenses

> **Click**   **Other Expenses** under Payroll.

On this screen, you must indicate whether expenses are calculated by percentage or by amount. The default Amount selection is correct for Gp Insurance, the single expense.

NOTES

NOTES

When the number of days accrued reaches the maximum, the Days Earned entries on the paycheques Entitlements tab screen will be zero.

NOTES

Refer to page 325 to review payroll linked accounts if necessary.

WARNING!

Sage 50 will not allow you to remove a linked account while it is being used as a linked account. When you try to remove an account, click OK in the Warning window to return to the Accounts window. First, turn the linking function off by deleting the account in the Linked Accounts window. Then delete the account balance and, finally, remove the account in the Accounts window. You cannot remove an account if it has a balance or if journal entries have been posted to it.

Defining Entitlements

Click   Entitlements under Payroll.

On this screen you can enter the rules for entitlements that apply to all or most employees. These will be added to new employee records as defaults.

Entitlements are usually linked to the number of hours worked. Employees at VeloCity are not entitled to take vacation time until they have worked for a certain period of time or to take paid sick leave immediately after being hired. The **Track Using % Hours Worked** determines how quickly entitlements accumulate. For example, 5 percent of hours worked yields about one day per month or 12 days of leave per year. VeloCity has **Maximums** for the number of days per year that an employee can take or accumulate. And finally, the days unused are not **cleared at the end of a year**. The number of days carried forward is still limited by the Maximum number of days available. The calculations are based on an eight-hour day as the default.

VeloCity gives salaried workers three weeks of vacation (8 percent) and allows a maximum of 25 days. Sick leave at 10 days per year is earned at the rate of 5 percent to a maximum of 15 days. Personal leave days (five days) accrue at the rate of 2.5 percent for a maximum of five days per year. VeloCity allows two of the three weeks of vacation time and five of the ten days of sick leave to be carried over to the next year; that is, they are not cleared at the end of the year. Personal leave days cannot be carried forward — the maximum is the same as the yearly allotment.

Click   the **Track Using % Hours Worked field for Vacation**.

Type   8 **Press** `tab` to advance to the Maximum Days field.

Type   25 **Press** `tab`.

Click   the **Track Using % Hours Worked field for Sick Leave**.

Type   5 **Press** `tab` to advance to the Maximum Days field.

Type   15 **Press** `tab`.

Click   the **Track Using % Hours Worked field for PersonalDays**.

Type   2.5 **Press** `tab` to advance to the Maximum Days field.

Type   5 **Press** `tab`.

Entering Payroll Linked Accounts

The following linked accounts are used by VeloCity for the Payroll Ledger for incomes and deductions:

PAYROLL LINKED ACCOUNTS

INCOMES

Principal Bank	1060 Bank: Niagara Trust Chequing		
Vac. Owed	2300 Vacation Payable	Advances & Loans	1220 Advances & Loans Receivable

Income

Vac. Earned	5300 Wages	Commission	5330 Commissions & Bonuses
Regular	5300 Wages	No. Clients	5330 Commissions & Bonuses
Overtime 1	5300 Wages	Bonus	5330 Commissions & Bonuses
Overtime 2	Not used	Tuition	5460 Employee Benefits
Salary	5320 Salaries	Travel Exp.	5350 Travel Expenses

DEDUCTIONS	**Linked Account**	**Payment Adjustment Account**
VRSP	2400 VRSP Payable	2400 VRSP Payable
Savings Plan	2410 Savings Plan Payable	2410 Savings Plan Payable
Garnishee	2430 Garnisheed Wages Payable	2430 Garnisheed Wages Payable

There are many linked accounts for payroll because each type of income, tax, deduction and expense that is used must be linked to a General Ledger account.

Click   **Linked Accounts** under Payroll, then **click Incomes**.

The names here are the ones you entered in the Names windows. If you deleted a name, it will not appear here.

The linked accounts for all types of income appear together on this first screen. You must identify a wage account for each type of employee payment used by the company, even if the same account is used for all of them. Once the Payroll bank account is identified as the same one used for Payables, the program will apply a single sequence of cheque numbers for all cheques prepared from the Payables and Payroll journals.

Type   the **account number** or **select** the **account** from the drop-down list.

Choose   **1060 Bank: Niagara Trust Chequing** for the Principal Bank field.

Press   (tab) to advance to the next linked account field.

Choose   **2300 Vacation Payable** for the Vac. Owed field.

Choose   **1220 Advances & Loans Receivable** for the Advances & Loans field.

Choose   **5300 Wages** for Regular and Overtime 1 and for Vacation Earned.

Choose   **5320 Salaries** for Salaries.

Choose   **5330 Commissions & Bonuses** for Commission, No. Clients and Bonus.

Choose   **5460 Employee Benefits** for Tuition.

Choose   **5350 Travel Expenses** for Travel Exp.

Click   **Deductions** so you can enter the next set of Payroll linked accounts.

Enter   the **linked payable** and **payroll adjustment accounts** for **VRSP**, **Savings Plan** and **Garnishee** from the chart on the previous page.

The following linked accounts are used for taxes and user-defined expenses:

PAYROLL LINKED ACCOUNTS CONTINUED

TAXES	Payables		Expenses		Payment Adjustment	
EI	2310	EI Payable	5410	EI Expense	5410	EI Expense
CPP	2320	CPP Payable	5420	CPP Expense	5420	CPP Expense
Tax	2330	Income Tax Payable			2330	Income Tax Payable
WSIB	2460	WSIB Payable	5430	WSIB Expense	5430	WSIB Expense
EHT	2380	EHT Payable	5440	EHT Expense	5440	EHT Expense
Not used Tax (Que.), QPP, QHSF, QPIP			**Not used** QPP, QHSF, QPIP		**Not used** Tax (Que.), QPP, QHSF, QPIP	

USER-DEFINED EXPENSES

	Payables		Expenses	Payment Adjustment
Gp Insurance	2420	Group Insurance Payable	5450 Gp Insurance Expense	5450 Gp Insurance Expense

Click   **Taxes** for the next set of Payroll linked accounts.

Enter   the **linked payables**, **expenses** and **payment adjustment accounts** for **EI**, **CPP**, **Tax**, **WSIB** and **EHT** from the chart above.

Click   **User-Defined Expenses** for the final Payroll linked accounts.

Enter   the **linked payable**, **expense** and **payment adjustment accounts** for **Gp Insurance** from the chart above.

Check   the **linked** payroll **accounts** against the charts on page 660 and this page.

CLASSIC VIEW
To add payroll linked accounts, you can right-click the Paycheques or the Payroll Cheque Run Journal icon in the Home window to select it. Click the Settings tool. Or, choose the Setup menu, and then choose Settings, Payroll and Linked Accounts.

If no Home window icon is selected, you can use the Settings tool's Select Setup drop-down list, choose Payroll and click Select.

NOTES
The deleted income and deduction names do not appear on the screens for linked accounts.

NOTES
You can add accounts from the Linked Accounts windows. Type a new number, press (enter) and choose to add the account.

NOTES
If you can use an account for more than one link, the account will be available in the drop-down list. Otherwise, once an account is selected as a linked account, it is removed from the list.

PRO VERSION

The Price List, Locations and Categories options are not available in the Pro version.

The FIFO method of costing is also not available in the Pro version.

Inventory & Services Ledger Settings

Click   Inventory & Services for the ledger option:

Click   Options:

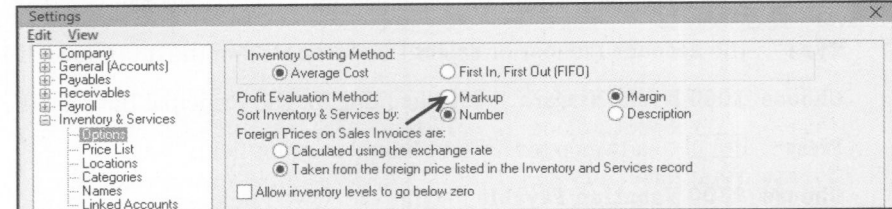

Inventory costs may be calculated in two ways. In the average cost method, costs are continually updated as you buy and sell at different prices. With the FIFO method, costs are tracked with the items and do not change for any one item — its historic purchase price remains as the cost price at the time of sale. VeloCity uses average costs.

Profits may be calculated on the basis of margin or markup. You can change the setting at any time, so you can prepare reports using both evaluation methods. The formulas for profit evaluation by margin and markup are as follows:

Margin = (Selling Price – Cost Price) x 100%/Selling Price

Markup = (Selling Price – Cost Price) x 100%/Cost Price

VeloCity uses the markup method of evaluating the profit on inventory sales, so we need to change the default setting.

Click   Markup to change the calculation method.

If you choose to sort Inventory Ledger items by description, the product name field will appear before the product number in the Inventory Ledger input forms, and inventory selection lists will be sorted alphabetically by name (read the margin Notes). When item numbers are not used, sorting by description will make it easier to find the item you want.

Because we added a foreign currency, the option to take foreign prices for sales from the Inventory Ledger or from the exchange rate is added. The default setting to use the foreign price in the Inventory Ledger Record is correct for VeloCity. With this option, you can switch pricing methods for individual items. If you choose the exchange rate method, you cannot choose different methods for different items.

The final option is to Allow Inventory Levels To Go Below Zero. VeloCity will choose this option to permit customer sales for inventory that is backordered.

Click   Allow Inventory Levels To Go Below Zero to select the option.

In the Premium version, you can create additional price lists and modify price lists from this settings screen. You can also set up the locations for inventory if you have more than one place where inventory is stored or sold.

Inventory Linked Accounts

VeloCity currently uses both linked accounts for inventory, the one for inventory adjustments or damaged merchandise and the one for additional item assembly costs. The linked accounts for the Inventory Ledger are listed here:

NOTES

The list of items in the Item Description field in the Sales and Purchases journals is always sorted by description. The Item Number field list in these journals is always sorted by number.

The choice you make on the Inventory Settings screen affects the selection lists in the Adjustments and Item Assembly journals, in the Inventory & Services window and in the Inventory & Services module window.

NOTES

Price lists are used in Chapter 18 to update prices. You can change one price relative to another for all items in a single step. Inventory locations are also covered in Chapter 18.

INVENTORY

Item Assembly Costs	5045 Item Assembly Costs
Adjustment Write-off	5040 Damaged Inventory

Click   **Linked Accounts** under Inventory & Services:

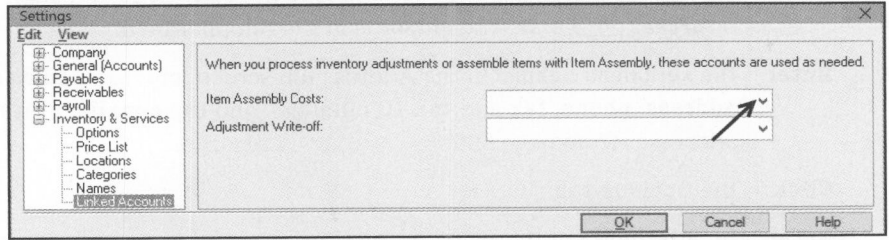

Type   the **account number** or **select** the **account** from the drop-down list.

Choose **Item Assembly Costs** as the Item Assembly Costs linked account.

Press   (tab). **Choose 5040 Damaged Inventory** as the Adjustment Write-off linked account.

Settings options for the Division module will be hidden if you chose to hide the module (User Preferences, View settings). Time and Billing, introduced in Chapter 18, has no settings options.

Click   **OK** to save the new settings.

You will get several confirmation messages. Because we deleted some payroll names, we are being warned that any accounts linked to these deleted fields will also be removed. The next message refers to the additional payroll names, and we are again being warned that their linked accounts will be removed. Refer to Chapter 9, page 327.

A second group of warnings relates to required account class changes for linked accounts. Refer to Chapter 7, pages 232–233.

Read   **each message carefully** and **click Yes** in response to return to the Home window.

Preparing the Subsidiary Ledgers

We have now completed the General Ledger setup, including

1. organizing all accounting reports and records
2. creating new accounts
3. identifying linked accounts for all ledgers
4. activating additional features and entering their linked accounts

The remaining steps involve setting up the records in the subsidiary ledgers:

5. inserting supplier, customer, employee and inventory information
6. entering historical startup information
7. printing reports to check the accuracy of your records

Preparing the Payables Ledger

Use VeloCity's Supplier Information on pages 626–627 to create the supplier records and add the outstanding historical invoices. If any information is missing for a supplier, leave that field blank. The first supplier, Complete Cycler Inc., is a foreign currency supplier.

CLASSIC VIEW
To add inventory linked accounts, you can right-click the Item Assembly or the Inventory Adjustments Journal icon in the Home window to select it. Click the Settings tool. Or, choose the Setup menu, and then choose Settings, Inventory & Services and Linked Accounts.

NOTES
To access the Division module options, refer to page 505.

WARNING!
Check your work carefully. Although you can change the designated linked accounts at any time, journal entries will be posted incorrectly if you do not have the correct linked accounts.

NOTES
For a review of the Payables Ledger setup, refer to page 233.

Entering Supplier Accounts

Click **Payables** in the Modules pane list.

Click the **Suppliers icon** 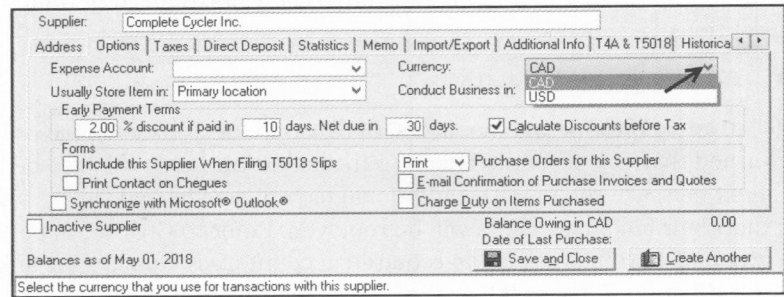 to open the Suppliers window.

Click the **Create Button** [Create] or **choose** the **File menu** and **click Create** or **press** [ctrl] + **N**. The cursor is in the Supplier field.

Enter the supplier's **name**. On the Address tab screen, enter the **contact**, **address**, **phone**, **fax** and **tax ID** numbers, and the **e-mail** and **Web site** addresses from page 626.

Click the **Options tab**.

Enter the **discounts**, if there are any, in the Terms fields, and the number of days in which the net amount is due. **Click Calculate Discounts Before Tax** if the discounts are before tax. Otherwise, leave the box unchecked.

Identifying Foreign Suppliers

Foreign suppliers are also identified on the Options tab screen.

Click the **Currency field list arrow**:

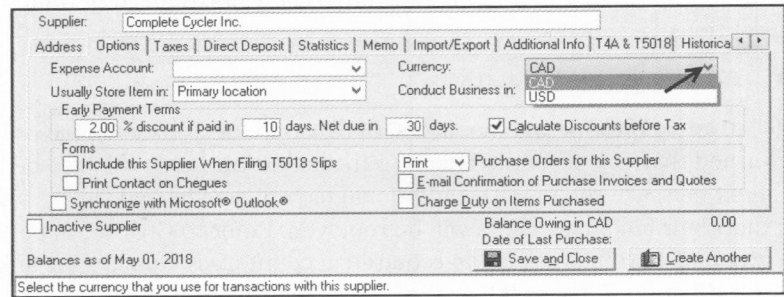

Click **USD**.

Click **Charge Duty On Items Purchased**.

You must activate this duty setting to make the duty fields in the Purchases Journal available for this supplier.

You can print the contact on cheques if this is appropriate for the supplier.

Enter the **default expense account** for the supplier if there is one.

Do not enter a default expense account for inventory suppliers — the linked asset account from the Inventory Ledger record is selected automatically by the program.

We will enter tax codes for all suppliers and customers later using the Assign Tax Codes feature in the Company Sales Tax Codes Settings (page 677). It is not necessary to change Tax Exempt entries. Leaving the setting at No will make all tax codes available. As long as the tax code in the journal is correct, taxes will be calculated correctly.

You do not need to enter any details on the Statistics, Memo and Import/Export tab screens.

The Balance Owing will be entered automatically by the program once you have entered historical invoices.

Correct any **errors** by returning to the field with the mistake, highlighting the errors and entering the correct information.

PRO VERSION
Remember that the term Vendors will replace Suppliers. Click Vendors in the Modules pane to change modules.

WARNING!
You cannot change the currency for a supplier or customer after entering historical invoices, so you must select the currency first. Otherwise, you must pay the invoices, clear paid transactions, remove the supplier and then re-create the supplier record from scratch.
After you enter historical invoices for a foreign supplier or customer, you cannot change the currency setting for the company, even if you delete the supplier.
You cannot access the duty fields in the Purchases Journal unless Charge Duty On Items Purchased is checked in the supplier's ledger.

NOTES
Leaving the code as No Tax and leaving the exempt status set at No will permit you to charge taxes if needed.
If taxes are not calculated correctly for a supplier or customer, check that the ledger entries for Tax Exempt are set to No.

NOTES
Year-to-date purchases and payments are not recorded because this is a new fiscal period.

Entering Historical Supplier Transactions

The chart on page 627 provides the information for this stage. Complete Cycler Inc. has an outstanding balance, so we must enter the historical transactions.

Click the **Historical Transactions tab**. **Click Save Now**. **Click Invoices**:

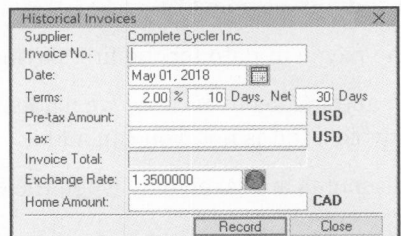

The Historical Invoices input screen for foreign suppliers has additional fields for the second currency information.

You can edit the payment terms for individual invoices if needed.

Enter **CC-918** as the **Invoice Number** and **Apr 28** as the invoice **Date**.

Press (tab). The Exchange Rate screen opens.

Enter **1.36** as the exchange rate and **click Make This The Default Rate For April 28**. **Click OK**.

Click the **Pre-Tax Amount field for USD**.

Type 3700 **Press** (tab) to advance to the Tax amount field for USD.

Type 481 **Press** (tab).

In the Home Amount field, $5 686.16 should be entered correctly automatically.

Click **Record**.

Repeat these steps to **enter other invoices** for this supplier, if there are any.

When you have recorded all outstanding invoices for a supplier,

Click **Close** to save the invoice.

You will return to the Historical Transactions tab screen. The invoices you entered have been added to the Balance fields. Balances are displayed in both currencies.

To enter the historical invoice for **Wheel Deals**, click Cancel if the exchange rate screen opens to close it without entering a new rate. Enter **$2 670** and **$347.10** as the **USD** pretax and tax amounts, and then enter **$4 090** as the **Home Amount**. Press (tab) and allow the program to recalculate the exchange rate. Do not save the revised exchange rate when prompted.

Historical invoices for home currency suppliers are recorded in the same way, except for the entry of the exchange rate. We will enter historical payments next.

Historical Payments

Click **Payments** on the Historical Transactions tab screen:

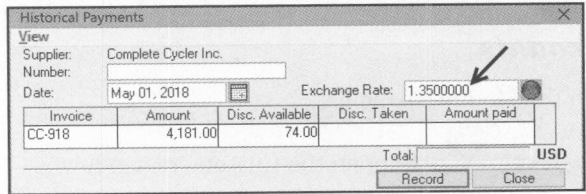

NOTES You can refer to page 238 to review entering historical supplier invoices and payments if necessary.

NOTES Because discounts from Complete Cycler Inc. are calculated before taxes, there are separate fields for pretax and tax invoice amounts.

WARNING! If you save an incorrect invoice amount, you must pay the invoice, clear paid invoices for the supplier (Home window, Maintenance menu), reset the payments for the year to zero (supplier's ledger, Statistics tab) and re-enter the outstanding invoices. Refer to page 249.

Historical payments for foreign suppliers have one additional field, the one for the exchange rate. You must enter an exchange rate for these payments — there is no field for the home currency amount.

> **Click**   the **Number field**.
>
> **Type**   344 (the **cheque number** for the first payment).
>
> **Press**   *tab* and **enter April 28** as the payment date for the first payment.

The exchange rate, 1.36, should be entered automatically because we made it the default rate for April 28 when we entered the invoice. If it is not, you can add it.

> **Skip**   the **Discount fields** because discounts are taken only when the early payment is a full payment.
>
> **Click**   the **Amount Paid column** (on the line for the invoice being paid).
>
> **Type**   2000 for the **payment amount**.
>
> **Press**   *tab* to advance to the next invoice if there is one. **Delete** any **amounts** or **discounts** that are not included in the payment.
>
> **Click**   **Record** to save the information and to display an updated statement for this supplier.
>
> **Repeat**   these steps to **enter other payments** to this supplier.

When you have recorded all outstanding payments for a supplier,

> **Click**   **Close** to return to the Payables Ledger for the supplier. The payment you have just entered has reduced the Balance amount.
>
> **Click**   the **Create tool** to display a new blank Payables Ledger screen.
>
> **Click**   the **Address tab**.
>
> **Repeat**   these procedures to **enter** the **remaining suppliers** and their **historical transactions** from pages 626–627.

If there are no historical invoices and payments,

> **Click**   **Create Another** to save the record and open a blank Payables Ledger window. **Click** the **Address tab**.
>
> **Display** or **print** the **Supplier List** and the **Supplier Aged Detail Report**, including terms, historical differences and foreign amounts. Compare these reports with the information on pages 626–627 to check the accuracy of your work.

Preparing the Receivables Ledger

Use VeloCity's Customer Information on pages 627–628 to create the customer records and add the outstanding historical invoices. Revenue accounts are added from the inventory records, so they are not needed in the customers' records. If any information is missing for a customer, leave that field blank.

Entering Customer Accounts

> **Click**   **Receivables** in the Modules pane list.
>
> **Click**   the **Customers icon** 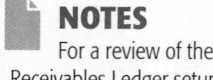 to open the Customers window.
>
> **Click**   ⧉ Create or **choose** the **File menu** and then **click Create**.

⚠ WARNING!
Remember not to include any discounts taken in the historical payments. If you do include them, the Payables Ledger will not be balanced and you will be unable to finish the history.
By clicking the Amount field directly, you can avoid including the discount.

NOTES
The Statistics tab screen has the summary amounts in both Canadian and US dollars.
The historical invoices and payments will be entered on the Statistics tab screen as Last Year's Purchases and Payments because we are starting a new fiscal period on May 1.

NOTES
For a review of the Receivables Ledger setup, refer to page 240.

The cursor is in the Customer field.

Enter   the customer's **name**. On the Address tab screen, enter the **contact**, **address**, **phone** and **fax numbers**, and the **e-mail** and **Web site addresses** according to page 627.

You can edit the default payment terms for individual customers or for individual historical invoices if necessary.

Click   the **Ship-To Address tab**.

The Mailing Address is already selected as the default ship-to address, so the same address will apply to both fields on invoices, orders and quotes.

Click   the **Options tab**.

Most entries on the Options tab screen are correct. Terms are entered from the default Receivables settings. Customer statements should be printed. Americas Vinelands Tours and Festival Tours are USD customers. All other customers are Canadian and use the home currency (CAD).

Choose USD from the Currency list for Americas Vinelands Tours (and for Festival Tours).

Choose Preferred from the Price List field list for **Americas Vinelands Tours** and for other preferred customers (the ones marked with * in the customer information chart on page 627) to change the price list for these customers.

Change the payment **terms** to **net 1** for **Cash and Interac** and **Visa Sales customers**.

The default code H is entered as the default tax code for all customers. We will change the codes for the USD customers from the Assign Tax Codes option.

Click   the **Statistics tab**.

Enter   the **credit limit**. Enter both CAD and USD limits for USD customers.

This is the amount that the customer can purchase on account before payments are required. If the customer goes beyond the credit limit, the program will issue a warning before posting an invoice.

The balance owing will be included automatically once you have provided the outstanding invoice information. If the customer has outstanding transactions, proceed to the next section on historical information. Otherwise,

Click   to save the information and advance to the next new Receivables Ledger input screen.

Click   the **Address tab**.

Entering Historical Customer Information

The chart on page 628 provides the information you need to complete this stage.

Enter   the customer's **name**, **address**, **options**, **taxes** and **credit limit**.

Click   the **Historical Transactions tab**. **Click Save Now**.

Click   **Invoices**.

Enter   the **invoice number**, **date** and **amount** for the first invoice. The default terms should be correct.

 NOTES
The preferred customers are
• Americas Vinelands Tours
• Backstage Tours
• Niagara Rapids Inn
• Park 'N Ride Tours

 WARNING!
Do not forget to remove the discount terms for cash and credit card customer sales. Changing the ledger records will make the sales invoice terms correct automatically.

NOTES
You can refer to page 243 to review entering historical customer invoices and payments if necessary.

 WARNING!
If you save an incorrect invoice amount, you must pay the incorrect invoice, clear paid transactions for the customer, then re-enter the customer's outstanding invoices. Refer to page 249.

Press `tab` to advance to the next field after entering each piece of information.

When all the information is entered correctly, you must save the customer invoice.

Click **Record** to save the information and to display another blank invoice for this customer.

Repeat these procedures to **enter** the **remaining invoices** for the customer, if there are any.

When you have recorded all outstanding invoices for a customer,

Click **Close** to return to the Historical Transactions window for the customer.

The invoices you entered have been added to the Balance field. Continue by entering payments received from this customer, if there are any, or proceed to enter the next customer.

Click **Payments** on the Historical Transactions tab screen.

Click the **Number field**.

Enter the **cheque number** for the first payment.

Press `tab` and **enter** the **payment date** for the first payment. Again, discounts apply only to full payments made before the due dates, so you should skip the Discount fields.

Click the **Amount Paid column** (on the line for the invoice being paid).

Enter the **payment amount**.

Press `tab` to advance to the next amount if other invoices are being paid. **Delete** any **amounts** or **discounts** that are not included in the payment.

Click **Record** to save the information and to display the updated balance for this customer.

Repeat these procedures to **enter** the **remaining payments** from the customer.

When you have recorded all outstanding receipts from a customer,

Click **Close** to return to the Receivables Ledger window for the customer.

The payment you entered has updated the customer's Balance field amount.

Click the **Create tool** 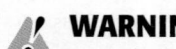 to open a new Receivables Ledger input screen.

Click the **Address tab** to prepare for entering other customers. After entering all customer records and historical data,

Click `Save and Close` (or ☒) after adding the last customer. **Close** the **Customers window** to return to the Home window.

Display or **print** the **Customer List** and the **Customer Aged Detail Report**, including terms and historical differences. Compare these reports with the information on pages 627–628 to check your work.

Preparing the Payroll Ledger

Use the VeloCity Employee Information Sheet, Employee Profiles and Additional Payroll Information on pages 628–630 to create the employee records and add historical information.

⚠️ **WARNING!**
Remember not to include any discounts taken in the historical payments. If you include them, the Receivables Ledger will not be balanced and you will be unable to finish the history.

📄 **NOTES**
For a review of the Payroll Ledger setup, refer to pages 327–337.

We will enter the information for VeloCity employee Dunlop Mercier.

Click   **Employees & Payroll** in the Modules pane list.

Click   the **Employees icon** [Employees] in the Home window.

Click   [Create] or **choose** the **File menu** and **click Create**.

Entering Personal Details for Employees

The Payroll Ledger new employee information form will open at the Personal information tab screen so you can begin to enter the employee record.

The Payroll Ledger has a large number of tabs for the different kinds of payroll information. The cursor is in the Employee field. By entering the surname first, your employee lists will be in correct alphabetic order.

Type   Mercier, Dunlop **Press** (tab).

Type   55 Trailview Rd. to enter the Street address.

The default city and province, those for the store, are correct.

Click   the **Postal Code field**. **Type** l0s1j0 **Press** (tab).

The program corrects the postal code format and advances to the Phone 1 field.

Type   9054681817

The default **Language Preference** is correctly set as English.

Click   the **Social Insurance Number (SIN) field**. You must use a valid SIN. The program has corrected the telephone number format.

Type   532548625 **Press** (tab).

The cursor advances to the Birth Date field. Enter the month, day and year using any accepted date format. Birth Date is a required field and it must be correct because it is linked to CPP calculations.

Type   9-18-85 **Press** (tab) **twice** to advance to the Gender field.

Choose **Male** from the drop-down list.

Press   (tab) to advance to the Hire Date field. This is the date the employee began working for VeloCity.

Type   1-6-14

The default entry for **Job Status** — Full time — is correct for all employees.

The next two fields will be used when the employee leaves the job — the date of termination and the reason for leaving that you can select from the drop-down list. The final option designates employees as active or inactive. All employees at VeloCity are active, so the default selection is correct.

We have not yet created job categories to identify salespersons, so we will assign employees to them later. The program will automatically enter the Date Last Paid.

Entering Employee Tax Information

Click   the **Taxes tab** to advance to the next set of employee details.

This screen allows you to enter income tax–related information for an employee, including the historical amounts for the year to date. Tax Table is a required field.

Click   the **Tax Table list arrow** for the list of provinces and territories.

NOTES
Social Insurance Number is not a required field until you are filing CRA reports. If you enter it, you must enter a valid number.
Birth Date is a required field — it is used to determine CPP eligibility and requirements.

NOTES
Refer to page 296 for more information about employee terminations.

NOTES
Refer to page 329 to review entering employee tax details.

Click	**Ontario**, the province of taxation for VeloCity employees.
Press	$\boxed{tab}$ to advance to the **Federal Basic Personal Amount field**.
Type	11474
Press	$\boxed{tab}$ to advance to the **Provincial Basic Personal Amount field**.
Type	10011

Gearie is the only employee with additional claim amounts. Schwinn is the only employee who chooses to have additional taxes withheld.

For **Gearie**, entering the **three federal and provincial claim amounts** from page 628 in their respective fields will provide the correct total, indexed and non-indexed amounts.

For **Schwinn**, click the **Additional Fed. Tax** field and type **50**.

If an employee is insurable by EI, you must leave the box for **Deduct EI** checked. The default EI contribution factor, 1.4, for VeloCity is correct. We entered it in the Payroll Taxes Settings window (page 659).

All employees at VeloCity make CPP contributions and pay income tax, so leave these check boxes selected. We will enter the historical income tax amounts next.

Click	the **Historical Amount field** for **Income Tax**.
Type	1668.29 **Press** $\boxed{tab}$ to advance to the EI Premiums Historical Amount field.
Type	232.97 to enter the amount of EI paid to date. **Press** $\boxed{tab}$ to move to the CPP Contributions Historical Amount field.
Type	547.31

Entering Income Amounts for Employees

We defined all the types of income for VeloCity in the Names, Incomes & Deductions setup (page 655). All employees use the following types of income, although not all will have regular amounts and not all will be used on all paycheques:
- Loans
- Benefits
- No. Clients
- Bonus
- Tuition
- Travel Exp.

For Mercier the following incomes are also used: Vacation (Vac.) Owed, Vacation (Vac.) Paid, Regular and Overtime 1.

For Gearie and Schwinn, Salary is used. For Gearie, Commission is also used. Because Quebec is not selected as the province of taxation, Benefits (Que) is not preselected. The checkmarks for Advances, Loans, Benefits and Vacation cannot be removed.

All the details you need to complete the Income tab chart are on pages 628–629.

Click the **Income tab**.

On the Income chart you can indicate the types of income that each employee receives (the **Use** column), the usual rate of pay for that type of income (**Amount Per Unit**), the usual number of hours worked (**Hours Per Period**), the usual number of pieces for a piece rate pay base (**Pieces Per Period**) and the amounts received this year before the earliest transaction date or the date used for the first paycheque (**Historical**

WARNING!
Enter employee historical payroll details carefully. You will be unable to edit these fields after finishing the history or after making Payroll Journal entries for the employee.
    They must also be correct because they are used to create T4s for tax reporting.

NOTES
The program skips the Quebec tax fields because no linked accounts were entered for them.

NOTES
Refer to page 331 if you need to review entering employee income details.

NOTES
The chart on pages 628–629 has the incomes that are used by an employee with a ✓ or an amount in the employee's column.

Amount). The **Year-To-Date (YTD) Amount** is added automatically by the program based on the historical amounts you enter and the paycheques entered in the program.

Checkmarks must be entered in the Use column for all fields that are needed in the Payroll journals, even if they will not be used on all paycheques.

Click   **Regular** in the Income column to select the line.

Press   (tab) to advance to the Amount Per Unit field where we need to enter the regular hourly wage rate.

Type   18 **Press** (tab) to advance the Hours Per Period field.

The usual number of work hours in the bi-weekly pay period is 80. You can change the default amount in the Payroll journals. Salaried workers normally work 150 hours each month.

Type   80 **Press** (tab) to advance to the Historical Amount field.

Historical income and deduction amounts for the year to date are necessary so that taxes and deductions can be calculated correctly and T4 statements will be accurate.

Type   11520 **Press** (tab).

The amount is entered automatically in the YTD column and the cursor advances to the Use column for Overtime 1.

Press   (tab) so you can enter the overtime hourly rate.

Type   27

Press   (tab) **twice** to advance to the Historical Amount field. There is no regular number of overtime hours.

Type   486

The next three income types do not apply to Mercier, so they should not be checked. The next income that applies is No. Clients, the piece rate method of pay. There is no historical amount, but we need to enter the rate or amount per unit (survey). The remaining incomes (No. Clients, Bonus and Travel Exp.) are correctly checked. There is no fixed amount per unit or period and there are no historical amounts.

Pressing the space bar when you are in the Use column will also add a ✓ or remove one if it is there. Pressing (↓) will move you to the next line in the same column.

Click   the **Use column beside Salary** to remove the ✓.

Click   the **Use column beside Commission** to remove the ✓.

Click   **No. Clients** in the Income column to select the line. **Press** (tab).

Type   10 to enter the amount received for each completed survey.

If employees have received vacation pay, enter this amount in the **Vac. Paid** field. Vacation pay not yet received is entered in the **Vac. Owed** field. Any loans (or advances) paid to the employees and not yet repaid are recorded in the **Loans** or (**Advances**) **Historical Amount** field. There is no record of advance or loan amounts recovered.

We need to add the historical loans, benefits and vacation amounts for Mercier. Mercier has $100 in loans not yet repaid, and he has not received all the vacation pay he has earned this year.

Scroll   **to the top** of the list so that the information for Loans is available.

Click   the **Historical Amount column beside Loans**.

NOTES
Checkmarks are added by default for all incomes, deductions and expenses that have linked accounts.

WARNING!
Do not click the Use column beside Regular or No. Clients for Mercier as that will remove these checkmarks.

NOTES
If you added a linked account for Overtime 2, it will have a ✓ in the Use column and you should remove it for all employees.

NOTES
Remember that commissions must be calculated manually and entered in the Payroll journals. The Commission field in the Payroll Ledger allows only a fixed amount, not a percentage of sales, as the entry.

NOTES
Employees may be paid yearly (1), semi-annually (2), monthly for 10 months (10), monthly (12), every four weeks (13), every two weeks for a 10-month year (22), twice a month (24), every two weeks (26) or weekly (52).

NOTES
When you select a specific account, all payroll expenses for that employee will be linked to the same account – the one you identify in this field. If you want to use different accounts for different wage expenses, you must use the linked accounts.

NOTES
Refer to page 333 to review entering employee deductions.

NOTES
For one-time changes, you can edit deduction amounts in the Payroll journals on the Deductions tab or the Deductions Details screen.
The Use column in the ledger record must be checked for the field to become available in the journal.

Type 100

Press (tab) to move to the Amount Per Unit column for Benefits. The group insurance premiums paid by the employer are employee benefits.

Type 16 **Press** (tab) to move to the Historical Amount for Benefits.

Type 128 **Press** (tab) to advance to the Historical Amount for Vac. Owed.

Type 706 **Press** (tab) to advance to the Historical Vac. Paid Amount.

Type 386

For **Schwinn**, click the Use column for Regular, Overtime 1 and Commission to remove the ✓. Enter the monthly salary and press (tab). Enter 150 as the number of hours worked in the pay period. Press (tab) and enter the historical amount. For No. Clients, enter 10 as the amount per unit. For Travel Exp., enter 120 as the historical amount. You cannot remove the ✓ for Vac. Owed and Vac. Paid, even if they are not used.

For **Gearie**, repeat these steps but leave Commission checked and enter the historical amount. For Tuition, enter the per period and historical amounts.

Pay Periods Per Year, another required field, refers to the number of times the employee is paid, or the pay cycle. Mercier is paid every two weeks, so 26 times per year.

Click the **list arrow** beside the field for **Pay Periods Per Year**.

Click **26**.

Retaining Vacation pay is normal for full-time hourly paid employees. Part-time and casual workers often receive their vacation pay with each paycheque because their work schedule is irregular. You will turn off the option to retain vacation when an employee receives the vacation pay, either when taking a vacation or when leaving the company (refer to page 275). If the employee is salaried and does not receive vacation pay, the option should also be turned off. For Mercier, or any employee who receives vacation pay, leave the option to Retain Vacation checked and type the vacation pay rate in the % field.

Double-click the **% field beside Vacation Rate**. **Type** 6

For **Schwinn** and **Gearie**, click Retain Vacation to remove the ✓.

Employee wages may all be linked to their individual and different linked expense accounts or to one single account. Wage expenses for all VeloCity employees are linked to the default accounts on page 660.

Entering Default Payroll Deduction Amounts

Click the **Deductions tab** to open the screen for payroll deductions.

On this screen you can indicate which deductions apply to the employee, the amount normally deducted and the historical amount — the amount deducted to date this year. All deductions are selected in the Use column. These are the deductions you entered previously (page 656).

By entering deduction amounts here, they will be included automatically on the Payroll Journal input forms. Otherwise, you must enter them manually in the journal for each pay period. Since all three employees participate in the VRSP and savings plans, you can enter the information here so that the deductions are made automatically. You should make permanent changes by editing the employee ledger record.

If you choose to calculate deductions as a percentage of gross pay in the Payroll Settings, the Percentage Per Pay Period fields will be available.

Click   **VRSP** in the Deduction column to select the line.

Press   (tab). You should enter the amount that is withheld in each pay period.

Type   50 **Press** (tab) to advance the cursor to the Historical Amount field.

Type   450 **Press** (tab) to advance the cursor to the Use column for Savings Plan.

Press   (tab). Enter the amount that is to be withheld in each pay period.

Type   50 **Press** (tab) to advance the cursor to the Historical Amount field.

Type   450 **Press** (tab) to update the YTD Amount and advance to the Use column for Garnishee.

Click   the **Use column for Garnishee** to remove the ✓. Mercier does not have wages withheld.

For **Schwinn**, enter 200 as the Amount and 800 as the YTD amount for Garnishee.

The remaining deductions are not used by VeloCity. Their names were deleted (page 656), so only the three we named appear in the ledger.

Entering WSIB and Other Expenses

Click   the **WSIB & Other Expenses tab**.

The user-defined expenses we created in the Additional Payroll Names screen (page 656) and the default WSIB rate (page 659) are entered on this screen.
In Ontario, WSIB (Workplace Safety and Insurance Board) is the name for the Workers' Compensation Board, so the tab is labelled WSIB. In other provinces, the tab label will be WCB & Other Expenses or the name selected on the Additional Payroll Names screen.
The default WSIB rate is entered from our setup information, but you can enter a different rate for an individual employee in this field. The rate is correct for Mercier.

For **Gearie**, enter 1.02 as the WSIB rate.

Other user-defined expenses are also added on this screen. VeloCity has only group insurance as a user-defined expense.

Click   the **Gp Insurance Amt. Per Period**. Enter the amount that the employer contributes in each pay period.

Type   16 **Press** (tab) to advance to the Historical Amount field.

Type   128

The remaining expense fields are not used by VeloCity at this time.

Entering Employee Entitlements

We entered the default rates and amounts for entitlements as Payroll Settings (page 660), but they can be modified in the ledger records for individual employees.
We must also enter the historical information for entitlements. This historical number will include any days carried forward from the previous periods. The number of days accrued cannot be greater than the maximum number of days defined for the entitlement for an employee. The number of Net Days Accrued, the amount unused and available for carrying forward, is updated automatically from the historical information and current payroll journal entries. Entitlements information is included in the chart on page 629.

NOTES
Refer to page 334 to review entering WSIB (WCB) details.

NOTES
The name WSIB in Ontario emphasizes safety rather than compensation for accidents. WSIB (or WCB) pays workers when they have been injured on the job and are unable to work.

NOTES
Refer to page 335 if you need to review entering employee entitlements.

NOTES
If employees take days before the sufficient number of hours worked have been accrued, the program will warn you. Then you can allow the entry for entitlements or not. This entry is similar to allowing customers to exceed their credit limits.

Click   the **Entitlements tab**.

You cannot enter information directly in the Net Days Accrued fields on the Entitlements tab screen.

Mercier receives vacation pay instead of paid time off, so the vacation entitlements details should be removed. The defaults for sick leave and personal days are correct.

Click   **8.00** in the **Track Using % Hours Worked field for Vacation**.

Press   del to remove the entry.

Press   tab to advance to the Maximum Days field.

Press   del to remove the entry.

Click   the **Historical Days field for Sick Leave**.

Type   12

Press   ↓ to advance to the Historical Days field for PersonalDays. The number of days is added to the Net Days Accrued.

Type   4   **Press** tab to enter the amount.

For **Gearie** and **Schwinn**, the default entries for tracking and maximum days are correct, but you must enter the Historical Days for each entitlement.

Entering Direct Deposit Information

NOTES
Refer to page 335 if you need to review entering direct deposit details.

Click   the **Direct Deposit tab**.

All three employees have elected to have their paycheques deposited directly to their bank accounts. On this screen we need to enter the bank account details. For each employee who has elected the direct deposit option, you must turn on the selection in the Direct Deposit Paycheques For This Employee check box. Then you must add the five-digit **Branch** or Transit **Number**, the three-digit **Bank Number**, the bank **Account Number** and finally the amount that is deposited, or the percentage of the cheque. Direct deposit information is included in the chart on page 629.

NOTES
All banks in Canada are assigned a three-digit bank number, and each branch has a unique five-digit transit number. Account numbers may range from five to twelve digits.

NOTES
The paycheque deposit may be split among multiple bank accounts by entering different percentages for the accounts.
To delete bank account details, click the Direct Deposit check box, change the deposit status to Inactive and then delete the bank information.

Click   the **Direct Deposit Paycheques For This Employee check box** to add a ✓.

Click   the **Branch No. field**.

Type   89008   **Press** tab to advance to the Institution No. field.

Type   102   **Press** tab to advance to the Account No. field.

Type   2998187   **Press** tab **twice** to advance to the Percentage field.

Type   100

The Memo tab will not be used at this time. You could enter a note with a reminder date to appear in the Daily Business Manager, for example, a reminder to issue vacation paycheques on a specific date or to recover advances.

Entering Additional Information

NOTES
Refer to page 336 to review entering additional information details for employees.

VeloCity has chosen to enter the name and phone number of the person to be contacted in case of an emergency involving the employee at work. We added the names for these fields in the Payroll Settings (page 656).

Click   the **Additional Info tab** to access the fields we added for the ledger when we entered Names.

You can indicate whether you want to display any of the additional information when the employee is selected in a transaction. We do not need to display the contact information in the Payroll Journal. Refer to the chart on page 629 for contact details.

Click   the **Emergency Contact field**.

Type   Adrian Ingles

Press   ⌨ *tab* **twice** to move to the Contact Number field.

Type   (905) 548-0301

Entering T4 and RL-1 Reporting Amounts

The next information screen allows you to enter the year-to-date EI insurable and pensionable earnings. By adding the historical amounts, the T4 slips prepared for income taxes at the end of the year and the Record of Employment termination reports will also be correct.

Because there are yearly maximum amounts for CPP and EI contributions, these historical details are also needed. Totals for optional deductions are also retained in the employee record. The amounts you need are in the chart on page 629.

Click   the **T4 and RL-1 Reporting tab** to open the next screen we need.

In the **Historical EI Ins. Earnings** field, you should enter the total earned income received to date that is EI insurable. The program will update this total every time you make payroll entries until the maximum salary on which EI is calculated has been reached. At that time, no further EI premiums will be deducted.

Pensionable Earnings are also tracked by the program. This amount determines the total income that is eligible for the Canada Pension Plan; CPP deductions will stop automatically when the maximum has been reached. The Pension Adjustment amount is used when the employee has a workplace pension program that will affect the allowable contributions for personal registered pension plans and will be linked with the Canada Pension Plan. Workplace pension income is reduced when the employee also has income from the Canada Pension Plan. Since VeloCity has no company pension plan, the Pension Adjustment amount is zero.

The T4 Employee Code applies to a small number of job types that have special income tax rules.

Click   the **Historical Amounts field for EI Ins. Earnings**.

Type   12392

Click   the **Historical Amounts field for Pensionable Earnings**.

Type   12520

Correct   any employee information **errors** by returning to the field with the error. **Highlight** the **error** and **enter** the **correct information**. **Click each tab** in turn so that you can check all the information.

When all the information is entered correctly, you must save the employee record.

Click   ▣ Create Another to save the record and open a new blank employee information form.

Click   the **Personal tab** so that you can enter address information.

Repeat   these procedures to **enter** other employee **records**.

Click   💾 Save and Close after entering the last record to save the record and close the Payroll Ledger.

NOTES
Additional information for other ledgers may also be displayed or hidden in journal transactions.

⚠ WARNING!
The Contact Number field is not predefined as a telephone number, so its format will not be corrected automatically by the program.

NOTES
Refer to page 337 if you need to review entering T4 and RL-1 reporting details.

NOTES
The EI Insurable amount is the total of gross wages, including overtime wages and vacation pay, but not benefits.
Pensionable earnings include these same incomes plus benefits.

NOTES
We will not use the remaining tax information fields for VeloCity. VeloCity does not have a company pension plan with regular payroll deductions, so there is no plan registration number. The Pension Adjustment amount is used when an employee contributes to a company pension plan and these payments reduce the amount the employee can contribute to a private registered pension plan. Income from company pension plans may also be reduced when CPP is collected at retirement.
CPP contribution rates are set federally.

NOTES
You can print these reports from the Reports menu in the Employees window.

NOTES
Refer to page 339 if you want to review the setup for job categories.

Display or **print** the **Employee List** and the **Employee Summary Report**. Compare them with pages 628–630 to check the accuracy of your work.

Close the **Employees window** to return to the Home window.

Entering Job Categories

Now that we have entered all the employees, we can set up job categories and indicate which employees are in each category.

Click the **Settings icon** . Then **click Payroll** and **Job Categories**.

On the Job Categories screen, you enter the category names and indicate whether the employees in each category submit time slips and whether they are salespersons. Categories may be active or inactive. We need a new category called Sales.

If you do not create categories, the employees in the default selection <None> are salespersons so they can still be selected in the Sales Journal.

Click the **Job Category field below <None>**.

Type Sales **Press** (tab) to add checkmarks to the next two columns and set the status to Active.

Click **Assign Job Categories** to change the screen.

The Sales category is selected and the screen is updated with employee names. Initially, all are Employees Not In This Job Category.

You can add employee names to the category by choosing an employee and clicking **Select** or by choosing **Select All**. Once employees are in a category (the column on the right), you can remove them. Select an employee and click **Remove** or click **Remove All** to move all names at the same time.

Click **Select All** to place all employees in the Sales category. **Click OK**.

Setting Up Payroll Remittances

Because we have entered all payroll settings and all suppliers, we can set up the payroll remittances information. This process has three steps: linking the suppliers to the taxes or deductions they receive, entering remittance frequency and entering the pay period end date for the next remittance. Refer to the chart on page 623 and the Accounting Procedures on page 635.

Click **Remittance** under **Payroll**.

All the payroll items that are linked to liability (remittance) accounts are listed: taxes, deductions and user-defined expenses. For each liability, we can select a supplier and enter the payment frequency and due date for the next payment.

NOTES
All payroll remittances are made monthly except those for EHT to the Minister of Finance and WSIB to the Workplace Safety and Insurance Board. These two remittances are made quarterly.
The end of the next remitting period for all suppliers is May 1.

Click the **List icon** in the Remittance Supplier column on the line for EI.

Click **Receiver General for Canada** in the list of suppliers that opens.

Click **Select** or **press** (enter) to return to the Remittance Settings screen with the cursor in the Remitting Frequency field for EI.

Choose Monthly from the Frequency drop-down list. **Press** (tab).

Type May 1

Enter   the remaining **Remittance Suppliers**, **Frequencies** and dates for the **End Of Next Remitting Period**. Refer to the chart on page 623.

For **EHT** and **WSIB**, select the **Quarterly Remitting Frequency**.

Assigning Sales Tax Codes

Instead of entering tax codes in the individual ledger records, we can assign them in groups with the Assign Tax Codes feature. You can use this feature to enter initial tax code settings, as we do here for suppliers, or to update tax codes, as we do here for clients.

Click   **Company**, **Sales Taxes** and **Tax Codes** to open the Settings window:

NOTES
You can also access the Assign Tax Codes screens from the Home window Maintenance menu.

Click   the **Assign Tax Codes** button below the list of codes:

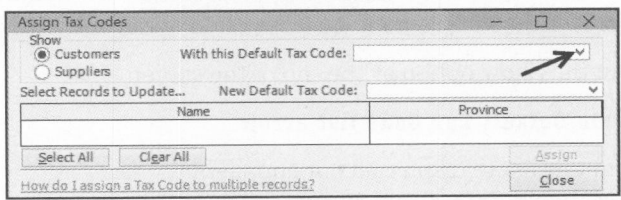

You can assign codes for suppliers and for customers. Customers are selected initially. None are listed because no tax code is selected. All customers were assigned the tax code H as part of the setup for the Receivables Ledger. As a result, showing all customers With This Default Tax Code (code H) will include all customers.

Choose H – HST @ 13% from the With This Default Tax Code drop-down list:

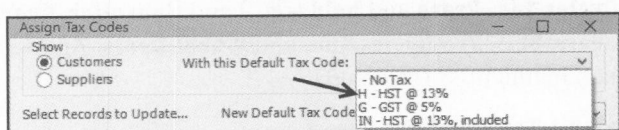

This will include all customers in the selection list:

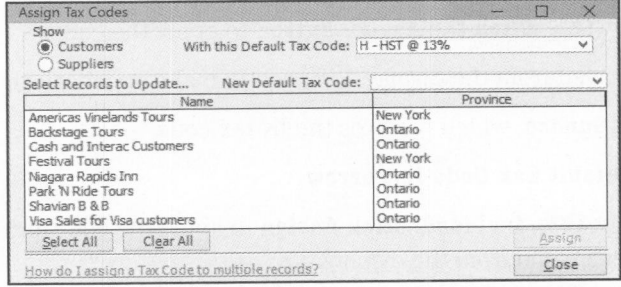

NOTES
If you already entered No Tax for the USD customers, they will not appear on this list.

The next step is to select the customers that require a different tax code.

You can select one customer, more than one customer or all customers (by clicking Select All). We need to select the two USD customers.

Click   **Americas Vinelands Tours**.

Press   and **hold** (ctrl) and then **click Festival Tours**. Both names are now highlighted and we are ready to choose a new default code for them.

Click   the **New Default Tax Code list arrow**:

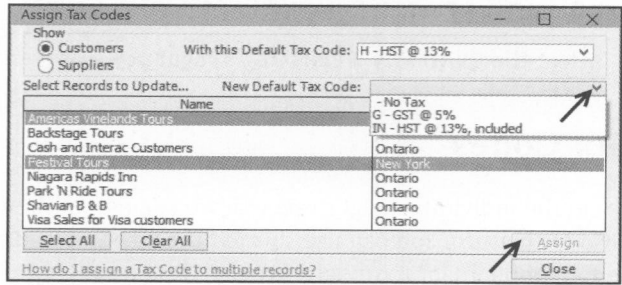

Our options are to change from code H to one of the codes not already applied. We can choose from No Tax, G and IN. USD customers do not pay taxes on exported goods.

Choose No Tax from the drop-down list. The Assign button becomes available.

Click   the **Assign button** below the list of names.

This will change the code for these two customers. Their names are removed from the list because they no longer have the tax code H — the one we chose.

The remaining customers stay on the list, so you can assign other tax codes if necessary. Tax code H is correct for the other customers, so we can continue by applying supplier tax codes. We have not entered any supplier tax codes yet, so the default entry will be No Tax. This is correct for the government agencies and payroll authorities.

Click   **Suppliers** in the Show option at the top of the screen.

Click   the **With This Default Tax Code list arrow**.

Select   **No Tax** from this list to display all our suppliers:

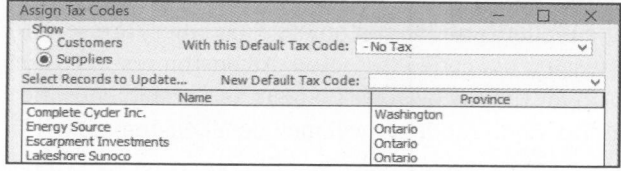

Click   **Complete Cycler Inc. Press** and **hold** ⌐ctrl⌐ and then **click Energy Source, Niagara Bell, Pro Cycles Inc.** and **Wheel Deals**. All five names should remain highlighted (selected).

Click   the **New Default Tax Code list arrow**.

We are changing from the code No Tax, so this is not on the drop-down list.

Click   **H – HST @ 13%. Click** the **Assign button** to apply the code.

The five names are removed from the display. We need to make one more change.

Click   **Lakeshore Sunoco**, which requires the IN tax code.

Click   the **New Default Tax Code list arrow**.

Click   **IN – HST @ 13%, included. Click Assign** to apply the code and remove the supplier's name from the display.

The remaining five suppliers are government agencies and payroll authorities for which the default No Tax code is correct.

Click   **Close** to save all the changes and return to the Tax Codes Settings.

Click   **OK** to save all the new settings and return to the Home window.

Preparing the Inventory Ledger

Use the VeloCity Inventory Information and chart on pages 630–631 to record details about the inventory items on hand.

Entering Inventory Records

The next set of keystrokes will enter the information for VeloCity's first inventory item, Bicycle Pump: standing model.

Click   **Inventory & Services** in the Modules pane list.

Click   the **Inventory & Services icon** . Again, with no inventory items on file, the icon window is empty.

Click   Create or **choose** the **File menu** and **click Create**:

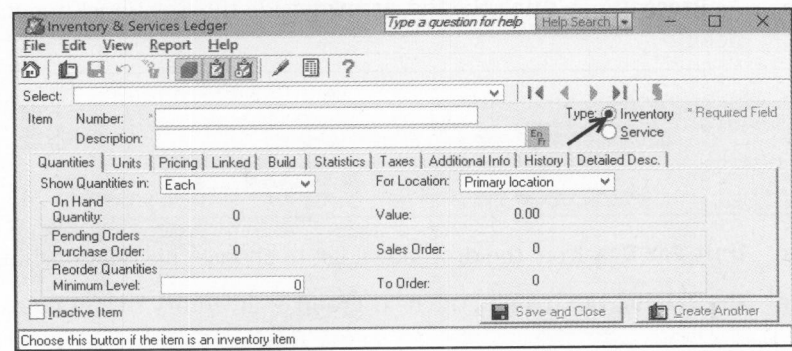

The cursor is in the Item Number field. Use this field for the code or number for the first item. When you sort inventory by description, the two item fields will be reversed — the Description field will appear first. Item Number is a required field.

Type   AC010 **Press** (tab) to advance to the Item Description field, the field for the name of the inventory item.

Type   Bicycle Pump: standing model

The Type is set correctly for this item as Inventory rather than Service.

The Show Quantities In field allows you to select the units displayed in the ledger. If you have entered different units for stocking, selling and buying, these will be available from the drop-down list. The Quantity On Hand and Value fields are updated by the program, as are the Purchase Orders and Sales Orders Pending.

Click   the **Minimum Level field**. Here you should enter the minimum stock level or reorder point for this inventory item.

Type   5

Click   the **Units tab** to advance to the next information screen:

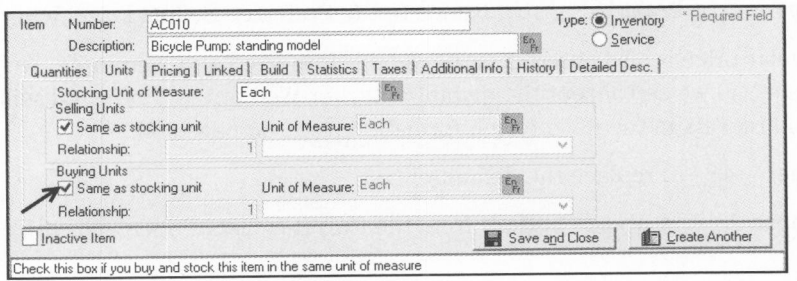

PRO VERSION
There isn't a Build tab in the Pro version, and only two show icons will be included in the tool bar. The Show Activities tool applies only to Premium features, and the Refresh tool is used with the multi-user option in Premium.

NOTES
If you hide the Inventory icon window (Setup menu, User Preferences, View), you will open this Inventory Ledger immediately when you click the Inventory & Services icon.

NOTES
The Item Description is not a required field, even when you sort by description.

WARNING!
Enter inventory details very carefully. You cannot remove an inventory record or change the Type if there is a quantity on hand. You must edit the History fields to reduce the quantity and value to zero. Then remove the item and re-enter all the details correctly.
Changing the Type requires an additional step. Close the ledger to save the changes in the history (with zero quantity). When you open the ledger again, you can edit the Type.

You can enter different units for items when the units for buying, stocking and selling differ. VeloCity uses the same units for stocking and selling but some buying units are different. For example, if items are purchased in dozens and stocked individually, the relationship is 12 to 1. The Stocking Unit must be changed. The bicycle pumps are purchased in boxes of four pumps and stocked and sold individually (unit).

Double-click the default entry **Each** for the Stocking Unit Of Measure.

Type   Unit

Click   **Same As Stocking Unit** in the **Buying Units section** to remove the ✓ and open the relationship fields. Here you should indicate how many stocking units are in each buying unit.

Press   (tab) to advance to the Unit Of Measure field.

Type   Box **Press** (tab) **twice** to advance to the Relationship field.

Type   4 **Press** (tab). **Click** the **list arrow** beside the Relationship number field:

Click   **Unit Per Box** from the drop-down list to choose this relationship.

Click   the **Pricing tab** to open the next group of inventory record fields:

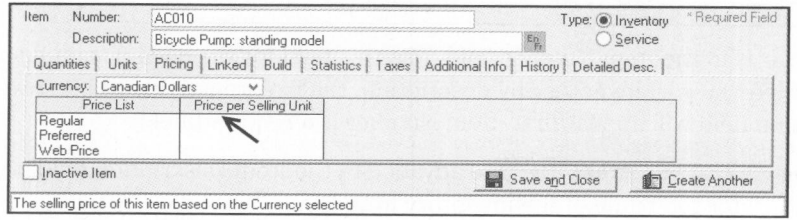

The Currency field and foreign price fields are available only if you indicated that inventory prices should be taken from the Inventory Ledger record and not calculated using the exchange rate. The pricing option appears on the Inventory Settings screen only after you enter foreign currency information for the company. Therefore, you must add and save currency information first. Taking prices from the ledger record is the default setting.

On the Pricing tab screen, you can enter regular, preferred and Web prices in the currencies that you have set up. If you created additional price lists, their names will also appear on this screen. The home currency (Canadian Dollars) is selected first.

Click   the **Regular Price Per Selling Unit field**. Here you should enter the selling price for this inventory item.

Type   50 **Press** (tab) to advance to the Preferred Selling Price field.

The regular price is also entered as the default Preferred and Web Price. We do not have Web sales, so we can accept the default entry for Web prices. Preferred selling prices are in brackets in the Inventory Information chart on page 630.

Type   45 to replace the default entry.

Choose United States Dollars from the Currency list to open USD price fields:

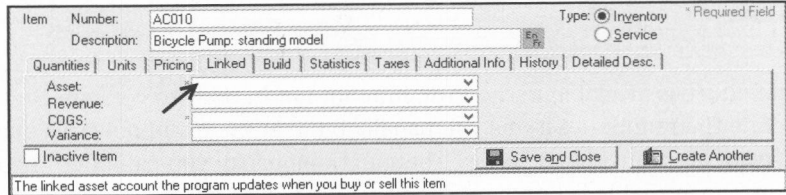

The pricing method is entered separately for each price. You can choose either Exchange Rate or Fixed Price for Regular, Preferred and Web prices.

Click   **Exchange Rate** beside Regular to change the entry to Fixed Price.

Press   (tab) to advance to the Regular Price Per Selling Unit field.

Type   37 **Press** (tab) to advance to the Pricing Method field.

Click   **Exchange Rate** to change the entry to Fixed Price.

Press   (tab) to advance to the Preferred Price Per Selling Unit field.

Type   33 **Press** (tab).

Click   the **Linked tab** to open the linked accounts screen for the item:

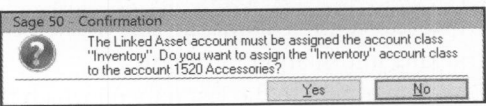

Click   the **Asset field list arrow**.

Here you must enter the **asset** account associated with the sale or purchase of this inventory item. All accessories in the Inventory chart on page 630 use account *1520*. All bicycles use *1540*, and the books use *1560* as the asset account. All available asset accounts are in the displayed list. Asset account is a required field.

Enter the account by clicking the list arrow and choosing from the drop-down account list, or

Type   1520 **Press** (tab).

The program asks you to confirm the account class change for account *1520*:

Click   **Yes** — you must accept the change in account class.

The cursor advances to the **Revenue** field. Here you must enter the revenue account that will be credited with the sale of this inventory item.

Again, you can display the list of revenue accounts by clicking the list arrow. Or,

Type   4020 **Press** (tab).

The cursor advances to the **COGS** field. Here you must enter the expense account to be debited with the sale of this inventory item, normally the *Cost of Goods Sold* account. VeloCity keeps track of each inventory category separately and has different expense accounts for each category. The appropriate expense account is updated automatically when an inventory item is sold. The COGS account is another required field.

NOTES
The ledger option to change the way foreign prices are calculated is available only when you selected Foreign Prices Are Taken From The Foreign Price Listed In The Inventory And Services Record as your Inventory Setting (page 662).

NOTES
Revenue and Variance accounts are not required fields for inventory items. Entering them in the ledger will add them automatically in the journal when the item is sold.

NOTES
If you add a new account at this stage, you can include an Opening Balance using the Add An Account wizard. Because the history is not finished, the Opening Balance field is added to the wizard.

Click the list arrow beside the field to display the available expense accounts.

Double-click **5050** or **type** 5050 **Press** ⌨tab⌨ to advance to the Variance field.

Click **Yes** to accept the account class change if prompted.

Sage 50 uses the **Variance** linked account when you restock oversold items. If there is a difference between the historical average cost of goods remaining in stock and the actual cost when the new merchandise is received, the price difference is charged to the variance expense account at the time of the purchase (refer to page 525). If you have not indicated a variance account, the program will ask you to identify one when you are entering the purchase that has a variance.

Type 5080 or **click** the **list arrow** and **choose** the **account**.

Click the **Build tab**.

Click **Yes** to accept the account class change and access the Build screen:

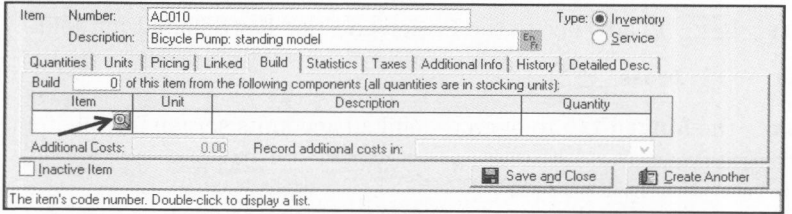

The Build feature is available in the Premium but not in the Pro version. On this screen you define the number of items you usually build at once and how this quantity is made or built from other inventory items. Then, in the journal, you can build the item by choosing it from the available list and entering the number of units you want to build at that time. This screen holds the components portion of the Item Assembly Journal.

Click the **Statistics tab** to open the next tab information screen:

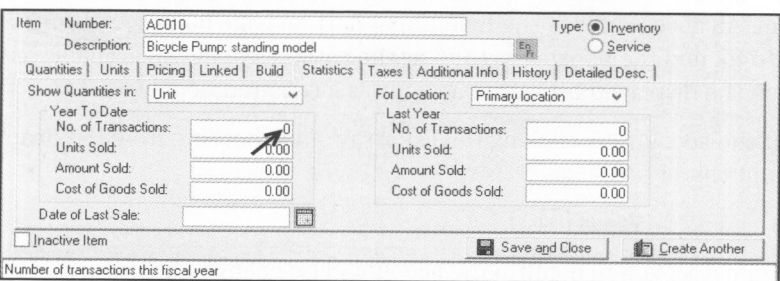

On this screen, you can enter historical information about the sale of the product. It would then be added to the inventory tracking information for reports.

The first activity field, the Date Of Last Sale, refers to the last date on which the item was sold. The next two sections contain information for the Year To Date and the previous year. Since VeloCity has not kept this information, you can skip these fields. Refer to page 372 in the Flabuless Fitness application (Chapter 10) for a more detailed description of these historical Statistics fields.

Click the **Taxes tab** to input the sales taxes relating to the inventory item:

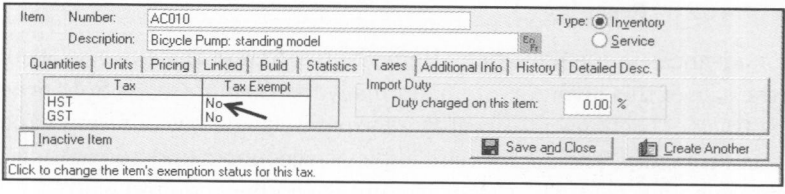

You can indicate whether the item is taxable for all the taxes you set up, GST and HST in this case. HST is charged on sales of all inventory items except for books, so the default entry No for **Tax Exempt** is correct for bicycle pumps.

The exemption settings in the ledger record do not control the tax code entered in the Sales Journal. They prevent a tax from being applied.

For **Books: Complete Bicycle Guide** and **Books: Endless Trails**, items BK010 and BK020, **click No** beside **HST** for Tax Exempt to change the entry to Yes.

Duty is also entered on this screen. You must activate the duty tracking option (page 651) before the duty rate field becomes available. Since no duty is charged on the imported inventory, you can leave the duty rate at 0%.

We have not added fields to the ledger record as we did for Payroll, so we can skip the **Additional Info** screen.

The next step is to add the opening historical balances for the inventory items.

> **Click** the **History tab**:

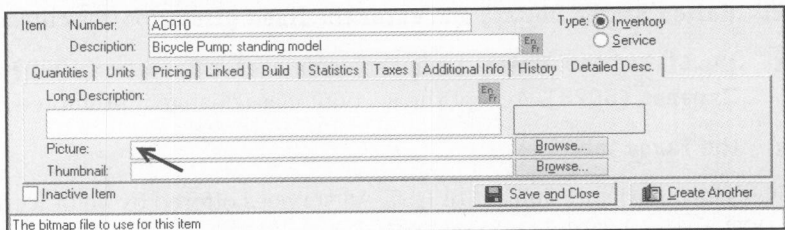

This screen has information about the starting quantities for the item at the time of conversion to Sage 50. The opening quantities and values are added to the Quantity On Hand and Value on the Quantities tab screen. History is entered in stocking unit quantities (the same as selling units for VeloCity).

> **Click** the **Opening Quantity field** to enter the opening level of inventory — the actual number of items available for sale.

> **Type** 10 **Press** [tab].

The cursor advances to the **Opening Value** field, where you should enter the actual total cost of the inventory on hand.

> **Type** 300

> **Click** the **Detailed Desc. tab**:

The final tab screen allows you to enter further descriptive information. This optional information provides a detailed description of the inventory item (up to 500 characters) as well as a picture in image file format.

> Type the detailed item description in the Long Description text box.

> **Click** **Browse** beside Picture. **Click This PC. Double-click C:, SageData16, LOGOS** and **PUMP.BMP** or **PUMP** to add the file name and picture.

> **Correct** any **errors** by returning to the field with the mistake. **Highlight** the **error** and **enter** the **correct information. Click** the different **tabs** to review all the information that you entered.

NOTES

To open the duty fields in the Purchases Journal, you must activate tracking of duty information and indicate in the supplier record that duty is charged on purchases from the supplier. Rates entered in the Inventory Ledger records will appear automatically in the Purchases Journal for those items. Duty rates can also be entered in the journal if you have not entered them in the ledger records.

NOTES

When you set up multiple locations, you can enter the quantity and value for items at each location. The Primary location is the default. In Chapter 18, we add a second location for VeloCity's second store, Ryder's Routes.

WARNING!

Enter inventory history details carefully. To change historical quantities, you must delete the history entries, save the item, then remove the item and re-enter it. Otherwise the cost information in journal entries will be incorrect.

The total opening value amounts for all items in an asset group must match the General Ledger asset account balance before you can finish entering the history.

NOTES

A picture file for the Bicycle Pump: standing model has been added to the SageData16\LOGOS folder with your other data files. We have not provided picture files for the remaining inventory items.

NOTES

Pictures using either .BMP or .JPG formats can be displayed on-screen for inventory items.

NOTES

An entry for each item is added to the Home window Inventory Item list pane as you create and save it.

PRO VERSION

pro The Time & Billing tab screen is used to set up Time & Billing, a feature that is not available in the Pro version. The Activity setting and Internal Service Activity also apply to the Time & Billing feature, so they do not appear on the Pro version screen.

NOTES

Enter USD prices because some United States customers will use these services in Canada and will pay taxes.

NOTES

Linked accounts for services are not required. However, adding them to the ledger record will have them entered into the journal automatically.

Click the **Quantities tab** to prepare for entering the next item. The quantity information (historical information) has been added.

Click [Create Another] to save the record and advance to a new input screen after you have added all the information.

Repeat these procedures to **enter** the **other** inventory **records** on page 630.

Entering Inventory Services

The final items on the inventory chart (page 631) are services that VeloCity provides. Entering services is similar to entering inventory, but there are fewer details.

You should have a blank Inventory & Services Ledger window open at the Quantities tab screen.

Click **Service** in the upper-right section of the screen to change the Type:

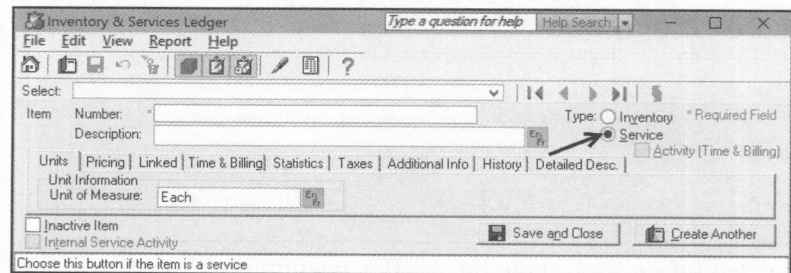

Some item details do not apply, so there are fewer tabs and fields for services. The Unit Of Measure and Selling Price have the same meaning for services as they do for inventory items. Because service items are not kept in stock or purchased, only the selling unit is applicable, there is no minimum quantity and the History fields are removed. Only expense and revenue accounts are linked for services, and even these are not required. The other two linked account fields do not apply and are removed for services. Remember to use *Revenue from Services* and *Cost of Services* as the linked accounts for inventory services.

Item Number is the only required field for service items.

Enter the **Item Number** and **Description** and the **Unit Of Measure**.

Click the **Pricing tab** and add **Regular** and **Preferred prices** in Canadian dollars. Select Canadian Dollars as the currency if necessary.

Select **United States Dollars** and **enter** the **fixed prices** for this currency.

Click the **Linked tab**. **Enter** the linked accounts for **Revenue (4040)** and **Expense (5075)**. Accept the account class change if prompted.

Click the **Taxes tab**.

Most services in Ontario are subject to HST. All services offered by VeloCity are not exempt from HST, so the default is correct at No.

Click [Create Another].

Click the **Units tab**. **Repeat** these procedures to **enter other service records**.

Click [Save and Close] after entering the last service record.

Close the **Inventory & Services window** to return to the Home window.

Display or **print** the **Inventory List**, **Summary**, **Quantity** and **Price Lists** reports. Compare them with the information on pages 630–631 to check them for accuracy.

Finishing the History

The last stage in setting up the accounting system involves finishing the history for each ledger. Before proceeding, you should check the data integrity (Home window, Maintenance menu) to learn whether there are any out-of-balance ledgers that will prevent you from proceeding. Correct these errors and then make a backup copy of the files.

You may also want to create a complete working copy of the not-finished files.

Making a Backup of the Company Files

Choose the **File menu** and **click Backup**, **click** the **Backup tool** or **click** the **Data Management icon** (Company module window) to start the Backup wizard.

Click **Browse** and **choose** the **data folder you want** for the not-finished backup of the data file.

Double-click the **File name field** in the Backup wizard screen.

Type NF-VELO

Click **OK** to create a backup copy of all the files for VeloCity.

The "NF" designates files as not finished to distinguish them from the ones you will work with to enter journal transactions. You will return to your working copy of the file so you can finish the history.

Changing the History Status of Ledgers to Finished

Refer to page 95 and page 249, respectively, for assistance with finishing the history and correcting history errors.

Choose the **History menu** and **click Finish Entering History**.

If your amounts, account types and linked accounts are correct, you will be warned that this step is not reversible and advised to back up the file first.

Click **Proceed** when there are no errors and you have backed up your files.

If you have made errors, you will not get the warning message. Instead Sage 50 will generate a list of errors.

Click **Print** so that you can refer to the list for making corrections.

Click **OK** to return to the Home window. **Make** the **corrections**, **replace** your **backup** file and then **try again** to finish the history.

Click **Proceed**.

The VeloCity files are now ready for you to enter transactions. The ledger icons in all module windows now appear without the open history icons. All the ledgers are ready for transactions.

Congratulations on reaching this stage! This is a good time to take a break.

Finish your **session**. This will give you an opportunity to read the next section and the instructions before starting the source document transactions.

WARNING!
Before adding passwords for practice, make a backup of your data file without passwords. You can restore this file to continue working if you forget your password or lock yourself out of the data file.
We strongly advise you not to set passwords for working copy data files used for tutorial purposes.

NOTES
Passwords have not been added to any data files for this text.

NOTES
You must work in single-user mode to set up passwords and users.

WARNING!
If you have forgotten your password, you will be unable to open the files. For this reason, you should
• keep the code in a safe place
• choose a code that is unique to you but easy for you to remember
• keep a backup copy of the unprotected files in a safe place

PRO VERSION
The Pro version does not have Time & Billing access rights.

NOTES
Passwords must be different for each person to serve their purpose of restricting access.

Entering Users and Security Passwords

Sage 50 allows you to set up passwords for different users. The password for the system administrator (sysadmin) controls access to the system or program. Passwords for other users control viewing and editing privileges for different ledgers, journals, reports and messages. If different employees work with different accounting records, they should have different passwords.

Restricting access by setting passwords is different from hiding ledgers using the Setup menu, User Preferences, View screen. Since the View preferences are unrestricted user settings, these hidden ledgers can be restored at any time by another user. Ledgers hidden by restricted access passwords can be accessed and restored only by opening the files with the system administrator (**sysadmin**) password and changing access rights.

Users and passwords are entered from the Setup menu in the Home window.

Choose the **Setup menu** and **click Set Up Users** to display the control window:

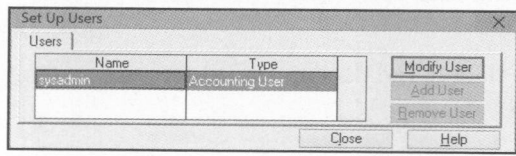

This Set Up Users window lists all users currently set up in the data files. Initially, the only user is sysadmin (system administrator). The highest level of access comes with the sysadmin password that allows the user to enter, use or modify any part of the data files, including creating users and setting passwords. The sysadmin password must be set before any other passwords can be set, so this user is selected initially. You can set up passwords for additional users to allow them access to different parts of the program. Begin by adding a password for sysadmin. You cannot change the sysadmin user name.

Click **Modify User** to open the Modify User password entry screen:

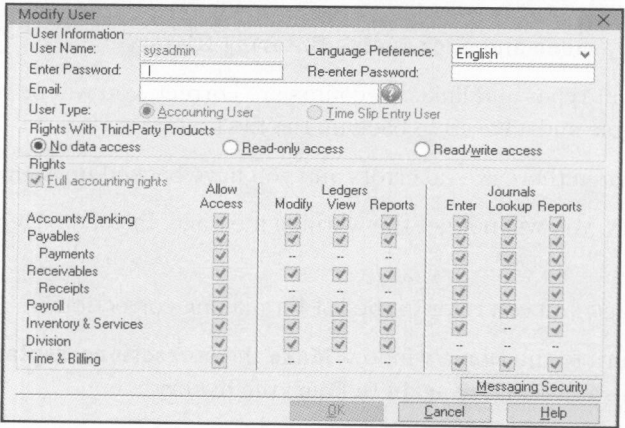

You cannot modify access privileges (or name) for the sysadmin because someone (the system administrator) must have full access to the data. All the Accounting Rights options are dimmed. The cursor is in the Enter Password field.

If you want **e-mail messages** from Sage also to go to an address other than the primary one connected with your Sage account, enter it in the E-mail field.

You can use up to seven letters and/or numbers as the code. Passwords are case sensitive — that is, ABC is different from Abc. If you enter a password with an upper case (capital) letter, you must use an upper case letter each time.

Type the **word** or **code** that you want as your password. For practice, choose a simple password such as your first name or your initials.

Press (tab) to advance to the next field, Re-enter Password.

For security reasons, the password is never revealed on the screen — an asterisk (*) or some other symbol will replace each letter or number that you type. As an added precaution, Sage 50 requires you to enter the code twice in exactly the same way.

Type the **password** or **code** again.

Access to **third-party products** can also be limited — the read/write access option provides the fullest level of access. No access — the highest security level — is selected by default. This is the only access setting you can modify for the sysadmin.

If the two password entries do not match, Sage 50 generates an error message when you close the Rights screen to save the user information.

Click OK and try re-entering the code again. If you still do not have a match, go back to the Enter Password field and type in the code. You may have mistyped the first entry. Then re-enter the password in the Re-enter Password field.

Click the **Messaging Security** button to open a screen with different types of Sage communications:

![Messaging Security dialog box](Messaging Security screen)

The drop-down list beside Full Messaging Rights allows full access or no access for each user. Support messages are always displayed. Click OK to return to the Add User screen. By default, the system administrator has full access to all types of messages.

Click **OK**. You will return to the Modify User screen. **Click OK** again to return to the Set Up Users screen.

If you have allowed read and write access to third-party products, and the password you entered is weak, the program will recommend selecting a more secure password.

For practice, you can click No to continue with the easy password.

The Add User button is now available. If you return to the Home window, there will be one password for the data files, the one for sysadmin.

You can now enter additional users.

Click **Add User** to open the new user setup screen:

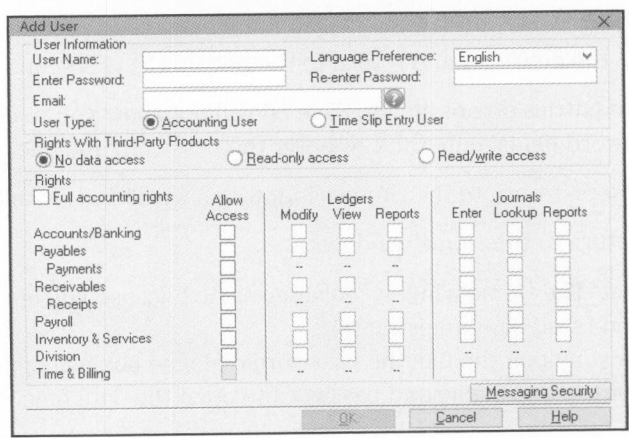

Adding Other Users

NOTES

You cannot add users until you have saved a password for sysadmin.

After you have added a password for the system administrator (sysadmin), you can set up additional users with unique passwords.

Each user can be allowed access to all parts of the program (full accounting rights) or access to only some of the ledgers and journals. Access to ledgers, journals and reports can be controlled separately. The Add User window should be open.

To give a user full access, click Full Accounting Rights below the Password and Third Party Rights sections. For each ledger and journal, you can allow the following: no access (no ✓ for Allow Access); modifying (editing) rights that include viewing; viewing rights only; or access to ledger reports. For journals, you can allow no access, enter rights (enter and look up transactions), lookup only or access to journal reports. Rights for each ledger and journal can be controlled separately, and each user may have different access rights. Each user must have a unique name and password.

Initially, the Add User options are given for an Accounting User for access to the ledgers and journals, but you can also restrict a user to accessing only the Time Slips. Refer to Appendix G for setting up time slip users.

The cursor should be in the User Name field.

> **Type**   the **name** of the first user.
>
> **Press**   ⌨tab⌨ **twice** to advance to the Enter Password screen.
>
> **Type**   the **word** or **code** that you want as your restricted usage password. You can use up to seven letters and/or numbers as the code.
>
> **Press**   ⌨tab⌨ to advance to the next field, Re-enter Password.
>
> **Type**   the **password** or **code** again.

Again, for security purposes, to be sure you entered the password that you intended, you must enter the same code twice. The E-mail address is optional — adding it will have product information sent to the user. The next step is defining the user's access rights.

> To allow access, click the check boxes beside the ledger name in the appropriate columns. For example, to allow viewing access only for the General Ledger, click the Allow Access check box beside Accounts/Banking. The program adds ✓s for all columns beside Accounts/Banking. Click Modify and Reports to remove those ✓. To allow no access, leave the Allow Access check box in the first column empty.

Similarly, you can restrict access to third-party information (such as Microsoft Office documents) and messages for each user. Passwords do not serve their purpose if the user cannot view reports in Sage 50 but can access and modify those reports in another program.

> **Click**   **OK** to save the new user and return to the Set Up Users screen.
>
> If the two password entries do not match, Sage 50 will not allow you to continue. Return to the password fields; enter and re-enter the password and click OK.

After entering all the users, return to the Home window to save all the changes.

> **Click**   **Close** to return to the Home window.

Nothing has changed yet. The Home window looks the same because you are using the program as the sysadmin (system administrator).

However, the next time you open the file, the password dialogue box will appear, and you will be required to enter the user name and password to open the data file:

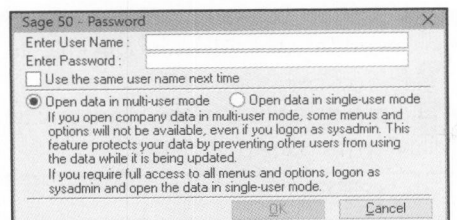

Type   the **user name**, either sysadmin or another user name. **Press** (*tab*).

Type   the **password** or **code** for this user.

Choose   the **Single-User** or **Multi-User Mode** for accessing the file. **Click OK**.

If you enter an incorrect code, nothing happens — the Password dialogue box remains open. If you enter the sysadmin user name and password, you will have full access to all parts of the program, including the security settings. If you have set passwords, you must enter the program using the sysadmin user name and password in order to change the security settings and user passwords. Other users can change their own passwords at any time; they cannot access the passwords for other users.

If you enter as a user other than the sysadmin and do not have full accounting rights, you will have restrictions in the Home window, like the one below. The following Classic view Home window illustrates restrictions for a user and the access rights allocated to that user:

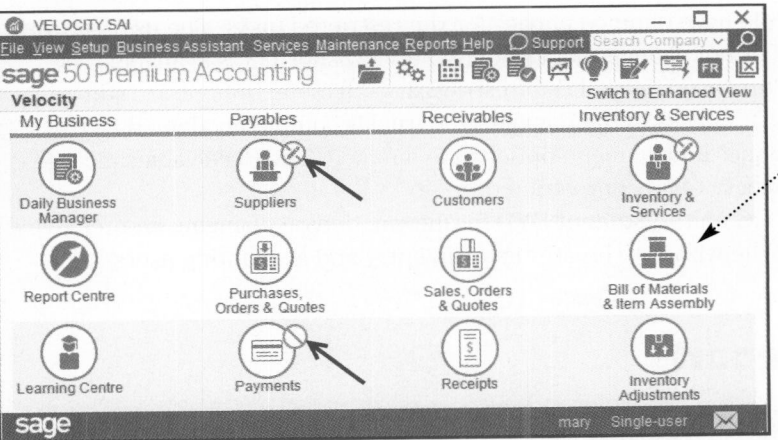

The user above can input normal sales journal entries and inventory entries, accept payments from customers and enter purchases. He/she cannot write cheques to suppliers, pay employees, reconcile accounts, make deposits or make General Journal entries.

The user does not have access to the General Ledger or journals, the Payroll Ledger or journals or to the Division Ledger — their icons are missing (no ✓ appears for these ledgers in the Allow Access settings of the Rights pane).

Only the Customers Ledger in this example can be modified. The ⊘ (**No Edit** symbol) on the Suppliers and Inventory & Services ledger icons means that these ledgers can be viewed but not edited (✓ for View, but not for Modify in the Rights pane). If you open these ledgers, all fields will be dimmed.

The **No Entry** symbol ⊘ on the Payments Journal indicates no access is permitted (the user cannot write cheques — there is no ✓ for Allow Access in the Rights pane). The Receivables (Customers & Sales) and Inventory journals are not restricted — no extra icon appears with them (✓ for Enter, Lookup and Reports in the Rights pane).

When access to reports is restricted for any journal or ledger (no ✓ for Reports in the Rights pane), those report menu options will be dimmed.

NOTES
Restricted menu options are directly related to the user's access rights.

The same set of access right restrictions is applied as in the previous illustration.

NOTES
Although users can change their own passwords, the sysadmin retains final control. He/she can still reset all passwords and remove users when necessary.

Several main menu options are also restricted. Only the system administrator can access the Set Up Users menu option after passwords are set. All users can change their own passwords.

The following composite screenshot of all drop-down lists in the Company and Payables windows in the Enhanced view indicates the same restrictions:

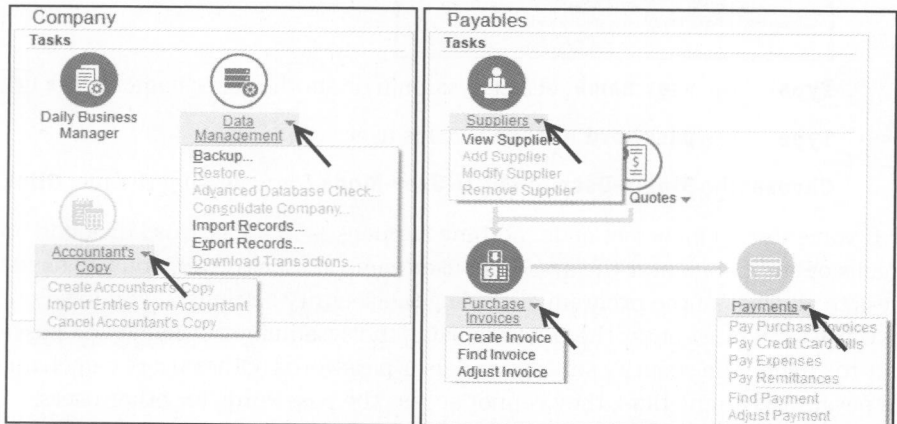

The Home window icons do not have symbols added. Modules the user cannot access — Banking and Payroll — are removed from the Modules pane list. The General Journal and Chart of Accounts icons are also removed from the Company window because the user is not permitted to access them. The three drop-down shortcuts lists for the Payables module have dimmed entries for the restricted tasks. The user can view the supplier records but not change them — only the View shortcut is available. The user's access to the Purchases Journal is unrestricted — all menu options are still available (not dimmed). Access to the Payments Journal is completely denied — the user cannot write cheques and all menu options are dimmed. The Receivables module is unchanged because access to it is unrestricted.

Refer to Appendix G on the Student DVD for information on changing and removing passwords, and using the wizard to create time-slip entry and accounting users.

Exporting Reports

NOTES
Integration with Microsoft Office software is described further in Appendix L on the Student DVD.

NOTES
Depending on your previous export selection, your default format and folder may be different from ours.

LOGOS may be entered in the Save In field if you did not change folder selections after adding the picture file.

NOTES
By default your working folder is selected, or the folder you opened most recently.

Sage 50 allows you to export reports to a specified drive and path. The files created by the program may then be used by spreadsheet or word processing programs. Exporting files will allow you to perform additional calculations and interpret data for reporting purposes. This process of integrating Sage 50 files with other software is an important step in making the accounting process meaningful.

The next set of keystrokes will export the opening Balance Sheet for VeloCity to a spreadsheet.

Display the **Balance Sheet** or the report you want to export.

Click the **Export Report tool** or **choose** the **File menu** and **click Export**:

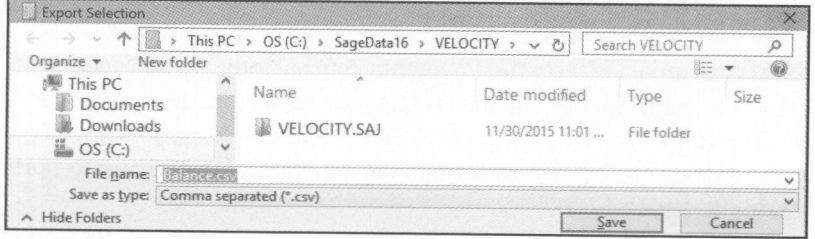

Click the **Save As Type list arrow** for the list of file types you can create:

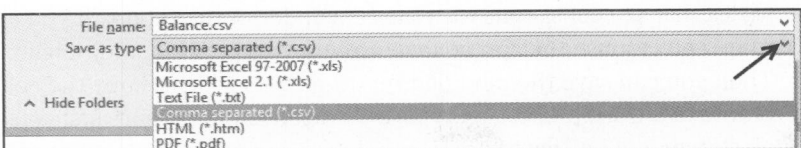

File formats available for export purposes include HTML for Web pages, Text for a word processing format file, Microsoft Excel Versions 97–2007 and 2.1, Comma Separated and PDF.

Click   **Microsoft Excel 97-2007** as the type for the Balance Sheet in the Save As Type field. Use the field list arrow to display the file type options if needed.

Choose the **location** for your exported file.

Click   the **File Name field list arrow** to access the folder you want.

Accept the default **file name**, or **type** the **name** you want for your file. The program assigns an extension to the file name so that Microsoft Excel will recognize the new file as an Excel file.

Click   **Save**. You will return to your displayed report.

To create a text file, click Text File. To generate a file that you can view with Acrobat Reader, but not modify, click PDF.

Any Sage 50 report that you have displayed can be opened directly as a Microsoft Excel spreadsheet. Formulas for totals and so on are retained and you can then use the spreadsheet file immediately.

Display the **Sage 50 report** you want to use in Excel.

Click   the **Open In Excel tool** or **choose** the **File menu** and **click Open In Microsoft Excel** to open the file name window:

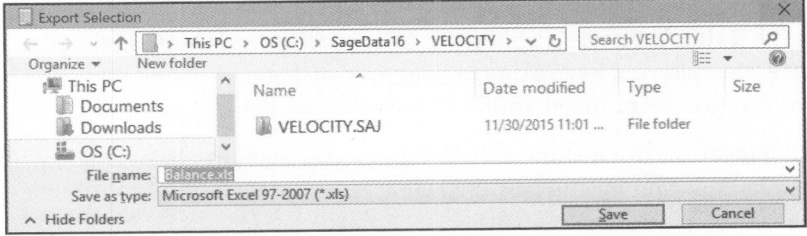

Choose a **location** for your spreadsheet data file.

Click   **Save** to open the spreadsheet. Your Sage 50 data file will remain open.

Close the **Excel file** when finished. You can now work with a report that you have exported.

Using Your Data Files and Reports with Other Software

Finish the session using Sage 50. Start the program you want to use with the exported file. Open the file you exported.

Some spreadsheet programs can open and convert a file that was saved in the format of a different program. For example, Microsoft Excel can open (or save) text files or Comma Separated Files. Simply choose the alternative file type in your Open File (or Save File) window. Click OK. Your exported file should replace the blank document screen.

Once you have exported a financial statement as a text file, you can include it in a written report prepared with any word processing program. You can then use the features of the word processing software to enhance the appearance of the statement

NOTES
The bank statements for this text were created by exporting the General Ledger reports as .CSV files to a spreadsheet, modifying the data and then copying the results to a word processing file.

NOTES
The .XLS format files retain the formulas from the Sage 50 reports while the .CSV files do not.

NOTES
The Open In Excel feature saves the Excel file before opening it, so you can return to it later.

NOTES
Be sure that the selected file type also matches the format of your exported file (e.g., .TXT for a text file, or .XLS for Excel).
Refer to the built-in help or program manuals if necessary for assistance with the third-party program.

NOTES
Comma Separated (*.CSV) format files opened in Excel and resaved as *.XLS files provide the best format and view for working with the files in Excel if you need to modify the file or add formulas.

using format styles that are consistent with the remainder of the report. If you exported a spreadsheet file, you can use the spreadsheet program to perform additional calculations. Then you can save the modified report as a text file or copy the cells you want to incorporate in a word processing report. We used exported spreadsheets to create the bank statements for this text.

When working with a spreadsheet program, you can use the calculation capabilities of the spreadsheet program to make comparisons between statements from different financial periods. You might also want to use the charting or graphing features to prepare presentation materials.

Exporting reports offers advantages over re-creating the statements — you save the time of retyping, and you ensure greater accuracy by avoiding errors while retyping.

SOURCE DOCUMENT INSTRUCTIONS

Instructions for May

1. **Enter** the **transactions** for May using all the information provided.

2. **Print** the following **reports**:
    a. Journal Entries (All Journals) for May, including foreign amounts, corrections and additional transaction details
    b. Customer Aged Detail Report for all customers for May
    c. General Ledger account reports for
        - Bank: Niagara Trust Chequing
        - Revenue from Sales
        - Sales Returns and Allowances
    d. Supplier Purchases Summary for Wheel Deals, all items, for May

3. **Export** the **Balance Sheet** as at May 31, 2018, to a spreadsheet application. **Calculate** the following **key ratios** in your spreadsheet:
    a. current ratio   b. quick ratio

4. **Set up** a **budget** for use in June and July and **enter amounts** based on expenses and revenues for May and for the first quarter.

Instructions for June

1. **Enter** the **transactions** for June using all the information provided.

2. **Print** the following **reports**:
    a. Journal Entries (All Journals) for June, including foreign amounts, corrections and additional transaction details
    b. Supplier Aged Detail Report for all suppliers for June
    c. Employee Summary Report for all employees for the pay period ending June 30, 2018
    d. Inventory Sales Summary Report (observe and report items that have not sold well over the two-month period)
    e. Customer Sales Summary (all customers, items and categories) for June

NOTES
The Premium version allows you to create Multi-Period Income Statements and Balance Sheets. Refer to Chapter 18, page 783.

3. **Export** the **Comparative Balance Sheet** for May 31 and June 30, 2018, to a spreadsheet application to use for three-month comparisons at the end of July.

4. **Compare** June's **performance against** May's budget **forecast**.

Instructions for July

1. **Enter** the **transactions** for July using all the information provided.

2. **Print** the following **reports**:
   a. Journal Entries (All Journals) for July, including foreign amounts, corrections and additional transaction details
   b. Trial Balance, Balance Sheet and Income Statement on July 31
   c. Inventory Statistics Report for Bicycles (All Journals) for July
   d. Bank Transaction Report for all bank accounts from May 1 to July 31

3. **Export** the **Balance Sheet** and **Income Statement** to a spreadsheet application. Combine the Balance Sheet with the comparative one for May and June. **Compare** first- and second-quarter figures, item by item, to assess the performance of VeloCity. You may want to use multi-period reports for this comparison.

4. **Make** a **backup copy** of your data files. **Advance** the **session date** to August 1, 2018, to start a new fiscal period.

5. **Print** the **Trial Balance**, **Balance Sheet** and **Income Statement** for August 1. **Compare** the end of July and the first of August **statements** and note the changes that result from Sage 50 closing the books for the new fiscal period.

PRO VERSION
Print the General Ledger Report for the bank accounts instead of the Bank Transaction Report.

⚠ WARNING!
Chapter 16, Case 8, in Appendix D on the Student DVD has the data you need to complete the bank account reconciliation for VeloCity. You must use your data files for July 31 to complete the reconciliation, so be sure to make a backup copy before you advance the session date to the new fiscal year.

SOURCE DOCUMENTS

SESSION DATE – MAY 15, 2018

1 | **Memo #5-1**   **Dated May 1, 2018**
Reverse the Accrued Wages adjustment from previous quarter. (Debit Accrued Wages and credit Wages expense account.)

2 | **Receipt #812**   **Dated May 1, 2018**
From Shavian B & B, cheque #147 for $4 429.60 in payment of account including $90.40 discount for early payment. Reference invoice #2191.

3 | **Payment Cheque #101**   **Dated May 2, 2018**
To Pro Cycles Inc., $5 960 in payment of account including $80 discount for early payment. Reference invoice #PC-618.

4 | **Purchase Order #38**   **Dated May 2, 2018**
Shipping date May 25, 2018
From Wheel Deals

25	CY020	Bicycle: Commuter Alum frame CX90	$ 9 750.00 USD
4	CY070	Bicycle: Youth YX660	640.00 USD
3	AC100	Trailer: third-wheel rider	330.00 USD
		Freight	200.00 USD
		HST	1 419.60 USD
		Total	$12 339.60 USD

Terms: 2/10, n/30. The exchange rate is 1.375.

5 | **Receipt #813**   **Dated May 2, 2018**
From Niagara Rapids Inn, cheque #73 for $5 537 in payment of account including $113 discount for early payment. Reference invoice #2194.

NOTES
Remember that receipts are deposited to Undeposited Cash and Cheques. This should be the default account.

NOTES
Edit the default purchase cost entered in the Amount field for all inventory purchases as required.

	Sales Order #248		**Dated May 2, 2018**
6	Delivery date May 6, 2018		

To Fallsview Riverside Resort (use Full Add for new customer)

1	AC010	Bicycle Pump: standing model	$ 50/ unit
2	AC020	Bicycle Pump: hand-held mini	80/ unit
10	AC030	Helmet	120/ helmet
9	AC040	Light: halogen	25/ unit
18	AC050	Light: rear reflector	15/ unit
9	AC060	Lock: kryptonite tube	70/ lock
2	AC070	Pannier: front wicker clip-on	80/ basket
2	AC080	Pannier: rear mesh	60/ basket
1	AC090	Trailer: 2-child closed	620/ unit
1	AC100	Trailer: third-wheel rider	260/ unit
1	CY010	Bicycle: Commuter Steel frame CX10	640/ bike
4	CY020	Bicycle: Commuter Alum frame CX90	960/ bike
4	CY040	Bicycle: Trail Alum frame TX560	1 220/ bike
2	CY090	Stationary Converter	870/ unit
		Freight (tax code H)	50
		HST	13%

Terms: 2/10, n/30.
Received cheque #96 for $3 000 as down payment (deposit #21) to confirm sales order.

	Payment Cheque #346	**Dated May 5, 2018**
7		

To Wheel Deals, $2 963.70 USD in payment of account including $53.40 discount for early payment. Reference invoice #WD-391. The exchange rate is 1.380.

	Memo #5-2	**Dated May 5, 2018**
8		

Re Damaged Inventory: Two (2) wicker panniers, item AC070, were crushed and damaged beyond repair. Adjust the inventory to recognize the loss.

	Sales Invoice #2470		**Dated May 5, 2018**
9			

To Fallsview Riverside Resort, to fill sales order #248

1	AC010	Bicycle Pump: standing model	$ 50/ unit
2	AC020	Bicycle Pump: hand-held mini	80/ unit
10	AC030	Helmet	120/ helmet
9	AC040	Light: halogen	25/ unit
18	AC050	Light: rear reflector	15/ unit
9	AC060	Lock: kryptonite tube	70/ lock
2	AC070	Pannier: front wicker clip-on	80/ basket
2	AC080	Pannier: rear mesh	60/ basket
1	AC090	Trailer: 2-child closed	620/ unit
1	AC100	Trailer: third-wheel rider	260/ unit
1	CY010	Bicycle: Commuter Steel frame CX10	640/ bike
4	CY020	Bicycle: Commuter Alum frame CX90	960/ bike
4	CY040	Bicycle: Trail Alum frame TX560	1 220/ bike
2	CY090	Stationary Converter	870/ unit
		Freight (tax code H)	50
		HST	13%

Terms: 2/10, n/30.

	Credit Card Purchase Invoice #NC-114	**Dated May 6, 2018**
10		

From Niagara Courier (use Full Add for new vendor), $500 plus $65 HST for prepaid advertisement to run over the next 12 weeks. Purchase invoice total $565 paid in full by Visa.

11 **Payment Cheque #347**   **Dated May 6, 2018**

To Complete Cycler Inc., $2 107 USD in payment of account including $74 discount for early payment. Reference invoice #CC-918. The exchange rate is 1.382.

12 **Memo #5-3**   **Dated May 7, 2018**

From Visa, received monthly credit card statement for $240 including $220 for purchases up to and including May 3 and $20 annual renewal fee. Submitted cheque #102 for $240 in full payment of the balance owing.

13 **Deposit Slip #18**   **Dated May 7, 2018**

Prepare deposit slip for all receipts for May 1 to May 7 to deposit the funds to Bank: Niagara Trust Chequing from Undeposited Cash and Cheques. The total deposit for the three cheques is $12 966.60.

14 **Receipt #814**   **Dated May 9, 2018**

From Backstage Tours, cheque #472 for $6 759.20 in payment of account including $180.80 discount for early payment. Reference invoice #2199.

15 **Credit Card Purchase Invoice #PS-1149**   **Dated May 10, 2018**

From Paper & Stuff (use Full Add for new vendor), $150 plus $19.50 HST for stationery and other office supplies for store. Purchase invoice total $169.50 paid in full by Visa.

16 **Credit Card Purchase Invoice #LS-612**   **Dated May 14, 2018**

From Lakeshore Sunoco, $92 including HST for gasoline purchase for delivery vehicle. (Use tax code IN.) Purchase invoice total paid in full by Visa.

17 **Employee Time Summary Sheet #14**   **Dated May 14, 2018**

For the Pay Period ending May 7, 2018
Dunlop Mercier worked 80 regular hours and 2 hours of overtime in the period. Recover $50 loan. Issue payroll deposit slip #DD25.

18 **Deposit Slip #19**   **Dated May 14, 2018**

Prepare deposit slip for all receipts for May 8 to May 14 to deposit the funds. One cheque for $6 759.20 is being deposited.

19 **Memo #5-4**   **Dated May 14, 2018**

Payroll Remittances: Use May 1 as the End of Remitting Period date to make the following payroll remittances in the Payments Journal. Read the margin Warning.

a) Record payment for EI, CPP and Income Tax Payable up to May 1 to the Receiver General for Canada. Issue cheque #103 in full payment.

b) Record payment for Garnisheed Wages Payable up to May 1 to the Receiver General for Canada. Issue cheque #104 in full payment.

c) Record payment for EHT Payable up to May 1 to the Minister of Finance. Issue cheque #105 in full payment.

d) Record payment for VRSP Payable up to May 1 to Manulife Financial. Issue cheque #106 in full payment.

e) Record payment for Savings Plan Payable up to May 1 to Escarpment Investments. Issue cheque #107 in full payment.

f) Record payment for Group Insurance Payable up to May 1 to Welland Insurance. Issue cheque #108 in full payment.

g) Record payment for WSIB Payable up to May 1 to Workplace Safety and Insurance Board. Issue cheque #109 in full payment.

 WARNING!

You may need to change the bank account for the payment to Visa. The USD bank account may remain selected after the US dollar payment.

 NOTES

All deposits are made to Bank: Niagara Trust Chequing from Undeposited Cash and Cheques.

NOTES

Paper & Stuff
Contact: Clip Papers
26 Pulp Ave.
Niagara on the Lake, ON
L0S 1J0
Terms: net 30
Tax code: H
Expense account: 1280

NOTES

Enter Memo #5-4A, Memo #5-4B and so on in the Reference Number and Comment fields for the payroll remittances.

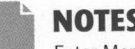 **WARNING!**

When you remit the payroll taxes to the Receiver General, the Pay Period date for Garnisheed Wages is updated to June 1 at the same time. You must change the date back to May 1 when making this remittance before paying the amounts to avoid including the amounts from the May 14 paycheque. Choose Yes to save the new dates when prompted.

Sage 50 groups the remittances to suppliers. To avoid this, you would need to create a separate supplier account for each remittance.

| 20 | **Memo #5-5** | **Dated May 14, 2018** |

Record payment for GST and HST for the period ending April 30 to the Receiver General for Canada. Issue cheque #110 in full payment.

| 21 | **Cash Purchase Invoice #ES-64329** | **Dated May 15, 2018** |

From Energy Source, $120 plus $15.60 HST paid for hydro service. Purchase invoice total $135.60. Terms: cash on receipt. Issue cheque #111 in full payment.

| 22 | **Receipt #815** | **Dated May 15, 2018** |

From Fallsview Riverside Resort, cheque #195 for $13 439.35 in payment of account including $335.50 discount for early payment. Reference invoice #2470 and deposit #21.

| 23 | **Purchase Order #39** | **Dated May 15, 2018** |

Shipping date May 20, 2018
From Complete Cycler Inc.

1	AC020	Bicycle Pump: hand-held mini	$ 360.00 USD
7	AC030	Helmet	3 045.00 USD
5	AC040	Light: halogen	360.00 USD
5	AC050	Light: rear reflector	250.00 USD
10	AC060	Lock: kryptonite tube	1 450.00 USD
		Freight	100.00 USD
		HST	723.45 USD
		Invoice total	$6 288.45 USD

Terms: 2/10, n/30. The exchange rate is 1.381.

| 24 | **Purchase Order #40** | **Dated May 15, 2018** |

Shipping date June 1, 2018
From Wheel Deals

4	AC090	Trailer: 2-child closed	$ 880.00 USD
4	AC100	Trailer: third-wheel rider	440.00 USD
20	CY020	Bicycle: Commuter Alum frame CX90	7 800.00 USD
		Freight	120.00 USD
		HST	1 201.20 USD
		Invoice total	$10 441.20 USD

Terms: 2/10, n/30. The exchange rate is 1.381.

SESSION DATE – MAY 31, 2018

| 25 | **Cash Purchase Invoice #NB-59113** | **Dated May 19, 2018** |

From Niagara Bell, $80 plus $10.40 HST paid for phone service. Purchase invoice total $90.40. Terms: cash on receipt. Issue cheque #112 in full payment.

| 26 | **Purchase Invoice #CC-2014** | **Dated May 20, 2018** |

From Complete Cycler Inc., to fill purchase order #39

1	AC020	Bicycle Pump: hand-held mini	$ 360.00 USD
7	AC030	Helmet	3 045.00 USD
5	AC040	Light: halogen	360.00 USD
5	AC050	Light: rear reflector	250.00 USD
10	AC060	Lock: kryptonite tube	1 450.00 USD
		Freight	100.00 USD
		HST	723.45 USD
		Invoice total	$6 288.45 USD

Terms: 2/10, n/30. The exchange rate is 1.383.

27
Credit Card Sales Invoice #2471   **Dated May 20, 2018**

To Visa Sales (sales summary)

Qty	Code	Description	Price	Amount
5	AC020	Bicycle Pump: hand-held mini	$ 80/ unit	$ 400.00
10	AC030	Helmet	120/ helmet	1 200.00
8	AC040	Light: halogen	25/ unit	200.00
8	AC050	Light: rear reflector	15/ unit	120.00
8	AC060	Lock: kryptonite tube	70/ lock	560.00
4	AC080	Pannier: rear mesh	60/ basket	240.00
1	AC090	Trailer: 2-child closed	620/ unit	620.00
1	AC100	Trailer: third-wheel rider	260/ unit	260.00
20	BK010	Books: Complete Bicycle Guide (code G)	40/ book	800.00
20	BK020	Books: Endless Trails (code G)	40/ book	800.00
1	CY030	Bicycle: Racer Ultra lite RX480	3 100/ bike	3 100.00
3	CY040	Bicycle: Trail Alum frame TX560	1 220/ bike	3 660.00
1	CY060	Bicycle: Mountain Carbon frame MX34	2 950/ bike	2 950.00
2	CY090	Stationary Converter	870/ unit	1 740.00
4	S010	Boxing for shipping	75/ job	300.00
4	S020	Maintenance: annual contract	110/ year	440.00
8	S030	Maintenance: complete tune-up	70/ job	560.00
20	S040	Rental: 1 hour	10/ hour	200.00
18	S050	Rental: 1 day	30/ day	540.00
14	S060	Repairs	45/ hour	630.00
		GST	5%	80.00
		HST	13%	2 303.60
		Total paid by Visa		$21 703.60

WARNING!
You must change the tax code for books (items BK010 and BK020) to G so that taxes will be correctly applied for these items.

28
Deposit Slip #20   **Dated May 21, 2018**

Prepare deposit slip for all receipts for May 15 to May 21 to deposit the funds. The total deposit for the single cheque is $13 439.35.

29
Cash Purchase Invoice #N-2018-1   **Dated May 23, 2018**

From Niagara Area Treasurer (use Full Add), $900 in full payment of first instalment of quarterly property tax assessment. Terms: EOM. Issued cheque #113 in full payment. Store as a monthly recurring entry. Recall the stored transaction to issue cheques #114 and #115 as postdated cheques for the next two instalments, dated June 23 and July 23.

30
Sales Invoice #2472   **Dated May 23, 2018**

To Park 'N Ride Tours (preferred customer)

1	AC010	Bicycle Pump: standing model	$ 45/ unit
2	AC020	Bicycle Pump: hand-held mini	70/ unit
10	AC030	Helmet	105/ helmet
6	AC040	Light: halogen	22/ unit
6	AC050	Light: rear reflector	12/ unit
6	AC060	Lock: kryptonite tube	65/ lock
2	AC070	Pannier: front wicker clip-on	75/ basket
1	AC100	Trailer: third-wheel rider	235/ unit
10	BK020	Books: Endless Trails (code G)	35/ book
2	CY020	Bicycle: Commuter Alum frame CX90	850/ bike
2	CY040	Bicycle: Trail Alum frame TX560	1 090/ bike
2	CY070	Bicycle: Youth YX660	420/ bike
6	S020	Maintenance: annual contract	100/ year
		GST	5%
		HST	13%

Terms: 2/10, n/30.

NOTES
Niagara Area Treasurer
Contact: Budd Jett
53 Price St.
Niagara Falls, ON L2K 2Z3
Tel: (905) 461-0063
Web: NAT.ca
Terms: net 1
Tax code: no tax (exempt)
Expense account: 5260

Use N-2018-2 and N-2018-3 as the invoice numbers for the postdated payments for property taxes.

NOTES
Remember to change the tax code for books to G.

Purchase Invoice #WD-364   **Dated May 26, 2018**

| 31 |

From Wheel Deals, to fill purchase order #38

25	CY020	Bicycle: Commuter Alum frame CX90	$ 9 750.00 USD
4	CY070	Bicycle: Youth YX660	640.00 USD
3	AC100	Trailer: third-wheel rider	330.00 USD
		Freight	200.00 USD
		HST	1 419.60 USD
		Total	$12 339.60 USD

Terms: 2/10, n/30. The exchange rate is 1.384.

Employee Time Summary Sheet #15   **Dated May 28, 2018**

| 32 |

For the Pay Period ending May 21, 2018
Dunlop Mercier worked 80 regular hours and 4 hours of overtime. Recover $50 loan. Issue payroll deposit slip #DD26.

Sales Invoice #2473   **Dated May 28, 2018**

| 33 |

To Backstage Tours (preferred customer)

20	AC030	Helmet	$105/ helmet
10	BK020	Books: Endless Trails (code G)	35/ book
10	S040	Rental: 1 hour	9/ hour
20	S050	Rental: 1 day	25/ day
		GST	5%
		HST	13%

Terms: 2/10, n/30.

NOTES
Remember to change the tax code for books to G.

Sales Return 2473-R   **Dated May 29, 2018**

| 34 |

Backstage Tours returned one damaged helmet (AC030) priced at $105 plus 13% HST. Total sales return amount $118.65 credited to account. Create new Subgroup Account 4070 Returns and Allowances. Terms: 2/10, n/30. Delete or change the comment.

Create an Adjustments Journal entry to write off the damaged helmet.

NOTES
Use the same payment terms for the return as for the sale so that the discount will be correctly reduced for the returned item.

Memo #5-6   **Dated May 29, 2018**

| 35 |

Transfer $21 000 USD to USD Chequing account: transfer $19 000 from Visa and Interac account and $2 000 from Savings account. The exchange rate is 1.385.

NOTES
Use the General Journal for the transfer of funds, or create two separate entries in the Transfers Journal.

Payment Cheques #348 and 349   **Dated May 29, 2018**

| 36 |

To Complete Cycler Inc., $6 177.15 USD in payment of account including $111.30 discount for early payment. Reference invoice #CC-2014.

To Wheel Deals, $12 121.20 USD in payment of account including $218.80 discount for early payment. Reference invoice #WD-364.

The exchange rate is 1.385.

Cash Purchase Invoice #PMC-55   **Dated May 29, 2018**

| 37 |

From Pedlar Maintenance Co. (use Full Add), $300 plus $39 HST paid for cleaning and maintenance of premises. Terms: cash on receipt. Issue cheque #116 for $339 in full payment. The company bills monthly for its services, so store the entry as a monthly recurring transaction. You will need to change the bank account if you use the Payments Journal for this entry.

NOTES
Pedlar Maintenance Co.
Contact: Moe Pedlar
890 Braker St.
Niagara on the Lake, ON
L0S 1J0
Tel: (905) 468-2331
Terms: net 1
Tax code: H
Expense account: 5240

Bank Debit Memo #91431   **Dated May 31, 2018**

| 38 |

From Niagara Trust, authorized withdrawals were made from the chequing account on our behalf for the following:
Bank service charges: $55
Mortgage payment: $1 480 interest and $220 principal reduction
Bank loan payment: $420 interest and $480 principal reduction

39

Credit Card Purchase Invoice #LS-6533   Dated May 31, 2018

From Lakeshore Sunoco, $69 including HST for gasoline (tax code IN) and $80 plus $10.40 HST for oil change (tax code H). Purchase invoice total $159.40 charged to Visa account.

40

Memo #5-7   Dated May 31, 2018

Prepare the payroll for the two salaried employees, Pedal Schwinn and Shimana Gearie. Add 2 percent of revenue from services for May as a commission to Gearie's salary. Issue payroll deposit slips #DD27 and #DD28.

SESSION DATE – JUNE 15, 2018

41

Receipt #816   Dated June 1, 2018

From Backstage Tours, cheque #434 for $3 222.78 in payment of account including $65.77 discount for early payment. Reference sales invoice #2473 and 2473-R.

42

Purchase Invoice #WD-1804   Dated June 1, 2018

From Wheel Deals, to fill purchase order #40
From Wheel Deals

4	AC090	Trailer: 2-child closed	$ 880.00	USD
4	AC100	Trailer: third-wheel rider	440.00	USD
20	CY020	Bicycle: Commuter Alum frame CX90	7 800.00	USD
		Freight	120.00	USD
		HST	1 201.20	USD
		Invoice total	$10 441.20	USD

Terms: 2/10, n/30. The exchange rate is 1.385.

43

Sales Invoice #2474   Dated June 1, 2018

To Festival Tours (monthly recurring sale)

40	S040	Rental: 1 hour	$ 7/ hour	USD
20	S050	Rental: 1 day	22/ day	USD
		HST	13%	

Terms: 2/10, n/30. The exchange rate is 1.385.

44

Cash Purchase Invoice #WI-6921   Dated June 2, 2018

From Welland Insurance, $2 592 (including PST) for six months of insurance coverage. Invoice total $2 592. Issued cheque #117 in payment.

45

Sales Invoice #2475   Dated June 2, 2018

To Americas Vinelands Tours (USD preferred customer, no delivery charge)

2	AC020	Bicycle Pump: hand-held mini	$ 54/ unit	USD
20	AC030	Helmet	80/ helmet	USD
6	AC040	Light: halogen	16/ unit	USD
6	AC050	Light: rear reflector	10/ unit	USD
6	AC060	Lock: kryptonite tube	47/ lock	USD
20	BK010	Books: Complete Bicycle Guide	27/ book	USD
20	BK020	Books: Endless Trails	27/ book	USD
8	CY010	Bicycle: Commuter Steel frame CX10	430/ bike	USD

Terms: 2/10, n/30 and free delivery. The exchange rate is 1.386.

46

Receipt #817   Dated June 5, 2018

From Americas Vinelands Tours, cheque #198 for $6 532.68 USD in payment of account, including $133.32 discount for early payment. Reference invoice #2475. The exchange rate is 1.387.

NOTES

Enter the two items purchased from Lakeshore Sunoco on separate lines because you need different tax codes for them.

NOTES

You must calculate the amount of the commission manually and then enter the amount in the journal.

NOTES

Using the same payment terms for the return as for the sale ensured that the discount would be correctly reduced for the returned item.

NOTES

Because the services for Festival Tours were provided in Canada, HST is charged. Change the tax code to H.

NOTES

PST is charged on insurance in Ontario. PST paid is not refundable, so there is no need to track it or record it separately. It will be included with the amount for Prepaid Insurance.

NOTES

Taxes are not charged on exported goods or on freight for foreign customers.

47	**Deposit Slip #21** **Dated June 5, 2018**

Prepare deposit slip for all receipts for May 29 to June 5 to deposit the funds. The total deposit for the single cheque is $3 222.78.

48	**Receipt #818** **Dated June 7, 2018**

From Festival Tours, cheque #1257 for $797.33 USD in payment of account, including $16.27 early payment discount. Reference invoice #2474. The exchange rate is 1.388.

49	**Credit Card Purchase Invoice #LS-6914** **Dated June 8, 2018**

From Lakeshore Sunoco, $69 including HST for gasoline. Purchase invoice total $69 charged to Visa account.

50	**Memo #6-1** **Dated June 9, 2018**

From Visa, received monthly credit card statement for $985.90 for purchases up to and including June 3. Prepare cheque #118 for $985.90 to pay the Visa bill.

51	**Credit Card Sales Invoice #2476** **Dated June 9, 2018**

To Visa Sales (sales summary)

Qty	Code	Description	Price	Amount
1	AC010	Bicycle Pump: standing model	$ 50/ unit	$ 50.00
8	AC030	Helmet	120/ helmet	960.00
8	AC040	Light: halogen	25/ unit	200.00
8	AC050	Light: rear reflector	15/ unit	120.00
8	AC060	Lock: kryptonite tube	70/ lock	560.00
2	AC090	Trailer: 2-child closed	620/ unit	1 240.00
12	BK010	Books: Complete Bicycle Guide (code G)	40/ book	480.00
24	BK020	Books: Endless Trails (code G)	40/ book	960.00
5	CY020	Bicycle: Commuter Alum frame CX90	960/ bike	4 800.00
2	CY050	Bicycle: Mountain Alum frame MX14	1 850/ bike	3 700.00
1	CY070	Bicycle: Youth YX660	460/ bike	460.00
6	S010	Boxing for shipping	75/ job	450.00
12	S020	Maintenance: annual contract	110/ year	1 320.00
20	S040	Rental: 1 hour	10/ hour	200.00
20	S050	Rental: 1 day	30/ day	600.00
20	S060	Repairs	45/ hour	900.00
		GST	5%	72.00
		HST	13%	2 022.80
		Total paid by Visa		$19 094.80

52	**Payment Cheque #350** **Dated June 9, 2018**

To Wheel Deals, $10 256.40 USD in payment of account including $184.80 early payment discount. Reference invoice #WD-1804. The exchange rate is 1.388.

53	**Sales Order #249** **Dated June 12, 2018**

Delivery Date: June 14, 2018
From Shavian B & B

16	AC030	Helmet	$120/ helmet
10	AC040	Light: halogen	25/ unit
10	AC050	Light: rear reflector	15/ unit
10	AC060	Lock: kryptonite tube	70/ lock
1	AC090	Trailer: 2-child closed	620/ unit
1	AC100	Trailer: third-wheel rider	260/ unit
7	CY020	Bicycle: Commuter Alum frame CX90	960/ bike
3	CY070	Bicycle: Youth YX660	460/ bike
10	S020	Maintenance: annual contract	110/ year
		HST	13%

Terms: 2/10, n/30.

Purchase Invoice #PC-1031   **Dated June 12, 2018**

From Pro Cycles Inc.

2	AC010	Bicycle Pump: standing model	$ 240.00
1	AC020	Bicycle Pump: hand-held mini	500.00
6	AC030	Helmet	3 600.00
5	AC040	Light: halogen	500.00
5	AC050	Light: rear reflector	350.00
5	AC060	Lock: kryptonite tube	1 000.00
10	AC070	Pannier: front wicker clip-on	500.00
10	AC080	Pannier: rear mesh	380.00
		Freight	140.00
		HST	937.30
		Invoice total	$8 147.30

Terms: 1/15, n/30.

Employee Time Summary Sheet #16   **Dated June 12, 2018**

For the Pay Period ending June 5, 2018
Dunlop Mercier worked 80 regular hours in the period (no overtime). He will receive $200 as a loan and have $50 recovered from each of the next four paycheques. Issue payroll deposit slip #DD29.

Receipt #819   **Dated June 13, 2018**

From Shavian B & B, cheque #284 for $2 000 as down payment (deposit #22) in acceptance of sales order #249.

Memo #6-2   **Dated June 14, 2018**

Record payment for GST and HST for the period ending May 31 to the Receiver General for Canada. Issue cheque #119 in full payment. Clear the tax reports up to May 31.

Memo #6-3   **Dated June 14, 2018**

Payroll Remittances: Make the following remittances for the period ending May 31. Choose Pay Remittance for payroll remittances.
a) Record payment for EI, CPP and Income Tax Payable for May to the Receiver General for Canada. Issue cheque #120 in full payment.
b) Record payment for Garnisheed Wages Payable for May to the Receiver General for Canada. Issue cheque #121 in full payment.
c) Record payment for VRSP Payable for May to Manulife Financial. Issue cheque #122 in full payment.
d) Record payment for Savings Plan Payable for May to Escarpment Investments. Issue cheque #123 in full payment.
e) Record payment for Group Insurance Payable for May to Welland Insurance. Issue cheque #124 in full payment.

Purchase Invoice #WD-3047   **Dated June 15, 2018**

From Wheel Deals

3	AC090	Trailer: 2-child closed	$ 660.00 USD
3	AC100	Trailer: third-wheel rider	330.00 USD
4	CY030	Bicycle: Racer Ultra lite RX480	4 480.00 USD
4	CY060	Bicycle: Mountain Carbon frame MX34	4 960.00 USD
4	CY090	Stationary Converter	960.00 USD
		Freight	200.00 USD
		HST	1 506.70 USD
		Invoice total	$13 096.70 USD

Terms: 2/10, n/30. The exchange rate is 1.3885.

NOTES

Enter Memo #6-3A, Memo #6-3B and so on in the Reference Number and Comment fields for payroll remittances.

⚠ WARNING!

Remember to reset the Pay Period date to June 1 for the second remittance to the Receiver General to avoid including the amounts from the June 12 paycheque.

	Sales Invoice #2477	**Dated June 15, 2018**	
	To Shavian B & B, to fill sales order #249		

60

16	AC030	Helmet	$120/ helmet
10	AC040	Light: halogen	25/ unit
10	AC050	Light: rear reflector	15/ unit
10	AC060	Lock: kryptonite tube	70/ lock
1	AC090	Trailer: 2-child closed	620/ unit
1	AC100	Trailer: third-wheel rider	260/ unit
7	CY020	Bicycle: Commuter Alum frame CX90	960/ bike
3	CY070	Bicycle: Youth YX660	460/ bike
10	S020	Maintenance: annual contract	110/ year
		HST	13%

Terms: 2/10, n/30.

61 **Memo #6-4**   **Dated June 15, 2018**

Old rental bicycles will be sold and replaced with new ones. Create new inventory item: CY200 Used Bicycles with a selling price of $200 each.
Enter an Inventory Adjustment to add 20 Used Bicycles (CY200) from Rental Bicycles asset account. The unit cost is $375. (Enter 20 as a positive quantity to increase the inventory. Change the default account to 1300.)

Enter an Inventory Adjustment to move 20 Bicycles (CY020) from inventory to Rental Bicycles asset account. Accept the default unit cost. (Enter a negative quantity to decrease the inventory. Change the default account to 1300.)

SESSION DATE – JUNE 30, 2018

62 **Memo #6-5**   **Dated June 16, 2018**

Transfer $18 000 USD to Bank: USD Chequing to cover cheque to Wheel Deals. Transfer $11 000 USD from 1120 Bank: Visa and Interac Account and $7 000 USD from 1080 Bank: Niagara Trust Savings. The exchange rate is 1.390.

63 **Payment Cheque #351**   **Dated June 16, 2018**

To Wheel Deals, $12 864.90 USD in payment of account including $231.80 discount for early payment. Reference invoice #WD-3047. The exchange rate is 1.390.

64 **Cash Purchase Invoice #NB-71222**   **Dated June 18, 2018**

From Niagara Bell, $95 plus $12.35 HST paid for phone service. Purchase invoice total $107.35. Terms: cash on receipt of invoice. Issue cheque #125 in full payment.

65 **Payment Cheque #126**   **Dated June 18, 2018**

To Pro Cycles Inc., $8 075.20 in payment of account including $72.10 discount for early payment. Reference invoice #PC-1031.

66 **Deposit Slip #22**   **Dated June 19, 2018**

Prepare deposit slip for the single cheque for $2 000 for June 13 to June 19.

67 **Cash Purchase Invoice #ES-79123**   **Dated June 20, 2018**

From Energy Source, $150 plus $19.50 HST paid for hydro service. Purchase invoice total $169.50. Terms: cash on receipt. Issue cheque #127 in full payment.

68 **Credit Card Purchase Invoice #M-1034**   **Dated June 21, 2018**

From Mountview Delivery (use Quick Add for the new supplier), $80 plus $10.40 HST paid for delivery services. Invoice total $90.40. Full amount paid by Visa. Enter tax code H for the purchase.

Sales Invoice #2478 — Dated June 22, 2018

To Candide's B & B (use Full Add for new customer)

2	AC020	Bicycle Pump: hand-held mini	$ 80/ unit
2	AC090	Trailer: 2-child closed	620/ unit
1	AC100	Trailer: third-wheel rider	260/ unit
20	BK020	Books: Endless Trails (code G)	40/ book
40	S050	Rental: 1 day	30/ day
	GST		5%
	HST		13%

Terms: 2/10, n/30.

69

Receipt #820 — Dated June 24, 2018

From Shavian B & B, cheque #391 for $12 506.94 in payment of account with $296.06 discount for early payment. Reference invoice #2477 and deposit #22.

70

Receipt #821 — Dated June 26, 2018

From Candide's B & B, cheque #532 for $3 990.36 in payment of account including $81.44 discount for early payment. Reference invoice #2478.

71

Memo #6-6 — Dated June 26, 2018

Add Charitable Donations as a payroll deduction. Since VeloCity will match employee donations, a user-defined expense is also needed.
Create new Group accounts:
    2440 Charitable Donations - Employee
    2450 Charitable Donations - Employer
    5390 Charitable Donations Expense
Add Donations as new name (Setup, Settings, Payroll, Names):
    for Deduction 4 on Names, Incomes & Deductions screen
    for User-Defined Expense 2 on Names, Additional Payroll screen
Deduction Settings (Payroll, Deductions):
    Deduct Donations by Amount After Tax, EI, CPP, EHT and Vacation Pay
Add new payroll linked accounts (under Payroll Settings):
    2440 for Employee Donations (Linked Accounts, Deductions)
    2450 for Employer Donations (Linked Accounts, User-Defined Expenses, Payables)
    5390 for Employer Donations (Linked Accounts, User-Defined Expenses, for Expenses and for Payment Adjustment)
Enter amounts in Payroll Ledger for Deductions and WSIB & Other Expenses:
    Gearie: Check Use for the deduction; enter $20 as the deduction and the expense amount per period
    Schwinn: Check Use for the deduction; enter $25 as the deduction and the expense amount per period

72

Employee Time Summary Sheet #17 — Dated June 26, 2018

For the Pay Period ending June 19, 2018
Dunlop Mercier worked 80 regular hours in the period and 2 hours of overtime. Recover $50 loan and issue payroll deposit slip #DD30.

73

Deposit Slip #23 — Dated June 26, 2018

Prepare deposit slip for all receipts for June 20 to June 26 to deposit the funds. The total deposit for two cheques is $16 497.30.

74

Cash Purchase Invoice #PMC-68 — Dated June 29, 2018

From Pedlar Maintenance Co., $330 plus $42.90 HST paid for maintenance. Terms: cash on receipt. Issue cheque #128 for $372.90 in payment. Recall the stored transaction. Edit the amount and store the changed entry.

75

NOTES
Remember to change the tax code for books to G.

NOTES
Candide's B & B
Contact: Candide Shaw
190 Playtime Circle
Niagara on the Lake, ON
L0S 1J0
Tel: (905) 468-5576
Terms: 2/10, n/30
Credit limit: $15 000
Tax code: H

NOTES
To add deductions, refer to
• page 655 for names
• page 659 for payroll deductions settings
• page 660 for linked accounts
• page 672 for entering the employee deduction
• page 673 for WSIB & other expense amounts

Debit Card Sales Invoice #2479   **Dated June 29, 2018**

76

To Bruno Scinto (Cash and Interac customer)

1	AC010	Bicycle Pump: standing model	$ 50/ unit	$ 50.00
2	AC030	Helmet	120/ helmet	240.00
2	AC040	Light: halogen	25/ unit	50.00
2	AC050	Light: rear reflector	15/ unit	30.00
2	AC060	Lock: kryptonite tube	70/ lock	140.00
2	CY030	Bicycle: Racer Ultra lite RX480	3 100/ bike	6 200.00
2	S020	Maintenance: annual contract	110/ year	220.00
	HST		13%	900.90
	Invoice total paid in full			$7 830.90

Debit card #5919 7599 7543 7777. Amount deposited to Visa and Interac account.

Credit Card Purchase Invoice #LS-7823   **Dated June 30, 2018**

77

From Lakeshore Sunoco, $115 including HST for gasoline and $80 plus $10.40 HST for tire repairs. Purchase invoice total $205.40 paid in full by Visa. (Remember to change the tax code for the tire repairs.)

NOTES

Remember to change the tax code for books to G.

Credit Card Sales Invoice #2480   **Dated June 30, 2018**

78

To Visa Sales (sales summary)

2	AC010	Bicycle Pump: standing model	$ 50/ unit	$ 100.00
2	AC030	Helmet	120/ helmet	240.00
2	AC040	Light: halogen	25/ unit	50.00
4	AC050	Light: rear reflector	15/ unit	60.00
20	AC060	Lock: kryptonite tube	70/ lock	1 400.00
8	AC080	Pannier: rear mesh	60/ basket	480.00
8	BK010	Books: Complete Bicycle Guide (code G)	40/ book	320.00
40	BK020	Books: Endless Trails (code G)	40/ book	1 600.00
2	CY030	Bicycle: Racer Ultra lite RX480	3 100/ bike	6 200.00
1	CY060	Bicycle: Mountain Carbon frame MX34	2 950/ bike	2 950.00
2	CY090	Stationary Converter	870/ unit	1 740.00
30	S040	Rental: 1 hour	10/ hour	300.00
40	S060	Repairs	45/ hour	1 800.00
	GST		5%	96.00
	HST		13%	1 991.60
	Total paid by Visa			$19 327.60

Purchase Invoice #WP-4489   **Dated June 30, 2018**

79

From Wellness in Print (use Full Add for new supplier)

150	BK010	Books: Complete Bicycle Guide	$3 000.00
200	BK020	Books: Endless Trails	4 000.00
	GST		350.00
	Purchase invoice total		$7 350.00

Terms: net 30 days.

NOTES

Wellness in Print
Contact: Slim Writer
29 Editorial Circle
Hamilton, ON L6G 2S6
Tel: (905) 488-1000
Terms: net 30
Tax code: G
Business No.: 813 276 490

Bank Debit Memo #96241   **Dated June 30, 2018**

80

From Niagara Trust, authorized withdrawals were made from the chequing account on our behalf for the following:

Bank service charges: $85
Mortgage payment: $1 470 interest and $230 principal reduction
Bank loan payment: $400 interest and $500 principal reduction

---

Memo #6-7   **Dated June 30, 2018**

81

Prepare the payroll salaries for Pedal Schwinn and Shimana Gearie. Gearie took one day of personal leave. Add 2 percent of service revenue for June as a commission to Gearie's salary. Issue payroll deposit slips #DD31 and #DD32.

Memo #6-8   **Dated June 30, 2018**

82

Prepare invoice #2481 to charge Park 'N Ride Tours $30.48 interest — 1.5% of the overdue amount. Terms: net 15.

SESSION DATE – JULY 15, 2018

Sales Invoice #2482   **Dated July 1, 2018**

83

To Festival Tours, recall stored entry

40	S040	Rental: 1 hour	$ 7/ hour	USD
20	S050	Rental: 1 day	22/ day	USD
	HST		13%	

Terms: 2/10, n/30. The exchange rate is 1.390.

Employee Time Summary Sheet #18   **Dated July 9, 2018**

84

For the Pay Period ending July 2, 2018
Dunlop Mercier worked 80 regular hours in the period (no overtime) and took one day of sick leave. Recover $50 loan and issue payroll deposit slip #DD33.

Receipt #822   **Dated July 9, 2018**

85

From Park 'N Ride Tours, cheque #1431 for $8 911.40 in payment of account. Reference invoices #2472 and #2481.

Memo #7-1   **Dated July 9, 2018**

86

From Visa, received monthly credit card statement for $364.80 for purchases made before July 3, 2018. Submitted cheque #129 for $364.80 in full payment of the balance owing.

Deposit Slip #24   **Dated July 9, 2018**

87

Prepare deposit slip for the single cheque for $8 911.40 being deposited.

Memo #7-2   **Dated July 14, 2018**

88

Record payment for GST and HST for the period ending June 30 to the Receiver General for Canada. Issue cheque #130 in full payment. Remember to clear the tax report up to June 30 after making the remittance.

Memo #7-3   **Dated July 14, 2018**

89

Payroll Remittances: Make the following payroll remittances for the pay period ending June 30 in the Payments Journal.
a) Record payment for EI, CPP and Income Tax Payable for June to the Receiver General for Canada. Issue cheque #131 in full payment.
b) Record payment for Garnisheed Wages Payable for June to the Receiver General for Canada. Issue cheque #132 in full payment.
c) Record payment for VRSP Payable for June to Manulife Financial. Issue cheque #133 in full payment.
d) Record payment for Savings Plan Payable for June to Escarpment Investments. Issue cheque #134 in full payment.
e) Record payment for Group Insurance Payable for June to Welland Insurance. Issue cheque #135 in full payment.
f) Record payment for Charitable Donations Payable for June to Canadian Cancer Society. Create a new supplier record and select Payroll Authority for the supplier. Choose the new supplier in the Payroll Remittance Settings screen for both Donations entries. Include employee and employer contributions in the remittance. Issue cheque #136 in full payment.

Enter Memo #7-3A, Memo #7-3B and so on in the Reference Number and Comment fields for the payroll remittances.

WARNING!
Remember to reset the Pay Period date to July 1 for the second remittance to the Receiver General to avoid including the amounts from the July 9 paycheque.

NOTES
You cannot create the new supplier from the Pay Remittance form in the Payments Journal – you must close the Remittance Journal.
Refer to page 676 for setting up payroll remittances.

NOTES

Remember to change the tax code for books to G.

90	**Credit Card Sales Invoice #2483**		**Dated July 14, 2018**	

To Visa Sales (sales summary)

5	AC020	Bicycle Pump: hand-held mini	$ 80/ unit	$ 400.00
14	AC030	Helmet	120/ helmet	1 680.00
21	AC040	Light: halogen	25/ unit	525.00
36	AC050	Light: rear reflector	15/ unit	540.00
4	AC060	Lock: kryptonite tube	70/ lock	280.00
3	AC080	Pannier: rear mesh	60/ basket	180.00
2	AC100	Trailer: third-wheel rider	260/ unit	520.00
18	BK010	Books: Complete Bicycle Guide (code G)	40/ book	720.00
35	BK020	Books: Endless Trails (code G)	40/ book	1 400.00
2	CY020	Bicycle: Commuter Alum frame CX90	960/ bike	1 920.00
6	CY040	Bicycle: Trail Alum frame TX560	1 220/ bike	7 320.00
2	CY070	Bicycle: Youth YX660	460/ bike	920.00
2	CY090	Stationary Converter	870/ unit	1 740.00
20	CY200	Used Bicycle	200/ bike	4 000.00
30	S020	Maintenance: annual contract	110/ year	3 300.00
		GST	5%	106.00
		HST	13%	3 032.25
		Total paid by Visa		$28 583.25

91	**Receipt #823**	**Dated July 15, 2018**

From Festival Tours, cheque #638 for $813.60 USD in payment of account. Reference invoice #2482. The exchange rate is 1.389.

92	**Memo #7-4**	**Dated July 15, 2018**

Transfer $30 000 from the Visa bank account to the savings account.
Transfer $20 000 from the Visa bank account to the CAD chequing account.

SESSION DATE – JULY 31, 2018

93	**Memo #7-5**	**Dated July 18, 2018**

Pay $8 000 to the Receiver General for Canada for quarterly instalment of business income tax. Issue cheque #137. Create new Group account 5550 Business Income Tax Expense. (Hint: Remember Business Income Tax Payable.)

94	**Memo #7-6**	**Dated July 18, 2018**

Create appropriate new Heading and Total accounts around the new Group account 5550 to restore the logical order of accounts.

95	**Cash Purchase Invoice #NB-86344**	**Dated July 18, 2018**

From Niagara Bell, $120 plus $15.60 HST paid for monthly phone service. Purchase invoice total $135.60. Terms: cash on receipt of invoice. Issue cheque #138 in full payment.

96	**Cash Purchase Invoice #ES-89886**	**Dated July 18, 2018**

From Energy Source, $140 plus $18.20 HST paid for hydro service. Purchase invoice total $158.20. Terms: cash on receipt. Issue cheque #139 in full payment.

97	**Sales Invoice #2484**	**Dated July 19, 2018**

To Fallsview Riverside Resort

4	CY020	Bicycle: Commuter Alum frame CX90	$960/ bike
30	S040	Rental: 1 hour	10/ hour
30	S050	Rental: 1 day	30/ day
		HST	13%

Terms: 2/10, n/30.

Cash Sales Invoice #2485 — Dated July 19, 2018

98

To Jim Ratter (choose Continue)

1	AC030	Helmet	$120/ helmet	$120.00
1	AC070	Pannier: front wicker clip-on	80/ basket	80.00
	HST		13%	26.00
	Invoice total paid in full with cheque #16			$226.00

Deposit Slip #25 — Dated July 23, 2018

99

Prepare deposit slip for single cheque totalling $226 to deposit funds.

Employee Time Summary Sheet #19 — Dated July 23, 2018

100

For the Pay Period ending July 16, 2018
Dunlop Mercier worked 80 regular hours in the period (no overtime) and took 1 day of sick leave. Recover $50 loan and issue payroll deposit slip #DD34.

Memo #7-7 — Dated July 25, 2018

101

Issue a cheque to Dunlop Mercier for vacation pay. Dunlop wants to pay for his upcoming vacation. Record 40 hours for this payment. Issue cheque #140. (Read the margin Warning.)

Credit Card Sales Invoice #2486 — Dated July 25, 2018

102

To Visa Sales (sales summary)

3	AC010	Bicycle Pump: standing model	$ 50/ unit	$ 150.00
14	AC030	Helmet	120/ helmet	1 680.00
12	AC040	Light: halogen	25/ unit	300.00
16	AC050	Light: rear reflector	15/ unit	240.00
8	AC060	Lock: kryptonite tube	70/ lock	560.00
2	AC070	Pannier: front wicker clip-on	80/ basket	160.00
3	AC090	Trailer: 2-child closed	620/ unit	1 860.00
1	AC100	Trailer: third-wheel rider	260/ unit	260.00
18	BK010	Books: Complete Bicycle Guide (code G)	40/ book	720.00
25	BK020	Books: Endless Trails (code G)	40/ book	1 000.00
3	CY010	Bicycle: Commuter Steel frame CX10	640/ bike	1 920.00
6	CY020	Bicycle: Commuter Alum frame CX90	960/ bike	5 760.00
6	CY070	Bicycle: Youth YX660	460/ bike	2 760.00
20	S020	Maintenance: annual contract	110/ year	2 200.00
12	S030	Maintenance: complete tune-up	70/ job	840.00
12	S060	Repairs	45/ hour	540.00
	GST		5%	86.00
	HST		13%	2 499.90
	Total paid by Visa			$23 535.90

Memo #7-8 — Dated July 25, 2018

103

Received Bank Debit Memo #99142 from Niagara Trust. Cheque #16 from Jim Ratter for $226.00 was returned as NSF. Prepare sales invoice #2487 to charge Ratter for the sales amount and add $50 in service charges for the cost of processing the cheque. Create new Group account 4220 Other Revenue. Terms: net 30. (Read the margin Notes.)

Purchase Order #41 — Dated July 25, 2018

104

Shipping date August 10, 2018
From Wheel Deals

10	AC070	Pannier: front wicker clip-on	$360.00 USD
10	AC080	Pannier: rear mesh	275.00 USD
	HST		82.55 USD
	Invoice total		$717.55 USD

Terms: 2/10, n/30. The exchange rate is 1.391.

WARNING! Remember to remove all wage and benefit amounts, deductions, user-defined expense amounts and entitlements for the vacation paycheque. Refer to page 275.

NOTES Remember to change the tax code for books to G.

NOTES You cannot reverse Ratter's NSF cheque or enter a negative receipt for it because it was a cash sale. You cannot adjust the invoice by changing the method of payment because there is no customer record.
Entering the bank account in the sales invoice for the amount of the NSF cheque will reverse the bank deposit and restore the accounts receivable.
Use Quick Add to create a new partial record for Jim Ratter. For the Ratter invoice, credit Niagara Trust Chequing account for $226, credit Other Revenue for $50, debit Accounts Receivable for $276. Refer to Accounting Procedures, page 633.

Purchase Order #42   Dated July 25, 2018

| 105 |

Shipping date August 10, 2018
From Pro Cycles Inc.

6	CY010	Bicycle: Commuter Steel frame CX10	$ 1 860.00
10	CY020	Bicycle: Commuter Alum frame CX90	5 400.00
4	CY030	Bicycle: Racer Ultra lite RX480	6 000.00
4	CY040	Bicycle: Trail Alum frame TX560	2 480.00
3	CY050	Bicycle: Mountain Alum frame MX14	2 790.00
4	CY060	Bicycle: Mountain Carbon frame MX34	6 880.00
6	CY070	Bicycle: Youth YX660	1 350.00
4	CY090	Stationary Converter	1 320.00
		Freight	200.00
		HST	3 676.40
		Invoice total	$31 956.40

Terms: 2/10, n/30. Edit the payment terms for this order.
Paid $5 000 deposit with cheque #141.

Purchase Order #43   Dated July 25, 2018

| 106 |

Shipping date August 10, 2018
From Complete Cycler Inc.

2	AC010	Bicycle Pump: standing model	$ 170.00 USD
1	AC020	Bicycle Pump: hand-held mini	360.00 USD
5	AC030	Helmet	2 175.00 USD
5	AC040	Light: halogen	380.00 USD
5	AC050	Light: rear reflector	250.00 USD
8	AC060	Lock: kryptonite tube	1 160.00 USD
		Freight	120.00 USD
		HST	599.95 USD
		Invoice total	$5 214.95 USD

Terms: 2/10, n/30. The exchange rate is 1.391.

NOTES

Use tax code IN for $226, the sale portion of the bad debt. Use No Tax as the code for the $50 handling charge. Remember to "pay" the account. Refer to Accounting Procedures, pages 633–634.

Memo #7-9   Dated July 27, 2018

| 107 |

Write off Jim Ratter's account because attempts to contact him were unsuccessful. The outstanding amount is considered a bad debt. Improved customer screening for payment by cheque will be implemented for new customers. (Read the margin Notes.)

Credit Card Purchase Invoice #LS-9855   Dated July 27, 2018

| 108 |

From Lakeshore Sunoco, $98 including HST paid for gasoline. Purchase invoice total $98 paid in full by Visa.

Cash Purchase Invoice #PMC-89   Dated July 29, 2018

| 109 |

From Pedlar Maintenance Co., $330 plus $42.90 HST paid for cleaning and maintenance of premises. Terms: cash on receipt. Issue cheque #142 for $372.90 in full payment. Recall stored transaction.

Bank Credit Memo #7642   Dated July 31, 2018

| 110 |

From Niagara Trust, semi-annual interest was deposited to bank accounts. $25 was deposited to chequing account and $845 to the savings account. Interest deposit includes the General Ledger Interest Receivable account balance $420.

Memo #7-10   Dated July 31, 2018

| 111 |

Prepare the payroll for Pedal Schwinn and Shimana Gearie, the salaried employees. Add 2 percent of service revenue for July as a commission to Gearie's salary. Issue payroll deposit slips #DD35 and #DD36.

Memo #7-11   **Dated July 31, 2018**

| 112 |

Prepare separate payroll cheques to pay all employees for completed surveys and quarterly bonuses. Withhold 10 percent income tax. (Read the margin Notes.)

    Gearie $300 bonus, 20 completed client surveys, $50 income tax
    Schwinn $250 bonus, 28 completed client surveys, $53 income tax
    Mercier $250 bonus, 26 completed client surveys, $51 income tax
Issue cheques #143, #144 and #145.

Memo #7-12   **Dated July 31, 2018**

| 113 |

Increase the allowance for doubtful accounts by $500 (credit entry) in preparation for the next fiscal period. (Refer to the Accounting Procedures on pages 633–634.)

Bank Debit Memo #143661   **Dated July 31, 2018**

| 114 |

From Niagara Trust, authorized withdrawals were made from the chequing account on our behalf for the following:
    Bank service charges: $75
    Mortgage payment: $1 450 interest and $250 principal reduction
    Bank loan payment: $380 interest and $520 principal reduction

Memo #7-13   **Dated July 31, 2018**

| 115 |

Increase the salaries and wages for all employees to begin with their next paycheques in July. Gearie and Shimana will receive an additional $100 per month. Mercier will be paid $20 per hour for his regular hours, and $30 per hour for his overtime hours.

Memo #7-14   **Dated July 31, 2018**

| 116 |

Prepare quarterly adjusting entries for depreciation on fixed assets using the following amounts:

Computer equipment	$ 550
Furniture & fixtures	80
Service tools	120
Retail premises	2 450
Van	1 875

Memo #7-15   **Dated July 31, 2018**

| 117 |

Prepare adjusting entries for the following:

Office supplies used	$ 190
Bicycle repair parts used	200
Prepaid insurance expired	2 016
Prepaid advertising expired	680
Payroll liabilities accrued for Mercier	720

Create a new Group expense account 5255 Repair Parts Used.

REVIEW

The Student DVD with Data Files includes Review Questions and Supplementary Cases for this chapter that encourage group work and report analysis. The DVD also includes bank reconciliation and online banking for this chapter.

NOTES
Use the Paycheques Journal to enter the piece rate pay and bonuses.
- Enter the piece rate pay and bonus amounts.
- On the Income tab screen, remove all hours, wage, salary and benefit amounts.
- Do not remove the Vacation Earned amount for Mercier.
- On the remaining tab screens, remove entitlement hours and deduction and user-defined expense amounts.
- Click the Taxes tab.
- Click the Enter Taxes Manually tool so that you can edit the income tax amounts.
- Enter the income tax amount. Do not change the EI or CPP amounts.
- Click Enter Taxes Automatically after creating the bonus cheques.

Stratford Country Inn

After completing this chapter, you should be able to

OBJECTIVES

- *plan* and *design* an accounting system for a small business
- *prepare* a conversion procedure from manual records
- *understand* the objectives of a computerized accounting system
- *create* company files
- *set up* company accounts
- *assign* appropriate account numbers and account classes
- *choose* and *enter* appropriate settings for all ledgers
- *create* supplier, guest, employee and inventory records
- *enter* historical data and account balances in all ledgers
- *finish* entering historical data to prepare for journal entries
- *enter* accounting transactions from realistic source documents

COMPANY INFORMATION

Company Profile

Stratford Country Inn is situated in Ontario just outside the Stratford city limits, close to Stratford Festival Theatres. The Inn has room for approximately 50 guests, with additional cots available for families who want to share rooms with their children. In addition to the theatre, which attracts most of the guests, the Inn has facilities for rowing and canoeing on the small lake area near the Thames River, and a forested area nearby is used for lovely summer walks or cross-country skiing in winter. Boxed lunches are available for picnics on the waterfront before theatre events or for afternoons in the park, and fixed price dinners are offered in the dining room. Many guests stay for several days at a time.

For an additional cost, a private consultant will pamper the guests with aromatherapy sessions. The consultant pays the Inn for use of her studio.

Guests come from near and far, and even a few American theatre groups have become regular visitors. The Inn prepares invoices and accepts payments in United States dollars for US accounts. For groups and clubs, the Inn bills the entire group as a single client. Most individual guests pay by Visa or MasterCard. All

> **NOTES**
> Stratford Country Inn
> 100 Festival Road
> Stratford, ON
> N5A 3G2
> Tel 1: (519) 222-6066
> Tel 2: (888) 272-6000
> Fax: (519) 272-7960
> Business No.: 767 698 321

> **NOTES**
> For the accommodation business, the terms Guest and Supplier replace Customer and Vendor.

guests pay HST on the services provided by the Inn and GST on the historic books. Regular guests, clubs, groups or agencies that reserve blocks of theatre tickets and accommodation have credit accounts. Groups place a deposit to confirm their accommodation. For groups that are offered preferred rates, no deposits are required. In the event of overbooking, guests who cannot be placed at the Inn are put up at a nearby bed and breakfast at the Inn's expense.

The grounds of the Inn include conference rooms for discussions and debates about theatre performances and related topics. Buses take guests to the theatre and return them to the Inn on a scheduled basis. Meals can be included for those who want an all-inclusive package. The Inn's dining room caters to its full accommodation guests as well as non-resident guests.

The owner, manager and desk attendant look after the front office. The owner also provides tours of the main theatre district that include backstage access. Five additional staff members cater to the other needs of the guests.

Accounts payable have been set up for food supplies, a maintenance contract (a cleaning crew vacuums the Inn), maintenance and repairs (electrical and carpentry work), linen supplies for kitchen and guest rooms and laundry services for towels and bedding.

By June 30, the Inn was ready to convert its accounting records to Sage 50 and had gathered the following reports to make the conversion:

- Chart of Accounts
- Post-Closing Trial Balance
- Supplier Information
- Guest Information
- Employee Information and Profiles
- Inventory and Services Information

PRO VERSION
pro The terms Customer and Vendor will replace the terms Guest and Supplier.

CHART OF ACCOUNTS

STRATFORD COUNTRY INN

ASSETS
Bank: Stratford Trust CAD Chequing
Bank: Stratford Trust USD Chequing
Bank: Credit Card
Accounts Receivable
Advances and Loans Receivable
Purchase Prepayments
Prepaid Advertising
Prepaid Insurance
Food Inventory
Linens & Towels
Blankets & Bedding
Supplies: Computer
Supplies: Office
Supplies: Dining Room
Supplies: Washroom
Books
Computer Equipment
Accum Deprec: Computers
Furniture & Fixtures ▶

▶Accum Deprec: Furn & Fix
Vehicle
Accum Deprec: Vehicle
Country Inn & Dining Room
Accum Deprec: Inn & Dining Room
Grounds & Property

LIABILITIES
Bank Loan
Accounts Payable
Prepaid Sales and Deposits
Credit Card Payable
Vacation Payable
EI Payable
CPP Payable
Income Tax Payable
EHT Payable
Group Insurance Payable
Tuition Fees Payable
WSIB Payable
GST Charged on Sales ▶

▶GST Paid on Purchases
HST Charged on Services
HST Paid on Purchases
Mortgage Payable

EQUITY
E. Prospero, Capital
Current Earnings

REVENUE
Revenue from Books
Revenue from Inn
Revenue from Dining Room
Revenue from Tours
Rental Fees
Other Revenue
Exchange Rate Differences

EXPENSE
Advertising & Promotion
Bank Charges and Card Fees
Cost of Books Sold
Cost of Services ▶

▶COGS: Food
Depreciation: Computers
Depreciation: Furn & Fix
Depreciation: Vehicle
Depreciation: Inn & Dining Room
Purchase Discounts
Interest Expense: Loan
Interest Expense: Mortgage
Hydro Expenses
Maintenance & Repairs
Overflow Accommodation
Telephone Expense
Vehicle Expenses
Wages: Management
Wages: General
Wages: Dining Room
EI Expense
CPP Expense
WSIB Expense
EHT Expense
Tuition Fees Expense

NOTES: Use appropriate account numbers and add subgroup totals, headings and totals to organize your Chart of Accounts as necessary. Remember to add a test balance account for the setup.

POST-CLOSING TRIAL BALANCE

STRATFORD COUNTRY INN

June 30, 2018	Debits	Credits			Debits	Credits
Bank: Stratford Trust CAD Chequing	$47 703		▶	Accum Deprec: Vehicle		$ 10 000
Bank: Stratford Trust USD Chequing				Country Inn & Dining Room	$400 000	
(2 200 USD)	3 000			Accum Deprec: Inn & Dining Room		20 000
Bank: Credit Card	12 000			Grounds & Property	200 000	
Accounts Receivable (deposit)		$ 1 000		Bank Loan		25 000
Advances and Loans Receivable	250			Accounts Payable		8 068
Prepaid Advertising	50			Credit Card Payable		395
Prepaid Insurance	400			Vacation Payable		5 725
Food Inventory	1 650			EI Payable		3 127
Linens & Towels	2 000			CPP Payable		6 694
Blankets & Bedding	3 000			Income Tax Payable		8 778
Supplies: Computer	400			EHT Payable		577
Supplies: Office	500			Group Insurance Payable		330
Supplies: Dining Room	800			WSIB Payable		1 631
Supplies: Washroom	250			GST Charged on Sales		310
Books	4 000			GST Paid on Purchases	200	
Computer Equipment	4 000			HST Charged on Services		5 970
Accum Deprec: Computers		1 200		HST Paid on Purchases	3 700	
Furniture & Fixtures	38 000			Mortgage Payable		300 000
Accum Deprec: Furn & Fix		4 200		E. Prospero, Capital		368 898
Vehicle	50 000	▶			$771 903	$771 903

SUPPLIER INFORMATION

STRATFORD COUNTRY INN

Supplier Name (Contact)	Address	Phone No. Fax No.	E-mail Web Site	Terms Tax ID
Avon Maintenance Services (Ken Sparkles)	66 Kleen Road Stratford, Ontario N5A 3C3	Tel: (519) 272-4611 Fax: (519) 272-4813	avonservices.com	net 30 631 393 461
Bard's Linen & Towels (Jason Bard)	21 Venice Street Stratford, Ontario N5A 4L2	Tel: (519) 271-2273 Fax: (519) 271-9333	bard@bards.com bards.com	2/10, n/30 after tax 763 271 673
Bell Canada (Bea Heard)	30 Whisper Road Stratford, Ontario N5A 4N3	Tel: (519) 273-2355	bheard@bell.ca bell.ca	net 1 634 345 373
Minister of Finance				net 1
Perth County Hydro (Wynd Mills)	66 Power Road Stratford, Ontario N5A 4P4	Tel: (519) 272-6121	perthenergy.com	net 1 721 431 214
Receiver General for Canada				net 1
Stratford Service Centre (A.L.L. Ledfree)	33 MacBeth Avenue Stratford, Ontario N5A 4T2	Tel: (519) 271-6679 Fax: (519) 276-8822	ledfree@ssc.com ssc.com	net 1 634 214 211
Tavistock Laundry Services (Martin Tavistock)	19 Merchant Road Stratford, Ontario N5A 4C3	Tel: (519) 271-7479 Fax: (519) 271-7888	tavistock.com	net 30 639 271 343
Tempest Food Wholesalers (Vita Minns)	35 Henry Avenue Stratford, Ontario N5A 3N6	Tel: (519) 272-4464 Fax: (519) 272-4600	vita@tempest.com tempest.com	net 30 673 421 936
Travellers' Life				
Workplace Safety & Insurance Board				
Zephyr Advertising Agency (Tom DeZiner)	32 Portia Blvd. Stratford, Ontario N5A 4T8	Tel: (519) 271-6066 Fax: (519) 271-6067	tom@westwinds.com westwinds.com	net 1 391 213 919

LIST OF REMITTANCE SUPPLIERS

STRATFORD COUNTRY INN

Remittance Supplier	Payroll Remittance	Frequency	Next Pay Period Ending Date
Receiver General for Canada	EI, CPP and Income Tax	Quarterly	Jul 1
Workplace Safety & Insurance Board	WSIB	Quarterly	Jul 1
Minister of Finance	EHT	Quarterly	Jul 1
Travellers' Life	group insurance	Quarterly	Jul 1

OUTSTANDING SUPPLIER INVOICES

STRATFORD COUNTRY INN

Supplier Name	Terms	Date	Inv/Chq No.	Amount	Total
Avon Maintenance Services	net 30	June 7/18	AM-68	$565	
	net 30	June 14/18	AM-85	565	
	net 30	June 21/18	AM-101	565	
	net 30	June 28/18	AM-127	565	
			Balance owing		$2 260
Tavistock Laundry Services	net 30	June 8/18	TL-693	$904	
	net 30	June 22/18	TL-742	904	
			Balance owing		$1 808
Tempest Food Wholesalers	net 30	June 23/18	TF-113	$2 000	
	net 30	June 30/18	TF-183	2 000	
			Balance owing		$4 000
			Grand Total		$8 068

GUEST INFORMATION

STRATFORD COUNTRY INN

Guest Name (Contact)	Address	Phone No. / Fax No.	E-mail / Web Site	Terms / Credit Limit
Festival Club of Rosedale (Jane Birken)	3 Rosedale Valley Rd. Toronto, Ontario M5G 3T4	Tel: (416) 482-6343	janebir@conundrum.com	net 5 $10 000
Hamlet Holiday Agency (Ron Doleman)	60 Tibault Avenue Stratford, Ontario N5A 3K3	Tel 1: (519) 272-6461 Tel 2: (800) 777-7777	rdoleman@hamlet.com hamlet.com	net 5 $10 000
* Metro Arts Appreciation Group (R. Downey)	4400 Yonge St. North York, Ontario M6L 3T4	Tel: (416) 923-8142	RDowney@artnet.com artnet.com	net 5 $10 000
* NY Friends of Shakespeare (J. Monte)	33 16th Avenue Buffalo, NY 13002	Tel 1: (716) 755-4992 Tel 2: (888) 755-5000	monte@aol.com	net 5 $10 000 (USD)
Waterloo University Literary Club (T. Fornello)	88 College Rd. Waterloo, Ontario N2A 3F6	Tel: (519) 431-6343	fornello4@uwo.ca	net 5 $10 000

NOTES: * indicates preferred price list guest

OUTSTANDING GUEST INVOICES

STRATFORD COUNTRY INN

Guest Name	Terms	Date	Inv/Chq No.	Total
Hamlet Holiday Agency	net 30	June 30/18	Deposit #40 (Chq 317; enter a negative invoice)	$1 000

EMPLOYEE INFORMATION SHEET

STRATFORD COUNTRY INN

	Owen Othello	Clara Claudius	Mary MacBeth	Hedy Horatio	Juliet Jones	Shelley Shylock	Bud Romeo
Position	Manager Male, full time	Clerk Female, full time	Cook Female, full time	Waiter Female, full time	Concierge Female, full time	Waiter Female, full time	Service Male, full time
Social Insurance No.	691 113 724	873 863 211	284 682 556	294 654 421	177 162 930	891 263 634	254 685 829
Address	38 Falstaff St. Stratford, ON N5A 3T3	147 King Henry St. Mary's, ON N4X 1B2	3 Bard Cr. Stratford, ON N5A 6Z8	17 Elizabeth St. Stratford, ON N5A 4Z1	5 Capella Cres. Stratford, ON N5A 5M1	29 Avon St. Stratford, ON N5A 5N5	42 Hosteller St. New Hamburg, ON N0B 2G0
Telephone	(519) 272-2191	(519) 373-6495	(519) 277-1338	(519) 278-5343	(519) 273-9122	(519) 273-5335	(519) 381-3738
Date of Birth (mm-dd-yy)	6-29-78	4-21-71	8-3-76	12-3-83	1-25-77	3-12-87	5-27-76
Date of Hire (mm-dd-yy)	3-1-09	5-2-02	6-1-12	6-1-14	1-1-13	1-1-16	12-16-11
Federal (Ontario) Tax Exemption - TD1							
Basic Personal	$11 474 (10 011)	$11 474 (10 011)	$11 474 (10 011)	$11 474 (10 011)	$11 474 (10 011)	$11 474 (10 011)	$11 474 (10 011)
Other Indexed	–	–	$13 595 (8 500)	–	$25 387 (18 107)	–	$11 474 (8 500)
Other Non-indexed	$5 520 (5 688)	–	–	$4 360 (4 528)	–	$11 260 (11 852)	–
Total Exemptions	$16 994 (15 699)	$11 474 (10 011)	$25 069 (18 511)	$15 834 (14 539)	$36 861 (28 118)	$22 734 (21 863)	$22 948 (18 511)
Additional Federal Tax	–	–	–	$50	–	$50	–
Employee Taxes							
Historical Income Tax	$4 594.20	$2 642.94	$3 132.22	$2 678.00	$1 437.67	$1 521.88	$1 550.12
Historical EI	$451.20	$360.96	$478.01	$321.62	$446.29	$189.54	$358.54
Historical CPP	$1 294.44	$863.76	$1 172.08	$818.09	$1 088.36	$599.87	$857.35
Employee Income							
Loans: Historical	–	–	–	$100.00	–	–	$150.00
Benefits: Historical	$4 400.00	–	–	$3 240.00	–	$7 540.00	–
Vacation Pay Owed	–	–	$1 525.18	$1 026.48	$1 424.28	$604.80	$1 144.26
Regular Wage Rate	–	–	$24.00/hr	$16.00/hr	$22.00/hr	$14.00/hr	$18.00/hr
No. Hours per Period	160	160	80	80	80	80	80
Wages: Historical	–	–	$24 960.00	$16 640.00	$22 880.00	$10 080.00	$18 720.00
Overtime 1 Wage Rate	–	–	$36.00/hr	$24.00/hr	$33.00/hr	$21.00/hr	$27.00/hr
Overtime 1: Historical	–	–	$468.00	$468.00	$858.00	$168.00	$351.00
Regular Salary	$4 000/mo.	$3 200/mo.	–	–	–	–	–
Salary: Historical	$24 000.00	$19 200.00	–	–	–	–	–
Commission	1% (Revenue from Inn)	–	–	–	–	–	–
Pay Periods	12	12	26	26	26	26	26
Vacation Rate	4 weeks	4 weeks	6% retained	6% retained	6% retained	6% retained	6% retained
Wage Account	Management	General	Dining Room	Dining Room	General	Dining Room	General
Deductions							
Group Insurance	$30.00	$60.00	$30.00	$15.00	$30.00	$15.00	$30.00
Insurance: Historical	$180.00	$360.00	$390.00	$195.00	$390.00	$195.00	$390.00
WSIB and User-Defined Expenses							
WSIB Rate	2.55	2.55	1.70	1.70	2.55	1.70	2.55
Tuition: Historical	$4 400.00	–	–	$3 240.00	–	$7 540.00	–
Entitlements (Rate, Maximum Days, Clear, Days Accrued)							
Vacation	8%, 30, No, 20	8%, 30, No, 20	–	–	–	–	–
Sick Leave	5%, 15, No, 9	5%, 15, No, 7	5%, 15, No, 8	5%, 15, No, 9	5%, 15, No, 10	5%, 15, No, 3	5%, 15, No, 8
T4 and RL-1 Reporting							
EI Insurable Earnings	$24 000.00	$19 200.00	$25 428.00	$17 108.00	$23 738.00	$10 248.00	$19 071.00
Pensionable Earnings	$28 400.00	$19 200.00	$25 428.00	$20 348.00	$23 738.00	$17 788.00	$19 071.00
Withheld	$6 519.84	$4 227.66	$5 172.31	$4 012.71	$3 362.32	$2 506.29	$3 156.01
Net Pay	$17 480.16	$14 972.34	$20 255.69	$13 195.29	$20 375.68	$7 741.71	$16 064.99

Payroll Information

General Payroll Information   E. Prospero, the owner, has arranged group insurance for his employees, and all employees have elected to join the plan. As entitlements, all staff may take 10 days' sick leave per year, and the vacation allowances are quite generous for the industry — four weeks of paid vacation for salaried staff after three years of service and 6 percent for all hourly paid employees. As an additional benefit, employees are reimbursed for their tuition fees on completion of eligible courses. Salaried employees are paid monthly, and hourly employees are paid every two weeks. All employees work full time, are eligible for EI and pay CPP and income tax; the EI factor is 1.4. The Inn pays 0.98 percent of payroll for EHT, the provincial health tax. WSIB rates vary for different types of work performed by the employees of the Inn.

Wage expenses for the manager, the dining room staff and the remaining general employees are tracked separately in three different payroll expense accounts.

Employee Profiles and TD1 Information

E. Prospero   owns the Inn and oversees all activities. Together with family members, he fills in where needed. He does not collect a salary and is not recorded as an employee.

Owen Othello   is the salaried manager for the Inn. He welcomes guests, instructs other employees and discusses issues, problems and plans with the owner. He is single and studies part time in an MBA program. One night a week he commutes to Toronto. An education allowance — $140 per month federal and $161 provincial — and $4 400 for tuition increase his basic tax claim amounts. Othello is the salesperson for all sales, and beginning in July he will receive a commission of 1 percent of the revenue from the Inn.

Clara Claudius   has been with the Inn the longest and works as the desk attendant. Although her primary job is reservations clerk, she also performs the accounting for the Inn. She too is salaried. Because her husband is also fully employed, she uses the basic single tax claim amounts plus the federal claim for her dependent child.

Mary MacBeth   works as the cook in the dining room. As a single parent with three dependent children, she claims the spousal equivalent for tax purposes for one child and the federal child credit for the other two. She is paid at an hourly rate of $24 per hour for the first 40 hours each week and $36 per hour after that.

Hedy Horatio   divides her time between waiting tables and helping the cook for her pay at the rate of $16 per hour plus $24 per hour for overtime hours. She studies part time at Conestoga College in the chef training program. The $3 240 tuition fee and the education tax claims — $140 per month federal and $161 provincial — supplement her basic single tax claim.

Juliet Jones   deals with requests from guests, working as the concierge and arranging for room service. She lives with and cares for her father and therefore has the eligible dependant claim plus a caregiver claim. She also has the age deduction transferred from her father ($7 125 federal and $4 888 provincial) to supplement her basic single tax claim. Her hourly wage rate is $22 for the first 40 hours each week and $33 for additional hours.

Shelley Shylock   waits tables in the dining room at the Inn. During the summer and festival months, she works full time for the Inn at the rate of $14 per hour and $21 for hours beyond the first 40 each week. She is a full-time student at the University of Waterloo and works part time until summer. The education deduction of $465 ($539 provincial) per month plus tuition fees at $7 540 supplement her tax claim amounts.

NOTES
Enter entitlements as Payroll Settings and edit records for each employee as needed.

Tuition is a user-defined payroll expense and taxable benefit. The benefits for Othello, Horatio and Shylock have already been paid, so only historical amounts are entered.

Remember that WSIB is the name for WCB in Ontario.

NOTES
The claim amounts subject to indexing do not include education and tuition amounts. The amount subject to indexing is used by the program to update claim amounts when a new tax table is introduced, based on the government indexing rate.

NOTES
Education amounts include the monthly allowance for textbooks.

Bud Romeo takes care of room service requests and also handles the baggage for the guests. He is married with two dependent children, so he has the spousal claim amount in addition to the basic single amount and federal child claim. He too is paid hourly at the rate of $14 per hour and $21 per hour for the time beyond 40 hours per week.

INVENTORY AND SERVICES INFORMATION

STRATFORD COUNTRY INN

Description	Min Stock	CAD Prices Reg (Pref)	USD Prices Reg (Pref)	Unit	Qty on Hand	Total (Cost)	Taxes
Books: Total asset value $4 000 (Linked Accounts: Books, Revenue from Books, Cost of Books Sold)							
Two Stratfords: England and Ontario	5	$80 ($70)	$65 ($55)	each	20	$1 000	G
Annotated Plays of Shakespeare	5	80 (70)	65 (55)	each	40	2 000	G
History of Stratford Country Inn	5	50 (45)	40 (35)	each	40	1 000	G
Services: Rooms (Linked Accounts: Revenue from Rooms, Cost of Services)							
Single Room		$150 ($130)	$120 ($105)	room/night			H
Double Room		200 (175)	160 (145)	room/night			H
Services: Meals (Linked Accounts: Revenue from Dining Room, Cost of Services)							
Boxed Lunch		$30 ($25)	$23 ($18)	meal			H
Dinner - Prix Fixe		$70 ($65)	56 (48)	meal			H
Services: Tours (Linked Accounts: Revenue from Tours, Cost of Services)							
Guided Tour		$500 ($450)	$400 (350)	tour			H

INSTRUCTIONS

⚠ WARNING!
Save your work and make backups frequently.

⚠ WARNING!
Remember to use a Test Balance account or the Retained Earnings account to check the Trial Balance before finishing the history for the General Ledger. Print the appropriate reports to check your work as you enter the company data.

📄 NOTES
Guests from the United States pay taxes on their Ontario purchases because the services and goods are consumed in Ontario.

pro PRO VERSION
Remember that the terms Vendors and Customers will replace Suppliers and Guests.

1. Use all the information presented in this application to set up the company accounts for Stratford Country Inn in Sage 50 using the following steps:
   a. Create company files in a new data folder for storing the company records.
   b. Enter the company information. Start a new fiscal period on July 1, 2018, and finish the period on September 30, 2018. Choose Accommodation as the industry.
   c. Enter names and printer information.
   d. Prepare the settings by changing the default settings as necessary.
   e. Organize the Balance Sheet and Income Statement accounts.
   f. Create accounts to correspond to your Balance Sheet and Income Statement. Add appropriate account numbers and types.
   g. Set up currency information for the USD transactions. The exchange rate on June 30 is 1.35.
   h. Change the account class for bank and credit card accounts and set up the cheque sequence.
   i. Enter linked accounts for the ledgers and credit cards. The fee is 2.75 percent.
   j. Enter sales tax information and create tax codes for GST @ 5%, refundable, and HST @ 13%, refundable. Reports should be available for both taxes.
   k. Enter guest, supplier, employee and inventory information. The tax code for all suppliers and guests is H, except for the payroll remittance suppliers and for Tempest Food Wholesalers, which supplies tax exempt foods.
   l. Enter historical balances in all ledgers.
   m. Create two Job Categories: Sales (employees in this category are salespersons) and Other (employees in this category are not salespersons). Assign Othello to Sales and all other employees to the Other category.

4

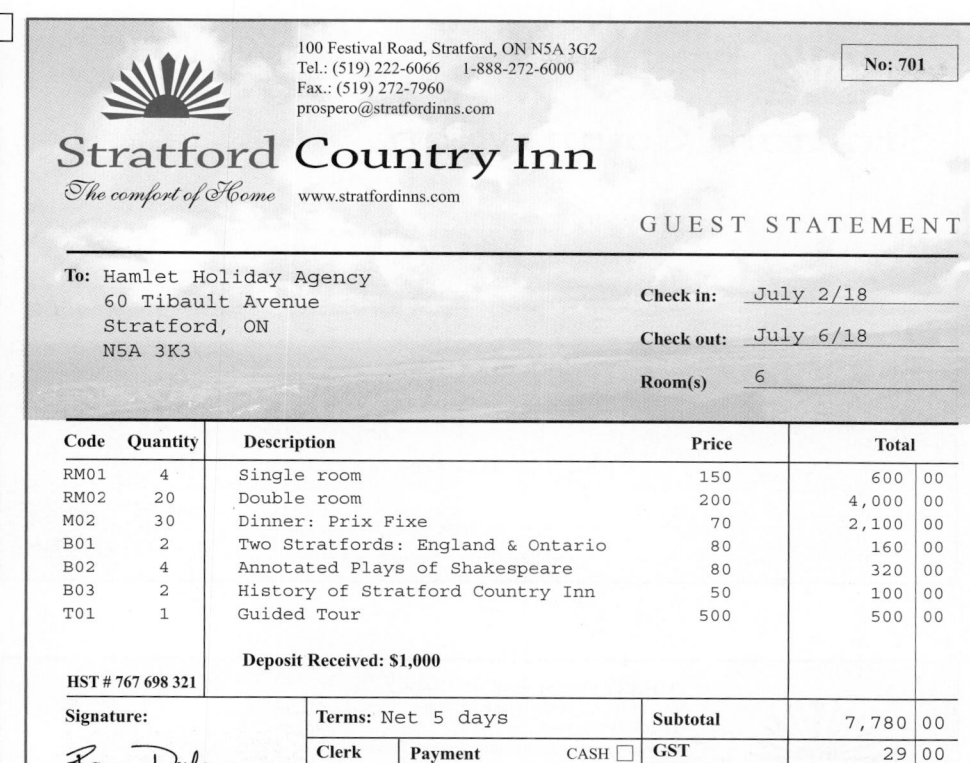

100 Festival Road, Stratford, ON N5A 3G2
Tel.: (519) 222-6066   1-888-272-6000
Fax.: (519) 272-7960
prospero@stratfordinns.com

No: 701

Stratford Country Inn

The comfort of Home   www.stratfordinns.com

GUEST STATEMENT

To: Hamlet Holiday Agency
60 Tibault Avenue
Stratford, ON
N5A 3K3

Check in: July 2/18
Check out: July 6/18
Room(s): 6

Code	Quantity	Description	Price	Total	
RM01	4	Single room	150	600	00
RM02	20	Double room	200	4,000	00
M02	30	Dinner: Prix Fixe	70	2,100	00
B01	2	Two Stratfords: England & Ontario	80	160	00
B02	4	Annotated Plays of Shakespeare	80	320	00
B03	2	History of Stratford Country Inn	50	100	00
T01	1	Guided Tour	500	500	00

Deposit Received: $1,000

HST # 767 698 321

Signature:

Ron Doleman

Terms: Net 5 days				
Clerk CC	**Payment Method:**	CASH ☐ CHEQUE ☐ ON ACCOUNT ☑	**Subtotal**	7,780	00
			GST	29	00
			HST	936	00
			BALANCE	$7,745	00

5

Waterloo University Literary Club
88 College Road
Waterloo, ON N2A 3F6

No: 413

Date 2 0 1 8 0 7 0 6
       Y Y Y Y M M D D

Pay to the order of Stratford Country Inn $ 1,000.00

——————— One Thousand ————————————————— 00/100 **Dollars**

WT Waterloo Trust
550 King Street
Waterloo, ON N2A 3F8

T. Fornelle
Chair

⑆⑈ 60431 ⑈ 105 ⑈ 413

Re: Deposit #41 — booking rooms in Inn   No: 413
Receipt #55 $1,000.00   July 6, 2018

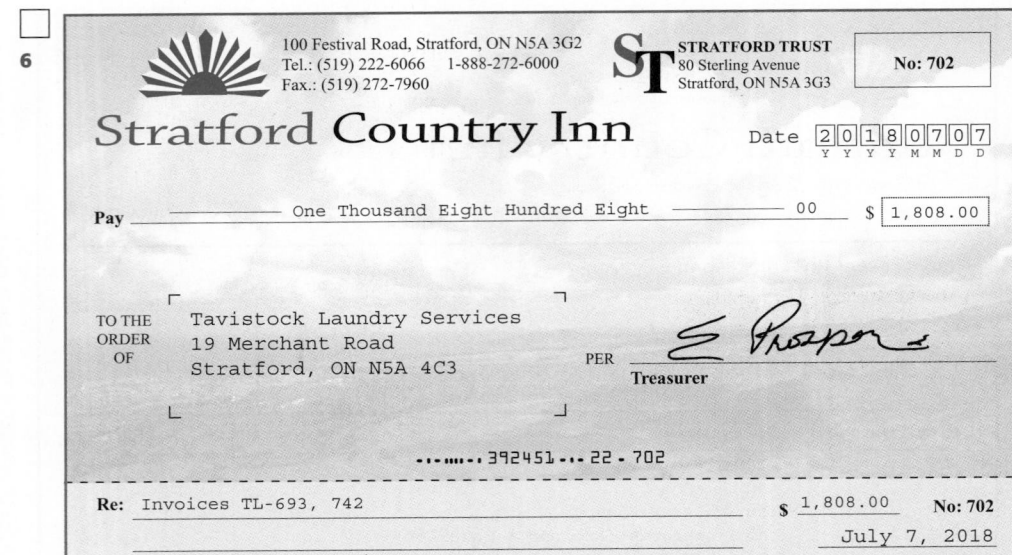

6

100 Festival Road, Stratford, ON N5A 3G2
Tel.: (519) 222-6066   1-888-272-6000
Fax.: (519) 272-7960

STRATFORD TRUST
80 Sterling Avenue
Stratford, ON N5A 3G3

No: 702

Stratford Country Inn

Date [2][0][1][8][0][7][0][7]
Y Y Y Y M M D D

Pay ———————— One Thousand Eight Hundred Eight ———————— 00 $ 1,808.00

TO THE
ORDER
OF

Tavistock Laundry Services
19 Merchant Road
Stratford, ON N5A 4C3

PER _E Prospero_
Treasurer

⑈⑈⑈ 392451 ⑈⑈ 22 - 702

Re: Invoices TL-693, 742 _____ $ 1,808.00   No: 702
_____   July 7, 2018

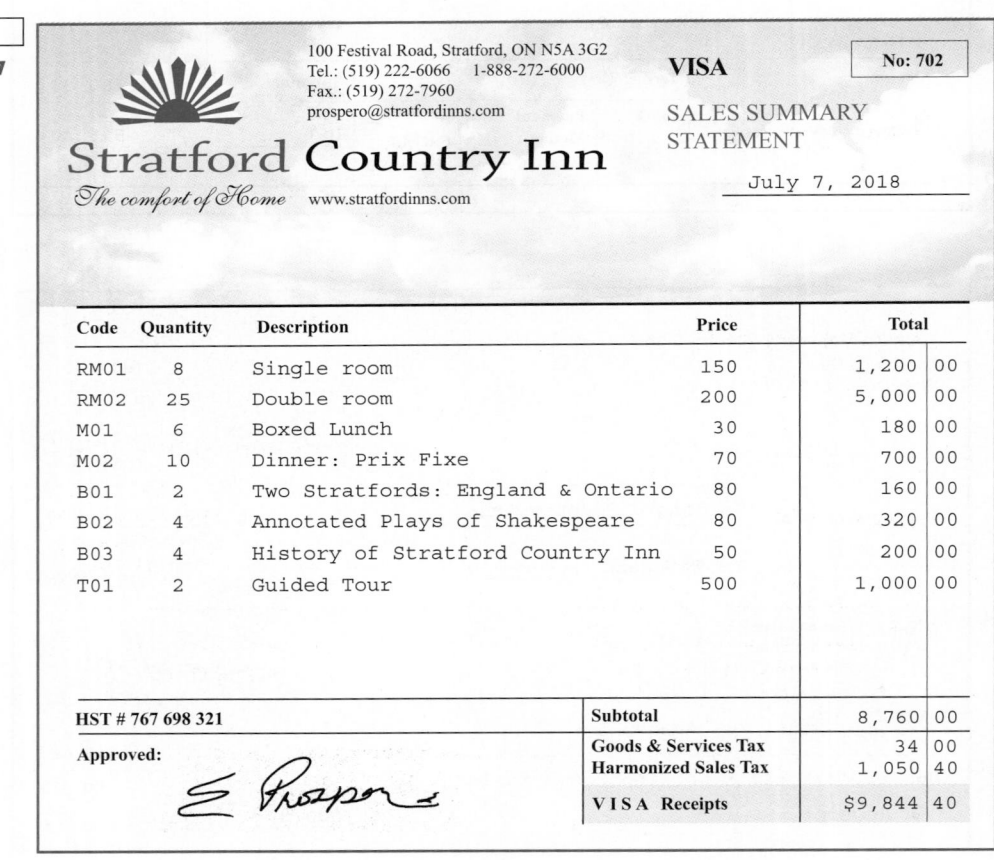

7

100 Festival Road, Stratford, ON N5A 3G2
Tel.: (519) 222-6066   1-888-272-6000
Fax.: (519) 272-7960
prospero@stratfordinns.com

VISA

No: 702

Stratford Country Inn
The comfort of Home   www.stratfordinns.com

**SALES SUMMARY
STATEMENT**

July 7, 2018

Code	Quantity	Description	Price	Total	
RM01	8	Single room	150	1,200	00
RM02	25	Double room	200	5,000	00
M01	6	Boxed Lunch	30	180	00
M02	10	Dinner: Prix Fixe	70	700	00
B01	2	Two Stratfords: England & Ontario	80	160	00
B02	4	Annotated Plays of Shakespeare	80	320	00
B03	4	History of Stratford Country Inn	50	200	00
T01	2	Guided Tour	500	1,000	00

HST # 767 698 321	Subtotal	8,760	00
	Goods & Services Tax	34	00
Approved: _E Prospero_	Harmonized Sales Tax	1,050	40
	V I S A Receipts	$9,844	40

8

Sold to: Stratford Country Inn
100 Festival Road
Stratford, ON
N5A 3G2

TEMPEST
Food Wholesalers

Telephone:
(519) 272-4464
Fax:
(519) 272-4600
Website:
www.tempest.com

35 Henry Avenue
Stratford, ON N5A 3N6

Billing Date: July 8, 2018
Invoice No: TF-284
Customer No.: 3423
Customer Copy

Date	Description	Charges	Payments	Amount
July 8/18	Fish and Meats	1000.00		1000.00
	Fresh Fruits	200.00		200.00
	Fresh Vegetables	200.00		200.00
	Dry Goods	200.00		200.00
	Dairy Products	200.00		200.00
	Baking Goods	200.00		200.00
	Recurring bi-weekly billing			

Terms: Net 30 days | Subtotal | 2000.00
HST #673 421 936
Signature: E Prosper
Overdue accounts are subject to 16% interest per year

HST 13% exempt
Owing 2000.00

9

Invoice No: TL-798
Date: July 8, 2018
Customer: Stratford Country Inn
100 Festival Road
Stratford, ON
N5A 3G2
Phone: (519) 222-6066

TAVISTOCK LAUNDRY Services

19 Merchant Road
Stratford, ON
N5A 4C3

Phone: (519) 271-7479
Fax: (519) 271-7888
www.tavistock.com

HST #639 271 343

Code	Description	Price	Amount
C-11	10 Loads Sheets	40.00	400.00
C-14	5 Loads Pillow Covers	20.00	100.00
C-20	15 Loads Towels	20.00	300.00
	Recurring bi-weekly billing		

Overdue accounts are subject to a 2% interest penalty per month | Sub-total | 800.00
Terms: Net 30 days | HST | 104.00
Signature: E Prosper | Total | 904.00

10

100 Festival Road, Stratford, ON N5A 3G2
Tel.: (519) 222-6066   1-888-272-6000
Fax.: (519) 272-7960

ST **STRATFORD TRUST**
80 Sterling Avenue
Stratford, ON N5A 3G3

No: 703

Stratford Country Inn

Date | 2 | 0 | 1 | 8 | 0 | 7 | 0 | 9 |
Y Y Y Y M M D D

Pay ——————————— Four Thousand ——————————— 00 $ 4,000.00

TO THE
ORDER
OF

Tempest Food Wholesalers
35 Henry Avenue
Stratford, ON N5A 3N6

PER *E Prosper*
Treasurer

⑈⑈⑈⑈ 392451⑈⑈ 22 · 703

Re: Invoices TF-113, 183 ————————————— $ 4,000.00   No: 703
—————————————————————————— July 9, 2018

11

Hamlet Holiday Agency
60 Tibault Avenue,
STRATFORD, ON N5A 3K3

SB Scotia Bank
44 Welland Avenue
STRATFORD, ON N5A 3F6

No: 349

Date | 2 | 0 | 1 | 8 | 0 | 7 | 1 | 0 |
Y Y Y Y M M D D

Pay ——— Seven thousand, seven hundred & forty-five——— 00 $ 7,745.00

TO THE
ORDER
OF

Stratford Country Inn
100 Festival Road
Stratford, ON N5A 3G2

PER *Ron Doleman*
Treasurer

⑈⑈⑈ 64299 ⑈ 168 ⑈ 349

Re: Invoice #701 & Cheque #317   No: 349
Receipt #56 $7,745.00   July 10, 2018

12

100 Festival Road, Stratford, ON N5A 3G2
Tel.: (519) 222-6066   1-888-272-6000
Fax.: (519) 272-7960

ST **STRATFORD TRUST**
80 Sterling Avenue
Stratford, ON N5A 3G3

No: 704

Stratford Country Inn

Date 2 0 1 8 0 7 1 0
Y Y Y Y M M D D

Pay ——————— Two Thousand Two Hundred Fourteen ——————— 80 — $ 2,214.80

TO THE
ORDER
OF

Bard's Linen & Towels
21 Venice Street
Stratford, ON N5A 4L2

PER _E Prospero_
Treasurer

···......392451···22-704

Re: Invoice BLT-64, Discount taken $45.20 $ 2,214.80   No: 704
                                                 July 10, 2018

13

STRATFORD SERVICE CENTRE

33 MacBeth Avenue
Stratford, ON N5A 4T2
Tel: (519) 271-6679
Fax: (519) 276-8822
www.ssc.com

Date: July 11, 2018   **Invoice:** 1143

Customer: Stratford Country Inn
               100 Festival Road
               Stratford, ON
               N5A 3G2

Phone: (519) 222-6066

HST #634 214 211

Code	Description	Price	Amount
M-114	Lube, Oil and Filter	40.00	40.00
XF-1	Fuel	120.00	120.00
		Sub-total	160.00

APPROVAL	CUSTOMER COPY				
EP	Cash	VISA	On Account	HST	20.80
		✓		Owing	180.80

14

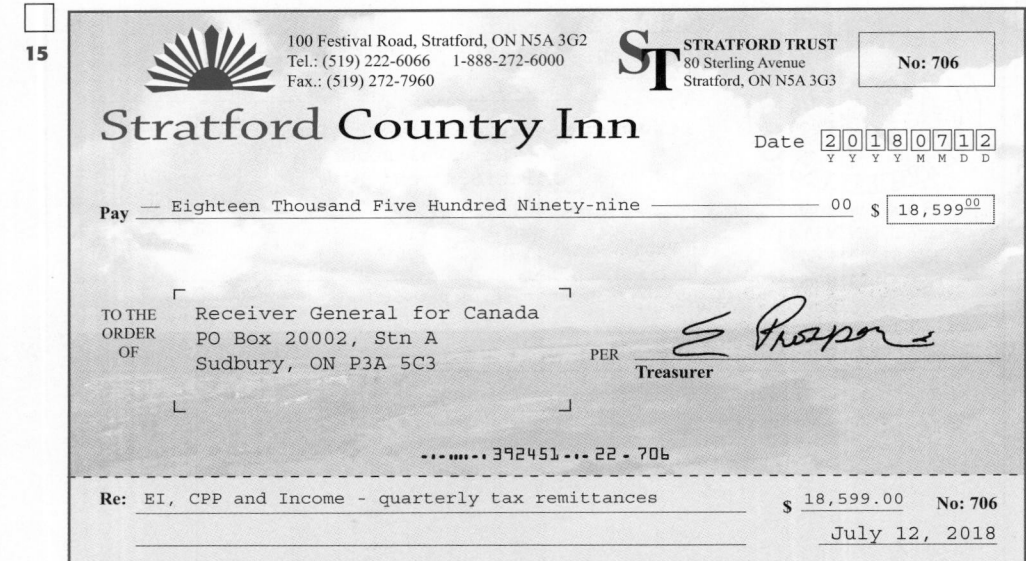

100 Festival Road, Stratford, ON N5A 3G2
Tel.: (519) 222-6066   1-888-272-6000
Fax.: (519) 272-7960

STRATFORD TRUST
80 Sterling Avenue
Stratford, ON N5A 3G3

No: 705

Stratford Country Inn

Date 2 0 1 8 0 7 1 2
Y Y Y Y M M D D

Pay ———— Two Thousand Three Hundred Eighty ———— 00 $ 2,380.00

TO THE ORDER OF
Receiver General for Canada
PO Box 20002, Stn A
Sudbury, ON P3A 5C3

PER E Prosper
Treasurer

392451 22 - 705

Re: HST and GST Remittance for June 30 $ 2,380.00   **No: 705**
July 12, 2018

15

100 Festival Road, Stratford, ON N5A 3G2
Tel.: (519) 222-6066   1-888-272-6000
Fax.: (519) 272-7960

STRATFORD TRUST
80 Sterling Avenue
Stratford, ON N5A 3G3

No: 706

Stratford Country Inn

Date 2 0 1 8 0 7 1 2
Y Y Y Y M M D D

Pay — Eighteen Thousand Five Hundred Ninety-nine ———— 00 $ 18,599.00

TO THE ORDER OF
Receiver General for Canada
PO Box 20002, Stn A
Sudbury, ON P3A 5C3

PER E Prosper
Treasurer

392451 22 - 706

Re: EI, CPP and Income - quarterly tax remittances $ 18,599.00   **No: 706**
July 12, 2018

16

100 Festival Road, Stratford, ON N5A 3G2
Tel.: (519) 222-6066   1-888-272-6000
Fax.: (519) 272-7960
prospero@stratfordinns.com

No: 703

Stratford Country Inn
The comfort of Home   www.stratfordinns.com

GUEST STATEMENT

To: Waterloo University
Literary Club
88 College Road
Waterloo, ON
N2A 3F6

Check in: July 9/18

Check out: July 13/18

Room(s) 8

Code	Quantity	Description Transaction	Price	Total	
RM01	16	Single room	150	2,400	00
RM02	24	Double room	200	4,800	00
M01	7	Boxed Lunch	30	210	00
M02	16	Dinner: Prix Fixe	70	1,120	00
B01	1	Two Stratfords: England & Ontario	80	80	00
B02	2	Annotated Plays of Shakespeare	80	160	00
B03	1	History of Stratford Country Inn	50	50	00
T01	1	Guided Tour	500	500	00
		Deposit Received: $1,000			

HST # 767 698 321

Signature: *J. Fornello*

Terms: Net 5 days

Clerk CC	**Payment Method:** CASH ☐ CHEQUE ☐ ON ACCOUNT ☑	

	Subtotal	9,320	00
	GST	14	50
	HST	1,173	90
	BALANCE	$9,508	40

17

100 Festival Road, Stratford, ON N5A 3G2
Tel.: (519) 222-6066   1-888-272-6000
Fax.: (519) 272-7960
prospero@stratfordinns.com

VISA

No: 704

Stratford Country Inn
The comfort of Home   www.stratfordinns.com

SALES SUMMARY STATEMENT

July 14, 2018

Code	Quantity	Description	Price	Total	
RM01	7	Single room	150	1,050	00
RM02	12	Double room	200	2,400	00
M01	10	Boxed Lunch	30	300	00
M02	40	Meals	70	2,800	00
B01	2	Two Stratfords: England & Ontario	80	160	00
B02	3	Annotated Plays of Shakespeare	80	240	00
B03	3	History of Stratford Country Inn	50	150	00
T01	1	Guided Tour	500	500	00

HST # 767 698 321

Approved: *E. Prospero*

	Subtotal	7,600	00
	Goods & Services Tax	27	50
	Harmonized Sales Tax	916	50
	VISA Receipts	$8,544	00

18

100 Festival Road, Stratford, ON N5A 3G2
Tel.: (519) 222-6066   1-888-272-6000
Fax.: (519) 272-7960
prospero@stratford.com

ET27

Stratford Country Inn

The comfort of Home   www.stratfordinns.com

**EMPLOYEE TIME
SUMMARY SHEET**

| Pay period ending: | July 14, 2018 | | Paycheque date: | July 14, 2018 |

Name of Employee	Regular hours	Overtime hours	Sick days
☐ Horatio, Hedy	80	0	0
☐ Jones, Juliet	80	0	1
☐ MacBeth, Mary	80	2	0
☐ Romeo, Bud	80	2	0
☐ Shylock, Shelley	80	2	0

Memo: Issue cheques #707 to #711
Recover $100 loan from Horatio and Romeo

19

**AVON
Maintenance
Services**
66 Kleen Road, Stratford, ON N5A 3C3
Telephone (519) 272-4611
Fax: (519) 272-4813
www.avonservices.com

Invoice No:	AM-184
Date:	July 15, 2018
Sold to:	Stratford Country Inn
	100 Festival Road
	Stratford, ON
	N5A 3G2
Phone:	(519) 222-6066

Code	Service Description		Price
KX-55	Vacuum Premises	*	1100.00
	Floor Polishing		
	Washroom Cleaning		
	Maintenance and Repairs		
	Recurring bi-weekly billing		
	* new price as described		
	in our previous notice		

Signature: *E Prospero*

| **Terms:** Net 30 days | | **HST** | 143.00 |
| **HST #631 393 461** | | **Amount owing** | 1243.00 |

20

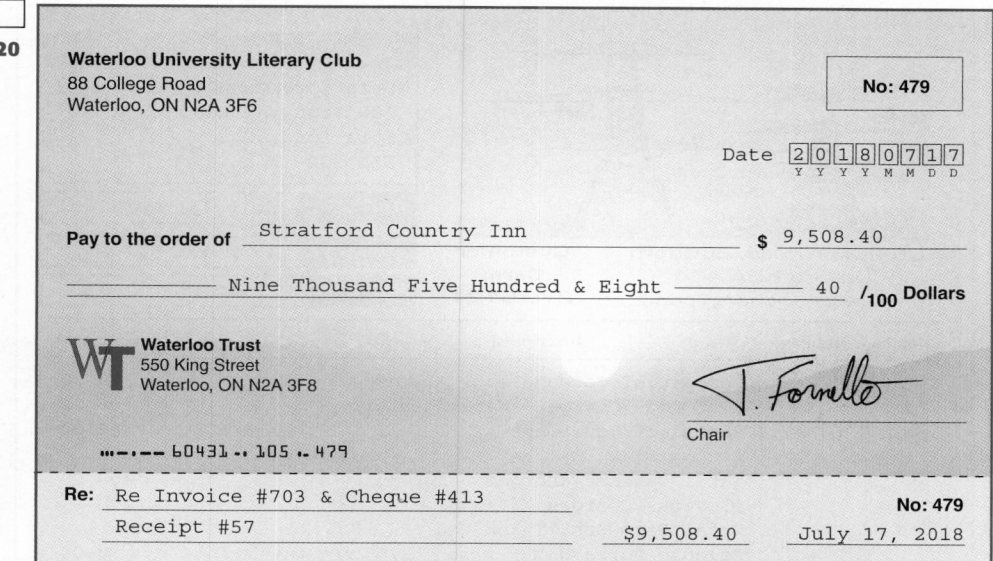

Waterloo University Literary Club
88 College Road
Waterloo, ON N2A 3F6

No: 479

Date 2 0 1 8 0 7 1 7
Y Y Y Y M M D D

Pay to the order of   Stratford Country Inn $ 9,508.40

——————— Nine Thousand Five Hundred & Eight ——————— 40 /100 Dollars

WT **Waterloo Trust**
550 King Street
Waterloo, ON N2A 3F8

Chair

⑆⑈⑆ 60431 ⑆ 105 ⑆ 479

Re: Re Invoice #703 & Cheque #413   **No: 479**
     Receipt #57 $9,508.40   July 17, 2018

21

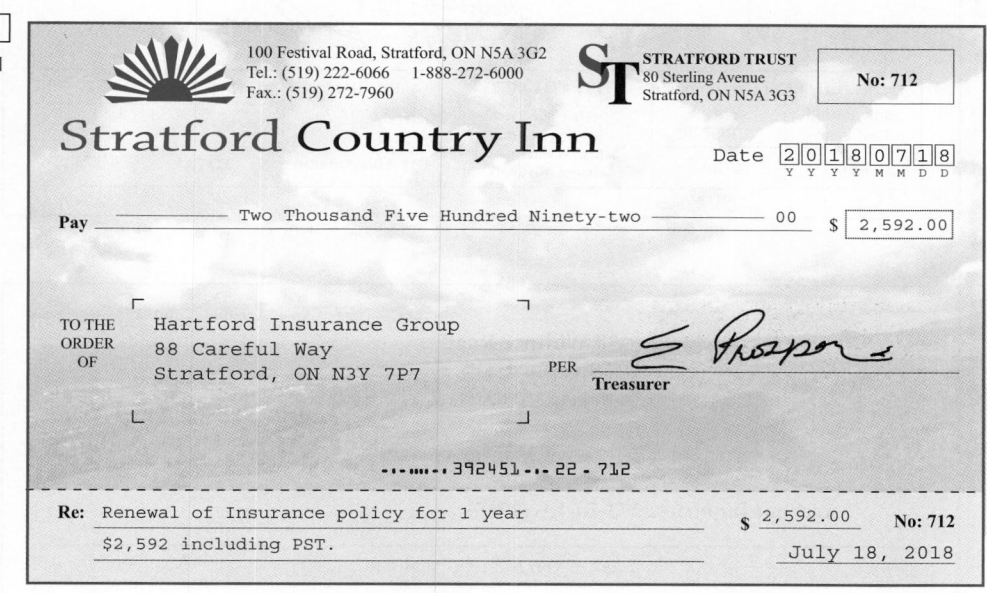

100 Festival Road, Stratford, ON N5A 3G2
Tel.: (519) 222-6066   1-888-272-6000
Fax.: (519) 272-7960

ST **STRATFORD TRUST**
80 Sterling Avenue
Stratford, ON N5A 3G3

No: 712

Stratford Country Inn

Date 2 0 1 8 0 7 1 8
Y Y Y Y M M D D

Pay ——————— Two Thousand Five Hundred Ninety-two ——————— 00 $ 2,592.00

TO THE
ORDER
OF
    Hartford Insurance Group
    88 Careful Way
    Stratford, ON N3Y 7P7   PER **Treasurer**

⑆⑈⑆ 392451 ⑆ 22 - 712

Re: Renewal of Insurance policy for 1 year $ 2,592.00   No: 712
     $2,592 including PST.   July 18, 2018

22

PERTH COUNTY HYDRO
66 Power Road, Stratford,
Ontario N5A 4P4
www.perthenergy.com

Customer
Care:
272-6121

	CUSTOMER NAME / SERVICE ADDRESS
	Stratford Country Inn 100 Festival Road Stratford, ON N5A 3G2

Date:	July 18, 2018
Account No:	3921 462 513
Invoice No:	37232

Months	Reading	Description	Net Amount
1	86527	Commercial Consumption	300.00
1		Flat Rate Charge — Water Heaters	60.00
1		Rental of Equipment	40.00
		Total Current Charges	400.00
		Previous Charges 385.20	
		Total Payments, Thank You 385.20	
		Balance Forward	0.00
		Adjustments	0.00

Paid in Full with cheque #713 for $452 07/18/18 E. Prosper

Average Daily KWh Consumption		HST #721 431 214	Due Date	HST 13%	52.00
Same Period Last Year	This Bill	After due date, a 1.5% monthly late payment interest charge will apply.	July 25/18		
269	258		Pay This Amount ▶	TOTAL	452.00

23

30 Whisper Road
Stratford, ON
N5A 4N3

www.bell.ca

Account Inquiries: 273-BELL (2355)

Account Number
519-222-6066

Account Address

Stratford Country Inn
100 Festival Road
Stratford, ON
N5A 3G2

July 18, 2018

ACCOUNT SUMMARY

```
Current Charges
    Monthly Services (June 12 to July 12)          240.00
    Equipment Rentals                               50.00
    Chargeable Messages                             30.00
    HST 634 345 373                                 41.60
Total Current Charges                              361.60

Previous Charges
    Amount of Last Bill                            323.00
    Payment Received June 19 — Thank You           323.00
    Adjustments                                      0.00
    Balance Forward                                  0.00
```

Paid in Full — chq #714 — 07/18/18 E. Prosper

Invoice: BC-66431	PLEASE PAY THIS AMOUNT UPON RECEIPT ▬▶	$361.60

24

Stratford Country Inn

100 Festival Road, Stratford, ON N5A 3G2
Tel.: (519) 222-6066   1-888-272-6000
Fax.: (519) 272-7960
prospero@stratfordinns.com

The comfort of Home   www.stratfordinns.com

No: 705

GUEST STATEMENT

To: NY Friends of Shakespeare
33 16th Avenue
Buffalo, NY
13002

Check in: July 17/18
Check out: July 20/18
Room(s) 9

Code	Quantity	Description	Price	Total	
RM01	6	Single room	105	630	00
RM02	21	Double room	145	3,045	00
M01	20	Boxed Lunch	18	360	00
M02	16	Dinner: Prix Fixe	48	768	00
B01	2	Two Stratfords: England & Ontario	55	110	00
B03	4	History of Stratford Country Inn	35	140	00
T01	1	Guided Tour	350	350	00
		**Preferred customer - no deposit required			

HST # 767 698 321   Exchange rate: 1.335 CAD

Signature: *J.Monte*

Terms: Net 5 days

Clerk CC	**Payment Method:**	CASH ☐ CHEQUE ☐ ON ACCOUNT ☑

Subtotal	5,403	00
GST	12	50
HST	669	89
BALANCE	USD $6,085	39

25

Festival Club of Rosedale
3 Rosedale Valley Rd.
Toronto, Ontario
M5G 3T4

No: 61

Date | 2 0 1 8 0 7 2 0 |
Y Y Y Y M M D D

Pay to the order of   Stratford Country Inn $ 1,000.00

One Thousand ———————————————— 00 /100 **Dollars**

R B **Royal Bank**
56 Bloor Street
Toronto, ON M5N 3G7

Jane Birker
Chairperson

⑈⟨—— 34298 ⟩⟨021⟩⟨061

Re: Deposit #42 — booking rooms in Inn

$1,000.00   July 20, 2018

No: 61

26

STRATFORD TRUST
80 Sterling Avenue
Stratford, ON N5A 3G3

VISA

Statement Period M D Y		Account Number	Account Enquiries	Daily Interest Rate	Annual Interest Rate
From 06/15/18 To 07/15/18		4512 6221 1384 6201	1-800-272-VISA	.05068%	18.5%

Trans. Date	Post Date	Particulars	Amount	Bus. Exp.
06 13	06 16	Stratford Service Centre, Stratford, ON	85.00	EP
06 18	06 21	Office Supplies Unlimited, Stratford, ON	88.00	EP
06 25	06 27	Stratford Service Centre, Stratford, ON	133.00	EP
06 28	06 30	Bullrich Dept. Store #32, Stratford, ON	113.00	EP
06 28	06 30	Bullrich Dept. Store #32, Stratford, ON	-24.00	EP
07 11	07 13	Stratford Service Centre, Stratford, ON	180.80	EP
06 20	06 20	Payment — Thank You	-422.00	EP

Balance $575.80 paid in Full by cheque #715 E Prospero July 21/18

Credit Limit	Opening Balance	Total Credits	Total Debits	Your New Balance
8500.00	422.00	446.00	599.80	575.80

Available Credit	Payment Due Date Month Day Year	Overlimit or Past Due	Current Due	Minimum Payment	Payment Amount
7924.20	07/24/18		57.00	57.00	575.80

27

100 Festival Road, Stratford, ON N5A 3G2
Tel.: (519) 222-6066   1-888-272-6000
Fax.: (519) 272-7960
prospero@stratfordinns.com

Stratford Country Inn
The comfort of Home   www.stratfordinns.com

VISA   No: 706

SALES SUMMARY STATEMENT

July 21, 2018

Code	Quantity	Description	Price	Total	
RM01	4	Single room	150	600	00
RM02	18	Double room	200	3,600	00
M01	8	Boxed Lunch	30	240	00
M02	22	Meals	70	1,540	00
B01	2	Two Stratfords: England & Ontario	80	160	00
B02	5	Annotated Plays of Shakespeare	80	400	00
B03	3	History of Stratford Country Inn	50	150	00
T01	1	Guided Tour	500	500	00

HST # 767 698 321

Subtotal	7,190	00
Goods and Services Tax	35	50
Harmonized Sales Tax	842	40
VISA Receipts	$8,067	90

Approved: *E Prospero*

28

Sold to: Stratford Country Inn
100 Festival Road
Stratford, ON
N5A 3G2

TEMPEST
Food Wholesalers

35 Henry Avenue
Stratford, ON N5A 3N6

Telephone:
(519) 272-4464
Fax:
(519) 272-4600
Website:
www.tempest.com

Billing Date: July 22, 2018
Invoice No: TF-344
Customer No.: 3423
Customer Copy

Date	Description	Charges	Payments	Amount
July 22/18	Fish and Meats	1000.00		1000.00
	Fresh Fruits	200.00		200.00
	Fresh Vegetables	200.00		200.00
	Dry Goods	200.00		200.00
	Dairy Products	200.00		200.00
	Baking Goods	200.00		200.00
	Recurring bi-weekly billing			

Terms: Net 30 days

Subtotal		2000.00

HST #673 421 936

Signature: *E Prosper*

Overdue accounts are subject to 16% interest per year

HST 13%		exempt
Owing		2000.00

29

Invoice No: TL-841
Date: July 22, 2018
Customer: Stratford Country Inn
100 Festival Road
Stratford, ON
N5A 3G2

Phone: (519) 222-6066

TAVISTOCK
LAUNDRY
Services

19 Merchant Road
Stratford, ON
N5A 4C3

Phone: (519) 271-7479
Fax: (519) 271-7888
www.tavistock.com

HST #639 271 343

Code	Description		Price	Amount
C-11	10 Loads Sheets	*	45.00	450.00
C-14	5 Loads Pillow Covers		20.00	100.00
C-20	15 Loads Towels		20.00	300.00
	Recurring bi-weekly billing			
	* new prices			

Overdue accounts are subject to a 2% interest penalty per month

Sub-total		850.00

Terms: Net 30 days

HST		110.50

Signature: *E Prosper*

Total		960.50

30

Zephyr Advertising Agency
32 Portia Blvd.
Stratford, ON
N5A 4T2

Telephone (519) 271-6066
Fax (519) 271-6067
www.westwinds.com
orders: contact tom@westwinds.com

Stratford Country Inn
100 Festival Road
Stratford, ON
N5A 3G2

ZA - 6998

Date	Description	Charges	Amount
July 23, 2018	Brochures & Flyers	300.00	300.00
	Paid in full cheque # 716 July 23/18 E Prosper		
		HST	39.00
HST # 391 213 919	**Terms:** Cash on Receipt	**Total**	339.00

31

NY Friends of Shakespeare
33 16th Avenue,
Buffalo, NY 13002

No: 181

Date 2 0 1 8 0 7 2 4
     Y Y Y Y M M D D

Pay to the order of Stratford Country Inn $ 6,085.39 (USD)

─────── Six thousand, eighty-five ─────── 39 /100 **Dollars**

CB **Chase Bank**
4 12th Avenue
Buffalo, NY 13002

J.Monte

⑈⦙⦙ 93937 ⦙ 301 ⦙ 181

- -

Re: Re Invoice #705: Receipt #59   **No: 181**

U.S. Currency. Currency Exchange 1.331 Cdn. $6,085.39 (USD)   July 24, 2018

32

33 MacBeth Avenue
Stratford, ON N5A 4T2
Tel: (519) 271-6679
Fax: (519) 276-8822
www.ssc.com

Date: July 25, 2018	Invoice: 1207

Customer:	Stratford Country Inn 100 Festival Road Stratford, ON N5A 3G2
Phone:	(519) 222-6066

HST #634 214 211

Code	Description	Price	Amount
R-69	Transmission—overhaul	500.00	500.00
XF-1	Fuel	100.00	100.00
		Sub-total	600.00

APPROVAL	CUSTOMER COPY				
EP	Cash	VISA	On Account	HST	78.00
		✓		Owing	678.00

33

100 Festival Road, Stratford, ON N5A 3G2
Tel.: (519) 222-6066   1-888-272-6000
Fax.: (519) 272-7960
prospero@stratfordinns.com

No: 707

Stratford Country Inn

The comfort of Home   www.stratfordinns.com

GUEST STATEMENT

To: Metro Arts Appreciation Group 4400 Yonge Street North York, ON M6L 3T4	Check in:	July 23/18
	Check out:	July 26/18
	Room(s)	10

Code	Quantity	Description	Price	Total	
RM01	6	Single room	130	780	00
RM02	24	Double room	175	4,200	00
M01	10	Boxed Lunch	25	250	00
M02	16	Meals	65	1,040	00
B01	1	Two Stratfords: England & Ontario	70	70	00
B02	4	Annotated Plays of Shakespeare	70	280	00
B03	1	History of Stratford Country Inn	45	45	00
T01	1	Guided Tour	450	450	00
		**Preferred Customer - no deposit required			

HST # 767 698 321

Signature:	Terms: Net 5 days		Subtotal	7,115	00
R. Downs	Clerk	Payment Method:	CASH ☐ CHEQUE ☐	GST HST	19 75 873 60
	CC		ON ACCOUNT ☑	**BALANCE**	**$8,008** 35

34

100 Festival Road, Stratford, ON N5A 3G2
Tel.: (519) 222-6066   1-888-272-6000
Fax.: (519) 272-7960
prospero@stratford.com

ET28

Stratford Country Inn
The comfort of Home   www.stratfordinns.com

E M P L O Y E E   T I M E
S U M M A R Y   S H E E T

Pay period ending: July 28, 2018		Paycheque date: July 28, 2018	
Name of Employee	**Regular hours**	**Overtime hours**	**Sick days**
☐ Horatio, Hedy	80	2	0
☐ Jones, Juliet	76	4	0
☐ MacBeth, Mary	80	0	0
☐ Romeo, Bud	80	0	1
☐ Shylock, Shelley	80	2	0

Memo: Issue cheques #717 to #721
Recover $50 loan from Romeo

35

100 Festival Road, Stratford, ON N5A 3G2
Tel.: (519) 222-6066   1-888-272-6000
Fax.: (519) 272-7960
prospero@stratfordinns.com

VISA   No: 708

Stratford Country Inn
The comfort of Home   www.stratfordinns.com

SALES SUMMARY
STATEMENT

July 28, 2018

Code	Quantity	Description	Price	Total	
RM01	7	Single room	150	1,050	00
RM02	14	Double room	200	2,800	00
M01	35	Boxed Lunch	30	1,050	00
M02	20	Dinner: Prix Fixe	70	1,400	00
B01	3	Two Stratfords: England & Ontario	80	240	00
B02	5	Annotated Plays of Shakespeare	80	400	00
B03	6	History of Stratford Country Inn	50	300	00
T01	2	Guided Tour	500	1,000	00

HST # 767 698 321		Subtotal	8,240	00
Approved:		**Goods and Services Tax**	47	00
		Harmonized Sales Tax	949	00
E Prospero		**V I S A Receipts**	$9,236	00

36

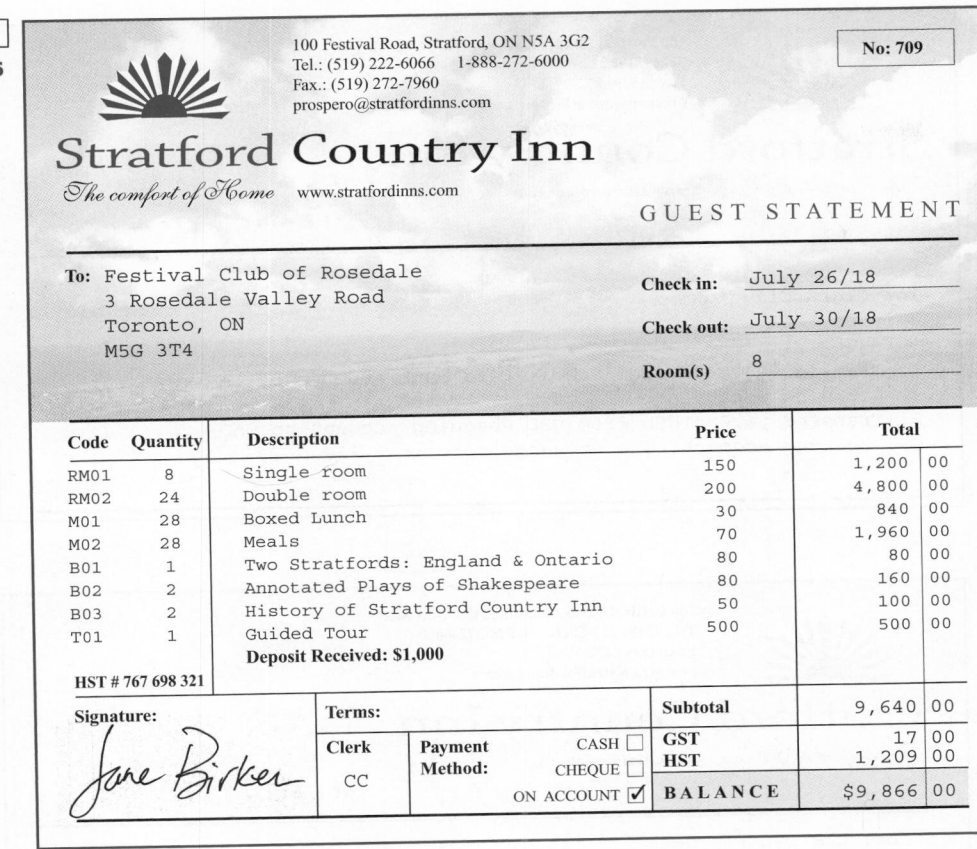

100 Festival Road, Stratford, ON N5A 3G2
Tel.: (519) 222-6066   1-888-272-6000
Fax.: (519) 272-7960
prospero@stratfordinns.com

No: 709

Stratford Country Inn

The comfort of Home   www.stratfordinns.com

GUEST STATEMENT

To: Festival Club of Rosedale
    3 Rosedale Valley Road
    Toronto, ON
    M5G 3T4

Check in: July 26/18

Check out: July 30/18

Room(s)   8

Code	Quantity	Description	Price	Total	
RM01	8	Single room	150	1,200	00
RM02	24	Double room	200	4,800	00
M01	28	Boxed Lunch	30	840	00
M02	28	Meals	70	1,960	00
B01	1	Two Stratfords: England & Ontario	80	80	00
B02	2	Annotated Plays of Shakespeare	80	160	00
B03	2	History of Stratford Country Inn	50	100	00
T01	1	Guided Tour	500	500	00
		Deposit Received: $1,000			

HST # 767 698 321

Signature: *Jane Birker*

Terms:			Subtotal	9,640	00
Clerk	Payment Method:	CASH ☐	GST	17	00
CC		CHEQUE ☐	HST	1,209	00
		ON ACCOUNT ☑	**BALANCE**	**$9,866**	**00**

37

Hamlet Holiday Agency
60 Tibault Avenue
STRATFORD, ON N5A 3K3

SB **Scotia Bank**
44 Welland Avenue
STRATFORD, ON N5A 3F6

No: 393

Date | 2 0 1 8 0 7 3 1 |
Y Y Y Y M M D D

Pay ———————— One thousand ———————— 00 $ | 1,000.00 |

TO THE
ORDER
OF
    Stratford Country Inn
    100 Festival Road
    Stratford, ON N5A 3G2

PER *Ron Derleman*

⑈⑈·⑈⑈ 64299·· 168 ·· 393

Re: Deposit #43 — booking rooms in Inn   No: 393

$1,000.00   July 31, 2018

38

100 Festival Road, Stratford, ON N5A 3G2
Tel.: (519) 222-6066   1-888-272-6000
Fax.: (519) 272-7960
prospero@stratfordinns.com

Stratford Country Inn

The comfort of Home   www.stratfordinns.com

M E M O # 3 1

From: the owner's desk
To: Clara Claudius
July 31, 2018

1. Transfer $40,000 from Credit Card Bank account to CAD
   Chequing account.
2. Transfer $6,000 USD from USD Chequing account to CAD
   Chequing account. The exchange rate is 1.324.

39

100 Festival Road, Stratford, ON N5A 3G2
Tel.: (519) 222-6066   1-888-272-6000
Fax.: (519) 272-7960
prospero@stratfordinns.com

Stratford Country Inn

The comfort of Home   www.stratfordinns.com

M E M O # 3 2

From: the owner's desk
To: Clara Claudius
July 31, 2018

1. Pay salaried employees Clara Claudius and Owen Othello. Add
   sales commission (1% Revenue from Inn) to Othello's salary.
   Issue cheques #722 and #723.

2. Pay quarterly balances owing as at July 1:
   a) To Minister of Finance (EHT), cheque #724
   b) Workplace Safety and Insurance Board (WSIB), cheque #725
   c) Travellers' Life (Group Insurance), cheque #726

3. Prepare adjusting entries for the following:
   a) Write off $216 of Prepaid Insurance
   b) Write off $50 of Prepaid Advertising
   c) Depreciation on Country Inn & Dining Room $600
      Depreciation on Computers $200
      Depreciation on Furniture & Fixtures $600
      Depreciation on Vehicles $800
   d) Food Inventory on hand $1 395

R E V I E W

The Student DVD with Data Files includes a
comprehensive supplementary case for this chapter and
bank reconciliation.

Part 3
Advanced Premium Features

OBJECTIVES

After completing this chapter, you should be able to

- **set up** inventory service activities for time and billing
- **update** prices from Inventory Settings
- **enter** employee time slips
- **import** time slip activities to prepare employee paycheques
- **import** time slip activities to prepare customer invoices
- **display** and **print** time and billing reports
- **set up** additional currencies
- **build** new inventory from Inventory Ledger record details
- **set up** multiple inventory locations
- **add** inventory locations to journal entries
- **transfer** inventory between locations
- **understand** related accounts for multiple fiscal periods
- **display** and **print** multi-period financial reports

COMPANY INFORMATION

Time and Billing Profile

Ryder's Routes, under the management of Steve Ryder and VeloCity, provides bicycle tour guide services in Canada and internationally to travel companies wanting to add cycling to their group package tours. Tour guides will also service the guests' bicycles while on tour. Guests may rent bicycles for their trips or ship their own bicycles. To accommodate this new service, Ryder will invoice customers using the Time & Billing module. After modifying the service records to price the services according to the time taken to complete the work and adding the new services, the company can track the work performed by each employee for each customer.

Additionally, Ryder has contracted with new suppliers and customers in Europe. No duty is charged on imported exercise equipment.

In August, Ryder's Routes began providing guided tours in addition to the existing services for the bicycles it sells. Services are billed in three ways: at an

hourly rate, at a flat rate regardless of the time required to complete the work and at no charge for repairs to bicycles under warranty. All tour and service work will be managed from Ryder's Routes, a new store near the VeloCity showroom. For convenience, Ryder's Routes will also sell bicycle accessories. Other inventory can be transferred to Ryder's Routes as needed. Separate inventory locations will be set up for the two stores so that Ryder can track the inventory at each location.

Ryder hired two new employees: Yvonne Leader will serve as tour guide and Moishe Alee will work as the primary sales associate in the new store.

The company's fiscal period will be reduced to one month and cash sales summaries will be entered at the end of the month to reduce the number of source documents.

NOTES
Sales and services provided by Ryder's Routes in Canada will have HST added. Tour guide services that are provided outside of Canada (in Europe or the United States) will not be taxable. The location of this service, not the home country of the customer, determines the taxability.

KEYSTROKES

Modifying Company Information

Changing Fiscal Dates

Open   **SageData16\RYDER\RYDER** to access the data files for this chapter and **accept August 1, 2018** as the session date.

Click   **Company** in the Modules pane list to open the Company window.

Enter   the **adjustment** for accrued wages and then **change** the **fiscal dates**.

NOTES
If you are working from the backup files, restore SageData16\RYDER1.CAB or RYDER1 to SageData16\RYDER\RYDER.

Memo #8-1	**Dated August 1, 2018**

Prepare an adjusting entry to reverse the year-end adjustment for $720 for accrued payroll. (Debit Accrued Wages and credit Wages.)

Memo #8-2	**Dated August 1, 2018**

Change the company fiscal dates. The new fiscal end is August 31, 2018. Change the company name to VeloCity - Ryder's Routes

NOTES
The wage expense credit entry that reverses the accrued payroll ensures that the correct amount from this pay period will be assigned to the previous fiscal period, adhering to the principle of recording expenses in the period in which they were incurred.

Click   the **Settings icon** [Settings], then **click Information**, or **choose** the **Setup menu** and **click Settings**, **Company** and **Information**:

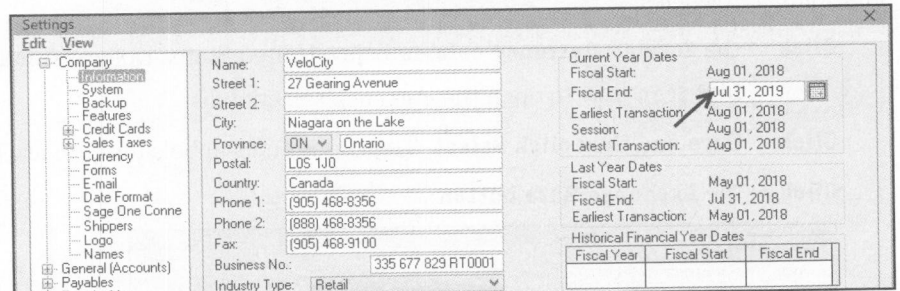

Most fiscal dates cannot be changed. Only the fiscal end can be edited. After starting a new fiscal period, the fiscal end is updated to one year past the new fiscal start because this period is most commonly used. Ryder's Routes, however, will use a one-month fiscal period to allow for more frequent performance review.

Drag through Jul 31, 2019 in the Fiscal End field.

Type   08-31-2018

Drag through VeloCity in the Name field.

Type `VeloCity - Ryder's Routes`

Leave the Settings window open so you can add the currency.

Adding a Foreign Currency

The Premium version of Sage 50 allows more than one foreign currency. Setting up additional currencies is similar to adding the first one. We will add the euro as the second foreign currency because a new supplier in Germany will provide some inventory items and European tours have been negotiated.

✓
3

Memo #8-3   **Dated August 1, 2018**

Add the euro as a foreign currency to prepare for transactions with customers and suppliers in Europe. The linked account for exchange rate differences is 4120 and the exchange rate on August 1 is 1.42.

Change the account number for 1150 Net Bank to 1190 to accommodate the new bank account for foreign currency transactions.

Create a new Subgroup account, 1150 Bank: Euro Chequing. 1150 is a Bank class account and the next cheque number is 101.

Add 1150, the new bank account, as the linked account for Payables and Receivables bank transactions in euros.

Click **Currency** to open the Currency Settings window:

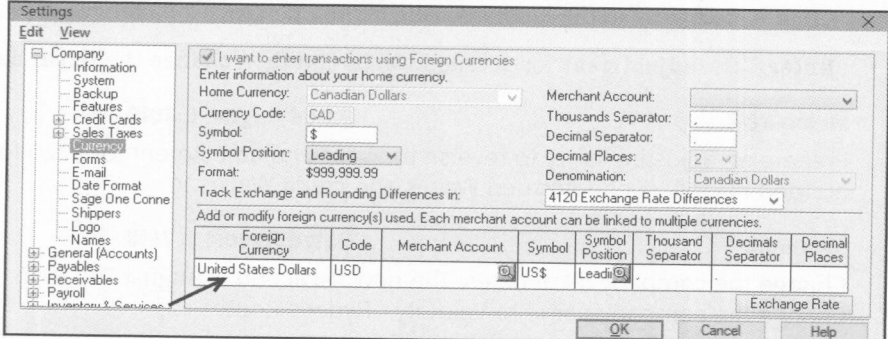

The currency added previously and its linked account for exchange rate differences are entered. You can select a different linked account, but you must use the same linked account for all currencies.

Click the **Foreign Currency column** below United States Dollars. **Click** the **List icon** 🔍 to open the currency selection list.

Click **Euro** and then **click Select**. The codes and symbols for euro are added.

Click the **Exchange Rate button**:

Euro is selected as the currency because the cursor was on this line in the previous screen. All other currencies you entered will be available from the Select A Foreign Currency drop-down list. You can add exchange rates for any of them.

Click the **Date column**. **Type** `Aug 1`

NOTES

If you choose United States Dollars from the Select A Foreign Currency list, you will open a screen with all the dates and exchange rates you have already saved as default rates.

Press ⌨ `tab` to move to the Exchange Rate column. **Type** `1.42`

Click **Display A Reminder If The Exchange Rate Is**.

The ✓ is added and we will accept the default **One Day** as our reminder period.

Click **OK** to return to the Settings. **Click OK** to return to the Home window.

NOTES
If you continue directly to the next Settings screen (for Linked Accounts) from the currency settings, you will be prompted to save the currency settings. Click OK to save the settings and continue.

Adding a Foreign Bank Account

Before using the currency in transactions, we need to create a new Bank class account for euro transactions.

Click the **Chart of Accounts icon** to open the Accounts window.

Double-click 1150 Net Bank. Click 1150, the account number. **Type** `1190` to change the account number.

Click the **Create tool** to open a new ledger window and **add** the new account **1150 Bank: Euro Chequing**.

Click **Subgroup Account** to change the Type if necessary.

Click the **Class Options tab**. **Choose Bank** from the Account Class drop-down list.

Click the **Currency list arrow** to access the options:

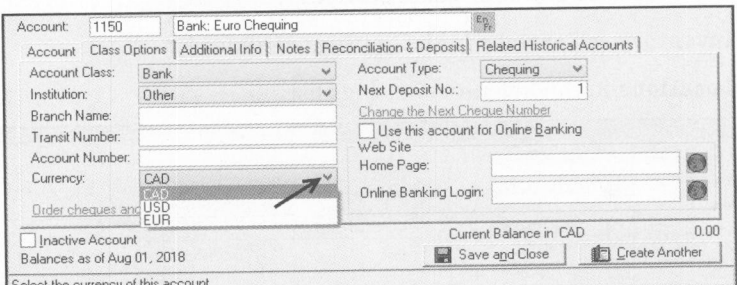

Click **EUR**. **Click** the **Save tool** before adding the cheque number.

Click **Change The Next Cheque Number** to open the Reports & Forms settings.

Click the **Next Cheque No. field** near the bottom of the form.

Type `101` **Click OK** to save the number and return to the ledger window.

Close the **Ledger window** and then **close** the **Accounts windows**.

Adding Linked Bank Accounts

We need to identify the new account as the linked account for euro transactions.

Click the **Settings icon**. Then **choose Payables** and **Linked Accounts**:

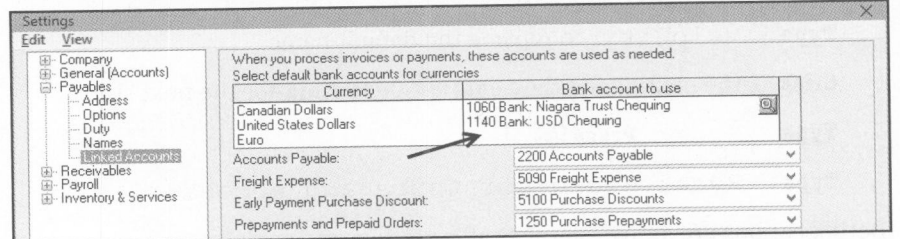

NOTES
You can click the Create tool in the Accounts window or in any ledger account window to open a new account ledger record window.

NOTES
Refer to page 648 for a review of setting up a bank account for a foreign currency.

NOTES
You can create the new account at this stage too. But you must remember to choose Subgroup as the account type and Bank as the class. Once you select the Bank class, you can choose the currency.

NOTES

Undeposited Cash and Cheques is defined as a Canadian Cash account, so it is included with the linked account selection list for euros. You cannot use the USD chequing account for euro transactions — it is not on the list of available accounts.

Click   the **Bank Account To Use column** beside Euro.

Click   the **List icon** . Only the Canadian and euro cash or bank accounts can be selected as the linked euro currency bank account.

Double-click 1150. Press (tab).

Click   **Receivables** and **Linked Accounts**.

Click   the **Bank Account To Use column** beside Euro.

Type   1150 **Press** (tab). Leave the Settings window open.

Entering Inventory Locations

Before leaving the Settings window, we will add the two stores as the locations for the business and for inventory. Items can be purchased for and sold from either store. Adjustments can also be made for the separate locations. The number of items in each store can, therefore, be monitored. If needed, items can be transferred from one location to another.

✓	**Memo #8-4**	**Dated August 1, 2018**
4		

Set up inventory locations for the two stores: VeloCity and Ryder. The VeloCity store is the primary location for inventory and the Ryder store is the secondary location for accessories and tour guide services.

Click   **Inventory & Services** in the Settings modules list.

NOTES

Click the ⊟ button beside modules to collapse the expanded lists.

Click   **Locations** in the Inventory settings list:

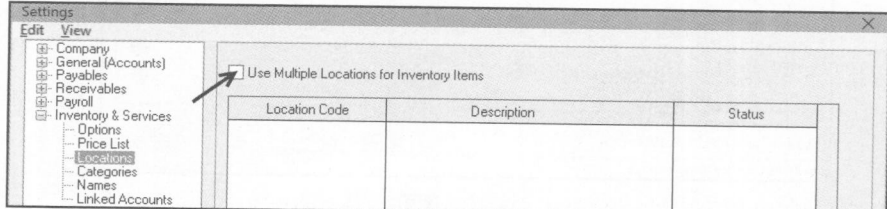

Click   **Use Multiple Locations For Inventory Items** to activate the option:

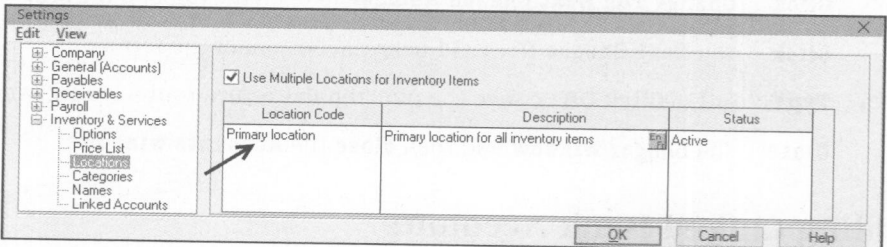

The Code, Description and Status fields are now available; we can enter the two stores. We will accept the default description for the first location.

Press   (tab) **twice** to select Primary Location.

Type   VeloCity to replace the default name.

Click   the next line of the **Location Code field** for the next store.

Type   Ryder **Press** (tab).

Type   Ryder Store for tours and accessories

Both locations are active, so the Status settings are correct.

Click   **OK** to return to the Home window.

Click   **Inventory & Services** in the Modules pane list.

Click   **AC010 Bicycle Pump: standing model** in the Home window Inventory Item list.

The Quantities tab screen includes a For Location field.

Click   the **For Location field list arrow**:

Item	Number:	AC010				Type:	⦿ Inventory
	Description:	Bicycle Pump: standing model			Fr Fr	○ Service	

Quantities | Units | Pricing | Linked | Build | Statistics | Taxes | Additional Info | Detailed Desc.

Show Quantities in: unit   For Location: All Locations

		All Locations
On Hand Quantity:	9	Value: VeloCity / Ryder
Pending Orders Purchase Order:	8	Sales Order: 0
Reorder Quantities Minimum Level:	5	To Order: 0

☐ Inactive Item   💾 Save and Close

The location in which the quantities on this tab are shown

The two locations you entered are on the drop-down list.

Choose   **VeloCity** from the For Location drop-down list to display the quantity at that store. **Choose Ryder** from the For Location drop-down list.

Initially, all the stock is at the primary location, the VeloCity store. The quantity at the VeloCity store is the same as the quantity for the All Locations selection. The quantity at the Ryder store is zero.

Close   the **Ledger window** to return to the Inventory & Services module window.

Time and Billing

Many businesses that provide services use time as the basis for billing customers. Law firms, consulting businesses and service businesses that complete maintenance and repair work are just a few examples. In addition, these businesses may keep track of how much time each employee spends on a particular job and then compare this with the standard number of hours expected for that type of work. Some jobs can be billed at a flat rate and some, such as warranty repairs or work performed for other departments of the same company, may be provided at no charge. In each of these cases, it is still important to know how much time was spent on the job. Businesses might also want to track non-billable and non-payroll times, such as for lunch breaks, when an employee is at a customer site.

The Time & Billing module in Sage 50 tracks these kinds of activities by integrating the Payroll, Inventory and Sales ledgers.

Setting Up Time and Billing Activities

Before recording the services provided by employees to customers, that is, filling in time slips, we must modify the service records to apply time and billing. First we will create the new services. We will work from the Inventory module. It should still be open.

Choose   **Add Inventory & Service** from the Inventory & Services icon drop-down shortcuts list to open a new record for inventory.

NOTES
Prices for tour guide services are group rates based on groups of 10 to 15 cyclists. Smaller and private groups may be served, but the rates will be the same. USD and euro prices will be added later.

☑ **Memo #8-5**   **Dated August 1, 2018**

5   Create the new records described in the chart below to add services and include Time & Billing information:

Item	Description	Selling Price Reg (Pref)	Unit	Related to Time?	Billable?	Billing Basis	Rate	Payroll
S070	Tour Guide: Hour	$150 ($120)	Hour	Yes	billable	billable time	per hour	Regular
S080	Tour Guide: Day	640 (560)	Day (8 hours)	Yes	billable	billable time	per day	Regular
S100	Warranty Repairs	0 (0)	Service Call	No	non-billable			Regular

Linked accounts for tours: Revenue: 4050 Revenue from Tours (new Subgroup account)
               Expense: 5075 Cost of Services
Linked accounts for repairs: Revenue: 4040 Revenue from Services; Expense: 5075 Cost of Services
Taxes: Charge HST on services provided in Canada. International tour guide services will be exempt from HST.

Type   S070 **Press** (tab). **Type** Tour Guide: Hour **Press** (tab).

Click   **Service** as the Type of item to modify the form for service items:

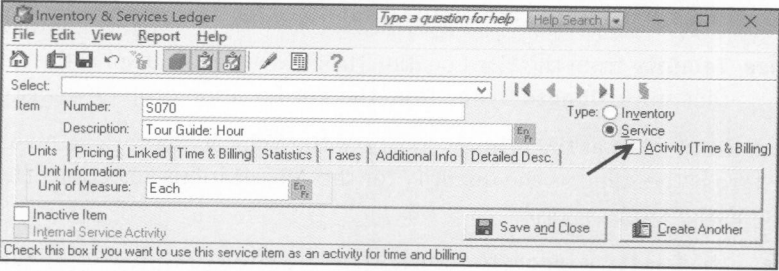

The Units tab window opens, and Activity is available as an option under Service.

Click   **Activity (Time & Billing)** to add a ✓.

This selection will open the fields related to time and billing on the Time & Billing tab. The Units information is now dimmed and the Required Field indicator (*) is added back to the screen. We will enter units on the Time & Billing tab screen, as instructed by the message that appears on the screen after we choose Activity. The Internal Service Activity option becomes available because this also applies to the Time & Billing module. We will enter the other item information first.

NOTES
Businesses often track the number of hours of service provided internally to other departments in the company as a way of monitoring internal efficiency or tracking departmental costs. They may monitor the time even if there is no charge for the service to the other department.

Click   the **Pricing tab** to open the Canadian dollar (home currency) price list.

Click   the **Regular Price Per Selling Unit field**.

Type   150 **Press** (tab) to advance to the Preferred Selling Price field.

Type   120

Click   the **Linked tab**.

Click   the **Revenue account field**. We will add the new account.

Type   4050 Revenue from Tours **Press** (tab) and **click Add** to start the Add An Account wizard with the name and number added.

Click   **Next three times** to accept the defaults to access the **Subgroup And Group Accounts** screen.

Click   **Yes** because this account is a Subgroup account.

Accept the **remaining defaults** to finish creating the account.

Click   the **Expense field** and **type** 5075

Click   the **Time & Billing tab** to access the next group of fields to be set up:

⚠ **WARNING!**
If you do not change the account type to Subgroup Account, the accounts will not be in logical order, and you will be unable to display some reports.
You can make the correction later from the General Ledger to restore the logical account order.

This screen has all the details that relate to the Time & Billing module. We must define the unit that the price is based on, indicate whether the unit is based on time and then add the relationship between the time and the unit of measure. Each is not recognized as a unit related to time, so the check box is empty.

Click   the **list arrow beside Each** in the Unit Of Measure field.

Click   **Hour**.

This Unit is automatically recognized as related to time, and the Relationship fields are now dimmed because we have already indicated a time unit. The next three fields define the **Billing & Payroll Options**:

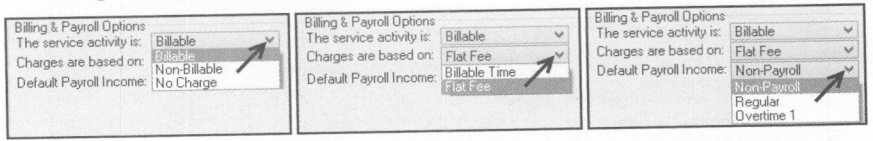

Billable is selected as the default for the service activity, and this is correct. Instead, an activity may be Non-Billable or there may be No Charge for the activity. Charges can be based on a Flat Fee or on Billable Time. Tour guide work is based on billable time.

The next option allows the time worked on the activity to be applied to an employee's paycheque. You can choose whether the time should be charged to the default payroll income account or to overtime. The non-payroll option may be selected if the work is completed by salaried employees. All services offered by Ryder's Routes are provided by the regular employees at the regular hourly wage rate.

Click   **Flat Fee** in the Charges Are Based On field or its list arrow.

Click   **Billable Time** to change the entry.

Click   **Non-Payroll** in the Default Payroll Income field or its list arrow.

Click   **Regular** to complete the Time & Billing tab screen:

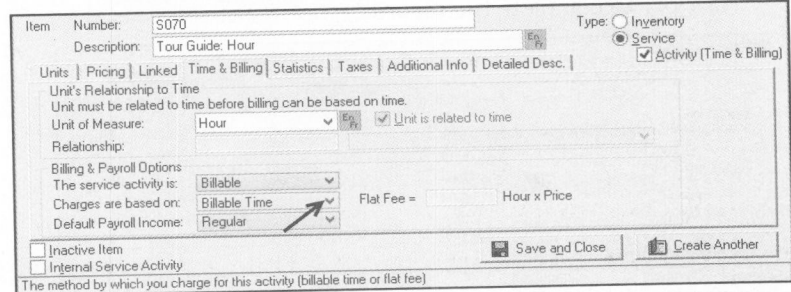

Click   the **Taxes tab**. You can accept the defaults. HST is charged, so the service is not tax exempt for HST.

Click   [Create Another] to save the record.

You are now ready to enter the next service. Service and Activity (Time & Billing) remain selected from the previous entry and are correct.

Type   S080 as the Number and Tour Guide: Day as the Description.

Click   the **Pricing tab** and **type** 640 as the Regular Price Per Selling Unit and 560 as the Preferred Price.

Click   the **Linked tab** and **enter 4050** as the Revenue account and **5075** as the Expense account.

Click   the **Time & Billing tab**. **Enter Day** as the Unit Of Measure.

NOTES

Day is not automatically recognized as a unit of time. Hours and minutes are the only default time units in the program.

This service requires additional information to indicate how many hours, or units of time, are in the day. The service will still be billed at an hourly rate, but Ryder's Routes charges a lower rate when a longer time period is purchased. Day as the unit is not automatically recognized as a unit related to time.

Click   **Unit Is Related To Time** to add a ✓ and open the Relationship fields.

Each day is based on eight billable hours of activity, so the relationship should be entered as eight hours per day. The Relationship field is a required field when the unit is not Hour or Minute and you indicate that it is related to time.

Click   the **first Relationship field**. **Type** 8

Click   the **list arrow beside the second Relationship field**:

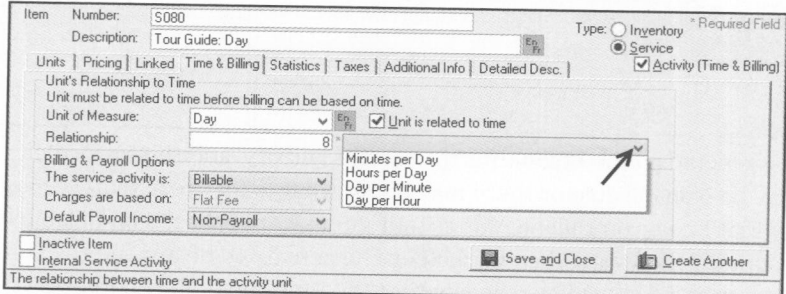

From the drop-down list, you can choose a relationship based on the number of hours or minutes per unit, or the number of units per hour or minute.

Click   **Hours Per Day**.

The next option is correct — the activity is Billable. However, it is charged on the basis of time, not at a flat rate. We need to change the entry for Charges Are Based On.

Click   **Flat Fee** in the Charges Are Based On field or its list arrow.

Click   **Billable Time** and then **choose Regular** as the Default Payroll Income category to complete the record:

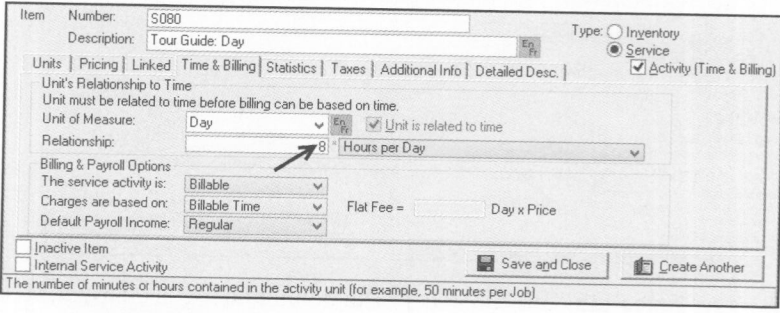

Click   Create Another   to save the record.

The final service is provided at no charge to customers, but it is entered as an inventory item so that the time spent on warranty repairs can be monitored. The price will be entered as zero.

Type   `S100` as the Number and `Warranty Repairs` as the Description.

Click   the **Pricing tab**. Do not enter any prices for the warranty service so that the prices will remain at zero.

Click   the **Linked tab** and **enter 4040** as the Revenue account and **5075** as the Expense account.

Click   the **Time & Billing tab**. **Enter Service Call** as the Unit Of Measure.

The service call for warranty work is not related to time because there is no charge for this service. We must indicate that the work is not billable. In addition, employees are paid at their usual wage rate for completing warranty work, even though the customer does not pay, so we must change the payroll category.

Click   the **list arrow beside Billable**. **Click Non-Billable** to change the entry.

Choose Regular as the Default Payroll Income category to complete the record:

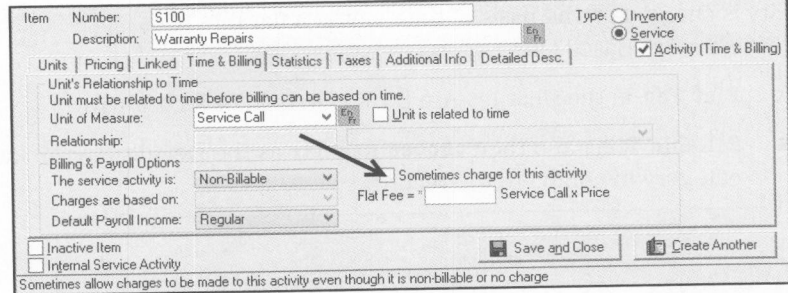

Another option for services that are normally not billed is to **sometimes charge**. When you choose the No Charge or Non-Billable options, this category becomes available. The pricing options are the same as for billable activities. You can relate the unit to time and enter the number of hours or minutes per unit, or enter a flat fee for the exceptional price. Prices are taken from Price fields on the Pricing tab screen.

Click   Save and Close to save the record and return to the Inventory & Services module window.

Adding Time and Billing Information to Services

You are now ready to edit the remaining service records to apply time and billing.

> ✓
> 6
>
> **Memo #8-6**   **Dated August 1, 2018**
>
> Edit the remaining service inventory records to add Time & Billing information. Then change the Canadian dollar prices and add foreign currency prices for services.

Item	Unit	Related to Time?	Relationship	Billable?	Billing Basis	Payroll
S010	box	yes	30 minutes/box	billable	billable time	Regular
S030	tune-up	no		billable	flat rate: 1 tune-up × price	Regular
S060	hour	yes		billable	billable time	Regular

Scroll   down the Inventory Item list in the Inventory & Services module window.

Click   **S010 Boxing for shipping** in the Home window list of items and services to open the record.

Click   the **Time & Billing tab** to open the Time & Billing screen.

NOTES
Sales of annual service contracts and rentals are not entered as service activities — there is no service time associated with them.

NOTES

When the relationship entry is 30 minutes per unit with the ledger price based on units, the charge in the Time Slip, which is based on the number of hours, would be for two boxes when you enter one hour.

Alternatively, you could enter 2 in the Relationship field and select "2 box per hour."

All the fields are dimmed because we still need to mark the service as an activity for time and billing.

> **Click**   **Activity (Time & Billing)** to open the extra fields.
>
> **Type**   box as the Unit Of Measure.

Again, as a unit, box is not automatically related to time.

> **Click**   **Unit Is Related To Time** to add a ✓ and open the Relationship fields.

Each boxing job is based on 30 minutes of billable time, so the relationship is entered as 30 minutes per box. This is the average time required to box one bicycle.

> **Click**   the **first Relationship field**. **Type** 30
>
> **Click**   the **list arrow beside the second Relationship field**.
>
> **Click**   **Minutes Per Box**.

The activity is charged on the basis of time, not at a flat rate, so we need to change the entry for Charges Are Based On.

> **Click**   **Flat Fee** in the Charges Are Based On field or its list arrow.
>
> **Click**   **Billable Time** and then **choose Regular** as the Default Payroll Income category to complete the record:

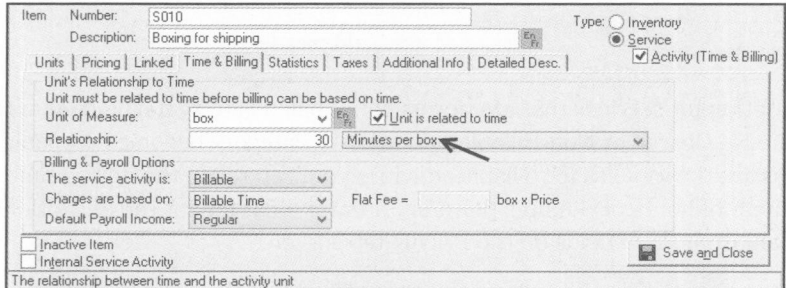

> **Click**   the **Next Item tool** ▶ **twice** to open the record for S030 Maintenance: complete tune-up.
>
> **Click**   **Activity (Time & Billing)** to change the item type.
>
> **Type**   tune-up as the Unit Of Measure.

The service is priced at a flat rate, so the unit is not related to time. Tune-up is not recognized as a unit of time, so the ✓ is not added. Billable is also the correct choice, but we need to enter the rate. By default, charges are based on a Flat Fee when the unit is not related to time, and the entry Flat Fee is dimmed. Flat Fee = ___ tune-up × Price is entered as the field label. This means that we must enter a number, not a price. The price will be calculated as the number of completed tune-ups multiplied by the price that is taken from the Pricing tab fields.

The flat rate for this service is one times the price; each tune-up is priced at $70 ($65 for preferred customers).

> **Click**   the **field beside Flat Fee =**.
>
> **Type**   1
>
> **Choose**   **Regular** as the Default Payroll Income category to update the Time & Billing screen:

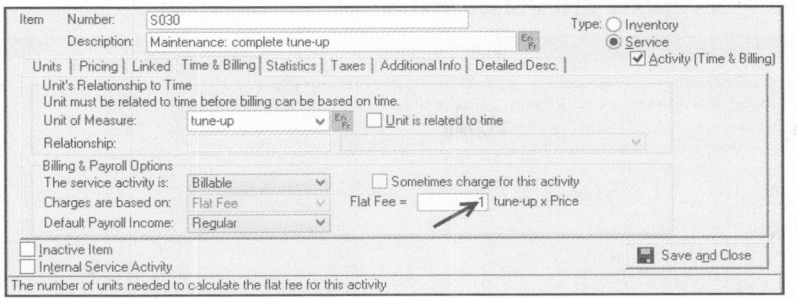

Click   the **Next Item tool** ▶ (three times) to open the record for **S060 Repairs**.

Click   **Activity (Time & Billing)**.

Again, because Hour is the unit, it is automatically related to time and most of the default details are correct.

Choose   **Regular** as the Default Payroll Income category.

Click   🖫 Save and Close to save the record and return to the Inventory & Services module window.

We will now edit the prices for these services using the Update Price Lists feature in the Inventory Settings window. You should still be in the Inventory Home window.

Updating Service Activity Prices

The Premium version allows you to define additional price lists and to update all prices from one screen. This feature is available as one of the settings for the Inventory Ledger. You can change individual item prices from this location or, if prices are raised by a fixed amount or percentage for one or more items or services, you can make the price changes globally. You can also set the prices in one list relative to the prices in another list by indicating the increase or decrease. All activity prices that require updating are listed in the following chart (the remaining prices are unchanged):

Item	Canadian Prices		USD Prices			Euro Prices		
	Reg	(Pref)	Reg	(Pref)		Reg	(Pref)	
S010	$ 80	($ 70)	$60	($ 52)	fixed price	€ 52	(€ 48)	fixed price
S060	50	(40)	35	(33)	fixed price	N/A	N/A	
S070	150	(120)	120	(110)	fixed price	100	(90)	fixed price
S080	640	(560)	480	(440)	fixed price	440	(410)	fixed price

Click   the **Settings icon** 🛠 Settings. **Click Price List** to open the Price List Settings:

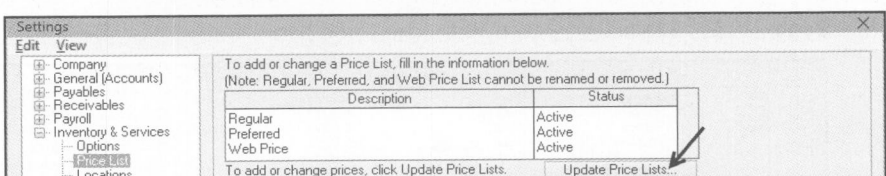

On this screen, you can define new price lists. You cannot remove or modify the three predefined price list names. If you want to create a new price list, you can type the new price list name below Web Price in the Description column and click Update Price Lists to open the item list. We need to update Regular and Preferred prices.

NOTES
The Flat Fee rate is a required field when the Flat Fee method of pricing is selected. Refer to the screenshot at the top of page 745.

NOTES
The remaining services (rentals and annual service contract) cannot be related to a specific amount of employee time, so they are not marked as activities.

NOTES
Price increases and decreases may be entered as amounts or percentages relative to the reference price.

NOTES
Foreign currency prices are not needed for services provided only in Canada to Canadian customers. The remaining services do not apply to customers in Europe.

NOTES
You can also access the Update Price Lists screens from the Home window Maintenance menu.

NOTES
If you have different units for stocking and selling, you can select the unit as well. The Unit field has a List icon.

Click an item to select it. Then click the List icon that opens beside the entry in the Unit column for the different units you can choose.

NOTES
You can select individual items by clicking the Select column beside the item. Click the column for the next item you want to change, and so on. Pressing the space bar when the cursor is in the Select column will also add the checkmark and select an item.

Then apply the change rules you want to only the selected items. For example, you could select items S010 and S060 and then apply the rule to increase these prices by a fixed amount of $5. We apply change rules to edit prices on page 775.

Click   the **Update Price Lists button**:

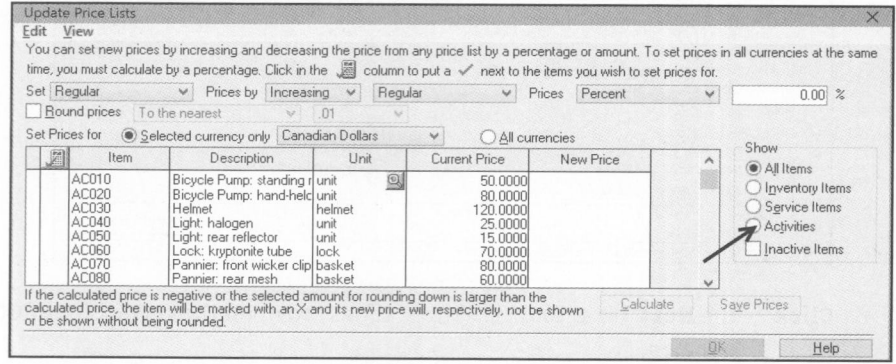

The inventory list opens with all items and services listed in Canadian regular prices. You can display All Items, Inventory Items only, Service Items only or Activities only.

You can select the items whose prices you want to update globally. You can set the prices in one list relative to another list by increasing or decreasing the reference prices by a fixed percentage or amount. Then you can round off the prices to the nearest unit — ranging from 0.0001 dollar to 1 000 dollars. You can make the price changes for one currency or for all currencies at the same time. You can also enter or edit individual prices in the new price column, so you can use this list to enter price changes manually for several inventory items on a single screen, without opening each ledger record separately.

You can Round Prices if you want to work with even amounts. Choose the direction for rounding off the price — up to the nearest, down to the nearest or to the nearest unit. Choose the nearest unit you want to round to from the drop-down list.

We will work from the smaller list of Activities. When you are changing a large number of prices, it is more efficient to work from the Update Price List screen.

Click   **Activities** under Show on the right-hand side of the screen:

	Item	Description	Unit	Current Price	New Price	Show
	S010	Boxing for shipping	box	75.0000		○ All Items
	S030	Maintenance: complete	tune-up	70.0000		○ Inventory Items
	S060	Repairs	Hour	45.0000		○ Service Items
	S070	Tour Guide: Hour	Hour	150.0000		● Activities
	S080	Tour Guide: Day	Day	640.0000		☐ Inactive Items
	S100	Warranty Repairs	Service Call	0.0000		

If the calculated price is negative or the selected amount for rounding down is larger than the calculated price, the item will be marked with an X and its new price will, respectively, not be shown or be shown without being rounded.   Calculate   Save Prices   OK   Help

The list now has the Canadian dollar Regular prices for all activities. We will edit these first. We will change the prices directly by entering the revised price in the New Price column. The prices for S010 and S060 have changed.

Click   **S010** and **press** (tab) until the cursor is in the New Price column.

Type   80

Press   (↓) **twice** to place the cursor in the New Price column for activity S060.

Type   50 **Press** (tab) to update the price list:

	Item	Description	Unit	Current Price	New Price	Show
	S010	Boxing for shipping	box	75.0000	80.0000	○ All Items
	S030	Maintenance: complete	tune-up	70.0000		○ Inventory Items
	S060	Repairs	Hour	45.0000	50.0000	○ Service Items
	S070	Tour Guide: Hour	Hour	150.0000		● Activities
	S080	Tour Guide: Day	Day	640.0000		☐ Inactive Items
	S100	Warranty Repairs	Service Call	0.0000		

If the calculated price is negative or the selected amount for rounding down is larger than the calculated price, the item will be marked with an X and its new price will, respectively, not be shown or be shown without being rounded.   Calculate   Save Prices   OK   Help

Now we will update USD regular prices.

Click **Canadian Dollars** in the Selected Currency Only field:

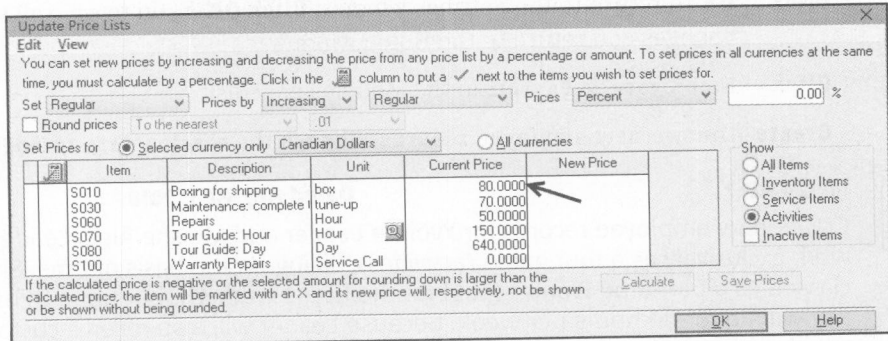

Select **United States Dollars**. Sage 50 provides a warning:

Before we continue, we need to save the new Canadian dollar prices.

Click **No** to return to the Canadian Dollars price list. **Click Save Prices**. The new prices move to the Current Price column:

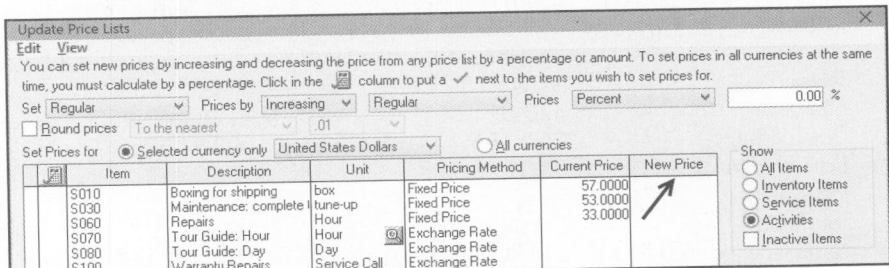

Click **Canadian Dollars** again in the Selected Currency Only field and **select United States Dollars** to view the prices in United States Dollars:

We need to change the prices for S010 and S060, as we did for Canadian Dollar prices, and we need to add prices for the new service activities.

Click **S010** and **press** (tab) until the cursor is in the New Price column.

Type 60

Press (↓) **twice** to place the cursor in the New Price column for activity S060.

Type 35

Click **Exchange Rate** for item S070 to change the entry to Fixed Rate.

Press (tab) to advance to the New Price column. **Type** 120

Click **Exchange Rate** for item S080 to change the entry to Fixed Rate.

Press (tab) to advance to the New Price column. **Type** 480

Click **Save Prices**. The new prices move to the Current Price column.

We can now update the Preferred USD prices.

Click   **Regular** in the Set field to open the drop-down list:

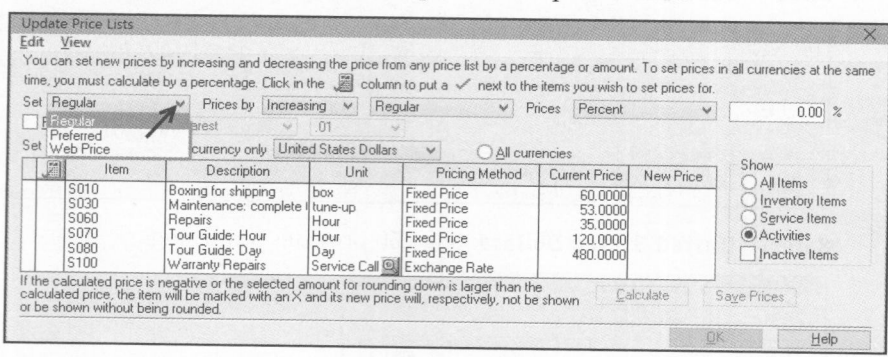

Click   **Preferred**. **Enter** the **preferred prices** for United States dollars. **Enter** the **regular** and **preferred prices** for euros from the chart on page 749. Remember to **click Save Prices** after each set. Read the margin Notes.

Click   **OK** to return to the Settings window. **Click OK** again to save all the changes and return to the Home window.

Click   **Employees & Payroll** in the Modules pane list.

Create   the **two new employee records**. **Change** the **session date to August 14**.

Memo #8-7   **Dated August 1, 2018**

Create new employee records for Yvonne Leader and Moishe Alee. Leader will work exclusively as a tour guide (activities), billing on the basis of time. She is classed as a part-time worker (paid for the hours worked), but her minimum pay will be for 20 hours per week. Because Leader will also receive customer tips that she tracks on her own, she will pay additional taxes each pay period. Alee will be paid a monthly salary as a full-time sales assistant in the new store.

	Leader, Yvonne (Female)	Alee, Moishe (Male)
Address:	499 Itinerant Dr.	551 Spoker Dr.
	Mt. Hope, ON L0R 1W0	St. Catharines, ON L2V 8H3
Telephone	(905) 418-7192	(905) 688-9101
SIN	420 011 009	128 663 887
Date of Birth	06-23-85	08-31-87
Date of Hire	08-01-18	08-01-18
Job Category	Sales	Sales
Tax Table	Ontario	Ontario
Basic Indexed: Fed (Prov)	$11 474 ($10 011)	$11 474 ($10 011)
Additional Federal Tax	$50 per week	
Regular Wage	$24/hour	N/A
# hours:	20 hours (part time)	150 hours (full time)
	(min hours in paycheque)	
Overtime Wage	$36/hour	N/A
Salary	N/A	$3 380/month
Do not use	Salary, Commission	Regular, Overtime
Pay Period:	Weekly (52 per year)	Monthly (12 per year)
Vacation:	4% Retained	3 weeks (0%, not retained)
Record Wage Expenses in:	Payroll linked accounts	Payroll linked accounts
WSIB Rate:	1.29	1.29
Vacation	delete entry	8%, 25 days max
Sick Leave	5%, 15 days max	5%, 15 days max
Personal Days	2.5%, 5 days max	2.5%, 5 days max
Direct Deposit	100% of paycheque to	100% of paycheque to
	branch #89008	branch #67752
	institution #102	institution #102
	account #341002	account #198823

NOTES
To enter the euro prices, first save the US prices, then select Euro as the currency and Regular as the price list. Enter the prices on page 749. Click Save Prices. Select Preferred as the price list and enter the preferred prices from page 749. Click Save Prices.

NOTES
Refer to pages 327–337 if you need assistance with entering the new employees. There is no historical information for the new employees.

Leader and Alee will not receive the group insurance benefit or the piece rate pay (No. Clients) or Bonus initially. Those benefits will apply after they finish the probationary work period. They also have no additional deductions at this time for VRSP, Savings Plan, Donations or Garnishee.

Preparing Time Slips

After setting up the service records to mark the activities and enter billing information, you can track the amount of time that each employee works for each customer at each activity by completing time slips.

Time slips for employees like the following one for Mercier may be entered from the Employees & Payroll module window or from the Receivables module window:

✓ **TIME SLIP #1**   **DATED AUGUST 7, 2018**

8   For Dunlop Mercier

Customer	Item	Actual Time	Billable Time	Billable Amount	Taxable	Payroll Time
Cathedral Tours	S010	3 hours	2.5 (5 boxes)	€ 260.00	yes	3 hours
Niagara Rapids Inn*	S060	4 hours	3.5 hours	$140.00	yes	4 hours
Niagara Rapids Inn*	S030	2 hours	2 hours	$65.00	yes	2 hours
Niagara Rapids Inn*	S100	4 hours	—	—	yes	4 hours
Festival Tours	S100	2 hours	—	—	yes	2 hours

Click   the **Time Slips icon** in the Receivables module Tasks pane or in the Employees & Payroll module Tasks pane:

The Time Slips Journal opens. All the tool icons in this window are the same as those found in other journals. Also, as in other journals, employees can be selected from a drop-down list and List icons are available for many of the fields.

Many features in other journals are also available for time slips. You can access these options from the tool buttons as you do in other journals or from the Time Slip menu. For example,

- Click the Store tool ⬇️ and enter a name and frequency to store the time slip as a recurring transaction.
- Click the Look Up Time Slip tool 🔲 to look up a time slip just as you look up purchases or sales invoices.
- Click the Adjust Time Slip tool 🔲 to adjust a time slip after recording. You cannot adjust a time slip for selecting the wrong employee.

The Time Slip number is updated automatically by Sage 50. Its starting number is taken from the Forms Settings, just like the next number for other forms. If the Time & Billing module is not hidden, the Next Number field for Time Slips is included in the Forms Settings screen. The number is correct.

The first time slip is for Mercier. His first job was completed for Cathedral Tours, a new regular-price customer in Europe. Use Full Add for the new customer.

Click   the **Employee list arrow** and **choose Dunlop Mercier**.

Enter   **August 7** in the Date field for the Time Slip.

Click   the **Customer field** and **type** `Cathedral Tours` **Press** tab .

Add   the **complete record** details for the new customer.

Click   the **Item field List icon** 🔍 to open the Select Activity list:

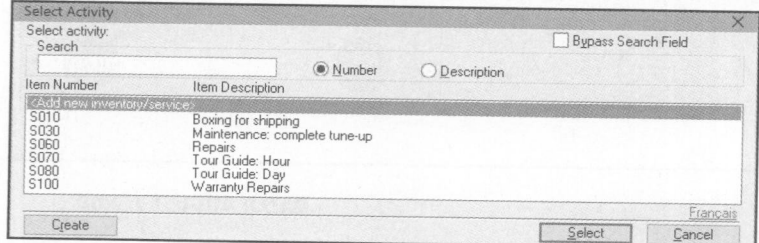

All services for which you selected Activity as the type of Service and added time and billing details will be on this list. Other services and inventory will not be included.

Double-click   S010 Boxing for shipping to add it to the journal.

The Item and Description fields are the usual ones for inventory and service transactions. The next field, **Billing Status**, is completed from the Time & Billing tab details in the ledger record. Usually the defaults are correct, but you can change them if needed. The Billing Status field has a List icon and a selection list. Activities may be Billable, Non-Billable or provided at No Charge.

If an activity is billable, you can use the **Timer** in this window to track the time worked on the activity. Some businesses track all time spent for a customer. For example, if a customer phones for advice, and telephone advice is a billable activity, you can start the timer at the beginning of the phone call and then stop it at the end to have an accurate measure of the duration of the call.

To use the timer, click the **Start** button. The counter will keep time in seconds until you click the **Stop** button. You can use this measurement as the actual time. Select the customer in the Customer column and enter the activity.

To apply the time to a customer, click the **Stopwatch icon** ⏱ or click the **Apply Time** button. The stopwatch time will be entered in the Actual Time column.

Time is entered as the number of hours, minutes and seconds (hhmmss). You can also enter the times as decimal amounts, such as 2.75 for two hours and 45 minutes. The simplest way to explain the format for entering time is with a few examples. The following chart summarizes the examples and outlines some of the rules:

EXAMPLES OF TIME ENTRIES IN THE TIME SLIPS JOURNAL

Entering This Number	Records This Time	Displays in Journal as
1 or 01 or 100 or 10000	Records 1 hour	01:00:00
001 or 0001 or 000100	Records 1 minute	00:01:00
00001 or 000001	Records 1 second	00:00:01
130 or 0130 or 013000	Records 1.5 hours (1 hour and 30 minutes)	01:30:00
0110 or 110 or 11000	Records 1 hour and 10 minutes	01:10:00
1030 or 103000	Records 10 hours and 30 minutes	10:30:00
11515 or 011515	Records 1 hour, 15 minutes and 15 seconds	01:15:15
995959	Records 99 hours, 59 minutes and 59 seconds	99:59:59

RULES FOR TIME ENTRIES IN THE TIME SLIPS JOURNAL

- You can enter up to six digits (hhmmss). A one- or two-digit number is always interpreted as the number of hours (zero minutes, zero seconds). The remaining missing digits are always assumed to be zero.
- For a three-digit entry, the first number represents hours and the next two represent the minutes.
- For a four-digit number, the first two numbers represent hours and the next two represent minutes.
- For a five-digit number, the first number represents the number of hours, the next two, minutes, and the final two, seconds.
- For a six-digit entry, the first two numbers represent hours, the next two, minutes, and the last two, seconds.
- You can omit seconds and minutes if they are zero. Leading zeros are not needed for hours.
- The times allowed on a line for one activity range from the shortest time of 1 second, entered as 000001 or 00001, to the longest, 99 hours, 59 minutes and 59 seconds, entered as 995959.

There are three columns for time: the **Actual Time** spent at the activity, the **Billable Time** or amount of time that the customer pays for, and the **Payroll Time** or hours the employee is paid for. Sometimes the customer is billed for fewer hours than the job actually required. For example, if an estimate has been given and the work is much more complex than anticipated, a business will usually not bill the customer for the full amount in the interest of good customer relations. At other times, the customer may be charged for more time than the activity requires. For example, a job may have a minimum time component, such as one hour of labour. Most companies will want to keep track of all times so that they can revise their prices to reflect their true costs.

Mercier spent 3 hours packing the five boxes (actual time); the customer will pay for 2.5 hours of work (billable time for five boxes); and Mercier will be paid for 3 hours of work for this job (payroll time).

> **Click**   the **Actual Time field**.
>
> **Type**   3 **Press** ⌈tab⌋ to update the time slip:

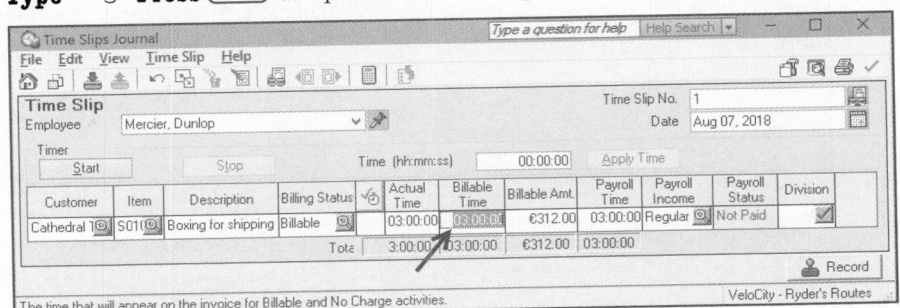

The program enters 03:00:00, the actual time, as the billable time and the payroll time. The price (**Billable Amt.**) is the billable time multiplied by the price from the ledger — €52 per box (half-hour). The currency is added for foreign currency amounts.

For this customer, five bicycles were packed for shipping. Recall that we entered 30 minutes as the usual time (or 0.5 hours) for the job. The hourly rate was determined as the Selling Price divided by the usual number of hours, that is, €52 (for 30 minutes) divided by 0.5, or €104 per hour. Thus the amount for 2.5 hours is 2.5 × €104, or €260.

The **Payroll Status** is Not Paid. You can edit the billable time, the billable amount, the payroll time and payroll income category for individual activities. We need to change the billable time to 2.5 hours, 2 hours and 30 minutes. The billable time is already selected.

Type   230 or 2.5 **Press** (tab) to update the billable amount to €260.

Click   the **Customer list icon** 🔍 and **select Niagara Rapids Inn** for the second activity.

Click   the **Item list icon** 🔍 and **select S060 Repairs**.

Click   the **Actual Time column**.

Type   4 **Press** (tab). **Type** 330 to update the Billable Time and Amount.

Repair service work is billed at a straight hourly rate, so the amount is the billable time multiplied by the hourly rate for the preferred customer.

Click   the **Customer list icon** 🔍 on the next line. **Select Niagara Rapids Inn** again.

Click   the **Item list icon** 🔍 and **select S030 Maintenance: complete tune-up**.

Click   the **Actual Time column**. **Type** 2 **Press** (tab).

This time the flat rate of $65 is entered for the preferred price customer and you cannot edit the billable time. However, you can edit the billable amount.

Click   the **Customer list icon** 🔍 and **select Niagara Rapids Inn** for the fourth activity.

Click   the **Item list icon** 🔍 and **select S100 Warranty Repairs**.

Click   the **Actual Time column**.

Type   4 **Press** (tab). No amount is entered because the activity is non-billable, but the hours are added to the employee's payroll time.

Click   the **Customer list icon** 🔍 and **select Festival Tours**.

Click   the **Item list icon** 🔍 and **select S100 Warranty Repairs**.

Click   the **Actual Time column**.

Type   2 **Press** (tab) to complete the entry:

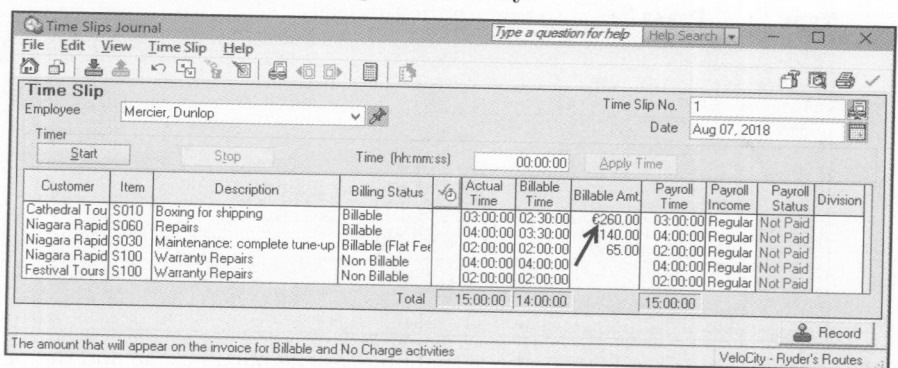

Check   the **time slip** carefully before recording and **correct mistakes**.

You can also allocate time slip details to divisions — on the basis of either percent or time (from the Division settings, as on page 505) and on the basis of actual, billable or payroll time (from the Allocate Based On drop-down list in the next screen).

Click the Division column for the activity line to open the Allocation screen:

Division Allocation - Time Slips					✕
Edit View					
☐ Apply this allocation to entire transaction					
Allocate based on: Actual Time ▾					
Total available:	03:00:00	02:30:00	260.00	03:00:00	100.00
Division	Actual Time	Billable Time	Billable Amt. (€)	Payroll Time	%
🔍					
Total allocated:	00:00:00	00:00:00	0.00	00:00:00	0.00
				OK	Cancel

Choose the basis of allocation and division. Enter the time or percentage allocated to the division for that activity. Click OK to return to the journal when finished.

Click   the **Record button** [🖊 Record] to save the entry.

Complete Time Slip #2 and then **close** the **Time Slips Journal**.

☐
9

TIME SLIP #2				DATED AUGUST 7, 2018		
For Yvonne Leader						
Customer	Item	Actual Time	Billable Time	Billable Amount	Taxable	Payroll Time
Cathedral Tours	S080	13 hours	12 hours	€ 660.00	no	13 hours
Cathedral Tours	S070	3 hours	2 hours	€ 200.00	no	3 hours
Festival Tours	S080	8 hours	8 hours	USD $480.00	yes	8 hours
Niagara Rapids Inn*	S070	4 hours	3.5 hours	$420.00	yes	4 hours

Add   a **shortcut** for the **Time Slips Journal**. **Choose Create Time Slip** under the Time & Billing heading.

Paying Employees from Time Slips

After filling in the time slips, we use them to prepare paycheques.

☑
10

Employee Time Summary Sheet #20   **Dated August 7, 2018**
For the Pay Period ending August 7, 2018
Use time slips to prepare the paycheque for Yvonne Leader. Issue deposit slip #37.
Pay Dunlop Mercier for 80 regular hours in the period and 2 hours of overtime.
Recover $50 loaned and issue deposit slip #38.

Open   the **Payroll Journal**.

Enter   **August 7** as the Cheque Date and the Period Ending date.

Choose Leader from the Employee list and **press** (tab) to enter her information:

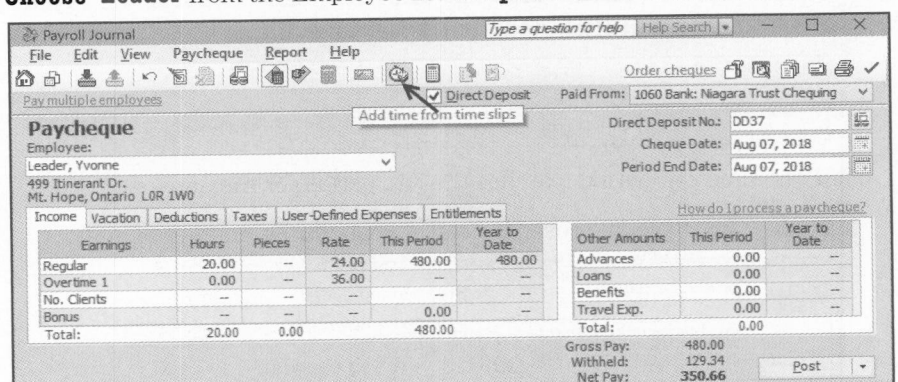

When activities are set up in the Inventory and Services Ledger and time slips are entered for employees, Sage 50 tracks the hours worked so you can use the summary of these time slips to prepare paycheques.

NOTES
You can allocate on the basis of actual, billable or employee time, or on a percentage basis. You can choose separately for each activity or apply the same allocation to the entire time slip.

NOTES
The successful recording confirmation message does not include a journal entry number.

NOTES
Service items S070 and S080 are not taxed when they are provided outside of Canada. They are deemed to be part of the tour. Services provided in Canada are taxable.
The * indicates that preferred customer prices apply.

NOTES
You can also add time slips information in the Payroll Cheque Run Journal by selecting the employees and clicking the Add Time tool button or by choosing Add Time From Time Slips from the Payroll menu. The option to increase the number of hours to those in the ledger record must be applied the same way — to all employees or to none of them.

NOTES

The Time Slip tool remains
unavailable until you select an
employee.

We will use this method to prepare the paycheque for the new employee, Yvonne Leader, because these activities are her primary responsibility. We are using the Payroll Journal to demonstrate the Sage 50 options for processing time slips.

> **Click**   the **Add Time From Time Slips tool** 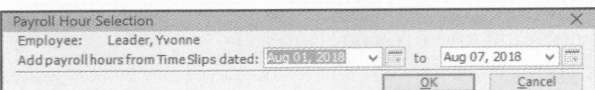 or **choose** the **Paycheque menu** and **click Add Time From Time Slips**.

The Payroll Hour Selection screen opens:

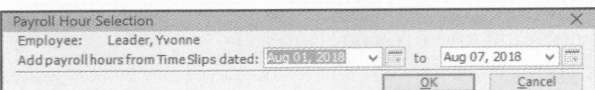

When you choose Pay Employee From Time Slip from the Employees & Payroll module Time Slips icon, a Search window opens. After you select the employee, the Payroll Hour Selection screen opens with the Payroll Journal in the background.

You should enter the dates for the time slips that apply to this pay period. Leader has worked for one week; therefore, you should include the time slips up to August 7.

These dates are entered as the defaults because we already entered August 7 as the period ending date and August 1 is the date Leader was hired.

> **Click**   **OK** to return to the journal.

The number of hours is updated and the journal entry is completed:

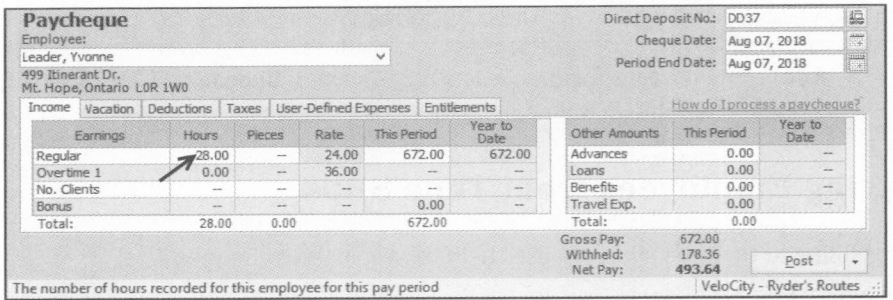

You can edit the number of hours as usual if necessary, and you can add advances or other deductions if they are appropriate.

> **Review** the **journal entry** and, when you are certain it is correct,

> **Click**   **Post** to save the transaction. **Click Yes** to continue.

> **Choose**   **Mercier** from the Employee list and press `tab` to enter his default payroll information.

> **Click**   the **Add Time From Time Slips tool** 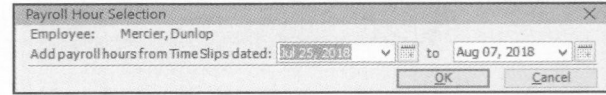 or **choose** the **Paycheque menu** and **click Add Time From Time Slips**:

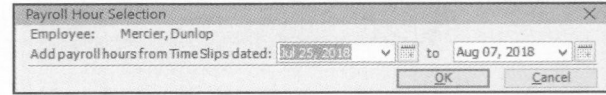

Again, the time slip period matches the pay period for the employee.

> **Click**   **OK**. Sage 50 presents a warning about the number of hours:

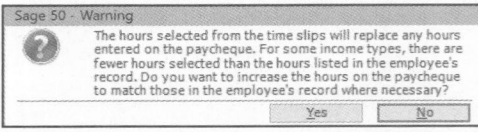

WARNING!

You must complete the step
of adding time from the time slips.
If you do not, the payroll status for
these activities will remain as Not
Paid and the employee could be
incorrectly paid a second time for
the same work.

You must also complete this
step before adding overtime
hours.

For Mercier, the hours worked exceed the hours on his time slip for the various customer jobs because he also performs other duties at the store. You have the option of

accepting the Time Slip information or increasing the hours to match the default in the employee records. For Mercier, the Payroll Ledger entry is the correct one.

Click   **Yes** to increase the number of hours and return to the journal. The number of Regular hours remains unchanged at 80 hours.

Enter   the **dates** for the paycheque.

Click   the **Overtime 1 field**. **Type** 2 to add the overtime hours.

Click   the **Loans field** and **accept** the **default** $50 remaining to be repaid.

Review the **journal entry** and make corrections if necessary.

Click   Post. **Click Yes** to continue and save the transaction.

Close   the **Payroll Journal**.

The program will update the Payroll Hours Selection dates for the next paycheque and the Payroll Status on these Time Slips.

Open   the **Time Slips Journal** from the shortcut or from the icon.

Click   the **Look Up Time Slips tool** .

Type   2 in the Time Slip Number field. **Click OK** to open Leader's time slip.

The time slip information has Paid in the Payroll Status column for each job completed by this employee, indicating that the employee has been paid for the work on this time sheet. You cannot use this time slip information for payroll again.

Click   the **Look Up Time Slips tool** and **type** 1 in the Time Slip Number field. **Click OK** to review Mercier's time slip.

His payroll status is also marked as Paid because we added time from the time slips, even though the hours were not used to determine his pay.

Close   the **Time Slips Journal**.

Preparing Sales Invoices from Time Slips

When sales invoices are prepared for mailing to customers, the service activities completed for this customer from time slips for all employees can be added directly to the invoices without re-entering each activity.

Click   **Receivables** in the Modules pane list, if necessary.

Click   the **Sales Invoices icon** to open the Sales Journal.

Sales Invoice #2488   **Dated August 7, 2018**

To Cathedral Tours: Complete sales invoice for € 1 120 plus HST from time slip activities. Include all activities to date. Enter H as the tax code for S010. Sales invoice total € 1 153.80. Terms: 2/10, n/30. The exchange rate is 1.44.

Choose **Cathedral Tours** as the customer. Invoice and Pay Later are correct.

Enter   **August 7, 2018** as the invoice date and **1.44** as the **exchange rate**.

Time slip activities may be entered using the tool icon or the Sales menu option:

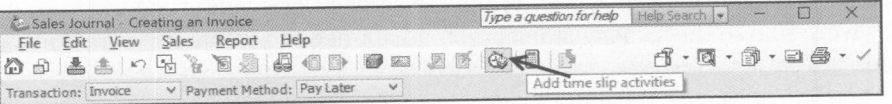

NOTES
When you add time slip hours in the Payroll Run Journal, you must do so for all selected employees. You cannot choose individual employees for this. You get the confirmation message about number of hours being increased, but again, it will apply to all employees.

NOTES
When you use the time slip number to look up the time slip, the Previous and Next tools will not be available.
You can Search All Employees in the Search lookup window and click OK to list all the time slips and then select one, as we did in other journals. This approach will make the Next and Previous tools available.

NOTES
From the Receivables module Time Slips icon shortcuts list, you can choose Create Invoice From Time Slip. After choosing the customer from the Select Customer screen, the Service Activities Selection screen on page 760 opens for that customer.

NOTES

If necessary, scroll or change the column width to include all the columns.

NOTES

Selecting non-billable activities will include Warranty Repair hours on the selection list. Non-billable activities are not added to the sales invoice.

NOTES

Clicking ⬚, the Add Activity column heading, will select all the activities in the list. Then you can click any activity to deselect it if you need to.

WARNING!

Enter tax codes on sales invoices for foreign customers carefully. Refer to the Time Slip if necessary.

NOTES

You can edit the amount billed to the customer in the Sales Journal by changing the Amount or the Price. You can also choose a different account number for the sales.

NOTES

If the information in the time slip was incorrect, close the Sales Journal without posting the invoice and adjust the time slip. Then re-enter the sales invoice.

Click the **Add Time Slip Activities tool** ⬚ or **choose** the **Sales menu** and **click Add Time Slip Activities** to open the activities list for this customer:

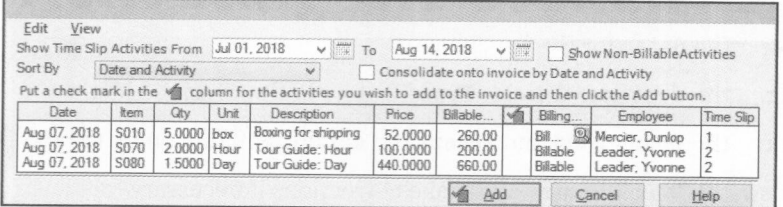

Services provided to the customer by all employees will be listed, and you can also include Non-Billable Activities by clicking its check box. You may need to scroll to include information in all columns. You can Sort the list By Date And Activity, the default, By Employee And Activity or By Activity. You can also Consolidate the list By Date And Activity, combining the amounts for each activity recorded for the same date. You can select all the activities for the invoice or omit some if they are incomplete or come after the billing date. All activities should be included on the invoice for Cathedral Tours.

Enter   **Aug 1 2018** and **Aug 7 2018** as the date range in the Show Time Slip Activities From and To date fields.

Click   the **Add Activity column** ⬚ for the first activity, S010. Only activities with a ✓ in this column are added to the sales invoice.

Click   the **Add Activity column** ⬚ for the remaining activities.

Click   the **Add button** ⬚ Add to return to the Sales Journal.

The activities are now added to the journal.

Taxes are charged on the boxing service for Canadian customers on European tours because the work was completed in Canada, so we need to change this tax code entry.

Double-click the **blank Tax code field for item S010**, and **choose H** as the code to complete the entry:

The Quantity refers to the units in the ledger — for S010, the customer pays for five completed units or boxes at one-half hour each. On the time sheet, we entered 230 (or 2.5) as the billable time. The 12 hours of tour guide service are entered as 1.5 days, the unit in the ledger. You can add other regular services or inventory to the sales invoice if they were sold to the same customer; you do not need to create a separate invoice for them.

You should review the journal entry before posting it.

Choose the **Report menu** and **click Display Sales Journal Entry**:

Account Number	Account Description	Foreign A...	Debits	Credits
	VeloCity - Ryder's Routes			
	Sales Journal Entry 08/07/2018 (J4)			
1200	Accounts Receivable	€1,153.80	1,661.47	-
2650	GST/HST Charged on Sales	€33.80	-	48.67
4040	Revenue from Services	€260.00	-	374.40
4050	Revenue from Tours	€860.00	-	1,238.40
1 Euro equals 1.4400000 Canadian Dollars			1,661.47	1,661.47

The journal entry is like other sales journal entries.

Close the **report** when you have finished viewing it and **make corrections** if necessary.

To correct the activities, click [icon] to return to the Service Activities Selection list. Previously selected activities have Invoiced in the Billing Status column.

Clicking the Add Activity column [icon] will add the ✓ and restore the status to Billable so you can select a different group of activities.

Click [Post] to save the journal entry.

Enter the next **four transactions**.

Sales Invoice #2489   **Dated August 7, 2018**

12 To Niagara Rapids Inn: Complete sales invoice for $625 plus HST from time slip activities. Include all activities to date. Sales invoice total $706.25. Terms: 2/10, n/30.

Sales Invoice #2490   **Dated August 7, 2018**

13 To Festival Tours: Complete sales invoice for $480 USD from time slip activities. Include all activities to date. No tax is charged for tours in the United States. Sales invoice total $480 USD. Terms: 2/10, n/30. The exchange rate is 1.376.

Receipt #825   **Dated August 7, 2018**

14 From Fallsview Riverside Resort, cheque #1628 for $5 695.20 in full payment of account. Reference sales invoice #2484.

Memo #8-8   **Dated August 7, 2018**

15 From Visa, received monthly credit card statement for $98 for purchases made before August 1, 2018. Submitted cheque #146 for $98 in full payment.

Building New Inventory

Instead of assembling inventory using the Item Assembly method, you can set up the inventory assembly components in the ledger record and then use this information to build an item using the Bill of Materials method. We will create the new inventory Promotional Safety Package, including the items or materials that make up the package.

Memo #8-9   **Dated August 7, 2018**

16 Create a new inventory record for a Promotional Safety Package that bundles several popular accessories. Create new linked Asset account: 1510 Promotions.

Item: AP100 Promotional Safety Package
Unit: package
Minimum: 0
Linked accounts: Asset 1510 Promotions; Revenue 4020; COGS 5050

Currency	CAD	USD	Euro
Regular Selling Price	$375	$280	€260
Preferred Selling Price	$350	$255	€240
Tax exempt: No			

NOTES
Selecting non-billable activities will add Warranty Repairs to the selection lists for Niagara Rapids Inn and Festival Tours. However, this service will not be added to the invoice.

NOTES
Click the Exchange Rate tool or type in the new rate for the sale to Festival Tours. The option to change the rate will not open automatically.

NOTES
The regular selling price for the Promotional Safety Package would be $405.

Build Components: use 1 of each   AC020 Bicycle Pump: hand-held mini
                                        AC030 Helmet
                                        AC040 Light: halogen
                                        AC060 Lock: kryptonite tube
                                        AC070 Pannier: front wicker clip-on
                        and 2 of   AC050 Light: rear reflector

Choose   **Inventory & Services** from the Modules pane list.

Choose   **Add Inventory & Service** from the Inventory & Services icon shortcuts list to open the Inventory Ledger for new Service Activity items. The cursor is in the Item Number field.

Type   AP100 **Press** (tab).

Type   Promotional Safety Package

Click   **Inventory** as the Type to modify the form for the inventory item.

The Units tab screen is displayed. All units are the same for this package.

Double-click   **Each** and **type** package

Click   the **Quantities tab**. The Minimum level is correct at 0.

Click   the **Pricing tab** to access the price fields.

On the Pricing tab screen, you can enter regular and preferred prices in all the currencies that you have set up. Canadian prices are given initially.

Click   the **Regular Price Per Selling Unit field**.

Type   375 **Press** (tab) to advance to the Preferred Price field.

Type   350

Choose   **United States Dollars** from the Currency list.

Foreign prices for Ryder's Routes are fixed, so we need to change the default setting. Clicking the entry will change the setting.

Click   **Exchange Rate** beside Regular to change the setting to Fixed Price.

Press   (tab) to advance to the Regular Selling Price for United States Dollars.

Type   280 **Press** (tab) to advance to the Preferred Pricing Method.

Click   **Exchange Rate** to change the setting to Fixed Price. **Press** (tab).

Type   255

Choose   **Euro** from the currency list.

Click   **Exchange Rate** beside Regular to change the setting to Fixed Price.

Press   (tab) to advance to the Regular Price for Euro.

Type   260 **Press** (tab) to advance to the Preferred Pricing Method.

Click   **Exchange Rate** to change the setting. **Press** (tab). **Type** 240

Click   the **Linked tab** to open the Linked Accounts screen.

Click   the **Asset field**.

Type   1510 Promotions **Press** (tab). We need to add the account.

Click   **Add** and **press** (tab) to open the Add Account wizard.

Accept the remaining **defaults** for the account and **click Yes** to change the account class.

Press `tab` to advance to the Revenue account field.

Type 4020 **Press** `tab` to advance to the COGS account field.

Type 5050

The variance linked account is not needed — the package will not be oversold.

Click the **Taxes tab** to open the list of sales taxes relating to the inventory.

The default entry No for Tax Exempt is correct — HST is charged on the sale of this item. Duty is not charged on this item because it is not purchased.

Click the **Build tab** to access the information screen we need for entering the assembly or building components for inventory items:

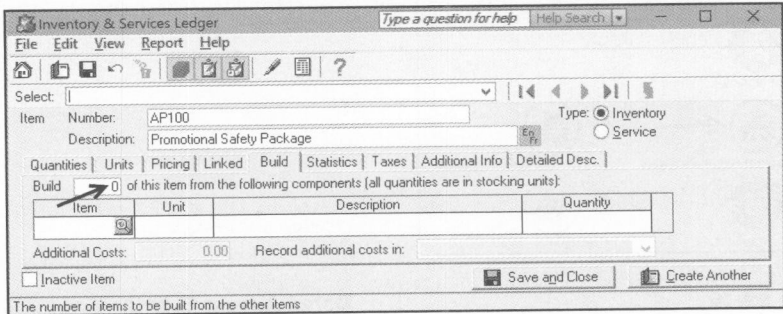

NOTES
You can mark the new inventory as exempt for GST, but you do not need to do so.

NOTES
This screen is similar to the upper Components section of the Item Assembly Journal (page 376), but you cannot enter unit costs for the components.

On this screen, we enter the relationship between the new inventory and its components — that is, how many new items we are building and how many of each input item this number of units requires. This is very similar to the Item Assembly Journal, except that we are only defining the building process at this stage. The actual building or assembly still takes place in the journal. One package is created from this set of accessories — we are defining the rules for building one package.

Click the **Build field** to enter the default number of packages being assembled from this set of components.

Type 1 **Press** `tab` to advance to the Item (number) field.

Click the **List icon** and **select AC020 Bicycle Pump: hand-held mini** to enter the first item.

The cursor advances to the Quantity field after entering the unit and description. Here you need to enter the number of pumps included in each Promotional Safety Package. We are defining the unit relationship between the assembled item and its components. One component item is used to make the package.

Type 1 **Press** `tab` to advance to the second Item line.

Enter the **next four components** and **enter 1** as the quantity for each. For **A050, enter 2** as the quantity.

The **Additional Costs** and its linked account field (**Record Additional Costs In**) became available once we entered the number of units to build. These fields have the same meaning as they do in the Item Assembly Journal. However, in the Bill of Materials method, costs are entered in the ledger record and separate assembly linked accounts can be defined for each item. There are no additional costs associated with creating the package, so we should leave these fields blank.

Click the **Quantities tab**.

NOTES
In the Pro version, there is one linked Item Assembly Costs account for the ledger, and it is entered on the Inventory Linked Accounts screen. This linked account is used for all Build From Item Assembly transactions in both Pro and Premium versions.

In the Premium version, you can enter a different linked account for additional costs for each item you build. These different linked accounts will be used for Build From Bill Of Materials transactions.

The quantity on hand remains at zero until we build the item in the journal. Quantities for the component items also remain unchanged.

Correct any **errors** by returning to the field with the mistake. **Highlight** the **error** and **enter** the **correct information**. **Click** the different **tabs** to check all the information that you entered.

Click [Save and Close] to save the record.

Building an Inventory Item in the Journal

The quantity of Promotional Safety Packages is still zero. In order to create stock of the package for sale, we must build the item in the Bill Of Materials & Item Assembly Journal:

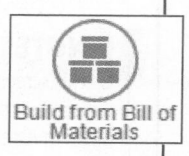
Build from Bill of Materials

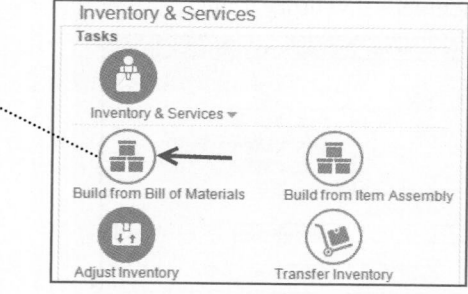

✓
17 **Memo #8-10** **Dated August 7, 2018**

Build five (5) packages of the new item Promotional Safety Package (AP100).

Click the **Build From Bill Of Materials icon** to open the journal:

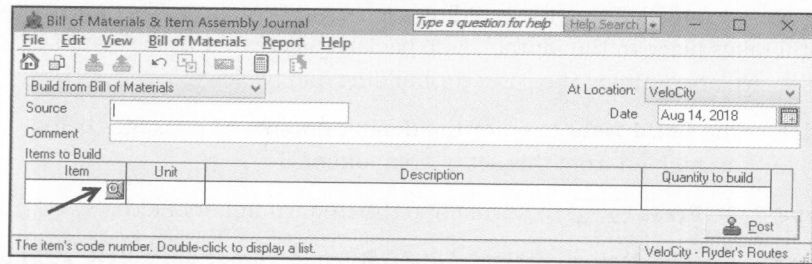

In the Premium version, you can assemble new inventory items either by using the Item Assembly method that we used in previous applications or the Bill of Materials method that follows.

The journal resembles the lower half of the Build From Item Assembly Journal screen, the Assembled Items section, but without components and costs (refer to page 375). Information for the upper half of the Item Assembly screen — for components and costs — is located in the ledger record. The default location is VeloCity.

Click the **Source field**.

Type Memo 8-10 **Press** (tab) to advance to the Date field.

Type 8-7 **Press** (tab) **twice** to advance to the Comment field.

Type Create promotional packages **Press** (tab). The cursor moves to the Item field.

Click the **List icon** to open the selection list:

NOTES
Built items may also be purchased if this is appropriate. They are available for selection in the Purchases Journal.

Classic **CLASSIC VIEW**
Click the Bill Of Materials &

Item Assembly icon
to open the journal. Choose Build From Bill Of Materials from the Build drop-down transactions list if necessary.

NOTES
Remember that you can choose Build From Item Assembly or Build From Bill Of Materials from the transactions drop-down list once the journal is open (refer to page 375).

NOTES
The additional costs and the components information are taken from the ledger record — the Build tab screen details. Item cost, as usual, is the average cost for each component because we selected this method for the company file (refer to page 662).

All items for which you have added build information will be listed on this screen. Because we have entered these details only for the Promotional Safety Package, it is the only one listed. You cannot create a new item from this Select screen.

Double-click AP100 to add it to the journal.

The unit and description are added for the package and the default quantity is 1. These details are taken from the ledger record. The quantity is selected, so we can change it. We are creating five packages.

Type   5   to complete the journal entry:

If you have other items to build, you can continue by choosing the items and entering a quantity for each of them.

Review your **work** before posting the transaction.

Choose the **Report menu** and **click Display Bill Of Materials & Item Assembly Journal** to display the journal transaction:

VeloCity - Ryder's Routes			
Bill of Materials & Item Assembly Journal Entry (08/07/2018 (J9)			
Account Number	Account Description	Debits	Credits
1510	Promotions	1,119.83	-
1520	Accessories	-	1,119.83
Additional Date:	Ref. Number:	1,119.83	1,119.83

The asset account balances have been updated by the transaction, just as they are in an Item Assembly transaction. Compare this journal entry with the one on page 377. The inventory quantities are also updated from the transaction — the quantity of packages increases and the quantities for the component accessory items decrease. Additional costs, if any, would be credited to the linked cost account for the package and debited to the assembled item asset account.

Close   the **journal display** and **make corrections** if necessary.

If there is not enough inventory of any item in stock to complete the build, Sage 50 will ask you to reduce the quantity to build:

Click OK and reduce the number of units you are building.

Click   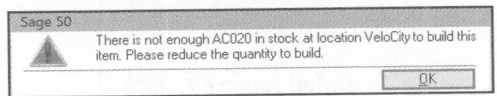   to save the entry. **Close** the **advisor** about low inventory.

Click the Item List icon — the number of promotional packages has been changed to five. Click Cancel to close this screen without making a selection.

You can now sell the package just like any other inventory item.

Multiple Levels of Build

You can use a built item just like any other single inventory item. The process is the same when you are selling the item or using it as a component to build other inventory. We created an additional built item to illustrate the multiple build — we include the next two screenshots for information only.

Nested building components are common in construction work. When you use a built item as a component for a second-stage build, you select it on the Build tab screen just like other inventory. When you are building the new second-stage item in the Bill of Materials Journal, the built component may be out of stock. In this case, Sage 50 offers to build the missing item when you try to post the entry:

NOTES

If there are further layers of building nested in a transaction, Sage 50 will offer to build the necessary components at each stage in the same way to complete the initial transaction.

The multiple build option lets you build the final items and allow Sage 50 to complete the intermediate builds.

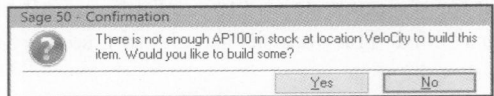

You can now automatically build the primary item, the built component, as part of the same journal transaction.

Click Yes to continue with the additional build:

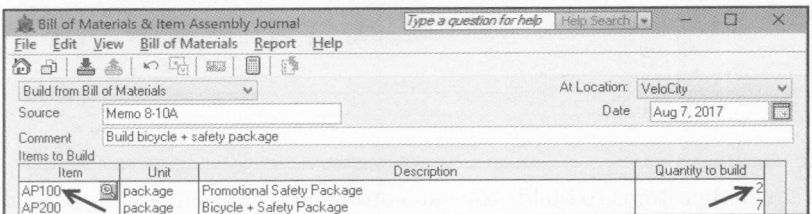

Sage 50 will add the out-of-stock built item to the journal as the first item to build. The number of units built will be those required to complete the secondary build.

Close the **Journal**.

Transferring Inventory between Locations

NOTES

Transfers may also be made when the item a customer wants is not located at the store the customer is visiting.

Items can be transferred from one location where the stock is available or stored to another. In Sage 50, the option to transfer items is available in the Inventory Adjustments & Transfers Journal, accessed from the Transfer Inventory icon:

CLASSIC VIEW

Click the Inventory Adjustments & Transfers icon

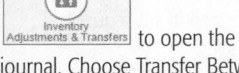

to open the journal. Choose Transfer Between Locations from the drop-down transactions list if necessary.

✓ 18

Memo #8-11   **Dated August 7, 2018**

The Ryder store is preparing for its official opening. Transfer the following inventory items from the VeloCity store to the Ryder store:

5	AP100	Promotional Safety Package
10	AC030	Helmet
10	AC040	Light: halogen
20	BK010	Books: Complete Bicycle Guide
20	BK020	Books: Endless Trails

Click   the **Transfer Inventory icon** to open the journal with Transfer Between
Locations, the type of transaction we need, already selected:

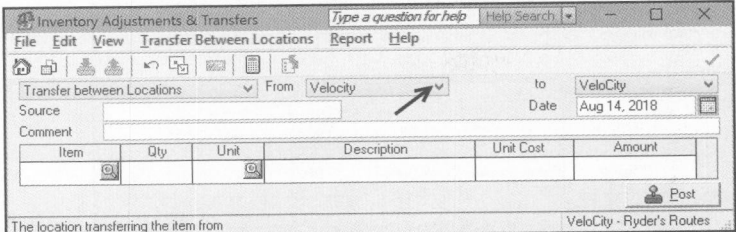

This is the same journal we used for other inventory adjustments in previous
chapters, but now there is no field for account numbers. When multiple locations are
used, transfers between locations are made in this journal. You can select the type of
transaction from the transactions drop-down list:

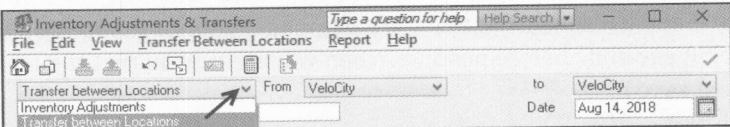

We need to indicate the direction of the transfer, in this case from the VeloCity store
to the Ryder store. VeloCity is the default location for both fields because it is the
primary location. This is correct as the From location.

Click   the **From** drop-down list arrow — both locations are listed.

Click   the **To** drop-down list arrow:

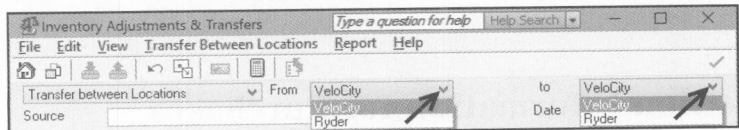

Both locations are available in both lists. You can make transfers to and from either
location.

Click   **Ryder** to add the second location for the To field.

As for other types of transactions, we need to enter the date, the source and a
comment. Then we will enter the items that are being moved.

Click   the **Source field**.

Type   Memo 8-11 **Press** (tab) to move to the Date field.

Enter   **August 7** as the date of the inventory move.

Click   the **Comment field**.

Type   Move inventory to Ryder store

Press   (tab) to advance to the Item code field. A list of items is available, as it
is for inventory fields in other journals.

You can access the inventory list by pressing (enter) in the Item field, clicking the
List icon or double-clicking the field.

Click   the **List icon** and **select AP100**, the first item on the transfer list.

Press   (tab) to move to the Qty (quantity) field.

Type   5

NOTES
Both locations are listed in
the From and the To location
drop-down lists because items may
be transferred from either location
to the other.

Enter the **remaining items** in the same way to complete the entry:

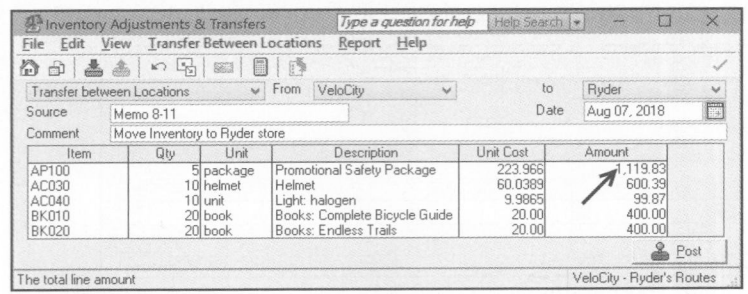

When you record (post) the transfer, the inventory at the two locations will be updated — the quantity at the VeloCity store is reduced and the quantity at the Ryder store is increased. You can verify that the changes have been made by accessing the ledger records for the items and choosing the locations on the Quantity tab screen. However, no journal entry results from this transaction and you cannot look up or adjust the entry, so check it carefully before posting. When you are certain that the transaction is correct, you must save it.

Click [🔖 Post] to save the entry. **Close** the **journal** to return to the Inventory Home window.

CORRECTING THE INVENTORY TRANSFER AFTER POSTING

To correct the transfer after posting, **repeat** the original **transfer** but **reverse** the **direction** of the **transfer** of goods — enter the original From location in the To location field and the original To location in the From location field. Refer to Appendix C, page A–27.

Adding Location Information for Purchases

Now that we have multiple locations for inventory, we must indicate which location the inventory is taken from or sent to when we make purchases, sales and adjustments. By choosing the correct location, we can accurately keep track of the quantity on hand at each store.

The purchase order from Complete Cycler Inc. was delivered to the Ryder store.

✓ **Purchase Invoice #CC-3775**   **Dated August 10, 2018**
19
    From Complete Cycler Inc. to fill purchase order #43
    All items shipped to Ryder store location

2	AC010	Bicycle Pump: standing model	$ 170.00 USD
1	AC020	Bicycle Pump: hand-held mini	360.00 USD
5	AC030	Helmet	2 175.00 USD
5	AC040	Light: halogen	380.00 USD
5	AC050	Light: rear reflector	250.00 USD
18	AC060	Lock: kryptonite tube	2 610.00 USD
		Freight	120.00 USD
		HST	788.45 USD
		Invoice total	$6 853.45 USD

Terms: 2/10, n/30. The exchange rate is 1.385.

Open the **Purchases Journal** (click the Create Purchase Invoice shortcut).

Choose PO #43 in the Order No. field and **press** [tab].

The order is placed on-screen as an invoice:

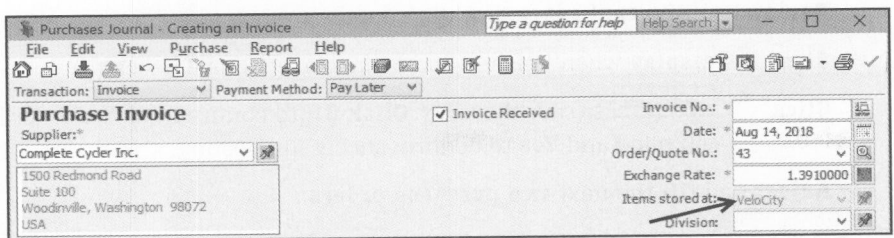

When the order was entered, locations were not set up, so the location field (**Items Stored At**) is dimmed and unavailable. VeloCity, the primary location, is entered, and this is not correct. We need to edit the order to change the location before filling it. We must also change the quantity ordered for item AC060.

Choose **Order** from the Transaction drop-down list to restore the purchase order. **Click Yes** to confirm that you are discarding the invoice.

Choose **PO #43** in the Order No. field list. **Press** ⸢tab⸣ to place the order on the screen. The fields are still dimmed and cannot be edited.

Click the **Adjust Purchase Order tool** , or **choose** the **Purchase menu** and **click Adjust Purchase Order** or **press** ⸢ctrl⸣ + **A**.

Click the **Items Stored At drop-down list arrow**:

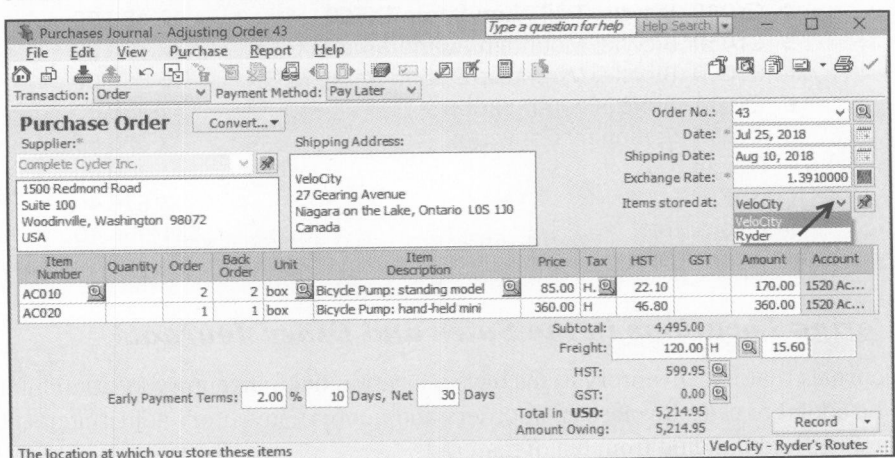

Click **Ryder. Enter Aug 10 18** as the order date. If you do not change the date, Sage 50 will warn you because we do not allow dates before August 1:

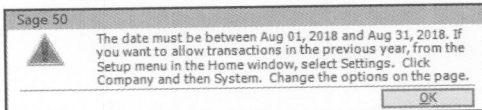

Enter **1.385** as the exchange rate when prompted to change the rate.

Click **8**, the order quantity for AC060 and **type** 18 **Press** ⸢tab⸣. We can now fill the order.

Choose **Invoice** from the Transaction drop-down list or **choose Convert This Purchase Order To A Purchase Invoice** from the Convert drop-down list.

Click **Yes** to confirm that you are changing the order to an invoice.

Click the **Fill Backordered Quantities tool** [icon], or **choose** the **Purchase menu** and **click Fill Backordered Quantities**. **Add CC-3775** as the invoice number and **Aug 10** as the invoice date to complete the transaction.

⚠ WARNING!
You must change the date for the purchase order. The original purchase order was placed on July 25. You cannot continue with this date because it precedes August 1, the start of the fiscal period and the date in the Do Not Allow Transactions Dated Before (Company, System Settings) field.

📄 NOTES
If the Exchange Rate screen opens again, click Cancel because we already entered the date for August 10.

NOTES
Location details are not included in the journal entry, but the inventory records will be correctly updated.

NOTES
Add Ryder as the location. Enter August 10 as the Order Date to adjust purchase order #41. Fill the order and add WD-4558 as the invoice number.

NOTES
Remember to change the payment method to Pay Later when you fill the order from Pro Cycles Inc.
Because you are not adjusting the order, you can leave the original order date unchanged.

NOTES
Location information may also be entered on the Options tab screens in supplier ledger records (Usually Store Item In field) and customer ledger records (Usually Ship Item From field).

Review your **journal entry**. Location details are not added to the journal entry.

Close the **display** when finished and make corrections if necessary.

Click [Post] to save the entry. **Click OK** to confirm that the order has been filled and **Yes** to confirm successful posting.

Adjust and **fill** the next **two purchase orders**.

20

Purchase Invoice #WD-4558	**Dated August 10, 2018**

From Wheel Deals to fill purchase order #41
All items shipped to Ryder store location

10	AC070	Pannier: front wicker clip-on	$360.00 USD
10	AC080	Pannier: rear mesh	275.00 USD
		HST	82.55 USD
		Invoice total	$717.55 USD

Terms: 2/10, n/30. The exchange rate is 1.385.

21

Purchase Invoice #PC-3877	**Dated August 10, 2018**

From Pro Cycles Inc. to fill purchase order #42 for VeloCity store

6	CY010	Bicycle: Commuter Steel frame CX10	$ 1 860.00
10	CY020	Bicycle: Commuter Alum frame CX90	5 400.00
4	CY030	Bicycle: Racer Ultra lite RX480	6 000.00
4	CY040	Bicycle: Trail Alum frame TX560	2 480.00
3	CY050	Bicycle: Mountain Alum frame MX14	2 790.00
4	CY060	Bicycle: Mountain Carbon frame MX34	6 880.00
6	CY070	Bicycle: Youth YX660	1 350.00
4	CY090	Stationary Converter	1 320.00
		Freight	200.00
		HST	3 676.40
		Invoice total	$31 956.40

Terms: 2/10, n/30.

Entering Locations in the Sales and Other Journals

All journals that use inventory items have a location field. Inventory location information can be added to sales invoices (and orders and quotes), inventory adjustments, item assemblies and building from bill of materials.

---

22 ✓

Sales Invoice #2491	**Dated August 10, 2018**

To Candide's B & B (from VeloCity store)

8	AC030	Helmet	$120/ helmet
4	AC060	Lock: kryptonite tube	70/ lock
4	CY020	Bicycle: Commuter Alum frame CX90	960/ bike
		HST	13%

Terms: 2/10, n/30.

Open the **Sales Journal** and **click** the **Ship From list arrow**:

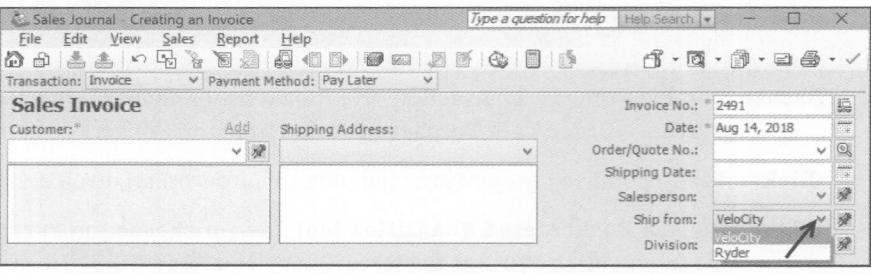

Choose VeloCity. **Enter** the remaining details for **Sales invoice #2491**. **Review** and then **post** the **entry**. **Close** the **Sales Journal**.

The location selection is also available in the Inventory Adjustments and Bill Of Materials & Item Assembly journals from the At Location drop-down list:

If the location you chose does not have any stock of an item needed to complete the build or assembly, Sage 50 provides an error about the insufficient inventory:

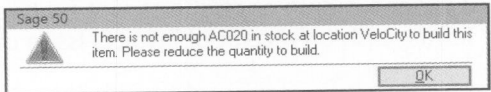

Click OK. In this case, you must first transfer or purchase the required item.

Enter the **remaining transactions** for August up to Memo #8-18.

23

Memo #8-12	**Dated August 14, 2018**

Remittances: Use the August 1 balances to make the following remittances in the Payments Journal. (Read margin Notes and Warning.)

a) Record payment for GST and HST for July to the Receiver General for Canada. Issue cheque #147 in payment.

b) Record payment for Garnisheed Wages Payable for July to the Receiver General for Canada. Issue cheque #148 in full payment.

c) Record payment for EI, CPP and Income Tax Payable for July to the Receiver General for Canada. Issue cheque #149 in full payment.

d) Record payment for EHT Payable for July for the quarter to the Minister of Finance. Issue cheque #150 in payment.

e) Record payment for VRSP Payable for July to Manulife Financial. Issue cheque #151 in payment.

f) Record payment for Savings Plan Payable for July to Escarpment Investments. Issue cheque #152 in payment.

g) Record payment for Group Insurance Payable for July to Welland Insurance. Issue cheque #153 in payment.

h) Record payment for Charitable Donations Payable for July to Canadian Cancer Society (employer and employee contributions). Issue cheque #154 in payment.

i) Record payment for WSIB Payable for the quarter to the Workplace Safety & Insurance Board. Issue cheque #155 in payment.

24

Purchase Invoice #ABS-7597	**Dated August 14, 2018**

From ABS International (use Full Add for new foreign supplier)

10 CY040	Bicycle: Trail Alum frame TX560	€ 3 800.00
	Freight	100.00
	HST	507.00
	Purchase invoice total	€ 4 407.00

The duty rate for these items is 0%.
Terms: net 30. The exchange rate is 1.425.
Change the default amounts.
All items shipped to the VeloCity store.

NOTES
Choose Previous Year in the report options window to make the July 31 balances available for sales tax amounts.
Choose Pay Remittance to remit payroll taxes and deductions.
Clear the GST and HST reports for July 31.

⚠ WARNING!
Remember to reset the Pay Period date to August 1 for the second remittance to the Receiver General to avoid including the amounts from the August 7 paycheque.

NOTES
Use Full Add for the new supplier because you need to add currency information.
ABS International
Contact: Derek Rad
Schumacher Str. 96
55123 Mainz, Germany
Tel: (49-6131) 468 913
Fax: (49-6131) 468 248
Currency: Euro
Terms: net 30
Tax code: H

SESSION DATE – AUGUST 31, 2018

25
Sales Order #250 & Deposit #23   **Dated August 16, 2018**
Delivery date August 24, 2018 (from VeloCity store).
From Park 'N Ride Tours. Special volume discounts will apply.
20 AC030   Helmet $100/ helmet
10 AC060   Lock: kryptonite tube   60/ lock
10 CY040   Bicycle: Trail Alum frame TX560   900/ bike
    HST   13%
Terms: 2/10, n/30. Change all prices for this order.
Deposit cheque #438 for $5 000 received with order.

26
Receipt #826   **Dated August 18, 2018**
From Candide's B & B, cheque #614 for $5 625.59 in payment of account
including $114.81 discount for early payment. Reference sales invoice #2491.

27
Cash Purchase Invoice #NB-00124   **Dated August 20, 2018**
From Niagara Bell, $220 plus HST for one month of phone service for two stores.
Purchase invoice total $248.60. Terms: cash on receipt of invoice. Issue cheque
#156 in full payment.

28
Deposit Slip #26   **Dated August 21, 2018**
Prepare deposit slip for $16 320.79 for cheques received in previous two weeks.

29
Cash Purchase Invoice #ES-93215   **Dated August 21, 2018**
From Energy Source, $310 plus HST for hydro service for two stores. Purchase
invoice total $350.30. Terms: cash on receipt of invoice. Issue cheque #157 in full
payment.

30
Memo #8-13   **Dated August 21, 2018**
Transfer 10 helmets (item A030) and 30 kryptonite tube locks (item AC060)
from Ryder to the VeloCity store.
Build five AP100 Promotional Safety Packages at the Ryder store location.

NOTES
The * indicates preferred customer prices apply.

NOTES
Use Full Add for the new customer in Europe so you can add the currency and price list:

New preferred price customer:
Gallery Tours
21 Via Della Mosca
50122 Florence, Italy
Tel: 055 282 691
Currency: Euro
Terms: 2/10, n/30
Tax Code: No tax
Credit Limit: $10 000 CAD
(€ 6 000)

NOTES
You cannot change the billable time for S030 because a flat rate is charged, the equivalent of one hour.

31   **TIME SLIP #3**   **DATED AUGUST 21, 2018**
For Dunlop Mercier

Customer	Item	Actual Time	Billable Time	Billable Amount	Taxable	Payroll Time
Cathedral Tours	S010	8 hours	8 (16 boxes)	€ 832.00	yes	8 hours
Gallery Tours*	S010	4 hours	4 (8 boxes)	€ 384.00	yes	4 hours
Park 'N Ride Tours	S100	2 hours	2 hours	–	N/A	2 hours
Backstage Tours*	S030	1.5 hours	N/A	$65.00	yes	1.5 hours
Backstage Tours*	S060	4 hours	4 hours	$160.00	yes	4 hours
Americas Vinelands Tours*	S080	8.5 hours	8 hours	USD $440.00	yes	8.5 hours

32   **TIME SLIP #4**   **DATED AUGUST 21, 2018**
For Yvonne Leader

Customer	Item	Actual Time	Billable Time	Billable Amount	Taxable	Payroll Time
Backstage Tours*	S070	4 hours	4 hours	$480.00	yes	4 hours
Backstage Tours*	S080	9 hours	8 hours	$560.00	yes	9 hours
Gallery Tours*	S070	3.5 hours	3 hours	€ 270.00	no	3.5 hours
Gallery Tours*	S080	26 hours	24 hours	€ 1 230.00	no	26 hours
Cathedral Tours	S070	6 hours	6 hours	€ 600.00	no	6 hours
Cathedral Tours	S080	17 hours	16 hours	€ 880.00	no	17 hours

Employee Time Summary Sheet #21   **Dated August 21, 2018**

33

For the Pay Period ending August 21, 2018
Edit the employee record for Yvonne Leader. Leader will be paid every two weeks (26 pay periods per year) and her minimum number of hours will be 40. If her contract hours from time slips are less than 40 hours, she will be paid for 40 hours. Change the Additional Federal Tax amount to $100.
Use time slips to prepare the bi-weekly paycheque for Yvonne Leader for the actual number of hours worked. Issue deposit slip #39.

Dunlop Mercier worked 80 regular hours in the period and 4 hours of overtime. Issue deposit slip #40 in payment. (Add time from time slips but choose Yes to use regular hours when prompted.)

NOTES
Pay Periods and Hours are entered on the Income tab and Additional Federal Tax on the Taxes tab of the Employee Ledger record.

Sales Invoice #2492   **Dated August 21, 2018**

34

To Cathedral Tours: Complete sales invoice for €2 312 plus HST from time slip activities. Include all activities to date. Enter H as the tax code for item S010. Sales invoice total €2 420.16. Terms: 2/10, n/30. The exchange rate is 1.415.

NOTES
Enter tax codes for foreign customers carefully.

Sales Invoice #2493   **Dated August 21, 2018**

35

To Backstage Tours: Complete sales invoice for $1 265 plus HST from time slip activities. Include all activities to date. Sales invoice total $1 429.45. Terms: 2/10, n/30.

Sales Invoice #2494   **Dated August 21, 2018**

36

To Gallery Tours: Complete sales invoice for €1 884 plus HST from time slip activities. Enter H as the tax code for item S010. Include all activities to date. Sales invoice total €1 933.92. Terms: 2/10, n/30. The exchange rate is 1.415.

Sales Invoice #2495   **Dated August 21, 2018**

37

To Americas Vinelands Tours: Complete sales invoice for $440 USD plus HST from time slip activities. Change the tax code for S080 to H. Include all activities to date. Sales invoice total $497.20 USD. Terms: 2/10, n/30. The exchange rate is 1.379.

NOTES
The tour for Americas Vinelands Tours is taxable because it is provided in Canada for the US customer.

Credit Card Purchase Invoice #LS-12331   **Dated August 24, 2018**

38

From Lakeshore Sunoco, $125 including HST paid for gasoline and $380 plus HST for vehicle repairs. Purchase invoice total $554.40 paid in full by Visa. Use tax code IN for the gasoline purchase and tax code H for the repairs.

NOTES
Do not forget to change the payment method for invoice #2496.

Sales Invoice #2496   **Dated August 28, 2018**

39

To Park 'N Ride Tours, to fill sales order #250 (VeloCity store)

20	AC030	Helmet	$100/ helmet
10	AC060	Lock: kryptonite tube	60/ lock
10	CY040	Bicycle: Trail Alum frame TX560	900/ bike
	HST		13%

Terms: 2/10, n/30. Remember to change the payment method to Pay Later.

TIME SLIP #5   **DATED AUGUST 31, 2018**

40

For Dunlop Mercier

Customer	Item	Actual Time	Billable Time	Billable Amount	Taxable	Payroll Time
Shavian B & B	S010	2 hours	2 (4 boxes)	$320.00	yes	2 hours
Shavian B & B	S100	3 hours	–	–	yes	3 hours
Niagara Rapids Inn*	S030	2 hours	2 hours	$65.00	yes	2 hours
Niagara Rapids Inn*	S060	4 hours	4 hours	$160.00	yes	4 hours
Americas Vinelands Tours*	S010	2 hours	2 (4 boxes)	USD $208.00	yes	2 hours
Americas Vinelands Tours*	S060	4 hours	4 hours	USD $132.00	yes	4 hours

☐	**TIME SLIP #6**				**DATED AUGUST 31, 2018**		
41	For Yvonne Leader						
	Customer	Item	Actual Time	Billable Time	Billable Amount	Taxable	Payroll Time
	Backstage Tours*	S070	5 hours	4.5 hours	$540.00	yes	5 hours
	Backstage Tours*	S080	15 hours	16 hours	$1 120.00	yes	15 hours
	Festival Tours	S070	4 hours	3 hours	USD $360.00	yes	4 hours
	Festival Tours	S080	12 hours	12 hours	USD $720.00	yes	12 hours
	Americas Vinelands Tours*	S070	2.5 hours	2 hours	USD $220.00	yes	2.5 hours
	Americas Vinelands Tours*	S080	8 hours	8 hours	USD $440.00	yes	8 hours

☐ **Sales Invoice #2497**   **Dated August 31, 2018**

42 To Shavian B & B: Complete sales invoice for $320 plus HST from time slip activities. Include all activities to date. Sales invoice total $361.60. Terms: 2/10, n/30.

☐ **Sales Invoice #2498**   **Dated August 31, 2018**

43 To Niagara Rapids Inn: Complete sales invoice for $225 plus HST from time slip activities. Include all activities to date. Sales invoice total $254.25. Terms: 2/10, n/30.

☐ **Sales Invoice #2499**   **Dated August 31, 2018**

44 To Americas Vinelands Tours: Prepare sales invoice for $1 000 USD plus HST from time slip activities for all activities to date. All activities are taxable (tax code H). Sales invoice total $1 130.00 USD. Terms: 2/10, n/30. The exchange rate is 1.383.

☐ **Sales Invoice #2500**   **Dated August 31, 2018**

45 To Backstage Tours: Sales invoice for $1 660 plus HST from time slip activities for all activities to date. Sales invoice total $1 875.80. Terms: 2/10, n/30.

☐ **Credit Card Sales Invoice #2501**   **Dated August 31, 2018**

46 To Visa Sales (sales summary). Sold from VeloCity store.

NOTES

Remember to change the tax code for books to G.

12	AC040	Light: halogen	$ 25/ unit	$ 300.00
12	AC060	Lock: kryptonite tube	70/ lock	840.00
2	AC100	Trailer: third-wheel rider	260/ unit	520.00
18	BK010	Books: Complete Bicycle Guide (code G)	40/ book	720.00
25	BK020	Books: Endless Trails (code G)	40/ book	1 000.00
6	CY020	Bicycle: Commuter Alum frame CX90	960/ bike	5 760.00
2	CY030	Bicycle: Racer Ultra lite RX480	3 100/ bike	6 200.00
2	CY050	Bicycle: Mountain Alum frame MX14	1 850/ bike	3 700.00
1	CY060	Bicycle: Mountain Carbon frame MX34	2 950/ bike	2 950.00
6	CY070	Bicycle: Youth YX660	460/ bike	2 760.00
2	CY090	Stationary Converter	870/ unit	1 740.00
10	S020	Maintenance: annual contract	110/ year	1 100.00
	GST		5%	86.00
	HST		13%	3 363.10
	Total paid by Visa			$31 039.10

☐ **Bank Debit Memo #120092**   **Dated August 31, 2018**

47 From Niagara Trust, authorized withdrawals were made from the chequing account on our behalf for the following:

Bank service charges	$ 55
Mortgage interest payment	1 450
Mortgage principal reduction	250
Bank loan interest payment	380
Bank loan principal reduction	520

48

Debit Card Sales Invoice #2502   **Dated August 31, 2018**

To Interac customers (sales summary). Sold from Ryder store.

10	AP100	Promotional Safety Packages	$375/ unit	$3 750.00
10	AC030	Helmet	$120/ helmet	1 200.00
6	S030	Maintenance: complete tune-up	70/ job	420.00
6	S060	Repairs	50/ hour	300.00
14	BK020	Books: Endless Trails (code G)	40/ book	560.00
	GST		5%	28.00
	HST		13%	737.10
	Total paid by Interac			$6 995.10

WARNING!
This is the first sale from the Ryder store, so you must change the default location.

49

Memo #8-14   **Dated August 31, 2018**

Prepare the payroll for Pedal Schwinn, Shimana Gearie and Moishe Alee, the salaried employees. Add 2 percent of service revenue for August as a commission to Gearie's salary. Issue deposit slips #41, #42 and #43.

NOTES
Remember to change the tax code for books to G.

50

Memo #8-15   **Dated August 31, 2018**

Interest earned but not yet received for bank accounts for August is $180.

51

Memo #8-16   **Dated August 31, 2018**

Prepare month-end adjusting entries for depreciation on fixed assets using the following amounts:

Computer equipment	$180
Service tools	40
Furniture & fixtures	25
Retail premises	810
Van	625

52

Memo #8-17   **Dated August 31, 2018**

Prepare end-of-period adjusting entries for the following:

Office supplies used	$ 100
Repair parts used	90
Prepaid insurance expired	672
Prepaid advertising expired	100
Payroll liabilities accrued	1 540

Updating Inventory Prices

At the end of the month, inventory prices will be adjusted. Rather than changing each record for regular and preferred prices in both Canadian and US dollars, we will use the Update Price List method that we used earlier to edit the activity prices. This method is more efficient when many prices must be changed or when they are changed by a fixed amount or percentage. In this case, we are changing all prices by fixed percentages. The Update Price Lists feature also allows us to round off the prices automatically.

53 ✓

Memo #8-18   **Dated August 31, 2018**

With two stores open and increased expenses, the prices for all inventory items will be raised. All regular Canadian prices will increase by 10 percent and all US regular prices will increase by 5 percent. All new preferred prices (Canadian and US) will be 15 percent lower than the new regular prices. All prices are rounded up to the nearest five dollar amount.

Click   the **Settings icon** .

Click   **Inventory & Services** and then **click Price List**.

Click   **Update Price Lists**. **Click Inventory Items** to list only the items we need. Prices for services are not changing.

Click   the **select item column heading** to select all items:

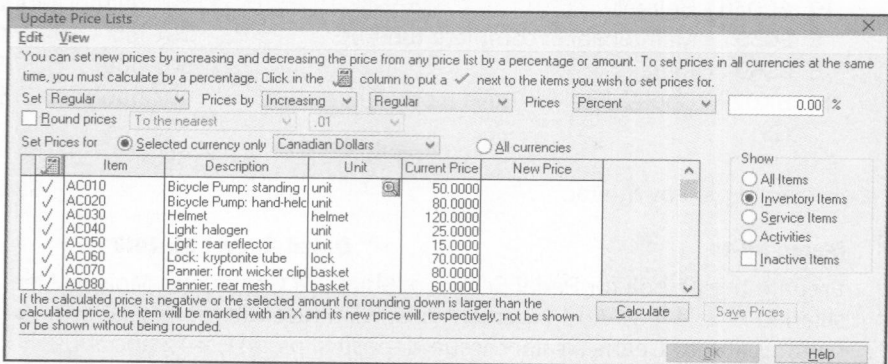

The upper part of the screen has the rules for the change. We can change any price list by increasing or decreasing the prices from another price list by a percentage or a fixed amount. These options are available from the respective drop-down lists:

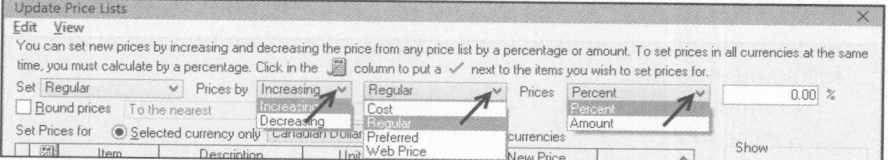

We are increasing Canadian Regular prices by a fixed percentage, so these entries are already correct. We are rounding the new prices up to the nearest five dollar amount. First, we need to enter the percentage of the increase.

Click   **0.00 in the % field**. **Type** 10

Press   tab to move to the check box for rounding.

Click   the **Round Prices check box** to add a ✓ and open the field we need.

Again, we have some options. You can round up, round down or round to the nearest amount. We want to round up to the nearest five dollar amount. To the nearest and one cent (.01) are the default entries. The units range from one ten-thousandth of a dollar (.0001) to one thousand dollars (1 000.00). These two selections are made from their respective drop-down lists:

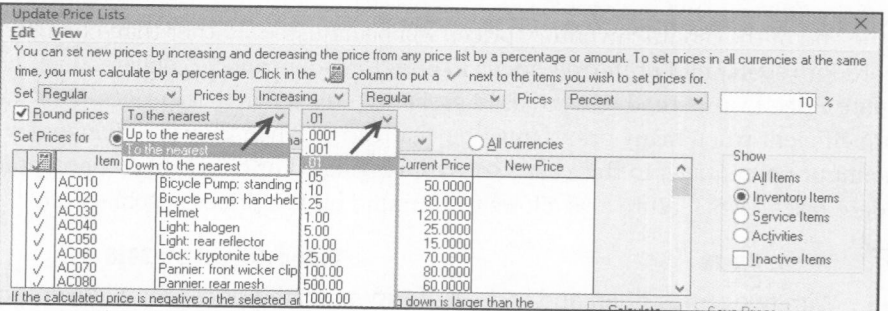

Click   **To The Nearest** to open the rounding options list and **choose Up To The Nearest**.

Click   **.01** to open the selection list and **choose 5.00** (five dollars) as the amount to complete the selection of options:

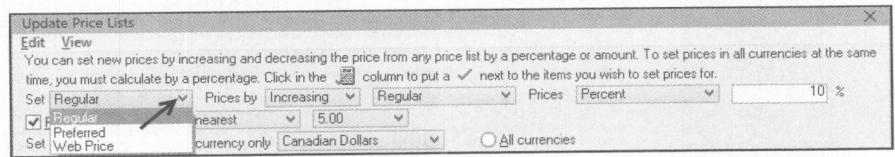

We do not want to increase prices for books or for AP100, the new promotion item, so we will deselect them. In this way, the change rules will not apply to these items.

Click   the Select column for AP100 to remove the ✓.

Press   ⊥ to remove the ✓ for BK010. **Press** ⊥ to remove the ✓ for BK020.

Click   **Calculate** to update the prices and add them to the New Price column.

Click   **Save Prices** to transfer the new prices to the Current Price column.

We will set the preferred prices relative to the new regular prices, decreasing them by 15 percent and rounding up to the nearest $5.00. We need to change the selected price list, the direction of the change and the percentage.

Click   **Regular** in the Set field:

> **NOTES**
> You could also calculate new prices for the AP100 and the book items and then change the prices after calculating but before saving.
> Until you save the new prices, you can edit individual amounts.

Choose **Preferred**. **Click Increasing** in the Prices By field and **choose Decreasing**. Regular is correct as the reference price list.

Click   **10** in the % field and **type** 15

Click   the **Select column** for **AP100**, **BK010** and **BK020**.

The remaining options are correct, so your selections are completed:

Click   **Calculate** to update the prices and add them to the New Price column.

Click   **Save Prices** to transfer the new prices to the Current Price column.

You can now change the prices for US dollars.

Click   **Canadian Dollars** in the Selected Currency Only field:

Choose United States Dollars.

Now apply the changes to the US dollar regular and preferred prices. First, increase the regular prices by 5 percent and round up to the nearest $5.00. Change the preferred prices by decreasing the regular prices by 15 percent and rounding up to the nearest $5.00 amount. The prices for AP100, BK010 and BK020 will not be changed.

NOTES
You can update the euro prices in the same way, by selecting euro as the currency. You can also update the prices for all currencies at the same time when the same updating rule applies to them all. You can, of course, adjust individual prices after.

Remember to **calculate** and then **save each price set**.

Click **OK** to return to the Settings screen and **click OK** again to return to the Home window.

Displaying Time and Billing Reports

The various Time and Billing reports provide different ways of organizing the same information. You can view the reports by customer, by employee or by activity.

Customer Time and Billing Report

NOTES
Sorting and filtering are not available for Time and Billing reports, but you can choose the columns to include in the report.

Click the **Report Centre icon** in the Home window. **Click Time & Billing**. **Click** the ⊞ beside **Billing**, **Payroll** and **Purchases** to expand the list of available reports:

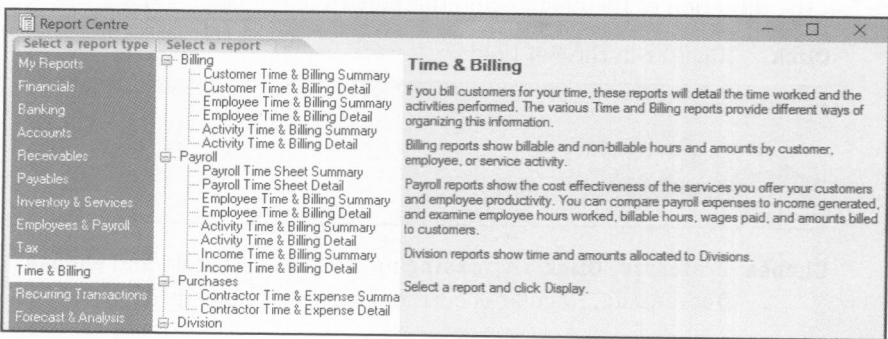

NOTES
Contractor Time & Billing reports (under Purchases) and Division reports do not apply to Ryder's Routes.

Click **Customer Time & Billing Summary** under **Billing**. **Click Modify This Report**:

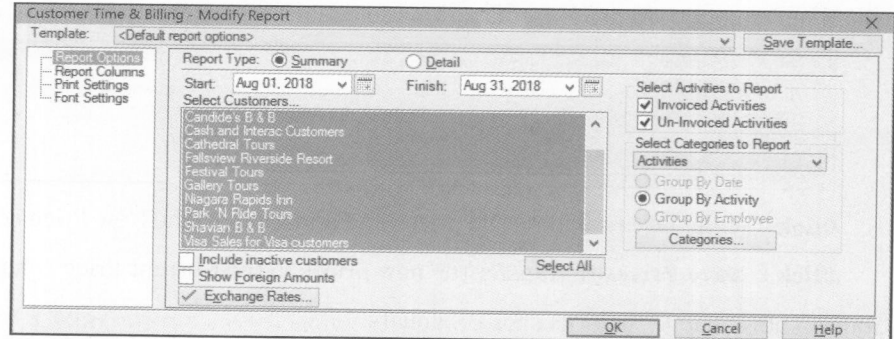

NOTES
From the Home window, choose the Reports menu, then choose Time & Billing. Click Billing and click Time By Customer to open the report options.

NOTES
Time and Billing reports can include a large amount of information. A good way to understand these reports is to prepare a very complete report. For example, select the Detail Report, choose all employees, click all Details and Activities and choose Activities and Customers as the categories for the report. Then choose all service activities from the next list. Print the report. Click the Modify tool or choose Modify Report from the Options menu in the report. Compare this report with the Summary Report for the same details and categories.

Time and Billing reports by customer provide the time and billed amounts organized by customer. Summary and Detail reports are available. **Detail** reports include a report line for each activity or employee on each time slip, while the **Summary** reports have only the totals for each selected category (activity or employee). You can select one or more customers for inclusion in the report. The reports will include columns for several billing details — actual time spent on activities, billable time, billable percentage (the proportion of the total time worked for which the customer was charged), billable amounts and invoiced amounts. In addition, if you changed the prices for any of the service activities in the Sales Journal, the report will include these changes as amounts written down or up. In the report, the invoiced amounts will then be different from the billable amounts. The effective billable percentage provides the relation between the invoiced amount and the billable amount. The non-billable time, no-charge time and amounts written down or up as percentages of the billable amounts are not in the default report, but you can add them by customizing the report columns. The default columns

may also be removed, and the report details can be grouped by date, by activity or by employee.

You can include **invoiced activities** (bills have been sent) or **uninvoiced activities** (bills have not been created and sent) or both.

The next decision for the report relates to the **categories** you want to include. You can report on the time spent according to the **activities** performed for the customer or according to the **employee** who completed the work or both. In all cases, the categories are included for each customer you selected.

Enter   **Start** and **Finish dates** for the report.

Choose   the **customers** for the report. **Press** and **hold** ⌨ctrl and **click** the **customer names** to begin a new selection. **Click Select All** to include (or remove) all customers.

Choose   the **invoicing details** for the report. **Click** a **detail** to remove a ✓ or to add it.

Click   the **Select Categories To Report list arrow** to select activities or employees or both.

Click   the **Categories button** to open the secondary selection list.

If you choose Activities as the category, you will list the activities:

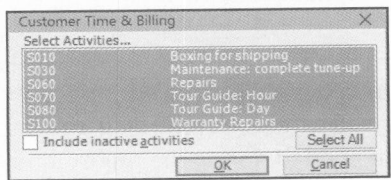

If you choose Employees as the category, you must select from the Employee list. If you choose both Activities and Employees, you must choose from lists for both.

Initially, all activities are selected, and clicking will change the selection. The Select All button acts like a toggle switch. To begin a new selection of activities,

Click   **Select All** to clear all selections.

Press   and **hold** ⌨ctrl and **click** the **activities** you want in the report to begin a new selection. **Click Select All** to include (or remove) all activities.

Click   **OK** to return to the report options screen.

Click   **OK** to generate the report.

The report has the amount of time worked for each customer according to the activity, employee or both, depending on the category you selected.

Close   the **report** when you have finished.

Employee and Activity Time and Billing Reports

The other two Time and Billing reports are similar to the Time by Customer Report, except that they organize the amounts by employee or by activity. The first options screen for the **Employee Time & Billing Report** (Summary or Detail) will include the Employee list, and the second selection screen will list the customers, the activities or both, depending on the category you choose. The Time by Employee Report has the time and billed amounts for each employee for each customer, each activity or both, depending on the categories you choose.

Similarly, the first options screen for the **Activity Time & Billing Report** (Summary or Detail) will include the Activity list, and the second selection screen will list the customers, the employees or both, depending on the categories you choose. The Time by Activity Report has the time and the billed amounts for each activity for each customer or by each employee or both, depending on the categories you choose.

Other report options are the same as they are for the Time by Customer Report, and both reports are available as a Summary or a Detail report.

Payroll Time Sheet Reports

The Time Sheet Report provides a summary of the hours of each income category that is on the time sheets. The number of hours of non-payroll, regular payroll and overtime for each employee can be included.

Click   **Payroll Time Sheet Summary** under **Payroll**. **Click Modify This Report**:

The **Summary** Report will provide the total number of hours in each payroll category (Non-payroll, Regular and Overtime 1 — the payroll category in the ledger record for the activity) for each employee selected for each time period during the report interval. The **Detail** Report will provide the number of hours in each payroll category for each time sheet.

You can customize the report by selecting columns for the payroll category. Non-payroll, Regular and Overtime 1 columns may be included or omitted.

Enter   **Start** and **Finish dates** for the report.

Choose   the **employees** for the report. **Press** and **hold** ⌈ctrl⌋ and **click** the **employee names** to begin a new selection. **Click Select All** to include (or remove) all employees.

Click   **OK** to display the report.

Close   the **report** when you have finished.

Employee Time and Billing Payroll Reports

The remaining Payroll Time reports provide information about the cost effectiveness of the service activities by comparing the labour costs with the income generated — the amount billed to the customer. Employee productivity is also measured by examining the actual hours, billable hours, payroll hours, wages paid and invoiced amounts.

Click   **Employee Time & Billing Summary** under **Payroll**.

Click   **Modify This Report**:

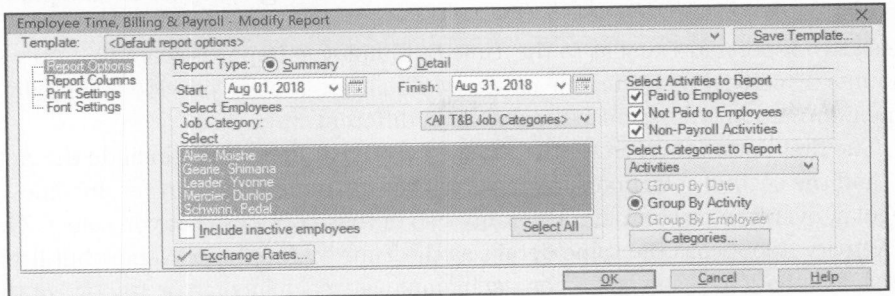

Summary and Detail reports are available. The **Detail** report includes a report line for each time sheet entry, while the **Summary** report includes only the totals for each selected category. You can select one or more employees for inclusion in the report. The reports will include several time and billing **details** — actual time spent on activities, payroll time, billable time, billable amounts, the actual payroll expense and the productivity ratio (the billable amount compared to the payroll expense) can be included. The effective productivity ratio percentage is the relation between the invoiced amount and the payroll expense amount. Payroll percentage (payroll time as a proportion of actual time) and billable percentage (the proportion of the total time worked for which the customer was charged) can be added to the report when you customize the report by selecting these time and billing details (report columns). The default report columns may be included or removed.

The report can include **activities** for which you have **paid** the employees, activities that have **not yet been paid**, activities that are **non-payroll** or all three payroll details.

The next decision for the report relates to the **categories** you want to include. You can report on the time spent according to the **activity** performed by the employee, according to the **customer** for whom the work was completed, according to the **income** (that is, regular, non-payroll or overtime) or any two of these three categories. In all cases, the categories are given for each employee you selected.

When you choose two categories for the report, you can group report details by one of them — select from date, activity, customer or income.

Enter   **Start** and **Finish dates** for the report.

Choose   the **employees** for the report. **Press** and **hold** ⌨ctrl⌨ and **click** the **employee names** to begin a new selection. **Click Select All** to include (or remove) all employees.

Choose   the **payroll status details**. **Click** a **detail** to add or to remove a ✓.

Choose   the **categories** for the report from the Select Categories To Report drop-down list.

Click   the **Categories button** to open the secondary selection list.

If you select the Activities category, you will list all services defined as activities in the ledger.

Choose   the **activities** for the report. **Press** and **hold** ⌨ctrl⌨ and **click** the **activity names** to begin a new selection. **Click Select All** to include (or remove) activities.

Click   **OK** to return to the report options screen.

Click   **OK** to open the report. By default the report will print in landscape orientation (sideways on the page) so that all details can fit on a line.

Close   the **report** when you have finished.

NOTES
If you select Customers or Income as the category, you will open selection lists for each category. If you selected two categories, you can choose from selection lists for both categories.

NOTES
The August 31 report for Ryder informs us that both employees have been partially paid for their time sheet entries — the August 31 time sheet has not yet been added to their paycheques. The same report for August 21 lists all time sheet activities as paid.

Activity and Income Time and Billing Payroll Reports

These two reports are similar to the Time by Employee Report except that they organize amounts by activity or by income category. The three reports provide essentially the same information but organize the details in different ways.

The first options screen for the **Time by Activity Report** will include the Activity list, and the second selection screen will list the customers, employees, incomes (regular, overtime or non-payroll) or any two of these options that you select. The Time by Activity Report has the same details as the Time by Employee Report but lists them for each activity for each customer, each employee, each income or any two of these options.

Similarly, the first options screen for the **Time by Income Report** will provide the income list, and the second selection screen will list the customers, employees, activities or any two of these three options. The Time by Income Report has the same details as the Time by Employee Report but lists them for each activity for each customer, each employee, each activity or any two of these options.

Other report options are the same as they are for the Time by Employee Report, and both reports are available as a Summary or a Detail report.

Multiple Fiscal Periods and Reports

After you have accumulated two fiscal periods of financial data, you can produce historical reports for these additional periods. Data for the current and previous years are always available, unless you have cleared the information.

Prepare a **list** of inventory items that should be ordered for each location.

Choose the **Maintenance menu** and **click Start New Year** to begin a new fiscal year.

Choose Yes when asked if you want to Back Up Your Data Files Before Beginning The New Fiscal Year and follow the backup instructions.

Choose No when asked if you want to clear the old data.

The Update Locking Date screen opens.

Enter 09/01/18 as the new date. **Click OK** to update the earliest transaction.

Choose the **Setup menu**, then **click Settings**, **Company** and **Information**:

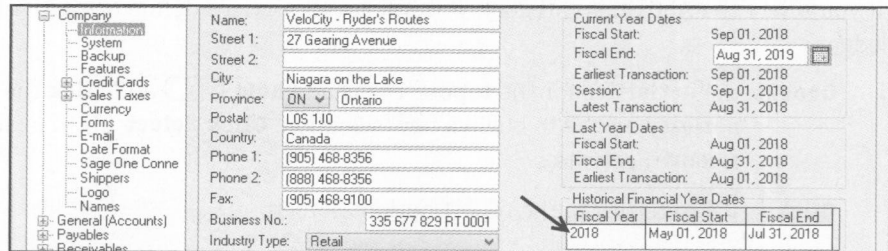

The first fiscal period, May 1 to July 31, 2018, is now listed in the section for Historical Financial Year Dates.

NOTES
Financial reports for August:
- Income Statement
- Balance Sheet
- Trial Balance
- Supplier and Customer Aged reports
- Employee Summary Report
- Inventory Summary and Inventory Quantity Detail reports, including location

NOTES
The Pro version stores up to seven years of historical financial data; the Premium version stores up to 99 years of data.

Drag through Aug 31, 2019, the Fiscal End date.

Type 09-30-18 **Click OK** to save the date and return to the Home window.

Multi-Period Financial Reports

Multiple-period reports are available for the Balance Sheet, Income Statement and Trial Balance. All are accessed from the Financials list of reports.

Click the **Report Centre icon**.

Click **Financials** to expand this list of reports.

Click the ⊞ beside **Balance Sheet**, **Income Statement** and **Trial Balance** to expand the Select A Report list. **Click Multi-Period** under **Balance Sheet**:

NOTES
From the Home window, choose the Reports menu, Financials, Multi-Period Reports, and click Balance Sheet, Income Statement or Trial Balance.

Click **Modify This Report**:

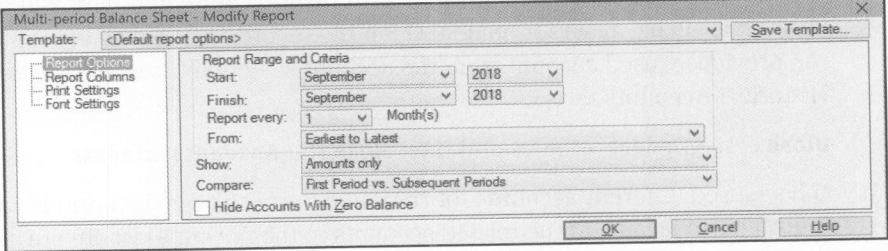

NOTES
Dates before the previous fiscal period that are eligible for the report will be those in the Historical Financial Year Dates section of the Company Information screen on page 782.

From the Home window, choose the Reports menu, then choose Financials and Multi-Period Reports and click Balance Sheet to access the report options.

The regular financial reports available in comparative form compare two fiscal periods or dates. Reports for the previous fiscal period are also available in regular reports. The multi-period reports include more than two periods and can even include multiple fiscal periods before the previous one.

For VeloCity and Ryder's Routes, monthly data can be viewed in a single report for May, the first month for which we entered data in Sage 50, to August.

There are several options for displaying the report. You can have the balances for each month for any interval ranging from one to twelve months. The report can be ordered from the earliest period to the latest, or from latest to earliest. You can include Amounts Only, Difference In Percentage or Difference In Amounts, just as you do for regular comparative reports. And you can compare the first period with each subsequent period, or you can compare each period with subsequent periods.

After choosing the options for the report,

Click **OK** to open the report.

> **Close**   the **report** when you have finished.

The **Income Statement** and **Trial Balance** are available for the same periods as the Balance Sheet. They have the same report options. To generate these reports,

> **Click**   **Multi-Period** under **Income Statement** (or **Trial Balance**) and then **click Modify This Report**.

> **Choose** the **report options** and **click OK**.

> **Close**   the **report** when you have finished. **Close** the **Report Centre**.

Related Historical Accounts

Because we have advanced to the next (third) fiscal period, we can create the list of related accounts. You can access and edit the related historical accounts in the General Ledger record for the account in the Related Historical Accounts tab screen.

> **Click**   the **Chart of Accounts icon** in the Company module window.

> **Double-click**   an **account** to open its General Ledger record.

> **Click**   the **Related Historical Accounts tab** to list the accounts used in previous periods.

If an account currently being used has a different name and number than the account used for the same purpose in a previous period, you can link them.

Each account has itself as the related historical account if it has been used for more than two fiscal periods. Each account can be related to only one account. Therefore, if the account is already related to itself, you cannot select it again.

> Open the record for the (old) previously used account. Delete the account listed as the related account in the Related Historical Accounts tab. This will make the account available again for linking. Open the record for the new account. Choose the previously used account from the account selection list in the Related Historical Accounts tab.

> **Close**   the **Ledger window** and then **close** the **Accounts window**.

If you have used different accounts for the same purpose over the periods and you have related them, you can add the related accounts to the Account List. To create the report of related account numbers,

> **Choose** the **Reports menu**, then **choose Lists** and **click Accounts**.

> **Click**   **Include Related Historical Accounts** and then **click OK**.

The report will list all General Ledger accounts with the current information and the accounts that were used for those same purposes in previous fiscal periods — the information that is stored in the General Ledger Related Historical Accounts tab fields.

> **Close**   the **report** when you have finished.

> **Close**   the **Home window** to exit the Sage 50 program.

REVIEW

The Student DVD with Data Files includes Review Questions and Supplementary Cases for this chapter.

Able & Associates

OBJECTIVES

After completing this chapter, you should be able to

- **activate** departmental accounting
- **create** departments
- **add** departments to accounts, vendors and clients
- **add** departments in journal entries
- **apply** line discounts in sales journal entries
- **display** and **print** department reports

COMPANY INFORMATION

Company Profile

NOTES

Able & Associates Inc.
88 Practice Blvd.
Huntsville, ON P1H 1T2
Tel: (705) 463-2145
Fax: (705) 465-1110
Business No.: 167 344 577

Able & Associates Inc. is a partnership of two chartered accountants, Count and Memor Able. They began their practice in Huntsville, Ontario, two years ago, shortly after receiving their C.P.A. designations. They each invested capital to start up the office. By relying extensively on electronic communications, remote access to client computers and frequent phone calls, they are able to serve clients throughout a large geographic area. Only occasional on-site meetings are required, and local clients often come to their office. Most of their revenue comes from auditing and preparing regular financial statements and income tax returns for small business clients. They share office space and office expenses, including a full-time office assistant. Count works in the office full time, but Memor is there only three days a week, spending the other two days working in a small family business. Thus, they allocate their joint expenses using a 60/40 percent division.

Most of the clients have contracts with Able & Associates and pay fees on a monthly basis. These clients are entitled to a discount of 2 percent of their fees if they pay within 10 days of the invoice date. Full payment is requested within 30 days. One-time clients do not receive discounts. Some regular vendors also offer discounts for early payment.

On March 31, at the end of the fiscal period, they decided to use the departmental accounting feature in Sage 50 to track their financial performance. Payroll taxes were remitted at year-end. To prepare for allocating opening account balances to departments, all opening account balances were transferred to

NOTES
For this professional service business, the terms Client and Vendor are used.

unallocated accounts in the corresponding financial statement section. The following business information was used to set up the accounts:

- Chart of Accounts
- Post-Closing Trial Balance and Statement of Opening Account Balances
- Vendor Information
- Client Information
- Employee Information
- Accounting Procedures

CHART OF POSTABLE ACCOUNTS

ABLE & ASSOCIATES INC.

ASSETS
10800 Bank: Chequing
11000 Investments
11200 Prepaid Association Dues
11400 Prepaid Subscriptions
11600 Prepaid Insurance
12000 Accounts Receivable
13400 Office Supplies
14400 Office Equipment
14800 Office Furniture
15000 Library ▶

▶**LIABILITIES**
21000 Bank Loan
22000 Accounts Payable
22500 Visa Payable
23000 EI Payable
23100 CPP Payable
23200 Income Tax Payable
24200 WSIB Payable
26500 HST Charged on Services
26700 HST Paid on Purchases

EQUITY
34500 Invested Capital: C. Able ▶

▶34800 Invested Capital: M. Able
35500 Retained Earnings
36000 Current Earnings

REVENUE
41000 Revenue from Services
41500 Revenue from Interest
41800 Other Revenue
42000 Sales Discounts

EXPENSE
51200 Association Dues
51300 Bank and Card Fees ▶

▶51400 Interest Expense
51500 Insurance Expense
51600 Publicity and Promotion
51800 Purchase Discounts
52000 Subscriptions
52200 Telephone Expense
52400 Rent
54000 Salaries
54100 EI Expense
54200 CPP Expense
54300 WSIB Expense

NOTES: The Chart of Accounts includes only postable accounts and the Current Earnings account. Able & Associates use five-digit account numbers for the General Ledger accounts.

POST-CLOSING TRIAL BALANCE

ABLE & ASSOCIATES INC.

April 1, 2018	Debits	Credits			Debits	Credits
10800 Bank: Chequing	$ 21 300		▶	21000 Bank Loan		$ 15 000
11000 Investments	44 000			22000 Accounts Payable		2 260
11200 Prepaid Association Dues	2 800			22500 Visa Payable		1 400
11400 Prepaid Subscriptions	1 500			26500 HST Charged on Services		2 200
11600 Prepaid Insurance	4 500			26700 HST Paid on Purchases	$ 1 640	
12000 Accounts Receivable	2 260			34500 Invested Capital: C. Able		33 000
13400 Office Supplies	1 800			34800 Invested Capital: M. Able		22 000
14400 Office Equipment	12 000			35500 Retained Earnings		28 740
14800 Office Furniture	8 000				$104 600	$104 600
15000 Library	4 800	▶				

STATEMENT OF ACCOUNT OPENING BALANCES

ABLE & ASSOCIATES INC.

April 1, 2018	Debits	Credits			Debits	Credits
19500 Unassigned Assets	$102 960	▶		29500 Unassigned Liabilities		$ 19 220
				39500 Unassigned Capital		83 740
					$102 960	$102 960

NOTES: The true account balances for the regular postable accounts are in the Trial Balance. The three unassigned accounts in the Statement of Opening Balances are temporary holding accounts. The temporary balance in these accounts is the sum of all balances for that section of the Balance Sheet (which temporarily have zero balances). These balances will be transferred back to the regular accounts to set up the departmental opening balances.

VENDOR INFORMATION

ABLE & ASSOCIATES INC.

Vendor Name (Contact)	Address	Phone No. Fax No.	E-mail Web Site	Terms Tax ID
Bell Canada (Yap Long)	500 Central Line Huntsville, Ontario P1F 2C2	Tel: (705) 466-2355	yap.l@bell.ca bell.ca	net 1
Muskoka Maintenance (M. Handimann)	72 Spoiler St. Huntsville, Ontario P1P 2B8	Tel: (705) 469-0808 Fax: (705) 469-6222	handimann@yahoo.com	2/10, n/30 295 416 822
Northlands Office Mgt. (Hi Bilding)	59 Condor St. Huntsville, Ontario P1D 4F4	Tel: (705) 283-9210 Fax: (705) 283-2310	bilding@northlands.com	net 1
Office Plus (B. Laser)	4 Paper Corners Huntsville, Ontario P1E 1G1	Tel: (705) 466-3335	officeplus.ca	1/15, n/30 822 101 500
Receiver General for Canada	Sudbury Tax Services Office PO Box 20004 Sudbury, ON P3A 6B4	Tel 1: (800) 561-7761 Tel 2: (800) 959-2221	cra-arc.gc.ca	net 1

OUTSTANDING VENDOR INVOICES

ABLE & ASSOCIATES INC.

Vendor Name	Terms	Date	Invoice No.	Amount	Total
Office Plus	1/15, n/30	Mar. 21/18	OP-2339	$2 260	$2 260

CLIENT INFORMATION

ABLE & ASSOCIATES INC.

Client Name (Contact)	Address	Phone No. Fax No.	E-mail Web Site	Terms Credit Limit
Adrienne Aesthetics (Adrienne Kosh)	65 Bytown Ave. Ottawa, Ontario K2C 4R1	Tel 1: (613) 722-9876 Tel 2: (613) 722-8701 Fax: (613) 722-8000	a.kosh@adrienneaesthetics.com adrienneaesthetics.com	2/10, n/30 $10 000
Dorfmann Design (Desiree Dorfmann)	199 Artistic Way, Unit 500 Hamilton, Ontario L8T 3B7	Tel: (905) 642-2348 Fax: (905) 642-9100	dd@dorfmann.com dorfmann.com	2/10, n/30 $10 000
Gorgeous Gifts (Gitte Gurlosi)	600 First St. Huntsville, Ontario P1L 2W4	Tel: (705) 462-1203 Fax: (705) 462-3394	gg@ggifts.com ggifts.com	2/10, n/30 $10 000
Truman Tires (Tyrone Truman)	600 Westminster St. London, Ontario N6P 3B1	Tel: (519) 729-3733 Fax: (519) 729-7301	tt@trumantires.com trumantires.com	2/10, n/30 $10 000

OUTSTANDING CLIENT INVOICES

ABLE & ASSOCIATES INC.

Client Name	Terms	Date	Invoice No.	Amount	Total
Adrienne Aesthetics	2/10, n/30	Mar. 25/18	843	$2 260	$2 260

EMPLOYEE INFORMATION SHEET

ABLE & ASSOCIATES INC.

Tryin, Reelie (Office Assistant)

Social Insurance No.	429 535 644	Total Federal (Ontario) Tax Exemption - TD1	$11 474 (10 011)
Address	200 Water St. #301	Employee Income (Reg. hours)	
	Huntsville, Ontario P1H 2L8	Salary	$3 800 /month (150 hours)
Telephone	(705) 446-2190		
Date of Birth (mm-dd-yy)	04-04-84	WSIB Rate	0.89
EI, CPP & Income Tax	Calculations are built into the Sage 50 program.		

NOTES

Able & Associates Inc. pays GST at the rate of 5 percent on subscriptions to professional journals and other books purchased for the business.

Accounting Procedures

Taxes (HST)

Able & Associates Inc. is a professional service business using the regular method of calculating HST. HST, at the rate of 13 percent, is charged on all services and paid on purchases. The difference between the HST charged and HST paid is remitted to the Receiver General for Canada quarterly.

Departments

Able & Associates has two departments, one for each partner. The division of most assets is 60 percent and 40 percent, to be consistent with their initial investments in the partnership and their time in the office.

Discounts for Early Payments

Able & Associates offers discounts to regular clients if they pay their accounts within 10 days. Full payment is expected in 30 days. No discounts are allowed on partial payments. Additional discounts are applied occasionally for clients in special circumstances. These are entered as line discounts for the sales.

Some vendors with whom Able & Associates has accounts set up also offer discounts for early payments.

INSTRUCTIONS

1. **Set up two departments** for Able & Associates.

2. **Record entries for the source documents** in Sage 50. Transactions indicated with a ✓ in the completion box beside the source document have step-by-step keystroke instructions.

3. **Print** the following **reports** after you have finished making your entries. Instructions for departmental reports begin on page 804.

   a. Comparative Balance Sheet with Departments for April 1 and April 30
   b. Income Statement with Departments for April 1 to April 30
   c. Departmental Income Statement
   d. Journal Report for April 1 to April 30 for all journals

KEYSTROKES

Departmental Accounting

Most companies are divided into departments, such as sales, marketing, service, finance, human resources and manufacturing. And most companies want to track the costs and performance of these departments separately. The departmental accounting feature in Sage 50 permits more detailed company reporting and analysis.

Unlike projects that work only through journal entries, departments are connected to all ledgers and journals. Departments can be associated with individual accounts, vendors and clients, and you can choose departments for accounts in journal entries.

Each account may be used exclusively by one department or by more than one department. For example, automotive parts in a car dealership will be used by the service department but not by the human resources or sales departments. Other accounts, such as a bank account, may be connected to all departments. Similarly, individual vendors, such as a car-parts vendor, may be linked to a specific department while others, such as utility providers, are linked to all departments. Clients, too, may be connected to specific departments. When you set up these connections, the departmental links are added to journal entries automatically, and you can generate detailed reports with departmental information.

Departmental account balances are generated when you add departmental information to journal entries, but they cannot be added as opening account balances in the ledgers. Therefore, ideally, you will add departmental information when you create company files so that you can have departmental information for all accounts. You can also choose to use departments only for Income Statement accounts and start using departments at the beginning of a fiscal period when these accounts have zero balances.

Setting Up Departments

Open `SageData16\ABLE\ABLE`. **Enter April 30, 2018** as the session date.

The history for the company files is not finished. Some linked accounts are missing and the ledgers are not balanced. (Read the margin Notes.)

Creating Departments

Before using departmental accounting, you must activate the feature and create the departments. The feature is not turned on by default, and you can add departments to an existing Sage 50 data file.

<table>
<tr><td>✓
1</td><td>**Memo #1**
Create two departments for Able & Associates: 1001: C. Able and 2001: M. Able</td><td align="right">**Dated April 1/18**</td></tr>
</table>

Click the **Settings icon** and **General (Accounts)** and **Departments**:

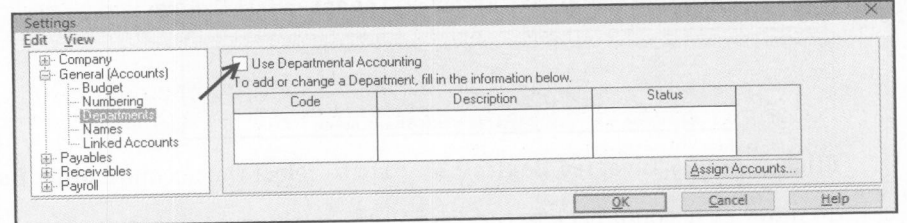

Click   **Use Departmental Accounting**. Sage 50 warns you about this step:

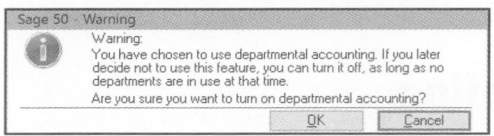

Adding departments is not a reversible step, unless the departments have not yet been used.

Click Cancel if you are not working with a separate copy of the data file. Make a backup first.

Click   **OK** to return to the Departments Settings screen.

For each department you want, you must assign a four-digit code and a name.

Click   the **Code field**.

Type   1001 **Press** (tab) to advance to the Description field. The Status is automatically set as Active.

Type   C. Able

Unused departments can have their status set to Inactive by clicking Active.

Click   the **Code field** on the next line. **Type** 2001

Press   (tab) to advance to the Description field. **Type** M. Able

Click   the **Assign Accounts button** to open the next screen:

From this screen, you can indicate which accounts use the departments. The cursor was on M. Able in the previous screen, so this department is selected. You can select departments from the drop-down list in the Department field.

Initially, all accounts use all departments. From this window, you can select accounts that are to be removed for a department.

The two investment accounts are separated according to the partner, so we should assign each one only to its correct department. That is, we can remove *34500 Invested Capital: C. Able* for M. Able and remove *34800 Invested Capital: M. Able* for C. Able. We are working with the M. Able department first.

Scroll down   the list of Accounts That Use This Department.

Click   **34500 Invested Capital: C. Able** to select the account.

Click   **Remove**. The account moves to the list of Accounts That Do Not Use This Department on the left-hand side of the screen.

Click   the **Department list arrow** and **choose 1001 C. Able**:

Click   **34800 Invested Capital: M. Able** to select the account. **Click Remove**.

To move an account back to the "Use" list, click it again and then click Select.

Click an account that you want to change and then press and hold ⌷ctrl⌷. Click each account you want until all the accounts you want are included.

Click the Remove button to shift the selected accounts to the other column.

Click Remove All to shift all the accounts to the "Do Not Use" column.

If only a few accounts use a department, it is easier to place them all on the "Do Not Use" side and then move the few to the "Use" side.

Reverse this procedure to move an account from the "Do Not Use" to the "Use" side. Click the account on the "Do Not Use" side and then click the Select button.

Click   **OK** to return to the Settings window. **Click OK** to return to the Home window.

Adding Departments to Accounts

Instead of adding department information to accounts from the Department Information window, you can add departments in the account ledger record directly.

✓	**Memo #2** **Dated April 1/18**
2	Assign accounts to departments. Invested Capital accounts are used by the department named in the account. All other accounts are used by both departments.

Click   **Company** in the Modules Pane list. **Click** the **Chart of Accounts icon**.

Double-click 34500 Invested Capital: C. Able in the list of accounts to open the General Ledger.

A new tab, Departments, has been added to the ledger record.

Click   the **Departments tab** to open the new screen:

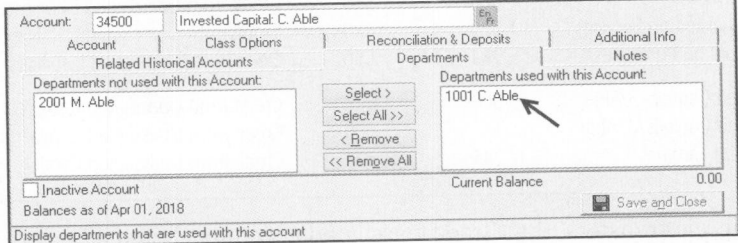

Department 2001 M. Able is located on the left-hand side under **Departments Not Used With This Account** because we moved it earlier on the Settings screen. The **Departments Used With This Account** column has 1001 C. Able in it.

On this screen, you can designate the departments that the account uses. You can modify these selections at any time. This screen is the same as the one for Department Information, except that now we are selecting the department instead of the account. However, in the General Ledger, you change the information for only one account at a time.

Click a department to select it or press ⌷ctrl⌷ and click more than one department if you want to select additional departments. Clicking Select will add the department to the account. Clicking Remove will remove a selected department from the account and place it on the "Not Used" side. Remove All and Select All will move all departments at once to the other side.

Close   the **Ledger window**. **Close** the **Accounts window**.

NOTES
You can also create a View Accounts shortcut (Banking Module) that will open the Accounts window. Double-click the account you need.

Adding Opening Departmental Balances

When you create a new company data file and add General Ledger accounts, you must enter the opening account balances as well, but you cannot split these balances among the departments. However, when you are entering transactions and have set up departments, you can choose a department from any Account field that allows you to select an account. We will use this approach to enter the opening departmental balances for all accounts. Initially we placed the total for all Balance Sheet accounts in the "unassigned" placeholder accounts for each section. When we transfer these amounts back to their appropriate accounts through General Journal entries, we can also assign departments.

✓ 3 | **Memo #3**   **Dated April 1/18**

Assign departmental opening account balances by transferring the unassigned balances from the chart below. Add linked accounts and then finish the history.

Account	Department Amounts 1001: C. Able	2001: M. Able	Source
10800 Bank: Chequing	$ 12 780	$ 8 520	Debit from Unassigned Assets
11000 Investments	26 500	17 500	Debit from Unassigned Assets
11200 Prepaid Association Dues	1 400	1 400	Debit from Unassigned Assets
11400 Prepaid Subscriptions	900	600	Debit from Unassigned Assets
11600 Prepaid Insurance	2 700	1 800	Debit from Unassigned Assets
12000 Accounts Receivable	2 260		Debit from Unassigned Assets
13400 Office Supplies	1 080	720	Debit from Unassigned Assets
14400 Office Equipment	7 200	4 800	Debit from Unassigned Assets
14800 Office Furniture	4 000	4 000	Debit from Unassigned Assets
15000 Library	2 400	2 400	Debit from Unassigned Assets
21000 Bank Loan	9 000	6 000	Credit from Unassigned Liabilities
22000 Accounts Payable	1 356	904	Credit from Unassigned Liabilities
22500 Visa Payable	840	560	Credit from Unassigned Liabilities
26500 HST Charged on Services	1 320	880	Credit from Unassigned Liabilities
26700 HST Paid on Purchases	984	656	Debit from Unassigned Liabilities
34500 Invested Capital: C. Able	33 000		Credit from Unassigned Capital
34800 Invested Capital: M. Able		22 000	Credit from Unassigned Capital
35500 Retained Earnings	17 244	11 496	Credit from Unassigned Capital

After entering the transfers, the three Unassigned accounts should all have zero balances and your Trial Balance should match the one on page 786.

Click the **General Journal icon** .

Enter Memo 3A as the Source, and **enter April 1** as the date.

Click the **Comment field** and **type** Transfer opening asset account balances to departments

Click the **Account field List icon** 🔍. The modified Select Account list opens.

Each account has a ⊞ icon added to indicate additional information is available. When you click the ⊞, all departments used by that account will be listed, so you can select a department for the transaction.

Click the ⊞ icon beside **10800 Bank: Chequing**:

The modified list now has the departments connected with the account.

Bank: Chequing has both departments available for a journal transaction. If you click the ⊞ beside *34500 Invested Capital: C. Able*, you can select only the one department that we assigned to it.

Click   **10800 - 1001 Bank: Chequing - C. Able**.

Click   **Select** to return to the journal with the cursor in the Debits field.

Type   12780 to enter the portion of the asset for this department.

Click   the **Account field List icon** again.

Double-click **10800 - 2001 Bank: Chequing - M. Able**. The cursor advances to
              the Credits field.

Type   −8520 (add a minus sign to the amount). **Press** ⌨(tab). The amount
              moves to the Debits column because we typed the minus sign.

Click   the **Account field** and **type** 19500

Press   ⌨(tab) to enter the total balance for the asset as a credit entry.

Accounts with departments all use the same format: account number, space, hyphen, space, department number. We can use this format to enter account numbers directly in a journal without using the Select Account list. You can omit the spaces when typing these numbers; Sage 50 will add them.

Click   the **Account field** on the next blank line.

Type   11000−1001

Press   ⌨(tab) to enter the account and advance to the Debits field.

Type   26500

Click   the **Account field** and **type** 11000−2001

Press   ⌨(tab) and **type** −17500 to move the amount to the Debits field.

Click   the **Account field** and **type** 19500 **Press** ⌨(tab) to enter the credit
              amount. **Press** ⌨(tab) again to update the totals.

At this stage, your journal entry should look like the one below:

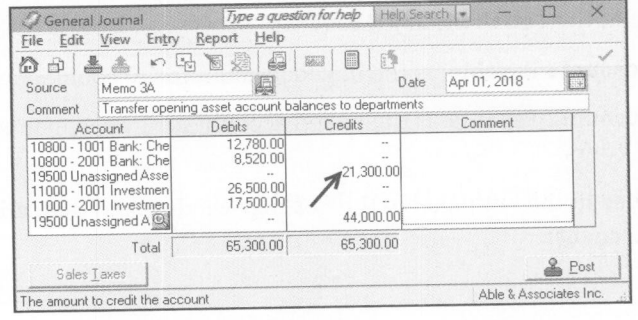

Before continuing, we will review the journal entry.

Press `ctrl` + **J** to open the journal display:

Account Number	Account Description	Debits	Credits
	Able & Associates Inc.		
	General Journal Entry 04/01/2018 (J1)		
10800 - 1001	Bank: Chequing - C. Able	12,780.00	-
10800 - 2001	Bank: Chequing - M. Able	8,520.00	-
19500	Unassigned Assets	-	21,300.00
11000 - 1001	Investments - C. Able	26,500.00	-
11000 - 2001	Investments - M. Able	17,500.00	-
19500	Unassigned Assets	-	44,000.00
Additional Date:	Additional Field:	65,300.00	65,300.00

The journal entry is different from the usual one in one significant way — we were able to divide the balance in each asset account between the two departments. These separate amounts can be added to the standard financial reports and will enable us to produce separate reports for each department.

Close the **journal display**.

Enter the **remaining asset account balance transfers** from memo #3 on page 792.

Review the **journal entry** again to verify that the total debits and credits match the initial account balance for *Unassigned Assets*.

Post the **journal entry** after entering all the asset account balances.

Enter the **liability account balance transfers** from memo #3 on page 792 as the second journal entry.

Review the **transaction** and then **post** it when the amounts are correct.

Enter the **capital account balance transfers** from memo #3 on page 792 as the third journal entry.

Review the **transaction** and then **post** it when the amounts are correct.

Close the **General Journal** to return to the Company module window.

Compare your **Trial Balance** with the one on page 786 and make corrections if needed.

If you entered the amounts correctly, the account balances for *Accounts Receivable* and *Accounts Payable* should match the historical invoice balances. However, before we can finish the history, we must add the missing essential linked accounts.

Finishing the History

Because we needed to access *Accounts Receivable* and *Accounts Payable* as postable accounts in the General Journal, we did not enter them as linked accounts. To finish the history, you must add these essential linked accounts.

Click the **Settings icon** [Settings]. **Click Payables** in the left panel of the Settings window and then **click Linked Accounts**.

Enter **22000 Accounts Payable** as the linked account for Accounts Payable.

Enter **22000 Accounts Payable** as the linked account for Prepayments and Prepaid Orders.

Click **Receivables** in the left panel of the Settings window and then **click Linked Accounts**.

NOTES
Do not enter sales tax information when prompted for the HST accounts (click Yes to confirm that you do not want to add sales tax details).

NOTES
Remember you can adjust General Journal entries after posting. Refer to page 45.

WARNING!
If you try to finish the history now, you will get the error message that the essential linked accounts are missing.

NOTES
Prepayments and deposits are not used, but linked accounts for them are required. Therefore, we can use Accounts Payable and Accounts Receivable.

Enter   **12000 Accounts Receivable** as the linked account for Accounts Receivable.

Enter   **12000 Accounts Receivable** as the linked account for Deposits and Prepaid Orders.

Click   **OK** to save the settings.

Choose the **History menu** and **click Finish Entering History**.

Click   **Backup** and continue to back up the not-finished file. **Click OK** when the backup is complete.

Click   **Proceed** to finish the history.

Adding Departments to Client Records

If some clients or vendors deal with only one department, you can add this information to the ledger record. C. Able has Adrienne Aesthetics as an exclusive client, and Dorfmann Design deals only with M. Able.

<table>
<tr><td>✓
4</td><td>**Memo #4**</td><td>**Dated April 1/18**</td></tr>
</table>

Clients: Assign C. Able to Adrienne Aesthetics and M. Able to Dorfmann Design. The remaining clients are associated with both departments.

Click   **Receivables** in the Modules pane list. **Click Adrienne Aesthetics** in the Clients List pane to open the record at the Address tab screen.

A Department field is added to the Address tab screen.

Click   the **Department list arrow** for the drop-down list of departments:

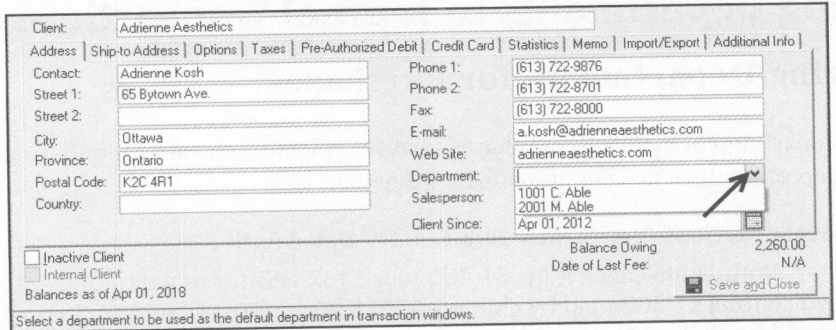

Click   **1001 C. Able** to select the department.

Next we need to select the departmental revenue account as the client's default.

Click   the **Options tab** so you can change the default revenue account.

Click   the **Revenue Account field list arrow** for the expanded account list:

Each account has three numbers associated with it — one for the main account and one for each department. By selecting the departmental account in the ledger record, department information will be added as the default when you sell to this client.

Choose 41000 - 1001 Revenue from Services - C. Able from the Account list.

> **⚠ WARNING!**
> Make a backup copy of the not-finished file so you can correct opening balance amounts later if necessary.

> **📄 NOTES**
> If a client or vendor is used by more than one department, you should not add a department to the record.

> **📄 NOTES**
> Another field is added to the ledger record – the Standard Discount field. Entering a rate in this field will add it to the Sales Journal automatically as the line discount rate (refer to page 799). You can still change the line discount rate in the journal.

Click   the **Next Client tool** 🔳 to open the record for Dorfmann Design.

Choose   **41000 - 2001 Revenue from Services - M. Able** from the Revenue Account list.

Click   the **Address tab** and **enter 2001 M. Able** in the Department field.

Click   🖫 Save and Close .

The remaining clients work with both departments, so we cannot add one department exclusively for them.

Adding Departments to Vendor Records

If a vendor is connected exclusively with one department, you can add the department to the vendor record, just as you do for clients. At this time, all vendors are used by both departments, so we will not add departments to the records.

> If you want to add departments to vendor records, open the Payables module window and then open the vendor record. The Department field has been added to the Address tab screen.
>
> Click the Department field list arrow and click the department you want from this list.
>
> On the Options tab screen, choose the departmental account as the default for expenses.
>
> Repeat this procedure for other vendors. Close the last vendor record.

Adding Departments to Journal Transactions

Entering Departments for Purchases

Adding departmental details to purchases involves selecting the appropriate General Ledger departmental subaccount instead of the main one.

NOTES
You can also enter this purchase in the Payments Journal as an Other Payment. Enter the amounts and choose the departmental accounts in the same way as described here.

✓	**Cheque Purchase Invoice #NO-2018-4** **Dated April 3/18**
5	From Northlands Office Mgt., $1 400 plus $182 HST for rental of office suite. Invoice total $1 582 paid by cheque #3011. $840 (60 percent) of the expense should be assigned to C. Able and $560 (40 percent) to M. Able.

Before proceeding, you should create shortcuts for the journals in other modules.

Create   **shortcuts** to Create and Pay Vendor Invoices, to Create Paycheques and to Create General Journal Entries.

Click   the **Create Vendor Invoices shortcut** to open the journal.

Choose   **Northlands Office Mgt.** as the vendor. **Press** ⌷tab⌷ . The default general Rent account and tax code are added from the vendor's record.

Choose   **Cheque** from the Payment Method list.

Enter   **April 3** as the payment date.

Click   the **Amount field. Type** 840 **Press** ⌷tab⌷ .

Click   the **List icon** 🔳 beside *Rent* in the Account field to open the Select Account screen. **Click** the ⊞ icon beside **52400 Rent**:

Department subaccounts are added, just as they were in the General Journal.

Click **52400 - 1001 Rent - C. Able**. **Press** (enter) to add the account for C. Able's share.

Click the **Amount field** on the second journal line. **Type** 560

Press (tab). **Click** the **Account field List icon**.

Choose **52400 - 2001 Rent - M. Able**. **Press** (enter) to add the account for M. Able's share.

Enter line **Descriptions** and **Source** information to complete the entry.

Choose the **Report menu** and **click Display Payments Journal entry**:

Account Number	Account Description	Debits	Credits
Able & Associates Inc. Expenses Journal Entry 04/01/2018 (J4)			
26700	HST Paid on Purchases	182.00	-
52400 - 1001	Rent - C. Able	840.00	-
52400 - 2001	Rent - M. Able	560.00	-
10800	Bank: Chequing	-	1,582.00
Additional Date:	Additional Field:	1,582.00	1,582.00

The rental expense amount has been shared between the two departments, but the other amounts have not. Because no single department is linked to the vendor, and the other accounts for the transaction are not accessible, they remain unallocated.

Close the **journal display** to return to the journal.

Click the **Paid From bank account list arrow**:

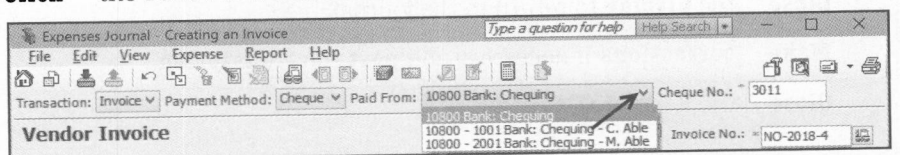

You can change the default bank account for this payment, but you can choose only one account for the single cheque. A complete allocation requires access to both bank department subaccounts. Therefore, you cannot allocate the bank amount.

Make **corrections** if necessary. **Post** the **transaction** and **close** the **journal**.

Entering Departments for Receipts

Receipt #48   **Dated April 4/18**

From Adrienne Aesthetics, cheque #3101 for $2 214.80, including $45.20 discount in full payment of invoice #843. Assign all amounts to C. Able.

Restore the **Receivables module** as the Home window if necessary.

Click the **Receipts Journal icon** to open the journal.

Choose **Adrienne Aesthetics**. **Press** (tab) to add the outstanding invoice.

Enter Apr 4 -18 as the date and **enter** 3101 as the client's cheque number.

Accept the **discount taken** and **amount received**.

NOTES
You can create separate bank accounts that link to the different departments.
You could also make separate payment journal entries for each department amount. This will allow you to choose the associated departmental bank account number, but not the department for tax accounts.

Press ⌨ *ctrl* **+ J** to review the transaction.

All amounts are allocated to C. Able except the bank account amount. The accounts are allocated because we set up a unique department link for the client in the ledger record. The allocated amounts are those for the default linked accounts for the journal. In this case, we can also allocate the bank amount because only one department is involved and we can select the account.

Close   the **display** to return to the journal.

Click   the **Deposit To bank account list arrow**:

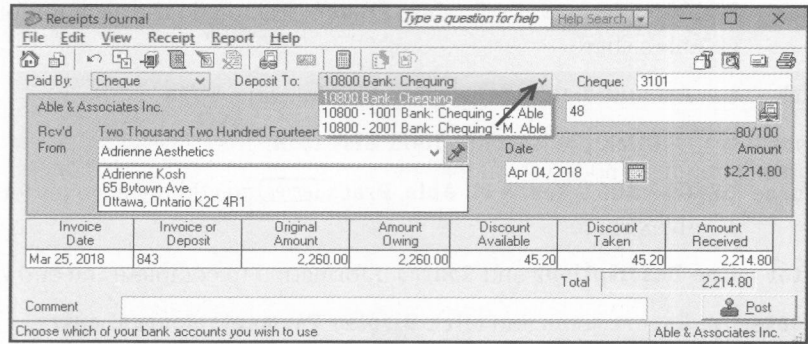

Click   **10800 - 1001 Bank: Chequing - C. Able** to update the journal entry.

Press ⌨ *ctrl* **+ J** to review the transaction:

Able & Associates Inc. Receipts Journal Entry 04/04/2018 (J5)			
Account Number	Account Description	Debits	Credits
10800 - 1001	Bank: Chequing - C. Able	2,214.80	-
42000 - 1001	Sales Discounts - C. Able	45.20	-
12000 - 1001	Accounts Receivable - C. Able	-	2,260.00
Additional Date:	Additional Field:	2,260.00	2,260.00

The entry is now completely allocated and it is correct. All amounts, including the discount, are attributed to C. Able's department.

Close   the **display** to return to the journal.

Make   **corrections** if necessary and **post** the **transaction**.

Close   the **Receipts Journal**.

Entering Departments for Sales with Line Discounts

Click   the **Client Invoices icon** [Client Invoices ▾] to open the Fees Journal.

> ✓
> 7
>
> **Sales Invoice #851**   **Dated April 4/18**
>
> To Adrienne Aesthetics, $5 800 plus HST for auditing financial statements and $900 plus HST for monthly accounting fee. Invoice total $7 243.30. Terms: 2/10, n/30. Additional 5 percent discount applies to the fee for auditing, by special arrangement with client. Adrienne Aesthetics is C. Able's client.

Choose Adrienne Aesthetics. **Press** ⌨ *tab* to add the client's record details.

Enter   **April 4** as the date. This time the default revenue account is correct:

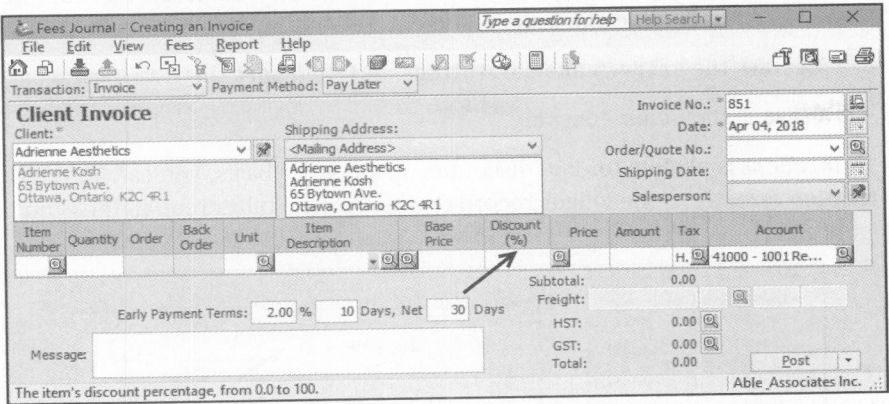

The department subaccount is taken from the record because a single department is linked to the client and we added the department subaccount as the default revenue account.

Two columns — **Base Price** and **Discount %** — have been added to the journal. These fields allow us to add discounts that apply only to a single invoice line, so you can enter different discount rates for each invoice line. Able & Associates offers some clients additional discounts. For part of this invoice, a 5 percent discount applies.

Entering Line Discounts

Click   the **Item Description field**.

Type   `prepare audited financial statements`

Press   ⌨ tab ⌨ to advance to the Base Price field.

Type   `5800`

Press   ⌨ tab ⌨ to advance to the Discount % field.

Type   `5`

Press   ⌨ tab ⌨ to apply the amount of the discount — $290.00.

The new discounted unit price, $5 510, has been added to the Price field, but the Amount field is still blank. To enter the amount automatically, you must enter the quantity for the line.

Click   the **Quantity field**. **Type** 1 **Press** ⌨ tab ⌨ to update the line.

The discounted amount, $5 510, is now entered as the amount.

Press   ⌨ ctrl ⌨ + **J** to review the transaction as we have entered it so far:

Account Number	Account Description	Debits	Credits
Able & Associates Inc. Fees Journal Entry 04/04/2018 (J6)			
12000 - 1001	Accounts Receivable - C. Able	6,226.30	
26500 - 1001	HST Charged on Services - C. Able	-	716.30
41000 - 1001	Revenue from Services - C. Able	-	5,510.00
Additional Date:	Additional Field:	6,226.30	6,226.30

Again, all amounts are allocated correctly because we have linked a single account and department to the record. The discount is taken directly to reduce revenue; it is not linked to the sales discount account used for early payments.

Close   the **display** to return to the journal and complete the entry.

Click   the **Item Description field**. **Type** `monthly fee`

Click   the **Amount field**. No discount applies to this service.

Type   `900`

Press ⌨ *tab* **twice** to add the tax code and advance to the Account field. The default account should be entered automatically.

Review the **entry**, **make corrections** and then **post** the **transaction**.

Close the **Sales Journal**.

If the client is eligible for line discounts on a regular basis, you can add that information directly to the ledger record on the Options tab screen in the Standard Discount field:

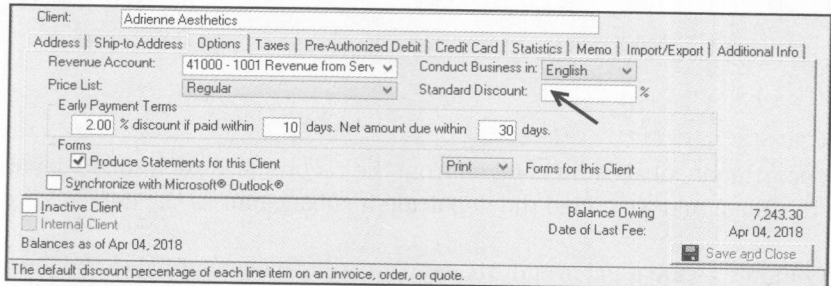

Continue with the **transactions** up to the payroll entry on April 30.

8 | **Payment Cheque #3012** — **Dated April 5/18**
To Office Plus, $2 237.40, including $22.60 discount in full payment of invoice #OP-2339. (You cannot assign these amounts — read the margin Notes.)

9 | **Cash Sales Invoice #852** — **Dated April 10/18**
To Truman Tires, $1 000 plus $130 HST for monthly fee for accounting assistance. Assign $600 (60%) of the fee to C. Able and $400 (40%) to M. Able. Received cheque #2900 for $1 107.40 in full payment, including 2% discount for early payment. (Read the margin Notes.)

10 | **Sales Invoice #853** — **Dated April 14/18**
To Dorfmann Design, $5 000 plus HST for preparing special financial reports for potential investors and $700 plus HST for monthly accounting fee. Invoice total $5 876 (with discount). Terms: 2/10, n/30. Additional 10 percent discount applies to the fee for preparing financial reports. Assign 100% of all amounts to M. Able.

11 | **Sales Invoice #854** — **Dated April 20/18**
To Gorgeous Gifts, $3 000 plus $390 HST for assistance with response to Canada Revenue Agency audit and $500 plus $65 HST for monthly accounting fee. Invoice total $3 955. Terms: 2/10, n/30. Assign $1 800 plus $300 (60%) of revenue amounts to C. Able and $1 200 and $200 (40%) to M. Able.

12 | **Cash Purchase Invoice #BC-233008** — **Dated April 22/18**
From Bell Canada, $400 plus $52 HST for monthly telephone and Internet service for one multi-line office telephone, two mobile phones and networked Internet service. Invoice total $452 paid by cheque #3013. Assign $240 (60%) of expense amount to C. Able and $160 (40%) to M. Able.

13 | **Purchase Invoice #OP-5102** — **Dated April 25/18**
From Office Plus, $3 000 plus $390 HST for new boardroom table and chairs (Office Furniture account). Invoice total $3 390. Terms: 1/15, n/30. Assign $1 800 (60%) of the asset account amount to C. Able and $1 200 (40%) to M. Able. (Read the margin Notes.)

14	**Cash Sales Invoice #855** **Dated April 28/18** To various one-time clients, $6 000 plus $780 HST for personal income tax preparation. Total cash received, $6 780, deposited to bank account. Assign $3 600 (60%) of revenue amount to C. Able and $2 400 (40%) to M. Able.
15	**Memo #5** **Dated April 28/18** Remit the HST owing to the Receiver General as at March 31. Issue cheque #3014. Assign $1 320 for HST Charged on Services and $984 for HST Paid (60% of HST amounts) to C. Able and $880 for HST Charged on Services and $656 for HST Paid (40%) to M. Able.

Entering Departments for Payroll Transactions

Payroll amounts are allocated to departments differently than amounts in other journals. If an employee works only with one department, you can add the department to the employee's ledger record.

✓ **16**	**Memo #6** **Dated April 30/18** Prepare payroll for Tryin, office assistant. Issue cheque #3015. Assign 60% of all amounts to C. Able and 40% to M. Able.

Click   the **Create Paycheque shortcut** to open the journal.

Choose   **Tryin, Reelie. Press** <u>tab</u> to add the employee's default record details.

All Payroll Journal accounts are linked accounts, so you cannot choose the department subaccounts to enter allocations. Instead, you can open the Department Allocation screens from the Paycheque menu:

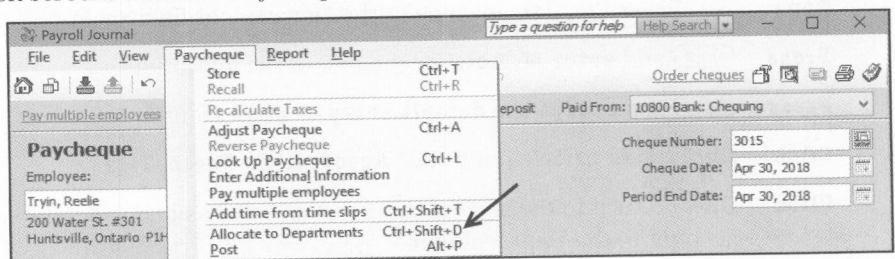

NOTES
Allocate To Departments is also available in the Payroll Run Journal from the Payroll menu. You can allocate for each employee separately.

You can also use the Departments tool:

Choose   the **Paycheque menu** and **click Allocate To Departments**, or

click   the **Allocate Account Amounts To Departments tool** .

Both methods will open the Allocation screen:

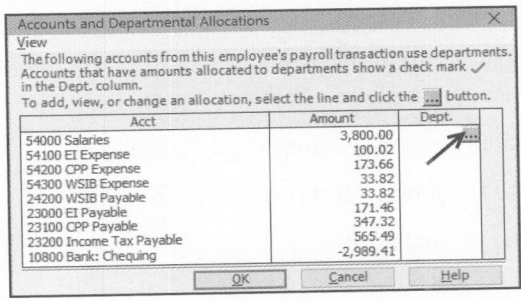

All accounts used in the journal entry are listed, and you can allocate one or more of them, or all, in the same way, or you can use different percentages or amounts.

Click the **Department Detail button** (in the Dept. column) for Salaries:

This screen is similar to the one we use to enter division allocations (refer to page 509). You can select one or more departments for each journal entry amount. And you can apply the same allocation to all accounts, just as we did for divisions in Chapter 13 (pages 515–517). Payroll amounts for the Ables are allocated by percentage, but you can allocate by amount if you prefer. You do not need to allocate the entire amount for an account. We want the same breakdown to apply to all amounts.

Click the **Department List icon** 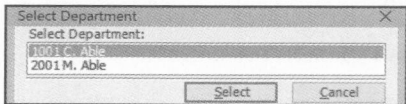 to open the selection list for departments:

Click **1001 C. Able**. **Click Select** to add the department.

Press (tab) to advance to the % (percentage) field.

Type 60 **Press** (tab) to advance to the Department field again.

Press (enter) and **enter M. Able** for the rest of the allocation.

Press (tab) and **accept** the **default entry** — 40 percent.

Click **Apply This Allocation To All Accounts By Percentage**.

Click **OK** to return to the account list screen. A ✓ has been added to each account in the Dept. column.

Click **10800 Bank: Chequing** to select the account line. The Detail button now appears on this line.

Click the **Dept. Detail button** 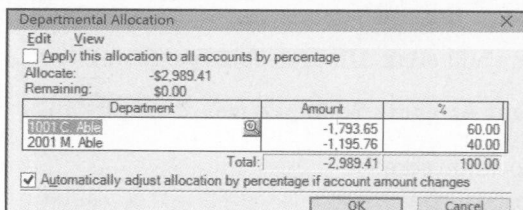 for this account:

The same 60–40 allocation is applied. But in this window, you have the option to change the allocation for the single account without affecting the others.

Click **OK** to accept the amounts already entered (or Cancel).

Click **OK** again to return to the journal and review the entry.

Press (ctrl) + **J** to view the journal entry:

Able & Associates Inc. Payroll Journal Entry 04/30/2018 (J15)		Debits	Credits
Account Number	Account Description		
54000 - 1001	Salaries - C. Able	2,280.00	-
54000 - 2001	Salaries - M. Able	1,520.00	-
54100 - 1001	EI Expense - C. Able	60.01	-
54100 - 2001	EI Expense - M. Able	40.01	-
54200 - 1001	CPP Expense - C. Able	104.20	-
54200 - 2001	CPP Expense - M. Able	69.46	-
54300 - 1001	WSIB Expense - C. Able	20.29	-
54300 - 2001	WSIB Expense - M. Able	13.53	-
10800 - 1001	Bank: Chequing - C. Able	-	1,793.65
10800 - 2001	Bank: Chequing - M. Able	-	1,195.76
23000 - 1001	EI Payable - C. Able	-	102.88
23000 - 2001	EI Payable - M. Able	-	68.58
23100 - 1001	CPP Payable - C. Able	-	208.39
23100 - 2001	CPP Payable - M. Able	-	138.93
23200 - 1001	Income Tax Payable - C. Able	-	339.29
23200 - 2001	Income Tax Payable - M. Able	-	226.20
24200 - 1001	WSIB Payable - C. Able	-	20.29
24200 - 2001	WSIB Payable - M. Able	-	13.53
Additional Date:	Additional Field:	4,107.50	4,107.50

All amounts are automatically applied in the 60–40 ratio for the two departments.

Close   the **display** to return to the journal.

Make   **corrections** if necessary and **post** the **transaction**.

Close   the **Paycheques Journal**.

Enter   the final **two General Journal entries** with allocations for all accounts.

Memo #7   **Dated April 30/18**

17

The following transactions appeared on the monthly bank statement for the Bank: Chequing account. Assign 60% of all amounts to C. Able and 40% to M. Able.

	Amounts for C. Able	Amounts for M. Able
Bank charges $60	$ 36	$ 24
Bank loan principal $300	180	120
Bank loan interest $200	120	80
Interest on chequing account $60	36	24
Interest from investments $180	108	72
Bank net withdrawal $320	192	128

NOTES
If you credit (or debit) the bank account for each charge (or deposit) amount separately, you will not enter the final net withdrawal amounts.

Memo #8   **Dated April 30/18**

18

Enter the adjustments for supplies used and prepaid expenses expired in April. Assign all amounts as indicated in the following summary. Create new Group Expense account 52600 Supplies Used.

	Amounts for C. Able	Amounts for M. Able
Office Supplies $100	$ 60	$ 40
Prepaid Insurance $500	300	200
Prepaid Association Dues $400	200	200
Prepaid Subscriptions $250	150	100

Handling Unallocated Amounts

We saw that the amounts for some accounts in the journals were not allocated. Most of the affected accounts are Balance Sheet accounts, and many users prefer to apply departmental accounting only to Income Statement accounts to avoid these incomplete entries. Unallocated amounts can also leave Departmental Balance Sheets out of balance since some amounts will not be included. For example, in a purchase of assets, the asset account was allocated but the HST account was not.

To prepare complete Departmental reports without unallocated amounts, you can enter General Journal adjusting entries to transfer the balances from the main account to the correct departmental subaccount. Clearly this could be a time-consuming exercise, as you would have to first determine all the appropriate amounts. Furthermore, the linked *Accounts Receivable* and *Accounts Payable* accounts are not accessible as postable accounts, so you would still be unable to allocate these amounts. For this exercise, we will not enter the adjustments for unallocated amounts.

NOTES
In the Accountant Edition of Sage 50, all accounts are available for posting. Your accountant would be able to make these adjustments for you by working with an Accountant's Copy of your data file. Refer to Chapter 12.

Departmental Reports

Many of the standard Sage 50 reports can have department information added to them. In addition, the primary financial statements — the Balance Sheet, Income Statement and Trial Balance — are available as departmental reports. As before, we will work from the Report Centre.

Click the **Report Centre icon** in the Home window.

Click **Financials** to open the list of financial reports.

Click the ⊞ beside **Balance Sheet** to expand this list.

Click the ⊞ beside **Income Statement** to expand this list.

Click the ⊞ beside **Trial Balance** to expand this list:

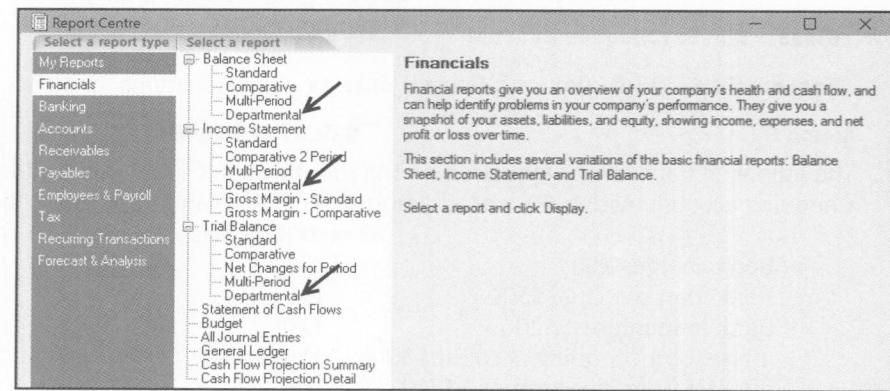

You can prepare a Departmental version of each of these reports.

Displaying Departmental Balance Sheets

If you want Balance Sheet information for each department, you should prepare the Departmental Balance Sheet.

NOTES
Including unallocated amounts — those not assigned to departments — and totals will provide balanced reports.

Click **Departmental** under **Balance Sheet**. **Click Modify This Report**:

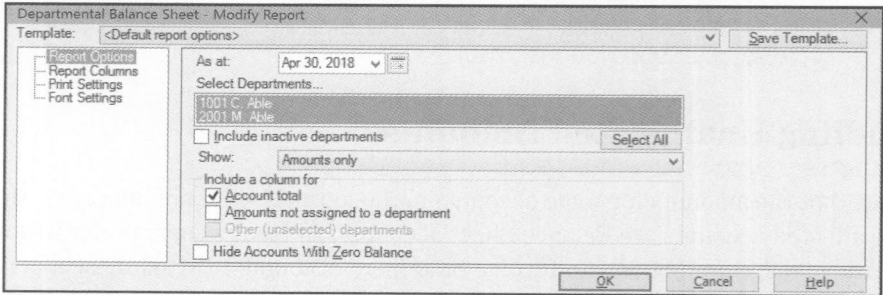

From the Home window, choose the Reports menu, then choose Financials and Departmental Reports and click Balance Sheet to open the report options.

You can report on one or more departments or all departments. The departmental amounts are in separate columns with headings, so you have a complete Balance Sheet for each department you selected. Remember that the Balance Sheet for each department separately may not balance if some amounts were not allocated. Adjustment amounts are added to the report for these imbalances.

Reports can include **Amounts** only or each amount as a **Percentage Of The Total**. You can also add **extra columns** for the total amount for each account, for amounts that

are not assigned to any department and for the total amount for other departments not included in the report.

> **Choose** the **departments** you want to include.
>
> **Choose** the **Amounts** or **Percentage** option.
>
> **Choose** the **additional columns** you want.
>
> **Enter** the **date** for the report and **click OK**.
>
> **Close** the **display** when you have finished.

Departmental Income Statement and Trial Balance Reports

Departmental Income Statements and Departmental Trial Balances are also available. The Departmental Income Statement is probably the most frequently used of these reports.

For both reports, select the departments to include in the report and choose whether you want to include amounts that are not assigned to a department. You can include amounts only or add the percentage of the total amount in your reports. In other respects, these reports are like the standard non-departmental reports.

Adding Departments to Other Reports

Many other reports allow departmental details to be added after you set up and use departments. **Journal reports** automatically include the department number with the account numbers if you have added that information to the journal transaction.

The **Balance Sheet**, **Income Statement**, **Trial Balance** and **General Ledger** all have a **Show Departments** check box added. Division reports also have this option.

> **Access** the **report options** in the usual way from the Report Centre or from the Reports menu.

The Balance Sheet Report Options window, for example, has the Show Departments option added:

> **Click** **Show Departments** to have the details added to the report.
>
> **Click** the **Select Departments button** to open the department list:

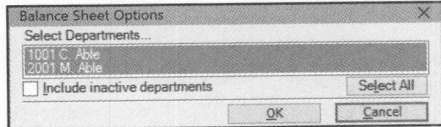

> **Select** the **departments** you want to add to the report.
>
> **Click** **OK** to return to the initial Balance Sheet Options window.
>
> **Choose** other **report options** in the usual way and **click OK** to open the report.
>
> **Close** the **display** when you have finished.

Department information can also be added to client and vendor reports. The Vendor Aged and Aged Overdue reports and the Pending Purchase Order Report allow you to

group the vendors by department for the report. The Client Aged and Aged Overdue reports and the Pending Sales Order Report have the same option for grouping clients by department.

The Vendor Aged Report Modify Report screen has this option:

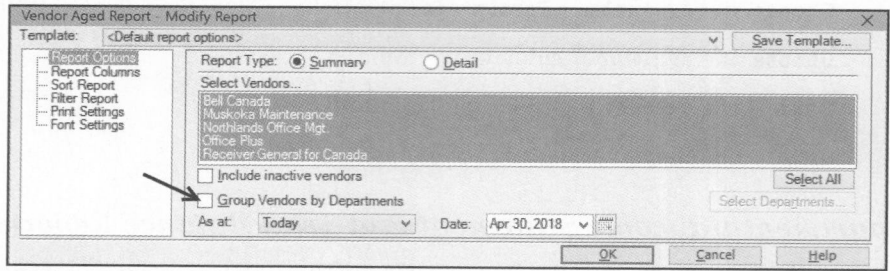

Click   **Group Vendors By Departments** to select the option.

Click   the **Select Departments button** to open the department list.

Select   the **departments** you want to add to the report.

You can include or omit vendors that do not have an assigned department.

Click   **OK** to return to the Vendor Aged Report options screen.

Choose   other **report options** in the usual way.

Click   **OK** to open the report.

Close   the **display** when you have finished.

Close   the **Report Centre** if it is open.

R E V I E W

The Student DVD with Data Files includes Review Questions and Supplementary Cases for this chapter.

Part 4
Appendices

Downloading, Installing and Activating the Student Version of Sage 50

Downloading the Sage 50 Student Program

STUDENT VERSION
The Student version is a single-user program.

NOTES
Your Internet screens will depend on the version of Windows and the Internet browser you are using. In addition, Web sites are updated regularly — always read and follow the instructions provided for you.
We used Windows 10 and Google Chrome for the screens in this Appendix.

WARNING!
If you have previously installed Sage 50, or an earlier Sage 50 Accounting Student version, you must uninstall that program before you can install the 2016 Sage 50 program. Use the Control Panel Programs – Uninstall A Program function to uninstall the program properly.
Refer to Using This Book, page xiii, for more information about different versions and the limitations of the Student version.

NOTES
You can complete your program registration before downloading the program. In this way, you will have the activation codes when you reach that stage (refer to page A–9).

NOTES
Sage 300 ERP is another Sage program that has a student version.
Farther down on this same Web page, you will find links for Support and Help as well as Training and Certification.

Most steps for installing the program are the same for all versions. The boxed notes on pages A–3 – A–4 outline the procedures for the retail Premium and Pro versions, including CD installation, registration and Payroll activation.

The Sage 50 Premium Student version is available only as a download.

Start your **computer** and open your **Internet browser** window.

Type `sage.com/ca/about-us/education` in the Web address field. **Press** (enter):

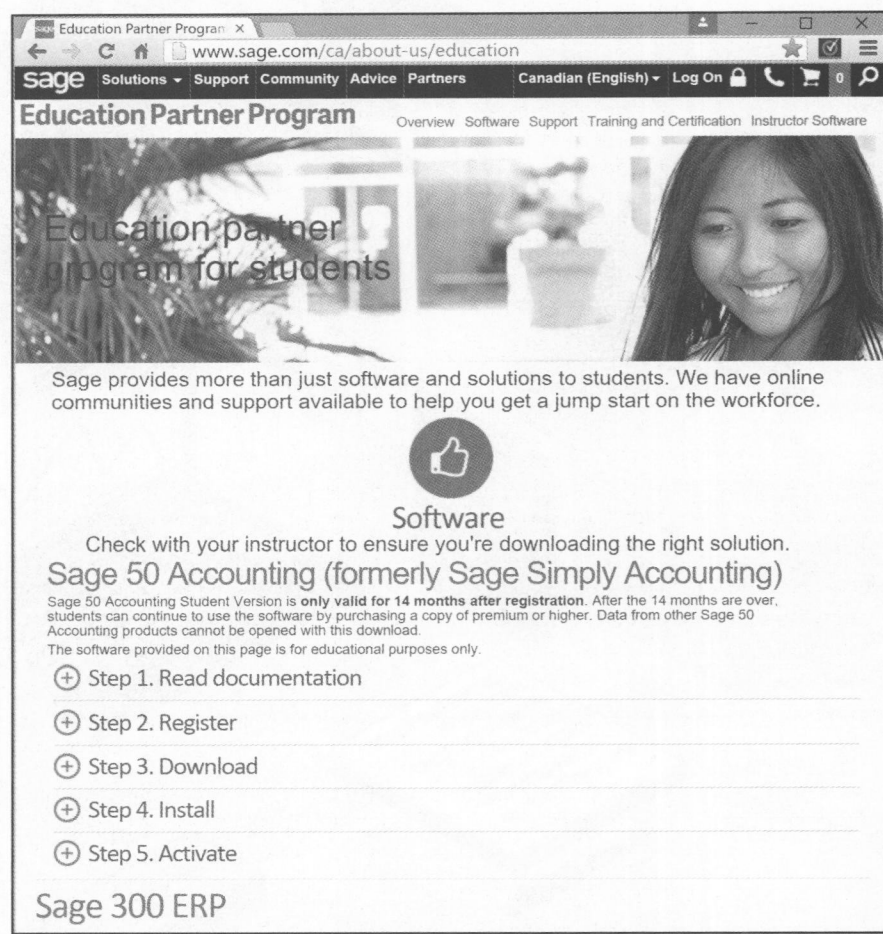

Click **each step** to expand it (refer to page A–4) and read all instructions.

INSTALLING SAGE 50 RETAIL VERSION

If you have an active licence for Sage 50, you can install the 2016.2 program by **downloading** the **update** for your current installation. You can install this new release only from the latest release, so you must first update your current program (choose Check For Updates under the Help menu in the Home window). Your registration and activation information will be taken from your current installation. The 2016 program will be installed in a folder separate from the 2015 program.

INSTALLING SAGE 50 FROM THE PROGRAM CD

Insert the **Sage 50 program CD** in the CD/DVD drive. The Installation screen should open immediately. If it does not, in the **Windows Search field**, **type setup.EXE**. **Click** the entry that matches the program on your Sage 50 disk in the CD drive. On the **desktop** screen, **right-click** the **Start menu icon** and **choose Run**. **Type D:\Setup\setup.EXE** or **click Browse** to locate the program. Then **click This PC** or Computer and double-click the **Sage 50 CD**, double-click the **Setup** folder and **double-click setup** (or **setup.EXE**).

INSTALLING FROM A NEW DOWNLOAD

Download the **Sage 50** program from the Sage Web site **<sage.com/ca/sage-50-accounting/>**. **Double-click** the **Buy Now** or **Try It Free** option. **Select Try** or **Buy** and then **choose** the **version** you want from lower down on the Web page. **Choose Save File** when prompted and then choose to **Run** the program if you get an additional security message. **Click** the icon for the Download Manager that was placed on your desktop.

You can **choose** the **location** for the program files that will be extracted. **Accept** the **default location** or **choose** another **location**. Make a note of the location for later. **Click Save** to start the Sage Download Manager.

When you are ready to install the program, find the file you downloaded in the location you selected. **Double-click** the **program** icon or the **Sage folder** and **program** icon (or filename **sa_20162cp1.EXE**) to begin the installation. You will be asked to enter the location for the installer control files. **Accept** the **default location** or **click Browse** and **choose** another **location**.

Click Next. You will open the Sage 50 Installation screen on page A–7. **Click Install Sage 50** and follow the steps on the following pages until the registration screen opens, advising that you have XX days remaining (until the trial version expires).

REGISTERING AND ACTIVATING SAGE 50

Until you register and activate the program, you will be allowed to use the program for a limited number of days. The key code for each copy of the program is unique and applies only to that serial number.

Have your product serial number ready for the registration. You can **register online** or **by telephone**. The telephone number is provided. To register online, start your Internet connection. **Click** the **Register Online link** on the registration information screen. Follow the instructions provided. **Print** a copy of the **codes screen** for reference.

When you register **by telephone**, you will **provide** the **serial number** from your online purchase, program package or CD and **receive** an **account ID number**, a **key code number** and a **payroll ID number**. These numbers will be linked to the serial number you provided and cannot be used for a different copy of the program.

If you chose **Remind Me Later, open any data file, choose** the **Help menu** and **click Enter Key Code**. This reminder message will appear each time you start the program until you complete the activation.

To **retrieve** the **key code online**, the default selection, start your Internet connection and **click OK**. You will be connected to the Sage 50 Web site and the account ID and serial number will be uploaded from your program to create a key code. The **key code** will be **added** to your program **automatically**.

If you have already registered and have the activation codes, **click Activate Now**. **Enter** your **Company Name** and the **account ID** provided by Sage for the program you have registered. To **enter** the code on this screen **manually, click Use This Key Code** to open the Key Code fields. **Enter** the **Key Code** provided by Sage for this program. Enter all names and numbers exactly as they are given to you, including spaces and punctuation. The key code is not case sensitive. If you make a mistake, the program will warn you and you can re-enter the details.

Click OK. When you have completed the registration, Sage 50 will confirm that activation was successful. **Click OK** to continue to the Sage 50 Welcome/Select Company screen (refer to page A–9).

NOTES
From the Computer window, you can right-click D: and click Open Autoplay and Run Launch.EXE to start the auto-run feature and open the Installation options screen.

WARNING!
Do not remove the program CD before clicking Exit on the opening Sage 50 Installation screen (refer to the screenshot on page A–7).

NOTES
When you download the retail version, only the latest release will be available and it will be later than release 2016.2, the one we used for this text.

NOTES
The default installation destination folder will be Sage 50 Premium Accounting or Sage 50 Pro Accounting.

NOTES
If you purchased the program by downloading it, your serial number and key codes will be e-mailed to you. You can copy and paste them into the appropriate fields on the activation screen.

STUDENT VERSION
The serial number for all copies of the Student version is 242P1U2-1000011.

NOTES
The letters o and i are not used in serial numbers, key codes or Payroll IDs.

NOTES
If you have not activated the program yet, you can do so from the Help menu. Choose Enter Key Code from the Help menu to open the You Have XX Days Remaining screen.

NOTES
If you have an existing account with Sage, registration may be completed automatically. You must still activate the program.

⚠ WARNING!
Do not download program updates automatically. If you download program updates, you may download a later version than the one we use and your payroll amounts may be different from the ones we provide. Payroll tables are updated every six months and the Release number is linked to payroll tax table dates. After updating, you will no longer be able to open these data files with Release 2016.2. Refer to page 80.

⚠ WARNING!
This Web page has links for downloading several Sage programs. Make sure that you choose 2016.2 in Step 3, the Download step.

NOTES
The arrows on this screenshot point to key parts of this Web page that you will need.

REGISTERING AND ACTIVATING SAGE 50 CONTINUED

Click Open Sample Company. Click OK to continue to the Session Date window. **Click OK** to accept the default session date. The session date is explained in Chapter 3 when you need to enter transactions.

With an open Internet connection, you can now view a short video to learn more or access this video later from the Help menu. These are some of the options on the Getting Started screen. **Click Close** to close the Getting Started window. For now, you can close any information screens about Sage services that pop up.

UNLOCKING SAGE 50 PAYROLL

You should unlock and activate the Payroll module before proceeding.

Choose the **Help menu** and **click Unlock Auto Payroll.** An information screen about payroll services for Sage 50 opens, advising that you need a payroll ID and subscription to the Sage 50 Payroll Plan — a fee-based service — to use the payroll features in the program. To learn more about the payroll plan or to subscribe, **click Tell Me More.**

Click Enter Payroll ID. You must enter the account payroll ID numbers provided for your program registration.

The default selection is to **retrieve** the **payroll ID online.** Be sure that your Internet connection is open. **Click** the **Account ID field** and **type** your **account number. Click OK.** The **payroll ID** will be **downloaded directly** to your program.

If you have the number already, you can enter it **manually. Click Use This Payroll ID** to make this selection. **Click** the **Payroll ID field** and **type** the **number** provided, exactly as it is given to you. The code is not case sensitive. **Click OK.**

When Sage 50 confirms that activation is successful, **click OK** to continue.

After you have activated your program and unlocked payroll, you can retrieve these codes automatically by selecting the online options if you need to reinstall the program.

The expanded instructions are combined here:

Education Partner Program

⊕ Step 1. Read documentation

⊖ Step 2. Register
1. Click the **Register** button. **Note**: Make sure to select the correct product.

   `Register`

2. Complete **all fields** in the registration form.
3. Select the **certify acknowledgement** check box and click **Submit**.

   You will receive an email with your activation code for the installed .

⊖ Step 3. Download
Do not download any product updates for the Student or Education versions unless you are advised to do so by an instructor.
1. Select which software to download.

   `2016.2` `2015.0` `2014.1` `2013`

2. Click **Save File** from the download screen.
3. Click **Run** from the Open file screen.
4. Click **Exit** when download is complete.

⊖ Step 4. Install
If you have previously installed any version of Sage 50 Accounting on your computer (including a 30-day trial), please uninstall that version, run the Student Version Utility, and then install the Student Version of Sage 50 Accounting.

1. Click **Install Sage 50** from the Sage launch screen.
2. Choose preferred **language** from the Install Wizard drop-down list and click **OK**.
3. Select **Yes** (recommended) and click **Next** begin installation.

   Note: If you are using Windows Firewall your firewall will automatically be configured.
4. Enter your **serial number**.
5. Click **I Agree** from the License agreement screen.
6. Click **Next** to accept the installation location.
7. Click **Install** from the Installation Summary screen and the installation progress begins.
8. Select to **launch program** and click **Finish** from the Installation finished window to activate your software.

   Note: You must register before activating your to receive an email with your activation key code.

⊖ Step 5. Activate
You must activate your software before you can use the program.
1. Launch **Sage 50 Accounting** .
2. Click **Activate Now**.
3. Enter the **activation key code** from the registration email and click **OK** to activate your software.

By registering first, you will have the key code you need to activate the program after you finish the installation.

Registering the Student Version

Click   **Register** in **Step 2 number 1**.

> **Sage 50**
> formerly Simply Accounting
>
> www.sage.com/ca/sage-50-accounting/lp/keyregstudent
>
> ### Sage 50 Accounting—Student Version Registration
>
> Register your copy of Sage 50 Premium Accounting-Student Version (formerly Sage Simply Accounting Premium - Student Version). Sage is committed to providing students with the necessary tools to be successful in the classroom—and in the workplace!
> *Please note that if you select the wrong version, you will not be able to activate your software. If you are not sure which version you are using, right click on the logo on your desktop, view the Properties tab, and note the version information.*
>
> Product Version: *   ○ Version 2016 (Premium)
>   ○ Version 2015 (Premium)
>   ○ Version 2014 (Premium)
>   ○ Version 2013 (Premium)
>
> First Name: *
> Last Name: *
> Email Address: *   Product activation information will be sent to your email address
>
> Address: *
> Address Cont.:
> Postal Code: *
> City:
> Province: *
> Phone Number: *
> Name of school: *
> Type of school: *   [-- ▼]
>   If you selected "Other", please specify:
>
> Province in which the school is located: *   [-- ▼]
>
> City in which the school is located: *
>
> Course of study: *   [-- ▼]
>   If you selected "Other", please specify:
>
> ☐ Keep me informed about special news and offers. You can withdraw at any time.
>
> [Submit]

All fields are **required** for your registration. First you should choose the version you are registering. Several versions of Sage 50 are registered on this page, so you must choose the right one.

Click   **Version 2016 (Premium)**.

Enter   **your own first and last name** and **e-mail address** in the appropriate fields.

Enter   your **address** (**street**, **postal code**, **city** and **province**) and **phone number**.

Enter   the name of **your school**, and select the **type of school** and **province** from the drop-down lists.

Enter   the **city** your school is located in and **select** the **course of study** from the drop-down list.

Click   **Submit** when you have finished.

Sage 50 provides a message confirming the successful registration:

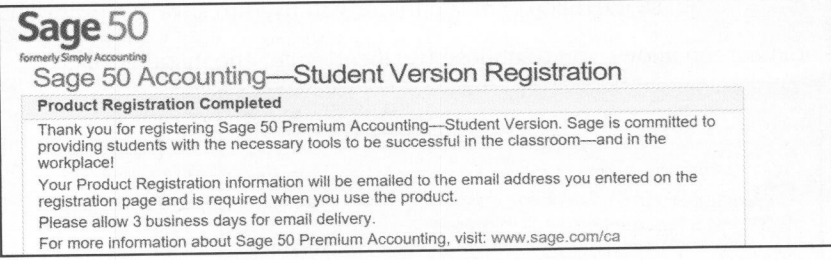

> **Sage 50**
> formerly Simply Accounting
>
> ### Sage 50 Accounting—Student Version Registration
>
> **Product Registration Completed**
>
> Thank you for registering Sage 50 Premium Accounting—Student Version. Sage is committed to providing students with the necessary tools to be successful in the classroom—and in the workplace!
>
> Your Product Registration information will be emailed to the email address you entered on the registration page and is required when you use the product.
>
> Please allow 3 business days for email delivery.
>
> For more information about Sage 50 Premium Accounting, visit: www.sage.com/ca

You should receive an e-mail shortly with your activation code. You will return to the instruction page.

Click   **2016.2** in **Step 3. Download, number 1** on the Sage Education Partner Program home page (on page A–4). This link will use the Download Manager as in the following steps.

If you get a security warning asking for permission, you should allow the program (the Download Manager) to make changes to your computer.

Next you should save the downloaded Sage 50 program. You will be asked to choose a location:

Accept   the **default location**, **choose** another **location** or **click** the **Make New Folder** option to **make** a **new folder**. We used Desktop as the location.

Click   **Save** to continue after making your choices.

Make a note of the location you selected in case you need to reinstall the program. In this way, you will not need to download the program again.

While the program is downloading, you may have a progress bar or a progress wheel like the one in the lower left-hand corner of the Google Chrome screen with Windows 10:

After the program has finished downloading, an icon has been placed on the desktop or in the folder you selected.

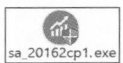

If you are viewing the folder contents in detail or list view, the program name will be **sa_20162cp1** — or **sa_20162cp1.EXE** if you show file extensions, as we do.

Installing Sage 50

Double-click   the **Sage 50 program installation icon** on your desktop, or in the lower left-hand corner of the Web page, or the program name sa_20162cp1.EXE (or sa_20162cp1) in the folder you used to save the program.

The next screen allows you to choose the location for the installer files:

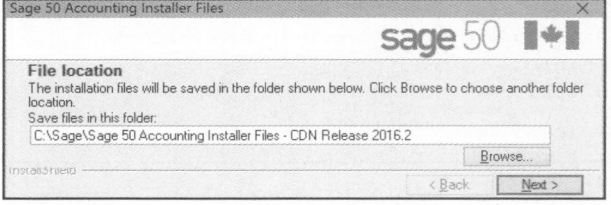

If you have any other programs running, close them before installing Sage 50.

Accept the **default** location and then **click Next** to open the Installation options:

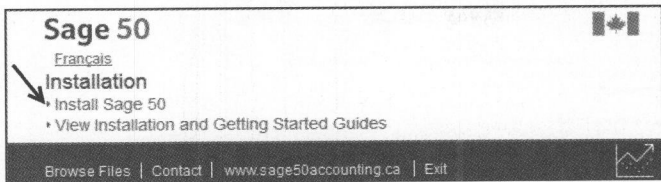

Click   **Install Sage 50**. Wait for the Select A Language To Use With This Installation screen to appear:

Click   your **language preference** from the drop-down list and **click OK**.

The next screen relates to the firewall you are using:

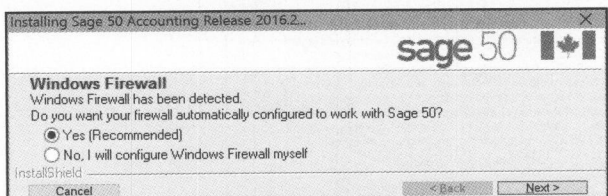

If you use the Windows Firewall, you should allow the firewall settings to be updated automatically.

Click   **Next** to continue.

If you click No, or if Windows is not your default firewall, your screen will list all the programs for which you must modify the firewall settings. We include all these programs on the following screenshot:

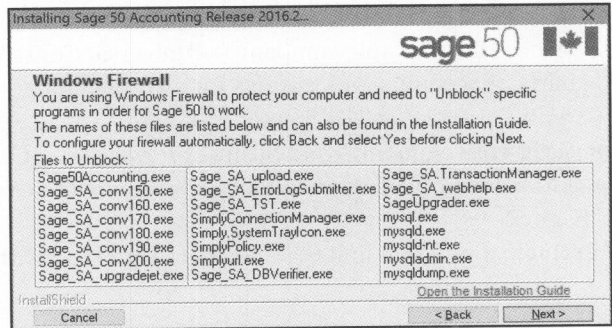

You can make a list of these programs now or view them in the Help information when you search for Firewall.

You are now ready to begin installing the program:

The default option, **Typical**, will provide all the basic components you need. You should choose the Advanced option only if you want to omit some features. Leave the

WARNING!
You must configure your firewall program to allow access to all the programs listed on this screenshot.

NOTES
If Sage 50 provides a run-time error message about the Connection Manager when you attempt to open a Sage 50 data file, you may need to start the Connection Manager program and/or configure your firewall settings manually to allow access. The programs listed are those required for Windows 10.
A complete list of the programs your firewall must not block is also available from the Help menu when you enter Firewall in the Search field (refer to Chapter 1, page 16).

default selection unchanged.

> **NOTES**
> Each copy of the retail version has a unique serial number.

    Click   **Next**. The next step requires you to enter the serial number:

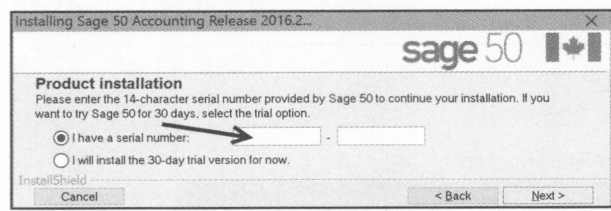

The cursor is in the Serial Number field, ready for you to enter the number.

    Type   `242P1U2-1000011` when you are prompted to enter the serial number. (This serial number applies to all copies of the Student version.)

> **NOTES**
> The retail Premium version will have Installing Sage 50 Premium Accounting Release 2016.2 in the title bar after you enter the unique serial number.

    Click   **Next** to advance to the licence agreement:

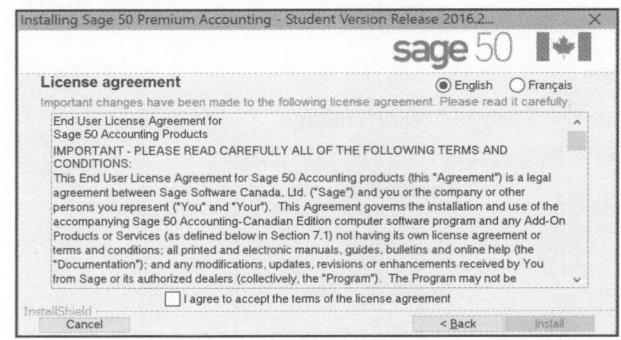

Not accepting the agreement will cancel the installation procedure. You must accept the agreement to install the program.

> **PRO VERSION**
> The title bar will have Installing Sage 50 Pro Accounting Release 2016.2 after you enter the unique serial number.

    Read   the **agreement** and **click I Agree**. Then **click Install** to continue.

By default, the program and all components will be included as follows:

> **NOTES**
> For older or 32-bit Windows programs, the Sage program will be placed in the Program Files folder.

- **Sage 50 Program**: the program that you will need to perform the accounting transactions for your company (installed to C:\Program Files (X86)\Sage\Sage 50 Premium Accounting Version 2016).
- **Sample Data**: complete records for a sample company — Universal Construction.
- **Templates**: predefined charts of accounts and settings for a large number of business types.
- **Customizable Forms**: a variety of commonly used business forms and reports.
- **Microsoft Office Documents**: a variety of Microsoft Office documents designed for integrated use with Sage 50.
- **Add-in for Microsoft Outlook**: a program link that connects your data with Microsoft Outlook.

The option to start the program is selected next:

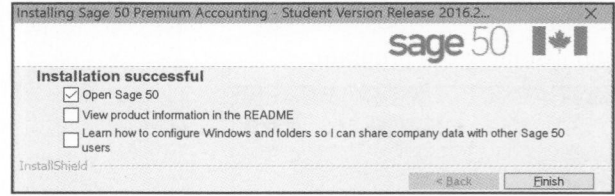

    Click   **Finish** to close this screen. **Click Exit** to close the initial installation screen.

The installation process has placed a shortcut on your desktop ![Sage 50 Premium Accounting Version 2016]. This icon is used to start the Sage 50 program.

Activating the Student Version

At this point, the Welcome page will open to allow you to continue with the activation. You must activate the Student version before you can use it — there is no trial period:

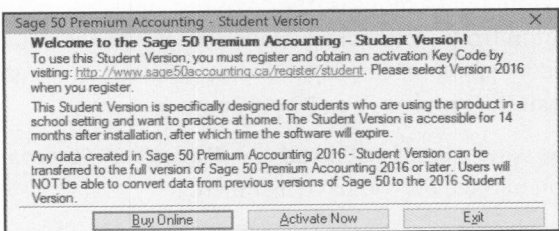

If you have not yet received the e-mail from Sage with the serial number and key code, wait for them. When they arrive, keep these numbers for reference.

If you did not complete the Registration step earlier (page A–5), click the underlined link on the Welcome screen above to open the screen on page A–5, enter the required information, submit the form, click Exit and wait for your e-mail from Sage. After you receive the codes, double-click the Sage 50 Premium icon on your desktop to open the Welcome screen again.

Write down the **23-character key code** from your e-mail message — you will enter this on the Activation screen. The name and serial number you provided are also included.

You can copy and paste the information from your e-mail into the activation fields.

Click the **Activate Now button** to open the Student Version Activation screen:

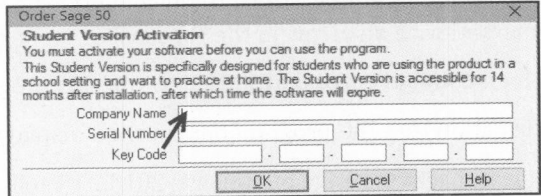

Type **your name** in the Company Name field. **Press** ⌨tab to advance to the Serial Number field.

Type 242P1U2-1000011 (This is the serial number for all copies of the Student version program.)

Press ⌨tab to advance to the **first Key Code field**.

Type the **23-character key code** from the e-mail message you received.

Click **OK**. Your Sage 50 Welcome screen opens:

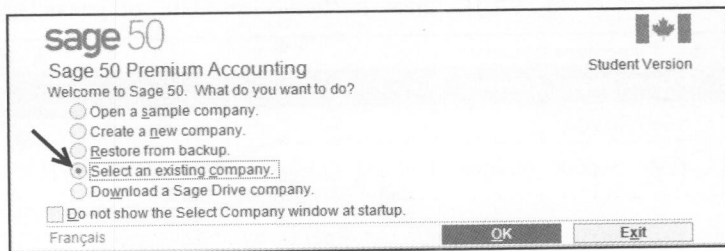

You can now use the program for 14 months.

If you do not activate the program immediately, the activation screen will open each time you start the Sage 50 program; you will be unable to open a data file.

NOTES
The activation message warns that you can use the program for only 14 months and you will not be able to open data from previous versions of Sage 50.
You do not need a payroll account or ID to use the Student version. Payroll is already unlocked or activated.

STUDENT VERSION
The Student version must be registered and activated before you can use the program. You can use the link in Step 2: Register on the Web site <sage.com/ca/about-us/education> to obtain the key code you will need to activate the Student version. Refer to page A–4.

NOTES
Instructions for starting Sage 50 are included in Chapter 1 of this text, beginning on page 8.
The retail versions can be used before activation (trial period). The message with the number of days remaining before activation is required will open each time you start the program until you have activated the program. The Student version will open with the Welcome/Activation screen on this page and you cannot continue before activating the program.

Student Version Expired Error Message

When you try to activate the Student version, Sage may generate a message that the Student version or the data has expired and you can no longer use it.

If you have not used the program for 14 months, the "expired" message may be triggered by registry file information from a previous installation. If you get this message, you may have previously installed a version of the Sage 50 program. You must uninstall that program before you can install the current Sage 50 program.

Click   **Exit** to close this window and **uninstall** the **Student 2015 version** and any other version of Sage 50 you have installed.

Use   the **Control Panel, Programs – Uninstall A Program** function to uninstall the program properly.

If you have already uninstalled all other Sage 50 programs and you still get this message when you try to activate the 2016 Student version, you will need to uninstall the 2016 Student version program. Click the **Student Version Utility** link to download StudentVerCleanUp.ZIP. Double-click the StudentVerCleanUp folder to open it, and then double-click StudentVerCleanUp.EXE to run the program and clear your registry information.

Uninstall the **Sage 50 2016 Student version program**.

Start   your **Internet connection** and **open** your **Web browser** if necessary.

Type   `na.sage.com/ca/about-us/education` in the Web address field. **Press** ⌈enter⌉.

Click   **Step 4. Install** and then **click** the **Student Version Utility program link** in the introductory paragraph of Step 4 to download this program to your desktop (marked with an arrow in the screenshot on page A–4).

Double-click the **desktop icon StudentVerCleanUp.EXE** to run this program.

Click   **OK** when the confirmation that the program has finished displays.

You should now be able to install and activate Sage 50 Release 2016.2 by following the instructions on page A–6.

Online Help for Students

Students needing help with the program should work with their instructor. Additional help for students is available online on the Sage 50 Student Forum.

Open   your **Internet browser**.

Type   `sagecity.na.sage.com` in the address bar and **press** ⌈enter⌉:

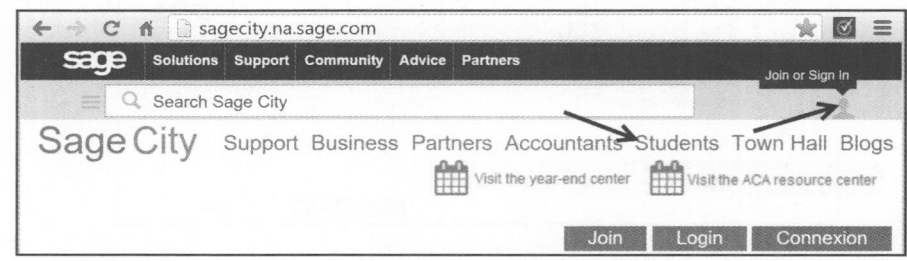

Click   **Students** in the home page header bar to access the open student site.

From this page you can access student forums, view learning videos, open the knowledge base for a variety of Sage programs, send an email to Sage and download the Sage 50 program.

Click   Forums. To continue, you must join the forum group:

Click   This Group Requires Membership For Participation - Click To Join. Or,

Click   the avatar and **Join Or Sign In**, or **click** the **Join** or the **Log On button** on the previous page.

These steps will open the Sign In page:

Enter   your email address and password and **click Sign In**.

If you are not yet a member, you must first join the forum.

Click   Join Here on the Sign In page and **complete** the **form** as instructed.

Click   Join Now to complete the registration.

Click   Forums. You now have access to additional information.

The inclusion of a link for **job opportunities** is an important addition to the SageCity, Students Web site. This link has information about job opportunities with Sage as well as jobs posted by accountants.

NOTES
Your name and e-mail address will not be displayed for other members; only your user name will appear on the screen.

Click   the **New button**:

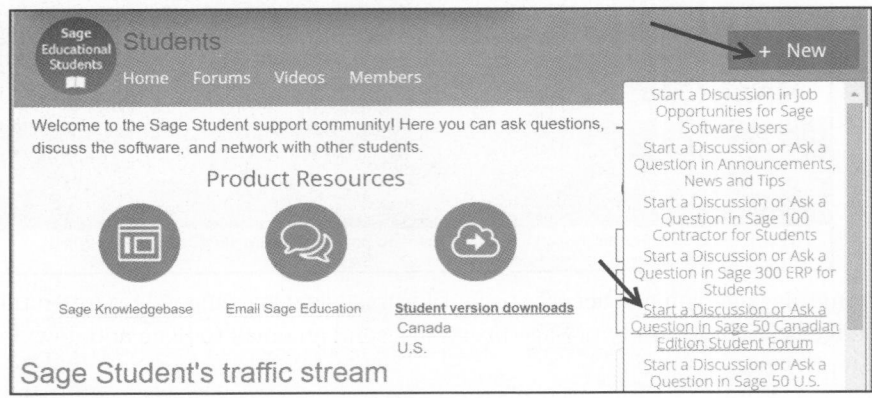

A drop-down list of Sage student forums in which you can participate appears.

Click   **Start A Discussion Or Ask A Question In Sage 50 Canadian Edition Student Forum** to continue:

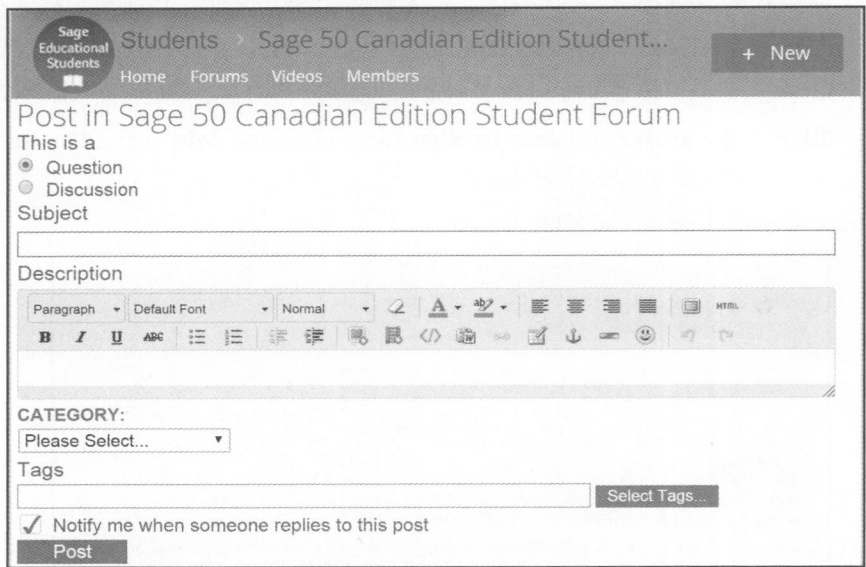

Choose   **Question** or **Discussion** to indicate which you are entering.

Type   your **question** in the Subject text box.

Provide   **additional information** in the Description text box and choose the Category that applies from the drop-down list.

Click   **Post** to submit your question.

Your question and responses to it will appear on the forum page for Sage 50 Canadian Edition with your user name, or you can choose to be notified. Your Notification icon will indicate that you have a reply.

You can also reply to discussions posted by other members.

Click   the **avatar** and **click Sign Out** to end your session:

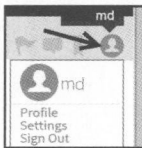

Shortcuts & Terminology

KEYBOARD SHORTCUTS

Using the Keyboard Instead of a Mouse

NOTES
The illustration in Chapter 1, page 13, shows several keyboard alternative commands in the pull-down Entry menu.

All Windows software applications are designed to be used with a mouse. However, there may be times when you prefer to use keyboard commands. And, if the mouse itself is inoperative, the keyboard alternatives may prevent you from losing data. A few basic principles will help you understand how they work. Some commands are common to more than one Windows software program. For example, ⌈ctrl⌉ + **C** (press and hold the Control key while you press C) is the copy command and ⌈ctrl⌉ + **V** is the paste command. Any selected text or image will be copied or pasted when you use these commands.

Pressing ⌈alt⌉ accesses the first menu bar item. Then press the arrow keys, ⌈↑⌉ and ⌈↓⌉, to move up and down through the pull-down menu choices of a highlighted menu item, or ⌈←⌉ and ⌈→⌉ to go back and forth to other menu items. Some menu choices have direct keyboard alternatives or shortcuts. If the menu item has an underlined letter, pressing ⌈alt⌉ together with the underlined letter will access that option directly. For example, ⌈alt⌉ + **F** (press and hold ⌈alt⌉ while you press F) accesses the File pull-down menu. Then pressing O (the underlined letter for Open) will give you the dialogue box for opening a new file. Some tool buttons and menu choices in Sage 50 have a direct keyboard command. When available, these direct keystrokes are given with the tool button name or to the right of a menu choice. For example, ⌈alt⌉ + ⌈f4⌉ is the shortcut for closing the active window or exiting from the Sage 50 program when the Home window is the active window.

To cancel a menu display, press ⌈esc⌉.

To choose or open a highlighted or selected button, press ⌈enter⌉.

When input fields are displayed in a Sage 50 window, press ⌈tab⌉ to move to the next field or ⌈shift⌉ and ⌈tab⌉ together to return to the previous field. The ⌈tab⌉ key is used frequently in this workbook as a quick way to accept input, advance the cursor to the next field and highlight field contents to prepare for editing. Using the mouse while you input information requires you to remove your hands from the keyboard, while the ⌈tab⌉ key does not.

A summary of keyboard shortcuts used in Sage 50 is included on page A–14. Additional shortcuts using more than two keys, such as ⌈ctrl⌉ + ⌈shift⌉ + **A** for Allocate, are also available. They are displayed in pull-down menus or with the tools for those commands.

NOTES
The same shortcuts in Sage 50 may have different functions, depending on the window you start from.

SUMMARY OF BASIC KEYBOARD SHORTCUTS

Shortcut	Resulting Action
ctrl + A	**Adjust,** begin the Adjust a Posted Entry function.
ctrl + B	Bring the **Home window** to the front.
ctrl + C	**Copy** the selected text.
ctrl + E	Look up the **previously posted invoice** (from a journal lookup window).
ctrl + F	**Search,** begin the search function.
ctrl + J	**Display** the **journal entry** report.
ctrl + K	**Track shipment** from a previously posted invoice lookup screen.
ctrl + L	Look up a **previously posted transaction** (from the journal window).
ctrl + N	Look up the **next posted invoice** (from a journal lookup window).
ctrl + N	Open a **new record** window (from a ledger icon or ledger record window).
ctrl + P	**Print,** open the print dialogue box.
ctrl + R	**Recall** a stored journal entry (from a journal window when an entry is stored).
ctrl + R	**Remove** the account record or remove the quote or order (from a ledger, quote or order window).
ctrl + S	Access the **Save As** function from the Home window (Home window, File menu) to save the data file under a new name. Keep the new file open.
ctrl + S	**Save** changes to a record; keep the ledger window open (from any ledger window).
ctrl + T	**Store** the current journal entry (open the Store dialogue box).
ctrl + V	**Paste** the selected text at the cursor position.
ctrl + X	**Cut** (delete) the selected text.
ctrl + Z	**Undo** the most recent change.
alt + C	**Create another** record; save the record you are creating and open a new record form to create another new record.
alt + N	**Save and close;** save the new record and close the ledger.
alt + P	**Post** the journal entry or record the order or quote.
alt + f4	**Close** the active window (if it has a close button). Close the program if the Home window is active.
alt + the underlined character on a button	**Select** the button's action. An alternative to clicking the button and/or pressing enter.
alt	Access the first item on the **menu bar.**
tab	Advance the cursor to the **next field.**
shift + tab	Move the cursor to the **previous field.**
Click	**Move** the cursor or **select** an item or entry.
shift + Click	**Select all** the items between the first item clicked and the last one.
ctrl + Click	**Select** this item **in addition** to ones previously selected.
enter	**Choose** the selected item or action.
Double-click	**Select** an entire word or field contents. In fields with lists, open the selection list.
→	**Move right** to the next icon to select it or to the next character in text.
←	**Move left** to the next icon to select it or to the next character in text.
↓	**Move down** to the next icon or entry in a list to select it.
↑	**Move up** to the previous icon or entry in a list to select it.

ACCOUNTING VS. NON-ACCOUNTING TERMS

We have used accounting terms in this workbook because they are familiar to students of accounting and because we needed to provide a consistent language for the book. The most frequently used non-accounting terms are included here for reference and comparison, in case you want to leave the non-accounting terms selected (Home window, Setup menu, User Preferences, Options screen — refer to page 80).

The chart shows the terms used for the Pro version and for the Premium version when the Other Industry type is selected. For other industries in the Premium version, the terms in the chart on page A–16 — Terminology Used for Different Types of Industries — will replace the Non-accounting Terms for Payables and Receivables. For example, the terms Providers and Expenses or Supporters and Revenues may be used. The term Suppliers generally replaces Vendors.

SUMMARY OF EQUIVALENT TERMS

MAJOR TERMS	ACCOUNTING TERMS	NON-ACCOUNTING TERMS
	Journal Entries	Transaction Details
	Payables	Vendors & Purchases
	Receivables	Customers & Sales
	Post	Process

DETAILED LIST: LOCATION	ACCOUNTING TERMS	NON-ACCOUNTING TERMS
Setup menu – Settings screen	Payables	Vendors & Purchases
	Receivables	Customers & Sales
Setup menu, User Preferences, View screen – Modules/Pages	Payables (Classic View)	Vendors & Purchases
	Receivables (Classic View)	Customers & Sales
Graphs menu	Payables	Unpaid Purchases
	Receivables	Unpaid Sales
Reports menu and Report Centre – Financials	General Ledger	Transactions by Account
Report Centre – Financials	All Journal Entries	All Transactions
Reports menu and Report Centre	Payables	Vendors & Purchases
	Receivables	Customers & Sales
Reports menu	Journal Entries	Transaction Details
Reports menu – Management Reports	Payables	Vendors & Purchases
	Receivables	Customers & Sales
All Icon window menus	Journal	Transactions
Accounts ledger window	General Ledger	Chart of Accounts Records
Vendors ledger window	Payables Ledger	Vendor Records
Customers ledger window	Receivables Ledger	Customer Records
All journals (button and menu)	Post	Process

INDUSTRY TYPES AND TERMS

In the Premium version, the terms and labels change when you select different types of industries (Setup menu, Settings, Company, Information screen — refer to pages 74–76). The chart on the following page summarizes the terms you will see when you apply different industry types. You can change the default industry terminology on the Settings, Names screens for the Payables and Receivables modules.

TERMINOLOGY USED FOR DIFFERENT TYPES OF INDUSTRIES

INDUSTRY — TERMS OR LABELS USED IN RECEIVABLES LEDGER

INDUSTRY	Customers	Sales Invoices	Sales Quotes	Sales Orders	Sales Journal – Invoice
Pro version (all)	Customers	Sales Invoices	Sales Quotes	Sales Orders	Sales Journal – Invoice
Premium Version					
Accommodation	Guests	Charges	Sales Quotes	Sales Orders	Sales Journal – Charge
Agriculture	Customers	Customer Invoices	Customer Quotes	Customer Orders	Revenues Journal – Invoice
Construction/Contractor	Customers	Bills	Estimates	Contracts	Sales Journal – Bill
Educational Service	Clients	Statements	Client Quotes	Client Orders	Fees Journal – Statement
Entertainment	Customers	Sales Invoices	Sales Quotes	Sales Orders	Sales Journal – Invoice
Food & Beverage	Guests	Charges	Sales Quotes	Sales Orders	Sales Journal – Charge
Manufacturing/Industrial	Customers	Sales Invoices	Sales Quotes	Sales Orders	Sales Journal – Invoice
Medical/Dental	Patients	Statements	Patient Quotes	Patient Orders	Fees Journal – Statement
Non-Profit	Supporters	Statements	Supporter Quotes	Supporter Orders	Revenues Journal – Statement
Other	Customers	Sales Invoices	Sales Quotes	Sales Orders	Sales Journal – Invoice
Personal Service	Clients	Client Invoices	Client Quotes	Client Orders	Revenues Journal – Invoice
Professional Service	Clients	Client Invoices	Client Quotes	Client Orders	Fees Journal – Invoice
Real Estate/Property	Clients	Statements	Client Quotes	Client Orders	Revenues Journal – Statement
Retail	Customers	Sales Invoices	Sales Quotes	Sales Orders	Sales Journal – Invoice
Service	Clients	Client Invoices	Client Quotes	Client Orders	Revenues Journal – Invoice
Transportation	Customers	Sales Invoices	Sales Quotes	Sales Orders	Sales Journal – Invoice

INDUSTRY — TERMS OR LABELS USED IN PAYABLES LEDGER

INDUSTRY	Vendors	Purchase Invoices	Purchase Quotes	Purchase Orders	Purchases Journal – Purchase Invoice
Pro version (all)	Vendors	Purchase Invoices	Purchase Quotes	Purchase Orders	Purchases Journal – Invoice
Premium Version					
Accommodation	Suppliers	Invoices	Purchase Quotes	Purchase Orders	Purchases Journal – Invoice
Agriculture	Suppliers	Purchase Invoices	Purchase Quotes	Purchase Orders	Purchases Journal – Invoice
Construction/Contractor	Suppliers	Invoices	Quotes	Orders	Purchases Journal – Invoice
Educational Service	Suppliers	Invoices	Purchase Quotes	Purchase Orders	Purchases Journal – Invoice
Entertainment	Suppliers	Supplier Invoices	Supplier Quotes	Supplier Orders	Expenses Journal – Invoice
Food & Beverage	Suppliers	Invoices	Purchase Quotes	Purchase Orders	Purchases Journal – Invoice
Manufacturing/Industrial	Suppliers	Purchase Invoices	Purchase Quotes	Purchase Orders	Purchases Journal – Invoice
Medical/Dental	Suppliers	Invoices	Supplier Quotes	Supplier Orders	Expenses Journal – Invoice
Non-Profit	Providers	Invoices	Provider Quotes	Provider Orders	Expenses Journal – Invoice
Other	Vendors	Purchase Invoices	Purchase Quotes	Purchase Orders	Purchases Journal – Invoice
Personal Service	Suppliers	Supplier Invoices	Supplier Quotes	Supplier Orders	Expenses Journal – Invoice
Professional Service	Vendors	Vendor Invoices	Vendor Quotes	Vendor Orders	Expenses Journal – Invoice
Real Estate/Property	Suppliers	Invoices	Supplier Quotes	Supplier Orders	Expenses Journal – Invoice
Retail	Suppliers	Purchase Invoices	Purchase Quotes	Purchase Orders	Purchases Journal – Invoice
Service	Suppliers	Supplier Invoices	Supplier Quotes	Supplier Orders	Expenses Journal – Invoice
Transportation	Vendors	Purchase Invoices	Purchase Quotes	Purchase Orders	Purchases Journal – Invoice

Terms for Project   Project (for Other, Service, Personal Service, Professional Service, Transportation and all industries in Pro version), Division (for Accommodation, Education, Entertainment, Food, Manufacturing and Retail), Crops (for Agriculture), Job Site (for Construction), Partner (for Medical), Fund (for Non-Profit), Property (for Real Estate)

Correcting Errors after Posting

We all make mistakes. This appendix outlines briefly the procedures you need to follow for those rare occasions when you have posted a journal entry incorrectly and you need to reverse it manually. In most cases, you can use the Adjust Journal Entry or Reverse Entry procedures to make corrections.

Obviously, you should try to detect errors before posting. Reviewing journal entries should become routine practice. The software also has built-in safeguards that help you avoid mistakes. For example, outstanding invoices cannot be overpaid, and employee wages and payroll deductions are calculated automatically. Furthermore, names of accounts, customers, vendors, employees and inventory items appear in full, so that you can check your journal information easily.

Before making a reversing entry, consider the consequences of not correcting the error. For example, misspelled customer names may not be desirable, but they will not influence the financial statements. After making the correction in the ledger, the newly printed statement will be correct (the journal will retain the original spelling). Sometimes, however, the mistake is more serious. Financial statements will be incorrect if amounts or accounts are wrong. Payroll tax deduction amounts will be incorrect if a wage amount or linked account is incorrect. GST/HST and PST remittances may be incorrect as a result of incorrect tax codes or sales or purchase amounts. Discounts will be incorrectly calculated if an invoice or payment date is incorrect. Some errors also originate from outside sources. For example, purchase items may be incorrectly priced by the vendor.

For audit purposes, prepare a memo explaining the error and the correction procedure. A complete reversing entry is often the simplest way to make the corrections for a straightforward audit trail. With the one-step reversing entry feature from the Adjust Entry or Lookup window in Sage 50, the reversing entry is made automatically. This feature is available for General Journal entries, paycheques, sales, purchases, receipts and most payments. Choose Adjust Invoice from the pull-down menu under the corresponding transaction menu, or click the Adjust Invoice tool in the journal. Then make the corrections if possible, or choose Reverse Entry from the pull-down menu under the corresponding transaction menu or click the Reverse tool. Under all circumstances, you should follow generally accepted accounting principles. Sage 50 will create the reversing entry automatically. Reports will include the correct entries after you post the adjusted journal entry. Including the original and reversing entries in reports is optional.

However, this feature is not available for all journals. And when the journal entry deposit account for a receipt is not the bank account (because the deposit was made later), you need to reverse a receipt manually to record an NSF cheque. In this appendix we will illustrate the procedure for reversing entries in all journals.

Reversing entries in all journals have several common elements. In each case, you should use an appropriate source number that identifies the entry as reversing (e.g., add ADJ or REV to the original source number). You should use the original posting date and terms, and add a comment. Make the reversing entry as illustrated on the following pages. Display the journal entry, review it carefully and,

NOTES

Adjusting entry procedures are provided on the following pages:

page 45 – General Journal
page 127 – Purchases
page 129 – Other Payments
page 137 – Payments
page 182 – Sales
page 273 – Paycheque
page 293– Payroll Run Entry
Reversing entry procedures are explained on
page 47 – General Journal
page 139 – Purchases
pages 175 and 605
            – Receipts
page 275– Payroll
page 249 – Historical
            invoices

when you are certain it is correct, post it. Next, you must enter the correct version of the transaction as a new journal entry with an appropriate identifying source number (e.g., add COR to the original source number).

Reversing entries are presented for each journal. The screenshots have only the transaction portion because the remaining parts of the journal screen do not change. The original and reversing entry screens and their corresponding journal displays are included. Explanatory notes appear beside each set of entries.

GENERAL JOURNAL

Use the same accounts and amounts in the reversing entry as in the original entry.

Accounts that were debited originally should be credited, and accounts that were credited originally should be debited.

Click the Sales Taxes button if you used this screen. Choose the tax code and, if necessary, enter the Amount Subject To Tax with a minus sign.

Repeat the allocation using the original percentages.

The General Journal display basically looks the same as the journal input form.

You can use the Adjust Entry or Reverse Entry features instead. Refer to page 45 and page 47.

PURCHASES JOURNAL

The only change you must make is that positive amounts in the original entry become negative amounts in the reversing entry (place a minus sign before the amount in the Amount field).

Similarly, negative amounts, such as for GST/HST Paid in GST/HST remittances, must be changed to positive amounts (remove the minus sign).

If freight was charged, enter the amount of freight with a minus sign.

Use the same accounts and amounts in the reversing entry as in the original entry. Tax amounts change automatically.

Repeat the allocation with the original percentages.

You can use the Adjust Invoice and Reverse Invoice options instead (page 127 and page 139). Reversing a paid invoice will generate a credit note.

Remember to "pay" the incorrect and reversing invoices to remove them from the Payments Journal and later clear them.

GENERAL JOURNAL: Original Entry

Account	Debits	Credits	Comment	Allo
1360 Paint & Supplies	200.00	--	paint supplies	
2670 GST Paid on Purchases	10.00	--	GST @ 5%	
2120 A/P - Western Sky Interic	--	210.00	terms: net 20	
Total	210.00	210.00		

Reversing Entry

Account	Debits	Credits	Comment	Allo
2120 A/P - Western Sky Interic	210.00	--	reversing A/P amount	
1360 Paint & Supplies	--	200.00	reversing supplies amount	
2670 GST Paid on Purchases	--	10.00	reversing GST amount	
Total	210.00	210.00		

PURCHASES JOURNAL (NON-INVENTORY): Original Entry

Item Number	Quantity	Order	Back Order	Unit	Item Description	Price	Tax	HST	Amount	Account	Divisions
					office repairs		H	30.00	200.00	5280 Repairs...	[Multiple Divisions]

Subtotal: 200.00
Freight:
Early Payment Terms: 1.00 % 15 Days, Net 30 Days
HST: 30.00
Total: 230.00

Purchases Journal Entry 06/07/2018 (J15)					
Account Number	Account Description	Division	Debits	Credits	Division Amt
2670	HST Paid on Purchases		30.00	-	
5280	Repairs & Maintenance		200.00	-	
		- Store Sales			160.00
		- Design			40.00
2200	Accounts Payable		-	230.00	
Additional Date:	Additional Field:		230.00	230.00	

Reversing Entry

Item Number	Quantity	Order	Back Order	Unit	Item Description	Price	Tax	HST	Amount	Account	Divisions
					reversing repairs		H	-30.00	-200.00	5280 Repairs...	[Multiple Divisions]

Subtotal: -200.00
Freight:
Early Payment Terms: 1.00 % 15 Days, Net 30 Days
HST: -30.00
Total: -230.00

Purchases Journal Entry 06/07/2018 (J16)					
Account Number	Account Description	Division	Debits	Credits	Division Amt
2200	Accounts Payable		230.00	-	
2670	HST Paid on Purchases		-	30.00	
5280	Repairs & Maintenance		-	200.00	
		- Store Sales			-160.00
		- Design			-40.00
Additional Date:	Additional Field:		230.00	230.00	

PAYMENTS JOURNAL — OTHER PAYMENTS: Original Entry

Acct	Description	Amount	Tax	HST	Allo
5290 Utilities	telephone services	210.00	H	31.50	✓

Subtotal	210.00
Tax	31.50 🔍
Total	241.50

Payments Journal Entry 06/07/2018 (J16)

Account Number	Account Description	Division	Debits	Credits	Division Amt
2670	HST Paid on Purchases		31.50	-	
5290	Utilities Expenses		210.00	-	
		- Store Sales			126.00
		- Design			63.00
		- Planting			21.00
1050	Bank: Chequing CAD		-	241.50	
Additional Date:	Additional Field:		241.50	241.50	

Reversing Entry

Acct	Description	Amount	Tax	HST	Allo
5290 Utilities	reversing telephone entry	-210.00	H	-31.50	✓

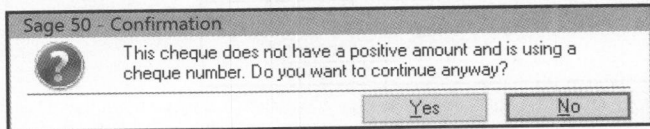

Subtotal	-210.00
Tax	-31.50 🔍
Total	-241.50

Payments Journal Entry 06/08/2018 (J18)

Account Number	Account Description	Division	Debits	Credits	Division Amt
1050	Bank: Chequing CAD		241.50	-	
2670	HST Paid on Purchases		-	31.50	
5290	Utilities Expenses		-	210.00	
		- Store Sales			-126.00
		- Design			-63.00
		- Planting			-21.00
Additional Date:	Additional Field:		241.50	241.50	

Sage 50 - Confirmation

? This cheque does not have a positive amount and is using a cheque number. Do you want to continue anyway?

[Yes] [No]

PAYROLL REMITTANCES: Original Entry

Remitting Frequency:	Monthly 🔍		End of Remitting Period:	Jun 01, 2018 📅

Remittance	Amount Owing	Payment Adjustment Account	Payment Adjustment	Payment Amount
RRSP	500.00	2400 RRSP Payable		500.00
			Total	500.00

Payments Journal Entry

		Account Number	Account Description	Debits	Credits
06/01/2018	(J18)	Memo 6, Capital Trust : RRSP remittance			
		2400	RRSP Payable	500.00	-
		2200	Accounts Payable	-	500.00
06/14/2018	(J19)	584, Capital Trust : RRSP remittance			
		2200	Accounts Payable	500.00	-
		1050	Bank: Chequing CAD	-	500.00
Additional Date:	Additional Field:			1,000.00	1,000.00

Reversing Entry

Remitting Frequency:	Monthly 🔍		End of Remitting Period:	Jun 01, 2018 📅

Remittance	Amount Owing	Payment Adjustment Account	Payment Adjustment	Payment Amount
RRSP	0.00	2400 RRSP Payable		-500.00
			Total	-500.00

OTHER PAYMENTS

The only change you must make is that positive amounts in the original entry become negative amounts in the reversing entry (place a minus sign before the amount in the Amount field).

Similarly, negative amounts, such as for GST/HST Paid in GST/HST remittances, must be changed to positive amounts (remove the minus sign).

Use the same accounts and amounts in the reversing entry as in the original entry. Tax amounts change automatically.

Repeat the allocation with the original percentages.

You can use the Adjust Invoice and Reverse Invoice options instead (page 129).

If Sage 50 generates a message about using the next cheque number with a negative amount, click No and enter a memo number or other reference in the Cheque Number field.

PAYROLL REMITTANCES

Payroll remittances are reversed in the same way as other payments. Enter the same cheque date and End Of Remitting Period date as you did for the original transaction and then enter the original amounts with a minus sign added.

Enter a memo number or other reference in the Cheque Number field to avoid using a cheque number for a negative amount.

You can also adjust and reverse these payments automatically. Open the Remittance Journal and search for the remittance you want. From the Adjust window, you can make changes or use the Reverse tool to reverse the entry completely.

PAYMENTS

Click ▦, the Include Fully Paid Invoices tool button.

The change you must make is that positive amounts in the original entry become negative amounts in the reversing entry.

If a discount was taken, click the Discount Taken field on the invoice line for the payment being reversed. Type the discount amount with a minus sign. Press `tab` to enter the payment amount. The minus sign will be added.

If no discount was taken, click the Payment Amount field on the invoice line for the payment being reversed. Type a minus sign and the amount.

Click No if Sage 50 provides the warning about posting a negative cheque amount and enter another reference number instead. This will restore the original balance owing for the invoice.

You can also use the Adjust Payment tool or the Reverse Payment feature. (Refer to page 137 and page 175.)

If you have already cleared the paid invoice, prepare a new Purchases Journal entry for the amount of the payment (non-taxable) to restore the balance owing. Enter a positive amount in the Amount field for the amount of the cheque and the Bank account in the Account field (to avoid entering the expense twice). On the next line, enter the discount amount (positive) with the Purchase Discounts account in the Account field. This will debit the Bank and Purchase Discounts accounts and credit Accounts Payable.

CREDIT CARD PAYMENTS

Enter the same amounts as in the original entry.

Add a minus sign to the Additional Fees And Interest amount and to the Payment Amount in the reversing entry.

Enter a memo number or other reference in the Cheque Number field to avoid using a cheque number for a negative amount.

Payments Journal Entry

	Account Number	Account Description	Debits	Credits
06/01/2018 (J20)		Memo 6A, Capital Trust : Reversing RRSP remittance		
	2200	Accounts Payable	500.00	-
	2400	RRSP Payable	-	500.00
06/14/2018 (J21)		584R, Capital Trust : Reversing RRSP remittance		
	1050	Bank: Chequing CAD	500.00	-
	2200	Accounts Payable	-	500.00
Additional Date:	Additional Field:		1,000.00	1,000.00

PAYMENTS: Original Entry

Due Date	Invoice or Prepayment	Original Amount	Amount Owing	Discount Available	Discount Taken	Payment Amount
Jul 31, 2018	GF-7880	460.00	460.00	13.80	13.80	446.20
					Total	446.20

Payments Journal Entry 06/04/2018 (J21)

Account Number	Account Description	Debits	Credits
2200	Accounts Payable	460.00	-
1050	Bank: Chequing CAD	-	446.20
5270	Purchase Discounts	-	13.80
Additional Date:	Additional Field:	460.00	460.00

Reversing Entry

Due Date	Invoice or Prepayment	Original Amount	Amount Owing	Discount Available	Discount Taken	Payment Amount
Jul 26, 2018	GF-1142	900.00	0.00	0.00		
Jul 31, 2018	GF-7880	460.00	0.00	0.00	-13.80	-446.20
					Total	-446.20

Payments Journal Entry 06/06/2018 (J22)

Account Number	Account Description	Debits	Credits
1050	Bank: Chequing CAD	446.20	-
5270	Purchase Discounts	13.80	-
2200	Accounts Payable	-	460.00
Additional Date:	Additional Field:	460.00	460.00

CREDIT CARD PAYMENTS: Original Entry

Credit Card Payable Account Balance:	630.00
Additional Fees and Interest:	60.00
Payment Amount:	460.00

Payments Journal Entry 06/05/2018 (J23)

Account Number	Account Description	Debits	Credits
2250	Credit Card Payable	400.00	-
5160	Credit Card Fees	60.00	-
1050	Bank: Chequing CAD	-	460.00
Additional Date:	Additional Field:	460.00	460.00

Reversing Entry

Credit Card Payable Account Balance:	230.00
Additional Fees and Interest:	-60.00
Payment Amount:	-460.00

Payments Journal Entry 06/05/2018 (J24)

Account Number	Account Description	Debits	Credits
1050	Bank: Chequing CAD	460.00	-
2250	Credit Card Payable	-	400.00
5160	Credit Card Fees	-	60.00
Additional Date:	Additional Field:	460.00	460.00

INVENTORY PURCHASES: Original Entry

Item Number	Quantity	Order	Back Order	Unit	Item Description	Price	Tax	HST	Amount	Account	Divisions
PL06	20			each	Plant: annual 15 cm	9.00	H	27.00	180.00	1360 Plants ...	
PS10	20			bag	Topsoil: 50 litre bag	4.00	H	12.00	80.00	1360 Plants ...	

Subtotal: 260.00
Early Payment Terms: ___ % ___ Days, Net 60 Days
Freight: 50.00 H   7.50 ✓
HST: 46.50
Total: 356.50

Purchases Journal Entry 06/07/2018 (J25)

Account Number	Account Description	Division	Debits	Credits	Division Amt.
1360	Plants and Soil		260.00	-	
2670	HST Paid on Purchases		46.50	-	
5100	Freight Expense		50.00	-	
		- Planting			50.00
2200	Accounts Payable		-	356.50	
Additional Date:	Additional Field:		356.50	356.50	

Reversing Entry

Item Number	Quantity	Order	Back Order	Unit	Item Description	Price	Tax	HST	Amount	Account	Divisions
PL06	-20			each	Plant: annual 15 cm	9.00	H	-27.00	-180.00	1360 Plants ...	
PS10	-20			bag	Topsoil: 50 litre bag	4.00	H	-12.00	-80.00	1360 Plants ...	

Subtotal: -260.00
Early Payment Terms: ___ % ___ Days, Net 60 Days
Freight: -50.00 H   -7.50 ✓
HST: -46.50
Total: -356.50

Purchases Journal Entry 06/09/2018 (J26)

Account Number	Account Description	Division	Debits	Credits	Division Amt.
2200	Accounts Payable		356.50	-	
1360	Plants and Soil		-	260.00	
2670	HST Paid on Purchases		-	46.50	
5100	Freight Expense		-	50.00	
		- Planting			-50.00
Additional Date:	Additional Field:		356.50	356.50	

SALES JOURNAL (INVENTORY AND NON-INVENTORY): Original Entry

Item Number	Quantity	Order	Back Order	Unit	Item Description	Price	Amount	Tax	Account	Divisions
FA06	2			each	End table: Cast Aluminum	95.00	190.00	H	4020 Revenue ...	Store Sales
FA07	2			each	Bench: Cast Aluminum	185.00	370.00	H	4020 Revenue ...	Store Sales
					custom design work		400.00	H	4040 Revenue ...	Design

Subtotal: 960.00
Early Payment Terms: 2.00 % 15 Days, Net 30 Days
Freight: 100.00 H   15.00 ✓
HST: 159.00
Total: 1,219.00

Sales Journal Entry 06/06/2018 (J27)

Account Number	Account Description	Division	Debits	Credits	Division Amt.
1200	Accounts Receivable		1,219.00	-	
5070	Cost of Goods Sold		440.00	-	
		- Store Sales			440.00
1400	Patio Furniture		-	440.00	
2650	HST Charged on Sales		-	159.00	
4020	Revenue from Store Sales		-	560.00	
		- Store Sales			560.00
4040	Revenue from Services		-	400.00	
		- Design			400.00
4100	Revenue from Delivery		-	100.00	
		- Store Sales			100.00
Additional Date:	Additional Field:		1,659.00	1,659.00	

INVENTORY PURCHASES

Change positive quantities in the original entry to negative ones in the reversing entry (place a minus sign before the quantity in the Quantity field).

Similarly, change negative quantities, such as for returns, to positive ones (remove the minus sign).

Add a minus sign to the freight amount if freight is charged.

Use the same accounts and amounts in the reversing entry as in the original entry. Tax amounts are corrected automatically.

Repeat the allocation using the original percentages.

You can use the Adjust Invoice and Reverse Invoice options instead (page 127 and page 139).

Remember to "pay" the incorrect and reversing invoices to remove them from the Payments Journal and later clear them.

SALES JOURNAL

For inventory sales, change positive quantities in the original entry to negative ones in the reversing entry (place a minus sign before the quantity in the Quantity field). Similarly, change negative quantities, such as for returns, to positive ones (remove the minus sign).

For non-inventory sales, change positive amounts in the original entry to negative amounts in the reversing entry (place a minus sign before the amount in the Amount column).

Add a minus sign to the freight amount if freight is charged. Add the salesperson.

Use the same accounts and amounts in the reversing entry as in the original entry, and the same method of payment.

Repeat the allocation using the original percentages.

You can use the Adjust Invoice and Reverse Invoice options instead (page 182). Reversing a paid invoice will generate a credit note.

Remember to "pay" the incorrect and reversing invoices to remove them from the Receipts Journal and later clear them.

Reversing Entry

Item Number	Quantity	Order	Back Order	Unit	Item Description	Price	Amount	Tax	Account	Divisions
FA06	-2			each	End table: Cast Aluminum	95.00	-190.00	H	4020 Revenue...	Store Sales
FA07	-2			each	Bench: Cast Aluminum	185.00	-370.00	H	4020 Revenue...	Store Sales
					reverse design charge		-400.00	H	4040 Revenue...	Design

Subtotal: -960.00
Freight: -100.00 H   -15.00
Early Payment Terms: 2.00 % 15 Days, Net 30 Days   HST: -159.00
Total: -1,219.00

Sales Journal Entry 06/09/2018 (J28)

Account Number	Account Description	Division	Debits	Credits	Division Amt
1400	Patio Furniture		440.00	-	
2650	HST Charged on Sales		159.00	-	
4020	Revenue from Store Sales		560.00	-	
		- Store Sales			-560.00
4040	Revenue from Services		400.00		
		- Design			-400.00
4100	Revenue from Delivery		100.00		
		- Store Sales			-100.00
1200	Accounts Receivable		-	1,219.00	
5070	Cost of Goods Sold		-	440.00	
		- Store Sales			-440.00
Additional Date:	Additional Field:		1,659.00	1,659.00	

NOTES
The Cost of Goods Sold amounts may have changed if you are using the average cost method and other transactions with different prices have taken place since the original sale. You cannot edit these amounts in the Sales Journal.

DEPOSITS or PREPAYMENTS: Original Entry

Invoice Date	Invoice or Deposit	Original Amount	Amount Owing	Discount Available	Discount Taken	Amount Received
Jun 09, 2018	170	2,438.00	2,438.00	42.40		

Deposit Reference No. 81   Deposit Amount 1,200.00
Total 1,200.00

DEPOSITS
You cannot enter a negative amount in the Deposit field, so you must "pay" the deposit.
Click the Payment Amount field for the Deposit line and press `tab`. Deposit amounts are included in red type under the heading Deposits.

Receipts Journal Entry 06/09/2018 (J30)

Account Number	Account Description	Debits	Credits
1050	Bank: Chequing CAD	1,200.00	-
2150	Prepaid Sales and Deposits	-	1,200.00
Additional Date:	Additional Field:	1,200.00	1,200.00

Reversing Entry

Invoice Date	Invoice or Deposit	Original Amount	Amount Owing	Discount Available	Discount Taken	Amount Received
Jun 09, 2018	170	2,438.00	2,438.00	42.40		
	Deposits					
	81	1,200.00	1,200.00			1,200.00

Deposit Reference No. 81-REV   Deposit Amount 0.00
Total -1,200.00

Receipts Journal Entry 06/09/2018 (J31)

Account Number	Account Description	Debits	Credits
2150	Prepaid Sales and Deposits	1,200.00	-
1050	Bank: Chequing CAD	-	1,200.00
Additional Date:	Additional Field:	1,200.00	1,200.00

NOTES
When you post the transaction, you will be asked to confirm that you want to make the payment to the customer — you are returning the deposit. Click Yes to continue.

Sage 50 - Confirmation
The total of the deposits being used is more than the total of the invoices being paid. This means that you are about to give the difference back to the customer in cash. Do you want to continue?

Yes   No

RECEIPTS WITH DEPOSITS: Original Entry

Invoice Date	Invoice or Deposit	Original Amount	Amount Owing	Discount Available	Discount Taken	Amount Received
Jun 09, 2018	170	2,438.00	2,438.00	42.40	42.40	2,395.60
	Deposits					
	82	1,100.00	1,100.00			1,100.00

Deposit Reference No.	83		Deposit Amount	0.00
			Total	1,295.60

Receipts Journal Entry 06/11/2018 (J33)

Account Number	Account Description	Debits	Credits
1050	Bank: Chequing CAD	1,295.60	-
2150	Prepaid Sales and Deposits	1,100.00	-
4150	Sales Discounts	42.40	-
1200	Accounts Receivable	-	2,438.00
Additional Date:	Additional Field:	2,438.00	2,438.00

Reversing Entry

Invoice Date	Invoice or Deposit	Original Amount	Amount Owing	Discount Available	Discount Taken	Amount Received
Jun 09, 2018	170	2,438.00	0.00	0.00	-42.40	-2,395.60
	Deposits					
	82	1,100.00	0.00			-1,100.00

Deposit Reference No.	82-REV		Deposit Amount	0.00
			Total	-1,295.60

Receipts Journal Entry 06/11/2018 (J34)

Account Number	Account Description	Debits	Credits
1200	Accounts Receivable	2,438.00	-
1050	Bank: Chequing CAD	-	1,295.60
2150	Prepaid Sales and Deposits	-	1,100.00
4150	Sales Discounts	-	42.40
Additional Date:	Additional Field:	2,438.00	2,438.00

PAYROLL JOURNAL: Original Income Tab Entry

Earnings	Hours	Pieces	Rate	This Period	Year to Date		Other Amounts	This Period	Year to Date
Regular	75.00	--	20.00	1,500.00	19,000.00		Advances	0.00	--
Overtime 1	4.00	--	30.00	120.00	720.00		Loans	100.00	100.00
Plantings	--	200.00	0.50	100.00	525.00		Benefits	50.00	50.00
Bonus	--	--	--	100.00	100.00				
Tuition	--	--	--	100.00	700.00				
Total:	79.00	200.00		1,920.00			Total:	150.00	

Income | Vacation | Deductions | Taxes | User-Defined Expenses | Entitlements — How do I process a paycheque?

Gross Pay: 1,970.00
Withheld: 476.39
Net Pay: **1,543.61**   Post ▾

Reversing Income Tab Amounts

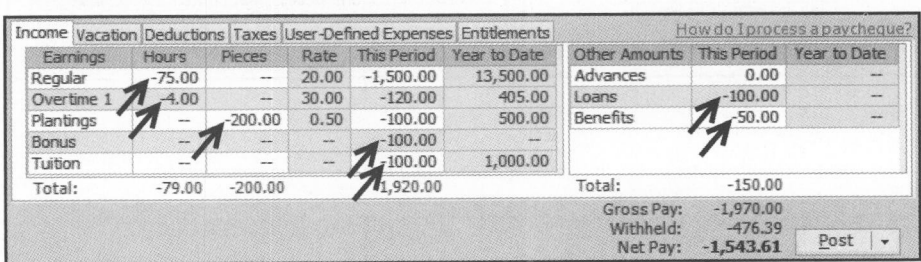

Earnings	Hours	Pieces	Rate	This Period	Year to Date		Other Amounts	This Period	Year to Date
Regular	-75.00	--	20.00	-1,500.00	13,500.00		Advances	0.00	--
Overtime 1	-4.00	--	30.00	-120.00	405.00		Loans	-100.00	--
Plantings	--	-200.00	0.50	-100.00	500.00		Benefits	-50.00	--
Bonus	--	--	--	-100.00	--				
Tuition	--	--	--	-100.00	1,000.00				
Total:	-79.00	-200.00		-1,920.00			Total:	-150.00	

Income | Vacation | Deductions | Taxes | User-Defined Expenses | Entitlements — How do I process a paycheque?

Gross Pay: -1,970.00
Withheld: -476.39
Net Pay: **-1,543.61**   Post ▾

RECEIPTS

Click 🗎, the Include Fully Paid Invoices tool.

Change positive amounts in the original entry to negative amounts in the reversing entry.

If a discount was taken, click the Discount Taken field on the invoice line for the receipt being reversed. Type the discount amount with a minus sign. Press tab to enter the payment amount. The minus sign will be added. Type a minus sign and enter the amount for the deposit.

If no discount was taken, click the Amount Received field on the invoice line for the receipt being reversed. Type a minus sign with the invoice receipt amount and with the deposit amount.

This will restore the original balance owing for the invoice, including the deposit.

You can use the Adjust Receipt and Reverse Receipt options instead (page 175).

If an NSF cheque uses a different bank account from the deposit entry, you must reverse the receipt manually. Choose the Bank account in the Deposit To field (page 605).

If you have already cleared the invoice, make a new Sales Journal entry for the payment amount (non-taxable) to restore the balance owing. Enter both the cheque and discount amounts as positive amounts and enter the Bank and Sales Discounts accounts instead of Revenue. Enter any deposit amounts as negative using the Prepayments linked account to create a debit entry and restore the deposit.

PAYROLL JOURNAL

Redo the original incorrect entry but DO NOT POST IT!

Click the Enter Taxes Manually tool to open all the deduction fields for editing.

Type a minus sign in front of the number of hours (regular and overtime) or in front of salary, commission and bonus amounts and piece rate quantity. Press tab to update all amounts, including vacation pay (change them to negative amounts). ▶

▶For the Advances and Loans fields, change the sign for the amount. Advances and loans should have a minus sign in the reversing entry and advances and loans recovered should be positive amounts.

Add a minus sign to the Benefits amount.

Click the Deductions tab and edit each deduction amount by typing a minus sign in front of it.

Click the Taxes tab. Check the amounts for CPP, EI and Tax with the original journal entry because these amounts may be incorrect (the employee may have reached the maximum contribution since the original entry or may have entered a different tax bracket). Change the amounts to match the original entry if necessary. The Employee Detail Report will provide the amounts entered for each paycheque.

Click the User-Defined Expenses tab. Change the original positive amounts to negative amounts by adding a minus sign.

Click the Entitlements tab. Add a minus sign to the number of hours worked. You cannot enter a negative number for Days Taken and earned. Add the number of days taken to the Days Earned amount. Add the number of days earned to the Days Taken amount.

Repeat the allocation with the original percentages and post.

Remember to click the Calculate Taxes Automatically button before you make the correct payroll entry.

The year-to-date balances will be restored.

You can use the Adjust Cheque option or Reverse Cheque instead to reverse and correct the Paycheque or Payroll Run journal entry (refer to page 273 and page 293). Using the reverse cheque approach may be safer, as payroll transactions are complex.

Enter a memo number or other reference in the Cheque or Deposit Number field to avoid using a cheque number for a negative amount.

Original Payroll Vacation Tab Entry

Income	Vacation	Deductions	Taxes	User-Defined Expenses	Entitlements			How do I process a paycheque?

	This Period		Year to Date		
Type	Hours	Amount	Hours	Amount	
Balance Forward (as of Jan 01, 2018)	--	--	--	--	
Vacation Earned	--	103.20	--	1,014.70	
Vacation Paid *	0.00	0.00	--	--	* These hours are recorded as EI Insurable Hours
Vacation Owed	--	--	--	1,014.70	

Reversing Vacation Tab Amounts

Income	Vacation	Deductions	Taxes	User-Defined Expenses	Entitlements			How do I process a paycheque?

	This Period		Year to Date		
Type	Hours	Amount	Hours	Amount	
Balance Forward (as of Jan 01, 2018)	--	--	--	--	
Vacation Earned	--	-103.20	--	808.30	
Vacation Paid *	0.00	0.00	--	--	* These hours are recorded as EI Insurable Hours
Vacation Owed	--	--	--	808.30	

Original Entries for Deductions and Taxes Tabs

Income	Vacation	Deductions	Taxes	User-Defined Expenses	Entitlements

Deduction	This Period	Year to Date
RRSP	50.00	600.00
Union Dues	15.37	164.54
Total:	65.37	

Income	Vacation	Deductions	Taxes	User-Defined Expenses	Entitlements

Tax	This Period	Year to Date
CPP	90.85	857.62
EI	34.22	382.49
Tax	285.95	2,469.83
Total:	411.02	

Reversing Amounts for Deductions and Taxes Tabs

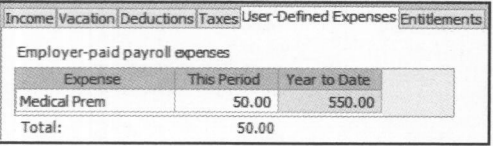

Income	Vacation	Deductions	Taxes	User-Defined Expenses	Entitlements

Deduction	This Period	Year to Date
RRSP	-50.00	500.00
Union Dues	-15.37	133.80
Total:	-65.37	

Income	Vacation	Deductions	Taxes	User-Defined Expenses	Entitlements

Tax	This Period	Year to Date
CPP	-90.85	675.92
EI	-34.22	314.05
Tax	-285.95	1,897.93
Total:	-411.02	

Original Entries for User-Defined Expenses and Entitlements Tabs

Income	Vacation	Deductions	Taxes	User-Defined Expenses	Entitlements

Employer-paid payroll expenses

Expense	This Period	Year to Date
Medical Prem	50.00	550.00
Total:	50.00	

Income	Vacation	Deductions	Taxes	User-Defined Expenses	Entitlements

Hours worked this period: 75.00

Entitlement	Days Earned	Days Taken	Net Days Accrued
Vacation	0.00	0.00	0.00
Sick Days	0.50	1.00	6.50
PersonalDays	0.25	1.00	3.25

Reversing Amounts for User-Defined Expenses and Entitlements Tabs

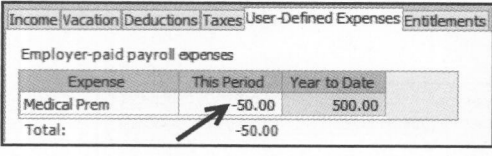

Income	Vacation	Deductions	Taxes	User-Defined Expenses	Entitlements

Employer-paid payroll expenses

Expense	This Period	Year to Date
Medical Prem	-50.00	500.00
Total:	-50.00	

Income	Vacation	Deductions	Taxes	User-Defined Expenses	Entitlements

Hours worked this period: -75.00

Entitlement	Days Earned	Days Taken	Net Days Accrued
Vacation	0.00	0.00	0.00
Sick Days	1.00	0.50	7.00
PersonalDays	1.00	0.25	4.00

Original Payroll Journal Entry

Payroll Journal Entry 06/14/2018 (J35)

Account Number	Account Description	Debits	Credits
1230	Advances & Loans Receivable	100.00	-
5450	Vacation Pay Expense	103.20	-
5470	General Wages	1,620.00	-
5480	Piece Rate Wage Expense	100.00	-
5490	Commissions and Bonuses	100.00	-
5500	Tuition Expense	100.00	-
5510	EI Expense	47.91	-
5520	CPP Expense	90.85	-
5530	WCB Expense	97.13	-
5550	Medical Expense	50.00	-
1050	Bank: Chequing CAD	-	1,543.61
2300	Vacation Payable	-	103.20
2310	EI Payable	-	82.13
2320	CPP Payable	-	181.70
2330	Income Tax Payable	-	285.95
2400	RRSP Payable	-	50.00
2420	Union Dues Payable	-	15.37
2450	Medical Payable	-	50.00
2460	WCB Payable	-	97.13
Additional Date:	Additional Field:	2,409.09	2,409.09

Reversing Payroll Journal Entry

Payroll Journal Entry 06/14/2018 (J36)

Account Number	Account Description	Debits	Credits
1050	Bank: Chequing CAD	1,543.61	-
2300	Vacation Payable	103.20	-
2310	EI Payable	82.13	-
2320	CPP Payable	181.70	-
2330	Income Tax Payable	285.95	-
2400	RRSP Payable	50.00	-
2420	Union Dues Payable	15.37	-
2450	Medical Payable	50.00	-
2460	WCB Payable	97.13	-
1230	Advances & Loans Receivable	-	100.00
5450	Vacation Pay Expense	-	103.20
5470	General Wages	-	1,620.00
5480	Piece Rate Wage Expense	-	100.00
5490	Commissions and Bonuses	-	100.00
5500	Tuition Expense	-	100.00
5510	EI Expense	-	47.91
5520	CPP Expense	-	90.85
5530	WCB Expense	-	97.13
5550	Medical Expense	-	50.00
Additional Date:	Additional Field:	2,409.09	2,409.09

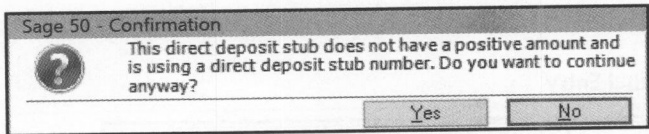

Sage 50 - Confirmation

This direct deposit stub does not have a positive amount and is using a direct deposit stub number. Do you want to continue anyway?

| Yes | No |

NOTES

When you are reversing a payroll entry, you must confirm that you are using a cheque or direct deposit number for a negative amount.

Click No. Enter a memo number or other reference in the Cheque or Deposit Number field instead.

ITEM ASSEMBLY JOURNAL

Re-enter the assembly as you did originally.

Type a minus sign in front of each quantity in the Qty field in both the Assembly Components and Assembled Items sections.

Also type a minus sign in front of the amount for Additional Costs.

If you know the original unit costs and they have changed, you can enter the cost amounts from the original item assembly in the reversing entry.

ITEM ASSEMBLY JOURNAL: Original Entry

Assembly Components

Item	Qty	Unit	Description	Unit Cost	Amount
SH01	20	each	Shrubs: 50 cm	6.00	120.00
PL06	20	each	Plant: annual 15 cm	9.00	180.00
				Additional Costs	200.00
				Total	500.00

Assembled Items

Item	Qty	Unit	Description	Unit Cost	Amount
S100	10	Each	Planting Special	50.00	500.00
				Total	500.00

Bill of Materials & Item Assembly Journal Entry 06/13/2018 (J38)

Account Number	Account Description	Debits	Credits
1510	Promotions	500.00	-
1360	Plants and Soil	-	180.00
1380	Shrubs	-	120.00
5060	Assembly Costs	-	200.00
Additional Date:	Additional Field:	500.00	500.00

Reversing Entry

Assembly Components

Item	Qty	Unit	Description	Unit Cost	Amount
SH01	-20	each	Shrubs: 50 cm	6.00	-120.00
PL06	-20	each	Plant: annual 15 cm	9.00	-180.00
				Additional Costs	-200.00
				Total	-500.00

Assembled Items

Item	Qty	Unit	Description	Unit Cost	Amount
S100	-10	Each	Planting Special	50.00	-500.00
				Total	-500.00

Bill of Materials & Item Assembly Journal Entry 06/14/2018 (J39)

Account Number	Account Description	Debits	Credits
1360	Plants and Soil	180.00	-
1380	Shrubs	120.00	-
5060	Assembly Costs	200.00	-
1510	Promotions	-	500.00
Additional Date:	Additional Field:	500.00	500.00

ADJUSTMENTS JOURNAL

Change the sign for the quantity in the Qty field (positive to negative or negative to positive).

If you know the original unit costs and they have changed, you can enter the cost amounts from the original adjustments entry in the reversing entry.

Repeat the allocation using the original percentages.

ADJUSTMENTS JOURNAL: Original Entry

Item	Qty	Unit	Description	Unit Cost	Amount	Acct	Allo
PL01	-12	each	Plant/ground cover: 5 l	10.00	-120.00	5110 Inventory Losses	√
				Total	-120.00		

Inventory Adjustments Journal Entry 06/14/2018 (J40)

Account Number	Account Description	Division	Debits	Credits	Division Amt.
5110	Inventory Losses	- Planting	120.00	-	120.00
1360	Plants and Soil		-	120.00	
Additional Date:	Additional Field:		120.00	120.00	

Reversing Entry

Item	Qty	Unit	Description	Unit Cost	Amount	Acct	Allo
PL01	12	each	Plant/ground cover: 5 l	10.00	120.00	5110 Inventory Losses	√
				Total	120.00		

Inventory Adjustments Journal Entry 06/14/2018 (J41)

Account Number	Account Description	Division	Debits	Credits	Division Amt.
1360	Plants and Soil		120.00	-	
5110	Inventory Losses	- Planting	-	120.00	-120.00
Additional Date:	Additional Field:		120.00	120.00	

TRANSFER FUNDS JOURNAL: Original Entry

Currency:	DKK ▼ Exchange Rate: 0.2000000
Transfer from:	1050 Bank: Chequing CAD
Transfer to:	1060 Bank Account: DKK
Amount:	10,000.00 **DKK**
Comment:	Transfer funds to cover payments

Reversing Entry

Currency:	DKK ▼ Exchange Rate: 0.2000000
Transfer from:	1060 Bank Account: DKK
Transfer to:	1050 Bank: Chequing CAD
Amount:	10,000.00 **DKK**
Comment:	Reversing funds transfer

General Journal 06/14/2018 to 06/14/2018

Account Number	Account Description	Debits	Credits	Foreign A...
06/14/2018 J42 FundsTransfer, Transfer funds to cover payments				
1060	Bank Account: DKK	2,000.00	-	Dkr10.000,00
1050	Bank: Chequing CAD	-	2,000.00	Dkr10.000,00
1 Danish Kroners equals 0.2000000 Canadian Dollars				
06/14/2018 J43 FundsTransfer, Reversing funds transfer				
1050	Bank: Chequing CAD	2,000.00	-	Dkr10.000,00
1060	Bank Account: DKK	-	2,000.00	Dkr10.000,00
1 Danish Kroners equals 0.2000000 Canadian Dollars		4,000.00	4,000.00	

TRANSFER INVENTORY JOURNAL: Original Entry

Transfer between Locations ▼   From VeloCity ▼   to Ryder ▼
Source: Memo 22   Date: Aug 14, 2018
Comment: Transfer inventory to create extra packages

Item	Qty	Unit	Description	Unit Cost	Amount
AC010	5	unit	Bicycle Pump: standing model	30.00	150.00
BK010	20	book	Books: Complete Bicycle Guide	20.00	400.00

Reversing Entry

Transfer between Locations ▼   From Ryder ▼   to VeloCity ▼
Source: Memo 23   Date: Aug 14, 2018
Comment: Reverse inventory transfer

Item	Qty	Unit	Description	Unit Cost	Amount
AC010	5	unit	Bicycle Pump: standing model	30.00	150.00
BK010	20	book	Books: Complete Bicycle Guide	20.00	400.00

NOTES

In this example the positive amount is associated with the recovery of losses.

TRANSFER FUNDS JOURNAL

The easiest way to reverse the transfer is to enter the same amounts but switch the bank accounts. Enter the original Transfer From account in the Transfer To field. Enter the original Transfer To account in the Transfer From field.

There is no journal entry to review. The reversal will be part of the General Journal Report. Our screenshot has the two related General Journal Report entries.

For foreign currency transfers, use the same exchange rate for both the original and the reversing transfer.

You can also use the Adjust Entry or Reverse Entry procedure for the transfer in the General Journal. When you look up transactions, the transfer entry is included. You can select it and then adjust it or reverse it like any other General Journal transaction (refer to page 45 and page 47).

TRANSFER INVENTORY JOURNAL

You cannot enter a negative quantity in the Transfer Inventory Journal.

Enter the transaction in the same way as the original one with one change — switch the locations for the From and To fields. Enter the original From location in the To field and the original To location in the From field.

No journal entry results from this transaction. However, the inventory ledger records will be updated for both locations.

If costs have changed, you can enter the costs from the original transfer entry if you know them.

BILL OF MATERIALS JOURNAL

Change the sign for the quantity in the Quantity To Build field (positive to negative or negative to positive).

Notice that the journal entries are the same as those for the Item Assembly Journal transactions on page A–26.

Costs may have changed since you entered the original transaction when you are using the average cost of goods method. You cannot change the unit costs in the Bill of Materials method.

BILL OF MATERIALS JOURNAL: Original Entry

Items to Build

Item	Unit	Description	Quantity to build
AP100	package	Promotional Safety Package with Bike	3

Bill of Materials & Item Assembly Journal Entry 08/14/2018 (J14)

Account Number	Account Description	Debits	Credits
1510	Promotions	2,051.45	-
1520	Accessories	-	671.45
1540	Bicycles	-	930.00
5045	Item Assembly Costs	-	450.00
Additional Date:	Ref. Number:	2,051.45	2,051.45

Reversing Entry

Items to Build

Item	Unit	Description	Quantity to build
AP100	package	Promotional Safety Package with Bike	-3

Bill of Materials & Item Assembly Journal Entry 08/14/2018 (J15)

Account Number	Account Description	Debits	Credits
1520	Accessories	671.45	-
1540	Bicycles	930.00	-
5045	Item Assembly Costs	450.00	-
1510	Promotions	-	2,051.45
Additional Date:	Ref. Number:	2,051.45	2,051.45

A

abbreviations, 2, 75
Able & Associates Inc.
    accounting procedures, 788
    client records, adding departments to,
        795–796
    company information, 785–788
    department reports, 804–806
    discounts for early payments, 788
    instructions, 788
    opening departmental balances, 792–794
    questions and cases, A–72 – A–73
    setting up departments, 789–791
access rights, 688, 689
accommodation business, 710
    see also Stratford Country Inn
account balances
    historical account balances, 92–95, 641–642
    opening balance, 92, 217, 792–794
    opening departmental balances, 792–794
    Test Balance Account, 217
account classes
    bank accounts, 218–220, 221
    credit card accounts, 219
    default selection, 44, 92
    defining, 642
    expense accounts, 219–220
    generally, 218
    Gross Margin Income Statement, 396–397
    recording changes in, 219
account groups, 86
account input fields, 80
Account List, 60–61
Account List Report, 61
account numbers
    adding from Setup Guide, 91
    changing account numbers, 95
    changing after posting, 44
    expanded account numbering, 215, 225
    extra digits, use of, 80
    four-digit account numbers, 39
    no number entered, 91
    number of digits, 79
    Numbering option, 79
    in Premium version, 39
    in Pro version, 79
account reconciliation
    Account Reconciliation Journal, 590–599
    bank statement reconciliation, 588–598
    cheque number as source code for cash
        expenses and revenues, 76–77
    clearing account reconciliation data, 614–615
    credit card accounts, 599
    generally, 585
    linking reconciliation accounts, 586–588

naming reconciliation accounts, 586–588
online reconciliation, 579, 585
turning on feature, 585–586
Account Reconciliation Journal, 590–599, 609–610
Account Reconciliation Report, 610–611
Account reports, 54
    see also general reports
Accountant Edition, 487, 803
accountants, 491
accountant's copy, 487–488
accountant's journal entries, 491–493
accounting
    accounting terms, 80, A–15
    accounting transactions, summary of, A–236
    accrual-basis accounting, 76, A–234 – A–235
    basic accounting, review of, A–225 – A–236
    cash-basis accounting, 76, A–117 – A–140,
        A–234 – A–235
    generally accepted accounting principles
        (GAAP), A–232 – A–234
accounting entity, A–232
accounts
    see also Chart of Accounts; specific accounts
    account classes. See account classes
    account numbers. See account numbers
    account types, 44, 84
    Add an Account wizard, 221, 222, 681
    allocation of balance, 45
    Check Validity of Accounts tool, 90
    departments, adding, 791
    editing from Accounts window, 90
    financial statement, omission from, 45
    historical account balances, 92–95
    new accounts. See new accounts
    organization of accounts, 39, 84, 85
    postable accounts, 86
    preset accounts, 90
    record balances, 80
    removal, if linked, 226
    Skeleton accounts, 87
    zero balances, 45
Accounts Ledger, 43
Accounts window, 89–91
Accounts window reports menu, 54
accrual-basis accounting, 76, A–234 – A–235
activation of program, A–3 – A–4, A–9 – A–12
Activity Time and Billing Payroll Reports, 782
Activity Time and Billing Reports, 779–780
Add An Account wizard, 221, 222, 587, 681
Add Users wizard, A–100 – A–104
adjusting entries. See adjustments
Adjusting General Journal screen, 47
adjustments
    see also corrections; corrections after posting;
        corrections before posting; reversals
    bad debts, 633–634
    and Balance Sheet, 100
    cash purchases, 127, 138
    closing adjusting entries, 100–101
    corrections after posting, A–26 – A–27
    and Income Statement, 100
    inventory adjustments, 366–368
    payroll, 281, 284
    payroll entries, 273–275
    payroll remittances, 280, 281
    Payroll Run entry, 293–295
    posted entry, 45–48
    posted invoice, 127–129
    posted payment, 137–139
    posted Revenues Journal entry, 182–183
    posting of adjusted entries, 47
    prepayments, 431

sales quotes, 415–416
shortcuts, 46
showing or omitting in reports, 59
time slips, 756, 760
year-end adjusting entries, 491
advancing the session date, 48–50
Advice, 19–20, 81
Aged Detail Report, 249
Aged Overdue Payables Reports, 146–147
Aged Overdue Receivables Reports, 192–193
aging of accounts, 631–632
Air Care Services
    accounting procedures, 204–205
    backup of company files, 246–247
    bank accounts, account class, 218–220
    company files, creating, 206–210
    company information, 199–204, 212
    company logo, 214–215
    credit cards, 219, 220–222
    customers in Receivables Ledger, entering,
        240–243
    default comments, 214, 231
    default settings, changing, 211–215
    discount settings, 230–231
    expense accounts, 219–220
    General Ledger, 215, 225
    general linked accounts, 225–226
    historical client information, 243–246
    historical invoices, correction of, 249–251
    historical supplier information, 238–240
    instructions, 206
    journal entries, preparing for, 246–248
    ledgers, preparing, 215–245
    linked accounts, 225–232
    open-invoice accounting for payables and
        receivables, 204
    opening account balances, 217
    payables, 226–228
    printer defaults, changing, 215
    questions and cases, A–38 – A–42
    receivables, 228–233
    sale of services, 205
    sales taxes, 222–225
    suppliers in Payables Ledger, entering,
        233–238
    the system, preparing, 210–215
    working with unfinished history, 247–248
Alberta
    see also Air Care Services; Helena's Academy;
        Muriel's Murals
    provincial medical plan premiums, 261, 269
    PST (Provincial Sales Tax), 30
allocations
    apply allocations, 80
    balance of account, 45
    Balance Sheet accounts, 507, 544
    cost allocations, 507–511
    departments, and unallocated amounts, 803
    division reports, 542–546
    divisions, 503–507
    freight expenses, 512–513
    Inventory Adjustments Journal, 504
    from Journal Division field, 520–522
    other journals, 533–535
    Payroll Journal, 533–535
    project allocation option, 216
    revenue amounts, 515–517
    in Sales Journal, 513–522
Allowance for Doubtful Accounts, 634
allowances, 633
alternative commands, 40
alternative instructions or commands, 6

alternative terms, 12
Andersson Chiropractic Clinic
  accounting procedures, 403–404
  additional transaction information, entering, 412–413
  company information, 400–404
  customer deposits, entering, 417–419
  Daily Business Manager, 435–447
  debit card sale transactions, 427–429
  deposits with sales orders, 426–427
  fees (sales) due, 440–441
  instructions, 404–405
  journal reports, displaying additional information, 450
  opening data files, 405
  patient (sales) orders due, 441–442
  payments due, 437–438
  payments from line of credit, 411–412
  Pending Patient (Sales) Orders, 449–450
  Pending Supplier (Purchase) Orders, 449
  prepayment to supplier, 409–413
  purchase orders, 407–409, 419–422, 429–431
  purchase orders due, 442–443
  purchase quote, 405–407, 422
  questions and cases, A–49 – A–50
  receipts for sales with deposits on orders, 434–435
  receipts on accounts with deposits, 424–426
  recurring transactions, removing, 443–444
  recurring transactions due, 438–440
  removal of quotes and orders, 448–449
  reports, displaying, 449–450
  revenue and expense accounts, 404
  sales orders, 416–417, 423–424
  sales orders with deposits, 431–435
  sales quotes, 413–417, 424
Assign Tax Codes, 223, 664, 677–678
audit trail, A–231
automatic advice, 19–20, 81
automatic backups, 77
automatic credit notes, 384
automatic updates, 80
automatically clearing data, 616–617
automatically save changes, 80

B
backing up. *See* backup files
backordered quantities, 419, 421, 430
backup files
  after advancing session date, 48–50
  automatic backups, 77
  backing up your work, 22–23
  backup message, 49
  backup options, 77, 212
  Backup tool, 22
  Backup Wizard, 22

and CDs or DVDs, 246
company files, 246–247, 685
default setting, 102
for different stages, 50
making a backup copy, 95
opening from backup, 24–26
reminders, 77
restoring, 24–26
settings, changing, 638
starting from, 70
updating the backup name, 50
Balance Sheet
  adjusting entries, 100
  allocations, 507, 544
  cash-basis *vs.* accrual-basis, A–139 – A–140
  Comparative Balance Sheet, 56
  Departmental Balance Sheet, 804–805
  display, 55–57
  exporting, 690
  generally, 55–56, A–225 – A–227
  single Balance Sheet only, 57
Bank Account Transactions Report, 149, 588–590
bank accounts
  account class, 218–220, 221
  adding currency to, 648–649
  bank account numbers, 523
  Bank class accounts, 218
  banking reports. *See* banking reports
  Cash class accounts, 218
  foreign bank accounts, 741
  group deposits, 593–594
  importing bank statements, A–141 – A–145
  linked accounts, and additional currencies, 232
  linking to, with the Web icon, A–146
  multiple bank accounts, 117, 126
  online banking, A–141 – A–146, A–203 – A–211
  reconciliation. *See* account reconciliation; bank statement reconciliation
  Sage One, A–203 – A–211
  Transfer Funds Journal, 480–481
  updating settings, 648–650
bank deposit slips, 577–584, 594–595
bank services, 26, 109
bank statement reconciliation
  Account Reconciliation Journal, 590–599
  adding account statement journal entries, 596–599
  bank statement and transaction report, comparison of, 588–590
  credit card bank account, 599
  deposit slip details, 594–595
  group deposits, 593–594
  marking journal entries as cleared, 592–596
  NSF cheques, marking, 595–596
  NSF service charges, 597
  reconciling the account, 590–592
  showing corrections, 593
Banking module, 38, 480
banking reports
  Account Reconciliation Journal, 609–610
  Account Reconciliation Report, 610–611
  Bank Account Transactions Report, 588–590
  Deposit Slip Journal, 610
  Deposit Slip Report, 611–612
  displaying, 609–612
  generally, 54
  printing, 612
  Reconciliation Transaction Report, 611
batch printing, 119, 213, 567–568
bilingual, 78, 83
Bill of Materials & Item Assembly Journal, 374–379, 764–766, A–28

Bill of Materials method, 761–766
Billable Time, 745
bills. *See* sales invoices
bonuses, 657, 658
bookmark, 39
British Columbia, 30
Budget Income Statements, 569–570
budget reports
  Budget Income Statements, 569–570
  displaying, 558
  effective use of, 569
  Income Statement reports, 557
  printing, 570
  setup options, 79
budgets
  adding budget amounts to divisions, 559–560
  budget amounts, changing, 566
  budget frequencies, changing, 567
  budgeting feature, turning on, 553–554
  copying budget amounts, 558
  General Ledger, budget amounts in, 556–558
  postable revenue and expense accounts, 557
  reports. *See* budget reports
  setting a budget, 554–556
  setting up, 553–558
  Total Budgeted Amount, 558
  updating budgets, 566–567
Business Advice, 19
Business Assistant menu, 19
business entity concept, A–232
business number, 212
Business Reports option, 58

C
Calendar icon, 21, 37, 208
calendar year, new, 307–308
Canada Revenue Agency, 92, 212, 269, 292, 299, A–157 – A–173
Cancel button, 37
capital accounts, 124, 227
cases, A–29 – A–73
cash-based accounting reports
  Unpaid Expense Transactions Reports, A–137
  Unpaid Revenue Transactions Reports, A–138
cash-basis accounting, 76, A–117 – A–140, A–234 – A–235
cash-basis accounting reports, A–136 – A–140
Cash Flow Projection Reports, 196
cash flow reports, 195–196
cash purchases, 119–121, 126–127, 127, 129, 138
cash sales, 156, 168–170
changing dates, 47, 48–50
charities, 68
  see also Love It Again
Chart of Accounts
  see also accounts
  Account List, 60–61
  Accounts window, 89–91
  adding a new account, 43
  creating, 89–92
  displaying, 60
  generally, 60
  organization of accounts, 84, 85
Check Validity of Accounts tool, 90
Checklists
  accessing, 81
  in Classic View, 489
  Day-End Procedures, 489
  end-of-month procedures, 612–618
  Fiscal Year-End Procedures, 489
  printing task list, 612
  reminders, 81
Cheque Log Reports, 149, 609

customer reports
Aged Overdue Receivables Reports, 192–193
Client Aged Reports, 191–192
Client/Customer Lists, 191
Client Revenues Reports, 193
Customer Analysis Report, 398
Customer Sales Reports, 396
displaying, 190–194
printing, 197–198
Receipts Journal, 194
Revenues (Sales) Journal, 193–194
Customer Sales Reports, 396
Customer Time and Billing Report, 778–779
customers
adding new customer, 170–175
addresses, 171–173, 241
Clients window, 178
credit limit, 175, 243
credit note, 182
departments, adding, 795–796
deposits, 417–419, 424–426
editing customer information, 177–180
editing records from Setup Guide, 179–180
entering in Receivables Ledger, 240–243,
666–667
foreign customers, 468–472
Full Add, 171
Grouped Client Lists, 191
historical customer information, 243–246,
667–668
importing transactions, A–149 – A–152
inactive, 617
Internal Client option, 171, 172
Internal Customer option, 241
late payments, 20
mailing labels, 197–198
multiple addresses, 172
One-Time Customer, 428
paid client transactions, clearing, 613–614
partial payments (cash-basis accounting),
A–135 – A–136
preferred customers, 379–380
in Pro version, 10
Quick Add, 170
removal of records, 617–618
reports. *See* customer reports
salespeople, adding to customer records,
342–343
saving customer record without historical
information, 246
saving new customer account, 175
ship-to-address, 172, 242
tax status, 174
customizing
accessing saved reports, A–83 – A–84
forms, 4, A–97 – A–98

journals, 83, 162
Microsoft Office documents, A–175 – A–183
orders, 165
print options, A–84 – A–86
Quote form, 423
removal of customization details, A–86
removal of report templates, A–87
reports, 62, A–75 – A–88
sales invoices, 161–162, A–89 – A–98

D

Daily Business Manager
in Classic View, 436
fees (sales) due, 440–441
Memo tab screen, 125, 237
patient (sales) orders due, 441–442
payments due, 437–438
posting from, 445–446
in Pro version, 436
purchase orders due, 442–443
quick access, 15
recurring transactions, removing, 443–444
recurring transactions due, 438–440
reminders, 81
working with, 435–447, 436–448
damaged files, 24
data files
backing up. *See* backup files
default location, 9, 24
exporting data, A–147 – A–149
file names and locations, 3
generally, 2
importing data, A–147, A–149 – A–152
installing your data, 4–6
ledger used, 3
opening a data file, 8–15, 36–38, 110, 157, 405,
456, A–104– A–106, A–116 – A–117
opening from backup, 24–26
with other software, 691–692
read-only files, 4
Short Date Format, 21
Short Date Separator, 21
sizes of, 48
dates
Additional information feature, 42
advancing the session date, 48–50
Calendar icon, 21, 37, 208
changing dates, 47, 48–50
date order, 76
Earliest Transaction date, 75–76, 208
edited date, correcting entries, 129
fiscal end date, 75
fiscal start date, 75, 95, 104
formats, 20–21, 78, 214, 639
later dates, working with, 48
long dates, 21, 158, 214
no practical restrictions, 75
in Payroll Journal, 266
Period Ending date (payroll), 266
postdated transactions, 56
session date. *See* session date
settings, 20–21, 639
short dates, 21, 214
Windows settings, 25
year. *See* year
Day-End Procedures, 489
debit cards, 222, 427–429
debits, 41, 114, 118, 160, 167, 793, A–228 – A–231
debits, pre-authorized, 523–524, 526–528
Deductions and Expenses Reports, 305
defaults
backups, 102
changing default settings, 73–80, 211–215
comments, 214, 231

company defaults, 638–640, 643–650
date, 43, 214
expense accounts, 124, 137
file locations, 9, 24
forms, 213, 638–639
general defaults, 79–80
General Ledger settings, 650
ledger settings, 650–663
names, changing, 639–640
payables default settings, 226–227, 650–652
payroll, 320–324, 655–661
printer defaults, 83–84, 215
receivables default settings, 229–230, 653–655
reports, 54, 56, 58
revenue account, 158
system defaults, 76–77
tax code, 230
tax rates, 659
Departmental Balance Sheet, 804–805
Departmental Income Statement, 805
Departmental Trial Balance, 805
departments
adding to accounts, 791
adding to other reports, 805–806
client records, adding to, 795–796
creating departments, 789–791
department reports, 804–806
departmental accounting, 789
Departmental Balance Sheet, 804–805
Departmental Income Statement, 805
Departmental Trial Balance, 805
finishing the history, 794–795
journal transactions, adding to, 796–803
line discounts, 799–800
opening departmental balances, 792–794
Payroll Journal, 801–803
Pro version, not available in, 79
Purchases Journal, 796–797
Receipts Journal, 797–798
Sales Journal, 798–800
setting up, 789–791
unallocated amounts, 803
Deposit Slip Journal, 610
Deposit Slip Report, 611–612
deposit slips, 577–584, 594–595
deposits
bank deposit slips, 577–584, 594–595
corrections to, 411, A–22
customer deposits, 417–419, 424–426
group deposits, 593–594
pre-authorized deposits, 522–524
receipts for sales with deposits on orders,
434–435
receipts on accounts with deposits, 424–426
sales order with deposits, 431–435
with sales orders, 426–427
desktop shortcut, 6
detail reports
Account Reconciliation Report, 610
Activity Time and Billing Reports, 779–780
Aged Overdue Payables Reports, 146–147
Aged Overdue Receivables Reports, 193
Cash Flow Projection Reports, 196
Client Aged Reports, 192
Client Revenues Reports, 193
Customer Sales Reports, 396
Customer Time and Billing Report,
778–779
Deposit Slip Report, 612
Division Income Reports, 543–544
Employee Reports, 304
Employee Time and Billing Payroll Reports,
781
Inventory Purchases Detail Report, 395

foreign currency
     adding, 643–644, 740–741
     additional currencies, and linked accounts,
          232
     bank accounts, adding to, 648–649
     exchange rate reports, 490
     exchange rates, 469, 471, 477, 478, 479, 644,
          666
     multiple foreign currencies, 740–741
     setup, 664
     suppliers' use of, 236
     transferring foreign funds, 480–481
foreign customers
     exchange rates, 469, 471
     HST, 620
     receipts, entering, 470–472
     sales to, 468–470
foreign purchases. *See* foreign suppliers
foreign suppliers
     exchange rates, 477, 478, 479
     foreign supplier record, 476–478
     and GST, 477
     historical invoices for, 664
     historical payments, 666
     identifying, 664
     import duties, 511–512
     import duty remittances, 536
     payments to, 471, 478–480
     purchases from, 476–478
forms
     batch printing, 213
     cheque Form settings, 219
     commonly used forms, 4
     company address, adding, 213
     customizing, 4, A–97 – A–98
     default form, location of, 163
     default settings, 213, 638–639
     Form Numbers, 213
     Forms folder, 215
     language, 78
     payroll form settings, 327
     verify sequence numbers, 213
freight expenses, 356, 364, 455–456, 502, 512–513,
          632
French, 78, 504
Full Add, 120, 171
future-dated transactions, 104, 295–296

G

General Journal
     Adjust Journal Entry, 39
     Banking module, 38
     corrections after posting, A–18
     corrections before posting, 42–43
     displaying, 61–62
     entering transactions, 38–43

     importing transactions, A–152 – A–156
     opening, 13
     posting, 43
     vs. Receivables, for sales entries, 167
     vs. Revenues Journal, for sales, 160
     Reverse Entry tool, 47
     review of entry, 42–43
     sales taxes, entering, 132–134
     year-end adjusting entries, 491
General Ledger
     budget amounts, entering, 556–558
     changing settings, 225
     editing General Ledger accounts, 88–89
     finishing General Ledger history, 95–96
     General Ledger Report, 59–60
     general linked accounts, 650
     linked accounts, 650
     modifying accounts in, 216
     new accounts, 91–92, 216–217, 640–642
     preparing, 87, 215, 640–642
     report, 466, 589
     settings, 650
general reports
     see also reports; specific reports
     Account List Report, 61
     Balance Sheet, 55–57
     Chart of Accounts, 60
     displaying general reports, 53
     General Journal, 61–62
     General Ledger Report, 59–60
     generally, 53
     Income Statement, 57–58
     Trial Balance, 58–59
generally accepted accounting principles (GAAP),
          A–232 – A–234
Getting Started screen, 10, 210
GIFI code, 44, 92
GIFI reports, A–157 – A–159
going-concern assumption, A–232
Goods and Services Tax. *See* GST (Goods and
          Services Tax)
Groen Fields
     accounting procedures, 109
     adjusting a posted invoice, 127–129
     adjusting a posted payment, 137–139
     cash purchases, entering, 119–121
     company information, 106–109
     Continue feature, and new suppliers, 131–132
     discounts, 129–132
     instructions, 110
     new supplier record, adding, 122–127
     opening data files, 110
     payments, accounting for, 116–119
     purchases, accounting for, 110–114
     questions and cases, A–34 – A–35
     recurring journal entry, 115–116
     reversing a posted purchase entry, 139–140
     sales taxes in General Journal, 132–134
     shortcuts, creating, 132–134
     stored entries, 135–136, 140–144
     supplier information, editing, 136–137
     supplier reports, 144–150
Gross Margin Income Statement, 396–397
group deposits, 593–594
Grouped Client Lists, 191
Grouped Division List, 543
Grouped Employee List, 303
Grouped Inventory Lists, 389
Grouped Supplier Lists, 145–146
GST (Goods and Services Tax)
     see also taxes
     administering the GST, 26–27
     bank and financial institution services, 26
     changes in rules, 27

     collection, 25
     definition of GST, 25–26
     exporting GST returns, A–159 – A–163
     foreign suppliers and, 477
     GST Paid on Purchases account, 26
     on imported and exported goods, 26
     input tax credit, 26
     insurance, 30
     other calculation methods, 27
     and other provincial (retail) sales taxes, 30
     paying the GST, 26
     Quick Method, 27
     refunds, calculation of, 28
     registration, 25
     regular method, 26–27
     remittances, calculation of, 27
     remittances, making, 466–467
     rent on business property, 26
     service business, 156
     setup, 222–225
     tax exempt goods and services, 26
     visitors, and GST refund, 26
     zero rated goods and services, 25

H

health care premiums. *See* medical premiums
Helena's Academy
     accounting procedures, 262–263
     adjusting payroll entries, 273–275, 293–295
     company information, 257–263
     instructions, 263
     payroll cheque run, 283–289
     payroll entitlements, 270–273
     payroll remittances, 263, 279–283
     payroll reports, 298–303
     payroll transactions, entering, 264–270
     questions and cases, A–43 – A–44
     termination of employee, 296–297
     vacation pay, releasing, 275–279
Help features, 15–19
Help menu, 16
Help Welcome screen, 16
hide
     effect of hiding, 81
     icons for modules or pages, 81
     journals for hidden modules, 149
     quantity inventory details, 366
     Select Company window, 83
     total inventory details, 366
     unused ledgers, and history, 248
historical cost, A–232 – A–233
historical transactions
     correction of historical invoices, 240, 249–251
     EI insurable earnings, 337
     employee year-to-date historical amounts, 302
     finishing departmental history, 794–795
     finishing payroll history, 340–341
     finishing the history, 95–96, 685, 794–795
     historical account balances, 92–95, 641–642
     historical client information, 243–246
     historical customer information, 667–668
     historical payments, 665–666
     historical supplier information, 238–240
     historical supplier transactions, 665
     Inventory Ledger, 372
     ledger status, changing to finished, 685
     outstanding historical difference, 240
     related historical accounts, 784
     sales invoices, 230
     saving customer record without historical
          information, 246
     working with unfinished history, 247–248
Home window, 10, 11, A–145
hourly paid employees, 266

essential linked accounts, 232
foreign currency transactions, 741–742
General Ledger, 650
general linked accounts, 225–226, 650
income linked accounts, 325
inventory, 371, 662–663, 763
inventory losses, 367
Linked Accounts Setting screen, 317
linked revenue account, 371
new accounts, creating, 650
payables linked accounts, 114, 227–228, 652
payroll, 324–327, 660–661
prepayments, 228
receivables, 160–161, 231–233, 654–655
reconciliation accounts, 586–588
removal, restricted, 226
Retained Earnings, 641
setup, 225–232
tax accounts, 228
taxes, 223
unused taxes, 326
variance linked account, 682
logo, 78–79, 214–215, 215, 639, 690
Long Date Format, 21, 158, 214
Look Up An Invoice tool, 472–476
lookup data
clearing, 615–616
deposit slip lookup data, clearing, 616
for other payments, clearing, 616
Lookup tool, 117, 139, 176
lost files, 24
Love It Again
accounting procedures, 68
Chart of Accounts, creating, 89–92
closing, 101–104
company files, creating, 69–73
company information, 65–68, 74–76
default settings, changing, 73–80
financial statements, format of, 85–86
finishing General Ledger history, 95–96
finishing the history, 95–96
general defaults, 79–80
General Ledger, 87–89, 91–92
historical account balances, 92–95
instructions, 69
ledgers, preparing, 84–95
making a backup copy, 95
printer defaults, 83–84
questions and cases, A–32 – A–33
Skeleton starter files, defining, 84
starting a new fiscal period, 101–104
the system, preparing, 73–84
system defaults, 76–77
transactions for earlier fiscal period, 104–105
user preference settings, 80–82
view menu settings, 82–83

view settings, 81
lower Tasks pane, 12

M
mailing labels
client, 197–198
employee mailing labels, 302–303
printing, 150–151, 197–198, 302–303
suppliers, 150–151
main menu bar, 10
Maintenance menu, 48, 249
Manitoba
see also Flabuless Fitness; Phoebe's Photo
Studio
PST (Provincial Sales Tax), 30, 156
manuals, 4
Maple Leaf Rags Inc.
accountant's copy, 487–488, 491
accountant's journal entries, importing,
491–493
accounting procedures, 455–456
company information, 451–456
credit card bill payments, 460–463
exchange rate reports, 490
foreign customers, 468–472
foreign suppliers, 476–480
instructions, 456
looking up and tracking purchases, 476
looking up invoices to track shipments,
472–476
monitoring routine activities, 488–490
opening data files, 456
questions and cases, A–50 – A–54
supplier's Web site, accessing, 463–465
tax remittances, 465–468
tracking sales shipments, 457–460
transferring foreign funds, 480–481
margin, 662
markup, 662
matching principle, A–233
materiality principle, A–233 – A–234
maximizing the Home window, 38
medical benefits, 268, 319
medical companies, 406, 421
see also Andersson Chiropractic Clinic
medical contributions, 269
medical premiums, 268
messages, 20
Microsoft Excel, 687, 691, 692, A–156,
A–182 – A–183
Microsoft Excel language option, 80
Microsoft Office
customized documents, A–175 – A–183
integration with, A–175 – A–183
Microsoft Outlook, 124, 173, 242, 475
Microsoft Word, 687, A–175 – A–183
minimize button, 38
Modify This Report option, 56, 57
Modules pane, 12
monetary principle, A–232
monitoring routine activities, 488–490
month-end procedures. See end-of-month
procedures
multi-period financial reports, 783–784
multi-period reports, 53
multi-user mode
accessing files, A–104– A–105
accounting users, adding, A–102– A–104
Add Users wizard, A–100 – A–104
budget features, 554
finishing a session, A–111
modifying users, A–109– A–110
refresh data, 39, 80, A–107
Refresh tool, 39, A–107

removing users, A–110 A–111
restrictions, A–106
and setup, 73
and starting new fiscal period, 101
switching to, A–99 – A–104
time slip entry users, adding, A–101 – A–102
working in, A–106– A–107
multiple quantities, 112
Muriel's Murals
accounting procedures, 36
adjusting a posted entry, 45–48
advancing the session date, 48–50
company information, 34–36
displaying general reports, 53–63
drill-down reports, 62–63
finishing a session, 64
General Journal transactions, entering, 38–43
instructions, 36
new account, adding, 43–45
opening data files, 36–38
questions and cases, A–30 – A–31
My Business tab, 15
MYOB, A–156

N
negative numbers
in Credits and Debits fields, 41
damaged inventory, 366
employee advances that are repaid, 286
in Purchases Journal, 113
in Sales Journal, 159
Net Days field, 124, 179, 235
new accounts
adding a new account, 43–45
in General Ledger, 91–92
"on the fly" creation, 247
required fields, 91
wizard, 44–45
New Brunswick, 28, 109
new calendar year, 307–308
Newfoundland and Labrador, HST in, 28
non-accounting terms, A–15
non-billable activities, 760
non-postable accounts, 558
non-profit organizations, 68
see also Love It Again
Northern Lights
accounting procedures, 315–316
company information, 309–316
Employee Ledger records, 327–338
finishing payroll history, 340–341
instructions, 316
job categories, 339–340
linking remittances to suppliers,
338–339
payroll setup, 316–343
questions and cases, A–44 – A–46
salesperson reports, 349–350
Northwest Territories, 30
Notes tab, 91, 92
Nova Scotia, 28
see also Groen Fields; Shady Corners
NSF cheques, 155, 175–177, 501, 595–596, 597,
605–606, A–120 – A–122,
A–129 – A–131
Numbering option, 79
Nunavut, 30

O
objectivity principle, A–232 – A–233
online banking, A–141 – A–146
see also Sage One
online help, 16, A–10 – A–12
online reconciliation, 579, 585

receivables. *See* sales
Receivables Ledger
   customer accounts, entering, 240–243,
      666–667
   default comments, 231, 653–654
   default settings, 229–230
   discount settings, 230–231, 653
   historical customer information, 667–668
   linked accounts, 160, 232–233, 654–655
   preparing, 666–668
   receivables terminology, changing, 654
   settings, 229–230, 653–655
   Statistics tab, 243
   Taxes tab, 242–243
   terminology, changing, 231
Receivables module window, 12
Receiver General for Canada, 25, 280, 282,
      338, 459
recognition principle, A–233
Reconciliation & Deposits Journal, 578–584
Reconciliation and Deposits Journal, 38
Reconciliation Transaction Report, 611
Record of Employment (ROE), A–168 – A–173
Record of Employment Report, 298–299
recurring transactions
   due, and Daily Business Manager, 438–440
   Payroll Journal entries, 270
   purchases, 115–116
   Random frequency, 150
   recurring frequency options, 115
   Recurring Transactions Report, 149–150
   removing, 443–444
   sales, 181–182
Recurring Transactions Report, 149–150
Refresh Lists option, 80
Refresh tool, 39, 91, 136, 164
registered charities, 68
   see also Love It Again
registration
   details, 16
   instructions, A–3 – A–4, A–5 – A–6
   registration screen, 8
   Student version, A–5 – A–6
   validation codes, 8
Related Tasks pane, 13
Relevé 1 Slips, 299, 300, 675–676
reminders, 77, 81
Remittance Journal, 280
removal
   alternative to records removal, 617
   customer records, 617–618
   customization details, A–86
   of linked accounts, 226
   orders, 448–449
   quotes, 448–449
   recurring transactions, 443–444

report templates, A–87
   supplier records, 617–618
reports
   see also specific reports
   accessing saved reports, A–83 – A–84
   Account reports, 54
   Accounts window reports menu, 54
   accounts with zero balances, 45
   all journal entries, in single report, 148, 194
   analysis, 53
   Banking reports, 54
   banking reports, 609–612
   budget reports, 569–570
   cash-basis accounting reports, A–136 – A–140
   cash flow reports, 195–196
   columns, A–76 – A–77
   commonly used reports, 4
   corrections, showing or omitting, 59, 61–62,
      148, 177
   customer reports, 190–194
      see also customer reports
   customization, 62, A–75 – A–88
   defaults, 54, 56, 58
   department reports, 804–806
   departments, adding, 805–806
   division reports, 542–546
   drill-down reports, 62–63
   exchange rate reports, 490
   exporting reports, 690–691
   filtering, 62, A–78 – A–84
   Financial reports, 54, 55
   Find in This Report option, 61
   Forecast and Analysis Reports, 397–399
   general reports, 53–63
   groups, A–81 – A–83
   inventory reports, 388–397
   journal reports, additional information in, 450
   Modify This Report option, 56, 57
   multi-period reports, 53, 783–784
   multiple fiscal periods, 782–784
   orders, 449–450
   and other software, 691–692
   payroll reports, 303–307
   previous fiscal periods, 53
   printing, 63
   Recently Viewed Reports, 13
   related historical accounts, 784
   Remittance Report, 281–282
   removal of customization details, A–86
   removal of report templates, A–87
   Report Centre, 13, 15, 54–55, 145
   Reports drop-down list, 13
   Reports menu, 53–54
   Reports pane, 13, 54–55
   Sage One, A–215 – A–216
   salesperson reports, 349–350
   searching in a report, A–87 – A–88
   sorting, A–77 – A–78
   supplier reports. *See* supplier reports
   tax reports, 194–195
   template, A–80 – A–81, A–86 – A–87
   This Week To Date option, 78
   time and billing reports, 778–782
   zero balances, 91
Restore wizard, 24
restoring from backup, 24–26
retail industry, 358
retail sales taxes. *See* PST (Provincial Sales Tax)
Retained Earnings accounts, 87, 225, 641
returns
   automatic credit notes, 384
   generally, 356
   purchase returns, 382–384
   sales returns, 380–382

revenue accounts, 158, 159, 173, 242, 371, 557
revenue amounts, allocation of, 515–517
revenues. *See* sales
Revenues Journal, 193–194
   see also Sales Journal
   adjusting entries, 182–183
   corrections, 161
   vs. General Journal, for sales, 160
   posting, 163–164
   review of entry, 160–161
reversals
   see also adjustments
   NSF cheques, 175–177, 605–606
   paycheques, 275
   posted purchase entry, 139–140
   Reverse Entry tool, 47
   reversing entry after posting, 47
   sales invoices, 381
review questions, A–29 – A–73
ROEs (Records of Employment), A–168 – A–173
ROI (return on investment), 398
rounding errors, 160, 459
routine activities, monitoring, 488–490
RST (Retail Sales Tax). *See* PST
      (Provincial Sales Tax)
RT extension, 212
Ryder's Routes
   company information, 739–740
   fiscal dates, changing, 739–740
   foreign bank account, adding, 741
   foreign currency, adding, 740–741
   inventory locations, entering, 742–743
   inventory prices, updating, 775–778
   linked bank accounts for foreign currency
      transactions, 741–742
   multiple fiscal periods, and reports, 782–784
   new inventory, building, 761–766
   questions and cases, A–70 – A–72
   service activity prices, updating, 749–752
   services, adding time and billing to, 747–749
   time and billing profile, 738–739
   time and billing reports, displaying, 778–782
   time and billing setup, 743–747
   time slips, 753–757
   transfer of inventory between locations,
      766–771

S
Sage 50
   see also Premium version; Pro version
   About Sage 50 screen, 16
   activation, A–3 – A–4, A–9 – A–12
   Advice, 19–20
   Classic View. *See* Classic View
   components, 4
   CRA reports, filing, A–157 – A–173
   Dashboard, 10–11
   desktop shortcut, 6
   downloading, A–2 – A–4
   Enhanced View, 12–13
   exporting records, A–148 – A–149
   generally, 4
   Help features, 15–19
   Home window, 10, 11
   Home window tool, 13
   importing records, A–154 – A–156
   installation, A–3, A–6 – A–8
   linking Sage One and Sage 50 files,
      A–217 – A–224
   vs. manual system, 53
   messages, 20
   Microsoft Office, integration with,
      A–175 – A–183
   and other software, 691–692

Inventory & Services Ledger, 662–663, 679–684
job categories, 676
ledger default settings, entering, 650–663
Manager's Report on Sage 50, 621
new accounts, creating, 640–642
Payables Ledger, 650–652, 663–666
Payroll Ledger, 655–661, 668–676
payroll remittances, 676–677
printer settings, 649–650
questions and cases, A–59 – A–67

Receivables Ledger, 653–655, 666–668
sales taxes, 645–648
security passwords, 686–690
subsidiary ledgers, preparing, 663–684
the system, preparation of, 637–640
tax codes, entering, 646–648
users, entering, 686–690
vendors. *See* suppliers
view
    see also display
    change view menu settings, 82–83
    change view settings, 81
    View Entries By, 46
    viewing options, 8, 25
Village Galleries
    accounting procedures, 552–553
    batch printing, 567–568
    budget amounts, 566
    budget reports, 569–570
    budgeting feature, turning on, 553–554
    budgets, setting up, 553–558
    company information, 547–553
    General Ledger, budget amounts in, 556–558
    instructions, 553
    questions and cases, A–56 – A–57
    setting a budget, 554–556
    updating budgets, 566–567
VRSP (voluntary registered pension plans), 321, 658

W
warnings, 105
WCB/WSIB, 269, 319, 323, 334–335, 673
Web sites, 463–465, 644
Week Begins On, 78
Windows 10, 5, 7, 13
Windows Calculator tool, 40, 274
Windows Copy command, 23
Windows desktop, 13, 14
WSIB (Workplace Safety and
        Insurance Board), 659

Y
year
    approaching year-end, 20
    four-digit year, 21
    future year, paycheques for,
        295–296
    new calendar year, 307–308
    posting to wrong year, 105
year-end adjusting entries, 491
Year End Review (PIER) Reports, 306
year-to-date insurable earnings, 299
Yukon, 30, 315
    see also Northern Lights

Z
zero balances, 91, 217
zero rated goods and services, 25, 109

n. Set up Payroll Remittances. Add the supplier and remittance frequency and enter July 1, 2018, as the end date of the next remitting period.

o. Back up your files.

p. Finish entering the history for all ledgers and finish your session.

2. Using the information provided, enter the source documents for July using Sage 50.

3. After you have completed your entries, print the following reports:
   a. Journal Entries (All Journals) from July 1 to July 31, 2018
   b. Supplier Aged Detail Report for all suppliers on July 31, 2018
   c. Guest Aged Detail Report for all guests on July 31, 2018
   d. Employee Summary (all employees) for the pay period ending July 31, 2018
   e. Income Statement for the period ending July 31, 2018

SOURCE DOCUMENTS

Create new accounts or supplier and guest records as needed for the source documents that follow. Change session dates as needed.

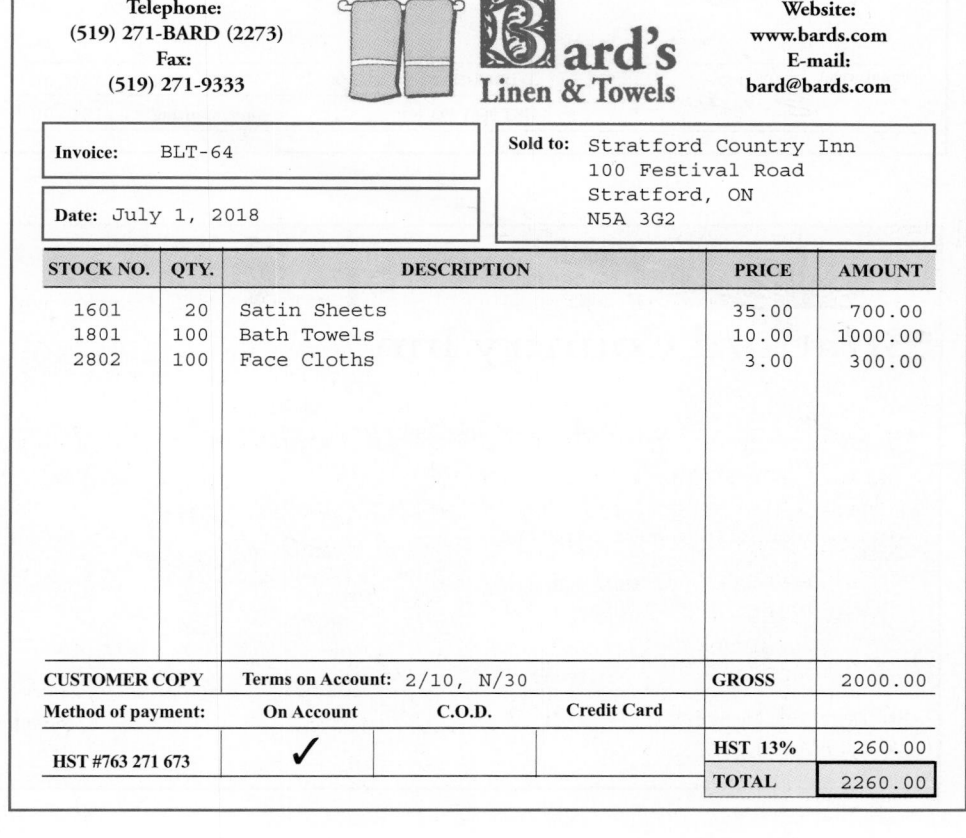

1

Telephone: (519) 271-BARD (2273) Fax: (519) 271-9333	**B ard's** Linen & Towels	Website: www.bards.com E-mail: bard@bards.com

Invoice: BLT-64	Sold to: Stratford Country Inn 100 Festival Road Stratford, ON N5A 3G2

Date: July 1, 2018

STOCK NO.	QTY.	DESCRIPTION	PRICE	AMOUNT
1601	20	Satin Sheets	35.00	700.00
1801	100	Bath Towels	10.00	1000.00
2802	100	Face Cloths	3.00	300.00

CUSTOMER COPY	Terms on Account: 2/10, N/30		GROSS	2000.00
Method of payment:	On Account ✓	C.O.D.	Credit Card	
HST #763 271 673			HST 13%	260.00
			TOTAL	2260.00

2

AVON Maintenance Services
66 Kleen Road, Stratford, ON N5A 3C3
Telephone (519) 272-4611
Fax: (519) 272-4813
www.avonservices.com

Invoice:	AM-148
Date:	July 1, 2018
Sold to:	Stratford Country Inn
	100 Festival Road
	Stratford, ON
	N5A 3G2
Phone:	(519) 222-6066

Code	Service Description	Price
KX-55	Vacuum Premises Floor Polishing Washroom Cleaning Maintenance and Repairs Recurring bi-weekly billing	1000.00

Signature: *E. Prosper*		
Terms: Net 30 days	**HST**	130.00
HST #631 393 461	**Amount owing**	1130.00

3

100 Festival Road, Stratford, ON N5A 3G2
Tel.: (519) 222-6066   1-888-272-6000
Fax: (519) 272-7960

STRATFORD TRUST
80 Sterling Avenue
Stratford, ON N5A 3G3

No: 701

Stratford Country Inn

Date 2 0 1 8 0 7 0 5
Y Y Y Y M M D D

Pay ———————— Two Thousand Two Hundred Sixty ———— 00 $ 2,260.00

TO THE
ORDER
OF
Avon Maintenance Services
66 Kleen Road
Stratford, ON N5A 3C3

PER *E. Prosper*
Treasurer

⑆392451⑆ 22 · 701

Re: Invoices AM-68, 85, 101, 127 $ 2,260.00   **No: 701**

July 5, 2018